Stephans' Railroad Directory

Volume 3B

Railroad/ Railfan 1929-1987

COMPILED BY KAREN & EARL STEPHANS

TIOGA PUBLICATIONS   NEW YORK

COPYRIGHT (C) 1988
BY KAREN & EARL STEPHANS
ALL RIGHTS RESERVED

Reproduction or translation of any part of this work beyond that permitted by Sections 107 and 108 of the 1976 United States Copyright Act without the permission of the copyright owner is unlawful. Requests for permission or further information should be addressed to the Permissions Department, Tioga Publications 101 N. Fenton Road Chenango Forks, NY 13746.

Stephans'
Railroad
Directory

Volume 3A

Railroad/ Railfan

Stephans'
Railroad
Directory

Volume 3B

Railroad/ Railfan

Library of Congress Cataloging in Publications Data:

Stephans, Earl
    Stephans' Railroad Directory Volume 3

    "RAILFAN/RAILROAD" 1929-1987

    1: Index to "RAILFAN/RAILROAD" MAGAZINE
    2: Model Railroads
    3: Prototype Railroads
    4: Railroad History
    5: Railroad Drawings-Plans-Specifications
    6: Model Building Techniques

Library of Congress Catalog Number   86-90268
ISBN   0-9616890-0-5

CONSIST	PAGE
OPERATING INSTRUCTIONS (UBRI)	004
THE SOURCE (HISTORY)	006
LOCOMOTIVES	008
EXTRAS	180
RENT-A-KID PHOTO COPIES	257
PASSENGER EQUIPMENT	258
DISPATCHERS REPORT	277
FREIGHT CARS	278
NON-REVENUE EQUIPMENT	286
DEADHEADS	299
PART A TRACTION	300
PART B STRUCTURES, SIGNALS & VEHICLES	340
PROTOTYPE MODELING IDEAS	370
RAILROAD ROSTERS AND HISTORIES	376
MODEL LAYOUTS	482
RAIL LITERATURE REVIEWS	484
GENERAL RAILROADING	514
APPENDIX	A1
HISTORICAL SOCIETIES & MAGAZINES	B1
CATEGORY INDEX	C1

See page C5

BILL OF LADING
STRUCTURES, SIGNALS & VEHICLES

This section contains the six subsections of Bridges and Tunnels, Commercial Buildings, Railroad Structures, Signals, Vehicles and General Structures. Bridges and Tunnels are self-explanatory. Commercial structures include stores, factories, houses, etc. Railroad structures are depots and stations, line side buildings, roundhouses, platforms, water towers, servicing facilities and the like. Signals are signals, both electrical and mechanical, signs, telltales, etc. Vehicles are all other conveyances, cars, trucks, roadwork equipment, barges, tugboats, etc. General structures is the catch-all.

Prototype data includes articles and specifications on the real thing. In some instances there are photographs with these articles that did not get special billing in the photograph section. The plans and drawings are just that. The plans are listed twice: once alphabetically and once by road. The photo section shows details or unusual photos of interest to the researcher. Finally, the model section highlights exceptional models and tells how to build/kitbash/rebuild your own "gems".

The descriptor line includes the description. If a road, geographical location, or year built is available it is included.

MANIFEST
STRUCTURES, SIGNALS & VEHICLES

DETAILED CONSIST	PAGE
BRIDGE & TUNNEL PROTOTYPE DATA	341
COMMERCIAL BUILDING PROTOTYPE DATA	342
RAILROAD STRUCTURE PROTOTYPE DATA	342
SIGNAL PROTOTYPE DATA	343
VEHICLE PROTOTYPE DATA	345
STRUCTURE, SIG & VEHIC PROTO DATA BY RD	345
RAILROAD STRUCTURE PLANS	348
BRIDGE & TUNNEL PHOTOS	348
BRIDGE & TUNNEL PLANS	348
SIGNAL PLANS	348
RAILROAD STRUCTURE PHOTOS	349
COMMERCIAL BUILDING PHOTOS	349
SIGNAL PHOTOS	356
VEHICLE PHOTOS	358
STRUCTURE, SIGNAL & VEHICLE PHOTO BY RD	359
RAILROAD STRUCTURE MODELS	368
COMMERCIAL BUILDING MODELS	368
VEHICLE MODELS	368
BRIDGE & TUNNEL MODELS	368
SIGNAL MODELS	368

Railroad/Railfan

STRUCTURES VEHICLES & SIGNALS

STRUCTURE, SIGNAL & VEHICLE PROTOTYPES	M	Y	P
* BRIDGE PROTOTYPE DATA *			
ASPEN TUNNEL UP WYOMING	11	47	89
BASCULE JACKNIFE BRIDGE CP UNIQUE CONST	01	78	12
BIG BEND TUNNEL: C&O	03	41	71
BOONE VIADUCT C&NW HIGHEST DOUBLE DECK	06	34	87
BRIDGE CN QUEBEC BRIDGE HISTORY OF	05	48	63
BRIDGE MKT POSEY HOLE DATA	09	47	73
BRIDGE NC&SL DIXIE LINE BRIDGE/HISTORY	06	46	71
BRIDGE NYNH&H BUZZARD BAY MA VERTICAL LI	07	52	65
BRIDGE POTOMAC RIVER RF&P BRIEF HISTORY	08	34	85
BRIDGE PRR ROCKVILLE BRIDGE AT HARRISBUR	06	46	73
BRIDGE SOO ST CROIX RIVER ARCH BRIDGE	06	53	59
BRIDGE SP PIT RIVER BRIDGE CALIFORNIA	07	42	69
BRIDGE T&NO SINGLE-LEAF BASCULE BEAUMONT	08	52	67
BRIDGES IN GENERAL	05	37	43
BRIDGES IN GENERAL 1	01	48	08
BRIDGES IN GENERAL 2	02	48	10
BRIDGES: 1ST IRON RAIL RR BRIDGE P&R	08	51	69
BRIDGES: 1ST IRON/1ST STEEL	06	59	36
BRIDGES: 280,000 IN THE US AND CANADA	05	37	43
BRIDGES: BUILT ON PONTOONS	08	51	67
BRIDGES: IRON ON PRR	02	44	56
BRIDGES: LOW SPOTS AT ENDS	03	47	129
CASCADE TUNNEL AIR COOLING GN	02	57	32
CASCADE TUNNEL GN.	11	49	48
COVERED BRIDGES	04	41	126
COVERED BRIDGES: 1941/LIST BY ROADS	04	43	128
COVERED RAILROAD BRIDGES: MORE	07	43	143
EMERGENCY RAILROAD BRIDGE-POTOMAC DESTRO	02	47	125
FR FOREIGN RAILROAD BRIDGES & TUNNELS	10	39	85
FR ENGLAND TANFIELD ARCH HISTORY	11	52	119
FR FRANCE: VIADUCT FADES 400' ABOVE	10	39	85
FR GERMAN RAILWAY TUNNEL	01	54	60
FR SCOTLAND FORTH BRIDGE	10	36	77
FR SNO FADES VIADUCT FRANCE-HIGHEST BRID	11	76	42
FR TUNNEL PROPOSED ENGLAND TO FRANCE	02	30	384
FR TUNNEL PROPOSED UNDER GILBALTER STRAI	02	30	380
GREEN RIVER BRIDGE L&N'S LARGEST	12	33	141
HELL GATE BRIDGE CONSTRUCTION NYNH&H	04	37	138
HIGH BRIDGE CNO&TP (SOUTHERN) DANVILLE K	06	77	53
HIGH BRIDGE S 1230' KENTUCKY RIVER	12	58	44
HOOSAC TUNNEL	04	36	52
HOOSAC TUNNEL HISTORY B&M	06	55	35
INTERNATIONAL RY BRIDGE PAINTED 2 COLORS	02	58	45
IRON CLAD RAILROAD BRIDGE, THE FIRST	08	51	68
IRON RAILROAD BRIDGES--READERS COMMENTS	05	67	32
KINZUA BRIDGE SHORT HISTORY	11	65	23
LETHBRIDGE VIADUCT CP 5327'	07	45	79
LIST OF TUNNELS OVER 1 MILE LONG N AMER	06	46	41
LONG BRIDGE PENNSYLVANIA--EMERGENCY XING	12	46	68
LONGEST & SHORTEST TUNNELS IN US	08	62	30
LONGEST RAIL TUNNEL LIST	04	60	30
LONGEST RAIL TUNNELS READER QUESTION	08	63	31
LONGEST TUNNELS IN THE US	05	66	33
NATURAL TUNNEL V&SW	08	50	53
NEW LONDON-GROTON BRIDGE OPENING	10	77	54
NEW YORK SUBWAY TUNNEL CONSTRUCTION	05	85	25
NICHOLSON BRIDGE DL&W CONCRETE ARCH	10	46	54
NSO 5 MILE BRIDGE ALBERMARIE SOUND NC	01	39	61
NYNH&H BRIDGE ACRSOSS HUDSON POUGHKEEPSI	08	31	45
PASS/FRT STATION BALTIMORE MD "OLDEST"	01	31	284
PECOS HIGH BRIDGE SP---HISTORY	07	49	42
PECOS RIVER BRIDGE (SP)	07	49	42
PECOS RIVER BRIDGE SP DATA	09	45	53
POTOMAC RIVER BRIDGE REPLACEMENT PRR	09	45	60
POUGHKEEPSIE BRIDGE: ITS HISTORY	04	44	73
QUEBEC BRIDGE CN	03	30	597
QUEBEC BRIDGE ON CN	05	48	63
RAIL BRIDGES AND NAVIGABLE RIVERS	10	68	08
RICHMONDS TRIPLE CROSSING	11	83	34
SALT LAKE FILL SP.	08	57	18
SALVAGING C&NW BRIDGE SHAWANO-OCONTO JCT	07	38	123
SAVAGE MD IRON BRIDGE B&O OLDEST IN US	02	67	26
SKEW ARCH BRIDGE ELIZABETH NJ	01	67	30
SNO BART LONGEST UNDER WATER TRANS TUBE	07	69	34
SNO BOX CAR FRAMES AS LOGGING BRIDGES	08	76	09
SNO BUZZARDS BAY LIFT BRIDGE PC	04	75	11
SNO CN LETHBRIDGE VIADUCT (HIGHEST)	05	76	24
SNO CN ST CLAIR TUNNEL	06	73	48
SNO CN ST JOHN RIVER BRIDGE	03	78	09
SNO CONNAUGHT TUNNEL CP LONGEST	06	76	50
SNO CP REPLACEMENT OF MOUNTAIN CREEK BRI	02	78	09
SNO EL NICHOLSON BRIDGE	06	62	43
SNO ENLARGING TUNNELS WITHOUT BLASTING	01	76	08
SNO FIRST BIG US TUNNEL B&M HOOSAC	05	72	56
SNO FIRST ELECTRICS IN HOOSAC TUNNEL B&M	01	75	55
SNO FIRST RAILWAY BRIDGE	04	73	48
SNO GEORGETOWN LOOP HIGH BRIDGE	09	84	29
SNO KINZUA VIADUCT REOPENED	11	87	38
SNO LAST STEAM THROUGH HOOSAC NKP #759	03	74	34
SNO LIST OF TUNNELS & THEIR OPENINGS	09	76	51
SNO LONGEST COVERED RR BRIDGE	08	71	44
SNO LONGEST RR BRIDGE "HUEY LONG"	07	72	62
SNO LONGEST RR TUNNELS (US & CANADA)	09	74	42
SNO MKT POSEY HOLE BRIDGE PROJECT	05	76	25
SNO MOFFAT TUNNEL	09	49	57
SNO MOFFAT TUNNEL BEGUN 1923	07	74	39
SNO NATURAL RR TUNNEL OF S IN VA	07	73	39
SNO NIAGARA GORGE RAIL SUSPENSION BRIDGE	07	76	50
SNO NYC DRAW BRIDGE NEVER OPENED-70 YEAR	11	72	08
SNO P&BPR TOLL BRIDGE CHARGES FOR LOCOS	11	66	38
SNO PC ROCKVILLE BRIDGE LONGEST STONE AR	04	72	66
SNO POUGHKEEPSIE BRIDGE BUILT 1886	10	74	45
SNO POUGHKEEPSIE BRIDGE REOPENING	08	76	50
SNO PRE STRESSED CONCRETE BRIDGES	03	71	60
SNO QUEBEC BRIDGE CN ST LAWRENCE RIVER	10	76	47
SNO REMOVAL OF ELECTRIC WIRE IN HOOSAC T	09	77	53
SNO SMITHFIELD ST BRIDGE REHABILITATION	12	76	45
SNO SOO BRIDGE AT ST CROIX RIVER	09	75	59
SNO SOO ST CROIX RIVER BRIDGE	04	70	34

Stephans' Railroad Directory

Railroad/Railfan

STRUCTURES VEHICLES & SIGNALS

STRUCTURE, SIGNAL & VEHICLE PROTOTYPES	M	Y	P
SNO SP PECOS RIVER BRIDGE (300' HIGH)	11	75	42
SNO SP TUNNEL ENLARGEMENTS 1968	03	68	26
SNO SP WORLDS LONGEST BRIDGE	06	69	39
SNO ST LAWRENCE BRIDGE CN LONGEST CANTIL	11	74	51
SNO SWING DRAW BRIDGE SPAN GN PUGET SOUN	04	55	35
SNO TUNNEL LISBON CT N&WO OLDEST TUNNEL	10	76	47
SNO TUNNEL TRACK-PANS	03	76	56
SNO TUNNELS AND THEIR ROADS	05	78	55
SNO VICTORIA BRIDGE MONTREAL CANADA	06	78	56
SNO WELDED BOX GIRDER BRIDGES-CONTINUOUS	03	71	60
SPIRAL TUNNEL CP MT OGDEN BC	05	74	12
ST CLAIR TUNNEL GT BUILT 1880-1891	10	45	51
STAMPEDE PASS TUNNEL NP	01	79	43
STARUCCA VIADUCT ERIE 1200' DATA	08	40	63
STARUCCA VIADUCT ERIE NEAR SUSQUEHANNA P	02	46	107
STEEL ACROSS THE RIVERS PART 2 BRIDGES	02	48	10
STEEL ACROSS THE RIVERS: BRIDGES	01	48	08
STONE ARCH BRIDGE PRR/STEEL TRUSS DOUBLE	02	35	84
STONE ARCH BRIDGES ON PRR	08	78	54
TRUSS RAILROAD BRIDGE SHORT DISCUSSION	03	78	52
TUNKHANNOCK VIADUCT DL&W--HISTORY	02	34	86
TUNNEL BIG BEN C&O HINTON/CLIFTON FORGE	08	34	84
TUNNEL CN MOUNT ROYAL TUNNEL HISTORY/DAT	08	51	66
TUNNEL CN ST CLAIR	01	42	63
TUNNEL D&SL MOFFAT TUNNEL	09	31	187
TUNNEL DANGERS IN EARLY YEARS	08	69	56
TUNNEL DL&W OXFORD TUNNEL: DIMENSIONS	07	36	87
TUNNEL HOOSAC B&M ITS HISTORY	06	55	35
TUNNEL HOOSAC TUNNEL ELECTRIFIED	05	43	90
TUNNEL IC EDGEWOOED CUT-OFF	03	47	73
TUNNEL REMOVAL ON US ROADS	12	65	27
TUNNELS GREAT MOUNTAIN TUNNELS	01	30	247
TUNNELS HISTORY OF/STORIES OF	06	46	10
TUNNELS IN GENERAL	01	30	247
VIADUCT: DECK PLATE GIRDER ERIE DATA	10	40	68
WORLDS LONGEST RR/HIWAY BRIDGE N ORLEANS	06	36	80

* COMERCIAL STRUCTURE PROTOTYPE DATA *

	M	Y	P
ABANDONED RAILROAD STRUCTURES-OTHER USES	01	39	137
HARVEY HOUSES	04	58	44
LOCKPORT NY UNION STATION HISTORY/NOW RE	01	75	52
MRS HOWARDS HOTEL ROWLESBURG WV B&O	SU	75	64R
RAILWAY INN: BABAHATCHIE	02	43	106
SNO PRINCE OF WALES HOTEL GN	03	76	56

* RAILROAD STRUCTURE PROTOTYPE DATA *

	M	Y	P
BLOW-DOWN SHED NP BILLINGS MONTANA	08	54	42
BLOW-DOWN SHEDS FOR STEAM LOCOS	02	78	50
BROAD STREET STATION PRR PHILA PA	05	67	16
CAB SIGNALS & HOW THEY WORK	05	72	59
CATENARY POLES: PRR NUMBERING SYSTEM	02	36	85
CATLLE GUARDS	01	30	208
CLAMSHELL LOADING OF COAL CHUTES MP	08	75	05
CLEBURNE SHOPS OF ATSF	02	78	55
COACH-CABOOSE BECOMES BROSELEY DEPOT	01	43	82
COALING STATION C&O (MODERN)	09	47	74
COVERED TURNTABLE READER INFORMATION	05	66	55
COVERED TURNTABLES--MORE READER COMMENTS	06	66	61
DEPOT B&O "POINT OF ROCKS" HISTORICAL IN	12	78	47
DIESEL SHOP AMTRAK COLLINWOOD OHIO	08	77	55
DROP PITS INSIDE ROUNDHOUSES	06	32	339
ELECTRIC CAR FERRY ON OHIO RIVER	02	77	56
ELECTRONIC TRACK SCALE	01	54	67
ENGINEHOUSE LIST (UP)	06	71	59
ERIE JERSEY CITY DEPOT CONSTRUCTION	02	60	32
FIRST TURNTABLES	05	78	55
FR FOREIGN RAILROAD PHOTOS	05	39	89
FR ITALY MILAN CENTRAL STATION--LARGEST	05	53	64
FR LONDON MIDLAND & SCOTTISH RY STATION	05	39	89
GEODESIC DOME REPAIR SHOP OF UNION TANK.	02	59	06
GIRDER TURN TABLES	01	30	208
GRAIN ELEVATOR WSH WEEHAWKEN NJ DATA	07	42	66
GRAND CENTRAL TERMINAL NEW YORK CITY NY,	06	50	12
GRAND CENTRAL TERMINAL NYC	09	78	24
GRAND CENTRAL TERMINAL NYC NEW YORK NY	08	65	27
GRAND CENTRAL TRIAPARTITE AGREEMENT (NY)	05	72	56
HARBORSIDE COAL LOADER ON CNJ	11	51	42
HOSPITAL FOR WHEELS (CR)	07	77	56
INGLEWOOD STATION INGLEWOOD CA ATSF	03	48	69
KING STREET STATION SEATTLE WA	01	52	32
LASALLE STREET STATION RI CHICAGO IL	10	70	22
LIST OF PASSENGER STATIONS 1946 & ROADS	11	71	31
LIST OF STATIONS ON NATIONAL REGISTER	12	76	49
LOCOMOTIVE WASHING MACHINE PRR	03	48	60
MEMORIES OF OLD BENICIA DEPOT SP	05	68	18
MEXICO CITY TERMINAL	12	69	16
MULE OR BARNEY CAR PUSHER PRR LI YARD	05	67	52
NO DIESELS GRAND CENTRAL/PRR IN NEW YORK	04	39	76
OIL COLLECTION PANS FOR DIESEL TERMINALS	03	74	48
OLDEST RAILROAD TICKET OFFICE NC&F	05	31	284
ONE STOP DIESEL SERVICING FACILITY	08	67	31
PASSENGER ELEVATOR ELD WEEHAWKEN NJ	08	51	95
PASSENGER STATION GRAND CENTRAL NYC DATA	08	31	46
PASSENGER STATION TYPE DEFINITIONS	01	65	29
PASSENGER STATIONS: 50,000	03	41	06
PASSENGER TERMINALS IN CHICAGO ILL	02	36	87
PENN STATION-MANHATTAN MONUMENT	08	71	28
PORTABLE CAR WASHER C&NW	04	46	63
RADAR SPEED DETECTORS ON THE RAILROADS	04	61	35
RAILROAD DEPOTS--6 SHORT CLIPS ABOUT	02	38	124
RAILROAD STATION CHAPEL PHILADELPHIA PA	02	35	43
RAILROAD STATION OWNED BY AGENT LV	11	36	138
RAILROAD STATIONS AS HISTORICAL LANDMARK	10	75	58
REDBALL TERMINAL PRR ENOLA PA	11	41	06
ROMANCE OF STATION BELLS	12	50	70
ROUNDHOUSE TRACTOR	07	53	06
ROUNDHOUSES--WORLD'S LARGEST	03	33	94
SAND TOWER FOR DIESELS	02	56	38
SAND TOWER FOR DIESELS BY ROSS &WHITE CO	02	56	38
SHEDS: "BUSH TRAINSHED"	09	45	60

Stephans' Railroad Directory

Railroad/Railfan

STRUCTURES VEHICLES & SIGNALS

STRUCTURE, SIGNAL & VEHICLE PROTOTYPES	M	Y	P
SINGLE ENGINE HOUSE PRR: DIMENSIONS	01	37	88
SIZES OF WAITING ROOMS IN NY & PHILY	12	60	30
SNO "BUSH TRAINSHED" DL&W	09	75	58
SNO ARMSTRONG TURNTABLES	11	72	54
SNO AUTOMATIC ENGINE WASHERS	01	66	24
SNO AUTOMATIC YARD EJ&W KIRK INDIANA	04	56	43
SNO B&M USE OF WATER SCOOPS 1887	07	75	52
SNO B&O: WORLDS OLDEST STATION	06	67	35
SNO B&O:FIRST RR STATION IN WASHINGTN DC	04	64	28
SNO B&O:STATION WHEELING W VA	04	62	46
SNO BIRM:OWNS TEMINAL STATION BIRMINGHAM	08	69	27
SNO BUMPING POSTS: MADE OF WOOD/STEEL	12	55	38
SNO COALING DOCK CN TEESWATER ONTARIO	10	59	08
SNO COST TO ELIMINATE GRADE CROSSINGS	10	73	58
SNO CP FACILITY AGINCOURT ONT	09	75	56
SNO DEPOT PRR BALTIMORE MD	08	57	44
SNO DEPOT V&T CARSON CITY NV NOW MASONIC	04	55	75
SNO DIESEL SERVICING CENTER OF E IN OHIO	12	44	43
SNO DIESEL TRACK PANS	02	75	51
SNO FREIGHT YARD AT CONWAY PA PRR	04	56	37
SNO GAVIN YARD GN AT MINOT ND	10	58	06
SNO GM&O PASSENGER STATION MOBILE AL	10	62	35
SNO GN:DIESEL SERVICE FACILITY HAVRE MT	05	69	31
SNO GRADE CROSSINGS OF STEEL	01	72	54
SNO HUMP YARDS	10	74	45
SNO IC BURNSIDE SHOPS MIDWEST LARGEST	08	76	50
SNO IRON RATS ON GRAND CENTRAL TERMINAL	08	65	19
SNO MILLION DOLLAR STATION B&A WORCESTER	05	76	25
SNO MILW:LARGEST ROUNDHOUSE LOCATIONS	12	72	59
SNO NYC:ABANDONING SYRACUSE TERMINAL	08	65	20
SNO NYNH&H: RUBBER GRADE CROSSINGS	11	70	42
SNO PAY RAILROAD TOILETS PRR 1910	11	75	46
SNO PC DEPOT LANCASTER PA DETERIORATION	08	74	44
SNO PC STATION WATERBURY CT ITALIAN TOWE	02	76	45
SNO PRR:EAGLES FROM PENN STA DISPOSITION	05	67	28
SNO R TIDEWATER TERMINAL AT PORT RICHMON	06	58	39
SNO RUBBER GRADE CROSSINGS	02	69	06
SNO SP:SNOWSHED VENTILATION	05	73	35
SNO STATION PHILADELPHIA PA B&O	08	76	51
SNO STATION PRR NORTHCUMBERLAND PA	02	59	37
SNO SUBURBAN STATION GN EDMONDS WA	06	57	40
SNO TRACK PANS FOR WATER PICKUP	07	74	41
SNO TRACK SCALE	01	46	60
SNO TRAIN SHEDS FOR PASSENGERS	02	66	28
SNO UP:LONGEST TURNTABLE IN US	04	67	28
SNO WATER TOWERS ON ATSF	12	54	09
STANDARD RAILROAD YARD	12	45	62
STATION B&O CAMDEN STN BALTIMORE MD	01	53	54
STATION C&O PRINCE WV RADIANT HEATED DAT	07	47	69
STATION CLEVELAND OHIO'S SKYSCRAPER	06	51	19
STATION HOUSTON UNION--ITS HISTORY	09	52	14
STATION NASHVILLE UNION STATION:CORRECT	04	49	132
STATION NEW ORLEANS UNION STN (5 ROADS)	04	48	71
STATION P&R SANBURY PA 1ST ELECTRIC LITE	06	58	34
STATION PRR LEVITTOWN PA	03	53	61
STATION PRR PITTSBURG PA MOST TRAINS/DAY	06	76	54
STATION SERVING MOST ROADS SL MO UNION	01	78	47
STATION ST LOUIS UNION-SERVES 17 ROADS/T	06	54	56
STATION TOLEDO OHIO DATA	08	58	40
STATIONS BETWEEN NY & MANHATTAN BEACH	08	32	57
STATIONS BUILT OVER BROOKS	05	44	126
STATIONS LV 4 ERECTED AT EASTON PA	06	44	124
STATIONS NEW AND OLD (CB&Q) PHOTO ESSAY	12	54	26
STATIONS ON NYBR&J	02	33	87
STATIONS WITH STREET NUMBERS	05	43	138
STATIONS: 5 UNUSUAL WITH DRAWINGS	09	37	101
SUNNYSIDE YARD PRR	05	48	10
TANK CAR REPAIR BLDG UTCC DOME SHAPED	02	59	06
THE "DEEPO" RAILROAD STATION MEMORIES	04	46	108
THREE LEVEL RAILROAD STATIONS	01	69	33
TRACK SCALE BALDWIN SR-4 ELECTRONIC DATA	01	54	67
TRAIN ORDER STATION ATSF VICTORVILLE	08	48	28
TRAINSHED-LAST READING TERMINAL PHILA PA	03	85	32
TURNTABLE: ON ITS WAY OUT??	05	55	13
TURNTABLES-LARGEST 135' NP	02	39	91
TURNTABLES: REPLACING	08	43	146
TURNTABLES: SMALL/BRANCH LINES HAND-OPER	09	38	55
TURNTABLES: THEIR HISTORY	04	43	08
UNION STATION HOUSTON TX	09	52	14
UNION STATION LOUISVILLE KY L&N	11	67	17
UNION STATION ST LOUIS MO ERECTED 1875	02	47	10
UNION STATIONS COUNTRY WIDE	11	71	24
UNION STATIONS: WHO OWNS?	05	37	38
UNION TERMINAL CLEVELAND OH	06	51	18
UP AMES MONUMENT	11	36	27
VANISHING WATER TANKS	06	63	13
WATER STOPS FOR STEAM LOCOS	10	55	12
WATER TANKS & COLUMNS	10	55	12
WATER TANKS OF DL&W WOODEN & STEEL	05	31	243
WATER TOWER (TWIN SPOUT) C&A FRANCIS MO	08	66	31
WATER TOWER-TWO SPOUT-READER INFORMATION	05	66	55
WATER TOWERS STILL STANDING	10	63	42
WATER TRACK PANS ADDITIONAL LOCATIONS	01	70	09
WELDING TORCHES IN ENGINE SHOPS	05	45	54
WINDMILL USED TO PUMP WATER UP	03	34	96

SIGNAL PROTOTYPE DATA

	M	Y	P
5 WAYS OF SIGNALLING THE SAME TRAIN MOVE	04	41	44
ABSOLUTE-PERMISSIVE BLOCK SIGNAL SYSTEM	12	29	97
AUTO CONTROL FOR SPEED (LIGHT SENSOR)	02	30	467
AUTO TRAIN OPERATION CN GREAT SLAVE LAKE	04	69	29
AUTOMATIC BLOCK SIGNALS:DIAGRAM/HOW WORK	03	34	84
AUTOMATIC INTERLOCKING MACHINE: HOW IT W	12	55	40
AUTOMATIC SIGNALING	01	47	50
AUTOMATIC TRAIN CONTROL	02	42	38
AUTOMATIC TRAIN CONTROLS	02	30	385
AUTOMATIC TRAIN CONTROLS.	07	43	64
BALL SIGNALS: UPPER NEW ENGLAND	09	45	88
BANJO SIGNALS	07	54	59
BLOCK SIGNALS: AUTOMATIC	03	30	574

Railroad/ Railfan

STRUCTURES VEHICLES & SIGNALS

STRUCTURE, SIGNAL & VEHICLE PROTOTYPES	M	Y	P
BLOCK SIGNALS: WITH 2 OR 3 SIGNAL ARMS	06	32	339
BLUE & PURPLE LIGHT SIGNIFICANCE	04	66	10
BROADWAY CROSSING IC MEMPHIS TN	03	72	07
BUSIEST MANUALLY OPERATED CROSSING OHIO	10	43	94
CAB SIGNALS AND TRAIN CONTROL	04	60	33
CAB SIGNALS-EARLY	10	52	48
CATENARY W/LEFT-HANDED SEMAPHORES NYNH&H	04	59	50
COLOR LIGHT SIGNALS B&M	04	34	82
COLOR LIGHT SIGNALS-ERIE	08	32	55
CROSSING SIGNAL SP	05	31	279
CTC DEFINITION	06	62	45
CTC SIGNAL OPERATION READER INFO ATSF	04	78	56
DWARF SEMAPHORE SIGNAL	10	32	346
DWARF SIGNAL	12	31	94
DWARF SIGNAL LIGHT: RED OR PURPLE	10	34	84
DWARF SIGNAL-WHAT IS IT?	07	77	48
EARLY CAB SIGNALS PRR	01	53	123
ELEVATION MARKER ERIE	12	47	82
FIRST INTERLOCKING SIGNAL SYSTEM DISCUSS	09	66	33
FIRST SIGNAL SYSTEMS IN US (NC&F)	04	66	34
FLAG SIGNALS ON STEAM LOCOMOTIVES	04	60	30
FLAG SIGNALS ON STEAM LOCOMOTIVES.	04	66	37
FLAGMAN REQUIREMENTS FOR STOPPED TRAINS	10	65	27
FLAGS ABOVE CLASSIFICATION LIGHTS	07	34	88
FLAGS PRR	12	31	91
FLAGS: WHITE/GREEN	09	38	58
FLAGS: WHITE/GREEN DESIGNATIONS	11	38	71
FLANGER SIGN	12	36	51
FLANGER SIGN CGW FAIRBANKS IA PHOTO	02	56	42
FLANGER SIGN: DESCRIBED/PURPOSE	03	46	74
FR FOREIGN RAILROAD	03	39	36
FR ENGLAND: FOG SIGNALMEN	03	39	36
FR SEMAPHORE SIGNALS GN IN ENGLAND	08	33	130
FUSEE AND TORPEDOS	08	51	12
FUSEE RULES FOR SLOW MOVING TRAINS	01	78	06
FUSEE-15 MINUTE RED/GREEN/WHITE	08	56	39
GALLOWS TYPE SIGNAL DESCRIPTION	06	66	33
GRADE CROSSING DEFINITION	10	34	81
HIGHBALL SIGNAL B&M/MC WAUMBEK JCT NH	07	71	06
HIGHBALL SIGNALS WHITEFIELD NH B&M/MC	05	71	40
HOBO SIGN LANGUAGE	04	67	30
HOME SIGNAL & DISTANT SIGNALS	03	71	60
INTERLOCKING	08	42	85
INTERLOCKING MACHINE	07	39	109
INTERLOCKING SIGNAL DESCRIPTION	03	37	60
LAMP/SIGNAL MARKERS ON CABOOSES	08	35	87
LANTERN GLOBE COLOR DISCUSSION	11	68	36
LANTERN STORY: WHALE-OIL TO ELECTRIC	09	76	11
LEFT-HANDED SIGNALING ADVANTAGES L&N	11	66	39
LIGHT SIGNALS ON REAR OF TRAIN RULES	04	66	38
MANUAL BLOCK SIGNALS ON CB&Q	05	66	35
MARKERS (REAR SIGAL LAMPS)	08	35	81
MARKERS: THEIR HISTORY/TYPES	06	59	26
OWL-FACED SIGNALS OF H&M MECHANISM & OPR	11	64	36
PARTLY COLORED LANTERN GLOBES READER INF	10	62	36

STRUCTURE, SIGNAL & VEHICLE PROTOTYPES	M	Y	P
POSITION TYPE SIGNAL PRR	12	31	91
PUZZLING SIGNAL SET UP-MP LITTLE ROCK AK	06	60	42
RAILROAD CROSSING SIGN CNE SALISBURY CT	07	49	130
RAILROAD SIGNALS IN GENERAL	10	37	04
RAILWAY FUSEE-COMPOSITION OF	05	37	37
RAILWAY FUSEE: WARNING SIGNAL/COMPOSITIO	05	37	37
REAR MARKERS IN FOUR-TRACK OPERATIONS	04	37	48
RED BLOCK SIGNAL SYSTEM DESCRIBED	05	53	64
RED DESIGNATION ON PRR REPLACING 3 YELLO	08	63	31
SEARCHLIGHT SIGNAL 1ST USED ON GT 1920	10	52	67
SEARCHLIGHT SIGNALS(PRE-CRACKING ROUNDEL	11	46	66
SEMAPHORE ELECTRICALLY OPERATED JCE	08	43	137
SEMAPHORE PROBLEMS	08	39	113
SEMAPHORE SIGNAL ORIGIN	06	49	64
SEMAPHORE SIGNAL POSITIONS	10	56	46
SEMAPHORE SIGNALS-SQUARE VS POINTED ENDS	08	38	90
SEMAPHORE UPPER QUADRANT PHOTO	10	47	64
SEMAPHORES NYNH&H (LEFT-HANDED) PHOTO	02	59	31
SIGN "STOP, LOOK, LISTEN" ORIGINATION	08	49	51
SIGN "W": WHISTLE FOR A GRADE CROSSING	01	36	86
SIGN: NC WARNING SIGN	02	47	61
SIGNAL B&M LANTERN IN BALL SIGNAL DATA	01	55	38
SIGNAL BANJO (ENCLOSED DISK BLOCK) DATA	10	50	136
SIGNAL BLOCK SIGNAL RULES DEFINITIONS	10	56	47
SIGNAL BRIDGE: WHAT IS IT??	11	54	36
SIGNAL CIRCUITS DETECT PARTED RAILS	09	72	54
SIGNAL CROSS-BUCK SIGN ORIGIN	11	54	33
SIGNAL FLAGS FRISCO--HOW THEY ARE MADE	05	31	247
SIGNAL MAINTAINERS (SP)	08	46	07
SIGNALING & ELECTRONICS 1	10	47	63
SIGNALING & ELECTRONICS 2	11	47	78
SIGNALING AN INTERLOCKED TERMINAL	04	40	110
SIGNALS: AUTOMATIC BLOCK	01	35	87
SIGNALS: BALL-TYPE STILL IN USE?	02	58	40
SIGNALS: BANJO TYPE (FIRST AUTO SIGNAL)	07	54	59
SIGNALS: CALL-ON	11	37	50
SIGNALS: DEVELOPMENT/TYPES/WAY THEY WORK	10	37	05
SIGNS: UNOFFICIAL HAND SIGNALS	11	41	25
SLOW SPEED BOARDS	11	37	50
SNO "STOP, LOOK, LISTEN" SIGN	06	44	82
SNO "STOP, LOOK, LISTEN" SIGN	06	44	82
SNO B&M: BALL SIGNALS IN USE 1965	10	65	28
SNO B&M:ANOTHER HIGHBALL SIGNAL	07	71	06
SNO BART AUTOMATIC RUNNING SYSTEM	05	73	60
SNO BURNING COLORS OF FUSEES 1903	07	74	03
SNO CAB SIGNALS	10	73	58
SNO CENTRALIZED TRAFFIC CONTROL	06	73	48
SNO CENTRALIZED TRAFFIC CONTROL ON SP	11	44	100
SNO CN: CTC INSTALLED BOSTON BAR	02	68	31
SNO CTC INSTALLATIONS ON CN	12	44	43
SNO CV:SIGNALING TYPES USED	10	68	34
SNO DEADMAN'S THROTTLE	06	57	43
SNO DEVICE DETECTS OBSTRUCTIONS OF TRACK	06	57	43
SNO EARLY CCT INSTALLATIONS	07	66	38
SNO ELECTRIC AUTO BLOCK SIGNALS C&NW	05	54	82

Railroad/Railfan

STRUCTURES   VEHICLES   & SIGNALS

STRUCTURE, SIGNAL & VEHICLE PROTOTYPES	M	Y	P
SNO FIRST CTC INSTALLATIONS (NYC)	09	74	43
SNO FIRST SEARCHLIGHT SIGNAL GT 1920	05	75	51
SNO FIRST SWITCH LAMPS IN US	05	75	52
SNO GREEN & WHITE FLAGS ON LOCOS	10	74	46
SNO HIGH BALL TERM	06	74	21
SNO ILLUMINATED TRACK DIGRAMS FOR DISPAT	08	66	31
SNO LOCOMOTIVE FLAG MEANINGS	02	72	61
SNO POWER INTERLOCKING	08	66	31
SNO RAILROAD LANTERNS	12	67	25
SNO SEMAPHORE INVENTION	07	74	40
SNO SIGNAL DWARF: LIGHT SIGNAL	03	55	30
SNO SIGNAL SYSTEM ATSF AT CAJUN PASS	06	44	83
SNO SIGNALS: COLOR LIGHT ON LV	06	45	59
SNO STRANGE LAMPS ON NYNH&H MT VERNON NY	11	73	02
SNO TERM "30" ENDING MESSAGES	11	72	54
SNO THIN PAPER FOR TRAIN ORDERS	10	72	53
SNO TORPEDOES: 2 SIGNAL REDUCE SPEED	08	56	44
SNO WHISTLE SIGNALS OF STEAM & DIESELS	08	65	21
SNO WORKING OF AUTO BLOCK SIGNALS	05	72	57
STANDARD TRAIN COMMUNICATION SIGNALS	10	45	49
STATION ORDER BOARD: SEMAPHORE	10	34	81
STOP LOOK LISTEN/RAILROAD CROSSING SIGNS	11	39	77
STOP SIGNALS AT NIGHT FOR FLAG STOPS	08	63	33
STOP, LOOK AND LISTEN SLOGAN	02	36	84
SWITCH LAMPS: HISTORY	04	51	72
SWITCH LOCKS S WHY NUB AT BOTTOM?	12	43	76
SWITCH STANDS-VARIOUS ROADS-DRAWINGS	09	43	96
SWITCH: ELECTRIC-USED BY STREET RAILWAYS	03	39	71
TELEGRAPH CODES FOR TRAIN CONTROL 1910	10	78	48
TELEGRAPH KEY, SOUNDER AND RELAYS	08	72	58
TELEPHONE DISPATCHING OF TRAINS	06	77	52
TISSUE PAPER USED FOR TRAIN ORDERS	07	38	76
TRACK TORPEDOES	06	50	36
TRACK WASHOUTS AND SIGNAL DESIGNATION AD	01	73	61
TRACKSIDE SIGNAL HISTORY	08	57	20
TRAIN COMMUNICATION SIGNALS	10	45	47
TRAIN CONTROL: INTERMITTENT/CONTINOUS	01	36	82
TRAIN HOOP ORDERS	09	41	19
TRAIN-ORDER CRANES--HOW THEY WORK	10	54	40
TRAIN-ORDER STAND FOR HIGH SPEEDS	06	46	68
TRAINMAN SIGNALS HAND/FLAG/LAMP	06	34	85
TRAINMAN'S HAND LANTERN SIGNALS	08	56	41
TRAINMAN'S HAND LANTERN: LANGUAGE OF OWN	01	53	34
TWIN ORDER BOARDS CV/B&M MILLERS FALL MA	08	46	91
WHISTLE BLASTS FOR GRADE CROSSINGS	10	71	45
WHISTLE CODES	12	42	70
WHISTLE SIGNAL FOR HIGHWAY CROSSINGS	05	39	68
WHISTLE SIGNALS	12	42	70
WHISTLE SIGNALS OF STEAM & DIESEL LOCOS	08	65	20
WHISTLE SIGNALS USED BY LOCOMOTIVES	02	32	328
WHISTLE SIGNALS.	05	45	30
WHISTLE SIGNALS: 4 OR 5 LONG BLASTS	07	36	83
WHISTLE SIGNALS: 4 SHORT BLASTS	04	66	34
WHISTLE SIGNALS: CHART OF	04	40	79
WHISTLE SIGNALS: CHART OF WHISTLE SIGNAL	05	55	35

STRUCTURE, SIGNAL & VEHICLE PROTOTYPES	M	Y	P
WHISTLE SIGNALS: COMMUNICATING	06	40	71
WHISTLE SIGNALS: DRAWING/HOW THEY WORK	01	55	37
WHISTLE SIGNALS: FLAGMAN	04	32	68
WIG WAG SIGNAL INVENTOR J HUGHSON	04	77	51
YARD SWITCH MACHINE: WHAT IS IT?	08	57	44
YELLOW FLAG SIGNALS & BLUE FLAGS	06	63	25

* VEHICLE PROTOTYPE DATA *

	M	Y	P
1957 PONTIAC STN WAGON HIGHWAY-RAILCAR	02	58	40
BRUCK: COMBINATION BUS-TRUCK GN	08	56	41
CAR FERRIES C&O: SS BADGER & SS SPARTAN	02	53	57
CAR FERRY C&O PERE MARQUETTE LENGTHENED	10	53	70
CAR FERRY GT "LANSDOWNE" CORRECT	07	46	57
CAR FERRY PM #10 BUILT IN 1945 DATA	06	46	74
CHESSIE'S FAIRBANKS-MORSE TUG FAIRWELL	07	84	34
EVANS AUTO-RAILER: HISTORY/DATA	08	42	94
FERRY BOAT DL&W SPECIFICATIONS	06	59	38
GN STEAMSHIP HISTORICAL INFORMATION	12	78	47
QUEBEC'S NEW RAIL FERRY	04	78	54
RAILWAY FERRIES-93 YEARS ON SF BAY	01	65	13
RIVER BOATS USE AFTER CAR FERRYS READER	12	72	11
ROUNDHOUSE TRACTOR	07	53	06
RUBBER TIRED SWITCHERS B&O--PC	02	78	50R
SIDE-WHEEL TRAIN FERRY "LANSDOWNE" GT	03	46	75
SIDEWHEELER "PELICAN" COMMENTS	07	67	34
SNO AA:CAR FERRIES	03	72	63
SNO CHESSIE MARINE FLEET	11	75	41
SNO CP: SHIPS ON THE GREAT LAKES	06	77	51
SNO CP: STEAMBOAT "PRINCESS MARGUERITE"	03	75	11
SNO CP: STEAMSHIP "PRINCESS OF ARCADIA"	06	75	30
SNO CP: VICTORIA-SEATTLE STEAMSHIPS	02	78	50
SNO IC:CAR FERRY "PELICAN"	05	67	28
SNO NP:TACOMA TRAIN-FERRY	02	72	62
SNO SH&P: SIDEWHEELER "PELICAN"	07	67	35
SNO W&BA: CAR FERRY SUSQUEHANNA (FIRST)	02	78	49
SNO WP&Y STERNWHEELER FERRYS DISPOSITION	09	74	44
STEAM WAGONS IN THE WEST	11	40	84
SWITCHMOBILE PRR 4 WHEEL DIESEL SWITCH	12	56	32
TRAIN FERRIES	11	54	10
TUGBOAT E "ROCHESTER" DIESEL TUG	02	47	66
TUGBOAT NYC #25 PAINTED GRAY	01	53	61
TUGBOAT NYNH&H TRANSFER #21 W/RADAR EQUI	03	48	58
VELOCIPEDE/HANDCARS/PUSHCARS	07	40	70

RD	STRUCTURE, SIGNAL & VEHICLE PROTOS BY RD	M	Y	P
A	DIESEL SHOP AMTRAK COLLINWOOD OHIO	08	77	55
AA	SNO AA:CAR FERRIES	03	72	63
ATSF	CLEBURNE SHOPS OF ATSF	02	78	55
	CTC SIGNAL OPERATION READER INFO ATSF	04	78	56
	TRAIN ORDER STATION ATSF VICTORVILLE	08	48	28
	INGLEWOOD STATION INGLEWOOD CA ATSF	03	48	69
	SNO WATER TOWERS ON ATSF	12	54	09
	HARVEY HOUSES	04	58	44
	SNO SIGNAL SYSTEM ATSF AT CAJUN PASS	06	44	83

Railroad/Railfan

STRUCTURES, VEHICLES & SIGNALS

RD	STRUCTURE, SIGNAL & VEHICLE PROTOS BY RD	M	Y	P
B&A	SNO MILLION DOLLAR STATION B&A WORCESTER	05	76	25
B&M	SNO FIRST BIG US TUNNEL B&M HOOSAC	05	72	56
	SNO B&M:ANOTHER HIGHBALL SIGNAL	07	71	06
	HIGHBALL SIGNAL B&M/MC WAUMBEK JCT NH	07	71	06
	SNO B&M USE OF WATER SCOOPS 1887	07	75	52
	SNO FIRST ELECTRICS IN HOOSAC TUNNEL B&M	01	75	55
	SNO REMOVAL OF ELECTRIC WIRE IN HOOSAC T	09	77	53
	TUNNEL HOOSAC B&M ITS HISTORY	06	55	35
	SIGNAL B&M LANTERN IN BALL SIGNAL DATA	01	55	38
	HOOSAC TUNNEL HISTORY B&M	06	55	35
	SNO B&M: BALL SIGNALS IN USE 1965	10	65	28
	COLOR LIGHT SIGNALS B&M	04	34	82
B&O	MRS HOWARDS HOTEL ROWLESBURG WV B&O	SU	75	64R
	SNO B&O: WORLDS OLDEST STATION	06	67	35
	SAVAGE MD IRON BRIDGE B&O OLDEST IN US	02	67	26
	RUBBER TIRED SWITCHERS B&O--PC	02	78	50R
	DEPOT B&O "POINT OF ROCKS" HISTORICAL IN	12	78	47
	SNO STATION PHILADELPHIA PA B&O	08	76	51
	STATION B&O CAMDEN STN BALTIMORE MD	01	53	54
	SNO B&O:FIRST RR STATION IN WASHINGTN DC	04	64	28
	SNO B&O:STATION WHEELING W VA	04	62	46
	PASS/FRT STATION BALTIMORE MD "OLDEST"	01	31	284
BART	SNO BART AUTOMATIC RUNNING SYSTEM	05	73	60
	SNO BART LONGEST UNDER WATER TRANS TUBE	07	69	34
BIRM	SNO BIRM:OWNS TEMINAL STATION BIRMINGHAM	08	69	27
C&A	WATER TOWER (TWIN SPOUT) C&A FRANCIS MO	08	66	31
C&EI	1957 PONTIAC STN WAGON HIGHWAY-RAILCAR	02	58	40
C&NW	SNO ELECTRIC AUTO BLOCK SIGNALS C&NW	05	54	82
	SALVAGING C&NW BRIDGE SHAWANO-OCONTO JCT	07	38	123
	PORTABLE CAR WASHER C&NW	04	46	63
	BOONE VIADUCT C&NW HIGHEST DOUBLE DECK	06	34	87
C&O	CAR FERRIES C&O: SS BADGER & SS SPARTAN	02	53	57
	CAR FERRY C&O PERE MARQUETTE LENGTHENED	10	53	70
	COALING STATION C&O (MODERN)	09	47	74
	STATION C&O PRINCE WV RADIANT HEATED DAT	07	47	69
	BIG BEND TUNNEL: C&O	03	41	71
	TUNNEL BIG BEN C&O HINTON/CLIFTON FORGE	08	34	84
CB&Q	STATIONS NEW AND OLD (CB&Q) PHOTO ESSAY	12	54	26
	MANUAL BLOCK SIGNALS ON CB&Q	05	66	35
CGW	FLANGER SIGN CGW FAIRBANKS IA PHOTO	02	56	42
CHESS	CHESSIE'S FAIRBANKS-MORSE TUG FAIRWELL	07	84	34
	SNO CHESSIE MARINE FLEET	11	75	41
CN	SNO CN ST CLAIR TUNNEL	06	73	48
	SNO CN: CTC INSTALLED BOSTON BAR	02	68	31
	QUEBEC'S NEW RAIL FERRY	04	78	54
	AUTO TRAIN OPERATION CN GREAT SLAVE LAKE	04	69	29
	SNO ST LAWRENCE BRIDGE CN LONGEST CANTIL	11	74	51
	SNO CN ST JOHN RIVER BRIDGE	03	78	09
	SNO CN LETHBRIDGE VIADUCT (HIGHEST)	05	76	24
	SNO QUEBEC BRIDGE CN ST LAWRENCE RIVER	10	76	47
	BRIDGE CN QUEBEC BRIDGE HISTORY OF	05	48	63
	QUEBEC BRIDGE ON CN	05	48	63
	TUNNEL CN MOUNT ROYAL TUNNEL HISTORY/DAT	08	51	66
	SNO CTC INSTALLATIONS ON CN	12	44	43
	SNO COALING DOCK CN TEESWATER ONTARIO	10	59	08
	TUNNEL CN ST CLAIR	01	42	63
	QUEBEC BRIDGE CN	03	30	597
CNE	RAILROAD CROSSING SIGN CNE SALISBURY CT	07	49	130
CNJ	HARBORSIDE COAL LOADER ON CNJ	11	51	42
CNO&TP	HIGH BRIDGE CNO&TP (SOUTHERN) DANVILLE K	06	77	53
CP	SNO CP: STEAMBOAT "PRINCESS MARQUERITE"	03	75	11
	SNO CP: STEAMSHIP "PRINCESS OF ARCADIA"	06	75	30
	SNO CP: SHIPS ON THE GREAT LAKES	06	77	51
	SNO CP: VICTORIA-SEATTLE STEAMSHIPS	02	78	50
	SNO CP FACILITY AGINCOURT ONT	09	75	56
	SPIRAL TUNNEL CP MT OGDEN BC	05	74	12
	BASCULE JACKNIFE BRIDGE CP UNIQUE CONST	01	78	12
	SNO CP REPLACEMENT OF MOUNTAIN CREEK BRI	02	78	09
	SNO CONNAUGHT TUNNEL CP LONGEST	06	76	50
	LETHBRIDGE VIADUCT CP 5327'	07	45	79
CR	HOSPITAL FOR WHEELS (CR)	07	77	56
CV	SNO CV:SIGNALING TYPES USED	10	68	34
	TWIN ORDER BOARDS CV/B&M MILLERS FALL MA	08	46	91
D&RGW	SNO MOFFAT TUNNEL BEGUN 1923	07	74	39
D&SL	TUNNEL D&SL MOFFAT TUNNEL	09	31	187
DL&W	FERRY BOAT DL&W SPECIFICATIONS	06	59	38
	WATER TANKS OF DL&W WOODEN & STEEL	05	31	243
	SNO "BUSH TRAINSHED" DL&W	09	75	58
	NICHOLSON BRIDGE DL&W CONCRETE ARCH	10	46	54
	TUNKHANNOCK VIADUCT DL&W--HISTORY	02	34	86
	TUNNEL DL&W OXFORD TUNNEL: DIMENSIONS	07	36	87
E	TUGBOAT E "ROCHESTER" DIESEL TUG	02	47	66
	ERIE JERSEY CITY DEPOT CONSTRUCTION	02	60	32
	KINZUA BRIDGE SHORT HISTORY	11	65	23
	SNO R TIDEWATER TERMINAL AT PORT RICHMON	06	58	39
	SNO DIESEL SERVICING CENTER OF E IN OHIO	12	44	43
	STARUCCA VIADUCT ERIE NEAR SUSQUEHANNA P	02	46	107
	ELEVATION MARKER ERIE	12	47	82
	VIADUCT: DECK PLATE GIRDER ERIE DATA	10	40	68
	STARUCCA VIADUCT ERIE 1200' DATA	08	40	63
	COLOR LIGHT SIGNALS-ERIE	08	32	55
EJ&W	SNO AUTOMATIC YARD EJ&W KIRK INDIANA	04	56	43
EL	SNO EL NICHOLSON BRIDGE	06	62	43
ELD	PASSENGER ELEVATOR ELD WEEHAWKEN NJ	08	51	95
FRIS	SIGNAL FLAGS FRISCO--HOW THEY ARE MADE	05	31	247
GM&O	SNO GM&O PASSENGER STATION MOBILE AL	10	62	35
GN	BRUCK: COMBINATION BUS-TRUCK GN	08	56	41
	GN STEAMSHIP HISTORICAL INFORMATION	12	78	47
	SNO GN:DIESEL SERVICE FACILITY HAVRE MT	05	69	31
	SNO PRINCE OF WALES HOTEL GN	03	76	56
	CASCADE TUNNEL GN.	11	49	48
	SNO GAVIN YARD GN AT MINOT ND	10	58	06
	SNO SWING DRAW BRIDGE SPAN GN PUGET SOUN	04	55	35
	SNO SUBURBAN STATION GN EDMONDS WA	06	57	40
	CASCADE TUNNEL AIR COOLING GN	02	57	32
GT	SIDE-WHEEL TRAIN FERRY "LANSDOWNE" GT	03	46	75
	CAR FERRY GT "LANSDOWNE" CORRECT	07	46	57
	SNO FIRST SEARCHLIGHT SIGNAL GT 1920	05	75	51
	SEARCHLIGHT SIGNAL 1ST USED ON GT 1920	10	52	67
	ST CLAIR TUNNEL GT BUILT 1880-1891	10	45	51

STEPHANS' RAILROAD DIRECTORY

Railroad/ Railfan

STRUCTURES VEHICLES & SIGNALS

RD	STRUCTURE, SIGNAL & VEHICLE PROTOS BY RD	M	Y	P
H&M	OWL-FACED SIGNALS OF H&M MECHANISM & OPR	11	64	36
IC	BROADWAY CROSSING IC MEMPHIS TN	03	72	07
	SNO IC BURNSIDE SHOPS MIDWEST LARGEST	08	76	50
	SNO IC:CAR FERRY "PELICAN"	05	67	28
	TUNNEL IC EDGEWOOED CUT-OFF	03	47	73
JCE	SEMAPHORE ELECTRICALLY OPERATED JCE	08	43	137
L&N	SNO PRE STRESSED CONCRETE BRIDGES	03	71	60
	ONE STOP DIESEL SERVICING FACILITY	08	67	31
	UNION STATION LOUISVILLE KY L&N	11	67	17
	LEFT-HANDED SIGNALING ADVANTAGES L&N	11	66	39
	GREEN RIVER BRIDGE L&N'S LARGEST	12	33	141
LV	RAILROAD STATION OWNED BY AGENT LV	11	36	138
	STATIONS LV 4 ERECTED AT EASTON PA	06	44	124
	SNO SIGNALS: COLOR LIGHT ON LV	06	45	59
MC	HIGHBALL SIGNALS WHITEFIELD NH B&M/MC	05	71	40
MILW	SNO MILW:LARGEST ROUNDHOUSE LOCATIONS	12	72	59
MKT	SNO MKT POSEY HOLE BRIDGE PROJECT	05	76	25
	BRIDGE MKT POSEY HOLE DATA	09	47	73
MP	CLAMSHELL LOADING OF COAL CHUTES MP	08	75	05
	PUZZLING SIGNAL SET UP-MP LITTLE ROCK AK	06	60	42
N&WO	SNO TUNNEL LISBON CT N&WO OLDEST TUNNEL	10	76	47
NC&F	FIRST SIGNAL SYSTEMS IN US (NC&F)	04	66	34
	OLDEST RAILROAD TICKET OFFICE NC&F	05	31	284
NC&SL	BRIDGE NC&SL DIXIE LINE BRIDGE/HISTORY	06	46	71
NKP	SNO LAST STEAM THROUGH HOOSAC NKP #759	03	74	34
NP	SNO NP:TACOMA TRAIN-FERRY	02	72	62
	STAMPEDE PASS TUNNEL NP	01	79	43
	BLOW-DOWN SHEDS FOR STEAM LOCOS	02	78	50
	BLOW-DOWN SHED NP BILLINGS MONTANA	08	54	42
	TURNTABLES-LARGEST 135' NP	02	39	91
NSO	NSO 5 MILE BRIDGE ALBERMARIE SOUND NC	01	39	61
NYBR&J	STATIONS ON NYBR&J	02	33	87
NYC	TUGBOAT NYC #25 PAINTED GRAY	01	53	61
	SNO NYC DRAW BRIDGE NEVER OPENED-70 YEAR	11	72	08
	SNO FIRST CTC INSTALLATIONS (NYC)	09	74	43
	GRAND CENTRAL TERMINAL NYC	09	78	24
	GRAND CENTRAL TERMINAL NYC NEW YORK NY	08	65	27
	SNO NYC:ABANDONING SYRACUSE TERMINAL	08	65	20
NYC&HR	GRAND CENTRAL TRIAPARTITE AGREEMENT (NY)	05	72	56
NYNH&H	TUGBOAT NYNH&H TRANSFER #21 W/RADAR EQUI	03	48	58
	SNO STRANGE LAMPS ON NYNH&H MT VERNON NY	11	73	02
	SNO NYNH&H: RUBBER GRADE CROSSINGS	11	70	42
	BRIDGE NYNH&H BUZZARD BAY MA VERTICAL LI	07	52	65
	HELL GATE BRIDGE CONSTRUCTION NYNH&H	04	37	138
	CATENARY W/LEFT-HANDED SEMAPHORES NYNH&H	04	59	50
	SEMAPHORES NYNH&H (LEFT-HANDED) PHOTO	02	59	31
	NYNH&H BRIDGE ACRSOSS HUDSON POUGHKEEPSI	08	31	45
O&M	THE "DEEPO" RAILROAD STATION MEMORIES	04	46	108
P&BPR	SNO P&BPR TOLL BRIDGE CHARGES FOR LOCOS	11	66	38
P&R	BRIDGES: 1ST IRON RAIL RR BRIDGE P&R	08	51	69
	STATION P&R SANBURY PA 1ST ELECTRIC LITE	06	58	34
PC	SNO PC ROCKVILLE BRIDGE LONGEST STONE AR	04	72	66
	SNO BUZZARDS BAY LIFT BRIDGE PC	04	75	11
	SNO PC DEPOT LANCASTER PA DETERIORATION	08	74	44
	SNO PC STATION WATERBURY CT ITALIAN TOWE	02	76	45
PM	CAR FERRY PM #10 BUILT IN 1945 DATA	06	46	74
PRR	SWITCHMOBILE PRR 4 WHEEL DIESEL SWITCH	12	56	32
	PENN STATION-MANHATTAN MONUMENT	08	71	28
	MULE OR BARNEY CAR PUSHER PRR LI YARD	05	67	52
	SNO PRR:EAGLES FROM PENN STA DISPOSITION	05	67	28
	BROAD STREET STATION PRR PHILA PA	05	67	16
	SNO PAY RAILROAD TOILETS PRR 1910	11	75	46
	STONE ARCH BRIDGES ON PRR	08	78	54
	STATION PRR PITTSBURG PA MOST TRAINS/DAY	06	76	54
	SUNNYSIDE YARD PRR	05	48	10
	LOCOMOTIVE WASHING MACHINE PRR	03	48	60
	EARLY CAB SIGNALS PRR	01	53	123
	STATION PRR LEVITTOWN PA	03	53	61
	SINGLE ENGINE HOUSE PRR: DIMENSIONS	01	37	88
	BRIDGES: IRON ON PRR	02	44	56
	BRIDGE PRR ROCKVILLE BRIDGE AT HARRISBUR	06	46	73
	SNO FREIGHT YARD AT CONWAY PA PRR	04	56	37
	SNO STATION PRR NORTHCUMBERLAND PA	02	59	37
	SNO DEPOT PRR BALTIMORE MD	08	57	44
	RED DESIGNATION ON PRR REPLACING 3 YELLO	08	63	31
	NO DIESELS GRAND CENTRAL/PRR IN NEW YORK	04	39	76
	POTOMAC RIVER BRIDGE REPLACEMENT PRR	09	45	60
	REDBALL TERMINAL PRR ENOLA PA	11	41	06
	FLAGS PRR	12	31	91
	POSITION TYPE SIGNAL PRR	12	31	91
	STONE ARCH BRIDGE PRR/STEEL TRUSS DOUBLE	02	35	84
	RAILROAD STATION CHAPEL PHILADELPHIA PA	02	35	43
	CATENARY POLES: PRR NUMBERING SYSTEM	02	36	85
R	TRAINSHED-LAST READING TERMINAL PHILA PA	03	85	32
RF&P	BRIDGE POTOMAC RIVER RF&P BRIEF HISTORY	08	34	85
RI	LASALLE STREET STATION RI CHICAGO IL	10	70	22
S	SNO NATURAL RR TUNNEL OF S IN VA	07	73	39
	HIGH BRIDGE S 1230' KENTUCKY RIVER	12	58	44
	SWITCH LOCKS S WHY NUB AT BOTTOM?	12	43	76
SH&P	SNO SH&P: SIDEWHEELER "PELICAN"	07	67	35
	SIDEWHEELER "PELICAN" COMMENTS	07	67	34
SOO	SNO SOO BRIDGE AT ST CROIX RIVER	09	75	59
	SNO SOO ST CROIX RIVER BRIDGE	04	70	34
	BRIDGE SOO ST CROIX RIVER ARCH BRIDGE	06	53	59
SP	SNO SP:SNOWSHED VENTILATION	05	73	35
	SNO SP TUNNEL ENLARGEMENTS 1968	03	68	26
	MEMORIES OF OLD BENICIA DEPOT SP	05	68	18
	SNO SP WORLDS LONGEST BRIDGE	06	69	39
	SNO SP PECOS RIVER BRIDGE (300' HIGH)	11	75	42
	PECOS RIVER BRIDGE (SP)	07	49	42
	SNO CENTRALIZED TRAFFIC CONTROL ON SP	11	44	100
	SIGNAL MAINTAINERS (SP)	08	46	07
	SALT LAKE FILL SP.	08	57	18
	PECOS HIGH BRIDGE SP---HISTORY	07	49	42
	BRIDGE SP PIT RIVER BRIDGE CALIFORNIA	07	42	69
	PECOS RIVER BRIDGE SP DATA	09	45	53
	CROSSING SIGNAL SP	05	31	279
T&NO	BRIDGE T&NO SINGLE-LEAF BASCULE BEAUMONT	08	52	67
UP	CAB SIGNALS & HOW THEY WORK	05	72	59
	ENGINEHOUSE LIST (UP)	06	71	59

Stephans' Railroad Directory

Railroad/Railfan

STRUCTURES VEHICLES & SIGNALS

RD	STRUCTURE, SIGNAL & VEHICLE PROTOS BY RD	M	Y	P
	SNO UP:LONGEST TURNTABLE IN US	04	67	28
	UP AMES MONUMENT	11	36	27
	ASPEN TUNNEL UP WYOMING	11	47	89
	WINDMILL USED TO PUMP WATER UP	03	34	96
UTCC	TANK CAR REPAIR BLDG UTCC DOME SHAPED	02	59	06
	GEODESIC DOME REPAIR SHOP OF UNION TANK.	02	59	06
V&SW	NATURAL TUNNEL V&SW	08	50	53
V&T	SNO DEPOT V&T CARSON CITY NV NOW MASONIC	04	55	75
W&BA	SNO W&BA: CAR FERRY SUSQUEHANNA (FIRST)	02	78	49
WP&Y	SNO WP&Y STERNWHEELER FERRYS DISPOSITION	09	74	44
WSH	GRAIN ELEVATOR WSH WEEHAWKEN NJ DATA	07	42	66

STRUCTURE, SIGNAL & VEHICLE PLANS

* BRIDGE PLANS *

	M	Y	P
BRIDGE PLANS HOWE THROUGH TRUSS BRIDGE	03	55	48
BRIDGES: DRAWBRIDGES (3 TYPES) DRAWINGS	02	48	19
CONCRETE OVERPASS PLANS	12	53	102
GIRDER BRIDGE PLANS	11	32	546
GIRDER BRIDGE/ABUTMENT PLANS	10	54	48
TRESTLE LOW, SINGLE TRACK DRAWING	01	33	103

* RAILROAD STRUCTURE PLANS *

	M	Y	P
COMBINATION FREIGHT/PASS STN MKT PLAN	09	32	225
COMBINATION STATION MKT DRAWING	09	32	227
ELEVATED WATCHMAN'S TOWER PLANS	10	53	99
GALLOWS TURNTABLE PLANS	05	55	78
SIGNAL TOWER PLANS..	09	50	103
STATION: CB&Q LA CROSSE WI DRAWING	03	41	28
STATIONS 5 UNUSUAL DRAWINGS	09	37	101
TANK CAR REPAIR BUILDING UTCC FLOOR PLAN	02	59	08
TOOL HOUSE AND HAND CAR PLANS	03	42	42
TRAIN SHED 1890'S PLANS	03	54	72
TRAIN SHED OPEN-AIR PLANS	05	54	86
WATER TANK AND TOWER PLAN	06	33	129
WATER TOWER PLANS	10	55	54
WAY STATION PLANS	12	39	52

* SIGNAL PLANS *

	M	Y	P
HIGH SPEED DELIVERY FORK DRAWING	12	39	124
INTERLOCKING: MANUAL DRAWING	08	42	87
SEMAPHORE STD 3 POSITION DRAWING	04	33	126
SIGNAL BRIDGE DRAWING	01	34	125
STANDARD TRAIN ORDER HOOP DRAWING	12	39	124

BRIDGE & TUNNEL PHOTOS

* BRIDGE PHOTOS *

	M	Y	P
BASCULE BRIDGE GN PHOTO	05	37	54
BERGEN TUNNEL PORTAL DL&W 1908 PHOTO	07	85	37
BRIDGE & TRESTLE CP PERRY SOUND ONT PHOT	03	70	18
BRIDGE BAR AROOSTOOK RIVER ASHLAND ME PH	10	76	16
BRIDGE CONSTRUCTION CROOKED RIVER OR PHO	08	77	61
BRIDGE CP SUMMERLAND BC PHOTO	03	76	32
BRIDGE IC CAIRO IL MODERNIZATION PHOTOS	07	52	112
BRIDGE NC&SL DIXIE LINE BRIDGE JOHNSVILE	06	46	72
BRIDGE NYC HARLEM RIVER NEW/OLD PHOTOS	09	51	60

BRIDGE & TUNNEL PHOTOS

	M	Y	P
BRIDGE NYNH&H BUZZARD BAY CADE COD MA PH	02	48	18
BRIDGE NYNH&H BUZZARD BAY VERTICAL LIFT	07	52	64
BRIDGE NYS&W: 1872/1894/1934 PHOTO	03	39	138
BRIDGE PIER UNDER CONSTRUCTION IC PHOTO	11	67	13
BRIDGE PIERS WINOOSKI RIVER GEORGIA VT P	09	67	01
BRIDGE SJ&LC WOODEN COVERED BRIDGE PHOTO	03	47	108
BRIDGE T&WE PIONEER OHIO COAL-TRUCK LOAD	12	43	132
BRIDGE: 2-HINGED STEEL ARCH NYC HELL GAT	01	48	09
BRIDGE: ARCH-TYPE CATENARY NYNH&H PHOTO	02	59	31
BRIDGE: CANTILEVER HIGH BRIDGE BC CANADA	01	48	25
BRIDGE: CENTER-SPANNED LOUISVILLE OH PHO	01	48	22
BRIDGE: DECK ARCH: STONEY CREEK BC PHOTO	01	48	28
BRIDGE: SINGLE TRACK ST LAWRENCE RIVER	01	48	30
BRIDGE: STARRUCA LANESBORO PA PHOTO	01	48	12
BRIDGE: TIMBER GENESEE RIVER PHOTO	01	48	18
BRIDGE: WTC/CO&C ERECTED IN 1940 PHOTO	05	41	59
CANTILEVER BRIDGE MONONGAHELA RIVER PA	06	37	45
COVERED BRIDGE B&M HENNIKER NH PHOTO	08	41	125
COVERED BRIDGE LC&SJ HARDWICK VT PHOTO	08	75	25
COVERED BRIDGE RU SHOREHAM VERMONT PHOTO	06	57	21
COVERED BRIDGE SJ&LC WOLCOTT VT. PHOTO	10	75	37
COVERED BRIDGE SJ&LCO WOLCOTT VT PHOTO	04	68	60
COVERED BRIDGE SJ&LCO WOLCOTT VT. PHOTO	01	80	25
COVERED RAILROAD BRIDGE SP OREGON 1920	09	41	121
DRAWBRIDGE INTERIOR FAM PHOTO	08	78	33
DRAWBRIDGE SE ST JOHNS QUEBEC 1882 PHOT	08	43	149
DROP-BOTTOM BRIDGE P&F PHOTO	08	43	131
FOUR TRACK VIADUCT NYC PHOTO	05	31	167
FR FOREIGN RAILROAD	02	38	22
FR CHAUMONT VIADUCT EASTERN FRANCE PHOTO	05	68	16
FR ENGLAND 3 LEVEL CROSSING AT CHESTER P	02	56	36
FR FRENCH CHAUMONT VIADUCT 2269' PHOTO	03	78	32
FR GARABIT VIADUCT FRANCE PHOTO	07	70	17
FR GERMANY DOUBLE STONE ARCH BIETIGEIM P	02	68	12
FR ITALY'S RR BRIDGES REBUILDING PHOTO	11	48	98
FR MOSCOW SUBWAY STATIONS PHOTOS	02	38	22
FR SWITZERLAND RHAETIAN RY LANDWASSE VIA	10	31	427
FR SWITZERLAND STEFFENBACK BRIDGE PHOTO	08	31	45
HELL-GATE BRIDGE NYNH&H PHOTO	05	37	55
KOHISLA TRESTLE CN BRITISH COLUMBIA PHOT	12	66	01
LIFT BRIDGE AT BALLARD WASHINGTON PHOTO	03	79	26R
LIFT BRIDGE HAND OPERATED CLEVELAND OHIO	01	40	57
LOGGING RAILRWAY BRIDGE PHOTO	05	41	60
MILES GLACIER BRIDGE CR&NW PHOTO	05	39	126
MONTREAL RIVER DAM/BRIDGE ALGC PHOTO	10	76	05
MOUNTAIN CREEK BRIDGE CP ROGERS PASS BC	02	78	10
NORTH FORK BRIDGE WP PHOTO	05	79	22
PEACE RIVER BRIDGE BCRW BEFOR/AFTER FIRE	03	80	23
PECOS RIVER BRIDGE SP PHOTO	11	75	42
PIPE TUNNEL CP NEWPORT VT PHOTO	05	70	14
RARITAN BAY NJ BRIDGE PRR PHOTO	03	84	67
RICHMONDS TRIPLE CROSSING OVER THE YEARS	11	83	34
SAMSON OF THE CIMMARON RI PHOTO	07	45	97
SIBLEY BRIDGE ATSF OVER MISSOURI RIVER P	08	71	54
SIMPLE-SPAN BRIDGE AL 700' NENANA AL PHO	08	36	121

Stephans' Railroad Directory

Railroad/Railfan

STRUCTURES   VEHICLES   & SIGNALS

BRIDGE & TUNNEL PHOTOS	M Y P
SLIDE SHEDS CN LYTTON BC PHOTO	11 86 44
SP MARTINEZ-BENICIA BRIDGE 5603' PHOTO	01 31 246
STARUCCA VIADUCT PENNSYLVANIA PHOTO	06 59 14
STARUCCA VIADUCT LANESBORO PA EL & DH	05 76 65
STEEL ARCH BRIDGE NIAGARA GORGE 1897 PHO	07 76 50
STEEL ARCH/CANTILEVER/TRESTLE LS&I PHOTO	08 37 54
STONE ARCH BRIDGE GN MINNEAPOLIS MN PHOT	12 78 24
STONE ARCH BRIDGE PRR (STONE/TIMBER) PHO	04 46 36
SWING BRIDGE CAPR CLEARWATER RIVER ID PH	12 77 23R
SWING BRIDGE DECATUR AL DETAIL PHOTO	09 71 19
THOMAS VIADUCT B&O BALTIMORE MD PHOTO	09 77 02
THOMAS VIADUCT B&O BALTIMORE MD. PHOTO	SP 77 37R
THREE LEVEL RAILWAY CROSSING RICHMOND VA	11 30 597
TOPLESS TUNEL CP PALLISER BC	11 73 03
TRESTLE STRONG MAINE PHOTO	09 35 52
TRESTLE AT SCRANTON PA DL&W 1866N PHOTO	08 34 134
TRESTLE BRIDGE N&W PHOTO	05 37 52
TRESTLE CB&Q NEAR MT PLEASANT PHOTO	07 52 129
TRESTLE SD&AE "SHORTEST LINE EAST" PHOTO	05 53 55
TRI-LEVEL BRIDGES RICHMOND VA PHOTO	12 66 21
TRILEVEL BRIDGE RICHMOND VA PHOTO	11 78 48
TRIPLE CROSSING RICHMOND VA DIESEL PHOTO	11 83 01
TRUS BRIDGE RU NEW HAVEN VT PHOTO	12 75 37
TUNNEL HAS ONE PORTAL SP SUMMIT OREGON	04 31 119
TUNNEL PITTSBURG TROLLEY SYSTEM PHOTO	04 70 42
TUNNEL PORTALS PRR GALLITZEN PA PHOTO	11 77 62
TUNNEL V&T SUTRO TUNNEL PHOTO	07 45 54
TWIN TUNNELS CP AGASSIZ BC PHOTO	01 76 49
VERTICAL LIFT BRIDGE TROY NY PHOTO	05 37 57
WROUGHT IRON TRUSS BRIDGE N&W 1886-1931	05 37 49

STRUCTURE, SIGNAL & VEHICLE PHOTOS	M Y P
# COMMERCIAL STRUCTURE PHOTOS #	
BEER PLANT (MEXICO) PHOTO	05 53 54
BREWERY COORS GOLDEN COLORADO PHOTO	01 85 39
COACH/BAGGAGE MC #509 USED AS TOWN HALL	08 48 63
COURTHOUSE SQUARE TALBOTTON GA PHOTO	07 43 105
DINER SP PHOTO	09 51 138
DRYING PLANT L&MA PHOTO	07 52 54
EAMES VACUUM BRAKE FACTORY KALAMAZOO MI	10 42 61
FERRY EXCHANGE HOTEL PORT COSTA CA 1917	01 67 46
FIRE-BELL FROM LOCO TIRE STEPNEY CT PHOT	12 70 31
GASOLINE FILLING STATION PHOTO	08 43 85
GRAIN ELEVATOR CN WAINRIGHT CANADA PHOTO	03 65 35
HARVEY HOUSE ATSF SYRACUSE KS 1890 PHOTO	04 75 13
HARVEY HOUSES (OLD AND NEW) PHOTO	04 58 44
HOTEL DELANCEY O&K CANNEL CITY KY PHOTO	08 52 47
LIMESTONE WASHER ASN&L LITHONIA GA PHOTO	04 66 56
MAYER FEED MILL LESTER PRAIRIE MN PHOTO	W 75 44R
MILE "0" MARKER ALASKA HI-WAY PHOTO	01 54 10
ONE ROOM SQUARED LOGS SCHOOL HOUSE PHOTO	11 51 37
PALACE HOTEL F&CC (BRICK & WOOD) PHOTO	08 58 28
POST OFFICE WHEELER SPRINGS CA (SMALLEST	02 49 108
POST OFFICE/SECOND HAND STORE F&CC PHOTO	08 58 24
POTATO WAREHOUSE BAR HOVEY & CO PHOTO	12 38 12
RAILWAY INN: BABAHATCHIE PHOTO	02 43 112
RICH RUN MINE WIDEN W VA 1926 PHOTO	08 62 17
RICHMOND LOCOMOTIVE WORKS 1900 PHOTO	09 69 18
ROGERS LOCOMOTIVE WORKS 1901? PHOTO	02 46 99
SALOON-GENERAL STORE U DRAGON UT PHOTO	06 60 20
SILK LOADING PLATFORMS SEATTLE WA PHOTO	04 65 15
SOD HUT CB&Q PHOTO	11 51 34
STORE HUDSON'S BAY COMPANY CHURCHILL CAN	06 54 29
STREET SCENE ELIZABETH NJ 1904 PHOTO	01 71 16
TRAIN COACH MOTEL SIOUX FALLS SD 1975 PH	06 76 58
VENERABLE CHURCH TALBOTTON GA PHOTO	07 43 106

# RAILROAD STRUCTURE PHOTOS #	
ALCO ERECTING SHOP INTERIOR 1948 PHOTO	11 77 55
ASH PITS D&H ONEONTA NY YARD 1922 PHOTO	06 63 22
BACKSHOP (STEAM) CB&Q INTERIOR 1900 PHOT	09 77 35
BACKSHOP INTERIOR SP SACRAMENTO CA PHOTO	04 66 25
BAGGAGE STN/LUNCH ROOM/DINING ROOM ATSF	02 45 92
BARREL TRANSFER D&RGW PHOTO	08 41 23
BENICIA DEPOT SP BENICIA CA PHOTO	05 68 19
BLOCK OFFICE "RK" P&WRR ROCK POINT PA PH	02 73 11
BLOW-DOWN SHED FOR STEAM LOCOS NP PHOTO	02 78 50
BLOW-DOWN SHED NP BILLINGS MONTANA PHOTO	08 54 42
BOX CAR STATION INT ATSF GLENDORA CA '45	11 72 31
BOXCAR DEPOT CN ARNOLDS COVE NF PHOTO	02 61 28
BOXCAR STATION SP #23907 PORT CHICAGO CA	11 69 25
BRICK DEPOT BR&P E SALAMANCA NY PHOTO	09 43 14
BROAD STREET STATION PRR AFTER FIRE PHOT	01 75 53
BROOKS LOCOMOTIVE WORKS 1888 WOOD CUT	08 70 19
BUCKET COAL HOIST CP CHIPMAN NB 1959 PHO	11 76 36
C&E STATION CASSVILLE, MISSOURI PHOTO	11 30 494
CABOOSE/TEMP STATION CP #436709 PHOTO	05 74 12

Railroad/ Railfan

STRUCTURES VEHICLES & SIGNALS

STRUCTURE, SIGNAL & VEHICLE PHOTOS		M	Y	P
CAR BARN & OFFICE CSCO WOOSTER OH	PHOTO	10	68	30
CAR BARN BERY (FIREPROOF)	PHOTO	04	53	88
CAR BARN CNYE BUILT IN 1907	PHOTO	08	56	68
CAR BARN CNYEA SOUTH LA PORTE IND	PHOTO	05	33	81
CAR BARN CSCO SEVILLE JUNCTION	PHOTO	05	52	87
CAR BARN CTR OIL CITY PA	PHOTO	12	50	90
CAR BARN NCT GLENBOROUGH CA	PHOTO	12	44	83
CAR REPAIR SHOP CP CALGARY ALB INTERIOR		05	75	10
CAR REPAIR SHOPS "UNION DOME" UTCC	PHOTO	08	58	44
CAR SHOP PRR INDIANAPOLIS	PHOTO	04	46	29
CAR SHOP SP DUNSMUIR CA 1913	PHOTO	01	69	20
CATTLE LANE KNOX RAILROAD MAINE	PHOTO	03	33	137
CLASSIFICATION YARD BN MINNEAPOLIS MN PH		01	77	09
COACH YARD LOUISVILLE UNION STATION PHOT		11	67	21
COAL CHUTE RU RUTLAND VT	PHOTO	08	46	20
COAL DOCK PRR MARION OHIO 1952	PHOTO	12	64	20
COAL DUMPING PIER PRR	PHOTO	11	39	88
COAL TOWER (WOOD) NORTH WALPOLE NH	PHOTO	12	70	13
COAL TOWER D&RGW CHAMA NM	PHOTO	11	72	16
COAL TOWER DW&P	PHOTO	04	58	45
COAL TOWER IC DYERSBURG TENN	PHOTO	09	44	65
COAL TOWER RU RUTLAND VERMONT	PHOTO	04	70	26
COALING DOCK (SMALL) CP TEESWATER ONT PH		05	76	29
COALING DOCK UP CHEYENNE WY 1959	PHOTO	10	74	56
COALING PLANT 400 TON CONCRETE CP	PHOTO	07	50	34
COALING STATION CONCRETE UP HANNA WY PH		04	45	72
COALING STATION MODERN C&O CLIFTON FORGE		09	47	74
COALING STATION N&W BLUEFIELD WV	PHOTO	07	54	20
COALING STATION N&W BLUEFIELD WV.	PHOTO	08	64	16
COALING STATION PRR PITTSBURGH PA	PHOTO	10	41	60
COALING STATION WM ELKINS WV	PHOTO	09	50	28
COALING TIPPLE AKRON OHIO	PHOTO	05	78	17
COALING TOWER B&O BENWOOD W VA	PHOTO	05	87	32
COALING TOWER C&NW CLYMAN JCT WI 1974 PH		08	74	22
COALING TOWER CB&Q GALESBURG IL	PHOTO	06	65	57
COALING TOWER CP ST LUC YARD MONTREAL PH		10	58	40
COALING TOWER L&MA	PHOTO	07	52	52
COALING TOWER MONON	PHOTO	11	68	61
COALING TOWER UP CHEYENNE WY 1959	PHOTO	02	78	56
COALING TOWER UP HANNA WY	PHOTO	04	74	28
COMBINATION STATION EV&I ELNORA IN	PHOTO	02	66	13
COMBINATION STATION MKT DUBLIN, TEXAS		09	32	229
CONCRETE COAL TRAIN LOADING SILO C&WY PH		08	71	66
CONCRETE RETARDER TOWER C&O VA	PHOTO	02	59	41
CONTROL BUILDING CP	PHOTO	01	51	139
CONTROL HOUSES B&M MECHANICSVILLE NY (2)		11	44	53
CONTROL SIGNAL & OFFICE B&O WASHINGTN PA		10	37	23
CONTROL TOWER CP COTE ST LUC MONTREAL PH		10	54	40
CONVEYOR BELT CPA	PHOTO	08	57	18
COVERED PLATFORM D&LC MALONE NY 1910 PHO		12	64	34
COVERED TURNTABLE NP EASTON WASH	PHOTO	02	66	17
CP YARDS ROSEBURG OR (WOODBURNING DAYS)		05	34	82
CROSSING TOWER MILW A-5	PHOTO	03	43	25
DEOPT MP HERRINGTON KS	PHOTO	12	77	12
DEPOT AB&C (NEXT OT TAL DEPOT)	PHOTO	07	43	110

STRUCTURE, SIGNAL & VEHICLE PHOTOS		M	Y	P
DEPOT ATSF PERRIS CALIF 1892	PHOTO	09	42	139
DEPOT ATSF ARCADIA CA BUILT 1895	PHOTO	09	75	10
DEPOT ATSF PERRIS CA 1891	PHOTO	11	73	28
DEPOT ATSF SWEETWATER TEXAS	PHOTO	11	49	110
DEPOT ATSF TOPEKA KS 1876	PHOTO	12	64	14
DEPOT B&ML KNOX (OLD FREIGHT HOUSE) PHO		10	40	15
DEPOT B&ML THORNDIKE	PHOTO	10	40	18
DEPOT BAR GUILFORD	PHOTO	12	35	63
DEPOT BCF&NB NORTH FOXBORO MASS	PHOTO	05	73	54
DEPOT BCR&N CEDAR RAPIDS IOWA	PHOTO	05	45	86
DEPOT BUILT WITH LOGS GRAND PRE NOVA SCO		06	40	127
DEPOT C&GR COLUMBUS	PHOTO	08	44	21
DEPOT C&O FOSTORIA OHIO	PHOTO	08	77	28
DEPOT C&O RUTHVEN ONTARIO	PHOTO	01	76	44
DEPOT CA&E GLEN ELLYN ILL	PHOTO	01	46	105
DEPOT CBELT GRENNWAY ARKANSAS	PHOTO	05	54	102
DEPOT CCC&SL MILFORD IN 1913	PHOTO	03	76	03
DEPOT CL ELKHORN CITY KY	PHOTO	12	53	18
DEPOT CORNWALL BRIDGE CT	PHOTO	03	73	17
DEPOT CP ONAWA	PHOTO	02	44	12
DEPOT CV MILLERS FALLS MASS	PHOTO	05	78	24R
DEPOT CV/B&M MILLERS FALLS MASS	PHOTO	08	46	91
DEPOT DSP&P COMO CO 1946	PHOTO	10	73	20
DEPOT FRAME MILW ONEIDA JCT IOWA	PHOTO	04	41	15
DEPOT FRT & PASS V&T VIRGINIA CITY	PHOTO	07	45	54
DEPOT GEORGIA WINTERVILLE	PHOTO	SU	76	49R
DEPOT GN EPHRATA WASHINGTON OLD AND NEW!		12	43	122
DEPOT GT EDWARDSBURG MI 1908	PHOTO	12	75	13
DEPOT GTW W/3 STEM LOCOS 1956	PHOTO	04	66	54
DEPOT HAMMONDSPORT NY	PHOTO	01	68	63
DEPOT HU FARMINGTON	PHOTO	10	44	115
DEPOT IC GIBSLAND LOUISIANA	PHOTO	04	78	45R
DEPOT INTERIOR B&O NEW ALBANY IN	PHOTO	02	60	15
DEPOT KCE RANDOLPH MAINE	PHOTO	09	35	43
DEPOT KCN&FS SULPHUR SPRINGS ARK	PHOTO	10	47	18
DEPOT L&HR GREAT MEDOWS NJ	PHOTO	W	74	22R
DEPOT L&N OPDYKE IL W/GINGERBREAD	PHOTO	12	54	29
DEPOT LI FLATBUSH AVENUE TERMINAL	PHOTO	01	43	34
DEPOT LI WOODSIDE NY	PHOTO	01	43	22
DEPOT LOUDON PARK CEMETERY PRR	PHOTO	06	60	23
DEPOT LV FLEMINGTON JCT PA	PHOTO	08	77	31R
DEPOT LV&T RHYOLITE NV	PHOTO	10	76	02
DEPOT M&SL REDWOOD MINNESOTA	PHOTO	04	58	25
DEPOT MICHC PEACOCK MI	PHOTO	10	52	18
DEPOT N&SL NORFOLK NY 1971	PHOTO	08	74	34
DEPOT N&W BLUE RIDGE VA	PHOTO	SP	75	64R
DEPOT NEZ&I	PHOTO	01	54	73
DEPOT NP BILLINGS MONT	PHOTO	10	41	125
DEPOT NP DETROIT LAKES MINN	PHOTO	10	44	11
DEPOT NP LOMBARD MONTANA	PHOTO	10	40	122
DEPOT NY&GL FORREST HILLS NJ	PHOTO	09	72	11
DEPOT NYNH&H CANAAN CONN	PHOTO	02	67	18
DEPOT NYNH&H NEW CANAAN CT 1959	PHOTO	04	75	46
DEPOT NYNH&H TARKIN RI	PHOTO	05	73	54
DEPOT NYS&W STILLWATER NJ	PHOTO	09	78	33R

Railroad/ Railfan

STRUCTURES VEHICLES & SIGNALS

STRUCTURE, SIGNAL & VEHICLE PHOTOS	M Y P
DEPOT O&K HELECHAWA KY PHOTO	08 52 37
DEPOT OCO KNEELAND STREET BOSTON MA PHOT	09 42 44
DEPOT OCO MASSACHUSETTS 1880? PHOTO	10 75 33
DEPOT OF ALASKA RAILROAD NEAR FAIRBANKS	10 34 42
DEPOT PH&NW COURT ST DEPOT HURON MICH	09 43 154
DEPOT PRR HARRISBURG PA PHOTO	04 46 27
DEPOT PRR ELIDA OHIO PHOTO	08 57 33
DEPOT R BYCOT PA TINY STATION! PHOTO	03 43 118
DEPOT READING SUNBURY PA PHOTO	02 67 58
DEPOT RI ELLSWORTH MN--X DOODLEBUG #9012	04 66 20
DEPOT S BLACKVILLE SC 1970 PHOTO	01 73 01
DEPOT SAL ZELLWOOD FL 1975 PHOTO	08 77 16
DEPOT SJ&LC EAST SWANTON VT PHOTO	08 75 24
DEPOT SJ&LCO JOHNSON VT PHOTO	01 80 30
DEPOT SP DALLAS TEXAS CIRCA 1903 PHOTO	04 77 18
DEPOT SP NILES CA 1941 PHOTO	04 71 38
DEPOT SP SALTON CA 1919 PHOTO	08 66 28
DEPOT SR&RL RANGELEY MAINE PHOTO	09 35 54
DEPOT T&T RHYOLITE PHOTO	04 53 117
DEPOT TAL (NEXT TO AB&C DEPOT) PHOTO	07 43 110
DEPOT TAT OFFICE/CAR BARN/STABLE PHOTO	02 46 21
DEPOT UC OGDEN UTAH PHOTO	02 45 26
DEPOT UP NYSSA OREGON PHOTO	12 54 37
DEPOT V&T GOLD HILL PHOTO	01 55 12
DEPOT VER NORTH BENNINGTON VT PHOTO	SU 75 27R
DEPOT W&A ATLANTA UNION DEPOT GA PHOTO	12 45 12
DEPOT WP BERRY CREEK PHOTO	04 44 22
DEPOT/ENGINEHOUSE OB&PA OGDENSBURG VT PH	F 75 31R
DEPOT/GENERAL OFFICES SNO SILVERTON PHOT	06 58 24
DEPOT/HARVEY HOUSE ATSF LA JUNITA CO PHO	04 46 73
DIESEL HOUSE CNW PHOTO	12 54 43
DIESEL PART CONVEYOR MAZE L&N PHOTO	11 68 16
DIESEL SANDING FACILITY ACL WAYCROSS GA	03 65 45
DIESEL SERVICE FACILITY ATSF ARGENTINE K	04 69 14
DIESEL SERVICE FACILITY LV SAYRE PA 1972	06 75 20
DIESEL SERVICE PLANT CP ALYTH YD INTER P	06 66 51
DIESEL SERVICING FACILITY EL HORNELL NY	12 76 66
DIESEL SERVICING MULTIPLE FACILITY PC PH	01 69 13
DIESEL SHOP BARSTOW CA ATSF PHOTO	01 84 40
DIESEL SHOP INTERIOR A COLLINWOOD OH PHO	08 77 55
DIESEL SHOP INTERIOR ATSF CLEBURNE TX PH	05 85 46
DIESEL SHOP INTERIOR C&O RUSSEL KY PHOTO	12 67 14
DIESEL SHOP INTERIOR NH NEW HAVEN CT PHO	12 87 55
DIESEL SHOP INTERIOR W/PLATFORMS GN PHOT	04 74 57
DIESEL TRACK PANS FOR YARD POLUTION CONT	11 72 59
DISPATCHER'S OFFICE MACKINAW JCT PHOTO	04 38 126
DUAL WATER TANKS L&N NEW MEMPHIS IL PHOT	08 63 31
DURAND DEPOT T&SB DURAND MI PHOTO	03 84 45
ELEVATED STATION BMTA CHARLESTOWN MA PHO	01 76 27
ELEVATOR O&LC (500,000 BUSHEL CAP) PHOTO	01 47 21
ENG HOUSE/WOOD WATER TANK DL&W ITHACA NY	05 31 241
ENGINE HOUSE A&MR ARCATA PHOTO	06 53 37
ENGINE HOUSE A&STAB PHOTO	08 72 57
ENGINE HOUSE D&CA DIAMOND SPRG CALIF PHO	05 41 57
ENGINE HOUSE DL&W ITHACA NY PHOTO	06 65 14

STRUCTURE, SIGNAL & VEHICLE PHOTOS	M Y P
ENGINE HOUSE DL&W ITHACA NY 1907 PHOTO	02 55 76
ENGINE HOUSE DL&W ITHACA NY 1907 PHOTO	06 76 48
ENGINE HOUSE GF SAN GABRIEL CA PHOTO	10 41 46
ENGINE SHED TM PARIS TX PHOTO	10 63 23
ENGINE TERMINAL B&O IVY CITY WASH DC PHO	01 66 41
ENGINE TERMINAL CN TORONTO CANADA PHOTO	05 71 17
ENGINE TERMINAL CNJ BETHLEHAM PA 1937 PH	11 70 23
ENGINE TERMINAL MC RIGBY YARD PORTLAND M	07 78 41R
ENGINE TERMINAL PARKWATER WA BN (VOLCANO	11 80 02
ENGINE TERMINAL RG DURANGO COLORADO PHOT	10 77 43R
ERECTING ROOM INTERIOR LV SAYRE PA PHOTO	01 65 25
ERECTING SHOP FLOOR ATSF PHOTO	02 71 31
ERECTING SHOP INTERIOR L&N S LOUISVILLE	11 64 20
ERECTING SHOP INTERIOR SP LOS ANGELES CA	07 66 22
ERECTING SHOP INTERIOR SP SACRAMENTO CA	07 66 24
ERECTION HALL INTERIOR R PHOTO	05 78 34R
FLAG STOP CV VERNON VT PHOTO	08 46 25
FR FOREIGN RAILROAD PHOTOS	03 38 78
FR AUSTRALIA FLINDERS ST STN MELBOURNE P	05 48 46
FR BRITISH RYS: SMALLEST STATION PHOTO	08 58 46
FR FRENCH INDO-CHINA STATION PHOTO	03 41 35
FR FRENCH SWITCH SHANTY PHOTO	05 37 126
FR INDIA CAWNPUR STATION LUCKNOW PHOTO	01 51 32
FR INDIAS CHITTARANJAN LOCO WORKS INT PH	07 72 25
FR INDO-CHINA RAILWAY STATION	12 31 94
FR LENINGRAD STATION MOSCOW PHOTO	05 46 49
FR NICARAGUA LARGE OPEN STATION CORINTO	06 30 403
FR NORWAY STATION IN HELL PHOTO	02 32 329
FR PALESTINE: STATION SIGN IN 3 LANGUAGE	07 41 67
FR PHILIPPINES HONDAGUA STATION PHOTO	06 32 420
FR PORTO RICO FUELING STATION AMER RR PH	03 38 78
FR REPAIR SHOP IN THE SUDAN AFRICA PHOTO	01 75 03
FR ROUNDHOUSE GUATEMALA CITY GUATEMALA P	06 65 59
FR RUSSIA STATION AT TAEKTER PHOTO	10 51 109
FR RUSSIA: MOSCOW TERMINAL PHOTO	05 46 44
FR RUSSIAN STATION LENINGRAD PHOTO	04 52 58
FR SPANISH RAILWAY SIGNAL TOWER PHOTO	07 47 69
FR STONE ROUNDHOUSE IN BRAZIL PHOTO	08 76 34
FR SUBWAY STATION VIENNA AUSTRIA PHOTO	02 64 24
FR SUBWAY STATION WEST BERLIN GERMANY PH	02 64 24
FR TRANS-SIBERIAN RY WAY STATION PHOTO	05 46 45
FR WATER TOWER CHRISTCHURCH NEW ZEALAND	10 78 08
FR WOOD & WATER STOP WNAG PO THAILAND PH	05 73 40
FREIGHT CAR REPAIR PLANT PRR HOLLIDAYSBU	08 53 59
FREIGHT CAR SCALES (AUTOMATIC) B&O PHOTO	02 66 30
FREIGHT DEPOT C&NW ELLSWORTH IA PHOTO	11 43 112
FREIGHT DEPOT ERIE BINGHAMTON NY PHOTO	SP 76 28R
FREIGHT DEPOT MP EXTENDS INTO 2 STATES	04 31 06
FREIGHT HOUSE NA WATERWAYS PHOTO	01 54 26
FREIGHT TERMINAL (ROUND) CNJ BRONX NY PH	04 64 27
FUELING & WATERING DIESEL FACILITY RF&P	04 71 51
FUELING FACILITY D&RGW (DIESEL) PHOTO	04 67 40
GALLOWS TURNTABLE SP LAWS CA 1952 PHOTO	05 78 54
GANTRY CRANE 50 TON L&N ATLANTA GA YARD	05 68 28
GANTRY CRANE BEDT PHOTO	06 52 37

Railroad/Railfan

STRUCTURES VEHICLES & SIGNALS

STRUCTURE, SIGNAL & VEHICLE PHOTOS	M	Y	P
GANTRY CRANE MP PIGGYBACK OPERATIONS	12	56	31
GANTRY FOR LOADING TRAILERS ON FLAT CARS	08	64	30
GENERAL OFFICE TP&W "WINDOWLESS" PHOTO	12	55	41
GENERAL OFFICES A&A PHOTO	02	54	52
GENERAL OFFICES D&H ALBANY NY PHOTO	04	47	26
GENERAL OFFICES EBT ORBISONIA PA PHOTO	W	75	27R
GENERAL OFFICES GEORGIA CAR & LOCO WORKS	09	47	79
GINGERBREAD DEPOT PC STRAFFORD PA PHOTO	10	72	42
GRAIN LOADERS RI PHOTO	11	72	15
GREENHOUSE GN MONROE OREGON PHOTO	06	54	97
HACK SHED UP #3303 (LA&SL) RHYOLITE NV P	10	76	03
HAND COALING STATION CP 1959 PHOTO	10	69	24
HEADQUARTERS MINNESOT TRANSFER CO PHOTO	05	54	61
HEADQUARTERS V NEW RIVER DIVISION PHOTO	04	39	26
HIGH BRIDGE S KENTUCKY RIVER	12	58	44
HORSECAR BARN SCHENECTADY NY 1888 PHOTO	04	69	44
HOSPITAL MKT DENISON HOSP FOR EMPLOYEES	07	48	34
HUMP YARD CONTROL TOWER PHOTO	08	30	88
HUMP YARD RETARDER NOISE SHED CN PHOTO	08	73	21
HYDRAULIC RAM FOR CAR MOVING IN YARD PHO	02	66	31
ICING MACHINE ATSF CALWA CALIFORNIA PHOT	02	57	43
INDIANAPOLIS UNION DEPOT 1 1859 PHOTO	04	62	21
INDIANAPOLIS UNION STATION 2 1880 PHOTO	04	62	26
INTERCHANGE TOWER D&H BINGHAMTON NY PHOT	SP	76	29R
INTERLOCKING PLANT D&H SCHOHARIE JCT NY	04	47	22
INTERLOCKING TOWER STERLING OH CHESSIE P	05	82	28
LIMA ERECTING SHOPS INTER & EXTERIOR PHO	08	74	29
LOCO ERECTION SHOP INTERIOR PRR ALTOONA	12	63	28
LOCO REPAIR SHOP INTERIOR CP ANGUS SHOP	03	67	39
LOCOMOTIVE SHED CN HALIBURTON ONTARIO PH	04	68	14
LOCOMOTIVE SHOP CN CHARLOTTETOWN PEI CAN	10	77	23R
LOCOMOTIVE SHOP INTERIOR P&LE 1904 PHOTO	06	62	35
LOCOMOTIVE SHOPS L&N 1865 PHOTO	11	64	18
LOCOMOTIVE WASHER UP PORTLAND OR 1970 PH	04	74	03
MACHINE SHOPS TM TERREL TX PHOTO	10	63	23
MAIL CRANE PHOTO	06	46	104
MAIL CRANE NYNH&H NIANTIC CT 1944 PHOTO	04	78	10
MAIL PICK-UP POLE (STEEL) ERIE PHOTO	04	58	47
MAIL/BAGGAGE ELEVATOR PHOTO	10	40	125
MCMYLER LOADER CNJ TERMINAL PHOTO	03	46	17
MD CABIN C&O MEADOW CREEK WVA PHOTO	05	85	03
MICROWAVE REPEATER STATION ATSF TEXAS	02	56	31
MISSION TOWER LOS ANGELES PASSENGER TERM	09	46	53
MULE OR BARNEY PHOTO PRR LI YARD PHOTO	05	67	52
MULTI-CUPOLA ENGINEHOUSE PRR HARRISBURG	04	46	25
MUSHROOM WATER TOWER O&LC CHURUBUSCO NY	12	64	34
NEW CLARK JUNCTION TOWER CTA CHICAGO IL	02	77	23
OCTAGONAL DEPOT D&H FT EDWARD NY 1976 PH	10	76	20
OIL TANK SP LAWS CALIFORNIA PHOTO	12	62	10
OIL WELL NP RICHEY MONTANA PHOTO	05	53	13
ORE CAR SHAKER CN PORT ARTHUR ONT PHOTO	07	72	39
ORE DUMPERS LAKEFRONT DOCK & TERMINAL CO	11	53	29
ORE UNLOADER B&LE AT CONNEAUT DOCK PHOTO	05	52	26
PADUCAH SHOPS IC INTERIOR PHOTO	SP	75	39R
PASSENGER & FREIGHT STN BALTIMORE MD.	01	31	284
PASSENGER DEPOT 1ST ATSF NEWTON KANSAS	04	31	02
PASSENGER STATION ATSF NEWTON KANSAS	04	31	03
PASSENGER STATION C&W CHICAGO IL ETCHING	11	43	87
PASSENGER STATION E GEAUGA LAKE OH PHOTO	06	61	52
PASSENGER STATION INTERIOR SP PASADENA P	04	64	16
PENN STATION INTERIOR NY NY PHOTO	11	64	66
PIGGYBACK TERMINAL CP AIR VIEW PHOTO	11	74	19
PIGGYBACK TERMINAL L&N ATLANTA GA PHOTO	05	68	15
PLATFORM SHELTER LI PHOTO	08	49	21
POLLING POCKET USE MC&SA PHOTO	08	66	16
PSTC ARDMORE JUNCTION INTERCHANGE PHOTO	10	55	45
PUMP HOUSE DL&W LINCOLN PARK NJ PHOTO	10	55	14
PUMP HOUSE DL&W LINCOLN PARK NJ PHOTO	05	31	247
RADAR TRAINMASTER SPEED-DETECTOR PHOTO	04	61	36
RAIL BOARDING HOUSE D&RGW SARGENTS CO PH	09	74	21
RAILRETARDER L&N ATLANTA GA PHOTO	05	78	04
RAILROAD CONSTRUCTION ENGINEER'S OFFICE	04	45	49
RAILROAD SHOPS LV SAYRE PA 1904 PHOTO	01	65	21
RAILWAY EXPRESS OFFICE SUFFERN NY PHOTO	12	50	25
RICHMOND CA TERMINAL ATSF PHOTO	07	86	48
ROBINS CAR SHAKEOUT L&MA PHOTO	07	52	55
ROBINS CAR SHAKEOUT L&MA PHOTO	07	52	57
ROOFED OVER WOOD STATION E SOUTHFIELD NY	02	60	19
ROTARY COAL DUMP YARD C&O NEWPORT NEWS V	05	78	32
ROTARY DUMPER W/RECEIVING BINS URR ETCHI	12	57	47
ROUND FREIGHT HOUSE CNJ BRONX TERMINAL	03	46	30
ROUND STATION C&O SOUTH LYONS MI PHOTO	03	71	14
ROUNDHOUSE & TABLE READING PA 1931 PHOTO	12	61	20
ROUNDHOUSE & TURNTABLE E SALAMANCA NY'47	12	69	26
ROUNDHOUSE A&PA NEEDLES CA 1890 PHOTO	04	34	85
ROUNDHOUSE ATLANTA GA AFTER SHERMAN 1864	11	32	479
ROUNDHOUSE ATLANTA GA AFTER SHERMAN PHOT	09	77	28
ROUNDHOUSE B&H BRIDGTON MAINE PHOTO	09	35	45
ROUNDHOUSE B&O MARTINSVILLE WV (1ST) PHO	11	44	112
ROUNDHOUSE C&O CLIFTON FORGE VA 1949 PHO	03	66	62
ROUNDHOUSE CPM&O SIOUX CITY IA PHOTO	04	55	42
ROUNDHOUSE D&RG SALIDA CO 1906 PHOTO	08	75	32
ROUNDHOUSE DSP&P COMO CO 1946 PHOTO	10	73	24
ROUNDHOUSE FLOODED CB&Q HANNIBAL MO 1947	03	76	42
ROUNDHOUSE FOREMAN'S OFFICE ACL PHOTO	01	55	37
ROUNDHOUSE FRISCO MONETT MO 1940 PHOTO	11	78	50
ROUNDHOUSE L&R ABANDONED ENGINE HOUSE PH	07	39	129
ROUNDHOUSE LS&MS NORWALK OHIO PHOTO	12	35	82
ROUNDHOUSE M&A HARRISON PHOTO	06	48	23
ROUNDHOUSE MC SOUTH RIGBY ME PHOTO	01	75	58
ROUNDHOUSE MCRI (WOODEN) PHOTO	10	50	51
ROUNDHOUSE NEEDLES CA 1890 & 1940 PHOTO	01	84	39
ROUNDHOUSE PRR NEWARK NJ AIR VIEW PHOTO	02	76	36
ROUNDHOUSE R READING PA PHOTO	06	76	49
ROUNDHOUSE RUINS D&H BINGHAMTON NY 1974	03	76	26
ROUNDHOUSE S JOHN SEIVER TENNESSEE PHOTO	11	77	32
ROUNDHOUSE SP (TAYLOR) PHOTO ESSAY	01	48	40
ROUNDHOUSE SP SACRAMENTO CA 1870 PHOTO	07	66	18
ROUNDHOUSE SP WEST OAKLAND CA 1904 PHOTO	07	66	20
ROUNDHOUSE SPM GUADALAJARA PHOTO	02	48	44

STRUCTURES VEHICLES & SIGNALS

STRUCTURE, SIGNAL & VEHICLE PHOTOS		M	Y	P
ROUNDHOUSE SR&RL PHILLIPS MAINE	PHOTO	12	55	30
ROUNDHOUSE UP GREEN RIVER WY	PHOTO	08	77	26
ROUNDHOUSE UP POCATELLO 1929	PHOTO	12	66	45
ROUNDHOUSE V&T CARSON CITY NEVADA	PHOTO	10	78	19
SAND HOUSE & TOWER SAL PORTSMOUTH VA	PHO	11	68	19
SAND HOUSE & TOWER V SEWELLS POINT VA	PH	11	68	20
SAND HOUSE MONON	PHOTO	11	68	61
SAND HOUSE NOW PART OF COALING STATION		03	42	65
SAND SPOUT WOOD NORFOLK VA YARD V	PHOTO	11	68	16
SAND TOWER (DIESEL) NDEM VERACRUZ MEX	PH	05	74	08
SAND TOWER DIESEL ROSS & WHITE CO	PHOTO	02	56	38
SAND TOWERS A IVY CITY WASHINGTON DC '75		11	75	45
SANDING TOWER RIGBY ENGINE HOUSE ME B&M		10	77	47
SCRAP YARD UP OMAHA NEBRASKA	PHOTO	07	77	32
SECTION HOUSE CN JOYBERT QUEBEC	PHOTO	03	33	139
SERVICING STEAM CLOSE-UP SP SAN FRANCISC		05	55	66
SHACK L&N FOR RADIO BROADCOASTS		04	37	119
SHOPS & YARD READING PA 1930 ARIAL PHOTO		12	61	22
SHOPS ATSF SAN BERNADINO CA INTERIOR '72		05	72	01
SHOPS IOWA EMERY IOWA	PHOTO	02	65	36
SIDE PORTER PIGGY BACK LOADER WP OAKLAND		05	73	14
SIGNAL TOWER (FRAME) LV GENEVA JCT NY	PH	08	69	41
SIGNAL TOWER (SHORE) FRANKFORT JCT PA	PH	04	75	19
SIGNAL TOWER NY&LB "S6" SEA GRIT	PHOTO	07	52	38
SIGNAL TOWER NYC (HUFF) WELLINGTON OH'51		11	76	23
SIGNAL TOWER P&R PHOENIXVILLE PA	PHOTO	04	56	74
SIGNAL TOWER PC "SHORE" FRANKFORD JCT PA		11	73	15
SIGNAL TOWER PC BRYN MAWR PA 1974	PHOTO	06	74	08
SIGNAL TOWER PRR HUNT TOWER	PHOTO	08	73	34
SIGNAL TOWER R "LIGHTHOUSE" OCTAGON SHAP		10	54	80
SIGNAL TOWER SP NILES CA	PHOTO	04	71	41
SIGNAL TOWER SP REDWOOD JCT CA	PHOTO	01	65	33
SMOKE DUCT ON NYC	PHOTO	05	37	38
SNO MISSION TOWER ATSF/SP/UP PHOTO ESSAY		09	46	53
STATION (UNION) MERIDIAN MISS 1937 PHOTO		04	74	60
STATION A&SU AT COBLESKILL NY	PHOTO	04	47	19
STATION ACL NORFOLK VA	PHOTO	03	41	16
STATION ACL SUTHERLAND FL	PHOTO	03	41	10
STATION ACL WEST PALM BEACH	PHOTO	01	52	20
STATION AL CHICALOON AL	PHOTO	07	31	492
STATION AND OUTHOUSE RGS OPHIR	PHOTO	03	53	69
STATION AT N. WHITEFIELD MAINE WW&F		03	35	38
STATION AT RELAY MASS B&O 1870 & 1935		05	35	134
STATION ATSF EDELSTEIN	PHOTO	06	45	66
STATION ATSF GRAND CANYON AZ	PHOTO	03	41	14
STATION ATSF INGLEWOOD 1887	PHOTO	11	47	138
STATION ATSF INGLEWOOD 1887-1947	PHOTO	03	48	70
STATION ATSF NEWTON	PHOTO	06	42	08
STATION ATSF OTTAWA JUNCTION	PHOTO	01	49	34
STATION ATSF SAN MARCIAL NM	PHOTO	03	42	61
STATION AVI WICHITA KANSAS	PHOTO	07	49	91
STATION B&LE ALBION	PHOTO	05	52	19
STATION B&M NORTH CONWAY NH	PHOTO	02	76	23
STATION B&M TAUNTON MASS BUILT IN 1865		12	50	76
STATION B&M/CV JOINT EFFORT VT	PHOTO	03	41	12

STRUCTURE, SIGNAL & VEHICLE PHOTOS		M	Y	P
STATION B&ML (1870/1900)	PHOTOS	10	40	11
STATION B&MR LINCOLN NEBRASKA	PHOTO	03	49	38
STATION B&O PASS/FRT MOUNT CLARE	PHOTO	03	47	17
STATION B&O SILVER SPRING MD	PHOTO	12	54	30
STATION BELL ACL WILMINGTON NC	PHOTO	06	36	130
STATION BOSTON SOUTH 1900	PHOTO	08	73	18
STATION BU&NW WASHINGTON IOWA	PHOTO	03	49	39
STATION C&E CASSVILLE	PHOTO	04	51	127
STATION C&GR WEST POINT	PHOTO	08	44	21
STATION C&O WILLIAMSBURG VA	PHOTO	03	41	20
STATION C&S GUNNISON CO 1946	PHOTO	10	73	24
STATION CB&Q (OLD AND NEW)	PHOTOS	12	54	26
STATION CB&Q CRESTON IOWA	PHOTO	04	73	30
STATION CB&Q GALESBURG IL CORRECTION	PHO	07	49	138
STATION CB&Q GALESBURG ILLINOIS	PHOTO	03	49	40
STATION CB&Q LA CROSSE WISCONSIN	PHOTO	03	49	36
STATION CGW FORT DODGE IA 1951	PHOTO	12	54	31
STATION CGW KANSAS CITY, MO	PHOTO	11	43	78
STATION CMI DIVIDE COLORADO	PHOTO	09	42	149
STATION CN BONADVENTURE STN MONTREAL	PHO	11	53	119
STATION CN EDMONTON	PHOTO	01	54	30
STATION CN JOLIETT QUEBEC 1939	PHOTO	01	70	21
STATION CN MONTREAL BONAVENTURE STN	DRAW	12	47	29
STATION CN PARK AVE STN MONTREAL	PHOTO	02	32	333
STATION CN TORONTO UNION STATION	PHOTO	12	47	19
STATION COL JEFFERSON CO	PHOTO	05	42	133
STATION CP AGASSIZ BC (BRICK)	PHOTO	04	73	24
STATION CP DORVAL QUEBEC 1957	PHOTO	10	69	04
STATION CP PARK AVE MONTRAL	PHOTO	03	41	27
STATION CSS&SB GARY	PHOTO	02	53	12
STATION D&H COBLESKILL NY	PHOTO	02	65	15
STATION D&H LAKE GEORGE NY	PHOTO	12	54	32
STATION D&H OLD UNION STA ALBANY NY	PHOT	04	69	14
STATION D&H SCHOHARIE JUNCTION NY	PHOTO	04	47	22
STATION D&RGW SILVERTON STATION	PHOTO	06	54	53
STATION DENVER CO	PHOTO	07	47	122
STATION DL&W BINGHAMTON NY	PHOTO	10	75	59
STATION DL&W WAYSISSING?	PHOTO	01	30	167
STATION DSP&P LEADVILLE CO 1929	PHOTO	12	33	46
STATION E BOGATA NJ 1909	PHOTO	06	72	51
STATION E ELMIRA NY 1885	PHOTO	07	31	491
STATION E ELMIRA NY 1900	PHOTO	01	73	47
STATION E SUSQUEHANNA PA	PHOTO	03	41	24
STATION EN PALISADE NEVADA	PHOTO	01	39	122
STATION FEC MIAMI FL 1930	PHOTO	04	75	28
STATION FJ&G GLOVERSVILLE NY 1954	PHOTO	06	68	59
STATION GN EPHRATA WASHINGTON	PHOTO	12	54	34
STATION GN FORT BENTON MONTANA	PHOTO	01	40	123
STATION GN SAUK CENTER MINNESOTA	PHOTO	06	54	100
STATION GTW SARANAC MI 1906	PHOTO	05	69	17
STATION HAR HARTWELL GA	PHOTO	01	47	72
STATION HOUSE ERIE	PHOTO	02	41	92
STATION IC ROCKFORD STATION (OLD)	PHOTO	12	54	33
STATION INTERIOR P&LE PITTSBURG PA	PHOTO	11	76	38
STATION IRY LOCKPORT NY	PHOTO	10	58	45

Railroad/Railfan

353

STRUCTURES VEHICLES & SIGNALS

STRUCTURE, SIGNAL & VEHICLE PHOTOS		M	Y	P
STATION IT MIDWEST TERMINAL BLDG	PHOTO	03	41	07
STATION KANSAS CITY MO	PHOTO	07	47	122
STATION L&N DEATSVILLE ALABAMA	PHOTO	08	42	47
STATION LI (OLD & NEW) MONTAUK NY	PHOTO	09	46	128
STATION LI COLD SPRING HARBOR	PHOTO	08	49	21
STATION LI HEMPSTEAD NY TEMPORARY	PHOTO	11	42	139
STATION LIG	PHOTO	05	52	44
STATION LV ALLENTOWN PA	PHOTO	05	44	127
STATION LV SAYRE PA 1973	PHOTO	12	73	18
STATION LVT SELLERSVILLE PA	PHOTO	09	42	102
STATION M&U UNIONVILLE NY	ETCHING	08	47	123
STATION MILW KILBOURN WISCONSIN	PHOTO	12	54	35
STATION MILW RONDOUT	PHOTO	03	53	41
STATION MKT PARSONS KAN (REPLICA)	PHOTO	07	48	13
STATION MKT PARSONS KANSAS	PHOTO	12	51	49
STATION MOVA SAYLESVILLE RI	PHOTO	08	49	71
STATION MP CRETE NE 1889	PHOTO	04	73	29
STATION MP ST LOUIS FREIGHT STN	PHOTO	05	52	67
STATION N&BF WATSESSING AVE (COAL YARD)		02	41	134
STATION N&W WIRTZ VA	PHOTO	08	64	23
STATION NB&T WEIR BRANCH 1850-66	PHOTO	08	31	46
STATION NEW ORLEANS PASSENGER TERMINAL		09	54	04
STATION NP FARGO ND	PHOTO	03	41	21
STATION NP FARGO ND WITH PARK	PHOTO	12	54	33
STATION NP/GN SEATTLE WA	PHOTO	07	47	123
STATION NT PARK PA (STONE)	PHOTO	04	45	101
STATION NYC CARYL NY 1942	PHOTO	08	68	26
STATION NYC GRAND CENTRAL TERMINAL	PHOTO	11	50	30
STATION NYC WEST SHORE STN HAVERSTRAW NY		04	47	51
STATION NYCE 89TH STREET STATION	PHOTO	06	56	22
STATION NYNH&H BRIDGEPORT CT 1977	PHOTO	08	77	15
STATION NYO&W WICKHAM AVE MIDDLETOWN NY		09	46	28
STATION NYP&B PARK SQUARE BOSTON MA PHOT		09	42	51
STATION O&K CANNEL CITY KY	PHOTO	08	52	36
STATION OCEAN SHORE RY FARALLONE CITY CA		12	35	69
STATION OGDEN UNION STATION	PHOTO	07	53	24
STATION P&F PIONEER STATION	PHOTO	08	43	132
STATION P-D TYRONE NM	PHOTO	05	53	104
STATION PC (BRICK) WALLINGFORD PA 1972 P		10	73	17
STATION PC MOORESTOWN NJ (NOW ANTIQUES)		03	74	17
STATION PC STRAFFORD PA (GINGERBREADY) P		12	72	03
STATION PEOP SANDUSKY	PHOTO	11	51	83
STATION PRR BROAD ST STATION PHIL PA PHO		05	67	16
STATION PRR DOVER DELAWARE	PHOTO	03	41	20
STATION PRR MILLVILLE PA 1913	PHOTO	11	74	12
STATION PRR NEW YORK NY	PHOTO	12	54	31
STATION PRR NORRISTOWN PA	PHOTO	03	41	29
STATION PRR TOLEDO OH 1948	PHOTO	04	71	16
STATION PRSL ATLANTIC CITY	PHOTO	07	45	95
STATION PRSL MILLVILLE NJ	PHOTO	06	42	129
STATION R GINGERBREAD BYCOT PA	PHOTO	08	54	14
STATION R GOTHIC 3 STORY HOPEWELL NJ PHO		05	74	43
STATION R PHILADELPHIA PA	PHOTO	05	44	25
STATION R ROBESONIA PA 1952	PHOTO	11	74	20
STATION R RYDAL PA 1973	PHOTO	06	73	15
STATION RGS OPHIR	PHOTO	10	50	19
STATION RI LASALLE STREET CHICAGO IL PHO		10	70	23
STATION RU (SMALL FRAME) CHATHAM NY PHO		08	46	12
STATION SAL CAMDEN SC	PHOTO	03	41	32
STATION SAL STONO SC	PHOTO	04	53	27
STATION SAL TAMPA UNION STATION	PHOTO	04	53	26
STATION SAL WEST PALM BEACH FL	PHOTO	03	41	32
STATION SALTON CALIFORNIA--THE LOWEST!		08	37	130
STATION SAN DIEGO GINGERBREAD ARCHITECTU		06	57	80
STATION SCL PUNTA GORDA FL	PHOTO	11	70	01
STATION SIRT STATEN ISLAND BEF/AFTER CLE		08	72	38
STATION SN WOODLAND CALIFORNIA	PHOTO	02	57	42
STATION SP CASCADE SUMMIT	PHOTO	01	53	55
STATION SP DUNSMUIR CA 1915	PHOTO	01	69	22
STATION SP MESA/COLLIDGE ARIZONA	PHOTO	06	41	121
STATION SP NILES CA 1910	PHOTO	04	71	40
STATION SP OWENYO	PHOTO	02	59	26
STATION SP PORT CHICAGO CA 1972	PHOTO	09	72	33
STATION SP PORT CHICAGO CA AFTER EXPLOSI		11	69	24
STATION SP SALTON CA 1912 LOWEST ELEVATI		10	78	50
STATION SP SALTON CALIFORNIA	PHOTO	06	56	44
STATION SP SANTA SUSANA CA 1947	PHOTO	11	76	28
STATION SPM NOGALES (STUCCO)	PHOTO	02	48	49
STATION SSP FREIGHT & SUB-STATION TULSA		03	53	83
STATION ST LOUIS UNION MEDIEVAL TYPE PHO		06	54	56
STATION ST LOUIS UNION TERMINAL	PHOTO	04	47	124
STATION STONE & BRICK CA&E ELMHURST ILL		01	46	104
STATION STOP SSP TULSA	PHOTO	03	53	91
STATION T&T SILVER LAKE CA	PHOTO	11	40	136
STATION TBRR CRANE'S MASS PRIOR 1863 PHO		08	31	46
STATION TWIN CITIES UNION STATION	PHOTO	02	54	25
STATION UDEY MERIDA CENTRAL STATION 1920		06	68	18
STATION UNION PASSENGER TERM NEW ORLEANS		12	54	36
STATION UNION STATION ATCHISON KS PHOTO		12	54	37
STATION UNION TERMINAL CINCINNATI OH PHO		12	54	30
STATION UP LAS VEGAS NV	PHOTO	03	41	23
STATION UP/MILW SEATTLE WA	PHOTO	07	47	123
STATION V&T VIRGINIA CITY NEVADA	PHOTO	09	41	09
STATION W ST LOUIS MO	PHOTO	02	47	22
STATION W ST LOUIS MO	PHOTO	03	41	15
STATION W TRUSEDALE MO	PHOTO	04	73	31
STATION W&NB (OLD HUNTING LODGE)	PHOTO	08	50	130
STATION W/POST OFFICE & FEED STORE LV PH		11	36	138
STATION WJ&S MILLVILLE NJ IN 1875	PHOTO	12	54	28
STATION WJ&S PASSENGER MILLVILLE NJ PHOT		02	46	86
STATION WM OWNINGS MILLS BALTIMORE MD PH		09	50	31
STATION WM THOMAS WV (BRICK)	PHOTO	09	68	18
STATION WO WOODSTOCK VT 1893	PHOTO	07	33	35
STATION Y&MV VICKSBURG MISS	PHOTO	03	41	08
STATION/GENERAL OFFICES EBT PA	PHOTO	08	41	15
STATION/OFFICE BUILDING/HARVEY HOUSE		04	46	72
STATION/OFFICES OR&LC HONOLULU	PHOTO	10	46	90
STATIONARY BOILER NKP 2-8-0 #803 1947 PH		11	74	58
STEAM ENGINE SERVICE FACILITY N&W	PHOTO	08	64	17
STEAM FUNNEL C&S DENVER CO	PHOTO	05	40	92

Stephans' Railroad_Directory

Railroad/Railfan

STRUCTURES VEHICLES & SIGNALS

STRUCTURE, SIGNAL & VEHICLE PHOTOS	M	Y	P
STEAM FUNNEL C&S DENVER CO 1939 PHOTO	10	73	20
STEAM FUNNEL MILW PHOTO	02	41	127
STEAM LOCOMOTIVE SCALE BALDWIN EDDYSTONE	08	31	39
STEEL WATER TOWER ATLANTA GA PHOTO	10	66	15
STONE DEPOT CLIFTON-ALDAN PA PC 1972 PHO	08	72	36
STONE WATER TANK DRAWING ERIE PHOTO	06	76	49
STORAGE SHED (X STATION) C&S PHOTO	02	45	130
STORE ROOM B&O MT CLARE SHOPS PHOTO	02	57	47
STUB STATION T&T 42ND ST NY NY PHOTO	01	78	61
SUBWAY STATION NYCTA PHOTO	02	64	24
SWITCH TOWER PC OLD SAYBROOK CT 1973 PHO	02	74	13
TANK CAR REPAIR BLDG UUTCC BATON ROUGE L	02	59	06
TENDER COAL LOADER (MANUAL) B&ML PHOTO	06	60	25
TENDER COAL LOADER WHT WINNIPEG MAN PHOT	06	60	24
TENDER COALING (MANUAL) STATION CP PHOTO	06	60	26
TENDER TRACKSIDE TANK NP SEATTLE WA PHOT	10	55	19
TERMINAL EL HOBOKEN NJ INTERIOR PHOTO	01	80	67
TERMINAL IT CHICAGO IL PHOTO	01	73	34
TERMINAL P&R PHILADELPHIA PA PHOTO	03	33	90
TERMINAL PRR ENOLA YARD ENOLA PA PHOTO	11	41	06
TERMINAL PRR W PHILADELPHIA PA 1876 ETCH	06	34	04
TERMINAL SCHEN & HVRY SARATOGA SPRINGS	02	45	105
THAWING SHEDS CNJ PHOTO	11	51	53
TICKET OFFICE EDAVILLE RAILROAD PHOTO	05	47	58
TICKET OFFICE INTERIOR RU SHELBURNE VT P	11	64	35
TICKET OFFICE NP CURB-SERVICE ST PAUL PH	08	57	43
TICKET OFFICE PRR NEW CASTLE DE PHOTO	06	54	69
TICKET OFFICE-OLDEST IN US NEW CASTLE DE	05	31	284
TIE-TREATING PLANT ATSF SOMERVILLE TX PH	11	75	30
TINY RAILROAD DEPOT MORGANTOWN PA PHOTO	11	65	25
TOWER BRB&L LYNN MASS PHOTO	01	40	74
TOWER D&RGW JACK'S CABIN PHOTO	10	53	29
TOWER DL&W MANUNKA CHUNK TOWER PA PHOTO	05	47	72
TOWER ELMORA TOWER S ELIZABETH NJ PHOTO	01	80	35
TOWER LV MOUNTAINTOP PA PHOTO	03	68	15
TOWER N&W MODERN PHOTO	09	44	28
TOWER N&W BLUEFIELD PHOTO	09	44	19
TOWER NKP XN LEIPSIC OHIO PHOTO	05	80	39
TOWER PRSL WINSLOW JCT PA PHOTO	08	67	21
TOWER T&NO #32 PHOTO	02	52	36
TRAILER GANTRY CRANE PRR KEARNEY NJ PHOT	06	66	60
TRAIN SHED & STATION CV ST ALBANS VT PHO	08	63	04
TRAIN SHED (BRICK) CV ST ALBANS VT 1928	06	76	51
TRAIN SHED B&M SALEM MASS PHOTO	11	73	27
TRAIN SHED PRR BROAD ST STN PHILA PA PHO	05	67	17
TRAIN SHED PRR COLUMBUS OHIO PHOTO	04	46	28
TRAIN SHED READING TERMINAL PHILA PA PHO	03	85	32
TRAIN SHED V&T VIRGINIA CITY PHOTO	01	55	15
TRAIN-ORDER STATION CN MINE CENTRE ONT P	04	75	19
TRANSFER TABLE NP (S TACOMA WASH) PHOTO	04	40	75
TRAVELIFT CRANE ATSF HOBART YARD LA CAL	04	67	34
TROLLEY STATION CTR COCHRAN PHOTO	12	50	86
TROLLEY STATION RT&C WARREN ME 1901 PHOT	02	71	43
TROLLEY STOP WALKER CALIFORNIA 1938 PHOT	05	66	61
TURNTABLE "GALLOWS" IC PHOTO	08	43	154

STRUCTURE, SIGNAL & VEHICLE PHOTOS	M	Y	P
TURNTABLE B&O IVY CITY, WASHINGTON DC PH	05	78	55
TURNTABLE C&O DETROIT MI 1953 PHOTO	04	72	51
TURNTABLE CNJ BETHLEHEM YARDS PA PHOTO	02	66	57
TURNTABLE D&H COLONIE SHOPS 1928 PHOTO	06	63	17
TURNTABLE D&RG SALIDA CO 1906 PHOTO	08	75	32
TURNTABLE MP PHOTO	05	70	30
TURNTABLE NCN GRASS VALLEY CALIF PHOTO	05	43	144
TURNTABLE R STRASBURG PA PHOTO	09	75	25
TURNTABLE READING HELLERTOWN PA PHOTO	11	69	28
TURNTABLE ST JOHNSBURY VT CP 1974 PHOTO	06	75	18
TURNTANLE MON SOUTH BROWNSVILLE PA 1972	10	72	59
TWIN WATER TOWERS ACL WAYCROSS GA PHOTO	10	64	28
UNION DEPOT TERRE HAUTE IN PHOTO	11	71	26
UNION STATION ATLANTA GA 1930 PHOTO	11	71	28
UNION STATION CHICAGO IL PHOTO	11	71	30
UNION STATION DENVER CO PHOTO	09	48	25
UNION STATION MILW GREAT FALLS MT PHOTO	11	71	31
UNION STATION MILW MILWAUKEE WI 1886 PHO	11	71	29
UNION STATION ST LOUIS PHOTO	02	47	10
UNION STATION ST LOUIS MO PHOTO	11	71	28
UNION STATION W PITTSBURGH PA PHOTO	11	71	26
UNION STATION WASHINGTON DC 1907 PHOTO	11	71	28
UNION STATION YARDS NASHVILLE TN PHOTO	02	66	15
VIADUCT AND ELEVATOR ELD AT WEEHAWKEN NJ	08	51	94
VISITORS CENTER UP BAILEY YARD N PLATTE	09	74	09
WAITING ROOM NSUB CAR #2626 PHOTO	08	52	94
WAITING STATION CSS&SB LYDICK IN PHOTO	02	53	34
WAREHOUSE BEDT PHOTO	06	52	41
WARMING HOUSE MC WATERVILLE ME PHOTO	08	47	133
WATCHMAN'S TOWER (X MILW & RI) 8 SIDED P	08	69	35
WATCHMAN'S TOWER CNS&M SOUTH UPTON PHOTO	10	53	78
WATCHMAN'S TOWER L&N PHOTO	04	76	31
WATCHMAN'S TOWER PE AMOCO PHOTO	07	54	57
WATCHMAN'S TOWER PE WATTS PHOTO	08	54	63
WATER & SAND SERVICE FACILITY UP PHOTO	02	70	01
WATER COLUMN ATSF PHOTO	10	55	22
WATER COLUMN CNJ CLOSE UP PHOTO	10	55	21
WATER COLUMN DL&W LINCOLN PARK NJ PHOTO	10	55	14
WATER PLUG C&O CHARLOTTESVILLE VA PHOTO	07	75	24
WATER PLUG CN ST ANNE DE BELLEVUE QUE	04	76	54
WATER SCOOPING TRACK PANS NYC CLINTON NY	11	69	19
WATER SOFTENER UDEY PHOTO	06	68	19
WATER SOFTENING PLANTS URY PHOTO	06	50	50
WATER SPOUT CN PALMERSTON ONT PHOTO	08	60	52
WATER SPOUT N&W DISPUTANTA VA 1950 PHOTO	04	68	27
WATER SPOUTS GN BIEBER CA PHOTO	02	32	397
WATER STOP PHOTO ESSAY	08	60	52
WATER STORAGE: TOWERS/TANK/WINDMILL/CARS	03	40	106
WATER TANK BAR OAKFILED MAINE PHOTO	12	38	09
WATER TANK B&ML PHOTO	10	40	12
WATER TANK CN PINE RIVER TO DAUPHIN PHOT	04	31	09
WATER TANK CN POINT ST CHARLES QUEBEC PH	10	63	42
WATER TANK CP (ENCLOSED) HEXAGONAL PHOTO	10	63	42
WATER TANK D&N PHOTO	09	43	114
WATER TANK D&RGW NEEDLETON CO PHOTO	06	69	16

Railroad/Railfan

STRUCTURES VEHICLES & SIGNALS

STRUCTURE, SIGNAL & VEHICLE PHOTOS	M	Y	P
WATER TANK DL&W ITHACA NY (TALL THIN) PH	06	65	14
WATER TANK DL&W WOODEN LINCOLN PARK NJ	06	54	87
WATER TANK M&U SERVICED 2 TRACKS PHOTO	10	55	19
WATER TANK NP MILES CITY MONTANA PHOTO	01	55	31
WATER TANK OPEN TOP NATIONAL CITY CALIF	07	45	101
WATER TANK PGE W/ENCLOSED SUBSTRUCTURE	10	55	19
WATER TANK RGS PHOTO	10	50	18
WATER TANK RGS RIDGWAY YARDS PHOTO	03	53	75
WATER TANK RGS STONER'S TANK PHOTO	10	55	15
WATER TANK RU BENNINGTON VT PHOTO	10	63	42
WATER TANK SAL PORTSMOUTH VA 1951 PHOTO	11	68	19
WATER TANK SOO HANKINSON ND PHOTO	12	64	36
WATER TANK SP PHOTO	02	59	29
WATER TANK SP KEELER CA 1959 PHOTO	08	60	55
WATER TANK SP LAWS CALIFORNIA PHOTO	12	62	10
WATER TANK SP OLD TANK CAR PHOTO	08	54	10
WATER TANK SQUARE WOODEN GCO TOPTON NC P	01	76	10
WATER TANK TM COMMERCE TX PHOTO	10	63	23
WATER TANK TRIO L&N WORTHVILLE KY PHOTO	06	63	13
WATER TANK TWINS R WEST FALLS PA PHOTO	10	63	42
WATER TANK TWO-SPOUT UP MILFORD UT PHOTO	04	67	66
WATER TANK WP VIRGILIA PHOTO	08	45	98
WATER TOWER (ENCLOSED) CNJ HOPATCONG JCT	07	65	18
WATER TOWER (ICE COVERED) WP WENDOVER UT	12	66	17
WATER TOWER (SQUARE) EBT SALTILLO PA PHO	04	67	08
WATER TOWER (TWO SPOUT) CBL POWERS OR PH	07	66	50
WATER TOWER A&A (BEING MOVED) PHOTO	02	54	58
WATER TOWER A&WP HOGANVILLE GA 1971 PHOT	10	78	08
WATER TOWER ACL LEESBURG FL PHOTO	03	77	23
WATER TOWER BAR OAKFIELD MAINE PHOTO	12	57	21
WATER TOWER BELOW SEA LEVEL SP SALTON CA	08	66	28
WATER TOWER BN MERRITT WASHINGTON PHOTO	09	72	17
WATER TOWER BRICK & WOOD NYC MT HOPE NY	04	64	19
WATER TOWER C&GR PHOTO	08	44	15
WATER TOWER C&TS LOS PINO CO 1970 PHOTO	01	74	40
WATER TOWER CASS (X C&O) CASS WV PHOTO	05	65	15
WATER TOWER CB&Q FERRYVILLE WIS PHOTO	08	64	55
WATER TOWER CGA 188' FOR FIRE PROTECTION	10	55	14
WATER TOWER CN POINT ELLICE YARD BC PHOT	02	67	54
WATER TOWER CN TORONTO CANADA PHOTO	05	71	17
WATER TOWER CNJ ATLANTIC HIGHLANDS NJ PH	11	70	21
WATER TOWER CP DUNCAN/COWICHAN BRANCH PH	08	64	55
WATER TOWER D&RGW (ICE COVERED) BOND COL	08	64	55
WATER TOWER D&RGW GRAND JCT COLORADO PHO	11	64	34
WATER TOWER D&RGW SARGENTS CO PHOTO	09	74	22
WATER TOWER D&SL UTAH JCT COLORADO PHOTO	10	63	42
WATER TOWER DL&W LINCOLN PARK NJ PHOTO	10	55	14
WATER TOWER DL&W WOODEN IN 1907 PHOTO	02	55	76
WATER TOWER E (STONE) 1853 PHOTO	01	33	39
WATER TOWER ENCLOSED CP SCOTT JCT QUE PH	02	65	01
WATER TOWER ET&WNC ELIZABETHTON TN PHOTO	06	66	34
WATER TOWER GN CLOQUET MINN PHOTO	06	65	04
WATER TOWER L&N NORTON VA 1949 PHOTO	11	64	16
WATER TOWER M&E WHIPPANY NJ PHOTO	08	64	55
WATER TOWER MILW DAVIS JCT IL PHOTO	08	64	55

STRUCTURE, SIGNAL & VEHICLE PHOTOS	M	Y	P
WATER TOWER NP BEMIDJI MN PHOTO	03	72	12
WATER TOWER NP MILES CITY MT PHOTO	01	76	31
WATER TOWER NYNH&H OCTAGON SOUTHINGTON	01	53	132
WATER TOWER R GORDON PA PHOTO	08	64	55
WATER TOWER RG CRESCO COLORADO PHOTO	04	64	01
WATER TOWER SOO NEW RICHMOND WI 1955 PHO	06	73	18
WATER TOWER SP CASMALIA CAL PHOTO	12	63	17
WATER TOWER UP TINTIO UT 1960 PHOTO	12	72	64
WATER TOWER WP FEATHER RIVER CANYON CA P	08	65	20
WATER TOWER-TWIN SPOUT-AB ALAMEDA CA PHO	04	66	47
WATER TOWER-TWIN SPOUT-D&RGW DURANGO CO	04	66	46
WATER TOWER-TWIN SPOUT-PRR SANDUSKY O PH	04	66	46
WATER TOWER-TWO SPOUTED INS ELNORA IN PH	02	66	13
WATER TOWERS-TWO SPOUT-REASONS FOR PRACT	04	66	48
WAY STATION CBELT OPDYKE ILL PHOTO	02	42	15
WAY STATION INGLEWOOD CA PHOTO	06	54	85
WAY STATION PRL&P ROTHE PHOTO	07	45	118
WHEAT EMPTYING PLATFORM RI PHOTO	04	52	79
WHISTLING HOIST LIFTS LOCOS 9' (JACK)PHO	03	40	75
WINDOW-WASHING MACHINE A ALBUQUERQUE NM	11	76	14
WOOD SIGNAL TOWER B&O #MN MT VERNON OH P	09	65	15
WOOD WATER TANK DL&W ITHACA NY 1907 PHOT	06	76	48
YARD OFFICE D&H CARBONDALE PA PHOTO	02	69	24
YARD OFFICE NKP PINE VALLEY OHIO PHOTO	01	79	63R
YARD OFFICE SP SUISIN CALIFORNIA PHOTO	10	58	24
YARD OFFICE TOWER S CHATTANOOGA TN PHOTO	12	55	18
YARD OFFICE/GENERAL OFFICE NC&SL PHOTO	12	45	33
YARD SCENE L&WV SCRANTON PA PHOTO	10	72	03
YARD SCRANTON PA DL&W IN DIAMOND STACK D	09	77	60
YARD TOWER ATSF BARSTOW CA PHOTO	11	78	02
YARD TOWER CBELT/T&NO SHREVEPORT LA PHOT	10	58	23

*   SIGNAL PHOTOS   *

	M	Y	P
A-C COLOR LIGHT SIGNALS W/AUTO TRAIN CON	08	38	08
A-C COLOR SIGNAL W/ AUTO TRAIN CONTROL	02	30	387
ATC SIGNALS ON S ASHEVILLE NC PHOTO	01	79	20
AUTOMATIC BLOCK SIGNAL IT PHOTO	01	40	11
BALL & LANTERN SIGNAL MC WHITEFIELD NH P	04	74	30
BALL SIGNAL B&M PHOTO	12	38	144
BALL SIGNAL B&M UNION TERMINAL PORTLAND	09	45	88
BALL SIGNAL B&M BERLIN NH PHOTO	SP	75	32R
BALL SIGNAL B&M WHITE RIVER JCT VT 1925	10	75	02
BALL SIGNAL MC CRAWFORD NOTCH NH PHOTO	07	78	64R
BALL SIGNAL MC/B&M WHITEFIELD NH PHOTO	05	84	46
BALL SIGNAL PORTLAND YARDS PHOTO	04	38	125
BALL SIGNAL RUTLAND BELLOWS FALLS VT PHO	05	79	42
BALL SIGNAL SRV STRONG ME PHOTO	11	31	488
BALL SIGNAL W DANVILLE JCT ILL PHOTO	08	31	97
BALL SIGNALS NORTH BENNINGTON VT PHOTO	09	39	72
BALL SIGNALS SOUTHERN LEXINGTON KY PHO	09	40	59
BANJO SIGNAL PHOTO	10	37	07
BANJO TYPE SIGNAL R PHOTO	05	44	33
BANNER SIGNAL NYNH&H 1880'S PHOTO	09	47	133
BLOCK SIGNAL LYNCHBURG VA PHOTO	10	37	11
CAB SIGNAL PANEL SB&LT PHOTO	10	52	48

STRUCTURES VEHICLES & SIGNALS

STRUCTURE, SIGNAL & VEHICLE PHOTOS	M	Y	P
CHAIN PULLEY SIGNAL CN WINNIPEG PHOTO	12	32	102
COLOR LIGHT SIGNAL S ASHVILLE NC PHOTO	10	37	18
CROSSBUCK NY&LB "LOOK OUT FOR THE LOCO"	07	52	35
CROSSING GATE L&N DETAIL PHOTO	04	76	31
CROSSING SIGN BAR BARBER-POLE"LOOK LISTE	08	45	81
CROSSING SIGN MILW ALUMINUM ALLOY PHOTO	02	56	37
CROSSING SIGN SYC SYLVANIA GA UNUSUAL PH	08	56	04
CROSSING SIGNAL PHOTO	06	58	37
CTC SYSTEM SIGNAL MILW PHOTO	08	60	13
DIGITAL HOT BOX INDICATOR L&N AUSTERLIZ	09	71	14
DISTANT SIGNAL C&NW AT ELBURN PHOTO	08	51	26
DWARF SIGNAL PHOTO	10	37	13
DWARF SIGNAL PRR 1968 PHOTO	11	70	14
FIELD TELEPHONING (UNIQUE METHOD) PHOTO	11	72	18
FIVE TRACK SEMAPHORE SIGNAL BRIDGE CNJ P	08	66	34
FLOODLIGHT TOWER E MARION YARDS PHOTO	01	49	64
FR FOREIGN RAILROADS	05	45	84
FR BRITISH SIGNAL GANTRY W/44 SEMAPHORES	06	58	15
FR LONDON MIDLAND & SCOTTISH SIGNAL TOWR	08	42	90
FR NETHERLAND RAILWAYS FOG SIGNALS PHOTO	03	53	24
FR TRINIDAD: CROSSING GATE & SIGNAL PHOT	05	45	84
GRADE CROSSING CN BI-LINGUAL SIGN PHOTO	03	65	33
GRADE CROSSING SIGN GILA BEND AZ TC&GB P	04	67	39
HALL TYPE SIGNAL PHOTO	10	37	10
HAND-OPERATED CROSSING GATES NYC/CNE PHO	06	41	25
HARP SWITCH STAND PHOTO	10	69	13
HIGH TARGET SIGNAL CNJ CARTERET PHOTO	03	46	35
HIGH TENSION WIRE GANTRY R PHILADELPHIA	11	68	24
HIGHBALL SIGNAL B&M WHITEFIELD NH PHOTO	07	66	40
HIGHBALL SIGNAL B&M/MC WHITFIELD NH PHOT	05	71	41
HIGHBALL SIGNAL MC WAUMBEK JCT NH PHOTO	07	71	06
HIGHBALL SIGNAL P&R WILMINGTON DE PHOTO	05	44	32
HIGHBALL SIGNAL READING PHOTO	02	38	123
HIGHBALL SIGNAL RU BELLOWS FALLS VT PHOT	04	70	23
HIGHBALL SIGNAL S PHOTO	05	40	139
MULTI TRACK SIGNAL BRIDGE E JERSEY CITY	07	74	33
OLD-TIME CROSSING GATE AND WATCHMAN ETCH	10	37	25
ORDER BOARD (OLD STYLE) CN ARNOLDS COVE	02	61	28
ORDER BOARD CP DORVAL QUE 1974 PHOTO	05	75	16
ORDER BOARD POST SP SANTA SUSANA CA 1947	11	76	28
ORDER BOARD SJ&LC JOHNSON VT PHOTO	10	42	59
ORDER BOARD: SWIFT TYPE PHOTO	08	57	21
ORDER CRANE MILW COMUS MINN PHOTO	09	42	60
ORDER HOOPS IC IN IOWA PHOTO	09	72	15
OSPREY NEST ON TELEGRAPH POLE CP BANFF A	02	75	19
OVERHEAD INDICATOR (TROLLEY) PHOTO	08	47	100
POSITION LIGHT SIGNAL PHOTO	10	37	15
POSITION LIGHT SIGNALS LV CONWAY PA PHOT	10	37	04
RAIL CROSSING SIGN MARTISCO NY NYC	05	81	34
RAIL CROSSING SIGN WP FREMONT CA 1970 PH	11	76	43
RAIL CROSSING SIGN WP OROVILLE CA PHOTO	08	70	21
RAILROAD CROSSING SIGN ATSF PHOTO	01	54	116
SEARCH LIGHT SIGNAL D&H CARBONDALE PA PH	02	69	18
SEARCHLIGHT SIGNAL DETAIL LV BATAVIA NY	04	75	20
SEARCHLIGHT SIGNAL PC OVERBROOK PA REAR	11	75	02

STRUCTURE, SIGNAL & VEHICLE PHOTOS	M	Y	P
SEARCHLIGHT TYPE COLOR LIGHT SIGNAL PHOT	10	37	22
SEMAPHORE (BACK SIDE) S RALEIGH NC PHOTO	09	74	44
SEMAPHORE BRIDGE (12 UNITS) DL&W HOBOKEN	06	65	21
SEMAPHORE C&O & GTW SOUTH LYONS MI PHOTO	03	71	14
SEMAPHORE D&H AT YD PHOTO	06	63	15
SEMAPHORE D&H CARBONDALE PA PHOTO	02	69	18
SEMAPHORE E GRAHAN NY PHOTO	12	76	30
SEMAPHORE IN DANGER POSITION PHOTO	08	57	22
SEMAPHORE NKP CONTINENTAL OHIO 1958 PHOT	08	60	64
SEMAPHORE NORTH FREEDOM WI PHOTO	09	75	35
SEMAPHORE NORTH FREEDOM WI MUSEUM PHOTO	06	76	65
SEMAPHORE NP AT LIVINGSTON MONTANA PHOTO	06	57	76
SEMAPHORE P&WRR ROCK POINT PA PHOTO	04	54	06
SEMAPHORE PAIR MONTAGUE CA 1973 PHOTO	08	74	52
SEMAPHORE PAIR CB&Q MENDOTA IL PHOTO	08	65	01
SEMAPHORE SIGNAL	10	37	05
SEMAPHORE SIGNAL (2 ARM) C&NW MAYFAIR IL	10	37	12
SEMAPHORE SIGNAL (STANDARD) MAST PHOTO	10	37	23
SEMAPHORE SIGNAL SCL PUNTA GORDA FL PHOT	11	70	01
SEMAPHORE SP MEDFORE OREGON PHOTO	05	42	131
SEMAPHORE WITH HAND LANTERN PHOTO	06	42	86
SEMAPHORE YD TOWER ERIE ARARAT PA PHOTO	02	69	19
SIGN "TRAIN" SUMMIT CA YARD ATSF PHOTO	02	66	59
SIGNAL (DOUBLE SEARCHLIGHT) EL PHOTO	10	72	65
SIGNAL (STOP OR GO) NLW&P PHOTO	09	46	129
SIGNAL 2 ARM L&W 1905 PHOTO	09	47	133
SIGNAL 3 POSITION L&HR PHOTO	09	47	133
SIGNAL ATOMIC POWERED SWITCH LAMP PHOTO	08	57	29
SIGNAL ATSF #11632 PORT CHICAGO CA 1968	11	72	30
SIGNAL AUTO BLOCK MKT DALLAS DIV PHOTO	07	48	32
SIGNAL AUTOMATIC COLOR-LIGHT IC PHOTO	08	57	25
SIGNAL B&M LANTERN IN BALL SIGNAL PHOTO	01	55	38
SIGNAL BANJO R PHOTO	09	47	133
SIGNAL BANJO TYPE PHOTO	07	54	59
SIGNAL BANJO TYPE WM BRANTSVILLE PA PHOT	10	59	16
SIGNAL BLOCK SIGNAL SYSTEM OF CN PHOTOS	05	55	41
SIGNAL BRIDGE (FOUR TRACK) NYC PHOTO	10	37	14
SIGNAL BRIDGE (ODD) PC BALTIMORE MD PHOT	09	69	41
SIGNAL BRIDGE AT PLAINFIELD STN PHOTO	12	58	40
SIGNAL BRIDGE B&M BOSTON MASS PHOTO	02	55	19
SIGNAL BRIDGE C&NW 4 TRACK PHOTO	08	51	23
SIGNAL BRIDGE LV TREICHLER PA PHOTO	08	69	40
SIGNAL BRIDGE N&W ROANOKE VA PHOTO	02	71	08
SIGNAL BRIDGE NKP LITTLE FALLS NY PHOTO	08	69	01
SIGNAL BRIDGE PC ZOO INTERLOCKING PHILY	08	75	01
SIGNAL BUCKET B&M BELLOWS FALLS VT PHOTO	02	43	58
SIGNAL C&O COLOR LIGHT BIG SANDY DIVISIO	12	55	15
SIGNAL COMBINATION BALL & ORDER BOARD PH	08	57	26
SIGNAL D&H PHOTO	04	70	01
SIGNAL DISC CUPOLA MOUNTED ATSF PHOTO	04	45	75
SIGNAL DWARF PHOTO	03	55	30
SIGNAL GANTRY D&H STARRUCCA PA PHOTO	11	75	36
SIGNAL HALL R READING PENNSYLVANIA PHOTO	04	41	49
SIGNAL HIGHBALL B&M NASHUA NH PHOTO	08	46	89
SIGNAL HIGHBALL TYPE PORTLAND TERMINAL P	09	54	27

Railroad/ Railfan

STRUCTURES VEHICLES & SIGNALS

STRUCTURE, SIGNAL & VEHICLE PHOTOS	M	Y	P
SIGNAL IC AUTOMATIC BLOCK SIGNAL PHOTO	10	54	53
SIGNAL INDICATIONS DIAGRAMS	04	59	40
SIGNAL LANTERN B&M NASHUA NH PHOTO	02	76	09
SIGNAL LANTERN TYPE BALL PHOTO	08	57	26
SIGNAL LIGHT REAR VIEW MILW PLUMMER JCT	07	66	42
SIGNAL POSITION LIGHT N&W PHOTO	10	47	63
SIGNAL PRSL SIGNAL #C119 IN MIDDLE TRACK	04	57	40
SIGNAL TARGET 2 & 3 POSITION ARMS PHOTO	08	49	27
SIGNAL TARGET IN 2 DIFFERNT POSITIONS PH	08	57	22
SIGNAL TOWER AND SWITCH PHOTO	10	37	19
SIGNAL TOWER NEAR CN STATION WINNIPEG	12	32	102
SIGNAL TOWER P&R PHOTO	10	37	09
SMASHBOARD PATH NEWARK NJ PHOTO	02	70	13
SOLAR COLLECTOR FOR TRACK SIGNAL CONTROL	03	76	58
SPEED LIMIT BOARD UP SPOKANE WA PHOTO	06	53	19
STRANGE SIGNAL C&O FOSTORIA OHIO PHOTO	08	77	28
SWITCH AND COLOR LIGHT SIGNAL HOOSICK NY	10	37	20
SWITCH STANDS VARIOUS ROADS SKETCHINGS	09	43	96
SWITCH-STAND CN (WOODEN) PHOTO	02	58	65
THREE LIGHT SIGNALS (3) R JENKINTOWN PA	03	75	27
TILTING CROSSBAR SIGNAL PHOTO	10	37	08
TORPEDOES: JAXON FOIL/BEMISDERER'S BULL	08	56	45
TRACKMAN SIGNALS PHOTO	09	52	143
TRAIN ORDER BOARD W&LE COSCHOCTON OH PHO	02	74	20
TRAIN ORDER BRACKET SP PHOTO	09	44	105
TRAIN ORDER CRANE MILW COMUS MINN PHOTO	10	54	40
TRAIN ORDER HOOPS DRAWING	09	41	21
TRAIN ORDER POST PHOTO	02	48	134
TRAIN ORDER POST SP MARION OREGON PHOTO	09	41	21
TRIANGULAR COLOR LIGHT SIGNALS P&PU ILL	10	37	24
TRIPOD-TELEGRAPH POLES CN PHOTO	12	58	45
TROLLEY SIGNAL TAT PHOTO	06	56	65
WHISTLE POSTS ACL (NEW) PHOTO	06	48	55
WIG-WAG CROSSING SIGNAL PHOTO	10	64	34
WIG-WAG SIGNAL SP CROSSING PHOTO	05	65	44
WINDMILL TOWER SIGNAL P&R PHOENIXVILLE P	05	44	32
YARD SWITCH MACHINE PHOTO	08	57	44

VEHICLE PHOTOS	M	Y	P
# VEHICLE PHOTOS #			
0-4-0 LOCOMOTIVE STEAM CARRIAGE 1836 PHO	03	34	138
AM ELECTRIC POWER DRAG LINE ARTIST CONCE	02	68	36
BAGGAGE WAGON A NILES MI 1974 PHOTO	11	74	18
BAGGAGE WAGON ALLIANCE NB 1969 CB&Q PHOT	02	76	20
BAGGAGE WAGON CN OSHAWA ONTARIO PHOTO	03	68	66
BAGGAGE WAGON JOLIET IL PHOTO	07	72	04
BAGGAGE WAGON PC NEW LONDON CT PHOTO	05	70	20
BAGGAGE WAGON SP OAKLAND CA 1955 PHOTO	05	74	06
BAGGAGE WAGONS CB&Q ALLIANCE NE 1969 PHO	08	71	25
BARGE UNLOADING NY HARBOR PHOTO	04	76	32
BOAT TRAIN NYNH&H "PRISCILLA" PHOTO	08	78	54
BUS MP "GOOSE CREEK" PHOTO	05	48	64
BUS NOPS #1001 FRENCH QUARTER TROLLEY PH	11	81	52

VEHICLE PHOTOS	M	Y	P
BUS REO? 1925 PHOTO	04	66	27
C47 ATSF SKYWAY GLENDALE CAL PHOTO	11	85	58
C54 ATSF SKYWAY DOUGLAS PHOTO	11	85	59
CAR FERRIES AA #1, #2 PHOTO	12	32	38
CAR FERRIES AA #4, #5 PHOTO	12	32	41
CAR FERRY "CITY OF MIDLAND 41" PHOTO	11	54	13
CAR FERRY "FLINT & PERE MARQUETTE 4" PHO	11	54	13
CAR FERRY "PERE MARQUETTE 17" PHOTO	11	54	66
CAR FERRY "PERE MARQUETTE 18" PHOTO	11	54	66
CAR FERRY "SEATRAIN HAVANA" PHOTO	12	52	126
CAR FERRY C&O "BADGER" LUDINGTON MI 1964	08	75	04
CAR FERRY C&O "CITY OF MIDLAND" PHOTO	07	50	136
CAR FERRY C&O "SS BADGER", "SS SPARTAN"	02	53	56
CAR FERRY CN "ABEGWEIT" PHOTO	08	47	62
CAR FERRY CN "HURON OF SARNIA"WINDSOR ON	04	71	65
CAR FERRY CN "LANDSDOWNE" WINDSOR ONTARI	02	71	20
CAR FERRY CONTRA COSTA PHOTO	10	47	111
CAR FERRY IC #B106 SIDE WHEELER "PELICAN	09	72	16
CAR FLOAT EAST RIVER NY 1961 PHOTO	05	76	25
CAR FLOAT PRR CAPTAIN EDWARD RICHARDSON	05	49	52
CAR FLOAT WP #3 PHOTO	03	51	21
CARFERRY W "DETROIT" WINDSOR ONT 1957 PH	10	73	19
CART ELMHURST DAIRY PHOTO	08	52	18
CASE 6 WHEEL MOTOR BUS 1920 PHOTO	08	76	54
CATENARY REPAIR TRUCK TORONTO CAN 1921 P	03	71	38
CIRCUS WAGON PHOTO	07	75	15
CIRCUS WAGONS PHOTO	02	30	331
COAL CONVEYOR ST THOMAS CANADA CN PHOTO	06	64	23
CSLS 1943 WHITE BUS RED/CREAM 1987 PHOTO	12	87	76
DEPOT BUS "HOTEL OSBORN" EUGENE OR 1913	02	73	36
DIESEL TANK TRUCK FIELD REFULER	10	72	35
DIESEL TRAIN FERRY WP "LAS PLUMAS" PHOTO	01	65	16
DRAG LINE "BIG MUSKIE" WORLDS LARGEST PH	08	69	21
ELECTRIC CAR FERRY "RAMON" PHOTO	03	51	20
ELECTRIC ICING MACHINE ATSF	02	41	140
FERRY CNJ "ELIZABETH" PHOTO	07	52	42
FERRY CNJ "QUEEN ELIZABETH" PHOTO	09	51	58
FERRY NYC "WEEHAWKEN" PHOTO	10	59	17
FERRY PRSL "MILLVILLE" PHOTO	08	67	20
FERRY SN "RAMONA" PITTSBURG CA PHOTO	05	67	41
FERRY WP "LAS PLUMAS" PHOTO	08	59	38
FR CONTAINER CARS	08	42	94
FR SAHARA'S 6 WHEELED CARS	03	30	570
GAS-BATTERY-ELECTRIC SWITCHER PRR #444 P	02	78	53R
GOULDSBORO STEEL TRANSFER CAR FERRY PHOT	10	38	63
HIGHWAY INSPECTION CAR C&NW PHOTO	12	56	35
HYDROAEROPLANE FAIRCHILD AERIAL SURVEYS	04	50	49
ICEBREAKER CN "ABEGWEIT" PHOTO	08	59	25
INTERURBAN TRAIN FERRY SN "RAMON" PHOTO	12	38	142
MAIL TRUCK #5890 INDIANAPOLIS IN 1931 PH	12	68	04
OIL-BURNING STEAM TUG NYC #18 PHOTO	03	41	96
PACKARD MOTOR CARS INSPECTS RIGHT OF WAY	08	36	76
PASSENGER TRAIN FERRY SN PHOTO	12	40	132
RAIL FERRY "CHIEF WAWATAM" SOO PHOTO	SP	76	45R
RAIL FERRY ATSF "OCEAN WAVE" 1905 PHOTO	01	65	14

Railroad/Railfan

STRUCTURES VEHICLES & SIGNALS

VEHICLE PHOTOS	M	Y	P
RAIL FERRY ATSF "SAN PABLO" PHOTO	01	65	14
RAIL FERRY CN "SEASPAN GREG" VICTORIA BC	09	78	53R
RAIL FERRY TO PRINCE EDWARD ISLAND CN PH	10	77	20R
RAILROAD BARGE IT&B "ISLAND SPRUCE"	09	65	30
RUBBER TIRED SWITCHER PC #3 PHOTO	02	78	51R
RUBBER TIRED SWITCHER B&O DT1 PHOTO	02	78	50R
SNO CAR FERRIES "HURON" & "LANSDOWNE"	04	74	44
SP (PACIFIC MOTOR TRUCKING CO) TRUCK PHO	08	50	22
STEAMSHIP "ASHBURY PARK" CNJ PHOTO	07	52	41
STEAMSHIP "SANDY HOOK" CNJ PHOTO	07	52	40
STRIPPING SHOVEL NP PHOTO	02	31	335
SWITCHMOBILE PRR 4 WHEEL/DIESEL PHOTO	12	56	33
TANK-TRUCK TRANSFERS MALT BOXCAR TO BREW	01	40	54
TOWER TRUCK WINNIPEG CANADA 1915 PHOTO	06	71	53
TRAILER SPOTTER FOR PIGGYBACK SERVICE	02	58	29
TRAIN FERRY SP "SIERRA NEVADA" PHOTO	01	65	17
TRAIN FERRY SP 7189 TON 1914 PHOTO	06	41	24
TRAIN FERRY W "WINDSOR" DETROIT RIVER 57	06	70	17
TRAINFERRY SN "RAMON" PHOTO	01	65	13
TRANS-PACIFIC STEAMER "MINNESOTA" PHOTO	02	37	48
TRUCK CONSUMER-FARMER MILK PHOTO	01	47	16
TUG "CHESSIE" FIRST NEW TUG IN 25 YEARS	05	84	27
TUG ATSF "EDWARD A ENGLE" PHOTO	11	84	51
TUG ATSF "JOHN HAYDEN" PHOTO	11	84	51
TUG ATSF "PAUL HASTINGS" RICHMOND CA PHO	11	84	50
TUG BOAT MORRIS CANAL PHOTO	08	46	40
TUG CHESSIE "MI DUNN", "J SPEED GREY" PH	07	84	35
TUG E "SCRANTON" EAST RIVER NY 1961 PHOT	05	76	25
TUGBOAT "DAVID WINTON" WOOD-BURNER STERN	06	54	33
TUGBOAT B&O PHOTO	08	59	23
TUGBOAT BEDT PHOTO	06	52	34
TUGBOAT BEDT "INVADER" PHOTO	06	52	38
TUGBOAT CMFG PHOTO	10	53	60
TUGBOAT MILW "CHRISTINE ROSS" PHOTO	08	57	15
TUGBOAT NA "CLEARWATER" DIESEL PHOTO	01	54	19
TUGBOAT NA "NORTHLAND ECHO" PHOTO	01	54	16
TUGBOAT PRR "AMBOY" PHOTO	08	59	19
TUGBOAT R "SHAMOKIN" PHOTO	02	54	73
TUGBOAT W/BOXCARS & GONDOLAS PHOTO	02	59	14
VELOCIPEDE PHOTO	08	57	64
VELOCIPEDE BY SHEFFIELD CAR CO ETCHING	06	59	73

RD	STRUCTURE, SIGNAL & VEHICLE PHOTOS BY RD	M	Y	P
A	BAGGAGE WAGON A NILES MI 1974 PHOTO	11	74	18
	WINDOW-WASHING MACHINE A ALBUQUERQUE NM	11	76	14
	DIESEL SHOP INTERIOR A COLLINWOOD OH PHO	08	77	55
	SAND TOWERS A IVY CITY WASHINGTON DC '75	11	75	45
A&A	GENERAL OFFICES A&A PHOTO	02	54	52
	WATER TOWER A&A (BEING MOVED) PHOTO	02	54	58
A&MR	ENGINE HOUSE A&MR ARCATA PHOTO	06	53	37
A&PA	ROUNDHOUSE A&PA NEEDLES CA 1890 PHOTO	04	34	85
A&STAB	ENGINE HOUSE A&STAB PHOTO	08	72	57
A&SU	STATION A&SU AT COBLESKILL NY PHOTO	04	47	19
A&WP	WATER TOWER A&WP HOGANVILLE GA 1971 PHOT	10	78	08
AA	CAR FERRIES AA #1, #2 PHOTO	12	32	38
	CAR FERRIES AA #4, #5 PHOTO	12	32	41
AB	WATER TOWER-TWIN SPOUT-AB ALAMEDA CA PHO	04	66	47
AB&C	DEPOT AB&C (NEXT OT TAL DEPOT) PHOTO	07	43	110
ACL	TWIN WATER TOWERS ACL WAYCROSS GA PHOTO	10	64	28
	ROUNDHOUSE FOREMAN'S OFFICE ACL PHOTO	01	55	37
	WATER TOWER ACL LEESBURG FL PHOTO	03	77	23
	STATION ACL SUTHERLAND FL PHOTO	03	41	10
	STATION ACL NORFOLK VA PHOTO	03	41	16
	STATION BELL ACL WILMINGTON NC PHOTO	06	36	130
	DIESEL SANDING FACILITY ACL WAYCROSS GA	03	65	45
	STATION ACL WEST PALM BEACH PHOTO	01	52	20
	WHISTLE POSTS ACL (NEW) PHOTO	06	48	55
AL	SIMPLE-SPAN BRIDGE AL 700' NENANA AL PHO	08	36	121
	STATION AL CHICALOON AL PHOTO	07	31	492
	DEPOT OF ALASKA RAILROAD NEAR FAIRBANKS	10	34	42
ALGC	MONTREAL RIVER DAM/BRIDGE ALGC PHOTO	10	76	05
ASN&L	LIMESTONE WASHER ASN&L LITHONIA GA PHOTO	04	66	56
ATSF	TUG ATSF "JOHN HAYDEN" PHOTO	11	84	51
	TUG ATSF "EDWARD A ENGLE" PHOTO	11	84	51
	TUG ATSF "PAUL HASTINGS" RICHMOND CA PHO	11	84	50
	RAIL FERRY ATSF "OCEAN WAVE" 1905 PHOTO	01	65	14
	RAIL FERRY ATSF "SAN PABLO" PHOTO	01	65	14
	ELECTRIC ICING MACHINE ATSF PHOTO	02	41	140
	SIBLEY BRIDGE ATSF OVER MISSOURI RIVER P	08	71	54
	C47 ATSF SKYWAY GLENDALE CAL PHOTO	11	85	58
	C54 ATSF SKYWAY DOUGLAS PHOTO	11	85	59
	SNO MISSION TOWER ATSF/SP/UP PHOTO ESSAY	09	46	53
	HARVEY HOUSES (OLD AND NEW) PHOTO	04	58	44
	SIGN "TRAIN" SUMMIT CA YARD ATSF PHOTO	02	66	59
	WATER COLUMN ATSF PHOTO	10	55	22
	TRAVELIFT CRANE ATSF HOBART YARD LA CAL	04	67	34
	SIGNAL ATSF #11632 PORT CHICAGO CA 1968	11	72	30
	BOX CAR STATION INT ATSF GLENDORA CA '45	11	72	31
	ERECTING SHOP FLOOR ATSF PHOTO	02	71	31
	DEPOT ATSF PERRIS CA 1891 PHOTO	11	73	28
	SHOPS ATSF SAN BERNADINO CA INTERIOR '72	05	72	01
	YARD TOWER ATSF BARSTOW CA PHOTO	11	78	02
	RICHMOND CA TERMINAL ATSF PHOTO	07	86	48
	DIESEL SHOP INTERIOR ATSF CLEBURNE TX PH	05	85	46
	TIE-TREATING PLANT ATSF SOMERVILLE TX PH	11	75	30
	ROUNDHOUSE NEEDLES CA 1890 & 1940 PHOTO	01	84	39
	DIESEL SHOP BARSTOW CA ATSF PHOTO	01	84	40
	DEPOT ATSF ARCADIA CA BUILT 1895 PHOTO	08	75	10

Stephans' Railroad Directory

Railroad/Railfan

STRUCTURES VEHICLES & SIGNALS

RD	STRUCTURE, SIGNAL & VEHICLE PHOTOS BY RD	M	Y	P
	HARVEY HOUSE ATSF SYRACUSE KS 1890 PHOTO	04	75	13
	STATION ATSF NEWTON PHOTO	06	42	08
	STATION ATSF SAN MARCIAL NM PHOTO	03	42	61
	DIESEL SERVICE FACILITY ATSF ARGENTINE K	04	69	14
	STATION ATSF EDELSTEIN PHOTO	06	45	66
	SIGNAL DISC CUPOLA MOUNTED ATSF PHOTO	04	45	75
	BAGGAGE STN/LUNCH ROOM/DINING ROOM ATSF	02	45	92
	DEPOT ATSF PERRIS CALIF 1892 PHOTO	09	42	139
	PASSENGER DEPOT 1ST ATSF NEWTON KANSAS	04	31	02
	PASSENGER STATION ATSF NEWTON KANSAS	04	31	03
	STATION ATSF GRAND CANYON AZ PHOTO	03	41	14
	STATION ATSF INGLEWOOD 1887 PHOTO	11	47	138
	DEPOT/HARVEY HOUSE ATSF LA JUNITA CO PHO	04	46	73
	STATION/OFFICE BUILDING/HARVEY HOUSE	04	46	72
	DEPOT ATSF TOPEKA KS 1876 PHOTO	12	64	14
	ICING MACHINE ATSF CALWA CALIFORNIA PHOT	02	57	43
	MICROWAVE REPEATER STATION ATSF TEXAS	02	56	31
	STATION ATSF OTTAWA JUNCTION PHOTO	01	49	34
	DEPOT ATSF SWEETWATER TEXAS PHOTO	11	49	110
	STATION ATSF INGLEWOOD 1887-1947 PHOTO	03	48	70
	RAILROAD CROSSING SIGN ATSF PHOTO	01	54	116
AVI	STATION AVI WICHITA KANSAS PHOTO	07	49	91
B&H	ROUNDHOUSE B&H BRIDGTON MAINE PHOTO	09	35	45
B&LE	ORE UNLOADER B&LE AT CONNEAUT DOCK PHOTO	05	52	26
	STATION B&LE ALBION PHOTO	05	52	19
B&M	COVERED BRIDGE B&M HENNIKER NH PHOTO	08	41	125
	SIGNAL B&M LANTERN IN BALL SIGNAL PHOTO	01	55	38
	SIGNAL BRIDGE B&M BOSTON MASS PHOTO	02	55	19
	HIGHBALL SIGNAL B&M/MC WHITFIELD NH PHOT	05	71	41
	BALL SIGNAL B&M BERLIN NH PHOTO	SP	75	32R
	HIGHBALL SIGNAL B&M WHITEFIELD NH PHOTO	07	66	40
	TRAIN SHED B&M SALEM MASS PHOTO	11	73	27
	SANDING TOWER RIGBY ENGINE HOUSE ME B&M	10	77	47
	SIGNAL LANTERN B&M NASHUA NH PHOTO	02	76	09
	STATION B&M NORTH CONWAY NH PHOTO	02	76	23
	BALL SIGNAL MC/B&M WHITEFIELD NH PHOTO	05	84	46
	BALL SIGNAL B&M WHITE RIVER JCT VT 1925	10	75	02
	SIGNAL BUCKET B&M BELLOWS FALLS VT PHOTO	02	43	58
	BALL SIGNAL B&M PHOTO	12	38	144
	BALL SIGNAL B&M UNION TERMINAL PORTLAND	09	45	88
	STATION B&M/CV JOINT EFFORT VT PHOTO	03	41	12
	CONTROL HOUSES B&M MECHANICSVILLE NY (2)	11	44	53
	SIGNAL HIGHBALL B&M NASHUA NH PHOTO	08	46	89
	STATION B&M TAUNTON MASS BUILT IN 1865	12	50	76
B&ML	STATION B&ML (1870/1900) PHOTOS	10	40	11
	WATER TANK B&ML PHOTO	10	40	12
	DEPOT B&ML KNOX (OLD FREIGHT HOUSE) PHO	10	40	15
	DEPOT B&ML THORNDIKE PHOTO	10	40	18
	TENDER COAL LOADER (MANUAL) B&ML PHOTO	06	60	25
B&MR	STATION B&MR LINCOLN NEBRASKA PHOTO	03	49	38
B&O	TUGBOAT B&O PHOTO	08	59	23
	THOMAS VIADUCT B&O BALTIMORE MD PHOTO	09	77	02
	THOMAS VIADUCT B&O BALTIMORE MD. PHOTO	SP	77	37R
	RUBBER TIRED SWITCHER B&O DT1 PHOTO	02	78	50R
	FREIGHT CAR SCALES (AUTOMATIC) B&O PHOTO	02	66	30
	ENGINE TERMINAL B&O IVY CITY WASH DC PHO	01	66	41
	TURNTABLE B&O IVY CITY, WASHINGTON DC PH	05	78	55
	COALING TOWER B&O BENWOOD W VA PHOTO	05	87	32
	ROUNDHOUSE B&O MARTINSVILLE WV (1ST) PHO	11	44	112
	CONTROL SIGNAL & OFFICE B&O WASHINGTN PA	10	37	23
	STATION AT RELAY MASS B&O 1870 & 1935	05	35	134
	STATION B&O PASS/FRT MOUNT CLARE PHOTO	03	47	17
	STORE ROOM B&O MT CLARE SHOPS PHOTO	02	57	47
	WOOD SIGNAL TOWER B&O #MN MT VERNON OH P	09	65	15
	DEPOT INTERIOR B&O NEW ALBANY IN PHOTO	02	60	15
	STATION B&O SILVER SPRING MD PHOTO	12	54	30
BAR	BRIDGE BAR AROOSTOOK RIVER ASHLAND ME PH	10	76	16
	POTATO WAREHOUSE BAR HOVEY & CO PHOTO	12	38	12
	WATER TANK BAR OAKFILED MAINE PHOTO	12	38	09
	CROSSING SIGN BAR BARBER-POLE"LOOK LISTE	08	45	81
	DEPOT BAR GUILFORD PHOTO	12	35	63
	WATER TOWER BAR OAKFIELD MAINE PHOTO	12	57	21
BCF&NB	DEPOT BCF&NB NORTH FOXBORO MASS PHOTO	05	73	54
BCR&N	DEPOT BCR&N CEDAR RAPIDS IOWA PHOTO	05	45	86
BCRW	PEACE RIVER BRIDGE BCRW BEFOR/AFTER FIRE	03	80	23
BEDT	TUGBOAT BEDT PHOTO	06	52	34
	TUGBOAT BEDT "INVADER" PHOTO	06	52	38
	WAREHOUSE BEDT PHOTO	06	52	41
	GANTRY CRANE BEDT PHOTO	06	52	37
BERY	CAR BARN BERY (FIREPROOF) PHOTO	04	53	88
BMTA	ELEVATED STATION BMTA CHARLESTOWN MA PHO	01	76	27
BN	WATER TOWER BN MERRITT WASHINGTON PHOTO	09	72	17
	DIESEL TRACK PANS FOR YARD POLUTION CONT	11	72	59
	CLASSIFICATION YARD BN MINNEAPOLIS MN PH	01	77	09
	ENGINE TERMINAL PARKWATER WA BN (VOLCANO	11	80	02
BR&P	BRICK DEPOT BR&P E SALAMANCA NY PHOTO	09	43	14
BRB&L	TOWER BRB&L LYNN MASS PHOTO	01	40	74
BU&NW	STATION BU&NW WASHINGTON IOWA PHOTO	03	49	39
C&E	C&E STATION CASSVILLE, MISSOURI PHOTO	11	30	494
	STATION C&E CASSVILLE PHOTO	04	51	127
C&GR	DEPOT C&GR COLUMBUS PHOTO	08	44	21
	STATION C&GR WEST POINT PHOTO	08	44	21
	WATER TOWER C&GR PHOTO	08	44	15
C&NW	HIGHWAY INSPECTION CAR C&NW PHOTO	12	56	35
	COALING TOWER C&NW CLYMAN JCT WI 1974 PH	08	74	22
	FREIGHT DEPOT C&NW ELLSWORTH IA PHOTO	11	43	112
	SEMAPHORE SIGNAL (2 ARM) C&NW MAYFAIR IL	10	37	12
	SIGNAL BRIDGE C&NW 4 TRACK PHOTO	08	51	23
	DISTANT SIGNAL C&NW AT ELBURN PHOTO	08	51	26
C&O	CAR FERRY C&O "SS BADGER", "SS SPARTAN"	02	53	56
	CAR FERRY C&O "CITY OF MIDLAND" PHOTO	07	50	136
	CAR FERRY C&O "BADGER" LUDINGTON MI 1964	08	75	04
	TRI-LEVEL BRIDGES RICHMOND VA PHOTO	12	66	21
	ROUNDHOUSE C&O CLIFTON FORGE VA 1949 PHO	03	66	62
	SIGNAL C&O COLOR LIGHT BIG SANDY DIVISIO	12	55	15
	DIESEL SHOP INTERIOR C&O RUSSEL KY PHOTO	12	67	14
	ROUND STATION C&O SOUTH LYONS MI PHOTO	03	71	14
	SEMAPHORE C&O & GTW SOUTH LYONS MI PHOTO	03	71	14
	TURNTABLE C&O DETROIT MI 1953 PHOTO	04	72	51
	ROTARY COAL DUMP YARD C&O NEWPORT NEWS V	05	78	32

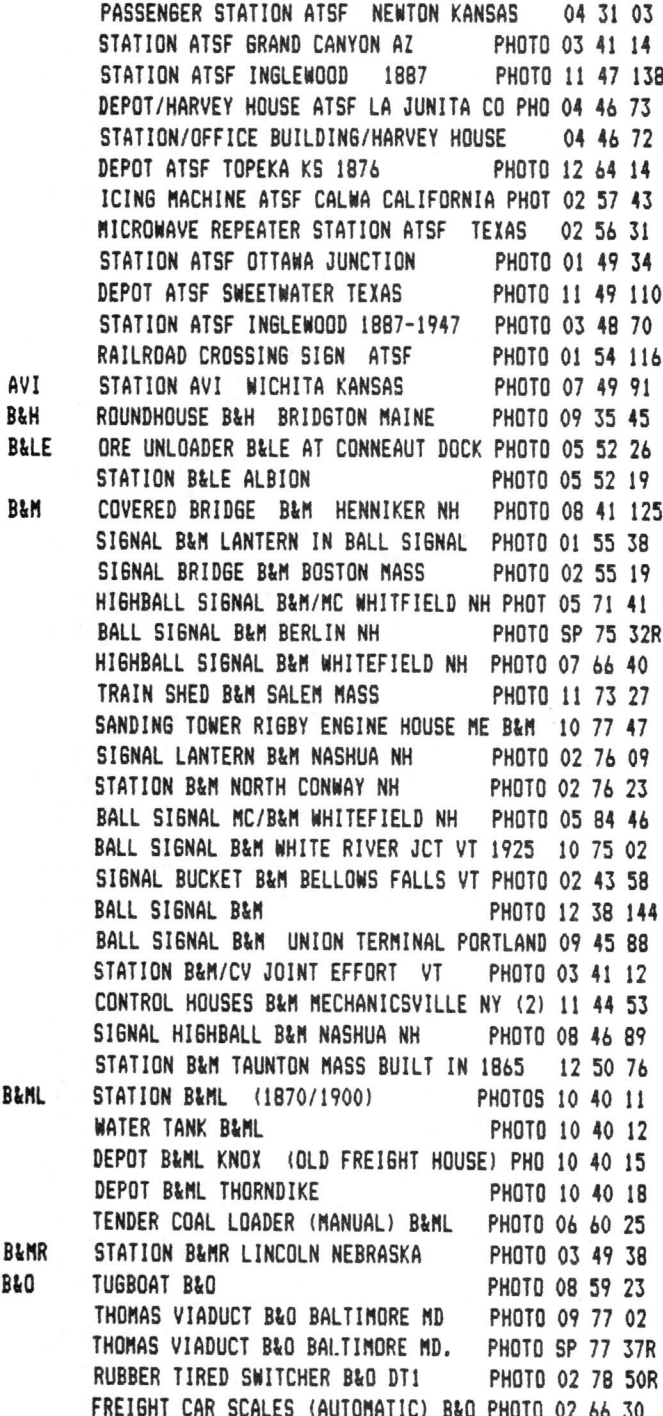

Stephans' Railroad Directory

Railroad/Railfan

STRUCTURES VEHICLES & SIGNALS

RD	STRUCTURE, SIGNAL & VEHICLE PHOTOS BY RD	M	Y	P
	DEPOT C&O FOSTORIA OHIO PHOTO	08	77	28
	STRANGE SIGNAL C&O FOSTORIA OHIO PHOTO	08	77	28
	DEPOT C&O RUTHVEN ONTARIO PHOTO	01	76	44
	MD CABIN C&O MEADOW CREEK WVA PHOTO	05	85	03
	WATER PLUG C&O CHARLOTTESVILLE VA PHOTO	07	75	24
	STATION C&O WILLIAMSBURG VA PHOTO	03	41	20
	COALING STATION MODERN C&O CLIFTON FORGE	09	47	74
	CONCRETE RETARDER TOWER C&O VA PHOTO	02	59	41
C&S	STEAM FUNNEL C&S DENVER CO 1939 PHOTO	10	73	20
	STATION C&S GUNNISON CO 1946 PHOTO	10	73	24
	STORAGE SHED (X STATION) C&S PHOTO	02	45	130
	STEAM FUNNEL C&S DENVER CO PHOTO	05	40	92
C&TS	WATER TOWER C&TS LOS PINO CO 1970 PHOTO	01	74	40
C&WY	CONCRETE COAL TRAIN LOADING SILO C&WY PH	08	71	66
CA&E	DEPOT CA&E GLEN ELLYN ILL PHOTO	01	46	105
	STATION STONE & BRICK CA&E ELMHURST ILL	01	46	104
CAPR	SWING BRIDGE CAPR CLEARWATER RIVER ID PH	12	77	23R
CASS	WATER TOWER CASS (X C&O) CASS WV PHOTO	05	65	15
CB&Q	BAGGAGE WAGONS CB&Q ALLIANCE NE 1969 PHO	08	71	25
	BAGGAGE WAGON ALLIANCE NB 1969 CB&Q PHOT	02	76	20
	TRESTLE CB&Q NEAR MT PLEASANT PHOTO	07	52	129
	WATER TOWER CB&Q FERRYVILLE WIS PHOTO	08	64	55
	STATION CB&Q CRESTON IOWA PHOTO	04	73	30
	BACKSHOP (STEAM) CB&Q INTERIOR 1900 PHOT	09	77	35
	ROUNDHOUSE FLOODED CB&Q HANNIBAL MO 1947	03	76	42
	STATION CB&Q LA CROSSE WISCONSIN PHOTO	03	49	36
	STATION CB&Q GALESBURG ILLINOIS PHOTO	03	49	40
	STATION CB&Q GALESBURG IL CORRECTION PHO	07	49	138
	SEMAPHORE PAIR CB&Q MENDOTA IL PHOTO	08	65	01
	COALING TOWER CB&Q GALESBURG IL PHOTO	06	65	57
	STATION CB&Q (OLD AND NEW) PHOTOS	12	54	26
CBELT	YARD TOWER CBELT/T&NO SHREVEPORT LA PHOT	10	58	23
	WAY STATION CBELT OPDYKE ILL PHOTO	02	42	15
	DEPOT CBELT GRENNWAY ARKANSAS PHOTO	05	54	102
CBL	WATER TOWER (TWO SPOUT) CBL POWERS OR PH	07	66	50
CCC&SL	DEPOT CCC&SL MILFORD IN 1913 PHOTO	03	76	03
CGA	WATER TOWER CGA 188' FOR FIRE PROTECTION	10	55	14
CGW	PASSENGER STATION CGW CHICAGO IL ETCHING	11	43	87
	STATION CGW KANSAS CITY, MO PHOTO	11	43	78
	STATION CGW FORT DODGE IA 1951 PHOTO	12	54	31
CHESS	TUG CHESSIE "MI DUNN", "J SPEED GREY" PH	07	84	35
	TUG "CHESSIE" FIRST NEW TUG IN 25 YEARS	05	84	27
	INTERLOCKING TOWER STERLING OH CHESSIE P	05	82	28
CHW	DIESEL HOUSE CHW PHOTO	12	54	43
CL	DEPOT CL ELKHORN CITY KY PHOTO	12	53	18
CMFG	TUGBOAT CMFG PHOTO	10	53	60
CMI	STATION CMI DIVIDE COLORADO PHOTO	09	42	149
CN	CAR FERRY CN "ABEGWEIT" PHOTO	08	47	62
	ICEBREAKER CN "ABEGWEIT" PHOTO	08	59	25
	COAL CONVEYOR ST THOMAS CANADA CN PHOTO	06	64	23
	CAR FERRY CN "LANDSDOWNE" WINDSOR ONTARI	02	71	20
	CAR FERRY CN "HURON OF SARNIA" WINDSOR ON	04	71	65
	RAIL FERRY TO PRINCE EDWARD ISLAND CN PH	10	77	20R
	RAIL FERRY CN "SEASPAN GREG" VICTORIA BC	09	78	53R
	BAGGAGE WAGON CN OSHAWA ONTARIO PHOTO	03	68	66
	KOHISLA TRESTLE CN BRITISH COLUMBIA PHOT	12	66	01
	SLIDE SHEDS CN LYTTON BC PHOTO	11	86	44
	TRIPOD-TELEGRAPH POLES CN PHOTO	12	58	45
	SWITCH-STAND CN (WOODEN) PHOTO	02	58	65
	STATION CN BONADVENTURE STN MONTREAL PHO	11	53	119
	SIGNAL BLOCK SIGNAL SYSTEM OF CN PHOTOS	05	55	41
	ENGINE TERMINAL CN TORONTO CANADA PHOTO	05	71	17
	WATER TOWER CN TORONTO CANADA PHOTO	05	71	17
	LOCOMOTIVE SHOP CN CHARLOTTETOWN PEI CAN	10	77	23R
	WATER TOWER CN POINT ELLICE YARD BC PHOT	02	67	54
	LOCOMOTIVE SHED CN HALIBURTON ONTARIO PH	04	68	14
	HUMP YARD RETARDER NOISE SHED CN PHOTO	08	73	21
	ORE CAR SHAKER CN PORT ARTHUR ONT PHOTO	07	72	39
	WATER PLUG CN ST ANNE DE BELLEVUE QUE	04	76	54
	STATION CN JOLIETT QUEBEC 1939 PHOTO	01	70	21
	TRAIN-ORDER STATION CN MINE CENTRE ONT P	04	75	19
	CHAIN PULLEY SIGNAL CN WINNIPEG PHOTO	12	32	102
	SIGNAL TOWER NEAR CN STATION WINNIPEG	12	32	102
	SECTION HOUSE CN JOYBERT QUEBEC PHOTO	03	33	139
	STATION CN PARK AVE STN MONTREAL PHOTO	02	32	333
	WATER TANK CN PINE RIVER TO DAUPHIN PHOT	04	31	09
	STATION CN TORONTO UNION STATION PHOTO	12	47	19
	STATION CN MONTREAL BONAVENTURE STN DRAW	12	47	29
	WATER TANK CN POINT ST CHARLES QUEBEC PH	10	63	42
	GRADE CROSSING CN BI-LINGUAL SIGN PHOTO	03	65	33
	GRAIN ELEVATOR CN WAINRIGHT CANADA PHOTO	03	65	35
	ORDER BOARD (OLD STYLE) CN ARNOLDS COVE	02	61	28
	BOXCAR DEPOT CN ARNOLDS COVE NF PHOTO	02	61	28
	WATER SPOUT CN PALMERSTON ONT PHOTO	08	60	52
	STATION CN EDMONTON PHOTO	01	54	30
CNJ	STEAMSHIP "SANDY HOOK" CNJ PHOTO	07	52	40
	STEAMSHIP "ASHBURY PARK" CNJ PHOTO	07	52	41
	FERRY CNJ "ELIZABETH" PHOTO	07	52	42
	FERRY CNJ "QUEEN ELIZABETH" PHOTO	09	51	58
	FREIGHT TERMINAL (ROUND) CNJ BRONX NY PH	04	64	27
	TURNTABLE CNJ BETHLEHEM YARDS PA PHOTO	02	66	57
	WATER COLUMN CNJ CLOSE UP PHOTO	10	55	21
	FIVE TRACK SEMAPHORE SIGNAL BRIDGE CNJ P	08	66	34
	ENGINE TERMINAL CNJ BETHLEHAM PA 1937 PH	11	70	23
	WATER TOWER CNJ ATLANTIC HIGHLANDS NJ PH	11	70	21
	HIGH TARGET SIGNAL CNJ CARTERET PHOTO	03	46	35
	ROUND FREIGHT HOUSE CNJ BRONX TERMINAL	03	46	30
	MCMYLER LOADER CNJ TERMINAL PHOTO	03	46	17
	WATER TOWER (ENCLOSED) CNJ HOPATCONG JCT	07	65	18
	THAWING SHEDS CNJ PHOTO	11	51	53
CNS&M	WATCHMAN'S TOWER CNS&M SOUTH UPTON PHOTO	10	53	78
CNYE	CAR BARN CNYE BUILT IN 1907 PHOTO	08	56	68
CNYEA	CAR BARN CNYEA SOUTH LA PORTE IND PHOTO	05	33	81
COL	STATION COL JEFFERSON CO PHOTO	05	42	133
CP	MOUNTAIN CREEK BRIDGE CP ROGERS PASS BC	02	78	10
	TWIN TUNNELS CP AGASSIZ BC PHOTO	01	76	49
	BRIDGE CP SUMMERLAND BC PHOTO	03	76	32
	TOPLESS TUNEL CP PALLISER BC	11	73	03
	PIPE TUNNEL CP NEWPORT VT PHOTO	05	70	14
	BRIDGE & TRESTLE CP PERRY SOUND ONT PHOT	03	70	18

Railroad/ Railfan

STRUCTURES   VEHICLES   &   SIGNALS

RD	STRUCTURE, SIGNAL & VEHICLE PHOTOS BY RD	M	Y	P
	COALING TOWER CP ST LUC YARD MONTREAL PH	10	58	40
	WATER TOWER CP DUNCAN/COWICHAN BRANCH PH	08	64	55
	DIESEL SERVICE PLANT CP ALYTH YD INTER P	06	66	51
	LOCO REPAIR SHOP INTERIOR CP ANGUS SHOP	03	67	39
	BUCKET COAL HOIST CP CHIPMAN NB 1959 PHO	11	76	36
	STATION CP AGASSIZ BC (BRICK) PHOTO	04	73	24
	SOLAR COLLECTOR FOR TRACK SIGNAL CONTROL	03	76	58
	COALING DOCK (SMALL) CP TEESWATER ONT PH	05	76	29
	PIGGYBACK TERMINAL CP AIR VIEW PHOTO	11	74	19
	HAND COALING STATION CP 1959 PHOTO	10	69	24
	TURNTABLE ST JOHNSBURY VT CP 1974 PHOTO	06	75	18
	ORDER BOARD CP DORVAL QUE 1974 PHOTO	05	75	16
	CAR REPAIR SHOP CP CALGARY ALB INTERIOR	05	75	10
	OSPREY NEST ON TELEGRAPH POLE CP BANFF A	02	75	19
	CABOOSE/TEMP STATION CP #436709 PHOTO	05	74	12
	STATION CP DORVAL QUEBEC 1957 PHOTO	10	69	04
	STATION CP PARK AVE MONTRAL PHOTO	03	41	27
	DEPOT CP ONAWA PHOTO	02	44	12
	CP YARDS ROSEBURG OR (WOODBURNING DAYS)	05	34	82
	WATER TANK CP (ENCLOSED) HEXAGONAL PHOTO	10	63	42
	COALING PLANT 400 TON CONCRETE CP PHOTO	07	50	34
	WATER TOWER ENCLOSED CP SCOTT JCT QUE PH	02	65	01
	TENDER COALING (MANUAL) STATION CP PHOTO	06	60	26
	CONTROL BUILDING CP PHOTO	01	51	139
	CONTROL TOWER CP COTE ST LUC MONTREAL PH	10	54	40
CPA	CONVEYOR BELT CPA PHOTO	08	57	18
CPM&O	ROUNDHOUSE CPM&O SIOUX CITY IA PHOTO	04	55	42
CR&NW	MILES GLACIER BRIDGE CR&NW PHOTO	05	39	126
CSCO	CAR BARN & OFFICE CSCO WOOSTER OH PHOTO	10	68	30
	CAR BARN CSCO SEVILLE JUNCTION PHOTO	05	52	87
CSLS	CSLS 1943 WHITE BUS RED/CREAM 1987 PHOTO	12	87	76
CSS&SB	WAITING STATION CSS&SB LYDICK IN PHOTO	02	53	34
	STATION CSS&SB GARY PHOTO	02	53	12
CTA	NEW CLARK JUNCTION TOWER CTA CHICAGO IL	02	77	23
CTR	CAR BARN CTR OIL CITY PA PHOTO	12	50	90
	TROLLEY STATION CTR COCHRAN PHOTO	12	50	86
CV	TRAIN SHED (BRICK) CV ST ALBANS VT 1928	06	76	51
	DEPOT CV MILLERS FALLS MASS PHOTO	05	78	24R
	DEPOT CV/B&M MILLERS FALLS MASS PHOTO	08	46	91
	FLAG STOP CV VERNON VT PHOTO	08	46	25
	TRAIN SHED & STATION CV ST ALBANS VT PHO	08	63	04
D&CA	ENGINE HOUSE D&CA DIAMOND SPRG CALIF PHO	05	41	57
D&H	INTERCHANGE TOWER D&H BINGHAMTON NY PHOT	SP	76	29R
	OCTAGONAL DEPOT D&H FT EDWARD NY 1976 PH	10	76	20
	ROUNDHOUSE RUINS D&H BINGHAMTON NY 1974	03	76	26
	SIGNAL GANTRY D&H STARRUCCA PA PHOTO	11	75	36
	SIGNAL D&H PHOTO	04	70	01
	SEARCH LIGHT SIGNAL D&H CARBONDALE PA PH	02	69	18
	SEMAPHORE D&H CARBONDALE PA PHOTO	02	69	18
	YARD OFFICE D&H CARBONDALE PA PHOTO	02	69	24
	STATION D&H OLD UNION STA ALBANY NY PHOT	04	69	14
	INTERLOCKING PLANT D&H SCHOHARIE JCT NY	04	47	22
	STATION D&H SCHOHARIE JUNCTION NY PHOTO	04	47	22
	GENERAL OFFICES D&H ALBANY NY PHOTO	04	47	26
	ASH PITS D&H ONEONTA NY YARD 1922 PHOTO	06	63	22

RD	STRUCTURE, SIGNAL & VEHICLE PHOTOS BY RD	M	Y	P
	TURNTABLE D&H COLONIE SHOPS 1928 PHOTO	06	63	17
	SEMAPHORE D&H AT YD PHOTO	06	63	15
	STATION D&H COBLESKILL NY PHOTO	02	65	15
	STATION D&H LAKE GEORGE NY PHOTO	12	54	32
D&N	WATER TANK D&N PHOTO	09	43	114
D&RG	TURNTABLE D&RG SALIDA CO 1906 PHOTO	08	75	32
	ROUNDHOUSE D&RG SALIDA CO 1906 PHOTO	08	75	32
D&RGW	TOWER D&RGW JACK'S CABIN PHOTO	10	53	29
	WATER TOWER D&RGW (ICE COVERED) BOND COL	08	64	55
	WATER TOWER D&RGW GRAND JCT COLORADO PHO	11	64	34
	WATER TOWER-TWIN SPOUT-D&RGW DURANGO CO	04	66	46
	FUELING FACILITY D&RGW (DIESEL) PHOTO	04	67	40
	COAL TOWER D&RGW CHAMA NM PHOTO	11	72	16
	RAIL BOARDING HOUSE D&RGW SARGENTS CO PH	09	74	21
	WATER TOWER D&RGW SARGENTS CO PHOTO	09	74	22
	WATER TANK D&RGW NEEDLETON CO PHOTO	06	69	16
	BARREL TRANSFER D&RGW PHOTO	08	41	23
	STATION D&RGW SILVERTON STATION PHOTO	06	54	53
DL&W	TRESTLE AT SCRANTON PA DL&W 1866N PHOTO	08	34	134
	BERGEN TUNNEL PORTAL DL&W 1908 PHOTO	07	85	37
	ENGINE HOUSE DL&W ITHACA NY 1907 PHOTO	02	55	76
	WATER TOWER DL&W WOODEN IN 1907 PHOTO	02	55	76
	WATER TOWER DL&W LINCOLN PARK NJ PHOTO	10	55	14
	PUMP HOUSE DL&W LINCOLN PARK NJ PHOTO	10	55	14
	WATER COLUMN DL&W LINCOLN PARK NJ PHOTO	10	55	14
	YARD SCRANTON PA DL&W IN DIAMOND STACK D	09	77	60
	ENGINE HOUSE DL&W ITHACA NY 1907 PHOTO	06	76	48
	WOOD WATER TANK DL&W ITHACA NY 1907 PHOT	06	76	48
	STATION DL&W BINGHAMTON NY PHOTO	10	75	59
	ENG HOUSE/WOOD WATER TANK DL&W ITHACA NY	05	31	241
	PUMP HOUSE DL&W LINCOLN PARK NJ PHOTO	05	31	247
	STATION DL&W WAYSISSING? PHOTO	01	30	167
	TOWER DL&W MANUNKA CHUNK TOWER PA PHOTO	05	47	72
	ENGINE HOUSE DL&W ITHACA NY PHOTO	06	65	14
	WATER TANK DL&W ITHACA NY (TALL THIN) PH	06	65	14
	SEMAPHORE BRIDGE (12 UNITS) DL&W HOBOKEN	06	65	21
	WATER TANK DL&W WOODEN LINCOLN PARK NJ	06	54	87
DSP&P	DEPOT DSP&P COMO CO 1946 PHOTO	10	73	20
	ROUNDHOUSE DSP&P COMO CO 1946 PHOTO	10	73	24
	STATION DSP&P LEADVILLE CO 1929 PHOTO	12	33	46
DW&P	COAL TOWER DW&P PHOTO	04	58	45
E	TUG E "SCRANTON" EAST RIVER NY 1961 PHOT	05	76	25
	STARUCCA VIADUCT PENNSYLVANIA PHOTO	06	59	14
	MAIL PICK-UP POLE (STEEL) ERIE PHOTO	04	58	47
	FREIGHT DEPOT ERIE BINGHAMTON NY PHOTO	SP	76	28R
	FIELD TELEPHONING (UNIQUE METHOD) PHOTO	11	72	18
	STONE WATER TANK DRAWING ERIE PHOTO	06	76	49
	SEMAPHORE E GRAHAN NY PHOTO	12	76	30
	STATION E ELMIRA NY 1900 PHOTO	01	73	47
	STATION E BOGATA NJ 1909 PHOTO	06	72	51
	MULTI TRACK SIGNAL BRIDGE E JERSEY CITY	07	74	33
	ROUNDHOUSE & TURNTABLE E SALAMANCA NY'47	12	69	26
	SEMAPHORE YD TOWER ERIE ARARAT PA PHOTO	02	69	19
	WATER TOWER E (STONE) 1853 PHOTO	01	33	39
	STATION E ELMIRA NY 1885 PHOTO	07	31	491

Stephans' Railroad Directory

Railroad/Railfan

STRUCTURES VEHICLES & SIGNALS

RD	STRUCTURE, SIGNAL & VEHICLE PHOTOS BY RD	M	Y	P
	STATION HOUSE ERIE PHOTO	02	41	92
	STATION E SUSQUEHANNA PA PHOTO	03	41	24
	FLOODLIGHT TOWER E MARION YARDS PHOTO	01	49	64
	PASSENGER STATION E GEAUGA LAKE OH PHOTO	06	61	52
	ROOFED OVER WOOD STATION E SOUTHFIELD NY	02	60	19
EBT	GENERAL OFFICES EBT ORBISONIA PA PHOTO	W	75	27R
	WATER TOWER (SQUARE) EBT SALTILLO PA PHO	04	67	08
	STATION/GENERAL OFFICES EBT PA PHOTO	08	41	15
ED	TICKET OFFICE EDAVILLE RAILROAD PHOTO	05	47	58
EL	STARUCCA VIADUCT LANESBORO PA EL & DH	05	76	65
	SIGNAL (DOUBLE SEARCHLIGHT) EL PHOTO	10	72	65
	DIESEL SERVICING FACILITY EL HORNELL NY	12	76	66
	TERMINAL EL HOBOKEN NJ INTERIOR PHOTO	01	80	67
ELD	VIADUCT AND ELEVATOR ELD AT WEEHAWKEN NJ	08	51	94
EN	STATION EN PALISADE NEVADA PHOTO	01	39	122
ET&WNC	WATER TOWER ET&WNC ELIZABETHTON TN PHOTO	06	66	34
EV&I	COMBINATION STATION EV&I ELNORA IN PHOTO	02	66	13
F&CC	PALACE HOTEL F&CC (BRICK & WOOD) PHOTO	08	58	28
	POST OFFICE/SECOND HAND STORE F&CC PHOTO	08	58	24
FAM	DRAWBRIDGE INTERIOR FAM PHOTO	08	78	33
FEC	STATION FEC MIAMI FL 1930 PHOTO	04	75	28
FJ&G	STATION FJ&G GLOVERSVILLE NY 1954 PHOTO	06	68	59
FRIS	ROUNDHOUSE FRISCO MONETT MO 1940 PHOTO	11	78	50
G	DEPOT GEORGIA WINTERVILLE PHOTO	SU	76	49R
	ROUNDHOUSE ATLANTA GA AFTER SHERMAN PHOT	09	77	28
GCO	WATER TANK SQUARE WOODEN GCO TOPTON NC P	01	76	10
GF	ENGINE HOUSE GF SAN GABRIEL CA PHOTO	10	41	46
GMT	COAL TOWER (WOOD) NORTH WALPOLE NH PHOTO	12	70	13
GN	STONE ARCH BRIDGE GN MINNEAPOLIS MN PHOT	12	78	24
	BASCULE BRIDGE GN PHOTO	05	37	54
	MAYER FEED MILL LESTER PRAIRIE MN PHOTO	W	75	44R
	DIESEL SHOP INTERIOR W/PLATFORMS GN PHOT	04	74	57
	DEPOT GN EPHRATA WASHINGTON OLD AND NEW!	12	43	122
	STATION GN FORT BENTON MONTANA PHOTO	01	40	123
	WATER SPOUTS GN BIEBER CA PHOTO	02	32	397
	WATER TOWER GN CLOQUET MINN PHOTO	06	65	04
	STATION GN EPHRATA WASHINGTON PHOTO	12	54	34
	GREENHOUSE GN MONROE OREGON PHOTO	06	54	97
	STATION GN SAUK CENTER MINNESOTA PHOTO	06	54	100
GT	DEPOT GT EDWARDSBURG MI 1908 PHOTO	12	75	13
GTW	DEPOT GTW W/3 STEM LOCOS 1956 PHOTO	04	66	54
	STATION GTW SARANAC MI 1906 PHOTO	05	69	17
HAR	STATION HAR HARTWELL GA PHOTO	01	47	72
HU	DEPOT HU FARMINGTON PHOTO	10	44	115
IC	BRIDGE PIER UNDER CONSTRUCTION IC PHOTO	11	67	13
	CAR FERRY IC #B106 SIDE WHEELER "PELICAN	09	72	16
	BRIDGE IC CAIRO IL MODERNIZATION PHOTOS	07	52	112
	PADUCAH SHOPS IC INTERIOR PHOTO	SP	75	39R
	ORDER HOOPS IC IN IOWA PHOTO	09	72	15
	DEPOT IC GIBSLAND LOUISIANA PHOTO	04	78	45R
	TURNTABLE "GALLOWS" IC PHOTO	08	43	154
	COAL TOWER IC DYERSBURG TENN PHOTO	09	44	65
	SIGNAL AUTOMATIC COLOR-LIGHT IC PHOTO	08	57	25
	SIGNAL IC AUTOMATIC BLOCK SIGNAL PHOTO	10	54	53
	STATION IC ROCKFORD STATION (OLD) PHOTO	12	54	33
INS	WATER TOWER-TWO SPOUTED INS ELNORA IN PH	02	66	13
IOWA	SHOPS IOWA EMERY IOWA PHOTO	02	65	36
IRY	STATION IRY LOCKPORT NY PHOTO	10	58	45
IT	TERMINAL IT CHICAGO IL PHOTO	01	73	34
	AUTOMATIC BLOCK SIGNAL IT PHOTO	01	40	11
	STATION IT MIDWEST TERMINAL BLDG PHOTO	03	41	07
IT&B	RAILROAD BARGE IT&B "ISLAND SPRUCE"	09	65	30
KCE	DEPOT KCE RANDOLPH MAINE PHOTO	09	35	43
KCN&FS	DEPOT KCN&FS SULPHUR SPRINGS ARK PHOTO	10	47	18
KN	CATTLE LANE KNOX RAILROAD MAINE PHOTO	03	33	137
L&HR	DEPOT L&HR GREAT MEDOWS NJ PHOTO	W	74	22R
	SIGNAL 3 POSITION L&HR PHOTO	09	47	133
L&MA	ROBINS CAR SHAKEOUT L&MA PHOTO	07	52	57
	ROBINS CAR SHAKEOUT L&MA PHOTO	07	52	55
	DRYING PLANT L&MA PHOTO	07	52	54
	COALING TOWER L&MA PHOTO	07	52	52
L&N	WATER TOWER L&N NORTON VA 1949 PHOTO	11	64	16
	LOCOMOTIVE SHOPS L&N 1865 PHOTO	11	64	18
	ERECTING SHOP INTERIOR L&N S LOUISVILLE	11	64	20
	DIGITAL HOT BOX INDICATOR L&N AUSTERLIZ	09	71	14
	COACH YARD LOUISVILLE UNION STATION PHOT	11	67	21
	PIGGYBACK TERMINAL L&N ATLANTA GA PHOTO	05	68	15
	GANTRY CRANE 50 TON L&N ATLANTA GA YARD	05	68	28
	DIESEL PART CONVEYOR MAZE L&N PHOTO	11	68	16
	RAILRETARDER L&N ATLANTA GA PHOTO	05	78	04
	WATCHMAN'S TOWER L&N PHOTO	04	76	31
	CROSSING GATE L&N DETAIL PHOTO	04	76	31
	STATION L&N DEATSVILLE ALABAMA PHOTO	08	42	47
	SHACK L&N FOR RADIO BROADCOASTS	04	37	119
	DUAL WATER TANKS L&N NEW MEMPHIS IL PHOT	08	63	31
	WATER TANK TRIO L&N WORTHVILLE KY PHOTO	06	63	13
	DEPOT L&N OPDYKE IL W/GINGERBREAD PHOTO	12	54	29
L&R	ROUNDHOUSE L&R ABANDONED ENGINE HOUSE PH	07	39	129
L&N	SIGNAL 2 ARM L&N 1905 PHOTO	09	47	133
L&WV	YARD SCENE L&WV SCRANTON PA PHOTO	10	72	03
LC&SJ	COVERED BRIDGE LC&SJ HARDWICK VT PHOTO	08	75	25
LI	DEPOT LI FLATBUSH AVENUE TERMINAL PHOTO	01	43	34
	DEPOT LI WOODSIDE NY PHOTO	01	43	22
	STATION LI HEMPSTEAD NY TEMPORARY PHOTO	11	42	139
	STATION LI (OLD & NEW) MONTAUK NY PHOTO	09	46	128
	STATION LI COLD SPRING HARBOR PHOTO	08	49	21
	PLATFORM SHELTER LI PHOTO	08	49	21
LIG	STATION LIG PHOTO	05	52	44
LS&I	STEEL ARCH/CANTILEVER/TRESTLE LS&I PHOTO	08	37	54
LS&MS	ROUNDHOUSE LS&MS NORWALK OHIO PHOTO	12	35	82
LV	STATION W/POST OFFICE & FEED STORE LV PH	11	36	138
	DEPOT LV FLEMINGTON JCT PA PHOTO	08	77	31R
	TOWER LV MOUNTAINTOP PA PHOTO	03	68	15
	STATION LV SAYRE PA 1973 PHOTO	12	73	18
	DIESEL SERVICE FACILITY LV SAYRE PA 1972	06	75	20
	SEARCHLIGHT SIGNAL DETAIL LV BATAVIA NY	04	75	20
	SIGNAL BRIDGE LV TREICHLER PA PHOTO	08	69	40
	SIGNAL TOWER (FRAME) LV GENEVA JCT NY PH	08	69	41
	STATION LV ALLENTOWN PA PHOTO	05	44	127
	POSITION LIGHT SIGNALS LV CONWAY PA PHOT	10	37	04

Railroad/ Railfan

STRUCTURES VEHICLES & SIGNALS

RD	STRUCTURE, SIGNAL & VEHICLE PHOTOS BY RD	M	Y	P
	RAILROAD SHOPS LV SAYRE PA 1904 PHOTO	01	65	21
	ERECTING ROOM INTERIOR LV SAYRE PA PHOTO	01	65	25
LV&T	DEPOT LV&T RHYOLITE NV PHOTO	10	76	02
LVT	STATION LVT SELLERSVILLE PA PHOTO	09	42	102
M	SAND HOUSE MONON PHOTO	11	68	61
	COALING TOWER MONON PHOTO	11	68	61
M&A	ROUNDHOUSE M&A HARRISON PHOTO	06	48	23
M&E	WATER TOWER M&E WHIPPANY NJ PHOTO	08	64	55
M&SL	DEPOT M&SL REDWOOD MINNESOTA PHOTO	04	58	25
M&U	WATER TANK M&U SERVICED 2 TRACKS PHOTO	10	55	19
	STATION M&U UNIONVILLE NY ETCHING	08	47	123
MC	COACH/BAGGAGE MC #509 USED AS TOWN HALL	08	48	63
	HIGHBALL SIGNAL MC WAUMBEK JCT NH PHOTO	07	71	06
	ENGINE TERMINAL MC RIGBY YARD PORTLAND M	07	78	41R
	BALL SIGNAL MC CRAWFORD NOTCH NH PHOTO	07	78	64R
	ROUNDHOUSE MC SOUTH RIGBY ME PHOTO	01	75	58
	BALL & LANTERN SIGNAL MC WHITEFIELD NH P	04	74	30
	WARMING HOUSE MC WATERVILLE ME PHOTO	08	47	133
	SIGNAL HIGHBALL TYPE PORTLAND TERMINAL P	09	54	27
MC&SA	POLLING POCKET USE MC&SA PHOTO	08	66	16
MCRI	ROUNDHOUSE MCRI (WOODEN) PHOTO	10	50	51
MEL	DRAG LINE "BIG MUSKIE" WORLDS LARGEST PH	08	69	21
MICHC	DEPOT MICHC PEACOCK MI PHOTO	10	52	18
MILW	TUGBOAT MILW "CHRISTINE ROSS" PHOTO	08	57	15
	WATER TOWER MILW DAVIS JCT IL PHOTO	08	64	55
	UNION STATION MILW MILWAUKEE WI 1886 PHO	11	71	29
	UNION STATION MILW GREAT FALLS MT PHOTO	11	71	31
	SIGNAL LIGHT REAR VIEW MILW PLUMMER JCT	07	66	42
	CROSSING TOWER MILW A-5 PHOTO	03	43	25
	WATCHMAN'S TOWER (X MILW & RI) 8 SIDED P	08	69	35
	ORDER CRANE MILW COMUS MINN PHOTO	09	42	60
	STEAM FUNNEL MILW PHOTO	02	41	127
	DEPOT FRAME MILW ONEIDA JCT IOWA PHOTO	04	41	15
	CROSSING SIGN MILW ALUMINUM ALLOY PHOTO	02	56	37
	CTC SYSTEM SIGNAL MILW PHOTO	08	60	13
	TRAIN ORDER CRANE MILW COMUS MINN PHOTO	10	54	40
	STATION MILW KILBOURN WISCONSIN PHOTO	12	54	35
	STATION MILW RONDOUT PHOTO	03	53	41
MKT	COMBINATION STATION MKT DUBLIN, TEXAS	09	32	229
	STATION MKT PARSONS KANSAS PHOTO	12	51	49
	STATION MKT PARSONS KAN (REPLICA) PHOTO	07	48	13
	SIGNAL AUTO BLOCK MKT DALLAS DIV PHOTO	07	48	32
	HOSPITAL MKT DENISON HOSP FOR EMPLOYEES	07	48	34
MON	TURNTABLE MON SOUTH BROWNSVILLE PA 1972	10	72	59
MOVA	STATION MOVA SAYLESVILLE RI PHOTO	08	49	71
MP	BUS MP "GOOSE CREEK" PHOTO	05	48	64
	STATION MP CRETE NE 1889 PHOTO	04	73	29
	DEOPT MP HERRINGTON KS PHOTO	12	77	12
	TURNTABLE MP PHOTO	05	70	30
	FREIGHT DEPOT MP EXTENDS INTO 2 STATES	04	31	06
	GANTRY CRANE MP PIGGYBACK OPERATIONS	12	56	31
	STATION MP ST LOUIS FREIGHT STN PHOTO	05	52	67
N&BF	STATION N&BF WATSESSING AVE (COAL YARD)	02	41	134
N&SL	DEPOT N&SL NORFOLK NY 1971 PHOTO	08	74	34
N&W	WROUGHT IRON TRUSS BRIDGE N&W 1886-1931	05	37	49

RD	STRUCTURE, SIGNAL & VEHICLE PHOTOS BY RD	M	Y	P
	TRESTLE BRIDGE N&W PHOTO	05	37	52
	COALING STATION N&W BLUEFIELD WV. PHOTO	08	64	16
	STEAM ENGINE SERVICE FACILITY N&W PHOTO	08	64	17
	STATION N&W WIRTZ VA PHOTO	08	64	23
	DEPOT N&W BLUE RIDGE VA PHOTO	SP	75	64R
	WATER SPOUT N&W DISPUTANTA VA 1950 PHOTO	04	68	27
	SIGNAL BRIDGE N&W ROANOKE VA PHOTO	02	71	08
	RAILROAD CONSTRUCTION ENGINEER'S OFFICE	04	45	49
	TOWER N&W MODERN PHOTO	09	44	28
	TOWER N&W BLUEFIELD PHOTO	09	44	19
	SIGNAL POSITION LIGHT N&W PHOTO	10	47	63
	COALING STATION N&W BLUEFIELD WV PHOTO	07	54	20
NA	TUGBOAT NA "NORTHLAND ECHO" PHOTO	01	54	16
	TUGBOAT NA "CLEARWATER" DIESEL PHOTO	01	54	19
	FREIGHT HOUSE NA WATERWAYS PHOTO	01	54	26
NB&T	STATION NB&T WEIR BRANCH 1850-66 PHOTO	08	31	46
NC&SL	BRIDGE NC&SL DIXIE LINE BRIDGE JOHNSVILLE	06	46	72
	YARD OFFICE/GENERAL OFFICE NC&SL PHOTO	12	45	33
NCN	TURNTABLE NCN GRASS VALLEY CALIF PHOTO	05	43	144
NCT	CAR BARN NCT GLENBOROUGH CA PHOTO	12	44	83
NDEM	SAND TOWER (DIESEL) NDEM VERACRUZ MEX PH	05	74	08
NEZ&I	DEPOT NEZ&I PHOTO	01	54	73
NKP	STATIONARY BOILER NKP 2-8-0 #803 1947 PH	11	74	58
	TOWER NKP XN LEIPSIC OHIO PHOTO	05	80	39
	YARD OFFICE NKP PINE VALLEY OHIO PHOTO	01	79	63R
	SIGNAL BRIDGE NKP LITTLE FALLS NY PHOTO	08	69	01
	SEMAPHORE NKP CONTINENTAL OHIO 1958 PHOT	08	60	64
NLW&P	SIGNAL (STOP OR GO) NLW&P PHOTO	09	46	129
NOPS	BUS NOPS #1001 FRENCH QUARTER TROLLEY PH	11	81	52
NP	STRIPPING SHOVEL NP PHOTO	02	31	335
	COVERED TURNTABLE NP EASTON WASH PHOTO	02	66	17
	WATER TANK NP MILES CITY MONTANA PHOTO	01	55	31
	TENDER TRACKSIDE TANK NP SEATTLE WA PHOT	10	55	19
	WATER TOWER NP BEMIDJI MN PHOTO	03	72	12
	BLOW-DOWN SHED FOR STEAM LOCOS NP PHOTO	02	78	50
	WATER TOWER NP MILES CITY MT PHOTO	01	76	31
	DEPOT NP BILLINGS MONT PHOTO	10	41	125
	TRANSFER TABLE NP (S TACOMA WASH) PHOTO	04	40	75
	DEPOT NP LOMBARD MONTANA PHOTO	10	40	122
	STATION NP FARGO ND PHOTO	03	41	21
	DEPOT NP DETROIT LAKES MINN PHOTO	10	44	11
	STATION NP/GN SEATTLE WA PHOTO	07	47	123
	SEMAPHORE NP AT LIVINGSTON MONTANA PHOTO	06	57	76
	TICKET OFFICE NP CURB-SERVICE ST PAUL PH	08	57	43
	STATION NP FARGO ND WITH PARK PHOTO	12	54	33
	OIL WELL NP RICHEY MONTANA PHOTO	05	53	13
	BLOW-DOWN SHED NP BILLINGS MONTANA PHOTO	08	54	42
NSUB	WAITING ROOM NSUB CAR #2626 PHOTO	08	52	94
NT	STATION NT PARK PA (STONE) PHOTO	04	45	101
NY&GL	DEPOT NY&GL FORREST HILLS NJ PHOTO	09	72	11
NY&LB	SIGNAL TOWER NY&LB "SG" SEA GRIT PHOTO	07	52	38
	CROSSBUCK NY&LB "LOOK OUT FOR THE LOCO"	07	52	35
NYC	FERRY NYC "WEEHAWKEN" PHOTO	10	59	17
	OIL-BURNING STEAM TUG NYC #18 PHOTO	03	41	96
	BRIDGE NYC HARLEM RIVER NEW/OLD PHOTOS	09	51	60

Stephans' Railroad Directory

Railroad/Railfan

STRUCTURES VEHICLES & SIGNALS

RD	STRUCTURE, SIGNAL & VEHICLE PHOTOS BY RD	M	Y	P
	FOUR TRACK VIADUCT NYC PHOTO	05	31	167
	ORE DUMPERS LAKEFRONT DOCK & TERMINAL CO	11	53	29
	WATER TOWER BRICK & WOOD NYC MT HOPE NY	04	64	19
	HYDRAULIC RAM FOR CAR MOVING IN YARD PHO	02	66	31
	STATION NYC CARYL NY 1942 PHOTO	08	68	26
	SIGNAL TOWER NYC (HUFF) WELLINGTON OH '51	11	76	23
	RAIL CROSSING SIGN MARTISCO NY NYC	05	81	34
	WATER SCOOPING TRACK PANS NYC CLINTON NY	11	69	19
	HAND-OPERATED CROSSING GATES NYC/CNE PHO	06	41	25
	SIGNAL BRIDGE (FOUR TRACK) NYC PHOTO	10	37	14
	SMOKE DUCT ON NYC PHOTO	05	37	38
	STATION NYC WEST SHORE STN HAVERSTRAW NY	04	47	51
	STATION NYC GRAND CENTRAL TERMINAL PHOTO	11	50	30
NYCE	STATION NYCE 89TH STREET STATION PHOTO	06	56	22
NYCTA	SUBWAY STATION NYCTA PHOTO	02	64	24
NYNH&H	BOAT TRAIN NYNH&H "PRISCILLA" PHOTO	08	78	54
	BRIDGE NYNH&H BUZZARD BAY VERTICAL LIFT	07	52	64
	BRIDGE NYNH&H BUZZARD BAY CADE COD MA PH	02	48	18
	BRIDGE: ARCH-TYPE CATENARY NYNH&H PHOTO	02	59	31
	HELL-GATE BRIDGE NYNH&H PHOTO	05	37	55
	DEPOT NYNH&H CANAAN CONN PHOTO	02	67	18
	DEPOT NYNH&H TARKIN RI PHOTO	05	73	54
	MAIL CRANE NYNH&H NIANTIC CT 1944 PHOTO	04	78	10
	STATION NYNH&H BRIDGEPORT CT 1977 PHOTO	08	77	15
	DIESEL SHOP INTERIOR NH NEW HAVEN CT PHO	12	87	55
	DEPOT NYNH&H NEW CANAAN CT 1959 PHOTO	04	75	46
	BANNER SIGNAL NYNH&H 1880'S PHOTO	09	47	133
	WATER TOWER NYNH&H OCTAGON SOUTHINGTON	01	53	132
NYO&W	STATION NYO&W WICKHAM AVE MIDDLETOWN NY	09	46	28
NYP&B	STATION NYP&B PARK SQUARE BOSTON MA PHOT	09	42	51
NYS&W	BRIDGE NYS&W: 1872/1894/1934 PHOTO	03	39	138
	DEPOT NYS&W STILLWATER NJ PHOTO	09	78	33R
O&K	HOTEL DELANCEY O&K CANNEL CITY KY PHOTO	08	52	47
	DEPOT O&K HELECHAWA KY PHOTO	08	52	37
	STATION O&K CANNEL CITY KY PHOTO	08	52	36
O&LC	MUSHROOM WATER TOWER O&LC CHURUBUSCO NY	12	64	34
	COVERED PLATFORM O&LC MALONE NY 1910 PHO	12	64	34
	ELEVATOR O&LC (500,000 BUSHEL CAP) PHOTO	01	47	21
OB&PA	DEPOT/ENGINEHOUSE OB&PA OGDENSBURG VT PH	F	75	31R
OCO	DEPOT OCO MASSACHUSETTS 1880? PHOTO	10	75	33
	DEPOT OCO KNEELAND STREET BOSTON MA PHOT	09	42	44
OR&LC	STATION/OFFICES OR&LC HONOLULU PHOTO	10	46	90
OS	STATION OCEAN SHORE RY FARALLONE CITY CA	12	35	69
P&F	DROP-BOTTOM BRIDGE P&F PHOTO	08	43	131
	STATION P&F PIONEER STATION PHOTO	08	43	132
P&LE	STATION INTERIOR P&LE PITTSBURG PA PHOTO	11	76	38
	LOCOMOTIVE SHOP INTERIOR P&LE 1904 PHOTO	06	62	35
P&PU	TRIANGULAR COLOR LIGHT SIGNALS P&PU ILL	10	37	24
P&R	TERMINAL P&R PHILADELPHIA PA PHOTO	03	33	90
	WINDMILL TOWER SIGNAL P&R PHOENIXVILLE P	05	44	32
	HIGHBALL SIGNAL P&R WILMINGTON DE PHOTO	05	44	32
	SIGNAL TOWER P&R PHOTO	10	37	09
	SIGNAL TOWER P&R PHOENIXVILLE PA PHOTO	04	56	74
P&WRR	BLOCK OFFICE "RK" P&WRR ROCK POINT PA PH	02	73	11
	SEMAPHORE P&WRR ROCK POINT PA PHOTO	04	54	06
P-D	STATION P-D TYRONE NM PHOTO	05	53	104
PATH	SMASHBOARD PATH NEWARK NJ PHOTO	02	70	13
PC	BAGGAGE WAGON PC NEW LONDON CT PHOTO	05	70	20
	RUBBER TIRED SWITCHER PC #3 PHOTO	02	78	51R
	STONE DEPOT CLIFTON-ALDAN PA PC 1972 PHO	08	72	36
	GINGERBREAD DEPOT PC STRAFFORD PA PHOTO	10	72	42
	STATION PC STRAFFORD PA (GINGERBREADY) P	12	72	03
	STATION PC (BRICK) WALLINGFORD PA 1972 P	10	73	17
	SIGNAL TOWER PC "SHORE" FRANKFORD JCT PA	11	73	15
	SIGNAL TOWER PC BRYN MAWR PA 1974 PHOTO	06	74	08
	SEARCHLIGHT SIGNAL PC OVERBROOK PA REAR	11	75	02
	TOWER ELMORA TOWER S ELIZABETH NJ PHOTO	01	80	35
	SIGNAL BRIDGE PC ZOO INTERLOCKING PHILY	08	75	01
	SWITCH TOWER PC OLD SAYBROOK CT 1973 PHO	02	74	13
	STATION PC MOORESTOWN NJ (NOW ANTIQUES)	03	74	17
	DIESEL SERVICING MULTIPLE FACILITY PC PH	01	69	13
	SIGNAL BRIDGE (ODD) PC BALTIMORE MD PHOT	09	69	41
PE	TROLLEY STOP WALKER CALIFORNIA 1938 PHOT	05	66	61
	WATCHMAN'S TOWER PE AMOCO PHOTO	07	54	57
	WATCHMAN'S TOWER PE WATTS PHOTO	08	54	63
PEOP	STATION PEOP SANDUSKY PHOTO	11	51	83
PGE	WATER TANK PGE W/ENCLOSED SUBSTRUCTURE	10	55	19
PH&NW	DEPOT PH&NW COURT ST DEPOT HURON MICH	09	43	154
PM	CAR FERRY "PERE MARQUETTE 18" PHOTO	11	54	66
	CAR FERRY "PERE MARQUETTE 17" PHOTO	11	54	66
PRL&P	WAY STATION PRL&P ROTHE PHOTO	07	45	118
PRR	SWITCHMOBILE PRR 4 WHEEL/DIESEL PHOTO	12	56	33
	TUGBOAT PRR "AMBOY" PHOTO	08	59	19
	CAR FLOAT PRR CAPTAIN EDWARD RICHARDSON	05	49	52
	RARITAN BAY NJ BRIDGE PRR PHOTO	03	84	67
	TUNNEL PORTALS PRR GALLITZEN PA PHOTO	11	77	62
	GAS-BATTERY-ELECTRIC SWITCHER PRR #444 P	02	78	53R
	STONE ARCH BRIDGE PRR (STONE/TIMBER) PHO	04	46	36
	GANTRY FOR LOADING TRAILERS ON FLAT CARS	08	64	30
	TRAILER GANTRY CRANE PRR KEARNEY NJ PHOT	06	66	60
	WATER TOWER-TWIN SPOUT-PRR SANDUSKY O PH	04	66	46
	MULE OR BARNEY PHOTO PRR LI YARD PHOTO	05	67	52
	TRAIN SHED PRR BROAD ST STN PHILA PA PHO	05	67	17
	STATION PRR BROAD ST STATION PHIL PA PHO	05	67	16
	STREET SCENE ELIZABETH NJ 1904 PHOTO	01	71	16
	STATION PRR TOLEDO OH 1948 PHOTO	04	71	16
	SIGNAL TOWER PRR HUNT TOWER PHOTO	08	73	34
	ROUNDHOUSE PRR NEWARK NJ AIR VIEW PHOTO	02	76	36
	STATION PRR MILLVILLE PA 1913 PHOTO	11	74	12
	DWARF SIGNAL PRR 1968 PHOTO	11	70	14
	BROAD STREET STATION PRR AFTER FIRE PHOT	01	75	53
	COALING STATION PRR PITTSBURGH PA PHOTO	10	41	60
	TERMINAL PRR ENOLA YARD ENOLA PA PHOTO	11	41	06
	COAL DUMPING PIER PRR PHOTO	11	39	88
	STATION PRR DOVER DELAWARE PHOTO	03	41	20
	STATION PRR NORRISTOWN PA PHOTO	03	41	29
	TERMINAL PRR W PHILADELPHIA PA 1876 ETCH	06	34	04
	CAR SHOP PRR INDIANAPOLIS PHOTO	04	46	29
	TRAIN SHED PRR COLUMBUS OHIO PHOTO	04	46	28
	DEPOT PRR HARRISBURG PA PHOTO	04	46	27

Stephans' Railroad Directory

Railroad/ Railfan

STRUCTURES VEHICLES & SIGNALS

RD	STRUCTURE, SIGNAL & VEHICLE PHOTOS BY RD	M	Y	P
	MULTI-CUPOLA ENGINEHOUSE PRR HARRISBURG	04	46	25
	COAL DOCK PRR MARION OHIO 1952 PHOTO	12	64	20
	DEPOT PRR ELIDA OHIO PHOTO	08	57	33
	LOCO ERECTION SHOP INTERIOR PRR ALTOONA	12	63	28
	DEPOT LOUDON PARK CEMETERY PRR PHOTO	06	60	23
	STATION PRR NEW YORK NY PHOTO	12	54	31
	FREIGHT CAR REPAIR PLANT PRR HOLLIDAYSBU	08	53	59
	TICKET OFFICE PRR NEW CASTLE DE PHOTO	06	54	69
PRSL	FERRY PRSL "MILLVILLE" PHOTO	08	67	20
	TOWER PRSL WINSLOW JCT PA PHOTO	08	67	21
	STATION PRSL MILLVILLE NJ PHOTO	06	42	129
	STATION PRSL ATLANTIC CITY PHOTO	07	45	95
	SIGNAL PRSL SIGNAL #C119 IN MIDDLE TRACK	04	57	40
PSTC	PSTC ARDMORE JUNCTION INTERCHANGE PHOTO	10	55	45
R	TUGBOAT R "SHAMOKIN" PHOTO	02	54	73
	WATER TOWER R GORDON PA PHOTO	08	64	55
	DEPOT READING SUNBURY PA PHOTO	02	67	58
	HIGH TENSION WIRE GANTRY R PHILADELPHIA	11	68	24
	ROUNDHOUSE R READING PA PHOTO	06	76	49
	STATION R RYDAL PA 1973 PHOTO	06	73	15
	STATION R ROBESONIA PA 1952 PHOTO	11	74	20
	TRAIN SHED READING TERMINAL PHILA PA PHO	03	85	32
	TURNTABLE READING HELLERTOWN PA PHOTO	11	69	28
	ERECTION HALL INTERIOR R PHOTO	05	78	34R
	TURNTABLE R STRASBURG PA PHOTO	09	75	25
	THREE LIGHT SIGNALS (3) R JENKINTOWN PA	03	75	27
	STATION R GOTHIC 3 STORY HOPEWELL NJ PHO	05	74	43
	DEPOT R BYCOT PA TINY STATION! PHOTO	03	43	118
	SIGNAL HALL R READING PENNSLYVANIA PHOTO	04	41	49
	HIGHBALL SIGNAL READING PHOTO	02	38	123
	BANJO TYPE SIGNAL R PHOTO	05	44	33
	STATION R PHILADELPHIA PA PHOTO	05	44	25
	SIGNAL BANJO R PHOTO	09	47	133
	WATER TANK TWINS R WEST FALLS PA PHOTO	10	63	42
	SHOPS & YARD READING PA 1930 ARIAL PHOTO	12	61	22
	ROUNDHOUSE & TABLE READING PA 1931 PHOTO	12	61	20
	SIGNAL TOWER R "LIGHTHOUSE" OCTAGON SHAP	10	54	80
	STATION R GINGERBREAD BYCOT PA PHOTO	08	54	14
REA	RAILWAY EXPRESS OFFICE SUFFERN NY PHOTO	12	50	25
RF&P	FUELING & WATERING DIESEL FACILITY RF&P	04	71	51
RG	WATER TOWER RG CRESCO COLORADO PHOTO	04	64	01
	ENGINE TERMINAL RG DURANGO COLORADO PHOT	10	77	43R
RGS	WATER TANK RGS STONER'S TANK PHOTO	10	55	15
	STATION RGS OPHIR PHOTO	10	50	19
	WATER TANK RGS PHOTO	10	50	18
	WATER TANK RGS RIDGWAY YARDS PHOTO	03	53	75
	STATION AND OUTHOUSE RGS OPHIR PHOTO	03	53	69
RI	SAMSON OF THE CIMMARON RI PHOTO	07	45	97
	DEPOT RI ELLSWORTH MN--X DOODLEBUG #9012	04	66	20
	GRAIN LOADERS RI PHOTO	11	72	15
	STATION RI LASALLE STREET CHICAGO IL PHO	10	70	23
	WHEAT EMPTYING PLATFORM RI PHOTO	04	52	79
RT&C	TROLLEY STATION RT&C WARREN ME 1901 PHOT	02	71	43
RU	COVERED BRIDGE RU SHOREHAM VERMONT PHOTO	06	57	21
	TRUS BRIDGE RU NEW HAVEN VT PHOTO	12	75	37
	TICKET OFFICE INTERIOR RU SHELBURNE VT P	11	64	35
	COAL TOWER RU RUTLAND VERMONT PHOTO	04	70	26
	HIGHBALL SIGNAL RU BELLOWS FALLS VT PHOT	04	70	23
	BALL SIGNAL RUTLAND BELLOWS FALLS VT PHO	05	79	42
	COAL CHUTE RU RUTLAND VT PHOTO	08	46	20
	STATION RU (SMALL FRAME) CHATHAM NY PHO	08	46	12
	WATER TANK RU BENNINGTON VT PHOTO	10	63	42
S	TRILEVEL BRIDGE RICHMOND VA PHOTO	11	78	48
	HIGH BRIDGE S KENTUCKY RIVER PHOTO	12	58	44
	YARD OFFICE TOWER S CHATTANOOGA TN PHOTO	12	55	18
	DEPOT S BLACKVILLE SC 1970 PHOTO	01	73	01
	ATC SIGNALS ON S ASHEVILLE NC PHOTO	01	79	20
	ROUNDHOUSE S JOHN SEIVER TENNESSEE PHOTO	11	77	32
	SEMAPHORE (BACK SIDE) S RALEIGH NC PHOTO	09	74	44
	HIGHBALL SIGNAL S PHOTO	05	40	139
	BALL SIGNALS SOUTHERN LEXINGTON KY PHO	09	40	59
	A-C COLOR LIGHT SIGNALS W/AUTO TRAIN CON	08	38	08
	COLOR LIGHT SIGNAL S ASHVILLE NC PHOTO	10	37	18
SAL	WATER TANK SAL PORTSMOUTH VA 1951 PHOTO	11	68	19
	SAND HOUSE & TOWER SAL PORTSMOUTH VA PHO	11	68	19
	DEPOT SAL ZELLWOOD FL 1975 PHOTO	08	77	16
	STATION SAL WEST PALM BEACH FL PHOTO	03	41	32
	STATION SAL CAMDEN SC PHOTO	03	41	32
	STATION SAL TAMPA UNION STATION PHOTO	04	53	26
	STATION SAL STONO SC PHOTO	04	53	27
SB&LT	CAB SIGNAL PANEL SB&LT PHOTO	10	52	48
SCHEN	TERMINAL SCHEN & HVRY SARATOGA SPRINGS	02	45	105
SCL	SEMAPHORE SIGNAL SCL PUNTA GORDA FL PHOT	11	70	01
	STATION SCL PUNTA GORDA FL PHOTO	11	70	01
SD&AE	TRESTLE SD&AE "SHORTEST LINE EAST" PHOTO	05	53	55
SE	DRAWBRIDGE SE ST JOHNS QUEBEC 1882 PHOT	08	43	149
SIRT	STATION SIRT STATEN ISLAND BEF/AFTER CLE	08	72	38
SJ&LC	BRIDGE SJ&LC WOODEN COVERED BRIDGE PHOTO	03	47	108
	COVERED BRIDGE SJ&LC WOLCOTT VT. PHOTO	10	75	37
	DEPOT SJ&LC EAST SWANTON VT PHOTO	08	75	24
	ORDER BOARD SJ&LC JOHNSON VT PHOTO	10	42	59
SJ&LCO	COVERED BRIDGE SJ&LCO WOLCOTT VT. PHOTO	01	80	25
	COVERED BRIDGE SJ&LCO WOLCOTT VT PHOTO	04	68	60
	DEPOT SJ&LCO JOHNSON VT PHOTO	01	80	30
SLV&TH	INDIANAPOLIS UNION STATION 2 1880 PHOTO	04	62	26
SN	TRAINFERRY SN "RAMON" PHOTO	01	65	13
	PASSENGER TRAIN FERRY SN PHOTO	12	40	132
	INTERURBAN TRAIN FERRY SN "RAMON" PHOTO	12	38	142
	FERRY SN "RAMONA" PITTSBURG CA PHOTO	05	67	41
	STATION SN WOODLAND CALIFORNIA PHOTO	02	57	42
SNO	DEPOT/GENERAL OFFICES SNO SILVERTON PHOT	06	58	24
SOO	RAIL FERRY "CHIEF WAWATAM" SOO PHOTO	SP	76	45R
	WATER TOWER SOO NEW RICHMOND WI 1955 PHO	06	73	18
	WATER TANK SOO HANKINSON ND PHOTO	12	64	36
SP	TRAIN FERRY SP "SIERRA NEVADA" PHOTO	01	65	17
	SP (PACIFIC MOTOR TRUCKING CO) TRUCK PHO	08	50	22
	TRAIN FERRY SP 7189 TON 1914 PHOTO	06	41	24
	BAGGAGE WAGON SP OAKLAND CA 1955 PHOTO	05	74	06
	SP MARTINEZ-BENICIA BRIDGE 5603' PHOTO	01	31	246
	TUNNEL HAS ONE PORTAL SP SUMMIT OREGON	04	31	119

366

Railroad/ Railfan

STRUCTURES VEHICLES & SIGNALS

RD	STRUCTURE, SIGNAL & VEHICLE PHOTOS BY RD	M	Y	P
	COVERED RAILROAD BRIDGE SP OREGON 1920	09	41	121
	PECOS RIVER BRIDGE SP PHOTO	11	75	42
	YARD OFFICE SP SUISIN CALIFORNIA PHOTO	10	58	24
	PASSENGER STATION INTERIOR SP PASADENA P	04	64	16
	ROUNDHOUSE SP SACRAMENTO CA 1870 PHOTO	07	66	18
	BACKSHOP INTERIOR SP SACRAMENTO CA PHOTO	04	66	25
	SERVICING STEAM CLOSE-UP SP SAN FRANCISC	05	55	66
	DEPOT SP SALTON CA 1919 PHOTO	08	66	28
	WATER TOWER BELOW SEA LEVEL SP SALTON CA	08	66	28
	ERECTING SHOP INTERIOR SP SACRAMENTO CA	07	66	24
	ERECTING SHOP INTERIOR SP LOS ANGELES CA	07	66	22
	ROUNDHOUSE SP WEST OAKLAND CA 1904 PHOTO	07	66	20
	STATION SP PORT CHICAGO CA 1972 PHOTO	09	72	33
	BENICIA DEPOT SP BENICIA CA PHOTO	05	68	19
	DEPOT SP NILES CA 1941 PHOTO	04	71	38
	STATION SP NILES CA 1910 PHOTO	04	71	40
	SIGNAL TOWER SP NILES CA PHOTO	04	71	41
	ORDER BOARD POST SP SANTA SUSANA CA 1947	11	76	28
	STATION SP SANTA SUSANA CA 1947 PHOTO	11	76	28
	GALLOWS TURNTABLE SP LAWS CA 1952 PHOTO	05	78	54
	STATION SP SALTON CA 1912 LOWEST ELEVATI	10	78	50
	DEPOT SP DALLAS TEXAS CIRCA 1903 PHOTO	04	77	18
	STATION SP PORT CHICAGO CA AFTER EXPLOSI	11	69	24
	BOXCAR STATION SP #23907 PORT CHICAGO CA	11	69	25
	SEMAPHORE SP MEDFORE OREGON PHOTO	05	42	131
	CAR SHOP SP DUNSMUIR CA 1913 PHOTO	01	69	20
	STATION SP DUNSMUIR CA 1915 PHOTO	01	69	22
	STATION SP MESA/COLLIDGE ARIZONA PHOTO	06	41	121
	TRAIN ORDER POST SP MARION OREGON PHOTO	09	41	21
	TRAIN ORDER BRACKET SP PHOTO	09	44	105
	WATER TANK SP LAWS CALIFORNIA PHOTO	12	62	10
	OIL TANK SP LAWS CALIFORNIA PHOTO	12	62	10
	STATION SP OWENYO PHOTO	02	59	26
	WATER TANK SP PHOTO	02	59	29
	STATION SP SALTON CALIFORNIA PHOTO	06	56	44
	SIGNAL TOWER SP REDWOOD JCT CA PHOTO	01	65	33
	WIG-WAG SIGNAL SP CROSSING PHOTO	05	65	44
	WATER TOWER SP CASMALIA CAL PHOTO	12	63	17
	ROUNDHOUSE SP (TAYLOR) PHOTO ESSAY	01	48	40
	WATER TANK SP KEELER CA 1959 PHOTO	08	60	55
	STATION SP CASCADE SUMMIT PHOTO	01	53	55
	DINER SP PHOTO	09	51	138
	WATER TANK SP OLD TANK CAR PHOTO	08	54	10
SPM	ROUNDHOUSE SPM GUADALAJARA PHOTO	02	48	44
	STATION SPM NOGALES (STUCCO) PHOTO	02	48	49
SR&RL	ROUNDHOUSE SR&RL PHILLIPS MAINE PHOTO	12	55	30
	DEPOT SR&RL RANGELEY MAINE PHOTO	09	35	54
SRV	BALL SIGNAL SRV STRONG ME PHOTO	11	31	488
SSP	STATION STOP SSP TULSA PHOTO	03	53	91
	STATION SSP FREIGHT & SUB-STATION TULSA	03	53	83
SYC	CROSSING SIGN SYC SYLVANIA GA UNUSUAL PH	08	56	04
T&NO	TOWER T&NO #32 PHOTO	02	52	36
T&SB	DURAND DEPOT T&SB DURAND MI PHOTO	03	84	45
T&T	STATION T&T SILVER LAKE CA PHOTO	11	40	136
	DEPOT T&T RHYOLITE PHOTO	04	53	117
T&WE	BRIDGE T&WE PIONEER OHIO COAL-TRUCK LOAD	12	43	132
TAL	DEPOT TAL (NEXT TO AB&C DEPOT) PHOTO	07	43	110
TAT	STUB STATION TAT 42ND ST NY NY PHOTO	01	78	61
	DEPOT TAT OFFICE/CAR BARN/STABLE PHOTO	02	46	21
	TROLLEY SIGNAL TAT PHOTO	06	56	65
TBRR	STATION TBRR CRANE'S MASS PRIOR 1863 PHO	08	31	46
TC&GB	GRADE CROSSING SIGN GILA BEND AZ TC&GB P	04	67	39
TM	MACHINE SHOPS TM TERREL TX PHOTO	10	63	23
	ENGINE SHED TM PARIS TX PHOTO	10	63	23
	WATER TANK TM COMMERCE TX PHOTO	10	63	23
TP&W	GENERAL OFFICE TP&W "WINDOWLESS" PHOTO	12	55	41
TTCO	CATENARY REPAIR TRUCK TORONTO CAN 1921 P	03	71	38
U	SALOON-GENERAL STORE U DRAGON UT PHOTO	06	60	20
UC	DEPOT UC OGDEN UTAH PHOTO	02	45	26
UDEY	WATER SOFTENER UDEY PHOTO	06	68	19
	STATION UDEY MERIDA CENTRAL STATION 1920	06	68	18
UP	ROUNDHOUSE UP POCATELLO 1929 PHOTO	12	66	45
	WATER TANK TWO-SPOUT UP MILFORD UT PHOTO	04	67	66
	WATER TOWER UP TINTIO UT 1960 PHOTO	12	72	64
	HACK SHED UP #3303 (LA&SL) RHYOLITE NV P	10	76	03
	COALING TOWER UP CHEYENNE WY 1959 PHOTO	02	78	56
	SCRAP YARD UP OMAHA NEBRASKA PHOTO	07	77	32
	ROUNDHOUSE UP GREEN RIVER WY PHOTO	08	77	26
	VISITORS CENTER UP BAILEY YARD N PLATTE	09	74	09
	COALING DOCK UP CHEYENNE WY 1959 PHOTO	10	74	56
	WATER & SAND SERVICE FACILITY UP PHOTO	02	70	01
	LOCOMOTIVE WASHER UP PORTLAND OR 1970 PH	04	74	03
	COALING TOWER UP HANNA WY PHOTO	04	74	28
	COALING STATION CONCRETE UP HANNA WY PH	04	45	72
	STATION UP LAS VEGAS NV PHOTO	03	41	23
	STATION UP/MILW SEATTLE WA PHOTO	07	47	123
	DEPOT UP NYSSA OREGON PHOTO	12	54	37
	SPEED LIMIT BOARD UP SPOKANE WA PHOTO	06	53	19
URR	ROTARY DUMPER W/RECEIVING BINS URR ETCHI	12	57	47
URY	WATER SOFTENING PLANTS URY PHOTO	06	50	50
UTCC	CAR REPAIR SHOPS "UNION DOME" UTCC PHOTO	08	58	44
	TANK CAR REPAIR BLDG UUTCC BATON ROUGE L	02	59	06
V	SAND SPOUT WOOD NORFOLK VA YARD V PHOTO	11	68	16
	SAND HOUSE & TOWER V SEWELLS POINT VA PH	11	68	20
	HEADQUARTERS V NEW RIVER DIVISION PHOTO	04	39	26
V&T	TUNNEL V&T SUTRO TUNNEL PHOTO	07	45	54
	DEPOT V&T GOLD HILL PHOTO	01	55	12
	TRAIN SHED V&T VIRGINIA CITY PHOTO	01	55	15
	ROUNDHOUSE V&T CARSON CITY NEVADA PHOTO	10	78	19
	DEPOT FRT & PASS V&T VIRGINIA CITY PHOTO	07	45	54
	STATION V&T VIRGINIA CITY NEVADA PHOTO	09	41	09
VER	DEPOT VER NORTH BENNINGTON VT PHOTO	SU	75	27R
W	CARFERRY W "DETROIT" WINDSOR ONT 1957 PH	10	73	19
	TRAIN FERRY W "WINDSOR" DETROIT RIVER 57	06	70	17
	UNION STATION W PITTSBURGH PA PHOTO	11	71	26
	STATION W TRUSEDALE MO PHOTO	04	73	31
	BALL SIGNAL W DANVILLE JCT ILL PHOTO	08	31	97
	STATION W ST LOUIS MO PHOTO	03	41	15
	STATION W ST LOUIS MO PHOTO	02	47	22
W&A	DEPOT W&A ATLANTA UNION DEPOT GA PHOTO	12	45	12

Stephans' Railroad Directory

Railroad/Railfan

STRUCTURES VEHICLES & SIGNALS

RD	STRUCTURE, SIGNAL & VEHICLE PHOTOS BY RD	M	Y	P
W&LE	TRAIN ORDER BOARD W&LE COSCHOCTON OH PHO	02	74	20
W&NB	STATION W&NB (OLD HUNTING LODGE) PHOTO	08	50	130
WHT	TENDER COAL LOADER WHT WINNIPEG MAN PHOT	06	60	24
WJ&S	STATION WJ&S PASSENGER MILLVILLE NJ PHOT	02	46	86
	STATION WJ&S MILLVILLE NJ IN 1875 PHOTO	12	54	28
WM	STATION WM THOMAS WV (BRICK) PHOTO	09	68	18
	SIGNAL BANJO TYPE WM BRANTSVILLE PA PHOT	10	59	16
	STATION WM OWNINGS MILLS BALTIMORE MD PH	09	50	31
	COALING STATION WM ELKINS WV PHOTO	09	50	28
WO	STATION WO WOODSTOCK VT 1893 PHOTO	07	33	35
WP	FERRY WP "LAS PLUMAS" PHOTO	08	59	38
	DIESEL TRAIN FERRY WP "LAS PLUMAS" PHOTO	01	65	16
	CAR FLOAT WP #3 PHOTO	03	51	21
	NORTH FORK BRIDGE WP PHOTO	05	79	22
	WATER TOWER (ICE COVERED) WP WENDOVER UT	12	66	17
	RAIL CROSSING SIGN WP FREMONT CA 1970 PH	11	76	43
	SIDE PORTER PIGGY BACK LOADER WP OAKLAND	05	73	14
	RAIL CROSSING SIGN WP OROVILLE CA PHOTO	08	70	21
	WATER TANK WP VIRGILIA PHOTO	08	45	98
	DEPOT WP BERRY CREEK PHOTO	04	44	22
	WATER TOWER WP FEATHER RIVER CANYON CA P	08	65	20
WTC	BRIDGE: WTC/CO&C ERECTED IN 1940 PHOTO	05	41	59
WW&F	STATION AT N. WHITEFIELD MAINE WW&F	03	35	38
Y&MV	STATION Y&MV VICKSBURG MISS PHOTO	03	41	08

STRUCTURE, SIGNAL & VEHICLE MODELS	M	Y	P
BRIDGE MODELS			
BRIDGE CONSTRUCTION HOWE THROUGH TRUSS	03	55	44
BUILD A MODEL RAILROAD BRIDGE	11	32	546
CONCRETE OVERPASS CONSTRUCTION	12	53	100
GIRDER BRIDGE/ABUTMENT CONSTRUCTION	10	54	49
OVERPASS CONCRETE TYPE CONSTRUCTION	12	53	100
TRESTLE AND BRIDGE PIERS CONSTRUCTION	12	54	50
TRESTLE LOW, SINGLE TRACK TO BUILD	01	33	103
TRESTLE ON A CURVE CONSTRUCTION	08	53	94
COMMERCIAL STRUCTURE MODELS			
DEFENSE INDUSTRY CONSTRUCTION	10	41	111
RAILROAD STRUCTURE MODELS			
COMBINATION STATION MKT CONSTRUCTION	09	32	225
ELEVATED WATCHMAN'S TOWER CONSTRUCTION	10	53	96
GALLOWS TRUNTABLE CONSTRUCTION	05	55	76
MID-VICTORIAN RAILROAD DEPOT CONSTRUCION	10	45	132
OLDTIME SIGNAL TOWER CONSTRUCTION	09	50	103
OPEN AIR TRAIN SHED CONSTRUCTION	05	54	84
ROUNDHOUSE CONSTRUCTION	09	34	94
TRAIN SHED OPEN AIR CONSTRUCTION	05	54	84
TRAINSHED OF 1890 CONSTRUCTION	03	54	70
TURNTABLE GALLOWS FRAME CONSTRUCTION	05	55	76
WATER TANK CONSTRUCTION	06	33	127
WATER TOWER CONSTRUCTION	10	55	54
WAY STATION CONSTRUCTION	12	39	49
YARD: FREIGHT/COACH/ENGINE CONSTRUCTION	08	39	111

STRUCTURE, SIGNAL & VEHICLE MODELS	M	Y	P
SIGNAL MODELS			
AUTOMATIC SIGNALING: CONSTRUCTION	03	39	109
BANJO SIGNAL CONSTRUCTION	08	42	110
BLOCK SIGNALS CONSTRUCTION	07	34	123
SEARCHLIGHT SIGNAL CONSTRUCTION	04	39	110
SEMAPHORE CONSTRUCTION	04	39	110
SEMAPHORE SIGNAL STD THREE POSITION TYPE	04	33	126
SIGNAL BRIDGE CONSTRUCTION	01	34	125
SIGNS: RIGHT OF WAY/MILE BOARDS/SPEED/ET	06	40	61
TWO-RAIL AUTOMATIC SIGNALING CONSTRUCTIO	01	40	63
VEHICLE MODELS			
TUG CONSTRUCTION	03	41	97

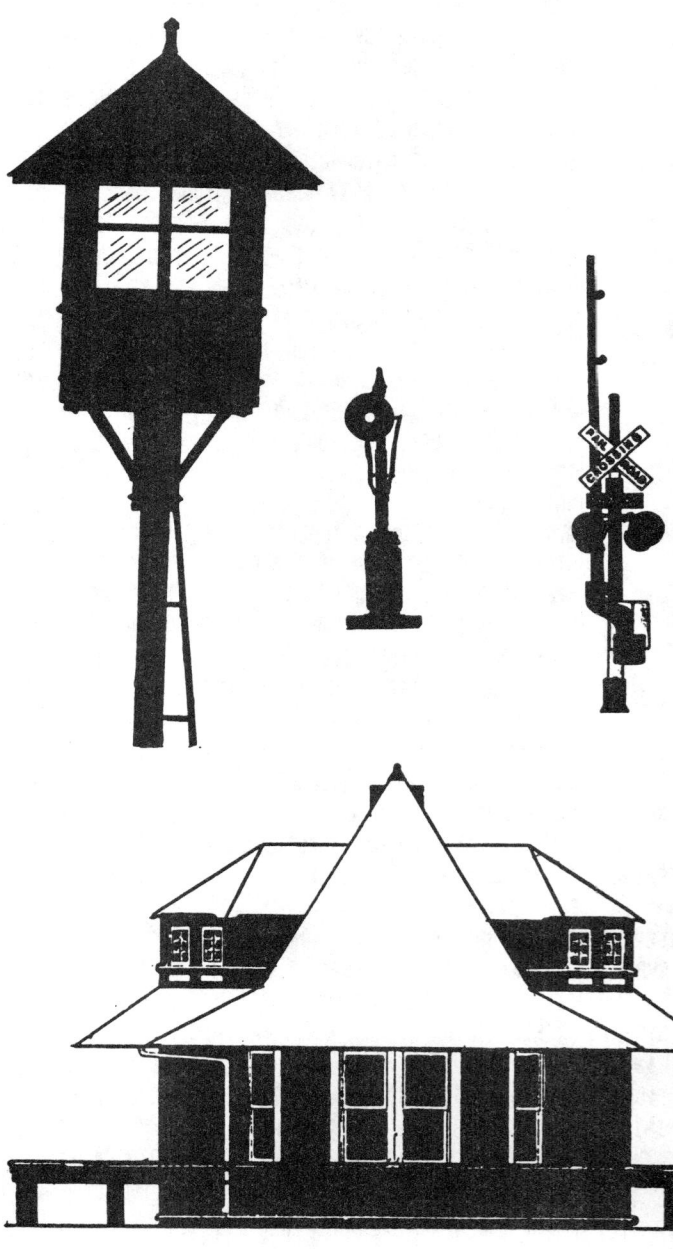

Railroad/Railfan

FRIENDS OF THE EAST ROAD TOP

THE EAST BROAD TOP RAILROAD:

Only one visit to the East Broad Top Railroad is enough to realize how special this important National Historic Landmark should be to anyone who loves the rails. The East Broad Top at Rockhill Furnace, Pennsylvania, is one of the very few places left in North America where you still can see—virtually intact, on the spot where it started over a century ago—a narrow gauge, steam-powered railroad, authentic to its last original detail.

Rails for the East Broad Top were laid down in 1872. For the next 84 years, the railroad hauled coal, timber, and gannister rock down from the mountains. In April 1956, with coal no longer profitable, the EBT shut down. The men just put down their tools, dropped the fires, locked the doors, and went home.

The EBT slept, just as it was left, until 1960 when its new owners, Kovalchick Salvage Company, reopened five miles of the mainline to tourists. Today, thanks to the Kovalchick family, the EBT survives to be enjoyed, much as it was left in 1956, the oldest narrow gauge railroad east of the Rocky Mountains. Today, the East Broad Top encompasses a picture of turn-of-the-century railroading, complete down to the stub switches and overhead belt machine shop.

FRIENDS OF THE EBT - PRESERVATION PLUS:

We believe the EBT is a unique historical resource worth saving for future generations to appreciate and enjoy. We are Friends of the East Broad Top, Inc., a group of railfans and modelers committed to repaying the enjoyment we have drawn from the EBT by preserving the railroad's history and encouraging full restoration of the amazingly still-intact 30-mile mainline.

- We actively encourage dialogue within the community of government, industry, public, and private groups interested in assuring preservation of the EBT for the future.

- We have an active program to preserve, restore, and reconstruct EBT equipment and structures. All members are welcome to participate in this work.

- Our magazine, *The TIMBER TRANSFER*, provides a lively forum for articles on history, modeling, and preservation of the EBT, including plans and photos often published for the first time.

- We have a growing archive of EBT historical material and a Plan Service for the benefit of our members at nominal cost.

- Our cooperation with manufacturers continues to promote production of many, heretofore unavailable, EBT-prototype model railroad kits and locomotives.

- Friends of the EBT sponsors special events on the railroad for our members.

Friends of the East Broad Top is a 501 (c) (3) nonprofit corporation, not affiliated with the East Broad Top Railroad or its parent company.

AN INVITATION:

We welcome the company of all who share our enthusiasm for the East Broad Top Railroad. Our membership is nationwide and international. We invite you to join us by filling out and sending in the application on the back of this brochure.

P.S. A membership in Friends of the EBT makes an imaginative gift that lasts all year.

FRIENDS OF THE EAST BROAD TOP, INC. MEMBERSHIP APPLICATION
INTRODUCED BY "STEPHANS' RAILROAD DIRECTORY"

YOUR NAME: _____   GIFT TO: NAME: _____

ADDRESS: _____   ADDRESS: _____

(CITY) _____ (STATE) _____   (CITY) _____ (STATE) _____

(ZIP CODE) _____ (COUNTRY) _____   (ZIP CODE) _____ (COUNTRY) _____

MEMBERSHIP CATEGORIES:

- REGULAR — $15.00 (US) _____
- SENIOR CITIZEN (Over age 65) — 7.50 (US) _____
- FULL-TIME STUDENT — 7.50 (US) _____
- SUSTAINING — 50.00 (US) _____
- LIFE — 300.00 (US) _____

TOTAL ENCLOSED: _____

PLEASE MAIL WITH CHECK OR MONEY ORDER (US FUNDS) TO

Friends of The East Broad Top
C/O Frederick H. Fisher
PO Box 551
Riverside, NJ 08075
U.S.A.

Continued on page 481

BILL OF LADING — PROTOTYPE EXAMPLES

The Prototype Section concerns itself with things the real railroads do that modelers can follow. It includes items that do not seem like what a prototype would do. The descriptor line defines the contents as best it can.

MANIFEST — PROTOTYPE EXAMPLES

DETAILED CONSIST	PAGE
PROTOTYPE TRACKWORK	371
SPECIAL CARS & TRAINS	372
PROTOTYPE SPEED & SCHEDULES	373
GENERAL PROTOTYPE DATA	375

Railroad/Railfan

PROTOTYPE

PROTOTYPE MISCELLANEOUS INFORMATION	M	Y	P
★ PROTOTYPE TRACK EXAMPLES ★			
3 TIE SUPPORTED JOINT VS 2-TIE SUSPENDED	03	38	57
ANTI-CREEPERS: METAL CLIPS UNDER RAILS	08	35	83
ASPHALT ROADBED	06	40	73
AUTOMATIC CLASSIFICATION YARDS	10	58	20
B&M HOTBOX DETECTOR AYER MASS PHOTO	10	59	39
BACK TO BACK TUNNELS S OLD FORT NC PHOTO	01	71	08
BLOCK DERAIL: HAYES (USED ON SIDE TRACK)	04	35	86
BRITISH TRACK UNLIKE AMERICAN	06	34	26
CATENARY INSTALLATION BM&LP PHOTO	08	74	23
CATENARY WIRES PRR NEW BRUNSWICK NJ PHOT	12	54	17
CEMENT RAODBED PM PHOTO	11	31	464
CONCRETE ROADBED	11	31	595
CONCRETE TIE SYSTEM FROM SWEDEN ON NYC	02	67	13
CONCRETE TIES/WOOD BLOCKS/SPIKES PRR	10	33	46
CROSSTIE PERSERVATION: EARLY	12	50	57
CROSSTIES	02	73	49
CROSSTIES: THEIR HISTORY	06	52	44
CURVATURE OF TRACK	05	32	178
DETERMINING PROTOTYPE TRACK CURVATURE	04	66	38
DROP PITS INSIDE ROUNDHOUSES	06	32	339
ELECTRIFIED TRACKAGE EAST VS WEST	02	39	93
ELECTRONIC YARDMASTER	03	55	43
ENOLA YARD PRR ENOLA PA	11	41	06
EXPANSION OF MILE LONG RAILS	08	38	93
FIXING SUN KINKED RAILS	05	67	08
FLYING SWITCH	12	54	41
FORMULA FOR ELEVATIONS OF OUTER RAILS	07	40	65
FR FOREIGN RAILROADS	03	31	570
FR SNO EUROPEAN TRACK GAUGES	02	73	49
FR TRINIDAD GOV'T RAILWAYS: BALLAST	03	31	570
GATEWAY YARD YOUNGSTOWN OH P&LE	10	58	18
HORSESHOE CURVE ON PRR DETAILS	10	60	32
HORSESHOE CURVE ON SP WHY NEEDED	02	61	30
HOTBOX DETECTIVE	10	57	42
HOW MANY TIES IN A MILE OF TRACK?? 3000	03	48	59
LAP SIDING	06	37	60
LASER TRACK INSPECTOR	01	70	36
LAYING WELDED RAIL	07	67	32
LOOP TRACKAGE CHICAGO ILLINOIS PHOTO	02	78	01
MECHANICAL DANDY DANCER	02	31	406
MILE LONG RAILS AND EXPANSION	12	37	54
MONTREAL YARD MONTREAL CANADA CP	07	50	32
PREPARING TRACK FOR HIGH SPEED TRAINS	01	43	73
PRESSURE WELDING RAIL	06	49	63
RAIL "SUN KINKS"	10	54	40
RAIL AND FLANGE LUBRICATOR TYPE MC PHOTO	12	59	35
RAIL BONDING	02	46	62
RAIL CONDITIONING VS SAND	06	57	40
RAIL CROSS SECTIONS THROUGH THE YEARS	02	73	49
RAIL DEFECTS	07	34	57
RAIL EXPANSION IN THE DESERT ON ATSF	06	72	08
RAIL FAILURES	11	38	12
RAIL JOINT-DE ARMAS EVENRAIL JOINT	08	32	57
RAILROAD TIES/WEIGHT OF RAIL	11	34	89

PROTOTYPE MISCELLANEOUS INFORMATION	M	Y	P
RAILS	11	38	07
RAILS 141/152/159/164 POUNDS	03	32	520
RAILS COLD WEATHER SNAPS	06	55	33
RAILS CONTINUOUS WELDED--ADVANTAGES	02	57	39
RAILS ON CURVES GREASED	12	38	70
RETARDER-EQUIPPED HUMP B&M MECHANICSVILLE	08	30	84
ROSEVILLE YARD ROSEVILLE CA SP	10	40	46
RT: RAILROAD TRACK TERMS	02	45	70
RT: DEGREE OF CURVES	07	47	64
RT: SIX DEGREE CURVE	02	45	70
RUBBER CUSHIONED RAILROAD TIE PLATE	09	53	68
RUSSIAN TRACK REPAIR 1 MI IN 4 HRS	02	73	05
SAGA OF HIGH-T (RAIL)	12	65	18
SCISSORS SWITCH TRACKWORK SHORT NOTE	09	71	39
SHOP-FABRICATED PANELIZED SWITCH PRR PHO	07	66	30
SNO 52-POUND RAILS: DESCRIBED	08	59	36
SNO ATSF RULING GRADES	04	78	11
SNO B&O:MORE ON STEEP GRADES	02	62	51
SNO BETTER TRACK NEED AND ACTIONS	05	75	51
SNO BOWL TRACKS	07	74	39
SNO BUMPING POSTS: MADE OF WOOD/STEEL	12	55	38
SNO CHECK IRONS IN TIE ENDS	03	75	12
SNO COLD WEATHER: CONTRACTS RAILS	08	57	39
SNO CONCRETE & LAMINATED WOOD TIES ON CN	12	73	11
SNO CONTINOUS WELDED RAIL	08	55	40
SNO CROSSTIE LIFE	07	73	39
SNO DOUBLE WYE FT COLLINS CO BN/C&S/D&CH	06	71	12
SNO DUAL-CONTROL SWITCH	10	55	32
SNO EARLY CROSSTIE TREATMENT METHODS	02	76	46
SNO ELEVATION MARKERS ON CURVE TIES	06	74	04
SNO EXPANSION OF WELDED RAIL	07	70	54
SNO FEEDER LINE	06	57	44
SNO FIRST "T" RAIL ROLLING DISPUTE	06	70	62
SNO FLAWS IN RAILS: HOW DETECTED	12	56	33
SNO GUARD RAIL TYPES	06	74	20
SNO HOOK HEAD SPIKES	12	75	57
SNO INTERCHANGE TRACK	06	57	44
SNO LARGEST TRACK ABANDONMENTS MKT	03	71	60
SNO OH: ABBREV FOR OPEN HEARTH/MANUFACTU	10	56	41
SNO OILED TRACK ON PRR CURVES ROCK PT PA	08	71	09
SNO PC: MILEPOST MARKINGS ON MAIN LINES	05	73	37
SNO POOR TRACK CONDITIONS	01	75	04
SNO RAIL CURVATURE MEASUREMENT	11	68	35
SNO RAIL EXPANSION IN THE DESERT	06	72	08
SNO RAILROAD SPIKES: SPENCER-SPIKE NEW!	08	59	10
SNO REBUILD OF GEORGRTOWN LOOP UP	09	76	47
SNO SAFETY TRACKS	08	76	52
SNO SLIP SWITCH WORKINGS	08	74	56
SNO SUN KINKS	06	74	20
SNO SWITCH TYPE CONSTRUCTION	12	76	28
SNO SWITCHBACK TRACKS	08	75	57
SNO SWITCHES: HOW PROTECTED AGAINST ICE	06	55	33
SNO T-RAILS: FIRST USED IN 1831	12	58	36
SNO TIE PLATE N&W	12	44	42
SNO TIE PLATES: WHAT ARE THEY?	08	59	38

Railroad/Railfan

PROTOTYPE

PROTOTYPE MISCELLANEOUS INFORMATION	M	Y	P
SNO TIES: WOODEN VS STEEL COST/WEAR	03	55	65
SNO TRACK EXPANSION & CONTRACTION	07	73	39
SNO TRACK SCOOP NYC&HR	06	45	61
SNO U SHAPED RAILS/CAST IRON RAILS CP	04	56	09
SNO WELDING RAIL ON SITE TECHNIQUES	07	72	09
SNO WHY TWO SPIKES IN 4 HOLE TIE PLATES	09	76	51
SNO YARD SWITCHES & GUARD RAILS	02	57	42
SPIKES: HOOK-HEADED RAILROAD	06	57	42
SPOTBOARD: GUIDE USED FOR EVEN ROADBED	10	57	44
STANDARD GAGE: WHY 4 FEET 8.5 INCHES??	10	47	69
STREAMLINING THE TRACK	01	43	73
STUB SWITCH C&S IDAHO SPRINGS CO PHOTO	09	54	28
STUB SWITCH OBJECTIONS	11	64	34
STUB SWITCH PHOTO ON D&RGW	11	64	34
STUB SWITCH-3 WAY D&RGW COLORADO CITY CO	03	66	13
STUB SWITCHES: MANUAL HOW THEY OPERATE	09	54	28
STUB TURNOUT & OLD TIME CROSSING	06	42	110
SWITCH PROTECTOR ON CN	05	77	09
SWITCHBACK	01	33	102
SWITCHBACKS: TRACK ARRANGEMENT	08	39	67
THIRD RAIL CROSSING DEVELOPMENT	03	31	598
THIRD RAIL WITH COVER PHOTO	12	68	39
THREE LEVEL CROSSING RICHMOND VA	06	55	36
THREE WAY SWITCH D&RGW COLORADO CITY CO	04	67	32
THREE-THROW SPLIT POINT SWITCHES	10	33	48
TIES	03	46	108
TIES/GAGE/BALLAST/RAILS	09	37	11
TRACK & ROADBED	09	39	08
TRACK AND CATENARY MT VERNON JCT NY PHOT	11	78	65
TRACK CURVATURE EXPRESSED AND MEASURED	08	72	58
TRACK CURVE LAYING BY DEGREE	09	65	30
TRACK FOR RUBBER TIRED METRO MONTREAL CA	08	68	63
TRACK IMPROVEMENT PHOTO ESSAY	07	48	53
TRACK INITIALS & NUMBERS: WHAT THEY MEAN	01	44	40
TRACK RELOCATION ENGINEERING PROBLEM	08	75	05
TRACK WITH CONCRETE TIES PORT SUTTON FL	05	65	43
TRACKAGE RIGHTS	10	41	24
TRIPLE STUB SWITCH D&CA DIAMOND SPRINGS	05	78	02
WEEDS ARE HARMFUL	01	39	63
WELDED RAIL'S WHY & HOW?	07	78	04
WELDED RAIL: LENGTH/EXPANSION CONTROLLED	05	44	78
WELDED RAIL: REPAIRS	05	38	75
WELDING TRACK ON SITE ON ATSF	07	72	09
WHARTON SWITCH:WHAT IS IT-HOW DOES IT WO	12	61	57
WOODEN CROSS-TIES	09	46	89
WYE IN A TUNNEL SP CASCADE MTS OR PHOTO	05	78	53
WYE WP KEDDIE CAL (INCOMPLETE?)	10	64	15
* SPECIAL CARS & TRAINS *			
844 TO NEW ORLEANS UP WORLDS FAIR SPECIA	09	84	48
AMBASSADOR, THE NORTHERN NEW ENGLAND	08	47	89
AMBULANCE TRAIN	07	37	16
BROADWAY LTD CELEBRATES 75TH YEAR PRR	09	77	38
BUFFALO HUNTING EXCURSIONS	11	30	536
CALIFORNIA ZEPHYR WP	11	49	15
CAMPAIGN TRAINS	02	53	39
CATENARY MAINTENANCE TRAIN	10	39	40
CATHEDRAL CAR	03	38	126
CATTLE TRAIN OPERATIONS	12	49	16
CHESSIE STEAM SPECIAL (150 ANNIV B&O)	10	77	14R
CIRCUS TRAIN	02	30	330
CIRCUS TRAIN "JOHN ROBINSON" PHOTO	08	75	17
CIRCUS TRAIN RB&BB	01	78	08
CIRCUS TRAIN BARABOO WI 1966 PHOTO	08	66	16
CIRCUS TRAIN IS ROLLING	09	71	12
CIRCUS TRAIN MORE!	04	56	28
CIRCUS TRAIN PHOTO ESSAY	03	69	16
CIRCUS TRAIN PHOTO MILWAUKEE WI	07	66	01
CIRCUS TRAIN SLEEPING ARRANGEMENTS	08	54	45
CIRCUS TRAIN.	07	34	38
CIRCUS TRAIN...	07	46	12
CIRCUS TRAINS & WRECKS	02	65	12
CIRCUS TRAINS: 100 YEARS	04	56	12
CITRUS FRUIT TRAIN FEB 14 1942 CALIF-ARI	03	53	62
CITY OF NEW ORLEANS (IC) TRAIN	12	47	37
CONSIST OF SP 1984 WORLDS FAIR DAYLIGHT	09	84	54
CORN TRAIN, THE (OHIO VALLEY TO KANSAS)	12	48	14
CPM&O "DAN PATCH" PRIVATE CAR	08	54	30
DEATH VALLEY SCOTTY SPECIAL	07	31	561
DUDE TRAIN OF OCO 1884	06	75	30
ERIE'S "STRAWBERRY TRAIN"	11	44	51
FIRST CIRCUS TRAIN IN US: 1860 NY CIRCUS	07	47	67
FIRST PRESIDENTIAL FUNERAL TRAIN	06	66	32
FLORIDA SPECIAL SHORT HISTORY	05	78	57
FLYING DUDE-TRAIN FOR WEALTHY NYNH&H	05	65	22
FR FOREIGN RAILROADS	08	44	62
FR FRENCH TRAIN "MERCI" TOUR IN US 1948	09	68	29
FR ITALY HOSPITAL TRAINS PHOTO	08	44	62
FR SNO ORIENT EXPRESS	10	76	14
FR SPAIN: TALGO TRAIN PHOTO	10	54	64
FREEDOM TRAIN	SU	75	14R
FREEDOM TRAIN IN LA GRANGE	F	75	14R
FREEDOM TRAIN IS HEADING WESTWARD	06	75	47
FREEDOM TRAIN OF 1947	12	47	06
FREEDOM TRAIN OF 1947	10	75	04
FREEDOM TRAIN OF 1947.	05	48	104
FREEDOM TRAIN PHOTO CONTEST WINNERS	10	77	28R
FREEDOM TRAIN READING T1 POWER	W	76	51R
FREEDOM TRAIN-INSIDE DISPLAYS	W	75	60R
FREEDOM TRAIN-NIGHT RIDE	11	75	20
FREEDOM TRAIN-ON THE ROAD WITH SP #4449	W	75	36R
FREEDOM TRAIN: 2-10-4 T&P #610 POWER	SU	76	14R
FREEDOM TRAIN: DOYLE MCCORMACK INTERVIEW	F	75	46R
FUNERAL TRAIN CHURCHILL, WINSTON	10	65	24
FUNERAL TRAIN DAVIS, JEFFERSON	02	46	95
FUNERAL TRAIN DAVIS, JEFFERSON 1893	12	62	22
FUNERAL TRAIN FOR BETTY THE DOG LI	02	58	44
FUNERAL TRAIN FOR DOG "BETTY II"	09	67	26
FUNERAL TRAIN FOR PET DOG	05	40	110
FUNERAL TRAIN GARFIELD 1881	12	62	23

PROTOTYPE

PROTOTYPE MISCELLANEOUS INFORMATION	M	Y	P
FUNERAL TRAIN GRANT AUG 1885	12	62	21
FUNERAL TRAIN GRANT, U.S.	09	35	56
FUNERAL TRAIN HARDING 1923	12	62	24
FUNERAL TRAIN LINCOLN ABRAHAM	04	46	26
FUNERAL TRAIN LINCOLN, ABRAHAM	02	45	138
FUNERAL TRAIN LINCOLN-7 CARS PAINTED BLK	12	62	18
FUNERAL TRAIN MCKINLEY	08	49	132
FUNERAL TRAIN MCKINLEY 1901	12	62	23
FUNERAL TRAIN ROOSEVELT	08	49	132
FUNERAL TRAIN ROOSEVELT (FDR) 1945	12	62	26
FUNERAL TRAIN ROOSEVELT, FRANKLIN PHOTO	11	45	22
GARBAGE TRAIN OF SAN FRANCISCO (WP)	03	69	06
GE "MORE POWER TO AMERICA" TRAIN SPECIAL	08	50	138
GM "TRAIN OF TOMORROW" SOLD TO UP	10	50	132
GREAT DAYS OF CIRCUS TRAINS	07	75	10
HEARTLAND SPECIAL REAGAN PRESIDENTIAL TR	01	85	33
HOSPITAL CAR	12	30	49
HOSPITAL ON WHEELS PHOTO ESSAY	09	45	104
HOSPITAL TRAIN	05	44	06
HOSPITAL TRAIN INTRODUCTION	10	77	55
JARRETT AND PALMER SPECIAL	09	32	191
LAST RUN MP "TEXAS EAGLE"	01	71	38
LI CIRCUS TRAIN NEWARK TO WESTBURY	01	51	73
LINDBERGH NEWSREEL TRAIN	08	31	75
LINDBERGH SPECIAL: A CREW MEMBER RECALLS	09	68	24
NEW ENGLANDS "GHOST TRAIN"	01	74	11
ODD RUN TRAINS--PUBLIC HANGING	12	60	06
OLD DOMINION RF&P	02	48	72
PENNSYLVANIA SPECIAL (PRR)	04	72	29
PICNIC TRAINS	10	75	12
PREAMBLE EXPRESS	W	75	16R
PREAMBLE EXPRESS-AMERICAN FREEDOM ADVANC	10	74	54
PRESIDENT TAFT'S SPECIAL TRAIN SP #2244	06	55	68
PRESIDENT'S SPECIAL	11	45	08
PRESIDENTIAL TRAIN TRAVEL	08	56	12
PRESIDENTIAL TRAIN TRAVEL,	02	53	38
PRESIDENTIAL TRAIN TRAVEL.	05	31	212
PRIVATE CARS	11	39	06
PRIVATE CARS ON SHORT LINES	12	59	19
PROSPERITY SPECIAL TRAIN OF 1922	01	47	26
PRR LINDBERGH SPECIAL	02	55	28
RACE HORSE TRANSPORTATION.	08	54	20
RAIL-GRINDER TRAIN IC	08	57	42
RELIEF TRAIN UP BRIDAL VEIL OR 1884 PHOT	12	70	04
RINGLING BROS B&B CIRCUS TRAIN PHOTO	12	78	62
SARAH BERNHARDT SPECIAL TRAIN	12	32	36
SCHOOL CARS IN CANADA	06	31	332
SENATOR HOWARD BAKER WHISTLE-STOP SPECIA	03	73	50
SHRINE SPECIAL TRAIN 1	12	50	38
SILK TRAIN READER INFORMATION	06	65	07
SILK TRAINS--NO DELAYS	04	65	13
SILK TRAINS: FASTER THAN PASSENGER TRAIN	12	59	33
SILK TRAINS: THEIR HISTORY	02	56	39
SILK TRANSPORT TRAIN	10	30	326
SNO "STATE" NAMED TRAINS	06	69	40
SNO "TALCUM POWDER SPECIAL" LI	04	75	11
SNO AL CAPONE'S TRAIN TRIP TO PRISON	11	66	38
SNO ATSF: CALIFORNIA LIMITED 1892-1938	07	68	27
SNO C&EI:EGYPTIAN ZIPPER PASSENGER TRAIN	09	70	30
SNO CALIFORNIA ZEPHYR BEGIN-END SERVICE	11	76	43
SNO CB&Q: ORIENTAL LIMITED	02	67	25
SNO CIRCUS AND CARNIVAL TRAINS	08	73	08
SNO CIRCUS TRAINS IN 1964	11	64	36
SNO CIRCUS TRAINS: LONGEST RUN	09	54	28
SNO CN:BLUEBERRY SPECIAL	11	70	60
SNO CP: "THE DOMINION" ENDING SERVICE	01	76	40
SNO CP: CANADIAN SILK TRAINS	06	77	10
SNO DEATH VALLEY SCOTTY RUN OF 1905	03	74	35
SNO DL&W: PHOEBE SNOW	11	67	08
SNO DL&W: PHOEBE SNOW TRAIN NAME ORIGIN	10	69	35
SNO E:MIDLANDER TRAIN	09	71	39
SNO EXECUTION TRAINS OF 1860'S	07	70	54
SNO FIRST CIRCUS TRAINS	02	74	52
SNO FREEDOM TRAIN: WHAT HAPPENED TO IT?	02	65	31
SNO GN: "ORIENTAL LIMITED"	07	78	56
SNO IC: "GREEN DIAMOND"	03	78	51
SNO MP: "SUNSHINE SPECIAL"	02	71	36
SNO NEWSPAPER SPECIAL (TORONTO GLOBE)	06	75	29
SNO NYNH&H: "FEDERAL EXPRESS" PRE-HELLGA	12	76	25
SNO NYP&B: NAME TRAIN "DOLLY VARDEN"	04	68	27
SNO PAY TRAINS	08	55	42
SNO POTUS--PRESIDENTIAL CAR/TRAIN	10	71	44
SNO PRESIDENTIAL CARS-GLEN SPRINGS & MAG	04	68	27
SNO PRIVATE CAR "HARRY TRUMAN" SOLD	07	69	08
SNO PRIVATE CAR "RAMBLER" (H FLANDERS)	04	67	10
SNO PRR: "SPIRIT OF ST LOUIS" TRAIN	01	65	29
SNO PRR: CONGRESSIONAL LIMITED	08	70	34
SNO PRR: THE TRAIN "NELLIE BLY"	06	78	56
SNO RB&BB CIRCUS TRAIN MAKE UP	07	67	33
SNO REXALL TRAIN	05	69	30
SNO RI: "SILVIS ROCKET"	04	68	60
SNO SAL: "SILVER METEOR"	12	70	44
SNO SILK TRAINS	02	59	40
SNO SILK TRAINS: READER INFORMATION	06	65	07
SNO STEAMBOAT EXPRESS FRL	10	76	46
SNO TRAINS NAMED "BULLET"	04	69	29
SPACE SHUTTLE EXPRESS ATSF BARSTOW CA	09	82	26
SPECIAL TRAINS: FLAGS/BUNTING/BLACK CREP	06	58	26
TRAIN X	10	52	120
TRAINS OF TOMORROW GMD 4 DIESEL CARS	09	47	132
TROOP TRAINS: HISTORY OF RAILWAY TROOP	01	41	27
WHISTLE STOPPING-JOHN ANDERSON CAMPAIGN	05	81	28
WRECKING TRAIN	11	43	09
YELLOW JACKET TRAIN M&LB 1898 PHOTO	10	48	55
ZOOLINER PORTLAND OREGON ZOO PHOTO	06	59	37

♦ SPEED & SCHEDULES ♦

	M	Y	P
72" DRIVING WHEEL TURNS PER MINUTE-30 MI	12	29	99
AMERICA'S UNOFFICAIAL TRAIN-SPEED RECORD	10	55	30
AMERICAS FASTEST TRAINS	06	33	44

PROTOTYPE

PROTOTYPE MISCELLANEOUS INFORMATION	M	Y	P
ANNUAL SPEED SURVEY 1937	04	38	06
ANNUAL SPEED SURVEY 1938	02	39	07
ANNUAL SPEED SURVEY 1939	01	40	06
ANNUAL SPEED SURVEY 1940	01	41	08
ANNUAL SPEED SURVEY 1941	01	42	95
ANNUAL SPEED SURVEY 1942	03	43	10
ANNUAL SPEED SURVEY 1943	03	44	66
ANNUAL SPEED SURVEY 1945	03	46	40
ANNUAL SPEED SURVEY 1946	04	47	78
ANNUAL SPEED SURVEY 1947	04	48	06
ANNUAL SPEED SURVEY 1948	04	49	08
ANNUAL SPEED SURVEY 1949	04	50	14
ANNUAL SPEED SURVEY 1950	04	51	19
ANNUAL SPEED SURVEY 1951	04	52	14
ATSF "CHIEF"-SPEED/LOCOS USED	05	31	279
AUTOMATIC TRAIN CONTROL	02	30	385
AUTOMATIC TRAIN CONTROL.	02	42	38
AVERAGE SPEEDS-EMPIRE ST/BROADWAY/20TH C	02	31	441
BLOCK SIGNAL RULES	10	56	47
BN SPOKANE DIVISON FREIGHT TRAINS	12	87	53
CANADIAN PACIFIC EAST BOUND TRANSCONTINE	02	37	76
CHICAGO TO MILWAUKEE SPEED RUN 1934 MILW	11	34	34
COAST TO COAST IN 90 MINUTES PANAMA	12	45	89
CTC CENTRALIZED TRAFFIC CONTROL.	10	42	54
DISPLAY OF SIGNALS	06	50	56
DISTANCE COVERED BY LOCO PULLING A TRAIN	12	29	99
EMPLOYEES TIMETABLES	06	42	81
FAST RUN: REASON FOR MILEAGE DIFFERENCES	02	39	89
FASTEST COAST TO COAST--CR & ATSF	11	87	40
FASTEST TRAINS ON VARIOUS ROADS	02	32	327
FIRST MILE A MINUTE RUNS	06	61	35
FR FOREIGN RAILROADS	06	51	139
FR CHINESE TIMECARD	06	51	139
FR FASTEST TRAIN IN WORLD	07	32	510
FR FRENCH WIN WORLD'S TRAIN-RECORD SPEED	08	55	03
FR GERMAN SPEED RUN OF 1902	11	31	565
FR TOP SPEED OF FRENCH TRAINS	02	68	30
FROM PACIFIC TO ATLANTIC IN 100 MINUTES	02	32	334
GN HILL'S RECORD BREAKING TRIP	04	31	123
GN SILK RUNS--2 A DAY APART SET RECORDS	04	31	122
HAND SIGNALS FOR RAILROADS	11	41	25
HIGH-SPEED SCHEDULES MAY 1942	05	42	149
IC RACES AIRPLANE 1910 AND WINS	06	58	34
INTERLOCKING SIGNALS	08	42	85
LIST OF AGGREGATE MILEAGE/SPEED/MO POWER	04	38	19
LIST OF NON-STOP MILE-A-MINUTE IN N AMER	04	38	09
LIST OF NONSTOP RUNS BY ROAD AND MILEAGE	02	39	11
MAXIMUM SPEED ON RAILROADS	08	30	91
MILE A MINUTE RUNS IN NORTH AMERICA	10	36	20
MILE POSTS TO TELL SPEED OF LOCOMOTIVE	05	32	178
MILE-A-MINUTE RUNS IN NORTH AMERICA	02	39	07
MILE-A-MINUTERS	01	40	06
MILE-A-MINUTERS 1940-41 WINTER	05	41	132
MILE-A-MINUTERS: MORE	05	40	95
MOTOR-CAR RUN IN CANADA: FASTEST	12	43	79

PROTOTYPE MISCELLANEOUS INFORMATION	M	Y	P
NEW YORK TO CHICAGO--FASTEST TIME	11	31	491
NEW YORK TO SAN FRANCISCO IN 81.5 HOURS	09	32	191
NON-STOP STEAM RUNS: LONGEST	11	41	44
NORTH AMERICA'S MILE-A-MINUTE TRAIN RUNS	04	38	07
NYC #999/ACL/R SPEED RECORDS	09	33	44
NYO&W FAST FREIGHT AW-2 SCHEDULE	11	41	50
OLDEST TIMETABLES IN AMERICA	10	33	54
PACEMAKER: FIRST RUN NYC	10	46	62
PASSENGER TRAIN SPEED & SCHEDULE HISTORY	01	50	10
PASSENGER TRAIN SPEEDS 1899-1949	01	50	35
PLANT SYSTEM SPEED RUN IN 1901.	09	30	218
PLOTTING NEW TIMETABLES	05	42	56
PRR "PENNSYLVANIA SPECIAL" FASTEST STEAM	08	57	30
PRR/R 60 MPH	02	31	441
RADIO COMMUNICATIONS IN RAILROADING	05	30	246
READING: JULY 20 1904 FASTEST TIME	05	33	77
REMOTE CONTROL TRAIN DISPATCHING	10	30	379
SMOKE ORDERS	10	57	74
SPEED OF LOCO DEPENDS ON...	02	32	330
SPEED RUNS OF THE NINETEENTH CENTURY	09	36	17
SPEED TIMING OF "BOARDWALK FLYER"	01	39	21
SPEED TIMING OF "CHAMPION"	03	40	80
SPEED TIMING OF "CONGRESSIONAL"	02	40	78
SPEED TIMING OF "CRUSADER" (READING)	05	40	29
SPEED TIMING OF "DETROIT ARROW"	07	39	77
SPEED TIMING OF "HIAWATHA" MILW	05	39	70
SPEED TIMING OF "MERCURY"	09	39	53
SPEED--PRR/B&O/NYC/P&R/CNJ	11	30	598
SPEED-MAIN FACTORS IN	11	31	485
TABLE FOR SPEED	02	33	80
TFO TIMING THE FAST ONES	09	39	53
TFO ANN RUTLEDGE B&O	11	39	29
TFO BOARDWALK FLYER	01	39	21
TFO BURLINGTON-ROCK ISLAND STREAMLINERS	12	40	50
TFO CHAMPION	03	40	80
TFO CONGRESSIONAL PRR	02	40	78
TFO CRUSADER READING LINES	05	40	29
TFO DETROIT ARROW	07	39	77
TFO MERUCRY NYC	09	39	53
TIME SCHEDULE OF FPL	01	47	84
TIME TABLE WNC 1861	12	43	12
TIMETABLE EASTERN RAILROAD 1852	01	55	34
TIMETABLE FUNERAL TRAIN PRES DAVIS	02	46	95
TIMETABLE GEORGIA RAILROAD 1845	01	50	66
TIMETABLE HBRR "THE PAS-CHURCHILL"	06	54	18
TIMETABLE ILLINOIS CENTRAL RAILROAD	06	42	82
TIMETABLE L&N 1877	09	32	233
TIMETABLE MICHIGAN SOUTHERN 1844	11	38	112
TIMETABLE SP "PRESIDENT'S SPECIAL" 1901	11	45	43
TIMETABLE WW&F SEPT 29 1930	09	35	49
TIMETABLES	06	35	40
TIMETABLES 1	05	51	24
TIMETABLES 2	06	51	36
TRACKSIDE SIGNAL HISTORY	08	57	20
TRAIN COMMUNICATION SYSTEMS	10	44	55

Railroad/ Railfan

PROTOTYPE

PROTOTYPE MISCELLANEOUS INFORMATION	M	Y	P
TRAIN MARKERS.	06	59	26
TRAIN ORDER HOOPS	09	41	18
TRAIN TELEPHONES	09	30	165
TRAIN TELEPHONES.	02	42	54
USM CHATTANOOGA & ATLANTA LINE 1863 TIME	11	48	30
B&O ELLWOOD CITY PA 1910 SABATOGE WRECK	05	71	05
BOILER EXPLOSION NYNH&H DECEMBER 1890	08	34	41
BOX CAR OVER STREET WRECK PHOTO	09	76	31
WRECK "NATIONAL LIMITED" 1960	09	70	08

*   GENERAL PROTOTYPE DATA   *

	M	Y	P
CAR TRUCK HISTORY	06	42	98
CLEANING UP WRECKS ON ICG	01	77	10
COLORS OF CONDUCTORS LANTERN GLOBES	06	62	44
CRACKED WHEELS--MARKING WHILE HOT	08	61	10
ELECTRONIC HOTBOX DETECTOR OPERATION	02	62	49
FIRST AUTOMATIC COUPLERS	08	61	34
FORM 19 VERSUS FORM 31 DIFFERENCES	11	38	72
KATY FLOOD SIGNALS	01	77	50
LOGGING RAILROADS	08	55	12
RUBBER TIRED TRACTORS FOR HARBOR SWITCHI	02	78	50R
SETTING AIR BRAKES (SPEED OF EXECUTION)	02	62	48
SNO LINK PIN COUPLERS	01	65	30
TENNESSEE'S RAILROADS IN 1930 LIST	01	77	51
TIMETABLES OLD AND NEW	06	35	40
TRACKMAN ON RAIL GANG	12	78	08
WESTINGHOUSE NON-AUTO AIR BRAKE 1869 DRA	11	30	530
WESTINGHOUSE PLAIN AUTO AIR BRAKE DRAW	11	30	531
WESTINGHOUSE QUICK ACTION AUTO AIR BRAKE	11	30	534
WORLDS SLOWEST TRAIN A&GWW "GOLD RUSH LT	03	31	527

Dispatchers Report continued

notify everyone who buys a book direct and everyone who registers their book with us (If you didn't buy it direct, a postcard with your name and address will do.) of a pre-publish special for them when the new book is sent to the printer. This will guarantee delivery to you in 4-6 weeks.

We feel the index project is worthwhile and plan to continue through all the magazines we can find. We also have some special topical indexes on the back burner. Watch for them.

Finally we are always open to ideas on how to do this job better. Please share your ideas with us.

Railroad/ Railfan

BILL OF LADING — RAILROAD HISTORIES & ROSTERS

Railroad Histories, Short Notes (SNO:), and Rosters are articles on specific railroads. In some instances they are they result of researching "The Olden Days" of the road, in some instances they are current happenings at the time of publication, which are now history. Short notes are differentiated from histories in that the article runs from a sentence to a short paragraph or two. Not a lot of information, but maybe just what YOU are looking for! The descriptor line contains the road abbreviation plus an idea of the subject matter contained in the article. The Roster listings show locomotives or rolling stock of the various roads or builders. The descriptor line includes the road, type of equipment and dates covered when available.

MANIFEST — RAILROAD HISTORIES & ROSTERS

DETAILED CONSIST	PAGE
ROSTERS BY ROAD	377
HISTORY OF...	406
HISTORY OF... SHORT NOTES	416
WRECKS AND DISASTERS	474
RAILROAD MAPS BY ROAD	478
HISTORY OF... SHORT NOTES ADDITIONS	480

Railroad/Railfan

RAILROAD HISTORIES & ROSTERS

ROSTERS BY RAILROAD	M	Y	P
ROSTER OF 2-8-4 VAN SWERINGEN BERKSHIRES	09	84	36
ROSTER OF 2-8-4 VAN SWERINGENS-PRESERVED	09	84	39
ROSTER OF 4-6-6-4 LOCOMOTIVES	10	64	25
ROSTER OF A RDC CARS	01	80	53
ROSTER OF A&A LOCOMOTIVES 3-1969	08	69	50
ROSTER OF A&A LOCOMOTIVES 4-1974	03	75	47
ROSTER OF A&A LOCOMOTIVES 6-1974	12	75	53
ROSTER OF A&A LOCOMOTIVES 7-1963	02	64	52
ROSTER OF A&BB DIESEL LOCOS-ALL TIME	01	84	50
ROSTER OF A&BB LOCOMOTIVES 1960	06	60	56
ROSTER OF A&BB LOCOMOTIVES 5-1974	03	75	44
ROSTER OF A&BB LOCOMOTIVES 6-1969	12	69	44
ROSTER OF A&D LOCOMOTIVES 1-1964	08	64	36
ROSTER OF A&D LOCOMOTIVES 4-1969	04	75	48
ROSTER OF A&D LOCOS: DIESELS (7)	09	52	59
ROSTER OF A&EC DIESELS W/SPECS	02	78	49
ROSTER OF A&EC LOCOMOTIVES 1-1960	10	62	53
ROSTER OF A&EC LOCOMOTIVES 1-1964	08	64	36
ROSTER OF A&EC LOCOMOTIVES 11-1974	04	75	48
ROSTER OF A&EC LOCOMOTIVES 3-1969	10	69	50
ROSTER OF A&EC LOCOS: DIESEL	12	56	29
ROSTER OF A&J LOCOMOTIVES 10-1965	02	66	54
ROSTER OF A&J LOCOMOTIVES 12-1970	05	71	57
ROSTER OF A&J LOCOMOTIVES 1971	03	75	45
ROSTER OF A&LM DIESEL LOCOMOTIVES	01	81	52
ROSTER OF A&LM LOCOMOTIVES 11-1974	03	75	47
ROSTER OF A&LM LOCOMOTIVES 12-1963	06	64	48
ROSTER OF A&LM LOCOMOTIVES 12-1964	05	65	50
ROSTER OF A&LM LOCOMOTIVES 3-1968	06	68	50
ROSTER OF A&LM LOCOMOTIVES 6-1971	03	72	58
ROSTER OF A&LM STEAM LOCOS 1961	02	61	56
ROSTER OF A&ML LOCOMOTIVES 12-1966	05	67	54
ROSTER OF A&MR LOCOMOTIVES 11-1974	03	75	47
ROSTER OF A&MR LOCOMOTIVES 3-1964	08	64	60
ROSTER OF A&MR LOCOMOTIVES 3-1967	06	67	50
ROSTER OF A&MR LOCOMOTIVES 6-1971	03	72	59
ROSTER OF A&N LOCOMOTIVES 10-1964	02	65	54
ROSTER OF A&N LOCOMOTIVES 12-1971	03	75	45
ROSTER OF A&N LOCOMOTIVES 3-1972	10	72	44
ROSTER OF A&N LOCOMOTIVES 6-1967	11	67	46
ROSTER OF A&N STEAM LOCOS 1961	02	61	56
ROSTER OF A&NR LOCOMOTIVES 11-1974	03	75	46
ROSTER OF A&NR LOCOMOTIVES 3-1970	11	70	40
ROSTER OF A&NR LOCOMOTIVES 7-1966	09	66	46
ROSTER OF A&NR STEAM LOCOS 1961	02	61	56
ROSTER OF A&O LOCOMOTIVES 11-1974	03	75	47
ROSTER OF A&R LOCOMOTIVES 1-1964	08	64	36
ROSTER OF A&R LOCOMOTIVES 3-1969	10	69	50
ROSTER OF A&R LOCOMOTIVES 8-1974	03	75	44
ROSTER OF A&R STEAM LOCOS 1961	02	61	56
ROSTER OF A&S LOCOMOTIVES 3-1965	09	65	54
ROSTER OF A&S LOCOMOTIVES 6-1968	02	69	46
ROSTER OF A&S LOCOMOTIVES 9-1967	03	68	52
ROSTER OF A&S LOCOMOTIVES 9-1972	01	73	52
ROSTER OF A&S LOCOMOTIVES 9-1973	06	74	52
ROSTER OF A&S LOCOMOTIVES 9-1973	03	75	46
ROSTER OF A&S LOCOS: DIESELS 1959	10	59	71
ROSTER OF A&SO LOCOMOTIVES	03	75	44
ROSTER OF A&SO LOCOMOTIVES 3-1970	11	70	40
ROSTER OF A&SO LOCOMOTIVES 7-1966	09	66	46
ROSTER OF A&SO LOCOS: (ONE 2-8-2)	10	48	128
ROSTER OF A&SRR (OWNS NO LOCOS) 1964	02	65	54
ROSTER OF A&SRR LOCOMOTIVES 3-1972	10	72	44
ROSTER OF A&SRR LOCOMOTIVES 5-1967	04	75	48
ROSTER OF A&SRR LOCOMOTIVES 6-1967	11	67	46
ROSTER OF A&SS LOCOMOTIVES 11-1974	03	75	45
ROSTER OF A&STAB LOCOMOTIVES 1-1961	02	62	30
ROSTER OF A&STAB LOCOMOTIVES 10-1964	12	64	32
ROSTER OF A&STAB LOCOMOTIVES 10-1966	02	67	48
ROSTER OF A&STAB LOCOMOTIVES 12-1970	07	71	52
ROSTER OF A&STAB LOCOMOTIVES 12-1971	08	72	57
ROSTER OF A&STAB LOCOMOTIVES 6-1967	10	67	50
ROSTER OF A&STAB LOCOMOTIVES 8-1974	04	75	47
ROSTER OF A&STAB LOCOS: DIESEL	08	52	103
ROSTER OF A&W LOCOMOTIVES 11-1974	03	75	44
ROSTER OF A&W LOCOMOTIVES 7-1965	01	66	66
ROSTER OF A&W LOCOMOTIVES 9-1970	05	71	58
ROSTER OF A&WE LOCOMOTIOVES 1-1964	08	64	36
ROSTER OF A&WE LOCOMOTIVES 3-1969	10	69	50
ROSTER OF A&WE LOCOMOTIVES 8-1974	04	75	48
ROSTER OF A&WE STEAM LOCOS 1961	02	61	56
ROSTER OF A&WP LOCOMOTIVES 1-1961	02	62	30
ROSTER OF A&WP LOCOMOTIVES 10-1966	02	67	48
ROSTER OF A&WP LOCOMOTIVES 12-1970	07	71	52
ROSTER OF A&WP LOCOMOTIVES 12-1974	04	75	47
ROSTER OF A&WP LOCOMOTIVES 3-1972	10	72	44
ROSTER OF A&WP LOCOMOTIVES 6-1967	11	67	46
ROSTER OF A&WP LOCOMOTOIVES 10-1964	02	65	54
ROSTER OF A&WP LOCOS	12	39	112
ROSTER OF A&WP LOCOS: STEAM/DIESEL-ELECT	07	52	110
ROSTER OF A&WRY (OWNS NO LOCOMOTIVES)'66	05	67	54
ROSTER OF A&WRY LOCOMOTIVES 6-1971	03	72	58
ROSTER OF AA LOCOMOTIVES 1960	06	60	56
ROSTER OF AA LOCOMOTIVES 3-1965	06	65	55
ROSTER OF AA LOCOMOTIVES 5-1974	03	75	46
ROSTER OF AA LOCOMOTIVES 6-1968	10	68	38
ROSTER OF AA LOCOMOTIVES 6-1969	12	69	44
ROSTER OF AA LOCOMOTIVES 6-1973	03	74	46
ROSTER OF AA LOCOS	09	42	76
ROSTER OF AB LOCOMOTIVES 3-1964	08	64	60
ROSTER OF AB LOCOMOTIVES 3-1967	06	67	50
ROSTER OF AB LOCOMOTIVES 6-1971	03	72	59
ROSTER OF AB LOCOMOTIVES 8-1971	03	75	45
ROSTER OF AB&C LOCOS	09	40	68
ROSTER OF AC&HB LOCOS	01	34	93
ROSTER OF AC&HB LOCOS: DIESEL-ELECTRICS	11	54	46
ROSTER OF AC&Y LOCOMOTIVES 1960	06	60	56
ROSTER OF AC&Y LOCOMOTIVES 6-1969	12	69	44
ROSTER OF AC&Y LOCOMOTIVES 8-1974	03	75	44
ROSTER OF AC&Y LOCOS	12	32	106

Railroad/Railfan

RAILROAD HISTORIES & ROSTERS

ROSTERS BY RAILROAD	M	Y	P
ROSTER OF AC&Y LOCOS: STEAM/DIESEL-ELECT	02	55	46
ROSTER OF ACL LOCOMOTIVES	12	38	113
ROSTER OF ACL LOCOMOTIVES 5-1965	11	65	26
ROSTER OF ACL LOCOS	07	33	84
ROSTER OF ACL LOCOS	03	47	119
ROSTER OF ACL LOCOS: DIESEL 1958	04	59	70
ROSTER OF ACL LOCOS: NEW PASS/FRT LOCOS	09	35	83
ROSTER OF AD&N (OWNS NO LOCOMOTIVES)1963	06	64	48
ROSTER OF AD&N LOCOMOTIVES 11-1974	04	75	47
ROSTER OF AD&N LOCOMOTIVES 12-1966	05	67	54
ROSTER OF AD&N LOCOMOTIVES 6-1971	03	72	58
ROSTER OF AE&FR LOCOMOTIVES 8-1974	04	75	48
ROSTER OF AE&FR LOCOMOTIVES 9-1967	03	68	52
ROSTER OF AE&FR LOCOMOTIVES 9-1972	01	73	52
ROSTER OF AGR LOCOMOTIVES	11	78	48R
ROSTER OF AGS LOCOS: PART 1 (S)	06	38	80
ROSTER OF AGS LOCOS: PART 2	07	38	134
ROSTER OF AL LOCOMOTIVES 12-1963	06	64	39
ROSTER OF AL LOCOMOTIVES 6-1970	03	71	49
ROSTER OF AL LOCOS	08	39	26
ROSTER OF AL LOCOS: 21! WITH DATA	05	34	87
ROSTER OF AL LOCOS: STEAM/DIESEL-ELECTRI	10	54	37
ROSTER OF AL LOCOS: TYPES IN SERVICE	01	37	89
ROSTER OF AL&M LOCOMOTIVES 3-1973	07	73	58
ROSTER OF AL&S LOCOMOTIVES 3-1966	05	66	48
ROSTER OF AL&S LOCOMOTIVES 6-1974	03	75	45
ROSTER OF AL&S LOCOMOTIVES 9-1969	03	70	62
ROSTER OF ALC STEAM LOCOS 1961	02	61	56
ROSTER OF ALCO DEMONSTRATORS	02	65	33
ROSTER OF ALCO HH LOCOMOTIVES ADDS	10	74	56
ROSTER OF ALEX LOCOMOTIVES 1-1964	08	64	36
ROSTER OF ALEX LOCOMOTIVES 3-1969	10	69	50
ROSTER OF ALEX LOCOMOTIVES 8-1974	03	75	45
ROSTER OF ALGC LOCOMOTIVES 10-1965	02	66	54
ROSTER OF ALGC LOCOMOTIVES 12-1970	05	71	57
ROSTER OF ALGC LOCOMOTIVES 6-1974	03	75	45
ROSTER OF ALM LOCOMOTIVES 3-1964	08	64	60
ROSTER OF ALM LOCOMOTIVES 3-1967	06	67	50
ROSTER OF ALM LOCOMOTIVES 6-1971	03	72	59
ROSTER OF ALM LOCOMOTIVES 6-1974	03	75	45
ROSTER OF AMC LOCOMOTIVES 11-1974	03	75	46
ROSTER OF AMC LOCOMOTIVES 3-1964	08	64	60
ROSTER OF AMC LOCOMOTIVES 3-1967	06	67	50
ROSTER OF AMC LOCOMOTIVES 6-1971	03	72	59
ROSTER OF AMC STEAM LOCOS 1961	02	61	56
ROSTER OF AN LOCOMOTIVES 10-1964	12	64	32
ROSTER OF AN LOCOMOTIVES 12-1971	08	72	57
ROSTER OF AN LOCOMOTIVES 12-1971	03	75	47
ROSTER OF AN LOCOMOTIVES 6-1967	10	67	50
ROSTER OF APA DIESEL LOCOMOTIVES	07	79	51
ROSTER OF APA LOCOMOTIVES 10-1963	04	64	35
ROSTER OF APA LOCOMOTIVES 12-1966	04	67	39
ROSTER OF APA LOCOMOTIVES 3-1971	10	71	46
ROSTER OF APA LOCOMOTIVES 5-1974	03	75	46
ROSTER OF APA LOCOMOTIVES 7-87	10	87	50
ROSTER OF APT (OWNS NO LOCOMOTIVES)1964	02	65	54
ROSTER OF APT LOCOMOTIVES 11-1967	11	67	46
ROSTER OF APT LOCOMOTIVES 3-1972	10	72	44
ROSTER OF ARR LOCOS (B&O)	06	34	90
ROSTER OF ARR LOCOS-PACIFIC TYPES 4-6-2	11	32	474
ROSTER OF ARR LOCOS: NOT CLASS A-E (B&O)	07	34	83
ROSTER OF ASM&L LOCOMOTIVES 10-1964	02	65	54
ROSTER OF ASM&L LOCOMOTIVES 3-1972	10	72	44
ROSTER OF ASM&L LOCOMOTIVES 6-1967	11	67	46
ROSTER OF ASM&L LOCOMOTIVES 6-1971	04	75	47
ROSTER OF AT&N LOCOMOTIVES 1-1961	02	62	30
ROSTER OF AT&N LOCOMOTIVES 10-1966	02	67	48
ROSTER OF AT&N LOCOMOTIVES 12-1970	07	71	52
ROSTER OF AT&N LOCOMOTIVES 6-1974	03	75	44
ROSTER OF ATC (OWNS NO LOCOMOTIVES)1964	02	65	54
ROSTER OF ATC LOCOMOTIVES 3-1972	10	72	44
ROSTER OF ATC LOCOMOTIVES 5-1964	04	75	48
ROSTER OF ATC LOCOMOTIVES 6-1967	11	67	46
ROSTER OF ATR LOCOMOTIVES 8-1974	04	75	48
ROSTER OF ATSF CF7 DISPOSITIONS	05	85	50
ROSTER OF ATSF DIESEL-ELECTRIC ROAD LOCO	10	41	74
ROSTER OF ATSF FREIGHT LOCOS	06	37	113
ROSTER OF ATSF FT RENUMBERINGS	08	71	58
ROSTER OF ATSF LOCO: STEAM 1949	10	50	109
ROSTER OF ATSF LOCOMOTIVES 1-1965	12	65	58
ROSTER OF ATSF LOCOMOTIVES 3-1970	08	71	54
ROSTER OF ATSF LOCOMOTIVES ADDS	04	71	66
ROSTER OF ATSF LOCOS	07	33	85
ROSTER OF ATSF LOCOS PART 3	07	37	113
ROSTER OF ATSF LOCOS-CONCLUSION	08	37	61
ROSTER OF ATSF LOCOS-INCLUDING SUBSIDIAR	05	37	83
ROSTER OF ATSF LOCOS: BRIEF W/ DATA	06	34	89
ROSTER OF ATSF LOCOS: STEAM/DIESEL 1959	08	59	64
ROSTER OF ATSF LOCOS: TANDEM LOCOS	06	36	86
ROSTER OF ATSF LOCOS: WITH DATA	07	34	94
ROSTER OF ATSF PART 1: DIESEL 1949	11	50	116
ROSTER OF ATSF SKYWAY AIR FLEET	11	85	58
ROSTER OF ATSF STEAM LOCOS 1961	02	61	56
ROSTER OF AU LOCOMOTIVES 12-1966	05	67	54
ROSTER OF AU LOCOMOTIVES 6-1971	03	72	58
ROSTER OF AU LOCOMOTIVES 9-1967	04	75	48
ROSTER OF AUPD (NO MOTIVE POWER)	06	60	56
ROSTER OF AUPD (OWNS NO LOCOMOTIVES)1969	12	69	44
ROSTER OF AUPD LOCOMOTIVES 1975	03	75	44
ROSTER OF AUSC (OWNS NO LOCOMOTIVES)1964	02	65	54
ROSTER OF AUSC (OWNS NO LOCOMOTIVES)1967	11	67	46
ROSTER OF AUSC LOCOMOTIVES 3-1972	10	72	44
ROSTER OF AUSC LOCOMOTIVES 5-1967	04	75	48
ROSTER OF AV LOCOMOTIVES 11-1962	08	63	60
ROSTER OF AV LOCOMOTIVES 3-1968	07	68	57
ROSTER OF AV LOCOMOTIVES 3-1973	06	73	11
ROSTER OF AV LOCOMOTIVES 8-1974	06	75	64
ROSTER OF AW LOCOMOTIVES 10-1965	03	66	59
ROSTER OF AW LOCOMOTIVES 12-1963	06	64	48
ROSTER OF AW LOCOMOTIVES 1975	03	75	47

Railroad/Railfan

RAILROAD HISTORIES & ROSTERS

ROSTERS BY RAILROAD	M	Y	P
ROSTER OF AW LOCOMOTIVES 3-1969	01	70	10
ROSTER OF AW LOCOS: NOW KCS	04	57	74
ROSTER OF AW STEAM LOCOMOTIVES-ALL TIME	01	76	56
ROSTER OF AW&W LOCOMOTIVES 5-1974	03	75	45
ROSTER OF AW&W LOCOMOTIVES 6-1962	12	62	60
ROSTER OF AW&W LOCOMOTIVES 9-67	02	68	62
ROSTER OF B&A LOCOS	01	33	102
ROSTER OF B&A LOCOS: PART 1 NYC	05	40	81
ROSTER OF B&A LOCOS: PART 2 NYC	06	40	113
ROSTER OF B&A LOCOS: STEAM/DIESEL 1949	02	50	90
ROSTER OF B&AN LOCOMOTIVES 11-1974	04	75	48
ROSTER OF B&AN LOCOMOTIVES 3-1968	09	68	44
ROSTER OF B&AN LOCOMOTIVES 3-1973	01	74	45
ROSTER OF B&AN LOCOMOTIVES 6-1964	11	64	62
ROSTER OF B&CH LOCOMOTIVES 11-1974	04	75	49
ROSTER OF B&E (OWNS NO LOCOMOTIVES) 1968	09	68	44
ROSTER OF B&E LOCOMOTIVES 3-1964	04	75	49
ROSTER OF B&E LOCOMOTIVES 3-1973	01	74	45
ROSTER OF B&E LOCOMOTIVES 6-1964	11	64	62
ROSTER OF B&GA LOCOS	12	43	91
ROSTER OF B&H LOCOS	11	38	133
ROSTER OF B&HA LOCOMOTIVES 11-1974	04	75	49
ROSTER OF B&HA LOCOMOTIVES 3-1969	08	69	50
ROSTER OF B&HA LOCOMOTIVES 6-1974	12	75	53
ROSTER OF B&HA LOCOMOTIVES 7-1963	02	64	52
ROSTER OF B&HA LOCOS	01	41	136
ROSTER OF B&HS LOCOMOTIVES 10-1973	05	74	59
ROSTER OF B&HS LOCOMOTIVES 3-1965	08	65	65
ROSTER OF B&HS LOCOMOTIVES 6-1968	03	69	38
ROSTER OF B&HS LOCOMOTIVES 7-1973	06	75	53
ROSTER OF B&HS STEAM LOCOS 1961	02	61	57
ROSTER OF B&IR LOCOMOTIVES 12-1967	05	68	52
ROSTER OF B&LE LOCOMOTIVES	05	38	68
ROSTER OF B&LE LOCOMOTIVES CORRECTTIONS	07	38	79
ROSTER OF B&LE LOCOMOTIVES 10-1973	04	75	50
ROSTER OF B&LE LOCOMOTIVES 1960	06	60	56
ROSTER OF B&LE LOCOMOTIVES 3-1966	05	66	48
ROSTER OF B&LE LOCOMOTIVES 6-1969	12	69	44
ROSTER OF B&LE LOCOMOTIVES 9-1969	03	70	62
ROSTER OF B&LE LOCOS: STEAM/DIESEL-ELECT	10	51	97
ROSTER OF B&LE REMAINING F7 LOCOS 3-82	07	82	47
ROSTER OF B&M LOCOMOTIVES 9-1965	03	66	61
ROSTER OF B&M LOCOS	04	33	88
ROSTER OF B&M LOCOS: NAMED ENGINES	01	46	13
ROSTER OF B&M LOCOS: STEAM	01	46	100
ROSTER OF B&M LOCOS: STEAM/DIESEL	10	56	55
ROSTER OF B&M LOCOS: STEAM/DIESEL CORREC	02	57	55
ROSTER OF B&ML LOCOMOTIVES 11-1962	08	63	60
ROSTER OF B&ML LOCOMOTIVES 3-1968	07	68	57
ROSTER OF B&ML LOCOMOTIVES 3-1973	06	73	11
ROSTER OF B&ML LOCOMOTIVES 8-1974	04	75	50
ROSTER OF B&ML LOCOS	02	34	87
ROSTER OF B&N LOCOMOTIVES 12-1963	06	64	48
ROSTER OF B&N LOCOMOTIVES 12-1966	05	67	54
ROSTER OF B&N LOCOMOTIVES 2-1971	04	75	49
ROSTER OF B&N LOCOMOTIVES 6-1971	03	72	58
ROSTER OF B&O DIESEL LOCOS (ALL TIME)	01	66	40
ROSTER OF B&O LOCOMOTIVES 1963 REVISION	12	63	61
ROSTER OF B&O LOCOMOTIVES 9-1961	04	62	32
ROSTER OF B&O LOCOS	06	34	90
ROSTER OF B&O LOCOS NOT CLASS A-E	07	34	83
ROSTER OF B&O LOCOS PART 1: STEAM	11	48	112
ROSTER OF B&O LOCOS PART 2: ELECTRIC/GAS	12	48	80
ROSTER OF B&O LOCOS PART 2: STEAM/DIESEL	12	48	80
ROSTER OF B&O LOCOS: RENUMBERING/RECLASS	10	57	58
ROSTER OF B&O LOCOS: STEAM/GAS/ELECT/DIE	12	53	71
ROSTER OF B&O STEAM LOCOS 1961	02	61	56
ROSTER OF B&OCT LOCOMOTIVES 6-1962	12	62	60
ROSTER OF B&OCT LOCOMOTIVES 9-1967	02	68	62
ROSTER OF B&OCT LOCOMOTIVES 9-1967.	03	68	52
ROSTER OF B&OCT LOCOMOTIVES 9-1972	01	73	52
ROSTER OF B&OCT LOCOMOTIVES 9-1974	04	75	49
ROSTER OF B&OCT LOCOS (B&O)	06	34	90
ROSTER OF B&OCT LOCOS: NOT CLASS A-E(B&O	07	34	83
ROSTER OF B&OCT LOCOS: STEAM/DIESEL	12	48	84
ROSTER OF B&OCT LOCOS: STEAM/DIESEL 1959	10	59	71
ROSTER OF B&S LOCOMOTIVES 1-1975	04	75	51
ROSTER OF B&S LOCOMOTIVES 3-1965	09	65	54
ROSTER OF B&S LOCOMOTIVES 6-1968	02	68	46
ROSTER OF B&S LOCOMOTIVES 9-1973	06	74	52
ROSTER OF B&S STEAM LOCOS 1961	02	61	56
ROSTER OF B&SQ LOCOS (B&O)	06	34	90
ROSTER OF B&SQ LOCOS: NOT CLASS A-E (B&O	07	34	83
ROSTER OF B&SR LOCOS: STEAM TANKS	12	55	33
ROSTER OF BA&P LOCOMOTIVES 11-1974	06	75	55
ROSTER OF BA&P LOCOMOTIVES 12-1968	05	69	50
ROSTER OF BA&P LOCOMOTIVES 7-1965	12	65	28
ROSTER OF BALDWIN DEMONSTRATORS	02	65	33
ROSTER OF BAM LOCOMOTIVES 11-1974	04	75	49
ROSTER OF BAR LOCOMOTIVES 6-1970	04	71	52
ROSTER OF BAR LOCOMOTIVES 8-1965	02	66	53
ROSTER OF BAR LOCOS	02	35	88
ROSTER OF BAR LOCOS: DIESEL	12	57	26
ROSTER OF BAR LOCOS: STEAM/DIESEL	01	50	104
ROSTER OF BBRR (OWNS NO LOCOMOTIVES)1966	02	67	48
ROSTER OF BBRR LOCOMOTIVES 12-1970	07	71	52
ROSTER OF BBRR LOCOMOTIVES 8-1974	04	75	51
ROSTER OF BC&G LOCOMOTIVES (ALL TIME)	08	62	20
ROSTER OF BC&G MOTOR CARS ALL TIME	08	62	20
ROSTER OF BC&G ROLLING STOCK ALL TIME	08	62	20
ROSTER OF BC&G STEAM LOCOS 1961	02	61	57
ROSTER OF BCH&P LOCOMOTIVES 10-1965	02	66	54
ROSTER OF BCH&P LOCOMOTIVES 11-1970	06	75	54
ROSTER OF BCH&P LOCOMOTIVES 12-1970	05	71	57
ROSTER OF BCR LOCOMOTIVES 2-1969	06	75	55
ROSTER OF BCR LOCOMOTIVES 3-1969	08	69	50
ROSTER OF BCR LOCOMOTIVES 6-1974	12	75	53
ROSTER OF BCR LOCOMOTIVES 7-1963	02	64	52
ROSTER OF BCYR LOCOMOTIVES 11-1974	06	75	54
ROSTER OF BE&M LOCOMOTIVES 1-1964	08	64	36

Railroad/Railfan

RAILROAD HISTORIES & ROSTERS

ROSTERS BY RAILROAD	M	Y	P
ROSTER OF BE&M LOCOMOTIVES 10-1969	04	75	49
ROSTER OF BE&M LOCOMOTIVES 3-1969	10	69	50
ROSTER OF BEC LOCOMOTIVES 3-1966	05	66	48
ROSTER OF BEC LOCOMOTIVES 8-1974	04	75	50
ROSTER OF BEC LOCOMOTIVES 9-1969	03	70	62
ROSTER OF BEDT LOCOMOTIVES 3-1969	08	69	50
ROSTER OF BEDT LOCOMOTIVES 3-1969	06	75	54
ROSTER OF BEDT LOCOMOTIVES 6-1974	12	75	53
ROSTER OF BEDT LOCOMOTIVES 7-1963	02	64	52
ROSTER OF BEDT STEAM LOCOS 1961	02	61	57
ROSTER OF BEEC LOCOMOTIVES 6-1970	02	71	59
ROSTER OF BEEC LOCOMOTIVES 7-1966	12	66	54
ROSTER OF BEEC LOCOMOTIVES 7-1970	04	75	50
ROSTER OF BELT LOCOMOTIVE 7-1966	09	66	46
ROSTER OF BELT LOCOMOTIVES 3-1970	11	70	40
ROSTER OF BELT LOCOMOTIVES 8-1974	04	75	50
ROSTER OF BFR LOCOS	02	36	84
ROSTER OF BHC LOCOMOTIVES 3-1966	08	66	64
ROSTER OF BHC LOCOMOTIVES 11-1974	06	75	53
ROSTER OF BHC STEAM LOCOS 1961	02	61	56
ROSTER OF BI&S LOCOMOTIVES 1-1961	02	62	30
ROSTER OF BI&S LOCOMOTIVES 9-1966	04	75	51
ROSTER OF BI&S STEAM LOCOS 1961	02	61	56
ROSTER OF BIRM LOCOMOTIVES 10-1966	02	67	48
ROSTER OF BIRM LOCOMOTIVES 12-1970	07	71	53
ROSTER OF BIS LOCOMOTIVES 1-1961	02	62	30
ROSTER OF BIS LOCOMOTIVES 10-1966	02	67	48
ROSTER OF BIS LOCOMOTIVES 12-1970	07	71	52
ROSTER OF BIS LOCOMOTIVES 3-1975	06	75	52
ROSTER OF BL LOCOS	11	43	122
ROSTER OF BL2 LOCOMOTIVES BY ROAD	04	60	29
ROSTER OF BM&E LOCOMOTIVES 10-1965	03	66	59
ROSTER OF BM&E LOCOMOTIVES 3-1969	01	70	10
ROSTER OF BM&E LOCOMOTIVES 9-1965	04	75	49
ROSTER OF BMT LOCOMOTIVES 3-1975	06	75	53
ROSTER OF BN ALCO LOCOSMOTIVES VANCOUVER	03	79	24R
ROSTER OF BN LOCOMOTIVES 12-1970	09	71	54
ROSTER OF BN LOCOMOTIVES ADDITIONS	10	71	66
ROSTER OF BN(M) LOCOMOTIVES 1-1975	06	75	55
ROSTER OF BORC LOCOMOTIVES	11	78	49R
ROSTER OF BOW LOCOMOTIVES 3-1964	06	75	53
ROSTER OF BOW: COMPLETE	09	47	61
ROSTER OF BOYC STEAM LOCOS 1961	02	61	56
ROSTER OF BOYN LOCOMOTIVES 3-1965	06	65	55
ROSTER OF BOYN LOCOMOTIVES 6-1968	10	68	38
ROSTER OF BOYN LOCOMOTIVES 6-1973	03	74	46
ROSTER OF BOYNE LOCOMOTIVES 11-1974	06	75	53
ROSTER OF BR&P LOCOS (B&O)	06	34	90
ROSTER OF BR&P LOCOS: NOT CLASS A-E (B&O	07	34	83
ROSTER OF BR&W LOCOMOTIVES 3-1974	10	74	48
ROSTER OF BR&W LOCOMOTIVES 9-1974	06	75	53
ROSTER OF BRB&L LOCOMOTIVES (ALL-TIME)	01	75	19
ROSTER OF BRB&L LOCOS: ALL-TIME STEAM	05	55	31
ROSTER OF BRC LOCOMOTIVES 11-1974	04	75	50
ROSTER OF BRC LOCOMOTIVES 9-1967	03	68	52

ROSTERS BY RAILROAD	M	Y	P
ROSTER OF BRC LOCOMOTIVES 9-1972	01	73	53
ROSTER OF BRC LOCOS: ALL-TIME	06	58	69
ROSTER OF BRC LOCOS: SEE JUNE 1958 1959	10	59	71
ROSTER OF BRI STEAM LOCOS 1961	02	61	57
ROSTER OF BUSH DIESEL-ELECTRIC SWITCHERS	10	41	72
ROSTER OF BUSH LOCOMOTIVES 3-1969	08	69	50
ROSTER OF BUSH LOCOMOTIVES 3-1969	06	75	55
ROSTER OF BUSH LOCOMOTIVES 6-1974	12	75	54
ROSTER OF BUSH LOCOMOTIVES 7-1963	02	64	52
ROSTER OF BW&PS LOCOS	04	42	68
ROSTER OF BYNC LOCOMOTIVES 11-1974	06	75	54
ROSTER OF BYRY LOCOMOTIVES 11-1974	06	75	54
ROSTER OF C ALL TIME	09	68	46
ROSTER OF C LOCOMOTIVES 12-1974	10	75	44
ROSTER OF C LOCOMOTIVES 3-1968	09	68	44
ROSTER OF C LOCOMOTIVES 3-1973	01	74	45
ROSTER OF C LOCOMOTIVES 6-1964	11	64	62
ROSTER OF C&A STEAM LOCOMOTIVES 1926	10	66	51
ROSTER OF C&BL 1977	04	77	56
ROSTER OF C&BL LOCOMOTIVES 3-1966	05	66	48
ROSTER OF C&BL LOCOMOTIVES 9-1969	03	70	63
ROSTER OF C&C LOCOMOTIVES 5-1975	10	75	44
ROSTER OF C&CV 1977	04	77	56
ROSTER OF C&CV LOCOMOTIVES 6-1974	12	75	54
ROSTER OF C&E EQUIPMENT: 1896 OPENING	09	48	138
ROSTER OF C&EI LOCOMOTIVES 12-1967	04	68	46
ROSTER OF C&EI LOCOMOTIVES 12-1971	05	72	63
ROSTER OF C&EI LOCOMOTIVES 4-1966	09	66	50
ROSTER OF C&EI LOCOMOTIVES 6-1962	12	62	48
ROSTER OF C&EI LOCOS	06	33	92
ROSTER OF C&EI LOCOS: DIESEL	09	50	81
ROSTER OF C&GR DIESEL LOCOMOTIVES	W	74	45R
ROSTER OF C&GR LOCOMOPTIVES 10-1973	05	74	59
ROSTER OF C&GR LOCOMOTIVES 11-1975	11	75	52
ROSTER OF C&GR LOCOMOTIVES 3-1965	08	65	65
ROSTER OF C&GR LOCOMOTIVES 6-1969	03	69	38
ROSTER OF C&GR LOCOS	12	40	69
ROSTER OF C&GR STEAM LOCOS 1961	02	61	58
ROSTER OF C&GT LOCOMOTIVES 10-1965	02	66	54
ROSTER OF C&GT LOCOMOTIVES 11-1974	06	74	56
ROSTER OF C&GT LOCOMOTIVES 12-1970	05	71	57
ROSTER OF C&H LOCOMOTIVES 3-1966	05	66	48
ROSTER OF C&H LOCOMOTIVES 7-1969	10	75	45
ROSTER OF C&H LOCOMOTIVES 9-1969	03	70	63
ROSTER OF C&I LOCOMOTIVES 3-1966	05	66	48
ROSTER OF C&I LOCOMOTIVES 3-1975	06	75	56
ROSTER OF C&I LOCOMOTIVES 9-1969	03	70	62
ROSTER OF C&IM LOCOMOTIVES 9-1967	03	68	52
ROSTER OF C&IM LOCOMOTIVES 9-1972	01	73	53
ROSTER OF C&IM LOCOMOTIVES1-1975	11	75	49
ROSTER OF C&IM LOCOS: DIESELS 1959	10	59	71
ROSTER OF C&IM LOCOS: STEAM	07	54	82
ROSTER OF C&IW LOCOMOTIVES 6-1972	11	75	51
ROSTER OF C&IW LOCOMOTIVES 9-1967	03	68	52
ROSTER OF C&IW LOCOMOTIVES 9-1972	01	73	53

Railroad/Railfan

RAILROAD HISTORIES & ROSTERS

ROSTERS BY RAILROAD	M	Y	P
ROSTER OF C&IW LOCOS: DIESEL/ELECTRIC	02	58	77
ROSTER OF C&IW LOCOS: DIESELS 1959	10	59	71
ROSTER OF C&LC LOCOMOTIVES	10	65	54
ROSTER OF C&LC LOCOMOTIVES 4-1973	06	75	55
ROSTER OF C&LC LOCOMOTIVES 6-1968	10	68	38
ROSTER OF C&LC LOCOMOTIVES 6-1973	03	74	46
ROSTER OF C&LE ALL CAR TYPES	05	68	36
ROSTER OF C&M LOCOS	01	36	89
ROSTER OF C&MI LOCOMOTIVES 7-1975	11	75	51
ROSTER OF C&MI LOCOS: 1 DIESEL 1959	10	59	72
ROSTER OF C&N LOCOMOTIVES 1-1960	10	62	53
ROSTER OF C&N LOCOMOTIVES 1-1964	08	64	36
ROSTER OF C&N LOCOMOTIVES 12-1969	05	70	50
ROSTER OF C&N LOCOMOTIVES 12-1974	10	75	43
ROSTER OF C&N LOCOMOTIVES 3-1966	06	66	48
ROSTER OF C&N LOCOMOTIVES 3-1969	10	69	50
ROSTER OF C&N LOCOMOTIVES 6-1970	04	71	51
ROSTER OF C&N LOCOMOTIVES 7-1966	10	66	52
ROSTER OF C&NW LOCOMOTIVES	12	34	87
ROSTER OF C&NW LOCOMOTIVES 3-1972	09	72	56
ROSTER OF C&NW LOCOMOTIVES 4-1966	11	66	58
ROSTER OF C&NW LOCOMOTIVES MASSIVE CORRE	11	72	56
ROSTER OF C&NW LOCOS	05	33	74
ROSTER OF C&NW LOCOS CORRECTION (11-66)	03	67	62
ROSTER OF C&NW LOCOS: 4-4-2 TYPE D CLASS	01	42	64
ROSTER OF C&NW LOCOS: STEAM/DIESEL	08	48	108
ROSTER OF C&NW LOCOS: STEAM/DIESEL 1958	06	59	61
ROSTER OF C&NW ROAD SWITCHERS	08	77	45R
ROSTER OF C&NW STEAM LOCOS 1961	02	61	57
ROSTER OF C&O LOCOMOTIVES	10	44	60
ROSTER OF C&O LOCOMOTIVES 6-1926	12	66	58
ROSTER OF C&O LOCOS	08	34	91
ROSTER OF C&O LOCOS: STEAM	05	48	120
ROSTER OF C&O LOCOS: STEAM CORRECTIONS	09	48	132
ROSTER OF C&O LOCOS: STEAM/DIESELS	02	59	64
ROSTER OF C&O STEAM LOCOS 1961	02	61	57
ROSTER OF C&PA ABANDONED 1970	04	77	57
ROSTER OF C&PA LOCOMOTIVES 3-1966	05	66	50
ROSTER OF C&PA LOCOMOTIVES 9-1969	03	70	63
ROSTER OF C&PI LOCOMOTIVES	SU	75	23R
ROSTER OF C&PI LOCOMOTIVES 11-1963	08	63	60
ROSTER OF C&PI LOCOMOTIVES 6-1970	12	70	56
ROSTER OF C&PI LOCOMOTIVES 7-1975	11	75	51
ROSTER OF C&S LOCOMOTIVES 10-1970	06	71	37
ROSTER OF C&S LOCOMOTIVES 7-1972	02	73	46
ROSTER OF C&S LOCOMOTIVES 9-1966	03	67	64
ROSTER OF C&S LOCOS: STEAM/DIESEL	06	58	46
ROSTER OF C&S LOCOS: STEAM/WITH OTHER #S	09	54	40
ROSTER OF C&S LOCOS:4-6-0/2-8-0 LOCOS	01	33	101
ROSTER OF C&S STEAM LOCOMOTIVES ALL TIME	03	76	45
ROSTER OF C&S STEAM LOCOS 1961	02	61	58
ROSTER OF C&TS LOCOMOTIVES	11	78	31R
ROSTER OF C&WC LOCOMOTIVES 12-1974	10	75	45
ROSTER OF C&WC LOCOMOTIVES 3-1972	10	72	44
ROSTER OF C&WC LOCOMOTIVES 6-1967	11	67	46
ROSTER OF C&WC LOCOS	06	41	65
ROSTER OF C&WI LOCOMOTIVES 6-1975	11	75	50
ROSTER OF C&WI LOCOMOTIVES 9-1967	03	68	52
ROSTER OF C&WI LOCOMOTIVES 9-1972	01	73	54
ROSTER OF C&WI LOCOS: DIESELS 1959	10	59	71
ROSTER OF C&WY LOCOMOTIVES 10-1970	06	71	37
ROSTER OF C&WY LOCOMOTIVES 3-1967	07	67	64
ROSTER OF C&WY LOCOMOTIVES 5-1966	11	66	62
ROSTER OF C&WY LOCOMOTIVES 6-1975	11	75	52
ROSTER OF C&WY LOCOMOTIVES 7-1964	10	64	62
ROSTER OF C&WY LOCOMOTIVES 9-1971	07	72	59
ROSTER OF C&Y DIESEL LOCOMOTIVES	SU	76	32R
ROSTER OF C&Z STEAM LOCOMOTIVES	10	73	35
ROSTER OF C&Z STEAM LOCOMOTIVES 1961	06	61	26
ROSTER OF C415 ALCO LOCOMOTIVES	09	84	42
ROSTER OF C430 ALCO LOCOS 1986	05	86	40
ROSTER OF CA&E LOCOS: SEE AUG 1959 1959	10	59	71
ROSTER OF CA&E MU CARS/FRT/WORK EQUIPMEN	08	59	75
ROSTER OF CAD LOCOMOTIVES 10-1964	04	65	53
ROSTER OF CAD LOCOMOTIVES 11-1974	06	75	56
ROSTER OF CAD LOCOMOTIVES 12-1967	05	68	52
ROSTER OF CAD LOCOMOTIVES 3-1973	10	73	61
ROSTER OF CAN STEAM LOCOMOTIVES 1920	07	66	57
ROSTER OF CAPR (OWNS NO LOCOMOTIVES)1967	12	67	48
ROSTER OF CAPR LOCOMOTIVES 10-1964	01	65	63
ROSTER OF CAPR LOCOMOTIVES 6-1970	06	71	37
ROSTER OF CAPR LOCOMOTIVES 6-1972	11	72	56
ROSTER OF CAPR LOCOMOTIVES 8-1964	06	75	56
ROSTER OF CARB LOCOMOTIVES 10-1963	04	64	35
ROSTER OF CARB LOCOMOTIVES 12-1974	10	75	43
ROSTER OF CARB LOCOMOTIVES 3-1970	12	70	60
ROSTER OF CARR LOCOMOTIVES 10-1964	04	65	53
ROSTER OF CARR LOCOMOTIVES 12-1967	05	68	52
ROSTER OF CARR LOCOMOTIVES 3-1973	10	73	61
ROSTER OF CARS LOCOMOTIVES 1-1964	08	64	36
ROSTER OF CARS LOCOMOTIVES 5-1975	10	75	43
ROSTER OF CART LOCOMOTIVES 12-1970	05	71	57
ROSTER OF CART LOCOMOTIVES 12-1974	10	75	43
ROSTER OF CASS LOCOS & ITS PREDECESSORS	05	65	21
ROSTER OF CAW LOCOMOTIVES 12-1969	05	70	50
ROSTER OF CAW LOCOMOTIVES 3-1966	06	66	48
ROSTER OF CAW LOCOMOTIVES 5-1975	10	75	43
ROSTER OF CB DIESEL LOCOMOTIVES	01	85	45
ROSTER OF CB&Q LOCOMOTIVES 6-1966	01	67	37
ROSTER OF CB&Q LOCOMOTIVES AS OF BN MERG	12	72	52
ROSTER OF CB&Q LOCOS	09	36	87
ROSTER OF CB&Q LOCOS W/DRIVERS/TF/DATA	06	34	88
ROSTER OF CB&Q LOCOS: DIESEL-ELECT PASS	11	41	49
ROSTER OF CB&Q LOCOS: STEAM/DIESEL	06	58	44
ROSTER OF CB&Q LOCOS: STEAM/DIESEL/GAS-E	10	49	109
ROSTER OF CB&Q STEAM LOCOS 1961	02	61	57
ROSTER OF CBE LOCOS	11	36	54
ROSTER OF CBE LOCOS: 7	07	34	92
ROSTER OF CBELT LOCOMOTIVES 1-1957	08	60	61
ROSTER OF CBELT LOCOMOTIVES 10-1969	04	70	54

Railroad/ Railfan

RAILROAD HISTORIES & ROSTERS

ROSTERS BY RAILROAD	M	Y	P
ROSTER OF CBELT LOCOS	02	47	111
ROSTER OF CBELT LOCOS: CORRECTIONS	06	47	135
ROSTER OF CBELT LOCOS: STEAM/DIESEL	07	53	96
ROSTER OF CBELT LOCOS: STEAM/DIESEL CORR	01	54	113
ROSTER OF CBELT ST LOUIS SO.WESTERN LOCO	09	32	197
ROSTER OF CBT EQUIPMENT: ALL-TIME	07	44	128
ROSTER OF CC&O LOCOS: STEAM/DIESEL	01	51	111
ROSTER OF CCC&SL LOCOS: PART 1 NYC	05	40	81
ROSTER OF CCC&SL LOCOS: PART 2 NYC	06	40	113
ROSTER OF CCR LOCOMOTIVES 3-1975	06	75	56
ROSTER OF CCT DIESEL LOCOMOTIVE ALL-TIME	11	79	26
ROSTER OF CCT LOCOMOTIVES 1-1975	10	75	44
ROSTER OF CCT LOCOMOTIVES 3-1964	08	64	60
ROSTER OF CCT LOCOMOTIVES 3-1967	06	67	50
ROSTER OF CCT LOCOMOTIVES 6-1971	03	72	59
ROSTER OF CCW LOCOMOTIVES 10-1964	02	65	58
ROSTER OF CCW LOCOMOTIVES 5-1975	10	75	44
ROSTER OF CF LOCOMOTIVES 1-1964	08	64	36
ROSTER OF CF LOCOMOTIVES 3-1969	10	69	50
ROSTER OF CGA LOCOMOTIVES	12	32	42
ROSTER OF CGA LOCOMOTIVES 6-1971	01	72	11
ROSTER OF CGA LOCOMOTIVES 7-1966	12	66	30
ROSTER OF CGA LOCOS	12	30	66
ROSTER OF CGA LOCOS: DIESELS	12	58	73
ROSTER OF CGA LOCOS: STEAM/DIESEL	06	48	117
ROSTER OF CGR LOCOS: NOW OWNED BY CN	05	35	87
ROSTER OF CGW LOCO RENUMBER CORRECTIONS	02	74	60
ROSTER OF CGW LOCOMOTIVES 1-1972	12	73	60
ROSTER OF CGW LOCOMOTIVES 8-1962	02	63	53
ROSTER OF CGW LOCOS	07	39	121
ROSTER OF CH-P LOCOMOTIVES 4-1964	10	64	30
ROSTER OF CHSC (OWNS NO LOCOMOTIVES)1966	08	66	64
ROSTER OF CHTR LOCOMOTIVES 1-1960	10	62	53
ROSTER OF CHTR LOCOMOTIVES 5-1975	10	75	45
ROSTER OF CHTT LOCOMOTIVES 5-1975	11	75	50
ROSTER OF CHTT LOCOMOTIVES 9-1967	03	68	52
ROSTER OF CHTT LOCOMOTIVES 9-1972	01	73	53
ROSTER OF CHTT LOCOS: DIESELS 1959	10	59	71
ROSTER OF CHUT LOCOS: STEAM	06	58	69
ROSTER OF CHV LOCOMOTIVES 1-1961	02	62	30
ROSTER OF CHV LOCOMOTIVES 10-1964	02	65	54
ROSTER OF CHV LOCOMOTIVES 10-1966	02	67	48
ROSTER OF CHV LOCOMOTIVES 12-1970	07	71	53
ROSTER OF CHV LOCOMOTIVES 12-1974	10	75	45
ROSTER OF CHV LOCOMOTIVES 3-1972	10	72	44
ROSTER OF CHV LOCOMOTIVES 6-1967	11	67	46
ROSTER OF CHV STEAM LOCOS 1961	02	61	57
ROSTER OF CHW LOCOMOTIVES 10-1975	10	75	45
ROSTER OF CHW LOCOMOTIVES 6-1970	04	71	51
ROSTER OF CHW LOCOMOTIVES 7-1966	10	66	52
ROSTER OF CI LOCOMOTIVES 12-1974	10	75	45
ROSTER OF CI LOCOMOTIVES 3-1972	10	72	44
ROSTER OF CI LOCOMOTIVES 6-1967	11	67	46
ROSTER OF CIN LOCOMOTIVES 5-1975	10	75	44
ROSTER OF CIN LOCOMOTIVES 6-1962	12	62	60
ROSTER OF CIN LOCOMOTIVES 9-1967	02	68	62
ROSTER OF CINCINNATI CAR CURVED LTWT CAR	06	46	128
ROSTER OF CITC LOCOMOTIVES 5-1975	10	75	44
ROSTER OF CIUT LOCOMOTIVES 1960	06	60	56
ROSTER OF CIUT LOCOMOTIVES 6-1969	12	69	46
ROSTER OF CK&S (OWNS NO LOCOMOTIVES)1968	10	68	39
ROSTER OF CK&S 1977	04	77	56
ROSTER OF CK&S LOCOMOTIVES 12-1965	04	66	58
ROSTER OF CK&S LOCOMOTIVES 9-1969	02	70	50
ROSTER OF CK&S STEAM LOCOS 1961	02	61	58
ROSTER OF CK&SA LOCOMOTIVES 3-1965	06	65	55
ROSTER OF CK&SA LOCOS: PART 1 NYC	05	40	81
ROSTER OF CK&SA LOCOS: PART 2 NYC	06	40	113
ROSTER OF CL LOCOMOTIVES 1-1964	08	64	36
ROSTER OF CL LOCOMOTIVES 10-1964	04	65	52
ROSTER OF CL LOCOMOTIVES 12-1967.	05	68	52
ROSTER OF CL LOCOMOTIVES 12-1969	05	70	50
ROSTER OF CL LOCOMOTIVES 12-1969	07	70	41
ROSTER OF CL LOCOMOTIVES 3-1966	06	66	48
ROSTER OF CL LOCOMOTIVES 3-1966	08	66	64
ROSTER OF CL LOCOMOTIVES 3-1969	10	69	50
ROSTER OF CL LOCOMOTIVES 3-1975	11	75	52
ROSTER OF CL LOCOMOTIVES 6-1970	04	71	51
ROSTER OF CL LOCOMOTIVES 7-1966	10	66	52
ROSTER OF CL LOCOS	01	34	130
ROSTER OF CL&C LOCOMOTIVES 11-1962	08	63	60
ROSTER OF CL&C LOCOMOTIVES 12-1968	05	69	50
ROSTER OF CL&C LOCOMOTIVES 12-1973	08	74	55
ROSTER OF CL&C LOCOMOTIVES 1963 REVISION	12	63	61
ROSTER OF CL&C LOCOMOTIVES 7-1975	11	75	51
ROSTER OF CLI LOCOMOTIVES 1-1964	08	64	36
ROSTER OF CLIF LOCOMOTIVES 2-1975	11	75	51
ROSTER OF CLIF LOCOMOTIVES 3-1969	10	69	50
ROSTER OF CLIF STEAM LOCOS 1961	02	61	58
ROSTER OF CLRR LOCOMOTIVES 3-1969	10	69	50
ROSTER OF CLRR LOCOMOTIVES 4-1969	06	75	56
ROSTER OF CLRT EQUIPMENT	02	58	72
ROSTER OF CM ABANDONED 1965	04	77	57
ROSTER OF CM LOCOMOTIVES 10-1964	01	65	63
ROSTER OF CM STEAM LOCOS 1961	02	61	58
ROSTER OF CM&L LOCOMOTIVES 3-1966	06	66	48
ROSTER OF CMI LOCOMOTIVES (ALL TIME)	07	76	59
ROSTER OF CMI LOCOS	08	42	42
ROSTER OF CMI LOCOS: ALL-TIME	08	36	88
ROSTER OF CN 4-8-2 CLASS U 6000 SERIES	06	65	61
ROSTER OF CN CENTURY LOCOMOTIVES	09	82	54
ROSTER OF CN ELECTRIC LOCOMOTIVES 7-1966	07	67	64
ROSTER OF CN ELECTRIC LOCOS CORRECTIONS	09	67	46
ROSTER OF CN ELECTRIC MOTIVE POWER & CAR	04	58	37
ROSTER OF CN LOCOMOTIVES	01	33	102
ROSTER OF CN LOCOMOTIVES 1 1-1971	11	71	54
ROSTER OF CN LOCOMOTIVES 11-1965	04	66	62
ROSTER OF CN LOCOMOTIVES 1963 REVISIONS	12	63	61
ROSTER OF CN LOCOMOTIVES 2 1-1971	12	71	40
ROSTER OF CN LOCOMOTIVES 2-1963	12	63	34

STEPHANS' RAILROAD DIRECTORY

Railroad/Railfan

RAILROAD HISTORIES & ROSTERS

ROSTERS BY RAILROAD	M	Y	P
ROSTER OF CN LOCOMOTIVES UPDATE	05	72	63
ROSTER OF CN LOCOS	10	32	352
ROSTER OF CN LOCOS PART 1 STEAM	11	47	124
ROSTER OF CN LOCOS PART 2: STM/DIESEL/EL	12	47	115
ROSTER OF CN LOCOS W/PREV OWNERS/DATA	06	34	89
ROSTER OF CN LOCOS: CORRECT 12/35 PG 86	03	36	87
ROSTER OF CN LOCOS: FROM CV & GTW	03	43	105
ROSTER OF CN LOCOS: PART 1 (2601 LOCOS)	09	37	83
ROSTER OF CN LOCOS: PART 2	10	37	124
ROSTER OF CN LOCOS: PART 3	11	37	77
ROSTER OF CN LOCOS: PART 4 CONCLUSIONS	12	37	77
ROSTER OF CN LOCOS: RENUMBERING	06	57	68
ROSTER OF CN LOCOS: STEAM/ELECTRIC/DIESE	10	53	38
ROSTER OF CN LOCOS:4-6-4T/4-6-0/2-8-0	11	32	475
ROSTER OF CN MONTREAL ELECTRICS	11	80	48
ROSTER OF CN MU CARS 7-1966	07	67	64
ROSTER OF CN&L LOCOMOTIVES 12-1969	05	70	50
ROSTER OF CN&L LOCOMOTIVES 2-1975	11	75	52
ROSTER OF CN&L LOCOS	06	33	88
ROSTER OF CN: LOCOS OWNED BY C&R PREVIOU	05	35	87
ROSTER OF CNJ LOCOMOTIVES	06	35	135
ROSTER OF CNJ LOCOMOTIVES 1930	01	68	52
ROSTER OF CNJ LOCOMOTIVES 2-1961	08	61	52
ROSTER OF CNJ LOCOMOTIVES 2-1966	08	66	34
ROSTER OF CNJ LOCOMOTIVES 7-1971	04	72	62
ROSTER OF CNJ LOCOS	12	32	106
ROSTER OF CNJ LOCOS: DIESELS (8) EMPLOYE	03	48	64
ROSTER OF CNJ LOCOS: STEAM/DIESEL	08	51	109
ROSTER OF CNO&TP LOCOMOTIVES 1-1960	10	62	53
ROSTER OF CNO&TP LOCOS: PART 1 (5)	06	38	80
ROSTER OF CNO&TP LOCOS: PART 2	07	38	134
ROSTER OF CNS&M LOCOS: SEE AUG 1959 1959	10	59	71
ROSTER OF CNS&M MU CARS/FRT LOCOS 1959	08	59	75
ROSTER OF CNY LOCOMOTIVES 4-1974	10	75	44
ROSTER OF CNY LOCOMOTIVES 6-1974	12	75	54
ROSTER OF CO&C LOCOMOTIVES 1-1975	11	75	52
ROSTER OF CO&C LOCOMOTIVES 3-1962	08	62	29
ROSTER OF CO&C LOCOMOTIVES 6-1970	06	71	37
ROSTER OF CO&CO 1977	04	77	57
ROSTER OF CO&CO DIESEL LOCOMOTIVES	05	83	36
ROSTER OF CO&CO LOCOMOTIVES 10-1973	05	74	59
ROSTER OF CO&CO LOCOMOTIVES 12-1969	07	70	41
ROSTER OF CO&CO LOCOMOTIVES 3-1966	08	66	64
ROSTER OF CO&CO LOCOMOTIVES 6-1968	03	69	38
ROSTER OF COMMON CARRIER STEAM POWER '61	02	61	56
ROSTER OF CONW 1977	04	77	56
ROSTER OF CORN ABANDONED 1965	04	77	57
ROSTER OF CORN LOCOMOTIVES 3-1966	05	66	48
ROSTER OF COUS LOCOMOTIVES 12-1969	05	70	50
ROSTER OF COUS LOCOMOTIVES 3-1966	06	66	48
ROSTER OF COUS LOCOMOTIVES 9-1969	11	75	52
ROSTER OF CP 3-1963	02	64	60
ROSTER OF CP CENTURY LOCOMOTIVES	09	82	54
ROSTER OF CP CLASS G5 PACIFICS	03	79	32R
ROSTER OF CP LOCOMOTIVES	09	47	123
ROSTER OF CP LOCOMOTIVES 12-1965	06	66	50
ROSTER OF CP LOCOMOTIVES 4-1971	02	72	27
ROSTER OF CP LOCOMOTIVES UPDATE	05	72	63
ROSTER OF CP LOCOS	02	33	129
ROSTER OF CP LOCOS--LIGHT OF LANTERN	07	32	511
ROSTER OF CP LOCOS-ESQUIMALT & NANAIMO	02	33	129
ROSTER OF CP LOCOS-MONTREAL & ATLANTIC	02	33	129
ROSTER OF CP LOCOS: (QUEBEC CENTRAL)	01	40	115
ROSTER OF CP LOCOS: ADDITIONS	03	54	18
ROSTER OF CP LOCOS: ADDS/CORRECTIONS	03	54	16
ROSTER OF CP LOCOS: STEAM/DIESEL	09	53	33
ROSTER OF CP LOCOS:4-6-0/4-6-4	11	32	475
ROSTER OF CP PACIFIC LOCOMOTIVES	03	79	62R
ROSTER OF CP STEAM LOCOMOTIVES 7-1929	05	66	40
ROSTER OF CP VERMONT LOCOMOTIVES	09	80	52
ROSTER OF CP&LT LOCOMOTIVES 3-1964	08	64	60
ROSTER OF CP&LT LOCOMOTIVES 3-1967	06	67	50
ROSTER OF CP&LT LOCOMOTIVES 3-1975	06	75	56
ROSTER OF CP&LT LOCOMOTIVES 6-1971	03	72	59
ROSTER OF CP-F 1977	04	77	57
ROSTER OF CP-F LOCOMOTIVES 12-1963	06	64	48
ROSTER OF CP-F LOCOMOTIVES 12-1966	05	67	54
ROSTER OF CP-F LOCOMOTIVES 6-1971	03	72	58
ROSTER OF CPM&O LOCOS	03	37	73
ROSTER OF CPM&O LOCOS: STEAM/DIESEL-ELEC	04	55	41
ROSTER OF CPR LOCOMOTIVES 12-1965	04	66	58
ROSTER OF CPR LOCOMOTIVES 9-1969	02	70	50
ROSTER OF CPTE (OWNS NO LOCOMOTIVES)1968	03	68	52
ROSTER OF CPTE LOCOMOTIVES 9-1967	11	75	50
ROSTER OF CPTE LOCOMOTIVES 9-1972	01	73	54
ROSTER OF CPTE LOCOS: OWNS NO EQUIPMENT	10	59	71
ROSTER OF CR&I LOCOMOTIVES 1-1975	11	75	50
ROSTER OF CR&I LOCOMOTIVES 9-1967	03	68	52
ROSTER OF CR&I LOCOMOTIVES 9-1972	01	73	54
ROSTER OF CR&I LOCOS: DIESELS 1959	10	59	71
ROSTER OF CR&I LOCOS: PART 1 NYC	05	40	81
ROSTER OF CR&I LOCOS: PART 2 NYC	06	40	113
ROSTER OF CR&IC LOCOMOTIVES 10-1964	02	65	58
ROSTER OF CR&IC LOCOMOTIVES 1972	05	73	56
ROSTER OF CR&IC LOCOMOTIVES 5-1975	10	75	44
ROSTER OF CR&IC LOCOMOTIVES 6-1967	01	68	56
ROSTER OF CRA ABANDONED 1973	04	77	57
ROSTER OF CRA LOCOMOTIVES 3-1965	06	65	55
ROSTER OF CRA LOCOMOTIVES 6-1968	10	68	39
ROSTER OF CRA LOCOMOTIVES 6-1973	03	74	46
ROSTER OF CRA STEAM LOCOS 1961	02	61	58
ROSTER OF CRI LOCOMOTIVES 3-1966	05	66	48
ROSTER OF CRI LOCOMOTIVES 7-1969	10	75	45
ROSTER OF CRI LOCOMOTIVES 9-1969	03	70	63
ROSTER OF CS&CC LOCOS	08	35	87
ROSTER OF CSF&E LOCOS: STEAM	08	56	43
ROSTER OF CSL LOCOMOTIVES 2-1975	11	75	50
ROSTER OF CSL LOCOMOTIVES 9-1967	03	68	54
ROSTER OF CSL LOCOMOTIVES 9-1972	01	73	54
ROSTER OF CSL LOCOS: DIESELS 1959	10	59	71

RAILROAD HISTORIES & ROSTERS

ROSTERS BY RAILROAD	M	Y	P
ROSTER OF CSS&SB FREIGHT MOTORS	01	79	53R
ROSTER OF CSS&SB LOCOMOTIVES 6-1962	12	62	60
ROSTER OF CSS&SB LOCOMOTIVES 9-1967	02	68	62
ROSTER OF CSS&SB LOCOMOTIVES 9-1967.	03	68	54
ROSTER OF CSS&SB LOCOMOTIVES 9-1972	01	73	54
ROSTER OF CSS&SB LOCOS: SEE AUG 1959	10	59	71
ROSTER OF CSS&SB MU CARS	01	79	53R
ROSTER OF CSS&SB MU CARS 6-1962	12	62	60
ROSTER OF CSS&SB MU CARS/FRT LOCOS 1959	08	59	75
ROSTER OF CUST (OWNS NO LOCOMOTIVES)1966	06	66	48
ROSTER OF CUST (OWNS NO LOCOMOTIVES)1968	03	68	54
ROSTER OF CUST LOCOMOTIVES 12-1969	05	70	50
ROSTER OF CUST LOCOMOTIVES 9-1972	01	73	54
ROSTER OF CUST LOCOS: OWNS NO EQUIP 1959	10	59	71
ROSTER OF CUT LOCOMOTIVES 1-1975	11	75	51
ROSTER OF CUT LOCOMOTIVES 1960	06	60	56
ROSTER OF CUT LOCOMOTIVES 6-1969	12	69	46
ROSTER OF CUT LOCOS: PART 1 NYC	05	40	81
ROSTER OF CUT LOCOS: PART 2 NYC	06	40	113
ROSTER OF CUY LOCOMOTIVES 1960	06	60	56
ROSTER OF CUY LOCOMOTIVES 6-1969	12	69	46
ROSTER OF CV (O&LC DIV) ALL TIME	04	63	58
ROSTER OF CV DIESEL LOCOMOTIVES	03	79	50R
ROSTER OF CV LOCOMOTIVES	08	47	117
ROSTER OF CV LOCOMOTIVES 11-1962	08	63	60
ROSTER OF CV LOCOMOTIVES 12-1968	05	69	50
ROSTER OF CV LOCOMOTIVES 12-1971	06	72	50
ROSTER OF CV LOCOMOTIVES 12-1973	08	74	55
ROSTER OF CV LOCOMOTIVES 12-1974	10	75	45
ROSTER OF CV LOCOMOTIVES 2-1967	08	67	64
ROSTER OF CV LOCOMOTIVES 3-1969	08	69	50
ROSTER OF CV LOCOMOTIVES 6-1968	09	68	50
ROSTER OF CV LOCOMOTIVES 6-1970	12	70	56
ROSTER OF CV LOCOMOTIVES 6-1973	10	73	13
ROSTER OF CV LOCOMOTIVES 7-1963	02	64	52
ROSTER OF CV LOCOS	12	35	88
ROSTER OF CV LOCOS BUILT BY CV SHOPS	10	62	06
ROSTER OF CV LOCOS OWNED BY CN	02	38	60
ROSTER OF CV LOCOS: TRANSFERRED TO CN	03	43	105
ROSTER OF CV RAILCARS	05	79	37
ROSTER OF CV STEAM LOCOMOTIVES 1945-60	05	79	35
ROSTER OF CVL 1977	04	77	57
ROSTER OF CW LOCOMOTIVES 11-1974	06	75	56
ROSTER OF CW LOCOMOTIVES 3-1964	08	64	60
ROSTER OF CW LOCOMOTIVES 3-1967	06	67	50
ROSTER OF CW LOCOMOTIVES 6-1971	03	72	59
ROSTER OF CW LOCOS	03	40	131
ROSTER OF CW LOCOS: CORRECTION 02-36	04	36	94
ROSTER OF CWP&S LOCOMOTIVES 9-1967	03	68	54
ROSTER OF CWP&S LOCOMOTIVES 9-1972	01	73	54
ROSTER OF CWP&S LOCOS: DIESELS 1959	10	59	71
FR ROSTER OF ANDORRA-ESCATRON (SPAIN)	03	85	57
FR ROSTER OF BALDWIN LOCOS IN BRAZIL	08	76	37
FR ROSTER OF EFDTC (BRAZILIAN RAILROAD)	09	79	47
FR ROSTER OF GRAND CAVALCADE (ENGLAND)	01	81	25
FR ROSTER OF LOCOMOTIVES IN BRAZIL	08	63	18
FR ROSTER OF LOCOMOTIVES IN BRAZIL 1972	08	72	25
FR ROSTER OF LONDON TRANSPORT (STEAM)	07	71	42
FR ROSTER OF SPAIN-PONFERRADA-VILLABLINO	01	85	29
FR ROSTER OF STEAM IN COSTA RICA 1973	10	73	37
FR ROSTER OF STEAM IN EL SALVADOR 1973	10	73	36
FR ROSTER OF STEAM IN GUATEMALA 1973	10	73	36
FR ROSTER OF STEAM IN HONDURAS 1973	10	73	37
FR ROSTER OF STEAM IN NICARAGUA 1973	10	73	37
FR ROSTER OF STEAM LOCOMOTIVES IN INDIA	07	72	27
FR ROSTER OF TURKISH RAILROAD STEAM LOCO	06	77	31
FR ROSTER S AFRICA'S 4-8-2 CLASS 19D	SU	75	30R
ROSTER OF D LOCOMOTIVES 12-1970	05	71	57
ROSTER OF D LOCOMOTIVES 8-1975	10	77	34
ROSTER OF D&GRW STEAM LOCOS 1961	02	61	58
ROSTER OF D&H LOCOMOTIVES	04	47	117
ROSTER OF D&H LOCOMOTIVES 7-1966	02	67	49
ROSTER OF D&H LOCOMOTIVES 8-1972	04	73	61
ROSTER OF D&H LOCOMOTIVES CORRECTION	06	73	64
ROSTER OF D&H LOCOS	11	36	125
ROSTER OF D&H LOCOS BUILT D&H SHOPS	06	63	17
ROSTER OF D&H LOCOS: #1400/#1401/#1402	06	36	85
ROSTER OF D&H LOCOS: DIESELS	04	59	58
ROSTER OF D&IR ALL TIME STEAM LOCOMOTIVE	10	61	26
ROSTER OF D&M 1977	04	77	59
ROSTER OF D&M LOCOMOTIVES 3-1965	06	65	55
ROSTER OF D&M LOCOMOTIVES 6-1968	10	68	39
ROSTER OF D&M LOCOMOTIVES 6-1973	03	74	46
ROSTER OF D&M LOCOS	06	42	79
ROSTER OF D&MM 1977	04	77	57
ROSTER OF D&MM LOCOMOTIVES 3-1969	08	69	50
ROSTER OF D&MM LOCOMOTIVES 6-1974	12	75	54
ROSTER OF D&MM LOCOMOTIVES 7-1963	02	64	52
ROSTER OF D&MM LOCOS	01	41	136
ROSTER OF D&MM STEAM LOCOS 1961	02	61	58
ROSTER OF D&NE LOCOMOTIVES 3-1965	07	65	53
ROSTER OF D&NE LOCOMOTIVES 5-1975	10	77	35
ROSTER OF D&NE LOCOMOTIVES 6-1968	12	68	48
ROSTER OF D&NE LOCOMOTIVES 6-1973	11	73	62
ROSTER OF D&NE STEAM LOCOS 1961	02	61	58
ROSTER OF D&R 1977	04	77	58
ROSTER OF D&R LOCOMOTIVES 12-1963	06	64	48
ROSTER OF D&R LOCOMOTIVES 12-1966	05	67	54
ROSTER OF D&R LOCOMOTIVES 6-1971	03	72	58
ROSTER OF D&R STEAM LOCOS 1961	02	61	58
ROSTER OF D&RGW DIESEL LOCOMOTIVES 8-63	07	76	43
ROSTER OF D&RGW DIESEL LOCOS 8-1963	04	64	34
ROSTER OF D&RGW LOCOMOTIVES 11-1966	04	67	40
ROSTER OF D&RGW LOCOS	02	37	89
ROSTER OF D&RGW LOCOS PURCHASED FROM N&W	10	45	49
ROSTER OF D&RGW LOCOS: STEAM/DIESEL	04	51	107

Stephans' Railroad Directory

384

Railroad/Railfan

RAILROAD HISTORIES & ROSTERS

ROSTERS BY RAILROAD	M	Y	P
ROSTER OF D&RGW STEAM LOCOMOTIVES	04	66	48
ROSTER OF D&RGW STEAM LOCOS 8-1963	04	64	34
ROSTER OF D&S LOCOMOTIVES 1-1964	08	64	37
ROSTER OF D&S LOCOMOTIVES 3-1969	10	69	50
ROSTER OF D&S LOCOMOTIVES 5-1975	10	77	35
ROSTER OF D&SL LOCOS	03	41	84
ROSTER OF D&TS LOCOMOTIVES 1960	06	60	56
ROSTER OF D&TSL	04	77	59
ROSTER OF D&TSL DIESEL LOCOMOTIVES	07	81	46
ROSTER OF D&TSL LOCOMOTIVES 3-1965	06	65	55
ROSTER OF D&TSL LOCOMOTIVES 6-1968	10	68	39
ROSTER OF D&TSL LOCOMOTIVES 6-1969	12	69	46
ROSTER OF D&TSL LOCOMOTIVES 6-1973	03	74	46
ROSTER OF D&TSL STEAM LOCOMOTIVES	07	81	55
ROSTER OF DA LOCOMOTIVES 10-1965	02	66	54
ROSTER OF DA LOCOMOTIVES 12-1970	05	71	57
ROSTER OF DA LOCOS	09	47	127
ROSTER OF DA LOCOS: ADDITIONS	03	54	18
ROSTER OF DA LOCOS: CORRECTIONS	09	53	119
ROSTER OF DA LOCOS: STEAM	09	53	39
ROSTER OF DA LOCOS: STEAM	05	53	68
ROSTER OF DA&W 1977	04	77	58
ROSTER OF DE 1977	04	77	58
ROSTER OF DE LOCOMOTIVES 3-1965	06	65	55
ROSTER OF DE LOCOMOTIVES 6-1968	10	68	39
ROSTER OF DE LOCOMOTIVES 6-1973	03	74	46
ROSTER OF DE&CI LOCOMOTIVES 1972	05	73	56
ROSTER OF DK&S (OWNS NO LOCOMOTIVES)1963	06	64	48
ROSTER OF DK&S LOCOMOTIVES 12-1966	05	67	54
ROSTER OF DK&S LOCOMOTIVES 6-1971	03	72	58
ROSTER OF DL&W EQUIPMENT	06	58	67
ROSTER OF DL&W LOCOS	08	33	47
ROSTER OF DL&W LOCOS: STEAM/DIESEL	04	48	122
ROSTER OF DL&W NAMED STEAM LOCOS BY DIV	10	61	44
ROSTER OF DL&W:ELECTRICS	07	81	51
ROSTER OF DM&CI 1977	04	77	59
ROSTER OF DM&CI LOCOMOTIVES 10-1964	02	65	58
ROSTER OF DM&CI LOCOMOTIVES 6-1967	01	68	56
ROSTER OF DM&IR ALL TIME STEAM LOCOMOTIV	10	61	33
ROSTER OF DM&IR LOCOMOTIVES 1-1973	07	73	59
ROSTER OF DM&IR LOCOMOTIVES 7-1962	02	63	35
ROSTER OF DM&IR LOCOS	08	38	85
ROSTER OF DM&IR LOCOS: STEAM	12	51	102
ROSTER OF DM&IR LOCOS: STEAM FROM EJ&E	04	49	64
ROSTER OF DM&IR LOCOS: STEAM/DIESEL	10	56	58
ROSTER OF DM&IR STEAM LOCOS 1961	02	61	59
ROSTER OF DM&N ALL TIME STEAM LOCOMOTIVE	10	61	29
ROSTER OF DMTC (OWNS NO LOCOMOTIVES)1964	02	65	58
ROSTER OF DMTC (OWNS NO LOCOMOTIVES)1967	01	68	56
ROSTER OF DMTC LOCOMOTIVES 1972	05	73	56
ROSTER OF DMU 1977	04	77	59
ROSTER OF DMU LOCOMOTIVES 6-1967	01	68	56
ROSTER OF DMV LOCOMOTIVES 10-1964	02	65	58
ROSTER OF DMV LOCOMOTIVES 1972	05	73	56
ROSTER OF DOS LOCOMOTIVES 9-1969	03	70	63
ROSTER OF DOS LOCOS (ABANDONED 1964)	10	77	35
ROSTER OF DPE LOCOS	08	43	88
ROSTER OF DPL MOTOR CARS, TRAILERS, LOCO	09	82	42
ROSTER OF DQ&E 1977	04	77	58
ROSTER OF DQ&E LOCOMOTIVES 12-1963	06	64	48
ROSTER OF DQ&E LOCOMOTIVES 12-1966	05	67	54
ROSTER OF DQ&E LOCOMOTIVES 6-1971	03	72	58
ROSTER OF DRI&N 1977	04	77	58
ROSTER OF DRI&N LOCOMOTIVES 10-1964	02	65	58
ROSTER OF DRI&N LOCOMOTIVES 1972	05	73	56
ROSTER OF DRI&N LOCOMOTIVES 9-1967	03	68	54
ROSTER OF DRI&N LOCOMOTIVES 9-1972	01	73	54
ROSTER OF DRI&N LOCOS: 7 DIESELS 1959	10	59	72
ROSTER OF DRI&NW LOCOMOTIVES 6-1967	01	68	56
ROSTER OF DSS&A LOCOS	08	32	130
ROSTER OF DSS&A LOCOS: STEAM/DIESEL	12	50	110
ROSTER OF DT 1977	04	77	59
ROSTER OF DT LOCOMOTIVES 3-1965	06	65	55
ROSTER OF DT LOCOMOTIVES 6-1968	10	68	39
ROSTER OF DT LOCOMOTIVES 6-1974	03	74	46
ROSTER OF DT&I LOCOMOTIVES 12-1966	05	67	55
ROSTER OF DT&I LOCOMOTIVES 12-1972	09	73	35
ROSTER OF DT&I LOCOMOTIVES 9-1961	02	62	10
ROSTER OF DT&I LOCOMOTIVES ADDS	12	73	61
ROSTER OF DT&I LOCOS	05	42	97
ROSTER OF DT&I LOCOS:STEAM/DIESEL-ELECTR	10	52	98
ROSTER OF DUD&T LOCOMOTIVE 7-1975	10	77	35
ROSTER OF DUD&T LOCOMOTIVES 3-1965	07	65	53
ROSTER OF DUD&T LOCOMOTIVES 6-1968	12	68	48
ROSTER OF DUD&T LOCOMOTIVES 6-1973	11	73	62
ROSTER OF DUSC (NO LOCOMOTIVES) 1964	08	64	37
ROSTER OF DUTR (OWNS NO LOCOMOTIVES)1964	10	64	62
ROSTER OF DUTR (OWNS NO LOCOMOTIVES)1967	07	67	64
ROSTER OF DUTR LOCOMOTIVES 9-1971	07	72	59
ROSTER OF DV&S 1977	04	77	58
ROSTER OF DV&S LOCOMOTIVES 12-1963	06	64	48
ROSTER OF DV&S LOCOMOTIVES 12-1966	05	67	54
ROSTER OF DV&S LOCOMOTIVES 6-1971	03	72	58
ROSTER OF DW&P LOCOMOTIVES 3-1965	07	65	53
ROSTER OF DW&P LOCOMOTIVES 5-1975	10	77	35
ROSTER OF DW&P LOCOMOTIVES 6-1968	12	68	48
ROSTER OF DW&P LOCOMOTIVES 6-1973	11	73	62
ROSTER OF DW&P LOCOS: PART 1	09	37	82
ROSTER OF DW&P LOCOS: PART 2	10	37	124
ROSTER OF DW&P LOCOS: PART 3	11	37	77
ROSTER OF DW&P LOCOS: PART 4	12	37	77
ROSTER OF E LOCOMOTIVES	10	32	350
ROSTER OF E LOCOS	10	35	88
ROSTER OF E LOCOS SOLD TO NYS&W	11	43	122
ROSTER OF E LOCOS: STEAM/DIESEL/GAS-ELEC	05	49	110
ROSTER OF E STEAM LOCOMOTIVES 1919	01	66	54
ROSTER OF E&LS LOCOMOTIVES 3-1965	06	65	55
ROSTER OF E&LS LOCOMOTIVES 6-1968	10	68	39
ROSTER OF E&LS LOCOMOTIVES 6-1973	03	74	47
ROSTER OF E&LS LOCOMOTIVES 7-1975	10	77	37

Railroad/ Railfan

RAILROAD HISTORIES & ROSTERS

ROSTERS BY RAILROAD	M	Y	P
ROSTER OF E&LS STEAM LOCOS 1961	02	61	59
ROSTER OF E&M LOCOMOTIVES 12-1969	05	70	50
ROSTER OF E&M LOCOMOTIVES 2-1977	10	77	36
ROSTER OF E&M LOCOMOTIVES 3-1966	06	66	48
ROSTER OF E&M STEAM LOCOS 1961	02	61	59
ROSTER OF E&MO LOCOMS (ABANDONDED 1961)	10	77	37
ROSTER OF E&N LOCOMOTIVES 10-1965	02	66	54
ROSTER OF E&N LOCOMOTIVES 12-1970	05	71	57
ROSTER OF EC&H LOCOMOTIVES 4-1976	10	77	35
ROSTER OF ECRY (OWNS NO LOCOMOTIVES)1964	08	64	37
ROSTER OF ED&W LOCOMOTIVES 12-1963	06	64	48
ROSTER OF ED&W LOCOMOTIVES 12-1966	05	67	54
ROSTER OF ED&W LOCOMOTIVES 2-1971	10	77	37
ROSTER OF ED&W LOCOMOTIVES 6-1971	03	72	58
ROSTER OF EEC LOCOMOTIVES 3-1966	05	66	50
ROSTER OF EEC LOCOMOTIVES 6-1975	10	77	36
ROSTER OF EEC LOCOMOTIVES 9-1969	03	70	63
ROSTER OF EJ&E LOCOMOTIVES 6-1962	12	62	60
ROSTER OF EJ&E LOCOMOTIVES 9-1967	02	68	62
ROSTER OF EJ&E LOCOMOTIVES 9-1967	03	68	54
ROSTER OF EJ&E LOCOMOTIVES 9-1972	01	73	55
ROSTER OF EJ&E LOCOS: DIESELS 1959	10	59	72
ROSTER OF EJ&E LOCOS: STEAM--TO DM&IR	04	49	64
ROSTER OF EJ&S LOCOS (ABANDONDED 1961)	10	77	36
ROSTER OF EJ&S STEAM LOCOS 1961	02	61	59
ROSTER OF EJR&T LOCOMOTIVES 10-1976	10	77	35
ROSTER OF EJR&T LOCOMOTIVES 3-1969	07	69	48
ROSTER OF EJR&T LOCOMOTIVES 3-1974	10	74	48
ROSTER OF EJR&T LOCOS: 2 DIESELS	02	59	44
ROSTER OF EL LOCOMOTIVES 12-1972	08	72	53
ROSTER OF EL LOCOMOTIVES 2-1961	10	61	18
ROSTER OF EL LOCOMOTIVES 8-73 CORRECTION	10	73	64
ROSTER OF EL LOCOMOTIVES ADDS	12	73	61
ROSTER OF ELECTRIC STREET CAR BUILDERS	01	78	44
ROSTER OF EMD DEMONSTRATORS	02	65	33
ROSTER OF EPUP (OWNS NO LOCOMOTIVES)1966	09	66	46
ROSTER OF EPUP LOCOMOTIVES 3-1970	11	70	40
ROSTER OF ERC&L LOGGING LOCOS ALL TIME	08	62	20
ROSTER OF ESL&C LOCOMOTIVES ALL TIME	08	62	51
ROSTER OF ESLJ LOCOMOTIVES 10-1976	10	77	37
ROSTER OF ESLJ LOCOMOTIVES 9-1967	03	68	54
ROSTER OF ESLJ LOCOMOTIVES 9-1972	01	73	54
ROSTER OF ESLJ LOCOS: DIESELS 1959	10	59	72
ROSTER OF ET&WNC LOCOMOTIVES 12-1969	07	70	41
ROSTER OF ET&WNC LOCOMOTIVES 3-1966	08	66	64
ROSTER OF ET&WNC LOCOMOTIVES 7-1975	10	77	36
ROSTER OF ET&WNC STEAM LOCOS 1961	02	61	59
ROSTER OF ETE LOCOMOTIVES 10-1965	02	66	54
ROSTER OF ETE LOCOMOTIVES 12-1970	05	71	57
ROSTER OF ETE LOCOMOTIVES 6-1975	10	77	37
ROSTER OF EV LOCOMOTIVES 3-1966	05	66	50
ROSTER OF EV LOCOMOTIVES 6-1975	10	77	37
ROSTER OF EV LOCOMOTIVES 9-1969	03	70	63
ROSTER OF EW LOCOMOTIVES 12-1971	06	72	50
ROSTER OF EW LOCOMOTIVES 3-1968	09	68	44
ROSTER OF EW LOCOMOTIVES 3-1973	01	74	45
ROSTER OF EW LOCOMOTIVES 3-1973	10	77	35
ROSTER OF EW LOCOMOTIVES 6-1964	11	64	62
ROSTER OF EW LOCOS: 2 DIESELS 1959	08	59	55
ROSTER OF F&C LOCOMOTIVES 10-1964	04	65	53
ROSTER OF F&C LOCOMOTIVES 12-1967	05	68	52
ROSTER OF F&C LOCOMOTIVES 3-1973	10	73	61
ROSTER OF F&C LOCOMOTIVES 4-1977	01	78	55
ROSTER OF F&CRR LOCOMOTIVES 8-1975	01	78	57
ROSTER OF F&PR LOCOMOTIVES 12-1963	06	64	48
ROSTER OF F&PR LOCOMOTIVES 12-1966	05	67	54
ROSTER OF F&PR LOCOMOTIVES 6-1971	03	72	58
ROSTER OF F&PR LOCOMOTIVES 8-1975	01	78	56
ROSTER OF F&PR STEAM LOCOS 1961	02	61	59
ROSTER OF FBL LOCOMOTIVES 10-1966	02	67	48
ROSTER OF FC DIESEL LOCOS 7-87	10	87	38
ROSTER OF FC&GO LOCOMOTIVES 7-1975	01	78	55
ROSTER OF FC&GU LOCOMOTIVES 10-1973	05	74	59
ROSTER OF FC&GU LOCOMOTIVES 3-1965	08	65	65
ROSTER OF FC&GU LOCOMOTIVES 6-1968	03	69	38
ROSTER OF FCAP LOCOMOTIVES 4-1973	02	74	11
ROSTER OF FCM STEAM LOCOS 1961	06	61	26
ROSTER OF FDC&P LOCOMOTIVES 4-1967	08	67	64
ROSTER OF FDES LOCOMOTIVES 10-1964	04	65	36
ROSTER OF FDES LOCOMOTIVES 7-1973	01	74	45
ROSTER OF FDES LOCOMOTIVES CORRECTION	05	74	59
ROSTER OF FDM&S LOCOMOTIVES 10-1964	02	65	58
ROSTER OF FDM&S LOCOMOTIVES 1972	05	73	56
ROSTER OF FDM&S LOCOMOTIVES 6-1967	01	68	56
ROSTER OF FDM&S LOCOMOTIVES 7-1975	01	78	56
ROSTER OF FDP LOCOMOTIVES 3-1967	09	67	65
ROSTER OF FDP LOCOMOTIVES 6-1964	11	64	57
ROSTER OF FDP STEAM LOCOMOTIVES	10	73	35
ROSTER OF FE LOCOMOTIVES 10-1976	01	78	55
ROSTER OF FE LOCOMOTIVES 12-1964	05	65	50
ROSTER OF FE LOCOMOTIVES 3-1968	06	68	50
ROSTER OF FE LOCOMOTIVES 3-1973	07	73	58
ROSTER OF FE STEAM LOCOS 1961	02	61	59
ROSTER OF FEC DINING CARS: STD/STAINLESS	02	49	60
ROSTER OF FEC LOCOMOTIVES 6-1973	11	73	60
ROSTER OF FEC LOCOMOTIVES CORRECTION	03	74	64
ROSTER OF FEC LOCOS	03	34	141
ROSTER OF FEC LOCOS: DIESELS 1959	12	59	44
ROSTER OF FEC LOCOS: STEAM AND DIESEL	01	48	90
ROSTER OF FERD LOCOMOTIVES 10-1976	01	78	55
ROSTER OF FERD LOCOMOTIVES 6-1962	12	62	60
ROSTER OF FERD LOCOMOTIVES 9-1967	02	68	63
ROSTER OF FJ&G LOCOMOTIVES 10-1976	01	78	56
ROSTER OF FJ&G LOCOMOTIVES 3-1969	08	69	50
ROSTER OF FJ&G LOCOMOTIVES 6-1974	12	75	54
ROSTER OF FJ&G LOCOMOTIVES 7-1963	02	64	54
ROSTER OF FJ&G LOCOS: 4 STEAM LOCOS	02	36	86
ROSTER OF FM DEMONSTRATORS	02	65	33
ROSTER OF FMSR (OWNS NO LOCOMOTIVES)1964	12	64	32
ROSTER OF FMSR LOCOMOTIVES 12-1971	08	72	57

Railroad/Railfan

RAILROAD HISTORIES & ROSTERS

ROSTERS BY RAILROAD	M	Y	P
ROSTER OF FMSR LOCOMOTIVES 6-1967	10	67	50
ROSTER OF FOR LOCOMOTIVES 10-1976	01	78	54
ROSTER OF FOR LOCOMOTIVES 11-1962	08	63	60
ROSTER OF FOR LOCOMOTIVES 6-1968	09	68	50
ROSTER OF FOR LOCOMOTIVES 6-1973	10	73	13
ROSTER OF FP&E LOCOMOTIVES 1960	06	60	56
ROSTER OF FP&E LOCOMOTIVES 3-1977	10	77	37
ROSTER OF FP&E LOCOMOTIVES 6-1969	12	69	47
ROSTER OF FR LOCOMOTIVES (FINAL)	06	67	50
ROSTER OF FR STEAM LOCOS 1961	02	61	59
ROSTER OF FRIS LOCOMOTIVES 10-1959	04	60	59
ROSTER OF FRIS LOCOS	11	34	41
ROSTER OF FRIS LOCOS: STEAM/DIESEL	07	48	98
ROSTER OF FRRY (ABANDONED 1966)	01	78	54
ROSTER OF FRRY LOCOMOTIVES 3-1964	08	64	60
ROSTER OF FS&VB LOCOMOTIVES 10-1965	03	66	59
ROSTER OF FS&VB LOCOMOTIVES 12-1966	05	67	54
ROSTER OF FS&VB LOCOMOTIVES 3-1969	01	70	10
ROSTER OF FSBC LOCOMOTIVES 7-1975	01	78	55
ROSTER OF FSS&RI STEAM LOCOS 1961	02	61	59
ROSTER OF FSUD (OWNS NO LOCOMOTIVES)1965	06	65	55
ROSTER OF FSUD (OWNS NO LOCOMOTIVES)1968	10	68	39
ROSTER OF FSUD LOCOMOTIVES 6-1973	03	74	47
ROSTER OF FSUD LOCOS (ABANDONDED 1965)	01	78	56
ROSTER OF FUDY LOCOMOTIVES 7-1975	01	78	56
ROSTER OF FW&D LOCOMOTIVES 7-1967	12	67	48
ROSTER OF FW&D LOCOMOTIVES 7-1973	12	73	54
ROSTER OF FW&D LOCOS: STEAM/DIESEL	06	58	47
ROSTER OF FW&D LOCOS: STEAM/DIESEL-ELECT	10	55	29
ROSTER OF FW&D STEAM LOCOS 1961	02	61	59
ROSTER OF FWB LOCOMOTIVES 3-1970	11	70	40
ROSTER OF FWB LOCOMOTIVES 7-1975	01	78	56
ROSTER OF FWB LOCOS: (TWO DIESELS)	10	48	128
ROSTER OF FWP LOCOMOTIVES 7-1966	09	66	46
ROSTER OF G LOCOMOTIVES 10-1964	02	65	56
ROSTER OF G LOCOMOTIVES 11-1976	03	78	55
ROSTER OF G LOCOMOTIVES 3-1972	10	72	45
ROSTER OF G LOCOMOTIVES 6-1967	11	67	46
ROSTER OF G LOCOS	12	39	112
ROSTER OF G LOCOS: STEAM/DIESEL-ELECTRIC	07	52	111
ROSTER OF G&F LOCOMOTIVES	06	41	62
ROSTER OF G&F LOCOMOTIVES 10-1964	02	65	56
ROSTER OF G&F LOCOMOTIVES 10-1976	03	78	54
ROSTER OF G&F LOCOMOTIVES 12-1969	05	70	50
ROSTER OF G&F LOCOMOTIVES 3-1966	06	66	48
ROSTER OF G&F LOCOMOTIVES 3-1972	10	72	44
ROSTER OF G&F LOCOMOTIVES 6-1967	11	67	46
ROSTER OF G&F LOCOS	03	33	93
ROSTER OF G&F LOCOS: STEAM/DIESEL-ELECTR	06	55	79
ROSTER OF G&GE LOCOS (ABANDONED 1960)	01	78	57
ROSTER OF G&GE LOCOS: 2 DIESELS 1959	10	59	72
ROSTER OF G&J LOCOMOTIVES 10-1977	10	78	57
ROSTER OF G&J LOCOMOTIVES 3-1969	08	69	50
ROSTER OF G&J LOCOMOTIVES 6-1974	12	75	54
ROSTER OF G&J LOCOMOTIVES 7-1963	02	64	52

ROSTERS BY RAILROAD	M	Y	P
ROSTER OF G&N DIESEL LOCOMOTIVES	SP	77	23R
ROSTER OF G&N LOCOMOTIVES 12-1969	05	70	50
ROSTER OF G&N LOCOMOTIVES 3-1966	06	66	48
ROSTER OF G&N LOCOMOTIVES 6-1977	03	78	57
ROSTER OF G&U LOCOMOTIVES 11-1962	08	63	60
ROSTER OF G&U LOCOMOTIVES 6-1968	09	68	50
ROSTER OF G&U LOCOMOTIVES 6-1973	10	73	13
ROSTER OF G&U LOCOMOTIVES 9-1976	03	78	56
ROSTER OF G&W DIESELS 1985	03	86	45
ROSTER OF G&WY LOCOMOTIVES 11-1976	03	78	54
ROSTER OF G&WY LOCOMOTIVES 3-1969	08	69	50
ROSTER OF G&WY LOCOMOTIVES 6-1974	12	75	54
ROSTER OF G&WY LOCOMOTIVES 7-1963	02	64	54
ROSTER OF G&WY LOCOS	01	41	136
ROSTER OF GAS&C LOCOMOTIVES 10-1964	02	65	56
ROSTER OF GAS&C LOCOMOTIVES 10-1976	03	78	55
ROSTER OF GAS&C LOCOMOTIVES 3-1972	10	72	45
ROSTER OF GAS&C LOCOMOTIVES 6-1967	11	67	46
ROSTER OF GB&W LOCOMOTIVES 3-1965	07	65	53
ROSTER OF GB&W LOCOMOTIVES 6-1968	12	68	48
ROSTER OF GB&W LOCOMOTIVES 6-1973	11	73	62
ROSTER OF GB&W LOCOMOTIVES 6-1977	03	78	57
ROSTER OF GB&W LOCOMOTIVES 7-1965	01	66	66
ROSTER OF GB&W LOCOS	07	42	152
ROSTER OF GC&E LOCOS	10	33	88
ROSTER OF GC&WR LOCOS	03	39	121
ROSTER OF GCH LOCOMOTIVES	11	78	52R
ROSTER OF GCO LOCOMOTIVES 1-1964	08	64	37
ROSTER OF GCO LOCOMOTIVES 9-1977	03	78	55
ROSTER OF GCO STEAM LOCOS 1961	02	61	59
ROSTER OF GCW LOCOMOTIVES 10-1964	04	65	36
ROSTER OF GCW LOCOMOTIVES 11-1972	03	78	55
ROSTER OF GCW LOCOMOTIVES 12-1967	04	68	48
ROSTER OF GCW LOCOMOTIVES 12-1972	08	73	13
ROSTER OF GE DEMONSTRATORS	02	65	33
ROSTER OF GFC LOCOMOTIVES 10-1965	02	66	54
ROSTER OF GFC LOCOMOTIVES 12-1970	05	71	57
ROSTER OF GFC LOCOMOTIVES 9-1970	03	78	55
ROSTER OF GH&H LOCOMOTIVES 3-1970	11	70	40
ROSTER OF GH&H LOCOMOTIVES 7-1966	09	66	46
ROSTER OF GH&H LOCOMOTIVES 8-1975	01	78	57
ROSTER OF GM&N LOCOS FRT/PASS/SWITCHERS	05	34	137
ROSTER OF GM&O LOCOMOTIVES 5-1962	02	63	30
ROSTER OF GM&O LOCOMOTIVES 8-1964	02	65	64
ROSTER OF GM&O LOCOMOTIVES 9-1973	06	74	50
ROSTER OF GM&O LOCOMOTIVES CORRECTION	09	74	33
ROSTER OF GM&O LOCOS: DIESEL	11	51	110
ROSTER OF GMI (OWNS NO LOCOMOTIVES) 1967	11	67	46
ROSTER OF GMI LOCOMOTIVES 10-1964	02	65	56
ROSTER OF GMI LOCOMOTIVES 3-1972	10	72	44
ROSTER OF GMI LOCOMOTIVES 8-1975	01	78	57
ROSTER OF GMT LOCOMOTIVES	F	75	25R
ROSTER OF GMT LOCOMOTIVES 6-1970	12	70	56
ROSTER OF GMT LOCOMOTIVES 9-1976	03	78	57
ROSTER OF GN FREIGHT DIESELS ORIGINAL #S	04	74	55

Railroad/Railfan

RAILROAD HISTORIES & ROSTERS

ROSTERS BY RAILROAD	M	Y	P
ROSTER OF GN LOCOMOTIVES	01	49	82
ROSTER OF GN LOCOMOTIVES (NOTES TO 2-68)	04	68	48
ROSTER OF GN LOCOMOTIVES 10-1962	06	63	46
ROSTER OF GN LOCOMOTIVES 10-1973	04	74	54
ROSTER OF GN LOCOMOTIVES 1968	02	68	63
ROSTER OF GN LOCOMOTIVES CORRECTION 1962	08	63	56
ROSTER OF GN LOCOMOTIVES CORRECTIONS	06	74	51
ROSTER OF GN LOCOS	08	35	89
ROSTER OF GN LOCOS (ROAD RENUMBERING)	06	68	66
ROSTER OF GN LOCOS RENUMBER & DISPOSITON	04	74	56
ROSTER OF GN LOCOS: ELECTRIC W/SPECIFICA	12	57	55
ROSTER OF GN LOCOS: STEAM/DIESEL-ELECTRI	02	57	34
ROSTER OF GN STEAM LOCOS 1961	02	61	60
ROSTER OF GN&A LOCOMOTIVES 12-1963	06	64	48
ROSTER OF GN&A LOCOMOTIVES 12-1966	05	67	54
ROSTER OF GN&A LOCOMOTIVES 2-1971	03	78	56
ROSTER OF GN&A LOCOMOTIVES 6-1971	03	72	59
ROSTER OF GNO LOCOMOTIVER 10-1976	03	78	55
ROSTER OF GNO LOCOMOTIVES 10-1964	02	65	56
ROSTER OF GNO LOCOMOTIVES 3-1972	10	72	45
ROSTER OF GNO LOCOMOTIVES 6-1967	11	67	46
ROSTER OF GNO STEAM LOCOS 1961	02	61	59
ROSTER OF GOT LOCOMOTIVES 10-1976	03	78	56
ROSTER OF GP LOCOMOTIVES 6-1975	03	78	57
ROSTER OF GP30 EMD LOCOMOTIVES	01	87	48
ROSTER OF GRR (ABANDONDONED 1962)	03	78	56
ROSTER OF GRRY (OWNS NO LOCOMOTIVES)1965	02	66	54
ROSTER OF GRRY LOCOMOTIVES 12-1970	05	71	57
ROSTER OF GRRY LOCOS: ELECTRICS	09	53	40
ROSTER OF GS&F LOCOMOTIVES 1-1960	10	62	53
ROSTER OF GS&F LOCOMOTIVES 10-1976	03	78	56
ROSTER OF GS&F LOCOS: PART 1 (S)	06	38	80
ROSTER OF GS&F LOCOS: PART 2	07	38	134
ROSTER OF GSW LOCOMOTIVES 3-1970	11	70	40
ROSTER OF GSW LOCOMOTIVES 7-1966	09	66	46
ROSTER OF GT LOCOMOTIVES 1-1975	03	78	56
ROSTER OF GT LOCOMOTIVES 3-1968	07	68	57
ROSTER OF GT LOCOS: PART 1	09	37	82
ROSTER OF GT LOCOS: PART 2	10	37	124
ROSTER OF GT LOCOS: PART 3	11	37	77
ROSTER OF GT LOCOS: PART 4	12	37	77
ROSTER OF GT STEAM LOCOMOTIVES SINCE '23	06	60	44
ROSTER OF GTN LOCOMOTIVES 1-1977	03	78	54
ROSTER OF GTN LOCOMOTIVES 3-1970	11	70	40
ROSTER OF GTN LOCOMOTIVES 7-1966	09	66	46
ROSTER OF GTP STEAM LOCOMOTIVES	07	66	53
ROSTER OF GTW LOCOMOTIVES 6-1968	10	68	39
ROSTER OF GTW LOCOMOTIVES 6-1973	03	74	46
ROSTER OF GTW LOCOS: PART 1	09	37	82
ROSTER OF GTW LOCOS: PART 2	10	37	124
ROSTER OF GTW LOCOS: PART 3	11	37	77
ROSTER OF GTW LOCOS: PART 4	12	37	77
ROSTER OF GTW LOCOS: TRANSFERRED TO CN	03	43	105
ROSTER OF GTW STEAM LOCOS 1961	02	61	59
ROSTER OF GUSC LOCOMOTIVES 3-1969	10	69	50

ROSTERS BY RAILROAD	M	Y	P
ROSTER OF GUSR (OWNS NO LOCOMOTIVES)1964	08	64	37
ROSTER OF GW LOCOMOTIVES 10-1976	03	78	57
ROSTER OF GW LOCOMOTIVES 3-1967	07	67	64
ROSTER OF GW LOCOMOTIVES 7-1964	10	64	62
ROSTER OF GW LOCOMOTIVES 9-1971	07	72	59
ROSTER OF GW STEAM LOCOS 1961	02	61	60
ROSTER OF GWH LOCOMOTIVES 3-1970	11	70	40
ROSTER OF GWH LOCOMOTIVES 7-1966	09	66	46
ROSTER OF GWH LOCOMOTIVES 8-1975	01	78	57
ROSTER OF GWS STEAM LOCOMOTIVES	03	72	22
ROSTER OF GWWD LOCOMOTIVES 10-1965	02	66	54
ROSTER OF GWWD LOCOMOTIVES 6-1977	03	78	57
ROSTER OF H&B LOCOMOTIVES 12-1969	05	70	50
ROSTER OF H&B LOCOMOTIVES 1977	10	78	57
ROSTER OF H&B LOCOMOTIVES 3-1966	06	66	48
ROSTER OF H&B STEAM LOCOS 1961	02	61	60
ROSTER OF H&BV LOCOS: PART 1 (MP)	03	38	60
ROSTER OF H&BV LOCOS: PART 2	04	38	67
ROSTER OF H&E (OWNS NO LOCOMOTIVES) 1965	03	66	59
ROSTER OF H&E LOCOMOTIVES 11-1977	10	78	58
ROSTER OF H&E LOCOMOTIVES 3-1969	01	70	10
ROSTER OF H&F EQUIPMENT	03	45	111
ROSTER OF H&F LOCOMOTIVES 10-1977	10	78	57
ROSTER OF H&N LOCOMOTIVES 10-1964	04	65	36
ROSTER OF H&N LOCOMOTIVES 11-1977	10	78	59
ROSTER OF H&N LOCOMOTIVES 12-1967	04	68	48
ROSTER OF H&N LOCOMOTIVES 12-1972	08	73	13
ROSTER OF H&NE LOCOMOTIVES 11-1977	10	78	58
ROSTER OF H&NE LOCOMOTIVES 7-1965	01	66	66
ROSTER OF H&NE LOCOMOTIVES 9-1970	05	71	58
ROSTER OF H&NRY LOCOS (ABANDONED 1951)	10	78	58
ROSTER OF H&S LOCOMOTIVES 1-1961	02	62	32
ROSTER OF H&S LOCOMOTIVES 10-1966	02	67	48
ROSTER OF H&S LOCOMOTIVES 11-1977	10	78	57
ROSTER OF H&S LOCOMOTIVES 12-1970	07	71	53
ROSTER OF HANC LOCOMOTIVES 10-1977	10	78	57
ROSTER OF HANC LOCOMOTIVES 3-1965	09	65	54
ROSTER OF HAR LOCOMOTIVES 10-1964	02	65	56
ROSTER OF HAR LOCOMOTIVES 11-1977	10	78	58
ROSTER OF HAR LOCOMOTIVES 3-1972	10	72	45
ROSTER OF HAR LOCOMOTIVES 6-1967	11	67	48
ROSTER OF HB&T LOCOMOTIVES	01	79	25R
ROSTER OF HB&T LOCOMOTIVES 3-1970	11	70	40
ROSTER OF HB&T LOCOMOTIVES 7-1966	09	66	46
ROSTER OF HBLR (OWNS NO LOCOMOTIVES)1964	08	64	60
ROSTER OF HBLR (OWNS NO LOCOMOTIVES)1967	06	67	50
ROSTER OF HBLR LOCOMOTIVES 6-1971	03	72	59
ROSTER OF HC LOCOS: ELECTRIC	11	46	107
ROSTER OF HC LOCOS: STEAM	11	46	107
ROSTER OF HER EQUIPMENT: COMPLETE	09	47	109
ROSTER OF HES LOCOMOTIVES 12-1963	06	64	48
ROSTER OF HES LOCOMOTIVES 12-1964	05	65	50
ROSTER OF HES LOCOMOTIVES 12-1966	05	67	54
ROSTER OF HES LOCOMOTIVES 3-1968	06	68	50
ROSTER OF HES LOCOMOTIVES 3-1971	10	78	58

STEPHANS'_RAILROAD_DIRECTORY

388

Railroad/Railfan

RAILROAD HISTORIES & ROSTERS

ROSTERS BY RAILROAD	M	Y	P
ROSTER OF HES LOCOMOTIVES 3-1973	07	73	58
ROSTER OF HES LOCOMOTIVES 6-1971	03	72	59
ROSTER OF HI (OWNS NO LOCOMOTIVES) 1964	08	64	60
ROSTER OF HI (OWNS NO LOCOMOTIVES) 1967	06	67	50
ROSTER OF HI LOCOMOTIVES 6-1971	03	72	59
ROSTER OF HIL LOCOMOTIVES 9-1977	10	78	58
ROSTER OF HNS LOCOS: PART 1 (MP)	03	38	60
ROSTER OF HNS LOCOS: PART 2	04	38	67
ROSTER OF HPT&D LOCOMOTIVES 1-1964	08	64	37
ROSTER OF HPT&D LOCOMOTIVES 10-1977	10	78	58
ROSTER OF HPT&D LOCOMOTIVES 3-1969	10	69	50
ROSTER OF HRRR LOCOS: PHOTO ESSAY	03	51	27
ROSTER OF HS LOCOS	11	42	150
ROSTER OF HS LOCOS (INC HOBART ESTATE)	12	39	118
ROSTER OF HS LOCOS: #3-#10	12	37	57
ROSTER OF HSH LOCOMOTIVES 11-1977	10	78	58
ROSTER OF HSH LOCOMOTIVES 3-1969	07	69	48
ROSTER OF HSH LOCOMOTIVES 3-1974	10	74	48
ROSTER OF HSH LOCOS: 2 DIESELS	02	59	44
ROSTER OF HT&W LOCOMOTIVES 11-1962	08	63	60
ROSTER OF HT&W LOCOMOTIVES 1963 REVISION	12	63	61
ROSTER OF HT&W LOCOMOTIVES 6-1968	09	68	50
ROSTER OF HT&W LOCOMOTIVES 6-1970	12	70	56
ROSTER OF HT&W LOCOMOTIVES 6-1973	10	73	13
ROSTER OF HT&W LOCOS (ABANDONED 1971)	10	78	59
ROSTER OF HTR LOCOS (ABANDONED)	10	78	57
ROSTER OF HV LOCOS-NOW BELONG TO C&O	01	39	64
ROSTER OF I FREIGHT & SERVICE MOTORS	08	68	33
ROSTER OF I PASSENGER MOTORS	08	68	32
ROSTER OF I-GN LOCOS: PART 1 (MP)	03	38	60
ROSTER OF I-GN LOCOS: PART 2	04	38	67
ROSTER OF IC LOCOMOTIVES 9-1967	03	68	58
ROSTER OF IC LOCOMOTIVES AS MERGER ICG	07	74	50
ROSTER OF IC LOCOMOTIVES CORRECTION	09	74	33
ROSTER OF IC LOCOS PART 1	12	36	116
ROSTER OF IC LOCOS PART 1: STEAM	05	51	118
ROSTER OF IC LOCOS PART 2	01	37	82
ROSTER OF IC LOCOS PART 2: STEAM/DIESEL	06	51	104
ROSTER OF IC LOCOS: STEAM/DIESELS	02	58	75
ROSTER OF IC STEAM LOCOS 1961	02	61	60
ROSTER OF ICG LOCOMOTIVES 12-1973	09	74	29
ROSTER OF ICG LOCOMOTIVES CORRECTIONS	11	74	56
ROSTER OF ICO STEAM LOCOMOTIVES 1910	08	66	50
ROSTER OF IHB LOCOMOTIVES 11-1977	10	78	60
ROSTER OF IHB LOCOMOTIVES 6-1962	12	62	60
ROSTER OF IHB LOCOMOTIVES 9-1967	03	68	55
ROSTER OF IHB LOCOMOTIVES 9-1967	02	68	62
ROSTER OF IHB LOCOMOTIVES 9-1972	01	73	56
ROSTER OF IHB LOCOS: DIESELS 1959	10	59	72
ROSTER OF IHB LOCOS: PART 1 NYC	05	40	81
ROSTER OF IHB LOCOS: PART 2 NYC	06	40	113
ROSTER OF IM&C LOCOMOTIVES	11	78	53R
ROSTER OF IN LOCOMOTIVES 9-1967	03	68	54
ROSTER OF IN LOCOMOTIVES 9-1972	01	73	55
ROSTER OF IN LOCOS (MERGED ATSF 1975)	10	78	60
ROSTER OF IN LOCOS: 6 DIESELS 1959	10	59	72
ROSTER OF INN LOCOMOTIVES 9-1967	02	68	63
ROSTER OF INN LOCOS (PURCHASED BY NJI&I)	10	78	61
ROSTER OF INTER LOCOMOTIVES 11-1977	07	78	62
ROSTER OF INTER LOCOMOTIVES 6-1970	04	71	51
ROSTER OF INTER LOCOMOTIVES 7-1966	10	66	52
ROSTER OF INTERURBANS IN CHICAGO	08	59	75
ROSTER OF IOWA LOCOMOTIVES 10-1964	02	65	58
ROSTER OF IOWA LOCOMOTIVES 1972	05	73	56
ROSTER OF IOWA LOCOMOTIVES 2-1976	07	78	62
ROSTER OF IOWA LOCOMOTIVES 6-1967	01	68	56
ROSTER OF IOWAT LOCOMOTIVES 10-1964	02	65	58
ROSTER OF IOWAT LOCOMOTIVES 11-1977	07	78	62
ROSTER OF IOWAT LOCOMOTIVES 1972	05	73	56
ROSTER OF IOWAT LOCOMOTIVES 6-1967	01	68	57
ROSTER OF IR LOCOMOTIVES 1-1978	07	78	62
ROSTER OF IR LOCOMOTIVES 3-1966	05	66	50
ROSTER OF IR LOCOMOTIVES 9-1969	03	70	63
ROSTER OF IRCA LOCOS: STEAM	08	48	48
ROSTER OF IRRC DIESEL LOCOMOTIVES	07	84	54
ROSTER OF IT LOCOMOTIVES 3-1965	09	65	55
ROSTER OF IT LOCOMOTIVES 6-1968	02	69	48
ROSTER OF IT LOCOMOTIVES 8-1977	10	78	60
ROSTER OF IT LOCOMOTIVES 9-1967	03	68	54
ROSTER OF IT LOCOMOTIVES 9-1972	01	73	55
ROSTER OF IT LOCOMOTIVES 9-1973	06	74	52
ROSTER OF IT LOCOS: DIESELS 1959	10	59	72
ROSTER OF IT LOCOS: ELECTRIC/DIESEL	04	53	101
ROSTER OF IU LOCOMOTIVES 11-1977	10	78	61
ROSTER OF IU LOCOMOTIVES 6-1962	12	62	60
ROSTER OF IU LOCOMOTIVES 9-1967	02	68	63
ROSTER OF J&E LOCOMOTIVES 9-1967	03	68	55
ROSTER OF J&E LOCOS: OWNS 2 UNITS 1959	10	59	72
ROSTER OF J&SC LOCOMOTIVES 3-1966	05	66	50
ROSTER OF J&SC LOCOMOTIVES 8-1969	07	78	63
ROSTER OF J&SC LOCOMOTIVES 9-1969	03	70	64
ROSTER OF J-PRR LOCOMS (ABANDONED 1954)	07	78	63
ROSTER OF JS LOCOS (ABANDONED 1959)	07	78	63
ROSTER OF JT LOCOMOTIVES 10-1964	12	64	32
ROSTER OF JT LOCOMOTIVES 11-1977	07	78	65
ROSTER OF JT LOCOMOTIVES 12-1971	08	72	57
ROSTER OF JT LOCOMOTIVES 6-1967	10	67	50
ROSTER OF JUD (OWNS NO LOCOMOTIVES) 1968	03	68	55
ROSTER OF JUD LOCOMOTIVES 9-1972	01	72	56
ROSTER OF JUD: OWNS NO MOTIVE POWER '59	10	59	72
ROSTER OF JUDC (OWNS NO LOCOMOTIVES)1965	09	65	55
ROSTER OF JUDC LOCOMOTIVES 6-1968	02	69	48
ROSTER OF JUDC LOCOMOTIVES 9-1973	06	74	52
ROSTER OF JW&N LOCOS (ABANDONED 1949)	07	78	63
ROSTER OF K&IT LOCOMOTIVES 1-1978	07	78	65
ROSTER OF K&IT LOCOMOTIVES 10-1964	04	65	53
ROSTER OF K&IT LOCOMOTIVES 12-1967	05	68	52
ROSTER OF K&IT LOCOMOTIVES 3-1973	10	73	61
ROSTER OF K&IT LOCOMOTIVES 6-1962	12	62	61
ROSTER OF K&IT LOCOMOTIVES 9-1967	02	68	63

Railroad/ Railfan

RAILROAD HISTORIES & ROSTERS

ROSTERS BY RAILROAD	M	Y	P
ROSTER OF K&MR&T (OWNS NO LOCOS) 1965	09	65	55
ROSTER OF K&MR&T LOCOMOTIVES 12-1972	08	73	13
ROSTER OF K&MR&T LOCOMOTIVES 6-1968	02	69	48
ROSTER OF K&MR&T LOCOMOTIVES 9-1973	06	74	52
ROSTER OF K&T LOCOMOTIVES 1-1978	07	78	64
ROSTER OF K&T LOCOMOTIVES 10-1964	04	65	53
ROSTER OF K&T LOCOMOTIVES 12-1967	05	68	52
ROSTER OF K&T LOCOMOTIVES 3-1973	10	73	62
ROSTER OF K&T STEAM LOCOS 1961	02	61	61
ROSTER OF KAC LOCOMOTIVES 6-1970	02	71	59
ROSTER OF KAC LOCOMOTIVES 7-1966	12	66	54
ROSTER OF KAC LOCOMOTIVES 7-1966	07	78	63
ROSTER OF KC LOCOS (ABANDONED 1964)	07	78	64
ROSTER OF KC&IAL LOCOS: NOW KCS	04	57	74
ROSTER OF KC&IAL STEAM LOCOMOTIVES-ALL T	01	76	56
ROSTER OF KC&NW LOCOMOTIVES 1-1978	07	78	64
ROSTER OF KC&NW LOCOMOTIVES 6-1970	02	71	59
ROSTER OF KC&NW LOCOMOTIVES 7-1966	12	66	54
ROSTER OF KCC LOCOMOTIVES 12-1977	07	78	64
ROSTER OF KCC LOCOMOTIVES 3-1965	09	65	55
ROSTER OF KCC LOCOMOTIVES 6-1968	02	69	48
ROSTER OF KCC LOCOMOTIVES 9-1973	06	74	52
ROSTER OF KCM&O LOCOS	04	40	117
ROSTER OF KCS 3-1963	02	64	62
ROSTER OF KCS DIESEL LOCOMOTIVES 12-1973	01	76	59
ROSTER OF KCS LOCOMOTIVES 12-1967	06	68	31
ROSTER OF KCS LOCOS	04	39	121
ROSTER OF KCS LOCOS: STEAM ALL-TIME	04	57	74
ROSTER OF KCS LOCOS: STEAM/DIESEL	06	52	100
ROSTER OF KCS STEAM LOCOMOTIVES-ALL TIME	01	76	56
ROSTER OF KCT LOCOMOTIVES 10-1964	04	65	36
ROSTER OF KCT LOCOMOTIVES 11-1977	07	78	64
ROSTER OF KCT LOCOMOTIVES 12-1967	04	68	48
ROSTER OF KCT LOCOMOTIVES 12-1972	08	73	13
ROSTER OF KCT LOCOMOTIVES 3-1965	09	65	55
ROSTER OF KCT LOCOMOTIVES 6-1968	02	69	48
ROSTER OF KCT LOCOMOTIVES 9-1973	06	74	53
ROSTER OF KGB&W LOCOMOTIVES 7-1965	01	66	66
ROSTER OF KGB&W LOCOMOTIVES 9-1970	05	71	58
ROSTER OF KGB&W LOCOS (MERGED 1969 GB&W)	07	78	65
ROSTER OF KL&L LOCOMOTIVES 3-1962	08	62	29
ROSTER OF KL&L STEAM LOCOS 1961	02	61	61
ROSTER OF KLN LOCOMOTIVES 9-1969	02	70	50
ROSTER OF KO&G LOCOMOTIVES 10-1964	04	65	36
ROSTER OF KO&G LOCOMOTIVES 10-1965	03	66	59
ROSTER OF KO&G LOCOMOTIVES 12-1967	04	68	48
ROSTER OF KO&G LOCOMOTIVES 12-1972	08	73	13
ROSTER OF KO&G LOCOMOTIVES 3-1969	01	70	10
ROSTER OF KO&G LOCOMOTIVES 3-1970	11	70	40
ROSTER OF KO&G LOCOMOTIVES 6-1968	02	69	48
ROSTER OF KO&G LOCOMOTIVES 7-1966	09	66	46
ROSTER OF KO&G LOCOMOTIVES 9-1973	06	74	52
ROSTER OF KO&G LOCOS (MERGED 1970 T&P)	07	78	63
ROSTER OF KSPS LOCOMOTIVES 1-1978	07	78	64
ROSTER OF KSPS LOCOMOTIVES 12-1967	04	68	48
ROSTER OF KSPS LOCOMOTIVES 12-1972	08	73	13
ROSTER OF KSPS LOCOMOTIVES 3-1965	09	65	55
ROSTER OF KSPS LOCOMOTIVES 6-1968	02	69	48
ROSTER OF KSPS LOCOMOTIVES 9-1973	06	74	52
ROSTER OF KUDC (OWNS NO LOCOMOTIVES)1964	02	65	58
ROSTER OF KUDC LOCOMOTIVES 1973	05	73	56
ROSTER OF KUDC LOCOMOTIVES 6-1967	01	68	56
ROSTER OF L&A DIESEL LOCOMOTIVES 12-1973	01	76	59
ROSTER OF L&A LOCOMOTIVES 12-1967	06	68	31
ROSTER OF L&A LOCOS	05	41	49
ROSTER OF L&A LOCOS: STEAM/DIESEL	06	52	102
ROSTER OF L&AL LOCOMOTIVES 3-1969	08	69	50
ROSTER OF L&BR LOCOMOTIVES 3-1969	08	69	50
ROSTER OF L&BR LOCOMOTIVES 6-1974	12	75	55
ROSTER OF L&BR LOCOMOTIVES 7-1963	02	64	54
ROSTER OF L&BR STEAM LOCOS 1961	02	61	61
ROSTER OF L&C DIESEL LOCOMOTIVES	01	79	55
ROSTER OF L&C LOCOMOTIVES 12-1969	05	70	50
ROSTER OF L&C LOCOMOTIVES 3-1966	06	66	48
ROSTER OF L&H LOCOS	02	42	83
ROSTER OF L&HR DIESEL LOCOMOTIVES	W	74	23R
ROSTER OF L&HR LOCOMOTIVES (NOW CONRAIL)	01	79	52
ROSTER OF L&HR LOCOMOTIVES 3-1966	05	66	50
ROSTER OF L&HR LOCOMOTIVES 3-1969	07	69	48
ROSTER OF L&HR LOCOMOTIVES 3-1969	08	69	50
ROSTER OF L&HR LOCOMOTIVES 3-1974	10	74	48
ROSTER OF L&HR LOCOMOTIVES 6-1974	12	75	54
ROSTER OF L&HR LOCOMOTIVES 7-1963	02	64	54
ROSTER OF L&HR LOCOS: DIESELS	02	59	44
ROSTER OF L&HR LOCOS: STEAM	12	58	71
ROSTER OF L&MA (ABANDONED 1964)	01	79	55
ROSTER OF L&MA (ABANDONED 1969)	12	69	47
ROSTER OF L&MA LOCOMOTIVES 1960	06	60	56
ROSTER OF L&N LOCOMOTIVE UPDATES	07	69	56
ROSTER OF L&N LOCOMOTIVES 1-1968	07	68	46
ROSTER OF L&N LOCOMOTIVES 1-1974	11	74	54
ROSTER OF L&N LOCOMOTIVES 7-1964	12	64	50
ROSTER OF L&N LOCOMOTIVES CORRECTIONS	01	75	64
ROSTER OF L&N LOCOMOTIVES TO M	SU	75	43R
ROSTER OF L&N LOCOS	01	36	89
ROSTER OF L&N LOCOS: DIESELS	10	58	72
ROSTER OF L&N LOCOS: STEAM/DIESEL	06	49	113
ROSTER OF L&N LOCOS: WHEEL ARRANGEMENTS	04	40	80
ROSTER OF L&NE (ABANDONED)	01	79	52
ROSTER OF L&NE (NOW CONRAIL)	01	79	52
ROSTER OF L&NE LOCOMOTIVES	03	33	94
ROSTER OF L&NE LOCOMOTIVES 3-1966	05	66	50
ROSTER OF L&NE LOCOMOTIVES 3-1969	07	69	48
ROSTER OF L&NE LOCOMOTIVES 3-1974	10	74	48
ROSTER OF L&NE LOCOMOTIVES 9-1969	03	70	64
ROSTER OF L&NE LOCOS	11	46	113
ROSTER OF L&NE LOCOS: DIESELS	02	59	44
ROSTER OF L&NE: DIESEL FRIEGHT LOCOS	07	49	67
ROSTER OF L&NO DIESEL LOCOMOTIVES	01	79	55
ROSTER OF L&NO LOCOMOTIVES 7-1965	01	66	66

Stephans' Railroad Directory

Railroad/Railfan

RAILROAD HISTORIES & ROSTERS

ROSTERS BY RAILROAD	M	Y	P
ROSTER OF L&NO LOCOMOTIVES 9-1970	05	71	58
ROSTER OF L&NO STEAM LOCOS 1961	02	61	61
ROSTER OF L&NW LOCOMOTIVES	04	78	49R
ROSTER OF L&NW LOCOMOTIVES 12-1963	06	64	48
ROSTER OF L&NW LOCOMOTIVES 12-1964	05	65	50
ROSTER OF L&NW LOCOMOTIVES 12-1966	05	67	54
ROSTER OF L&NW LOCOMOTIVES 3-1968	06	68	50
ROSTER OF L&NW LOCOMOTIVES 3-1973	07	73	58
ROSTER OF L&NW LOCOMOTIVES 4-1978	11	78	59
ROSTER OF L&NW LOCOMOTIVES 6-1971	03	72	59
ROSTER OF L&PB DIESEL LOCOMOTIVES	01	81	52
ROSTER OF L&PB LOCOMOTIVES 12-1963	06	64	48
ROSTER OF L&PB LOCOMOTIVES 12-1967	05	67	54
ROSTER OF L&PB LOCOMOTIVES 4-1978	11	78	59
ROSTER OF L&PB LOCOMOTIVES 6-1971	03	72	59
ROSTER OF L&PS LOCOMOTIVES 10-1965	02	66	54
ROSTER OF L&PS LOCOS (SOLD TO CN 1966)	11	78	57
ROSTER OF L&WRR (OWNS NO LOCOS) 1964	02	65	56
ROSTER OF L&WRR LOCOMOTIVES 3-1972	10	72	45
ROSTER OF L&WRR LOCOMOTIVES 6-1967	11	67	48
ROSTER OF L&WV EQUIPMENT	03	51	90
ROSTER OF L&WV LOCOMOTIVES 3-1966	05	66	50
ROSTER OF L&WV LOCOMOTIVES 9-1969	03	70	64
ROSTER OF L&WVA LOCOMOTIVES 6-1969	12	69	47
ROSTER OF L&WVR (NO MOTIVE POWER)	06	60	56
ROSTER OF LA&L LOCOMOTIVES 1-1978	11	78	57
ROSTER OF LA&L LOCOMOTIVES 6-1974	12	75	54
ROSTER OF LA&S LOCOMOTIVES	01	79	51
ROSTER OF LA&SL LOCOMOTIVES	05	33	84
ROSTER OF LA&SL LOCOS	07	47	115
ROSTER OF LA&SO LOCOMOTIVES	01	79	52
ROSTER OF LA&SO LOCOMOTIVES 1-1964	08	64	37
ROSTER OF LA&SO LOCOMOTIVES 3-1969	10	69	50
ROSTER OF LAJ LOCOMOTIVES 2-1978	11	78	58
ROSTER OF LAJ LOCOMOTIVES 3-1964	08	64	60
ROSTER OF LAJ LOCOMOTIVES 3-1967	06	67	50
ROSTER OF LAJ LOCOMOTIVES 6-1971	03	72	60
ROSTER OF LAUPT (OWNS NO LOCOS) 1964	08	64	60
ROSTER OF LAUPT (OWNS NO LOCOS) 1967	06	67	50
ROSTER OF LAUPT LOCOMOTIVES 6-1971	03	72	60
ROSTER OF LC&M LOCOMOTIVES 3-1969	08	69	50
ROSTER OF LC&M LOCOMOTIVES 6-1974	12	75	54
ROSTER OF LC&M LOCOMOTIVES 7-1963	02	64	54
ROSTER OF LC&M LOCOMOTIVES ABANDONDED 68	01	79	51
ROSTER OF LD&R (OWNS NO LOCOMOTIVES)1964	04	65	36
ROSTER OF LD&R (OWNS NO LOCOMOTIVES)1968	04	68	48
ROSTER OF LD&R LOCOMOTIVES 12-1972	08	73	13
ROSTER OF LD&RT (NO MOTIVE POWER)	06	60	56
ROSTER OF LD&RT LOCOMOTIVES 6-1969	12	69	47
ROSTER OF LE LOCOMOTIVES 12-1964	05	65	50
ROSTER OF LE LOCOMOTIVES 3-1968	06	68	50
ROSTER OF LE LOCOMOTIVES 3-1973	07	73	58
ROSTER OF LE LOCOMOTIVES 4-1978	11	78	59
ROSTER OF LE STEAM LOCOMOTIVES 1962	04	63	35
ROSTER OF LE STEAM LOCOS 1961	02	61	61
ROSTER OF LE&E (NO MOTIVE POWER)	06	60	56
ROSTER OF LE&E LOCOMOTIVES 6-1969	12	69	47
ROSTER OF LE&E LOCOS	02	36	90
ROSTER OF LE&E LOCOS: PART 1 NYC	05	40	81
ROSTER OF LE&E LOCOS: PART 2 NYC	06	40	113
ROSTER OF LE&E LOCOS: STEAM CORRECT 1/49	11	49	103
ROSTER OF LE&FW LOCOMOTIVES	01	79	51
ROSTER OF LE&FW LOCOMOTIVES 6-1962	12	62	61
ROSTER OF LE&FW LOCOMOTIVES 9-1967	02	68	63
ROSTER OF LE&N LOCOMOTIVES 10-1965	02	66	54
ROSTER OF LE&N LOCOMOTIVES 12-1970	05	71	57
ROSTER OF LE&N LOCOS: ELECTRICS	09	53	40
ROSTER OF LEF&C LOCOMOTIVES	01	79	51
ROSTER OF LEF&C LOCOMOTIVES 3-1966	05	66	50
ROSTER OF LEF&C LOCOMOTIVES 9-1969	03	70	64
ROSTER OF LH&SL LOCOS	01	36	89
ROSTER OF LI DIESEL LOCOS 8-1962	04	63	25
ROSTER OF LI ELECTRIC PASSENGER EQUIPMEN	07	50	114
ROSTER OF LI LOCOMOTIVES 1-1960	08	60	36
ROSTER OF LI LOCOMOTIVES 1-1978	11	78	57
ROSTER OF LI LOCOMOTIVES 1963 REVISION	12	63	61
ROSTER OF LI LOCOMOTIVES 3-1969	08	69	54
ROSTER OF LI LOCOMOTIVES 6-1974	12	75	54
ROSTER OF LI LOCOS	05	36	89
ROSTER OF LI LOCOS: ADDITION (4-6-0'S)	12	49	107
ROSTER OF LI LOCOS: DIESEL (PASS/FRT)	05	51	52
ROSTER OF LI LOCOS: PARTIAL	05	34	87
ROSTER OF LI LOCOS: STEAM/DIESEL/ELECTRI	09	49	95
ROSTER OF LI PASSENGER EQUIPMENT 8-1963	04	63	25
ROSTER OF LI&M (MERGED INTO C&NW 1958)	01	79	52
ROSTER OF LI&M LOCOS: DIESELS 1958	06	59	64
ROSTER OF LIMA-HAMILTON DIESEL LOCOS	W	74	52R
ROSTER OF LIMA-HAMILTON LOCOS-2ND OWNERS	W	74	56R
ROSTER OF LM LOCOMOTIVES 12-1964	05	65	50
ROSTER OF LM LOCOMOTIVES 3-1968	06	68	50
ROSTER OF LM LOCOMOTIVES 3-1973	07	73	58
ROSTER OF LM LOCOMOTIVES 4-1978	11	78	59
ROSTER OF LNA&C LOCOMOTIVES 6-1962	12	62	61
ROSTER OF LNA&C LOCOMOTIVES 6-1978	11	78	60
ROSTER OF LNA&C LOCOMOTIVES 9-1967	02	68	63
ROSTER OF LOD LOCOS	11	43	122
ROSTER OF LOP&G (MERGED INTO LOP&SG '71)	01	79	52
ROSTER OF LOP&G LOCOMOTIVES 1-1960	10	62	53
ROSTER OF LOP&G LOCOMOTIVES 10-1964	12	64	32
ROSTER OF LOP&G LOCOMOTIVES 12-1971	08	72	57
ROSTER OF LOP&G LOCOMOTIVES 6-1967	10	67	50
ROSTER OF LOP&SG LOCOMOTIVES	01	79	53
ROSTER OF LOS LOCOMOTIVES 1-1960	10	62	53
ROSTER OF LOS LOCOMOTIVES 12-1964	05	65	50
ROSTER OF LOS LOCOMOTIVES 3-1968	06	68	51
ROSTER OF LOS LOCOMOTIVES 3-1973	07	73	58
ROSTER OF LOS LOCOMOTIVES 4-1978	11	78	60
ROSTER OF LP&N LOCOMOTIVES 1-1978	11	78	58
ROSTER OF LP&N LOCOMOTIVES 12-1965	04	66	58
ROSTER OF LP&N LOCOMOTIVES 3-1962	08	62	29

Railroad/Railfan

RAILROAD HISTORIES & ROSTERS

ROSTERS BY RAILROAD	M	Y	P
ROSTER OF LP&N LOCOMOTIVES 6-1970	06	71	37
ROSTER OF LP&N LOCOMOTIVES 9-1969	02	70	50
ROSTER OF LS&B LOCOMOTIVES	01	79	51
ROSTER OF LS&B LOCOMOTIVES 9-1967	03	68	55
ROSTER OF LS&B LOCOMOTIVES 9-1972	01	73	56
ROSTER OF LS&B LOCOS: STEAM/DIESEL 1959	10	59	72
ROSTER OF LS&I DIESEL LOCOMOTIVES	01	79	54
ROSTER OF LS&I DIESEL LOCOMOTIVES	07	85	53
ROSTER OF LS&I LOCOMOTIVES 3-1965	06	65	55
ROSTER OF LS&I LOCOMOTIVES 6-1968	10	68	39
ROSTER OF LS&I LOCOMOTIVES 6-1973	03	74	47
ROSTER OF LS&I STEAM LOCOS 1961	02	61	61
ROSTER OF LSEL CORRECTIONS (5-68)	08	68	36
ROSTER OF LSEL FREIGHT & PASSENGER MOTOR	04	68	37
ROSTER OF LST&T DIESEL LOCOMOTIVES	01	79	54
ROSTER OF LST&T LOCOMOTIVES 7-1965	01	66	66
ROSTER OF LST&T LOCOMOTIVES 9-1970	05	71	58
ROSTER OF LT DIESEL LOCOMOTIVES	01	79	55
ROSTER OF LT LOCOMOTIVES 1960	06	60	56
ROSTER OF LU&N LOCOMOTIVES 6-1968	10	68	38
ROSTER OF LU&N LOCOMOTIVES 6-1973	03	74	47
ROSTER OF LU&N LOCOMOTIVES 6-1978	11	78	60
ROSTER OF LV LOCOMOTIVES	10	34	83
ROSTER OF LV LOCOMOTIVES 1-1968	05	68	33
ROSTER OF LV LOCOMOTIVES 1-1974	12	74	51
ROSTER OF LV LOCOMOTIVES 6-1959	02	60	57
ROSTER OF LV LOCOMOTIVES CORRECTIONS	02	75	64
ROSTER OF LV LOCOMOTIVES UPDATE (5-68)	07	68	66
ROSTER OF LV LOCOS	04	35	89
ROSTER OF LV LOCOS: RECLASSIFICATIONS	08	49	110
ROSTER OF LV LOCOS: STEAM/DIESEL/GAS-ELE	07	49	103
ROSTER OF LVRC DIESEL LOCOMOTIVES	05	80	29
ROSTER OF M LOCOMOTIVES 10-1959	04	60	58
ROSTER OF M LOCOMOTIVES 6-1968	02	69	44
ROSTER OF M LOCOMOTIVES TO L&N	SU	75	43R
ROSTER OF M LOCOS	01	33	130
ROSTER OF M LOCOS: STEAM/DIESEL	02	49	67
ROSTER OF M&A LOCOS	07	36	88
ROSTER OF M&BA LOCOMOTIVES 11-1962	08	63	60
ROSTER OF M&BA LOCOMOTIVES 1963 REVISION	12	63	61
ROSTER OF M&BA LOCOMOTIVES 6-1970	12	70	56
ROSTER OF M&BIG LOCOMOTIVES 1-1961	02	62	32
ROSTER OF M&BIG LOCOMOTIVES 10-1966	02	67	48
ROSTER OF M&BIG LOCOMOTIVES 10-1973	05	74	59
ROSTER OF M&BIG LOCOMOTIVES 12-1970	07	71	53
ROSTER OF M&BIG LOCOMOTIVES 3-1965	08	65	65
ROSTER OF M&BIG LOCOMOTIVES 6-1968	03	69	38
ROSTER OF M&BL LOCOMOTIVES 10-1964	12	64	32
ROSTER OF M&BL LOCOMOTIVES 12-1971	08	72	57
ROSTER OF M&BL LOCOMOTIVES 6-1967	10	67	50
ROSTER OF M&BL LOCOS (ABANDONED 1976)	11	78	61
ROSTER OF M&E LOCOMOTIVES 3-1969	07	69	48
ROSTER OF M&E LOCOMOTIVES 3-1974	10	74	49
ROSTER OF M&E LOCOS: 1 DIESEL	02	59	44
ROSTER OF M&E LOCOS: 5 LOCOS (4 USED)	06	35	85

ROSTERS BY RAILROAD	M	Y	P
ROSTER OF M&E LOCOS: CORRECTIONS	09	35	87
ROSTER OF M&ET DIESEL LOCOMOTIVES	11	79	46
ROSTER OF M&ET LOCOMOTIVES 3-1964	08	64	60
ROSTER OF M&ET LOCOMOTIVES 3-1967	06	67	50
ROSTER OF M&ET LOCOMOTIVES 6-1971	03	72	60
ROSTER OF M&ET LOCOS	11	42	151
ROSTER OF M&G DIESEL LOCOMOTIVES	11	79	46
ROSTER OF M&G LOCOMOTIVES 1-1961	02	62	32
ROSTER OF M&G LOCOMOTIVES 10-1966	02	67	48
ROSTER OF M&G LOCOMOTIVES 12-1970	07	71	53
ROSTER OF M&G STEAM LOCOS 1961	02	61	61
ROSTER OF M&HM LOCOMOTIVES 6-1968	10	68	39
ROSTER OF M&HM LOCOMOTIVES 6-1973	03	74	47
ROSTER OF M&IB&B LOCOMOTIVES 3-1965	09	65	55
ROSTER OF M&IB&B LOCOS: 1 DIESEL 1959	10	59	72
ROSTER OF M&LB EQUIPMENT	10	48	55
ROSTER OF M&LS LOCOMOTIVES 3-1965	06	65	55
ROSTER OF M&LS LOCOMOTIVES 6-1968	10	68	39
ROSTER OF M&LS LOCOMOTIVES 6-1973	03	74	47
ROSTER OF M&LS LOCOMOTIVES 6-1978	11	78	60
ROSTER OF M&NE LOCOMOTIVES 6-1962	12	62	61
ROSTER OF M&NF LOCOMOTIVES 10-1964	04	65	53
ROSTER OF M&NF LOCOMOTIVES 12-1967	05	68	52
ROSTER OF M&NF LOCOMOTIVES 3-1973	10	73	62
ROSTER OF M&NF STEAM LOCOS 1961	02	61	61
ROSTER OF M&NJ LOCOMOTIVES 3-1969	08	69	52
ROSTER OF M&NJ LOCOMOTIVES 6-1974	12	75	55
ROSTER OF M&NJ LOCOMOTIVES 7-1963	02	64	54
ROSTER OF M&NRY LOCOS (ABANDONED 1955)	11	78	60
ROSTER OF M&O LOCOS 1934	09	34	88
ROSTER OF M&PP LOCOMOTIVES 3-1967	07	67	64
ROSTER OF M&PP LOCOMOTIVES 7-1964	10	64	62
ROSTER OF M&PP LOCOMOTIVES 9-1971	07	72	59
ROSTER OF M&PP LOCOMOTIVES 9-1971	11	78	61
ROSTER OF M&PP STEAM LOCOS 1961	02	61	61
ROSTER OF M&SL GAS-ELECTRIC CARS	04	44	57
ROSTER OF M&SL LOCOMOTIVES	04	44	56
ROSTER OF M&SL LOCOS	03	35	81
ROSTER OF M&SV DIESEL LOCOMOTIVES	07	79	30
ROSTER OF M&SV LOCOMOTIVES 10-1973	05	74	59
ROSTER OF M&SV LOCOMOTIVES 3-1965	08	65	65
ROSTER OF M&SV LOCOMOTIVES 6-1968	03	69	38
ROSTER OF M&WE LOCOMOTIVES 9-1967	02	68	63
ROSTER OF M&WR LOCOS	04	33	97
ROSTER OF M&WR LOCOS W/FORMER B&M NUMBER	10	33	48
ROSTER OF M-I LOCOMOTIVES 3-1960	08	60	29
ROSTER OF M-I LOCOMOTIVES 3-1965	09	65	55
ROSTER OF M-I LOCOMOTIVES 6-1968	02	69	48
ROSTER OF M-I LOCOMOTIVES 9-1967	03	68	55
ROSTER OF M-I LOCOMOTIVES 9-1972	01	73	56
ROSTER OF M-I LOCOMOTIVES 9-1973	06	74	53
ROSTER OF M-I LOCOS: DIESELS 1959	10	59	72
ROSTER OF M-I LOCOS: PART 1 (MP)	03	38	60
ROSTER OF M-I LOCOS: PART 2	04	38	67
ROSTER OF MA LOCOMOTIVES 10-1963	04	64	35

Railroad/Railfan

RAILROAD HISTORIES & ROSTERS

ROSTERS BY RAILROAD	M	Y	P
ROSTER OF MA LOCOMOTIVES 12-1966	04	67	39
ROSTER OF MA LOCOMOTIVES 2-1971	11	78	60
ROSTER OF MA LOCOMOTIVES 3-1971	10	71	46
ROSTER OF MA STEAM LOCOS 1961	02	61	61
ROSTER OF MA&CR LOCOMOTIVES 3-1965	07	65	53
ROSTER OF MA&CR LOCOMOTIVES 6-1968	12	68	48
ROSTER OF MA&CR LOCOMOTIVES 6-1973	11	73	62
ROSTER OF MA&PA	09	32	234
ROSTER OF MA&PA LOCOMOTIVES 3-1966	05	66	50
ROSTER OF MA&PA LOCOMOTIVES 3-1968	09	68	44
ROSTER OF MA&PA LOCOMOTIVES 3-1973	01	74	45
ROSTER OF MA&PA LOCOMOTIVES 6-1964	11	64	62
ROSTER OF MA&PA LOCOMOTIVES 9-1969	03	70	64
ROSTER OF MA&PA LOCOS	12	33	92
ROSTER OF MAT LOCOMOTIVES 12-1970	05	71	57
ROSTER OF MAT: COMPLETE	05	47	82
ROSTER OF MATE LOCOMOTIVES 3-1969	08	69	50
ROSTER OF MATE LOCOMOTIVES 6-1974	12	75	54
ROSTER OF MATE LOCOMOTIVES 7-1963	02	64	54
ROSTER OF MC LOCOMOTIVES	07	78	42R
ROSTER OF MC LOCOMOTIVES 1-1968	09	68	48
ROSTER OF MC LOCOMOTIVES 11-1964	04	65	49
ROSTER OF MC LOCOMOTIVES 5-1974	01	75	58
ROSTER OF MC LOCOS	01	47	107
ROSTER OF MC LOCOS 1932	05	32	212
ROSTER OF MC LOCOS: STEAM LOCOS SCRAPPED	07	49	64
ROSTER OF MC LOCOS: STEAM/DIESEL	06	53	104
ROSTER OF MC LOCOS: STEAM/DIESELS	10	58	68
ROSTER OF MC STEAM LOCOMOTIVES	09	78	38R
ROSTER OF MC STEAM LOCOS 1961	02	61	61
ROSTER OF MC U18B NAMED LOCOMOTIVES	07	78	42R
ROSTER OF MC&SA LOCOMOTIVES 3-1970	11	70	41
ROSTER OF MC&SA LOCOMOTIVES 7-1966	09	66	47
ROSTER OF MC&SA STEAM LOCOS 1961	02	61	61
ROSTER OF MCKC LOCOMOTIVES 3-1966	05	66	50
ROSTER OF MCKC LOCOMOTIVES 9-1969	03	70	64
ROSTER OF MCO LOCOMOTIVES 3-1966	05	66	50
ROSTER OF MCO LOCOMOTIVES 9-1969	03	70	64
ROSTER OF MCRI LOCOMOTIVES 3-1964	08	64	60
ROSTER OF MCRI LOCOMOTIVES 3-1967	06	67	50
ROSTER OF MCRI LOCOMOTIVES 6-1971	03	72	60
ROSTER OF MCRI LOCOS	10	36	71
ROSTER OF MD&S LOCOMOTIVES 6-1978	11	78	60
ROSTER OF MD&W DIESEL LOCOMOTIVES	07	79	29
ROSTER OF MD&W LOCOMOTIVES 3-1965	07	65	53
ROSTER OF MD&W LOCOMOTIVES 6-1968	12	68	48
ROSTER OF MD&W LOCOMOTIVES 6-1973	11	73	62
ROSTER OF MER&L PASSENGER EQUIPMENT	04	43	141
ROSTER OF MERY (OWNS NO LOCOMOTIVES)1965	07	65	53
ROSTER OF MERY LOCOMOTIVES 6-1968	12	68	48
ROSTER OF MERY LOCOMOTIVES 6-1973	11	73	62
ROSTER OF MEXICAN STEAM INDUSTRIAL LINES	10	73	35
ROSTER OF MEXICAN STEAM LOCOMOTIVES 1961	06	61	26
ROSTER OF MEXICAN STEAMERS DISPLAY/OPERA	01	71	31
ROSTER OF MEXP DIESEL LOCOMOTIVES	11	79	46
ROSTER OF MEXP LOCOMOTIVES 10-1973	05	74	59
ROSTER OF MEXP LOCOMOTIVES 3-1965	08	65	65
ROSTER OF MEXP LOCOMOTIVES 6-1968	03	69	38
ROSTER OF MF LOCOMOTIVES 7-1966	12	66	54
ROSTER OF MF STEAM LOCOS 1961	02	61	61
ROSTER OF MFG LOCOMOTIVES 2-1978	11	78	61
ROSTER OF MFG LOCOMOTIVES 3-1965	09	65	55
ROSTER OF MFG LOCOMOTIVES 6-1968	02	69	48
ROSTER OF MFG LOCOMOTIVES 9-1972	01	73	56
ROSTER OF MFG LOCOMOTIVES 9-1973	06	74	53
ROSTER OF MFG LOCOS: DIESELS 1959	10	59	72
ROSTER OF MH LOCOMOTIVES 12-1965	04	66	58
ROSTER OF MH LOCOMOTIVES 9-1969	02	70	50
ROSTER OF MHM LOCOMOTIVES 3-1969	07	69	48
ROSTER OF MHM LOCOMOTIVES 3-1974	10	74	49
ROSTER OF MHM LOCOS: OWNS NO MOTIVE POWR	02	59	44
ROSTER OF MI DIESEL LOCOMOTIVES	07	79	30
ROSTER OF MI LOCOMOTIVES 10-1973	05	74	59
ROSTER OF MI LOCOMOTIVES 3-1965	08	65	65
ROSTER OF MI LOCOMOTIVES 6-1968	03	69	38
ROSTER OF MI STEAM LOCOS 1961	02	61	61
ROSTER OF MI&W LOCOS: #102/ #104	01	36	85
ROSTER OF MICHC LOCOS: PART 1 NYC	05	40	81
ROSTER OF MICHC LOCOS: PART 2 NYC	06	40	113
ROSTER OF MID LOCOMOTIVES 6-1969	12	69	47
ROSTER OF MIDC LOCOS: DIESEL	06	57	40
ROSTER OF MIDC LOCOS: STEAM ALL-TIME	06	57	40
ROSTER OF MIDC PASSENGER EQUIPMENT	12	35	87
ROSTER OF MIIR (OWNS NO LOCOMOTIVES)1968	12	68	48
ROSTER OF MIIR LOCOMOTIVES 6-1973	11	73	62
ROSTER OF MIL LOCOMOTIVES 10-1964	02	65	56
ROSTER OF MIL LOCOMOTIVES 3-1972	10	72	45
ROSTER OF MIL LOCOMOTIVES 6-1967	11	67	48
ROSTER OF MIL STEAM LOCOS 1961	02	61	61
ROSTER OF MILW LOCOMOTIVES 11-1965	07	66	42
ROSTER OF MILW LOCOMOTIVES 1939 RENUMBER	06	70	50
ROSTER OF MILW LOCOMOTIVES 5-1960	10	60	58
ROSTER OF MILW LOCOS	05	33	74
ROSTER OF MILW LOCOS: DIESEL/ELECTRIC	03	51	114
ROSTER OF MILW LOCOS: ELECTRIC	10	32	404
ROSTER OF MILW LOCOS: RENUMBERING	11	39	60
ROSTER OF MILW LOCOS: STEAM	10	32	402
ROSTER OF MILW LOCOS: STEAM	02	51	78
ROSTER OF MISSC LOCOMOTIVES 3-1965	08	65	65
ROSTER OF MISSC LOCOS	09	33	84
ROSTER OF MITR DIESEL LOCOMOTIVES	07	79	30
ROSTER OF MITR LOCOMOTIVES 3-1965	07	65	53
ROSTER OF MITR LOCOMOTIVES 6-1968	12	68	48
ROSTER OF MITR LOCOMOTIVES 6-1973	11	73	62
ROSTER OF MIV LOCOMOTIVES 10-1965	03	66	59
ROSTER OF MIV LOCOMOTIVES 12-1963	06	64	48
ROSTER OF MIV LOCOMOTIVES 12-1966	05	67	55
ROSTER OF MIV LOCOMOTIVES 12-1967	04	68	48
ROSTER OF MIV LOCOMOTIVES 6-1971	03	72	59
ROSTER OF MJ LOCOMOTIVES 1-1978	11	78	61

Railroad/Railfan

RAILROAD HISTORIES & ROSTERS

ROSTERS BY RAILROAD	M	Y	P
ROSTER OF MJ LOCOMOTIVES 9-1967	03	68	55
ROSTER OF MJ LOCOMOTIVES 9-1972	01	73	57
ROSTER OF MJ LOCOS: 2 UNITS 1959	10	59	72
ROSTER OF MKT LOCOMOTIVES 1962	06	63	58
ROSTER OF MKT LOCOMOTIVES 1963 REVISION	12	63	61
ROSTER OF MKT LOCOMOTIVES 4-1968	11	68	54
ROSTER OF MKT LOCOMOTIVES 8-1974	05	75	39
ROSTER OF MKT LOCOS "KATY"	10	34	46
ROSTER OF MKT LOCOS: STEAM/DIESEL	02	48	115
ROSTER OF MM LOCOMOTIVES 10-1965	02	66	54
ROSTER OF MM LOCOMOTIVES 12-1970	05	71	57
ROSTER OF MN&S AUTO RAILERS	08	43	89
ROSTER OF MN&S DIESEL LOCOMOTIVES	07	79	29
ROSTER OF MN&S DIESEL LOCOMOTIVES	07	82	54
ROSTER OF MN&S LOCOMOTIVES 3-1965	07	65	53
ROSTER OF MN&S LOCOMOTIVES 6-1968	12	68	48
ROSTER OF MN&S LOCOMOTIVES 6-1973	11	73	62
ROSTER OF MN&S LOCOS: ALL-TIME	08	43	88
ROSTER OF MN&S MOTOR CARS	09	82	45
ROSTER OF MN&S MOTOR COACHES	08	43	89
ROSTER OF MN&S STEAM LOCOMOTIVES	09	82	45
ROSTER OF MNJ LOCOS: PRIOR TO 1880	10	43	89
ROSTER OF MO LOCOS: STEAM TANKS	12	55	33
ROSTER OF MON LOCOMOTIVES 3-1966	05	66	50
ROSTER OF MON LOCOMOTIVES 6-1970	02	71	59
ROSTER OF MON LOCOMOTIVES 7-1966	12	66	54
ROSTER OF MON LOCOMOTIVES 9-1969	03	70	64
ROSTER OF MON LOCOS	12	33	131
ROSTER OF MONT LOCOMOTIVES 3-1966	05	66	50
ROSTER OF MONT LOCOMOTIVES 9-1969	03	70	64
ROSTER OF MOVA LOCOMOTIVES 11-1962	08	63	60
ROSTER OF MOVA LOCOMOTIVES 9-1969	04	70	52
ROSTER OF MOVA LOCOS: #3, #5	12	34	84
ROSTER OF MOW LOCOMOTIVES 12-1968	05	69	50
ROSTER OF MOW LOCOMOTIVES 7-1965	12	65	28
ROSTER OF MP LOCOMOTIVES (POST RENUMBER)	01	69	46
ROSTER OF MP LOCOMOTIVES (PRE RENUMBER)	01	69	43
ROSTER OF MP LOCOMOTIVES 3-1960	08	60	29
ROSTER OF MP LOCOMOTIVES POST '62 RENUM1	08	75	53
ROSTER OF MP LOCOMOTIVES POST '62 RENUM2	09	75	49
ROSTER OF MP LOCOMOTIVES POST 1974 RENUM	09	75	50
ROSTER OF MP LOCOMOTIVES PRE-1962 RENUMB	08	75	51
ROSTER OF MP LOCOS: PART 1	03	38	60
ROSTER OF MP LOCOS: PART 2	04	38	67
ROSTER OF MP LOCOS: STEAM/DIESEL	09	51	98
ROSTER OF MP STEAM LOCOMOTIVES 1906	03	66	34
ROSTER OF MPR&DE LOCOS	08	43	88
ROSTER OF MRW LOCOMOTIVES 1961	02	61	22
ROSTER OF MRW RAIL MOTOR CARS 1961	02	61	22
ROSTER OF MSRI STEAM LOCOS 1961	02	61	61
ROSTER OF MSRW EQUIPMENT	08	53	76
ROSTER OF MT&W LOCOMOTIVES 7-1965	01	66	66
ROSTER OF MT&W LOCOMOTIVES 9-1970	05	71	58
ROSTER OF MTA ALL CARS 1961	02	61	40
ROSTER OF MTA FP10 LOCOMOTIVES	07	83	30
ROSTER OF MTA: RAPID TRANSIT/SURFACE LIN	03	52	82
ROSTER OF MUS LOCOMOTIVES 12-1969	07	70	41
ROSTER OF MUS LOCOMOTIVES 3-1966	08	66	64
ROSTER OF MV LOCOMOTIVES 10-1964	04	65	36
ROSTER OF MW DIESEL LOCOMOTIVES	07	79	29
ROSTER OF MW LOCOS	08	43	89
ROSTER OF MW MOTOR CARS	09	82	44
ROSTER OF MW MOTOR COACHES	08	43	89
ROSTER OF MWCOG LOCOMOTIVES 12-1973	08	74	55
ROSTER OF N&B LOCOMOTIVES 3-1966	05	66	51
ROSTER OF N&B LOCOMOTIVES 9-1969	03	70	64
ROSTER OF N&B LOCOS	11	36	59
ROSTER OF N&PBL LOCOMOTIVES 6-1970	04	71	51
ROSTER OF N&PBL LOCOMOTIVES 7-1966	10	66	52
ROSTER OF N&PBL LOCOS: STEAM	09	52	107
ROSTER OF N&SL LOCOMOTIVES 3-1969	08	69	52
ROSTER OF N&SL LOCOMOTIVES 6-1974	12	75	55
ROSTER OF N&SL LOCOMOTIVES 7-1963	02	64	54
ROSTER OF N&SS LOCOMOTIVES 1960	06	60	56
ROSTER OF N&SS LOCOMOTIVES 6-1969	12	69	47
ROSTER OF N&W ELECTRIC LOCOS 9-1961	02	62	58
ROSTER OF N&W LOCOMOTIVES	09	44	121
ROSTER OF N&W LOCOMOTIVES (REVISIONS)	08	69	64
ROSTER OF N&W LOCOMOTIVES 1-1961	08	61	49
ROSTER OF N&W LOCOMOTIVES 12-1968	06	69	30
ROSTER OF N&W LOCOMOTIVES CORRECTION.	07	69	56
ROSTER OF N&W LOCOMOTIVES CORRECTIONS 3	11	69	64
ROSTER OF N&W LOCOMOTIVES CORRECTIONS..	09	69	60
ROSTER OF N&W LOCOS	03	36	91
ROSTER OF N&W LOCOS SOLD TO D&RGW	10	45	49
ROSTER OF N&W LOCOS: STEAM	02	53	85
ROSTER OF N&W LOCOS: STEAM/S-T-E/DIESEL	08	56	59
ROSTER OF N&W STEAM LOCOS 1961	02	61	62
ROSTER OF NA LOCOMOTIVES 1-1969	11	69	43
ROSTER OF NA LOCOMOTIVES 12-1964	06	65	54
ROSTER OF NA LOCOS	04	41	113
ROSTER OF NA LOCOS: STEAM	02	55	47
ROSTER OF NA&S (OWNS NO LOCOMOTIVES)1965	08	65	65
ROSTER OF NC LOCOS	01	33	100
ROSTER OF NC&SL LOCOS	10	39	90
ROSTER OF NC&SL LOCOS: DIESELS	10	58	73
ROSTER OF NC&SL LOCOS: STEAM/DIESEL	01	52	109
ROSTER OF NCL EQUIPMENT W/DISPOSITION	06	44	114
ROSTER OF NCL PASSENGER CARS	06	44	114
ROSTER OF NCN LOCOS	11	34	96
ROSTER OF NCN LOCOS: 4 SERVICEABLE	10	36	74
ROSTER OF NCO LOCOS	07	35	82
ROSTER OF NCO LOCOS: STEAM	10	55	62
ROSTER OF NCTC LOCOMOTIVES 12-1969	05	70	50
ROSTER OF NCTC LOCOMOTIVES 3-1966	06	66	48
ROSTER OF NDEM LOCOMOTIVES	10	73	34
ROSTER OF NDEM LOCOMOTIVES 7-1968	03	69	37
ROSTER OF NDEM STEAM LOCOS 1961 STD & NA	06	61	26
ROSTER OF NEZ LOCOMOTIVES 10-1964	01	65	63
ROSTER OF NEZ LOCOMOTIVES 6-1967	12	67	48

Railroad/Railfan

RAILROAD HISTORIES & ROSTERS

ROSTERS BY RAILROAD	M	Y	P
ROSTER OF NEZ LOCOMOTIVES 6-1972	11	72	56
ROSTER OF NEZ STEAM LOCOS 1961	02	61	62
ROSTER OF NF LOCOS	08	38	81
ROSTER OF NF&D LOCOMOTIVES 3-1969	10	69	52
ROSTER OF NF&D LOCOMOTIVES 6-1970	04	71	51
ROSTER OF NH&I LOCOMOTIVES 9-1969	03	70	64
ROSTER OF NJ LOCOMOTIVES 10-1965	02	66	55
ROSTER OF NJ LOCOMOTIVES 12-1970	05	71	57
ROSTER OF NJ LOCOMOTIVES 3-1969	08	69	52
ROSTER OF NJ LOCOMOTIVES 6-1974	12	75	55
ROSTER OF NJ LOCOMOTIVES 7-1963	02	64	54
ROSTER OF NJ LOCOS: 2 DIESELS	04	59	58
ROSTER OF NJ&NY LOCOMOTIVES 3-1969	07	69	48
ROSTER OF NJ&NY LOCOMOTIVES 3-1974	10	74	49
ROSTER OF NJ&NY LOCOMOTIVES 7-1963	02	64	54
ROSTER OF NJ&NY LOCOS: OWNS NO MOTIVE PO	02	59	44
ROSTER OF NJEL EQUIPMENT	06	58	67
ROSTER OF NJI&I LOCOMOTIVES 6-1962	12	62	61
ROSTER OF NJI&I LOCOMOTIVES 9-1967	02	68	63
ROSTER OF NJM LOCOMOTIVES	11	43	126
ROSTER OF NJM LOCOS	07	43	100
ROSTER OF NJM LOCOS: PRIOR TO 1880	10	43	98
ROSTER OF NJUN LOCOMOTIVES 3-1969	08	69	52
ROSTER OF NJUN LOCOMOTIVES 6-1974	12	75	55
ROSTER OF NJUN LOCOMOTIVES 7-1963	02	64	54
ROSTER OF NKP LOCOMOTIVES (FINAL)	07	77	52
ROSTER OF NKP LOCOS	10	47	119
ROSTER OF NKP LOCOS (NYC&ST.L.)	04	34	88
ROSTER OF NKP LOCOS: DIESEL	04	58	70
ROSTER OF NKP LOCOS: STEAM	04	58	67
ROSTER OF NKP LOCOS: STEAM/DIESEL-ELECTR	08	53	100
ROSTER OF NL&G LOCOMOTIVES	04	78	49R
ROSTER OF NL&G LOCOMOTIVES 12-1964	05	65	50
ROSTER OF NL&G LOCOMOTIVES 3-1968	06	68	51
ROSTER OF NL&G LOCOMOTIVES 3-1973	07	73	59
ROSTER OF NN LOCOMOTIVES 10-1963	04	64	35
ROSTER OF NN LOCOMOTIVES 10-1968	04	69	54
ROSTER OF NN STEAM LOCOS 1961	02	61	61
ROSTER OF NO LOCOMOTIVES 10-1964	04	65	36
ROSTER OF NO LOCOMOTIVES 10-1965	03	66	59
ROSTER OF NO&LC LOCOMOTIVES 12-1964	05	65	50
ROSTER OF NO&LC LOCOMOTIVES 3-1968	06	68	51
ROSTER OF NO&LC LOCOMOTIVES 3-1973	07	73	58
ROSTER OF NO&NE LOCOS: PART 1 (S)	06	38	80
ROSTER OF NO&NE LOCOS: PART 2	07	38	134
ROSTER OF NOPB LOCOMOTIVES 12-1964	05	65	50
ROSTER OF NOPB LOCOMOTIVES 3-1968	06	68	51
ROSTER OF NOPB LOCOMOTIVES 3-1973	07	73	58
ROSTER OF NOPS TROLLEYS	11	81	51
ROSTER OF NOT LOCOMOTIVES 12-1964	05	65	50
ROSTER OF NOT LOCOMOTIVES 3-1968	06	68	51
ROSTER OF NOT LOCOMOTIVES 3-1973	07	73	59
ROSTER OF NOT&M LOCOS: PART 1 (MP)	03	38	60
ROSTER OF NOT&M LOCOS: PART 2	04	38	67
ROSTER OF NOUPT LOCOMOTIVES 12-1964	05	65	50
ROSTER OF NOUPT LOCOMOTIVES 3-1968	06	68	51
ROSTER OF NOUPT LOCOMOTIVES 3-1973	07	73	59
ROSTER OF NP LOCOMOTIVES 1-1963	10	63	37
ROSTER OF NP LOCOMOTIVES 3-1969	09	69	62
ROSTER OF NP LOCOS	05	47	118
ROSTER OF NP LOCOS: PART 1	05	39	114
ROSTER OF NP LOCOS: PART 2 (CONCLUSION)	06	39	78
ROSTER OF NP LOCOS: STEAM/DIESEL-ELECTRI	12	56	46
ROSTER OF NP STEAM LOCOS 1961	02	61	62
ROSTER OF NPC LOCOS	08	55	48
ROSTER OF NPIER LOCOMOTIVES 11-1962	08	63	60
ROSTER OF NPIER LOCOMOTIVES 9-1969	04	70	52
ROSTER OF NPTR LOCOMOTIVES 9-1969	02	70	50
ROSTER OF NS LOCOS	11	40	77
ROSTER OF NS LOCOS:	08	55	48
ROSTER OF NS&W LOCOMOTIVES	SP	77	46R
ROSTER OF NS&W STEAM LOCOMOTIVES	09	70	24
ROSTER OF NSO LOCOMOTIVES 12-1968	12	69	37
ROSTER OF NSO LOCOMOTIVES 4-1962	10	62	06
ROSTER OF NSO LOCOS: STEAM/DIESEL	05	52	109
ROSTER OF NTRR (OWNS NO LOCOMOTIVES)1964	10	64	62
ROSTER OF NTRR (OWNS NO LOCOMOTIVES)1967	07	67	64
ROSTER OF NTRR LOCOMOTIVES 9-1971	07	72	59
ROSTER OF NTRY (OWNS NO LOCOMOTIVES)1966	10	66	52
ROSTER OF NTRY LOCOMOTIVES 6-1970	04	71	52
ROSTER OF NU&R LOCOMOTIVES 12-1964	05	65	50
ROSTER OF NU&R LOCOMOTIVES 3-1968	06	68	51
ROSTER OF NU&R LOCOMOTIVES 3-1973	07	73	58
ROSTER OF NWP (OWNS NO LOCOMOTIVES) 1964	08	64	60
ROSTER OF NWP LOCOMOTIVES 3-1967	06	67	50
ROSTER OF NWP LOCOMOTIVES 6-1971	03	72	60
ROSTER OF NWP LOCOS WITH HISTORIES	04	36	37
ROSTER OF NWP LOCOS: STD/NARROW GAGE	08	55	46
ROSTER OF NY&LB LOCOMOTIVES 3-1969	07	69	48
ROSTER OF NY&LB LOCOMOTIVES 3-1974	10	74	49
ROSTER OF NY&LB LOCOS: OWNS NO MOTIVE PO	02	59	44
ROSTER OF NY&OM LOCOS	07	43	100
ROSTER OF NY&V LOCOMOTIVES (ALL TIME)	06	65	54
ROSTER OF NYC DIESEL LOCOMOTIVES 12-1962	06	62	54
ROSTER OF NYC ELECTRIC LOCOS 12-1961	06	62	54
ROSTER OF NYC EQUIP: GRAND CENTRAL TERMI	12	58	34
ROSTER OF NYC LOCOMOTIVES	07	33	84
ROSTER OF NYC LOCOMOTIVES	11	32	475
ROSTER OF NYC LOCOMOTIVES READER UPDATE	10	62	59
ROSTER OF NYC LOCOS	01	33	101
ROSTER OF NYC LOCOS	08	33	90
ROSTER OF NYC LOCOS: 4-6-2 & 0-10-0	02	35	85
ROSTER OF NYC LOCOS: CORRECTION/ADDITION	04	56	56
ROSTER OF NYC LOCOS: DISTRIBUTION 1956	02	56	79
ROSTER OF NYC LOCOS: ELECTRIC/DIESEL-ELE	02	56	76
ROSTER OF NYC LOCOS: LE&E DIVISON STEAM	11	49	103
ROSTER OF NYC LOCOS: P&LE DIVISION	11	49	102
ROSTER OF NYC LOCOS: PART 1	05	40	81
ROSTER OF NYC LOCOS: PART 2	06	40	113
ROSTER OF NYC LOCOS: PART 3	07	40	84

Railroad/Railfan

RAILROAD HISTORIES & ROSTERS

ROSTERS BY RAILROAD	M	Y	P
ROSTER OF NYC LOCOS: PART 4	08	40	128
ROSTER OF NYC LOCOS: STEAM POST WAR RE-#	02	56	67
ROSTER OF NYC LOCOS: STEAM	12	55	68
ROSTER OF NYC MARINE EQUIPMENT	03	41	72
ROSTER OF NYC STEAM LOCOS 1961	02	61	61
ROSTER OF NYC&SL STEAM LOCOS 1961	02	61	61
ROSTER OF NYCRR LOCOMOTIVES (NONE)	04	64	54
ROSTER OF NYCRR LOCOMOTIVES 3-1969	08	69	52
ROSTER OF NYCRR LOCOMOTIVES 6-1974	12	75	55
ROSTER OF NYCS EQUIPMENT	06	57	64
ROSTER OF NYD LOCOMOTIVES 3-1969	08	69	52
ROSTER OF NYD LOCOMOTIVES 7-1963	02	64	54
ROSTER OF NYNH&H DIESEL LOCOS 10-1960	04	61	38
ROSTER OF NYNH&H ELECTRIC LOCOS 10-1960	04	61	38
ROSTER OF NYNH&H EQUIP: GRAND CENTRAL TE	12	58	34
ROSTER OF NYNH&H LOCO CORRECTION (4-69)	12	69	50
ROSTER OF NYNH&H LOCOMOTIVES	10	32	351
ROSTER OF NYNH&H LOCOMOTIVES	03	33	92
ROSTER OF NYNH&H LOCOMOTIVES 10-1968	04	69	52
ROSTER OF NYNH&H LOCOMOTIVES 10-1977	02	78	34
ROSTER OF NYNH&H LOCOMOTIVES UPDATE	07	69	58
ROSTER OF NYNH&H LOCOS	01	39	125
ROSTER OF NYNH&H LOCOS: ADDITIONS SINCE	03	43	102
ROSTER OF NYNH&H LOCOS: STEAM/DIESEL/ELE	02	52	94
ROSTER OF NYNH&H MU UNITS 10-1960	04	61	38
ROSTER OF NYO&W LOCOS PART 1 ALL-TIME	05	43	107
ROSTER OF NYO&W LOCOS PART 2 ALL-TIME	06	43	121
ROSTER OF NYO&W LOCOS PART 3 ALL-TIME	07	43	96
ROSTER OF NYO&W MOTIVE POWER 1932	04	32	36
ROSTER OF NYS&W (ERIE) STEAM LOCOS 1919	01	66	57
ROSTER OF NYS&W DIESEL LOCOMOTIVES 2-87	05	87	56
ROSTER OF NYS&W EQUIPMENT	04	41	73
ROSTER OF NYS&W LOCOMOTIVES 3-1969	07	69	50
ROSTER OF NYS&W LOCOMOTIVES 3-1974	10	74	49
ROSTER OF NYS&W LOCOS AND RAIL CARS	02	41	69
ROSTER OF NYS&W LOCOS: ALL-TIME	11	43	122
ROSTER OF NYS&W LOCOS: DIESELS 1958	02	59	44
ROSTER OF NYS&W LOCOS: ERIE RENUMBERED	11	43	126
ROSTER OF NYS&W LOCOS: HISTORICAL ROSTER	10	43	97
ROSTER OF NYS&W LOCOS: PRIOR TO 1890	10	43	98
ROSTER OF NYS&W STEAM LOCOS CORRECTION	05	66	55
ROSTER OF O&LC LOCOMOTIVES ALL TIME	04	63	58
ROSTER OF O&N LOCOMOTIVES 3-1969	08	69	52
ROSTER OF O&N LOCOMOTIVES 6-1974	12	75	55
ROSTER OF O&NW LOCOMOTIVES 12-1965	04	66	58
ROSTER OF O&NW LOCOMOTIVES 9-1969	02	70	50
ROSTER OF OB&PA LOCOMOTIVES	F	75	32R
ROSTER OF OB&PA LOCOMOTIVES 6-1974	12	75	55
ROSTER OF OC&E LOCOMOTIVES 12-1965	04	66	58
ROSTER OF OC&E LOCOMOTIVES 9-1969	02	70	50
ROSTER OF OCITY LOCOMOTIVES 10-1965	03	66	59
ROSTER OF OCJR (OWNS NO LOCOMOTIVES)1965	03	66	59
ROSTER OF OCJR LOCOMOTIVES 3-1969	01	70	10
ROSTER OF OL&B LOCOMOTIVES 12-1973	08	74	55
ROSTER OF OL&B LOCOMOTIVES 5-1965	11	65	55
ROSTER OF OL&B LOCOMOTIVES 9-1968	03	69	66
ROSTER OF ON LOCOMOITIVES 3-1969	01	70	46
ROSTER OF ON LOCOMOTIVES 3-1965	07	65	53
ROSTER OF ON LOCOS: ALL-TIME	01	55	44
ROSTER OF OP&E LOCOMOTIVES 12-1965	04	66	58
ROSTER OF ORW STREETCARS/INTERURBANS/OTH	06	45	81
ROSTER OF OSL LOCOMOTIVES	07	47	115
ROSTER OF OSL LOCOS	05	33	84
ROSTER OF OT LOCOMOTIVES 3-1964	08	64	60
ROSTER OF OT LOCOMOTIVES 3-1967	06	67	50
ROSTER OF OT LOCOMOTIVES 6-1971	03	72	60
ROSTER OF OUR&D LOCOMOTIVES (NONE) 1963	04	64	35
ROSTER OF OUR&D LOCOMOTIVES 3-1970	12	70	60
ROSTER OF OWR&N LOCOMOTIVES	07	47	115
ROSTER OF OWR&N LOCOS	05	33	84
ROSTER OF P&BR LOCOMOTIVES 3-1968	09	68	44
ROSTER OF P&BR LOCOMOTIVES 6-1964	11	64	62
ROSTER OF P&BRRR LOCOMOTIVES 3-1973	01	74	46
ROSTER OF P&D LOCOMOTIVES ALL TIME	08	62	51
ROSTER OF P&EA LOCOMOTIVES 6-1962	12	62	61
ROSTER OF P&EA LOCOMOTIVES 9-1967	02	68	63
ROSTER OF P&EA LOCOMOTIVES 9-1972	01	73	57
ROSTER OF P&EA LOCOS: DIESELS 1959	10	59	73
ROSTER OF P&EA LOCOS: PART 1 NYC	05	40	81
ROSTER OF P&EA LOCOS: PART 2 NYC	06	40	113
ROSTER OF P&F LOCOMOTIVES 1960	06	60	57
ROSTER OF P&F LOCOMOTIVES 6-1969	12	69	47
ROSTER OF P&IR (OWNS NO LOCOMOTIVES)1964	04	65	52
ROSTER OF P&IR LOCOMOTIVES 3-1973	10	73	62
ROSTER OF P&IR LOCOMOTIVES 9-1967	03	68	56
ROSTER OF P&IR LOCOMOTIVES 9-1972	01	73	57
ROSTER OF P&IR LOCOS: OWNS NO MOTIVE POW	10	59	73
ROSTER OF P&LE 134 LOCOS BUILT 1895-1915	06	62	36
ROSTER OF P&LE LOCOMOTIVES 1960	06	60	57
ROSTER OF P&LE LOCOMOTIVES 6-1969	12	69	47
ROSTER OF P&LE LOCOMOTIVES 9-1969	03	70	65
ROSTER OF P&LE LOCOS	02	36	90
ROSTER OF P&LE LOCOS: PART 1 NYC	05	40	81
ROSTER OF P&LE LOCOS: PART 2 NYC	06	40	113
ROSTER OF P&LE LOCOS: STEAM/DIESEL	11	49	102
ROSTER OF P&LE U28B DIESELS	11	86	54
ROSTER OF P&N DIESEL-ELECTRIC LOCOMOTIVE	03	65	52
ROSTER OF P&N ELECTRIC LOCOMOTIVES	03	65	52
ROSTER OF P&N LOCOMOTIVES 1-1964	08	64	37
ROSTER OF P&N LOCOMOTIVES 12-1969	05	70	50
ROSTER OF P&N LOCOMOTIVES 3-1966	06	66	48
ROSTER OF P&N LOCOMOTIVES 3-1969	10	69	52
ROSTER OF P&N LOCOMOTIVES CORRECTION	05	65	59
ROSTER OF P&N PASSENGER EQUIPMENT	03	65	52
ROSTER OF P&NW LOCOMOTIVES 12-1963	06	64	48
ROSTER OF P&NW LOCOMOTIVES 12-1966	05	67	55
ROSTER OF P&NW LOCOMOTIVES 6-1971	03	72	59
ROSTER OF P&NW STEAM LOCOS 1961	02	61	62
ROSTER OF P&OV LOCOMOTIVES 3-1966	05	66	51
ROSTER OF P&OV LOCOMOTIVES 9-1969	03	70	65

STEPHANS' RAILROAD DIRECTORY

Railroad/Railfan

RAILROAD HISTORIES & ROSTERS

ROSTERS BY RAILROAD	M	Y	P
ROSTER OF P&PU LOCOMOTIVES 9-1967	03	68	56
ROSTER OF P&PU LOCOMOTIVES 9-1972	01	73	57
ROSTER OF P&PU LOCOS: DIESELS 1959	10	59	73
ROSTER OF P&SR LOCOMOTIVES 3-1964	08	64	60
ROSTER OF P&SR LOCOMOTIVES 3-1967	06	67	51
ROSTER OF P&SR LOCOMOTIVES 6-1971	03	72	60
ROSTER OF P&SR LOCOS: DIESEL	08	58	69
ROSTER OF P&SR PASSENGER EQUIPMENT	05	48	100
ROSTER OF P&W LOCOMOTIVES 6-1973	10	73	13
ROSTER OF P&WV LOCOMOTIVES 1960	06	60	57
ROSTER OF P&WV LOCOS	01	35	88
ROSTER OF P&WV LOCOS: ISSUED MARCH 1949	12	49	106
ROSTER OF PA&AT LOCOMOTIVES 3-1969	07	69	50
ROSTER OF PA&AT LOCOMOTIVES 3-1974	10	74	49
ROSTER OF PA&MR LOCOMOTIVES 3-1966	05	66	51
ROSTER OF PA&MR LOCOMOTIVES 9-1969	03	70	65
ROSTER OF PAN LOCOS: STEAM/DIESEL	03	48	114
ROSTER OF PARR LOCOMOTIVES 3-1967	06	67	50
ROSTER OF PARR LOCOMOTIVES 6-1971	03	72	60
ROSTER OF PATH LOCOMOTIVES 7-1963	02	64	55
ROSTER OF PB LOCOMOTIVES 10-1973	05	74	59
ROSTER OF PB&NE LOCOMOTIVES 3-1966	05	66	51
ROSTER OF PB&NE LOCOMOTIVES 9-1969	03	70	64
ROSTER OF PC 1 ALL TIME	08	76	42
ROSTER OF PC 2 ALL TIME	09	76	20
ROSTER OF PC 3 ALL TIME	10	76	52
ROSTER OF PC 4 ALL TIME	11	76	50
ROSTER OF PC 5 ALL TIME	12	76	52
ROSTER OF PC 6 ALL TIME	01	77	58
ROSTER OF PC 7 ALL TIME	02	77	45
ROSTER OF PC LOCOS (ACTIVE UNITS) 2-75	12	76	51
ROSTER OF PC&N LOCOMOTIVES 3-1970	11	70	41
ROSTER OF PC&N LOCOMOTIVES 7-1966	09	66	47
ROSTER OF PC&Y LOCOMOTIVES 3-1966	05	66	51
ROSTER OF PC&Y LOCOMOTIVES 9-1969	03	70	65
ROSTER OF PC&Y LOCOS	09	43	137
ROSTER OF PCOA LOCOMOTIVES	08	33	90
ROSTER OF PCOA LOCOS	10	35	87
ROSTER OF PCOAST (OWNS NO EQUIPMENT)1962	08	62	29
ROSTER OF PCOAST LOCOMOTIVES 6-1970	06	71	37
ROSTER OF PCOAST LOCOS	03	34	88
ROSTER OF PE LOCOMOTIVES 3-1964	08	64	60
ROSTER OF PE LOCOS: DIESELS	08	58	69
ROSTER OF PERB LOCOMOTIVES 3-1970	11	70	41
ROSTER OF PETE LOCOMOTIVES 9-1967	03	68	56
ROSTER OF PETE LOCOMOTIVES 9-1972	01	73	57
ROSTER OF PETE LOCOS: 1 DIESEL 1959	10	59	73
ROSTER OF PEV LOCOMOTIVES 10-1964	12	64	32
ROSTER OF PGE LOCOMOTIVES 3-1965	08	65	54
ROSTER OF PGE LOCOMOTIVES 5-1969	11	69	43
ROSTER OF PGE LOCOS: ALL-TIME STEAM/DIES	03	55	39
ROSTER OF PGE LOCOS: STEAM/DIESEL	05	50	65
ROSTER OF PGE MOTIVE POWER	02	33	87
ROSTER OF PH&D LOCOMOTIVES 3-1965	06	65	55
ROSTER OF PH&D LOCOMOTIVES 6-1968	10	68	39
ROSTER OF PH&D LOCOMOTIVES 6-1973	03	74	47
ROSTER OF PHBL (OWNS NO LOCOMOTIVES)1966	05	66	51
ROSTER OF PHBL LOCOMOTIVES 9-1969	03	70	64
ROSTER OF PI LOCOMOTIVES 12-1969	05	70	50
ROSTER OF PI LOCOMOTIVES 3-1966	06	66	48
ROSTER OF PI&SH LOCOMOTIVES 3-1966	05	66	51
ROSTER OF PI&SH LOCOMOTIVES 9-1969	03	70	65
ROSTER OF PI&SH LOCOS: DIESELS	08	55	42
ROSTER OF PIT CARS AND BARNS IN USE	03	54	69
ROSTER OF PIT PASSENGER CARS	05	44	104
ROSTER OF PIT PASSENGER EQUIPMENT	05	44	104
ROSTER OF PIT PCC CARS (ALL TIME)	12	61	54
ROSTER OF PIT SERVICE CARS	12	61	54
ROSTER OF PM LOCOMOTIVES	01	33	102
ROSTER OF PM LOCOS	11	35	88
ROSTER OF PM&Y LOCOS	02	36	90
ROSTER OF POTB LOCOMOTIVES 9-1969	02	70	50
ROSTER OF PR LOCOS	01	41	136
ROSTER OF PR LOCOS (CORRECTION) LOCO #2	03	41	78
ROSTER OF PRES STEAM LOCOS 1961	02	61	62
ROSTER OF PRR ELECTRIC LOCOS ALL TIME	10	62	33
ROSTER OF PRR LOCOS	06	33	92
ROSTER OF PRR LOCOS 4-4-2/2-10-2/4-4-2	10	34	84
ROSTER OF PRR LOCOS ASSIGNED TO PRSL	08	67	23
ROSTER OF PRR LOCOS CLASS 65S CORREC DEC	02	40	122
ROSTER OF PRR LOCOS-MALLETS	01	33	100
ROSTER OF PRR LOCOS: CLASS 6B1/L5/O1/P5A	05	39	69
ROSTER OF PRR LOCOS: ELECTRIC	01	42	58
ROSTER OF PRR LOCOS: ELECTRIC ENGINE #S	10	42	61
ROSTER OF PRR LOCOS: PART 1	07	41	57
ROSTER OF PRR LOCOS: PART 2 (#1-#3499)	08	41	50
ROSTER OF PRR LOCOS: PART 3 (#3500-9999)	09	41	89
ROSTER OF PRR LOCOS: PART 4 0-4-0 TO 2-8	10	41	60
ROSTER OF PRR LOCOS: PART 5 2-10-2 THRU	11	41	77
ROSTER OF PRR LOCOS: STEAM/ELECT/DSL/GAS	12	54	22
ROSTER OF PRR LOCOS: STEAM/ELECTRIC	08	57	36
ROSTER OF PRR LOCOS: STREAMLINED ELECTRI	12	35	82
ROSTER OF PRR STEAM HOGS (CLASS R & H3)	12	74	61
ROSTER OF PRR STEAM LOCOS 1961	02	61	62
ROSTER OF PRR STEAM LOCOS NORTHUMBERLAND	10	63	31
ROSTER OF PRR: DIESEL-ELECTRIC LOCOS	08	57	55
ROSTER OF PRRCO STEAM LOCOMOTIVES	10	73	35
ROSTER OF PRSL DIESEL LOCOMOTIVES	08	67	23
ROSTER OF PRSL GAS-ELECTRIC CARS	12	41	59
ROSTER OF PRSL LOCOMOTIVES 3-1969	07	69	50
ROSTER OF PRSL LOCOMOTIVES 3-1974	10	74	49
ROSTER OF PRSL LOCOS	12	41	59
ROSTER OF PRSL LOCOS: DIESELS 1958	02	59	44
ROSTER OF PRV LOCOMOTIVES 10-1973	05	74	59
ROSTER OF PRV LOCOMOTIVES 3-1965	08	65	65
ROSTER OF PRV LOCOMOTIVES 6-1968	03	69	38
ROSTER OF PS&SV LOCOMOTIVES (ALL TIME)	05	86	54
ROSTER OF PSCT EQUIPMENT	06	58	67
ROSTER OF PSL LOCOS: 3 DIESELS 1959	10	59	73
ROSTER OF PST PASSENGER CARS 1960	12	60	54

Railroad/Railfan

RAILROAD HISTORIES & ROSTERS

ROSTERS BY RAILROAD	M	Y	P
ROSTER OF PST WORK CARS 1960	12	60	54
ROSTER OF PT LOCOMOTIVES	07	78	42R
ROSTER OF PT LOCOMOTIVES 11-1962	08	63	60
ROSTER OF PT LOCOMOTIVES 12-1965	04	66	58
ROSTER OF PT LOCOMOTIVES 3-1968	07	68	57
ROSTER OF PT LOCOMOTIVES 9-1969	02	70	50
ROSTER OF PT LOCOS	02	35	87
ROSTER OF PT LOCOS	09	46	98
ROSTER OF PT LOCOS: DIESELS	10	58	69
ROSTER OF PT STEAM LOCOMOTIVES	09	78	38R
ROSTER OF PTC SUBWAY CARS	04	58	62
ROSTER OF PTE LOCOMOTIVES 6-1967	10	67	50
ROSTER OF PTE LOCOMOTIVES 12-1971	08	72	57
ROSTER OF PTER LOCOMOTIVES 12-1965	04	66	58
ROSTER OF PTER STEAM LOCOS 1961	02	61	62
ROSTER OF PTO LOCOMOTIVES 3-1962	08	62	29
ROSTER OF PTO LOCOMOTIVES 6-1970	06	71	37
ROSTER OF PTR LOCOMOTIVES 12-1965	04	66	58
ROSTER OF PTR LOCOMOTIVES 3-1973	06	73	11
ROSTER OF PTR LOCOMOTIVES 9-1969	02	70	50
ROSTER OF PTRA (OWNS NO LOCOMOTIVES)1966	09	66	47
ROSTER OF PTRA LOCOMOTIVES 3-1970	11	70	41
ROSTER OF PUD&R (OWNS NO LOCOS) 1964	10	64	62
ROSTER OF PUD&R LOCOMOTIVES 3-1967	07	67	64
ROSTER OF PUD&R LOCOMOTIVES 9-1971	07	72	59
ROSTER OF PULLMAN CARS USED ON CRESCENT	10	77	55
ROSTER OF PVS LOCOMOTIVES 3-1970	11	70	41
ROSTER OF PVS LOCOMOTIVES 7-1966	09	66	47
ROSTER OF Q LOCOMOTIVES 3-1964	08	64	60
ROSTER OF Q LOCOMOTIVES 3-1967	06	67	51
ROSTER OF Q LOCOMOTIVES 6-1971	03	72	60
ROSTER OF Q STEAM LOCOS 1961	02	61	62
ROSTER OF QA&P (OWNS NO LOCOMOTIVES)1966	09	66	47
ROSTER OF QA&P LOCOMOTIVES 3-1970	11	70	41
ROSTER OF QC (NO LOCOMOTIVES 1962)	08	63	60
ROSTER OF QC LOCOMOTIVES 10-1965	02	66	55
ROSTER OF QC LOCOMOTIVES 12-1970	05	71	57
ROSTER OF QC LOCOMOTIVES 6-1970	12	70	56
ROSTER OF QC LOCOS	09	47	127
ROSTER OF QC LOCOS: #1-67	01	40	115
ROSTER OF QC LOCOS: ADDITIONS	03	54	18
ROSTER OF QC LOCOS: STEAM	09	53	39
ROSTER OF QNC&L LOCOMOTIVES 10-1965	02	66	55
ROSTER OF QNS&L LOCOMOTIVES 12-1970	05	71	57
ROSTER OF R LOCOMOTIVES 5-1969	11	69	46
ROSTER OF R LOCOMOTIVES 6-1961	12	61	30
ROSTER OF R LOCOS	01	33	100
ROSTER OF R LOCOS PART 1	01	38	73
ROSTER OF R LOCOS PART 2	02	38	118
ROSTER OF R LOCOS: 4-4-2 TYPES	02	33	81
ROSTER OF R LOCOS: PART 1	05	44	43
ROSTER OF R LOCOS: PART 2	06	44	115
ROSTER OF R LOCOS: STEAM/DIESEL	03	53	110
ROSTER OF R MU EQUIPMENT	08	58	52
ROSTER OF R STEAM LOCOS 1961	02	61	62
ROSTER OF R&R LOCOMOTIVES 12-1969	05	70	50
ROSTER OF R&R LOCOMOTIVES 3-1966	06	66	48
ROSTER OF R&R STEAM LOCOS 1961	02	61	63
ROSTER OF R&S LOCOMOTIVES 10-1965	02	66	55
ROSTER OF R&S LOCOMOTIVES 12-1970	05	71	58
ROSTER OF RF TANK CARS	01	30	209
ROSTER OF RF&P LOCOMOTIVES 3-1967	09	67	65
ROSTER OF RF&P LOCOMOTIVES 6-1970	04	71	52
ROSTER OF RF&P LOCOMOTIVES 7-1966	10	66	52
ROSTER OF RF&P LOCOS	11	32	554
ROSTER OF RF&P LOCOS: STEAM/DIESEL	03	52	102
ROSTER OF RG LOCOS: CORRECTIONS	02	43	139
ROSTER OF RG LOCOS: PART 1 MAR 1871-1942	12	42	127
ROSTER OF RG LOCOS: PART 2	01	43	104
ROSTER OF RG LOCOS: PART 3 NARROW GAGE	02	43	82
ROSTER OF RGC LOCOS: PART 1 (MP)	03	38	60
ROSTER OF RGC LOCOS: PART 2	04	38	67
ROSTER OF RI DIESEL-ELECTRIC EQUIPMENT	07	43	66
ROSTER OF RI LOCOMOTIVES	10	32	351
ROSTER OF RI LOCOMOTIVES 1-1966	01	67	41
ROSTER OF RI LOCOMOTIVES 12-1959	04	60	57
ROSTER OF RI LOCOMOTIVES 7-1972	03	73	60
ROSTER OF RI LOCOS	09	35	89
ROSTER OF RI LOCOS: DIESELS 1959	12	59	44
ROSTER OF RI LOCOS: STEAM/DIESEL	04	49	109
ROSTER OF RI MOTOR CARS	04	66	22
ROSTER OF RI STEAM LOCOMOTIVES 8-1912	04	66	59
ROSTER OF RIVT LOCOMOTIVES 1960	06	60	57
ROSTER OF RIVT LOCOMOTIVES 6-1969	12	69	48
ROSTER OF ROADS NOT IN OFFICIAL GUIDE 02	10	62	54
ROSTER OF ROADS NOT IN OFFICIAL GUIDE 03	12	62	54
ROSTER OF ROADS NOT IN OFFICIAL GUIDE 04	02	63	50
ROSTER OF ROADS NOT IN OFFICIAL GUIDE 06	06	63	60
ROSTER OF ROADS NOT IN OFFICIAL GUIDE 08	08	63	57
ROSTER OF ROADS NOT IN OFFICIAL GUIDE 09	10	63	58
ROSTER OF ROADS NOT IN OFFICIAL GUIDE 10	12	63	52
ROSTER OF ROADS NOT IN OFFICIAL GUIDE 11	02	64	38
ROSTER OF ROADS NOT IN OFFICIAL GUIDE RE	02	64	39
ROSTER OF ROCKRR (OWNS NO LOCOS) 1964	08	64	37
ROSTER OF ROCKRR LOCOMOTIVES 3-1969	10	69	52
ROSTER OF RR LOCOMOTIVES 3-1969	07	69	50
ROSTER OF RR LOCOMOTIVES 3-1974	10	74	49
ROSTER OF RR LOCOS: 6 DIESELS 1958	02	59	44
ROSTER OF RR LOCOS: 7 STEAM BALDWINS	03	35	89
ROSTER OF RRR LOCOMOTIVES 12-1966	05	67	55
ROSTER OF RRR LOCOMOTIVES 6-1971	03	72	59
ROSTER OF RRR STEAM LOCOS 12-1963	06	64	48
ROSTER OF RRR STEAM LOCOS 1961	02	61	62
ROSTER OF RS&P LOCOMOTIVES 3-1970	11	70	41
ROSTER OF RS&P LOCOMOTIVES 7-1966	09	66	47
ROSTER OF RS&S LOCOMOTIVES 3-1970	11	70	41
ROSTER OF RS&S LOCOMOTIVES 7-1966	09	66	47
ROSTER OF RT LOCOMOTIVES 6-1970	04	71	52
ROSTER OF RT LOCOMOTIVES 7-1966	10	66	52
ROSTER OF RTC EQUIPMENT	10	48	89

Railroad/ Railfan

RAILROAD HISTORIES & ROSTERS

ROSTERS BY RAILROAD	M	Y	P
ROSTER OF RTCM (OWNS NO LOCOMOTIVES)1965	07	65	53
ROSTER OF RTCM LOCOMOTIVES 6-1968	12	68	48
ROSTER OF RTCM LOCOMOTIVES 6-1973	11	73	62
ROSTER OF RU LOCOMOTIVES	08	46	33
ROSTER OF RU LOCOMOTIVES 11-1962	08	63	60
ROSTER OF RU LOCOMOTIVES 7-1963	02	64	55
ROSTER OF RU LOCOS	11	33	130
ROSTER OF RU LOCOS: DIESEL 1958	06	59	65
ROSTER OF RU STEAM LOCOMOTIVES 1946	04	70	26
ROSTER OF RV LOCOMOTIVES 3-1969	07	69	50
ROSTER OF RV LOCOMOTIVES 3-1974	10	74	49
ROSTER OF RV LOCOS: 2 DIESELS 1958	02	59	44
ROSTER OF S LOCOMOTIVES 1-1960	10	62	52
ROSTER OF S LOCOS PART 1: STEAM	03	50	105
ROSTER OF S LOCOS PART 2: DIESELS	04	50	114
ROSTER OF S LOCOS: 1905-14/1509/1516/	03	35	86
ROSTER OF S LOCOS: PART 1 INCL SUBSIDIAR	06	38	81
ROSTER OF S LOCOS: PART 2 INCL SUBSIDIAR	07	38	134
ROSTER OF S LOCOS: SOME SCRAPPED	04	41	46
ROSTER OF S&A LOCOMOTIVES 10-1964	02	65	56
ROSTER OF S&A LOCOMOTIVES 3-1972	10	72	46
ROSTER OF S&A LOCOMOTIVES 6-1967	11	67	48
ROSTER OF S&C LOCOMOTIVES 1-1961	02	62	32
ROSTER OF S&C LOCOMOTIVES 10-1966	02	67	48
ROSTER OF S&C LOCOMOTIVES 12-1970	07	71	53
ROSTER OF S&C STEAM LOCOS 1961	02	61	63
ROSTER OF S&H LOCOMOTIVES 3-1966	05	66	51
ROSTER OF S&H LOCOMOTIVES 9-1969	03	70	65
ROSTER OF S&L LOCOMOTIVES 10-1965	02	66	55
ROSTER OF S&L LOCOMOTIVES 8-1975	10	77	34
ROSTER OF S&L LOCOS: STEAM	06	56	69
ROSTER OF SAL LOCOS	05	35	89
ROSTER OF SAL LOCOS/RAILCARS 1958	06	59	69
ROSTER OF SAL LOCOS: DIESEL ELECTRICS	11	40	67
ROSTER OF SAL LOCOS: STEAM/DIESEL	09	48	114
ROSTER OF SAND LOCOMOTIVES 10-1964	02	65	56
ROSTER OF SAND LOCOMOTIVES 3-1972	10	72	46
ROSTER OF SAND LOCOMOTIVES 6-1967	11	67	48
ROSTER OF SAS LOCOS: PART 1 (MP)	03	38	60
ROSTER OF SAS LOCOS: PART 2	04	38	67
ROSTER OF SAU&G LOCOS: PART 1 (MP)	03	38	60
ROSTER OF SAU&G LOCOS: PART 2	04	38	67
ROSTER OF SB&RGV LOCOS: PART 1 (MP)	03	38	60
ROSTER OF SB&RGV LOCOS: PART 2	04	38	67
ROSTER OF SBC STEAM LOCOMOTIVES	10	73	35
ROSTER OF SBELT LOCOMOTIVES 3-1964	08	64	61
ROSTER OF SBELT LOCOMOTIVES 3-1967	06	67	51
ROSTER OF SBR LOCOMOTIVES 3-1969	08	69	52
ROSTER OF SBR LOCOMOTIVES 6-1974	12	75	55
ROSTER OF SBR LOCOMOTIVES 7-1963	02	64	55
ROSTER OF SBUF LOCOMOTIVES 3-1969	08	69	52
ROSTER OF SBUF LOCOMOTIVES 6-1974	12	75	55
ROSTER OF SBUF LOCOMOTIVES 7-1963	02	64	55
ROSTER OF SC&M LOCOMOTIVES 6-1970	02	71	59
ROSTER OF SC&M LOCOMOTIVES 7-1966	12	66	54

ROSTERS BY RAILROAD	M	Y	P
ROSTER OF SCA EQUIPMENT	04	48	98
ROSTER OF SCT LOCOMOTIVES 10-1964	02	65	58
ROSTER OF SCT LOCOMOTIVES 1972	05	73	56
ROSTER OF SCT LOCOMOTIVES 6-1967	01	68	57
ROSTER OF SCTC LOCOS: PART 1	09	37	82
* ROSTER OF SCTC LOCOS: PART 2	10	34	124
ROSTER OF SCTC LOCOS: PART 3	11	37	77
ROSTER OF SCTC LOCOS: PART 4	12	37	77
ROSTER OF SD&AE (OWNS NO LOCS) 1967	06	67	51
ROSTER OF SD&AE LOCOMOTIVES 6-1971	03	72	61
ROSTER OF SD&AE LOCOS	07	35	88
ROSTER OF SD&AE LOCOS CORRECTION	11	35	86
ROSTER OF SD&AE LOCOS: 6 DIESELS	12	55	38
ROSTER OF SD&AE LOCOS: STEAM/LEASED DIES	06	56	61
ROSTER OF SD&AE(OWNS NO LOCOMOTIVES)1964	08	64	60
ROSTER OF SEM PASSENGER CARS	11	47	115
ROSTER OF SEM WORK CARS	11	47	115
ROSTER OF SFB LOCOMOTIVES 6-1971	03	72	61
ROSTER OF SG LOCOMOTIVES 1-1960	10	62	53
ROSTER OF SG LOCOMOTIVES 10-1964	12	64	32
ROSTER OF SG LOCOMOTIVES 10-1964	02	65	56
ROSTER OF SG LOCOMOTIVES 12-1971	08	72	57
ROSTER OF SG LOCOMOTIVES 3-1972	10	72	46
ROSTER OF SG LOCOMOTIVES 6-1967	11	67	48
ROSTER OF SG LOCOMOTIVES 6-1967	10	67	50
ROSTER OF SH LOCOS: 2 SERVICEABLE	10	36	74
ROSTER OF SHORTLINE LOCOMOTIVES (A)	03	75	44
ROSTER OF SHORTLINE LOCOMOTIVES (A) CORR	05	75	64
ROSTER OF SHORTLINE LOCOMOTIVES (A-B)	04	75	47
ROSTER OF SHORTLINE LOCOMOTIVES (A-B) CO	06	75	64
ROSTER OF SHORTLINE LOCOMOTIVES (B-C)	06	75	52
ROSTER OF SHORTLINE LOCOMOTIVES (C)	10	75	43
ROSTER OF SHORTLINE LOCOMOTIVES (C-D)	04	77	56
ROSTER OF SHORTLINE LOCOMOTIVES (CH-CO)	11	75	49
ROSTER OF SHORTLINE LOCOMOTIVES (D-F)	10	77	34
ROSTER OF SHORTLINE LOCOMOTIVES (F-G)	01	78	54
ROSTER OF SHORTLINE LOCOMOTIVES (G)	03	78	54
ROSTER OF SHORTLINE LOCOMOTIVES (G-I)	10	78	57
ROSTER OF SHORTLINE LOCOMOTIVES (I-K)	07	78	62
ROSTER OF SHORTLINE LOCOMOTIVES (L)	01	79	51
ROSTER OF SHORTLINE LOCOMOTIVES (L-M)	11	78	57
ROSTER OF SHORTLINE LOCOMOTIVES (M)	07	79	29
ROSTER OF SHORTLINES IN ALABAMA	02	67	48
ROSTER OF SHORTLINES IN ALABAMA 1971	07	71	52
ROSTER OF SHORTLINES IN ALABAMA CORRECTI	05	67	53
ROSTER OF SHORTLINES IN ALASKA 1967	03	67	64
ROSTER OF SHORTLINES IN ARIZONA 1967	04	67	39
ROSTER OF SHORTLINES IN ARIZONA 1971	10	71	46
ROSTER OF SHORTLINES IN ARKANSAS	06	64	48
ROSTER OF SHORTLINES IN ARKANSAS 1967	05	67	54
ROSTER OF SHORTLINES IN ARKANSAS 1972	03	72	58
ROSTER OF SHORTLINES IN ARKANSAS ADDS	06	72	66
ROSTER OF SHORTLINES IN CALIFORNIA	08	64	60
ROSTER OF SHORTLINES IN CALIFORNIA 1967	06	67	50
ROSTER OF SHORTLINES IN CALIFORNIA 1972	03	72	59
* ROSTER OF SCTC: PART 2	10	37	124

Railroad/ Railfan

RAILROAD HISTORIES & ROSTERS

ROSTERS BY RAILROAD	M	Y	P
ROSTER OF SHORTLINES IN CALIFORNIA CORRE	11	64	62
ROSTER OF SHORTLINES IN CANADA	02	66	54
ROSTER OF SHORTLINES IN CANADA 1971	05	71	57
ROSTER OF SHORTLINES IN CANADA CORRECT	08	71	66
ROSTER OF SHORTLINES IN COLORADO	10	64	62
ROSTER OF SHORTLINES IN COLORADO 1967	07	67	64
ROSTER OF SHORTLINES IN COLORADO 1972	07	72	59
ROSTER OF SHORTLINES IN CONNECTICUT 1967	08	67	64
ROSTER OF SHORTLINES IN CONNECTICUT 1972	06	72	50
ROSTER OF SHORTLINES IN DELAWARE	11	64	62
ROSTER OF SHORTLINES IN DISTRICT OF COL.	09	67	65
ROSTER OF SHORTLINES IN DISTRICT OF COLU	08	59	55
ROSTER OF SHORTLINES IN FLORIDA 1967	10	67	50
ROSTER OF SHORTLINES IN FLORIDA 1972	08	72	57
ROSTER OF SHORTLINES IN FLORIDA REVISION	10	72	66
ROSTER OF SHORTLINES IN GEORGIA 1965	02	65	54
ROSTER OF SHORTLINES IN GEORGIA 1967	11	67	46
ROSTER OF SHORTLINES IN GEORGIA 1972	10	72	44
ROSTER OF SHORTLINES IN GEORGIA CORRECT	05	65	59
ROSTER OF SHORTLINES IN GEORGIA REVISION	12	72	66
ROSTER OF SHORTLINES IN IDAHO 1965	01	65	63
ROSTER OF SHORTLINES IN IDAHO 1967	12	67	48
ROSTER OF SHORTLINES IN IDAHO 1972	11	72	56
ROSTER OF SHORTLINES IN ILLINOIS	10	59	68
ROSTER OF SHORTLINES IN ILLINOIS 1967	03	68	52
ROSTER OF SHORTLINES IN ILLINOIS 1973	01	73	52
ROSTER OF SHORTLINES IN ILLINOIS CORREC1	03	73	62
ROSTER OF SHORTLINES IN ILLINOIS CORREC2	04	73	63
ROSTER OF SHORTLINES IN ILLINOIS CORREC3	05	73	62
ROSTER OF SHORTLINES IN INDIANA	12	62	60
ROSTER OF SHORTLINES IN INDIANA 1968	02	68	62
ROSTER OF SHORTLINES IN IOWA 1965	02	65	58
ROSTER OF SHORTLINES IN IOWA 1967	01	68	56
ROSTER OF SHORTLINES IN IOWA 1973	05	73	56
ROSTER OF SHORTLINES IN IOWA CORRECTIONS	05	65	59
ROSTER OF SHORTLINES IN KANSAS 1965	04	65	36
ROSTER OF SHORTLINES IN KANSAS 1968	04	68	48
ROSTER OF SHORTLINES IN KANSAS 1973	08	73	13
ROSTER OF SHORTLINES IN KANSAS ADDS	12	73	61
ROSTER OF SHORTLINES IN KANSAS CORRECTIO	10	73	64
ROSTER OF SHORTLINES IN KENTUCKY 10-1964	04	65	53
ROSTER OF SHORTLINES IN KENTUCKY 1968	05	68	52
ROSTER OF SHORTLINES IN KENTUCKY 1973	10	73	61
ROSTER OF SHORTLINES IN KENTUCKY ADDS	12	73	61
ROSTER OF SHORTLINES IN KENTUCKY ADDS	02	74	60
ROSTER OF SHORTLINES IN LOUISIANA 1965	05	65	50
ROSTER OF SHORTLINES IN LOUISIANA 1968	06	68	50
ROSTER OF SHORTLINES IN LOUISIANA 1973	07	73	58
ROSTER OF SHORTLINES IN MAINE 1968	07	68	56
ROSTER OF SHORTLINES IN MAINE 1973	06	73	11
ROSTER OF SHORTLINES IN MARYLAND	11	64	62
ROSTER OF SHORTLINES IN MARYLAND 1968	09	68	44
ROSTER OF SHORTLINES IN MARYLAND 1974	01	74	45
ROSTER OF SHORTLINES IN MARYLAND ADDITON	05	74	59
ROSTER OF SHORTLINES IN MASSACHUSETTS 68	09	68	50
ROSTER OF SHORTLINES IN MASSACHUSETTS 73	10	73	13
ROSTER OF SHORTLINES IN MASSACHUSETTS AD	02	74	60
ROSTER OF SHORTLINES IN MICHIGAN 1965	06	65	55
ROSTER OF SHORTLINES IN MICHIGAN 1968	10	68	39
ROSTER OF SHORTLINES IN MICHIGAN 1974	03	74	46
ROSTER OF SHORTLINES IN MINNESOTA 1965	07	65	53
ROSTER OF SHORTLINES IN MINNESOTA 1968	12	68	48
ROSTER OF SHORTLINES IN MINNESOTA 1973	11	73	62
ROSTER OF SHORTLINES IN MINNESOTA CORR 1	03	74	64
ROSTER OF SHORTLINES IN MINNESOTA CORR 2	01	74	64
ROSTER OF SHORTLINES IN MISSISSIPPI 1965	08	65	65
ROSTER OF SHORTLINES IN MISSISSIPPI 1969	03	69	38
ROSTER OF SHORTLINES IN MISSISSIPPI 1974	05	74	59
ROSTER OF SHORTLINES IN MISSOURI 1965	09	65	54
ROSTER OF SHORTLINES IN MISSOURI 1969	02	69	46
ROSTER OF SHORTLINES IN MISSOURI CORRECT	09	74	33
ROSTER OF SHORTLINES IN MONTANA 1965	12	65	28
ROSTER OF SHORTLINES IN MONTANA 1969	05	69	50
ROSTER OF SHORTLINES IN NEBRASKA 1965	11	65	55
ROSTER OF SHORTLINES IN NEBRASKA 1969	03	69	66
ROSTER OF SHORTLINES IN NEBRASKA 1974	08	74	55
ROSTER OF SHORTLINES IN NEW ENGLAND 1963	12	63	61
ROSTER OF SHORTLINES IN NEW HAMPSHIRE 69	05	69	50
ROSTER OF SHORTLINES IN NEW HAMPSHIRE 74	08	74	55
ROSTER OF SHORTLINES IN NEW HAMPSHIRE CO	11	74	56
ROSTER OF SHORTLINES IN NEW JERSEY	02	59	44
ROSTER OF SHORTLINES IN NEW JERSEY ADDS	09	69	60
ROSTER OF SHORTLINES IN NEW JERSEY 1969	07	69	48
ROSTER OF SHORTLINES IN NEW JERSEY 1974	10	74	48
ROSTER OF SHORTLINES IN NEW JERSEY CORRE	12	74	59
ROSTER OF SHORTLINES IN NEW JERSEY UPDAT	08	69	64
ROSTER OF SHORTLINES IN NEW MEXICO 1969	07	69	54
ROSTER OF SHORTLINES IN NEW YORK 1963	04	64	52
ROSTER OF SHORTLINES IN NEW YORK 1969	08	69	50
ROSTER OF SHORTLINES IN NEW YORK 1975	12	75	53
ROSTER OF SHORTLINES IN NEW YORK ADDS	11	69	64
ROSTER OF SHORTLINES IN NORTH CAROLINA	08	64	36
ROSTER OF SHORTLINES IN NORTH CAROLINA	10	69	50
ROSTER OF SHORTLINES IN OHIO	06	60	56
ROSTER OF SHORTLINES IN OHIO 1969	12	69	44
ROSTER OF SHORTLINES IN OHIO ADDS	03	70	54
ROSTER OF SHORTLINES IN OHIO CORRECTIONS	05	70	66
ROSTER OF SHORTLINES IN OKLAHOMA	03	66	59
ROSTER OF SHORTLINES IN OKLAHOMA 1970	01	70	10
ROSTER OF SHORTLINES IN OREGON 1966	04	66	58
ROSTER OF SHORTLINES IN OREGON 1970	02	70	50
ROSTER OF SHORTLINES IN PENNSYLVANIA	05	66	48
ROSTER OF SHORTLINES IN PENNSYLVANIA '70	03	70	62
ROSTER OF SHORTLINES IN PENNSYLVANIA COR	10	70	66
ROSTER OF SHORTLINES IN RHODE ISLAND '70	04	70	52
ROSTER OF SHORTLINES IN RHODE ISLAND ADD	07	70	60
ROSTER OF SHORTLINES IN SOUTH CAROLINA	06	66	48
ROSTER OF SHORTLINES IN SOUTH CAROLINA	05	70	50
ROSTER OF SHORTLINES IN SOUTH CAROLINA A	08	70	62
ROSTER OF SHORTLINES IN SOUTH DAKOTA '66	08	66	64

Railroad/Railfan

RAILROAD HISTORIES & ROSTERS

ROSTERS BY RAILROAD	M	Y	P
ROSTER OF SHORTLINES IN TENNESSEE 1966	08	66	64
ROSTER OF SHORTLINES IN TENNESSEE 1970	07	70	41
ROSTER OF SHORTLINES IN TEXAS 1966	09	66	46
ROSTER OF SHORTLINES IN TEXAS 1970	11	70	40
ROSTER OF SHORTLINES IN UTAH 1970	12	70	60
ROSTER OF SHORTLINES IN VERMONT 1970	12	70	56
ROSTER OF SHORTLINES IN VIRGINIA 1966	10	66	52
ROSTER OF SHORTLINES IN VIRGINIA 1971	04	71	51
ROSTER OF SHORTLINES IN VIRGINIA ADDS	02	71	66
ROSTER OF SHORTLINES IN VIRGINIA ADDS	07	71	66
ROSTER OF SHORTLINES IN WASHINGTON 1971	06	71	37
ROSTER OF SHORTLINES IN WASHINGTON DC'72	06	72	50
ROSTER OF SHORTLINES IN WEST VIRGINIA 66	12	66	54
ROSTER OF SHORTLINES IN WEST VIRGINIA 71	02	71	59
ROSTER OF SHORTLINES IN WISCONSIN	01	66	66
ROSTER OF SHORTLINES IN WISCONSIN 1971	05	71	58
ROSTER OF SHORTLINES IN WYOMING 1966	11	66	62
ROSTER OF SHORTLINES IN WYOMING 1971	06	71	37
ROSTER OF SHRT EQUIPMENT	05	49	83
ROSTER OF SHRT EQUIPMENT W/FORMER OWNERS	08	45	90
ROSTER OF SHRT PASSENGER CARS	08	45	90
ROSTER OF SI LOCOMOTIVES 3-1974	10	74	49
ROSTER OF SI LOCOMOTIVES 6-1974	12	75	55
ROSTER OF SIE LOCOMOTIVES 3-1964	08	64	60
ROSTER OF SIE LOCOMOTIVES 3-1967	06	67	51
ROSTER OF SIE LOCOMOTIVES 6-1971	03	72	61
ROSTER OF SIE LOCOS	11	42	150
ROSTER OF SIE LOCOS: STEAM	06	55	78
ROSTER OF SIE STEAM LOCOS 1961	02	61	63
ROSTER OF SIEV LOCOS: STEAM	10	55	62
ROSTER OF SIN LOCOMOTIVES 1972	05	73	56
ROSTER OF SIN LOCOMOTIVES 6-1967	01	68	57
ROSTER OF SIND LOCOMOTIVES 6-1962	12	62	61
ROSTER OF SIND LOCOMOTIVES 9-1967	02	68	63
ROSTER OF SIRT LOCOMOTIVES 3-1969	08	69	52
ROSTER OF SIRT LOCOMOTIVES 3-1969	07	69	50
ROSTER OF SIRT LOCOMOTIVES 3-1974	10	74	49
ROSTER OF SIRT LOCOMOTIVES 6-1974	12	75	55
ROSTER OF SIRT LOCOMOTIVES 7-1963	02	64	55
ROSTER OF SIRT LOCOS (B&O)	06	34	90
ROSTER OF SIRT LOCOS: DIESEL	12	48	84
ROSTER OF SIRT LOCOS: DIESELS 1958	02	59	44
ROSTER OF SIRT LOCOS: NOT CLASS A-E (B&O	07	34	83
ROSTER OF SIRT LOCOS: STEAM	02	43	59
ROSTER OF SIRY LOCOMOTIVES 10-1964	02	65	58
ROSTER OF SJ&GI LOCOS	05	33	84
ROSTER OF SJ&LC LOCOS	04	33	97
ROSTER OF SJ&LC LOCOS W/ORIGINAL B&M #S	03	33	88
ROSTER OF SJ&LC LOCOS: AFTER 1925	10	42	96
ROSTER OF SJ&LCO LOCOMOTIVES 11-1962	08	63	60
ROSTER OF SJ&LCO LOCOMOTIVES 6-1970	12	70	56
ROSTER OF SJ&LCO LOCOS 1963 REVISION	12	63	61
ROSTER OF SJ&LOC (LOATI & VT NORTHERN)	03	80	50
ROSTER OF SJ&LV DIESEL LOCOMOTIVES	01	80	28
ROSTER OF SJB LOCOMOTIVES 3-1960	08	60	29
ROSTER OF SJB LOCOMOTIVES 3-1965	09	65	55
ROSTER OF SJB LOCOMOTIVES 6-1968	02	69	48
ROSTER OF SJB LOCOMOTIVES 9-1973	06	74	53
ROSTER OF SJRT LOCOMOTIVES 1-1960	10	62	53
ROSTER OF SJT LOCOMOTIVES 3-1965	09	65	55
ROSTER OF SJT LOCOMOTIVES 6-1968	02	69	48
ROSTER OF SJT LOCOMOTIVES 9-1973	06	74	53
ROSTER OF SLB&M LOCOS: PART 1 (MP)	03	38	60
ROSTER OF SLB&M LOCOS: PART 2	04	38	67
ROSTER OF SLC LOCOMOTIVES 3-1967	07	67	64
ROSTER OF SLC LOCOMOTIVES 7-1964	10	64	62
ROSTER OF SLC LOCOMOTIVES 9-1971	07	72	59
ROSTER OF SLCUD LOCOMOTIVES (NONE) 1963	04	64	35
ROSTER OF SLCUD LOCOMOTIVES 3-1970	12	70	60
ROSTER OF SLG&W LOCOMOTIVES 10-1963	04	64	35
ROSTER OF SLG&W LOCOMOTIVES 3-1970	12	70	60
ROSTER OF SLV&TH 5-1917	04	62	29
ROSTER OF SLV&TH LOCOMOTIVES ALL TIME	08	62	51
ROSTER OF SLV&TH READER UPDATE	10	62	58
ROSTER OF SM LOCOMOTIVES 10-1964	02	65	56
ROSTER OF SM LOCOMOTIVES 3-1972	10	72	45
ROSTER OF SM LOCOMOTIVES 6-1967	11	67	48
ROSTER OF SMA LOCOMOTIVES 10-1963	04	64	35
ROSTER OF SMA LOCOMOTIVES 12-1966	04	67	39
ROSTER OF SMA LOCOMOTIVES 3-1971	10	71	46
ROSTER OF SMT STEAM LOCOS 1961	02	61	63
ROSTER OF SMV LOCOMOTIVES 3-1964	08	64	60
ROSTER OF SMV LOCOMOTIVES 3-1967	06	67	51
ROSTER OF SMV LOCOMOTIVES 6-1971	03	72	61
ROSTER OF SMV LOCOS: ALL-TIME/STEAM-DIES	06	56	45
ROSTER OF SMV STEAM LOCOS 1961	02	61	62
ROSTER OF SN LOCOMOTIVES 3-1964	08	64	60
ROSTER OF SN LOCOMOTIVES 3-1967	06	67	51
ROSTER OF SN LOCOMOTIVES 6-1971	03	72	60
ROSTER OF SNY LOCOMOTIVES 3-1969	08	69	52
ROSTER OF SNY LOCOMOTIVES 6-1974	12	75	55
ROSTER OF SNY LOCOMOTIVES 7-1963	02	64	55
ROSTER OF SOMRR LOCOMOTIVES 12-1971	06	72	50
ROSTER OF SOO LOCOMOTIVES	06	47	125
ROSTER OF SOO LOCOMOTIVES 5-1968	10	68	23
ROSTER OF SOO LOCOMOTIVES 6-1961	12	61	34
ROSTER OF SOO LOCOMOTIVES 6-1974	02	75	53
ROSTER OF SOO LOCOMOTIVES 9-1965	02	66	51
ROSTER OF SOO LOCOS	02	34	131
ROSTER OF SOO LOCOS--CLASS J/F2I/H1	02	33	86
ROSTER OF SOO LOCOS: CORRECTIONS	08	53	116
ROSTER OF SOO LOCOS: STEAM/DIESEL	05	53	106
ROSTER OF SOT LOCOMOTIVES 12-1973	08	74	55
ROSTER OF SOT LOCOMOTIVES 5-1965	11	65	55
ROSTER OF SOT LOCOMOTIVES 6-1968	03	69	66
ROSTER OF SOUTHERN SYSTEM LOCOMOTIVES 60	10	62	52
ROSTER OF SP 1984 WORLDS FAIR DAYLIGHT	09	84	54
ROSTER OF SP 2-6-0 MOGULS 1938	10	61	16
ROSTER OF SP LOCOMOTIVES	09	38	130
ROSTER OF SP LOCOMOTIVES	10	38	120

Railroad/ Railfan

RAILROAD HISTORIES & ROSTERS

ROSTERS BY RAILROAD	M	Y	P
ROSTER OF SP LOCOMOTIVES	11	38	120
ROSTER OF SP LOCOMOTIVES 1 12-1969	08	70	30
ROSTER OF SP LOCOMOTIVES 2	09	70	34
ROSTER OF SP LOCOMOTIVES 3 12-1969	10	70	40
ROSTER OF SP LOCOS	01	33	101
ROSTER OF SP LOCOS	12	33	94
ROSTER OF SP LOCOS CORRECTIONS	10	50	128
ROSTER OF SP LOCOS PART 1: STEAM	06	50	92
ROSTER OF SP LOCOS PART 2: STEAM/NARROW	07	50	98
ROSTER OF SP LOCOS PART 3: DIESELS	08	50	100
ROSTER OF SP LOCOS-CORRECTIONS	01	39	127
ROSTER OF SP LOCOS-NARROW GAGE	11	38	122
ROSTER OF SP LOCOS-SHOP ENGINES (MOW)	11	38	121
ROSTER OF SP LOCOS: "SUNSET LIMITED"	01	34	93
ROSTER OF SP LOCOS: ARTICULATED CORRECTI	09	35	87
ROSTER OF SP LOCOS: CAB-IN-FRONTS	03	55	19
ROSTER OF SP LOCOS: DIESELS TO NWP	08	55	48
ROSTER OF SP LOCOS: STEAM/DIESEL	08	58	65
ROSTER OF SP LOCOS:ARTICULATED	05	35	81
ROSTER OF SP LOCOS:DISPOSITION OF 3900 S	02	58	45
ROSTER OF SP STEAM LOCOS 1961	02	61	63
ROSTER OF SP&S LOCOMOTIVES 3-1970	11	70	52
ROSTER OF SP&S LOCOMOTIVES 6-1960	12	60	63
ROSTER OF SP&S LOCOS	03	39	118
ROSTER OF SP&S LOCOS: STEAM/DIESEL	11	52	39
ROSTER OF SPERRY DETECTOR CARS	01	79	31R
ROSTER OF SPI LOCOMOTIVES 10-1964	01	65	63
ROSTER OF SPI LOCOMOTIVES 3-1962	08	62	29
ROSTER OF SPI LOCOMOTIVES 6-1967	12	67	48
ROSTER OF SPI LOCOMOTIVES 6-1970	06	71	37
ROSTER OF SPI LOCOMOTIVES 6-1972	11	72	56
ROSTER OF SPI LOCOS: STEAM	03	49	100
ROSTER OF SPM LOCOS	02	41	117
ROSTER OF SPS DETECTOR CARS 6-1969	01	70	66
ROSTER OF SPUD LOCOMOTIVES 3-1965	07	65	53
ROSTER OF SPUD LOCOMOTIVES 6-1968	12	68	48
ROSTER OF SPUD LOCOMOTIVES 6-1973	11	73	62
ROSTER OF SR&N LOCOMOTIVES 3-1970	11	70	41
ROSTER OF SR&RL LOCOS	09	35	55
ROSTER OF SR&RL LOCOS: STEAM	12	55	33
ROSTER OF SRTC (OWNS NO LOCOMOTIVES)1964	02	65	56
ROSTER OF SRTC LOCOMOTIVES 3-1972	10	72	46
ROSTER OF SRTC LOCOMOTIVES 6-1967	11	67	48
ROSTER OF SS LOCOMOTIVES 12-1964	05	65	50
ROSTER OF SS LOCOMOTIVES 3-1968	06	68	51
ROSTER OF SS LOCOMOTIVES 3-1973	07	73	58
ROSTER OF SSD LOCOMOTIVES 3-1972	10	72	46
ROSTER OF SSD LOCOMOTIVES 6-1967	11	67	48
ROSTER OF SSL LOCOMOTIVES 3-1969	08	69	52
ROSTER OF SSL LOCOMOTIVES 6-1974	12	75	55
ROSTER OF SSL LOCOMOTIVES 7-1963	02	64	54
ROSTER OF SSLV LOCOMOTIVES 3-1967	07	67	64
ROSTER OF SSLV LOCOMOTIVES 7-1964	10	64	62
ROSTER OF SSLV LOCOMOTIVES 9-1971	07	72	59
ROSTER OF SSLV STEAM LOCOS 1961	02	61	63
ROSTER OF SSP LOCOMOTIVES 10-1965	03	66	59
ROSTER OF SSP LOCOMOTIVES 3-1969	01	70	10
ROSTER OF ST LOCOMOTIVES 12-1968	05	69	50
ROSTER OF ST LOCOMOTIVES 12-1973	08	74	55
ROSTER OF ST LOCOMOTIVES 6-1970	12	70	58
ROSTER OF ST&E LOCOMOTIVES 3-1964	08	64	61
ROSTER OF ST&E LOCOMOTIVES 3-1967	06	67	51
ROSTER OF ST&E LOCOMOTIVES 6-1971	03	72	61
ROSTER OF STEAM FAN TRIP LOCOS & SPECS	02	78	31R
ROSTER OF STEAM IN MEXICO & CENTRAL AMER	10	73	34
ROSTER OF STEAM SUPER-LOCOMOTIVES	10	66	19
ROSTER OF STEW LOCOMOTIVES 3-1966	05	66	51
ROSTER OF STEW LOCOMOTIVES 9-1969	03	70	66
ROSTER OF STREETCARS IN MEXICO CITY	10	68	29
ROSTER OF STRR LOCOMOTIVES 3-1966	05	66	51
ROSTER OF STRR LOCOMOTIVES 9-1969	03	70	66
ROSTER OF STRR STEAM LOCOS 1961	02	61	63
ROSTER OF SUGL LOCOS: PART 1 (MP)	03	38	60
ROSTER OF SUGL LOCOS: PART 2	04	38	67
ROSTER OF SURR (OWNS NO LOCOMOTIVES)1964	08	64	37
ROSTER OF SURR LOCOMOTIVES 3-1969	10	69	52
ROSTER OF SURY LOCOMOTIVES 3-1967	06	67	51
ROSTER OF SURY LOCOMOTIVES 6-1971	03	72	61
ROSTER OF SURY(OWNS NO LOCOMOTIVES)1964	08	64	61
ROSTER OF SUSC LOCOS	11	43	122
ROSTER OF SV LOCOS: 6 STEAM LOCOS	01	36	87
ROSTER OF SW&C LOCOMOTIVES	11	78	55R
ROSTER OF T LOCOMOTIVES 12-1969	07	70	41
ROSTER OF T LOCOMOTIVES 3-1966	08	66	64
ROSTER OF T&FS LOCOS: NOW PART OF KCS	04	57	74
ROSTER OF T&FS STEAM LOCOMOTIVES-ALL TIM	01	76	56
ROSTER OF T&GU (OWNS NO LOCOMOTIVES)1967	10	67	50
ROSTER OF T&GU LOCOMOTIVES 10-1964	12	64	32
ROSTER OF T&GU LOCOMOTIVES 12-1971	08	72	57
ROSTER OF T&N LOCOMOTIVES 3-1970	11	70	41
ROSTER OF T&N LOCOMOTIVES 7-1966	09	66	47
ROSTER OF T&NO LOCOS	03	42	132
ROSTER OF T&NO LOCOS CORRECTIONS	05	42	67
ROSTER OF T&NO LOCOS: DIESEL	08	58	69
ROSTER OF T&NON LOCOS	03	43	109
ROSTER OF T&P LOCOMOTIVES 1960	12	60	60
ROSTER OF T&P LOCOMOTIVES 2-1970	11	70	64
ROSTER OF T&P LOCOMOTIVES 3-1965	09	65	54
ROSTER OF T&P LOCOS	07	33	130
ROSTER OF T&P LOCOS: STEAM/DIESEL	10	48	126
ROSTER OF T&T LOCOS	11	42	152
ROSTER OF T&T LOCOS: 5 LOCOMOTIVES	07	35	86
ROSTER OF T-NMR (OWNS NO LOCS) 1966	09	66	47
ROSTER OF T-NMR LOCOMOTIVES (NONE) 1963	04	64	35
ROSTER OF T-NMR LOCOMOTIVES 3-1969	07	69	54
ROSTER OF T-NMR LOCOMOTIVES 3-1970	11	70	41
ROSTER OF TA&G LOCOMOTIVES 1-1961	02	62	32
ROSTER OF TA&G LOCOMOTIVES 10-1964	02	65	56
ROSTER OF TA&G LOCOMOTIVES 10-1966	02	66	48
ROSTER OF TA&G LOCOMOTIVES 12-1969	07	70	41

Railroad/ Railfan

RAILROAD HISTORIES & ROSTERS

ROSTERS BY RAILROAD	M	Y	P
ROSTER OF TA&G LOCOMOTIVES 12-1970	07	71	53
ROSTER OF TA&G LOCOMOTIVES 3-1966	08	66	64
ROSTER OF TA&G LOCOMOTIVES 3-1972	10	72	46
ROSTER OF TA&G LOCOMOTIVES 6-1967	11	67	48
ROSTER OF TA&W LOCOMOTIVES 1960	06	60	57
ROSTER OF TA&W LOCOMOTIVES 6-1969	12	69	48
ROSTER OF TACR STEAM LOCOMOTIVES	10	73	35
ROSTER OF TB LOCOMOTIVES 6-1962	12	62	61
ROSTER OF TB LOCOMOTIVES 9-1967	02	68	63
ROSTER OF TC LOCOMOTIVES 3-1970	11	70	41
ROSTER OF TC&GB LOCOMOTIVES 10-1963	04	64	35
ROSTER OF TC&GB LOCOMOTIVES 12-1966	04	67	39
ROSTER OF TC&GB LOCOMOTIVES 3-1971	10	71	46
ROSTER OF TCT LOCOMOTIVES 3-1970	11	70	41
ROSTER OF TCT LOCOMOTIVES 7-1966	09	66	47
ROSTER OF TEM LOCOS	07	38	79
ROSTER OF TENNC LOCOMOTIVES 10-1964	04	65	53
ROSTER OF TENNC LOCOMOTIVES 12-1967	05	68	52
ROSTER OF TENNC LOCOMOTIVES 12-1969	07	70	41
ROSTER OF TENNC LOCOMOTIVES 3-1966	08	66	64
ROSTER OF TENNC LOCOMOTIVES 3-1973	10	73	62
ROSTER OF TENNC LOCOS: STEAM/DIESEL	04	53	65
ROSTER OF TEXS LOCOS ALL TIME	05	84	51
ROSTER OF TF LOCOMOTIVES 1-1964	08	64	37
ROSTER OF TH&B LOCOMOTIVES	07	32	458
ROSTER OF TH&B LOCOMOTIVES 10-1965	02	66	55
ROSTER OF TH&B LOCOMOTIVES 12-1970	05	71	58
ROSTER OF TH&I LOCOMOTIVES ALL TIME	08	62	50
ROSTER OF TH&L LOCOMOTIVES ALL TIME	08	62	51
ROSTER OF THE SOUTHWEST LOCOS 10-1963	04	64	35
ROSTER OF TIV LOCOS	02	44	73
ROSTER OF TM STEAM LOCOMOTIVES	10	63	19
ROSTER OF TMB LOCOMOTIVES 3-1962	08	62	29
ROSTER OF TMB LOCOMOTIVES 6-1970	06	71	37
ROSTER OF TMEX LOCOMOTIVES 3-1970	11	70	41
ROSTER OF TMEX LOCOMOTIVES 7-1966	09	66	47
ROSTER OF TO&E LOCOMOTIVES 10-1965	03	66	59
ROSTER OF TO&E LOCOMOTIVES 3-1969	01	70	10
ROSTER OF TOV LOCOMOTIVES 10-1963	04	64	35
ROSTER OF TOV LOCOMOTIVES 3-1970	12	70	60
ROSTER OF TOV STEAM LOCOS 1961	02	61	63
ROSTER OF TP&W DIESEL LOCOMOTIVES 1983	09	83	53
ROSTER OF TP&W LOCOMOTIVES 10-1964	02	65	58
ROSTER OF TP&W LOCOMOTIVES 1972	05	73	57
ROSTER OF TP&W LOCOMOTIVES 6-1967	01	68	57
ROSTER OF TP&W LOCOMOTIVES 9-1967	02	68	63
ROSTER OF TP&W LOCOMOTIVES 9-1967	03	68	56
ROSTER OF TP&W LOCOMOTIVES 9-1972	01	73	57
ROSTER OF TP&W LOCOS: ADDITIONS	11	54	73
ROSTER OF TP&W LOCOS: DIESELS 1959	10	59	73
ROSTER OF TP&W LOCOS: STEAM/DIESEL	08	54	80
ROSTER OF TP&W STEAM LOCOS 1870	09	83	48
ROSTER OF TP&W STEAM POWER	09	83	47
ROSTER OF TPMP LOCOMOTIVES 12-1964	05	65	50
ROSTER OF TPMP LOCOMOTIVES 3-1968	06	68	52
ROSTER OF TPMP LOCOMOTIVES 3-1973	07	73	58
ROSTER OF TPT LOCOMOTIVES 3-1969	07	69	50
ROSTER OF TPT LOCOMOTIVES 3-1974	10	74	49
ROSTER OF TPT LOCOS: OWNS NONE 1958	02	59	45
ROSTER OF TRA LOCOMOTIVES 3-1965	09	65	55
ROSTER OF TRA LOCOMOTIVES 6-1968	02	69	48
ROSTER OF TRA LOCOMOTIVES 9-1967	03	68	56
ROSTER OF TRA LOCOMOTIVES 9-1972	01	73	57
ROSTER OF TRA LOCOMOTIVES 9-1973	06	74	53
ROSTER OF TRA LOCOS: DIESELS 1959	10	59	73
ROSTER OF TRASD LOCOMOTIVES 1-1961	02	62	32
ROSTER OF TRASD LOCOMOTIVES 10-1966	02	67	48
ROSTER OF TRASD LOCOMOTIVES 12-1970	07	71	53
ROSTER OF TRO LOCOMOTIVES 3-1964	08	64	61
ROSTER OF TRO LOCOMOTIVES 3-1967	06	67	51
ROSTER OF TRO LOCOMOTIVES 6-1971	03	72	61
ROSTER OF TRO LOCOMOTIVES ALL TIME	11	87	56
ROSTER OF TS LOCOMOTIVES 3-1964	08	64	61
ROSTER OF TS LOCOMOTIVES 3-1967	06	67	51
ROSTER OF TS LOCOMOTIVES 6-1971	03	72	61
ROSTER OF TSE LOCOMOTIVES 3-1970	11	70	41
ROSTER OF TSE LOCOMOTIVES 7-1966	09	66	47
ROSTER OF TSE STEAM LOCOS 1961	02	61	63
ROSTER OF TSU LOCOMOTIVES 10-1965	03	66	59
ROSTER OF TSU LOCOMOTIVES 3-1969	01	70	10
ROSTER OF TT LOCOMOTIVES 1960	06	60	57
ROSTER OF TT LOCOMOTIVES 6-1969	12	69	48
ROSTER OF TTCO EQUIPMENT	02	58	73
ROSTER OF TTRY (OWNS NO LOCOMOTIVES)1965	02	66	55
ROSTER OF TTRY LOCOMOTIVES 12-1970	05	71	58
ROSTER OF TUSCO(OWNS NO LOCOMOTIVES)1964	12	64	32
ROSTER OF TUSCO (OWNS NO LOCOMOTIVES)'67	10	67	50
ROSTER OF TUSCO LOCOMOTIVES 12-1971	08	72	57
ROSTER OF TUSK LOCOMOTIVES 1-1961	02	62	32
ROSTER OF TUST (OWNS NO LOCOMOTIVES)1963	06	64	48
ROSTER OF TUST (OWNS NO LOCOMOTIVES)1964	05	65	50
ROSTER OF TUST (OWNS NO LOCOMOTIVES)1966	09	66	47
ROSTER OF TUST LOCOMOTIVES 12-1966	05	67	55
ROSTER OF TUST LOCOMOTIVES 3-1968	06	68	51
ROSTER OF TUST LOCOMOTIVES 3-1970	11	70	41
ROSTER OF TUST LOCOMOTIVES 6-1971	03	72	59
ROSTER OF UDEY STEAM LOCOS 1961 STD & NA	06	61	26
ROSTER OF UF (NO LOCOMOTIVES 1962)	08	63	60
ROSTER OF UF LOCOMOTIVES 6-1968	09	68	50
ROSTER OF UF LOCOMOTIVES 6-1973	10	73	13
ROSTER OF UM&P LOCOMOTIVES 3-1966	05	66	52
ROSTER OF UM&P LOCOMOTIVES 9-1969	03	70	66
ROSTER OF UN LOCOMOTIVES 3-1966	05	66	52
ROSTER OF UN LOCOMOTIVES 9-1969	03	70	66
ROSTER OF UNION ARMY CIVIL WAR LOCOMOTIV	06	67	48
ROSTER OF UP 1939-46 "TRAIN" PASSENGER L	01	71	44
ROSTER OF UP LOCOMOTIVES	07	47	115
ROSTER OF UP LOCOMOTIVES 1-1970	01	71	42
ROSTER OF UP LOCOMOTIVES 7-1963	04	64	46
ROSTER OF UP LOCOMOTIVES POST 1948	01	71	45

Railroad/Railfan

RAILROAD HISTORIES & ROSTERS

ROSTERS BY RAILROAD	M	Y	P
ROSTER OF UP LOCOMOTIVES READER ADDS	05	71	66
ROSTER OF UP LOCOS	05	33	84
ROSTER OF UP LOCOS 1948-REBUILD PASS UNI	04	64	50
ROSTER OF UP LOCOS AFTER 1946 RENUMBERIN	01	71	45
ROSTER OF UP LOCOS AFTER 1948 RENUMBERIN	01	71	45
ROSTER OF UP LOCOS PRE 1939 PASS UNITS	04	64	48
ROSTER OF UP LOCOS PRE 1948 PASS UNITS	04	64	50
ROSTER OF UP LOCOS: DIESEL-ELECTRICS	05	39	64
ROSTER OF UP LOCOS: STEAM/DIESEL/GAS-TUR	12	57	73
ROSTER OF UP PASSENGER LOCOS (1963)	04	64	53
ROSTER OF UP PRE-1936 "M" PASSENGER LOCO	01	71	45
ROSTER OF UP STEAM LOCOS 1961	02	61	63
ROSTER OF URO LOCOMOTIVES 12-1965	04	66	58
ROSTER OF URO LOCOMOTIVES 9-1969	02	70	50
ROSTER OF URR LOCOMOTIVES 3-1966	05	66	52
ROSTER OF URR LOCOMOTIVES 9-1969	03	70	66
ROSTER OF URY LOCOS: STEAM/DIESEL	06	50	54
ROSTER OF URY STEAM LOCOMOTIVES	10	73	35
ROSTER OF URYT LOCOMOTIVES 12-1969	07	70	41
ROSTER OF URYT LOCOMOTIVES 3-1966	08	66	64
ROSTER OF USSC ATLANTIC CITY OPERATION	03	82	30
ROSTER OF USY&T LOCOMOTIVES 9-1967	03	68	56
ROSTER OF USY&T LOCOMOTIVES 9-1972	01	73	57
ROSTER OF USY&T LOCOS: OWNS NO MOTIVE PO	10	59	73
ROSTER OF UT LOCOMOTIVES 3-1965	09	65	55
ROSTER OF UT LOCOMOTIVES 6-1968	02	69	48
ROSTER OF UT LOCOMOTIVES 7-1966	09	66	47
ROSTER OF UT LOCOMOTIVES 9-1973	06	74	53
ROSTER OF UT STEAM LOCOS 1961	02	61	63
ROSTER OF UTAH DIESEL LOCOMOTIVES	W	76	46R
ROSTER OF UTAH LOCOMOTIVES 10-1963	04	64	35
ROSTER OF UTAH LOCOMOTIVES 3-1970	12	70	60
ROSTER OF UTAH LOCOS: 5 STEAM/4 DIESEL-E	02	56	43
ROSTER OF UTCO LOCOMOTIVES 3-1970	11	70	41
ROSTER OF UTRC LOCOS: OWNS NONE 1958	02	59	45
ROSTER OF V LOCOS (ALL-TIME)	04	37	71
ROSTER OF V LOCOS: CORRECTIONS	06	37	63
ROSTER OF V LOCOS: NORFOLK TO CHARLESTON	04	34	82
ROSTER OF V LOCOS: STEAM/ELECTRIC	07	51	106
ROSTER OF V&CS (OWNS NO LOCOMOTIVES)1964	08	64	37
ROSTER OF V&MA LOCOMOTIVES 1977	10	77	43
ROSTER OF V&S LOCOMOTIVES 12-1965	04	66	58
ROSTER OF V&S LOCOMOTIVES 9-1969	02	70	50
ROSTER OF V&T LOCOS: ALL-TIME STEAM	01	55	21
ROSTER OF V&T LOCOS: WITH THEIR HISTORY	09	41	14
ROSTER OF VA LOCOMOTIVES ALL TIME	08	62	52
ROSTER OF VBR ALL TIME STEAM LOCOMOTIVES	02	62	17
ROSTER OF VBR LOCOMOTIVES 6-1970	04	71	52
ROSTER OF VBR LOCOMOTIVES 7-1966	10	66	52
ROSTER OF VBR STEAM LOCOS 1961	02	61	63
ROSTER OF VC LOCOMOTIVES 6-1970	04	71	52
ROSTER OF VC LOCOMOTIVES 7-1966	10	66	52
ROSTER OF VCO LOCOMOTIVES 3-1964	08	64	61
ROSTER OF VCO LOCOMOTIVES 3-1967	06	67	51
ROSTER OF VCO LOCOMOTIVES 6-1971	03	72	61
ROSTER OF VCO STEAM LOCOS 1961	02	61	64
ROSTER OF VE LOCOMOTIVES 3-1964	08	64	61
ROSTER OF VE LOCOMOTIVES 3-1967	06	67	51
ROSTER OF VE LOCOMOTIVES 6-1971	03	72	61
ROSTER OF VE LOCOS: DIESELS	08	58	68
ROSTER OF VER LOCOMOTIVES	SU	75	23R
ROSTER OF VER LOCOMOTIVES 6-1970	12	70	58
ROSTER OF VS LOCOMOTIVES 10-1964	12	64	32
ROSTER OF VS LOCOMOTIVES 10-1964	02	65	56
ROSTER OF VS LOCOMOTIVES 12-1971	08	72	57
ROSTER OF VS LOCOMOTIVES 3-1972	10	72	46
ROSTER OF VS LOCOMOTIVES 6-1967	10	67	50
ROSTER OF VS LOCOMOTIVES 6-1967	11	67	48
ROSTER OF W LOCOMOTIVES	02	40	70
ROSTER OF W LOCOMOTIVES 11-1961	04	62	35
ROSTER OF W LOCOS	05	33	76
ROSTER OF W LOCOS: CLASS/WEIGHT/NUMBERS	04	33	97
ROSTER OF W LOCOS: CORRECTIONS	08	52	132
ROSTER OF W LOCOS: STEAM/DIESEL	04	52	113
ROSTER OF W&LE LOCOS	09	39	116
ROSTER OF W&LE LOCOS: STEAM/DIESEL 1949	05	50	122
ROSTER OF W&LE STEAM LOCOMOTIVES 1939	03	74	30
ROSTER OF W&NO LOCOMOTIVES 3-1969	07	69	50
ROSTER OF W&NO LOCOMOTIVES 3-1974	10	74	49
ROSTER OF W&NO LOCOS: 5 DIESELS 1958	02	59	45
ROSTER OF W&OD LOCOMOTIVES 6-1970	04	71	52
ROSTER OF W&OD LOCOMOTIVES 7-1966	10	66	52
ROSTER OF W&OV LOCOMOTIVES 12-1963	06	64	48
ROSTER OF W&OV LOCOMOTIVES 12-1966	05	67	55
ROSTER OF W&OV LOCOMOTIVES 6-1971	03	72	59
ROSTER OF W&Q LOCOS: STEAM	12	55	33
ROSTER OF W&SR LOCOMOTIVES 12-1963	06	64	48
ROSTER OF W&SR LOCOMOTIVES 12-1966	05	67	55
ROSTER OF W&SR LOCOMOTIVES 6-1971	03	72	59
ROSTER OF W&SR STEAM LOCOS 1961	02	61	64
ROSTER OF W&T LOCOMOTIVES 10-1964	02	65	56
ROSTER OF W&T LOCOMOTIVES 3-1972	10	72	46
ROSTER OF W&T LOCOMOTIVES 6-1967	11	67	48
ROSTER OF W&T STEAM LOCOS 1961	02	61	64
ROSTER OF W&WA LOCOMOTIVES 3-1966	05	66	52
ROSTER OF WA LOCOMOTIVES 1900-1962	08	63	63
ROSTER OF WA LOCOMOTIVES 9-1969	04	70	52
ROSTER OF WA&G LOCOMOTIVES 3-1966	05	66	52
ROSTER OF WA&G LOCOMOTIVES 3-1969	08	69	52
ROSTER OF WA&G LOCOMOTIVES 6-1974	12	75	55
ROSTER OF WA&G LOCOMOTIVES 7-1963	02	64	55
ROSTER OF WA&G LOCOMOTIVES 9-1969	03	70	66
ROSTER OF WAR LOCOMOTIVES 1-1964	08	64	37
ROSTER OF WAR LOCOMOTIVES 12-1970	07	71	53
ROSTER OF WAR LOCOMOTIVES 3-1969	10	69	52
ROSTER OF WARR 2-8-0 CLASS H10 LOCOS	07	82	38
ROSTER OF WARR LOCOMOTIVES 3-1966	05	66	52
ROSTER OF WARR LOCOMOTIVES 9-1969	03	70	66
ROSTER OF WAS LOCOMOTIVES 12-1969	05	70	50
ROSTER OF WAS LOCOMOTIVES 3-1966	06	66	48

RAILROAD HISTORIES & ROSTERS

ROSTERS BY RAILROAD	M	Y	P
ROSTER OF WASHT LOCOMOTIVES 12-1971	06	72	50
ROSTER OF WASHT LOCOMOTIVES 3-1967	09	67	65
ROSTER OF WASHT LOCOS: DIESELS CLASS RS1	08	59	55
ROSTER OF WB&E LOCOS	11	43	122
ROSTER OF WBT&S LOCOMOTIVES 3-1970	11	70	41
ROSTER OF WBT&S LOCOMOTIVES 7-1966	09	66	46
ROSTER OF WCRC LOCOMOTIVES 1-87	09	87	49
ROSTER OF WDT&S STEAM LOCOS 1961	02	61	64
ROSTER OF WF&O EQUIPMENT	11	48	87
ROSTER OF WF&O PASSENGER CARS	11	48	87
ROSTER OF WI&M LOCOMOTIVES 10-1964	01	65	63
ROSTER OF WI&M LOCOMOTIVES 3-1962	08	62	29
ROSTER OF WI&M LOCOMOTIVES 6-1967	12	67	48
ROSTER OF WI&M LOCOMOTIVES 6-1970	06	71	37
ROSTER OF WI&M LOCOMOTIVES 6-1972	11	72	56
ROSTER OF WI&M STEAM LOCOS 1961	02	61	64
ROSTER OF WI&W LOCOMOTIVES 6-1970	04	71	52
ROSTER OF WI&W LOCOMOTIVES 7-1966	10	66	52
ROSTER OF WINI LOCOMOTIVES 6-1970	02	71	59
ROSTER OF WINI LOCOMOTIVES 7-1966	12	66	54
ROSTER OF WINI STEAM LOCOS 1961	02	61	64
ROSTER OF WLOO LOCOMOTIVES 10-1964	02	65	58
ROSTER OF WLOO LOCOMOTIVES 1972	05	73	56
ROSTER OF WLOO LOCOMOTIVES 6-1967	01	68	57
ROSTER OF WM LOCOMOTIVES	10	46	121
ROSTER OF WM LOCOMOTIVES 12-1961	06	62	52
ROSTER OF WM LOCOMOTIVES 4-1970	02	71	49
ROSTER OF WM LOCOS	10	33	88
ROSTER OF WM LOCOS: ADDITIONAL COMMENTS	01	47	132
ROSTER OF WM LOCOS: STEAM/DIESEL	12	52	106
ROSTER OF WMW&N LOCOMOTIVES 3-1970	11	70	41
ROSTER OF WMW&N LOCOMOTIVES 7-1966	09	66	47
ROSTER OF WP DIESEL LOCOMOTIVES 1979	05	79	26
ROSTER OF WP EMD UNITS 1978	05	78	57
ROSTER OF WP LOCOMOTIVES	12	46	112
ROSTER OF WP LOCOMOTIVES 10-1960	04	61	60
ROSTER OF WP LOCOMOTIVES 4-1970	02	71	47
ROSTER OF WP LOCOS	06	32	330
ROSTER OF WP LOCOS: CORRECTION	04	53	138
ROSTER OF WP LOCOS: STEAM/DIESEL	01	53	100
ROSTER OF WP&Y LOCOMOTIVES 1-1971	09	71	53
ROSTER OF WP&Y LOCOMOTIVES 10-1965	02	66	55
ROSTER OF WP&Y LOCOMOTIVES 12-1963	06	64	39
ROSTER OF WP&Y LOCOMOTIVES 12-1970	05	71	58
ROSTER OF WP&Y LOCOMOTIVES 9-1966	03	67	64
ROSTER OF WP&Y LOCOS	10	40	55
ROSTER OF WP&Y LOCOS: ADDITIONAL INFORMA	08	56	73
ROSTER OF WP&Y LOCOS: STEAM/DIESEL-ELECT	04	56	69
ROSTER OF WP&Y STEAM LOCOS 1961	02	61	64
ROSTER OF WPA EQUIPMENT: PASS/WORK	09	49	85
ROSTER OF WPA LOCOS: ADDITIONS	01	50	91
ROSTER OF WPE LOCOMOTIVES 3-1966	05	66	52
ROSTER OF WPE LOCOMOTIVES 9-1969	03	70	66
ROSTER OF WRA LOCOMOTIVES 1-1961	02	62	32
ROSTER OF WRA LOCOMOTIVES 10-1966	02	67	48

ROSTERS BY RAILROAD	M	Y	P
ROSTER OF WRA LOCOS	12	39	112
ROSTER OF WRA LOCOS: STEAM/DIESEL-ELECTR	07	52	106
ROSTER OF WROM STEAM LOCOMOTIVES	10	73	35
ROSTER OF WRR (OWNS NO LOCOMOTIVES)1966	05	66	52
ROSTER OF WRR LOCOMOTIVES 9-1969	03	70	66
ROSTER OF WSS&YP LOCOMOTIVES 12-1968	05	69	50
ROSTER OF WSS&YP LOCOMOTIVES 7-1965	12	65	28
ROSTER OF WSSB LOCOMOTIVES 1-1964	08	64	37
ROSTER OF WSSB LOCOMOTIVES 3-1969	10	69	52
ROSTER OF WSTC (OWNS NO LOCOMOTIVES)1964	08	64	37
ROSTER OF WSTC LOCOMOTIVES 3-1969	10	69	52
ROSTER OF WUTR (OWNS NO LOCOMOTIVES)1964	04	65	36
ROSTER OF WUTR (OWNS NO LOCOMOTIVES)1967	04	68	48
ROSTER OF WUTR LOCOMOTIVES 12-1972	08	73	13
ROSTER OF WVN LOCOMOTIVES 6-1970	02	71	59
ROSTER OF WVN LOCOMOTIVES 7-1966	12	66	54
ROSTER OF WW&F LOCOS: STEAM	12	55	33
ROSTER OF WWV LOCOMOTIVES 12-1965	04	66	58
ROSTER OF WWV LOCOMOTIVES 3-1962	08	62	29
ROSTER OF WWV LOCOMOTIVES 6-1970	06	71	37
ROSTER OF WWV LOCOMOTIVES 9-1969	02	70	50
ROSTER OF WYS LOCOMOTIVES 3-1965	06	65	55
ROSTER OF WYS LOCOMOTIVES 6-1968	10	68	39
ROSTER OF WYS LOCOMOTIVES 6-1973	03	74	47
ROSTER OF WYT LOCOMOTIVES 3-1965	06	65	55
ROSTER OF WYT LOCOMOTIVES 6-1968	10	68	39
ROSTER OF WYT LOCOMOTIVES 6-1973	03	74	47
ROSTER OF Y LOCOMOTIVES 1-1964	08	64	37
ROSTER OF Y LOCOMOTIVES 3-1969	10	69	52
ROSTER OF Y&N LOCOMOTIVES 1960	06	60	57
ROSTER OF Y&N LOCOMOTIVES 6-1969	12	69	48
ROSTER OF Y&S LOCOMOTIVES 1960	06	60	57
ROSTER OF Y&S LOCOMOTIVES 6-1969	12	69	48
ROSTER OF Y&S LOCOMOTIVES 9-1969	03	70	66
ROSTER OF Y&SO LOCOMOTIVES 9-1966	03	67	64
ROSTER OF Y&SU (OWNS NO LOCOMOTIVES)1966	05	66	52
ROSTER OF YAV LOCOMOTIVES 3-1962	08	62	29
ROSTER OF YU LOCOMOTIVES 3-1967	06	67	51
ROSTER OF YV LOCOS: 8 LOCOMOTIVES	07	35	86
ROSTER OF YVT LOCOMOTIVES 6-1970	06	71	37
ROSTER OF YW LOCOMOTIVES 3-1964	08	64	61
ROSTER OF YW LOCOMOTIVES 6-1971	03	72	61
ROSTER OF YW STEAM LOCOS 1961	02	61	64
ROSTERS APPEARING IN RAILROAD MAGAZINE	10	38	61
ROSTERS IN RAILROAD MAG 1932-1955	03	55	74
ROSTERS IN RAILROAD MAG THRU 1942	02	43	61
ROSTERS IN RAILROAD MAGAZINE	06	40	74
ROSTERS INDEX TO ALL PUBLISHED IN RR MAG	12	41	84
ROSTERS OF LOCOMOTIVES IN RAILROAD MAG	08	47	65
ROSTERS OF LOCOS IN RAILROAD MAGAZINE	07	49	65
ROSTERS OF RAILROAD MAGAZINE (ALL TIME)	09	67	58

Stephans' Railroad Directory

Railroad/Railfan

RAILROAD HISTORIES & ROSTERS

HISTORY	M	Y	P
FR HISTORY OF AFRICA: SAHARA RAILWAY	03	30	562
FR HISTORY OF AFRICA: WHITE XPRESS DESER	03	30	562
FR HISTORY OF AUSTRALIAN RAILROADS	05	48	44
FR HISTORY OF AUSTRALIAN ROADS	11	30	538
FR HISTORY OF BURMA RAILWAYS	07	45	114
FR HISTORY OF CEYLON: NUWARA ELIYA LINE	12	36	21
FR HISTORY OF CHINESE RAILROAD	11	50	40
FR HISTORY OF COSTA RICA: NORTHERN RY	03	52	16
FR HISTORY OF COSTA RICA: NORTHERN RY	07	37	35
FR HISTORY OF CUBAN ROAD: HC	11	46	95
FR HISTORY OF DUTCH RAILWAYS: WARTIME	08	40	67
FR HISTORY OF ECUADOR: GUAYAQUIL & QUITO	11	35	91
FR HISTORY OF EGYPT	03	51	34
FR HISTORY OF EGYPT: SUDAN RAILWAYS	10	52	37
FR HISTORY OF ETHIOPIA RAILROAD	11	35	56
FR HISTORY OF EUROPE HI SPEED PASS TRAIN	06	30	442
FR HISTORY OF EUROPE: COMPAIGNE IN WAGON	05	30	218
FR HISTORY OF FEDERATED MALAY STATES RY	04	37	68
FR HISTORY OF FRENCH AUTORAILS	04	49	60
FR HISTORY OF INDIA'S RAILROADS	01	51	29
FR HISTORY OF IRANIAN STATE RY: CHAPLAIN	10	45	06
FR HISTORY OF IRELAND BALLYBUNION MONO	09	33	39
FR HISTORY OF IRELAND: LAST ELECT TRAMWY	12	57	27
FR HISTORY OF ITALIAN RAILWAYS: WAR-TORN	01	45	70
FR HISTORY OF JAPAN'S RAILROADS	06	49	72
FR HISTORY OF JAVA RAILWAYS	11	40	35
FR HISTORY OF MADEIRA-MAMORE RR: AMAZON	05	53	71
FR HISTORY OF NETHERLANDS RAILWAYS	03	53	15
FR HISTORY OF PAN:	02	32	334
FR HISTORY OF PERU: CENTRAL RAILWAY OF	04	40	82
FR HISTORY OF PERU: RAILROAD IN THE SKY	08	30	06
FR HISTORY OF PHILIPPINE RAILROAD	06	32	420
FR HISTORY OF RUSSIA'S RAILROAD	04	52	52
FR HISTORY OF RUSSIA: IRON SHUTTERS	10	51	107
FR HISTORY OF RUSSIAN RAILWAYS	07	37	119
FR HISTORY OF SIBERIAN EXILE SOVIET UNIO	04	30	88
FR HISTORY OF SWEDEN'S RAILWAYS	02	49	42
FR HISTORY OF SWEDEN: STOCKHOLM SUBWAY	11	53	32
FR HISTORY OF SWEDISH RAILWAYS	10	37	55
FR HISTORY OF SWEDISH RAILWAYS	06	56	33
FR HISTORY OF SWISS RAILWAYS	09	47	32
FR HISTORY OF TOKYO EXPRESS	12	46	48
FR HISTORY OF TRINIDAD GOV'T RAILWAY	03	31	568
FR HISTORY OF UK: BRISTOL & GLOUCESTER R	07	35	63
FR HISTORY OF UK: NOTTINGHAM & DERBYSHIR	07	51	83
FR HISTORY OF USSR: FRONTIER FOR BOOMERS	09	31	211
FR HISTORY OF VATICAN CITY RAILWAY	11	50	36
FR HISTORY OF WALES: FESTINIOG RAILWAY	07	38	56
HISTORY OF 2-6-0 LOCOMOTIVES (MOGULS)	05	36	41
HISTORY OF 2-8-2 LOCOMOTIVES (MIKADO)	08	37	41
HISTORY OF 2-8-2 LOCOS (MIKADOS)	12	59	24
HISTORY OF 4-4-0 LOCOS (EIGHT-WHEELERS)	02	57	18
HISTORY OF 4-4-2 LOCOMOPTIVES (ATLANTIC)	08	58	30
HISTORY OF 4-6-0 LOCOMOTIVES	09	36	65
HISTORY OF 4-6-0 LOCOS (TEN-WHEELERS)	06	57	25

HISTORY	M	Y	P
HISTORY OF 4-6-2 LOCOMOTIVES (PACIFICS)	02	58	18
HISTORY OF 4-6-2 LOCOMOTIVES (THE FIRST)	07	36	47
HISTORY OF 4-6-2 LOCOS (PACIFIC TYPE)	06	36	90
HISTORY OF 4-6-4 LOCOMOTIVES (HUDSON)	04	59	22
HISTORY OF 4-8-0 LOCOMOTIVES	03	37	28
HISTORY OF 4-8-2 LOCOMOTIVES (MOUNTAINS)	08	59	26
HISTORY OF 4-8-2 LOCOS (MOUNTIAN TYPE)	11	37	58
HISTORY OF 4-8-4 LOCOS (NORTHERN)	12	58	18
HISTORY OF A&A: 28 MILES/SHORT LINE/NYS	02	54	45
HISTORY OF A&A:USING STEAM AGAIN	02	63	44
HISTORY OF A&BB:A AND A COUPLE OF B'S	01	84	47
HISTORY OF A&BR: 1895-1936/ABANDONED	07	36	98
HISTORY OF A&FA: USES ONLY RAIL-BUSES	06	38	63
HISTORY OF A&LM: RIDE "CROSSETT MAN"	01	81	51
HISTORY OF A&LM:THE GATOR LINE	11	80	32
HISTORY OF A&MR	09	34	36
HISTORY OF A&MR: INCORP 1881	06	53	34
HISTORY OF A&MR: ODDEST GAGE!	01	37	69
HISTORY OF A&SU: GOULD & FISK RAID	03	33	16
HISTORY OF A: AMTRAKING ACROSS THE COUNT	11	76	10
HISTORY OF A: BUSINESS BOOMING PER FUEL	02	74	46
HISTORY OF A: COMMENTS ON PROBLEMS	09	71	30
HISTORY OF A: RETURN OF THE "CENTURY"?	SP	76	48R
HISTORY OF A: TURBO EMPIRE	SP	77	41R
HISTORY OF A: WINDS OF CHANGE	11	81	36
HISTORY OF A:1974 GROWTH	03	75	28
HISTORY OF A:AMTRAK TO SCRANTON	03	80	60
HISTORY OF A:IMPROVED SCHEDULE 1975	01	75	50
HISTORY OF A:PAST IMPERFECT-PAST PERFECT	10	77	13R
HISTORY OF A:PROBLEMS ON THE SP	06	75	42
HISTORY OF A:RDC'S AN ENDANGERED SPECIES	01	80	51
HISTORY OF A:RETURN OF"BROADWAY LIMITED"	09	72	50
HISTORY OF A:WANTS CONGRESSIONAL MONEY	01	72	43
HISTORY OF A:ZEPHYR GOES AMTRAK	09	83	32
HISTORY OF ABI: 1908/5 MILES/TEXAS/EQUIP	08	50	90
HISTORY OF ABSO:FROM CANOE TO AIRPLANE	04	50	46
HISTORY OF AC&HB: NORTH FROM THE SOO	02	50	08
HISTORY OF AC&Y: OHIO MIXED TRAIN	12	51	35
HISTORY OF ACL: THE BEE LINE/WESTERN DIV	10	46	12
HISTORY OF ADIR: ALCO EMPIRE	03	82	51
HISTORY OF AF: 2 CAR CABLE LINE/320'	11	41	39
HISTORY OF AGR: CREATURES OF BONE VALLEY	11	78	47R
HISTORY OF AGR: CRITTERS OF BONE READER	03	79	04R
HISTORY OF AL: 500 MILES/STANDARD GAGE	10	54	33
HISTORY OF ALCO: 100 YEARS PHOTO ESSAY	10	48	34
HISTORY OF ALCO: REPRINT/UPDATED INFORMA	10	48	27
HISTORY OF AMC: WHERE IS IT?	02	77	56
HISTORY OF AMC:BLUE BALDWINS	01	87	62
HISTORY OF AMERICAN LOCOMOTIVE COMPANY	05	37	07
HISTORY OF AMRL	09	34	36
HISTORY OF AP: FREAK MAIN LINE	10	31	393
HISTORY OF APA: ALL ALCO LINE	07	79	50
HISTORY OF APA:UPDATE ON THE APACHIE	10	87	50
HISTORY OF APDT: ALCO EMPIRE	03	82	57
HISTORY OF ATN: SMALL LINE/GOING STRONG	09	33	86

Railroad/ Railfan

RAILROAD HISTORIES & ROSTERS

HISTORY	M	Y	P
HISTORY OF ATSF: ATSF ENTERS SPACE AGE	09	82	26
HISTORY OF ATSF: CANYON WAR OF 1878	08	32	22
HISTORY OF ATSF: CITRUS REEFERS	12	48	18
HISTORY OF ATSF: CLEBURNE SHOPS	02	78	55
HISTORY OF ATSF: HARVEY GIRLS	08	69	10
HISTORY OF ATSF: INDIANS 1883	02	33	18
HISTORY OF ATSF: JOINT LINE	05	78	47R
HISTORY OF ATSF: LAND GRANT LEGEND	12	51	40
HISTORY OF ATSF: OTTAWA JUNCTION	01	49	33
HISTORY OF ATSF: RIO GRANDE DIVISION	03	32	507
HISTORY OF ATSF: SAN MARCIAL FLOOD	08	54	70
HISTORY OF ATSF: SUPER STEAM POWER	02	71	23
HISTORY OF ATSF: TUGS ON SF BAY	11	84	49
HISTORY OF ATSF:ACTION AT ABO	07	87	46
HISTORY OF ATSF:FLASH FLOOD AT MOJAVE GA	01	78	26
HISTORY OF ATSF:NEEDLES DISTRICT-DESERT	01	84	36
HISTORY OF ATSF:ROUGH, TOUGH TEHACHAPI L	04	69	32
HISTORY OF ATSF:SANTA FE SKYWAY SAGA	11	85	57
HISTORY OF ATSF:SANTA FE TO THE BAY	07	86	47
HISTORY OF AU: LESS THAN ONE MILE!	08	34	37
HISTORY OF AUTO-TRAIN: EXPANDING	09	73	39
HISTORY OF AVI: 1907/KANSAS/INTERURBAN	07	49	86
HISTORY OF B&A: HISTORY/ROSTER	06	36	87
HISTORY OF B&C: IOWA'S LAST NARROW GAGE	01	37	56
HISTORY OF B&FB: "PEG-LEG" RAILROAD	11	34	44
HISTORY OF B&H	09	35	41
HISTORY OF B&H: 1881 TO ?/16 MILES	09	35	45
HISTORY OF B&HA: ALCO EMPIRE	03	82	50
HISTORY OF B&LE: 214 MILES/RANKINGS	05	52	12
HISTORY OF B&M: BERLIN BRANCH	SP	75	32R
HISTORY OF B&M: DIESELS DOWN EAST	07	45	46
HISTORY OF B&M: HILLSBORO BRANCH	SU	76	18R
HISTORY OF B&M: HILLSBORO BRANCH READER	F	76	05R
HISTORY OF B&M: LINE OF THE MINUTE MAN	01	46	06
HISTORY OF B&M: MOGUL COUNTRY NOW DIESEL	03	54	33
HISTORY OF B&M:I REMEMBER STEAM DAYS	12	71	24
HISTORY OF B&M:REORGANIZATION COMPLETION	05	83	26
HISTORY OF B&ML	01	34	90
HISTORY OF B&ML: TOWN OPERATED STEAM RD	10	40	06
HISTORY OF B&ML: WHY WE'RE GOING DIESEL	12	48	48
HISTORY OF B&NW: TRAIL OF LONESOME PINE	09	82	30
HISTORY OF B&O: BRENWOODS EM1'S	W	76	18R
HISTORY OF B&O: CINCINNATIAN	06	47	08
HISTORY OF B&O: DANIEL WILLARD	01	30	321
HISTORY OF B&O: SAND PATCH HILL	11	78	20R
HISTORY OF B&O: STERLING OHIO RU TOWER	10	73	47
HISTORY OF B&O:BENWOOD W VA PHOTO	05	87	32
HISTORY OF B&O:KIMBALL, OHIO 1957	W	74	26R
HISTORY OF B&O:POWER OVER THE ALLEGHENIE	04	67	17
HISTORY OF B&S: STEAM POWER	10	59	20
HISTORY OF B&SR: NOW MAINE CENTRAL	09	35	49
HISTORY OF B&W: 36 MILES/33 CURVED MILES	04	35	33
HISTORY OF BA&P: COPPER HAULER	03	54	80
HISTORY OF BA&P: COPPER HAULER CORRECTIO	06	54	08
HISTORY OF BALDWIN DIESEL LOCOMOTIVES	10	72	58
HISTORY OF BALDWIN EDDYSTONE PLANT	08	31	33

HISTORY	M	Y	P
HISTORY OF BALDWIN LOCOMOTIVE WORKS	12	72	20
HISTORY OF BAR: MAINE/600+ MILES	12	57	19
HISTORY OF BAR: ROLLING IN THE MONEY	12	38	07
HISTORY OF BAR:PAINT SCHEME CHANGING	03	73	49
HISTORY OF BART:NEWEST & MOST MODERN	12	72	42
HISTORY OF BART:ROHR CAR BRAKING PROBLEM	06	72	40
HISTORY OF BBLR: ONE TOWN INTERURBAN	02	71	60
HISTORY OF BC&G:ENGINE SMOKE IN MTS	08	62	13
HISTORY OF BCE: EXPANDING ELECTRIC LINE	03	48	90
HISTORY OF BCO: FORMATION	11	82	22
HISTORY OF BCRW:BOOM BUILDING IN 1973	01	73	08
HISTORY OF BE&M: 4 CLASSES OF SERVICE/NC	03	49	64
HISTORY OF BEC	08	40	78
HISTORY OF BEDT: RAILROAD ACROSS RIVER	06	52	26
HISTORY OF BEDT:NY STILL HAS STEAM ROAD	04	61	13
HISTORY OF BELL GEARED LOCOS	02	46	57
HISTORY OF BERY: ASSOCIATION/HISTORY	04	53	78
HISTORY OF BERY: OPERATING MUSEUM	04	55	29
HISTORY OF BH&FP	02	39	67
HISTORY OF BHC: NARROW GAGE/S DAKOTA	08	59	44
HISTORY OF BLH:MERGER OF 1950	09	72	49
HISTORY OF BM&LP: WORLDS QUIETEST RR	09	73	28
HISTORY OF BM&LP:NEW POWERING CONCEPTS	05	74	39
HISTORY OF BMTC:BRIEF HISTORY	09	75	52
HISTORY OF BN: NORTHWEST FUNNEL	12	87	48
HISTORY OF BN: STEAM TODAY! 1979	07	79	38
HISTORY OF BN: TO GOODLAND KANSAS	05	82	53
HISTORY OF BN:ALLIANCE LINE	03	87	32
HISTORY OF BN:BIG GREEN ALCOS OF VANCOUV	03	79	20R
HISTORY OF BN:EVERGREN F UNITS	09	79	22
HISTORY OF BN:ORIN CUTOFF	05	80	48
HISTORY OF BORC:CREATURES OF BONE VALLEY	11	78	49R
HISTORY OF BOW: BUILT 1911/GA/12 MI/EQUI	09	47	61
HISTORY OF BR&E	11	38	58
HISTORY OF BR&W:GIRL ON A COAL PILE	01	79	08
HISTORY OF BRB&L: COMMUTERS NARROW-GAGE	01	75	14
HISTORY OF BRB&L: COMMUTERS' NARROW GAGE	05	55	26
HISTORY OF BRB&L: STEAM INTERURBAN LINE	01	37	70
HISTORY OF BREP:CREATURES OF BONE VALLEY	11	78	50R
HISTORY OF BRILL: BUILDER OF STREETCARS	02	48	92
HISTORY OF BROOKS LOCOMOTIVE WORKS	08	70	16
HISTORY OF BUDD COMPANY: PASSENGER CARS	10	49	13

Stephans' Railroad Directory

Railroad/Railfan

RAILROAD HISTORIES & ROSTERS

HISTORY	M	Y	P
HISTORY OF C&A: MEMORIES	05	37	87
HISTORY OF C&AM:"JOHN BULL" RESTORATION	01	82	38
HISTORY OF C&AM:JOHN BULL--150 YEARS	01	82	34
* HISTORY OF C&CA: INCORP 1830/NOW CMT	02	49	88
HISTORY OF C&E PRIVATELY OWNED STM LINE	11	30	494
HISTORY OF C&F: DIAMOND JO LINE	03	36	39
HISTORY OF C&GL	08	40	27
HISTORY OF C&GR: MISSISSIPPI DELTA ROAD	08	44	08
HISTORY OF C&GR: NOW ICG	W	74	41R
HISTORY OF C&GR:LAST BALDWIN ON THE DELT	07	84	30
HISTORY OF C&LC: MI SHORT LINE IN COLORA	05	82	50
HISTORY OF C&LE: GLORY DAYS	09	74	46
HISTORY OF C&LE: WORLD'S FASTEST INTERUR	01	34	79
HISTORY OF C&LE: TROLLEY--LONG HAUL COMBO	05	71	23
HISTORY OF C&NW: 100TH ANNIVERSARY	08	36	95
HISTORY OF C&NW: ALCO COUNTRY	08	77	43R
HISTORY OF C&NW: ALCO COUNTRY UPDATE	09	81	28
HISTORY OF C&NW: GALENA DIVISION/BUSIEST	08	51	22
HISTORY OF C&NW:PELLETS AND PULPWOOD	03	80	24
HISTORY OF C&O: KENOVA WV AND COAL	04	78	50R
HISTORY OF C&O:614 4-8-4 STEAMS FOR SAFE	01	81	45
HISTORY OF C&O:614 STEAMS FOR SAFETY 2	03	81	47
HISTORY OF C&O:LOCOMOTIVE AWARENESS	11	72	57
HISTORY OF C&O:THE LAST GREENBRIER 4-8-4	01	81	37
HISTORY OF C&S: DIAMOND JUBILEE	10	73	20
HISTORY OF C&S: JOINT LINE	05	78	47R
HISTORY OF C&S: NARROW GAGE	01	37	57
HISTORY OF C&S: RETURN OF GEORGETOWN LOOP	07	79	46
HISTORY OF C&SL: CANADA'S FIRST	06	32	325
HISTORY OF C&SL: CANADA'S FIRST RAILWAY	08	36	132
HISTORY OF C&TS: GOOD NEWS FROM NARROW G	11	78	30R
HISTORY OF C&WC:CAROLINA MIXED	11	86	38
HISTORY OF C&Y: THE OTHER DIVISIONS	SU	76	31R
HISTORY OF C&Y:THE JANSEN TURNS	SU	76	25R
HISTORY OF CA&C	01	37	67
HISTORY OF CA&C: 1880 NARROW GAGE	02	35	36
HISTORY OF CA&E:LAST DAYS OF "ROARIN' EL	12	77	28R
HISTORY OF CAB-IN-FRONT LOCOS (SP)	03	55	11
HISTORY OF CABOOSES	12	41	06
HISTORY OF CABOOSES	06	55	15
HISTORY OF CAD: KENTUCKY ROAD	08	68	56
HISTORY OF CAMELBACK LOCOMOTIVES	10	57	28
HISTORY OF CANADA RAILROADS PART 2	12	47	12
HISTORY OF CAPR: BORROWED STEAM	02	78	45R
HISTORY OF CAPR: FIRST DIVISION	12	77	18R
HISTORY OF CAPR: IDAHO'S PANHANDLE PIKE	12	52	17
HISTORY OF CAPR: LOG TRAINS	02	78	38R
HISTORY OF CAR FERRYING ACROSS GREAT LAK	11	54	10
HISTORY OF CARS: DAILY EXCEPT SUNDAY	10	52	112
HISTORY OF CASS:MOUNTAIN-CLIMBING SHAYS	05	65	13
HISTORY OF CASS:NEW LIFE FOR B&M BRANCH	05	83	48
HISTORY OF CB&Q WITH ROSTER OF LOCOS	09	36	87
HISTORY OF CB&Q: AURORA--1948	F	75	18R
HISTORY OF CB&Q: LAND GRANT LEGEND	11	51	30
HISTORY OF CB&Q:PIONEER ZEPHYR	06	74	44
* HISTORY OF C&CV: ALCO EMPIRE	03	82	54

HISTORY	M	Y	P
HISTORY OF CB: COORS AND A RAILROAD	01	85	37
HISTORY OF CBELT ST LOUIS SOUTHWESTERN	09	32	196
HISTORY OF CBELT: SAGA OF	05	54	94
HISTORY OF CBELT: SUPPLY TRAIN	04	54	64
HISTORY OF CC&N:NARROW GAUGE IN BIG WOOD	04	65	62
HISTORY OF CCT:THE TRACTION COMPANY	11	79	24
HISTORY OF CCW: 1910/IOWA/24 MILES	10	49	96
HISTORY OF CGA A BRIEF HISTORY	12	32	43
HISTORY OF CGA: A DREAM OF TWO CITIES	05	51	64
HISTORY OF CGA:FOUR SECTIONS OF #9	03	79	40R
HISTORY OF CGW: 1400 MILE RAILROAD	09	53	12
HISTORY OF CHESS: THE NEW IMAGE	07	73	35
HISTORY OF CHESS:KIMBALL, OHIO-1974	W	74	30R
HISTORY OF CHICAGO LOCOMOTIVE BUILDERS	03	73	26
HISTORY OF CIM: 1909 EXPERIMENT	12	67	60
HISTORY OF CL BRIEF! HISTORY 309 MILES	01	34	131
HISTORY OF CL: RUGGED ROUTE	12	53	16
HISTORY OF CL:A TRIP TODAY (1975)	08	75	47
HISTORY OF CLEVELAND OHIO TRACTION LINES	03	46	110
HISTORY OF CLRT:AIRPORTER	04	72	53
HISTORY OF CMFG: BABE IN THE WOODS	10	53	50
HISTORY OF CMI	11	32	487
HISTORY OF CMI:	12	30	90
HISTORY OF CMI: MEMORIES	08	42	06
HISTORY OF CMI: STANDARD GAGE	08	36	39
HISTORY OF CN: 23545 MILES!	11	47	12
HISTORY OF CN: DIESEL SERVICING	12	53	58
HISTORY OF CN: EXPANDS!	04	58	32
HISTORY OF CN: HUDSON BAY ROUTE	03	30	530
HISTORY OF CN: NEW 100 MILE BRANCH LINES	03	38	48
HISTORY OF CN: NORTH TO HUDSON BAY	03	30	530
HISTORY OF CN: PRINCE EDWARD ISLAND	10	77	18R
HISTORY OF CN: SENNETERRE-ROUYN LINE	06	41	36
HISTORY OF CN: SMITHERS DIVISION	05	50	16
HISTORY OF CN:CURTAIN CALL COVERED WAGON	07	86	40
HISTORY OF CN:DODSLAND & PORTER SUB DIV	05	84	30
HISTORY OF CN:EXPLORING FRASER CANYON	11	86	42
HISTORY OF CN:GREAT SLAVE LAKE BRANCH	09	65	16
HISTORY OF CN:MONTREALS ENDANGERED ELEC	11	80	46
HISTORY OF CNJ	03	33	92
HISTORY OF CNJ:	06	35	135
HISTORY OF CNJ: BIG MAC/MCMYLER DUMPER	11	51	43
HISTORY OF CNJ: CAMELBACKS	10	54	11
HISTORY OF CNJ: COAL AND COMMUTERS	03	46	10
HISTORY OF CNJ: STEAM DAYS	11	70	20
HISTORY OF CNJ:ASHLEY PLANES	02	70	40
HISTORY OF CNS&M: INTERURBAN/PASSENGERS	10	53	72
HISTORY OF CNY: ALCO EMPIRE	03	82	55
HISTORY OF CNYE: BEGAN 1906	12	56	41
HISTORY OF CNYEA	05	33	78
HISTORY OF CO&CO:BLUE/YELLOW & IN BLACK	05	83	35
HISTORY OF CO&E:THIS LITTLE PIGGY TO MKT	07	80	26
HISTORY OF COOKE LOCO WRKS: PATTERSON NJ	06	33	34
HISTORY OF CORREGIDOR: US OWNED/OPERATED	03	37	10
HISTORY OF COUPLERS	01	30	233

Railroad/ Railfan

RAILROAD HISTORIES & ROSTERS

HISTORY	M	Y	P
HISTORY OF CP "BATTLE OF FORT WAYNE"	05	34	90
HISTORY OF CP: ANGUS SHOPS/CAST IRON FRT	09	53	62
HISTORY OF CP: DIESELS ACROSS THE BORDER	09	50	32
HISTORY OF CP: HECTOR-FIELD ROUTE	06	30	321
HISTORY OF CP: KETTLE VALLEY DIVISION	08	50	28
HISTORY OF CP: LAST DAYS OF STEAM	10	69	18
HISTORY OF CP: MONTREAL HUMP RETAINER YD	07	50	32
HISTORY OF CP: OPERATED BUT NOT BUILT	06	30	321
HISTORY OF CP: STEEL ACROSS CANADA	08	33	80
HISTORY OF CP: THE BIG HILL	09	46	73
HISTORY OF CP:CP RAIL IN VERMONT	09	80	50
HISTORY OF CP:WHERE SD40-2S DONT ROAM BL	09	85	52
HISTORY OF CPA: GREAT SALT LAKE FILL	08	57	19
HISTORY OF CPR: TOWN OWNED ROAD	09	78	34R
HISTORY OF CPR:RAILWAY PAYS ITS BILLS	09	66	23
HISTORY OF CPR:TOWN MONEY MAKER	10	72	11
HISTORY OF CR: CONRAIL AND THE SHORTLINE	F	76	38R
HISTORY OF CR: FOUR TRACK FAREWELL	05	82	54
HISTORY OF CR: HERE COMES CONRAIL	SU	75	38R
HISTORY OF CR: PRO & CONRAIL	W	75	28R
HISTORY OF CR:BOXCAR NJ WEEKEND	W	76	30R
HISTORY OF CR:COMPUTER SIMULATION	02	76	04
HISTORY OF CR:CONRAILS PLEASANT SUPRISES	F	76	59R
HISTORY OF CR:NJUN CONRAILS TROLLEY	F	76	18R
HISTORY OF CRB&L: LOGGING ROAD	02	39	78
HISTORY OF CRI:FIVE ALCOS AND A MACK	05	79	49
HISTORY OF CRR&B: A DREAM OF 2 CITIES	05	51	64
HISTORY OF CRT: SOUTH SIDE ELEVATED LINE	12	36	119
HISTORY OF CRTA:CHICAGO'S NEW LOOK	05	78	40R
HISTORY OF CS&I: 1900	06	53	76
HISTORY OF CSCR: UP AND DOWN RAILWAY	04	52	93
HISTORY OF CSF&E: 24 MILE LOGGING PIKE	09	42	113
HISTORY OF CSO: MEMORIES	05	42	06
HISTORY OF CSO: RATHOLE DIVISION	01	39	07
HISTORY OF CSS&SB: MODERNIZED	04	57	50
HISTORY OF CSS&SB: SHORE LINE	02	53	10
HISTORY OF CSS&SB: STILL AN INTERURBAN	11	78	38R
HISTORY OF CSS&SB:THE 800'S GARY JOB	09	80	36
HISTORY OF CSS&SB:TRACKING SOUTH SHORE	01	79	47R
HISTORY OF CT UNDER CHICAGO STREETS	11	33	94
HISTORY OF CT: 1912/UNDERGROUND/NARROW G	01	50	84
HISTORY OF CTR: ELECTRIC STREET RY 1	11	50	88
HISTORY OF CTR: ELECTRIC STREET RY 2	12	50	82
HISTORY OF CV	12	35	88
HISTORY OF CV: BORDER LINE/FREIGHT RATE	08	47	08
HISTORY OF CV: ST ALBANS VERMONT	05	51	18
HISTORY OF CV:CENTRAL VERMONT STEAM	05	79	35
HISTORY OF CV:DYNAMIC PROPERTY	03	79	45R
HISTORY OF CV:THE OLD DAYS	10	76	06
HISTORY OF CVL: CLOSED FOR 1980 SEASON	09	80	63
HISTORY OF CVL:LONGEST STEAM RUN EAST OF	07	80	49
HISTORY OF D&BB:FROG WAR WITH PRR 1876	11	75	43
HISTORY OF D&CA: OWNED BY CALIF. DOOR CO	01	37	68
HISTORY OF D&H: CORRECTIONS	11	47	133
HISTORY OF D&H: INCREDIBLE ROAD	SU	75	60R
HISTORY OF D&H: ITS HISTORY/ITS FUTURE	04	47	06
HISTORY OF D&H: RETRACKING THE APOLLOS	F	76	51R
HISTORY OF D&H: WITH LOCOMOTIVE ROSTER	11	36	125
HISTORY OF D&H:117 YEARS OF STEAM POWER	06	63	14
HISTORY OF D&H:OWEGO CONNECTION	SP	76	18R
HISTORY OF D&H:STRANGERS IN SOUTH STATIO	04	78	29R
HISTORY OF D&I: ELECTRIC TROLLEY LINE	01	37	57
HISTORY OF D&M: MACKINAW DIVISION	07	78	53R
HISTORY OF D&MM:RETURN TO PROSPERITY	03	86	48
HISTORY OF D&N: RAILS RUST IN CATSKILLS	09	43	103
HISTORY OF D&RG: BUCKHORN FLAT/ROBBERY	12	48	86
HISTORY OF D&RG: GLORY DAYS	11	46	44
HISTORY OF D&RG: MY NARROW GAGE ALBUM	05	40	06
HISTORY OF D&RG: STANDARD & NARROW GAGE	04	36	91
HISTORY OF D&RGW: A WEEKEND ON THE D&RGW	10	53	19
HISTORY OF D&RGW: CANYON WAR OF 1878	08	32	22
HISTORY OF D&RGW: MARSHALL PASS LINE	F	76	42R
HISTORY OF D&RGW: NARROW GAUGE	07	32	495
HISTORY OF D&RGW: SILVERTON LINE	06	54	42
HISTORY OF D&RGW: SILVERTON/NARROW GAGE	06	55	40
HISTORY OF D&RGW: STANDARD GAGE	01	37	60
HISTORY OF D&RGW: THE SILVERTON LINE	06	69	13
HISTORY OF D&RGW:MONARCH MINUET	07	80	45
HISTORY OF D&SL: NOW MOFFATT DIV D&RGW	09	47	08
HISTORY OF D&TSL: NKP COLORS BUT GTW	07	81	40
HISTORY OF D&TSL:STEAM ON THE SHORE LINE	07	81	54
HISTORY OF D&WT: OHIO ROAD	01	77	51
HISTORY OF DARA: WELCOME DAKOTA RAIL	11	82	37
HISTORY OF DB&W: 1898-1919"SWITZERLAND T	07	41	47
HISTORY OF DCC&P: PROPOSED	09	33	78
HISTORY OF DIESEL LOCOMOTIVES	04	55	19
HISTORY OF DIESEL LOCOS: 33 YEARS	10	57	23
HISTORY OF DL&W: BIG EXPANSION	12	29	136
HISTORY OF DL&W:50 YEARS OF ELECTRICS	07	81	48
HISTORY OF DL&W:NAMED LOCOS BY DIVISION	10	61	44
HISTORY OF DM&IR: HEADACHE ON IRON RANGE	03	50	12
HISTORY OF DM&IR:GREAT DAYS OF STEAM	10	61	25
HISTORY OF DM&IR:STEAM DAYS	12	60	34
HISTORY OF DO: ALCO EMPIRE	03	82	53
HISTORY OF DO: EXPANDS 177.4 MILES	07	82	24
HISTORY OF DOUBLE-ENDED LOCOMOTIVES	04	58	26
HISTORY OF DPE: 1907 STEAM ONLY/NOW FRT	08	43	80
HISTORY OF DPE:RAILROAD NAMED FOR A HORS	08	65	13
HISTORY OF DPL: MOTOR CARS & STEAM	09	82	38
HISTORY OF DS: LUMBER NARROW GAGE ROAD	01	37	56
HISTORY OF DSP&P	12	34	46
HISTORY OF DSP&P: ALPINE PASS ROUTE	03	38	64
HISTORY OF DSP&P: ALPINE TUNNEL ROUTE	06	41	06
HISTORY OF DSP&P: NARROW GAGE ROAD	01	37	53
HISTORY OF DSP&P: SOUTH PARK'S LAST RUN	08	37	96
HISTORY OF DSS&A: A BRIEF HISTORY	08	32	131
HISTORY OF DSS&A: FINANCIAL STATUS	07	36	35
HISTORY OF DT&I: HENRY FORD'S RAILROAD	07	38	08
HISTORY OF DT&I: IRONTON RUN	SP	75	20R
HISTORY OF DUTCHESS (LOCOMOTIVE)	08	56	11

Stephans' Railroad Directory

Railroad/Railfan

RAILROAD HISTORIES & ROSTERS

HISTORY	M	Y	P
HISTORY OF E&K:MICHIGAN'S FIRST RAILROAD	10	34	35
HISTORY OF E&M:LAST ALL STEAM RR IN US	02	76	11
HISTORY OF E&M:WHAT'S IN A NAME?	SP	77	13R
HISTORY OF E&N: VANCOUVER ISLAND TODAY	09	78	49R
HISTORY OF E: FIGHTS FOR 6' GAUGE	01	33	36
HISTORY OF E: FLYING SAUCER	09	51	12
HISTORY OF E: GOULD-FISK RAID	03	33	16
HISTORY OF E: OPERATION ESCALATOR	10	51	40
HISTORY OF E: STEAM POWER	06	67	22
HISTORY OF E: THOSE BERKSHIRES	12	69	22
HISTORY OF E:CENTIPEDES 2-8-8-8-2	10	74	50
HISTORY OF E:DINING STATIONS	01	76	12
HISTORY OF E:MALLETS	06	70	30
HISTORY OF EB&L: LOGGING ROAD/NH/EQUIPME	01	48	118
HISTORY OF EBT: STORY & PHOTO ESSAY	07	51	46
HISTORY OF EBT: NARROW GAGE ROAD	01	37	49
HISTORY OF EBT: ORBISONIA OBSESSION	W	75	18R
HISTORY OF EBT: STANDARD GAGE CARS	03	34	131
HISTORY OF ED: LAST OF THE TWO-FOOTERS	05	47	54
HISTORY OF EI&TH	05	41	47
HISTORY OF EL: STERLING OHIO RU TOWER	10	73	47
HISTORY OF ELD: PASSENGER ELEVATOR	08	51	94
HISTORY OF EMT:LAST DAYS	09	83	28
HISTORY OF EN: COLLECTS FROM UNCLE SAM	02	38	26
HISTORY OF EN: NARROW GAGE ROAD	01	37	65
HISTORY OF EPCL: TEXAS/INTERN'L STREETCA	01	52	94
HISTORY OF ET&WNC: 50 YRS OLD 3' GAUGE	11	33	139
HISTORY OF ET&WNC: OLDEST NARROW GAGE RD	01	37	52
HISTORY OF F&C: KENTUCKY/BEGAN AS KM	08	50	38
HISTORY OF F&CC: BY A F&CC HOGGER	04	42	06
HISTORY OF F&CC: SHORTEST LIVED COLORADO	08	58	23
HISTORY OF FC:PINSLY COMES TO FLORIDA	10	87	36
HISTORY OF FDM&S: 150 MILE INTERURBAN	09	52	74
HISTORY OF FEC: KEY WEST BRANCH	12	33	132
HISTORY OF FEC: OVERSEAS EXTENSION	12	33	132
HISTORY OF FEC: PALM BEACH RAILS	01	52	14
HISTORY OF FJ&G: ALCO EMPIRE	03	82	55
HISTORY OF FJ&G:MOHAWK VALLEY SHORTLINE	01	69	34
HISTORY OF FPT: 1897-1946/PARK TROLLEY	12	46	98
HISTORY OF FRIS: JULY 4 1851 1ST RAILS	01	53	10
HISTORY OF FRIS:FAIRWELL FRISCO	11	80	51
HISTORY OF G&J: ALCO EMPIRE	03	82	56
HISTORY OF G&N: CAROLINA SWAMP RABBIT	12	49	38
HISTORY OF G&N: THE SWAMP RABBIT	SP	77	18R
HISTORY OF G&W: ALCO EMPIRE	03	82	46
HISTORY OF G&W:NEW & EXPANDING	03	86	44
HISTORY OF G: A YANKEE CORRECTIONS	03	50	138
HISTORY OF G: A YANKEE AND COTTON	01	50	56
HISTORY OF G: GEORGIA MIXES	SU	76	47R
HISTORY OF GAR:CREATURES OF BONE VALLEY	11	78	51R
HISTORY OF GAUGES IN THE UNITED STATES	12	31	80
HISTORY OF GB&W: BADGER STATE ROAD	11	51	14
HISTORY OF GCH:CREATURES OF BONE VALLEY	11	78	51R
HISTORY OF GIL:GUILFORD PREVIEW	05	83	31
HISTORY OF GM&O: REBEL ROUTE	01	45	06
HISTORY OF GM&O: THE FABULOUS FALKNER	03	54	22
HISTORY OF GMT: RUTLAND REVIVAL	F	75	23R
HISTORY OF GN: CANYON WAR	10	56	22
HISTORY OF GN: CASCADE TUNNEL/AIR-COOLIN	02	57	33
HISTORY OF GN: FOUNDED BY JIM HILL	02	37	34
HISTORY OF GN: GREENHOUSES	06	54	96
HISTORY OF GN: JAMES J HILL'S ADVENTURE	02	55	10
HISTORY OF GN: JIM HILL	12	78	20
HISTORY OF GN: LAND GRANT	10	51	68
HISTORY OF GN: ST CLOUD SHOPS/20 BOXCARS	08	53	50
HISTORY OF GN: THE "HUTCH" BRANCH	W	75	40R
HISTORY OF GN:ROAD DIESEL RENUMBERING	06	68	66
HISTORY OF GN:STEAMSHIP MINNESOTA & DAKO	12	78	47
HISTORY OF GRAHAM CUTOFF	09	51	42
HISTORY OF GRANT LOCO WRKS: PATTERSON NJ	06	33	34
HISTORY OF GT:125TH ANNIVERSARY	09	78	57
HISTORY OF GT:SOUTH PARIS SWITCHER	09	85	32
HISTORY OF GTW: D&TSL	07	81	40
HISTORY OF GVE: MONTANA'S ONLY INTERURBA	12	59	29
HISTORY OF GWS:GREATEST CONCENTRATION ST	03	72	22
HISTORY OF GWWD:MANITOBAS UNCOMMON CARRI	05	81	50
HISTORY OF H&H: 1904-1927 1 LOCO/1 MILE	10	33	48
HISTORY OF H&LB: THE PORTAGE RAILROAD	11	52	42
HISTORY OF H&M: STARTED 1874/DONE 1909	11	47	105
HISTORY OF H&S:ENTERPRISING ROAD	11	86	58
HISTORY OF H&W	02	41	73
HISTORY OF HALL & HALL: 1 MILE LONG	12	38	112
HISTORY OF HAR: OWNED BY CHAMBER OF COMM	01	47	60
HISTORY OF HB&IT	12	34	59
HISTORY OF HB&T:FOUR OWNERS	01	79	20R
HISTORY OF HC:RAILWAY THAT CHOCOLATE BLT	10	60	16
HISTORY OF HD: 1 MILE NARROW GAGE MICH	04	35	35
HISTORY OF HH: SAN FRANCISCOS OWN RR	02	74	49
HISTORY OF HINKLEY LOCOMOTIVE WORKS	06	44	81
HISTORY OF HL&T: WOODEN RAILWAY STILL!	07	35	79
HISTORY OF HM	06	41	26
HISTORY OF HOTS	03	36	39
HISTORY OF HY&T: PUMPKIN VINE	07	40	23
HISTORY OF IC: EVOLUTION OF LOGO	07	67	34
HISTORY OF IC: LAND GRANT LEGEND	08	51	28
HISTORY OF IC: LARRY DOWNS	12	32	107
HISTORY OF IC: LOCOMOTIVE NAMES	11	35	40
HISTORY OF IC: STRONGHOLD OF STEAM	06	52	13
HISTORY OF IC: WITH ROSTER	12	36	116
HISTORY OF IC:CASEY JONES LEGEND DEBUNKD	02	76	06
HISTORY OF IC:CASEY JONES WRECK REPORT	03	78	36
HISTORY OF IC:DAMAGES DUE TO C JONES WRE	07	66	40
HISTORY OF ICO:CAPSULE	01	79	42
HISTORY OF IL:FORGOTTEN NARROW GAUGE	10	64	18
HISTORY OF IM&C:CREATURES OF BONE VALLEY	11	78	52R
HISTORY OF IRCA: BANANA LINE/912 M/3' GA	08	48	36
HISTORY OF IRRC:NEW LIFE ON THE OLD ROCK	07	84	50
HISTORY OF IT: 171 MILE INTERURBAN	12	51	80
HISTORY OF IT: LONGEST INTERURBAN	05	55	42
HISTORY OF IUR: PERRY & COLFAX INTER/IA	05	51	94

Railroad/Railfan

RAILROAD HISTORIES & ROSTERS

HISTORY	M	Y	P
HISTORY OF IVT: 1907/"IVY WAY"/ILLINOIS	04	50	90
HISTORY OF J&W: AUTOMATED SHORT LINE	07	65	24
HISTORY OF JC&FR	12	58	26
HISTORY OF JOHNSON BAR	11	30	602
HISTORY OF JW&N: CHAUTAUQUA LAKE ROUTE	05	46	115
HISTORY OF K&O	10	30	353
HISTORY OF KAC&LC	03	77	47
HISTORY OF KCE	09	35	41
HISTORY OF KCE: 5 MILES 1890-1929	09	35	41
HISTORY OF KCS: 85% INCOME FROM FREIGHT	10	47	12
HISTORY OF KCS: STILLWELL, FOUNDER	04	57	32
HISTORY OF KCS: F UNITS OF SULPHUR SPRING	11	83	54
HISTORY OF KS: MODERN INTERURBAN	08	55	34
HISTORY OF KYRR: BIG NAME IN SMALL RAILWA	09	82	22
HISTORY OF L	07	39	65
HISTORY OF L&HR: POUGHKEEPSIE BRIDGE BUR	W	74	18R
HISTORY OF L&MA: LAKE ERIE LIMESTONE LIN	07	52	51
HISTORY OF L&N	01	36	89
HISTORY OF L&N: HOOK & EYE DIVISION	06	40	06
HISTORY OF L&N: MONON MERGER	SU	75	40R
HISTORY OF L&N: MULE	02	53	06
HISTORY OF L&N: SCOTTSVILLE BRANCH	03	76	46
HISTORY OF L&N: STEAM POWER	11	64	17
HISTORY OF L&N: U-BOATS OF DECOURSEY	05	81	45
HISTORY OF L&NW: SHORTLINE SKETCHBOOK	04	78	34R
HISTORY OF L&S: 7.5 MILES/HAULED GOLD &	04	42	70
HISTORY OF L&WV: THIRD RAIL INTERURBAN	03	51	80
HISTORY OF LA&A: ALCO EMPIRE	03	82	47
HISTORY OF LA: NARROW GAGE ROAD	01	37	54
HISTORY OF LATR: ADDITIONS/CORRECTIONS	04	54	103
HISTORY OF LATR: LARGE STREETCAR OPERATI	01	54	36
HISTORY OF LEBG&N: CROSSCOUNTRY INTERURB	06	52	77
HISTORY OF LI: CARS GET BEAUTY TREATMENT	01	71	40
HISTORY OF LI: GOES DIESEL	05	51	46
HISTORY OF LI: HISTORY & ROSTER	05	36	89
HISTORY OF LI: MARCH 1949 BANKRUPTCY	08	49	11
HISTORY OF LI: PASSENGER BUSINESS	01	43	12
HISTORY OF LIG: COMPLETED 1871/PA/16 MIL	05	52	43
HISTORY OF LIMA LOCOMOTIVE WORKS	02	73	53
HISTORY OF LIMA SUPER POWER LOCOS	08	74	24
HISTORY OF LISRY: FIRST RUNS 1888	06	68	40
HISTORY OF LK&W	05	35	72
HISTORY OF LOCOMOTIVE PLANTS	05	37	07
HISTORY OF LS&I: ALLIGATORS IN N WOODS	07	85	48
HISTORY OF LSEL: INTERURBAN	11	51	77
HISTORY OF LU&N: THE OTHER L&N	01	81	33
HISTORY OF LV: OWEGO CONNECTION	SP	76	18R
HISTORY OF LV: STEAM POWER	01	65	19
HISTORY OF LV: TRACKING THE APOLLOS	W	75	48R
HISTORY OF LV: WHEN STEAM RULED THE LV	08	69	36
HISTORY OF LV: BLACK DIAMOND LAST RUN	10	76	34
HISTORY OF LVRC: TODAYS VALLEY ROAD	05	80	26
HISTORY OF M	05	49	10
HISTORY OF M&A	01	41	65
HISTORY OF M&A: HISTORY AND ROSTER	07	36	88
HISTORY OF M&A: TURBULENT NORTH ARKANSAS	06	48	10
HISTORY OF M&BL: COMPLETED 1910/3 LOCOS	08	50	06
HISTORY OF M&E	11	40	71
HISTORY OF M&LB: STEAM DUMMY HISTORY	02	59	67
HISTORY OF M&LB: THE YELLOW JACKET	10	48	55
HISTORY OF M&NG	06	40	06
HISTORY OF M&OL PHOTO ESSAY	11	40	64
HISTORY OF M&ONE: 40 PROSPEROUS YEARS	04	41	06
HISTORY OF M&SL	05	36	33
HISTORY OF M&SL: BRIEF	03	35	80
HISTORY OF M&SL: FINANCIAL HISTORY	05	36	33
HISTORY OF M&SL: LONGEST RR RECEIVERSHIP	04	44	46
HISTORY OF M&U: 14 MILES/NY/EQUIPMENT	08	47	120
HISTORY OF M: EARLY DAYS	12	32	98
HISTORY OF MA: SMOKE OVER ARIZONA	06	62	21
HISTORY OF MABEL: PRIVATE TROLLEY	08	51	84
HISTORY OF MAINE'S TWO-FOOT GAGE	12	55	23
HISTORY OF MALLET (ARTICULATED) LOCOS	03	44	08
HISTORY OF MALLET LOCOMOTIVES	08	55	26
HISTORY OF MAN: SHORTEST STD GAGE/500'	06	38	124
HISTORY OF MANN BOUDOIR SLEEPING CAR	06	59	24
HISTORY OF MASON MACHINE WORKS	02	34	38
HISTORY OF MBTA: NEW CARS TO REPLACE PCC	10	71	50
HISTORY OF MC&I:	12	58	27
HISTORY OF MC&LM	01	34	90
HISTORY OF MC: BAR HARBOR MAINE	01	77	50
HISTORY OF MC: FIRST GENERATION DIESELS	09	78	45R
HISTORY OF MC: FROM SILVIS TO BANGOR	11	81	30
HISTORY OF MC: HISTORY HIGHLIGHTS	09	78	44R
HISTORY OF MC: PASSENGER SERVICE	09	78	46R
HISTORY OF MC: STEAM LOCOMOTIVES	09	78	37R
HISTORY OF MC: STILL INDEPENDENT & MAKIN	07	78	38R
HISTORY OF MC: DAVID FINK ON GUILFORD	05	83	28
HISTORY OF MCH: SOLD FOR SCRAP	12	37	59
HISTORY OF MCKEEN MOTOR CARS	01	51	14
HISTORY OF MCRI: 1897/LUMBER ROAD/43AD	10	50	42
HISTORY OF MCRI: STEAM RETURNS	11	82	28
HISTORY OF MEL: CREWLESS ELECTRICS	08	69	19
HISTORY OF MI: LONGEST ALL STEAM IN SOUTH	04	63	14
HISTORY OF MI: THE MISSISSIPPIAN TRADITIO	12	87	59
HISTORY OF MICHC: MACKINAW DIVISION	10	52	14
HISTORY OF MICHIGAN'S LUMBER PIKES	07	53	51
HISTORY OF MILW: ELECTRIFICATION ENDING	05	73	22
HISTORY OF MILW: OLYMPIAN PART 1	06	50	14
HISTORY OF MILW: OLYMPIAN PART 2	07	50	36
HISTORY OF MILW: OLYMPIC PENINSULA BRANC	03	50	40
HISTORY OF MILW: PUGET SOUND MARINE OPER	03	41	87
HISTORY OF MILW: SEA-GOING RAILROAD	03	41	87
HISTORY OF MILW: BANKRUPT	03	78	42
HISTORY OF MILW: ELECTRIFICATION	06	70	18
HISTORY OF MILW: ELECTRIFICATION PROBLEMS	12	75	07
HISTORY OF MILW: FAIRWELL TO 1ST GENERATI	02	78	18R
HISTORY OF MINE RAILROAD OPER-COAL FIELD	07	46	54
HISTORY OF MKT: KATY	07	48	08
HISTORY OF MKT: NEWS BUTCHER OF 1906	02	71	61

Railroad/Railfan

Stephans' Railroad Directory

RAILROAD HISTORIES & ROSTERS

HISTORY	M	Y	P
HISTORY OF MKT:100 YEARS OF MKT RAILROAD	12	70	20
HISTORY OF MKT:KATYS OKLAHOMA F'S	05	79	45
HISTORY OF MMI:LOOK LIKE WM OR BN OR GET	11	85	50
HISTORY OF MN&S: 1918/REORGANIZATION DPE	08	43	83
HISTORY OF MN&S: MOTOR CARS AND STEAM	09	82	38
HISTORY OF MN&S:BLUE DRAGON OF GOLDEN VA	07	82	48
HISTORY OF MO	09	35	41
HISTORY OF MO:	05	39	77
HISTORY OF MO: 6 MILES/1882-??/UNUSUAL!!	09	35	43
HISTORY OF MOBCH:CRITTERS OF BONE READER	03	79	04R
HISTORY OF MOBCH:CRITTERS OF BONE VALLEY	11	78	54R
HISTORY OF MONTANAS FIRST STREET CARS	10	64	32
HISTORY OF MOVA: SHORTEST STEAM/STD GAGE	08	49	68
HISTORY OF MP: COAL BURNING DAYS	08	69	10
HISTORY OF MP: MO PAC NAVY--PAPER MILL	01	83	51
HISTORY OF MP: MO-PAC'S NAVY	11	82	40
HISTORY OF MPR&DE: MOTOR CARS & STEAM	09	82	38
HISTORY OF MRC: 7/8 MILE/SINGLE-TRACKED	05	40	74
HISTORY OF MRS: ARMY RAILROADERS	02	43	24
HISTORY OF MSRW: TROLLEY/NEW HAMPSHIRE	08	53	64
HISTORY OF MSW: NARROW GAGE ROAD	01	37	70
HISTORY OF MT&L:STREETCAR RIOT 8-1919	08	75	46
HISTORY OF MT&MW: WORLDS CROOKEDEST PIKE	06	32	320
HISTORY OF MT: CARWAYS	01	55	40
HISTORY OF MT: RUBBER TIRED METRO	08	68	63
HISTORY OF MV: SALT SPRAY ON THE RAILS	08	43	08
HISTORY OF MWCOG:CHANGES ON MT WASHINGTO	03	84	49
HISTORY OF MWCOG:RAILWAY TO THE MOON	07	69	18
HISTORY OF N&SV: NARROW GAGE ROAD	01	37	46
HISTORY OF N&W	03	36	91
HISTORY OF N&W: BOAZ TO BLUE RIDGE	SP	75	24R
HISTORY OF N&W: COAL/2000 MI/HISTORY/MER	07	54	18
HISTORY OF N&W: COAL/ORE/GRAIN LEADER	10	73	07
HISTORY OF N&W: GAUGE CHANGING 1886	07	35	46
HISTORY OF N&W: GEARED FOR TONNAGE	09	44	08
HISTORY OF N&W: IT MERGER & SD39'S	09	82	50
HISTORY OF N&W: KENOVA WV AND COAL	04	78	50R
HISTORY OF N&W: KIMBALL, OHIO 1974	W	74	30R
HISTORY OF N&W: POCAHONTAS DIV MEMORIES	03	45	09
HISTORY OF N&W: STATION AGENT	07	54	71
HISTORY OF N&W: TIDEWATERS 251'S	07	82	31
HISTORY OF N&W:76 YEARS OF ROANOKE BUILT	08	64	13
HISTORY OF NA: 923 MILES/CANADA'S 3RD LA	01	54	10
HISTORY OF NARROW-GAGE ROADS: OBSOLETE	08	41	06
HISTORY OF NC&SL	07	35	37
HISTORY OF NC&SL: SCHOOL ON WHEELS	05	53	06
HISTORY OF NC&SL: CHATTANOOGA LOCOS	11	48	12
HISTORY OF NC&SL: LEASED W&A	12	45	08
HISTORY OF NC&SL: PADUCAH & MEMPHIS DIVS	09	50	06
HISTORY OF NC: NARROW GAGE ROAD	01	37	66
HISTORY OF NCI: TROLLEY DAYS	12	54	46
HISTORY OF NCN: NARROW GAGE ROAD	01	37	68
HISTORY OF NCO: COW-COUNTRY NARROW-GAGE	10	55	40
HISTORY OF NCRR: ALCO EMPIRE	03	82	53
HISTORY OF NEIP: NORTH AMERICA'S 1ST RY	05	42	25
HISTORY OF NEW ORLEANS TRACTION LINES	11	70	36
HISTORY OF NEW YORK LOCOMOTIVE WORKS	01	44	104
HISTORY OF NEZ&I: 1908-1944/DEPOT/EQUIP/	01	54	70
HISTORY OF NEZ:13 MILE ODD BALL SHORT LI	02	78	44R
HISTORY OF NF: NARROW GAGE RAILWAY	08	38	70
HISTORY OF NH&SL	10	41	72
HISTORY OF NI: 40 YEARS	02	54	77
HISTORY OF NJTR: WHITE FLAGS INTO OBLIVI	02	51	68
HISTORY OF NJUN: CONRAILS TROLLEY	F	76	18R
HISTORY OF NKP:KIMBALL, OHIO 1957	W	74	26R
HISTORY OF NL&G: SHORTLINE SKETCHBOOK	04	78	34R
HISTORY OF NN: ORGANIZED 1905/OPERATE 06	07	48	41
HISTORY OF NN: THE ELY ROUTE	09	52	36
HISTORY OF NNB&S: ONE MAN RAILROAD	03	55	22
HISTORY OF NOPB: CITY OWNED RAILROAD	12	67	18
HISTORY OF NOPS: O-K LINE	09	51	79
HISTORY OF NOPS: ST CHARLES LINE	11	81	42
HISTORY OF NP: IRON SPKIE AT GOLD CREEK	12	33	84
HISTORY OF NP: LAKE SUPERIOR TO PUGET SO	05	47	12
HISTORY OF NP: LAND GRANT	09	51	64
HISTORY OF NP: OIL BONANZA	05	53	12
HISTORY OF NP: STAMPEDE PASS SWITCHBACK	04	37	28
HISTORY OF NP: SWEETMAN 1ST CONDUCTOR	04	40	72
HISTORY OF NP: WASHINGTON TERRITORY	09	37	31
HISTORY OF NP: YELLOWSTONE LOCOMOTIVES	12	29	100
HISTORY OF NP:DEATH OF MONTESANO WA DEPO	05	71	51
HISTORY OF NP:PIONEER DAYS	02	63	20
HISTORY OF NP:REBUILDING STEAM LOCOS	02	72	22
HISTORY OF NPC: INCORP 1871/CALIF/NARROW	01	54	82
HISTORY OF NPC: SLIM GAUGE	10	67	53
HISTORY OF NRR: SALT SPRAY ON THE RAILS	08	43	08
HISTORY OF NS&W:STEAM ROAD	09	70	19
HISTORY OF NSC&T: INTERURBAN	02	52	75
HISTORY OF NSC&T: INTERURBAN LINE/CANADA	06	50	84
HISTORY OF NWP: CALIFORNIA/REDWOOD EMPIR	08	53	33
HISTORY OF NWP: WITH HISTORY OF LOCOS	04	36	37
HISTORY OF NY&LB: THE LONG BRANCH ROUTE	07	52	30
HISTORY OF NY&LE:ALCO EMPIRE	03	82	44
HISTORY OF NY&O	04	33	94
HISTORY OF NYC: 100 YEARS OF STEAM	09	53	44
HISTORY OF NYC: CLASS I RAILROAD	11	50	15
HISTORY OF NYC: COMMUTING	12	51	14
HISTORY OF NYC: DISTRIBUTION OF LOCOS	02	56	79
HISTORY OF NYC: NY CITY STREET TRACKAGE	07	30	562
HISTORY OF NYC: PUTNAM DIVISION	01	49	48
HISTORY OF NYC:GRAND CENTRAL STATION	08	65	27
HISTORY OF NYCE: 66 MILES FOR A NICKEL	04	33	81
HISTORY OF NYCE: FORNEY/HOGGER/TALLOWPOT	04	31	49
HISTORY OF NYCE: THIRD AVENUE EL	06	56	13
HISTORY OF NYCS: ELEVATED LINES	02	52	28
HISTORY OF NYNH&H: ELECTRICS	04	59	48
HISTORY OF NYNH&H: ELECTRIFICATION 1	12	58	30
HISTORY OF NYNH&H: ELECTRIFICATION 2	02	59	30
HISTORY OF NYNH&H: ELECTRIFICATION PART1	04	75	40
HISTORY OF NYNH&H: ELECTRIFICATION PART2	05	75	24

Railroad/ Railfan

RAILROAD HISTORIES & ROSTERS

HISTORY	M	Y	P
HISTORY OF NYNH&H: FL9'S	12	77	36R
HISTORY OF NYNH&H: PELLEY BECOMES PRES	12	29	01
HISTORY OF NYNH&H: SHEPAUG BRANCH	04	48	46
HISTORY OF NYNH&H: TWILIGHT OF ELECTRICS	06	59	48
HISTORY OF NYNH&H:CENTER THIRD RAIL OPER	01	69	32
HISTORY OF NYO&W: SHAWANGUNK BARRIER	09	46	11
HISTORY OF NYS&W: NOTES FROM STOUDSBURG	W	76	13R
HISTORY OF NYS&W:BEFORE STACK TRAINS	07	87	34
HISTORY OF NYS&W:NOTES FROM STROUDSBURG,	12	77	13R
HISTORY OF NYS&W:NOTES FROM STROUDSBURG.	08	77	13R
HISTORY OF NYS&W: STACK TRAINS	05	87	44
HISTORY OF NYS&W:SUSQUEHANNA OVER STARUC	01	84	55
HISTORY OF O&K: KENTUCKY HOSPITALITY	08	52	32
HISTORY OF O&NW: OREGONS LAST LOGGERS	08	77	18R
HISTORY OF O&RV:1876 UP SUBSIDIARY	12	78	46
HISTORY OF OB&PA: RUTLAND REVIVAL	F	75	30R
HISTORY OF OC&E: OREGONS LAST LOGGERS	08	77	21R
HISTORY OF OCT:CHESTER COUNTY PA	09	84	30
HISTORY OF OILC: ELECTRIC STREET RAILWAY	11	50	88
HISTORY OF OILCR: WOODEN COACHES	12	56	38
HISTORY OF OKT: ELECTRIC LINE	09	51	78
HISTORY OF ONCE: ALCO EMPIRE	03	82	49
HISTORY OF ONE: ALCO EMPIRE	03	82	53
HISTORY OF ONG: THURSTON CO PEOPLE BUILD	09	37	32
HISTORY OF ONMI: ALCO EMPIRE	03	82	48
HISTORY OF OR&LC: 172 MILES	05	35	36
HISTORY OF OR&W: OHIO'S LAST NARROW GAGE	09	50	54
HISTORY OF OS: REBORN AFTER 15 YEARS	12	35	69
HISTORY OF OWR&N: TOLD BY PACIFIC XPRESS	11	42	06
HISTORY OF P&CS	11	35	111
HISTORY OF P&LE: GATEWAY YARD	10	58	18
HISTORY OF P&LE: TO BE AN INDEPENDENT	07	79	20
HISTORY OF P&LE:BUILT 134 LOCOMOTIVES	06	62	35
HISTORY OF P&LE: U28B "RIVER BOATS"	11	86	51
HISTORY OF P-D: GHOST STATION	05	53	104
HISTORY OF P: CAR HOUSE KIDS	07	53	70
HISTORY OF PAN	04	37	56
HISTORY OF PAP	03	39	123
HISTORY OF PASSENGER SERVICE	08	30	50
HISTORY OF PAT:STEEL CITY COMMUTING	11	81	33
HISTORY OF PATH:HUDSON TERMINAL	11	71	48
HISTORY OF PATH:TOKENS BACK TO COINS	02	72	46
HISTORY OF PAUL & BEGGS LOCO WORKS: NJ	06	33	34
HISTORY OF PAY CARS	02	56	20
HISTORY OF PC: PICTURESQUE PENN-CENTRAL	SU	76	34R
HISTORY OF PCOA: NARROW GAGE ROAD	01	37	69
HISTORY OF PCOAST: WASHINGTON TERRITORY	09	37	33
HISTORY OF PE: PASSENGER SERVICE	07	74	40
HISTORY OF PE: TWILIGHT	08	54	48
HISTORY OF PECO: CHARTERED 1887	10	42	105
HISTORY OF PGE: 44 YEARS TO COMPLETE	12	56	19
HISTORY OF PGE: BRITISH COLUMBIA	01	49	10
HISTORY OF PGE: JUDGEMENT DAY	02	31	407
HISTORY OF PIN:PINSLY-ALWAYS A CLASS ACT	10	87	60
HISTORY OF PIT: STEEL CITY TRACTION	03	54	63
HISTORY OF PPJ	04	33	94
HISTORY OF PPR: MONORAIL EXPERIMENT 1909	12	67	60
HISTORY OF PRIVATE CAR MINEOLA	02	56	46
HISTORY OF PRR: $45 MILLION RISK	11	67	60
HISTORY OF PRR: ATLANTIC TYPE LOCOS	03	52	30
HISTORY OF PRR: BOOKKEEPING & BUDGETING	02	31	370
HISTORY OF PRR: ELECTRIC LOCOMOTIVES	06	35	126
HISTORY OF PRR: ELECTRIFICATION	02	63	35
HISTORY OF PRR: FROG WAR	10	32	353
HISTORY OF PRR: GIANT LOCOMOTVIES	11	35	44
HISTORY OF PRR: LADY SWITCHTENDER	04	54	18
HISTORY OF PRR: LAKE CONEMAUGH DAM DISAS	06	49	13
HISTORY OF PRR: POPE'S CREEK LOCAL	07	54	46
HISTORY OF PRR: POWER PARADE	12	54	11
HISTORY OF PRR: SAGA OF OLD BROAD	05	67	16
HISTORY OF PRR: STEAM DAYS ON MIDDLE DIV	08	73	34
HISTORY OF PRR: SUNNYSIDE YARD	05	48	10
HISTORY OF PRR:FROG WAR 1876 WITH D&BB	11	75	43
HISTORY OF PRR:PENN STATION EAGLES DISPO	05	72	36
HISTORY OF PRR:PENN STATION NY	04	67	29
HISTORY OF PRR:PENNSY HOGS	11	74	38
HISTORY OF PRR:PENNSY PACIFICS	03	65	21
HISTORY OF PRR:STEAM ENGINES TO MUSEUMS	07	68	15
HISTORY OF PRR:THE PENNSYLVANIA SPECIAL	04	72	29
HISTORY OF PRRCO	08	30	115
HISTORY OF PRSL: STEAM DAYS ON SEASHORE	08	67	16
HISTORY OF PS	11	35	111
HISTORY OF PS&SV:MALLETS IN THE WOODS	05	86	51
HISTORY OF PSTC: 1848/RUNNING STRONG	10	55	44
HISTORY OF PSY: 4-6-0 LOCO #111	03	43	06
HISTORY OF PTR: WILLAMETTE VALLEY LINE	05	53	84
HISTORY OF PTR: WILLIAMETTE 05-53 CORREC	10	53	95
HISTORY OF PVRR: FORMATION	11	82	22
HISTORY OF QBRW: SHORT BRIDGE LINE	10	51	80
HISTORY OF QC	01	40	112
HISTORY OF QM&S	09	41	80
HISTORY OF QNS&L: 360 MILES/ORE CARRIER	04	50	46
HISTORY OF QNS&L: CAIN'S RAILROAD	10	49	42
HISTORY OF QT:QUABOAG AND THE QUASAR	01	87	56
HISTORY OF R&N: STEAM & JUICE	01	74	43
HISTORY OF R&N:READERS SUPPLEMENT	04	74	52
HISTORY OF R: DOODLEBUG RPO	09	79	38
HISTORY OF R: LARGEST ANTHRACITE CARRIER	05	44	08
HISTORY OF R:103 YEARS OF LOCO BUILDING	12	61	20
HISTORY OF R:LAST YEARS OF READING STEAM	11	68	23
HISTORY OF RAILPAX: AMTRAK PREDECESSOR	07	71	32
HISTORY OF RAILROAD MAGAZINE	01	73	02
HISTORY OF RBL	06	36	45
HISTORY OF RCBH&W: 35 MILES	01	34	94
HISTORY OF RCBH&W: RAPID CANYON/CROUCH L	03	48	34
HISTORY OF REA: FIGHT FOR SURVIVAL	12	50	20
HISTORY OF REA: WILLIAM HARNDEN FOUNDER	10	48	94
HISTORY OF RG: JOINT LINE	05	78	47R
HISTORY OF RG: WASATCH RANGE/SOLDIER SUM	01	46	91
HISTORY OF RGS: DEATH OF PHOTO ESSAY	03	53	66

Railroad/ Railfan

RAILROAD HISTORIES & ROSTERS

HISTORY	M	Y	P
HISTORY OF RGS: LAST RIGHTS FOR RGS	10	77	41R
HISTORY OF RI: LASALLE STREET STATION	10	70	22
HISTORY OF RI: REBUILT SYSTEM	10	51	14
HISTORY OF RI: THE LAST DAYS	05	82	38
HISTORY OF RI:BREAKUP OF THE ROCK	08	75	03
HISTORY OF RI:DOODLEBUGS	04	66	16
HISTORY OF RICHMOND LOCOMOTIVE WORKS	09	69	18
HISTORY OF ROB: NO LOCOS/NO ROLLING STOC	01	37	56
HISTORY OF ROCHESTER SUBWAY	10	48	84
HISTORY OF ROGERS LOCO WRKS: PATTERSON J	06	33	34
HISTORY OF ROGERS LOCOMOTIVE WORKS	02	46	99
HISTORY OF ROGERS, KETCHUM & GROSVENOR L	06	33	34
HISTORY OF RRR:IC HOGGER RIDES RRR	08	63	28
HISTORY OF RU: GREEN MOUNTAIN GATEWAY	06	57	19
HISTORY OF RU: GREEN MOUNTAIN ROAD	F	75	23R
HISTORY OF RU: GREEN MOUNTAIN ROUTE	08	46	12
HISTORY OF RU: OGDENSBURG BRIDGE & PORT	F	75	30R
HISTORY OF RU: STEAM POWER	04	70	20
HISTORY OF S&BL:RIDE BEHIND A WOODBURNER	05	76	37
HISTORY OF S&EG: ORGANIZED 1908	10	50	80
HISTORY OF S&L: 100% STEAM	04	60	16
HISTORY OF S: ASHEVILLE TRAINS	10	77	46R
HISTORY OF S: RAILS ACROSS BLUE RIDGE	12	43	08
HISTORY OF S: RAT-HOLE DIVISION	01	39	07
HISTORY OF S:ROYAL HUDSON SOUTH #2839	03	80	42
HISTORY OF SA&O: BAILEY'S RR BATTLE	09	46	06
HISTORY OF SAL	05	35	89
HISTORY OF SAL: FREIGHT/PASS/HISTORY/PHO	04	53	12
HISTORY OF SAL: WOOD PULP	04	52	63
HISTORY OF SAN FRANCISCO'S CABLE CARS	11	45	90
HISTORY OF SANT: ORGANIZED 1908	10	50	80
HISTORY OF SAV: 23 MILES	10	35	73
HISTORY OF SB&LT: OPENED 1871/NOW PRR	10	52	48
HISTORY OF SBUF: ALCO EMPIRE	03	82	45
HISTORY OF SCA: PENNSYLVANIA INTERURBAN	04	48	94
HISTORY OF SCHENECTADY LOCOMOTIVE WORKS	05	37	07
HISTORY OF SCS&PS: WASHINGTON TERRITORY	09	37	33
HISTORY OF SD&A: OLD ROAD	05	73	18
HISTORY OF SD&AE	07	35	88
HISTORY OF SD&AE:GOOD BY! ABANDONMENT	05	77	03
HISTORY OF SEM: TROLLEY TOWN USA	08	56	28
HISTORY OF SF:2-8-0 SF #204 "UNCLE DICK"	10	33	140
HISTORY OF SHEPV: INCORP 1869/NOW NYNH&H	04	48	46
HISTORY OF SHRT: ELECTRIC RAILWAYS	05	49	78
HISTORY OF SIGNALS	10	37	05
HISTORY OF SILV: MR BRADSHAW BUYS SILVER	11	81	38
HISTORY OF SILV: NARROW GAUGE IN ROCKIES	06	58	18
HISTORY OF SIRT: ISLAND ELECTRIC	07	49	10
HISTORY OF SJ&LC: 90 MILES/VERMONT	03	47	104
HISTORY OF SJ&LC:VERMONT VIGNETTES	08	75	24
HISTORY OF SJ&LCO:LOATI TO LAMOILLE VAL	03	80	48
HISTORY OF SJ&LCO:PORTLAND TO PINSLY	01	80	24
HISTORY OF SJ&LCO:TODAYS LAMOILLE VALLEY	05	80	26
HISTORY OF SL&N	07	41	66
HISTORY OF SLC: WHERE DOES IT RUN?	02	77	57

HISTORY	M	Y	P
HISTORY OF SLEEPING CARS	01	43	80
HISTORY OF SL&W: 1906/17 MILES/HI WATER	12	48	94
HISTORY OF SLI: THOUSAND ISLAND TROLLEY	06	69	37
HISTORY OF SLS&E	04	33	97
HISTORY OF SLV&TH:VANDALIA STORY	04	62	17
HISTORY OF SMS:SHE'LL BE COMIN' ROUND MT	06	72	24
HISTORY OF SN&M:PIONEER INTERURBAN LINE	07	68	62
HISTORY OF SN: PASSENGER SERVICE PHOTOS	12	40	132
HISTORY OF SNO: BUILT BY OTTO MEARS	02	41	76
HISTORY OF SOO: HAIL TO THE CHIEF FER	SP	76	45R
HISTORY OF SOO: SOUTH OF SCHILLER	SP	77	50R
HISTORY OF SOO: UNLUCKIEST BIG RAILROAD	09	38	07
HISTORY OF SOP	08	37	96
HISTORY OF SOS: CHARTERED 1903	06	51	90
HISTORY OF SP&S: JAN 31 1954 BIG LIFT OP	09	54	10
HISTORY OF SP&S: PRIDE OF THE NORTHWEST	11	52	17
HISTORY OF SP: CALLGIRLS	06	59	32
HISTORY OF SP: CANYON WAR	10	56	22
HISTORY OF SP: HUSTLING SHASTAS	07	52	14
HISTORY OF SP: IMPERIAL VALLEY	12	53	36
HISTORY OF SP: LAKEVIEW BRANCH	01	86	52
HISTORY OF SP: NARROW GAGE	02	59	26
HISTORY OF SP: NILES CA	04	71	38
HISTORY OF SP: OVERLAND LTD	03	30	573
HISTORY OF SP: PORT CHICAGO CALIFORNIA	11	69	24
HISTORY OF SP: SALT LAKE DIVISION	06	44	08
HISTORY OF SP: SIERRA NEVEDA MOUNTAIN DI	06	40	24
HISTORY OF SP: SP #X6264	08	54	77
HISTORY OF SP: SUNSET LIMITED	08	58	18
HISTORY OF SP:BUILT 248 ENGINES ITSELF	07	66	17
HISTORY OF SP:LIFE ON TRAIN-FERRIES	01	67	47
HISTORY OF SP:OLD DAYS AT DUNSMUIR DEPOT	01	69	18
HISTORY OF SP:RAILROADING BELOW SEA LEVE	08	66	22
HISTORY OF SP:ROSEVILLE YARD SACRAMENTO	10	71	28
HISTORY OF SPA: ROAD NEVER BUILT/NAMES	01	38	45
HISTORY OF SPC: PROJECTED 1875/NOW SP	12	44	68
HISTORY OF SPEN: FROM NOME TO NOWHERE	12	57	34
HISTORY OF SPM	02	48	34
HISTORY OF SPTA: TAKE OVER OF PTC	12	67	32
HISTORY OF SR&RL	09	35	41
HISTORY OF SR&RL: FAREWELL	11	35	134
HISTORY OF SR&RL: SANDY RIVER BLUES	11	31	536
HISTORY OF SR: OWNED BY CITY OF SEATTLE	02	37	58
HISTORY OF SRG:SOUTHERN RIO GRANDE	01	79	42
HISTORY OF SRV: AMERICA'S LONGEST 2' GAG	09	35	52
HISTORY OF SSP: TROLLEY/OKLAHOMA	03	53	81
HISTORY OF STEAM TURBINE LOCOS (N&W)	04	55	27
HISTORY OF STEPHENSON LOCOMOTIVE WORKS	04	36	44
HISTORY OF STREETCAR POST OFFICES	09	54	46
HISTORY OF STROMBECK-BECKER COMPANY	10	36	83
HISTORY OF STRR: 20 YEARS ON "ROAD TO PA	09	78	18R
HISTORY OF STRR: CHARTERED 1832/PA/4.5 M	11	47	70
HISTORY OF SUFT: BATTERY CARS	06	51	90
HISTORY OF SV: LAST NAR GAGE TO USE WOOD	01	37	69
HISTORY OF SW&C:CRITTERS OF BONE VALLEY	11	78	55R

STEPHANS' RAILROAD DIRECTORY

414

Railroad/ Railfan

RAILROAD HISTORIES & ROSTERS

HISTORY	M	Y	P
HISTORY OF SWS: INTERURBAN/OHIO/215 MILE	05	52	82
HISTORY OF T&CR	10	40	65
HISTORY OF T&GO: 102 MILES	11	35	83
HISTORY OF T&NO: T&NO JUCTION	02	52	34
HISTORY OF T&P: EARLY DAYS	10	34	126
HISTORY OF T&SB: PERSONAL SERVICE SHORT L	03	84	38
HISTORY OF T&T: SHORT HISTORY	06	35	87
HISTORY OF TAL: GEORGIA SHORT LINE/8 MIL	07	43	102
HISTORY OF TAT: ELEVATED	02	52	17
HISTORY OF TAUNTON LOCOMOTIVE WORKS	02	34	38
HISTORY OF TC&GB: GILA BEND MIXED	05	78	28R
HISTORY OF TC&GB: WHERE PASS RIDE THE CA	10	73	26
HISTORY OF TCTR: 12 MILE/INTERURBAN/	09	44	126
HISTORY OF TEM: 1948.	05	80	41
HISTORY OF TEM: NORTHERN CANADA/PHOTOS	06	48	32
HISTORY OF TERY: PRIVATE OWNED TROLLEY L	02	58	48
HISTORY OF TEXS: 1896 ORE--1976 TOUTISTS	05	84	48
HISTORY OF TEXS: CONVICTS BUILD THIS ROAD	05	74	26
HISTORY OF TI	12	38	65
HISTORY OF TIMETABLES PART 1	05	51	25
HISTORY OF TIMETABLES PART 2	06	51	36
HISTORY OF TIV: NARROW GAGE ROAD	01	37	51
HISTORY OF TIV: NARROW GAGE/PA/	02	44	62
HISTORY OF TLL: NARROW GAGE	01	37	56
HISTORY OF TM: HETTY GREEN'S RAILROAD	10	63	17
HISTORY OF TMEX: INTERN'L SWITCHING LINE	06	51	57
HISTORY OF TP&W FEB 14 1863	06	35	07
HISTORY OF TP&W: READERS COMMENTS	11	83	04
HISTORY OF TP&W: BIG STEAM ON TP&W	09	80	60
HISTORY OF TP&W: MOTIVE POWER	09	83	46
HISTORY OF TP&W: PRAIRIE MARKSMAN	01	84	34
HISTORY OF TP&W: THE TIP UP	07	83	43
HISTORY OF TRACKSIDE SIGNALS	08	57	20
HISTORY OF TRO: BALDWINS ON TRONA	11	87	51
HISTORY OF TTC: SERVES PEARL BEER	04	78	25R
HISTORY OF TURNTABLES	05	55	12
HISTORY OF TUS: STEAM TO DIESEL/8 MILES	01	49	88
HISTORY OF U: BAXTER PASS	07	40	73
HISTORY OF U: CROOKEDEST PIKE	01	33	33
HISTORY OF U: NARROW GAGE/CROOKEDEST RR	01	37	64
HISTORY OF U: NARROW GAUGE MEMORIES	06	60	16
HISTORY OF UC: BRIGHAM YOUNG'S ROAD	02	45	08
HISTORY OF UP	10	30	401
HISTORY OF UP	09	30	279
HISTORY OF UP: AMES MONUMENT	11	36	27
HISTORY OF UP: FLOOD OF 1938 CALIFORNIA	02	43	119
HISTORY OF UP: GAS-TURBINES	02	55	34
HISTORY OF UP: GEORGETOWN LOOP	07	79	41
HISTORY OF UP: GEORGETOWN LOOP	07	86	32
HISTORY OF UP: GRAND SCALE RR PICTURE	03	39	55
HISTORY OF UP: HOME BUILT ENGINES	08	67	34
HISTORY OF UP: INTO CHICAGO	04	78	18R
HISTORY OF UP: LARAMIE WY--1957	SP	76	51R
HISTORY OF UP: MONUMENT AT SHERMAN HILL	04	67	44
HISTORY OF UP: SEATTLE STATION CRISIS	01	52	32
HISTORY OF UP: STEEL TO THE PACIFIC	08	30	115
HISTORY OF UP: UNLIMITED POWER	02	51	18
HISTORY OF UP: YELLOWSTONE PARK/SNOWPLOW	02	54	64
HISTORY OF UP: COMPUTERS DONT RUN EVERYTH	11	78	12
HISTORY OF UP: DAVID NEUHARTS MOTIVE POWE	04	74	28
HISTORY OF URWO: SLOW TRAIN THRU ARKANSA	04	55	54
HISTORY OF URY: THE SISAL LINE	06	50	44
HISTORY OF USA: CAMP DIX RAILROAD	08	38	20
HISTORY OF USM: CIVIL WAR	11	53	56
HISTORY OF USM: RAILS FOR THE ARMY	12	52	42
HISTORY OF USN: RAILROAD INVOLVEMENT	11	49	38
HISTORY OF USSC: COVERED WAGONS TO ATLAN	03	82	28
HISTORY OF UTAH: UTAH PURE	W	76	44R
HISTORY OF V&T: 52 MILES	09	41	06
HISTORY OF V&T: 66 MILES 9 LOCOS 1 OWNER	12	33	95
HISTORY OF V&T: NEVADA NEGATIVE	07	49	28
HISTORY OF V&T: NEVADA'S GOLDEN RAILROAD	01	55	11
HISTORY OF V&T: REVIVAL	08	76	41
HISTORY OF V&T: SAGEBRUSH SHORTLINE	07	45	52
HISTORY OF V&T: NEVADAS GOLDEN RAILROAD	05	76	02
HISTORY OF V: TRANSPORTATION FACTORY	04	39	07
HISTORY OF V: BEFORE THE WIRES CAME DOWN	06	63	27
HISTORY OF VAL: ROBERT E LEE'S RAILROAD	08	66	18
HISTORY OF VAL: A VISIT TO CONNECTICUT	06	71	48
HISTORY OF VANDERBILT TENDERS	11	31	490
HISTORY OF VBR: STEAM TODAY 1961	02	62	13
HISTORY OF VER: RUTLAND REVIVAL	SU	75	18R
HISTORY OF VER: TENTH ANNIVERSARY	03	74	02
HISTORY OF VIA: BROCKVILLE	07	79	22
HISTORY OF VIA: TRAINS TO CHURCHILL	03	83	28
HISTORY OF VIA: VIA AND THE BUSMAN	03	82	22
HISTORY OF VIA: BATTLE OF THE "ATLANTIC"	01	86	57
HISTORY OF VIP: OHIO ISLAND RY	07	73	50
HISTORY OF VIRGINIA STREETCARS 1888-1949	03	50	72
HISTORY OF W&A: 4-4-0 #232 LOCOMOTIVE	01	38	118
HISTORY OF W&A: CHATTANOOGA LOCOS	11	48	12
HISTORY OF W&A: STATE OWNED RAILROAD	12	45	08
HISTORY OF W&LE: PINE VALLEY MALLETS	01	79	38R
HISTORY OF W&LE: STEAM DAYS	03	74	28
HISTORY OF W&NB	02	41	70
HISTORY OF W&NB: PICTURESQUE PASS ROUTE	01	52	46
HISTORY OF W&OD: NO TICKETS SOLD	10	49	72
HISTORY OF W&WA: NARROW GAGE ROAD	01	37	51
HISTORY OF WA&FC	06	38	63
HISTORY OF WARR: B&LE ERA	07	82	41
HISTORY OF WARR: PRR ERA	07	82	34
HISTORY OF WATERVILLE STREET RY GROUP	11	48	82
HISTORY OF WB&PL	03	39	62
HISTORY OF WCF&N: 98 MI/ELECTRIC/	04	49	84
HISTORY OF WCRC: SEMAPHORES & SEAHAWKS	09	87	46
HISTORY OF WEL	04	39	67
HISTORY OF WES: STEAM IN LOUISIANA	08	63	36
HISTORY OF WEST VIRGINIA TROLLEY LINES	09	48	106
HISTORY OF WHEELS	03	43	45
HISTORY OF WIN: 70 MILES/INDIANIA	12	52	80

Railroad/Railfan

RAILROAD HISTORIES & ROSTERS

HISTORY	M	Y	P
HISTORY OF WINANS LOCOMOTIVES	11	36	69
HISTORY OF WIS&S: NORTHERN BECOMES SOUTHE	01	82	49
HISTORY OF WM: FAREWELL CONNELLSVILLE	F	75	49R
HISTORY OF WM: LINCOLN RODE HERE/LOYALTY	09	50	11
HISTORY OF WM: MOUNTAIN CLIMBING STEAM	09	68	13
HISTORY OF WM: CLIMBING BLACK ROCK FORK	11	72	22
HISTORY OF WM: STEAM DAYS	06	64	28
HISTORY OF WNC: MURPHY BRANCH	06	49	32
HISTORY OF WNC: RAILS ACROSS BLUE RIDGE	12	43	08
HISTORY OF WO: LAST RUN AND MEMORIES	07	33	29
HISTORY OF WP&Y: COMPLETED 1900/NARROW G	04	56	48
HISTORY OF WP&Y: IRON TRAIL/GOLD COUNTRY	10	31	378
HISTORY OF WP&Y: AMAZING WHITE PASS	07	81	28
HISTORY OF WP&Y: MIXED TO WHITEHORSE	09	81	50
HISTORY OF WP: CALIFORNIA ZEPHYR	11	49	15
HISTORY OF WP: FIRE IN TUNNEL 9	05	54	65
HISTORY OF WP: MILPITAS F'S	W	76	37R
HISTORY OF WP: MILPITAS F'S ARE BACK	09	78	28R
HISTORY OF WP: OPERATION--TIDEWATER	03	51	16
HISTORY OF WP: FEATHER RIVER CANYON	05	79	23
HISTORY OF WP: SIERRA STORM (1952)	03	76	18
HISTORY OF WPA: ELECTRIC LINES	06	49	86
HISTORY OF WPC	04	38	122
HISTORY OF WR: FAILURE FROM THE BEGINNING	03	37	66
HISTORY OF WRB: SOLD FOR $301	01	39	29
HISTORY OF WSL: CALIFORNIA SHORTLINE	11	50	54
HISTORY OF WSL: PAUL BUNYAN'S TOOTHPICKS	06	59	18
HISTORY OF WSS&YP: ROCKLAND OIL ROAD	01	77	51
HISTORY OF WTC: SPRINGFIELD OREGON LINE	08	77	27R
HISTORY OF WTC: SYCAN OPERATION IN OREGON	08	77	25R
HISTORY OF WVA: STRANGE SAGA	01	83	26
HISTORY OF WVA: ORIGINAL BEGAN IN ILL	01	83	31
HISTORY OF WW&CR: WASHINGTON TERRITORY	09	37	35
HISTORY OF WW&F	09	35	41
HISTORY OF WW&F ABANDONED	03	35	39
HISTORY OF YW: SISKIYOU SHORTLINE	08	48	94

SHORT NOTES ON...	M	Y	P
FR AFRICA: STRIKE IN SUDAN	04	53	121
FR ARGENTINE GOV'T RR: SOUTHERNMOST	04	53	62
FR BRITISH RYS: NEW TANK LOCO	04	54	62
FR FRANCE/ITALY: PHOTO OF SOUPLER USED	10	58	41
FR SNO FOREIGN RAILROADS SHORT NOTES	04	32	71
FR SNO "BATTLE OF BRITAIN" TYPE LOCOMOTI	10	66	36
FR SNO 2-8-2 CONSTANT TORQUE LOCO NOTES	01	70	37
FR SNO AFRICA LIBERIA'S NARROW GAGE ROAD	03	51	57
FR SNO AFRICA: CONGO NARROW GAGE RAILROA	08	56	41
FR SNO AFRICA: FIRST RAILWAY LINE 1856	05	50	60
FR SNO AFRICAN COLONY ERITEA: RAILROAD	06	58	38
FR SNO AFRICAN REPUBLIC OF LIBERIA RR	11	50	138
FR SNO AMERICAN RR OF PORTO RICO-LOCOS	04	32	71
FR SNO ARGENTINE GOV'T RR/SINGLE TRACK	02	53	123

SHORT NOTES ON...	M	Y	P
FR SNO ARGENTINE RAILWAY SERVICE	06	58	36
FR SNO AUSTRALIA: BABY CLINIC ON RAILS	04	55	74
FR SNO AUSTRALIA: COMMONWEALTH RAILWAY	07	41	65
FR SNO AUSTRALIA: LAST HORSE CAR TRAM	05	55	52
FR SNO AUSTRALIA: LOCOS ELECTRIC	10	58	36
FR SNO AUSTRALIAN LOCOS: DIESELS--YES!	05	50	136
FR SNO AUSTRALIAN RAILWAY GAGES	02	44	57
FR SNO AUSTRALIAN RAILWAYS: NO DIESELS	01	50	139
FR SNO BELGIAN CONGO: RAIL TRANSPORTATIO	08	54	47
FR SNO BERMUDA RAILWAY	11	43	148
FR SNO BERMUDA RAILWAY: 1937-1948	06	48	57
FR SNO BOMBAY BARODA & CENTRAL INDIA RY	01	39	129
FR SNO BRAZIL GOV'T RY: MADEIRA-MAMORE	06	53	119
FR SNO BRAZIL: GAGES OF RAILWAYS	10	57	43
FR SNO BRAZIL: SAN JOSE TO CORUMBA	01	49	69
FR SNO BRITAIN: NEWCASTLE & CARLISLE RY	03	45	75
FR SNO BRITISH "OVERHEAD" PRIV OWNED ELE	10	56	19
FR SNO BRITISH "ROYAL SCOT": TO CANADA	01	34	41
FR SNO BRITISH LOCO #46202	02	53	134
FR SNO BRITISH LOCOMOTIVES: NO HEADLIGHT	07	36	83
FR SNO BRITISH LOCOS LACK OF LIGHTS/PILO	07	69	34
FR SNO BRITISH LOCOS: NO HEADLIGHTS	10	56	45
FR SNO BRITISH RAILWAYS GEOGRAPHIC STATI	10	69	35
FR SNO BRITISH RAILWAYS ON BELLS/WHISTLE	07	66	39
FR SNO BRITISH RAILWAYS: AC ELECTRICS	10	59	35
FR SNO BRITISH RAILWAYS: DIESEL SHUNTING	05	54	82
FR SNO BRITISH RAILWAYS: PASS TERMINAL	01	50	127
FR SNO BRITISH RAILWAYS: TRACK RENEWAL	11	48	59
FR SNO BRITISH RAILWYS: WOMEN ONLY TRAIN	03	54	20
FR SNO BRITISH RY: 2 DECK SUBURBAN CARS	03	52	58
FR SNO BRITISH RY: DIESELIZATION/MU TRAI	09	53	73
FR SNO BRITISH RY: TURBO-JET LOCO	08	52	63
FR SNO BRITISH RYS: 3 NEW FEEDING METHOD	04	52	128
FR SNO BRITISH RYS: CITY OF TRURO	10	57	40
FR SNO BRITISH: LOCOMOTIVE CLASSES	12	33	87
FR SNO CHINA: CONNECT WITH ASIA	06	52	62
FR SNO CHINESE: GOBI DESERT RAILWAY	04	59	56
FR SNO DANISH RAILWAY PHOTO ESSAY	06	44	102
FR SNO DANISH TRAM: COPENHAGEN	11	53	99
FR SNO DENMARK: DELAYED BY MOSQUITOS	10	55	36
FR SNO E GERMAN RR CONTROLLED BY RUSSIA	05	53	125
FR SNO EAST AFRICA: KENYA-UGANDA RY	10	53	110
FR SNO EAST AFRICAN RY: UGANDA	06	58	34
FR SNO EAST AFRICAN RYS: NO DIESELS	02	56	06
FR SNO EGYPTIAN RAILROAD: MUMMIES FUEL	04	53	129
FR SNO EGYPTIAN STATE RAILWAYS	05	47	130
FR SNO ELEPHANTS AS SWITCHERS	03	52	133
FR SNO ENGLAND GREAT WESTERN RY: INVALID	08	39	65
FR SNO ENGLAND: BLACKPOOL SYSTEM	12	51	91
FR SNO ENGLAND: CANTERBURY & WHITSTABLE	05	44	06
FR SNO ENGLAND: ROMENY HYTHE & DYMCHURCH	02	53	60
FR SNO ENGLISH CHANNEL: RAIL TUNNEL UNDR	04	68	26
FR SNO ENGLISH RAILWAYS: PHOTO ESSAY	05	49	70
FR SNO ETHIOPIA RAILROAD "TEST"	04	69	10
FR SNO EURAILPASS: UNIQUE NEW TICKET	02	59	69

STEPHANS' RAILROAD DIRECTORY

Railroad/Railfan

RAILROAD HISTORIES & ROSTERS

SHORT NOTES ON...	M	Y	P
FR SNO EUROPE: NO PILOTS ON LOCOMOTIVES	04	69	30
FR SNO EUROPEAN RAILROAD GAGES	05	44	78
FR SNO EUROPEAN RAILROADS	03	33	90
FR SNO EUROPEAN RYS: WHISTLES ON LOCOS	08	57	41
FR SNO FIJI ISLANDS: COLONIAL SUGAR REFI	08	56	43
FR SNO FIJI RAILWAY SOUTH PACIFIC	06	32	324
FR SNO FIRST RAILROADS IN AFRICA	02	70	41
FR SNO FIRST RAILROADS IN CHINA	02	70	41
FR SNO FIRST RAILROADS IN JAPAN	02	70	41
FR SNO FORMOSAN RAILWAYS SOUTH SEA	06	39	117
FR SNO FRANCE: ROBOT TRAIN	10	55	11
FR SNO FRENCH "MISTRAL"	01	70	36
FR SNO FRENCH NAT'L RR: "MISTRAL"	06	53	59
FR SNO FRENCH NAT'L RR: MILEAGE/FREIGHT	04	59	35
FR SNO FRENCH NAT'L RRS: MISTRAL	08	57	39
FR SNO FRENCH NAT'L RYS: "PENDULUM" PASS	12	57	38
FR SNO FRENCH NATIONAL RAILROADS	09	52	133
FR SNO FRENCH NATIONAL RY: STEAM LOCO #	12	56	06
FR SNO FRENCH RAILROADS: BEING ELECTRIFI	03	55	31
FR SNO GERMAN CAPTURED RR EQUIPMENT	11	52	126
FR SNO GERMAN NATIONAL RAILROAD	06	59	36
FR SNO GERMAN RAILWAYS: CONDITIONS	05	55	35
FR SNO GERMANY'S WUPPERTAL MONORAIL	07	51	59
FR SNO GREAT BRITAIN: LLANDUDNO & COLWYN	06	55	46
FR SNO GREAT BRITAIN: LMS RAILWAY	11	34	42
FR SNO GREAT WESTERN OF ENGLAND	09	34	87
FR SNO HONG KONG: DOUBLE DECK TROLLEYS	06	53	91
FR SNO HONG KONG: IMPROVEMENTS	02	54	92
FR SNO ICELANDS RAILROAD	04	74	04
FR SNO INDIA: WORLD'S BROADEST RAILS	11	44	52
FR SNO ISRAEL'S RAILROADS	07	70	54
FR SNO ITALIAN RAILROADS	08	59	37
FR SNO ITALIAN STATE RAILWAYS: 2 ELECTRI	12	53	67
FR SNO ITALIAN STATE RAILWAYS: ETR MEANS	02	56	39
FR SNO JAPAN: 135 STREET RAILWAY SYSTEMS	01	39	130
FR SNO JAPAN: 1ST LINE BUILT IN 1872	04	50	74
FR SNO JAPAN: 3' GAGE ENOSHIMA-KAMAKURA	10	55	51
FR SNO JAPAN: GOV'T OWNED/PASS REVENUE	12	53	65
FR SNO JAPAN: SUBWAYS OF TOKYO/OSAKA	06	40	102
FR SNO JAPAN: TOKYO GOV'T MONORAIL	08	58	53
FR SNO JAPAN: TOYIO-CARRYING CAIN TO	02	45	44
FR SNO JAPANESE RAILWAY SYSTEM	10	56	46
FR SNO JAPANESE RY: BEGAN 1870/MILEAGE	10	58	35
FR SNO JAPANESE RYS: SHARE BERTHS	08	57	45
FR SNO JAPANESE TROLLEYS	08	51	88
FR SNO JAPANS CROWD "PUSHERS"	06	69	39
FR SNO KOREAN NATIONAL RAILROAD	05	52	133
FR SNO KOREAN TROLLEY LINES	06	52	85
FR SNO LAPLAND: ARTIC ELECTRIC RAILWAY	10	39	69
FR SNO LARGE THREE CYLINDER LOCOMOTIVES	02	67	54
FR SNO LIBERIA: 5 TRACKMAN FROM B&O HELP	11	51	121
FR SNO LOCOMOTIVE "CORNWALL" READER INFO	01	70	37
FR SNO LONDON MIDLAND & SCOTTISH RAILWAY	12	51	64
FR SNO MADEIRA-MAMORE RY (BOLIVA-BRAZIL)	10	31	429
FR SNO NAPLES: VESUVIUS RAILWAY	01	45	61
FR SNO NETHERLANDS RAILWAYS: 100 YEARS	10	39	77
FR SNO NETHERLANDS RY: ELECTRIC LOCOS	04	50	74
FR SNO NEW ZEALAND "OPPOSSUM"/HORSE TRAI	08	53	124
FR SNO NILAGIRI EXPRESS (INDIA) COG RY	09	69	08
FR SNO ORIENT EXPRESS	02	67	25
FR SNO PARIS METRO: RUBBER WHEEL TIRES	04	52	78
FR SNO PARIS-LYONS-MEDITERRANEAN RR HIST	12	65	28
FR SNO PERUVIAN CENTRAL	08	35	85
FR SNO PHILLIPPINES: NO STEAM LOCOS	10	58	36
FR SNO REPUBLIC OF COLOMBIA	06	52	67
FR SNO ROME: VATICAN RAILROAD/1934	08	36	74
FR SNO ROYAL SCOT: INAUGURATED 1848	09	52	61
FR SNO RUSSIA: CREW INCENTIVES	07	50	135
FR SNO RUSSIA: MEDAL = PAY	07	52	126
FR SNO RUSSIA: TRANS-SIBERIA RAILROAD	02	32	329
FR SNO RUSSIA: TRANS-SIBERIAN RAILWAY	07	52	69
FR SNO RUSSIAN RAILROAD MILES OF TRACK	07	66	38
FR SNO RUSSIAN ROADS	06	31	443
FR SNO RUSSIAN RRERS LEARNING FROM US GI	09	73	12
FR SNO SAUDI ARABIA: TO BE COMPLETED '51	10	50	57
FR SNO SNOW PROBLEMS ON TOKAIDO LINE	08	68	30
FR SNO SPANISH TALGO TRAINS	01	53	59
FR SNO ST LAURENT-ST JEAN LINE FR GUIANA	11	34	88
FR SNO SWEDISH STATE RY: ORDERS NEW ELEC	04	59	56
FR SNO SWISS ALPS: FURKA-OBERALP LINE	12	57	46
FR SNO SWISS FEDERAL RAILROADS	08	52	61
FR SNO SWISS FEDERAL RAILROADS	03	43	122
FR SNO SWISS: WATER POWERED CABLE CAR	12	70	44
FR SNO SWITZERLAND: DEVELOPED NEW SNOPLO	12	49	57
FR SNO SWITZERLAND: GYRO RAILBUSES	07	52	66
FR SNO SWITZERLAND: JUNGFRAU RAILWAY	11	53	46
FR SNO TOKAIDO SHOWING PROFIT IN YEAR 2	01	69	31
FR SNO TOKYO STREETCAR LINES	08	69	32
FR SNO URUGUAY: FULLY DIESELIZED	05	55	33
FR SNO URUGUAY: STD GAGE/1861 MI/DIESELI	10	57	42
FR SNO USSR RAILWAYS: MILES/GAGES	10	55	37
FR SNO USSR: 75000 MILES/4000 ELECTRIFIE	10	58	35
FR SNO USSR: ROBOT TRAINS	10	58	08
FR SNO VENEZUELA: MICROWAVE CHANNELS	02	54	73
FR SNO VENEZUELA: PRINCIPAL RAILROADS	08	54	43
FR SNO VIET-NAM RAILWAYS	03	65	45
FR SNO VIETNAM: RAILROADING IN	10	66	34
FR SNO VIETNAM: RAILWAYS	05	66	33
FR SNO VIETNAMESE NATIONAL RAILWAY	11	67	08
FR SNO WALES: FESTINIOG RAILWAY	01	47	134
FR SNO WALES: OLDEST PASSENGER RAILWAY	10	58	38
FR SNO WORLDS HIGHEST COG RAILWAY	09	66	32
FR SNO WW I ARMISTICE CAR	12	67	25
FR SWEDISH RYS: CONCRETE TIES/HULA-HULA	10	58	33
SNO "PEG LEG" RR OF WATERPORT NY 1890	06	63	25
SNO A&A: BA&A BECAME IN 1917	12	40	65
SNO A&A: INCORP 1917/ABSORBED BA&A/EQUIP	05	45	65
SNO A&A: LOCOS: NOW 2 DIESELS	06	54	114
SNO A&BUF: 1836-1850/NOW B&ROCH	11	43	61
SNO A&BUF: BECAME PART OF B&ROCH IN 1850	09	53	44

Railroad/ Railfan

RAILROAD HISTORIES & ROSTERS

SHORT NOTES ON...	M	Y	P
SNO A&CJ: SUBSIDIARY OF B&O	10	40	70
SNO A&CRY: ORGANIZED 1890/STEAM DUMMY RD	09	52	83
SNO A&D: INCORP 1894/105 MILES/S LEASED	09	52	61
SNO A&D: JULY 1 1949-NOW INDEPENDENT	08	49	132
SNO A&D: LEASED BY S	03	41	77
SNO A&D: NARROW GAGE	06	31	443
SNO A&DA: DISPATCHER'S MEMORIES/HISTORY	05	48	128
SNO A&E: 1924/ACQUIRES PART OF CP&STL	07	36	85
SNO A&E: FROM CP&SL 1924	06	75	29
SNO A&E: SUCCESSOR TO CP&SL/NOW IT	11	39	91
SNO A&EC: 94 MILES/NORTH CAROLINA/DIESEL	01	47	125
SNO A&EC: COMPLETELY DIESELIZED	12	56	29
SNO A&EC: EMBLEM CHANGING	12	46	85
SNO A&EC: ORGANIZED APPROX 1937	08	58	41
SNO A&EL: ORGANIZED IN 1838	06	32	339
SNO A&ES: BUILT 1889	08	74	56
SNO A&FA: OPERATED UNTIL 1936/RAILBUSES	03	50	77
SNO A&FL: BECAME PART OF G&F IN 1907	06	41	61
SNO A&FL: BECAME PART OF G&F IN 1927	03	39	75
SNO A&FL: PURCHASED BY G&F IN 1907	03	36	83
SNO A&GU: LEASED BY MP	06	34	87
SNO A&GW: BECAME NYP&O/THEN ERIE	10	37	68
SNO A&GW: FAILED IN 1874	09	31	190
SNO A&GWW: BECAME NORTHERN ALBERTA RY	04	35	86
SNO A&GWW: INCORP IN 1909/MERGED IN 1930	04	34	84
SNO A&GWW: MERGED WITH ED&BC BECAME NA	01	73	60
SNO A&H: THIRD RAIL ELECTRIC	12	55	44
SNO A&LG: INCORP 1847/BECAME A&WP 1857	08	51	62
SNO A&LG: INCORP IN 1847/BECAME A&WP	09	35	85
SNO A&MR: HISTORY/MEMORIES	10	53	106
SNO A&MR: NAME CHANGED IN 1902	01	49	68
SNO A&MR: ORGAN 1881/OPEN 1893/NOW A&MR	01	49	68
SNO A&MR: RAIL ROAD (2 WORDS)	06	56	72
SNO A&MR: RENAMED 1902/WAS ARCATA TRANSP	01	49	68
SNO A&N: 1895/REORGANIZTION/NOW GS&G	09	46	91
SNO A&NC: CHARTERED 1852/A&EC LEASED RAI	08	58	41
SNO A&PA: CENTRAL DIVISION-112 MILES	11	34	90
SNO A&PA: CHARTERED IN 1866	12	38	70
SNO A&R: INCORP 1892/STD GAGE/EQUIPMENT	07	47	67
SNO A&ROC: BECAME PART OF R&SRR	09	53	44
SNO A&RS: ABSORBED BY FJ&G	04	52	105
SNO A&SCH: ABSORBED MH&H IN 1847	11	43	61
SNO A&SCH: WAS MH&H/BECAME NYC/NY	09	53	44
SNO A&SL: FIRST AMERICAN INTERNATIONAL	06	67	36
SNO A&SMT: BUILT 1898-1903/OWNED BY EP&S	02	48	129
SNO A&SO: ACQUIRED BY T&P IN 1927	10	42	63
SNO A&SSRY: BECAME PART OF LVT IN 1905	08	42	95
SNO A&STAB: 82 MILES/PASSENGER & FREIGHT	02	56	37
SNO A&STAB: AKA THE BAY LINE/PULLMAN SER	02	47	125
SNO A&STAB: MOTIVE POWER	08	51	65
SNO A&STAB: MOTIVE POWER OWNED BY	04	51	72
SNO A&STAB: SHORT HISTORY	11	77	25
SNO A&STL: BRIEF HISTORY	01	41	77
SNO A&STL: NOW PART OF NYC	12	35	40
SNO A&SY: CHARTERED 1834/26 MILES	11	43	61
SNO A&SYR: BECAME PART OF R&SRR IN 1850	09	53	44
SNO A&T: CHARTERED IN 1859/ BECAME ATSF	02	36	87
SNO A&U: 25 MILES/1 LOCO/8 CARS/NOW ATSF	10	35	84
SNO A&U: NOW ATSF	06	73	48
SNO A&V: INCORP 1889/LEASED BY Y&MV/141	11	36	55
SNO A&W: ABSORBED BY GB&W	11	51	24
SNO A&W: INCORP IN 1890/WISCONSIN/EQUIPM	07	35	85
SNO A&WE: 24 MILES/REVENUE INCREASED	05	52	127
SNO A&WF: 1925/REORGANIZATION/ABAN 1939	04	45	77
SNO A&WP: 1857/WAS A&LG/EQUIPMENT/MILES	08	51	62
SNO A&WP: 1947/RESULT OF NAME CHANGE	09	35	85
SNO A&WP: 227 MILES/53 LOCOS/EQUIPMENT	01	34	92
SNO A&WP: INCORP 1847	12	39	112
SNO A&WS: BECAME PART OF BOSTON & ALBANY	04	35	86
SNO A&Y: SUBSIDIARY OF SOUTHERN RAILWAY	02	32	333
SNO A: AMTRAK STEAM	06	72	60
SNO A: COST OF VARIOUS ROADS TO JOIN	12	71	56
SNO A: SHORT HISTORY ON CREATION-RAILPAX	08	71	22
SNO A: TURBOLINERS	10	76	46
SNO AA: ABSORBED TAA&C	07	53	53
SNO AA: BANKRUPTCY CAUSES	05	74	48
SNO AA: BRIEF HISTORY	08	66	32
SNO AA: CAR FERRY FLEET	02	55	75
SNO AA: CONTROLLED BY WABASH/FREIGHT ONL	06	55	34
SNO AA: INTER-LAKE CARRIER	09	42	77
SNO AB&A: "THE BEE LINE"/NOW AB&C	09	40	68
SNO AB&A: ACL TOOK CONTROL IN 1926	10	46	12
SNO AB&A: FOUNDED 1905/ACL PREDECESSOR	04	71	62
SNO AB&C: 1927	09	40	68
SNO AB&C: 637 MILES/75 LOCOS/CARS/VALUE	06	39	52
SNO AB&C: ACL PREDECESSOR WAS AB&A	04	71	62
SNO AB&C: REORGANIZATION OF AB&A	10	46	12
SNO AB&CL: OPENED 1895/OHIO/ELECTRIC	11	52	88
SNO AB&NW: NOW PART OF SOO	12	34	84
SNO AB&S: BECAME LSRR /THEN LSEL	11	51	78
SNO ABELT: LEASED BY MP	06	34	87
SNO ABS: CHARTERED IN 1892/NOW PSY	01	35	87
SNO AC&HB: ALGC IS SHORTENED NAME	01	72	56
SNO AC&HB: ALGOMA CENTRAL IS NOW AC&HB	07	35	84
SNO AC&HB: CHARTERED 1899	06	35	82
SNO AC&HB: MILES/BRANCHES/EQUIPMENT	01	34	93
SNO AC&HB: PREVIOULSY ALGC	06	38	72
SNO AC&HB: SAULT ST MARIE TO HEARST ONT	08	75	57
SNO AC&HR: 1901/ALGC BECOMES-NAME CHANGE	07	36	82
SNO AC&HR: MILES/EQUIPMENT/ NAME CHANGES	01	38	59
SNO AC&Y: 171 MILES/OHIO	02	55	46
SNO AC&Y: COMPLETELY DIESELIZED	10	54	42
SNO AC&Y: INCORP IN 1907/ROSTER/MILES	10	34	86
SNO AC&Y: PASSENGER SERVICE ABANDONED	09	52	121
SNO AC&Y: PROPOSED ADDITION	07	48	68
SNO ACL: 981 LOCOMOTIVES	09	32	236
SNO ACL: ABSORBED AB&A IN 1926	10	46	12
SNO ACL: BRANCHLINE TRAINS WITHDRAWN?	02	51	130
SNO ACL: BRIDGE SPAN SCRAPPED	02	50	136
SNO ACL: BRIEF HISTORY-ORIG LINE CHARTER	03	66	28

Stephans' Railroad Directory

Railroad/Railfan

RAILROAD HISTORIES & ROSTERS

SHORT NOTES ON...	M	Y	P
SNO ACL: BUYS 5 TWIN-UNIT DINING CARS	09	51	61
SNO ACL: CONSOLIDATIONS OF SMALLER ROADS	01	33	98
SNO ACL: DIESEL-ELECTRIC EQUIPMENT	01	47	52
SNO ACL: FAYETTEVILLE CUT-OFF	06	77	51
SNO ACL: LIST OF ROADS CONTROLLED 1940	05	75	51
SNO ACL: LIST OF ROADS CONTROLLED BY	06	39	52
SNO ACL: MERGED WITH SF&W IN 1902/NOW PS	12	40	62
SNO ACL: MERGER WITH SAL & HISTORY	11	71	38
SNO ACL: NEW LAND FROM CALOOSAHATCHEE RI	01	34	74
SNO ACL: NO MORE MAN IN FRONT OF TRAIN	06	52	131
SNO ACL: PALMDALE TO EVERGALDES/PASS SER	10	57	41
SNO ACL: PLANT SYSTEMS NOW PART OF	12	37	54
SNO ACL: SECONDARY FLAGMAN	06	47	85
SNO ACL: SF&W JOINS IN 1902	12	73	52
SNO ACL: STANDARD GAUGE SOUTH OF WILMING	09	78	63
SNO ACL: STREAMLINED DINING CAR NAMES	03	50	60
SNO ACL: SYSTEM B	07	39	11
SNO ACL: UNUSUAL WATERSHED DOTHAN AL	05	51	129
SNO ACL: WILMINGTON TO NEWBERN NC	03	41	72
SNO ACLC: BECAME ACL 1900 NOW SCL	06	73	49
SNO ACLV: R-P NAME CHANGE 1900 NOW SCL	06	73	49
SNO ACR: MULES RELIEF LOCOMOTIVE	08	39	64
SNO ACRR: 1901 TO 1933	07	38	76
SNO ACRR: BECAME PART OF PRSL IN 1933	04	39	74
SNO ACRR: NOW PART OF READING COMPANY	01	33	98
SNO ACRR: SHORT HISTORY/ NARROW GAGE/ETC	09	33	47
SNO ACRR: SUBSIDIARY OF P&R	11	44	55
SNO ACSR: BECAME ACSRY 1892	08	74	56
SNO ACSRY: FORMED 1892 DIED 1949	08	74	56
SNO ACT: 7 MILES/BRILLINERS TO BUSES	12	50	94
SNO ACT: MAJOR REPAIR JOB	05	55	49
SNO ADAMS EXPRESS CO	11	64	36
SNO ADD: LEASED TO RUTLAND	08	46	17
SNO AE: APACHE INDIANS GET FREE RIDES	05	34	14
SNO AEA: BECAME NEW MEXICO CENTRAL 1908	11	34	94
SNO AF&N: INCORP 1889/BECAME A&N IN 1895	09	46	91
SNO AF: FARE RAISED/NEW OWNERS	02	54	91
SNO AF: INCLINE RAILWAY BRIEF HISTORY	11	65	38
SNO AF: PILE-SUPPORTED LINE PHOTO	04	53	92
SNO AJ&N: MERGED WITH ANO IN 1913	05	35	83
SNO AK&MO: BILOXI BLUES	10	87	48
SNO AK&N: 1896/BECAME PART OF L&N	05	54	79
SNO AKAC: ORGAN 1909 RECEIVERSHIP 1925	05	72	56
SNO AL&H: 1855/BECAME W&OD	04	46	115
SNO AL&SA: COMPLETED IN 1851/BECAME C&A	04	55	34
SNO AL&SE: INCORP 1902/OPERATED BY FB&S	08	55	46
SNO AL: 1915/21 LOCOS/EQUIPMENT	12	35	85
SNO AL: 521 MILES/GOV'T OWNED/EQUIPMENT	07	32	509
SNO AL: ABSORBED TANANA VALLEY	01	47	57
SNO AL: GOV'T SURPLUS ROLLING STOCK PURC	03	47	74
SNO AL: HITTING MOOSE	08	71	11
SNO AL: OWNED BY US GOV'T	08	54	121
SNO AL: OWNED BY US GOV'T/FINANCIAL	09	40	64
SNO AL: OWNERSHIP TRANSFERRED TO STATE	07	85	28
SNO AL: PASSENGER TRAIN TRAFFIC	11	70	42

SHORT NOTES ON...	M	Y	P
SNO AL: SOLVES TRUCK PROBLEM	06	40	102
SNO AL: STANDARD GAGE ROAD	01	32	258
SNO ALB: CHARTERED 1863 AS HORSE CAR LIN	12	55	44
SNO ALBS: 1.68 MILES/OWNED BY A&N	09	46	91
SNO ALCO: 9 ORIGNAL PLANTS	07	37	57
SNO ALCO: ACQUIRES COOKE LOCO WORK/ROGER	09	32	233
SNO ALCO: BOMBARDIER ACQUIRES ALCO	07	84	26
SNO ALCO: NAMES AND LOCOATIONS OF PLANTS	06	34	85
SNO ALCO: RHODE ISLAND LOCOMOTIVE WORKS	07	33	84
SNO ALCO: RICHMOND PLANT	04	33	96
SNO ALCO: TAKES OVER RI LOCO WORKS	05	37	35
SNO ALEX: FOUNDED 1887 AS ST&W	02	69	32
SNO ALGC: "BLACK BEAR ROUTE"	04	64	28
SNO ALGC: 21 GP7 ROAD SWITCHERS/STEAM SC	10	55	36
SNO ALGC: ESTABLISHED 1889/BECAME AC&HB	10	71	44
SNO ALGC: INCORP 1899/NAME CHANGE 1901	01	38	59
SNO ALGC: INCORP IN 1899/324 MILES	07	36	82
SNO ALGC: NOW AC&HB	07	35	84
SNO ALGC: NOW KNOWN AS AC&HB/ITS ROUTES	06	38	72
SNO ALGC: READER MEMORIES	12	43	131
SNO ALTA: TRAMWAY/NARROW GAGE/UTAH ROAD	02	34	88
SNO ALV	09	33	136
SNO ALY: NEW LOGGING ROAD!	03	86	28
SNO AMC: INCORP 1908/CALIFORNIA/12 MILES	07	37	55
SNO AMERICAN EXPRESS CO HISTORY	11	64	36
SNO AMID: CHARTERED IN 1887/NOW PSY	01	35	87
SNO AMID: NOW PART OF PLANT SYSTEMS	12	37	54
SNO AN: BUILT 1907/PASS SERVICE ENDS '51	08	56	42
SNO AND&K: WAS AW&G	11	50	99
SNO AND: HAD 8 LOCOS IN 1871	06	33	92
SNO ANO: 1912-1920/NARROW GAGE TO STD	05	35	83
SNO ANTV: TAKEN OVER IN 1910	03	37	61
SNO AP&J: TROLLEY LINE/22 MILE/ABANDONED	04	35	85
SNO APC: ABSORBED TR&U APPROX 1935	01	49	90
SNO APC: ROADS ABSORBED BY APC	05	51	102
SNO APC: SOLD STREETCARS TO MTWC	01	49	91
SNO APRY: 9 MILES	04	34	86
SNO AR&E: BUILT 1888/PART BECAME EP&W	10	55	37
SNO AR&S: BECAME EP&S IN 1900	01	37	88
SNO AR&S: TO EP&S IN 1900	04	75	12
SNO AR: ALBERTA GOVERNMENT LINE 1967	06	67	36
SNO ARC: CHARTERED IN 1905 3' GAGE	06	33	89
SNO ARC: CHARTERED IN 1905/3' GAGE/16 MI	03	34	86
SNO ARC: GEARED LOCOS	01	39	65
SNO ARC: NARROW GAE/COLORADO/ABANDONED	01	54	107
SNO ARC: ORGANIZED 1913 KNOWN AS G&GP	12	73	52
SNO ARC: ORGANIZED IN 1913/3' GAGE/1 LOC	11	38	73
SNO ARR&N:	11	33	89
SNO ARR: 1929/FORECLOSURE C&A/PART B&O	04	55	35
SNO ARR: B&O TAKES OVER IN 1931	07	43	66
SNO ARR: EQUIP RENUMBERED/RECLASSIFIED	10	32	349
SNO ARR: MERGER WITH GM&O	10	46	83
SNO ARR: NON-ARTICULATED DIESEL LOCO	02	48	79
SNO ARR: SECTIONS/HISTORY	08	46	58
SNO ARTC: ORGANIZED IN 1881/1902=A&MR	01	49	68

Railroad/Railfan

RAILROAD HISTORIES & ROSTERS

SHORT NOTES ON...	M	Y	P
SNO ASH&W: INCORP IN 1906/OHIO/22 MILES	07	36	85
SNO ASL: NOW PART OF WB&AE	03	32	522
SNO ASM&L: 8 MILES/2 SECTIONS/2 LOCOS/	03	36	83
SNO ASM&N: BECAME CGA	06	72	60
SNO ASO: OPENED 1904	12	72	59
SNO ASO: OPENED 1914/NOW ABANDONED/EQUIP	01	37	87
SNO ASRC: FORMED 1907/DIED 1925	12	76	46
SNO ASRY: OPPORTUNITY BRANCH LINE	01	49	92
SNO AT&F: 1891/PART OF TV&C	05	45	65
SNO AT&F: ACQUIRED REMAINING TV&C TRACKS	12	40	65
SNO ATR: MAKING MONEY?	04	76	53
SNO ATSF: PHOTO ESSAY	08	42	112
SNO ATSF: "SAINT & ANGEL"	06	37	60
SNO ATSF: 10 MEXICAN LABORERS FOUND IN C	01	53	135
SNO ATSF: 1ST CAST-STEEL FRAMES BY BALDW	10	50	62
SNO ATSF: 2-10-0 5000 SERIES LOCOS USED	02	41	72
SNO ATSF: 2-10-4 LOCOS VS DIESEL	09	48	133
SNO ATSF: 3800 SERIES LOCO HISTORY/DATA	01	50	48
SNO ATSF: 9000 OPERATED MILES	11	40	69
SNO ATSF: 9646 MILES/EQUIPMENT	03	32	521
SNO ATSF: AMARILLO-SLATON LINE/STEAM LOC	12	54	04
SNO ATSF: ARGENTINE YARD	09	70	30
SNO ATSF: ARIZONA & UTAH BECAME PART OF	10	35	84
SNO ATSF: BOOK OF THE MONTH PROGRAMS	02	53	134
SNO ATSF: BOUNDRIES OF BAKERSFIELD	02	41	69
SNO ATSF: CHANGES FROM AT&SF/REASONS	04	43	99
SNO ATSF: CHARTERED IN 1895	02	36	87
SNO ATSF: CLASS 3700 LOCOS/TYPES/BLDRS	04	44	72
SNO ATSF: CYRUS K HOLLIDY TRAIN/LOCOS	02	59	38
SNO ATSF: DIESEL-ELECTRIC LOCO HISTORY	05	54	79
SNO ATSF: DISPATCHER BUILT RELIGIOUS SIG	04	70	34
SNO ATSF: DIVISIONS	08	49	57
SNO ATSF: DUTCH CLOCK	08	49	54
SNO ATSF: EDWARDS AIR FORCE LINE RELOCAT	07	53	44
SNO ATSF: ELECTRONIC DEVICE STRAIN/STRES	02	47	63
SNO ATSF: FAREWELL TO MORSE!	10	76	09
SNO ATSF: FINANCIAL RECORDS	03	36	81
SNO ATSF: FIRST DIESEL FREIGHT RUN	10	65	27
SNO ATSF: GARDEN CITY	05	47	115
SNO ATSF: GAS TURBINE LOCO BALDWIN BUILT	06	47	137
SNO ATSF: GRADE REDUCTION AT CAJUN PASS	11	72	06
SNO ATSF: HIGH FREQUENCY TWO WAY RADIO	06	49	135
SNO ATSF: HISTORY OF SPECIFIC LOCOS/DATA	09	33	50
SNO ATSF: ICE MFG PLANT STATISTICS	03	53	140
SNO ATSF: ICE PACKS	10	50	64
SNO ATSF: INDIAN LABOR	02	53	128
SNO ATSF: INSIGNIA FOR PASSENGER CONDUCT	06	40	74
SNO ATSF: KANSAS CITY MEXICO & ORIENT	03	33	89
SNO ATSF: LARGEST DIESELIZED/600 HP SWIT	08	54	45
SNO ATSF: LEASES NEW MEXICO CENTRAL	11	34	94
SNO ATSF: LINES AND WHEN BUILT	09	34	84
SNO ATSF: LOCO #1468/DOODLEBUG #M180/	12	48	126
SNO ATSF: LOCO #1700/2 BUSY DIVISIONS	06	32	335
SNO ATSF: LOCO #3600,#22, #94, #95, #114	04	32	69
SNO ATSF: LOCO #3834 LOST!	04	33	130
SNO ATSF: LOCOS HAVE 2 STEAM DOMES	09	42	57
SNO ATSF: LONGEST SINGLE PROJECT IN 1937	05	38	73
SNO ATSF: MAIN LINE DIVISIONS	09	34	87
SNO ATSF: MAIN LINES	12	31	92
SNO ATSF: MAINLINE DIVISIONS 1930	11	74	52
SNO ATSF: MOTHER HUBBARD EXPERIMENT	08	74	56
SNO ATSF: MR HOOD/CONTRACT READER MEMOR	03	47	133
SNO ATSF: NAME ORIGIN--DEBATES	12	51	123
SNO ATSF: NEW TIMETABLES	08	48	126
SNO ATSF: PART OF A&PA BECOMES ATSF	12	38	70
SNO ATSF: ROYAL GORGE WAR	07	73	38
SNO ATSF: RR GHOST TOWN HOT SPRINGS NM	08	32	91
SNO ATSF: S4 LOCOMOTIVE OPERATION	06	72	27
SNO ATSF: SANTA CLAUS OF THE RAILS	01	42	49
SNO ATSF: SANTA FES RAILROADER TEST	09	86	28
SNO ATSF: SIGNAL SYSTEM AT CAJUN PASS	06	44	83
SNO ATSF: SILVER ROADBED	03	34	45
SNO ATSF: SOUTHERN CALIFORNIA RR NOW	08	34	85
SNO ATSF: SUPER CHIEF	06	51	68
SNO ATSF: SUPER-C SERVICE	11	68	34
SNO ATSF: TRACK MACHINES/THEIR HISTORY	12	44	10
SNO ATSF: VICTORVILLE TRAIN ORDER STATIO	08	48	28
SNO ATSF: WATER TOWERS/"PLUGS"	12	54	09
SNO ATSF: WHO NAMED IT?	07	51	123
SNO ATSF: WILLIAMSFIELD GETS WATER TANKS	08	53	123
SNO AU: SHORTEST RR/LESS THAN 1 MILE/ARK	01	37	87
SNO AUR: CHARTERED 1849/12 MI/NOW CB&Q	03	49	15
SNO AUS: BECAME PART OF G&F IN 1919	03	36	83
SNO AV&SB: LEASED BY C&GR/SALUDA MOUNTAI	11	44	13
SNO AV: PHOTO ESSAY	10	42	100
SNO AV: ELECTRIC LINE/32 MILES/EQUIPMENT	11	32	470
SNO AV: INCORPORATED 1902 OPENED 1911	04	76	53
SNO AV: MAINE INTERURBAN/BUILT 1907/EQUI	02	47	108
SNO AVOY: ABSORBED BY T&P IN 1900	10	42	63
SNO AW&B: ANNAPOLIS & ELK RIDGE REORGANI	06	32	339
SNO AW: ACQUIRED BY KCS IN 1935	09	40	63
SNO AW: BECAME PART OF KCS	04	57	74
SNO AY&C: LOCO #356 HISTORY	01	47	130
SNO AZ: BUILT, NEVER OPERATED	01	38	52
SNO B&A: 24 ACRE YARD--REMOVE TRACKS	07	53	118
SNO B&A: 402 MILES/EQUIPMENT	01	33	102
SNO B&A: 407 MILES/329 LOCOMOTIVES	01	32	261
SNO B&A: CHESTER & BECKET (MORE COMMENTS	07	35	87
SNO B&A: CHESTER & BECKET ARE STATIONS	05	35	86
SNO B&A: DERBY SHOPS AT MILO JCT ME	03	72	62
SNO B&A: DIESELIZATION OF FREIGHT SERVIC	08	47	61
SNO B&A: DIVISIONS	07	33	85
SNO B&A: FORMATION & SHORT HISTORY	09	78	64
SNO B&A: INCORP IN 1870/CONSOLIDATION	04	35	86
SNO B&A: SUBURBAN PASSENGERS	04	31	121
SNO B&AGA: RENAMED GNO	09	46	93
SNO B&AN: CHARTERED 1840	02	69	32
SNO B&AN: INTERURBAN PASS SERVICE WAR	07	49	92
SNO B&AN: INTERURBAN/25 MILE/	04	46	115
SNO B&AN: READERS WANT INTERURBAN SERVIC	10	49	102

Railroad/ Railfan

RAILROAD HISTORIES & ROSTERS

SHORT NOTES ON...	M	Y	P
SNO B&AN: USES OUR BUSES/NOT TRAINS	04	49	95
SNO B&ASL: STEAM/BECAME B&AN	04	46	115
SNO B&AT: 46 MILES	07	34	91
SNO B&AT: RENAMED 1890 FROM T&CV	01	73	61
SNO B&BE: INCORP 1901	08	53	81
SNO B&BED: 1876-1878/9 MILES/MASSACHUETT	06	36	81
SNO B&BI: CHARTERED 1876	12	55	24
SNO B&BI: OPENED 1877 FIRST 2' GAUGE	02	75	51
SNO B&BL: NOW PART OF MONON	05	49	26
SNO B&BL: THE "BEDFORD" LOCO 2-4-0 1875	08	37	53
SNO B&C: 3' GAGE/ABANDONED/IOWA	06	36	83
SNO B&C: BUILT 1879/36 MILE/3' /NOW MILW	07	48	67
SNO B&C: BUILT IN 1890/1933 NEW OWNERSHI	04	35	86
SNO B&CH: CHARTERED 1867/ABANDONED 1956	04	57	08
SNO B&CH: CONTROLLED BY LOCO INTERESTS	06	47	138
SNO B&CH: EQUIPMENT	06	33	92
SNO B&CH: LOCOS/ 1 LEFT/2 SOLD	07	49	131
SNO B&CV: 1917 CONSOLIDATION = WM	09	35	86
SNO B&CV: CONSOLIDATED WITH WM 1917	05	73	35
SNO B&D: NARROW & STD GAGE	04	42	71
SNO B&E: ACQUIRED MD&V IN 1923	04	35	83
SNO B&E: INCORP IN 1923	05	34	87
SNO B&E: MD&V & BC&A/9 LOCOS/8 PASS TRAI	09	31	190
SNO B&EA: OPENED BETWEEN 1905-10/NOW B&O	01	35	86
SNO B&ERIE: MERGED TO BECOME PART LS&MS	06	35	82
SNO B&FB: MONORAIL TYPE/IMPRACTICAL	11	54	36
SNO B&GA: 20 MILE ORE LINE/COMMON CARRIE	12	43	91
SNO B&GA: COPPER ORE-CARRYING RR/22 MILE	11	43	60
SNO B&GA: OWNED BY KENNECOTT COPPER CORP	07	40	68
SNO B&GR: PURCHASED TUS IN 1907	01	49	89
SNO B&H	03	33	136
SNO B&H: 2' GAGE ROAD/BUILT 1890'S/LOCOS	03	35	90
SNO B&H: B&SR RENAMED AS/DIED IN 1941	12	55	31
SNO B&H: CORRECTIONS TO OCT 1949	12	40	66
SNO B&H: INCORP 1927/MAINE/OWNED BY TOWN	10	40	71
SNO B&H: RAILCAR #3	01	39	135
SNO B&HA: 10 MILES/NOW PART OF ERIE	04	32	69
SNO B&HA: CONTROLLED BY ERIE	04	34	84
SNO B&HB: 1917 CONSOLIDATION = WM	09	35	86
SNO B&HB: CONSOLIDATED WITH WM 1917	05	73	35
SNO B&HBE: 1917 CONSOLIDATION = WM	09	35	86
SNO B&HBE: CONSOLIDATED WITH WM 1917	05	73	35
SNO B&HWE: 1917 CONSOLIDATION = WM	09	35	86
SNO B&L: 1ST SCHEDULED TRAIN SERVIC 1835	10	57	40
SNO B&L: B&M LEASED IN 1881	06	34	88
SNO B&L: CHARTERED 1836 CORRECTION	07	53	47
SNO B&L: CUMMUTATION SERVICE	01	53	59
SNO B&L: LEASES CMA IN 1886	03	34	89
SNO B&LAM: ORGANIZED 1875	04	74	43
SNO B&LAM: ORGANIZED IN 1876	05	33	76
SNO B&LAMV: CHARTERED IN 1889	05	33	76
SNO B&LE: INCORPORATED IN 1900	07	34	90
SNO B&LE: PREVIOUSLY KNOWN AS PB&LE	06	32	338
SNO B&LEH: 1881-1894/ 3' GAGE	11	33	91
SNO B&LEH: 1893/WAS MDCE/STANDARD GAGE	12	46	79
SNO B&LEH: BECAME PART OF MA&PA IN 1901	07	35	84
SNO B&LEH: BECAME PART OF MA&PA IN 1901	11	36	58
SNO B&LEH: MARYLAND DIVISION	11	33	91
SNO B&M: 4-8-2 4100 SERIES LOCO NAMES	11	41	51
SNO B&M: 92 PACIFIC LOCOS	08	32	57
SNO B&M: ABSORBED EASTERN RR OF MASSACHU	06	48	54
SNO B&M: ACQUIRED 4 PT LOCOS	07	51	129
SNO B&M: ACQUIRES VERMONT VALLEY IN 1877	05	36	82
SNO B&M: ACTON BRANCH IN 1896	07	34	90
SNO B&M: ASSUMED LEASE OF SUNCOOK VALLEY	01	34	88
SNO B&M: BORROWED EQUIPMENT 1940	12	66	31
SNO B&M: BOSTON & LOWELL BECAME PART OF	03	34	89
SNO B&M: BRIDGE REMONVED/MT WASHINGT COG	11	38	74
SNO B&M: BRIEF HISTORY	10	66	36
SNO B&M: CONTROLS PROFILE & FRANCONIA NO	06	32	335
SNO B&M: CUMMUTATION TICKETS	01	53	61
SNO B&M: DIESELIZATION--PROGRESS	12	53	65
SNO B&M: DIESELS SLASH COSTS	02	48	131
SNO B&M: FINANCIAL/MILEAGE/EQUIPMENT	03	35	90
SNO B&M: FIRST ELECTRICS THROUGH HOOSAC	01	75	55
SNO B&M: FIRST MILE A MINUTE RUN	06	71	44
SNO B&M: FLATCAR #33509 RETURNS 2 1/2 YR	11	51	127
SNO B&M: HOOSAC TUNNEL	06	55	35
SNO B&M: HOOSAC TUNNEL OVERHEAD WIRE REM	09	47	69
SNO B&M: IMPROVING PASSENGER SERVICE	11	54	72
SNO B&M: INCORP IN 1835, 1841, & 1843	06	34	88
SNO B&M: LEASES EASTERN RR IN 1884	12	33	93
SNO B&M: LOCO #622 SCRAPPED/#3713 DISPOS	10	58	36
SNO B&M: LOCOS LEASED TO DL&W	09	43	72
SNO B&M: LOCOS RENUMBERED	05	47	134
SNO B&M: LONG RULE NOT UNDERSTANDABLE	03	66	30
SNO B&M: MASSACHUETTS CETRAL DIVISION	02	40	118
SNO B&M: MOGULS/FREIGHT AND PASS SERVICE	08	50	134
SNO B&M: NAMED LOCOMOTIVES	12	71	30
SNO B&M: NUMBER OF STEAM/ELECTRIC LOCOS	06	31	444
SNO B&M: PURCHASES COACHES FROM PRR	04	41	49
SNO B&M: READ DOWN TABLES ONLY/MORE TRAI	01	53	131
SNO B&M: RPO SERVICE/WASHOUT JAN 1934	10	48	137
SNO B&M: SALES OF 2-10-2 LOCOMOTIVES	08	73	56
SNO B&M: SIGNAL HISTORY	03	53	136
SNO B&M: STEAM-OPERATED TRAIN/LOCO #3715	11	54	33
SNO B&M: SUBURBAN PASSENGERS	04	31	121
SNO B&M: TALGO TYPE TRAIN BUILT BY ACF	04	56	41
SNO B&MA: INCORP 1903/BECAME PI&SH	01	38	57
SNO B&MI: ALPHABET LINE	10	47	08
SNO B&ML: 33 MILES CHARTERED IN 1867	06	37	60
SNO B&ML: CHARTERED 1867/MAINE/33 MILES	07	53	48
SNO B&ML: CHARTERED IN 1867/33 MILES	01	34	90
SNO B&ML: COALING UP	03	55	25
SNO B&ML: INTERESTING TIDBITS!!	06	44	120
SNO B&ML: PAYING PASSENGER SERVICE	08	60	25
SNO B&ML: WHERE IS IT?	05	77	54
SNO B&MR: NOW PART OF CB&Q	08	34	87
SNO B&NM: MINNESOTA & INTERNAT'L ABSORBS	04	35	85
SNO B&NO: 1919/BECAME PART OF KW IN 1924	08	53	81

Railroad/ Railfan

STEPHANS_RAILROAD_DIRECTORY

RAILROAD HISTORIES & ROSTERS

SHORT NOTES ON...	M	Y	P
SNO B&NY: OPEN 1873/FROM NHM&W TO NYNH&H	10	75	52
SNO B&O&C: 1877/PART OF B&O/NEVER OWN CO	09	36	74
SNO B&O: 1000 HP SWITCHERS ORDERS-BLDRS?	04	48	75
SNO B&O: 1830-1950 MONT AIRY LOCAL	06	50	136
SNO B&O: 1ST PRES TO RIDE A TRAIN 1833	11	52	122
SNO B&O: 1ST TELEVISION BROADCAST 1948	02	49	61
SNO B&O: 2438 LOCOS	11	30	599
SNO B&O: 5 TRACK FOREMAN HELP LIBERIA	11	51	121
SNO B&O: 8 SENECA INDIANS LOCO ENGINEERS	03	53	123
SNO B&O: ACQUIRED LITTLE KANAWHA RR 1918	01	35	86
SNO B&O: ACQUIRES 2 ROADS (ZM&P/B&EA)	01	35	86
SNO B&O: ACQUIRES CH&D IN 1917	01	33	98
SNO B&O: ALL-ROOM SLEEPERS--NAMES	08	50	53
SNO B&O: ALLOWS PETS IN COACHES	02	53	129
SNO B&O: ARMOURED CAR FOR BRIDGE REPAIRS	05	46	76
SNO B&O: B&SQ MERGER	12	66	27
SNO B&O: BALTIMORE PITTSBURGH & CHICAGO	09	36	74
SNO B&O: BARR YARD CHICAGO COMMUNICATION	06	50	61
SNO B&O: BIG HILL	01	43	79
SNO B&O: BLACK RIVER TO ZANESVILLE LINE	12	55	38
SNO B&O: BRANCH LINE TO PERRY NY ABANDON	12	51	119
SNO B&O: BRIDAL COACH-AUG 1949 CORRECTIO	11	49	132
SNO B&O: BUDD RDC CARS	12	53	63
SNO B&O: BUFFALO ROCHESTER & PITTSBURGH	07	32	510
SNO B&O: BUYS MJK&R IN 1932	10	33	48
SNO B&O: CAMDEN STATION ALTERATIONS	01	53	54
SNO B&O: CHILDREN--HAZARDS RIGHT OF WAY	07	51	125
SNO B&O: CHRISTMAS TRADITION	01	55	04
SNO B&O: DAYTON & UNION NOW PART OF B&O	06	35	86
SNO B&O: DIESELS #51 ON DISPLAY	06	54	116
SNO B&O: ELECTRIC EXPERIMENTS 1851	10	74	45
SNO B&O: ELECTRIC LOCO PRIOR CIVIL WAR	05	43	89
SNO B&O: FIRST PASSENGER RAILROAD IN US	10	56	46
SNO B&O: FOUNDED IN 1828/1ST US RAILROAD	11	36	58
SNO B&O: GLENWOOD SHOPS DIESEL REPAIR	01	52	73
SNO B&O: GRADE CROSSING ACCIDENTS	02	50	133
SNO B&O: HIGHEST ALTITUDE/STEEPEST GRADE	10	61	42
SNO B&O: ILCHESTER TUNNEL	10	43	08
SNO B&O: IMPROVEMENTS/DIESEL FREIGHT SRV	09	48	80
SNO B&O: LIST OF ROADS CONTROLLED 1941	05	74	47
SNO B&O: LOCO #51 STREAMLINED DIESEL	02	54	119
SNO B&O: LOCOS #7400, #7450, #7109 DATA	01	34	88
SNO B&O: LOCOS AND CLASSIFICATIONS	02	31	441
SNO B&O: LORD AND LADY BALTIMORE SCRAPPD	02	50	127
SNO B&O: MARINE EQUIPMENT IN NY HARBOR	02	46	65
SNO B&O: MECHANICAL TRIMMERS-GRAIN LOADR	08	52	64
SNO B&O: MILL CREEK YARD--CINCINNATI OH	11	48	53
SNO B&O: MORSE VS TELEPHONE DISPATCHING	08	51	65
SNO B&O: MOTOR #10/FELLS POINT/HISTORY	01	54	75
SNO B&O: NEW BRIDGE AT PULASKI HIGHWAY	04	51	67
SNO B&O: NEW CHICAGO FREIGHT YRAD	08	49	56
SNO B&O: NUMBER PLATES GRADE-CROSSING SI	04	49	68
SNO B&O: NY WATER FLEET 1941	02	76	46
SNO B&O: OLD & NEW LETTERING	04	44	76
SNO B&O: OPENS TRANSPORTATION MUSEUM	10	53	123
SNO B&O: PHILA-CHICAGO DOUBLE TRACK MAIN	01	46	63
SNO B&O: PITTSBURGH PA TO WILLARD OHIO	10	40	69
SNO B&O: PREPARES FOR IRON ORE IMPORTS	09	51	57
SNO B&O: PRESIDENTIAL SERIES LOCOS	04	43	99
SNO B&O: RDC1 CARS (BUDD) WHERE USED	02	51	49
SNO B&O: REBUILD MAIN LINE--HURRICANE	07	74	47
SNO B&O: RECKLESS MOTORIST RECEIVE WARNI	04	50	127
SNO B&O: RECKLESS MOTORISTS	11	52	122
SNO B&O: RESTAURANT TACES/VARIES BY STAT	12	52	124
SNO B&O: RIVERVALE IN TRACK RE-ALIGNMENT	12	50	55
SNO B&O: ROADS IT CONTROLS	09	41	78
SNO B&O: ROYAL BLUE LAST RUN 1958	10	58	08
SNO B&O: ROYAL BLUE/ROYAL LIMITED	06	31	440
SNO B&O: ROYAL LIMITED OF 1898	11	74	51
SNO B&O: SIGNAL SYSTEM CHANGES	10	48	70
SNO B&O: SOC FOR PRESERVATION MEMORY STM	09	54	63
SNO B&O: SPRINGFIELD DIVISION	11	42	68
SNO B&O: STEWARDESS-NURSES	12	57	61
SNO B&O: TELEVISION ON THE TRAIN	02	49	61
SNO B&O: TRACKAGE 2, 3, 4	08	33	88
SNO B&O: TRANSPORTATION COMPANY LIST	03	78	52
SNO B&O: TUNNEL #1/CLARKSBURG WV	04	51	126
SNO B&O: TV RAILROADING	01	53	129
SNO B&O: USE OF ELECTRIC LOCOMOTIVES	05	66	33
SNO B&O: USES ELECTRICS THRU TUNNELS	12	32	103
SNO B&O: WHITE RIVER JUNCTION DIESEL LOC	05	45	59
SNO B&OCT	01	33	101
SNO B&OHT: PURCHASED CTT IN 1910	12	57	47
SNO B&OSW: CONSOLIDATION	01	35	87
SNO B&P: LEASED TO OC IN 1888	01	76	39
SNO B&P: SEEKONK CASE	04	48	105
SNO B&PIC: FIRST LOCOMOTIVE IN MAINE	05	78	57
SNO B&PITT: MERGED IN 1900 TO FORM PB&LE	07	34	90
SNO B&Q: 449 MILES/EQUIPMENT	01	42	65
SNO B&R: MERGED WITH RUTLAND	03	32	518
SNO B&ROCH: BECAME NYC	09	53	44
SNO B&ROCH: FORMED IN 1850/CONSOLIDATION	11	43	61
SNO B&SQ: 253 MILES/46 LOCOMOTIVES	01	32	261
SNO B&SQ: BRIEF HISTORY	12	66	27
SNO B&SQ: RAILROAD NOW PART OF B&O	10	35	84
SNO B&SQ: SHORT HISTORY	04	66	38
SNO B&SQU: RAILWAY NOW ABANDONED	10	35	84
SNO B&SR: 1880'S/2' GAGE/MAINE/21 MILES	12	55	29
SNO B&SR: BECAME BRIDGTON & HARRISON RY	03	35	90
SNO B&SW: ORGANIZED 1875/BECAME BZ&C	09	50	61
SNO B&W: REORGANIZED IN 1905 AS WR	06	36	80
SNO B&WE: "ROAD OF APOSTLES"/23 MI/TEXAS	08	55	40
SNO B&WEL: 1895-1898/9 MI/TROLLEY/VT	10	52	91
SNO B&WO: BOSTON'S FIRST TRAIN 1834	03	78	51
SNO BA&A: ATTICA & FREEDON BECAME 1894	12	40	65
SNO BA&A: ORGANIZED 1894/STANDARD GAGE	05	45	65
SNO BA&P: 1890 STYLE COMBINATION PASS CR	12	48	102
SNO BA&P: 1ST STEAM FRT/PASS TO ELECTRIF	10	33	49
SNO BA&P: 2 PASSENGER TRAINS	08	38	93
SNO BA&P: BRIEF HISTORY	05	77	53

RAILROAD HISTORIES & ROSTERS

SHORT NOTES ON...	M	Y	P
SNO BA&P: COMPLETED 1892-ELECTRIFIED '12	01	74	11
SNO BA&P: LARGEST ELECTRIC LINE MONTANA	10	34	83
SNO BA&P: ORE-CARRYING ROAD/NOW ELECTRIC	08	43	54
SNO BALDWIN LOCO WORKS: OWNERSHIP	11	68	34
SNO BALDWIN LOCOMOTIVE WORKS: DIESELS	12	56	35
SNO BALDWIN-LIMA-HAMILTON CORPORATION	04	51	138
SNO BALDWIN: PROSPEROUS YEAR	04	31	115
SNO BALT: #38 CAR LINE	04	53	96
SNO BALT: 329 MILES/EQUIPMENT	01	42	65
SNO BALT: CONVERSION	02	55	64
SNO BALT: CREDIT SLIPS/SLACK HOURS	09	54	51
SNO BALT: INTERURBANS/30+ LINES	04	46	115
SNO BALT: PCC CARS ON SUBURBAN LINE	11	50	96
SNO BAR: 614 MILES/EQUIPMENT	06	33	92
SNO BAR: COMMENTS BY FIREMAN	02	39	123
SNO BAR: COMMENTS BY MR. TODD'S CHILDREN	02	39	123
SNO BAR: READER/MEMORIES/TRUE TALES OF R	08	45	77
SNO BAR: STEAM LOCOS IN SERVICE/STORAGE	02	56	38
SNO BARN: INCORP IN 1866/BECAME TUCK	11	34	95
SNO BART: EARTHQUAKE DISCUSSION	07	71	46
SNO BAYT: 5.5 MILES/STANDARD GAGE/1 LOCO	12	29	97
SNO BB&BC: MEMORIES OF 1910-1911	01	47	131
SNO BB&K: ORGANIZED 1880/SOLD 1892/NARRO	09	54	28
SNO BBB&C: CHARTERED 1847 FIRST SW ROAD	12	73	51
SNO BBELT: CHARTERED 1889	12	46	80
SNO BBER: CHARTER 1889/ LEASED ACRR 1890	10	75	52
SNO BC&A: B&E ACQUIRES RAIL LINES IN '28	05	34	87
SNO BC&A: NOW PART OF...	09	31	190
SNO BC&F: TO OC 1883	01	76	39
SNO BC&FR: INCORP 1852/BECAME WM IN 1853	09	35	86
SNO BC&FR: INCORPORATED 1852 NOW WM	05	73	35
SNO BC&G: DEMISE	06	64	50
SNO BC&N: DE KALB LINE 1862	07	33	82
SNO BC&P: 1865	09	37	63
SNO BC&S: 41 MILES	04	31	122
SNO BC&SA: BRIEF HISTORY	10	65	27
SNO BC&SA: CHARTERED 1903/FLA TO GA	04	45	75
SNO BCE: OPEN OBSERVATION CARS/RAILFANS	01	51	96
SNO BCF&NB: NOW NYNH&H	05	73	54
SNO BCG&A	10	32	350
SNO BCL&P: REORGANIZATION	09	37	63
SNO BCR&M: BECAME BCR&N IN 1876	05	38	71
SNO BCR&M: FORMED 1874/TO BCR&N IN 1876	04	75	12
SNO BCR&N: ABSORBED BY RI IN 1902	01	49	41
SNO BCR&N: ORGANIZED 1876 TO RI 1903	04	75	12
SNO BCR&N: ORGANIZED 1876/532 MILES/EQUI	05	38	71
SNO BCR: INCORP 1869/TERMINAL SWITCHING	01	54	68
SNO BCR: INCORPORATED 1869 NOT BC&G	07	69	35
SNO BDAM: TENNESSEE/TUNNEL THRU ROCK 20'	06	41	28
SNO BE&NC: ACQUIRED BY V&SW IN 1899	12	38	69
SNO BE&W: ORGANIZED 1913/RAILS TORE UP	07	39	130
SNO BEAR: CHARTERED 1865/PA/BECAME S&AL	02	57	40
SNO BEC: 1892/REORGANIZATION/EQUIPMENT	12	41	78
SNO BED: ABSORBED BY HU&BT	07	32	508
SNO BED: CHARTERED 1858	03	68	25
SNO BED: CONSOLIDATED WITH H&BT IN 1864	05	37	40
SNO BED: CONSOLIDATED WITH H&BTM IN 1864	09	35	82
SNO BEDB: BECAME CTH&SE	07	46	52
SNO BEDT: TERMINALS OF 1951	05	76	25
SNO BELL: 326 MILES/EQUIPMENT	01	42	65
SNO BELL: RECONSTRUCT?	09	46	107
SNO BERS: FOLDED 1932	04	47	69
SNO BERY: EQUIPMENT/HISTORY	07	47	109
SNO BETHLEHEM TRANS CORP: RUNS 7 SHORTLI	06	42	92
SNO BF&N: MINNESOTA & INTERNAT'L LEASES	04	35	85
SNO BFR: "JAMES WHITCOMB RILEY" MAKE-UP	06	41	27
SNO BFR: CCC&SL NICK NAME	04	71	62
SNO BG	05	32	10
SNO BG:	11	32	473
SNO BG: ABSORBED BY LV&T IN 1914	10	49	131
SNO BG: CONTROLLED BY LV&T IN 1914	07	73	39
SNO BH&E: 1864/RECEIVERSHIP 1870/NOW NH	07	43	69
SNO BH&E: CHARTERED IN 1863/NOW NY&NE	08	34	85
SNO BH&E: FORM 1864 BECAME NY&NE & NERR	07	74	40
SNO BH&FP: CHARTERED 1881 NOW BN	08	73	57
SNO BH&FP: CHARTERED 1881 TO CB&Q 1900	12	75	58
SNO BH&FP: CHARTERED IN 1881/3' GAGE	06	38	76
SNO BHC: 3' GAGE/BUYS WP&Y #69 LOCO	04	56	69
SNO BHRR: NO HORSE CAR IN BROOKLYN	02	61	39
SNO BI&B: CHARTERED 1876 DIED 1878	05	73	35
SNO BI&S: INCORP 1924/48 MILES/ALA	11	36	57
SNO BI&S: SHORT HISTORY	01	65	31
SNO BIR: ALABAMA/PCC CARS/TROLLEY-BUS	12	49	79
SNO BIR: BUSES/RAIL LINES	11	47	112
SNO BIRT: SUBURBAN ROUTES TO BESSEMER/3	10	52	89
SNO BL&K: OPENED 1886/ENTERED PITTSBURGH	09	54	28
SNO BL&S: INCORPORATED 1883-NOW READING	06	67	35
SNO BL&YC: INCORP IN 1904/NOW C&I	02	35	83
SNO BLE&C: RECEIVERSHIP 1924	03	73	43
SNO BLISS: RIGA TO ADRIAN MICH	01	37	90
SNO BM&A: ORGANIZED IN 1901 BECAME LH&ND	07	72	62
SNO BM&A: ORGANIZED IN 1901/1912 NAME CH	06	35	82
SNO BM&LP: BIG FLOP PER "BUSINESS WEEK"	11	75	54
SNO BM&R: NOT JUST A BRANCH LINE ANYMORE	11	86	61
SNO BM: BEGAN 1836/BECAME PART OF LV	12	56	29
SNO BM: LV ACQUIRED IN 1864	08	46	43
SNO BMT&NB: INCORP IN 1894/NOW PAR OF LV	01	37	89
SNO BMT: ACQUIRED BY V&SW IN 1908	12	38	69
SNO BMT: BECAME SOUTHERN APPALACHIAN RY	09	70	33
SNO BMT: INCORP 1910/N CAROLINA/EQUIP/MI	09	53	69
SNO BMT: INCORP 1917/ACQUIRED L&N	02	36	85
SNO BMT: MERGED INTO V&SW 1908	05	74	46
SNO BMT: NOW YANCEY	12	55	39
SNO BMTC: SURFACE CARS	07	33	82
SNO BN&NL: MERGED 1869 TO N&WO TO NYNH&H	12	71	57
SNO BN: ANNUAL DIESEL FUEL BILLS	02	73	50
SNO BN: FORMATION 1970	09	74	43
SNO BN: HUMP YARD LOCATIONS	02	74	52
SNO BN: LINE MILEAGE (23,872.55)	12	70	44
SNO BN: WHY THE NAME BURLINGTON?	11	75	43

Railroad/ Railfan

Stephans' Railroad Directory

RAILROAD HISTORIES & ROSTERS

SHORT NOTES ON...	M	Y	P
SNO BO&W: 1908-1928/11 MILES/N CAROLINA	09	36	76
SNO BO&W: ORGANIZED 1908 DIED 1928	03	75	10
SNO BOD&B: CHARTER 1881 THEN BODRL 1895	12	74	57
SNO BOD&B: CHARTERD 1881/3' GAGE/NOW MLR	05	37	36
SNO BODRL: FROM BOD&B 1895 TO MLR	12	74	57
SNO BODRL: NAME CHANGE 1895/NOW MLR	05	37	36
SNO BOE: SHORT LINE STARTED 1966	06	67	36
SNO BOQUERON RAILROAD: PANAMA ROAD	08	39	73
SNO BP&C: ORGANIZED 1872/PART OF B&O	09	36	74
SNO BP&CT: SCRAPPED IN 1953/NAVY CONTROL	02	56	41
SNO BP&N: INCORPORATED 1909 BRIEF HISTOR	03	71	60
SNO BR&A: SOLD 1897/BECAME TF	01	36	81
SNO BR&B: ACL PREDECESSOR	04	71	62
SNO BR&E: 645 MILES FOR 87 CENTS	11	38	58
SNO BR&M: CONNECTED WITH READING	10	33	44
SNO BR&N: BRIEF HISTORY	09	65	38
SNO BR&P: CONDUCTOR MEMORIES/HISTORY	09	43	08
SNO BR&P: MALLETS BUILT BY ALCO	12	31	92
SNO BR&P: NOW PART OF B&O	06	55	35
SNO BR&PA: NOW PART OF B&O	07	32	510
SNO BR&WE: NOW PART OF PLANT SYSTEMS	12	37	54
SNO BR&WE: REORGANIZED IN 1882/NOW PSY	01	35	87
SNO BR: CHARTERED 1852/44 MILES/S CAROLI	05	39	65
SNO BR: TWO DIFFERENT ROADS W/SAME NAME	03	73	41
SNO BRB&BE: OPENED 1886/28 MILES/EQUIPME	12	41	78
SNO BRB&L: 3' GAGE/READER MEMORIES	04	47	135
SNO BRB&L: BRIEF HISTORY	08	65	21
SNO BRB&L: INCORP IN 1874/3' GAGE	10	34	87
SNO BRB&L: OPEN END TROLLEY CAR DATA	03	41	74
SNO BRB&L: ORGANIZED 1874/MASS/NARROW GA	06	50	64
SNO BRB&L: SOLD IN 1927/1927-8 ELECTIFIE	10	35	86
SNO BRB&L: WONDERLAND PARK/READER MEMORI	12	47	128
SNO BRC: FIRE DAMAGES LOCOS	10	58	10
SNO BRC: LEASES C&WI	07	34	90
SNO BRIGB: CHARTERED 1889/14 MILES	11	44	55
SNO BRIN: INCORP 1906/BECAME S&NW 1914	07	35	84
SNO BRIS: 1892-1930/2 LOCOS/7 CARS	03	33	94
SNO BRIS: CHARTERED IN 1890	03	35	87
SNO BRIS: CORRECTION--ABANDONED IN 1930	05	35	85
SNO BROOKS LOCO WORKS DUNKIRK NY	04	36	89
SNO BROOKS LOCOMOTIVE WORKS: NOV 1 1869	04	34	79
SNO BRTE: 1900/CONSOLIDATION OF 24 COMPA	11	49	85
SNO BRTE: 67 ABSORBED COMPANIES/9 LEASED	05	50	105
SNO BRW: DIESELIZATION PLANS	05	52	69
SNO BRW: SET SAFETY RECORD 1949	07	50	64
SNO BS&WA: NOW PART OF B&O	06	55	35
SNO BSL&PA: INCORP 1903/BECAME BSL&W	03	37	62
SNO BSL&W: LEASED BY MP	06	34	87
SNO BSL&W: NAME CHANGE 1904/83 MILES	03	37	62
SNO BT&P: FORMATION	01	87	40
SNO BTR&U: 1914 PURCHASED B&GR	01	49	89
SNO BU&BA: COMPLETED 1874/MAINE/NOW MC	06	40	73
SNO BU&NW: CHARTER 1875/NARROW/ NOW CB&Q	10	45	54
SNO BU&W: CHARTERED 1881/ABAND 1930/CB&Q	10	45	54
SNO BUCK&N: MERGED IN 1915	02	35	84

SHORT NOTES ON...	M	Y	P
SNO BUCKEYE STEEL CASTINGS COMPANY	10	39	85
SNO BUF&G: ACQUIRED BY LV IN 1889	08	46	43
SNO BUF&L: BECAME NYC	09	53	44
SNO BUMPING POSTS: MADE OF WOOD/STEEL	12	55	38
SNO BURI: 1930/5 YEARS EACH OPERATES	11	40	68
SNO BURI: 1930/T&BV BECAME	09	36	74
SNO BURI: EQUIPMENT/MILEAGES	03	38	54
SNO BURI: SUCCESSOR TO T&BV/2 OWNERS	03	49	14
SNO BURL: 1471 LOCOS	12	31	92
SNO BUTCO: LEASED TO FRISCO IN 1927	01	43	82
SNO BW&LE: ACQUIRED BY TH&B IN 1892	07	36	85
SNO BW&LE: BECAME TH&B IN 1891	08	51	64
SNO BW&PS: LEASED TO BW&S IN 1883	04	42	68
SNO BW&S: ABSORBED BW&PS IN 1883/	04	42	69
SNO BW&S: ABSORBED BY BRB&L IN 1891	10	34	87
SNO BW&S: ABSORBED BY BRB&L IN 1891	06	50	65
SNO BW: ROAD OF APOSTLES/TX/NAMED STATIO	10	57	41
SNO BWC: 2900 HOPPERS!	07	33	85
SNO BZ&C: BECAME OR&W 1903	06	73	48
SNO BZ&C: BECAME OR&W IN 1903	10	35	86
SNO BZ&C: CONSOLIDATED 1882/BECAME OR&W	09	50	62
SNO C&A: BECAME ARR	08	46	58
SNO C&A: REORGANIZATION IN 1861?/NAME CH	04	55	34
SNO C&AL: PROJECTED IN 1901	02	53	11
SNO C&AM: ABSORBED BY PRR	07	41	51
SNO C&AT: CHARTERED 1830/BLOCKS D&BB	03	53	62
SNO C&AT: CHARTERED 1852	10	57	38
SNO C&AT: NOW PART OF PRR	09	35	84
SNO C&B: INCORP 1896/CO DISSOLVED 1931	07	35	87
SNO C&BC: ORGANIZED 1879	06	38	76
SNO C&BCO: NEVER MUCH PAST PEMBERTON	04	49	128
SNO C&CA: INCORP 1830/26 MILES	10	36	74
SNO C&CA: INCORP 1830/26 MILES/HORSE PWR	09	54	30
SNO C&CF: 1915/CLEVELAND OHIO/ELECTRIC L	03	46	111
SNO C&CFE: 1897/TRACTION LINE/CLEVELAND	03	46	111
SNO C&CI: BECAME K&AR	11	72	56
SNO C&CON: ONCE A WOOD BURNING ROAD	08	46	17
SNO C&CR: SIX LOCOMOTIVES	07	31	538
SNO C&CRY: BECAME PART OF L&C	12	50	57
SNO C&CT	01	33	101
SNO C&CT: BECAME PART OF CTT IN 1897	12	57	47
SNO C&E: 5 MILES/1 LOCO/INDEPENDENTLY OW	06	32	337
SNO C&E: 5 MILES/MISSOURI/1 LOCO/RAILCAR	04	48	130
SNO C&E: ABANDONED/HOPE FOR NEW COMPANY	11	49	125
SNO C&E: READER MEMORIES 1892	09	48	137
SNO C&E: SERVICE ABANDONED/EQUIPMENT	07	49	129
SNO C&EE: 1900/CLEVELAND OHIO/ELECTRIC L	03	46	111
SNO C&EI: 15 DELUXE CABOOSES PLACED INTO	11	50	66
SNO C&EI: 939 MILES/EQUIPMENT	11	33	88
SNO C&EI: A BRANCH BECOMES C&IC	01	33	98
SNO C&EI: ABANDONED BRANCH/BECOMES CA&SO	01	36	85
SNO C&EI: ACQUIRED BY EI&TH SOLD TO BFR	12	73	54
SNO C&EI: CUTTING PASSENGER LOSSES	11	53	107

RAILROAD HISTORIES & ROSTERS

SHORT NOTES ON...	M	Y	P
SNO C&EI: EVANSVILLE TO YANKEETOWN LINE	01	53	57
SNO C&EI: JORDAN SPREADER	12	49	58
SNO C&EI: LAST STEAM/COMMUTER SERVICE	04	56	42
SNO C&EI: LEASES EVANSVILLE & TERRE HAUT	12	33	91
SNO C&EI: ORGANIZED 1877 & 1894 & 1920	05	41	44
SNO C&EI: RAILROAD TO RAILWAY IN 1920	12	33	91
SNO C&EI: RESERVED DINING CAR SEATS	05	55	63
SNO C&EI: TUESDAY IS "LADIES DAY"	02	55	06
SNO C&EI: WANSFORD FREIGHT YRAD	10	51	63
SNO C&EP: BECAME PART OF SF&W	12	40	61
SNO C&EP: CONSOLIDATED TO SF&W 1884	12	73	52
SNO C&ET: 1910/CLEVELAND OHIO/ELECTRIC L	03	46	111
SNO C&F: CHARTERED 1853/BECAME SLIM&S	01	36	81
SNO C&F: NOW PART OF READING	11	31	491
SNO C&F: ORG 1853 TO SLIM&S 1874	11	74	52
SNO C&F: ORGANIZED 1853/BECAME SLIM&S	10	40	68
SNO C&G: CHARTERED IN 1848/13 MI/EQUIPME	02	33	83
SNO C&GR: 168 MILES/EQUIPMENT	11	36	55
SNO C&GR: DEC 24 1928 SNOW STORM	01	43	137
SNO C&GR: DIESEL RETIREMENTS	09	83	26
SNO C&GR: TO ICG 1972 & FINAL DISPOSITIO	01	75	55
SNO C&GS: CHARTERED 1880/MERGES/REORGANI	06	38	76
SNO C&GU: BUILT 20 MILE 1901/CGA LEASED	07	54	60
SNO C&I: 50 MILES	04	34	84
SNO C&I: NAME CHANGE IN 1911/38 MI/EQUIP	02	35	83
SNO C&IAL: ABSORBED BY LNAC IN 1881	05	49	26
SNO C&IC: ABANDONED BRANCH OF C&EI	01	36	85
SNO C&IC: MERGED WITH C&EI IN 1894	05	41	44
SNO C&IC: MILEAGE/NAME CHANGES	06	38	76
SNO C&IC: TAKEN OVER BY CA&SO	01	33	98
SNO C&IM: 132 MILES/29 LOCOS/EQUIPMENT	09	34	84
SNO C&IM: 1905/ACQUIRES PART OF CP&STL	07	36	85
SNO C&IM: 1906/NAME CHANGE/ABSORBED/EQUI	09	47	73
SNO C&IM: 3 STYLES OF LETTERING	11	45	55
SNO C&IM: BRIEF HISTORY	11	78	47
SNO C&IM: ILLINOIS/130 MILES	07	54	81
SNO C&IM: PASS LINES/2-10-2/EX-WABASH SC	11	54	73
SNO C&IT: BECAME PART OF MONON	05	49	26
SNO C&L: BUILT 1886	11	71	39
SNO C&L: CHARTERED 1886/CALIF/3' GAGE/	03	37	61
SNO C&L: INCORP 1885/ABANDONED 1913	02	72	62
SNO C&LE: 1930/CONSOLIDATION	11	52	88
SNO C&LE: ELECTRIC LINE/OPERATES FROM TO	01	39	59
SNO C&LE: LIST-INTERURBANS ABSORBED BY	09	53	76
SNO C&LV: MERGED WITH RUTLAND IN 1901	03	32	518
SNO C&MH: ABSORBED BY CORNWALL RR 1856	12	37	55
SNO C&MO: LEASED BY B&M IN 1895	01	48	119
SNO C&MO: LEASED SUNCOOK VALLEY RR	01	34	88
SNO C&MV	05	34	83
SNO C&N: INCORP 1895/REORGANIZTION	12	35	87
SNO C&NE: ACQUIRED BY T&P IN 1926	10	42	63
SNO C&NO: MERGED WITH C&N IN 1910	12	35	87
SNO C&NP	01	33	101
SNO C&NP: BECAME PART OF CTT IN 1897	12	57	47
SNO C&NP: LEASED WC IN 1890	08	32	56
SNO C&NRR: OPENED 1838/TRAMWAY PRIMITIVE	12	49	54
SNO C&NW: "400" FIGURE EIGHT HEADLIGHT	11	37	50
SNO C&NW: "400" FLYER	04	35	87
SNO C&NW: "400" FLYER ADDITIONAL COMMENT	06	35	87
SNO C&NW: "400" LOCOS HAVE 2 HEADLIGHTS	04	37	49
SNO C&NW: "400" USES OIL/COAL BURNERS	05	36	81
SNO C&NW: "400"/OIL USED	11	35	85
SNO C&NW: 14 OPERATING DIVISIONS/LIST OF	09	40	64
SNO C&NW: 1810 COAL BURNING LOCOS	08	30	91
SNO C&NW: 1948 MAINTANNCE/IMPROVEMENT PL	08	48	62
SNO C&NW: 7873 MILES/781 LOCOS/MERGER??	04	56	41
SNO C&NW: ACQUIRES LI&M/DIESELIZATION	06	58	72
SNO C&NW: ASH PANS	07	49	131
SNO C&NW: BUDD RDC'S	10	50	61
SNO C&NW: DEATH TAKES HOLIDAY/READER MEM	07	46	92
SNO C&NW: DIVISIONS	08	49	57
SNO C&NW: DOLLY RUNS READER COMMENTS	09	71	09
SNO C&NW: DOUBLE DECK CENTER DOOR COACHS	03	54	120
SNO C&NW: ELECTRIC AUTO BLOCK SIGNALS	05	54	82
SNO C&NW: ELLSWORTH STATION/READER MEMOR	11	43	112
SNO C&NW: FE&MV NOW PART OF C&NW	02	38	57
SNO C&NW: FOREST PRODUCTS CALCULATOR	08	52	63
SNO C&NW: FRT/PASS SERVICE DIESELIZED	10	56	46
SNO C&NW: GASOLINE PROPELLED DOODLEBUG	08	53	123
SNO C&NW: INCORP IN 1859	04	34	79
SNO C&NW: INSTALLED MOVING PICTURES	09	32	233
SNO C&NW: INVENTION OF ENGINEERS CAP	02	70	10
SNO C&NW: LEFT HANDED RAILWAY	08	61	35
SNO C&NW: LOCOS #3002, #2802, #2803 RETI	11	51	65
SNO C&NW: LONGEST DOUBLE TRACK CTC INSTA	02	51	48
SNO C&NW: ONE AGENT HANDLES 2+ STATIONS?	04	58	08
SNO C&NW: OPERATE ON LEFT-HAND SIDE/WHY?	11	53	45
SNO C&NW: OPERATES MOTOR CARS ON BRANCHS	11	30	599
SNO C&NW: OPERATING DIVISIONS IN 1940	01	74	11
SNO C&NW: ORDERED 61 DIESELS FEB 1950	06	50	60
SNO C&NW: PACIFIC TYPE LOCOS PULL	03	36	84
SNO C&NW: PROVISO CAR REPAIR SHOP	11	46	66
SNO C&NW: REHABILITED DIESEL LOCO	12	57	57
SNO C&NW: RESPONSE 1 AGENT/2 STATIONS	08	58	10
SNO C&NW: RUN ON LEFT HAND TRACK	07	31	537
SNO C&NW: RUNS ON LEFT TRACK	05	38	76
SNO C&NW: SPIKELESS FUSES	05	51	136
SNO C&NW: SUICIDE OF RAILDAOG BEVERLY IA	06	46	06
SNO C&NW: TAKES OVER MATTOON RAILWAY	01	37	88
SNO C&NW: TELEGRAPHER CONTEST OF 1895	07	73	10
SNO C&NW: TRAIN INDICATOR BOARDS-CUSTOM	01	52	126
SNO C&NW: TRAIN INDICATOR BOARDS/TRACK16	04	52	131
SNO C&NW: TRAINS RUN ON LEFT HAND TRACKS	04	32	67
SNO C&NW: WHY IT IS A LEFT-HANDED LINE	12	65	28
SNO C&NWT: 1897/OPENED 1898/NOW DB&W	09	39	70
SNO C&NWT: CONSTRUCTED 1898/BECAME DB&W	09	36	74
SNO C&NWT: OPENED 1898 BECAME DB&W	10	74	46
SNO C&NWT: OPENED 1898 BECAME DB&W 1909	09	73	40
SNO C&NWT: OPENED 1898/3' GAGE/REORGANIZ	11	38	73
SNO C&O: 1950 200 TON COAL TRAIN	05	75	52

Stephans' Railroad Directory

Railroad/Railfan

RAILROAD HISTORIES & ROSTERS

SHORT NOTES ON...	M	Y	P
SNO C&O: 45 STEAM LOCOS ORDERED	04	48	76
SNO C&O: 70 TON HOPPER CARS ORDERED	04	47	53
SNO C&O: 825 MILES	08	38	90
SNO C&O: ABSORBED FLINT & PERE MARQUETTE	07	53	55
SNO C&O: AIRPLANE STYLE TRAY MEALS	04	52	127
SNO C&O: BEST IN THE EAST	06	56	04
SNO C&O: BIG BEND TUNNEL	03	41	71
SNO C&O: BIG SANDY DIV	05	35	83
SNO C&O: BRIEF HISTORY/EQUIPMENT/FINANCL	05	34	80
SNO C&O: CAR FERRY LENGTHENED	10	53	70
SNO C&O: CHARTERED AS C&O OF INDIANA	09	35	81
SNO C&O: CLASS H LOCOS/TRAIN CONTROL/ETC	05	34	82
SNO C&O: CONTROL FIGHT FOR CSS&SB	03	67	45
SNO C&O: CONVERSION OF OPEN SECTION PLMS	11	49	66
SNO C&O: EXPEDITER SCHEDULE	03	48	61
SNO C&O: FFV TRAIN/HOW GOT NAME	08	57	42
SNO C&O: HAMMOND-CINCINNATI RUN	03	50	134
SNO C&O: LIGHTNING TRAIN FINDER/TIMETABL	09	47	69
SNO C&O: LOCOS HAULING FAST FLYING VIRGI	02	34	86
SNO C&O: MERGED WITH PERE MARQUETTE	10	47	69
SNO C&O: MOUNTIAN SUB-DIVISION STRAIGHTE	04	48	72
SNO C&O: PASS TRAFFIC SALESMAN USE OTHER	02	54	72
SNO C&O: RENUMBERING SCHEME OF PM LOCOS	10	52	62
SNO C&O: REPLACED OPEN SECTION PULLMANS	02	51	52
SNO C&O: SEWELL VALLEY RR A BRANCH OF	08	39	68
SNO C&O: SMALLER RR COMPANIES OWNED BY	10	59	38
SNO C&O: SPANISH TRAIN--LIKES	07	48	65
SNO C&O: SPEEDWEST-FAST FREIGHT TRAIN	09	51	61
SNO C&O: STATION FORT MONROE	03	40	118
SNO C&O: TAKE YOUR CAR WITH YOU SERVICE	10	65	29
SNO C&O: THE VALLEY QUEEN TRAIN	06	50	133
SNO C&O: TIPPING RESTORED ON DINING CARS	10	50	127
SNO C&O: TRACE FORK SUBDIVISION EXTENSIO	08	48	60
SNO C&O: TRAIN CONTROLS	06	34	87
SNO C&O: TURNTABLE SPAN=BRIDGE MAINSTAY	07	51	127
SNO C&O: USING PASSENGER PLANE	12	55	04
SNO C&O: WALBRIDGE YARD/PRESQUE ISLE DOC	06	48	51
SNO C&OC: INCORP 1913/15 MILES/EQUIP/FIN	12	36	51
SNO C&PA: INCORP 1882/PENNSYLVANIA/EQUIP	03	37	61
SNO C&PE: 50 MILES/EQUIP/PASS & FRT SERV	02	40	121
SNO C&PE: BRIEF HISTORY	04	67	34
SNO C&PE: INCORP IN 1851/49 MILES/EQUIPM	05	36	82
SNO C&PI: 4 LOCOMOTIVES	08	32	53
SNO C&PM: 1942 MILITARY ROAD	07	67	33
SNO C&PS: BECAME PCOAST	02	37	80
SNO C&PS: INCORP IN 1880/BECAME PCOAST	12	36	50
SNO C&R: 1890-	05	34	132
SNO C&RBV: NOW PART OF IC	06	56	37
SNO C&RO: NOW PART OF C&A	11	47	67
SNO C&S: ACQUIRED BY CB&Q/744 MILES	03	49	14
SNO C&S: BUYS CS&CC IN 1905	03	32	520
SNO C&S: FORMED IN 1898/NOW PART OF CB&Q	09	54	40
SNO C&S: LAST NARROW GAGE ROUTE GONE!	12	43	43
SNO C&S: LOCO #12, #37 BY COOKE/ROUNDHOU	05	55	04
SNO C&S: NARROW GAGE/ORGANIZED IN 1871	01	39	63
SNO C&S: RESULT OF RECEIVERSHIP OF UPD&G	10	55	36
SNO C&S: SOUTH PARK LINE	02	33	85
SNO C&SE: BECAME CENTRAL INDIANA	11	38	72
SNO C&SE: BECAME CENTRAL INDIANA RY	01	36	85
SNO C&SL: 16 MILES/EARLY HISTORY	11	47	16
SNO C&SL: BRIEF HISTORY	08	66	31
SNO C&SL: CHARTERED 1832 OLDEST STEAM IN	11	76	42
SNO C&STL: SOLD AUGUST 1889 TO NYC	04	31	122
SNO C&SU: 1843/REORGANIZATION OF I&OS	02	42	48
SNO C&SWT: 1902/CONSOLIDATION OF LINES	05	52	88
SNO C&TOL: MERGED TO BECOME PART LS&MS	06	35	82
SNO C&TOM: RECEIVERSHIP 1880'S	04	47	108
SNO C&V: CHARTERED 1831/NOW PART OF IC	06	56	37
SNO C&WO: INCORP 1905/9 MILES/NOW CARR	11	34	96
SNO C&WC: 343 MILES/EQUIPMENT	12	31	96
SNO C&WC: CHARTERED 1896	06	41	64
SNO C&WI: INCORP IN 1879/EQUIPMENT/MILES	07	34	90
SNO C&WI: LIST OF ROADS CONTROLLED BY	09	39	72
SNO C&WIB: MERGED IN 1882 TO FORM C&WI	07	34	90
SNO C&WT: LAGRANGE ROUTE ABANDONED	06	48	101
SNO C&WV: ORGANIZED IN 1900/CONSOLDIATIO	06	35	85
SNO C&WY: INCORP 1899/STD GAGE/EQUIPMENT	01	47	56
SNO C&YR: INCORP IN 1909	02	34	85
SNO C&YR: SOLD AT RECEIVERS SALE 1922	11	50	126
SNO CA&C: BECAME N&CA	05	53	140
SNO CA&C: ONE HORSE PIKE	12	32	47
SNO CA&C: ORGANIZED IN 1880/37 GAGE/MILE	04	34	86
SNO CA&C: SILVER AND ITS PART IN BUILDIN	04	51	130
SNO CA&CH: ACQUIRED BY GN&A IN 1911	03	37	61
SNO CA&CIN: CONSOLIDATION	04	31	122
SNO CA&CIN: READER CORRECTION INFO	09	84	06
SNO CA&CL: ORGANIZED IN 1868	08	52	83
SNO CA&COL	05	34	83
SNO CA&E: ELECTRIC/SUNSET LINE	01	46	102
SNO CA&E: FINANCIAL	03	41	77
SNO CA&E: INTERURBAN LINE IN JEOPARDY	06	52	83
SNO CA&E: INTERURBAN LINE MAY EXPAND	04	52	103
SNO CA&M: ABSORBED BY SWS IN 1906	05	52	91
SNO CA&N: OPENED IN 1885/3'GAGE/22 MILES	08	31	47
SNO CA&SE: MERGED WITH CWP&S IN 1909	05	36	84
SNO CA&SO:	06	38	76
SNO CA&SO: ABANDONED/BRIEF HISTORY/MERGR	05	47	126
SNO CA&SO: ABANDONED/MOTIVE POWER	03	43	119
SNO CA&SO: INCORP 1922	01	33	98
SNO CA&SO: INCORP 1922/154 MI/EQUIPMENT	01	36	85
SNO CA&T: BECAME PARTA OF SLIM&S	01	36	81
SNO CA&T: ORG 1853 TO SLIM&S 1874	11	74	52
SNO CA&T: ORGANIZED 1853/BECAME SLIM&S	10	40	68
SNO CA: CONSOLIDATION OF SEVERAL ROADS	11	38	72
SNO CAD: OPENED 1901 BRIEF HISTORY	02	72	61
SNO CAI: CATSKILL MOUNTAIL RR LEASED	05	33	72
SNO CAL&N: ACQUIRED BY SF&N IN 1903/8 MI	08	55	45
SNO CALS: 7 MILES/ABANDONED ABOUT 1930	01	50	90
SNO CAM: ACQUIRED BY SF&N IN 1903/3 MILE	08	55	45
SNO CAM: STEAM ROAD THAT NEVER WAS	12	44	81

Stephans' Railroad Directory

Railroad/ Railfan

RAILROAD HISTORIES & ROSTERS

SHORT NOTES ON...	M	Y	P
SNO CAN: 735 LOCOS IN 1917 ABSORBD BY CN	10	33	46
SNO CAN: OPENED 1896 NOW CN	09	73	40
SNO CAN: SHORT HISTORY	08	78	54
SNO CAN: SHORT HISTORY/NOW PART OF CN	04	38	49
SNO CAN: TELEGRAPH POLES & NUMBERS	06	33	90
SNO CANO: 20 MILES/LEASED TO	01	35	82
SNO CANO: LEASED BY EC&N NOW LV	04	74	44
SNO CAPR: INCORP 1909/MILES/EQUIPMENT	09	42	62
SNO CAPR: MOTIVE POWER OWNED BY NP	11	35	85
SNO CAPR: OWNS NO EQUIPMENT	08	35	86
SNO CARB: INCORP 1922/5 MI/UTAH/NO EQUIP	09	34	85
SNO CAROLINA RR: ACTUALLY KCRR	05	73	36
SNO CARR: FREIGHT SUBSIDIARY OF L&N	12	57	46
SNO CARS: BRIEF HISTORY	08	67	31
SNO CART: CARTIER MINING QUEBEC	02	74	53
SNO CARTH: HORSEDRAWN /ROCHESTER NY/1833	10	48	84
SNO CAS: MERGED IN 1889 TO FROM SCAL	08	34	85
SNO CAYL: ORGANIZED IN 1867	01	35	82
SNO CAYS: ORGANIZED AS CAYUGA LAKE	01	35	82
SNO CAZS: 6 MILES/1 LOCO/WISCONSIN ROAD	06	32	335
SNO CB&C: FAILED DREAM/SOLD FOR JUNK	10	50	128
SNO CB&E: CONSOLIDATION 1896	05	52	85
SNO CB&KC: NOW PART OF CB&Q	08	34	87
SNO CB&Q: 1849-1949 PHOTO ESSAY	03	49	12
SNO CB&Q: 1105 MILES OF DOUBLE TRACK	10	31	429
SNO CB&Q: ACQUIRES DENVER UTAH & PACIFIC	06	33	89
SNO CB&Q: BIG HORN CANYON WY LINE RELOCA	12	48	73
SNO CB&Q: BOYSEN DAM RELOCATION	11	50	66
SNO CB&Q: CHICAGO-ST PAUL SERVICE	03	45	77
SNO CB&Q: CLASS TA/T2/T3 LOCO--DATA	04	33	96
SNO CB&Q: COMMUTERS/MODERNIZATION	03	52	136
SNO CB&Q: DATE WHEN CB&Q ENTERS NEBRASKA	11	33	91
SNO CB&Q: DOUBLE TRACK	05	44	79
SNO CB&Q: FIRST LIGHTWEIGHT PASS SERVICE	05	76	25
SNO CB&Q: FIRST MANUAL BLOCK SIGNALS	05	66	35
SNO CB&Q: FRANK HUGHES/COLCHESTER ILL	11	51	128
SNO CB&Q: LINES IT CONTROLS/MILEAGE	01	38	57
SNO CB&Q: MORNING & AFTERNOON ZEPHYRS	12	67	10
SNO CB&Q: NARROW GAGE IN IOWA	10	75	53
SNO CB&Q: OPEN LETTER TO MR. BUDD, PRES	07	47	48
SNO CB&Q: ROADS IN BURLINGTON SYSTEM/ROU	04	39	79
SNO CB&Q: ROADS WHICH ARE PART OF	08	34	87
SNO CB&Q: ROCK BALLAST PLANT/LA CROSSE D	06	45	61
SNO CB&Q: ST JOSEPH & DES MOINES NOW	10	36	70
SNO CB&Q: STEAM LOCOS LEFT IN SERVICE	11	54	34
SNO CB&Q: SUMMIT CUT	04	53	61
SNO CB&Q: SYNTHETIC FUEL FROM COAL	11	49	66
SNO CB&Q: THREE TRACK MAINLINE	10	61	40
SNO CB&SJ: CONSOLIDATED WITH SJ&CB 1868	07	32	509
SNO CBE&O: TRACTION COMPANY	05	52	85
SNO CBE: 1896-1935/28 MILES	11	36	54
SNO CBE: 1899-1935 PHOTO ESSAY	03	43	66
SNO CBE: INCORP IN 1896/29 MILES/EQUIPME	04	34	79
SNO CBE: LEASED WASHINGTON DIV	03	39	62
SNO CBELT: EMBLEM	05	54	99
SNO CBELT: GENEOLOGY OF	02	47	111
SNO CBELT: LOGO EVOLUTION	03	73	42
SNO CBELT: SHORT HISTORY	09	32	196
SNO CBELT: TRUE TALES	08	32	58
SNO CBER: BRIEF HISTORY	01	65	29
SNO CBSR: GLACE BAY NOVA SCOTIA	06	76	50
SNO CBT: 21 MILES/ABANDONED 1947	01	50	90
SNO CBT: INTERURBAN LINE/21 MILES	07	44	127
SNO CC&CS: KNOWN AS CRIPPLE CR SHORTLINE	02	41	74
SNO CC&CS: LEASED CS&CC	01	35	86
SNO CC&L: BECAME PART OF C&O AND NKP	09	35	81
SNO CC&O: BECAME CLINCHFIELD RR	11	39	89
SNO CC&O: NOW CLINCHFIELD RY/55 TUNNELS	07	31	538
SNO CC&P: FORMATION	12	87	44
SNO CC&RC: CHARTERED 1887/BECAME CO&G	03	55	29
SNO CC&RG: 1906/ RESULT OF REORGAINZATIO	11	35	85
SNO CC&S: 116 MILES/NOW PART OF W&LE	06	38	76
SNO CC&SR: PRIVATELY OWNED LUMBER ROAD	08	37	57
SNO CCAN: BECAME NORTHERN ALBERTA RY	04	35	86
SNO CCC&SL: NYC MERGER 1914	05	68	27
SNO CCE: 23 MILES/1912-1933/1 LOCO	01	36	85
SNO CCE: ACQUIRES SAN JUAN PACIFIC	07	33	82
SNO CCE: FROM SJP 1912 (SECOND CCE)	01	76	41
SNO CCE: INCORP 1912 CONTROLLED BY PPC	09	75	59
SNO CCE: INCORP IN 1912/ABANDONED	10	36	71
SNO CCE: INCORPORATED 1912 DIED 1933	11	72	54
SNO CCE: NO LONGER OPERATING	09	44	64
SNO CCE: OPENED 1861 TO CPA 1864 (FIRST)	01	76	41
SNO CCF&RG: INCORP 1906/REORGAN AS CC&RG	11	35	85
SNO CCRR: BECAME PART OF PRSL IN 1933	04	39	74
SNO CCRR: TO OC IN 1872	01	76	39
SNO CCSDRG: CHARTERED 1875/BECAME TMEX	02	46	61
SNO CCSR: 238 MILES/EQUIPMENT	01	42	65
SNO CCW: BUSINESS GOOD/CAR #53	12	50	93
SNO CCW: INCORP 1910/STD GAGE STEAM/ELEC	05	42	66
SNO CCW: PASS SERV ABANDONED/CAR #53	10	52	88
SNO CD&C: T EDISON'S FIRST JOB	01	78	46
SNO CD&M: BRIEF HISTORY OF BRIDGE & MUSE	12	65	36
SNO CD&M: CLOSED 1933	05	74	46
SNO CD&MI: ROCK ISLAND PREDECESSOR	04	71	62
SNO CD&V: SOLD IN 1877/BECAME C&EI	05	41	44
SNO CD&V: SOLD TO C&EI IN 1877	11	33	91
SNO CDR&N: ORGANIZED 1886/NARROW GAGE/FR	12	58	37
SNO CE&I: BECAME PART OF LVT IN 1905	08	42	95
SNO CE&W: CONSOLIDATION 1900	05	52	88
SNO CEAST: NOW PART OF CN/127 MILES	10	33	48
SNO CECR: BUILT 1892 ATSF 1901 END '60	11	75	44
SNO CET: BECAME SIOUX CITY TRACTION CO.	04	50	77
SNO CF&A: BECAME CF&SE IN 1905	07	35	84
SNO CF&E: 1901/CLEVELAND OHIO/ELECTRIC	03	46	111
SNO CF&N: BECAME D&S IN 1904	04	36	93
SNO CF&PG: CHARTERED 1876/BECAME F&NW	06	56	40
SNO CF&SE: INCORP IN 1905	07	35	84
SNO CF: 9 MILE INTERCHANGE ROAD/N CAROLI	10	44	89
SNO CG&C: PURCHASED BY CGN IN 1913	05	37	38

Stephans' Railroad Directory

Railroad/ Railfan

RAILROAD HISTORIES & ROSTERS

SHORT NOTES ON...	M	Y	P
SNO CG&C: STANDARD GAGE/47 MILES	07	34	87
SNO CG&ME: BUILT 1874-5/30"/NJ/BECAME R	06	43	135
SNO CG&P: CONSTRUCTION BEGAN IN 1886	05	45	120
SNO CGA: "NANCY HANKS II" STREAMLINER	12	54	08
SNO CGA: 1834 BEGINNINGS NOW S	06	72	60
SNO CGA: 20 MILE STRETCH BECOMES H&S	07	54	60
SNO CGA: DIESEL AND STREAMLINED EQUIPMEN	02	47	64
SNO CGA: MAN O'WAR	11	47	66
SNO CGA: MILEAGE	06	30	412
SNO CGA: NO NARROW GAGE BRANCH LINES	07	31	536
SNO CGA: RECEIVERSHIP 1933	02	76	47
SNO CGN: 1913-1934/CONSOLIDATION	05	37	38
SNO CGR: 1750 MILES	04	38	49
SNO CGR: MARITIME ROADS NOW CN	09	73	40
SNO CGR: NOW PART OF CN/425 LOCO IN 1917	10	33	46
SNO CGRT: RAPID TRANSIT LINE/INTERURBAN	12	46	105
SNO CGW: "REDBIRD" LOCO PAINTED RED	10	57	43
SNO CGW: "WHALEBELLIES"/ALL-WELDED HOPPR	04	50	72
SNO CGW: 1495 MILES/EQUIPMENT	07	33	84
SNO CGW: CHARTERED IN 1892/INCORP IN 1909	10	34	87
SNO CGW: COMPLETELY DIESELIZED	06	52	135
SNO CGW: DIESELS OWNED/ORDERED	09	49	55
SNO CGW: DIVISIONS (TWO)	03	35	85
SNO CGW: FLANGER SIGN	02	56	42
SNO CGW: MALLET LOCOS	04	44	76
SNO CGW: NUMBER OF LOCOMOTIVES OWNED	05	31	279
SNO CGW: SUCCEEDS CSP&KC IN 1892/REORGAN	03	34	86
SNO CGW: TAKES OVER WISCONSIN MINN & PAC	01	34	90
SNO CH&A: ACQUIRED BY ERIE IN 1881	10	37	69
SNO CH&B: BECAME PART OF WISCONSIN CENTR	08	32	56
SNO CH&B: SOLD IN 1890	01	33	101
SNO CH&D: NOW PART OF B&O	01	33	98
SNO CH&E: CHICAGO & ATLANTIC BECAME	10	37	69
SNO CH&L: BECAME CAROLINA &NORTH-WESTERN	12	35	87
SNO CH&M: TO C&NW 1864	12	76	28
SNO CH&NW: ABANDONED 1939	07	40	68
SNO CH&SO: NOW PART OF PLANT SYSTEMS	12	37	54
SNO CH&SO: REORGANIZED IN 1880/NOW PSY	01	35	87
SNO CHAT: OPERATED SARANAC & LAKE PLACID	04	47	21
SNO CHES: VIRGINIA'S FIRST ROAD	02	61	30
SNO CHESS: GROWTH BY ADDING EL EST	09	75	04
SNO CHESS: ROADS MAKING UP THE SYSTEM	03	76	56
SNO CHICAGO: 28 ROADS INTO, NOT 1 THRU	08	33	91
SNO CHSO: BECAME CTH&SE IN 1910	07	46	52
SNO CHT: 1903 TO 1925/26 MILES	11	37	50
SNO CHT: ELECTRIC LINE	05	46	115
SNO CHT: INCORPORATED 1903 DIED 1925	08	73	56
SNO CHV&T: PREDECESSOR TO HV	12	71	57
SNO CHVR: CHARTERED 1853 NOW PC	09	73	43
SNO CHW: INCORP IN 1900/NAME CHANGE 1895	07	34	91
SNO CHW: PURCHASED BY N&W/54 MILES	12	54	41
SNO CI&B: CONEY ISLAND AVE LINE	07	33	82
SNO CI&NW: 25 MILES/ROLLING STOCK	08	56	41
SNO CI: BRIEF HISTORY	03	78	51
SNO CILL: INCORP 1905/BECAME C&IM 1906	09	47	73

SHORT NOTES ON...	M	Y	P
SNO CIN&E: INCORP 1898/21 MILES/NOW IR&T	12	47	92
SNO CIN: $1 A YEAR PRESIDENT	12	52	124
SNO CIN: CHARTERED IN 1903/118 MILES	11	38	72
SNO CIN: INCORP 1903/ 52 MILES	01	36	85
SNO CINO: INCORP 1880/36 MILES	02	36	87
SNO CINO: OPENED IN 1881/BECAME CL&N	02	35	86
SNO CIRCUS ROUTE INTO NYC MADISON SQUARE	08	45	48
SNO CIRCUS TRAINS: FIRST OPERATED IN US	09	49	58
SNO CK&O: 1913 ORGANIZATION	05	69	30
SNO CK&O: BRIEF HISTORY	03	31	604
SNO CK&S: BRIEF HISTORY	10	77	55
SNO CK: INCORP 1911/EQUIPMENT /22 MILES	03	32	520
SNO CL&B: NEW LINE KAMMS CORNER TO ELYRI	05	52	85
SNO CL&C: PURCHASED CLAR	05	55	50
SNO CL&CA:	06	38	77
SNO CL&E: COMPLETED 1896	05	52	85
SNO CL&N: ACQUIRED BY PRR IN 1896	02	36	87
SNO CL&N: ACQUIRES MIDELTOWN & CINCINNAT	04	39	79
SNO CL&N: CONSOLIDATION	04	31	122
SNO CL&N: INCORP IN 1888/NOW PART OF PRR	02	35	86
SNO CL&SO: 27 MILE EXTENSION IN 1901	05	52	88
SNO CL&W: 200 MILES/BECAME B&O	11	36	58
SNO CL&WE: 1895-1899	05	34	82
SNO CL: 2 ROADS COMPRISE	11	39	89
SNO CL: 309 MILES/55 TUNNELS/NOW LEASED	07	31	538
SNO CL: 309 MILES/EQUIPMENT	12	31	96
SNO CL: FREIGHT ONLY ONLY	10	54	62
SNO CL: LEASED ROAD	11	70	42
SNO CL: PASSENGER COACH STILL RUNS	02	55	74
SNO CLA: 11 MILES	03	34	86
SNO CLAR: SHORT HISTORY NOW PART OF CL&C	12	60	30
SNO CLAR: SOLD TO CL&C	05	55	50
SNO CLOCKS AS LOCOMOTIVE STD EQUIPMENT	09	67	28
SNO CLRT: ELECTRIC CAR #0516 SOLD/NEW HO	10	53	93
SNO CLRT: NEW CARS	10	52	88
SNO CLRT: NEW SYSTEM ALMOST COMPLETE	03	55	42
SNO CLRT: SHAKER ANEXING & CAR STOP SIGN	08	73	50
SNO CLS&E: OPENED 1896	03	68	24
SNO CLS&SB: 1909/CHICAGO & AIRLINE BECAM	02	53	13
SNO CLS: OWNS 1.2 MILES OF TRACK	01	37	87
SNO CM&C: INCORP IN 1901/S CAROLINA/18 M	09	35	87
SNO CM&G: CHARTERED IN 1908/NOW MILW	02	33	83
SNO CM&P: NOW PART OF MILW	01	34	88
SNO CM&S: ERECTED 1897 BEREA TO MEDINA	05	52	88
SNO CM&W: FORMATION	09	87	33
SNO CM: INCORP 1921/6 MILES/IDAHO	04	36	93
SNO CMA: MASSC REORGANIZED AS CMA 1885	03	34	89
SNO CMI: 1906 DAYS	11	70	66
SNO CMI: 222 MILES/ROUTE	07	31	536
SNO CMI: 337 MILES/ABANDONED 1918/EQUIP	03	32	520
SNO CMI: ABANDONED IN 1918/EQUIPMENT	11	33	88
SNO CMI: ABSORBED CC&CS IN 1921	02	41	74
SNO CMI: MIDLAND MEMORIES/WRECKS	12	42	139
SNO CMI: TAKEN OVER BY MIDLAND TERMINAL	11	34	92
SNO CMSP: 1874/ BECAME MILWAUKEE ROAD	06	38	75

Railroad/ Railfan

RAILROAD HISTORIES & ROSTERS

SHORT NOTES ON...	M	Y	P
SNO CMSP: 1876/ CHICAGO ADDED TO MI&SP	06	50	23
SNO CMSP: FLOATING BRIDGES	12	43	78
SNO CMSP: MEMORIES OF THE OLD ST PAUL	12	43	44
SNO CMSP: MILWAUKEE & ST PAUL MERGES W/	01	34	90
SNO CMT: 3' GAGE/CHARTERED IN 1880	05	33	72
SNO CMT: ABSORBED CANAJOHARIE & CATSKILL	02	49	88
SNO CMT: BUILT IN 1880/3' GAGE/FOLLOWED	09	54	30
SNO CMT: CHARTERED 1880/NY/16 MILES/	03	43	105
SNO CMT: FORMED IN 1880	10	36	74
SNO CMT: ORGANIZED 1880/3' GAGE/NEW YORK	07	36	87
SNO CN&C: INTERSTATE TROLLEY SYSTEM KY	07	41	66
SNO CN: % NUMBER AFTER CLASSIFICATION	03	43	101
SNO CN: 102 MPH ON RAPIDO	02	68	32
SNO CN: 188 MILE BRANCH LINE/NEW STATION	12	54	08
SNO CN: 1920 "PEAVINE" ALBERTA	12	33	86
SNO CN: 3 ELECTRIC LOCOS MONTREAL TERMIN	04	51	71
SNO CN: 3126 LOCOMOTIVES	07	32	506
SNO CN: 4 MAJOR ROADS ABSORBED BY	10	33	46
SNO CN: 4500 HP ELECTRO-MOTIVE DIESELS	12	48	66
SNO CN: ABSORBING GT	07	77	49
SNO CN: ACQUIRED GT IN 1920	10	36	73
SNO CN: ACQUIRES GTP	02	78	49
SNO CN: ACQUIRING NF, TEN &QRL&P	10	78	47
SNO CN: ALASKA PIPELINE CONTRIBUTION	05	74	46
SNO CN: AUTO TRAIN OPERATION GREAT SLAVE	04	69	29
SNO CN: CANADA EASTERN/INTERCOLONIAL	10	33	48
SNO CN: COALING DOCK TEESWATER ONTARIO	10	59	08
SNO CN: COLONIAL SLEEPERS DESCRIBED	08	48	132
SNO CN: COMPLETES COAST TO COAST CTC	03	66	10
SNO CN: CONSOLIDATIONS/SUBSIDIARY	09	37	82
SNO CN: CORRECTION TO CANADA RAILROADS	03	48	130
SNO CN: CRYC & C&G NOW PART OF CN	02	33	83
SNO CN: CTC INSTALLATION	12	44	43
SNO CN: DENTIST OFFICE--NORTHERN ONTARIO	12	51	119
SNO CN: DIESEL CLASSIFICATIONS	02	61	36
SNO CN: DIESEL ELECTRIC LOCOS REPLACE ST	05	50	138
SNO CN: DIESEL LOCO NUMBERING CLASSIFICA	09	50	50
SNO CN: DIESEL POWER ORDER AUTUMN 1952	04	53	63
SNO CN: DIESEL-ELECTRICS EDMONTON-WINNIP	09	53	67
SNO CN: DIESELIZATION PROGRAM	04	49	67
SNO CN: DIESELS PROGRAM	07	49	63
SNO CN: DUPLEX ROOMETTE CARS	10	50	62
SNO CN: DW&P NOW PART OF CN	06	38	74
SNO CN: EMBLEM CHANGES	06	46	99
SNO CN: EXPERIMENTING W/COLOR DESIGNS	09	42	59
SNO CN: FERRYBOAT "ELIZABETH"	09	51	58
SNO CN: FINANCIAL RECORDS 1929-1934	12	35	80
SNO CN: GIFT TICKETS	08	52	67
SNO CN: GOV'T OWNED/LOSING MONEY	11	48	121
SNO CN: GRAND TRUCK NOW PART OF CN	01	34	88
SNO CN: GRAND TRUNK WESTERN/GRAND TRUNK	02	33	86
SNO CN: HARVEST EXCURSIONS	10	33	85
SNO CN: INTERNATIONAL LIMITED	06	31	441
SNO CN: KEY HARBOR BRANCH	06	35	82
SNO CN: KITTY FOX ONLY GIRL OPERATOR	03	55	36
SNO CN: LOCOMOTIVE GRAVEYARD	06	69	10
SNO CN: LOCOS TRANSFERRED FROM CV & GTW	02	74	52
SNO CN: LYN JUNCTION-WESTPORT ONT BRANCH	02	53	57
SNO CN: MAIN LINE STATIONS ALPHABETICAL	04	54	12
SNO CN: MARITIME ACTIVITIES-ATLANTIC PRO	03	74	34
SNO CN: MILEAGE OWNED IN UNITED STATES	06	38	72
SNO CN: MILEAGE/MOTIVE POWER	12	29	99
SNO CN: MONTREAL TO LAC REMI	12	40	59
SNO CN: MOUNT ROBSON	11	53	50
SNO CN: MOUNT ROYAL TUNNEL	08	51	66
SNO CN: NEW BRANCH LINE TO TERRACE	10	52	64
SNO CN: NEW CAR FERRY	08	47	61
SNO CN: NEW SLEEPER CAMPBELLTON	02	50	56
SNO CN: NEW TYPE OF SLEEPER ORDERED	06	54	111
SNO CN: NUMBER OF CARS IN YARDS	01	36	87
SNO CN: OLD INSIGNE	06	35	87
SNO CN: ORANGE CABOOSES	04	45	74
SNO CN: OWNS NA JOINTLY WITH CP	04	35	86
SNO CN: PIONEER PART OF LINE	03	52	54
SNO CN: PRINCE EDWARD ISLAND DIESELIZED	10	50	129
SNO CN: PURCHASED QRL&P	07	52	91
SNO CN: QRL&P MONTMORENCY DIVISON PURCHA	03	52	125
SNO CN: QUEBEC BRANCH	02	47	63
SNO CN: QUEBEC BRIDGE	05	48	63
SNO CN: QUEBEC BRIDGE/3 YEARS TO PAINT	03	30	597
SNO CN: QUEBEC CITY-LAKE ST JOHN LINE	12	55	37
SNO CN: RAIL PASSENGER SERVICE RETURNS	01	73	46
SNO CN: ROADS ACQUIRES AND DATES	09	35	84
SNO CN: ROADS INCORPORATED INTO	04	38	49
SNO CN: ROBOT POWER IN BC	04	75	38
SNO CN: ROYAL TRAIN/CAR FERRIES/DIESELS	04	48	127
SNO CN: RUNS IN 6 TIME ZONES	06	52	135
SNO CN: SLEEPING CAR MODERNIZATION	07	53	46
SNO CN: SMITHERS DIVISION/SUB-DIVISIONS	05	50	35
SNO CN: ST CANUT TO CUSHING JCT ABANDONE	08	45	51
SNO CN: ST CLAIR TUNNEL	01	42	63
SNO CN: TIMETABLES/TOWN NAMES	08	48	133
SNO CN: TRAINS TO HALIFAX NS	08	63	31
SNO CN: TWO WAY UNIT TRAINS	02	75	08
SNO CN: UNIT TRAINS	07	68	27
SNO CN: WHY IS IT IN THE RED	04	72	10
SNO CN: WORLD'S 3RD LARGEST RR SYSTEM	01	36	84
SNO CN: WWII PASSENGER PERFORMANCE	06	51	71
SNO CNE&W: MERGES WITH PBC 1892 NOW CNE	03	34	84
SNO CNE: 1899	03	34	84
SNO CNE: CHARTERED IN 1899/MILES/EQUIPMN	02	34	86
SNO CNE: NOW PART OF NYNH&H	03	38	57
SNO CNE: WHERE IT RUNS	03	35	88
SNO CNJ: 21 PACIFIC LOCOS/WEIGHT/TF	07	31	536
SNO CNJ: 691 MILES/EQUIPMENT	03	32	523
SNO CNJ: 8 DIESEL-ELECTRIC NAMED FOR EMP	03	48	63
SNO CNJ: ACQUIRES W&NO IN 1930	04	36	93
SNO CNJ: ASHLEY PLANE/USES-NOW DISMANTLE	12	50	137
SNO CNJ: BLUE COMET DERAILMENT/DISCONTIN	03	73	41
SNO CNJ: CLASS 820-830 LOCOS/WEIGHT/TF	07	31	536

Railroad/ Railfan

RAILROAD HISTORIES & ROSTERS

SHORT NOTES ON...	M	Y	P
SNO CNJ: COAL-BURNERS & OIL-ELECTRICS	06	31	441
SNO CNJ: CONSOLIDATION IN 1849	03	33	92
SNO CNJ: CONSOLIDATIONS	12	32	104
SNO CNJ: DIESELIZATION/14 DIESEL PURCHAS	12	48	66
SNO CNJ: GRADES	03	31	603
SNO CNJ: INCORP IN 1847/CONSOLIDATION/	08	34	86
SNO CNJ: LEASED 2-10-0 IN 1917-1918	08	58	44
SNO CNJ: LINE NOW ENDS AT HALEYVILLE NJ	06	50	129
SNO CNJ: OPERATES BLUE COMET	07	36	81
SNO CNJ: PURCHASED SOMERVILLE & EASTON	08	39	45
SNO CNJ: SHORT RANGE RADAR	08	52	131
SNO CNJ: SUNDAY ON THE OLD JERSEY CENTRL	05	39	27
SNO CNJ: TAXES	05	45	78
SNO CNJ: TIMETABLE SIMULARITY W/NY&LB	12	64	52
SNO CNJ: YARDS/ THE "BULLET"	04	31	121
SNO CNO&TP: BECAME PART OF S	06	44	81
SNO CNO&TP: BRIEF HISTORY	07	78	56
SNO CNO&TP: CHARTERED 1881 NOW S	11	73	57
SNO CNO&TP: CHARTERED 1881/NOW PART OF S	07	53	48
SNO CNO&TP: CHARTERED 1881/NOW SOUTHERN	04	36	94
SNO CNO&TP: RATHOLE DIVISION	02	64	34
SNO CNQ: FORMED IN 1906	12	40	59
SNO CNRY: KENTUCKY/BECAME CLINCHFIELD RR	11	39	89
SNO CNS&M: BUSES FOR INTERURBANS?	05	49	85
SNO CNS&M: CHICAGO CITY LIMITS	01	54	77
SNO CNS&M: ELECTROLINER	07	47	104
SNO CNS&M: FINANCIAL	03	41	77
SNO CNS&M: ONE TIME STEAM POWER	04	62	47
SNO CNW: BECAME PARTA OF NPC	09	40	66
SNO CNW: CHARTERED 1898/NOW PARTA OF NWP	08	55	45
SNO CNYE: PROJECTED/NEVER COMPLETED	03	44	115
SNO CNYS: 1900-1923/STD GAGE/EQUIP/MILES	02	54	75
SNO CO&E: END OF THE STEAM ERA	05	87	26
SNO CO&G: ABSORBED CC&RC IN 1894	03	55	29
SNO CO&G: ABSORBED HOTS IN 1902	12	44	45
SNO CO&G: LEASED TO RI IN 1904	06	30	411
SNO CO&L: AUTHORIZED 1889/2' GAGE/EQUIPM	01	41	74
SNO CO&L: CHARTERED 1882/STD GAGE/PENNSY	04	36	92
SNO CO&L: CHARTERED IN 1882/NOW PART PRR	03	35	87
SNO CO&O: CHARTERED 1853 (VIRGINIA)	08	75	58
SNO CO&SL: 1917 CONSOLIDATION = WM	09	35	86
SNO CO&SL: CONSOLIDATIONS WITH WM 1917	05	73	35
SNO CO&SO: 1902/34 MILES/EQUIP/ABANDONED	05	34	82
SNO CO&SW: CONSOLIDATIONS/NOW PART OF IC	06	58	36
SNO CO&W: INCORP 1896/LEASED BY CP/132 M	08	40	64
SNO CO: BUILT 1878/9 MI/NARROW GAGE/ARIZ	05	54	83
SNO COAL: STONE CANYON RR BECAME COAL	04	36	91
SNO COL&SE: 20 MILES/SHORTLINE/COLORADO	12	40	61
SNO COL&SE: 4 MILES/LOCO #2	08	49	135
SNO COL: BRIEF HISTORY	10	61	42
SNO COL: CHARTERED 1865/3' & STD GAGE	10	34	82
SNO COL: CHARTERED IN 1865/STD& 3' GAGE	03	34	86
SNO COL: ORGANIZED 1871/UP 1881 /C&S '00	12	74	58
SNO COLN: INCORP IN 1901/IOWA/7 MI/ABAND	01	35	85
SNO COLRR: 2.5 MILES/SHORT LINE/COLORADO	12	40	61
SNO COLRT: NEW TROLLEY LINE	12	54	49
SNO COLSC: 1925-1928/NO FARES/TROLLEY	12	49	79
SNO COLT: ABSORBED CR&LC	06	56	66
SNO COLT: DOUBLE DECKER	10	55	51
SNO COLV: ABSORBED BY CO&L IN 1886	03	35	87
SNO COLV: BECAME PART OF CO&L IN 1886	04	36	92
SNO CON: CONTROLLED NH TROLLEY LINES	04	47	64
SNO CONN: 1907/ABSORBED ELECTRC NH OWNED	04	47	63
SNO CONN: GASOLINE CONVERSIONS	01	53	87
SNO CONN: LAST DAYS OF BRANCH SERVICE	02	76	47
SNO CONN: OPEN CARS	04	43	147
SNO CONNC: CONNECTICUT CENTRAL FORMATION	10	87	34
SNO CONNR: LEASED BY B&M IN 1893	06	34	88
SNO CONV: SHORT HISTORY	01	66	28
SNO COOKE LOCOMOTIVE WORKS	09	32	233
SNO COR&E: PURCHASED YREKA RAILROAD	03	54	121
SNO COR: 1ST COMPLETE PASSENGER TRAIN	12	45	59
SNO CORN: 4 DIESEL ELECTRICS/NO MORE STE	08	50	134
SNO CORN: INCORP 1850/12 MILES/PA/EQUIPM	12	37	55
SNO CORN: NO PASSENGER SERVICE	10	39	87
SNO COW: OPENED IN 1871/NOW PART NYNH&H	03	38	58
SNO CP	10	38	37
SNO CP&A: MERGED TO BECOME PART OF LS&MS	06	35	82
SNO CP&LT: INCORP 1911/8 MILES/EUIPMENT	04	35	83
SNO CP&LT: INCORPORATED 1911	07	72	62
SNO CP&SG: CHARTERED IN 1899	07	34	87
SNO CP&SG: PURCHASED BY CGN IN 1913	05	37	38
SNO CP&SL: 234 MILE/EQUIPMENT/HISTORY	11	39	91
SNO CP&SL: INCORP 1909 RECEIVERSHIP 1923	06	75	29
SNO CP&SL: PART BECAME LI&M IN 1900	03	36	81
SNO CP&SS: ACQUIRED BY CP&SG	07	34	87
SNO CP&STL: ORGANIZED IN 1887	07	36	84
SNO CP: 0-10-0 SWITCHERS CLASS W1	08	58	45
SNO CP: 0-8-0/4-6-0 LOCO--DATA	12	32	105
SNO CP: 1ST CONTINENTAL RAILWAY	01	36	87
SNO CP: 2277 LOCOS/EQUIPMENT	07	32	510
SNO CP: 31 MILLION DOLLAR EQUIPMENT ORDR	08	48	63
SNO CP: 37 MILES OF NEW RAILWAY	01	52	124
SNO CP: 4 VARIETIES OF COLONIS CARS	04	53	138
SNO CP: ACQUIRES SPI IN 1917	03	36	86
SNO CP: BARGES ON KOOTENAY LAKE 1933	09	73	05
SNO CP: BRITISH COLUMBIA DISTRICT	04	33	94
SNO CP: BROCKSVILLE ONTATION TUNNEL	06	51	133
SNO CP: BUYS 57 MILES OF MC	05	74	46
SNO CP: BUYS TH&B	08	77	11
SNO CP: CALGARY ALBERTA DIESEL SERVICE P	05	52	68
SNO CP: CHRISTMAS TREES	01	55	04
SNO CP: CLASS 63/64/2231/2500/2665 DATA	12	31	92
SNO CP: COAST SERVICE	06	58	35
SNO CP: COLONIST CARS	12	52	132
SNO CP: COMBINATION SNOWPLOW & MELTER	12	55	35
SNO CP: COMPLETED FROM COAST TO COAST	05	66	33
SNO CP: CONVERSION FROM COAL TO OIL BURN	01	50	73
SNO CP: COUNTESS OF DUFFERIN HISTORY	02	44	101
SNO CP: DECAPODS CLASS R,S,T READER INFO	01	74	13

Railroad/ Railfan

RAILROAD HISTORIES & ROSTERS

SHORT NOTES ON...	M	Y	P
SNO CP: DIESEL LOCO NUMBERING CLASSIFICA	09	50	50
SNO CP: DIESEL SERVICE PLANT ALYTH YARDS	04	54	33
SNO CP: DIESELIZATION OF SCHREIBER DIV	10	76	46
SNO CP: DIESELIZATION PROGRAM	04	49	68
SNO CP: DISPOSITION OF "LAST CONT SPKIE"	06	75	08
SNO CP: DIVERSIFICATION OF CP LTD	12	76	27
SNO CP: DIVISIONS OF CROWSNEST PASS ROUTE	12	34	85
SNO CP: DOME CAR OBSERVATORY SLEEPER	02	54	107
SNO CP: EARLY DIESEL OPERATIONS	03	73	43
SNO CP: EARLY DIRECTION OF	09	49	33
SNO CP: ELECTRIFICATION REVELSTROKE BC	03	73	02
SNO CP: EQUIPMENT NUMBERS'68-NEW MARKING	01	69	31
SNO CP: FIRST TRANSCONTINENTAL LINE CAND	12	74	58
SNO CP: FLAME-HARDENED PISTON RING GROOV	02	46	65
SNO CP: FREIGHT TERMINAAL MONTREAL PLANS	03	48	62
SNO CP: HOTELS OWNED IN 1973	02	74	53
SNO CP: IMPORT WORKERS FROM ENGLAND 1907	04	69	08
SNO CP: KETTLE VALLEY RR LEASED TO CN	02	33	83
SNO CP: KICKING HORSE CANYON	12	59	33
SNO CP: LAKE SECTION CONSTRUCTION	01	78	47
SNO CP: LAST PUSHER STATION	06	77	09
SNO CP: LEASED DA	05	49	55
SNO CP: LEASES OTTAWA NORTHERN & WESTERN	04	33	95
SNO CP: LETHBRIDGE VIADUCT 5327' LONG	07	45	79
SNO CP: LIST OF SPECIFIC LOCOS & BUILDER	10	39	86
SNO CP: LOCO #969 CONVERTED TO WOODBURNR	04	57	08
SNO CP: LOCO CHANGES TRANSCONTINENTAL LT	01	52	71
SNO CP: LOCOMOTIVE NUMBERS/TYPES	06	32	339
SNO CP: LOCOS/TRACTIVE FORCE	07	38	77
SNO CP: MAY 1958 STRIKE	12	58	38
SNO CP: MILEAGE/MOTIVE POWER	12	29	99
SNO CP: MORANT PHOTOS PHOTO ESSAY	03	46	96
SNO CP: NEW DIESEL LOCOS ORDERED W/DATA	08	57	74
SNO CP: NEW EQUIP/ODD NAMES TIMETABLE/ME	01	48	134
SNO CP: OLD SIDING #29	09	78	63
SNO CP: OPERATION OSPREY	12	55	20
SNO CP: OWNS NA JOINTLY WITH CN	04	35	86
SNO CP: PASSENGER SERICE REDUCED KOOTENA	08	58	06
SNO CP: PASSENGER STEAM SHIP/CORRECT/ADD	11	50	134
SNO CP: PRIEST PRESIDENT FOR A DAY	01	72	54
SNO CP: PRIVATELY OWNED	10	31	423
SNO CP: PRIVATELY OWNED/MAKING MONEY	11	48	121
SNO CP: PURCHASED HEREFORD RY IN 1928	05	38	72
SNO CP: RAVENHEAD SUB-DIVISION	05	55	63
SNO CP: ROOMETTE CARS	06	45	61
SNO CP: SCHREIBER DIVISION DIESELIZATION	12	50	55
SNO CP: SELKIRK LOCOS	08	54	44
SNO CP: SINGLE TRACK/MEMORIES	02	44	08
SNO CP: SMITHS FALLS DIVISION	07	34	92
SNO CP: SNOW MELTER	09	51	60
SNO CP: SOAP SPECIAL	10	51	141
SNO CP: START OCEAN GOING SERVICE 1886	01	74	11
SNO CP: STEAM ENGINE CHANGES 1950	03	76	55
SNO CP: STEAM LOCOS REPLACED BY DIESEL-E	05	50	138
SNO CP: STEAMERS IN WW II	05	78	56
SNO CP: STEAMSHIP SERVICE	02	42	47
SNO CP: STRETCH OF TRACK IN US UNDER CP	03	44	99
SNO CP: U-SSHAPED RAILS/CAST IRON RAILS	04	56	09
SNO CP: UNUSUAL NAMES ON TIMETABLE	05	48	132
SNO CP: VANCOUVER ISLAND TERMINAL	06	50	62
SNO CPA: EIGHT 4-4-0'S AS S PLOW PUSHERS	12	65	16
SNO CPA: INCORP 1861 & 1899/NOW SP	10	55	37
SNO CPA: LEASED TO SP IN 1885	04	38	49
SNO CPA: SNOW 1890	02	48	65
SNO CPM&O: COMPLETE W/ROUTE MAP & ROSTER	03	37	72
SNO CPM&O: INCORP 1880 "OMAHA ROAD"	10	70	20
SNO CPM&O: KNOWN AS "OMAHA"	04	34	79
SNO CPM&O: OMAHA LINE/1617 MILES	04	55	41
SNO CPM&O: READER MEMORIES	09	47	135
SNO CPR: OREGON/SMALL FREIGHT LINE	07	53	49
SNO CR & ATSF: FASTEST COAST TO COAST	11	87	40
SNO CR&IC: 1904/"CRANDIC"/27 MILE/ELECTR	03	55	60
SNO CR&L: BECAME CONSOLIDATED RAILWAY CO	04	47	63
SNO CR&LC: BECAME COLUMBUS TRACTION CO	06	56	66
SNO CR&NW: ALASKA ROAD/196 MILES/EQUIPMN	03	35	84
SNO CR&NW: FINANCIAL/EQUIPMENT	11	36	58
SNO CR&NW: INCORP 1905/ALASKA/196 MILES	12	35	85
SNO CR&NW: LAST TRAIN 1938	03	66	30
SNO CR&NW: NOV 14 1938 LAST TRAIN	05	39	125
SNO CR&NW: SHORT HISTORY	05	65	44
SNO CR&S: BECAME C&A	06	72	60
SNO CR&SJ: 28 MILES/EQUIPMENT/ROSTER	12	32	104
SNO CR&W: BUILT 1907 (BEN HUR ROUTE)	12	75	58
SNO CR: CONRAIL IN CANADA	11	78	49
SNO CR: MAJOR SHOP LOCATIONS	06	78	57
SNO CR: OPERATING REGIONS & DIVISIONS	03	78	50
SNO CR: ROADS MELDED INTO CONRAIL	07	76	50
SNO CR: WHAT IS CONRAIL?	09	75	58
SNO CRA: 1899/NAME CHANGE/MILES/EQUIPMEN	03	49	60
SNO CRARK: INCORP IN 1906/11 MILES/ABAND	08	34	89
SNO CRESC: ORGANIZED IN 1865	08	52	83
SNO CRI: INCORP 1898/12 MILES/PA ROAD	02	43	61
SNO CRLI: STEWART RR NICK-NAME	11	73	59
SNO CRO: PHOTO ESSAY	02	38	54
SNO CRR&C: CHARTERED/CORPORATE TITLE	05	51	64
SNO CRRR: NARROW GAGE/ABANDONED 1916-17	11	46	51
SNO CRW: 32 MILES/EQUIPMENT	01	42	65
SNO CRY: 1869/DAYTON OHIO/STREETCAR LINE	02	48	98
SNO CRYC: NOW PART OF CN	02	33	83
SNO CRYOC: PROFILE MAP & SHORT HISTORY	12	63	62
SNO CS&CC	10	32	350
SNO CS&CC: CHARTERED 1897 TO F&CC 1919	11	73	58
SNO CS&CC: CHARTERED 1897/85 MILES/EQUIP	03	32	520
SNO CS&CC: CHARTERED 1897/BANKRUPT 1920	01	35	86
SNO CS&H	05	34	83
SNO CS&RB: MERGED IN 1889 TO FROM SCAL	08	34	85
SNO CS&STL: 1925/ACQUIRES PART OF CP&STL	07	36	85
SNO CS&STL: FROM CP&SL 1924	06	75	29
SNO CS&STL: ILLINOIS/86 MILES/ABANDONED	06	40	136
SNO CS&STL: SUCCESSOR TO CP&SL	11	39	91

Railroad/ Railfan

RAILROAD HISTORIES & ROSTERS

SHORT NOTES ON...	M	Y	P
SNO CS&U: INCORP 1909/BECAME SAU&G 1912	06	52	65
SNO CS&W: INCORP IN 1892	07	34	91
SNO CS: INCORP FEBRUARY 28 1868	04	31	121
SNO CSB&NI: NOW PART OF PRR	12	57	39
SNO CSB: INCORP 1873/2.5 MILES	04	31	122
SNO CSCR: 1877/INGENUITY	11	45	96
SNO CSCR: NOW SAN FRANCISCO MUNICIPAL RY	07	52	90
SNO CSF&E: STANDARD GAGE/LOGGING RD/CA	08	56	43
SNO CSHR: CABLE TRACTION/1ST CABLE RY	11	45	94
SNO CSL: 11 LOCOS 0-6-0/0-8-0 TYPES	07	31	538
SNO CSL: TRACKAGE/EQUIPMENT/DIVIDENDS	11	37	51
SNO CSLI: ADDITIONAL HISTORY	01	69	33
SNO CSLI: CANADA SOUTHERN BRIDGE LEASED	04	31	122
SNO CSLI: OWNED BY MICHC	10	58	39
SNO CSLI: PART OF MICHC (NYC SYSTEM)	06	58	34
SNO CSLI: TRAIN CONFISCATED FOR DEBT	12	70	54
SNO CSLS: 1110 MILES/EQUIPMENT	01	42	65
SNO CSO: BECAME CNO&TP IN 1881	07	53	48
SNO CSO: BEGUN 1869 BY CITY CINNACINNATI	04	36	94
SNO CSO: HIGH BRIDGE	06	44	81
SNO CSOR: JOINING NYC VIA MICHC	10	68	34
SNO CSP&FL: 177 MILES	04	34	79
SNO CSP&KC: BECAME PART OF CGW	09	53	17
SNO CSP&KC: INCORP IN 1886	10	34	87
SNO CSP&KC: ORGANIZED IN 1886	03	34	86
SNO CSRT: INCORPORATED IN 1888	06	53	76
SNO CSS&SB: EARLY DAYS	05	86	25
SNO CSS&SB: ELECTRIC LINE	10	45	94
SNO CSS&SB: FINANCIAL	03	41	77
SNO CSS&SB: FISCAL CRISIS AGAIN	01	87	34
SNO CSS&SB: SYSTEM WIDE RADIO HOOKUPS	11	49	84
SNO CSS&SB: TAKE OVER BY C&O	03	67	45
SNO CSW: 1922/REORGANIZATION	05	52	93
SNO CSX: ROADRAILER SERVICE	12	87	44
SNO CT&S: INCORP 1912/ARKANSAS/14 MILES	11	43	62
SNO CT&S: INCORPORATED 1913 TO RI 1931	03	74	34
SNO CT&V: NOW PART OF B&O	01	37	87
SNO CT&V: SHORT HISTORY	06	62	45
SNO CT: 2' GAGE/CHICAGO IL/SMALL FREIGHT	12	55	31
SNO CT: NARROW GAGE/62 MILES UNDER CHICA	01	37	89
SNO CTA: ABANDON PART OF SERVICE	04	52	104
SNO CTA: CHICAGO GOES UNDERGROUND	07	51	82
SNO CTA: GETTING 250 CARS	01	55	73
SNO CTA: PHOTOGRAPHIC STUDIOS	08	54	89
SNO CTA: SILVER & RED ARTICULATES	08	48	86
SNO CTC: 162 MILES/EQUIPMENT	01	42	65
SNO CTC: BELTSVILLE LINE/BENNING LINE	04	50	99
SNO CTC: BELTSVILLE SHUTTLE LINES	10	49	105
SNO CTC: FORMULA FOR CAR SCHEDULING	04	52	101
SNO CTC: MUSIC ALLOWED	02	53	81
SNO CTC: PULLED PLOW/READER MEMORIES	12	46	107
SNO CTCO: 15 MILES/PRIVATE RIGHT-OF-WAYS	08	47	96
SNO CTH&SE: 362 MILES/EQUIPMENT	10	33	44
SNO CTH&SE: INCORP 1910/STD GAGE/EQUIPME	07	46	52
SNO CTH&SE: LEASED BY MILW IN 1921	06	38	75

SHORT NOTES ON...	M	Y	P
SNO CTT	01	33	101
SNO CTT: ORGANIZED 1897/CONSOLIDATION	12	57	47
SNO CTV&W: BECAME CL&W/NOW B&O	11	36	58
SNO CUM: 32 MILES LONG	06	34	84
SNO CUM: CUMBERLAND COAL CO/RAILROAD CO	11	46	06
SNO CUMV: CHARTERED IN 1831/NOW PART PRR	12	34	83
SNO CUMV: HISTORY OF "PIONEEER" LOCO	09	42	59
SNO CUT: DISPOSTSION OF P1 ELECTRICS	06	71	44
SNO CUT: EXTENT OF ELECTRIFICATION	08	68	30
SNO CV&W: ORGANIZED 1896/BECAME C&E	04	48	130
SNO CV: 2-10-4 MOST POWERFUL STEAM 1940	12	74	58
SNO CV: 67 LOCOS	10	32	350
SNO CV: ABSORBS B&LAM	05	33	76
SNO CV: DISCONTINUED STEAM 1957	12	57	46
SNO CV: FOR SALE!	07	83	26
SNO CV: LOCOMOTIVE BUILDING	08	62	32
SNO CV: NOT FOR SALE	09	83	26
SNO CV: PART OF GRAND TRUNK CORP	12	77	45
SNO CV: ROSTER OF LOCOS/CLASS/DATE BUILT	10	59	08
SNO CV: SERVOCENTER	12	73	52
SNO CV: STEAM LOCOS STILL OPERATING	06	57	41
SNO CV: STORAGE BATTERY CARS/CLASS 700 L	01	55	37
SNO CVL: MAIDEN RUN 1975	12	75	07
SNO CVRY: CHARTERED 1871 TO CP 1883	08	76	60
SNO CVW&M: BECAME CINO/THEN NYC	08	44	129
SNO CW&E: BECAME LNP&W IN 1924	12	35	85
SNO CW&E: CHARTERED 1914/BECAME LNP&W	01	47	56
SNO CW&LE: INCORP 1903/37 MILES/EQUIPMEN	08	38	92
SNO CW&MV: 1890/1913 MILES/B&O PURCHASED	12	55	38
SNO CW&S: 1899-1902	05	34	82
SNO CW: COMPLETED 1912 PHOTO ESSAY	06	43	98
SNO CW: INCORP 1905/OWNED BY UNION LUMBR	02	36	87
SNO CW: INCORP 1905/STANDARD GAGE/EQUIPM	03	40	132
SNO CW: INCORP IN 1905/EQUIP/MILES/OWNED	03	35	87
SNO CW: SKUNKS	08	63	30
SNO CW: THE SKUNK	12	47	61
SNO CWP&S: INCORP 1909/13 MILES	05	36	84
SNO CWP&S: TWELVE 0-6-0 SWITCHERS	07	31	538
SNO CWU: TAKEN OVER BY C&WI IN 1912	07	34	90
SNO CWV: TO DA 1894	07	74	39
SNO CY&E: 1910/CLEVELAND OHIO/ELECTRIC L	03	46	111
SNO CYC: GRADED ROADBED SOLD TO CDR&N	12	58	37
SNO CYR&P: BECAME SPM IN 1909	02	41	117
SNO CYR&P: NOW PART OF SPM	05	51	74
SNO D&BB: 1870'S BEGAN LINE/C&AT PROBLEM	03	53	62
SNO D&C: INCORP IN 1866/SOLD IN 1876	04	34	85
SNO D&C: OPENED 1871/NOW PART OF NYNH&H	03	38	58
SNO D&CA: BUILT 1913	07	72	62
SNO D&CA: LUMBER ROAD/33 MILES/CALIFORNI	04	35	83
SNO D&E: ACQUIRED BY DELAWARE & NORTHERN	01	37	87
SNO D&E: BECAME DELAWARE & NORTHERN 1911	11	38	71
SNO D&E: BUILT IN 1907/LOCO #2, 3, 7, 10	09	34	85
SNO D&H: 150TH YEAR---BRIEF HISTORY	06	73	50
SNO D&H: 179 DIESEL LOCOS/NO STEAM	04	56	41
SNO D&H: 1899 NAME CHANGE/855 MILES	06	34	89

RAILROAD HISTORIES & ROSTERS

SHORT NOTES ON...	M	Y	P
SNO D&H: 7 YEARS OF CONTINUOUS RAILS	12	41	86
SNO D&H: 899 MILES/EQUIPMENT	04	33	94
SNO D&H: ABANDONED USE OF CAPROTTI VALVE	03	44	100
SNO D&H: D&HCC BECAME D&H	02	35	84
SNO D&H: DERECO HOLDING CO (N&W)	07	71	43
SNO D&H: EQUIPMENT	06	34	84
SNO D&H: HIGH-PRESSURE LOCOS	07	41	67
SNO D&H: MECHANICSVILLE/FORT EDWARD	08	40	64
SNO D&H: NO STEAM, 179 DIESELS	10	56	45
SNO D&H: NOT BEHIND IN MOTIVE POWER	01	34	89
SNO D&H: OWNED UNITED TRACTION & T&NE	12	55	46
SNO D&H: OWNS NAPIERVILLE JUNCTION RY	01	34	87
SNO D&H: POPPET VALVE LOCOS	06	47	135
SNO D&H: SUBSIDIARIES	04	47	24
SNO D&HCC: INCORP IN 1823/RENAMED 1899	06	34	89
SNO D&HCC: LEASED RENSSELAER & SARATOGA	02	35	84
SNO D&HG: SURVEYED 1826/SHORT HISTORY	12	43	74
SNO D&I: ELECTRIC RAILWAY/COLORADO	03	53	96
SNO D&IN: CAR #25 SOLD	10	50	88
SNO D&IN: COMPLETED IN 1907/17 MILES	02	38	59
SNO D&IR: "HIGHBALL" TRAMP TRAIN	01	31	246
SNO D&IR: OWNED BY DM&N	08	37	60
SNO D&LN: LIMA NORTHERN BECAME D&LN 1897	07	34	92
SNO D&M: 1894 TO? 242 MILES INCORP 1894	04	37	52
SNO D&M: INCORP 1894/197 MILES	10	35	86
SNO D&M: MICHIGAN MINE RAILROAD	06	42	77
SNO D&M: MODERNIZATION PROGRAM	05	47	68
SNO D&M: STARTED ABOUT 1878/LOGGING ROAD	12	56	30
SNO D&MM: 15 MILES/3 LOCOS/3 PASS CARS	04	32	69
SNO D&N: 4 LOCOS/TYPES	08	31	46
SNO D&N: INCORP 1911 TO SUCCEED D&E	11	38	71
SNO D&N: INCORP 1911/38 MILES/NY/EQUIPME	01	37	87
SNO D&N: INCORP IN 1911	11	38	73
SNO D&N: ORGANIZED IN 1911/1929 38 MI	09	34	85
SNO D&NE: INCORP 1898/MINNESOTA/58 MILES	02	37	78
SNO D&NE: INCORP IN 1898/58 MILES/EQUIPM	07	35	84
SNO D&NE: NOT OWNED BY DM&N! CORRECTION	08	37	60
SNO D&NM: 1898-1922/STD GAGE/EQUIP/MILES	04	53	61
SNO D&NM: CHARTERED 1898 DIED 1922	02	76	46
SNO D&NO: MERGED WITH FW&DC IN 1887	10	55	36
SNO D&NR: BECAME DANVILLE & WESTERN 1891	07	34	91
SNO D&NRY: ABSORBED BY T&P IN 1903	10	42	63
SNO D&NW: 57 MILES/EQUIPMENT	03	32	521
SNO D&R: CHARTERED 1883 AS RY TO RR 1900	12	76	27
SNO D&RG: 1870/NARROW GAGE/EQUIPMENT	11	49	135
SNO D&RG: 1890 OVERHAULING OF LOCO #42	05	54	120
SNO D&RG: LARGEST NARROW GAGE LOCO ORDER	02	62	48
SNO D&RG: LARGEST SINGLE ORDER OF LOCOS	01	46	61
SNO D&RG: MR. THOM MEMORIES	02	43	139
SNO D&RG: MY NARROW GAGE ALBUM PART 3	12	39	28
SNO D&RG: OPENED 1905/BECAME D&RGW 1920	04	51	71
SNO D&RG: ROLLING STOCK	02	43	58
SNO D&RG: ROLLING STOCK MANUFACTURERS	02	73	49
SNO D&RG: ROYAL GORGE WAR	07	73	38
SNO D&RG: STANDARD GAGE 1905 DURANGO CO	04	75	11
SNO D&RGS: 5 MILES OF TRACK NOT DISMANTL	05	54	80
SNO D&RGW NARROW GAUGE: FREIGHT OUTLOOK	11	69	29
SNO D&RGW: "INSPECTORS"-NOW IN JUNK YARD	07	45	75
SNO D&RGW: 3' GAGE BRANCH LINE	01	33	97
SNO D&RGW: 3' GAGE TRACK	05	35	86
SNO D&RGW: 826 MILES OF 3' TRACK	04	34	84
SNO D&RGW: ABANDONED LINES	01	55	64
SNO D&RGW: BLACK CANYON OF GUNNISON	08	56	39
SNO D&RGW: DELUXE PASSENGER TRAIN	05	50	76
SNO D&RGW: DURANGO & SILVERTON CO	12	71	57
SNO D&RGW: ENGINEER LOOKS BACK OVER YEAR	05	39	28
SNO D&RGW: FILED PETITION ABANDON PARTS	02	50	134
SNO D&RGW: INCORP 1920/ABSORBED D&RG	04	51	71
SNO D&RGW: LAST NARROW GAUGE REMOVED	11	85	34
SNO D&RGW: LEASES GOSHEN VALLEY IN 1927	09	34	86
SNO D&RGW: MARSHALL PASS	12	34	81
SNO D&RGW: MARSHALL PASS ROUTE	01	73	61
SNO D&RGW: MOFFATT DIVISON	09	47	08
SNO D&RGW: NARROW GAGE COMMON CARRIER	10	58	34
SNO D&RGW: NARROW GAGE ROAD	01	32	258
SNO D&RGW: NEW 42 MILE LINE	12	32	101
SNO D&RGW: NEW EMBLEM	09	49	127
SNO D&RGW: POWER & PROFIT 1975	11	75	43
SNO D&RGW: RUBBER-TIRED RAILBUS	03	38	56
SNO D&RGW: SILVERTON BRANCH PASS INCREAS	05	55	07
SNO D&RGW: SOME LINES ABANDONED/NARROW G	10	54	63
SNO D&RGW: STREAMLINER TRAINS	09	41	79
SNO D&RGW: TRACKS (CORRECTION) 04-36	06	36	86
SNO D&RIB: FORMED 1884 TO DRI&N 1898	07	75	54
SNO D&RIB: INCORPORATED IN 1884	10	33	46
SNO D&RIBT	10	33	46
SNO D&S: INCORP 1904/REORG/N CAROLINA	04	36	93
SNO D&SH: OPENED 1901/BECAME TEXTR	11	44	88
SNO D&SJ: MERGED WITH E&K TO BECOME MC	11	49	65
SNO D&SL: 1913/REORGANIZATION OF DN&P	03	41	82
SNO D&SL: 1913/REORGANZIATION 1925	12	34	83
SNO D&SL: 232 MILES/EQUIPMENT	06	33	92
SNO D&SL: INCORP 1925/232 MILES/58 LOCOS	02	36	89
SNO D&SL: MOFFAT TUNNEL AND VENTILATION	05	34	83
SNO D&SL: MOFFATT TUNNEL	05	33	70
SNO D&SL: MOFFATT TUNNEL	05	32	181
SNO D&SL: PROPOSED MERGER WITH RG	06	47	88
SNO D&SO: 24 MILES/ABANDONED	09	36	76
SNO D&SW: ABSORBED BY W&T IN 1907	04	40	77
SNO D&U: CHARTERED IN 1863/REORGANIZTION	06	35	86
SNO D&U: SHORT HISTORY	01	31	280
SNO D&WE: BOUGHT COLLINS & REIDSVILLE	05	34	132
SNO D&WV: CONSOLIDATED WITH W&T IN 1886	04	40	77
SNO D&XT: COMPETED W/RAPID TRANSIT OHIO	11	52	89
SNO D-M: OPENED 1882/NOW PART OF IC	05	45	61
SNO DA&F: BECAME PART OF G&F IN 1907	03	36	83
SNO DA&G: BECAME PART OF G&F IN 1907	06	41	61
SNO DA&G: BECAME PART OF G&F IN 1927	03	39	75
SNO DA&W: INCORP IN 1891/82 MILES	07	34	91
SNO DA&W: SUBSIDIARY OF SOUTHERN	10	47	60

Railroad/Railfan

RAILROAD HISTORIES & ROSTERS

SHORT NOTES ON...	M	Y	P
SNO DA: INCORP 1895/CONSOLIDATIONS	07	37	57
SNO DA: INCORP 1895/LEASED TO CP	05	49	54
SNO DA: INCORPORATED 1895 NOW CP	08	73	56
SNO DA: OPENED 1858 LEASED TO CP	07	74	39
SNO DAKR: (X-GN HUTCHINSON BRANCH)	03	86	29
SNO DAV&P: 1871 TO 1873/LEASED TO NYC&HR	11	37	51
SNO DAV&P: 1872 CONSOLIDATION	06	39	52
SNO DAV&P: CONSOLIDATION 1872 NOW NYC&HR	02	75	49
SNO DAVENPORT LOCO WORKS: BRIEF HISTORY	06	35	80
SNO DB&L: CHARTERED 1872/NOW PECO	10	42	105
SNO DB&MP: PM&Y PURCHASED IN 1882	01	43	83
SNO DB&W: 1909 FROM C&NWT REORGANIZATION	09	73	40
SNO DB&W: 1909-1917	09	39	70
SNO DB&W: 1909/REORGANIZATION	11	38	72
SNO DB&W: 3' GAGE/ABANDONED AFTER WAR/	09	36	73
SNO DB&W: FROM C&NWT 1897 ABANDONED 1917	06	74	21
SNO DBC&A: BECAME D&M IN 1894	10	35	86
SNO DBC&A: BECAME D&M IN 1894	04	37	52
SNO DBC&W: 1905-1925	03	34	87
SNO DBC&W: OPERATED 1910 TO 1951	04	74	45
SNO DC&S: ORGANIZED IN 1925/EQUIPMENT/MI	03	34	87
SNO DC: 1 LOCO/2 CARS	12	37	55
SNO DC: INCORP IN 1916/46 M/UTAH/WP OWNS	09	34	85
SNO DC: ORGANIZED 1916STD GAGE/EQUIPMENT	11	52	59
SNO DCT: SUBWAY PLANS	10	71	50
SNO DE: INCORP 1904/17 MILE/EQUIPMENT	06	47	87
SNO DE: TEMINAL RAILROAD/MICHIGAN/EQUIPM	07	40	68
SNO DE: WHERE IS IT?	02	61	32
SNO DER&I: NOW WABASH	07	44	62
SNO DERECO HOLDING CO EL/D&H/N&W	07	71	43
SNO DET: INCORPORATED 1905/EQUIPMENT	06	47	87
SNO DH&S: "HUCKLEBERRY LINE/MICH/NOW NYC	04	54	10
SNO DH&S: CHARTERED 1875/65 MILES	04	31	122
SNO DIESEL POOLING-CBELT--MP--PRR	05	67	29
SNO DK&S: 6 MILES/1 LOCOMOTIVE	11	32	473
SNO DK&S: 6 MILES/2 LOCOS/EQUIPMENT	12	31	94
SNO DL&A: SOUTH PARK LINE	02	33	85
SNO DL&B: INCORP 1854/NAME CHANGES/HISTO	04	46	60
SNO DL&C: BUILT 1897/ND/6 MILES/STD GAGE	12	38	72
SNO DL&G: TRUE TALES OF RAILS/MEMORIES	04	43	72
SNO DL&N: BRIEF HISTORY	12	61	58
SNO DL&N: STANDARD GAGE/6 MILES	12	38	72
SNO DL&NO: CHARTERED 1889/OHIO/23 MILES	04	39	79
SNO DL&W: "ROUTE OF PHOEBE SNOW"	08	54	45
SNO DL&W: 1ST INDIVIDUAL DRINKING CUPS	06	50	59
SNO DL&W: CONVERTING LOCOS	08	37	56
SNO DL&W: ELECTRIFIED SERVICE SUBURBN NJ	04	48	139
SNO DL&W: FERRY HAMBURG DISPOSITION	02	74	53
SNO DL&W: GILLESPIE SPECIAL	05	47	71
SNO DL&W: GRAVEL PLACE YARDS PHOTO ESSAY	03	40	134
SNO DL&W: HOBOKEN DEPOT & FERRY TERMINAL	11	45	53
SNO DL&W: LARGEST FREIGHT YARDS	12	35	81
SNO DL&W: LOCATION OF ENGINE HOUSES	02	62	49
SNO DL&W: LOCOS LEASED BY B&M	09	43	72
SNO DL&W: MARKINGS ON CERTAIN CARS	02	57	44
SNO DL&W: NICHOLSON BRIDGE	10	46	54
SNO DL&W: OXFORD TUNNEL	07	36	87
SNO DL&W: PEQUEST RIVER FILL	05	45	60
SNO DL&W: PHOEBE SNOW	10	57	39
SNO DL&W: PHOEBE SNOW ADS	01	45	78
SNO DL&W: USES ONLY DIESEL POWER	10	54	39
SNO DL&W: VULCLAIN COMPOUNDS #16 TO #693	12	58	37
SNO DLS&S: INCORP 1846/BECAME LV IN 1853	07	36	80
SNO DM&CI: PHOTO ESSAY	07	42	149
SNO DM&CI: DIESEL FREIGHT LINE	05	51	100
SNO DM&CI: WAS INTERURBAN RAILWAY	09	52	81
SNO DM&FD: BECAME PART OF RI	06	38	73
SNO DM&FD: M&SL BUYS DM&FD IN 1915	01	33	99
SNO DM&FD: WAS DMV NOW RI	01	73	60
SNO DM&IR: 569 MILES/15 DIESELS/EQUIPMEN	04	56	41
SNO DM&IR: CONSOLIDATIONS	08	38	85
SNO DM&MI: ORGANIZED 1870/C&NW ABSORBED	09	43	72
SNO DM&S: ABSORBED BY D&NR IN 1899	07	34	91
SNO DMU: INCORP IN 1884/EQUIPMENT/MILES	06	34	85
SNO DMV: OPENED 1869 BECAME DM&FD NOW RI	02	74	53
SNO DMV: OPENED 1869 NOW RI	01	73	60
SNO DMV: OPENED IN 1869	06	38	73
SNO DN&P: CHARTERED IN 1902/BECAME D&SL	12	34	83
SNO DN&P: ORGANIZED 1902/BECAME D&SL '13	03	41	82
SNO DN&P: ORGANIZED IN 1913/NOW D&SL	02	36	89
SNO DNS: PRIVATELY OWNED LUMBER ROAD	08	37	57
SNO DO: THE ROAD EXPANDS	07	82	24
SNO DP: DROPPED	11	32	470
SNO DPA: REORGANIZED IN 1904 AS MR&NW	12	53	69
SNO DPE: FREIGHT/PASSENGER/GAS-ELECTRICS	05	37	35
SNO DR&T: 165 STREETCARS	12	53	97
SNO DR&T: ORDERS 25 PCC CARS	02	43	145
SNO DRI&N: INCORP 1884/49 MILES/EQUIPMEN	10	33	46
SNO DRI&N: RENAMED 1898 FROM D&RIB	07	75	54
SNO DRL&W: SUBSIDIARY OF DW&P/1905/NAME	11	44	52
SNO DRRR: MERGED W/DEERFIELD VALLEY RR	06	35	82
SNO DS&M: OPENED 1872/32 MILES	08	51	68
SNO DS&M: ORGANIZED 1871 TO PD&E 1879	09	75	57
SNO DS&M: ORGANIZED 1871/NOW PD&E	08	38	92
SNO DSC&M: 39 MILES/EQUIPMENT/ 1906-	07	33	84
SNO DSH: INCORP 1873/CHANGED HANDS SEVER	11	50	130
SNO DSO: INCORP IN 1901/RESULT OF MERGER	07	34	92
SNO DSP&P: PHOTO ESSAY LAST OF THE DSP&P	11	38	66
SNO DSS&A: FINANCIAL	07	36	85
SNO DSS&A: FINANCIAL/STOCK	11	36	56
SNO DST: 437 MILES/EQUIPMENT	01	42	65
SNO DST: BAKER CAR LINE	08	52	93
SNO DST: PCC CARS VS BUSES	08	50	96
SNO DT&FW: 1887/MERGER OF FW&DC + D&NO	10	55	36
SNO DT&I: 1905/REORGANIZED IN 1914	07	34	92
SNO DT&I: CONTROLLED BY PENNROAD/69 LOCO	02	32	331
SNO DT&I: DISCONTINUED ELECTRIFICATION	04	32	72
SNO DT&I: DOUBLE TRACKED/OVAL CONCRETE P	11	41	49
SNO DT&I: ELECTRIC EQUIP JUNKED 1937	05	38	76
SNO DT&I: HENRY FORD BUYS	07	38	09

Railroad/Railfan

RAILROAD HISTORIES & ROSTERS

SHORT NOTES ON...	M	Y	P
SNO DT&I: INDUSTRIAL FREIGHT ROAD/H FORD	05	42	94
SNO DT&I: OWNED BY PENNROAD CORPORATION	05	33	72
SNO DT&I: SHORT HISTORY	10	63	31
SNO DT&M: ABSORBED BY LS&MS	06	35	82
SNO DT: 18 MILES/35 LOCOS/24 MISC CARSS	10	33	48
SNO DU&P: CHARTERED IN 1880/ 3' GAGE/48M	06	33	89
SNO DU&P: NARROW GAGE TO STD GAGE 1889	09	33	45
SNO DU&P: STANDARD GAGE IN 1889	12	33	90
SNO DU: OPENED 1892/NOW NYNH&H	03	38	58
SNO DUMMY STREET LOCOMOTIVES	01	33	138
SNO DV&RL: CHARTERED 1901/BECAME DRL&W	11	44	52
SNO DV&S: INCORP 1934/AR/18 MILES/EQUIPM	03	43	105
SNO DV&S: SHORT HISTORY	06	77	52
SNO DV: 1914-1931	10	33	45
SNO DV: ABANDONED 1931	06	74	20
SNO DV: ABANDONED IN 1931	12	34	84
SNO DV: NARROW GAGE/20 MI/ABANDONED 1931	11	32	474
SNO DV: OPENED 1914/ABANDONED 1931	10	57	42
SNO DVA: 13 MILES/RAILROAD TO RAILWAY/	01	34	92
SNO DVA: OPENED 1901/13 MILES/ABANDONED	10	37	72
SNO DVA: PENNY-PINCHING	10	33	80
SNO DVRR: MERGED WITH HT&W IN 1892/NOW	06	54	126
SNO DVRR: ORGANIZED TO BUILD 13 MILES	06	35	82
SNO DW&MR: BECAME RCBH&W/SOUTH DAKOTA	03	48	34
SNO DW&P: INCORP 1909/165 MILES/MINNESOT	11	44	52
SNO DW&P: INCORP 1909/173 MILES	06	38	74
SNO DW&P: TELEGRAPH INSTRU/MAN BLOCK SYS	07	36	84
SNO DW&PIT: BECAME DAV&P IN 1872	06	39	52
SNO DW&PIT: OPENED 1871 TO DAV&P 1872	02	75	49
SNO DW&W: PART OF GRAND TRUNK CORP	12	77	45
SNO DW: FORMATION	01	84	30
SNO DWAT: CHARTERED 1902/BECAME V 1907	04	59	38
SNO DWC: 3.3 MILES	06	38	76
SNO E&C: BECAME E&TH IN 1877	06	38	76
SNO E&G: 1886/KENTUCKY/11 MILE/NO EQUIPM	04	58	44
SNO E&I: CONTROL TO E&TH & C&EI & EI&TH	12	73	54
SNO E&K: 1836/1ST RR IN OHIO/32 MILE/	11	49	65
SNO E&K: OPENED 1836	03	76	56
SNO E&K: OPENED 1836/BRIEF HISTORY	04	70	34
SNO E&KR: BECAME PART OF NPC	09	40	65
SNO E&KR: BECAME PART OF NWP	08	55	45
SNO E&LS: INCORP 1898/REORGAN 1900/EQUIP	11	48	59
SNO E&LS: IRON ORE, ALCOS & MORE!	11	85	60
SNO E&LS: TRACKAGE/MICHIGAN/EQUIPMENT	04	53	63
SNO E&M: SHORTEST RR IN MICHIGAN!	02	47	123
SNO E&N: 22 LOCOMOTIVES	11	32	473
SNO E&NA: CHARTERED 1853/MAINE/MC 1882	01	44	43
SNO E&NA: CHARTERED IN 1850/MAINE/114 MI	11	34	92
SNO E&NA: INCORP 1851/COMPLETED 1860	05	51	62
SNO E&NA: LEASES BUCKSPORT & BANGOR 1874	06	40	73
SNO E&NC: BECAME V&SW 1899	05	74	46
SNO E&O: MERGED WITH TH&B IN 1915	07	36	85
SNO E&O: MERGED WITH TH&B IN 1915	08	51	64
SNO E&P: NARROW GAGE ROAD/BRIEF HISTORY	05	54	82
SNO E&P: SHORT HISTORY	02	61	30
SNO E&P: SHORT HISTORY	03	78	52
SNO E&PT: CHARTERED 1858 & BRIEF HISTORY	12	69	29
SNO E&S: 1831 NOW PART OF CNJ	03	33	92
SNO E&S: BECAME CNJ IN 1847	08	34	86
SNO E&S: CHARTERED 1831/SOLD 1849 S&EA	08	39	45
SNO E&S: CONSOLIDATION WITH S&EA	12	32	104
SNO E&TH: 1877/185 MILES WITH BRANCHES	06	38	76
SNO E&TH: CONTROL BY C&EI & EI&TH & BFR	12	73	54
SNO E&TH: GAINS CONTROL OF PD&E IN 1886	08	51	68
SNO E&TH: LEASES TO C&EI IN 1880	11	33	91
SNO E&TH: MERGED WITH C&EI IN 1911	05	41	44
SNO E&WC: 1913-1933/EQUIPMENT AS OF 1918	07	50	66
SNO E&WC: INCORPORATED 1913 PARENT SAL	07	72	62
SNO E&WC: STARTED 1913/FLORIDA/48 MILES	06	57	39
SNO E&WV: CHARTERED 1882 TO ERIE 1901	06	76	51
SNO E&WV: PURCHASED BY ERIE IN 1901	06	54	59
SNO E&WV: STD GAGE/NOW E/GRAVITY RR	04	48	127
SNO E: 250 CAR COAL TRAIN (MATT SHAY)	05	75	52
SNO E: 28 PASSENGER TRAINS REMOVED	03	51	131
SNO E: 2900 SERIES LOCOS RELEGATED	04	50	77
SNO E: 3RD RAIL	07	38	76
SNO E: 4-WAY RADIO INSTALLATION	01	49	62
SNO E: 5' GAGE TO STD GAGE IN 1882	10	39	85
SNO E: A&GW/NYP&O BECAME PART OF ERIE	09	31	190
SNO E: BATH & HAMMONDSPORT NOW PART OF	04	32	69
SNO E: BRANCHES/PASSENGER MOTIVE POWER	03	33	93
SNO E: BROAD VS STD GAGE PASSENGER CARS	03	44	101
SNO E: BUILDERS PLATES/NY TO CHICAGO TRA	10	32	350
SNO E: CAMELBACKS BY ALCO/REBUILT BY B	10	57	39
SNO E: CHARTER AMENDED	06	56	39
SNO E: DIESEL LOCOS	10	49	55
SNO E: DIESEL LOCOS IN SERVICE/ORDERED	07	47	64
SNO E: DIESEL SERVICING CENTER MARION OH	12	44	43
SNO E: ELECTIFIED BRANCH LINES	07	40	66
SNO E: ELECTRIFICATION	08	32	55
SNO E: EMBLEM/HISTORY OF EMBLEM	01	46	97
SNO E: ENTRANCE TO CLEVELAND UNION STN	12	48	70
SNO E: HISTORY OF 2-8-8-8-2 "MATT SHAY"	10	42	121
SNO E: LOCOS HISTORY W/PHOTOS	09	51	26
SNO E: LOCOS/FRT CARS/PASS CARS/GAS-ELEC	10	33	43
SNO E: MARINE EQUIPMENT OWNED	11	44	54
SNO E: MARINE FLEET SIZE 1940	08	75	56
SNO E: MFSE-15A NEW SYMBOLS	04	59	78
SNO E: MILK TRAINS	06	33	90
SNO E: MNRJ/NY&GL/M&GL NOW PART OF ERIE	04	36	90
SNO E: MOTHER HUBBARB TYPE MALLETS	12	56	30
SNO E: NAME CHANGES	10	37	68
SNO E: NEW DIESELS ORDERS ALCO VS EMD	08	48	60
SNO E: NEW YORK MARINE--HARBOR EQUIPMENT	04	49	69
SNO E: NYS&W AND WB&E BECAME PART OF	08	32	54
SNO E: NYS&W DIVISION	04	36	90
SNO E: ORDER OF THE RED SPOT	01	65	33
SNO E: ORBANIZED AS NEW YORK & ERIE	09	31	190
SNO E: PURCHASED E&WV IN 1901/LOCOS & CA	06	54	59
SNO E: RADIO ANTENNAE STEERING WHEEL	06	57	39

Railroad/ Railfan

435

RAILROAD HISTORIES & ROSTERS

SHORT NOTES ON...	M	Y	P
SNO E: RESCUES AIRLINE TRAVELERS BING NY	05	54	12
SNO E: RINGWOOD BRANCH	03	47	132
SNO E: STEEL PASSENGER CAR	10	48	130
SNO E: STRAWBERRY TRAIN	11	44	51
SNO E: TAKES OVER NYS&W IN 1900	11	34	93
SNO E: TESTS PLASTIC TIEPLATES	07	52	135
SNO E: TOUGH GOING	02	39	89
SNO E: TRAINS AND SPEEDS	07	32	512
SNO E: WHICH PARTS ELECTRIFIED	04	65	54
SNO EB&C: INCORPORATED 1892 & HISTORY	12	69	28
SNO EBRY: MERGED WITH C&EI IN 1911	05	41	44
SNO EBT: DOUBLE GAGE/33 MILE/PENNSYLVANI	09	39	72
SNO EBT: EQUIPMENT	12	40	65
SNO EC&N: 119 MILES	01	35	82
SNO EC&N: BECAME A BRANCH OF LV	05	53	62
SNO EC&N: LEASED CANO NOW LV	04	74	44
SNO ECRR: BRIEF HISTORY	12	62	31
SNO ED&BC: BECAME NORTHERN ALBERTA RY	04	35	86
SNO ED&BC: INCORP IN 1907/EQUIPMENT	04	34	84
SNO ED&BC: INCORPORATED 1907 NOW NA	01	73	60
SNO ED: MUSEUM ROAD	08	76	50
SNO EF: BECAME PART OF SF&W	12	40	61
SNO EFLORB: CONSOLIDATED TO SF&G 1884	12	73	52
SNO EG&S: ELYRIA TO GRAFTON/8 MILES	05	52	88
SNO EH: 1907-1929/3' & STD GAGE/UTAH/EQU	09	34	85
SNO EHWP: LUMBER ROAD BECAME O&NW	06	36	84
SNO EI&TH: CONSOLIDATIONS	06	38	76
SNO EI&TH: INCORP 1920/REORGANIZATION	05	41	47
SNO EI&TH: NOW PART OF THE BIG FOUR	12	31	96
SNO EI&TH: SOLD TO BFR LEASED TO NYC	12	73	54
SNO EJ&E: NEW DIESEL MOTIVE POWER	01	74	12
SNO EJ&E: NO STEAM SINCE 1948	08	56	38
SNO EJ&E: OFF-LINE AGENCY	07	52	127
SNO EJ&S: 18 MILES/EQUIPMENT/FINANCIAL	02	53	121
SNO EJ&S: INCORP 1901/19 MILES/EQUIPMENT	05	38	73
SNO EJ&S: INCORP 1901/MICHIGAN/19 MILES	03	39	74
SNO EJ&W: KIRK YARD GARY INDIANA AUTOMAT	04	56	43
SNO EJR&T: 4 MILES/6 OIL LOCOS/579 FRT	04	34	86
SNO EJR&T: INDUSTRIAL ROAD	02	59	44
SNO EKS: 36 MILE/BECAME EASTERN KENTUCKY	04	36	94
SNO EKS: RENAMED FROM EK	06	76	50
SNO EKY: INCORP 1870	04	36	94
SNO EKY: INCORPORATED 1870 TO EKS	06	76	50
SNO EL: DERECO HOLDING CO (N&W)	07	71	43
SNO EL: PASSING OF PHOEBE SNOW	03	67	58
SNO EL: REFRESHMENT CARS	05	71	52
SNO ELS: BECAME L&CRY/THEN LSEL	11	51	78
SNO EM&SW: MARION & EASTERN TAKES OVER	12	34	84
SNO EMRR: 3' GAGE/OPERATED BY W&NB	01	52	47
SNO EMT: OPENED 1948/52 MILES/EQUIPMENT	04	49	64
SNO EN: ABANDONED/JUNKED!	02	39	126
SNO ENY: ABANDONED IN 1929	12	55	48
SNO EORC: CALIFORNIA/2 DOUBLE-DECKERS	08	43	56
SNO EOT: 1902/CLEVELAND OHIO/ELECTRIC LI	03	46	111
SNO EP&S: BUILT BY AR&S IN 1888-89	10	55	37
SNO EP&S: GEOGRAPHIC LOCATION	11	77	24
SNO EP&S: INCORP 1900/CONSOLIDATIONS	01	37	88
SNO EP&S: INCORPORATED 1900 TO SP 1924	04	75	12
SNO EP&S: MERGED WITH SP IN 1924	02	48	129
SNO EP&S: MILEAGE/CORRECTIONS TO JAN '37	03	37	64
SNO EP: BECAME PART OF P&R IN 1869	12	59	34
SNO EPCL: BUYS 17 CARS FROM SDE	07	50	117
SNO EPS: .4 MILES/NO ROLLING STOCK	07	54	119
SNO EPS: SHORT HISTORY	08	61	35
SNO ER&E: ACQUIRED BY SF&N IN 1903/23 MI	08	55	45
SNO ERM: CHARTERED IN 1836/LEASED TO B&M	12	33	93
SNO ERM: NOW PART OF B&M	06	48	54
SNO ES&G: PREDESSOR TO R&N	04	74	52
SNO ES&N: OPENED 1889 ELECTRIFIED 1904	12	74	58
SNO ESL&S: BRIEF HISTORY	09	66	32
SNO ESL: LUCE LINES/INCORP 1908/	12	35	81
SNO ESP: "GENTLEMAN'S AGREEMENT"	06	48	19
SNO ESRY: INCORP 1908/NOW PART OF S 1909	03	40	76
SNO ET&G:	11	30	598
SNO ET&G: CHARTERED IN 1848/110 MILES	08	34	85
SNO ET&V	11	30	598
SNO ET&V: CHARTERED IN 1849/130 MILES	08	34	85
SNO ET&WNC: 1882/34 MILES OF TRACK	02	57	46
SNO ET&WNC: CHANGES	05	43	143
SNO ET&WNC: HAS GONE DIESEL!!!	04	68	56
SNO ET&WNC: NARROW GAGE PART STILL RUNS	02	48	133
SNO ET&WNC: NARROW GAGE/34 MILES	11	36	57
SNO ET&WNC: WANTS TO ABANDON NARROW GAGE	10	50	131
SNO ETCO: ORGANIZED 1865 THEN PRR 1920	05	75	51
SNO ETV&G: BRIEF HISTORY	01	66	27
SNO ETV&GA: CONSOLIDATION OF ET&V + ET&G	08	34	85
SNO ETV&GA: FORERUNNER OF SOUTHERN RY	11	30	598
SNO ETV&GA: LEASED/SOLD TO SOUTHERN RY	06	30	411
SNO EU: BEGAN 1903/2' GAGE/MAINE/P&R SUB	12	55	29
SNO EUC: 1882/1 EMPLOYEE/1.8 MILES	07	51	136
SNO EV&I: CONSOL FROM OTHERS 1885 - C&EI	07	73	39
SNO EV&I: FORMED 1885/CONSOLIDATION	06	38	76
SNO EV&I: PART OF BIG FOUR NOT C&EI! COR	08	38	94
SNO EV&I: REORGANIZED AS EI&TH IN 1920	05	41	47
SNO EV&P: PD&E TAKES OVER IN 1880	08	38	92
SNO EV&P: TO PD&E 1880 THEN IC/ICG	09	75	57
SNO EVERGREEN FREIGHT CAR CORPORATION	02	68	30
SNO EW&B: CONSOLIDATED TO EV&I TO C&EI	07	73	39
SNO EW&B: CONSOLIDATION 1885	06	38	76
SNO EW&STL: ORGANIZED 1853/BECAME TW&W	07	36	85
SNO EW&W: CONSOLIDATED TO EV&I 1885	12	73	53
SNO EW&W: NEVER BUILT	06	38	76
SNO EW&W: NEVER BUILT	07	73	39
SNO EW&W: NEVER BUILT/NOW PART OF C&EI	08	38	94
SNO EW: 1935/ACQUIRED CBE PHOTO ESSAY	03	43	66
SNO EW: PART OF CBE NOW EW	03	39	63
SNO F&C: EMBLEM	08	50	42
SNO F&C: FORMED 1927 FROM KM NOW PINSLEY	11	75	47
SNO F&C: LOCOS/READER MEMORIES	11	50	121
SNO F&C: RAILWAY TO RAILROAD IN 1927	12	33	93

RAILROAD HISTORIES & ROSTERS

SHORT NOTES ON...	M	Y	P
SNO F&C: WHISKEY RR OF THE WORLD	04	51	125
SNO F&CC: BECAME PART OF CC&CS IN 1921	02	41	74
SNO F&CC: LEASED CS&CC	01	35	86
SNO F&I: BUILT AS LE&W	08	36	75
SNO F&M: 1884	12	55	27
SNO F&M: TWO FOOT GAGE/READER MEMORIES	03	46	92
SNO F&N: NO MORE!	06	32	335
SNO F&NW: BRIEF HISTORY	10	77	54
SNO F&NW: REORGANIZED 6 TIMES/ABAND '55	06	56	40
SNO F&PM: BECAME PART OF C&O/LOGGING RD	07	53	55
SNO F&PM: NOW PART OF C&O	02	56	24
SNO F&W: 3' LINE/16 MILES	04	47	108
SNO F&WI: BECAME PART OF SAL	04	53	29
SNO F-MT: 10 MILES	04	46	115
SNO FAM: LINES THAT MAKE-UP	06	74	20
SNO FAMILY PLAN	02	53	135
SNO FARM: BRIEF HISTORY	04	78	54
SNO FB&S: BECAME PART OF NPC	09	40	66
SNO FB&S: BECAME PART OF NWP	08	55	45
SNO FB&S: SHORT HISTORY	07	77	48
SNO FC&P: NOW PART OF SAL	06	32	338
SNO FC: MAIL/EXPRESS/PASSENGER SERVICE	07	43	06
SNO FCMR: COLORADO ROAD/BIRNEYS	03	49	82
SNO FDM&S: BOXCARS/PASS SERVICE	12	52	99
SNO FDM&S: NEW AND OLD EMBLEM	06	54	124
SNO FDM&S: TO BECOME A FREIGHT LINE	03	55	58
SNO FDM&S: TROLLEY WIRE/DIESEL/ELECTRICS	10	54	70
SNO FDS: TROLLEY LINE/FDM&S GAINS CONTRL	09	52	83
SNO FE&MV: C&NW TAKES OVER IN 1903	04	34	79
SNO FE&MV: CHARTERED 1869 C&NW 1884	01	75	55
SNO FE&MV: CHARTERED 1869/MILES/EQUIPMEN	02	38	57
SNO FEC: 121 LOCOS/NOW IN RECEIVERSHIP	09	37	61
SNO FEC: 25 LOCOS REPOSSESSED/NOW WHERE	01	37	87
SNO FEC: 869 MILES/EQUIPMENT	12	31	96
SNO FEC: ABANDON SMYRNA-ORANGE CITY 1934	01	69	31
SNO FEC: FINANCIAL/GROSS REVENUES	09	36	73
SNO FEC: FLAGER SYSTEM MOTIVE POWER	01	48	88
SNO FEC: INCORP IN 1892	06	34	84
SNO FEC: LOCOS/ADDITIONAL CREWS	06	31	443
SNO FEC: NEW EMBLEM/CABOOSE COOKS	09	45	113
SNO FEC: NOW IN RECEIVERSHIP	08	36	74
SNO FEC: OIL-BURNER LOCOS	11	54	33
SNO FEC: OLD RAILS USED AS GUARD RAILS	04	43	136
SNO FEC: PARTIALLY DESTROYED BY HURRICAN	08	36	74
SNO FEC: STEAM LOCO DISPOSITION	10	61	44
SNO FEC: STEAM LOCOS REPRIEVED	07	53	117
SNO FERD: BUILT 1909/7 MILES/EQUIPMENT	03	40	120
SNO FERD: INCORP 1911/ INDIANA/7 MILES	12	40	62
SNO FERS: FISHER SYSTEM	10	73	46
SNO FIRT: PLANNED/NEVER BUILT	12	46	106
SNO FJ&G: 8 STEAM LOCOMOTIVES	06	32	337
SNO FJ&G: ABSORBED AMERSTDAM & ROCTON ST	04	52	105
SNO FJ&G: DEMISE	07	84	28
SNO FJ&G: ELECTRIC TO DIESELIZED STEAM	12	55	44
SNO FJ&G: INCORPORATED 1867	08	67	32
SNO FL&N: 1919/KENTUCKY/6 MI/1 LOCO/3 CA	07	35	84
SNO FLRR: BRIEF HISTORY	06	78	57
SNO FMC: 130 MILES/EQUIPMENT	10	50	60
SNO FMU: 2 MILE/SUMMER ONLY/5 CARS/1920	12	46	105
SNO FOP: CASTLETON-ON-HUDSON PHOTO ESSAY	12	49	82
SNO FOP: EQUIPMENT OWNED	12	49	82
SNO FP&P: ORANGE & FREDERICKSBURG ACQUIR	09	34	84
SNO FPL: MINNEAPOLIS/LESS THAN 2 MILES	01	47	81
SNO FPL: OPENED 1917	11	53	104
SNO FR: GEARED LOCOS	01	39	65
SNO FRANK: MERGED WITH CUMBERLAND VALLEY	12	34	83
SNO FRB: 5 MILES/MERGED W/SOUTHSIDE 1868	01	34	93
SNO FRIS: 1920 LEGAL CASE OF INJURED FIR	09	73	09
SNO FRIS: 5267 MILES/EQUIPMENT	07	33	84
SNO FRIS: A&PA CENTRAL DIVISION NOW PART	11	34	90
SNO FRIS: ABSORBED KCFS&M	06	48	16
SNO FRIS: ABSORBED KCFSG	09	54	37
SNO FRIS: BRIEF HISTORY ON ITS NAME	04	66	34
SNO FRIS: BULL MOOSE TRAIN ABANDONED	09	49	139
SNO FRIS: CENTRAL DIV OF A&PA	12	38	70
SNO FRIS: CENTRALIZED TRAFFIC CONTROL	11	51	62
SNO FRIS: DIESEL LOCOS	12	51	67
SNO FRIS: FULLY DIESELIZED	08	52	124
SNO FRIS: GOES COMPLETELY DIESEL	11	78	47
SNO FRIS: HOW IT GOT ITS NAME	10	57	41
SNO FRIS: JERRY KETCHUM-DEPOT PASS REPRE	05	48	106
SNO FRIS: KCM&B BECAME PART OF	03	54	29
SNO FRIS: LEASED TO ATSF 1890-1895	11	40	69
SNO FRIS: LINE EMBLEM SIGNIFICANCE	12	63	62
SNO FRIS: LIST OF ROADS THAT BECAME FRIS	06	78	57
SNO FRIS: LOCOS/MILEAGE/EQUIPMENT	12	31	91
SNO FRIS: OPERATES 20 MILE ARMY ROAD	02	42	44
SNO FRIS: OWNING X PRR POWER	09	78	64
SNO FRIS: RAIL LETTERS/NUMBERS	04	47	52
SNO FRR: LEASED BY B&M IN 1900	06	34	88
SNO FRR: NOW PART OF BOSTON & MAINE	12	35	39
SNO FRR: OIL LOCOS IN HOOSAC TUNNEL	05	74	47
SNO FRY: 24 MI/MISSISSIPPI/FREE RIDES	09	53	119
SNO FS&S: INCORP IN 1886 TO FRISCO	06	74	02
SNO FS&W: CHARTERED 1899/ABANDONED/10 LO	05	39	66
SNO FS&W: CLASS I ROAD/ASSETS/VALUATION	06	35	86
SNO FS&W: OPENED 1901/STD GAGE/EQUIPMENT	11	52	62
SNO FS: NOW PART OF PLANT SYSTEM	01	35	87
SNO FS: NOW PART OF PLANT SYSTEMS	12	37	54
SNO FSRY: FOUNDED 1890	08	74	56
SNO FV: 3 COAL BURNING LOCOS	03	30	574
SNO FV: SUBSIDIARY OF NYC	09	32	233
SNO FW&C	01	33	99
SNO FW&D: BRIEF HISTORY	09	77	54
SNO FW&D: TEXAS/902 MILES	10	55	36
SNO FW&DC: INCORP 1873/MERGED W/D&NO '87	10	55	36
SNO FW&DC: SUBSIDIARY OF CB&Q/OWNS WIV	03	49	14
SNO G&C: RE-INCORP IN 1889/NAME CHANGED	03	54	30
SNO G&F: 465 MILES/32 LOCOS	01	32	261
SNO G&F: INCORP 1906 & 1926/ACQUIRED...	03	39	75

Railroad/ Railfan

RAILROAD HISTORIES & ROSTERS

SHORT NOTES ON...	M	Y	P
SNO G&F: INCORP 1906 & 1926/ACQUISTIONS	03	36	83
SNO G&F: INCORP 1906/CONSOLIDATION	06	41	61
SNO G&FT: BECAME PART OF G&F IN 1920	03	36	83
SNO G&GE: 1 LOCO/1 PASS CAR/ETHERLY BRAN	12	31	97
SNO G&GE: 1 PASSENGER 1946/10 MILES/ILL	09	47	138
SNO G&GE: BRIEF HISTORY	02	67	27
SNO G&GE: REORGAN 1898/10 MILES/EQUIPMEN	02	36	87
SNO G&GP: 3' GAGE/COLORADO/ABANDONE 1918	08	33	88
SNO G&GP: ARGENTINE CENTRAL REOPENED AS	03	34	86
SNO G&GP: BUYS ARGENTINE CENTRAL	06	33	89
SNO G&GP: COLORADO/3' GAGE/1 GEARED LOCO	11	38	73
SNO G&HE: BECAME PART OF WPA IN 1910	10	55	52
SNO G&I: OPENED IN 1871	01	35	82
SNO G&IR: FIRST TRAIN 1903 1040 DAYS LAT	12	76	06
SNO G&M: LEASED BY PD&E	08	38	92
SNO G&MI: REORGANIZED IN 1863 AS D&U	06	35	86
SNO G&MIS: GETS IC TRACKAGE	11	85	34
SNO G&MV: ABSORBED BY WEST JERSEY RR	10	42	146
SNO G&N: 23 MILES/EQUIPMENT	06	33	92
SNO G&P: CHARTERED 1907/"T" SHAPED ROAD	08	41	71
SNO G&P: CHARTERED 1907/MONTANA/EQUIP/MI	06	39	56
SNO G&P: CHARTERED 1907/STD GAGE/EQUIPME	07	53	49
SNO G&ST: REORGANIZED 1923 DIED 1928	03	74	33
SNO G&SW: CHARTERED 1857 NOW C&NW	06	74	20
SNO G&SW: CHARTERED 1857/3' GAGE/2 LOCOS	08	38	92
SNO G&WY: CHARTERED 1899 BRIEF HISTORY	01	71	50
SNO G&WY: OWNED BY STERLING SALT CO	11	76	46
SNO G: GAINESVILLE JEFFERSON & SOUTHERN	01	35	85
SNO G: ORGANIZED 1833	12	39	112
SNO GARC: CHARTERED 1885/2 MI/ HORSE CAR	05	47	116
SNO GAS&C: 1922/50 MILES/GEORGIA/EQUIPME	04	48	72
SNO GAS&C: BRIEF HISTORY	03	78	53
SNO GAS&C: INCORP 1922/50 MILES/EQUIPMEN	09	35	87
SNO GATX: DEFINITION	07	65	31
SNO GAYP: INTERURBAAN FREIGHT MOTOR	12	54	62
SNO GB&E: CHARTERED BY COAL OPERATORS	04	59	39
SNO GB&LP: CHARTERED 1861/BECAME GB&W	11	51	16
SNO GB&W: 214 MILES	07	42	153
SNO GB&W: INCORP 1896/ACQUISITONS/EQUIPM	07	40	71
SNO GB&W: INCORP IN 1896/EQUIPMENT/FINAN	07	35	85
SNO GBW&SP: ACQUIRED BY GB&W IN 1896	07	35	85
SNO GBW&SP: FORECLOSURE 1896/NOW GB&W	07	40	71
SNO GC&C: 1917 CONSOLIDATION = WM	09	35	86
SNO GC&C: CONSOLIDATED WITH WM 1917	05	73	35
SNO GC&E: ORGANIZED 1910/74 + 18 MILES	05	36	82
SNO GC&E: ORGANIZED IN 1910 AS ASPULP CO	08	32	57
SNO GC&P: BECAME DAARIEN & WESTERN	05	34	132
SNO GC&SF: CHARTERED 1873 NOW ATSF	03	75	12
SNO GC&WR: BECAME PART OF SP&S IN 1943	02	50	58
SNO GC&WR: TO SP&S 1943	01	75	54
SNO GCL: ROADS THAT MADE UP HOLDIN CO	10	73	59
SNO GCO: BRIEF HISTORY ORIGINATED 1905	09	67	27
SNO GCRR: BECAME CC&CS	02	41	74
SNO GCT: 1888-1917/COLORADO/2' GAGE	12	55	31
SNO GCT: ACQUIRED BY GILPIN RR IN 1906	03	35	87
SNO GE&E: REORGANIZED IN 1898 AS G&GE	02	36	87
SNO GF&A: NOW PART OF SEABOARD AIR LINE	10	39	87
SNO GF&OD: W&OD ABSORBED IN 1911	05	35	86
SNO GF: PHOTO ESSAY	10	41	44
SNO GGA: 2-6-6-2 LARGE STEAM POWER	02	74	53
SNO GHE: STARTED 1911 ENDED 1936	08	75	57
SNO GI&A: ACQUIRED BY LV IN 1876	08	46	43
SNO GI&A: CONSOLIDATION/BANKRUPT 1875	01	35	82
SNO GI&S: 1876 REORGANIZATION	01	35	82
SNO GI: CHARTERED IN 1906/ACQUIRES GCT	03	35	87
SNO GIL: D&H JOINS GUILFORD TRANSPORTATI	05	84	28
SNO GJ&S: CHARTERED 1872 TO G 1884	10	73	59
SNO GJ&S: CHARTERED IN 1872/3' GAGE/52 M	01	35	85
SNO GL&S: FIRST RUN	01	87	38
SNO GL&W: 1901-1931	03	33	89
SNO GL&W: ORGANIZED 1901/MOSTLY PRIVATE	06	38	74
SNO GL: BECAME H&FS IN 1913	04	48	72
SNO GM&N: 1ST TRAIN HOSTESS	02	47	125
SNO GM&N: MERGED INTO GM&O 1940	07	68	27
SNO GM&O: ABSORBED ARR IN 1947	04	55	34
SNO GM&O: ACF DAYLINERS FOR ALTON ROUTE	10	48	71
SNO GM&O: HIGHWAY POST OFFICE	08	56	39
SNO GM&O: LITTLE REBEL	08	54	16
SNO GM&O: MERGER WITH ALTON	10	46	83
SNO GM&O: MOBILE & OHIO BECAME	04	54	10
SNO GM&O: PLANS TO ACQUIRE ALTON	08	45	45
SNO GMI: GAINESVILLE JEFFERSON & SOUTHER	01	35	85
SNO GN&A: 1922/CONSOLIDATIONS	03	37	61
SNO GN: 1151 LOCOS(STEAM/GAS-ELECT/ELECT	11	31	487
SNO GN: 1ST WESTERN ROAD W/OUT GOV'T AID	02	57	39
SNO GN: ACQUIRES MONTFORT & GATINEAU '03	12	40	59
SNO GN: BLIZZARD OF '49	12	49	28
SNO GN: BUTTE DIVISION/FIFTH SUBDIVISION	12	51	64
SNO GN: CASCADE MOUNTAIN TRACK RELOCATIO	08	50	120
SNO GN: CASCADE TUNNEL/RAIL DETERIORATIO	11	49	48
SNO GN: CASCADIAN DINING CARS REBUILT	02	55	30
SNO GN: CHARTERED 1889/NORTHWESTERN ROAD	07	36	82
SNO GN: CONTROLS VV&E	07	33	84
SNO GN: DIESEL PASSENGER LOCOS	05	48	62
SNO GN: DIVISIONS	03	35	85
SNO GN: DIVISIONS	05	46	76
SNO GN: ELECTRIC LOCOS/TOURIST SLEEPING	10	57	40
SNO GN: ELECTRIFICATION	11	30	600
SNO GN: ELECTRIFICATION STATUS 1961	02	61	28
SNO GN: EMD DIESELS ORDERED (12)	11	48	52
SNO GN: EXPANSION	01	51	131
SNO GN: FINANCIAL	07	34	89
SNO GN: FOSSTON BRANCH	03	37	61
SNO GN: GAVIN YARD AT MINOT ND	10	58	06
SNO GN: LEASES/W&SF (PREVIOUSLY SDCEN)	03	38	53
SNO GN: LOCOMOTIVES/CLASS/NUMBERS/WEIGHT	04	33	96
SNO GN: LOGO EVOLUTION	09	67	26
SNO GN: MERGER WITH NP	06	70	60
SNO GN: MILEAGE/SIGNALS/LOCO #2014/SPRAG	07	31	534
SNO GN: NAME-TRAINS	05	67	31

RAILROAD HISTORIES & ROSTERS

SHORT NOTES ON...	M	Y	P
SNO GN: NEW MERCHANDISE FREIGHT SERVICE	06	47	84
SNO GN: NO REORGANIZATIONS!/JIM HILL	03	35	85
SNO GN: ORIENTAL LIMITED	06	35	82
SNO GN: OWNERSHIP OF OTHER ROADS	04	60	29
SNO GN: PUGET SOUND SWING DRAW BRIDGE SP	04	55	35
SNO GN: PURPOSE OF 2-6-8-0 MALLETS	10	74	45
SNO GN: SANDON BC VIA K&SL	11	67	30
SNO GN: SEVEN MILLION DOLLAR TRAIN	07	47	80
SNO GN: SPM&M CORRECTION 07-36 PG 82	10	36	76
SNO GN: SUBURBAN STATION EDMONDS WA	06	57	40
SNO GN: THE "EMPIRE BUILDER" INAUG 1929	01	72	54
SNO GN: TRADEMARK APPEARS ON TENDERS	07	32	509
SNO GN: WILLIAM CROOKS LOCO	02	59	39
SNO GNC: TO CNQ 1906/CAN 1914/DOC 1917	07	75	52
SNO GNO: INCORP 1894/ACQUIRED B&AGA	09	46	93
SNO GO: BECAME PART OF T&GO 1905	07	37	53
SNO GO: BECAME PART OF T&GO IN 1905	11	35	83
SNO GO: BECAME T&GO IN 1905	01	41	73
SNO GOSH: INCORP IN 1918-19/9 MILES/UTAH	09	34	86
SNO GOVERNORS ISLAND RR: SCRAPPED	04	31	111
SNO GPEX: OWNS INSULATED MILK CARS	12	55	36
SNO GPT: PENSACOLA MOBILE & N ORLEANS BE	10	39	87
SNO GR&I: BRIEF HISTORY	03	67	31
SNO GR&I: NOW PART OF PRR/LOGGING ROAD	07	53	54
SNO GR&M: 1878/70 MILES/2 LOCOS	08	51	68
SNO GR&M: LEASED TO PD&E	09	75	57
SNO GR&NW: INCORP 1908	10	52	64
SNO GR: ACQUIRED BY MICHC	04	31	122
SNO GRA: FIRST ROAD TO USE SNOWPLOWS	08	65	19
SNO GRA: OPENED 1826 SHORT HISTORY	04	70	34
SNO GRA: STRAP RAIL/STONE RAIL/NOW HIWAY	06	54	10
SNO GRANT LOCOMOTIVE WORKS	09	32	233
SNO GRAY: BECAME PART OF S&NY IN 1903	12	35	85
SNO GRAY: MERGED WITH S&NY IN 1903	05	37	40
SNO GRAY: NOW PART OF S&NY	02	33	83
SNO GREYHOUND BUSSES: NYC/PRR FINANCIAL	01	40	55
SNO GRR: INCORP 1915/16 MILES/NY/EQUIPME	10	42	61
SNO GRRY: BIRNEY ONE MAN CAR	01	54	77
SNO GS&G: INCORP 1906/ONLY OPERATED A&N	09	46	91
SNO GS&G: RECEIVERSHIP 1933/36 MILES/EQU	10	39	85
SNO GS: 2 SMALL BALDWINS PURCHASED	12	48	126
SNO GSRY: LOGGING LINE/RI/EQUIPMENT	12	56	53
SNO GSSR: FOUNDED 1904 SOLD TO SLE 1916	03	74	33
SNO GSW: EXPECTED COMPLETE '58/TX/16.5 M	02	59	10
SNO GSW: WHOLLY-OWNED	06	59	35
SNO GT&W: PURCHASED BY FRISCO IN 1930	09	54	29
SNO GT: 1164 LOCOS/ABSORBED BY CN 1919	10	33	46
SNO GT: 4000+ MILES/CANADA & US	10	36	73
SNO GT: ACQUIRED CANADA ATLANTIC 1905	11	38	73
SNO GT: CHARTERED 1851/NOW PART OF CN	10	35	85
SNO GT: DEPOT NAMES ORDER BDS/CLASS 500	04	56	08
SNO GT: GRAND TRUNK WESTERN NOW PART OF	02	33	86
SNO GT: INCORP 1847/EARLY HISTORY	11	47	17
SNO GT: JULY 1857 1ST TRIP TO SARANAC MI	03	43	118
SNO GT: LINES THAT MAKE IT UP	12	77	45
SNO GT: MAINLINE	01	76	39
SNO GT: NORTH AMERICA'S 1ST INTERNATIONA	07	78	55
SNO GT: NORTHERN & NORTH-WESTERN 1888	01	35	85
SNO GT: ORIGINAL MAIN LINE	11	72	54
SNO GT: PART BECOMES CANADIAN NAT'L	01	36	84
SNO GT: ST CLAIR TUNNEL	10	45	51
SNO GT: TAKES OVER NORTHERN & NORTHWSTRN	01	34	88
SNO GT: THE THREAT	10	45	138
SNO GT: WHY THE TRAIN WAS LATE	02	45	74
SNO GTCO: CONSOLIDATION OF CN US ROADS	11	73	57
SNO GTI: STRIKE ACTIONS	01	87	40
SNO GTP: 1911 TORCHWOOD SASKATCHEWAN	05	72	11
SNO GTP: 260 LOCOS IN 1919 ABSORBD BY CN	10	33	46
SNO GTP: BECOMES PART OF CN	02	78	49
SNO GTP: BUILT IN 1905	11	47	19
SNO GTP: INCORP IN 1903/NOW PART OF CN	04	38	49
SNO GTP: INCORPORATED 1903 COMPLETED '14	09	73	40
SNO GTP: PROJECTED INTO ALASKA	07	35	81
SNO GTW: CASS CITY TO BAD AXE ABANDONED	02	52	129
SNO GTW: CHARTERED IN 1845	10	35	85
SNO GTW: CLASS I ROAD	12	73	52
SNO GTW: PART OF GRAND TRUNK CORP	12	77	45
SNO GTW: PART OF GRANT TRUNK SYSTEM/CN	02	33	86
SNO GTW: ROADS MERGED TO FORM GTW	04	78	55
SNO GTW: STEAM LOCOS/K4B/41%/AUX STACK	04	58	41
SNO GV&NW: INCORP IN 1912/BANKRUPT 1923	03	35	87
SNO GW: ABSORBED BY GT IN 1882	11	47	19
SNO GW: BRANCHES/EQUIPMENT/OWNERS GW SUB	02	38	57
SNO GW: SUBSIDIARY OF GWS	01	78	47
SNO H&BC: BECAME BOSTON & ALBANY	04	35	86
SNO H&BM: MERGED WITH L&M	03	48	23
SNO H&BTM: 1852 TO ? 74 MILES	05	37	39
SNO H&BTM: INCORP 1852/PENNSYLVANIA/MILE	09	35	82
SNO H&BV: LEASED BY MP	06	34	87
SNO H&CW: LEASES NEWBURGH DUCHESS & CONN	08	34	85
SNO H&DS: SOLD TO TH&B IN 1929	08	51	64
SNO H&E: OPENED 1912 TO KATY	04	76	54
SNO H&F: BECAME B&AN	04	46	115
SNO H&F: FORMED 1906/INTERURBAN LINE	03	45	107
SNO H&F: GENEALOGY OF H&F	03	45	110
SNO H&F: LAST TRIP/CARS 171, 172	07	54	99
SNO H&F: ROSTER/PART SERVICE ENDED	02	48	99
SNO H&FS: 60 MILES/GEORGIA ABANDONED ROA	05	34	132
SNO H&FS: INCORP 1896/SOLD 1922 TO GA&C	04	48	72
SNO H&FS: PORTION BECAME GA&C IN 1922	09	35	87
SNO H&FS: SHORT HISTORY	03	78	53
SNO H&L: OWNED BY NYS&W	05	34	82
SNO H&LR: EUREKA CALIFORNIA/2-4-2 #4 LOC	07	35	86
SNO H&M: EMBLEM	11	47	111
SNO H&M: PASSENGER SERVICE ONLY	05	52	99
SNO H&M: SUBWAY/PRIVATE ROW	02	59	44
SNO H&N: STARTED 1900 BRIEF HISTORY	07	70	39
SNO H&NE: 6 MILES/2 LOCOS/WISCONSIN ROAD	06	32	335
SNO H&NW: CHARTERED 1871 CONSOL TO N&NW	10	73	58
SNO H&NW: CHARTERED 1871/BECAME N&NW	01	35	85

Stephans' Railroad Directory

Railroad/Railfan

RAILROAD HISTORIES & ROSTERS

SHORT NOTES ON...	M	Y	P
SNO H&S: 20 MILES/660 HP DIESEL LOCO	07	54	60
SNO H&S: INCORPORATED 1953	09	76	51
SNO H&TC: CHARTERED 1848 NOW SP	09	73	42
SNO H&TC: CHARTERED IN 1848/SP (T&NO)	08	35	83
SNO H&W: 11 MILES/EQUIPMENT	08	32	57
SNO H&W: CHARTERED 1895/ VERMONT/7 MILES	02	41	73
SNO H&W: INCORP 1895/VT/10.5 MI/GRANITE	01	46	61
SNO H&W: INCORP IN 1894/BEING ABANDONED	03	35	87
SNO H&WH: CHARTERED 1859/BECAME CONN	04	47	64
SNO H&WI: 1892/MERGER OF DVRR AND HT&W	06	54	126
SNO HA&W: BRIEF HISTORY	03	78	53
SNO HALC: HALIFAX NOVA SCOTIA	10	54	44
SNO HAMP: BUILT 1913 NEVER OPERATED	08	73	57
SNO HAMP: NO TRAIN EVER RAN OVER!	01	35	83
SNO HAY: PRIVATELY OWNED QUARRY LINE	04	37	53
SNO HB&TD: ABSORBED BY E&KR	08	55	46
SNO HBRR: CONTROLLED BY CN	04	49	66
SNO HBRR: FULL-TIME BEAVER PATROL	08	51	128
SNO HCA&W: NOW PART OF MP	08	34	87
SNO HCO&W: LV LEASES 3 MILES OF TRACK	01	34	90
SNO HCR: MUSEUM ROUTE	05	76	25
SNO HCRR: MERGES WITH P&CRR IN 1889	03	34	84
SNO HCRR: NOW PART OF NYNH&H	03	38	57
SNO HE&WT: WANDERING GOATS	05	47	137
SNO HE: INCORP 1915/42 MILES/1 LOCO	02	39	91
SNO HE: INCORPORATED 1915 (WASH STATE)	07	73	38
SNO HE: OPENED 1894 READER INFORMATION	03	74	35
SNO HER: ABANDONED/28 MI/TROLLEY/ONTARIO	09	47	108
SNO HERE: CHARTERED 1887	05	38	72
SNO HES: CHICAGO MILL & LUMBER CO OPERAT	01	37	90
SNO HES: LUMBER ROAD/4 LOCOMOTIVES	11	32	472
SNO HESO: 4 LOCOS/151 CARS	11	36	53
SNO HF&W: 8 MILES/GEORGIA ABANDONED ROAD	05	34	132
SNO HH: 68 MILES/NOW MOTOR HIGHWAY	03	50	129
SNO HH: OWNED BY CITY OF SAN FRANCISCO	07	53	48
SNO HILLC: 25 MILES/1 LOCO/MINNESOTA	06	32	335
SNO HL&T: WOODEN RAILS	04	54	61
SNO HM&PLA: ABANDONED IN 1906/SHORT HIST	02	34	84
SNO HM&R: ABSORBED BY CONN	07	52	84
SNO HM: 11 MILES/3 LOCOS/8 MISC CARS	04	34	86
SNO HM: INCORP 1902/"HOBEKEN SHORE ROAD"	06	41	26
SNO HNS: INTERURBAN/RAILCARS	01	48	103
SNO HNS: LEASED BY MP	06	34	88
SNO HNS: RAIL BUSES	04	47	75
SNO HOBO: TOURIST ROAD INFORMATION	10	87	34
SNO HOPE: KNOWN AS WRB NOW NYNH&H	07	73	38
SNO HOTS: BEGAN 1875/BUILT BY DIAMOND JO	12	44	45
SNO HOTS: HOBO OUTWITS DIAMOND JOE	12	32	93
SNO HP&FV: CALIFORNIA ROAD/TROLLEY	08	43	56
SNO HPM: ABSORBED BY PRR	07	41	51
SNO HPT&D: INCORP IN 1923/34 MILES/EQUIP	02	34	85
SNO HPT&D: NO BONDED DEBTS/EQUIPMENT	11	50	126
SNO HR&B: CONSOLIDATED 1887 TO NY&MA	11	73	57
SNO HR&B: MERGED WITH PH&B IN 1875=NY&MA	02	35	85
SNO HRRR: 1851/HORSECAR LINE/EQUIPMENT	03	51	27
SNO HRRR: CONSOLIDATED WITH NYS&W 1893	11	34	93
SNO HRRR: INCORP 1846/144 MILES	11	43	62
SNO HRRR: MERGES WITH NYS&W IN 1893	05	34	82
SNO HS	09	37	63
SNO HS: 6 MILE/STANDARD GAGE/CALIFORNIA	10	36	74
SNO HS: 6.4MILES/ABANDONED DEC 1937	12	39	117
SNO HS: ABANDONED/LOCOS	10	37	73
SNO HS: HOBART ESTATE COMPANY AKA HS	12	37	57
SNO HS: NAME/GAGE CHANGES/ROSTER	12	37	57
SNO HSG&W: ACQUIRED IN 1911 BY GN&A	03	37	61
SNO HSH: SWITCHING ROAD	02	59	44
SNO HT&W: 2 ROADS MERGE INTO	06	35	82
SNO HT&W: 24 MILES/2 LOCOS/EQUIPMENT	06	33	92
SNO HT&W: INCORP 1886	07	41	67
SNO HT&W: MERGED WITH DVRR IN 1892/NAME	06	54	126
SNO HT&W: NOT ABANDONED	10	51	125
SNO HT&W: STD GAGE/LOCOS/25 MILES	04	33	97
SNO HT: 1903/CHOCALOTE LINE	08	47	94
SNO HT: TROLLEY FREIGHT SERVICE PHOTO ES	11	41	132
SNO HU&BT: CHARTERED & OPENED IN 1862/EQ	07	32	508
SNO HU: CROSS-ISLAND TROLLEY	10	44	112
SNO HV: INCORP 1899 TO C&O	12	71	57
SNO HV: LOSS OF TRAIN 1907	09	69	10
SNO HVE: LOW WATER	08	34	36
SNO HVRY: ABANDONED 1928	12	55	48
SNO HY&T: 1 LOCOMOTIVE/EQUIPMENT	01	33	100
SNO HY&T: 13 MILES/ILLINOIS/FREIGHT LINE	07	54	119
SNO HY&T: EQUIPMENT	04	33	95
SNO HY&T: HISTORY OF PUMPKIN VINE	09	69	30
SNO HY&T: PUMPKIN VINE/TO BE DISSOLVED	03	48	129
SNO I&A: OPENED IN 1874	01	35	82
SNO I&E: BECAME AMC IN 1908	07	37	55
SNO I&EV: CONSOLIDATION 1885	06	38	76
SNO I&M: CHARTERED 1889	07	75	52
SNO I&M: CHARTERED IN 1889	06	37	60
SNO I&ME: INTERURBAN/INDIANA	04	53	99
SNO I&N: ABSORBED BY GB&W	11	51	17
SNO I&N: ABSORBED BY GB&W IN 1914	07	40	72
SNO I&WN: CHARTERED 1907 NOW MILW (1916)	09	73	41
SNO I&WN: CHARTERED 1907 TO MILW 1914	12	74	58
SNO I&WN: CHARTERED IN 1907/MILEAGE	01	38	59
SNO I&WN: CHARTERED IN 1907/PART OF MILW	02	35	85
SNO I-GN: LEASED BY MP	06	34	87
SNO I: LIST-INTERURBANS ABSORBED BY	09	53	76
SNO I: REORGANIZED AS IN 1886	06	38	76
SNO IA&W: ACQUIRES WESTERN DIV NYWS&B	12	35	83
SNO IA&W: OLD NY&OM	11	72	54
SNO IB&T: INCORP 1902/BECAME MD&W	07	38	76
SNO IBT: 58 JORALEMON STREET/VENT	12	46	06
SNO IC&E: CONSOLIDATION OF 11 LINES	11	52	88
SNO IC&LRR: BECAME PART OF BIG FOUR	03	43	101
SNO IC&W: CONSOLIDATED WITH M&SL IN 1916	01	33	99
SNO IC: #X9151 JORDAN DITCHER & SPREADER	02	56	39
SNO IC: 1946 VERSUS 1941 COSTS	01	47	134
SNO IC: 1ST CHARTER OF COMPANY PART OF	10	56	47

Railroad/ Railfan

RAILROAD HISTORIES & ROSTERS

SHORT NOTES ON...	M	Y	P
SNO IC: BURMA ROAD	05	43	139
SNO IC: CAIRO BRIDGE/NEW RAILS	06	46	77
SNO IC: CHARTER DAYS	07	74	39
SNO IC: CHARTER LINES	02	70	41
SNO IC: CHARTERED 1851/ORIGINAL MAIN LIN	12	42	42
SNO IC: CITY OF NEW ORLEANS TRAIN	12	47	36
SNO IC: EDGEWOOD CUT-OFF (TUNNELS)	03	47	73
SNO IC: EDGEWOOED CUTOFF TUNNEL #2 7000'	03	49	60
SNO IC: ELECTRONIC "ENGINEER"	12	55	36
SNO IC: EXECUTIVE'S PHILOSOPHY	03	30	561
SNO IC: FINANCIAL RECORDS/VALUATION	03	36	83
SNO IC: FIRST ALL-ELECTRIC DINING CAR	06	49	128
SNO IC: GOING AFTER PASSENGERS	12	67	08
SNO IC: GREEN DIAMOND STREAMLINER	04	44	73
SNO IC: HIGH BROWN-FREIGHT TRAIN NICKNAM	05	48	65
SNO IC: LOCO #382 JINXED	08	55	43
SNO IC: LOCO #4919--NUMBER CHANGES	10	31	429
SNO IC: LOCO #640/EXTRA TALLOWPOT	07	47	126
SNO IC: MARINE DIVISON	09	54	27
SNO IC: MARKHAM YARD IMPROVEMENTS	09	49	54
SNO IC: MODERNIZES CAIRO IL BRIDGE	07	52	112
SNO IC: MOVING FLOUR IN BULK LOTS	08	53	109
SNO IC: ORG 1850/INCORP 1851/COMPLT 1856	03	50	59
SNO IC: PANAMA LIMITED GIVES WEATHER REP	01	39	129
SNO IC: PEKIN TO DECATUR SECTION	08	51	68
SNO IC: REBUILDING MANY OF ITS ENGINES	09	37	60
SNO IC: REDWOOD DISTRICT	03	68	24
SNO IC: RICHMOND CREEK VIADUCT	04	50	77
SNO IC: SERIES 1427 LOCO/CLASSIFICATION	05	31	279
SNO IC: STEAM POWER ON CHICAGO-N ORLEANS	10	54	06
SNO IC: SUBURBAN ELECTRIFICATION SYSTEM	06	43	65
SNO IC: TAKES OVER OHIO VALLEY IN 1897	12	33	91
SNO IC: TEST RUN/HEAVY LOADS	04	51	126
SNO IC: TRACKAGE AGREEMENTS TENN TO ALAB	06	46	74
SNO IC: TRACKSIDE GRAVES NEOGA IL	01	69	31
SNO IC: TRAILERAILS	11	48	56
SNO IC: UNUSUAL LAWSUIT/DERAILMENT	02	55	09
SNO IC: WINFILED BRANCH SOLD TO FRISCO	02	56	37
SNO IC6: LOSES TAX EXEMPT STATUS	08	76	09
SNO ICO: 500 MILE LINE/CANADA/EARLY HIST	11	47	19
SNO ICO: NOW PART OF CN/1154 MILES	10	33	48
SNO ICO: OWNED BY DOMINION GOV'T/NOW CN	10	34	86
SNO ICO: TRACKSIDE GRAVE	06	54	125
SNO ID&C: CONSTRUCTION 1872/BECAME C&IAL	05	49	26
SNO IH&IR: INDUSTRIAL ROAD	04	56	45
SNO IHB: 628 MILES/EQUIPMENT	12	31	96
SNO IHB: BLUE ISLAND IL FRT CLASSIF YARD	11	54	35
SNO IHB: DIESELIZATION/NYC AFFILATE	01	50	124
SNO IL: CHARTERED 1888/WASHINGTON/16 MIL	12	35	82
SNO IM&C: 35 MILES/PRIV ELECTRIC FREIGHT	12	46	106
SNO IM: 1874/CONSOLIDATION/173 MILES	03	39	75
SNO IM: 2 MILES/1 MAN PIKE PHOTO ESSAY	07	44	48
SNO IMT	01	33	102
SNO IMT: CHARTERED 1895/3' GAGE/CALIF/	05	36	84
SNO IN: CHICAGO FRT TERMINAL LINE	04	41	48
SNO IN: INCORP IN 1901/28 MI BELT LINE	11	35	85
SNO INMT: 1907-1935/26 MILES	03	36	83
SNO INMT: BECAME C&NWT 1897 TO DB&W '09	06	74	21
SNO INMT: DB&W CHARTERED AS	09	39	70
SNO INMT: INCORPORATED 1907 DIED 1935	06	73	48
SNO INMT: INCORPORATED 1907 DIED 1935	12	75	57
SNO INTER: INCORP IN 1896/61 MILES/EQUIP	08	34	90
SNO INTER: L&N AND S FIGHT FOR CONTROL	10	60	33
SNO IOWAC: MERGED WITH M&SL IN 1912	01	33	99
SNO IOWAC: MERGED WITH M&SL IN 1916	09	52	57
SNO IOWAC: ROUTE CORRECTION 9/1952	03	53	65
SNO IR&T: 1903/MERGER/CINCINNATI	12	47	92
SNO IR: 12 MILES/8 LOCOS/10 FREIGHT/LEAS	05	32	179
SNO IRR: BRIEF HISTORY	01	67	28
SNO IRT: AIR CONDITIONED SUBWAY TRAINS	04	54	60
SNO IRT: NY CITY/SUBWAY CARS	10	33	47
SNO IRT: SAFETY DEVICES	08	33	90
SNO IRT: SANDS ST STATION	12	71	57
SNO IRW: COLLEGE AVE RUN	05	53	102
SNO IRY: TROLLEY SYSTEM/BUFFALO NY	10	49	101
SNO ISM&E: LEASED BY MP	06	34	87
SNO ISO: CHARTERED 1908 DIED 1913	08	74	58
SNO ISO: CHARTERED 1908/24 MILES/EQUIPME	02	32	331
SNO ISRY: 12 MILES/ELECTRIC LINE	06	47	99
SNO ISTCC: ISTHAMUS CANAL COMMISSION PAN	09	72	53
SNO IT&B: SHORT HISTORY-CLASSIFIED AS RY	09	65	29
SNO IT: 530+ MILES/STEAM/ELECTRIC	11	36	57
SNO IT: CHANGES IN PASSENGER SCHEDULES	04	52	103
SNO IT: DONATES HEAVY WOODEN INTERURBAN	01	51	95
SNO IT: ELEVATED/SUBWAY LINES	06	47	103
SNO IT: LAST INTERURBAN PASSENGER TRAIN	09	53	91
SNO IT: MAY BE SOLD TO 8 RAILROADS	03	55	56
SNO IT: NEW EQUIPMENT ORDERED	03	47	93
SNO IT: ORIGINATED 1901	05	69	31
SNO IT: PASSENGER EQUIPMENT/SERVICE	07	50	115
SNO IT: PEORIA STATION/LINE ABANONDED	09	50	88
SNO IT: TRYING TO ABANDON PEORIA TERMINL	03	50	83
SNO IT: WANTS TO ABANDON 150 MILES	02	43	148
SNO IT: WANTS TO ABANDON PASS SERVICE	12	54	61
SNO ITAS: PURACHSED BY M&RR IN 1904	04	53	61
SNO ITCO: 1903-1910/EXPRESS PACKAGES	01	50	85
SNO ITH: 1.55 MILES/CONTROLLED BY CNYS	02	54	75
SNO ITH: RECEIVERSHIP BEFORE 1928	06	47	99
SNO IUR: BECAME DM&CI	09	52	81
SNO IV: CALIFORNIA/ABANDONED 1939	08	40	65
SNO IV: INCORP IN 1916/EQUIPMENT/MI/FINA	03	35	84
SNO J&A:	06	34	84
SNO J&C: 37 MILES/CONTROLLED BY ALTON	08	46	58
SNO J&H: 1925/ACQUIRES PART OF CP&STL	07	36	85
SNO J&H: FROM CP&SL 1924	06	75	29
SNO J&H: SUCCESSOR TO CP&SL/ABANDONED	11	39	91
SNO J&LP: CREATED 1842	08	52	83
SNO J&NW: INCORP 1899/TEXAS/EQUIPMENT	08	40	64
SNO J: JOINED TO FORM JM&I	12	33	34
SNO JA&F: FIRST IRON TANK CARS 1870	01	75	55

Railroad/ Railfan

RAILROAD HISTORIES & ROSTERS

SHORT NOTES ON...	M	Y	P
SNO JA&IR: BECAME PART OF FEC IN 1893	06	34	84
SNO JANNEY COUPLER: 1ST USED/INVENTED BY	02	32	327
SNO JC&A	07	38	75
SNO JC&LE: BECAME JW&N/NEW YORK	03	48	98
SNO JCE: "OLD SAL" LOCO #590	04	47	139
SNO JCE: ASHLEY PLANE	07	41	66
SNO JCE: LOCOS NAMED FOR RAILROAD MEN	03	47	132
SNO JCE: MAIN LINE ENGINE TERMINALS	01	47	52
SNO JCRR: ELECTRIC FREIGHT LINE 500'/MA	02	48	99
SNO JE&N: 1907/NOW SOUTHERN CAMBRIA RY	04	48	94
SNO JM&I	12	33	34
SNO JP: CHARTERED 1882/HORSECAR LINE/PA	05	48	94
SNO JR: CANAL & ROAD CO/WASHINGTON FOUND	11	36	58
SNO JS&AF: CHURCH AS A CARBARN	01	76	40
SNO JS: 3 LOCOS-#7511, #300, #7 DATA	10	57	22
SNO JSW: ILLINOIS ROAD	11	31	489
SNO JT&KW: PART NOW FEC/PART NOW ACL	08	37	59
SNO JTC: USES PCC CARS/ABSORBED ROADS	05	48	94
SNO JTT: INCORP/NAME CHANGED BEFORE CONS	04	48	94
SNO JVT: CITY SYSTEM/60 MILE/120 CARS	12	46	105
SNO JW&N: INTERURBAN/NY/ELECTRIFIED 1916	03	48	98
SNO K&AR: ALSO KNOWN AS KARSHNER RR	11	72	56
SNO K&AV: NOW PART OF MP	08	34	87
SNO K&DM: 1873/162 MILES	06	38	73
SNO K&DM: RI ACQUIRES IN 1878	11	33	91
SNO K&DM: WAS DMV NOW RI	01	73	60
SNO K&DR: 2' GAGE/MAINE	12	55	27
SNO K&IB: INCORP IN 1900/BECAME K&IT	08	35	87
SNO K&IT: CHARTERED 1900 BRIEF HISTORY	05	68	27
SNO K&N: ACQUIRED BY KCS IN 1935	09	40	63
SNO K&NL: MERGED TO BECOME PA&AT IN 1915	04	49	128
SNO K&OH	11	30	598
SNO K&SE: 1916-1934/16 MILES	07	34	91
SNO K&SEN: FOUNDED 1882 BRIEF HISTORY	03	70	37
SNO K&SID: 4 LOCOS/3 FRT CARS/STATIONS	07	32	509
SNO K&SID: FORMED IN 1919/ILLINOIS	04	39	76
SNO K&SID: INCORP 1919/MILES/EQUIPMENT	03	32	522
SNO K&SL: CHARTERED 1892 NOW CP	12	73	52
SNO K&SL: CHARTERED 1892/3' GAGE/NOW CP	06	32	335
SNO K&W: NOW PART OF CB&Q	08	34	87
SNO K&W: NOW PART OF CB&Q/NARROW TO STD	06	57	40
SNO K-HC: 3 LOCOS/STONE QUARRY RD/CALIF	04	33	93
SNO KA: DEMISE	10	66	08
SNO KAC&LC: 1889-1904/1 LOCO/6 CARS	03	33	94
SNO KAC&LC: 1889-1924/STEAM TO ELECTRIC	01	53	55
SNO KAC&LC: BRIEF HISTORY	01	67	29
SNO KAC&LC: INCORP IN 1889/6 MILES	05	33	73
SNO KATY: BARRIGER REBUILDING	08	67	06
SNO KATY: GRAVES AT MP 19-4 RED ROCK TX	02	62	50
SNO KB&TC: BECAME PART OF N&CRR IN 1902	05	42	63
SNO KC&B: ANNEXED INTO KCN 1897	08	73	56
SNO KC&E: FROM KCW&NW BECAME MP	11	74	52
SNO KC&IAL: BECAME PART OF KCS	04	57	74
SNO KC&IAL: BECAME PART OF KCS IN 1902	09	40	61
SNO KC&K: 1888-1899/PA/3' GAGE THEN STD	03	45	75
SNO KCC&S: OPENED 1885 LEASED FRIS 1923	08	75	57
SNO KCC&S: OPENED 1885/154 MILES/EQUIPME	09	44	64
SNO KCE: ABANDONED	11	32	470
SNO KCE: BUILT 1890/DIED 1929	12	55	30
SNO KCERY: UNION STN TO CHELSEY PARK	06	39	56
SNO KCFS&M: ABSORBED BY FRISCO	06	48	16
SNO KCFS&M: BRIEF HISTORY	08	65	19
SNO KCFS&M: CHARTERD 1901/LEASED TO FRIS	09	44	64
SNO KCFS&M: PLEASANT HILL BRANCH	06	47	140
SNO KCFS&S: ACQUIRED BY KCP&G IN 1893	09	40	60
SNO KCFSG: PART OF FRIS	05	45	60
SNO KCFSG: NOW PART OF FRISCO	09	54	37
SNO KCKV&W: ALL PASS EQUIP JUNKED	01	38	62
SNO KCKV&W: KAW VALLEY LINE/35 MILES/EQU	11	37	56
SNO KCM&B: BECAME PART OF FRISCO	03	54	29
SNO KCM&O: INCORP 1901/3 MINOR NAME CHAN	08	50	49
SNO KCM&O: INCORP 1901/SHORT HISTORY	04	40	117
SNO KCM&O: INCORP IN 1900/REORGANIZED	09	35	82
SNO KCM&O: NOW PART OF ATSF	03	33	89
SNO KCM&O: STILL INCOMPLETE	08	36	75
SNO KCM&O: US ROAD AND MEXICAN ROAD-2!!	11	34	93
SNO KCN&FS: CHARTERED 1887/NOW KCS	09	40	60
SNO KCN&FS: INCORP 1889	10	47	17
SNO KCN: CHARTERED IN 1893/ABANDONED	02	35	84
SNO KCN: CONSOLIDATIONS/162 MILES	08	38	92
SNO KCN: FROM KCW&NW TO MP 1910 DIED '18	11	74	52
SNO KCN: REORG KCW&NW AND KC&B 1897	08	73	56
SNO KCN: SHORT HISTORY	05	34	131
SNO KCP&G: 1893 NAME CHANGE/NOW KCS	09	40	60
SNO KCP&G: BECAME KANSAS CITY SOUTHERN	09	35	85
SNO KCP&G: INCORP 1893	10	47	18
SNO KCPS: 6 SERIOUS PROBLEMS FACING TRAN	04	55	62
SNO KCPS: 7 STREETCAR ROUTES	10	55	52
SNO KCRR: 1910-1929	10	36	70
SNO KCRR: KNOWN AS CAROLINA RAILROAD	05	73	36
SNO KCRR: OPENED IN 1907	10	31	427
SNO KCS&G: ACQUIRED BY KCS IN 1935	09	40	63
SNO KCS&GT: ACQUIRED BY KCS IN 1935	09	40	63
SNO KCS&M: CHARTERED 1881/FRIS ACQUIRES	05	45	60
SNO KCS: ACQUIRES KC ELEVATOR CO 1907	04	39	76
SNO KCS: INCORP 1900/MERGERS/CONSOLIDATO	09	40	60
SNO KCS: INCORP IN 1900/HISTORY/FINANCIL	09	35	85
SNO KCS: LOCOS #200-205 FORMER WABASH	11	42	67
SNO KCS: SHAYS ON FLAT LAND LINE	11	68	36
SNO KCS: STILWELL--LEGENDARY FIGURE	03	48	137
SNO KCSB: BECAME PART OF KCS IN 1902	09	40	61
SNO KCSJCB: NOW PART OF CB&Q	08	34	87
SNO KCSL&C: 161.9 MILES/ALTON CONTROLLED	08	46	58
SNO KCST: ACQUIRED BY KCS IN 1935	09	40	63
SNO KCW&NW: CHARTERED 1885 TO KCN TO MP	11	74	52
SNO KCW&NW: CONSOLIDATED WITH L&OL 1887	08	73	56
SNO KCW&NW: OPENED 1872 REORG KC&E TO MP	11	74	52
SNO KCW&NW: ORGANIZED 1885/REORGAN 1887	08	38	92
SNO KCW&NW: TAKEN OVER BY KC&N IN 1893	02	35	84
SNO KCW&NW: TWO RD SAME NAME 1885 & 1872	11	74	52

Railroad/ Railfan

RAILROAD HISTORIES & ROSTERS

SHORT NOTES ON...	M	Y	P
SNO KE: INCLINE RAILROAD AT UTAH-EMPLOYE	05	55	37
SNO KE: OWNS NEVADA NORTHERN	09	52	43
SNO KEWC: READER INFO-TWO ROADS 1900&30	07	76	52
SNO KGB&W: ABSORBED BY GB&W	11	51	24
SNO KGB&W: INCORP IN 1890/35 MILES	07	35	86
SNO KGJ&E: INCORP 1895/W VA ROAD/EQUIPME	04	35	83
SNO KICO: INCORP 1866	04	36	94
SNO KINL: REORGANIZED IN 1910 AS KCRR	10	36	70
SNO KISH: INCORP 1892/PA/16 MILES	12	37	56
SNO KLS&C: FREIGHT OPERATIONS START	12	87	44
SNO KLS&C: INCORP IN 1905/EQUIPMENT	06	35	86
SNO KLS&C: PART PM/PART ABANDONED	01	37	86
SNO KLS: 1917-1930/CALIFORNIA/18 MILES	12	36	52
SNO KM: CHARTERED IN 1888	12	33	93
SNO KM: ORGANIZED 1884/NOW F&C	08	50	38
SNO KM: PLANNED 1884 SOLD 1927 TO F&C	11	75	47
SNO KMRY: THREE NARROW GAGE LOCOS FOUND	05	55	64
SNO KN: ABANDONED	03	33	136
SNO KO&G: MIDLAND VALLEY CONSOLIDAT 1926	11	34	96
SNO KO&G: NO 2-8-0'S END IN EVEN NUMBER	01	43	136
SNO KS: AUTO COUPLERS/10 WHEEL LOCOS	06	33	90
SNO KS: ELECTRIC RAILWAY LINES	10	47	93
SNO KS: EMBLEM	12	55	51
SNO KURY: CHARTERED IN 1872/BECAME LEX&E	11	34	93
SNO KVRR: CHARTERED IN 1901	04	33	94
SNO KVRR: CHARTERED IN 1901/404 MILES	02	33	83
SNO KVRR: KIAMICHI VALLEY FORMATION	11	87	40
SNO KW: ABSORBED BERLIN & NORTHERN 1924	08	53	81
SNO KWE: 1899-1926/5 MILES/10 OPEN CARS	12	46	105
SNO KWNC: NAME CHANGE 1905/ABANDOND 1917	02	35	84
SNO KYRR: ACQUIRES RI TRACKAGE	11	85	34
SNO L&A: 1929	10	37	73
SNO L&A: CHARTERED 1902 & 1928	05	41	48
SNO L&A: DIESELS VERSUS STEAM TRAINS	06	52	131
SNO L&A: LEASED LOUISIANA RR & NAV CO	12	35	84
SNO L&AND: B&M LEASED IN 1874	06	34	88
SNO L&AT: ABSORBED BY L&N	11	46	08
SNO L&B: ELECTRIC SERVICE 1888	06	54	92
SNO L&BR: LOCO #S - YR BUILT/NY/10.5 MIL	01	43	136
SNO L&BV: INCORP IN 1909/ELECTRIC RAILWY	04	34	84
SNO L&C: INCORP 1896/29 MI/STD GAGE/EQUI	12	50	57
SNO L&C: SHORT LINE/SOUTH CAROLINA/STD G	06	47	129
SNO L&CRY: BECAME LSE IN 1901	03	37	62
SNO L&CRY: BECAME PART OF LSEL	11	51	78
SNO L&D: FORMATION	09	87	30
SNO L&DV: HIGH BRIDGE/BECAME CSO IN 1870	06	44	80
SNO L&E: 3' GAGE/OPENED ABOUT 1870/EQUIP	02	33	82
SNO L&ERR: BECAME LORAIN STREET RAILROAD	03	53	93
SNO L&F: CHARTERED 1847/NOW PART OF L&N	01	52	77
SNO L&FF: MERGED WITH L&F TO BECOME LC&L	01	52	77
SNO L&H: CHARTERED IN 1887/ 1887-1898	05	34	82
SNO L&H: TRI-STATE FREIGHT HAULER	02	42	81
SNO L&HR: 1891 TO ?/EQUIPMENT	02	32	333
SNO L&HR: 1968 OWNERS	10	68	34
SNO L&HR: BRIEF HISTORY	09	66	35
SNO L&HR: INCORPORATED IN 1882	11	33	88
SNO L&HR: MAINLINE OPERATION	02	59	44
SNO L&HR: NO CLASS LETTERS ON LOCOS	09	35	85
SNO L&HR: OPENED 1882/96 MILES	03	36	83
SNO L&HR: TRI-STATE ROAD	12	58	70
SNO L&K: INCORP 1869/NOW QC	01	40	112
SNO L&L: INCORP IN 1853/BECAME LIG 1871	02	35	86
SNO L&LA: STARTED 1853/SOLD 1871 TO LIG	05	52	43
SNO L&LA: SOLD IN 1871	01	53	128
SNO L&LO: CHARTERED 1907	04	59	38
SNO L&M: MERGED WITH H&BM	03	48	23
SNO L&M: NOW PART OF LV	03	35	85
SNO L&MA: 10 MILES/5 COAL BURNERS	03	30	574
SNO L&MA: INCORP 1886/OHIO/STD GAGE	05	50	60
SNO L&MA: MCKEEN CAR #5 NOW RESTAURANT	11	51	123
SNO L&MISS: NOW PART OF BIG 4	03	35	85
SNO L&MR: 101.7 MILES/ALTON CONTROLLED	08	46	58
SNO L&MRY: BECAME PART OF MONON	05	49	26
SNO L&N: 1358 LOCOS	11	30	599
SNO L&N: 1925 ATLANTA DIVISION	09	69	61
SNO L&N: ATLANTA TO KNOXVILLE BRANCH LIN	05	54	78
SNO L&N: BAGGAGE CHECKING FOR NEGROES	09	52	134
SNO L&N: CHANGED GAGES 1896-1900	09	53	68
SNO L&N: CONTROLLED BY ACL	09	38	56
SNO L&N: DEATH CHANGES A RAILROAD	11	46	06
SNO L&N: DIESEL/1 STEAM LOCO	08	57	43
SNO L&N: DONATES BELL TO ROCHESTER KY CH	04	51	126
SNO L&N: FIRST PASSENGER TRAIN	08	56	41
SNO L&N: LC&L BECAME PART OF L&N IN 1881	01	52	77
SNO L&N: LEASING "GENERAL"	07	67	32
SNO L&N: LEXINGTON & EASTERN/KENTUCKY UN	11	34	93
SNO L&N: LEXINGTON & OHIO NOW PART OF	01	46	63
SNO L&N: LOCO #1885 LEASED TO CARR	12	57	46
SNO L&N: LOCOS NAMED FOR OFFICIALS/CITIE	03	43	121
SNO L&N: MERGED WITH NC&SL/CHANGES	08	59	38
SNO L&N: MERGER WITH NC&SL	03	72	63
SNO L&N: MILEAGE	06	30	412
SNO L&N: ONE DAY TO STANDARD GAGE	07	51	65
SNO L&N: OWNED 17 4-4-0 TYPE LOCOMOTIVES	01	39	65
SNO L&N: RAIL-JEEP	11	50	139
SNO L&N: RAILWAY OPERATING BATTALION	07	46	103
SNO L&N: RELAY ALL MAIN LINE TRACK	02	53	128
SNO L&N: ROCKHOUSE CREEK BRANCH	01	48	76
SNO L&N: ROLLING STOCK & LOCOS OWNED	11	49	70
SNO L&N: SMOKE ELIMINATION DEVISE	03	45	74
SNO L&N: TAKE OVER OF C&EI CHICAGO-EVANS	09	69	10
SNO L&N: TWO TANKS USED ON FREIGHT LOCOS	12	40	61
SNO L&NE: ABSORBED PP&B IN 1895	12	35	83
SNO L&NE: BRIEF HISTORY	03	66	29
SNO L&NE: FREIGHT CARRIER/130.6 MILES	03	44	98
SNO L&NE: FREIGHT ROAD/127 MILES	02	45	69
SNO L&NE: MAIN LINES/TERMINAL	07	40	68
SNO L&NE: MAINLINE OPERATION	02	59	44
SNO L&NE: MILEAGE/BRANCHES	06	33	90
SNO L&OL: CONSOLIDATED INTO KCW&NW 1887	08	73	56

Railroad/ Railfan

STEPHANS' RAILROAD DIRECTORY

RAILROAD HISTORIES & ROSTERS

SHORT NOTES ON...	M	Y	P
SNO L&OL: MERGED WITH KC&NW	02	35	84
SNO L&OL: ORGANIZED 1886	08	38	92
SNO L&PS: 1ST DIESEL	01	55	75
SNO L&PS: CANADA'S OLDEST RAILWAY	07	53	118
SNO L&PS: CONNECTIONS/CORRECTIONS	05	50	136
SNO L&PS: HOW TO RUIN PASSENGER BUSINESS	04	55	63
SNO L&R: CHARTERED IN 1898/LEASED TO SP	03	35	87
SNO L&RNG: 5' 2.5" TRACK/NOT TO READING	12	39	110
SNO L&SQ: CNJ LEASES	03	33	92
SNO L&SQ: LEASED TO CNJ	12	36	51
SNO L&T: CHARTERED 1889 FROM LT&W TO UP	06	75	29
SNO L&T: CHARTERED 1899/57 MILES	03	37	61
SNO L&WV: "LAUREL LINE"/CHARTERED 1913	03	39	74
SNO L&WV: 3RD RAIL OPERATION 1903	09	76	52
SNO L&YFR: OPENED 1896/6 MILES/NEW YORK	02	37	76
SNO L-IC: ABORTED ROAD OF 1854	01	76	40
SNO L-IC: CALICO ROAD/UNUSUAL SETTLEMENT	12	50	51
SNO L: MY NARROW GAGE ALBUM PART 2	08	39	46
SNO LA&M: MILWAUKEE TO ST PAUL 1864	12	76	28
SNO LA&SL: 1916/RESULT OF NAME CHANGE	05	41	48
SNO LA&SL: DIESELIZATION	05	47	71
SNO LA&SL: FROM SPLASL 1916 TO UP 1921	09	75	58
SNO LA&SL: UP OWNS HALF	03	36	83
SNO LA: 3' GAGE/N CAROLINA/ PHOTO ESSAY	04	43	67
SNO LACK&M: NOW PART OF DL&W	03	35	85
SNO LAS&S: RECENTLY ABANDONED/SHORT HIST	07	36	85
SNO LATR: ABANDONED LINES	03	55	57
SNO LATR: DENIED ABANDONMENT	04	55	46
SNO LATR: MONORAIL SYSTEM	06	54	91
SNO LATR: PROPOSED RAPID TRANIST NETWORK	08	56	69
SNO LC&C: PROJECTED	11	48	23
SNO LC&L: CONSOLIDATION IN 1869	01	52	77
SNO LC&MI: NOW PART OF MILW	03	35	85
SNO LC&NW: 1919 NAME CHANGE/CP LEASES	04	34	84
SNO LC&SE: 42 MILES/3 LOCOS/WISCONSIN	06	32	335
SNO LC&SE: ORGANIZED 1904 TO MILW 1933	03	75	10
SNO LC&SE: ORGANIZED 1904/40 MILES/STD	03	50	60
SNO LCOL: 1890'S/13 MILES	05	52	85
SNO LE&N: IMPROVING LINES	08	52	92
SNO LE&W: BECAME PART OF NKP IN 1922	04	57	40
SNO LE&W: FREMONT & INDIANA BUILT AS	08	36	75
SNO LE: WHAT WILL HAPPEN TO LE?	06	62	24
SNO LEF&C: BRIEF HISTORY	01	68	27
SNO LEWMV: INCORP 1881 HALTED 1883/NO $	12	55	38
SNO LEX&E: REORGANIZED 1894/93 MI/EQUIP	11	34	93
SNO LF&D: 1891-1903/EQUIPMENT/NOW NYC	12	42	43
SNO LG&MR: BUILT 1876/1ST LOGGING ONLY R	07	53	52
SNO LH&NO: BRIEF HISTORY	02	67	25
SNO LH&NO: NAMED IN 1912 FROM BM&A	07	72	62
SNO LH&NO: ORGANIZED IN 1901/ABANDONED	06	35	82
SNO LH&SL: CHARTERED 1896 BRIEF HISTORY	04	68	27
SNO LHP&P:	11	33	90
SNO LHP&P: TAKEN OVER IN 1914	12	35	85
SNO LI&DE: BRIEF HISTORY & LEGENDS	12	61	60
SNO LI&M: ACQUIRED BY C&NW	06	58	72
SNO LI&M: INCORP 1900/51 MILES/EQUIPMENT	03	36	81
SNO LI&M: ORGANIZED BY CP&STL IN 1890	07	36	85
SNO LI&M: ROSTER/51 MILES/EQUIPMENT	05	35	87
SNO LI: PHOTO ESSAY	10	59	42
SNO LI: 33 ELECTRIC LOCOS NEAAR NY TERMI	12	29	98
SNO LI: 66 DIESELS FOR NON PASSENGER RUN	03	52	119
SNO LI: 99 LOCOMOTIVES/LINES	04	32	69
SNO LI: AIR-CONDITIONED PASSENGER CARS	10	55	31
SNO LI: ALL-STEEL PASS EQUIP GIBBS CARS	10	51	134
SNO LI: BOUGHT BY NEW YORK STATE	04	69	10
SNO LI: BRIEF NOTES	08	60	36
SNO LI: BUILT 1834/NOT ALWAYS COMMUTER	06	58	36
SNO LI: CAR FLOATS	10	51	62
SNO LI: COMMUTER VS PRR	09	49	127
SNO LI: DIESEL SELF-PROPELLED BUDD CARS	03	55	67
SNO LI: DOUBLE DECKERS OPEREATED MORE	12	52	123
SNO LI: DOUBLE-DECKERS	10	47	80
SNO LI: EARLY ELECTRIFICATION 19104	09	74	43
SNO LI: ELECTRIC TRAIN RUN	12	55	50
SNO LI: EMBLEM CHANGES	05	46	112
SNO LI: EMPLOYS 440 MEN	08	40	59
SNO LI: FASTEST COMMUTER LINE	04	58	72
SNO LI: FIRST ELECTRIC/1905	06	58	34
SNO LI: FREIGHT CARS???	08	56	45
SNO LI: HEMPSTEAD DEPOT	01	43	135
SNO LI: INCORP IN 1834/OWNED BY PRR	06	34	89
SNO LI: JUNK MUSEUM-GHOSTLY CARS	02	75	06
SNO LI: K-CARD	06	45	134
SNO LI: LARGEST COMMUTER ROAD/BANKRUPTCY	12	54	04
SNO LI: LARGEST STEAM LOCOMOTIVES	08	56	40
SNO LI: LEASES NYB&MB IN 1885	09	35	87
SNO LI: LEASES NYBR&J AND NY&MB 1882	03	74	33
SNO LI: LEASING 16 READING COACHES	10	53	69
SNO LI: LOCO #307 OLD & NEW	04	36	87
SNO LI: LOCOMOTIVES IN SERVICE	01	34	92
SNO LI: MICROWAVE-BEAM RADIO SYSTEM	01	49	66
SNO LI: MICROWWAVE-BEAM RADIO SYSTEM	01	49	66
SNO LI: MONTAUK BRANCH UNPROFITABLE	06	53	113
SNO LI: MORE READER MEMORIES	05	43	140
SNO LI: MOST PASSENGERS CARRIED	08	67	31
SNO LI: MURRY HILL WAITING ROOM RAZED	12	64	52
SNO LI: NERVE CENTER	05	77	47
SNO LI: NEW COLOR SCHEME	03	50	138
SNO LI: NEW YORK BAY RIDGE & JAMAICA RR	02	33	87
SNO LI: QUAINT BLOCK SPACING 1890	07	69	10
SNO LI: RAIL ROAD (2 WORDS)	06	56	71
SNO LI: READERS REMINISENCE	03	43	127
SNO LI: ROAD CAR NUMBERING	10	60	32
SNO LI: ROCKAWAY BEACH BRANCH	10	50	132
SNO LI: SHORT HISTORY	02	61	31
SNO LI: SHORT HISTORY OF LI	08	32	57
SNO LIC&MB: BECAME NYB&MB IN 1885	09	35	87
SNO LIC&MB: CONSOLIDATED 1885 LI LEASED	09	73	42
SNO LIC&MB: INCORP IN 1883	08	32	57
SNO LIG: 16 MILES/BEING ABANDONED	03	53	135

STEPHANS_RAILROAD_DIRECTORY

Railroad/Railfan

RAILROAD HISTORIES & ROSTERS

SHORT NOTES ON...	M	Y	P
SNO LIG: LATROBE & LIGONIER BECOMES 1871	02	35	86
SNO LJC&M: CHARTERED 1910/NEVER WAS	01	55	65
SNO LK: INCORP IN 1896/ACQUIRED BY B&O	01	35	86
SNO LLB&C: CHARTERED IN 1883	10	31	427
SNO LLB&C: CHARTERED IN 1883/NOW KWNC	02	35	84
SNO LMRR: INCORP 1834/OHIO/200 MILES	10	59	38
SNO LMRR: JOINED WITH MR&LE 1846	03	76	56
SNO LN: CHARTERED IN 1895/EQUIP/MILES	07	34	92
SNO LNA&C: SHORT HISTORY	08	78	44
SNO LNA&C: SUBSIDIARIES/ BECAME MONON	05	49	26
SNO LNA&CH: "LONG NARROW & CROOKED"	07	38	76
SNO LNA&S: ABSORBED NA&SA/BECAME MONON	05	49	25
SNO LNO&T: ORGANIZED 1884 NOW ICG	07	73	38
SNO LNO&T: ORGANIZED IN 1884/456 MILES	11	38	72
SNO LNP&W: INCORP 1924/111 MILES/EQUIPMN	12	35	85
SNO LNP&W: INCORP 1924/ACQUIRED CW&E	01	47	56
SNO LNP&W: INCORPORATED IN 1924	11	33	90
SNO LO&CH: BECAME PART OF SF&W	12	40	61
SNO LO&P: CHARTERED IN 1903/BECAME LOP&G	03	44	103
SNO LO&RB: BECAME PART OF SF&W	12	40	61
SNO LO&S: 3' GAGE/PENNSYLVANIA/28 MILES	03	36	81
SNO LODI: OWNED BY NYS&W	05	34	82
SNO LOP&G: ORGANIZED IN 1905/WOOD-BURNER	03	44	103
SNO LOR: 1903/REORGANIZATION OF P&HRC/EQ	06	45	60
SNO LOSRR: CHARTERED 1875/ NOW RW&O	02	37	78
SNO LOT&CH: CONSOLIDATED TO SF&W 1884	12	73	52
SNO LOU: CHARTERED 1853 TO VC	08	75	58
SNO LP&N: BUILT 1951	09	73	07
SNO LR&AV: 1877/BECAME CBELT NORTH SECTI	02	47	111
SNO LR&HS: INCORP 1892/24 MI/N CAROLINA	06	36	81
SNO LR&N		10	37	73
SNO LR&N: INCORP 1903	10	37	73
SNO LR&N: INCORP 1903 LEASED TO L&A	11	75	43
SNO LR&N: INCORP 1903/LEASED TO L&A	12	35	84
SNO LR&N: INCORPORATED 1903 BECAME L&A	11	72	55
SNO LR: ONE OF HIGHEST RR EAST OF ROCKIE	02	57	46
SNO LRRR: INCORP IN 1864/13 MILES/EQUIPM	06	33	91
SNO LRRY: MERGED INTO MONT 1917	02	72	61
SNO LRY: NEW PCC CARS TRADED	02	47	108
SNO LS&B: CHARTERED 1890/FRT/15 MI/EQUIP	10	52	62
SNO LS&B: DEMISE 3-25-86	07	86	30
SNO LS&I: INCORP 1923/MERGER/STD GAGE/EQ	10	47	70
SNO LS&M: CHARTERED 1857/BECAME SP&DUL	04	36	93
SNO LS&M: RESULT OF NAME CHANGE 1861	12	34	83
SNO LS&MS: ASHTABULA WRECK DECEMBER 1876	10	49	61
SNO LS&MS: BRIEF HISTORY	02	67	25
SNO LS&MS: BRIEF HISTORY	01	66	25
SNO LS&MS: CHARTERED IN 1869/CONSOLIDATI	06	35	82
SNO LS&MS: ENGINEER "FLYING DUTCHMAN"	09	73	40
SNO LS&MS: FAST MAIL/SCHEDULE	02	45	72
SNO LS&MS: LAKE SHORE TRAMP TRUST	06	35	79
SNO LS&MS: MAHONONG COAL 25 MILES BECOME	03	38	54
SNO LS&MS: MERGED WITH NYC IN 1914	08	53	63
SNO LS&MS: NYC MERGER 1914	05	68	27
SNO LS&MS: TO NYC IN 1914	03	76	57
SNO LS&TV: BECAME CL&W/NOW B&O	11	36	58
SNO LSE: INCORP 1901/CONSOLIDATIONS/EQUI	03	37	62
SNO LSEL: EQUIPMENT	06	33	90
SNO LSEL: GENEOLOGY CHART	11	51	73
SNO LSM&PC: INCORP 1886/HORSECAR LINE	03	53	98
SNO LSRR: REORGANIZED/BECAME LSEL	11	51	78
SNO LSRR: ABSORBED BY LSEL/RETAINED NAME	03	53	93
SNO LSRR: MERGED W/NI&SM 1869 TO LS&MS	03	76	57
SNO LSWC: FORMED BY BN/UP	08	71	06
SNO LT&W: CHARTERED 1879 TO L&T 1889	06	75	29
SNO LT&W: CHARTERED IN 1879/NOW L&T	03	37	61
SNO LV&T: BUILT IN 1905	05	32	180
SNO LV&T: CONSOLIDATED IN 1914	11	32	474
SNO LV&T: INCORP 1905/ABANDONED	11	38	71
SNO LV&T: INCORP 1905/ABANDONED/197 MILE	11	35	84
SNO LV&T: INCORP IN 1905/11 LOCOS	11	38	73
SNO LV&T: INCORPORATED 1905	07	73	39
SNO LV&T: TOOK OVER BG IN 1914	10	49	131
SNO LV&T: WHAT HAPPENED TO LOCOS	02	36	89
SNO LV: 100+ FEET ELECTRIFIED	04	59	34
SNO LV: 1853/ABSORBED DLS&S	07	36	80
SNO LV: ABSORBS UI&E	02	53	127
SNO LV: AUTO TRAIN CONTROLS	10	43	73
SNO LV: BEGAN AS BEAVER MEADOW RR 1836	12	56	29
SNO LV: BLACK DIAMOND EXPRESS	10	72	53
SNO LV: CENTENNIAL PHOTO ESSAY	08	46	41
SNO LV: COAL-BURNERS/GAS-ELECT/OIL=ELECT	06	31	441
SNO LV: COLOR LIGHT SIGNALS	06	45	59
SNO LV: DELANO (RAILROAD TOWN)	03	48	12
SNO LV: DIESEL LOCO CHIME WHISTLES	07	50	137
SNO LV: DLS&S NOT PREDECSSOR! CORRECTION	09	36	78
SNO LV: ELMIRA & CORTLAND BRANCH	05	53	62
SNO LV: FINANCIAL/EQUIPMENT	06	34	84
SNO LV: GENEVA ITHACA & SAYRE NOW PART	01	35	82
SNO LV: LAST VULCAN COMPOUND	08	58	45
SNO LV: LEASES HAYT'S CRN OVID & WILLARD	01	34	90
SNO LV: LEASES IRONTON RAILROAD	05	32	179
SNO LV: LEASES PEOPLES TRACK-3 MILES	01	34	90
SNO LV: LEASES STATE LINE & SULLIVAN RR	01	34	90
SNO LV: MILEAGE	01	34	90
SNO LV: NIAGARA FALLS YARD	10	54	39
SNO LV: RECLASSIFICATION PROGRAM	08	49	110
SNO LV: THEIR FIRST STREAMLINER	09	39	119
SNO LVT: PHOTO ESSAY	09	42	100
SNO LVT: ABANDONMENT BY 1905'S--BUSES	01	48	107
SNO LVT: CHARTERED 1905/REORGANIZATION	08	42	95
SNO LVT: INTERURBANS TO BUSES?	05	50	102
SNO LVT: LIBERTY BELL ROUTE	08	52	95
SNO LVT: LIBERTY BELL ROUTE SCRAPPED	04	52	105
SNO LVT: QUAKER CITY INTERURBANS ABANDON	01	50	90
SNO LW: OPERATED BY PE	02	34	84
SNO LWRY: WICKERSHAM WASHINGTON	09	76	52
SNO LX&E: ABSORBED BY L&N	11	46	08
SNO LX&E: CHARTERED 1872 AS UNION TO L&N	05	72	57
SNO LX&O: L&F PURCHASED	01	52	77

Railroad/ Railfan

RAILROAD HISTORIES & ROSTERS

SHORT NOTES ON...	M	Y	P
SNO LX&O: ORGANIZED 1831 NOW L&N	04	73	47
SNO LX&O: ORGANIZED 1831/HORSE-DRAWN RD	01	46	63
SNO LY&D: MERGED IN 1859	09	36	74
SNO M&AT	02	33	129
SNO M&AT: LEASED M&CR NOW CP	06	72	60
SNO M&BI: 97 MILES/GEORGIA/RY AND RR	03	53	64
SNO M&BI: CHARTERED 1896 FROM M&BI RR	04	75	11
SNO M&BIG: BRIEF HISTORY	08	77	57
SNO M&BIG: EMPLOYEE CHRISTMAS PRESENTS	04	54	117
SNO M&BR	11	30	598
SNO M&CH: TOOK OVER TVRR 1865	07	76	50
SNO M&CIN: BUILT 1890/CL&N ACQUIRED 1902	04	39	79
SNO M&CLRR: BECAME P&EAST IN 1907	10	36	70
SNO M&CR: SOLD 1880 NOW CP	06	72	60
SNO M&CRR: ABSORBED TVRR/BECAME S	12	51	65
SNO M&CRR: ORGANIZED IN 1883	08	33	88
SNO M&CT: INCORP 1871/BECAME PART OF S	03	54	24
SNO M&DC: INCORP IN 1924	08	34	85
SNO M&DSC: BEING ABANDONED/LOCOS	01	35	87
SNO M&DSC: INCORP IN 1932	08	34	85
SNO M&DSC: PART OF MD&V BECOMES M&DSC	04	35	83
SNO M&DU: INCORP 1885/BECAME MD&S 1890	07	35	86
SNO M&E: 1903/NAME CHANGE/WAS W&PR	12	52	69
SNO M&E: HISTORY OF ITS 5 LOCOS	06	35	85
SNO M&E: INCORP 1903/12 MILE/NEW JERSEY	11	40	71
SNO M&E: INCORP 1903/CONSOLIDATION/EQUIP	08	42	93
SNO M&E: INCORP IN 1903/CONSOLIDATION	04	35	87
SNO M&E: SWITCHING ROAD	02	59	44
SNO M&E: 11 MILES/5 LOCOS/10 FRT CARS	04	34	86
SNO M&F: 18 MILES/2 LOCOS	01	34	90
SNO M&GR: LOGGING ROAD/MICH/RENAMED/ABAN	07	53	55
SNO M&GRY: 1898/NAME CHANGE	12	40	59
SNO M&GRY: BANKRUPT 1903 SOLD TO GNC	07	75	52
SNO M&I: CHARTERED 1836/1ST IN INDIANIA	10	56	40
SNO M&I: JOINED WITH J TO FORM JM&I	12	33	34
SNO M&IRY: INCORP 1900/ CONTROLLED BY NP	04	35	85
SNO M&IRY: TURTLE RIVER MN AGENT 1901	08	73	03
SNO M&LF: ABSORBED BY T&P IN 1900	10	42	63
SNO M&ME: REORGANIZATION	12	31	96
SNO M&MF: NOT DEAD-FROM OWNER	07	75	47
SNO M&MF: TAKES OVER ABANDONED M&NF 1975	02	75	42
SNO M&MI: WISCONSINS FIRST ROAD	12	76	28
SNO M&NA: 368 MILES/EQUIPMENT	03	32	522
SNO M&NA: REORGANIZATION/1905	06	48	20
SNO M&NE: INCORP 1887/EQUIPMENT/MILEAGE	04	38	50
SNO M&NG: OWNED BY L&N	06	49	51
SNO M&O: OPENED 1861/NOW GM&O/STEEL RAIL	04	54	10
SNO M&OC: CHARTERED 1886/3'/35 MI/EQUIP	10	52	62
SNO M&ONE: 2 PASSENGER TRAINS DAILY	08	40	64
SNO M&ONE: 8 MILE/IOWA/MEMORIES	04	47	138
SNO M&ONE: 9 MILES/2 LOCOS/IOWA ROAD	06	32	335
SNO M&ONE: INCORP 1900/8 MILES/IOWA EQUI	02	37	77
SNO M&ONE: INCORP IN 1900/8 MILES/IOWA	09	34	82
SNO M&ONE: INCORP 1900/8 MI/EQUIP/FINANCL	08	34	86
SNO M&PAC: CHARTERED 1884-6/NOW SOO	12	34	84
SNO M&PAC: ORGANIZED IN 1853/6N LEASED	07	36	82
SNO M&PP: 9 MILE COG LINE	02	38	61
SNO M&PP: BECAME DIESELIZED 1950	09	50	46
SNO M&PP: NOW USES TWO DIESEL LOCOS	02	55	28
SNO M&QT: PART OF SOS BECAME	06	51	92
SNO M&RR: 1904-1932/STD GAGE/EQUIP/MILES	04	53	61
SNO M&RR: 63 MILES/EQUIPMENT	03	32	521
SNO M&RR: CHARTERED 1904/ABANDONED 1932	05	38	73
SNO M&RR: CHARTERED 1904 ABANDONED 1932	01	75	54
SNO M&SC: 63 MILES	11	37	53
SNO M&SC: DIESELIZED/GRANBY SERVICE	04	51	103
SNO M&SC: INCORP 1897/ELECTRIC/EQUIPMENT	11	36	58
SNO M&SC: BRIEF HISTORY AFTER FOLDING	06	61	34
SNO M&SCR: COMPLETED 1887/NOW PART OF SOO	12	34	84
SNO M&SL: "PEORIA GATEWAY LINE"	01	33	99
SNO M&SL: EQUIPMENT/LOCOMOTIVES	07	33	84
SNO M&SL: MERGED WITH IOWAC IN 1916	09	52	57
SNO M&SL: STOCKHOLDERS DISPUTE	03	54	125
SNO M&SL: TRAIN #70 "MALES ONLY"	01	43	137
SNO M&SLRY: BECAME SL&AD IN 1896	11	40	73
SNO M&SP: "PEORIA GATEWAY"	03	32	522
SNO M&SP: 1628 MILES/208 LOCOS/EQUIPMENT	05	34	85
SNO M&SV: 1 LOCO/21 MILES	11	38	70
SNO M&SW: BECAME PART OF G&F IN 1907	06	41	61
SNO M&SW: BECAME PART OF G&F IN 1927	03	39	75
SNO M&SW: IN 1907 BECAME PART OF G&F	03	36	83
SNO M&TI: NOW PART OF ROCK ISLAND	07	36	84
SNO M&U	10	33	43
SNO M&U: 1913/MU&WG REORGAZINED AS	11	41	52
SNO M&WB: MERGED WITH MERIDAN & CROMWELL	08	33	88
SNO M&WB: CHARTERED 1887 MERGED MW&CR '88	10	75	54
SNO M&WE: "THE BALL LINE" TERMINAL ROAD	02	43	140
SNO M&WE: INCORPORATED 1902	08	74	57
SNO M&WE: INCORP 1902/BALL MASON JARS OWN	12	41	76
SNO M&WR: 44 MILES	06	33	92
SNO M&WR: FIRST LOCO HISTORY	08	33	137
SNO M-I: "STE GENEVIEVE" TRANSFER STMBOA	10	51	63
SNO M: NEW ALBANY & SALEM NOW PART OF	10	56	45
SNO M: NOT CONTROLLED BY ANY OTHER ROAD	04	37	50
SNO M: SPECIAL WOMENS CAR	03	50	127
SNO M: SUBSIDIARIES	05	49	26
SNO MA&CR: INTERURBAN/MINNEAPOLIS/15 MI	03	53	97
SNO MA&E: INCORP IN 1913/LEASED TO MP	12	34	84
SNO MA&ME: NOW PART OF B&M	08	41	70
SNO MA&PA: 81 MILES/EQUIPMENT	05	32	183
SNO MA&PA: EMBLEM HISTORY	12	55	36
SNO MA&PA: INCORP IN 1911/CONSOLIDATION	07	35	84
SNO MA&PA: MARYLAND CENTRAL BECAME MA&PA	12	46	78
SNO MA&PA: ORGANIZED 1901/CONSOLIDATION	11	36	58
SNO MA&PA: CONSOLIDATION IN 1901 FORMS	12	33	92
SNO MA&S: INCORP 1911/ABAND 1937/STD GAG	02	52	57
SNO MA&W: INCORP 1914/ARIZONA/1 LOCO/2 C	01	37	87
SNO MAD: BEGAN 1904/6 MILES/MAINE/	12	55	29
SNO MAH: OHIO/38 MILES/PART NYC/MS&LS	03	38	54
SNO MAH: SHENANGO BRANCH LEASED 1889	12	34	85

Stephans' Railroad Directory

Railroad/Railfan

RAILROAD HISTORIES & ROSTERS

SHORT NOTES ON...	M	Y	P
SNO MAHANOY PLANE, PA: HOW NAME/RR/1931	01	34	93
SNO MAIL: RAILROADS VS AIRPLANES/QUANITY	03	32	517
SNO MAL: CONSOLIDATED W/GRAND TRUNK WEST	04	31	122
SNO MAN: 500' STANDARD GAGE/PRIVATE OWND	11	39	90
SNO MANHATTAN: CROSS-RIVER BRIDGE/TUNNEL	02	56	41
SNO MAR: NOW PART OF PRR	12	36	52
SNO MARTA: WINS GOLD STAR	07	82	20
SNO MASSC: BRANCH NOT DIVISION OF B&M	04	40	80
SNO MASSC: CHARTERED IN 1869/1869-1883	03	34	89
SNO MASSC: NOW PART OF B&M	02	40	118
SNO MAT: 3 MILE/CANADA/STANDARD GAGE	05	47	82
SNO MATT: CHARTERED IN 1895/58 MILES/EQU	08	34	85
SNO MATT: ORGANIZED 1895/LUMBER/WISCONSI	01	37	88
SNO MAX: PORTLAND WELCOMES MAX	03	87	24
SNO MBE: NOT RAPID TRANIST LINE/FLORIDA	12	46	105
SNO MC	06	33	92
SNO MC&C: INCORP IN 1900	09	32	233
SNO MC&FD: LEASED BY CGW	03	34	86
SNO MC&FD: LEASED IN 1901	10	34	87
SNO MC&LM: ORGANIZED 1870/ 4' 9.5" GAGE	01	34	90
SNO MC&LM: BRIEF HISTORY	02	66	29
SNO MC&LM: SHORT HISTORY	08	61	34
SNO MC&RR: CHARTERED 1881 MERGED MW&CR'88	10	75	54
SNO MC&SA: BRIEF HISTORY	02	64	36
SNO MC: 1121 MILES/200 LOCOS/EQUIPMENT	01	33	100
SNO MC: DIVISIONS	07	32	507
SNO MC: JACKSON MULTIPLE TAMPER	02	51	50
SNO MC: LEASED HEREFORD RY IN 1890	05	38	72
SNO MC: LEASED UPPER COOS RAILROAD	05	54	80
SNO MC: LEASES BELFAST & MOOSEHEAD LAKE	01	34	90
SNO MC: LEASES RF&RL IN 1907/ABANDONED??	03	35	87
SNO MC: MERGER OF E&K AND D&SJ	11	49	65
SNO MC: NEW DELUXE PASSENGER EQUIPMENT	02	48	74
SNO MC: NEW EMBLEM--PINE TREE SYMBOL	01	48	130
SNO MC: SLASHS PASSENGER FARES	06	51	132
SNO MC: TRACK PANS 1887	03	51	63
SNO MC: WARMING HOUSE	08	47	132
SNO MC: WASHINGTON COUNTY RR MERGES WITH	10	33	45
SNO MC: WATER SCOOPER MEMORIES	08	48	137
SNO MC: WOOD TO COAL BURNERS/LOCOS	10	57	38
SNO MC: CAMELBACK LOCOMOTIVES	07	65	31
SNO MCA: DISCONTINUED 1931/9 MILES	08	55	43
SNO MCA: INCORP 1874/L&N LEASED/STD GAGE	03	51	61
SNO MCCO: BECAME PART OF W&NO IN 1905	04	36	93
SNO MCCO: BECAME PART OF W&NO IN 1905	07	50	64
SNO MCH: BUILT 1818/PA/NOW ABANDONED	11	47	71
SNO MCH: 1818 LAID AS COAL ROAD-NO ENGINE	11	31	487
SNO MCI: 900 REVENUE CARS/OTHERS	04	51	102
SNO MCI: 91 PCC CARS	02	55	63
SNO MCL: WAS PE/SUBWAYS/BUSES	11	54	60
SNO MCOL: INCORP 1890/SERVE LUMBERING	12	40	59
SNO MCOL: INCORPORATED 1890 TO M&GRY 1898	07	75	53
SNO MCOR: FROM RRV 1920 FOLDED 1922	08	75	56
SNO MCR: ABANDONED/W VA/LOGGING ROAD	04	57	46
SNO MCRI: CALIFORNIA/NEW ROAD	02	55	74
SNO MCRI: INCORP 1897	10	36	71
SNO MCRI: INCORP 1897/61 MILES/EQUIPMENT	11	35	84
SNO MCRI: LOCOS #15, #17 SCRAPPED	08	50	124
SNO MCRY: 1882/NAME CHANGES/BECAME CGW	09	35	85
SNO MCRY: TO WM&P IN 1884	01	34	90
SNO MD&B: CHARTERED 1902	11	74	52
SNO MD&G: STANDARD GAGE MARBLE ROAD 1902	08	37	58
SNO MD&GU: TAKEN OVER BY GN&A IN 1922	03	37	61
SNO MD&S: 1890/94 MILES/GEORGIA ROAD	07	35	86
SNO MD&SC: SHORT HISTORY	07	65	41
SNO MD&V: BRIEF HISTORY/EQUIPMENT/MILEAG	04	35	83
SNO MD&V: CENTREVILLE BRANCH NOW B&E	05	34	87
SNO MD&V: FORMED IN 1905/72 MILES	08	34	85
SNO MD&V: NOW...	09	31	190
SNO MD&W: 40 MILES	07	38	76
SNO MD&W: 40 MILES/EQUIPMENT	03	32	521
SNO MD&W: MERGED WITH M&SL IN 1912	01	33	99
SNO MDCE: NARROW GAGE/BECAME MA&PA	12	46	78
SNO ME&W: LOGGING ROAD/MICHIGAN/ABANDOND	07	53	55
SNO ME: PRO-RAIL MANAGEMENT/NEW LIFE	01	50	87
SNO MEC: YEARS OF MOST TRACKAGE	12	68	30
SNO MEIGS: MONORAIL SYSTEM/1880	09	47	104
SNO MEP&P: ABSORBED BY T&P IN 1873	10	42	63
SNO MER&L: PHOTO ESSAY	04	43	138
SNO MER&T: 317 MILES/EQUIPMENT	01	42	65
SNO MFG: 31 MILES/8 LOCOS/EQUIPMENT	10	33	44
SNO MFG: CONSOLIDATION	04	31	122
SNO MFG: INCORP IN 1887/8 LOCOS	12	37	54
SNO MFG: RIVER TRANSFER SERVICE	01	55	37
SNO MFG: BRIEF HISTORY CHARTERED 1887	09	69	32
SNO MG: BUILT IN 1889/2' GAGE	12	50	138
SNO MG: PENNSYLVANIA/2' GAGE/STEAM STREE	12	55	31
SNO MG: SUBSIDIARY OF CO&L/1889-1889	04	36	92
SNO MGAP: CHARTERED IN 1850/MERGD W/O&AL	09	36	74
SNO MGAP: MERGED WITH O&AL IN 1867	12	55	35
SNO MGB&W: C&NW TAKES OVER IN 1909	04	34	79
SNO MH&H: BECAME A&SCH/THEN NYC	09	53	44
SNO MH&H: CORNERSTONE/RELIC	09	48	134
SNO MH&H: DEWITT CLINTON	11	39	88
SNO MH&H: STARTED 1830/BECAME PART NYC	02	57	43
SNO MH&H: CHARTERED 1826/BECAME A&SCH	11	43	61
SNO MH&H: FIRST PASSENGER TRAIN IN NY	02	67	26
SNO MH&H: FIRST TRAIN IN NY-DEWIT CLINTON	04	66	34
SNO MH&N: INCORPORATED 1890	11	72	56
SNO MHL: 2 MILE/NARROW GAGE/WOOD RAILS	10	56	39
SNO MHM: 3.6 MILES	02	59	44
SNO MHM: 4 MILES/CONTROLLED BY CNJ	04	34	86
SNO MHM: INCORP 1866/3 MILES/RAIL/CONTRO	07	50	64
SNO MHRR:	11	33	88
SNO MHRR: BECAME PART OF L&HR IN 1912	03	36	83
SNO MHV: BECAME PART OF NYC	09	53	44
SNO MI&L: CHARTERED IN 1901/EQUIPMENT	02	36	87
SNO MI&L: INCORP 1913/19 MILES/EQUIPMENT	04	33	95
SNO MI&MO: COMPLETED 1855/NOW PART OF RI	12	50	53
SNO MI&MO: OPENED 1855 NOW RI	01	76	40

Railroad/Railfan

RAILROAD HISTORIES & ROSTERS

SHORT NOTES ON...	M	Y	P
SNO MI&NW: CHARTERED 1843	02	55	14
SNO MI&PAC: STARTED IN 1853/NOW GN	03	35	85
SNO MI&SC: INCORP 1856/ABSORBED BY GN	07	36	82
SNO MI&SC: BECAME GREAT NORTHERN IN 1889	03	35	85
SNO MI&SP: BECAME CMSP IN 1876	06	50	23
SNO MI&SP: MINNESOTA CENTRAL RR PART OF	01	34	90
SNO MI&SP: ORGANIZED IN 1863	06	38	75
SNO MI&W: 4 LOCOS/ WHERE ARE THEY NOW?	03	36	87
SNO MI&W: NO LONGER OPERATING	09	44	65
SNO MI: STILL STEAM POWERED 1967	06	67	35
SNO MIBL: 175 FEET OF TRACK	08	32	30
SNO MIBL: 175 FEET OF TRACK	04	33	113
SNO MICHC: 12 ELECTRIC LOCOS	09	32	236
SNO MICHC: BOXCARS AND CANADIAN SOUTHER	11	41	50
SNO MICHC: NOW PART OF NYC/CHARTERD 1846	03	47	130
SNO MICHS: MERGED TO NI&SM 1855	03	76	57
SNO MICROWAVE RADIO RELAY SYSTEM	02	56	42
SNO MIDC: INCORP 1906/EQUIPMENT/78 MILES	06	57	40
SNO MIDC: BRIEF HISTORY	06	66	12
SNO MIDC: IMOPOSING NAME-SMALL RD	04	63	37
SNO MIDCO: MERGED IN 1881 TO FROM NYS&W	04	36	90
SNO MIDL: 1ST PULLMANS ON BRITISH ISLES	12	50	51
SNO MIDL: 70 MILES/GEORGIA ABANDONED ROA	05	34	132
SNO MIDL: ABSORBED MU&WG IN 1882	11	41	52
SNO MILEAGE OF LV/LACK	05	32	182
SNO MILEAGE/# OF LOCOS MKT/CP/NH/B&M/CN	03	32	522
SNO MILW: "HIAWATHA" LOCOS	11	35	82
SNO MILW: 10641 MILES/708 LOCOS/MERGER??	04	56	41
SNO MILW: 11242 MILES/1649 LOCOS/EQUIPMN	05	34	85
SNO MILW: 1718 LOCOS/"PIONEER LIMITED"	01	32	259
SNO MILW: 1ST PASSENGER TRAIN	08	35	86
SNO MILW: A SHORT HISTORY	10	32	412
SNO MILW: AIR LINE CLASSIFICATION	10	52	125
SNO MILW: ALL DOME LOUNGE CARS HIAWATHA	09	52	58
SNO MILW: ANDOVER-BRAMTON BRANCH ABANDON	11	41	49
SNO MILW: BELLEVUE & CASCADE A PART OF	04	35	86
SNO MILW: BELLEVUE & CASCADE BECAME PART	07	48	67
SNO MILW: BELLEVUE TO CASCADE IA ABANDON	06	36	83
SNO MILW: BELLEVUE-CASCADE BRANCH	11	33	90
SNO MILW: BRANCH LINES NOT OPERATED	08	40	64
SNO MILW: CHICAGO MILW & GARY LINE	02	33	83
SNO MILW: CHICAGO MILW & PUGET SOUND	01	34	88
SNO MILW: CHICAGO TERRE HAUTE & SOUTHEAS	10	33	44
SNO MILW: COOLS CARS WITH STEAM	01	35	86
SNO MILW: DIESELIZED/1 ELECTRIC LOCO	08	57	40
SNO MILW: DISCONTINUED PASS SERVICE MINN	10	33	46
SNO MILW: DIVISIONS	03	35	85
SNO MILW: DIVISIONS	11	45	53
SNO MILW: DIVISIONS IN 1930	10	73	58
SNO MILW: DIVISIONS.	11	49	71
SNO MILW: ELECTRIC LOCOS/STEAM LOCOS	01	37	86
SNO MILW: ELECTRIC POWER ON PASS SERVICE	11	30	600
SNO MILW: ELECTRIFICATION	11	50	137
SNO MILW: ELECTRIFIED MILES	08	37	59
SNO MILW: FIRE TRUCK TURNTABLE RIDE	08	51	131
SNO MILW: HIAWATHA EQUIPMENT WHEREABOUTS	02	69	33
SNO MILW: HIAWATHA TYPE LOCOS	03	36	84
SNO MILW: HIAWATHA USES 4-6-4 OR 4-4-2	05	36	81
SNO MILW: HIAWATHAS STREAMLINED PHOTOS	09	48	94
SNO MILW: KANSAS CITY MO BRIDGE SOLD	10	51	141
SNO MILW: LOCOS #10300, #10308 W	02	57	40
SNO MILW: LOMBARD MONT ONLY BY RR	10	40	122
SNO MILW: MILEAGE/SIGNALS/LOCO #2407	07	31	534
SNO MILW: NAME CHANGES/REVENUE/ORGANIZED	06	38	75
SNO MILW: NAROW GAGE BRANCH ABANDONED	08	33	121
SNO MILW: PASSENGER TRAINS NEW COLORS	10	56	76
SNO MILW: PIG'S EYE YARD	12	55	06
SNO MILW: POLES ON INSPECTION CAR	06	45	59
SNO MILW: RADIO OUTFITS	08	47	63
SNO MILW: RENUMBER LOCOS/WHY?	12	38	70
SNO MILW: REPLACEING STEAM POWER	05	51	137
SNO MILW: STATUS ON ELECTRIC DISTRICTS	08	68	30
SNO MILW: STEAM & ELECTRIC	01	37	89
SNO MILW: TAKES OVER DSC&M	07	33	84
SNO MILW: TAKES OVER I&WN IN 1916	02	35	85
SNO MILW: TIGER HOTEL BURKE IDAHO	08	54	18
SNO MILW: USE OF ELECTRIC POWER 1968	05	68	27
SNO MILW: VINING IA STATION CLOSED	07	52	133
SNO MILW: ELECTRIFICATION IN WASHINGTON S	03	70	37
SNO MILW: PASSENGER EQUIP LIVERY CHANGES	06	69	39
SNO MILWAUKEE INTERURBAN LINES	04	47	73
SNO MIND: CHICAGO & SOUTHWESTERN PREVIOU	11	38	72
SNO MINNC: ALWAYS PART OF MILW & ST PAUL	01	34	90
SNO MINV: MONTOUR OWNS COMMON STOCK	08	47	63
SNO MIT	11	33	88
SNO MIT: ABANDONMENT IN FUTURE	08	43	141
SNO MIT: BOUGHT CMI TRACK	09	31	189
SNO MIT: INCORP IN 1892/COLORADO MIDLAND	11	34	92
SNO MIT: INCORPORATED 1892	05	72	56
SNO MIV: 363 MILES/EQUIPMENT/MANAGEMENT	04	32	71
SNO MIV: INCORP 1903/COMPLETED 1906	08	56	38
SNO MIV: INCORP IN 1903/MILES/FINANCIAL/	11	34	96
SNO MJ&KC: BECAME GM&O	01	45	15
SNO MJ: BRIEF HISTORY	04	66	38
SNO MJK&R: ACQUIRED BY B&O	04	33	116
SNO MJK&R: SOLD TO B&O 1932/1 LOCO SCRAP	10	33	48
SNO MK&E: MERGED IN 1890/BECAME MKT	05	35	86
SNO MKT: 1799 MILES/EQUIPMENT	07	33	84
SNO MKT: AUTOMATIC FLOOD SIGNAL DEVICE	06	50	63
SNO MKT: DIVISIONS	11	34	94
SNO MKT: EMBLEM	01	53	43
SNO MKT: HOW MKT GOT ITS TRADEMARK	09	39	51
SNO MKT: INCORP IN 1899/CONSOLIDATION	05	35	86
SNO MKT: LARGEST ALL FREIGHT LINE 1965	10	65	28
SNO MKT: PAINTS CABOOSES YELLOW	12	41	81
SNO MKT: PASS/FRT LOCOS	04	38	52
SNO MKT: POSEY HOLE BRIDGE PROJECT	09	47	73
SNO MKT: RACE OF 1870	05	47	129
SNO MKT: RECORD BUILT SHOO-FLY	08	77	57
SNO MKT: SHORT-WAVE RADIO	04	48	66

STEPHANS' RAILROAD DIRECTORY

Railroad/Railfan

RAILROAD HISTORIES & ROSTERS

SHORT NOTES ON...	M	Y	P
SNO MKTX: 1389 MILES/EQUIPMENT	07	33	84
SNO MKTX: DIVISIONS	11	34	94
SNO ML&TC: 1905-1915/FLORIDA/10 MILES/7 T	12	46	105
SNO MLCO: MONTOUR RR SUBSIDIARY	11	77	26
SNO MLR: 3' GAGE/NAME CHANGES	05	37	36
SNO MLR: FROM BODRL	12	74	57
SNO MM&S: MERGED WITH LS&I IN 1923	10	47	70
SNO MM&W: 1902 LEASED TO NYNH&H	08	33	88
SNO MM&W: FORMED 1898 MERGED NYNH&H 1905	10	75	54
SNO MM: 6 MILES/2 LOCOS/1 MISC CA/6N CONT	07	32	511
SNO MMA: 1949/STANDARD GAGE	11	49	123
SNO MMI: THE ROAD GROWS	07	84	28
SNO MN&S: COMPLETELY DIESELIZED/BOXCARS	02	58	39
SNO MN&S: INCORP 1918/74 MI/EQUIPMENT	01	41	76
SNO MN&S: INCORP 1918/74 MILES/EQUIPMENT	12	35	80
SNO MN&S: NEVER AN ELECTRIC LINE	02	43	147
SNO MNJ: MERGED TO BECOME PART OF NYS&W	11	34	93
SNO MO: 2' GAGE/8 MILES/EQUIPMENT	11	32	470
SNO MO: 2' GAGE/MAINE/NOW ABANDONED	01	44	118
SNO MO: 3 PHOTOS/BRIEF HISTORY	02	40	124
SNO MO: 6 MILES/FREIGHT=SLATE/MAINE/2' G	12	55	29
SNO MO: ABANDONED 1944/EQUIPMENT WHERE?	06	59	37
SNO MO: BRIEF HISTORY/PHOTO ESSAY	02	42	22
SNO MO: INCORP 1882/MAINE/2' GAGE/FREIGH	10	40	70
SNO MO: MAINE/TWO BY SIX	10	59	35
SNO MO: NAR GAGE/1 FATAL ACCIDENT 37 YRS	10	31	427
SNO MO: NARROW GAGE/6.6 MILES/2 LOCOS	06	31	443
SNO MOMI: MAID OF THE MIST INCLINE	08	77	10
SNO MON: 178 MILES/EQUIPMENT	02	34	88
SNO MON: CORRECTION FEB 1934	04	34	86
SNO MON: INCORP IN 1900/55 LOCOS	02	35	84
SNO MONR: STILL ON PAAPER IN 1835	05	51	67
SNO MONS: TO DA 1905	07	74	39
SNO MONT: INCORP 1917/CONSOLIDATION/MILE	08	47	62
SNO MONT: SOLD RECENTLY	04	47	49
SNO MONT: SOLD TO P&LE	01	47	134
SNO MONT: 45 MILES/INCORP 1917 AS CONSOLI	10	37	69
SNO MONT: INCORPORATED 1913 CONTROLED PRR	02	72	61
SNO MONT: SHORT HISTORY	11	77	26
SNO MONTA: BUILT 1897-8/COPPER ORE HAULR	03	50	123
SNO MONTL: COLORADO NARROW GAGE/LOGGING	06	56	37
SNO MONTREAL & BYTOWN RY: BROAD GAGE LIN	11	33	79
SNO MORB: GOV MORRIS BUILT/2 M/NY&H OWNS	09	34	86
SNO MP&G: INCORP IN 1906/BECAME GN&A	03	37	61
SNO MP: 111 POWER DIESEL UNITS	01	48	73
SNO MP: 1155 LOCOMOTIVES	05	34	83
SNO MP: ABSORBED SLIM&S	06	48	16
SNO MP: AIRBRAKE INSTRUCTION CAR	02	49	64
SNO MP: CENTRAL KANSAS-COLORADO DIV	01	48	72
SNO MP: CENTRALIZED TRAFFIC CONTROL PLAN	05	49	55
SNO MP: CHARTERED 1849/OPENED 1852	01	36	81
SNO MP: DE SOTO NEW CAR CONSTRUCTION SHP	04	48	78
SNO MP: EAGLE MERCHANDISE CLEANED OUTSID	04	52	75
SNO MP: EAGLES (STREAMLINED PASS CARS)	02	49	96
SNO MP: FLAGGING--READER MEMORIES	08	47	129
SNO MP: GREAT RADIO INSTALLATION PROGRAM	08	51	67
SNO MP: IMPROVEMENT PROGRAM FOR 1951	07	51	68
SNO MP: LOCOMOTIVE NUMBERS/TYPES	03	33	89
SNO MP: MODERNIZED FRT/PASS SERVICE	06	59	10
SNO MP: NEW METHOD TO HAUL TRUCKS	12	56	28
SNO MP: ROADS ABSORBED BUT RETAIN IDENTI	06	34	87
SNO MP: ROADS TAKEN OVER SINCE 1912	09	34	84
SNO MP: ROADS WHICH ARE PART OF	08	34	87
SNO MP: ROADS WHICH BECAME PART OF	03	38	60
SNO MP: ST LOUIS FREIGHT TERMINAL	05	52	63
SNO MP: STYLIZED EAGLE LOGO PHOTO	01	69	17
SNO MP: TRAIN WASHER ST LOUIS PHOTO ESSY	05	49	77
SNO MP: WIDENED ROADBED	01	34	90
SNO MP: CONTROLED SLIM&S	11	74	52
SNO MP: RECEIVERSHP 1909 NEW MP 1917	11	74	52
SNO MPR&DE: 1907/ELECTRIC LINE/NOW DPE	08	43	80
SNO MPR&DE: BECAME PARAT OF MN&S	01	41	76
SNO MR&BT: BRIEF HISTORY CHARTERED 1890	10	69	34
SNO MR&BT: EARLY INFORMATION	01	70	37
SNO MR&LE: CHARTERED 1832/COMPLETED 1844	11	49	66
SNO MR&LE: CHARTERED 1832 OPENED 1835	03	76	56
SNO MR&NW: REORGANIZED IN 1909 AS RCBH&W	12	53	69
SNO MRCC: B&O AND B&SQ PREDECESSOR	04	71	62
SNO MRIL: LEASES LINE TO MCRI	10	36	71
SNO MRL&M: 33 MILES/EQUIPMENT	03	32	521
SNO MRL&M: INCORP 1904/33 MI/EQUIP/FINAN	08	35	83
SNO MRL: LOCOS/WEST VA/LOGGING ROAD	04	57	46
SNO MRNJ: OPENED IN 1874/41 MILES/	04	36	90
SNO MRS: CONDUCTS RAILWAY OPERATIONS	11	43	58
SNO MRS: IN ITALY PHOTO ESSAY	08	45	85
SNO MS&NI: BECAME LS&MS	08	53	63
SNO MS&NI: BECAME PART OF LS&MS	06	35	82
SNO MS&NI: PART OF OLD LS&MS	08	41	70
SNO MS: 1886-1941/EQUIPMENT	10	43	73
SNO MS: 1886/15 FRT CARS/7 MISC CARS	11	40	75
SNO MSCR&B: INCORP 1884/BECAME MS 1886	11	40	75
SNO MSCR&B: INCORP 1884/BECAME MS IN '86	10	43	73
SNO MSM&A: CHARTERED 1883/NOW SOO	12	34	83
SNO MSM&A: SUCCEEDED BY SOO LINE 1888	05	37	37
SNO MSOK: BECAME ORW/OKLAHOMA/1902-	06	45	78
SNO MSPR&D: DAN PATCH LINES/SOLD 1918	12	35	80
SNO MSRW: 4 MODERN CARS	11	53	103
SNO MSSRY: 1883/CABLE CARS	11	45	96
SNO MT&MW: CROOKEDEST RAILWAY IN WORLD	08	31	43
SNO MT&MW: RESULT OF NAME CHANGE 1913	05	37	37
SNO MT&MW: BUILT 1896 CROOKEDEST IN WORLD	10	71	45
SNO MT&W: INCORP 1912/WAS RY/EQUIPMENT	05	48	67
SNO MTA: EAST BOSTON EXPANSION	07	51	65
SNO MTA: EXTENSIONS/BRB&L LINES	12	54	49
SNO MTA: FOLLOWS BRB&L TRACKS INTO LYNN	03	55	60
SNO MTA: MILLIONS FOR HUB TRANSIT	09	46	107
SNO MTA: RAPID TRANSIT	12	51	88
SNO MTCE: BUILT 1900 DIED 1927	05	72	57
SNO MTCE: APPROX 1900/7 TO 1924	11	34	93
SNO MTCO: SUBSIDIARY OF B&M	03	54	125

Railroad/ Railfan

RAILROAD HISTORIES & ROSTERS

SHORT NOTES ON...	M	Y	P
SNO MTCO: TERMINAL RR OWNED BY B&M	09	37	65
SNO MTE&G: 3 MILES/MONCTON NB CANADA	01	50	90
SNO MTRR: INCORP IN 1907/STD GAGE/EQUIP	11	34	90
SNO MTU: INCLINE RAILROAD NO LONGER	02	51	138
SNO MTWC: PURCHASED APC STREETCARS/#'S	01	49	91
SNO MU&WG:	10	33	43
SNO MU&WG: CHARTERED 1881/BECAME MIDL	11	41	52
SNO MUN	09	32	234
SNO MUN: 1864/BECAME W&NB IN 1921	02	41	70
SNO MUN: ORGANIZED 1864/BECAME W&NB	01	52	48
SNO MUN: OPENED 1864 TO W&NB	07	75	53
SNO MV&MT: CHARTERED 1896/CALIFORNIA	05	37	37
SNO MV&MT: CHARTERED 1896 TO MT&MW 1913	06	75	30
SNO MV: FOUNDED 1874/3' GAGE/9 MI/SOLD	06	55	36
SNO MV: 3 FT GAGE OF MASS	03	69	23
SNO MVE: ABANDONED 1917/9 MILE	11	52	89
SNO MVRR: CONSOLIDATION/1870	07	32	509
SNO MVT: BECAME ILLINOIS TERMINAL SYSTEM	11	36	57
SNO MW&CR	08	33	88
SNO MW&CR: FORMED 1888 LEASED NY&NE 1892	10	75	54
SNO MW&S: INCORP 1909/MONTANA/26 MILES	01	37	87
SNO MW: 1924/1932 REORGANIZATION	12	35	81
SNO MW: CHARTERED IN 1853	01	33	99
SNO MWP: LARGEST W VA ELCTRIC SYSTEMS	09	48	108
SNO MXC: METAL CABS/WOODEN DESTROYED BY	01	44	39
SNO N&A: PHOTO ESSAY	02	51	16
SNO N&A: INCORP 1903/EQUIPMENT/11.5 MILE	12	45	64
SNO N&AT: 1900/ELECTRICALLY POWERED	12	54	58
SNO N&B: 12 MILES/5 LOCOS/6 CARS	11	31	491
SNO N&B: CHARTERED 1902/12 MILES/PENNSYL	09	36	76
SNO N&B: FREIGHT LINE/PA/8.5 MI/EQUIPMEN	09	52	124
SNO N&C: BECAME ACL 1900 NOW SCL	06	73	49
SNO N&CA: BECAME SP/WAS CA&C	05	53	140
SNO N&CH: "TENNESSEE" FIRST LOCO	02	52	56
SNO N&CH: CHARTERED 1845	11	48	23
SNO N&CRR: INCORP 1902/CONSOLIDATION	05	42	63
SNO N&K: BECAME PART OF N&CRR IN 1902	05	42	63
SNO N&L: INCORP 1835/B&L LEASED/B&M LEAS	02	40	122
SNO N&L: INCORPORATED 1835 NOW B&M	02	73	49
SNO N&LSRR: CHARTERED IN 1857	12	34	83
SNO N&M: CHARTERED 1900/8 MILES/NOW PRR	09	35	85
SNO N&M: INCORP 1900/NEW YORK/8 MILES	12	36	52
SNO N&NW: RESULT OF MERGER IN 1879	01	35	85
SNO N&NW: TAKEN OVER BY GT/THEN CN	01	34	88
SNO N&OV: REBUILT TO STANDARD GAGE 1893	12	54	58
SNO N&PB: MAHONE ROUTED FEDERAL TROOPS	10	57	76
SNO N&PBL: 9 ROAD CONTROL	09	52	106
SNO N&PMT: 1906/ABSORBED NR&LC	12	54	59
SNO N&PT: LEASED NEWPORT NEWS RY & LIGHT	03	50	75
SNO N&RRV: ABSORBED BY T&P IN 1901	10	42	63
SNO N&S: 1923 TO 1935/41 MILES	09	37	64
SNO N&S: INCORPORATED 1923 DIED 1935	03	75	12
SNO N&S: OLNY CLASS I ROAD TO BUILD STM	09	54	28
SNO N&SG: BECAME CGA	06	72	60
SNO N&SL: 18 MILES/EQUIPMENT	12	31	96
SNO N&SL: INCORP IN 1911/18 MILES/EQUIPM	08	35	83
SNO N&SP: BECAME PART OF G&F IN 1907	06	41	61
SNO N&SP: BECAME PART OF G&F IN 1907.	03	36	83
SNO N&SP: BECAME PART OF G&F IN 1927	03	39	75
SNO N&SV: NOW SUSQUEHANNA RIVER & WESTRN	07	32	510
SNO N&W: 100 YEARS OLD	12	38	131
SNO N&W: 4-8-4 CLASS J LOCO OPERATING SC	12	49	54
SNO N&W: BRIDGE #861 MAYBERRY WV	11	46	63
SNO N&W: BRYAN BEARD, PHOTOGRAPHER	04	56	04
SNO N&W: CINCINNATI TO PORTSMOUTH IMPROV	10	46	54
SNO N&W: COAL & WATER STOPS/CLASS J LOCO	03	52	56
SNO N&W: COINCIDENCES	03	43	120
SNO N&W: CONVERTS COAL TO OIL-BURNERS	05	47	68
SNO N&W: DERECO HOLDING CO (EL/D&H)	07	71	43
SNO N&W: DISPUTANTA VA	12	47	138
SNO N&W: FEB 11 1950 DIESEL LOCOS	07	50	128
SNO N&W: LIST OF LOCOS ORDERED IN 1949	05	50	65
SNO N&W: LOCOS ORDERED 2-8-8-2/2-6-6-4	09	48	78
SNO N&W: LONGEST STOPPAGE OF TRAFFIC	11	52	132
SNO N&W: LOW WATER ALARMS	02	56	38
SNO N&W: MODERNIZATION PROJECT	05	47	139
SNO N&W: NEW DIESEL-STEAM INFORMATION	12	58	36
SNO N&W: NEW STREAMLINE INTRODUCED	08	46	35
SNO N&W: OUTSTANDING SAFETY MEDALS	02	49	110
SNO N&W: OWNS 36 Y6 TYPE MALLETS	12	41	81
SNO N&W: POCAHONTAS DIVISION MEMORIES	04	45	39
SNO N&W: PURCHASED CHW	12	54	41
SNO N&W: PURCHASES 8 GENERAL PURPOSE LOC	10	55	04
SNO N&W: ROANOKE SHOP SMOKE ABATER	01	49	66
SNO N&W: SELLS LOCO #200-5 CLASS K3-RF&P	01	45	40
SNO N&W: SMOKE ABATER--HOW IT WORKS	01	49	66
SNO N&W: STEAM & DIESEL POWER--STATUS	08	58	39
SNO N&W: STEAM-TURBINE LOCO	04	55	27
SNO N&W: SWIFTEST TRAIN ON	09	38	56
SNO N&W: TIE PLATE	12	44	42
SNO N&WO: CHARTERED 1836 NOW NYNH&H	12	71	57
SNO N&WO: READER INFORMATION	06	72	62
SNO NA&B: OPENED 1873	01	73	60
SNO NA&B: OPENED IN 1876/24 M/ACTON ROAD	07	34	90
SNO NA&LE: INTERURBAN WITHIN CITY LIMITS	07	46	132
SNO NA&SA: 1847/FORERUNNER TO MONON	05	49	21
SNO NA&SA: COMPLETED 1854/NOW MONON	10	56	45
SNO NA: A&GWW AND ED&BC MERGED W IN 1930	04	34	84
SNO NA: INCORP IN 1929/OWNED BY CP & CN	04	35	86
SNO NANC: IN 1897 NRR BECAME NANC	02	35	84
SNO NAU: INCORP 1845/CONN/LEASED TO NH	12	56	30
SNO NBCC: CHARTERED 1858 BRIEF HISTORY	11	70	42
SNO NBL: ST AUGUSTINES HORSE CAR LINE	02	61	36
SNO NBP: 23 MILES/ST JOHN NB CANADA	01	50	90
SNO NC&SL: ABANDONMENT OF 16.5 MILES	01	51	132
SNO NC&SL: ABSORB NASHVILLE &CHATTANOOGA	02	52	56
SNO NC&SL: CAPSHAW BRANCH ABANDONED 1929	03	45	77
SNO NC&SL: DIESELIZED JAN 5 1953	08	56	38
SNO NC&SL: DIXIE LINE BRIDGE	06	46	71
SNO NC&SL: ETOWAH RIVER CUTOFF	12	49	59

Railroad/Railfan

RAILROAD HISTORIES & ROSTERS

SHORT NOTES ON...	M	Y	P
SNO NC&SL: FERRY TRANSFER SERVICE	08	32	53
SNO NC&SL: GRANDPA'S ROAD/1902 MEMORIES	05	52	134
SNO NC&SL: LONGEST RIVER TRANSPORT	10	50	56
SNO NC&SL: MERGED W/L&N/CHANGES	08	59	38
SNO NC&SL: MERGER WITH L&N	03	72	63
SNO NC&SL: OLD GABRIEL-NO MORE!	07	50	130
SNO NC&SL: WHEN TIME STOOD STILL	02	45	06
SNO NC: 3' GAGE/93 MILES	01	34	92
SNO NCE: NOW PART OF PRR	04	53	134
SNO NCN: INCORP 1874/3' NARROW GAGE/20 M	10	36	74
SNO NCN: INCORP IN 1874/3' GAGE/21 MILES	09	34	83
SNO NCO: BRIEF HISTORY	02	67	26
SNO NCO: CHARTERED 1888/3' GAGE/EQUIP/MI	07	35	82
SNO NCO: WHAT HAPPENED TO 3 LOCOS	10	55	36
SNO NCR: CHARTERED IN 1837	07	36	85
SNO NCR: COMPLETED 1842/1ST IN ILLINOIS	10	56	40
SNO NCRY: FAILED IN 1870'S/BECAME QMO&O	08	35	83
SNO NCST: CHARTERED 1901/13 MILES/TROLLY	05	48	94
SNO NCT: OPENED 1902/4 MILES	12	44	81
SNO ND&C: INCORP IN 1877/59 MILES/EQUIPM	04	34	85
SNO ND&C: STATE LINE CT TO NY NOW NH	08	34	85
SNO ND: 1907-1919/1 LOCO/1 PASS/2 FRT CR	04	33	94
SNO ND: INCORPORATED 1907 DIED 1919	02	74	52
SNO NDRY: INCORPORATED 1907--DIED 1910	09	72	53
SNO NE: THIRD-RAIL INTERURBAN/NOW SN	02	57	42
SNO NERR: ACQUIRED BY NHNH&H 1895	07	74	40
SNO NERR: LEASES N&WO 1869 TO NYNH&H	12	71	57
SNO NEZ: BACKGROUND	07	77	49
SNO NF&G: CHARTERED 1926/ABSORBED 3 ROAD	04	59	38
SNO NF: 1096 MILES/3'6" GAGE/LOCOMOTIVES	04	33	96
SNO NF: BECAME PART OF CN/700 MILES	01	50	126
SNO NF: DELUXE PASSENGER COACHES	10	49	55
SNO NFALLS	05	34	86
SNO NFL&P: 3 MILES/ST JOHNS CANADA	01	50	91
SNO NFWP&C:	05	34	86
SNO NGRR: SHORT HISTORY	06	67	08
SNO NH&I: BRIEF HISTORY	10	66	60
SNO NHM&W: CHARTERED 1867 TO B&NY 1873	10	75	52
SNO NHSL: INCORP 1923/ABSORBED SLE	10	41	72
SNO NHSL: INCORPORATED 1923 DIED 1929	10	74	46
SNO NI&N: LEASED BY MP	06	34	87
SNO NI&SM: FORMED FROM MICHS & NI 1855	03	76	57
SNO NIAGC	05	34	86
SNO NIPC: 60 MILES/NO EQUIPMENT	05	51	62
SNO NJ&NY: OWNED BY ERIE	02	59	44
SNO NJ&P: 1905 FORMED RESULT OF REORGANI	12	31	96
SNO NJ: QUEBEC ROAD/OWNED BY D&H/28 MILE	01	34	87
SNO NJER: MERGED IN 1881 TO FORM NYS&W	04	36	90
SNO NJI&I: 12 MILE BRANCH OF WABASH	12	46	82
SNO NJI&I: BRIEF HISTORY	04	62	44
SNO NJI&I: INDUSTRIES SERVED	08	70	35
SNO NJI&I: ORIGIN OF ITS NAME	06	62	06
SNO NJJ: ORGANIZED 1886/LEASED BY NYC	11	38	72
SNO NJM: CHARTERED 1870/88 MILES	04	36	89
SNO NJM: MOST NOW PART OF ERIE NYS&W LIN	04	36	90
SNO NJRT: POPOVER STOPOVERS	09	49	74
SNO NJS: ABSORBED BY CNJ	04	49	128
SNO NJUN: 44 MILE FREIGHT LINE	12	56	27
SNO NJUN: SHORT HISTORY	08	66	32
SNO NKP: "COMMERCIAL LIMITED" RUN	11	31	489
SNO NKP: 6 WHEELERS NUMBER CONVERSIONS	10	52	127
SNO NKP: ABSORBS TSL&W IN 1923	09	34	83
SNO NKP: CLEVELAND TO CHIGAO OVERNITE FR	03	47	70
SNO NKP: CLOVER LEAF DIVISION	10	53	68
SNO NKP: CONNEAUT OHIO /BUFFALO YARDS/	08	59	35
SNO NKP: DIESEL ROAD LOCOS	02	48	76
SNO NKP: DOUBLE TRACK MILEAGE	03	42	70
SNO NKP: HISTORY OF NAME	11	72	54
SNO NKP: HOW IT GOT ITS NAME	12	54	41
SNO NKP: HOW IT GOT ITS NAME!	11	38	72
SNO NKP: INCORP 1881/ROADS ABSORBED	04	57	40
SNO NKP: NAME ORIGIN	10	59	35
SNO NKP: NEW YORK CHICAGO & ST LOUIS	07	34	92
SNO NKP: OPERATED DINING CARS	08	49	139
SNO NKP: PORTIONS CENTRALIZED TRAFFIC CO	03	50	61
SNO NKP: VAN SWERINGEN EMPIRE BRIEF HIST	01	66	26
SNO NLACK: 1901	03	39	74
SNO NLL: CHARTERED 1873/ 39 MILES/	03	39	76
SNO NLW&P: SIGNAL AT WILLIMANTIC POSITIO	01	47	128
SNO NLW&S: CHARTERED 1847	03	72	63
SNO NM&C: ACQUIRED BY EP&S IN 1914	01	37	88
SNO NM&C: TO EP&S 1914	04	75	12
SNO NMC: ORGANIZED IN 1908/CONSOLDIATION	11	34	94
SNO NMICH: INCORP 1888/BECAME CRA 1899	03	49	60
SNO NMM: ORGANIZED 1904	03	74	34
SNO NMM: ORGANIZED IN 1904/1 LOCOMOTIVE	01	39	63
SNO NN&H: PURCHASED NNR&L	03	50	75
SNO NN: EMBLEM	09	52	52
SNO NN: INCORP 1905/EQUIPMENT/MILEAGE	04	38	51
SNO NN: INCORP 1906/NEVADA/141 MILES/EQU	01	40	51
SNO NN: INCORPORATED 1905	02	76	47
SNO NN: OWNED BY KENNECOTT COPPER CORP	07	40	68
SNO NN: PURCHASED BY LA DEPT OF WATER &	09	87	30
SNO NNB&S: INCORP 1909/16MILES/CANADA	05	54	12
SNO NNR&L: LEASED BY N&PT	03	50	75
SNO NNY: NOW RUTLAND/1ST REEFERS	02	52	55
SNO NO&C: 1901 REORGANIZED/WAS NO&C	08	52	85
SNO NO&C: 1835-1894/STREET RY/8 MILES	10	48	70
SNO NO&C: BEGAN 1835	08	52	82
SNO NOC&L: ORGANIZED IN 1883	08	52	83
SNO NOF: ABSORBED BY RV IN 1905	01	42	64
SNO NOF: ACQUIRED BY RAHWAY VALLEY RR	12	36	51
SNO NOH: NO LOCOMOTIVES	12	32	106
SNO NOH: OWNED BY AKRON CANTON& YOUNGSTO	10	34	86
SNO NOP: ABSORBED BY T&P IN 1881	10	42	63
SNO NOPB: ORGANIZED 1904/43 MI MAIN LINE	07	53	48
SNO NOPS: 6 TROLLEY ROUTES	08	49	99
SNO NOPS: READER COMMENTS ON VARIOUS LIN	11	49	85
SNO NOPS: USED NEUTRAL GROUND/ABSORPTION	08	52	85
SNO NOR&LC: 1905/WAS NEW ORLEANS RAILWAY	08	52	85

Railroad/Railfan

RAILROAD HISTORIES & ROSTERS

SHORT NOTES ON...	M	Y	P
SNO NORL: CONSOLIDATIONS	08	52	85
SNO NORTH: BECAME N&NW IN 1879	01	35	85
SNO NORY: LESES MC&LM/ NOW PART OF PRR	01	34	90
SNO NOT&P: LEASED BY MP	06	34	87
SNO NOY: LEASED TO THE RUTLAND	08	46	17
SNO NP&R: INCORPORATED 1880 NOW CP	06	72	60
SNO NP: 600 MEN RESTORED TO PAYROLL	01	31	285
SNO NP: ACQUIRES SP&DUL VARIOUS TIMES	04	36	93
SNO NP: BRAKEMAN'S FATE VEILED IN MYSTER	01	46	47
SNO NP: CAR FOR ICING EXPRESS REEFERS	08	39	67
SNO NP: CASCADE MOUNTAINS-NO CLICKETY CL	04	54	85
SNO NP: CLASS 3000 MALLETS/ROCKY MT DIV	06	32	337
SNO NP: DIVISIONS	03	35	85
SNO NP: EMBLEM (HISTORY OF)	12	76	03
SNO NP: EMBLEM ORIGIN	05	55	36
SNO NP: FARGO & SOUTHWESTERN BRANCH	11	33	89
SNO NP: FIFTY YEARS IN THE CAB/MEMORIES	10	44	08
SNO NP: FIRST LAKE TO SEA ROUTE	04	76	53
SNO NP: FIRST RAIL LAID 1870	02	57	44
SNO NP: HERALD	08	45	46
SNO NP: HOPPERS TUNNEL NOW DAYLIGHT	03	53	135
SNO NP: LEASES SLS&E IN 1892	04	33	97
SNO NP: LINES FINISHED	05	32	179
SNO NP: LOCO CLASSES/WEIGHTS/TRACTIVE FO	07	31	537
SNO NP: LOCOMOTIVES OWNED	05	47	67
SNO NP: LOMBARD MONT ONLY BY RR	10	40	122
SNO NP: MALLET LOCOS STILL IN USE	03	55	28
SNO NP: MERGER WITH GN PLANS TO 1893	06	70	60
SNO NP: MILEAGE/SIGNALS/SPRAGUE AUTO CON	07	31	534
SNO NP: MINNESOTA ROAD	02	55	14
SNO NP: MULLAN TUNNEL-NEW VENTILATION	06	49	62
SNO NP: N DAKOTA LINE RELOCATION	12	46	83
SNO NP: ORIGIN OF HERALD	03	74	33
SNO NP: PURCHASED CDR&N IN 1897	12	58	38
SNO NP: RADIO COMMUNICATION INSTALLATION	06	52	61
SNO NP: RADIO NETWORK INSTALLATION PROGR	09	53	71
SNO NP: RAIL MARKINGS	03	65	48
SNO NP: ST PAUL TO DULUTH LINE	12	34	83
SNO NP: TEST RUN OF EMD 4500 HP DIESELS	05	47	110
SNO NP: UNIQUE DEVICE TRACKS TRAINS	05	31	238
SNO NP: WHERE SOME LOCOS ARE USED NOW	12	55	35
SNO NP: WORDS ON RAILS MEAN	12	31	91
SNO NPA: CHARTERED 1852	02	52	58
SNO NPA: NO LOCOS/NO TRACK/NO CARS	08	51	129
SNO NPC: 4-4-0 LOCO #16, #18 LOCOS CORRE	04	54	16
SNO NPC: CHARTERED 1871/SOLD 1902 TO NS	09	40	65
SNO NPC: FIRST CAB-IN-FRONTIER	08	44	69
SNO NPC: INCORP 1871/BECAME NS IN 1902	08	55	46
SNO NPIER: INCORPORATED IN 1875/8 MILES	07	38	76
SNO NPIER: SHORT HISTORY	09	66	A8
SNO NPOLE: 60 MILES/SUSPENDED 1916-17	03	34	83
SNO NPRR: CHARTERED 1871 SOLD TO NS 1902	05	74	47
SNO NR&LC: DOUBLE TRACK/ABSORBS	12	54	58
SNO NRC: ABSORBED TS&LH IN 1858	11	47	20
SNO NRC: CONSOLIDATED 1879 TO N&NW	10	73	58

SHORT NOTES ON...	M	Y	P
SNO NRC: NOW PART OF CN	10	35	85
SNO NRNJ: OWNED BY ERIE/NO STEAM LOCOS	11	53	53
SNO NRR: OPENED 1881 BECAME NANC 1897	06	74	20
SNO NRR: OPENED IN 1881/ABANDONED 1917	02	35	84
SNO NRWM: PASSENGER TRAIN ONCE A MONTH	08	56	74
SNO NS&M: BECAME MONT 1913	02	72	61
SNO NS&M: BECAME PART OF MONTOUR RR	04	36	91
SNO NS&M: MERGED TO BECOME MONT/1917	08	47	63
SNO NS&M: SHORT HISTORY	11	77	26
SNO NS: 1902/SP OWNS/PART OF NWP	08	55	45
SNO NS: 805 MILES/EQUIPMENT	11	40	71
SNO NS: ALBEMARLE SOUND TRESTLE	10	53	68
SNO NS: FAILED IN 1870'S/BECAME QM0&0	08	35	83
SNO NS: NEW MANAGEMENT/READER COMMENTS	01	48	137
SNO NS: PURCHASED NPC IN 1902/NOW NWP	09	40	65
SNO NS: QM0&0 BECAME	03	52	54
SNO NS: STREAMLINED RAIL BUSES	09	53	67
SNO NSC&T: 5 PASSENGER CARS/EXRESS SERVI	01	51	97
SNO NSC&T: IMPROVEMENTS	12	52	95
SNO NSC&T: INCORP IN 1899/BRIEF HISTORY	05	34	86
SNO NSC&T: LINES STILL INSERVICE/BUS TRA	05	42	66
SNO NSC&TN: STOCK OWNED BY NSC&T	05	34	86
SNO NSC: 25 MILES/HALIFAX NS CANADA	01	50	91
SNO NSO: 42 MILES OF ELECTRIC ROAD	04	34	85
SNO NSO: 930 MILES/105 LOCOS/EQUIPMENT	01	34	92
SNO NSO: ACQUIRES SUFFOLK & CAROLINA	03	39	76
SNO NSRY: HALIFAX NOVA SCOTIA	10	54	44
SNO NST&PC: HALIFAX NOVA SCOTIA	10	54	44
SNO NSUB: 1935/UTILIZED MORRIS CANAL BED	10	40	66
SNO NT&NW: 1906/ABSORBED BY FDM&S	06	35	85
SNO NTRC: OPENED 1915 EASTERN END OF GTP	09	73	40
SNO NV: STOCK VALUE	04	37	53
SNO NW: LEASED TO NPC IN 1886	08	55	46
SNO NWL: CHANGED COLOR-COACHES & PULLMAN	11	31	491
SNO NWP: 441 MILES/61 LOCOMOTIVES	02	33	84
SNO NWP: ACQUIRES PETALUMA & SANTA ROSA	10	36	73
SNO NWP: ALL PURPOSE LOCO #99	04	68	26
SNO NWP: ALMOST ALL DIESEL/ORIGINAL EQUI	01	54	109
SNO NWP: BORROWED 12 WHEELERS FROM SP	12	55	38
SNO NWP: CONSOLIDATIONS	09	40	65
SNO NWP: EQUIPMENT	09	31	188
SNO NWP: EUREKA TO SAUSALITO RUNS	12	31	95
SNO NWP: INCORP 1907/CONSOLDIATIONS	08	55	45
SNO NWP: PT REYES BRANCH (NARROW GAGE)	12	34	82
SNO NWP: STEAM POWER IN 1920	08	78	56
SNO NWP: TUNNELS	04	49	133
SNO NWSOP: LINE WEST OF OCEAN VIEW	12	54	58
SNO NY&B: 1869/BECAME NYC PUTNAM DIVISIO	02	59	36
SNO NY&B: ORGANIZED IN 1869/NOW NYC&N	06	35	82
SNO NY&E: INCORP 1832/BECAME ERIE	10	37	68
SNO NY&E: MUST OPERATE IN NYS/AMENDED	06	56	39
SNO NY&E: ORGANIZED IN 1832	09	31	190
SNO NY&GL: 1878/REORGANIZATION OF M&GL	04	36	90
SNO NY&H: BUYS MORRIS BRANCH IN 1853	09	34	86
SNO NY&H: LEFT SIDE RAILROAD	01	68	27

Railroad/Railfan

RAILROAD HISTORIES & ROSTERS

SHORT NOTES ON...	M	Y	P
SNO NY&H: NEW YORK'S EARLIEST STREET RY	02	46	09
SNO NY&H: OPENED IN 1871	09	34	86
SNO NY&LB	03	33	92
SNO NY&LB: BRIEF HISTORY	02	62	51
SNO NY&LB: JOINTLY OWNED	02	59	44
SNO NY&LB: OWNED BY CNJ	11	36	58
SNO NY&M: BUILT LINE IN 1872	09	34	86
SNO NY&MA: ABSORBED BY P&E	04	34	85
SNO NY&MA: CONSOLIDATED 1887 HR&B PH&B	11	73	57
SNO NY&MB: BECAME NYB&MB IN 1885	09	35	87
SNO NY&MB: CONSOLIDATED THEN LI LEASED	09	73	42
SNO NY&MB: INCORP IN 1876	08	32	57
SNO NY&MB: LEASED TO LI 1882	03	74	33
SNO NY&NE: FORMED IN 1873/REORGANIZATION	08	34	85
SNO NY&NE: NOW PART OF NYNH&H	01	35	82
SNO NY&NE: NOW PART OF NYNH&H.	03	38	57
SNO NY&NE: NOW PART OF NYNH&H/GHOST TRAI	06	57	40
SNO NY&NE: OPENED 1882/NOW PART NYNH&H	03	38	58
SNO NY&O: CHARTER 1897 BANK 1900 TO NYC	05	75	51
SNO NY&O: CHARTERED 1897/BANKRUPT 1900	04	33	94
SNO NY&OM: AUBURN BRANCH	07	32	507
SNO NY&OM: BECAME NYO&W IN 1880	02	38	59
SNO NY&OM: OPERATED NEW JERSEY MIDLAND	04	36	89
SNO NY&OM: ORGANIZED 1866 BECAME NYO&W	11	72	54
SNO NY&OM: ORGANIZED 1866/BANKRUPT 1873	12	35	83
SNO NY&P: 57 MILES/EQUIPMENT	04	32	69
SNO NY&P: BRIEF HISTORY	06	67	34
SNO NY&QC: 1909	10	51	83
SNO NYA&L: CHARTERED 1900/IN 1914 CNYS	02	54	75
SNO NYB&J: BECAME NYB&MB 1885	09	35	87
SNO NYB&J: CONSOLIDATED 1885 LI LEASED	09	73	42
SNO NYB&MB: 1885 CONSOLIDATION/LI LEASED	09	35	87
SNO NYB&MB: BRANCH OF LONG ISLAND RR	08	32	57
SNO NYB&MB: BRIEF HISTORY	04	67	33
SNO NYB&MB: CONSOLIDATION THEN LI LEASE	09	73	42
SNO NYB&N: 1872/CONSOLIDATION	02	59	37
SNO NYBR&J: INCORP IN 1875	08	32	57
SNO NYBR&J: OPENED 1877 NY&MB LEASES '78	03	74	33
SNO NYBR&J: OPENED 1877/NARROW TO STD GA	02	33	87
SNO NYC&HR: ACQUIRED LS&MS IN 1898	06	35	82
SNO NYC&HR: ACQUIRED NYWS&B	02	38	61
SNO NYC&HR: ACQUIRED SL&AD IN 1898	11	40	73
SNO NYC&HR: ACQUIRES NYWS&B IN 1886	12	35	83
SNO NYC&HR: FIRST MAJOR CONSOLIDATIONS	05	42	63
SNO NYC&HR: LEASED DAV&P IN 1873	06	39	52
SNO NYC&HR: NEW YORK & HARLEM CONSOLIDAT	09	34	86
SNO NYC&HR: NOW PART OF NYC	12	35	39
SNO NYC&HR: RIVER DIVISION	12	33	93
SNO NYC&HR: TRACK SCOOP	06	45	61
SNO NYC&HR: W VANDERBLT QUOTES	08	63	30
SNO NYC&N: BRIEF HISTORY	02	67	26
SNO NYC&N: ORGANIZED IN 1878	06	35	82
SNO NYC&SL: NICKEL PLATE ROAD	11	38	72
SNO NYC: PHOTO ESSAY	04	49	78
SNO NYC: "RAILROAD COWBOYS" NO MORE	07	41	69
SNO NYC: 107 TON STEEL GIRDER TRANSPORTD	12	51	67
SNO NYC: 12,050 MILES/US LARGEST ROAD	07	32	506
SNO NYC: 20TH CENTURY LIMITED	05	43	89
SNO NYC: 225 HUDSON TYPE LOCOS/#S/WHERE	10	32	350
SNO NYC: 300 STEAM LOCOS SCRAPPED	12	52	124
SNO NYC: 406 PASSENGER STATIONS FOR SALE	12	56	07
SNO NYC: 503 STEAM LOCOS SCRAPPED 1945-	06	50	61
SNO NYC: 9 WHEELER LOCO	01	53	137
SNO NYC: ABSORBED ZANESVILLE & WESTERN	08	56	44
SNO NYC: ACQUIRES CONTROL OF RUTLAND '05	03	32	518
SNO NYC: ACQUIRES RAQUETTE LAKE RAILWAY	09	32	231
SNO NYC: AUTOMATIC TICKET-SELLING MACHIN	01	53	131
SNO NYC: BENTON HARBOR ROUNDHOUSE/MEMORI	01	48	132
SNO NYC: BLAUVELT NY STATION	08	53	117
SNO NYC: BRIEF HISTORY	05	40	81
SNO NYC: CAR-WASHING MACHINES HIGH BRIDG	12	50	55
SNO NYC: CATSKILL MOUNTAIN BRANCH (U&D)	01	33	97
SNO NYC: CATSKILL MT BRANCH OF RIVER DIV	07	36	86
SNO NYC: CLASS 5200 LOCO DRIVERS	08	31	46
SNO NYC: COLLECTOR SHOES	07	45	79
SNO NYC: COMMUTER TRAIN DELAYS EXPLAINED	05	54	120
SNO NYC: COMPLETELY DIESELIZED	10	57	40
SNO NYC: CTC SYSTEM	10	57	06
SNO NYC: DE-STREAMLINING LOCOS	11	48	123
SNO NYC: DEATH AVENUE NEW YORK	07	70	56
SNO NYC: DEWITT CLINTON CARS	01	49	118
SNO NYC: DIALING A DIESEL	01	55	37
SNO NYC: DIESEL LEVIATHANS	04	47	72
SNO NYC: DIESEL-ELCTRIC HUMP YARD SWITCH	08	46	57
SNO NYC: DIVISIONS	03	32	521
SNO NYC: DOUBLE ENDER	01	31	281
SNO NYC: DOUBLE TRACKING/FOUR TRACK MILE	10	55	32
SNO NYC: DOUBLE/TRIPLE/MAIN TRACKS	03	36	83
SNO NYC: ELEVATOR ALBANY NY 30 YRS TO FX	01	52	129
SNO NYC: EMPIRE STATE EXPRESS	10	72	53
SNO NYC: EQUIPMENT	06	34	84
SNO NYC: FEDERAL VALLEY LINES	09	32	233
SNO NYC: FIRST FLUORSCENT LIGHTING	01	74	12
SNO NYC: FOUR TRACK TWIN LIFT BRIDGE	11	53	112
SNO NYC: FREIGHT CAR/ "S" PRECEDING #	10	41	71
SNO NYC: FREIGHT CARS W/ LETTER S	07	46	54
SNO NYC: GOODBYE TO FERRIES PHOTO ESSAY	10	59	17
SNO NYC: GRADE CROSSING ELIMINATION PROJ	11	71	38
SNO NYC: GRAND CENTRAL TERMINAL	06	50	12
SNO NYC: GRAND CENTRAL TERMINAL-ELECTRIC	04	43	99
SNO NYC: HOSPITAL CAR/IRON LUNG/TRANSPOR	07	50	137
SNO NYC: HOT-BOX ALARM	03	47	71
SNO NYC: HOTBOX DETECTORS	04	59	38
SNO NYC: KILLS DEER--REEFERS DROP SALT	08	48	130
SNO NYC: LAST PASS TRAIN LEAVES SYRACUSE	10	54	06
SNO NYC: LAST STEAM & HUDSON TYPE	06	62	46
SNO NYC: LEASES DH&S FOR FREIGHT SERVICE	04	54	10
SNO NYC: LEASES OHIO CENTRAL LINES	03	33	94
SNO NYC: LIST OF RAILROADS CONSISTING OF	12	55	68
SNO NYC: LITTLE FALLS-DODGEVILLE BRANCH	12	42	43

Railroad/ Railfan

RAILROAD HISTORIES & ROSTERS

SHORT NOTES ON...	M	Y	P
SNO NYC: LIVERY ON FIRST 20TH CENTURY LT	10	68	35
SNO NYC: LOCOS USED/ELECTRIFICATION	08	32	53
SNO NYC: LONGEST PASS TRAINS/NEW YRS EVE	05	43	138
SNO NYC: MAGIC TRAY MEAL ON UPSTATE SPEC	05	52	136
SNO NYC: MARINE EQUIPMENT	03	41	72
SNO NYC: MARINE EQUIPMENT USED 1940	12	73	51
SNO NYC: MERGED WITH LS&MS IN 1914	08	53	63
SNO NYC: MICHC/BIG FOUR/NYC LOCOS RENUMB	04	37	52
SNO NYC: MICHIGAN CENTRAL DIV "WOLVERINE	07	54	60
SNO NYC: NEW YORK CITY COWBOY LOCATIONS	12	71	11
SNO NYC: NYC TO BUFFALO/ROADS ABSORBED	11	43	61
SNO NYC: NYC&HR CHANGES NAME TO NYC 1914	09	34	86
SNO NYC: NYWS&B NOW PART OF NYC	12	36	50
SNO NYC: ORDERS 387 DIESELS-EQUIP/BLDRS	08	51	65
SNO NYC: ORDERS DIESELS (111)	06	48	58
SNO NYC: ORDERS MORE DIESEL UNITS	11	47	88
SNO NYC: ORIGIN OF TERM REDCAPS	02	47	124
SNO NYC: ORIGNIAL EMBLEM	02	55	28
SNO NYC: OWNS 41 WRECKING CRANES	04	36	87
SNO NYC: OWNS NEW YORK & OTTAWA	04	33	94
SNO NYC: PACEMAKER FREIGHT SERIVE	08	46	60
SNO NYC: PACEMAKER FREIGHT SERVICE	08	49	58
SNO NYC: PETERS CREEK BRANCH	08	52	121
SNO NYC: PETTY LARCENY SELF SERVICE NEWS	07	52	127
SNO NYC: PITTSBURG & LAKE ERIE PART OF	01	34	88
SNO NYC: PITTSBURGH & LAKE ERIE PART OF	09	32	233
SNO NYC: PUTNAM DIV CONSTRUCTION DATE/MI	01	49	59
SNO NYC: PUTNAM DIV CONSTUCTION DATES/MI	10	49	59
SNO NYC: PUTNAM DIV/HARLEM DIVISION	09	34	86
SNO NYC: PUTNAM DIVISION CORRECTION	03	49	137
SNO NYC: PUTNAM DIVISION BEGINNINGS	02	59	36
SNO NYC: PUTNAM DIVISION/DIESELS	11	51	61
SNO NYC: ROADS COMPRISING NYC	04	33	96
SNO NYC: ROUNDHOUSES	10	54	41
SNO NYC: RW&O NOW PART OF NYC	09	37	65
SNO NYC: SEALED BEAM HEADLIGHTS	07	48	133
SNO NYC: SHENANGO BRANCH	12	34	85
SNO NYC: SOLD 36 PASSENGER STATIONS	10	58	36
SNO NYC: SOLD MOST OF STATIONS	06	59	08
SNO NYC: STAR/CIRCLE ON BOXCARS	12	47	79
SNO NYC: STEAM LOCO IDLE/BABY RACCOONS	01	53	125
SNO NYC: STEAMERS FOR DISPLAY	12	61	58
SNO NYC: STEAMERS/STORED WHERE/HOW MANY/	02	59	38
SNO NYC: STREAMLINED LOCOS (4)	03	37	60
SNO NYC: SUBSIDIARIES "S" FRT CARS WHY?	01	36	81
SNO NYC: SUBSIDIARIES LOCOS RENUMBERED	05	37	38
SNO NYC: SUBWAY-ELEVATED MILES	10	54	40
SNO NYC: TEN DIVISION NAMES	10	71	45
SNO NYC: TEN RR THAT MADE UP THE NYC	07	78	56
SNO NYC: TILLY FOSTER IRON MINE	01	53	63
SNO NYC: TIMETABLE OF FAST FREIGHT SYSTE	11	50	62
SNO NYC: TRACK RELOCATION	04	47	52
SNO NYC: TUGBOAT W/CHEVRON MARKINGS-SIGN	11	53	50
SNO NYC: TUGBOATS	01	53	61
SNO NYC: TWIN LIFT SPAN/BRONX 138TH STN	10	53	66
SNO NYC: WATER LEVEL ROUTE IMPROVEMENTS	06	51	72
SNO NYC: WEST SHORE DIV 1942	06	75	30
SNO NYC: WEST SHORE DIVISION	07	38	75
SNO NYC: WHITE STAR ON BOXCARS INDICATES	06	56	37
SNO NYC: YONKERS EDITORIAL	07	51	129
SNO NYCE: $400,000 PER MILE	07	40	71
SNO NYCE: 9TH AVE ELEVATED DISMANTLED	03	41	68
SNO NYCE: STEA/ELECTRIC/MAY BE ABANDONED	06	55	27
SNO NYCRR: SHORTEST CLASS 1 ROAD/CONNECT	10	36	69
SNO NYCS: BLUE LIGHT CORRECTION	06	58	73
SNO NYCS: BLUE LIGHTS = EMERGENCY EXITS	02	58	41
SNO NYCS: MILEAGE/PASSENGER CARS	10	56	40
SNO NYCS: NEW MOTORS FOR GE SUBWAY CARS	02	48	78
SNO NYCS: OPENED 1904/ADDED DIVISIONS	03	55	58
SNO NYCTA: 3 DIVISIONS/STATISTICS	08	45	49
SNO NYCTA: CAR #13 IN ARKANSAS/HISTORY	12	53	92
SNO NYCTA: HORIZONTAL CONVEYOR BELTS	02	55	43
SNO NYCTA: IMPROVING GRADUALLY	03	54	118
SNO NYCTA: KEROSENE LAMPS TO BE REPLACED	10	54	72
SNO NYCTA: LINKS 6TH AVE & BMT CULVER LI	06	54	91
SNO NYCTA: LOST AND FOUND SHOP	01	55	49
SNO NYCTA: THIRD-RAIL PHONE COMMUNICATIO	02	55	62
SNO NYLE&W: 1878 REORGANIZATION	10	37	69
SNO NYNH&H	03	33	92
SNO NYNH&H: "GHOST TRAIN"/"WHITE TRAIN"	12	31	93
SNO NYNH&H: 10 RECTIFER ELECTRIC LOCOS	06	53	59
SNO NYNH&H: 14" RULE	02	40	118
SNO NYNH&H: 2082 MILES/EQUIPMENT	07	33	84
SNO NYNH&H: 5 ELECTRIC FREIGHT LOCOS	01	43	81
SNO NYNH&H: ACQUIRED NY&NE	05	36	42
SNO NYNH&H: AIR-CONDITIONED	11	43	61
SNO NYNH&H: AUTO CONTROL/SELF-PROPELLED	04	56	04
SNO NYNH&H: BERLIN-MIDDLETOWN BRANCH	08	33	88
SNO NYNH&H: BOAT TRAIN FALL RIVER LINE	08	78	55
SNO NYNH&H: BOSTON TO HARLEM FRT TRAIN S	05	41	45
SNO NYNH&H: BOUGHT FIRST ELECT LINE 1895	04	47	64
SNO NYNH&H: BRIEF HISTORY CHARTERED 1872	04	69	30
SNO NYNH&H: CAPACITORS--WOODMONT TOWERS	11	48	53
SNO NYNH&H: COMMUTERS	10	51	63
SNO NYNH&H: CONSIST OF "ROGER WILLIAMS"	04	58	39
SNO NYNH&H: CUTS FARES	06	49	136
SNO NYNH&H: DANDURY BRANCH ELECTRIFICATI	07	76	51
SNO NYNH&H: DIESELIZATION MAYBROOK NY TO	11	47	83
SNO NYNH&H: DIESELIZED 1952/3 MIKADO	12	59	06
SNO NYNH&H: DISCONTINUED LINE/LOCOS	09	32	236
SNO NYNH&H: DRAWBRIDGE OPERATIONS	03	47	73
SNO NYNH&H: ELECTRIC LOCOS	06	31	444
SNO NYNH&H: ELECTRIFICATION READERS COMM	07	75	05
SNO NYNH&H: GASOLINE RAILCARS/GAS-ELECTR	11	40	71
SNO NYNH&H: GRAND CENTRAL TRAINS	05	44	77
SNO NYNH&H: INDUCTION TRAIN COMMUNICATIO	10	45	50
SNO NYNH&H: LAST PASSENGER SERV HARLEM	11	68	35
SNO NYNH&H: LAST STEAM POWER	09	74	42
SNO NYNH&H: LAST STEAM RUNS	06	65	38
SNO NYNH&H: LEASED OCO	02	59	37

Stephans_Railroad_Directory

Railroad/Railfan

RAILROAD HISTORIES & ROSTERS

SHORT NOTES ON...	M	Y	P
SNO NYNH&H: LEASES MM&W	08	33	88
SNO NYNH&H: LEASES OLD COLONY IN 1893	12	33	93
SNO NYNH&H: LINES/PREVIOUS OWNERS OF LIN	03	38	57
SNO NYNH&H: LIST OF PRESIDENTS	04	40	76
SNO NYNH&H: LOCOS NUMBERED 1000 TO 1095	04	31	121
SNO NYNH&H: M DUMPING EQUIPMENT	04	47	134
SNO NYNH&H: MERCHANTS LIMITED	04	44	77
SNO NYNH&H: MERGED WITH SL&N IN 1898	09	54	30
SNO NYNH&H: NANTASKET BRANCH ELECTRIFIED	12	44	46
SNO NYNH&H: NY&NE BECOMES PART OF NYNH&H	08	34	85
SNO NYNH&H: NY&NE NOW PART OF NYNH&H	01	35	82
SNO NYNH&H: NYC SELSS 1/2 INTEREST OF RU	03	32	518
SNO NYNH&H: PASS BUSINESS INCREASE	07	52	137
SNO NYNH&H: PROVIDENCE-WORCESTER LINE	06	52	67
SNO NYNH&H: RADAR-EQUIPPED TUGS	03	48	58
SNO NYNH&H: RENAISSANCE TWR WATERBURY CT	02	46	62
SNO NYNH&H: SHEPAUG BRANCH	11	47	129
SNO NYNH&H: SL&N MERGED WITH IN 1898	07	41	66
SNO NYNH&H: SOUTH STN BOSTON MA CHAPEL	03	55	69
SNO NYNH&H: STATE LINE CT TO NY/WAS ND&C	08	34	85
SNO NYNH&H: STRETCHES OF FREE TRACK	08	41	71
SNO NYNH&H: TRACKAGE	09	34	81
SNO NYNH&H: TROLLEYS ON THE TRACK	05	75	51
SNO NYNH&H: TUNNEL/HOUSATONIC RIV BRIDGE	10	47	125
SNO NYO&W: ACQUIRES PART OF NYWS&B	12	35	83
SNO NYO&W: CLOSE SHAVE--READER MEMORIES	08	47	125
SNO NYO&W: CREAMERIES/READER MEMORIES	01	47	136
SNO NYO&W: DIESELIZATION PLANS	02	47	122
SNO NYO&W: INCORP IN 1880/REV/EQUIP/MILE	02	38	59
SNO NYO&W: LOCOS LEASED TO OTHER ROADS	12	57	46
SNO NYO&W: MOUNTAIN ROAD	05	43	105
SNO NYO&W: SHAWANGUNK BARRIER:COMMENTS	01	47	126
SNO NYO: SUBURBAN CAR LINE/10 MILES	12	48	102
SNO NYP&B: BUILT 1884 NYNH&H LEASES 1889	09	76	52
SNO NYP&B: LEASES P&W TO NYNH&H 1892	12	75	56
SNO NYP&B: NOW PART OF NEW HAVEN	01	36	41
SNO NYP&C: TO BE "WORLD'S MOST MODERN RR	11	37	52
SNO NYP&N: NOW PART OF PRR	03	35	86
SNO NYP&O: A&GW REORGANIZED AS	09	31	190
SNO NYP&O: ATLANTIC & GREAT WESTERN BECO	10	37	68
SNO NYP&O: BRIEF HISTORY	07	65	31
SNO NYPO&D: NOW LEASED TO PRR	11	31	491
SNO NYR&M: NOW RUTLAND RAILROAD	04	40	79
SNO NYRY: INCORP 1909/STREET RY ROCHESTR	10	48	85
SNO NYRY: LOW LEVEL DOUBLE DECK TROLLEY	10	34	87
SNO NYS&W: 1ST CLASS I RR ALL DIESEL	10	45	49
SNO NYS&W: CONSOLIDATION 1893/EQUIP/MILE	05	34	82
SNO NYS&W: CONTROLLED BY ERIE	05	34	82
SNO NYS&W: CONTROLS WILKES BARRE & EASTR	08	32	54
SNO NYS&W: INCORPORATED 1893 BRIEF HISTO	10	70	20
SNO NYS&W: MAINLINE OPERATION	02	59	44
SNO NYS&W: NO LONGER IN RECEIVERSHIP	12	53	63
SNO NYS&W: RESULT OF CONSOLIDATION 1881	11	34	92
SNO NYS&W: ROADS WHICH MERGED TO FROM	04	36	90
SNO NYW&B: ORGANIZED IN 1910/ELECTRIC	02	41	71
SNO NYW&P: ACQUIRED BY NYC&N IN 1878	06	35	82
SNO NYW&R: JAMAICA BAY ROUTE	01	34	93
SNO NYWS&B: 1880/BANKRUPT 1886/NYC&HR	12	35	83
SNO NYWS&B: BUILT IN 1884	12	33	93
SNO NYWS&B: NOW WEST SHORE RAILROAD	02	40	121
SNO NYWS&B: ORGANIZED IN 1880/NOW NYC	12	36	50
SNO O&AL: CHARTERED IN 1849/NOW SOUTHERN	09	36	74
SNO O&AL: MERGED IN 1867 W/MANASSAS GAP	12	55	35
SNO O&E: LEASED HB&TD IN 1904/MERGED NWP	08	55	46
SNO O&ES: BOUGHT CALIFORNIA & NEVADA	08	31	47
SNO O&FRR: INCORP IN 1925	09	34	84
SNO O&G: NOW PART OF CN	03	52	125
SNO O&H: INCORP 1908/NOW SOUTHERN NY RY	11	37	53
SNO O&LC: CONSOLIDATED WITH RUTLAND 1901	08	46	17
SNO O&LC: MERGED WITH RUTLAND IN 1898	03	32	518
SNO O&M: "THE DEEPO"/READER MEMORIES	04	46	108
SNO O&M: ABSORBED PANA & SPRINGFIELD RR	11	42	68
SNO O&M: MERGED IN 1893 W/B&O SOUTHWESTR	01	35	87
SNO O&MV: BECAME SOUTHERN NEW YORK RAILW	11	37	53
SNO O&NW: DEMISE	07	84	28
SNO O&NW: INCORP 1934/OREGON/50 MILES	06	36	84
SNO O&PA: STARTED 1892 LOCATED CAMMAL PA	07	73	40
SNO O&PA: SUBSIDIARY OF SP	12	35	40
SNO O&SA: MULE CAR/ELECTRIFIED IN 1895	12	53	98
SNO O&W: ABSORBED BY W&T IN 1899	04	40	77
SNO O&WE: COMPLETED 1899	05	52	88
SNO O&WT: BECAME W&CR IN 1892	03	38	54
SNO O&WT: BUILT 1890 BECAME W&CR THEN NP	11	74	52
SNO O&WT: NOW PART OF NP	07	36	84
SNO OA&M: MERGER 1867/NOW PART OF S	12	55	35
SNO OC&A: CONSOLIDATION/OPENED 1865-66	09	37	63
SNO OC&FR: NAMED 1854 MERGER 1863 W/OC&N	01	76	39
SNO OC&N: TO OC 1872 (SECOND TIME)	01	76	39
SNO OC&P: BUILT IN 1865	01	33	97
SNO OC&RS: FOUNDED 1906/NOW SNY	11	37	53
SNO OC: LEASED TO NYNH&H 1893	01	76	39
SNO OCCRR: BECAME PART OF PRSL IN 1933	04	39	74
SNO OCITY: INCORP 1923	09	37	63
SNO OCO: 1ST TO USE CONTAINERS	06	51	71
SNO OCO: CHARTERED 1844 TO OC&FR	01	76	39
SNO OCO: DUDE TRAIN OF 1884	06	75	30
SNO OCO: DUDE TRAIN--SUBSRIBERS ONLY	10	52	67
SNO OCO: INCORP 1872//LEASED TO NYNH&H	02	59	37
SNO OCO: LEASES PLYMOUTH & MIDDLEBOROUGH	12	33	93
SNO OCRR	11	33	88
SNO OCRR: BECAME PART OF L&HR IN 1907	03	36	83
SNO OCS: INCORP 1908/EQUIPMENT	06	38	73
SNO OCS: INCORPORATED 1908 DIED 1926	10	72	53
SNO OCT: FORMATION	03	78	48
SNO OCT: FORMATION.	07	77	04
SNO OCT: FORMED 1976 X PC OCTORARO BRANC	12	76	59
SNO OE: INCORPORATED IN 1906	11	38	72
SNO OE: OWNED BY SP&S	01	75	54
SNO OER: FORMED 1907	11	52	88
SNO OER: LIST-INTERURBANS WHICH BECAME	09	53	76

Railroad/Railfan

RAILROAD HISTORIES & ROSTERS

SHORT NOTES ON...	M	Y	P
SNO OG&NE: ABSORBED BY T&P IN 1915	10	42	63
SNO OH&IN	01	33	99
SNO OH&MO: BERKEY TO MORENCI	01	37	89
SNO OH&MO: INCORP 1933/21 MILES OF T&WE	11	36	53
SNO OH&PA	01	33	99
SNO OHIO: ORGANIZED 1836/ON STILTS	12	49	55
SNO OHIOC: 800 MILES	04	33	94
SNO OHIOC: EMERGENCY FUEL (DEAD PIG)	01	33	48
SNO OKC&E: NOW PART OF CB&Q	08	34	87
SNO OKT: STANDARD GAGE	01	52	102
SNO ON: FORMERLY SVT	11	52	90
SNO ON&W: 38 MILES/EQUIPMENT	07	33	85
SNO ON&W: ABANDONED 1954/38 MI/TENNESSEE	07	54	115
SNO ON: 1946/WAS T&NON	05	51	61
SNO ON: NAME CHANGE 1946/WAS T&NON	01	55	43
SNO ONO: INCORP IN 1915/EQUIP/FINANCIAL	11	34	96
SNO OP&E: SHORT HISTORY	08	77	56
SNO OP: 5 MILE ROAD/"OREGON PONY" LOCO	11	34	91
SNO OR&LC: 1889/90 MILES	10	46	84
SNO OR&LC: BRANCH DISTRUCTION BY US NAVY	08	78	06
SNO OR&LC: OUT OF RY BUSINESS/SELLS EQUI	05	51	137
SNO OR&W: 3' GAGE/ABANDONED	06	32	336
SNO OR&W: BELLAIRE ZANESVILLE & CINCINNA	05	34	131
SNO OR&W: CHARTERED 1872 BRIEF HISTORY	08	69	26
SNO OR&W: CHARTERED 1903 RECEIVER / BZ&C	06	73	48
SNO OR&W: CHARTERED 1903/NOW ABANDONED	10	35	86
SNO OR&W: NARROW GAUGE OF PRR 1930	12	75	57
SNO ORL: ORGANIZED IN 1867	08	52	83
SNO ORRY: INCORP IN 1881/EQUIPMENT/MILE	04	34	84
SNO ORW: 78 MILES/INTERURBAN/HISTORY	06	45	78
SNO ORWO: SHANNON CONVENTION 1888 STRIKE	02	51	38
SNO ORY: RESUME RAIL OPERATIONS	03	51	128
SNO OS&H: BECAME NORTHERN RY IN 1858	01	35	85
SNO OS&H: FIRST LOCO "LADY ELGIN"	05	70	38
SNO OS&H: NAME CHANGED TO NRC 1858	10	73	58
SNO OS: COMPLETED IN 1909/MILES/EQUIPMEN	04	32	70
SNO OSA: 18 MILES/OKLAHOMA/1 LOCO/2 CARS	08	39	68
SNO OSC: BRIEF HISTORY	03	78	53
SNO OSGOOD BRADLEY CAR CO-TO SSC 1910	03	69	24
SNO OSL: ACQUIRED BY UP IN 1899	03	36	83
SNO OSL: MILES IN 1890	08	76	51
SNO OSL: SPLASL ACQUIRES PART ROADS FROM	05	41	48
SNO OSO: ORGANIZED IN 1881/ EQUIPMENT	07	34	92
SNO OSO: SPRINGFIELD SOUTHERN BECAME OSO	07	34	92
SNO OT: ONE DIESEL LOCO	09	50	91
SNO OTN&W: ABSORBS PONTIAC PACIFIC JCT	04	33	95
SNO OTN&W: LEASED TO CP 1902	09	74	43
SNO OTRY: OWNED BY SP&S	01	75	54
SNO OV: TAKEN OVER BY IC IN 1897	11	33	91
SNO OVER: INCORP 1904/BECAME TK&N 1912	02	36	85
SNO OWB&FL: NOW PART OF MONON	05	49	26
SNO OWR&N: ACQUIRED BY UP IN 1899	03	36	83
SNO OWR&N: OWNED BY UP	04	33	94
SNO OWR&N: SNOW PLOW AND YARD DALLES OR	01	76	41

SHORT NOTES ON...	M	Y	P
SNO P&AR: PART OF WP&Y/FREIGHT/PARLOR CO	03	55	65
SNO P&B: 1893-1903/EQUIPMENT	11	44	55
SNO P&B: OPENED 1893 FROM P&R DIED 1903	10	75	53
SNO P&BR: 95 MILE TERMINAL FREIGHT ROAD	10	55	36
SNO P&BRRR: FREIGHT TERMINAL ROAD/EQUIPM	06	42	92
SNO P&C: STARTED 1834/STATE-OWNED	05	54	122
SNO P&CA: PROJECTED TROLLEY LINE	10	48	67
SNO P&CE: ABSORBED BY PORTLAND IN 1901	07	53	76
SNO P&CF: CHARTERED 1838/FERRY SERVICE	08	52	131
SNO P&CRR: INCORP IN 1887	03	34	84
SNO P&CRR: PART ABANDONED/P&E/NYNH&H	03	38	58
SNO P&CS: PITTSBURGH RY WANTS TO ABANDON	08	54	91
SNO P&D: 7 1/2 MILES	08	51	68
SNO P&D: OPENED 1872/NOW PART OF IM	03	39	75
SNO P&E: CHARTERED 1866 BECAME PH&B 1875	11	73	57
SNO P&E: CHARTERED IN 1866/SOLD IN 1875	02	35	85
SNO P&E: CHARTERED IN 1893/40 MI/EQUIPMN	04	34	85
SNO P&E: OPENED 1872/NOW PART OF NYNH&H	03	38	57
SNO P&E: PART BECAME NYNH&H	03	38	58
SNO P&EA: 21 ROAD & YARD SWITCHING DIESE	02	52	56
SNO P&EA: 212 MILES	04	33	94
SNO P&EA: 212 MILES/EQUIPMENT	12	31	96
SNO P&EAST: INCORP 1907/OREGON/33 MILES	10	36	70
SNO P&ERR: CLOSED TRACK CIRCUIT 1ST USED	08	52	64
SNO P&ERR: EMPIRE LINE/FAST FREIGHT LINE	06	42	90
SNO P&F: INCORP 1933/PART OF T&WE BECOME	11	36	53
SNO P&F: ONLY 1/2 MILE NOT ABANDONED!	08	43	130
SNO P&F: PIONEER TO LAYETTE	01	37	89
SNO P&F: US SHORTEST COMMON CARRIER	05	74	46
SNO P&FN:	03	32	520
SNO P&FN: ALWAYS CONTROLLED BY B&M	06	32	335
SNO P&FN: STARTED 1880 DIED 1922 B&M CON	08	74	56
SNO P&FN: SUPPLEMENTAL READER INFORMATIO	09	75	60
SNO P&H: CHARTERED 1875/3'/PA/SOLD 1879	06	45	60
SNO P&HRC: CHARTERED 1880/OLD P&H/SOLD	06	45	60
SNO P&HT: LEASED BY UTRC	04	35	83
SNO P&HT: LEASED BY UTRC IN 1888	04	40	75
SNO P&HT: MERGED TO BECOME P&AT IN 1915	04	49	128
SNO P&I: 1846/BECAME LE&W/THEN NKP	04	57	40
SNO P&IN: INCORP 1899/90 MILES	10	33	45
SNO P&KC: 1872 OIL FIELDS	09	33	136
SNO P&LB: 1880 RAILWAY/MERGED 1883 RR	04	49	128
SNO P&LE: 15 DIESEL SWITCHERS ORDERED	09	47	131
SNO P&LE: CHARTERED IN 1875	12	38	69
SNO P&LE: CONTROLS MONTOUR RAILROAD	11	77	26
SNO P&LE: IDENTITY WIUTH PC	06	68	29
SNO P&LE: INDEPENDENT WITHIN NYC?	02	64	35
SNO P&LE: MARIETTA COLUMBUS & CLEVELAND	09	32	233
SNO P&LE: NYC OWNS 1/2 STOCK	02	36	90
SNO P&LE: ONE OF NYC LINES	01	34	88
SNO P&LT: SOLD AT AUCTION 1911	07	72	62
SNO P&LT: SOLD AT AUCTION/NOW CP&LT	04	35	83
SNO P&M: BRIEF HISTORY	12	65	27
SNO P&M: CHARTERED IN 1890	12	33	93
SNO P&MOR: BECAME MONT 1913	02	72	61

Railroad/ Railfan

RAILROAD HISTORIES & ROSTERS

SHORT NOTES ON...	M	Y	P
SNO P&MOR: MERGED IN 1917 TO BECOME MONT	08	47	63
SNO P&MP: SHORT HISTORY	08	65	20
SNO P&MR: BECAME PART OF MONTOUR RR	04	36	91
SNO P&MR: SHORT HISTORY	11	77	26
SNO P&N: 15 MILE FREIGHT ONLY LINE DIESL	02	55	64
SNO P&N: DISCONTINUE PASSENGER SERVICE?	06	47	104
SNO P&N: ELECTRIC LINE OF THE CAROLINAS	04	44	105
SNO P&N: NOSTALGIA	01	53	87
SNO P&NC: MERGED WITH PN&NY IN 1892	02	52	58
SNO P&NE: INCORPORATED 1890	07	72	63
SNO P&NW: INCORP IN 1890/33 MILES/EQUIP	03	34	85
SNO P&NY: OWNED BY NYS&W	05	34	82
SNO P&NYC: CONTROLLED BY LV	08	46	43
SNO P&NYC: NAMED 1866 BRIEF HISTORY	11	70	42
SNO P&O: MAINE & VERMONT DIVISIONS	03	33	137
SNO P&O: VERMONT DIV SOLD TO SJ&LC 1880	07	35	86
SNO P&R: 1833/1ST TRAIN 1839/	12	39	119
SNO P&R: 1883-1892/LEASES CNJ	03	33	92
SNO P&R: JULY 4 1912/HORSE KICKS CAR	06	47	140
SNO P&R: LEASES W&N IN 1900	07	34	87
SNO P&R: PANIC OF 1893	10	51	127
SNO P&R: SIGNALS--HALL AUTO/TURN TOWERS	03	42	69
SNO P&R: SINGLE TRACK RAILROADING	06	47	139
SNO P&RA: 2' GAGE/28 MILES/MAINE/MOUNTAI	12	55	29
SNO P&RF: 1900 RECOLLECTIONS	08	60	10
SNO P&RF: SHORT HISTORY	02	78	50
SNO P&RO: 1879 TO B&M AND ERM	07	74	40
SNO P&RO: 52 MILES/TODAY FREIGHT SERVICE	07	43	69
SNO P&ROAN: REGULATIONS	03	39	76
SNO P&S: REORGANIZED ALOT/ABANDON 1936	11	51	65
SNO P&SF: 1721 MILES/NO EQUIPMENT	12	31	96
SNO P&SI:	09	33	48
SNO P&SL: BOUGHT PENNSYLVANIA & DELAWARE	06	32	333
SNO P&SP: OPENED 1873/22 MNILES/EQUIPMEN	06	51	69
SNO P&SR: 43 MILES/6 LOCOS/EQUIPMENT	03	32	519
SNO P&SR: INCORP 1903/CONSOLIDATIONS	10	36	73
SNO P&SR: INCORP 1903/HISTORY/EQUIPMENT	05	48	99
SNO P&SR: LATER-DAY OPERATIONS	06	78	57
SNO P&SRR: SURVEYED 1865/EQUIPMENT	11	42	68
SNO P&SS:	09	33	48
SNO P&TH: OPENED 1874/NOW PART OF IM	03	39	75
SNO P&W: 1973 REVIVED AS COMMON CARRIER	05	73	08
SNO P&W: CHALLENGES PRR ON TRACK CONDITI	05	75	37
SNO P&W: INCORPORATED 1844 LEASED NYP&B	12	75	56
SNO P&WAL: BECAME PART OF L&HR	03	36	83
SNO P&WAT: CHARTERED 1852/NOW RW&O	02	37	78
SNO P&WAT: CHARTERED 1852/OPENED 1857	09	37	65
SNO P&WR: PSTC GAINED CONTROL OF IN 1948	08	54	95
SNO P&WRR: COMPLETED 1881/B&O ACQRD 1891	10	40	70
SNO P&WS: ABSORBED BY PSTC	08	54	94
SNO P&WV: FINANCIAL	12	36	51
SNO P&WV: MILES/CUTS/FILLS/BRIDGES/TUNNE	10	35	86
SNO P&WV: WPT BECAME P&WV	10	48	69
SNO P-C: MILITARY RAILROAD	04	42	23
SNO P-PJ: INCORPORATED 1880 TO OTN&W/CP	09	74	43
SNO PA&AT: 1915	04	40	75
SNO PA&AT: 1915/MERGERS	04	49	128
SNO PA&AT: 25 MILES/2 LOCOS/1 PASS CAR	04	34	86
SNO PA&D: INCORP 1873	06	32	333
SNO PA&D: INCORPORATED 1873 TO PO&NE/PRR	08	75	57
SNO PA&DEC: INCORP 1869/NOW PART OF IM	03	39	75
SNO PA&NY: 1915 REORGANIZATION/FORMS	12	31	96
SNO PAJR: BRIEF HISTORY	02	67	27
SNO PAJV: INCORP 1890/3' GAGE/40 MI/EQUI	02	36	84
SNO PAJV: INCORP IN 1890/1929 SOLD TO SP	06	35	82
SNO PAN: 1ST CONTINENTAL RR	01	36	87
SNO PAN: A PROFITABLE RAILROAD	10	76	13
SNO PAN: COAST TO COAST 90 MINUTES	12	45	89
SNO PAN: FINANCIAL	09	40	64
SNO PAN: LOCOS CORRECTIONS	12	48	125
SNO PAN: MANY LOCOS RETURNED TO US	07	48	127
SNO PAN: NOW PANAMA CANAL COMPANY	11	51	123
SNO PAN: READER MEMORIES/PHOTO NOTES	08	48	132
SNO PAS: 1836/"TAPEWORM"	07	42	64
SNO PAWN: ABSORBED BY C&IM IN 1906	09	47	73
SNO PB&E: ORGANIZED 1900 NEVER OPENED	10	73	58
SNO PB&E: ORGANIZED 1900/	06	38	77
SNO PB&E: ORGANIZED 1900/NEVER OPENED	06	38	77
SNO PB&LE: LEASED BY B&LE IN 1900	07	34	90
SNO PB&LE: NOW BESSEMER & LAKE ERIE	06	32	338
SNO PB&LE: ROADS MERGED TO FORM PB&LE	11	64	35
SNO PB&NE: INCORP 1910/LOCOS & BUILDERS	01	32	260
SNO PB&NE: INCORPORATED IN 1920/RUNS 4 M	01	34	92
SNO PB&W: NOW PART OF PRR	04	53	134
SNO PBC: MERGES W/CNE&W IN 1892 NOW CNE	03	34	84
SNO PBC: NOW PART OF NYNH&H	03	38	57
SNO PBRR: CHARTERED 1890/3' GAGE	03	36	81
SNO PC&N: 2 LOCOS/14 MILES/TEXAS	03	53	128
SNO PC&SL: NOW PART OF PRR	11	39	90
SNO PC&T: DISSOLVED IN 1916	10	40	70
SNO PC&Y: 10 MILE SWITCHING LINE	09	43	137
SNO PC&Y: 23 MILES/EQUIPMENT	12	31	96
SNO PC: EXECUTIVE SHAKEUP	09	70	09
SNO PC: RAILROADS OWNED	06	71	44
SNO PC: TRAINING ENGINEERS 1975	02	75	03
SNO PCC&SL: NAME CHANGED FROM PC&SL N/PC	09	73	43
SNO PCEC: 9 MILES/ABANDONED 1930	01	50	90
SNO PCOA: 3' GAGE/103 MILES/EQUIPMENT	09	32	235
SNO PCOA: 3' GAGE/76 MILES/7 LOCOS/DATA	08	33	90
SNO PCOA: ABANDONED 1934	05	34	131
SNO PCOA: CALIFORNIA ROAD	01	34	86
SNO PCOA: FINANCIAL	05	34	83
SNO PCOA: INCORP 1882/3' GAGE/CONSOLIDAT	10	35	87
SNO PCOA: INCORP IN 1882	06	34	88
SNO PCOA: WAS SLO&SM ABANDONED 1940 CA	05	76	26
SNO PCOAST: 1916/WASHINGTON/EQUIP/FINANC	12	36	50
SNO PCOAST: 54 MILES/EQUIPMENT	09	32	235
SNO PCOAST: PREDECESSORS	02	37	80
SNO PCOAST: WASHINGTON ROAD/54 MILES/9 L	01	34	86
SNO PCOAST: WASHINGTON/FREIGHT SERVICE	09	44	65

Railroad/ Railfan

RAILROAD HISTORIES & ROSTERS

SHORT NOTES ON...	M	Y	P
SNO PD&E: 1880/MERGERS	08	51	68
SNO PD&E: 257 MILES/COMPOSED OF SEVERAL	08	38	92
SNO PD&E: CONSOLIDATION 1879 PL&D/DS&M	09	75	57
SNO PD: CONSOLIDATION	04	31	122
SNO PE&NY: CHARTERED 1870	04	49	128
SNO PE&SS: ABSORBED BY PE&NY IN 1879	04	49	128
SNO PE: PHOTO ESSAY	01	41	114
SNO PE: 3 MORE RAIL PASS LINES TO END?	10	52	89
SNO PE: 6 LINES NOW BUSES/CHANGES	06	50	90
SNO PE: ABANDONED SOME PASS SERVCIE	09	50	88
SNO PE: BUSES REFUSED	06	55	46
SNO PE: GREASING TROLLEY CAR #00150	12	53	92
SNO PE: NOW METROPOLITAN COACH COMPANY	11	54	60
SNO PE: OUTRUN METROPOLITAN COACH LINES	01	55	73
SNO PE: OWNS VENICE SHORT LINE	06	48	99
SNO PE: PASADENA SL/SIERRA VISTA LOCAL	10	51	87
SNO PE: PASSENGER SERVICE SOLD	07	53	85
SNO PE: SIZE STATISTICS 1917	12	76	25
SNO PE: TROLLEY GREASER COMMENTS	05	54	110
SNO PECO: CHARTERED 1887/NOW SR&W (1903)	10	50	62
SNO PEI: BRIEF HISTORY	08	78	56
SNO PEMV: LEASED BY B&M IN 1895	01	48	119
SNO PENE: 35 CARS/2 STEAM LOCOS/FLORIDA	12	46	105
SNO PEOP: BECAME SN&SO/THEN LSEL	11	51	78
SNO PEOP: LV LEASES 3 MILES OF TRACK	01	34	90
SNO PEPC: INTERURBAN DIVISION	05	47	93
SNO PET: FIRST INTERSTATE RAILWAY	07	34	45
SNO PET: OPENED 1833	04	58	46
SNO PEXT: MERGED IN 1881 TO FORM NYS&W	04	36	90
SNO PFE: SUPER GIANT FREEZERS FOR FROZEN	04	54	114
SNO PFW&C: CONSOLIDATION OF SEVERAL ROAD	12	38	70
SNO PFW&C: INCORP IN 1862/PRR LEASED	11	32	474
SNO PFW&C: ORGANIZED IN 1856	01	33	98
SNO PG&E: SACRAMENTO ELECTRIC GAS & RY	09	40	141
SNO PGE: 1952 FIRST RUN TO PRINCE GEORG	03	53	130
SNO PGE: DIESEL COLORS/NAME	03	55	39
SNO PGE: EQUIPMENT	05	38	70
SNO PGE: EXPANSION PLAN	04	47	53
SNO PGE: EXPANSION--READER COMMENTS	04	49	132
SNO PGE: INCORP IN 1912	07	36	83
SNO PGE: RENAMED TO BRITISH COLUMBIA RY	02	72	05
SNO PGE: ROSTER/MILEAGE/EQUIPMENT/ROUTE	02	33	87
SNO PH&B: 1875-1887/BECAME NY&MA	02	35	85
SNO PH&B: INCORP IN 1866/BECAME P&E	04	34	85
SNO PH&B: REORGANIZED 1875 CONS NY&MA 87	11	73	57
SNO PH&WH: 17 MILES/ACQUIRD BY LV	08	46	43
SNO PHSR: UNUSUAL SHORT LINE	06	77	49
SNO PHV: ABANDONED IN 1868	01	33	97
SNO PI&RGV: 26 MILES/	10	39	87
SNO PI&RGV: ABANONED 1941/EBONY PILINGS	11	53	49
SNO PI&RGV: TEXAS/EBONY PILING	05	54	120
SNO PI&SH: 1910 NAME CHANGE/104 MILES	01	38	57
SNO PI: SOUTH CAROLINA/9.3 MILES/COMMON	01	55	61
SNO PIER: BUILT 1899 DIED 1905 1ST ELECT	10	76	46
SNO PIGR: 15 MILE/BUILT 1920/BECAME T&NC	01	39	60
SNO PIGR: 1906-1931/12 MILES/T&NC LEASED	09	36	76
SNO PIGR: INCORPORATED 1906 FOLDED 1931	10	75	53
SNO PIT: 13 YEAR BANKRUPTCY/NEW ORGANIZA	05	51	104
SNO PIT: 2 INTERURBAN LINES IN JEOPARDY	05	52	98
SNO PIT: 553 MILES/EQUIPMENT	01	42	65
SNO PIT: BIGGEST STREET CAR SYSTEM IN NA	12	61	55
SNO PIT: ELECTRIC/HORSE CARS/TROLLEYS	05	44	94
SNO PIT: INTERURBAN COMMUNICATION SYSTEM	03	49	81
SNO PIT: PCC CARS/NEW BRIDGE	10	51	86
SNO PL&D: 67 MILES/NOW PART OF IC	08	51	68
SNO PL&D: ORGANIZED 1867 TO PD&E 1879	09	75	57
SNO PL&D: ORGANIZED 1871/NOW PD&E	08	38	92
SNO PL&W: 1896/RESULT OF REORGANIZATION	09	35	83
SNO PL&W: INCORP 1896 & 1902/EQUIP/FINAN	04	41	49
SNO PLC: SF&N ACQUIRED IN 1903/MILEAGE	08	55	46
SNO PLZ&W: INCORP 1918/ILLINOIS/16 MILES	11	38	72
SNO PLZ&W: INCORPORATED 1918	03	73	42
SNO PLZ&W: INCORPORATED 1918 FROM WR&E	08	75	57
SNO PM&C: BECAME PL&W IN 1896	04	41	49
SNO PM&C: CONSOLIDIATES IN 1886	09	35	83
SNO PM&NO: 26 MILES/NOW GULF PORTS TERMI	10	39	87
SNO PM&Y: INCORP 1881/NOW NYC	01	43	82
SNO PM: "CITY OF MIDLAND"	08	41	69
SNO PM: BRIEF HISTORY	12	65	27
SNO PM: BRIEF HISTORY	04	64	28
SNO PM: CAR FERRY #10	06	46	74
SNO PM: CONCRETE ROADBED	05	39	69
SNO PM: MERGED WITH C&O IN 1947	10	47	69
SNO PM: OPERATED PART OF KLS&C	06	35	86
SNO PM: READERS REMINISCENCE	05	43	135
SNO PM: RENUMBERING SCHEME-NEW C&O #S	10	52	62
SNO PMID: MERGED IN 1881 TO FROM NYS&W	04	36	90
SNO PN&NY: INCORP 1876	02	52	58
SNO PNE: 16 MILES	05	37	35
SNO PNE: INCORPORATED 1910 TO SP 1934	05	75	51
SNO PO&D: INCORP 1924/793 MILES	04	31	122
SNO PO&NE: LEASED TO PRR (NOW PC)	08	75	58
SNO PO&NE: POMEROY & STATE LINE BECAME	06	32	333
SNO PO: AUTOGRAPHED LOCOMOTIVES	07	50	06
SNO PO: PURCHASED 2 NEW LOCOS	07	48	125
SNO PONT: CHARTERED 1830	07	73	39
SNO PONT: SHORT HISTORY	06	61	34
SNO PONT: SMOKY MARY PONT #142	07	32	509
SNO PORAM: BECAME PART OF W&NO IN 1905	07	50	64
SNO PORR: BECAME PART OF W&NO IN 1905	04	36	93
SNO POTCR: INCORP 1907/STD GAGE/EQUIPMEN	12	48	69
SNO POV&C: CONSTRUCTION STARTED 1947	06	47	90
SNO PP&B: BECAME L&NE IN 1895	06	68	29
SNO PP&B: OPENED 1890 BECAME L&NE	10	72	53
SNO PP&B: OPENED 1890/BANKRUPT 1891	12	35	83
SNO PP: 1859/BECAME SPA IN 1863	04	46	60
SNO PPCO: GRAVITY RAILROAD CAR	02	51	127
SNO PPJ: INCORPORATED IN 1880	04	33	94
SNO PPSC&T	05	34	86
SNO PR&A: BECAME PART OF C&WC IN 1896	06	41	64

Railroad/Railfan

RAILROAD HISTORIES & ROSTERS

SHORT NOTES ON...	M	Y	P
SNO PR&NE: RESULT OF CONSOLIDATION 1892	03	34	84
SNO PR&NE: SOLD UNDER FORECLOSURE	02	34	86
SNO PR&WC: BECAME PART OF C&WC IN 1896	06	41	64
SNO PRL&P: READER MEMORIES/INTERURBAN DI	07	45	118
SNO PRL&P: REORGANIZED AS PEPC	05	47	95
SNO PRL:	04	46	115
SNO PRR	01	33	99
SNO PRR: "ALLENTOWN ROUTE"	08	72	58
SNO PRR: "FOREIGN LINE" PASES NO MORE	02	55	09
SNO PRR: % OF FREIGHT/PASSENGER BUSINESS	12	46	75
SNO PRR: 124' SUPER FLATCAR DESCRIBED	05	53	60
SNO PRR: 1ST OIL-BURNING STEAM LOCO 1887	01	52	73
SNO PRR: 2-10-2 CLASS N1 LOCOS SCRAPPED	08	56	40
SNO PRR: 214 DIESEL LOCOS ORDERED	01	51	72
SNO PRR: 4 NEW ELECTRIC LOCOS--DATA	06	52	65
SNO PRR: 52 ELECTRIC LOCOS NEAR NY TERMI	12	29	98
SNO PRR: 6352 LOCOS	11	30	599
SNO PRR: ABANDONMENT OF LINE TO TOMS RIV	10	62	36
SNO PRR: ABSORBED GR&I	07	53	54
SNO PRR: ABSORBED M&I	10	56	40
SNO PRR: ACQUIRED ILLINOIS MIDLAND	03	39	75
SNO PRR: ADOPTED NUMBERING SYS FOR LOCOS	11	43	61
SNO PRR: AERO-TRAIN	04	56	04
SNO PRR: AEROTRAIN FAILURE	08	70	34
SNO PRR: AIRPLANE PASSENGER EXPERIMENT	05	69	30
SNO PRR: ALLENTOWN ROUTE	10	50	60
SNO PRR: AUTOMATIC FOOD-SERVICE CAR	05	54	122
SNO PRR: AUTOMATIC SPEED CONTROL	07	51	62
SNO PRR: BACK TO STEAM	06	57	37
SNO PRR: BALTIMORE & EASTERN A SUBSIDIAR	04	35	83
SNO PRR: BEST SAFETY RECORD	04	31	113
SNO PRR: BROAD STREET STATION TRAINS REM	09	51	61
SNO PRR: BURMA ROAD	03	43	126
SNO PRR: CAMELBACK LOCOS BUILT IN 1899	02	57	46
SNO PRR: CATENARY POLES/ELECTRIC LINES	02	36	85
SNO PRR: CENTENNIAL ALBUM PHOTO ESSAY	04	46	10
SNO PRR: CHARTERED 1823/ABSORBED/2677 MI	07	41	51
SNO PRR: CLASS A BOXCAR DESIGNATION	07	51	67
SNO PRR: CLASS E1 CAMELBACK LOCOS	10	54	39
SNO PRR: CLASS K4/K5 LOCO DRIVERS	08	31	46
SNO PRR: CLASS K4/PHILA STEAM/DIESEL-POW	10	54	07
SNO PRR: CLASS K4S/K5 LOCOS---DATA	10	31	423
SNO PRR: CLASS K5 STEAM LOCOS #5698-5699	08	56	39
SNO PRR: CLASS S2 STEAM TURBINE LOCO	11	47	84
SNO PRR: CLASS T1 4-4-4-4/661/DIESEL/ELE	12	57	41
SNO PRR: CLASS T1 LOCOS: WHERE ARE THEY?	09	54	29
SNO PRR: CLASSIFICATION SIGNALS ON LOCOS	02	42	44
SNO PRR: COAL INDUSTRY	07	47	130
SNO PRR: COMMERCIAL COMMUNICATIONS CIRCU	01	47	55
SNO PRR: COMMUNICATIONS	10	44	55
SNO PRR: COMPROMISE CARS	06	74	21
SNO PRR: CONEMAUGH DIVISION RELOCATION	10	49	53
SNO PRR: CONSOLIDATIONS OF SEVERAL DIVIS	02	50	59
SNO PRR: CONTROL OF B&O 1901	07	78	05
SNO PRR: CONTROLS TH&I/TH&P	12	33	91

SHORT NOTES ON...	M	Y	P
SNO PRR: CONWAY PA FREIGHT YARD	04	56	37
SNO PRR: CONWAY YARD PITTSBURGH PA	01	65	10
SNO PRR: CONWAY YARD/MCCLINTOCK MEMORIES	08	48	126
SNO PRR: CORNWALL & LEBANAON NOW PART OF	03	35	87
SNO PRR: CPT EDWARD RICHARDSON CAR FLOAT	05	49	51
SNO PRR: CUMBERLAND VALLEY NOW PART OF	12	34	83
SNO PRR: DELAWARE RIVER BRIDGE PROJECT	02	59	35
SNO PRR: DEPOT BURLINGTON NJ REPLACING	02	49	61
SNO PRR: DEPOT IN BALTIMORE MD	08	57	44
SNO PRR: DIAMOND RING LOST IN PEAR SHIPM	01	31	279
SNO PRR: DIESEL LOCO ON MADISON IN HILL	04	54	16
SNO PRR: DIVISIONS	02	38	58
SNO PRR: ELECTRIC LOCOMOTIVE CLASSES	08	33	91
SNO PRR: ELECTRIC LOCOS	12	47	52
SNO PRR: ELECTRIC MU COACH BUILDERS	11	64	36
SNO PRR: ELECTRIFICATION/LOCOMOTIVES	07	32	511
SNO PRR: ELECTRIFYING 1300 MILES	02	30	436
SNO PRR: ELIMINATED/CONSOLIDATED DIVISIO	02	51	50
SNO PRR: ENOLA YARD CAPACITY	05	43	89
SNO PRR: ENOLA YARD NAMING	06	60	29
SNO PRR: ENOLA YARD/ROCKVILLE BRIDGE PHO	07	46	59
SNO PRR: ENOLA YARDS= ALONE	10	55	32
SNO PRR: EXPERIMENTAL ELECTRIC FRT LOCOS	07	49	64
SNO PRR: FACSIMILE TELEGRAPHY RESERVATIO	10	53	71
SNO PRR: FIRST ELECTRIFIED	06	31	442
SNO PRR: FIRST SECTION OPENED	04	73	46
SNO PRR: FIRST SECTION OPENED	07	46	53
SNO PRR: FREIGHT SERVICE IMPROVEMENT	03	53	58
SNO PRR: GRAND RAPIDS DIVISON DIESELIZED	10	49	56
SNO PRR: HARBOR TUG "NEWARK"	05	50	62
SNO PRR: HOLLIDAYSBURG PA FRT CAR REPAIR	08	53	59
SNO PRR: HOTBOXES	10	53	122
SNO PRR: IMPROVEMENTS OF 1944	05	45	61
SNO PRR: IRON BRIDGES	02	44	56
SNO PRR: JAN 1951 STRIKE	08	53	79
SNO PRR: JEFFERSON MADISON & INADIANAPOL	12	33	34
SNO PRR: JEFFERSONIAN	04	58	46
SNO PRR: LARGEST DIESEL FLEET	03	50	58
SNO PRR: LARGEST TRAIN-COMMUNICATION SYS	11	52	138
SNO PRR: LAST SERVICING STEAM LOCOS	10	63	30
SNO PRR: LAST STEAM IN REVENUE	11	65	23
SNO PRR: LEASED PFW&C	11	32	474
SNO PRR: LEASED PO&NE	06	32	333
SNO PRR: LEASES WNY&P IN 1930	07	35	84
SNO PRR: LINDBERGH SPECIAL TRAIN	02	55	28
SNO PRR: LOCO #1178 CLASS O/P HISTORY/DA	10	51	134
SNO PRR: LOCO WASHING MACHINE SUNNYSIDE	03	48	60
SNO PRR: LOCOMOTIVE CLASS DIFFERENCES	06	58	39
SNO PRR: LOCOMOTIVES/CLASSES	03	33	94
SNO PRR: LOCOS #/CLASS IN NORTHUMBERLAND	06	59	34
SNO PRR: LOCOS PLACED IN SERVICE 1943	08	44	63
SNO PRR: LOCOS/VICE-PRESIDENTS/EQUIPMENT	10	59	38
SNO PRR: LONESOME TRAIN/LINCOLN FUNERAL	02	45	138
SNO PRR: LOW GRADE FREIGHT LINE PHILADEL	11	52	62
SNO PRR: MADISON HILL DIESEL/STEEPEST NA	06	54	56

Stephans' Railroad Directory

Railroad/Railfan

RAILROAD HISTORIES & ROSTERS

SHORT NOTES ON...	M	Y	P
SNO PRR: MARINE EQUIPMENT OWNED	07	45	75
SNO PRR: MU TYPE CARS	02	58	41
SNO PRR: MULE SHOE CURVE	12	68	30
SNO PRR: NARROW GAGE LINES	04	69	29
SNO PRR: NARROW GAGE LINES	04	31	120
SNO PRR: NARROW GAUGE LINES IN 1930	12	75	57
SNO PRR: NEW CABOOSES/ALL-STEEL/BAY WIND	02	57	06
SNO PRR: NEW JERSEY MEADOW ROUNDHOUSE	01	48	73
SNO PRR: NEW STATION AT LEVITTOWN PA	03	53	61
SNO PRR: NEW TRAIN BEING BUILT/DESCRIBED	06	55	67
SNO PRR: NORTH RIVER TUNNEL EXTENSIONS	11	53	51
SNO PRR: NORTHUMBERLAND PA OLD ENGINEHOU	02	59	37
SNO PRR: NORTHWESTERN OHIO NOW PART OF	01	34	90
SNO PRR: ORGANIZED 1847/FIRST PRESDIENT	02	37	79
SNO PRR: OWNS 4800 LOCOS	03	38	54
SNO PRR: OWNS 4800 LOCOS.	07	38	73
SNO PRR: OWNS LONG ISLAND RR	06	34	89
SNO PRR: OWNS OR CONTROLS (LIST OF RR)	11	36	53
SNO PRR: PA LIMITED/NY-CHICAGO LTD/SPECI	04	57	41
SNO PRR: PANHANDLE DIVISION IMPROVEMENTS	02	50	56
SNO PRR: PANHANDLE ROUTE IMPROVEMENTS	02	51	52
SNO PRR: PAOLIA PA STATION (NEW)	09	52	127
SNO PRR: PHILA-HARRISBURG EXT ELECTRIC	12	40	63
SNO PRR: PHILLY-HARRISBURG ELECTRIFICATI	05	74	47
SNO PRR: POT LUCK ENTREE	06	50	135
SNO PRR: POTOMAC RIVER BRIDGE REPLACEMEN	09	45	60
SNO PRR: PRINCETON BRANCH	04	55	62
SNO PRR: PROSPEROUS, DESPITE HARD TIMES	05	31	177
SNO PRR: PURCHASE GN STEAM LOCOMOTIVES	01	78	46
SNO PRR: PURCHASED OR&W IN 1907	09	50	56
SNO PRR: RADIO TELEPHONE INSTALL YORK PA	04	51	67
SNO PRR: RAHWAY NJ	07	40	67
SNO PRR: RAIL-GRINDING TRAINS	12	54	42
SNO PRR: RAILROAD TRACK TANKS FIRST USED	01	45	43
SNO PRR: REORGANIZING/NOW HAS DIVISIONS	02	56	06
SNO PRR: ROADS PRR CONTROLS OR OWNS	10	61	42
SNO PRR: ROCKVILLE BRIDGE AT HARRISBURG	06	46	73
SNO PRR: ROUNDHOUSE/YARD AT BRADFORD JCT	08	31	48
SNO PRR: RUBBER-TIRED STORAGE BAT#14379	06	58	39
SNO PRR: SELF-POWERED COMBINATION CARS	08	56	39
SNO PRR: SHIMMYSHAKER/"BIG BERTHA"	11	51	63
SNO PRR: SIMPLE/STANDARDIZED/NO BOOSTERS	03	39	71
SNO PRR: STATUS OF PRR-NYC MERGER	11	65	23
SNO PRR: STEAM LOCOS ON BRANCH LINES	06	54	117
SNO PRR: STEAM LOCOS STILL OPERATING	10	56	44
SNO PRR: TEST LAB AT ALTOONA PA	02	69	32
SNO PRR: TICKET PUNCHES	02	48	137
SNO PRR: TRACK CONSTRUCTION PROJECT	12	51	65
SNO PRR: TRACK VS LINE IN OPERATION	09	32	233
SNO PRR: TRACKLESS SWITCHERS	11	35	81
SNO PRR: TRAIN PHONE COLUMBUS TO SANDUSK	11	48	56
SNO PRR: TRAIN TELEPHONE COMMUNICATIONS	06	49	62
SNO PRR: TRAIN TELEPHONE SYSTEM	07	44	75
SNO PRR: TRAINS PULLED BY MOUNTAIN TYPES	06	31	443
SNO PRR: TRENTON BRANCH FREIGHT LINE	12	45	62

SHORT NOTES ON...	M	Y	P
SNO PRR: TUBULAR DESIGNED TRAIN ORDERED	08	55	41
SNO PRR: TWO METHODS OF PROMOTION	06	57	44
SNO PRR: TYPE 705 TICKET MACHINE	08	55	42
SNO PRR: UNION LINE TRADEMARK	09	32	234
SNO PRR: VANDALIA LINE BECOMS PART OF	11	33	88
SNO PRR: VARIOUS ROADS NOW PART OF PRR	05	34	85
SNO PRR: WARREN & FRANKLIN RY NOW PART	01	33	97
SNO PRR: WATER SLOP TEST FOR GOOD TRACK	10	32	331
SNO PRR: WAYNESBURG & WASHINGTON PART OF	06	32	336
SNO PRR: WHEEL BALANCE TESTS AUG 1948	02	49	59
SNO PRR: WHITE TRIANGLE CORRECT JULY P67	10	51	67
SNO PRR: WHITE TRIANGLE ON BOXCARS	10	56	40
SNO PRR: WORLD'S FASTEST STEAM LOCOMOTIV	08	57	30
SNO PRR: YEAR AROUND SANTA CLAUSES	10	44	144
SNO PRRCO: BECAME MISSOURI PACIFIC RY	01	36	81
SNO PRRCO: CHARTERED 1849 THEN MP(FIRST)	11	74	52
SNO PRSL: 1933 CONSOLIDATIONS	04	39	74
SNO PRSL: 1933/MERGER	12	41	57
SNO PRSL: ABANDONS SOME TACKAGE	02	43	138
SNO PRSL: ATLANTIC CITY RR BECAME IN '01	07	38	76
SNO PRSL: CONSOLIDATION OF PRR/R IN 1933	10	57	38
SNO PRSL: CONSOLIDATION OF TRACKS	07	36	81
SNO PRSL: DIESELIZAED/MAINTAIN STEAM FAC	04	59	06
SNO PRSL: DIESELS 6/DIESEL COACHES 6 BUD	09	51	126
SNO PRSL: JOINTLY OWNED/OPERATED SEPARAT	02	59	44
SNO PRSL: NELLIE BLY TRAIN RUNNING	10	55	59
SNO PRSL: ORDERS 6 16000 HP DIESEL LOCOS	05	53	133
SNO PRSL: WOODEN CARS BANISHED	07	49	95
SNO PRWM: NOW OWNED BY/PLANS FOR RECONST	01	55	36
SNO PS&LE: MERGED IN 1896 TO FORM PB&LE	07	34	90
SNO PS&N: 145 MILES ABANDONED	06	47	140
SNO PS&N: TRACKS TORN UP/READER MEMORIES	10	47	131
SNO PS&SL: MERGED WITH CHVR 1871 NOW PC	09	73	43
SNO PS: SF&W AND ACL MERGER 1902	12	40	62
SNO PSCT: DIESEL BUSES/TRACKLESS TROLLEY	08	50	98
SNO PSCT: HOBOKEN ELEVATED LINE	12	49	77
SNO PSCT: NJ STREET CARS/39 LINES	10	33	43
SNO PSCT: SURFACE TRANSP/SUBWAY/TROLLEYS	07	52	91
SNO PSIRY: INCLINE RAILWAY	06	77	52
SNO PSNJ: NEWARK SUBWAY/ORANGE LINE	12	50	94
SNO PSRR: 8 MILES/IRREGULAR SCHEDULE	01	36	87
SNO PSRR: BRIEF HISTORY STARTED 1906	02	68	37
SNO PSS: ACQUIRED BY BRB&L IN 1912	06	50	65
SNO PSTC: INTERURBAN/PHILADELPIA	10	50	84
SNO PSTC: RED ARROW LINES	08	54	94
SNO PSY: CONSOLIDATION OF MANY ROAD/LIST	01	35	87
SNO PSY: MAIL RUN RECORD HOLDER	07	77	48
SNO PSY: READER MEMORIES	05	43	141
SNO PSY: SOUTHERN RAILROADS	12	37	54
SNO PT&B: 1880 TO ? 156 MILES	09	37	63
SNO PT&PS: LEASED PTS 1914	11	76	42
SNO PT: NAME CHANGED 1911	09	46	94
SNO PTC: 750 MILES/EQUIPMENT	01	42	65
SNO PTC: BUYS USED PCC CARS & BUSES/ABAN	05	55	49
SNO PTC: ELECTRIC MONITOR/LESS DELAYS	10	51	87

Stephans' Railroad Directory

Railroad/Railfan

RAILROAD HISTORIES & ROSTERS

SHORT NOTES ON...	M	Y	P
SNO PTC: PAINT SCHEME CHANGES	11	52	101
SNO PTC: PRACTICE TRACK	10	45	103
SNO PTC: PURCHASING NEW EQUIPMENT	04	55	46
SNO PTC: WILLIAM PENN/TROLLEY	06	58	61
SNO PTO: FROM PT&PS 1945 TO MILW 1974	11	76	42
SNO PTR: BUYS 8 CARS FROM PE	10	53	95
SNO PTS: CHARTERED 1887	11	76	42
SNO PULLMAN "CHIEF" SERIES CARS: SEATING	10	45	54
SNO PULLMAN CARS: NAMES=INTERIOR ARRANGE	05	45	61
SNO PULLMAN COMPANY	05	33	70
SNO PULLMAN COMPANY CORPORATE STRUCTURE	03	76	10
SNO PULLMAN COMPANY:	06	39	52
SNO PULLMAN COMPANY: 1ST STEEL PULLMAN	01	43	81
SNO PULLMAN COMPANY: CAR NAMING	07	37	52
SNO PULLMAN COMPANY: PHYSICAL ASSETS	11	46	66
SNO PULLMAN COMPANY:9483 CARS/NAMES/DATA	07	32	506
SNO PULLMAN: LAUNDRY OPERATIONS	11	51	65
SNO PULLMAN: STANDARD CAR MFG CO/FUTURE	11	37	52
SNO PUSC: INCORP 1887/RENAMED AS PT 1911	09	46	94
SNO PVRY: BECAME NORTHERN ALBERTA RY	04	35	86
SNO PVS: ACQUIRED BY T&P IN 1927	10	42	63
SNO PVS: CHARTERED 1909/EQUIPMENT	12	54	42
SNO PW&B: 1851-52 LAID TRACKS ON ICE	02	59	35
SNO PW&B: 3 CYLINDER LOCOS	10	47	68
SNO PW&B: FIRST CAR FERRIES	10	58	38
SNO PW&B: SUSQUEHANNA CAR FERRY/1852 ICE	09	48	78
SNO PW&BRR: BRIEF HISTORY-OPEN COACHES	05	67	29
SNO PW&BRR: FORMED 1854 TO OCO 1891	07	75	53
SNO PW&O: INCORP 1886	12	55	38
SNO PX	06	33	89
SNO PY&A: SUBSIDIARY OF PC-INCORP 1906	01	69	32
SNO PY&C: EXTENDED IN 1884/BECAME B&O	10	40	70
SNO Q&B: 13 MILES/NEVER FINISHED	01	38	120
SNO Q&B: 15 MILES/1 LOCO/1 CAR	11	31	491
SNO Q&E: INCORP 1896/17 MI/STD GAGE/PA	12	52	69
SNO Q&LSJ: PURCHASED BY CN IN 1906	12	55	37
SNO Q: INCORP 1917/EQUIPMENT/MILEAGE	02	49	64
SNO QA&P: INCORP 1909	11	33	89
SNO QA: CHARTERED IN 1894/OPENED IN 1898	04	35	83
SNO QA: INCORP IN 1894	08	34	85
SNO QBRW: 1910-1943	04	43	146
SNO QC: 357 MILES/EQUIPMENT	05	38	74
SNO QC: 365 MILES/52 LOCOS/EQUIPMENT	01	33	102
SNO QC: BUSINESS CAR "SHERBROOKE"	07	51	137
SNO QC: ITS ROUTES	06	38	72
SNO QC: LOCO #42/HISTORY	06	52	129
SNO QC: QUEBEC CITY TO NEWPORT VT	08	75	57
SNO QM&S: CN ABSORBED NOT CP READER CORR	05	73	07
SNO QM&S: INCORP 1906/ABORBED BY CN/EQUI	09	41	80
SNO QM&S: INCORPORATED 1906 NOW CP	02	73	50
SNO QM&S: PURCHASED BY D&H 1906 SOLD '29	01	74	13
SNO QMO&O: BUILT IN LATE 1870'S	03	52	54
SNO QMO&O: CONSOLIDATION/NOW PART OF CP	08	35	83
SNO QMO&O: NOW CP	11	73	58
SNO QNS&L: 356 MILES/TRACK HOLDING UP??	03	55	69
SNO QNS&L: 360 MILES/NEW RAIL LINE	10	55	33
SNO QRL&P: INTERURBAN/CANADA	11	50	95
SNO QRL&P: MONTMORECNY DIV SOLD TO CN	03	52	125
SNO QRL&P: PURCHASED BY CN	07	52	91
SNO QSRY: BECAME PART OF QM&S IN 1906	09	41	80
SNO QSRY: MERGED WITH SS TO QM&S	02	73	50
SNO QW: ABSORBED BY QUINCY IN 1917	02	49	64
SNO R&A: ABSORBED JAMES RIVER CO/NOW C&O	11	36	58
SNO R&B: BECAME RUTLAND IN 1867	08	36	76
SNO R&CL: BRIEF HISTORY	04	67	34
SNO R&CL: LEASED TO NYO&W 1924	11	76	44
SNO R&CO: OPENED 1875/NOW PART OF NYNH&H	03	38	58
SNO R&D: 5' GAGE/NOW PART OF S	04	45	77
SNO R&D: ABSORBED BY S IN JULY 1894	11	44	14
SNO R&D: FORERUNNER OF SOUTHERN RAILWAY	11	30	598
SNO R&D: MAY 1 1886 ASSUMES OPER OF 2 RD	11	44	13
SNO R&DB: BECAME NEW JERSEY SOUTHERN	04	49	128
SNO R&ER: ABSORBED BY NYRY/INTERURBAN LI	10	48	85
SNO R&G: 50 MILES/GEORGIA ABANDONED ROAD	05	34	132
SNO R&GV: OWNED BY KENNECOTT COPPER CORP	07	40	68
SNO R&L: CHARTERED 1856/BECAME EP 1859	12	59	34
SNO R&N: CHARTERED 1909/JUNKED 1924/EQUI	01	32	263
SNO R&NO: CHARTERED 1909 SCRAPPED 1924	04	74	43
SNO R&P: PARTIALLY CONSTRUCTED	01	33	98
SNO R&PB	09	33	48
SNO R&S: INCORP 1911/QUEBEC/20 MILES	05	45	62
SNO R&SA: LEASED SARATOGA & SCHENECTADY	02	35	83
SNO R&SB: ABSORBED BY NYRY/40 MILES	10	48	85
SNO R&SRR: BECAME NYC	09	53	44
SNO R&SUB: ABSORBED BY NYRY/2 LINES	10	48	85
SNO R&W: CONSOLIDATED WITH N&SL IN 1908	08	35	83
SNO R&WAT: CHARTERED 1852/NOW RW&O	09	37	65
SNO R-P: CHARTERED 1836 NOW SCL	06	73	49
SNO R-P: CHARTERED 1836/FARES	10	51	133
SNO R: 200 MILES ELECTRIFIED	12	59	33
SNO R: ABSORBED D&BB	03	53	62
SNO R: ATLANTIC CITY RR NOW PART OF R	01	33	98
SNO R: B&O HAS CONTROLLING INTEREST	01	39	64
SNO R: BLUE LINE	05	66	14
SNO R: BRIEF HISTORY OF NEWTON BRANCH	10	60	31
SNO R: BUYS ATLANTIC CITY RAILROAD 1883	09	33	48
SNO R: CAMELBACKS	07	41	61
SNO R: CAR RETARDER INSTALLATION	06	52	61
SNO R: CATASAUQUA & FOGELVILLE NOW PART	11	31	491
SNO R: CATAWISSA BRANCH/LARGEST FILL	09	33	127
SNO R: CLASSIFICATION OF LOCOMOTIVES	10	33	48
SNO R: COAL & OIL BURNERS	06	31	441
SNO R: CONTROLLED ELECTRONICALLY FUTURE?	04	57	06
SNO R: CONTROLS STONE HARBOR RAILROAD	06	33	90
SNO R: CRUSADER INAUGURATED	03	71	60
SNO R: DEISEL LOCOS F3/F2/FT	08	53	115
SNO R: FIRST TRAIN PULLED BY HORSES	04	62	45
SNO R: FREIGHT YARDS	08	35	81
SNO R: HARBOR FLEET	06	46	73
SNO R: INSPECTION LOCO "BLACK DIAMOND"	09	49	133

Railroad/ Railfan

RAILROAD HISTORIES & ROSTERS

SHORT NOTES ON...	M	Y	P
SNO R: LEASES IRONTON RAILROAD	05	32	179
SNO R: LETTERS ON PILOT DECK DONATE HOUS	08	46	59
SNO R: LOCO CLASSIFICATION/INITIALS/	05	44	43
SNO R: LOCOMOTIVES BUILT BY READING	08	60	24
SNO R: MILES/LOCOS/EQUIPMENT	12	31	94
SNO R: NAVY=FLEET OF FLOATING EQUIPMENT	10	57	40
SNO R: NUMBER OF CARS IN YARDS	01	36	87
SNO R: OIL/GAS:ELECTRIC CARS/WHERE OPERA	04	42	66
SNO R: PHILA & READING NOW KNOWN AS R	06	34	89
SNO R: PORT RICHMOND TIDEWATER TERMINAL	06	58	39
SNO R: QUEEN OF THE VALLEY	02	50	56
SNO R: RADAR EQUIPMENT TESTING	04	46	63
SNO R: RUTHERFORD YARD HARRISBURG PA IMP	11	53	46
SNO R: SERIES 1700-1756 LOCO--DIMENSIONS	09	31	190
SNO R: SPEED RECORD OF 115 MPH IN 1904	04	66	36
SNO R: STAR ON CABOOSE	09	49	55
SNO R: STEAM LOCOS LEFT/LOCO #1026 #1027	06	56	40
SNO R: THERMAL RELAYS	08	57	70
SNO R: TYPES OF LOCOS	12	59	34
SNO RAP: MERGED TO BECOME IR&T	12	47	92
SNO RBC: WHY THEY GAVE UP RAIL TRANSPORT	08	60	24
SNO RC&B: INCORP 1862/HORSECAR LINE/NY	10	48	84
SNO RC&BT: BRIEF HISTORY	08	76	51
SNO RCBH&W: 1909-1948/REORGANIZATIONS/EQ	12	53	69
SNO RCR: INCORP IN 1913/ABANDONED 1932	05	36	82
SNO REA	12	37	52
SNO REA: 1968 OWNERSHIP & CONTROL	10	68	34
SNO REA: MOVES METEORITES	02	31	443
SNO REDR: MISSILE RAILROAD	12	61	58
SNO RF&P: 110 LOCOMOTIVES	04	32	72
SNO RF&P: BUYS N&W LOCOS #200-5 CLASS K3	01	45	40
SNO RF&P: INCORP 1834/441 MILES/EQUIPMEN	05	40	93
SNO RF&P: INCORP 1834/NO REORGANIZATIONS	12	57	45
SNO RF&P: INCORP 1834/OPENED 1836	05	35	87
SNO RF&P: JOINT CONTROLLING ROADS	02	67	26
SNO RF&RL: ORGANIZED IN 1894/MC LEASED	03	35	87
SNO RG: HOTROD/GENERATOR UNITS	11	53	51
SNO RG: PROPOSED MERGER WITH D&SL	06	47	88
SNO RGC: LEASED BY MP	06	34	87
SNO RGRR: CHARTERED 1870/BECAME PI&RGV	11	53	49
SNO RGS: EQUIPMENT/REVENUES	03	38	56
SNO RGS: LOCO #74, CABOOSE #0401 IN PARK	01	53	133
SNO RGS: OPENED 1892/EQUIPMENT/1932 EQUI	02	58	39
SNO RGS: PLANNED BY OTTOW MEARS	01	55	06
SNO RGS: SCRAPS SOLD	12	52	129
SNO RH&L: RED CROSS OWNS	05	47	130
SNO RI: "WOBBLIES" BEFORE WWI INCIDENTS	08	73	07
SNO RI: 4-4-0 #628 LOST IN QUICKSAND	05	34	134
SNO RI: ABSORBED CO&G	12	44	45
SNO RI: ABSORBED CO&G IN 1902	03	55	29
SNO RI: ABSORBED K&DM AND DM&FD	01	73	60
SNO RI: ACQUIRES CT&S 1931	03	74	34
SNO RI: ACQUIRES KEOKUK & DES MOINES	12	33	91
SNO RI: BURNS 100 BOXCARS A MONTH	11	50	139
SNO RI: CABOOSES W/CONDUCTORS NAMES	04	52	137
SNO RI: COFFEE & DONUT SERVICE	04	52	127
SNO RI: DENVER CUTOFF	06	51	71
SNO RI: DIESEL LOCOS	05	46	75
SNO RI: DIESEL-ELECTRIC LOCOS	10	41	71
SNO RI: FREE RIDES-SHOP TRAIN SPECIAL	11	51	125
SNO RI: GOLDEN STATE LIMITED	11	72	54
SNO RI: LOCO REBUILDING PROGRAM	12	45	61
SNO RI: LOCOMOTIVE CHANGES	09	42	57
SNO RI: MILES OF DOUBLE TRACK	10	31	429
SNO RI: OUT STATION REPORTS AUTO SIGNALS	08	46	61
SNO RI: PASSENGER TRAIN REVENUE	08	48	60
SNO RI: PASSENGER TRAINS	06	57	43
SNO RI: RADIO ON MAIN LINE FREIGHTS	10	51	63
SNO RI: RESEARCH LABORATORY	01	52	74
SNO RI: ROADS IN RI SYSTEM	04	39	79
SNO RI: ROCKET TRAINS DIESEL POWER	07	50	62
SNO RI: SAMSON OF THE CIMARRON	06	45	59
SNO RI: TYPES OF DIESELS USED ON ROCKETS	12	74	57
SNO RI: WHITE & BLACK RIVER BRANCH	09	45	57
SNO RIDP: MERGED TO BECOME PART OF JC&A	07	38	73
SNO RIS: 81 MILES	06	34	84
SNO RISR: BOUGHT NYP&B 1889 REOR UERC'21	09	76	52
SNO RL&NF: BECAME NYC	09	53	44
SNO RL: CHARTERED IN 1899	09	32	231
SNO RLC: BECAME PART OF JC&A	07	38	73
SNO RM&SF: 1915/NEW MEXICO/	02	35	86
SNO RM&SF: LEASED BY ATSF IN 1915	05	41	43
SNO RM&SF: OWNED BY ATSF	11	73	58
SNO RO&GV: DISCONTINUED 1871/STILL PROFI	11	48	132
SNO RO&SO: CREATION	11	86	34
SNO ROCH: ROCHESTER CITY & BRIGHTON BECA	10	48	84
SNO ROCHE: ABSORBED BY ROCHESTER RAILWAY	10	48	84
SNO ROCKRR: ACL ACQUIRES IN 1922	01	33	98
SNO ROR: ACQUIRED BY TOWNSVILLE RR 1910	09	36	76
SNO ROR: SOLD 1919 TO TOWN	03	76	56
SNO RPRY: BECAME SIOUX CITY TRACTION CO.	04	50	77
SNO RR&G: INCORP 1905/FAMILY ENTERPRISE	11	42	67
SNO RR: SHORTLINE	02	59	45
SNO RRV: OPENED 1891 THEN MCRY 1920	08	75	56
SNO RRY: INCORP IN 1871/4 MILES	01	34	92
SNO RS&P: INCORPORATED IN 1906 TEXAS RD	03	69	23
SNO RSR: ABANDONED/HISTORY/EQUIPMENT	05	52	96
SNO RTC: ABSORBED R&SB	10	48	87
SNO RTC: CITY OWNERSHIP LEADS TO PROBLEM	01	49	91
SNO RTOH: BUILT A LINE IN EARLY 1900'S	11	52	88
SNO RU: ABSORBED NNY	02	52	55
SNO RU: BARLOW PLAN/READER COMMENTS	05	47	125
SNO RU: COMPLETED IN 1849/MERGERS	03	32	518
SNO RU: CONTROLLED BY NYC/EQUIPMENT	06	38	75
SNO RU: IN THE DAYS OF STEAM POWER PHOTO	06	57	16
SNO RU: INCORP 1867	08	36	76
SNO RU: LOCOS RENUMBERED/NAME CHANGES	02	39	91
SNO RU: NEW YORK RUTLAND & MONTREAL BECA	04	40	79
SNO RV: PHOTO ESSAY	04	40	131
SNO RV: 7.1 MILW SHORTLINE	02	59	45

Stephans' Railroad Directory

Railroad/ Railfan

RAILROAD HISTORIES & ROSTERS

SHORT NOTES ON...	M	Y	P
SNO RV: INCORP 1904/11 MILES/NEW JERSEY	12	36	51
SNO RV: INCORP 1904/STD GAGE/11 MILE/EQU	01	42	64
SNO RVA: BUILT 1888/MILEAGE/EQUIPMENT	12	31	96
SNO RVA: OPENED 1891/BRIEF HISTORY	07	33	134
SNO RVA: ORGANIZED 1866 & BRIEF HISTORY	12	69	29
SNO RVAM: REORGANIZATION	12	31	96
SNO RW&O: 1885 REORGANIZED	02	36	84
SNO RW&O: INCORP IN 1861STORY	02	37	78
SNO RW&O: NOW PART OF NYC/1861 TO ?	09	37	65
SNO S&A: 1915 TO ? 145 MILES	04	37	51
SNO S&A: INCORP 1915/145 MILES/EQUIPMENT	07	35	84
SNO S&A: SHORT HISTORY	08	62	32
SNO S&AL: 1867/BECAME B&LE	02	57	40
SNO S&BV: PROJECTED/BECAME PL&W IN 1896	04	41	49
SNO S&CA: 1874 NAME CHANGE/3.5' GAGE/39M	03	39	76
SNO S&CRY: BUILT AROUND 1870	10	53	107
SNO S&CV: BUILT IN 1873	08	45	45
SNO S&EA: BECAME CNJ IN 1847	08	34	86
SNO S&EA: CHARTERED IN 1847	03	33	92
SNO S&EA: CONSOLIDATES WITH E&S	12	32	104
SNO S&EA: EARLY 1849 TO APRIL 1 1849	08	39	45
SNO S&ERY: INCORP IN 1905/UP 1921/ABANDO	02	35	87
SNO S&I: BECAME LSE IN 1901	03	37	62
SNO S&IE: NOW PART OF SC&P	04	32	71
SNO S&INT: BECAME LSEL	11	51	78
SNO S&J: 3' GAGE/LOGGING ROAD	10	50	60
SNO S&LP: COMPLETED 1893/D&H ABSORBED	04	47	21
SNO S&MP: NOW PERE MARQUETTE	06	45	13
SNO S&NE: 60'/3' 6" GAGE/1 FUNERAL CAR	05	53	96
SNO S&NW: INCORP 1906	04	37	51
SNO S&NW: RESULT OF NAME CHANGE 1914	07	35	84
SNO S&NY: 1903 TO ?/CONSOLIDATIONS	05	37	40
SNO S&NY: 6 LOCO/EQUIPMENT/2 TRAINS DALY	08	32	54
SNO S&NY: INCORP 1903/RESULT OF CONSOLID	12	35	85
SNO S&NY: INCORP IN 1903/67 MILES/EQUIPM	02	33	83
SNO S&PT: 1888-1889/CONNECTICUT/1.51 MIL	05	50	103
SNO S&R: INCORP 1848	11	43	61
SNO S&RRV:	10	37	73
SNO S&RRV: BECAME LR&N IN 1903	12	35	84
SNO S&RRV: BECAME LR&N THEN L&A	11	72	55
SNO S&RRV: TO LR&N 1903	11	75	43
SNO S&SO: 40 MILES/GEORGIA ABANDONED ROA	05	34	132
SNO S&SP: NOW PART OF PLANT SYSTEMS	12	37	54
SNO S&SP: REORGANIZED 1893/NOW PSY	01	35	87
SNO S&SRR: 25 MILE/GEORGIA ABANDONED ROA	05	34	132
SNO S&TI: ORGANIZED IN 1901/EQUIPMENT	05	34	83
SNO S&U: BECAME NYC	09	53	44
SNO S&U: CHARTERED 1836	11	43	61
SNO S&UD: BECAME NYC	09	53	44
SNO S&WW: ORGANIZED 1873/NOW PCOAST	02	37	80
SNO S: 2287 LOCOS/OFFICE	11	30	599
SNO S: 3 FOOT NARROW GAGE TRACK LOCATION	06	74	21
SNO S: 3' GAGE/WAS A&D	03	41	77
SNO S: 4-6-2 #1408 SAFETY/SPEED PERFORMA	04	41	55
SNO S: 7962 MILES/EQUIPMENT	05	34	83
SNO S: 95 TON ORE CARS ORDERED FROM PLM	01	54	68
SNO S: ABSORBED CNO&TP	07	53	48
SNO S: ABSORBS R&D IN JULY 1894	11	44	14
SNO S: ACQUIRED V&SW	09	46	08
SNO S: ATLANTIC & YADKIN PART OF	02	32	333
SNO S: CNO&TP NOW PART OF SOUTHERN	04	36	94
SNO S: COMPLETELY DIESELIZED	10	53	122
SNO S: COW CATCHER CATCHES COW	01	69	06
SNO S: CRESCENT LIMITED	09	35	86
SNO S: CUMBERLAND RIVER BRIDGE MOVED	10	51	67
SNO S: DUPLEX LOCOS	05	44	74
SNO S: ETV&GA BECOMES PART OF SOUTHERN	08	34	85
SNO S: FINANCED CUMBERLAND	11	46	06
SNO S: HARTWELL RAILWAY SOLD 1924	01	47	62
SNO S: KNOXVILLE & APPALACHIA SEPARATED	08	54	115
SNO S: LOCO #1102/OLD97	06	58	39
SNO S: M&CRR ABSORBED BY	12	51	65
SNO S: MEMPHIS & CHARLESTON RY NOW PART	03	54	24
SNO S: MILEAGE	06	30	412
SNO S: MURPHY LINE/LOCO 397	08	30	91
SNO S: NATURAL TUNNEL APPALACHIA VA	08	50	53
SNO S: O&AL MERGES	09	36	74
SNO S: OA&M BECAME PART OF SOUTHERN	12	55	35
SNO S: ORGANIZED 1894	10	56	41
SNO S: PULLMAN CAR NAMES	05	33	73
SNO S: QUEEN & CRESCENT ROUTE	06	57	41
SNO S: RAILROADS & TERMINALS OF THE S	05	78	57
SNO S: REVISED ITS DINING SEATING PROCED	04	54	16
SNO S: TOCCOA TO ELBERTON GA BRANCH	03	40	76
SNO SA&AP: NOW PART OF SP	11	31	491
SNO SA&AP: NOW PART OF T&NO	08	34	87
SNO SA&G: BECAME PART OF A&G/NOW ACL	01	37	85
SNO SA&O: ACQUIRED BY V&SW IN 1899	12	38	69
SNO SA&O: BECAME V&SW 1899	05	74	46
SNO SA&SC: CHARTERED IN 1833	02	35	83
SNO SAL:	12	37	55
SNO SAL: "AIR LINE" MEANING	07	67	32
SNO SAL: 639 LOCOS/OTHER EQUIPMENT	04	32	68
SNO SAL: CHARTERED 1900/CONTROLS	04	42	64
SNO SAL: DIVISIONS	08	38	93
SNO SAL: DIVISIONS IN 1938	02	75	49
SNO SAL: FINANCIAL/GROSS REVENUES	09	36	73
SNO SAL: FLORIDA CENTRAL & PENINSULAR	06	32	338
SNO SAL: FORMATION	08	78	55
SNO SAL: HELICOPTER WARNS MOTORISTS	08	59	10
SNO SAL: MERGER WITH ACL & HISTORY	11	71	38
SNO SAL: MILEAGE	06	30	412
SNO SAL: NOV 1896 SPEED RECORD TRAIN	01	74	13
SNO SAL: PHOSPHATE ROCK TRANSFER FACILIT	09	49	58
SNO SAL: RECEIVERSHIP/SEABOARD RY CO	05	44	78
SNO SAL: ROAD DIESEL FREIGHT LOCO ORDERD	02	46	65
SNO SAL: SILVER METEOR TRAIN MAKE-UP	11	40	71
SNO SAL: STEAM LOCO DISPOSITION	10	61	42
SNO SAL: WHAT'S IN A NAME?	06	64	36
SNO SAL: WHY AIR LINE IN NAME	02	60	35

Railroad/ Railfan

Stephans' Railroad Directory

RAILROAD HISTORIES & ROSTERS

SHORT NOTES ON...	M	Y	P
SNO SALEM: BECAME PART OF PL&W IN 1896	04	41	49
SNO SALV: PURCHASED BY CGN IN 1913	05	37	38
SNO SAND: 4 MILES/6 MILE EXTENSION BUILD	04	56	56
SNO SAND: BRIEF HISTORY/NEWSPAPER CLIPPI	02	47	126
SNO SAR&S: 1946/FORMERLY B&M'S SARATOGA	01	47	44
SNO SAR&S: WAS TROY SARATOGA & NORTHERN	05	47	131
SNO SARY: WAS BLACK MOUNTAIN RAILROAD	09	70	33
SNO SAS: LEASED BY MP	06	34	87
SNO SAU&G: 1912/NAME CHANGE/STD GAGE	06	52	65
SNO SAU&G: LEASED BY MP	06	34	87
SNO SAV: FIRST FAR WEST RAILROAD	06	60	28
SNO SAV: OPENED 1856 FIRST P COAST ROAD	12	73	51
SNO SB&NY: PART OF DL&W	09	42	60
SNO SB&NY: SHORT HISTORY	10	62	36
SNO SB&RGV: LEASED BY MP	06	34	88
SNO SBC: CONSTRUCT BEGAN 1937/OPENED '48	03	49	60
SNO SBR: SHORT HISTORY	11	64	34
SNO SBUF: SHORT HISTORY	08	62	31
SNO SC&F: MERGED WITH SPC 1887 NOW SP	09	73	42
SNO SC&F: MERGED WITH SPC IN 1887	10	35	87
SNO SC&M: 3 MILE/W VIRGINIA/DIESELIZED	06	58	36
SNO SC&MS: 1888 ELEVATED	06	76	51
SNO SC&MS: BUILT 1888	02	70	40
SNO SC&P: 1908-1910	07	33	82
SNO SC&PA: C&NW TAKES OVER IN 1901	04	34	79
SNO SC&PRR: PURCHASED BY WASHINTON CO RR	10	33	45
SNO SC&WI: MERGED IN 1882 TO FORM C&WI	07	34	90
SNO SC: BECAME COAL FIELDS RY	04	36	91
SNO SC: SUSPENDED IN 1912	11	33	92
SNO SCA&P: EQUIPMENT	04	32	71
SNO SCA: TROLLEY/PA/FASTEST 1910-1928	05	48	95
SNO SCAL: CONSOLIDATION IN 1889	08	34	85
SNO SCC&RR: REPLANTS FOREST WITH PINES	03	49	128
SNO SCEC: INCORP IN 1912 BUILT SJ&E	05	36	82
SNO SCERY: REORGANIZATION 1895	04	50	77
SNO SCH&T: BECAME NYC	09	53	44
SNO SCHEN: CITY LINES/INTERURBAN SERVICE	12	55	44
SNO SCHS: ORGANIZED IN 1866	08	52	83
SNO SCHUY: ABSORBED BY N&A IN 1905	12	45	64
SNO SCIR: ORGANIZED 1885 INCLINE ROAD	01	74	11
SNO SCIT: FORMED 1899/RESULT OF A MERGER	04	50	76
SNO SCL: 78.86 MILES OF STRAIGHT TRACK	01	69	59
SNO SCL: MERGER OF SAL & ACL 7-1-67	08	67	06
SNO SCL: NUMBERING BICENTENNIAL #1776	11	71	52
SNO SCO: CHARTERED IN 1846/NOW B&M	03	35	87
SNO SCP: 1879 HORSECARS/1887 GAS/STREETC	03	48	139
SNO SCPA: NEW MEXICO/30 YEARS/2' MINING	12	55	31
SNO SCPA: OLD MINING ROAD/61 MILES	12	37	54
SNO SCRT: BUILT 1888	02	70	40
SNO SCRT: CHARTERED 1888/ELEVATED/IOWA	04	50	76
SNO SCRY: CHARTERED IN 1884	03	34	86
SNO SD&A: BECAME SD&AE	05	73	18
SNO SD&A: CONTROLLED BY SP/EQUIPMENT	09	32	235
SNO SD&AE: READER INFORMATION	06	76	52
SNO SD&AE: SOLD TO MEXICAN GOVERNMENT	11	70	61
SNO SD&PM: COMPLETED IN 1871	09	34	86
SNO SDCEN: INCORP 1902 1906 TO W&SF	11	74	52
SNO SDCEN: INCORP 1902/EQUIP/NAME CHANGE	03	38	53
SNO SDE: 1891/NOW SAN DIEGO TRANSIT	07	49	94
SNO SDE: PCC CARS SOLD/ABANDONED 1949	07	50	117
SNO SDE: PCC CARS/CLASS 400 SCRAPPED	07	52	94
SNO SDT: SAN DIEGO ELECTRIC/PCC CARS SOL	07	49	94
SNO SDW: "ORPHAN RAILROAD"	04	38	122
SNO SE&P:	11	33	88
SNO SE&PH: BECAME PART OF L&HR IN 1912	03	36	83
SNO SE&PH: PENNSYLVANIA/.13 MILES/1889	03	47	138
SNO SEAST: GEORGIA/229 MILES/NEEDS FUNDS	07	52	112
SNO SEAT: INCORP 1931/CAR FERRY	09	40	59
SNO SEK: FORMATION	09	87	30
SNO SEM: BUYS YORK UTILITY EQUIPMENT	11	49	86
SNO SEM: MAINE/EQUIPMENT/PURPOSE	02	47	108
SNO SEM: POWER PLANT DONATED/100' TRACK	02	50	77
SNO SEMI-AUTOMATIC TELEGRAPH KEY: NEW!	01	50	131
SNO SEMIN:: MERGED IN 1890/BECAME MKT	05	35	86
SNO SESC: BECAME ACL 1900 NOW SCL	06	73	49
SNO SET&K: CHARTERED 1869/BECAME QC	01	40	112
SNO SET&K: INCORP IN 1869/BECAME QC	05	38	74
SNO SEWV: CHARTERED 1908	04	59	38
SNO SEWV: WEST VIRGINIA/BRANCH OF C&O	08	39	68
SNO SF&N: BECAME PART OF GN IN 1907	10	31	426
SNO SF&N: BECAME PART OF NPC	09	40	66
SNO SF&N: CHARTERED 1887 TO GN 1900	10	76	46
SNO SF&N: INCORP 1903/ATSF OWNS/MERGERS	08	55	45
SNO SF&NP: BECAME PART OF NPS	09	40	66
SNO SF&NP: CNW LEASED ALL SF&NP PROPERTY	08	55	46
SNO SF&NW: ABSORBED BY B&A IN 1880	04	35	86
SNO SF&S: BECAME LSEL	11	51	78
SNO SF&W: CONSOLIDATION 1884/NOW PSY	01	35	87
SNO SF&W: INCORP 1884/CONSOLIDATIONS	12	40	61
SNO SF&W: INCORPORATED 1884-PLANT SYSTEM	12	73	52
SNO SF&W: NOW PART OF PLANT SYSTEMS	12	37	54
SNO SF-S: CONSOLIDATED WITH SN	02	57	42
SNO SF-S: OWNS NEVADA COUNTY NARROW GAGE	09	34	83
SNO SF: WHY THE 0 IN LOCO NUMBERS?	11	34	91
SNO SFC&W: CHARTERED 1901 NOW SP	04	75	11
SNO SFC&W: CHARTERED 1901/EQUIP/NOW SP	02	54	74
SNO SFC: BECAME NEW MEXICO CENTRAL 1908	11	34	94
SNO SFCRR: STREETCAR/FARMINGTON MO/8 MIL	02	43	145
SNO SFM: OPENED CSCR	07	52	90
SNO SFM: PLANNED ABANDONMENT	06	47	103
SNO SFM: PROFITS INCREASE	01	53	84
SNO SFN&C: 46 MILES/3 LOCOMOTIVES	02	33	84
SNO SFN&C: INCORP IN 1911/40 MILES	06	36	80
SNO SFP: CONSTRUCTED 1913/TROLLEY/PA	05	48	95
SNO SFR&E: ACQUIRD BY RM&SF IN 1924	05	41	43
SNO SFRY: BUILT 1912 DIED 1944	11	75	42
SNO SFT&B: LEASED TO NPC IN 1889	08	55	46
SNO SFV&N: ACQUIRED BY SFN&C IN 1911	06	36	80
SNO SG&N: BECAME PART OF SNO IN 1910	06	36	80
SNO SG&NA: BECAME CGA	06	72	60

Railroad/ Railfan

RAILROAD HISTORIES & ROSTERS

SHORT NOTES ON...	M	Y	P
SNO SG: INCORP 1896/EQUIPMENT/MILES/MERG	03	47	74
SNO SG: INCORP 1896/USE WOOD-BURNERS	03	44	103
SNO SH&N: 40 YEARS IN RECEIVERSHIP	02	47	120
SNO SH&PE: ABSORBED BY C&IM IN 1936	09	47	73
SNO SH&W:	09	33	48
SNO SH: INCORP IN 1912	06	33	90
SNO SH: ORGANIZED IN 1912	09	33	48
SNO SHEP: 1873/BECAME SL&N IN 1887	11	47	129
SNO SHEP: 1873/REORGANIZATION/THEN SL&N	07	41	66
SNO SHEP: REORGANIZED 1873 SL&N	01	74	12
SNO SHEPV: CHARTER 1868 REORG 1873 SHEP	01	74	12
SNO SHEPV: CHARTERED 1868/REORG AS SL&N	09	54	30
SNO SHEPV: CHARTERED IN 1868/THEN SL&N	07	41	66
SNO SHEPV: INCORP 1869/BECAME SHEP	11	47	129
SNO SHRT: CONSTRUCTED IN 1920'S	11	52	90
SNO SHRT: NEW EQUIPMENT ORDERED	03	47	93
SNO SHRT: PAVING FOR PARKING MEDIANS	10	68	30
SNO SHRT: WELCOME BACK SHAKER RAPID	07	82	21
SNO SHT: ABSORBED BY STONE HARBOR	06	33	90
SNO SICT: 1890-99 ELEVATED/1895 ELECTRIC	06	48	100
SNO SICT: CHARTERED 1899	04	50	77
SNO SID&O: SPLIT IN 1919/YALE/WES/K&SID/	04	39	76
SNO SIE: CALIFORNIA/FREIGHT OPERATIONS	09	44	65
SNO SIE: FINANCIAL	05	34	83
SNO SIE: INCORP 1897/57 MILES	06	55	78
SNO SIE: INCORP IN 1897/EQUIPMENT/FINANC	08	35	82
SNO SILP: INCORP 1906/18 MILES/EQUIPMENT	08	38	91
SNO SILP: INCORPORATED 1906	08	74	57
SNO SILV: COLORADO/15 MILES/ABANDONED	06	36	80
SNO SILV: FOLDED AGAIN	01	43	133
SNO SIN: SHORT HISTORY & DEMISE	04	67	48
SNO SIND: BECAME CTH&SE IN 1910	07	46	52
SNO SINV: LOGGING ROAD/WESTERN PENNSYLVA	04	49	65
SNO SIRT: FARE JUGGLING	03	71	40
SNO SIRT: MAINLINE ROAD	02	59	45
SNO SIRT: NORTH SHORE LINE/EARLY HISTORY	08	53	78
SNO SIRT: RELIGION AND UNIONS	02	53	80
SNO SIRT: ROLLING STOCK/READER OPINIONS	10	49	104
SNO SIRY: BRIEF HISTORY	05	69	39
SNO SJ&CB: CONSOLIDATION WITH CB&SJ 1868	07	32	509
SNO SJ&DM: NOW PART OF BURLINGTON	10	36	70
SNO SJ&E: 1912-1931 53 MILES	05	36	82
SNO SJ&GI: 259 MILES/9 LOCOMOTIVES	01	32	261
SNO SJ&GI: UP OWNS SINCE 1918	03	36	83
SNO SJ&LC:	01	33	102
SNO SJ&LC: 96 MILES/EQUIPMENT	06	33	92
SNO SJ&LC: 96 MILES/EQUIPMENT.	03	38	54
SNO SJ&LC: CORPORATE HISTORY	03	74	34
SNO SJ&LC: INCORP IN 1880/EQUIP/MI/FINAN	07	35	86
SNO SJ&LE: NOW PART OF PLANT SYSTEMS	12	37	54
SNO SJ&LE: REORGANIZED 1896/NOW PSY	01	35	87
SNO SJ&M: NEW BRUNSWICK DIV OF E&NA	11	34	92
SNO SJ&O: 1912-1928/12 MILES/UTAH/EQUIPM	09	34	85
SNO SJ: ELECTRIC STREET RAILWAY/HISTORY	03	42	126
SNO SJE: 1900-1930/FLORIDA/5 MILES/6 CAR	12	46	106

SHORT NOTES ON...	M	Y	P
SNO SJP: CHARTERED IN 1907	07	33	82
SNO SJP: OPENED 1907 TO CCE 1912(SECOND)	01	76	41
SNO SJR:	09	33	48
SNO SJRY: FORMED 1908	12	76	46
SNO SJV: 27 MILES	09	37	64
SNO SJV: CHARTERED 1905 OPENED 1906	03	75	11
SNO SJV: CHARTERED 1905/DISMANTLED 1918	12	41	82
SNO SJV: CHARTERED IN 1905/3 LOCOS	07	31	533
SNO SKA: INCORP IN 1866/EQUIPMENT/MILES	04	34	85
SNO SL&A: BUILT IN 1853/EARLY HISTORY	11	47	17
SNO SL&AD: INCORP 1896/CONSOLIDATIONS	11	40	73
SNO SL&ARY: BECAME SL&AD IN 1896	11	40	73
SNO SL&C: BRIEF HISTORY	05	63	42
SNO SL&H: PROVIDES MOTOR COACH PASS SERV	06	37	63
SNO SL&IM: BECAME SLIM&S	01	36	81
SNO SL&IM: MERGED-CA&T AND C&F TO SLIM&S	02	73	49
SNO SL&IM: ORG 1853 TO SLIM&S 1874	11	74	52
SNO SL&IM: ORGANIZED 1853/BECAME SLIM&S	10	40	68
SNO SL&IM: SHORT HISTORY	02	62	53
SNO SL&IM: TRANSFER BOAT/4' 8.5" TRACK	04	54	10
SNO SL&IV: OPENED 1850	03	52	54
SNO SL&KC: MERGED IN 1890/BECAME MKT	05	35	86
SNO SL&LA: INTERURBAN TROLLEY LINE/16.3	05	41	48
SNO SL&N: 1887/BECAME PART OF NH IN 1898	11	47	129
SNO SL&N: 1887/REORGANIZATION	07	41	66
SNO SL&N: BLAKESLEE MEMORIES	08	48	128
SNO SL&N: LEASED TO NYNH&H 1898	01	74	12
SNO SL&N: REORGAN 1873/MERGED WITH NH	09	54	30
SNO SL&NA: ORGANIZED 1899	06	48	19
SNO SL&S: LV LESAES 24 MILES OF TRACK	01	34	90
SNO SL&SU: 1ST STREETCAR REGULAR MAIL RT	08	55	61
SNO SLA&T: REORGANIZATION/BECAME CBELT	02	47	111
SNO SLA&TH: THE CAIRO SHORT LINE	09	45	59
SNO SLB&M: LEASED BY MP	06	34	87
SNO SLE: INCORP 1905/MILES/EQUIPMENT	10	41	72
SNO SLE: INCORPORATED 1905 DIED 1919	10	74	46
SNO SLE: PURCHASES GSSR '16 BANKRPT 1919	03	74	33
SNO SLE: ROUTES WEST OF E LYME SUSPENDED	01	42	66
SNO SLER&W: CONTROLLED BY FS&W	11	52	62
SNO SLG&W: 16 MILE ROAD	12	77	46
SNO SLIM&S: BECAME MP	06	48	16
SNO SLIM&S: CHARTER 1874 FROM SLIM, C&F	11	74	52
SNO SLIM&S: CHARTERED 1874 NOW MP	02	73	49
SNO SLIM&S: CHARTERED 1874/695 MILES	01	36	81
SNO SLIM&S: CHARTERED 1874/695 MILES.	10	40	68
SNO SLKC&N: CONSOLIDATION 1879	07	36	85
SNO SLKC: ELECTRIC ROAD	11	33	91
SNO SLL&D: INCORP 1870 BY A&PA	09	36	73
SNO SLL&W: BUILT BY A&PA/NOW ATSF	09	36	73
SNO SLO&SM:	06	34	88
SNO SLO&SM: BECAME PCOA	05	76	26
SNO SLO&SM: BECAME PCOA IN 1882	10	35	87
SNO SLO: INCORP IN 1873	10	35	87
SNO SLOR: BRIEF HISTORY	03	67	31
SNO SLPS: 345 MILES/EQUIPMENT	01	42	65

Railroad/ Railfan

RAILROAD HISTORIES & ROSTERS

SHORT NOTES ON...	M	Y	P
SNO SLRM&P: ACQUIRED BY ATSF 1913	11	73	58
SNO SLRM&P: CHARTERED 1905/COAL MINING	05	41	43
SNO SLRM&P: LINE NEVER BUILT	02	35	85
SNO SLRM&P: TO ATSF 1912 NAME TO RM&SF	03	76	57
SNO SLS&BC: INCORP 1889/SOLD 1889	04	31	122
SNO SLS&E:	02	39	125
SNO SLS&E: CHARTER 1885 BECAME NP 1890'S	05	74	46
SNO SLS&E: CHARTERED IN 1885	04	33	97
SNO SLV&TH: CHARTERED IN 1865/158 MILES	11	33	88
SNO SLV: OLDEST IRRIGATION DITCH/LOCO/CH	01	54	122
SNO SLVS: 31 MILE/COLORADO/FRIEGHT LINE	12	53	117
SNO SM&H: BECAME SM&N/THEN SN&SO/ LSEL	11	51	78
SNO SM&N: OPENED 1893/OHIO INTERURBAN	11	52	88
SNO SMD: INCORP 1868/NOW WB&PL	03	39	62
SNO SMISS: INCORP 1894/NOW C&GR	11	36	55
SNO SMRR: INCORPORATED IN 1864/7.6 MILES	10	33	43
SNO SMS: LOCATION	08	76	51
SNO SMT: DISAGREEMENT SETTLED WITH PRAY	10	50	131
SNO SMV: 23 MILES	03	34	85
SNO SMV: INCORP 1911/23 MILES/CALIFORNIA	11	35	83
SNO SMV: INCORPORATED 1911 DIED 1950	04	76	53
SNO SMW: 23 MILE FREIGHT ROAD	07	45	16
SNO SN&S: BECAME LSE IN 1901	03	37	62
SNO SN&SO: BECAME LSEL	11	51	78
SNO SN: 1918/CONSOLIDATIONS/MERGERS	02	57	42
SNO SN: TRAIN FERRY "RAMON"	07	50	66
SNO SN: WP TRYING TO WRECK ROAD???	01	53	88
SNO SNE: INCORPORATED 1910	07	73	38
SNO SNE: INCORPORATED 1910/	05	39	66
SNO SNG: 1895-1932/3' GAGE/14 + 7 MILES	06	36	80
SNO SNG: NARROW GAGE MINING ROAD/RESUMES	11	37	57
SNO SNRY: BECAME PART OF G&F IN 1911	06	41	61
SNO SNW&L: BECAME HOBART SOUTHERN	12	37	57
SNO SNY: NAME CHANGES/MILEAGE/EQUIPMENT	11	37	53
SNO SNYP: 1916/BECAME SOUTHERN NY RY	11	37	53
SNO SOC: REORGANIZED AS SIERRA RAILROAD	09	44	65
SNO SOCA: 1ST TO CHANGE TO STANDARD GAGE	07	51	65
SNO SOCA: HISTORY TO SOUTHERN	10	68	34
SNO SOMRR: INCORP 1886/2 MILES	01	35	84
SNO SOMRR: SHORT HISTORY	06	61	39
SNO SOMRR: SOLD TO NYNH&H/LOCOS---WHERE?	03	35	90
SNO SONV: 1875/3' GAGE/NOW NWP	03	48	129
SNO SOO: ARCH BRIDGE ST CROIX RIVER	06	53	59
SNO SOO: BEMIDJI-SCHLEY MN LINE	12	55	35
SNO SOO: BUYS WC IN 1908	01	54	68
SNO SOO: DIESEL EQUIPMENT OWNED	08	48	63
SNO SOO: DIVISIONS	03	35	85
SNO SOO: DIVISIONS IN 1930	10	73	58
SNO SOO: HEAVIEST LOCO 4-8-2/UPKEEP LOCO	07	36	80
SNO SOO: INCORP IN 1888/ROADS CONSOLIDAT	12	34	83
SNO SOO: ORGANIZED IN 1883	09	31	187
SNO SOO: PRONOUNCIATION OF NAME/1888 TO?	05	37	37
SNO SOO: ST CROIX RIVER BRIDGE	05	50	60
SNO SOTC: ABSORBED BY T&P IN 1872	10	42	63
SNO SP&DUL: 1877 REORGANIZATION	12	34	83

SHORT NOTES ON...	M	Y	P
SNO SP&DUL: NP ACQUIRES DIFFERENT TIMES	04	36	93
SNO SP&O: CHARTERED IN 1871/REORGANIZED	01	36	84
SNO SP&P: BEGAN 1857 BECAME GN NOW BN	04	74	43
SNO SP&P: NOW GN	07	43	66
SNO SP&P: UNDEPENDABLE	02	55	13
SNO SP&S: 111 LOCOS	10	31	429
SNO SP&S: BUYS 2 LOCOS FROM GN	09	52	61
SNO SP&S: COOKING ON CABOOSES	05	46	135
SNO SP&S: INCORP 1905/EQUIPMENT/MILEAGE/	02	50	58
SNO SP&S: INCORPORATED 1905 TO GN/NP/BN	01	75	54
SNO SP&S: JOINTLY OWNED BY GN & NP	03	39	121
SNO SP: "CP HUNTINGTON"	08	43	58
SNO SP: "SHASTA DAYLIGHTS"	01	50	123
SNO SP: "THE LIFE LINE" BLOOD DONOR CAR	04	52	134
SNO SP: 100TH ANNIVERSARY	06	55	67
SNO SP: 2-6-0/4-4-2/0-6-0 LOCO TROUBLES	09	54	06
SNO SP: 200' BELOW SEA LEVEL SIGN	04	42	123
SNO SP: 24 LOCOS-1 TRAIN/TEHACHAPI MTNS	05	44	64
SNO SP: 3239 LOCOS/OFFICE	11	30	599
SNO SP: 4722 MILES	05	31	279
SNO SP: 48 MILE CUTOFF	06	58	10
SNO SP: 6000 HP EMD DIESELS/USE WHERE?	09	47	72
SNO SP: ABSORBED SFC&W	02	54	74
SNO SP: ACCUSED OF RUN DOWN PASS SERVICE	08	59	10
SNO SP: ACQUIRED CP&S IN 1924	01	37	88
SNO SP: ASSETS/VALUATION	11	36	57
SNO SP: ATLANTIC TYPE LOCOS #S/CLASS	10	54	06
SNO SP: BOUGHT PAJARO VALLEY RR IN 1929	06	35	82
SNO SP: CABOOSE REMINDS OF SAEFTY RESPON	03	53	134
SNO SP: CASCADE LINE	06	37	60
SNO SP: CASCADE TIME STEPPED UP	01	51	77
SNO SP: CENTRALIZED TRAFFIC CONTROL	11	44	100
SNO SP: CLOUDCROFT BRANCH	02	48	128
SNO SP: COAST DIVISION	02	54	115
SNO SP: COLTON-PALMDALE CUTOFF	10	67	06
SNO SP: COUNTRY'S LARGEST RAILROAD	10	35	83
SNO SP: DAYLIGHT INAUGURATED IN 1922	12	50	53
SNO SP: DAYLIGHT INTRODUCTION	08	72	58
SNO SP: DAYLIGHT LOCO #4459 CLASS GS5	10	50	56
SNO SP: ENGLEWOOD YARD HOUSTON TX	12	31	94
SNO SP: ENTERPRISES OWNED/CONTROLLED BY	06	36	80
SNO SP: FORMS/NO ADVERTISING VALUE	11	39	90
SNO SP: FOX FILM CORP USES LOCO/STATION	11	33	88
SNO SP: GOLDEN STATE BLUNT END REAR CAR	10	54	43
SNO SP: HIGH POINT OF STEAM POWER	07	78	55
SNO SP: HIGHEST & LOWEST POINTS	04	55	33
SNO SP: HORSESHOE CURVE EL PASO TX NEED	02	61	30
SNO SP: IMPACT REGISTER DEVICE	12	51	63
SNO SP: INSTRUCTION CAR	07	53	116
SNO SP: INTER-CALIFORNIA LINE	02	38	60
SNO SP: INTERURBAN SERVICE/STEAM	12	40	65
SNO SP: JULY 1891 HEAVY RAINSTORM WASHES	12	58	39
SNO SP: KEELER-LAWS BRANCH/NARROW GAGE	11	54	73
SNO SP: LAST STEAM RUNS	01	66	24
SNO SP: LAST STEAM USED & PURCHASED	11	78	47

Stephans' Railroad Directory

Railroad/Railfan

RAILROAD HISTORIES & ROSTERS

SHORT NOTES ON...	M	Y	P
SNO SP: LEASES LAKE TAHOE RY & TRANS CO	03	35	87
SNO SP: LOCO SANDERS CUT BACK ON DEPOSIT	10	56	39
SNO SP: LOCOMOTIVE TYPE/CLASS/TRACTIVE F	10	32	349
SNO SP: MCKEEN GAS CARS TRAINS USING	06	58	37
SNO SP: MINA BRANCH/LOCOS USED--DATA	07	35	83
SNO SP: NARROW GAGE	01	43	134
SNO SP: NEVADA & CALIFORNIA BRANCH	05	53	140
SNO SP: NO NAME TRAIN ORDER-COST CUTTING	01	76	39
SNO SP: NOW HAS GUARD DOGS	08	74	06
SNO SP: OLIVER MILLET LOUNGE CAR	04	48	134
SNO SP: OPERATES EP&S + CPA MILEAGE	10	55	37
SNO SP: OWENS VALLEY DIESELIZED/LOCOS WH	10	55	36
SNO SP: PACIFIC RAILROAD OF MEXICO	01	55	36
SNO SP: PASSENGER TRAIN DETERIORATION	05	68	08
SNO SP: PASSENGER TRAINS--ALL BUT 3 DIES	02	57	45
SNO SP: PECOS RIVER BRIDGE	09	45	53
SNO SP: PORTLAND DE-ELECTRICIFICATION	06	73	48
SNO SP: PROSPERITY SPECIAL-20 2-10-2 SHI	01	73	60
SNO SP: RADAR-TYPE EQUIPMENT	07	49	61
SNO SP: RAILROADING LADY	09	43	06
SNO SP: RAILROADS OWNED OR OPERATED BY	08	37	55
SNO SP: READER MEMORIES: FIRST TRIP	03	47	133
SNO SP: READERS MEMORIES	06	43	138
SNO SP: REMOTE CONTROL SNOW MELTERS	06	54	12
SNO SP: RIO GRANDE DIVISON CONVERTING LO	08	50	124
SNO SP: RUNAWAY	10	50	133
SNO SP: SA&AP/T&NO NOW PART OF SP	11	31	491
SNO SP: SACRAMENTO GENERAL SHOPS	10	46	53
SNO SP: SACRAMENTO GENERAL SHOPS/REPAIR	11	46	65
SNO SP: SALTON CA STATION	10	56	77
SNO SP: SIERRA ROUTE SNOWSHED/VENTS	08	44	65
SNO SP: SPM EXTENSION OF SP	02	41	117
SNO SP: STEAM LOCOS SCRAPPED/ #'S/TYPE	12	48	72
SNO SP: TAYLOR ROUND HOUSE PHOTO ESSAY	01	48	40
SNO SP: TAYLOR YARD IMPROVEMENTS	04	50	74
SNO SP: TUNNLES ELIMINATED	07	45	76
SNO SP: WHO BUILT CAB-IN-FRONTERS	12	56	28
SNO SP: WRECK OF DEC 9 1929	01	34	36
SNO SPA: 1863/NOW PA TURNPIKE	04	46	60
SNO SPA: CIRCA 1885	02	68	29
SNO SPC: CHARTERED 1876 LEASED TO SP '87	09	73	41
SNO SPC: CHARTERED 1876/MERGERS/NO SP	10	35	86
SNO SPEG: FORMATION	04	78	06
SNO SPEG: READER INFORMATION	09	85	05
SNO SPI: INCORP 1905/CP ACQUIRES 1917/EQ	03	36	86
SNO SPLASL: BRIEF HISTORY	09	69	32
SNO SPLASL: INCORP 1901 TO LA&SL 1916	09	75	58
SNO SPLASL: INCORP 1901/ACQUISITIONS	05	41	48
SNO SPLASL: READER INFORMATION	12	69	29
SNO SPM&M: M&PAC REORGANIZED AS	07	36	82
SNO SPM&M: GN TAKES OVER IN 1890	03	35	85
SNO SPM: CHARTERED 1909/SP EXTENSION	02	41	117
SNO SPM: CYR&P BECAME PART OF	05	51	74
SNO SPM: DIVISIONS	05	33	74
SNO SPMRY: FLORIDA/30 MILES	12	46	106
SNO SPMRY: NEW PCC STREAMLINERS TRIED	11	47	113
SNO SPRS: BECAME OHIO SOUTHERN IN 1881	07	34	92
SNO SPS: ITS HISTORY	02	53	64
SNO SPTEX: ABSORBED BY T&P IN 1872	10	42	63
SNO SPW: BECAME PART OF G&F IN 1911	03	36	83
SNO SPW: BECAME PART OF G&F IN 1911.	06	41	61
SNO SR&D:	11	30	598
SNO SR&ELK: TO B&O 1918	11	76	44
SNO SR&RL: 1908/2' GAGE/MERGERS	12	55	29
SNO SR&RL: ABANDONED IN MID '30'S	04	51	132
SNO SR&RL: BUILT IN 1877/2' GAGE/COMMON	01	55	35
SNO SR&RL: ENGINE 1, 2, 24 SPECIFICATION	09	73	41
SNO SR&RL: FAREWELL TO SANDY RIVER LINE	10	32	418
SNO SR&RL: SHORT HISTORY	02	34	88
SNO SR&SQ: LEASED TO NPC IN 1875	08	55	46
SNO SR&W:	07	32	510
SNO SR&W: 1903-1939/FORMERLY PECO	10	50	62
SNO SRDAC: EQUIPM BUILT 1901/1917-UNUSUA	12	48	102
SNO SRR: ABSORBED BY B&A IN 1889	04	35	86
SNO SRTM: RT METRO OPENS	07	87	26
SNO SRV: PURCHASED BEDFORD & BILLERICA	12	55	26
SNO SS&C: BRIEF HISTORY	02	67	26
SNO SS&S: INCORP 1886/3' GAGE/ABANDONED	09	36	76
SNO SS&S: INCORPORATED 1886 DIED 1930	07	75	52
SNO SS&S: NARROW-GAGE LINE	08	41	72
SNO SS&S: SLIM-GAGE	11	41	52
SNO SS: BECAME PART OF QM&S IN 1906	09	41	80
SNO SS: MERGED WITH QSRY TO QM&S	02	73	50
SNO SSLI: ROCKAWAY RAILWAY CO MERGED INT	01	34	92
SNO SSLV: 31.38 MILES LONG SHORT HISTORY	07	69	35
SNO SSNP: BECAME NORFOLK & WESTERN	07	54	21
SNO SSO&G: CHARTERED IN 1877/NOW PSY	01	35	87
SNO SSO&G: NOW PART OF PLANT SYSTEMS	12	37	54
SNO SSP: 1955 FAREWELL PASSENGER RUN	05	55	52
SNO SSP: 24 HOUR STREET CAR SERVICE	05	43	125
SNO SSP: SOLD TO DAWSON BUS CO/8 MILES	04	55	63
SNO SSRY: BECAME S&INT/THEN LSEL	11	51	78
SNO SSWR: HORSE-CARS TO CABLE CARS 1877	11	45	94
SNO ST&E: 22 MILES/1 LOCOMOTIVE	07	32	510
SNO ST&E: OLDEST LOCO IN REGULAR SERVICE	08	47	131
SNO ST: 7 MILES/EQUIPMENT	08	32	57
SNO ST: ELECTRIC LINE/FUTURE BRIGHT	05	55	50
SNO STAR UNION LINE: CHARTERED AS WI&TC	11	45	55
SNO STAT: ORGANIZED 1906	12	72	60
SNO STAT: ORGANIZED 1906/GEORGIA/EQUIPME	06	37	62
SNO STEAM VS GAS-ELECTRIC	08	33	87
SNO STER: LEASED BY NPC IN 1872	08	55	46
SNO STEW: 1875-1879/NOW LONG ISLAND RR	07	36	85
SNO STEWRR: BUILT 1875 NOW LI	05	73	35
SNO STL&A: BRIEF HISTORY	01	41	77
SNO STRR: 4.5 MILES/PASS SERVICE/EQUIPME	06	59	07
SNO STRR: COMMON CARRIER	02	61	31
SNO STRR: LITTLE FOUR MILE ROAD	06	33	54
SNO STRR: LOCATION	07	76	51
SNO STRR: OLDEST SHORTLINE/PENNSYLVANIA	05	52	128

Railroad/ Railfan

RAILROAD HISTORIES & ROSTERS

SHORT NOTES ON...	M	Y	P
SNO SUBT: INCORP 1899/32 MI/BECAME IR&T	12	47	92
SNO SU&L: LEASED BY MP	06	34	87
SNO SUNV: CHARTERED 1863/APPLIED ABANDON	02	53	58
SNO SUNV: CORRECTIONS FEB P58/P134	05	53	138
SNO SUNV: FAREWELL TRAIN/NEW HAMPSHIRE	05	53	68
SNO SUNV: NEW HAMPSHIRE ROAD/1863/22 MI.	01	34	88
SNO SURY: INCORP 1912 OWNED BY SP/ATSF	07	76	51
SNO SUSC: OWNED BY NYS&W	05	34	82
SNO SV&BT: 1855/WAS DL&B/BECAME P-P 1859	04	46	60
SNO SV&E: CHARTERED 1902/32 MILES	04	37	53
SNO SV&E: INCORP IN 1906 16 MILES	07	37	58
SNO SV&E: INCORPORATED 1906 DIED 1932	08	73	57
SNO SV&E: INCORPORATED 1906 DIED 1932	02	75	50
SNO SV&E: INCORPORATED 1906 DIED 1932.	11	75	41
SNO SV: 6 STEAM LOCOMOTIVES	01	36	87
SNO SV: INCORP 1890/3' GAGE/OREGON/62 MI	10	36	73
SNO SVAL: INCORP 1880/4 MILES/EQUIPMENT	02	40	122
SNO SVAL: ONE LOCO/NO ROLLING STOCK	10	41	76
SNO SVP: 1875-1875/MONORAIL	03	48	128
SNO SVT: BECAME OHIO MIDLAND	11	52	90
SNO SWITCH KEYS: BRASS--WHY?	04	59	38
SNO SWL: 3' GAGE/ 50 MILES	04	37	55
SNO SWNM: BECAME EP&S IN 1900	01	37	88
SNO SWNM: TO EP&S 1900	04	75	12
SNO SWRY: BECAME PART OF SL&AD IN 1896	11	40	73
SNO SY&B: 1886-1892/6 MILES	09	42	59
SNO SY&B: SHORT HISTORY	10	62	36
SNO SYC: BEGAN 1885/GEORGIA/15 MILES	08	54	114
SNO SYC: CHARTERED 1884 BRIEF HISTORY	03	70	38
SNO SYC: RY AFTER 1903 RR BEFORE 1903	09	69	32
SNO CT&V: VALLEY LINE READER INFORMATION	11	80	05
SNO T&AL: 24.5 MILES/ARKANSAS	01	30	209
SNO T&BV: BECAME BURI	03	49	14
SNO T&BV: CHARTERED 1902/BECAME BURI	11	40	68
SNO T&BV: INCORP 1902/1930 NAME CHANGE	09	36	74
SNO T&BV: NOW BURLINGTON-ROCK ISLAND	03	38	54
SNO T&C: BRIEF HISTORY	02	66	30
SNO T&C: BRIEF HISTORY CHARTERED 1885	03	66	27
SNO T&CR: CHARTERED 1895 RECEIVERSHP '99	04	74	44
SNO T&CR: CHARTERED 1895/145 MILES/EQUIP	10	40	65
SNO T&CR: SHORT HISTORY	04	65	56
SNO T&CV: CHARTERED 1883 THEN B&AT 1890	01	73	61
SNO T&CV: CHARTERED IN 1883/REORGAN 1890	07	34	90
SNO T&EA: INTERURBAN W/FREIGHT SERVICE	11	52	90
SNO T&EA: SHORT HISTORY	12	68	31
SNO T&FS: BECAME PART OF KCS	04	57	74
SNO T&FS: TEXAS LINE KANSAS CITY SOUTHER	09	35	85
SNO T&GO: 89 MILES/NEVADA	07	47	28
SNO T&GO: CONSOLIDATION 1905	07	37	53
SNO T&GO: INCORP 1905/CONSOLIDATION/MILE	12	35	83
SNO T&GO: INCORP 1905/NEVADA/STD GAGE/EQ	01	41	73
SNO T&GO: INCORP IN 1905/ASSETS/VALUATIO	06	35	86
SNO T&GW: ORGANIZED 1907/ABANDONED 1918	09	52	63
SNO T&ILL: ORGANIZED 1853/BECAME TW&W	07	36	85
SNO T&IRY: 1915 BRILL INTERURBAN FREIGHT	12	54	62

SHORT NOTES ON...	M	Y	P
SNO T&KW: FEC ACQUIRES IN 1899	06	34	84
SNO T&LC: ABSORBED BY T&CR	10	40	66
SNO T&LCR: SOLD TO T&CR	04	74	44
SNO T&LSC: INCORP 1863/BECAME CPM&O	04	55	41
SNO T&NC: LEASED PIGR UNTIL 1926	09	36	76
SNO T&NC: LEASED PIGR UNTIL 1926	10	75	53
SNO T&NC: PIGEON RIVER RR BECAME PART OF	01	39	61
SNO T&NE: 7.5 MILES/PRIVATE RIGHT OF WAY	12	55	44
SNO T&NO: MCKEEN GAS CARS USED ON BRANCH	06	58	37
SNO T&NO: NOW PART OF SP	11	31	491
SNO T&NO: ORGANIZED IN 1875	05	31	279
SNO T&NO: SINGLE-LEAF BASCULE TEXAS	08	52	67
SNO T&NO: STEAM LOCOS RETAINED SINCE DIE	02	56	38
SNO T&NO: TEXAS TRUNK RAILROAD BECAME	04	44	99
SNO T&NON: 443 MILES/63 LOCOS/EQUIPMENT	01	33	102
SNO T&NON: 63 LOCOS	09	32	236
SNO T&NON: ALWAYS GOV'T OWNED/LOCOS	02	36	85
SNO T&NON: AUTHORIZED 1902/CANADA/MI/EQU	07	40	68
SNO T&NON: AUTHORIZED 1902/MILES/EQUIPME	01	38	59
SNO T&NON: BECAME ON IN 1947	05	51	61
SNO T&NON: BUILT 1902/NAME CHANGED 1946	01	55	43
SNO T&NON: CANADIAN'S FOURTH LARGEST	03	43	109
SNO T&NON: LOCO TYPES/CLASS/DATA	04	32	73
SNO T&NV: 38 MILES/STANDARD GAGE/EQUIPME	12	32	105
SNO T&NV: DEMISE	11	86	36
SNO T&O: SEPARATE RAILROAD	07	51	128
SNO T&OC: FORECLOSURE	09	32	233
SNO T&P: 1872/ROADS ACQUIRED/BRIEF HISTO	10	42	63
SNO T&P: 1952 MILES	07	33	84
SNO T&P: 25 YEARS WITH NO PASS KILLED	06	50	137
SNO T&P: 60-70 PERCENT DIESELIZATION	01	50	126
SNO T&P: COACH #X473--ITS LIFE	05	51	139
SNO T&P: HEAVYWEIGHT RAIL 132 POUND	11	50	126
SNO T&P: JUKE BOX TRAIN CALLER	07	50	67
SNO T&P: LIST OF ROADS MAKING UP	09	74	43
SNO T&P: LOCO HEADLIGHTS ON DAY/NIGHT	11	49	127
SNO T&P: LOCO STILL IN QUICKSAND/65 YRS	12	41	70
SNO T&P: METAL HOODS/CLASSIFICATION FLAG	12	49	125
SNO T&P: MOVED 135 CIRCUS CARS IN 1 MONT	02	50	126
SNO T&P: NELLIE THE HORSE STILL USED	07	52	139
SNO T&P: RETIRED 71 STEAM LOCOS	04	50	129
SNO T&P: SELLS LAKE TO TOWN/DIESELIZED	09	52	130
SNO T&P: SIDE DOOR CABOOSES	05	54	123
SNO T&P: SPECIAL EDUCATIONAL TOURS	10	50	127
SNO T&P: STEAM GENERATOR CAR	04	51	68
SNO T&P: TAXLESS COMMUNITY	11	52	123
SNO T&P: TEENAGE SABOTAGE ATTEMPT	09	52	134
SNO T&P: TUMBLEWEED FENCES	06	65	09
SNO T&P: WRECK OF LOCO #642	12	54	72
SNO T&SL: MERGED AND BECAME CBELT	02	47	111
SNO T&SL: 1879/TYLER TAP RR RENAMED AS	02	47	111
SNO T&SM: 1ST ROAD CHARTERED IN FLORIDA	10	56	44
SNO T&ST: INCORP IN 1912/BECAME TS	12	35	85
SNO T&T: 5 LOCOS (#S/TYPES)/GAS-ELEC CAR	01	32	258
SNO T&T: ABSORBS/ABANDONED/CORRECTIONS	10	49	131

Railroad/ Railfan

RAILROAD HISTORIES & ROSTERS

SHORT NOTES ON...	M	Y	P
SNO T&T: INCORP 1904 143 MILES	07	37	53
SNO T&T: INCORP 1904/STD GAGE/HISTORY	09	52	63
SNO T&T: INCORP IN 1904	05	32	179
SNO T&T: INCORP IN 1904/NEVADA/EQUIPMENT	06	35	87
SNO T&TH: NOW PLANT SYSTEMS	01	35	87
SNO T&TO: IOWA/3.5 MILES	02	54	107
SNO T&WE: CORRECTIONS	01	37	89
SNO T&WE: 1915 BRILL INTERURBAN FREIGHT	12	54	62
SNO T&WE: 59 MILES/20 MILE BRANCH	01	37	89
SNO T&WE: INCORP 1924/REORGAN/31 MILES	11	36	53
SNO T&WS: BECAME CONSOLIDATED RAILWAY CO	04	47	65
SNO T-DR: FORMED 1911 RENAMED '15 TO DT&I	04	76	08
SNO T-F: ORIGINALLY STEAM/18 MILES	04	46	115
SNO T-NMR: ACQUIRED BY T&P IN 1928	10	42	63
SNO TA&G: CORRECTIONS	08	38	94
SNO TA&G: WHERE IS IT?	02	61	28
SNO TAA&C: BECAME AA/ABSORBED LG&MR 1886	07	53	53
SNO TAA&J: BUILT 1907	04	76	08
SNO TANDEM-COUMPOUND LOCOS: THE FIRST	01	50	76
SNO TANK-CAR HISTORY	10	48	69
SNO TANV: 45 MILES/NARROW GAGE/NOW AL	01	47	57
SNO TANV: ALASKA/NARROW GAGE/ABANDONED	12	35	85
SNO TAT: 26 MILE YONKERS	12	51	90
SNO TAT: 265 MILES/EQUIPMENT	01	42	65
SNO TAT: FIRST RPO CARS/READER MEMORIES	06	48	90
SNO TAT: GONE! DESCRIBED	10	55	52
SNO TC&D: 1ST LOCO IN ALABAMA	08	56	41
SNO TC&D: SECOND ALABAMA RAILROAD	06	61	36
SNO TC&D: TUSC RENAMED AS TC&D	12	51	65
SNO TC&OR: CONSOLIDATION	04	31	122
SNO TC&SL: CONSOLIDATED IN 1883	02	36	87
SNO TC&SL: RESULT OF MANY CONSOLIDATIONS	09	34	83
SNO TCRT: CONTROL CHANGES HANDS/POLICIES	02	51	76
SNO TCRT: STREETCARS DISAPPEARING/MEMORI	04	54	100
SNO TCS&D: ACQUIRED BY NYC	04	31	122
SNO TD&B: FORMED IN 1879	09	34	83
SNO TE: BRIEF HISTORY	12	64	54
SNO TE: INTERURBAN LINE	11	44	88
SNO TE: LARGEST ELECTRIC LINE IN TEXAS	10	34	83
SNO TEM: CORRECTIONS	07	38	79
SNO TEM: INCORPORATED IN 1885/113 MILES	05	38	74
SNO TEM: MOTOR CARS/4-4-0/"BRIDGE" ROAD	10	48	129
SNO TEM: OPENED IN 1889/CORRECTIONS/ROST	07	38	79
SNO TEM: SOLD 1950	04	50	121
SNO TENNC: 269 MILES/EQUIPMENT	05	32	181
SNO TENNC: BECAME PART OF N&CRR IN 1902	05	42	63
SNO TENNC: BRIEF HISTORY/EQUIPMENT	09	42	64
SNO TEXS: STATE RR IN 1984	05	84	62
SNO TEXSL: ACQUIRED BY T&P IN 1929	10	42	63
SNO TEXT: NOW T&NO	04	44	99
SNO TEXTR: BECAME TE	11	44	88
SNO TF&E: 1888 HORSE CARS/1892 TROLLEY/	04	39	139
SNO TF&F: PURCHASED LEB&N IN 1916	06	52	82
SNO TF&F: ROUTE/3 MILES TORN UP	10	52	91
SNO TF&N: BECAME PART OF LSE IN 1901	03	37	62
SNO TF&NK: BECAME LSEL	11	51	78
SNO TF: CHARTERED 1898/STD GAGE/58 MILES	04	59	35
SNO TF: INCORP 1898/58 MILES/5 LOCOS/EQU	01	36	81
SNO TH&B: COMPLETE TAKEOVER BY CP	11	77	25
SNO TH&B: INCORP 1891 ABSORBS/MERGERS/EQ	08	51	64
SNO TH&B: INCORP IN 1892	07	36	85
SNO TH&B: SOLD TO CP	08	77	11
SNO TH&I: LEASES VANDALIA IN 1880	12	33	91
SNO TH&P	05	34	83
SNO TH&P:	11	33	91
SNO TH&SE: CONSOLIDATED TO EV&I TO C&EI	07	73	39
SNO TH&SE: CONSOLIDATION 1885	06	38	76
SNO TIDE: CHARTERED 1904/BECAME V 1907	04	59	38
SNO TIDE: INCORP IN 1904/NAME CHANGE '07	05	34	85
SNO TIV: CHARTERED IN 1881/3' GAGE/13 MI	03	34	86
SNO TK&N: INCORP 1912/19 MILES/EQUIPMENT	02	36	85
SNO TLL: ABANDONED 1942/LOCO DISPLAY/6 M	06	54	116
SNO TLP&C: INCORPORATED 1892 BECAME T&CR	04	74	44
SNO TLP&CR: INCORP 1892/T&CR BUYS 1896	10	40	65
SNO TM&P: 1911-1918/3' GAGE/EQUIPMENT	08	49	54
SNO TM&P: INCORPORATED 1911 DIED 1918	09	74	42
SNO TMEX: 1881/NAME CHANGE CCSDRG	02	46	61
SNO TMEX: TEXAS/161 MILES/EQUIPMENT	10	39	85
SNO TOKIO EXPRESS: 3 ON US LINES	11	45	56
SNO TON: BECAME PART OF T&GO IN 1905	07	37	53
SNO TON: BECAME PART OF T&GO IN 1905	11	35	83
SNO TON: BECAME T&GO IN 1905	01	41	73
SNO TONAW: 1832-1850/NOW B&ROCH	11	43	61
SNO TONAW: BECAME PART OF B&ROCH IN 1850	09	53	44
SNO TOV: INCORP 1908/6 MILES/UTAH/EQUIPM	09	34	86
SNO TOWN: 1919-1933/11 MILES/N CAROLINA	09	36	76
SNO TOWN: INCORPORATED 1919 DIED 1933	03	76	56
SNO TP&W: 1880/REORGANIZATION/EQUIP/MILE	04	41	46
SNO TP&W: 2 STACK LOCOS-PURPOSE	01	51	75
SNO TP&W: 239 MILES/20 MONTHS OF STRIKES	11	47	87
SNO TP&W: BAD LUCK	11	52	137
SNO TP&W: FREIGHT ROAD/239 MILES	08	54	79
SNO TP&W: PRESIDENT ROB'T MCMILLAN INTER	07	83	54
SNO TP&WAR: CHARTERED 1863/OPENED 1868	04	41	46
SNO TP: INCORP 1871/BECAME T&P 1872	10	42	63
SNO TPT: INDUSTRIAL & SWITCHING ROAD	02	59	45
SNO TPT: SHORT HISTORY	09	66	33
SNO TR&U: 1915 NAME CHANGE OF BTR&U	01	49	90
SNO TRA: 1889 /95 STEAM, 31 DIESEL LOCOS	06	43	64
SNO TRAIN ROBBERY: WINSLOW AZ 1889	08	32	91
SNO TRO: INCORP 1913/33 MILES/CALIF/EQUI	01	38	58
SNO TROYC: 1889/MERGER OF 3 HORSECAR LIN	12	55	44
SNO TRSL: OPENED 1897/BOSTON MASS/SUBWAY	03	45	74
SNO TS&LH: CHARTERED 1849 THEN OS&H 1857	10	73	58
SNO TS&LH: CHARTERED IN 1849	01	35	85
SNO TS&LH: INCORP 1849 BECAME NRC 1858	11	47	20
SNO TS&N: ABSORBED BY T&P IN 1901	10	42	63
SNO TS&NO: INCORP 1873/STATION NAMES	05	47	131
SNO TS: INCORP 1912/3 LOCOS/EQUIPMENT	12	35	85
SNO TS: INCORPORATED 1912 OWNED BY WP	06	76	51

Railroad/Railfan

RAILROAD HISTORIES & ROSTERS

SHORT NOTES ON...	M	Y	P
SNO TSL	11	30	598
SNO TSL&C: BUILT 1846/BECAME PART OF NKP	04	57	40
SNO TSL&KC: 451 MILES/BECAME TSL&W	04	38	49
SNO TSL&KC: ORGANIZED 1866/CLOVER LEAF R	09	34	83
SNO TSL&KC: SOLD 1900/BECAME TSL&W	10	53	68
SNO TSL&W: 451 MILES	04	38	49
SNO TSL&W: CLOVER LEAF SYSTEM/LOCO USED	06	32	336
SNO TSL&W: CLOVER LEAF/INCORP 1900/CONSO	10	53	68
SNO TSL&W: INCORPORATED 1900 FROM TSL&KC	04	75	11
SNO TSL&W: REORGANIZATION OF TSL&KC 1900	09	34	83
SNO TT: CONTROLLED BY	06	38	73
SNO TT: INCORPORATED 1907 BRIEF HISTORY	06	70	62
SNO TTAP: INCORP 1871/EVENTUALLY CBELT	02	47	111
SNO TTC: HAULS BEER/1 MI/2 RDS SAME NAME	04	53	94
SNO TTCO: NEW SUBWAY SYSTEM	03	55	59
SNO TTCO: REFUGE FOR STREETCARS	02	53	77
SNO TTM: BUILT IN 1904/BECAME NNB&S	05	54	12
SNO TTY: ABSORBED BY CONNECTICUT COMPANY	04	47	63
SNO TU: SHORT HISTORY	09	33	131
SNO TUCK: 1880/29 MILES/EQUIP/NAME CHANG	11	34	95
SNO TUCK: BRIEF HISTORY	07	65	31
SNO TUCK: OPENED 1871/EQUIPMENT	07	54	60
SNO TUSC: CHARTERED 1830	12	51	65
SNO TUSC: CHARTERED 1830 TO TVRR 1847	07	76	50
SNO TUSC: FIRST ALABAMA RAILROAD	06	61	36
SNO TUV: 1891-1934/3' GAGE/PENNSLYVANIA	03	36	85
SNO TUV: 27 MILES/BUS LINE	05	34	132
SNO TV&C: 1881 MERGER/SOLD 1891/NOW AT&F	05	45	65
SNO TV&C: 1881/MERGER/STORMY CAREER	12	40	65
SNO TV&H: SHEFFIELD & TIONESTA TAKES OVE	05	34	83
SNO TV&SC: ABSORBED BY S&TI	05	34	83
SNO TV: BECAME TV&C IN 1881	12	40	65
SNO TV: CHARTERED 1880/3'/BECAME TV&C	05	45	65
SNO TVE: BECAME TV&C IN 1881	12	40	65
SNO TVE: BECAME TV&C IN 1881/MERGER	05	45	65
SNO TVRR: 1847/TC&D REORGANIZED	12	51	65
SNO TVRR: FROM TUSC 1847 TO M&CH 1866	07	76	50
SNO TW&W: REORGANIZED AS WABASH RAILWAY	07	36	85
SNO TW: CHARTERED 1875 DIED 1899	05	75	52
SNO TW: CHARTERED 1875/REORGANIZED 1880	03	52	56
SNO U&D: INCORP 1901/HISTORY/EQUIPMENT	01	33	96
SNO U&D: INCORP IN 1901/CONSOLIDATIONS	07	36	86
SNO U&D: LAST PASSENGER RUN/ PART OF NYC	08	54	10
SNO U&N: INCORP 1920/TEXAS/37 MILES/EQUI	09	39	71
SNO U&SRR: BECAME NYC	09	53	44
SNO U&SRR: CHARTERED 1833/78 MILES	11	43	61
SNO U: 3' GAGE/FINANCIAL/LARGEST ARTICUL	01	35	82
SNO U: BAXTER PASS/THE BIG HILL!	07	40	73
SNO UC&B: LEASED TO NYO&W 1924	11	76	44
SNO UC: DIVIDED UP BETWEEN UP & D&RGW	09	34	86
SNO UCRR: LEASED BY B&M	05	54	80
SNO UERC: FROM RISR REORGANIZATION 1921	09	76	52
SNO UERY: CARS TO MEXICO CITY	03	49	83
SNO UF: 2.5 MILE CONNECTING RR/MASSUCHUE	03	36	83
SNO UI&E: ABSORBED BY LV	02	53	127
SNO UI&E: NAME CHANGES/HISTORY	05	53	62
SNO UI&E: OPENED 1872 BECAME EC&N NOW LV	04	74	44
SNO UI&E: OPENED IN 1872/NOW PART OF LV	01	35	82
SNO UIRY: CABLE & TROLLEY/GOFFSTOWN NY	06	51	128
SNO UM: UNIVERSITY OWNED TROLLEY LINE	08	46	120
SNO UNIC: TO SP&S 1944	01	75	54
SNO UNION STAR LINE: (FAST FREIGHT LINE)	03	69	23
SNO UNO: COMPLETED 1874/NARROW GA/NOW UP	04	57	45
SNO UNTR: LINES IN 6 CITIES	12	55	43
SNO UNTR: RECHARTERED	12	58	29
SNO UP: "CITY OF SALINA" STRLINER SCRAPP	07	42	69
SNO UP: "SOUND-MAGAZINE" ADVERTISING	08	54	16
SNO UP: 1000 MI TREE--LANDMARK	04	73	46
SNO UP: 1000 MILE TREE	01	46	62
SNO UP: 4000 SERIES BIG BOYS/SPECIFICATI	12	56	32
SNO UP: 939 LOCOS/AUX TENDERS/ETC	11	30	599
SNO UP: ACQUISITIONS AND OWNERSHIPS	03	36	83
SNO UP: ARTICULATED LOCOS	06	44	85
SNO UP: ASPEN TUNNEL	11	47	89
SNO UP: BREDDLOVE HIGHBALLS DRAG	03	30	488
SNO UP: CITY OF PORTLAND-WHAT HAPPENED?	11	47	83
SNO UP: CITY OF SALINA 1ST STREAMLINED	08	55	43
SNO UP: DEPARTMENT STORE ON WHEELS	03	52	55
SNO UP: ELECTRON MICROSCOPE	02	56	43
SNO UP: EMBLEM--SHIELD/SLOGAN	08	56	40
SNO UP: EQUIPMENT ORDER NOV 1947	04	48	75
SNO UP: EXPERIMENTAL STEAM TURBINE-ELECT	04	57	45
SNO UP: FIRST LIQUID FUEL LOCOMOTIVES	05	68	26
SNO UP: FIRST TO BUILD RR INTO UTAH??	04	57	45
SNO UP: GAS-TURBINE ELCTRIC NOW PROPANE	08	53	57
SNO UP: GAS-TURBINE ELECTRIC LOCOS GE	07	51	67
SNO UP: HERALD EVOLUTION	02	74	06
SNO UP: ILWACO RY & NAV CO BECOMES PART	12	35	82
SNO UP: KELSO CA TRUE RAILROAD TOWN	11	75	10
SNO UP: LIVESTOCK SERVICE SLC TO LOS ANG	02	48	76
SNO UP: LOCO REVAMPS/SOME SCRAPPED	03	48	135
SNO UP: LOCOS BOARDED AT POCATELLO	04	50	132
SNO UP: MCKEEN MOTOR CAR	08	43	58
SNO UP: MERGED WITH DT&FW IN 1891	10	55	36
SNO UP: NAMES OF STREAMLINERS/DOMELINERS	06	56	41
SNO UP: NAMING OF TOWNS	02	48	134
SNO UP: NEW 42 MILE LINE WYOMING	06	52	60
SNO UP: NEW STYLE TICKETS	07	51	133
SNO UP: ORD BRANCH	12	47	138
SNO UP: ORDERS 15 GAS TURBINE ELECTRICS	04	53	63
SNO UP: ORDERS 35 DIESELS 1950	06	50	60
SNO UP: OWNS OREGON WASHINGTON RR & NAV	04	33	94
SNO UP: PACKET LINE ST JOE MO	07	78	55
SNO UP: PURCHASED LNP&W IN 1935	01	47	56
SNO UP: REPAINTING PASSENGER EQUIPMENT	08	52	127
SNO UP: ROCK ISLAND MERGER CONDITIONS	03	75	10
SNO UP: SAFETY SIDE LADDER TREADS	06	53	60
SNO UP: SHERMAN HILL	07	53	109
SNO UP: SOUTH TRACK HIGHER	10	38	56
SNO UP: STREAMLINERS REPAINTED ON RUN	06	40	60

470

Railroad/ Railfan

RAILROAD HISTORIES & ROSTERS

SHORT NOTES ON...	M	Y	P
SNO UP: TEN MILLION DOLLAR TRACK JOB	09	41	84
SNO UP: TOURIST SLEEPING CARS ELIMINATED	07	47	126
SNO UP: TRAIN CHANGES	06	36	79
SNO UP: TRANSPARENT BOXCAR	11	52	59
SNO UP: TRANSPARENT BOXCAR-REDUCE DAMAGE	03	53	134
SNO UP: TURKISH BATH FOR LOCOS	12	46	83
SNO UP: TYPES OF STEAM LOCOS OWNED BY	06	56	38
SNO UPCC: 1ST ELECTRIC MINE LOCO	11	48	57
SNO UPD&G: MERGER OF DT&FW + UP	10	55	36
SNO URR: 0-10-2 STEAM LOCOS-WHERE NOW?	07	50	62
SNO URR: 44.5 MILES/OWNED BY US STEEL	06	46	101
SNO URR: 46 MILES/EQUIPMENT	06	32	333
SNO URR: FULLY DIESELIZED	10	50	131
SNO URWO	04	33	94
SNO URWO: INCORPORATED 1896 NOW UP	09	72	52
SNO URWO: PURCHASED SEATTLE & WALLA WALL	02	37	80
SNO URY: 5 DIESELS/42 WOODBURNERS	12	57	40
SNO URY: BECAME FDES	10	73	35
SNO USA: DIESEL-ELECTRIC LOCOS/ALCO	11	53	45
SNO USAF: TEN MAN ROAD	05	78	16
SNO USN: 92 STEAM LOCOS/ELECT/OIL BURNER	12	33	94
SNO USN: EQUIPMENT LIST/TYPE/QUANITY	11	49	44
SNO USRA: MALLETS BUILT FOR	04	44	75
SNO UT&N: LONGEST 3' GAGE/NOW STD/NOW UP	10	55	31
SNO UT: BECAME PART OF KCS IN 1902	09	40	61
SNO UTA&M: TAKEN OVER IN 1910	03	37	61
SNO UTAH: INCORP 1912/COAL ROAD/99 MILES	02	34	86
SNO UTAHT: OWNED BY UTAH RAILWAY COMPANY	02	34	86
SNO UTCC	06	33	89
SNO UTDC: SKYTRAIN TO VANCOUVER	09	86	24
SNO UTRC: INCORP 1888/2 LOCOS/1 PASS CAR	04	40	75
SNO UTRC: INCORP IN 1888/25 MILES/EQUIPM	04	35	83
SNO UTRC: SWITCHING LINE/19 MILES	02	59	45
SNO UV&N: CHARTERED 1914/REORGAN 1940	06	54	59
SNO UV: CHARTERED 1890/INCORP 1904	09	34	85
SNO UW&PW: INCORP 1854/BECAME A&MR	06	56	72
SNO UW&PW: REALLY FIRST IN CALIFORNIA	10	60	35
SNO V&J: NOW PART OF IC	06	56	37
SNO V&MA: FIRST ROSTER INFORMATION	10	77	43
SNO V&SW: 1898/WAS SA&O	09	46	08
SNO V&SW: CHARTERED 1899 FROM SA&O/E&NC	05	74	46
SNO V&SW: CHARTERED IN 1899	12	38	69
SNO V&SW: CONTROLLED BY SOUTHERN	05	74	46
SNO V&T: 68 MILES/8 LOCOS/EQUIPMENT	02	33	80
SNO V&T: ADDITIONAL HISTORY	01	69	33
SNO V&T: CHARTERED 1869/67 MILES/EQUIPME	08	31	47
SNO V&T: DEPOT AT CARSON CITY NEVADA	01	55	66
SNO V&T: DEPOT CARSON CITY TO MASONIC LO	04	55	75
SNO V&T: INCORP IN 1905/EQUIPMENT/MILES	12	34	84
SNO V&T: NOT ABANDONED! CORRECT 02 PG133	04	42	117
SNO V&T: TO BE ABANDONED	11	48	134
SNO V&TEN: READERS HISTORY FORMED 1866	06	68	30
SNO V&TEN: READERS INFO CHARTERED 1848	10	68	36
SNO V&W: LEASED VIRGINIAN IN 1922	05	34	85
SNO V: 1907/CONSOLIDATION/MALLETS	04	59	37
SNO V: 800'S MOST POWERFUL LOCO'S BUILT	04	60	29
SNO V: BUILT TO HAUL SOFT COAL/NAME CHAN	04	37	71
SNO V: CLUB CARS	08	45	49
SNO V: ELECTRONIC TUBE ELECTRIC LOCOS	04	56	42
SNO V: NEW RECTIFIER LOCOS	06	57	42
SNO V: TIDEWATER RY NAME CHANGED TO V	05	34	85
SNO VA: LEASED TO TERRE HAUTE & INDIANAP	12	33	91
SNO VA: NOW PART OF PRR/0-4-0 TURTLE BAC	08	58	41
SNO VAC: CHARTERED IN 1887	09	38	56
SNO VAL: STAUNTON TO HARRISONBURG VA SLD	03	43	119
SNO VAL: TROLLEY	07	41	66
SNO VANDALIA LINE: SLV&TH CALLED THIS	11	33	88
SNO VC: FROM LOU	08	75	58
SNO VC: LOST ALL EQUIPMENT IN FIRE	12	49	129
SNO VC: NAME CHANGED IN 1926/38 MI/EQUIP	09	34	84
SNO VC: OPENED 1853 BRIEF HISTORY	06	70	62
SNO VC: SHORT HISTORY	08	63	30
SNO VC: SHORT HISTORY	05	65	42
SNO VCO: FINANCIAL	05	34	83
SNO VCO: INCORP 1911/CALIF/17 MILES/EQUI	02	38	61
SNO VCO: INCORP 1911/CALIF/22 MI/EQUIP/	08	35	82
SNO VCO: NOW ONLY OXNARD TO PT HUENENE	09	44	65
SNO VCO: STANDARD GAGE/WHEEL CHECKERS	12	51	69
SNO VCS&I: LAST NORTH DAKOTA ELECTRIC	08	77	57
SNO VE&PC: PRIVATE BUSES 1925	12	54	59
SNO VE&PC: VR&P BECAME IN THE 1920'S	03	50	75
SNO VEPCO: VIRGINIA STREET CAR LINE	03	50	75
SNO VIP: READER HISTORY ADDITIONS	03	74	55
SNO VIP: READER REMEMBERS EARLY YEARS	04	75	09
SNO VM&W: 40 MILES/GEORGIA ROAD/ABANDOND	05	34	132
SNO VM&W: CHARTERED 1906 (GEORGIA)	08	73	56
SNO VM&W: CHARTERED 1909	12	72	60
SNO VM&W: CHARTERED 1909/ABANDONED/EQUIP	06	37	62
SNO VPS: ABSORBED BY VEPCO IN 1944	03	50	75
SNO VR&P: OPERATED RICHMOND/PETERSBURG	03	50	75
SNO VS: BECAME PART OF G&F IN 1907	03	36	83
SNO VS: BECAME PART OF G&F IN 1907	06	41	61
SNO VS: BECME PART OF G&F IN 1927	03	39	75
SNO VSL: OWNED BY PE/VENICE CALIF	06	48	99
SNO VSP&S: TOURIST ROAD	03	71	60
SNO VT: BUS SUBSTITUTION	01	48	104
SNO VTC: BIBLE SERVICES ON SUNDAY	11	78	47
SNO VV&E: INCORP 1897 BRITISH COLUMBIA	07	33	84
SNO VV: CHARTERED 1848/24 MILES/VERMONT/	05	36	82
SNO VV: SUBSIDIARIES/OWNS	03	38	54
SNO VW&S: 33' LONG/FACTORY OWNED ROAD	11	39	90
SNO W&A: #3 "GENERAL" NEWS ACCOUNT	01	32	277
SNO W&A: 1837/NOW PART OF L&N/87 MILES	10	59	38
SNO W&A: BUILT 1841 NOW L&N BRIEF HISTOR	06	71	44
SNO W&AN: BECAME DA IN 1895	07	37	57
SNO W&AN: JOINED WITH Y&A TO DA 1894	07	74	39
SNO W&AN: MERGED W/Y&A TO FORM DA NOW CP	08	73	56
SNO W&AN: MERGED WITH Y&A IN 1894	05	49	53
SNO W&B	06	31	441
SNO W&BA: TRAINS ON ICE	02	78	49

Railroad/Railfan

RAILROAD HISTORIES & ROSTERS

SHORT NOTES ON...	M	Y	P
SNO W&BV: NOW PART OF PLANT SYSTEMS	01	35	87
SNO W&CB: ACQUIRED BY CBE IN 1896	11	36	54
SNO W&CB: SOLD IN 1895 TO CBE	04	34	79
SNO W&CE: BECAME CONSOLIDATED RAILWAY CO	04	47	65
SNO W&CR: CHARTERED 1892 FROM O&WT TO NP	11	74	52
SNO W&CR: CHARTERED 1892/EQUIPMENT/MILES	03	38	54
SNO W&FRY: OIL CITY TO OLEOPOLIS	01	33	97
SNO W&L: 20 MILES/2 LOCOS/EQUIPMENT	12	32	106
SNO W&LE: 1938 LAST PASS TRAIN	05	46	96
SNO W&LE: CHARTERED IN 1871/REORGANIZATI	05	34	82
SNO W&LE: INCORP IN 1916/512 MILES/EQUIP	02	35	87
SNO W&LE: NOW PART OF CC&S	06	38	76
SNO W&LE: SCRAPPING MOTIVE POWER PHOTOS	11	40	132
SNO W&M: READER INFORMATION	07	76	52
SNO W&M: TWO RAILROADS SAME NAME	09	66	35
SNO W&MV: BECAME MIDLAND VALLEY IN 1929	11	34	96
SNO W&MV: LEASED TO MIV IN 1910	08	56	38
SNO W&N: BRIEF HISTORY	04	66	35
SNO W&N: CHARTERED IN 1877	07	34	86
SNO W&NB: BRIEF HISTORY	06	62	46
SNO W&NB: BUILT IN 1865	09	32	234
SNO W&NB: INCORPORATED 1921 DIED 1938	07	75	53
SNO W&NB: NARROW GAGE	07	32	510
SNO W&NB: RY INCORP 1921/SUCCEEDED RR	02	41	70
SNO W&NO: 16 MILES/NO LOCOS/22 FRT CARS	04	34	86
SNO W&NO: INCORP 1905/CONSOLID/NOW CNJ	04	36	93
SNO W&NO: INCORP 1905/CONSOLIDATION/MILE	07	50	64
SNO W&NO: OWNED & OPERATED BY CNJ	02	59	45
SNO W&NO: OWNED AND OPERATED BY/LOCO	01	31	281
SNO W&O: CHARTERED 1903/BECAME WF&O/ELEC	11	48	85
SNO W&OD: 90 MILES/INTERURBAN/48 CARS	03	50	77
SNO W&OD: ELECTRIC LINE	04	46	115
SNO W&OD: ELECTRIC LINE/84 MILES	05	35	86
SNO W&OD: TRAIN #45 ABANDONED	12	51	119
SNO W&P: INCORP 1889 SOLD 1895 NY&NE	11	73	57
SNO W&P: INCORP IN 1889/ NY&NE PURCHASED	01	35	82
SNO W&POT: 1886/BECAME WB&PL	03	39	62
SNO W&PR: BECAME MORRISTOWN & ERIE	04	35	87
SNO W&PR: EASTERN EXTENSION OF W&PR	12	52	69
SNO W&Q: 1854-1911/NAME CHANGED/PROBLEMS	01	35	86
SNO W&Q: BECOMES WW&F	04	36	92
SNO W&Q: CHARTERED 1854/BECAME WW&F	12	55	30
SNO W&RL	09	33	48
SNO W&SF: 1906 FROM SDCEN/BECAME GN 1922	11	74	52
SNO W&SF: 1916 SOUTH DAKOTA CENTRAL RY	03	38	53
SNO W&SF: INCORPORATED 1902/NAME CHANGES	03	38	53
SNO W&SH: INCORP 1883/BECAME W&T IN 1884	04	40	77
SNO W&T: 1884/STANDARD GAGE/EQUIPMENT	04	40	77
SNO W&V: BECAME PART OF DAV&P IN 1872	06	39	52
SNO W&V: OPENED 1871 TO DAV&P 1872	02	75	49
SNO W&WA: 1875-1933/EQUIPMENT	05	35	85
SNO W&WA: 3' GAGE/OPENED IN 1877/NOW PRR	06	32	336
SNO W&WA: CORRECTIONS/ADDITITIONS/MEMORIE	03	55	70
SNO W&WA: DERAILMENT ON NEW TURNTABLE	06	72	08
SNO W&WA: INCORP 1875/3'ROAD	08	41	69
SNO W&WA: MOTHBALLING	03	76	10
SNO W&WA: NARROW GAGE IN PENNSYLVANIA	02	39	123
SNO W&WR: BECAME ACL 1900 NOW SCL	06	73	49
SNO W-BC: FORMED 1912/OPENED 1915	12	44	46
SNO W-BRY: NOW ONLY 2 ROUTES	01	48	104
SNO W-BS: TROLLEY/ND TO MINN/2 CARS	08	51	90
SNO W-W: 3 1/2 MILES/ABANDONED 1926	03	53	99
SNO W: 1877/REORGANIZED 1889	07	36	85
SNO W: CANNON BALL TRAIN	02	47	64
SNO W: DELMAR STATION ESCALATOR	06	48	50
SNO W: DETROIT-CHICAGO LINE/OPENED 1893	10	50	55
SNO W: FIRST ROAD DIESEL	02	78	50
SNO W: LAST STEAM OPERATION	10	54	09
SNO W: NO SLEEPER SERVICE	04	47	54
SNO W: NORTHERN CROSS BECAME PART OF	10	56	40
SNO W: SHORT LINE OPENED 1893	12	75	57
SNO WA&FC: ABSORBED BY WA&MV	03	50	76
SNO WA&G: "SOLE LEATHER LINE"	06	63	24
SNO WA&G: BRIEF HISTORY	12	66	27
SNO WA&G: FREIGHT LINE/NY/EQUIPMENT	10	59	35
SNO WA&MV: ELECTRIC LINE	03	50	76
SNO WA&P: CHARTERED 1831 NOW PC	09	73	43
SNO WA&SL: MERGED IN 1886	09	35	83
SNO WA&W: NOW PART OF PLANT SYSTEM	01	35	87
SNO WA&WA: NARROW GAUGE OF PRR 1930	12	75	57
SNO WA: BECAME PART OF L&HR	03	36	83
SNO WA: BECAME PART OF L&HR	02	32	333
SNO WA: INCORPORATED 1949	09	76	52
SNO WA: SHORTEST IN 1968	09	68	28
SNO WAL: SAL PREDECESSOR	04	71	62
SNO WARR: PRR ACQUIRED IN 1925	12	43	80
SNO WASHR: INCORP 1895/ PENNSYLVANIA/4 M	12	35	81
SNO WAT&R: CHARTERED 1832/NOW RW&O	02	37	78
SNO WAT: PHOTO ESSAY	07	42	93
SNO WAT: 5 MILES/RAILS TORN UP NOV 1954	02	55	06
SNO WAT: 6 MILES/1 LOCO/EQUIPMENT	06	33	92
SNO WAT: INCORP 1909/5 MILES/4 EMPLOYEES	02	36	84
SNO WAV: BRIEF HISTORY	08	65	21
SNO WAV: INCORPORATED 1866 BRIEF HISTORY	05	70	38
SNO WAV: ORGANIZED IN 1866/ERIE OPERATED	02	35	85
SNO WB&AE: 1907/BECAME ELECTRIFIED	06	32	339
SNO WB&AE: ANNAPOLIS SHORT LINE PART OF	03	32	522
SNO WB&E: CHARTERED 1892/8 MILES	01	42	65
SNO WB&E: CHARTERED 1892/NYS&W TAKES OVE	11	34	93
SNO WB&E: CHARTERED IN 1892	08	32	54
SNO WB&E: CHARTERED IN 1892/EQUIPMENT	06	33	89
SNO WB&E: OWNED BY NYS&W	05	34	82
SNO WB&E: SHORT HISTORY	07	65	31
SNO WB&PL: INCORP 1918/MARYLAND/24 MILES	06	36	84
SNO WB&S: ABANDONED 1943/TRACKS TORN UP	05	55	64
SNO WC	01	33	101
SNO WC&F: BECAME PART OF SF&W	12	40	61
SNO WC&F: CONSOLIDATED TO SF&W 1884	12	73	52
SNO WC&W: NOW PART OF MP	10	55	33
SNO WC: ACQUIRED BY SOO 1909	05	37	37

Railroad/Railfan

RAILROAD HISTORIES & ROSTERS

SHORT NOTES ON...	M	Y	P
SNO WC: CHICAGO HARLEM & BATAVIA/LEASED	08	32	56
SNO WC: PURCHASED BY SOO IN 1908/MI/BRAN	01	54	68
SNO WC: SOO LAKE STATES DIVISION ADDITIO	12	87	44
SNO WC: TAKEN OVER BY SOO IN 1909	12	34	84
SNO WCC: 1840 HOPPERS & GONDOLAS	07	33	85
SNO WCF&N: INTERURBAN LINE	02	55	64
SNO WCF&N: INTERURBAN/BUSES/TROLLEYS	08	50	96
SNO WCNS: TO DA 1894	07	74	39
SNO WCO: CHARTERED IN 1893/136 MILES	10	33	45
SNO WCRY: MERGED WITH SOUTH GEORGIA RY	03	47	74
SNO WCVMGS: 1859/RESULT OF CONSOLIDATION	09	36	74
SNO WDV: NARROW GAGE ROAD	10	33	44
SNO WELP: CONSOLIDATED WITH WV&FH 1891	11	48	85
SNO WES: FORMED IN 1919/ILLINOIS	04	39	76
SNO WESR: CONSOLIDATION	09	46	111
SNO WF&S: 176 MILES/TEXAS/7 WOMEN OWN	10	53	111
SNO WF&S: INCORPORATED 1907	08	67	32
SNO WFE: CHARTERED 1831/BECAME PART IC	10	56	47
SNO WG: MERGED IN 1881 TO FORM NYS&W	04	36	90
SNO WG: MERGED TO BECOME PART OF NYS&W	11	34	93
SNO WGB: ABSORBED BY GB&W	11	51	24
SNO WGB: ACQUIRED BY GB&W IN 1921	07	40	72
SNO WGB: ACQUIRED BYGB&W IN 1922	07	35	85
SNO WI&M: BRIEF HISTORY	02	64	34
SNO WI&M: INCORP 1905/49 MILES/EQUIPMENT	02	37	77
SNO WI&NE: PURCHASED IN 1886 BY CSP&KC	10	34	87
SNO WI&P: FIRST RAILROAD IN WV 1836	02	66	31
SNO WI&TC: CHARTERED 1863/STAR UNION LIN	11	45	55
SNO WI&W: BECAME WINONA RAILROAD	12	52	80
SNO WI&W: BUILT 1923/40 MILES/VIRGINIA	04	39	78
SNO WIL&R: BECAME W&N IN 1877	07	34	87
SNO WIN: RAILROAD HAD 4 DIFFERENT NAMES	09	53	82
SNO WIP: OPENED 1891/JOHNSTON PA	01	53	57
SNO WIPR: BECAME MORRISTOWN & ERIE	04	35	87
SNO WIV: OWNED BY FW&DC/234 MILES	03	49	14
SNO WJ&S: TRUE TALES OF THE RAILS	07	45	80
SNO WM&P: 1883/BECAME CGW	09	35	85
SNO WM&P: TAKES OVER MCRY IN 1884	01	34	90
SNO WM: CHARTERED IN 1853	06	38	77
SNO WM: CONTROL BY B&O/C&O	09	71	39
SNO WM: DIESELIZATION & END PASSENGER	10	69	34
SNO WM: INCORP 1910/REORG/CONSOLIDATION	09	35	86
SNO WM: INCORPORATED 1910	05	73	35
SNO WM: LEASES GREENBRIER CHEAT & ELK	05	36	82
SNO WM: LOCOS AND WHERE IN USE	04	49	67
SNO WM: WHERE 4-8-4'S WERE RUN	11	74	52
SNO WMCE: BRIEF HISTORY	04	67	56
SNO WNSP: 3 MILES/YARMOUTH NS CANADA	01	50	90
SNO WNY&P: INCORP IN 1895/REORGANIZATION	07	35	84
SNO WO&N: MERGED 1869 TO N&WO TO NYNH&H	12	71	57
SNO WO: 14 MILES/EQUIPMENT	08	32	57
SNO WORR: BRIEF HISTORY	09	77	02
SNO WP&C: 1901/BECME WB&PL	03	39	62
SNO WP&C: SUSPENDED IN 1917/NOW WB&PL	06	36	84
SNO WP&Y: PHOTO ESSAY	07	43	130
SNO WP&Y: 3' GAGE/ASSETS/EQUIP/FINANCIAL	11	36	58
SNO WP&Y: DEAD HORSE GULCH	12	59	33
SNO WP&Y: DIESEL-ELECTRIC LOCOS	03	55	64
SNO WP&Y: NARROW GAGE/MEMORIES	06	45	24
SNO WP&Y: WHITE PASS SHUTS DOWN	01	83	22
SNO WP: "CALIFORNIA ZEPHYRS" WITHDRAWN	05	50	126
SNO WP: 1903 ORGANIZED/OTHER HEADLINES	07	53	109
SNO WP: 70 CARS LEFT AT OROVILLE	08	48	138
SNO WP: ABSORBED DEEP CREEK RAILROAD	11	52	61
SNO WP: BRIEF HISTORY AT 75 YEARS	09	78	63
SNO WP: BUZZ-WAGON/PAY TRAIN/MOTOR 830 W	03	45	78
SNO WP: CALIFORNIA ZEPHYR PROBLEM	03	67	58
SNO WP: COMPARTMENTIZER BOXCAR	05	52	69
SNO WP: CTC INSTALLATIONS	11	50	69
SNO WP: EARLY STEAM POWER	12	73	52
SNO WP: FASTEST FREIGHT SPEED (AVERAGE)	04	51	130
SNO WP: FEATHER RIVER CANYON TOPOGRAPHY	08	65	19
SNO WP: FEATHER RIVER CANYON TRACKAGE	11	65	25
SNO WP: GOOD-BYE KEDDIE CALIFORNIA	01	75	03
SNO WP: GRADES	08	30	90
SNO WP: INCORP 1903	02	37	78
SNO WP: LARGEST MAINLINE MILEAGE CTC CON	07	53	47
SNO WP: LOCO NUMBERS AND BUILDERS	06	31	443
SNO WP: MAIN DIVISIONS/ROUNDHOUSES	10	34	84
SNO WP: MILITARY BLOOD PROCUREMENT CAR	06	51	132
SNO WP: NO CLEARANCE CAR	04	58	44
SNO WP: OPENED IN 1910/EQUIPMENT	12	31	95
SNO WP: OWNS DEEP CREEK RR	09	34	85
SNO WP: PHOTO-ELECTRIC RECORDER SIG FAIL	10	53	125
SNO WP: SW HAS NET LOSS/SHARES FACILITIE	01	53	88
SNO WPA: CORRECTIONS/READER MEMORIES	09	49	84
SNO WPA: 130 MILES/221 EMPLOYEES/EQUIPME	12	42	150
SNO WPA: 5 REMAINING LINES ABANDONED	05	52	96
SNO WPA: ABSORBED G&HE IN 1910	10	55	52
SNO WPA: RAPID DETERIORATION	02	52	82
SNO WPT: 60 MILES	10	48	69
SNO WR&E: BECAME PLZ&W IN 1918	11	38	72
SNO WR&E: TO PLZ&W 1918 RECEIVERS SALE	08	75	57
SNO WR: BRIEF HISTORY	04	67	34
SNO WR: CHARTERED 1867/ABANNDONED 1939	04	56	44
SNO WR: CHARTERED 1905/REORGAN/VERMONT	06	36	80
SNO WRA: (+ A&WP) MILEAGE/EQUIPMENT	09	35	85
SNO WRA: INCORP 1883	12	39	112
SNO WRA: PART OF ATLANTA & WEST POINT RR	01	34	92
SNO WRB: INCORPORATED 1872 NOW NYNH&H	07	73	38
SNO WRB: INCORPORATED IN 1874	11	38	70
SNO WRCO: WATERTOWN WI	03	76	11
SNO WRRR: 19 MILES/EQUIPMENT	08	32	57
SNO WRRR: 2 LOCOMOTIVES	08	32	53
SNO WRRR: SEVERAL! JUNE 48 CORRECTION	11	48	125
SNO WRTRR: SHORT HISTORY	04	60	32
SNO WSH: PREVIOUSLY CALLED NYWS&B	02	40	121
SNO WSL&P: 1879/RESULT OF CONSOLIDATION	07	36	85
SNO WSO: MERGED WITH RF&P IN 1920	05	40	93
SNO WSS&YP: INCORP IN 1910	09	38	58

Railroad/Railfan

RAILROAD HISTORIES & ROSTERS

SHORT NOTES ON...	M	Y	P
SNO WSSB: INCORP 1905/88 MILES/FREIGHT/E	03	46	74
SNO WSSB: OPENED 1910 BRIEF HISTORY	04	69	29
SNO WT&H: IN 1899 BECAME UNITED TRACTION	12	55	44
SNO WT: BUILT 1905/60 MILES	03	42	75
SNO WTC: DIESELS/1 STEAM LOCO #100	10	59	06
SNO WTC: STEAM LOCOS LOGGING SERVICE/WA	03	40	75
SNO WV&C: ORGANIZED 1911	07	75	52
SNO WV&C: ORGANIZED 1911/ABANDONED/EQUIP	06	37	62
SNO WV&F: 1891/CONSOLIDATION/1892 ELECTR	11	48	85
SNO WV&FH: 1888 HORSECARS/EQUIPMENT/3 MI	11	48	85
SNO WV&M: ABANDONED BEFORE 1895?/LOCO	01	35	85
SNO WV&M: CHARTERED IN 1842/MAINE LUMBER	11	34	92
SNO WVRY: WA&MV BECAME WVRY/BECAME BUS	03	50	76
SNO WW&F	03	33	136
SNO WW&F: 1900-1933/3' GAGE/DERAILMENT	01	35	86
SNO WW&F: ACQUIRED WISCASSET & QUEBEC	04	36	92
SNO WW&F: SHORT HISTORY	12	77	45
SNO WW&F: W&Q RENAMED AS/DIED 1933/WRECK	12	55	30
SNO WW&G: INCORP IN 1908/NO LINE OPERATE	06	34	87
SNO WWI: 8.5 MILES/ALABAMA ROAD	02	33	81
SNO WWV: SOON TO BE ABANDONED	04	50	98
SNO Y&A: BECAME DA IN 1895	07	37	57
SNO Y&A: JOINED WITH W&AN TO DA 1894	07	74	39
SNO Y&A: MERGED W/W&AN TO FORM DA NOW CP	08	73	56
SNO Y&A: MERGED WITH W&AN IN 1894/NOW DA	05	49	55
SNO Y&MV: 1892/NOW PART OF IC	11	38	72
SNO Y&MV: INCORPORATED 1892 TO IC 1946	11	75	44
SNO Y&MV: LEASES ALABAMA & VICKSBURG	11	36	55
SNO Y&MV: NAME CHANGED FROM LNO&T TO ICG	07	73	38
SNO Y&OR: ELECTRIC LINE/OHIO/7 MILES/	09	35	84
SNO Y&S: ABANDONED 1948	11	52	89
SNO Y&S: MONTOUR RR SUBSIDIARY	11	77	26
SNO Y&S: SOLD RECENTLY	04	47	49
SNO Y&S: SOLD TO THE PRR	01	47	134
SNO Y&S: STEAM TO INTERURBAN/NOW FREIGHT	02	48	98
SNO Y&SO: 15 MILES/SWITCHING LINE/FREIGH	08	56	40
SNO Y&SO: INDUSTRIAL LINE/15 MI/STD GAGE	09	52	57
SNO Y&SO: SHORT HISTORY	03	65	48
SNO Y&SU: INTERURBAN LINE/FREIGHT SERVIC	11	52	89
SNO Y: LOCAL RESIDENTS BUY BMT	12	55	39
SNO YALE: FORM IN 1919/ILLINIOS/	04	39	76
SNO YALE: ORGANIZED IN 1919	10	37	69
SNO YH&B: INCORP IN 1883/11 MILES/ABANDO	10	34	86
SNO YN&S: LINE NEVER OPERATED	08	37	60
SNO YOUNGSTOWN OH CENTER STREET CROSSING	10	43	94
SNO YREKA: NOW YW/8 MILES/EQUIPMENT	11	39	89
SNO YSO: PA DIV OF B&LEH BECAME Y&SO	11	33	91
SNO YSO: BECAME PART OF MA&PA IN 1901	11	36	58
SNO YSO: BECAME PART OF MA&PA IN 1901	07	35	84
SNO YSO: MERGED WITH B&LEH/BECAME MA&PA	12	46	79
SNO YSP: ACQUIRED BY MW&A IN 1909	01	37	87
SNO YUC: 2 MILE/ELECTRIC/MAINE/EQUIPMENT	07	49	95
SNO YUC: ELECTRIC EQUIPMENT NOW AT SEM	11	49	86
SNO YUC: MAINE ELECTRIC LINE	02	47	108
SNO YV: 78 MILES/EQUIPMENT	03	32	523
SNO YV: 8 LOCOS/253 FREIGHT/8 PASS CARS	04	37	49
SNO YV: COMPLETED IN 1907/LOCOMOTIVES	04	32	69
SNO YV: INCORP 1902/CALIFORNIA/EQUIPMENT	07	35	86
SNO YV: INCORP 1902/REORG 1934/CALIF/EQU	05	40	94
SNO YV: TRAINS/BUSES/EQUIPMENT	04	44	132
SNO YW: WAS YREKA RR	11	39	89
SNO Z&W: CONTROLLED BY T&OC/NYC ABSORBED	08	56	44
SNO ZM&P: OPENED BETWEEN 1905-10/NOW B&O	01	35	86

RAIL WRECKS AND DISASTERS	M	Y	P
0-4-0 HT&W #1 "READSBORO" DEERFIELD RIVE	11	35	115
15 KILLED BY RUNAWAY TENDER MARCH 2 1936	08	36	59
1937 JAN-JUNE: ONLY 1 RY PASSENGER KILLD	12	37	52
2 ENGINES PASS 1 TRACK BATAVIA NY 1885	05	32	179
4-6-2 PRR #3806 CLASS K4S MINSON NJ	11	43	60
A LOCO ON BOX CAR PLUG DOOR--FREAK ACCID	10	75	40
A&A SANDUSKY NY GRAVEL TRAIN WRECK	02	54	59
A&SU AND ERIE HARPURSVILLE NY 1869 WRECK	03	33	16
AL G BARNES CIRCUS TRAIN WRECK	09	40	22
ALBP SPRING 1943 DERAILMENT	01	44	125
AMTRAK VS BRAY BOULDER 3-8-82	01	83	44
AMTRAKS WORST WRECK BALTIMORE MD 1-4-87	05	87	30
ATSF "HORNY TOAD" WRECK 1917	07	33	73
ATSF #1207 IN TURNTABLE PIT 8-1939 PHOTO	04	65	64
ATSF #3834 2-10-2 FLOOD 10-1932 WOODFORD	02	71	28
ATSF 2-10-2 GR 2-10-2 #1405 NEAR DENVER?	08	66	33
ATSF MAJOVE GAP FLASH FLOOD	01	78	26
ATSF RIO GRANDE DIV AUGUST 1 1929 FLOOD	08	54	70
ATSF ROBINSON NM-GUILTY FIREMAN	07	77	10
ATSF SCHOMBERG NM 6-1920	08	75	02
ATSF SHATTUCK OK 10-1954 WRECK 1ST PERSO	07	78	08
ATSF SPRINGER NM 1917	04	75	04
ATSF WOODFORD CA OCTOBER 1 1932 FLOOD	04	33	130
ATSF WOODFORD STATION 1932 FLASH FLOOD	05	50	129
B&A NOV 9 1907 WEST BROOKFIELD MA	03	43	121
B&M CORNFIELD MEET #1021 & #???	05	46	100
B&M CORNFIELD MEET #1021 READER COMMENT	05	47	134
B&M TRESTLE COLLAPSE SEPT 1939	04	66	37
B&M WOODSVILLE NH UNIQUE DAYTIME WRECK	09	51	123
B&O "CAPITOL LIMITED" ALLISON PK PA 1932	09	32	232
B&O 1-1966 AT SEVENTEEN MILE GRADE	05	67	61
B&O COBURG IN FEBRUARY 1886 WRECK	08	33	133
B&O COBURG IN 1-1886 (NOT 2) READER INFO	01	74	04
B&O COBURG IN 2-1886 ENGINE ON ENGINE PH	11	73	32
B&O JAMES CREEK PA DEC 23 1903 WRECK	06	36	20
B&O SAND PAATCH PA DECEMBER 1912 WRECK	08	33	133
B&P FOREST HILLS MA MARCH 10 1887 WRECK	10	34	94
B&P RICHMOND SWITCH RI APRIL 19 1873 WRE	10	34	89
B&SQ DOUBLE-HEADER WRECK SEPT 11 1911	09	32	235
BAR #252 HITS #2644 MARCH 23 1945 MAINE	09	45	54
BARNUM & BAILEY CIRCUS TRAIN CLINTON IA	05	51	132
BC&M ASHLAND HILL NH 1882 PHOTO	11	75	61
BIG FOUR JAN 21 1893 WRECK	05	43	136
BN MANQUON IL 5-1972 "PHANTOM" PROCEED W	09	73	07

Railroad/Railfan

RAILROAD HISTORIES & ROSTERS

RAIL WRECKS AND DISASTERS	M	Y	P
BN MANQUON IL 5-1972 "PHANTOM" PROCEED W	09	73	07
BOILER EXPLOSION NYNH&H DECEMBER 1890	08	34	41
BOILER EXPLOSIONS--WHAT CAUSES	12	33	87
BOX CAR AFTER CARBOY OF NITRIC ACID FIRE	07	41	12
BOX CAR OVER STREET WRECK PHOTO	09	76	31
BROCKTON MA PLANNED WRECK 9-12-33	02	34	92
BRTS BROOKLY NY NOVEMBER 1 1918 WRECK	10	36	91
BURI "TEXAS ROCKET" DIESEL-ELECTRIC LOCO	06	43	56
C&A #205 LEXINGTON ILL OCT 9 1899 WRECK	09	33	129
C&AM NOVEMBER 9 1833 "FIRST" RR WRECK	02	47	64
C&AM BURLINGTON NJ 8-1855 (DR HEINEKEN)	10	73	58
C&NW #388 LOCO DERAILED-RAIL DEFECT 1880	05	46	105
C&NW WINFIELD IL 1943 WRECK	05	44	76
C&NW WRECK 1895 COLO, IOWA PHOTO	11	35	85
C&O GUYAN RIVER WV JANUARY 1913 WRECK	02	33	27
C&O HINTON WV OCTOBER 1890 WRECK	03	68	27
C&O JEFFERSON PARK HILL TUNNEL 10/2/1925	08	51	123
C&O STORY BEHIND "WRECK ON THE C&O"	11	67	30
C&S LOVELAND COLORADO FEB 24 1904 WRECK	08	49	89
CA&CH DURHAM NY 1840 WRECK PHOTO	12	68	31
CANADA'S BIGGEST RAIL ACCIDENT 6/29/1864	05	35	41
CB&Q KANSAS 1902 CIRCUS WRECK	04	61	35
CBELT DELTA MO 1915 CORN FIELD MEET CONS	12	73	12
CIM WRECK PHOTO	02	46	94
CIRCUS 1893 TYRONE PA (WALTER S MAIN C)	02	75	02
CIRCUS ELEPHANTS KILLED BY LOCOS	08	59	37
CIRCUS TRAINS & WRECKS	02	65	12
CIRCUS WRECK CAUSED BY KIDNEY PILLS	02	35	30
CIRCUS WRECK NEW BRUNSWICK CANADA 1930	04	56	22
CIRCUS WRECK REVELSTOKE BC AUG 11 1911	04	58	10
CIRCUS WRECKS AG BARNES 6-1930	09	67	27
CL ERWIN TENN SEPT 13 1916 ELEPHANT KILL	08	59	37
CMI FALL OF 1902 WRECK	02	43	132
CMI COLORADO SPRINGS CO SEPT 16 1902	06	40	74
CMI LOCO #22 1897/1902 WRECKS	04	49	57
CMI NEW CASTLE 8-1913 WRECK PHOTO	07	65	62
CMSP WISCONSIN 1890 PASSENGER & D-HEAD F	05	75	15
CN #78270 CABOOSE CAMPBELL SIDING	06	46	105
CN CIRCUS WRECK 1930	07	46	14
CN DUGALD MANITOBA SEPT 1947 KILLS 31	09	48	80
CN FRANK ALBERTA 1900 LAND SLIDE	12	33	140
CNE NEW HARTFORD CT 1916 WRECK	05	76	11
CNJ "BLUE COMET" DERAILMENT 8-1939	03	73	41
CNJ CARS GET RIDE IN NEW YORK HARBOR	05	31	249
COLLVER SPECIAL HIRAM GA JAN 7 1908	02	50	28
CP ALIX ALBERTA DECEMBER 1912 WRECK	01	34	136
CP CANAAN NB 1930 AG BARNES CIRCUS	12	75	10
CP GREELY BC AUGUST 1928 WRECK	02	73	31
CP ILLECILLEWEST BC CANADA MAR 2 1936 WR	08	36	59
CP KAM ONT 5-1973 READER INFORMATION	03	74	50
CP PERTH NB CANADA FREIGHT TRAIN CORNFIE	06	55	72
CP WRECK BEAVERMOUTH BC	10	72	04
CP&SL DOW ILL 3 ACCIDENTS/SAME LOCATION	02	39	127
CR SHARONVILLE OH 1976 WORK TRAIN/FREIGH	09	76	23
CSS&SB RUNNAWAY EXPLINATIONS 1967	06	68	37

RAIL WRECKS AND DISASTERS	M	Y	P
CSS&SB WRECK 1-21-85	07	85	24
CV BETHEL CT 1908 WRECK	05	76	12
CV BETHEL VT PHOTO	12	75	13
CV FREIGHT TRAIN DERAILMENT 1940	06	41	137
CV WOODSTOCK BRIDGE VT FEB 5 1887 WRECK	05	36	92
D&H #1510 LOCO JULY 1941 EXPLOSION	12	41	80
D&H COBLESKILL NY BOILER EXPLOSION 1941	02	65	13
D&H RAREST RAILROAD ACCIDENT	08	52	128
D&RGW 1926 WACO CO 30 DEAD	09	40	60
D&RGW CANON CITY CO JULY 1934 WRECK	12	34	86
D&RGW CLIFF SLIDE TWISTS RAILS	04	36	130
D&RGW WRECK 3-1906 PUEBLO COLORADO	08	69	26
DAY OF DISASTER--WASHINGTON DC 1-13-82	07	82	21
DERAILED TRAIN GREENDALE NY 1931	05	31	250
DERAILMENT MARYSVILLE ILL APRIL 29 1926	06	30	369
DL&W DELAWARE WATER GAP 5-1948 WRECK	04	65	08
DL&W DELAWARE WATER GAP MAY 15 1948 WREC	12	48	68
DL&W WRECK JUNE 16 1925 44 KILLED	03	36	130
DUNKIRK NY MOST WRECK PRONE CITY IN US	09	73	08
E #3306 CUBA JCT NY 1929	06	43	56
E BINGHAMTON NY SEPTEMBER 1933 WRECK	03	72	64
E EAST CORNING NY 1940'S WRECK	06	71	10
E GREAT BEND NY WASHOUT PHOTO	04	71	18
E PATTERSON NJ JUNE 16 1936 JUMPED TRACK	03	40	116
E WRECKS ON OLD ERIE (1860'S)	06	33	132
EC&N WRECK CAUSED BY BALL SIGNAL	09	33	62
EJ&E GARY INDIANA 4-1926 WRECK	02	71	10
ELKHORN FLOOD JUNE 22 1901	01	44	116
* EMSR REVERE MASS AUGUST 26 1871 WRECK	06	48	54
ERM REVERE MASS AUGUST 1871 WRECK	01	72	54
ERM REVERE MASS AUGUST 26 1871 WRECK	06	48	54
EXPLOSION AT BLACK TOM--$10,000,000 LOSS	06	30	370
F&CC ANACONDA JUY 2 1894 (2ND DAY OPERAT	08	58	25
FEC WRECK FEB 12 1934 JUPITER FLA PHOTO	12	35	139
FLOOD DAMAGE NWP 1965 EEL RIVER CANYON P	10	65	66
FR FOREIGN RAILROAD WRECK	07	31	535
FR CHINA GREAT BOLIVIAN TRAIN WRECK 1945	03	50	126
FR DUNDEE SCOTLAND TAY BRIDGE COLLAPSE	11	73	58
FR FRANCE LAGNY DECEMBER 24 1933	01	35	12
FR FRANCE MODANE 12-1917 WORST WRECK	10	77	24
FR FRENCH RR MODANE DEC 12 1917 WRECK	04	59	36
FR FRENCH WORST WRECK 12-1917 543 KILLED	09	70	31
FR ITALIAN TRAGEDY MARCH 2 1944	07	51	67
FR ITALY MODANE DECEMBER 12 1917 WRECK	01	35	06
FR ITALY TUNNEL DISASTER MARCH 1944	04	61	33
FR LONDON ENG 1931 "ROYAL SCOT"	02	74	53
FR LONDON MIDLAND & SCOTTISH "ROYAL SCOT"	07	31	535
FR MXC ENCARNACION MEXICO WRECK 9/23/07	09	49	96
FR SCOTLAND GRETNA GREEN MAY 22 1915	01	35	10
FR SCOTLAND TAY BRIDGE DEC 28 1879 WRECK	02	51	51
FR SCOTLAND TAY BRIDGE DEC 28 1879 WRECK	06	34	22
FR SNO WORST RAIL DISASTER ON RECORD '44	07	76	51
FR SWITZERLAND HEAD-ON COLLISION	07	51	128
FRD FAMOUS RAILROAD DISASTERS	05	34	89
FRD PRR PSOPECT PA WRECK OF 1872	05	34	89
* EMSR REVERE MA AUG 26 1871 WRECK	03	37	122

Railroad/ Railfan

475

RAILROAD HISTORIES & ROSTERS

RAIL WRECKS AND DISASTERS	M	Y	P
FRD WRECK AT TARIFFVILLE JAN 14 1878	07	36	90
FREAK WRECKS PILING LOCOMOTIVES	10	67	10
G&WE IVANHOE JUNE 1918 CIRCUS TRAIN WREC	10	68	06
GALVESTON TX FLOOD SEPTEMBER 8 1900	05	40	98
GN MOORHEAD MINN 1917 MURDER	04	58	38
GN WELLINGTON WASHINGTON MARCH 1 1910	04	49	123
GR&I SEPT 22 1901 MEETS FREIGHTER	02	44	84
GR&I SEPT 22 1901 HEAD-ON COLLISION	02	40	129
GT LINDSEY ONTARIO 1887 WRECK READER COM	11	78	49
GT PASSENGER TRAINS COLLIDE AUG 1904	05	36	136
GT SHERBROOKE QUE WRECK READER INFORMATI	09	78	12
GT WRECK (6-78) RICHMOND QUE 1984 READER	11	78	07
GTC 6-1869 BELOEIL BRIDGE QUEBEC WRECK	06	67	35
GTC BELOEIL QUEBEC JUNE 29 1864 WRECK	04	35	41
GTW BATTLE CREEK MI 1949 WRECK PHOTO	02	69	12
GTW LEPEER MI 1936 WRECK	12	71	35
GTW MERRITON ONTARIO 1892 WRECK	08	43	58
GTW SMITH CREEK MI 1-1968 WRECK	05	69	16
GTW WRECK DECEMBER 6 1913	10	36	134
GW JUMBO CIRCUS ELEPHANT CANADA SEP 1885	02	50	125
H&CW #10 CRASHED INTO FRAMINGTON RIVER	05	42	68
H&CW TARIFFVILLE CN JAN 14 1878 WRECK	07	36	90
HALIFAX HARBOR SHIP EXPLOSION 1917	08	74	38
HE&WT WORK TRAIN WRECK	01	70	58
HINCKLEY MN FIRE 9-1-1894	01	37	32
HOCKING VALLEY MOGUL BLOWS UP 1905	03	32	494
HV BUGGY WRECK REMEMBERED BY P SOUTHWORT	06	69	29
IC JULY 1940 SHREVEPORT LA IN CREEK	01	42	127
IC "PANAMA LIMITED NOV 04 1937 WRECK	08	38	10
IC "SEMINOLE" WRECK 1941	08	77	56
IC 5-1900 REPORT OF CASEY JONES WRECK	03	78	36
IC AND M-I AUGUST 16 1942 WRECK	12	42	44
IC DAMAGES DUE TO C JONES WRECK 1900	07	66	40
IC LOCO HITS 2 WOODEN WORKING CARS 1931	05	31	176
IC VAUGHN MO APRIL 30 1900 CASEY JONES W	11	54	38
ICG CHICAGO IL 10-1972	10	73	51
IOWA TERMINAL SHOPS FIRE 11-1967	03	68	33
JOHNSTOWN FLOOD PHOTO ESSAY	08	39	119
JOHNSTOWN PA FLOOD 5-31-1889	09	36	40
L&N "PAN AMERICAN LTD" MOBILE RIVER ALA	05	31	170
L&PS ST THOMAS ONTARIO 7-15-1887 WRECK	01	36	125
LAKE ERIE CAR FERRY MARQUETTE BESMER '09	07	75	08
LEAKING CARBOY OF NITRIC ACID--FIRE	06	30	372
LI BERLIN NY AUGUST 26 1893 WRECK	09	36	35
LI PASSENGER TRAIN AUG 26 1893 WRECK	09	36	34
LI SNOWPLOW AND COMBINATION CAR WRECK	01	43	28
LI WAVERLY LI NY 1875 WRECK	10	31	408
LI WESTBURY NY 1901 FIRST AUTO-TRAIN	09	76	05
LIQUOR TRAIN WRECK 1904	12	36	59
LS&MS ANGOLA NY DECEMBER 19 1867 WRECK	08	34	78
LS&MS ASHATBULA OHIO DECEMBER 29 1876 WR	09	34	40
LS&MS ASHTABULA DECEMBER 1876 WRECK	10	49	61
LS&MS ASHTABULA OH 12-1876 WRECK	04	71	62
LS&MS ASHTABULA OHIO DECEMBER 29 1876 WR	10	49	60
LS&MS ASHTABULA WRECK MORE COMMENTS	02	50	131

RAIL WRECKS AND DISASTERS	M	Y	P
LS&MS ASHTABULA WRECK: WOODEN RR BRIDGE	03	50	136
LS&MS ASHTBULA OHIO 1876 READER COMM	01	50	123
LS&MS KIPTON OHIO 1891 WRECK	01	66	18
LS&MS WATERLOO IN 7-1910	08	74	13
LSEL NOVEMBER 1951 MOTORMAN SAVES GIRL	09	52	93
LV MUD RUN PA OCTOBER 10 1888 COLLISION	07	35	32
M&O NOV 1940 PRATTVILLE ALABAMA	03	43	122
MAINE CENTRAL ENGINE HITS FREIGHT TRAIN	11	33	133
MALPAIS MEXICO WRECK 6-24-1881	03	36	51
MC AUG 31 1939 NEW GLOUCESTER MAINE	07	40	128
MC WINTER 1906-07 ONLY MAN TO LIVE MEMOR	07	48	137
MC WRECK 11-1907 DOVER FOXCROFT MAINE	09	69	13
MC WRECK JULY 21 1933	05	35	85
MEXICO'S VANISHED TRAIN 1888	08	37	95
MICHC JUNE XX 1918 CIRCUS WRECK	02	35	30
MILLION DOLLAR WRECK WELLINGTON MO 1931	10	44	121
MILW JUNE 13 1924 GREATEST MAIL ROBBERY	03	53	37
MILW SUPERIOR MICH MAY 31 1952 WRECK	10	53	71
MKT #368 HITS MULES 1912 MCALESTER OK	12	43	133
MKT #381 LOCO SPRING FLOOD DERAILS	11	45	140
MKT CRASH TX 1896 PLANNED WRECK	05	67	33
MKT EDDY TEXAS FEB 1882 WRECK PHOTO	08	63	33
MKT MCALESTER OK 1912 WRECK PHOTO	12	70	22
MKT ORANGE RIVER MO 1878 WRECK	05	33	135
MP 2-8-2 MP #1432 LOCO MAY 12 1934 WRECK	05	35	137
MP CHRIS LAVOO MURDER CASE	02	55	28
MP PAY CAR ACCIDENT WITNESS MEMORIES	01	47	128
MP TAFT LA 2-1973	02	74	05
MP WRECK 1930: MISREAD ORDERS	01	70	59
MT WASHINGTON COG WRECK 9-1967	01	68	56
MT&L MUSKEGON MI 8-1919 STREETCAR RIOT	08	75	46
N&W THAXTON VA JULY 2 1889 WRECK	03	36	70
N&W WRECK 6-1937 MAYBEURY WV	08	66	08
N&WO FOUR TRAIN WRECK DECEMBER 1891	02	61	32
NC&O #7 1898 WRECK PHOTO	05	68	22
NC&SL NASHVILLE TN 7-1918 WRECK 99 DIE	07	78	11
NC&SL NASHVILLE TN JULY 9 1918 LOCO #1,4	11	44	51
NC&SL WRECK HOOKER GA MARCH 1 1942	03	43	97
NC&SL WRECK JULY 9 1918 KILLS 99 PEOPLE	04	35	16
NKP SHOPS TENNESSEE JULY 9 1918 WRECK	02	58	41
NKP SILVER CREEK NY SEPT 14 1886 WRECK	11	34	66
NP BITTER ROOT CANYON FEBRUARY 1903	03	51	59
NP CLINTON MT NOVEMBER 10 1885 WRECK	03	41	56
NP COCOLALLA IDAHO 1910 WRECK #1504	01	49	111
NP FEBUARY 11 1903 SNOWSLIDE	03	51	59
NP WRECK 2-1903 ON S-BRIDGE	03	65	45
NP WRECK CAUSED BY ANIMALS (1920'S)	04	69	54
NPA AMBLER PA 7-1850 WRECK	07	78	07
NPC #14 LOCO AFTER EARTHQUAKE	03	36	86
NPR AMBLER PA JULY 17 1856 WRECK	02	35	44
NRR SOUTH BEACH JULY 23 1909 WRECK	07	44	110
NY&E MAST HOPE NY JULY 18969 WRECK	01	34	137
NY&NE EAST THOMPSON CN DECEMBER 4 1891 W	12	43	102
NYC 4-6-4 "WOLVERINE" CLASS J3A ROCHEST	08	45	48
NYC DENLEY NY 7-1908 "CLAYTON FLYER" WRE	02	64	36
✱ NC&SL NASHVILLE TN JULY 9 1918 WRECK	04	35	16

Railroad/Railfan

RAILROAD HISTORIES & ROSTERS

RAIL WRECKS AND DISASTERS	M	Y	P
NYC DIESEL LOCOMOTIVE FIRE	08	51	135
NYC MARCH 1916 "20TH CENTURY LTD" WRECK	01	72	54
NYC WRECK 1910 ALLIANCE & FREEBURG OHIO	11	35	86
NYC WRECK GLENVILLE NY 1920	04	78	10
NYC WRECK PROVIDENCE RI	07	32	512
NYC&H DUYVIL NY JAN 13 1882 WRECK	09	32	238
NYC&H SPUYTEN DUYVIL NY 1882 HUDSON RIVR	09	32	238
NYC&HR SPUYTEN DUYVIL NY JAN 13 1882 WRE	12	35	44
NYC&HR WRECK 2-1885 BATAVIA NY	01	68	30
NYC/NH PARK AVE TUNNEL 1902 AND 1904	03	49	60
NYC/NH WRECK JAN 1902 PARK AVE TUNNEL	04	70	34
NYCE 150TH STREET JUNE 8 1916 WRECK	06	56	27
NYNA NY CITY 9-1905 WRECK	06	70	40
NYNH&H JANUARY 10 1958 WRECK	06	59	50
NYNH&H LOCO WESTERLY RI JULY 10 1911 WRE	08	44	112
NYNH&H NEW HAMBURG NY FEBRUARY 1871 WREC	07	34	76
NYNH&H PLAINSVILLE CT LOCO #6 PHOTO	01	53	132
NYNH&H PLAINSVILLE CT MARCH 1889 WRECK	01	53	133
NYO&W #140, #177 AT PORT JERVIS NY	09	46	20
NYO&W #189 NEAR LITTLE FALLS TRESTLE	01	47	136
NYO&W #191 & UNMANNED LOCOMOTIVE WRECK	12	65	24
NYO&W FIRE-GUTTED COACH #1 1941	09	46	36
O&K FROZEN KY JANUARY 19 1910 1 KILLED	08	52	42
OCO MARLBORO JCT MASS 1886 WRECK	08	32	133
OCO FREAK WRECK 1898 MARLBORO JCT MASS	07	67	26
P&N SOUTH CAROLINA FEB 1941 WRECK	06	71	55
P&N SPARTANBURGH SC 12-1941 WRECK	09	71	47
P&RF CANTON MAINE 1910 WRECK	03	32	527
P&W CORNFIELD MEET 8 & 10 WHEELER PHOTO	10	78	48
P&WRR MARIENVILLE PA 1906 LOCO & COW MET	07	52	127
PC CLEVELAND OH 1974--RAN INTO BRIDGE WT	12	74	46
PCC&SL KINGS MILLS OH 1890 POWDER CAR DI	11	77	26
PENNSY LOCO DERAILED-SIDE ON COLLISION	04	31	16
PITTSBURGH TROLLEY DISASTER 12/24/1917	03	36	89
PM CABOOSE WRECK AUGUST 3 1941	12	41	25
PM ENGINE #167 1910 WRECK PHOTO	01	68	08
PM GRAND RAPIDS MICHIGAN DEC 25 1907	02	58	10
PM GRAND RAPIDS MICHIGAN DEC 26 1903	06	58	08
PRESIDENT ROOSEVELT SEPT 3 1902 WRECK	02	55	62
PRR JOHNSTOWN FLOOD MAY 21 1889	06	49	13
PRR JUNE 15 1945 BUFFALO DAY EXPRESS	05	46	76
PRR #1185 MCKEES ROCKS PA WRECK	09	44	114
PRR #443 LOCO HARRISBURG PA APPROX 1916	07	36	132
PRR ATLANTIC LOCO THRU DRAWBRIDGE/BOAT	07	50	66
PRR BROAD STREET STATION FIRE 6-1923	02	68	08
PRR FREIGHT WRECK SO ELIZABETH STN NJ	12	47	81
PRR HYDETOWN PA 1-1910 WRECK	02	69	10
PRR LONG BRANCH NJ SEPTEMBER 1901 WRECK	10	61	40
PRR MCCANN'S CROSSING MAY 30 1893 CIRCUS	05	50	133
PRR MU TRAIN WRECK 28 KILLED 1942	05	42	61
PRR TRAIN ROBBERY FOR $65 IN PENNIES	10	78	10
PRR WATERTANK NORTH MADISON IND FIRE '40	10	57	43
PRR WEST LIBERTY OHIO 1913 WRECK	11	45	53
PS&N SEPTEMBER 22 1912 WRECK	02	48	136
QUEBEC ONT CANADA BRIDGE WRECK 8-29-07	02	36	44

RAIL WRECKS AND DISASTERS	M	Y	P
R MEADOW TOWER NJ JULY 31 1896 WRECK	04	36	81
RAILROAD DISASTERS IN 1830-1840	02	33	68
RF&P WRECK 1-1970 (TRACK TYPE)	09	70	30
RI CIMARRON RIVER DOVER OK SEPT 18 1906	12	58	40
RI IN QUICKSAND READER INFORMATION	07	34	134
RI WRECK BY DRUNK ENGINEER	11	71	06
RT&C 1911 WRECK	12	71	46
S "FAT NANCY" DISASTER JULY 12 1888	01	40	129
S "ROYAL PALM" 12-1925 WRECK	03	67	32
S #1408 WRECK 1937	04	41	65
S #4578 SPARTANBURG SC WRECK	05	46	31
S #6942/CARS SANDERSVILLE JAN 1941 WRECK	03	44	122
S ALEXANDRIA VA 1906 "CANNON BALL" WRECK	01	33	76
S CHAPPELLIS SC 8-1930	12	74	24
S CHICKAMAUGA TN 9-1925 "DIXIE FLYER"	10	73	10
S DANVILLE VA 09/1903 WRECK OF "OLD 97"	01	34	37
S DANVILLE VA 1903 "OLD 97"	12	75	57
S DANVILLE VA 1903 "WRECK OF 97"	05	50	64
S DANVILLE VA WRECK OF OLD 97	12	52	63
S GLEN MARY TN 11-1929 "PONCE DE LEON"	10	73	10
S HATTIESBURG YARD WRECK 1910 PHOTO	11	77	14
S HIRAM GA JANUARY 7 1908 WRECK	02	50	28
S LAUREL MISSISSIPPI 1-1969 WRECK	07	70	58
S OLD 97 9-1903 DANVILLE VA WRECK PHOTO	04	65	50
S ROCKMART GA 12-1926 "ROYAL PALM"	10	73	10
S STATESVILLE NC AUGUST 1891 WRECK	02	33	26
S STONE CREEK GA 1896 (INTENTIONAL)	12	74	20
S STONE CREEK WRECK FEBRUARY 29 1896	04	51	74
S WASHOUT JANUARY 26 1937	08	40	137
S WRECK 9-1903 (OLD 97)	10	68	34
SCA BROOKDALE PA CAR #102, #104	04	48	96
SCA CONEMAUGH PA 3 HOUSES/1 SCHOOL DEM	04	48	97
SIRT FIRE JUNE 25 1946	12	46	130
SLKC&N 4 LOCOS ORRICK MO JUNE 14 1873	02	39	127
SLKC&N JUNE 14 1873 WRECK	12	41	77
SMITHVILLE OHIO DERAILMENT---FEAST	05	49	128
SN YOLO BYPASS JULY 1951	12	51	91
SNO ME&D:TRAIN ROBERY 1850	02	70	40
SNO MEXICAN WRECK AND ASLEEP ENGINEER	03	65	46
SNO NYC:WORST WRECK ON "20 CENTURY LTD"	01	72	54
SNO S: WRECK OF OLD 97 9-1903	11	69	29
SOCA 1832 1ST PASSENGER WRECK	06	47	90
SP DECEMBER 9 1929 WRECK	01	34	36
SP #1152 LOCO TUMBLES INTO WATER WRECK	01	43	141
SP #2451 HITS TRUCK OF SAND OCT 19 1935	06	37	138
SP #3690 LOCO MARCH 25 1938 WRECK	04	44	127
SP AUGUST 12 1939 SABOTAGED NEVADA	04	40	92
SP BEAUMONT TEXAS RUNAWAY WRECKS	03	53	125
SP BOILER EXPLOSION 11-1946 BOSQUE AZ	07	65	06
SP CASCO CA JULY 1947 FREIGHT TRAIN KILL	01	48	73
SP HARNEY NV AUGUST 12 1939 WRECK	04	40	92
SP LOCO EXPLOSION RICE HILL OREGON 1912	03	45	77
SP RICHVALE CA DEC 25 1931 WRECK	06	35	86
SP WOODEN TRESTLE BRIDGE COLLAPSE 1935	04	36	139
SP&S DESCHUTES RIVER JANUARY 31 1954	09	54	10

Railroad/Railfan

RAILROAD HISTORIES & ROSTERS

RAIL WRECKS AND DISASTERS	M	Y	P
SPARROW COLORADO HEAD-ON COLLISION 1906	08	50	135
STEEL CAR BULGES UNDER GAS PRESSURE	06	30	374
SUBWAY WRECK NOVEMBER 1 1918 97 KILLED	10	36	91
T&P CORN FIELD MEET 6-1903 JEFFERSON TX	08	65	17
T&P JEFFERSON TEXAS JUNE 4 1903 WRECK	04	55	44
T&P JEFFERSON TX JUNE 4 1903 WRECK	04	55	44
T&P SPRING 1885 WRECK	12	54	72
TP&W CHATSWORTH IL AUG 10 1887 WRECK	06	35	07
TP&W CHATSWORTH WRECK 8-1887	11	64	34
UNION STATION ROBBERY DURHAM NC	07	48	126
UP SMOKEY HILL DIV JUNE 1882 39 CARS!	02	39	127
V&M ATHOL MASSACHUETTS JUNE 1870 WRECK	03	34	82
V&M ROYALSTON MASS 1870 BRIDGE DISASTER	03	77	08
VERMONT FLOOD DAMAGE NOV 1947	08	47	89
W BEMENT IL 11-1904 WRECK	08	71	46
W WILLIAMSPORT IN 6-1924 OPEN SWITCH	05	76	24
W&LE BEACH CITY OH 7-1924	07	74	06
W-BRY APRIL 30 1939 TROLLEY/CAR COLLISIO	03	40	20
WC DUPLAINVILLE WISCONSIN 1898	09	48	135
WHAT ABOUT THAT WRECK?	03	48	10
WHEN BOILERS BLOW UP	06	37	06
WJ&S ATLANTIC CITY NJ OCT 28 1906 WRECK	12	36	120
WJ&S JULY 1896 EXCURSION TRAIN WRECK	11	51	133
WORLD'S THREE GREATEST RAILROAD WRECKS	01	35	06
WP KEDDIE CA JUNE '81 WRECK & COMMOTION	01	82	55
WP MCCLEAN CUT SPRING 1943 ROCK SLIDE	05	44	79
WRECK "NATIONAL LIMITED" 1960	09	70	08
WRECK AT ATLANTIC CITY NJ JULY 31 1896	04	36	81
WRECK PARADISE CA SUMMER 1909	04	78	10
WRECKS BEFORE SPEED GRAPHIC	03	55	32
WRECKS OF BYGONE DAYS	05	34	128
WW&F FREIGHT TRAIN DERAILS 1933	11	33	133

RAILROAD ROUTE MAPS	M	Y	P
FR FOREIGN RAILROAD ROUTES	05	48	49
FR ROUTE OF ETHIOPIA RAILROAD	11	35	56
FR ROUTE OF GUATEMALA RAILROADS	08	48	38
FR ROUTE OF JAPAN'S RAILROAD	06	49	73
FR ROUTE OF NETHERLAND RAILWAYS	03	53	16
FR ROUTE OF SWEDISH GOV'T RAILWAYS	06	56	35
FR ROUTE OF VICTORIAN GOV'T RAILWAYS	05	48	49
ROUTE OF 37 UNITED STATES STREAMLINERS	02	40	120
ROUTE OF A&GWW "GOLD RUSH LIMITED"	03	31	527
ROUTE OF A: INTERCITY PASSENGER ROUTES	07	76	53
ROUTE OF AA	09	42	77
ROUTE OF AB&C	10	46	17
ROUTE OF ABSO: PROPOSED ROUTE	04	50	50
ROUTE OF AC&HB	02	50	19
ROUTE OF AC&HB:	11	54	47
ROUTE OF AL	10	54	34
ROUTE OF ALBANY NY AREA STREETCARS/INTER	12	55	45
ROUTE OF ATSF	07	37	113
ROUTE OF AV	10	42	101
ROUTE OF AVI	07	49	89
ROUTE OF B&A	06	36	87
ROUTE OF B&BL	10	34	13

RAILROAD ROUTE MAPS	M	Y	P
ROUTE OF B&GA	12	43	91
ROUTE OF B&M: MOGUL COUNTRY LINE	03	54	41
ROUTE OF B&O: CINCINNATIAN	06	47	16
ROUTE OF B&O: CUMBERLAND DIVISION	06	47	19
ROUTE OF B&O: MONONGAH DIVISION	06	47	20
ROUTE OF B&O: OHIO DIVISION	06	47	23
ROUTE OF BAR	12	38	08
ROUTE OF BAR:	12	57	19
ROUTE OF BART NOV 1971	12	72	43
ROUTE OF BCE	03	48	91
ROUTE OF BEDT	06	52	35
ROUTE OF BERY	04	53	80
ROUTE OF BIR	11	47	112
ROUTE OF BM&LP: ARIZONA REMOTE ELECTRIC	09	73	29
ROUTE OF BR&P	09	43	12
ROUTE OF BZ&C: AROUND 1898	09	50	62
ROUTE OF C&CA	02	49	90
ROUTE OF C&F	03	36	39
ROUTE OF C&GR	08	44	12
ROUTE OF C&I: BATTERY AND ELECTRIC ROUTE	05	48	96
ROUTE OF C&LE	09	74	46
ROUTE OF C&LE:	05	68	36
ROUTE OF C&MRY	03	42	49
ROUTE OF C&O: "GEORGE WASHINGTON"	12	36	27
ROUTE OF C&O: MARQUETTE DISTRICT	07	50	136
ROUTE OF C&S: MAXIMUM EXTENT OF	10	73	20
ROUTE OF C&S: NARROW GAGE LINES	12	43	43
ROUTE OF C&TA	02	49	90
ROUTE OF C&WC	06	41	61
ROUTE OF CA&C	02	35	36
ROUTE OF CANYON WAR AFTERMATH 1931	10	56	27
ROUTE OF CAPR: 1ST-4TH DIVISION	12	52	19
ROUTE OF CAR FERRIES: GREAT LAKES	11	54	12
ROUTE OF CB&Q	09	36	87
ROUTE OF CB&Q:	03	49	14
ROUTE OF CB&Q: BIG HORN RELOCATION	11	50	68
ROUTE OF CBELT	05	54	97
ROUTE OF CBT	07	44	127
ROUTE OF CCW	10	49	98
ROUTE OF CGW	09	53	19
ROUTE OF CMI	11	32	487
ROUTE OF CMI: TOTAL MAIN LINE MILES 335	08	36	47
ROUTE OF CMT	02	49	90
ROUTE OF CN	11	47	14
ROUTE OF CN: SMITHERS DIVISION	05	50	18
ROUTE OF CNJ	06	35	135
ROUTE OF CNJ:	03	46	15
ROUTE OF CNS&M	10	53	74
ROUTE OF CNS&M: NORTH SHORE LINE	07	47	107
ROUTE OF CONN	04	47	65
ROUTE OF CP: KETTLE VALLEY LINE	08	50	31
ROUTE OF CPA: GREAT SALT LAKE FILL	08	57	19
ROUTE OF CPM&O	03	37	72
ROUTE OF CRB&L	02	39	80
ROUTE OF CSO: 27 TUNNELS	01	39	09

Railroad/Railfan

RAILROAD HISTORIES & ROSTERS

RAILROAD ROUTE MAPS	M	Y	P
ROUTE OF CSS&SB: DETOUR	04	57	51
ROUTE OF CSS&SB: ELECTRIC LINE	10	45	94
ROUTE OF CT: LOOP AREA	01	50	86
ROUTE OF CTCO	08	47	96
ROUTE OF CTR	11	50	90
ROUTE OF CV	12	35	88
ROUTE OF D&H	11	36	125
ROUTE OF D&H:	04	47	08
ROUTE OF D&M	06	42	77
ROUTE OF D&N	09	43	105
ROUTE OF D&RGW	07	32	495
ROUTE OF D&RGW: LITTLE GIANT #215-216	05	50	85
ROUTE OF D&RGW: SILVERTON BRANCH	06	55	42
ROUTE OF DAYLIGHT PASSENGER TRAIN	08	37	28
ROUTE OF DL&W: GIBSON TO BINGHAMTON	02	59	37
ROUTE OF DPE	08	43	81
ROUTE OF DSP&P: CONTINENTAL DIVIDE	04	55	51
ROUTE OF DSP&P: WITH ELEVATIONS	06	41	09
ROUTE OF DSS&A	08	32	130
ROUTE OF DT&I	05	42	95
ROUTE OF DT&I:	07	38	10
ROUTE OF E: GIBSON TO BINGHAMTON	02	59	37
ROUTE OF EARLY COLORADO RAILROADS: 1885	09	48	32
ROUTE OF EB&L: LUMBER ROAD/NEW HAMPSHIRE	01	48	125
ROUTE OF EPCL	01	52	96
ROUTE OF F&C	08	50	41
ROUTE OF F&CC	04	42	12
ROUTE OF FDM&S	09	52	76
ROUTE OF FEC: SEA-GOING RAILROAD	12	33	132
ROUTE OF FERRY LINES: SAN FRANCISCO BAY	08	59	24
ROUTE OF FES	11	50	90
ROUTE OF FPL	01	47	83
ROUTE OF FPT: FAIRMONT PARK	12	46	99
ROUTE OF FRIS	01	53	12
ROUTE OF G&F	06	41	61
ROUTE OF G&W: READERS MAP CORRECTION	07	86	04
ROUTE OF G: INCLUDING MONROE BRANCH(FRT)	01	50	67
ROUTE OF GB&W	11	51	21
ROUTE OF GB&W:	07	42	153
ROUTE OF GM&O	01	45	08
ROUTE OF GN	08	35	88
ROUTE OF GN GN-WP CONNECTION	12	31	92
ROUTE OF GN:	02	37	44
ROUTE OF GN: CASCADE MOUNTAIN LINE	08	50	121
ROUTE OF GN: EXTENSION	02	37	52
ROUTE OF GN: OLD MARCUS DIVISION	08	39	19
ROUTE OF H&F	03	45	108
ROUTE OF H&M	11	47	107
ROUTE OF H&M: HUDSON TUNNELS	06	58	66
ROUTE OF HALC IN 1949	10	54	46
ROUTE OF HBRR	06	54	16
ROUTE OF HC: ELECTRIC AND STEAM	11	46	106
ROUTE OF HIGH	04	40	61
ROUTE OF HT	08	47	96
ROUTE OF HU	10	44	112
ROUTE OF IC	12	36	116
ROUTE OF INTERCITY PASSENGER ROUTES 1974	10	74	15
ROUTE OF IT	12	51	82
ROUTE OF IVT	04	50	96
ROUTE OF J&SS	05	48	96
ROUTE OF JC&FR	12	58	27
ROUTE OF JCE	03	46	14
ROUTE OF JTC	05	48	96
ROUTE OF KCS	10	47	32
ROUTE OF KVRR	08	50	30
ROUTE OF L&A	10	47	32
ROUTE OF L&H	02	42	81
ROUTE OF L&N	01	36	89
ROUTE OF LATR	01	54	38
ROUTE OF LATR: PROPOSED RAPID TR NETWORK	08	56	69
ROUTE OF LEBG&N	06	52	78
ROUTE OF LI	01	43	12
ROUTE OF LI: BELMONT ROUTE	02	56	49
ROUTE OF LSEL	11	51	80
ROUTE OF M	05	49	20
ROUTE OF M&A	07	36	88
ROUTE OF M&A:	06	48	12
ROUTE OF M&LB	10	48	56
ROUTE OF M&ONE	04	41	10
ROUTE OF M&SL	03	35	80
ROUTE OF M&SL:	04	44	53
ROUTE OF M&U	08	47	122
ROUTE OF MAINE'S TWO FOOT GAGE TRACK	12	55	24
ROUTE OF MANHATTAN CROSS RIVER BRIDGE/TU	02	56	40
ROUTE OF MC&I:	12	58	27
ROUTE OF MCRI: CALIFORNIA	10	50	43
ROUTE OF MICHC: MACKINAW DIVISION	10	52	16
ROUTE OF MILE-A-MINUTE RUNS	10	36	22
ROUTE OF MKT: 1948 3252 MILES	07	48	19
ROUTE OF MN&S	08	43	81
ROUTE OF MO	02	42	22
ROUTE OF MV	08	43	10
ROUTE OF N&W	03	36	92
ROUTE OF NA	11	47	14
ROUTE OF NA	01	54	17
ROUTE OF NA:	02	55	47
ROUTE OF NARROW GAGE RDS MISSISSIPPI EAS	01	37	48
ROUTE OF NARROW GAGE ROADS 7 WEST STATES	01	37	53
ROUTE OF NARROW GAGUE ROADS IN MAINE	09	35	51
ROUTE OF NC&SL	11	48	14
ROUTE OF NC&SL: ATLANTA DIVISION CHANGES	11	48	18
ROUTE OF NC&SL: WILDERSVILE TO TIMBERLAK	11	48	38
ROUTE OF NCAM	05	48	96
ROUTE OF NCO	10	55	41
ROUTE OF NEW YORK STATE JUICE LINES	02	45	102
ROUTE OF NJTR	02	51	69
ROUTE OF NNB&S	03	55	23
ROUTE OF NOPS	09	51	78
ROUTE OF NP	05	47	24
ROUTE OF NP: STAMPEDE TUNNEL	04	37	29

Railroad/ Railfan

479

RAILROAD HISTORIES & ROSTERS

RAILROAD ROUTE MAPS	M	Y	P
ROUTE OF NRR	08	43	11
ROUTE OF NSC&T	06	50	87
ROUTE OF NSC&T:	02	52	76
ROUTE OF NWP	08	55	45
ROUTE OF NWP: ABANDONED 36" LINES	08	55	49
ROUTE OF NY&OM: STYLIZED MAP 1876	09	46	27
ROUTE OF NYC	11	50	16
ROUTE OF NYC AND LEASED/CONTROLLED LINES	06	40	112
ROUTE OF NYC IN 1853	09	53	52
ROUTE OF NYC: NEW YORK CITY VICINITY	12	51	16
ROUTE OF NYC: PUTNAM DIVISON	01	49	50
ROUTE OF NYCE: THIRD EL	06	56	23
ROUTE OF NYCS: PROPOSED	12	57	66
ROUTE OF NYNH&H: ELECTRIFICATION CT/RI/MA	12	58	33
ROUTE OF NYNH&H: ELECTRIC LINES	02	59	33
ROUTE OF NYNH&H: MAIN ROUTE/STONINGTON T	08	44	105
ROUTE OF NYO&W	05	43	105
ROUTE OF NYP&C	11	37	52
ROUTE OF NYS&W	04	41	73
ROUTE OF O&K	08	52	34
ROUTE OF OHIO TRACTION LINES	11	52	89
ROUTE OF OILC	11	50	90
ROUTE OF OKT	09	51	78
ROUTE OF ON	01	55	43
ROUTE OF OR&LC	05	35	37
ROUTE OF OS	12	35	69
ROUTE OF OTIS	02	49	90
ROUTE OF P&F: LAST HALF-MILE	08	43	130
ROUTE OF P&N	04	44	104
ROUTE OF P&SR	05	48	99
ROUTE OF P&WV	01	35	89
ROUTE OF PE: CORRECTED TO OCT 1943	01	44	94
ROUTE OF PECO	10	42	105
ROUTE OF PEPC	05	47	94
ROUTE OF PGE	01	49	15
ROUTE OF PGE	12	56	19
ROUTE OF PGE:	03	55	38
ROUTE OF PIT: INTERURBAN/ABANDONED/SUBUR	05	44	96
ROUTE OF PM	11	35	90
ROUTE OF PROSPERITY SPECIAL	01	47	29
ROUTE OF PRR: ELECTRIFIED TRACKAGE	01	42	56
ROUTE OF PRSL	12	41	58
ROUTE OF PTC	02	47	100
ROUTE OF PTR	05	53	88
ROUTE OF QC	01	40	112
ROUTE OF QNS&L: PROPOSED	10	49	45
ROUTE OF R&N: 1924	01	74	44
ROUTE OF RAILROADS IN RECEIVERSHIP	05	36	34
ROUTE OF RAILROADS INTO TWIN CITIES	02	54	18
ROUTE OF RCBH&W	03	48	41
ROUTE OF RI	09	35	90
ROUTE OF RU	06	57	20
ROUTE OF S&EG	10	50	82
ROUTE OF S: MURPHY BRANCH	06	49	51
ROUTE OF SAL	05	35	89

RAILROAD ROUTE MAPS	M	Y	P
ROUTE OF SAN FRANCISCO CABLE ST RAILROAD	11	45	95
ROUTE OF SANT	10	50	82
ROUTE OF SB&LT	10	52	50
ROUTE OF SCA	04	48	95
ROUTE OF SCA:	05	48	96
ROUTE OF SD&AE	07	35	88
ROUTE OF SFP	05	48	96
ROUTE OF S&N	06	58	21
ROUTE OF SILV	06	58	21
ROUTE OF SJ&LC	10	42	97
ROUTE OF SL&W	12	48	97
ROUTE OF SNO	06	58	21
ROUTE OF SOO	02	34	131
ROUTE OF SOUTH JERSEY RAPID 1959	05	65	35
ROUTE OF SP&S	11	52	18
ROUTE OF SPEN	12	57	35
ROUTE OF SPM	02	48	36
ROUTE OF SR AND CONNECTIONS	02	37	60
ROUTE OF STRR	11	47	71
ROUTE OF SWS	05	52	84
ROUTE OF T&T	12	44	53
ROUTE OF TAL: WITH DEPOTS/CROSSINGS/BRID	07	43	107
ROUTE OF TEM	06	48	35
ROUTE OF TH&B	07	32	459
ROUTE OF THE RU	01	47	15
ROUTE OF TIV	02	44	65
ROUTE OF U	01	33	34
ROUTE OF UC	02	45	24
ROUTE OF UDEY	06	68	19
ROUTE OF UP: GEORGETOWN LOOP REBUILD MAP	09	76	47
ROUTE OF URY	06	50	44
ROUTE OF V&T	07	45	55
ROUTE OF V&T 1949	01	55	10
ROUTE OF V: ELECTRIFIED DIV	04	39	31
ROUTE OF W&A	12	45	15
ROUTE OF W&OD	10	49	75
ROUTE OF WCF&N: 1897-1949 GROWTH	04	49	87
ROUTE OF WIN	12	52	83
ROUTE OF WM	09	50	29
ROUTE OF WNC: SWANNANOA ROUTE	12	43	14
ROUTE OF WP&Y	10	40	72
ROUTE OF WP&Y:	04	56	50
ROUTE OF WPA	06	49	88
ROUTE OF WPA CORRECTIONS	09	49	84
ROUTE OF WPA:	12	42	150
ROUTE OF WW&F	03	35	39

SHORT NOTE ADDITIONS	M	Y	P
SNO A: FIVE YEAR PLAN	02	78	49
SNO ALGC: LOCATIONS & BRIEF HISTORY	11	69	28
SNO ATSF: ENGINE THROWING A ROD	04	67	32
SNO C&MO: B&M LEASED IN 1895	06	34	88
SNO C&O: JEFFERSON PARK HILL TUNNEL	08	51	123
SNO LCO: FORMATION	02	78	52
SNO NYC "TWENTIETH CENTURY LTD"--COAL	02	32	327
SNO NYC: TWENTIETH CENTURY LIMITED	08	31	47

Railroad/Railfan

HISTORICAL SOCIETY & MAGZINE LIST

BALTIMORE & OHIO HISTORICAL
PO BOX 13578
BALTIMORE MD 21203

BOSTON & MAINE HISTORICAL
PO BOX 2362 HARWOOD STN
LITTLETON MA 01460

BURLINGTON ROUTE HISTORICAL
PO BOX 60525
LAGRANGE IL 60525

CHESAPEAKE & OHIO HISTORICAL
PO BOX 417
ALDERSON W VA 24910

CHICAGO & NORTHWESTERN
17004 LOCUST DRIVE
HAZEL CREST IL 60429

ERIE LACKAWANNA HISTORICAL
22 DUQUESNE CT
NEW CASTLE DE 19720

EXTRA 2200 SOUTH
PO BOX 41417
CINCINNATI OH 45241

FINE SCALE MODELER
1027 N SEVENTH ST
MILWAUKEE WI 53233

FREIGHT CAR JOURNAL
PO BOX 1458
MONROVIA CA 91016

FRIENDS OF EBT
736 SHAW AVE
LANSDALE PA 19446

GULF MOBILE & OHIO
PO BOX 24
BEDFROD PARK IL 60499

HERALD, THE
PO BOX 2171
CUMBERLAND MD 21503

LOCO & RAILWAY PRESERVATION
PO BOX 246
RICHMOND VT 05477

LOCOMOTIVE QUARTERLY
PO BOX 383
MT VERNON NY 10552

MAINLINE MODLER
51155 MONTICELLO DR
EDMONDS WA 98020

MO PAC HISTORICAL SOCIETY
116 N SECOND ST APT 1
DUPO IL 62239

MODEL RAILROADING
2901 BLAKE ST
DENVER CO 80205

MODEL TECH
BOX 286
CADILLAC MI 49601

MOTIVE POWER REVIEW
PO BOX 2096
COVINA CA 91722

MOUNTAIN STATE RR & HIST
PO BOX 89
CASS WV 24927

NARROW GAUGE & SHORT LINE
PO BOX 26
LOS ALTOS CA 94023

NAT'L RAILWAY HISTORICAL
PO BOX 58153
PHILA PA 19102

NATIONAL MODEL RAILROAD ASS
4121 CROMWELL ROAD
CHATTANOOGA TN 37421

NEW HAVEN (NYNH&H)
13 FRANKLIN ST
NORTH HAVEN CT 06473

NICKEL PLATE ROAD (NKPHTS)
PO BOX 29822
ST LOUIS MO 63129

NORTHERN PACIFIC RY HS
10 32ND AVE NE
FARGO ND 58102

NYC HEADLIGHTS
PO BOX 745
MENTOR OH 44061

O SCALE NEWS   48/FT
6514 NORTH 11TH ST
PHIAL PA 19126

ONTARIO & WESTERN RY HISTOR
BOX 713
MIDDLETOWN NY 10940

PACIFIC COAST LOGGING HIST
4928 NORTH FRACE ST
TACOMA WA 98407

PACIFIC RAILNEWS
PO BOX 6128
GLENDALE CA 91205

PASSENGER TRAIN JOURNAL
PO BOX 6128
GLENDALE CA 91205

PENNSYLVANIA RR TECH & HIST
PO BOX 389
UPEER DARBY PA 19082

PHILA CHAPTER PRRT&HS
137 STOCKTON RD
BRYN MAWR PA 19010

PROTOTYPE MODELER
PO BOX 6128
GLENDALE CA 91205

BILL OF LADING   MODEL LAYOUTS

This section covers layouts and the basic building of them. The sub-categories include Model Trackwork (including switch machines), Prototype Trackwork, Layout Design, Layout Operation, Layout Plans, Layout Building, Scenery, and Layout Visits. All are self-explanatory.

Layout building concerns itself with all aspects of layout construction. The operation section will give you ideas on what to do with or how to run your pike when it is finished.

This section also includes the electrical aspects of model railroading as well as a few technique tips.

MANIFEST   MODEL LAYOUTS

DETAILED CONSIST	PAGE
LAYOUT OPERATION	483
LAYOUT PLANS	483
LAYOUT DESIGN	483
LAYOUT BUILDING	483
LAYOUT VISITS	483
MODEL TRACKWORK	483
GENERAL ELECTRONICS	483
SCENERY	483

Railroad/Railfan

MODEL LAYOUTS

MODEL LAYOUTS	M	Y	P
LAYOUT DESIGN			
LAYING OUT A MINIATURE PIKE	07	36	139
RAILROADS IN MINIATURE-MANY SCALES/USES	09	31	176
LAYOUT TRACK PLANS			
GARDEN RAILROAD TRACK PLANS	10	46	110
MODEL TRACK BUILDING			
DOUBLE SLIP SWITCH CONSTRUCTION	03	33	79
DOUBLE SLIP SWITCH PLANS	03	33	80
SPIRAL CURVES	11	37	110
TRACK HOW TO MAKE MODEL TRACK	06	34	129
TRACKWORK CONSTRUCTION	05	42	87
UNIT CONSTRUCTION FOR LAYOUT BUILDING	04	41	97
ELECTRICAL ITEMS			
CURRENT DISTRIBUTION ON MODEL RAILROADS	07	34	123
RAILROAD SCANNER REVIEW REGENCY ELECTRON	SP	75	08R
SCENERY MODELING			
BUILD YOUR OWN SCENERY	06	55	56
MOUNTAIN SCENERY TO BUILD	03	37	138
SCENERY FOR MODEL RAILROADS	07	32	501
LAYOUT CONSTRUCTION			
BUILD A MODEL RAILROAD	12	34	137
CATENARY WIRE CONSTRUCTION FOR LAYOUTS	01	43	99
ELECTRIFYING A MODEL RAILROAD	06	32	369
FOUR-TRACK PASSENGER TERMINAL LAYOUT	02	39	108
INSTALLATION OF SWITCH MACHINES	11	54	43
LAYING LOWER-LEVEL TRACK	08	54	84
LAYOUT PROBLEMS	01	37	111
MODEL PAINTING HINT: DARKENED SHADES	05	40	68
PORTABLE FOUNDATION CONSTRUCTION	07	54	88
REMOTE CONTROL CABINET	02	55	48
RIGHT-OF-WAY REALISM FOR YOUR LAYOUTS	10	42	115
TRAIN CONTROL IN MODEL RAILROADING	01	40	63
TWO RAIL OPERATIONS IN MODEL RAILROADING	09	39	108
UPPER LEVEL PLATFORM CONSTRUCTION	09	54	52
WIRING YOUR CIRCUITS	01	55	50
LAYOUT OPERATIONS			
NUMBERING RAILROAD EQUIPMENT	08	39	113
OPERATING YOUR LAYOUT BY TIMETABLE	06	39	107
SOUND EFFECTS FOR YOUR LAYOUT	11	41	108
LAYOUT VISITS			
BACKYARD PIKE THAT WENT TO THE FAIR	02	40	87
BIG 7 ROUTE MARSHALL	09	36	134
CECILWOOD VEST POCKET RY FULL SIZE	02	32	401
FLORISTS' LIMITED--DELIVERS INV/MESSAGES	04	37	77
LIVE STEAMERS IN THE PARLOR	08	49	36
LIVE STEAMERS IN THE PARLOR PART 2	09	49	60
MIDGET ISLAND RAILROAD NEW BRUNSWICK	03	40	93
MINIATURE RR DESIGNED BY ENG. KOVALSKY	04	31	83

MODEL LAYOUTS	M	Y	P
PLYWOOD EMPIRE ROUTE APT SIZED 1890'S	06	54	85
RENSSELAER CENTRAL 9.5" STUDENTS	03	39	60
SEVEN MINUTE SPRING RY 1 1/2" SCALE	02	32	400

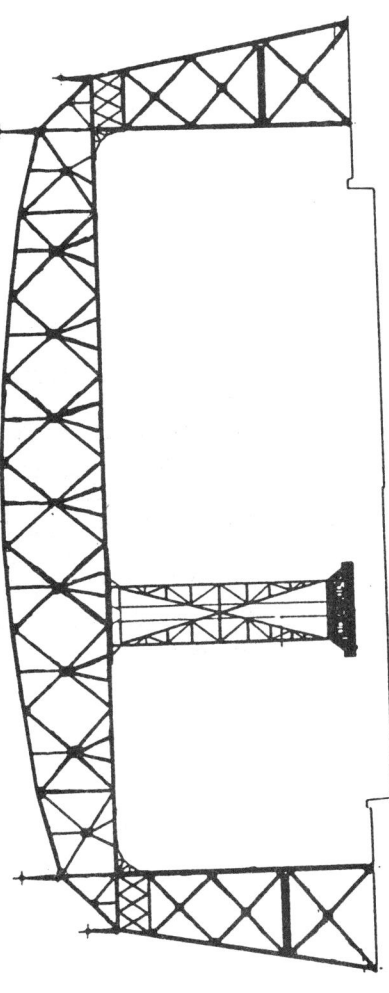

BILL OF LADING — LITERATURE REVIEWS

Literature Reviews has three sub categories. Prototype books are about real railroads. Modeling books are about models and model aspects of railroading. Videos list video tapes as they are released. The descriptor lists the full title of the entry. If space permits the author (or publisher) is listed at the end of the line.

MANIFEST — LITERATURE REVIEWS

DETAILED CONSIST	PAGE
PROTOTYPE BOOK REVIEWS	485
PROTOTYPE BOOK REVIEWS BY ROAD	505
VIDEO REVIEWS	512
MODELING BOOK REVIEWS	512

Railroad/Railfan

LITERATURE REVIEWS

RAILROAD PROTOTYPE BOOKS	M	Y	P
'RITIN' AND RAILIN' (B&O) PEPPER	11	74	59
100 YEARS OF CAPITAL TRACTION: STREETCAR	10	73	46
100 YEARS OF RAILROAD CARS LUCAS	08	59	67
100 YEARS OF STEAM LOCOS LUCAS	12	57	33
20TH CENTURY:GREATEST TRAIN IN THE WORLD	12	62	46
36 MILES OF TROUBLE (WR) MORSE	01	74	61
36 MILES OF TROUBLE (WR) MORSE	12	59	55
4-8-4 PICTORIAL WEYNER	11	73	60
400 STORY (C&NW) SCRIBBINS	11	82	19
400,000 MILES BY RAIL BLANTON	12	72	54
45 MILES TO YESTERDAY--DURANGO-SILVERTON	07	72	60
50 BEST OF B&O BARR	08	77	61
50 BEST OF B&O #3 KELLY	06	78	61
50 BEST OF B&O 2 HARWOOD	12	77	60
50 BEST OF B&O. BARR	10	77	10R
5:10 TO SUBURBIA OLMSTED	SP	76	10R
6000 & 7000 SERIES CARS ON EMSR CUMMINGS	08	65	63
76 YEARS OF PEORIA STREETCARS	07	65	41
80 YEARS OF TRANSPORTATION PROGRESS	04	58	48
90 YEARS OF BUFFALO RAILWAYS GORDON	09	70	44
94 YEARS OF ROCHESTER RAILWAYS GORDON	01	76	28
AAR RESEARCH ACTIVITIES 1956 ASSN OF AME	06	57	67
ABANDONED RAILROADS OF BEDFORD (IN) SULZ	08	60	51
ABOVE THE CIVIL WAR: STORY OF THADDEUS L	11	67	59
ABOVE THE CLAMOR BAKER	07	47	127
ACE CORSON,RAILROADER: 1878-1960 DESMOND	02	65	61
ACE ENGINEMAN MCKILLOP	10	63	40
ACROSS NEW YORK BY TROLLEY QP#4	SU	76	08R
ACROSS NY BY TROLLEY KRAMER	04	76	57
ACROSS NY BY TROLLEY:3RD AVE RAILWAY SYS	09	84	16
ADARONDACK VISTAS GARDNER	04	75	62
ADVENTURE UNDERGROUND:STORY OF WORLDS TU	10	62	37
ADVENTURES OF ALF WILSON (CIVIL WAR REP)	01	73	59
AGE OF STEAM, A CLASSIC ALBUM OF AMER RR	12	57	33
AGE OF STEAM, THE BEEBE & CLEGG	02	58	74
ALASKA RAILROAD FITCH	02	68	59
ALASKA RAILROAD IN PICTURES PRINCE	07	66	46
ALASKAS RAILROAD BUILDER:MIKE HENLEY HER	08	60	51
ALBUM OF WESTERN LOCOMOTIVES DUNSCOMB	08	60	51
ALCO ROTARY PLOW 1909 (REPRINT)	01	74	61
ALCO USRA LOCOMOTIVES 1919 REPRINT	01	74	61
ALGOMA EASTERN RAILWAY WILSON	04	78	61
ALL ABOARD! HISTORY OF RR IN MICHIGAN	03	70	52
ALL THE LIVE LONG DAY EVANS	04	69	50
ALL TIME INDEX 1929-69:RR TR RMC MR WAYN	03	71	58
ALL TIME INDEX REVISED WAYNER	10	78	65
ALLEGHENY: LIMAS FINEST HUDDLESTON	05	85	17
ALLONG THE IRIN TRAIL RICHARDSON	12	66	51
ALONG AN OPEN TRACK KOCHANEK	01	73	58
ALONG THE LACKAWANNA-A PICTORIAL REVIEW	07	76	60
ALONG THE LINE:INTERURBAN TO CLINTON--IN	10	76	56
AMBASSADOR ON RAILS FAUT	01	50	121
AMERICAN DIESEL LOCOMOTIVE ROBERTS	03	78	48
AMERICAN HERITAGE HISTORY OF RR IN AMERI	12	75	60
AMERICAN LOCOMOTIVE ENGINEERING COMPANIO	09	70	50

RAILROAD PROTOTYPE BOOKS	M	Y	P
AMERICAN LOCOMOTIVES:ENGINEERING HISTORY	10	68	48
AMERICAN ORIGINAL, THE PCC CAR KASHIN	07	87	18
AMERICAN RAILROAD (1874 HARPERS REPRINT)	08	72	63
AMERICAN RAILROAD JOURNAL V2 1967-68	12	68	58
AMERICAN RAILROAD JOURNAL:1966 DUKE	05	66	46
AMERICAN RAILROAD NETWORK 1861-90 TAYLOR	02	57	71
AMERICAN RAILROAD PASSENGER CAR WHITE	09	78	58
AMERICAN RAILROADS FRANCIS	08	70	52
AMERICAN RAILROADS DEBATE HANDBK 1939-40	01	40	57
AMERICAN RAILROADS-CHI HIST OF AMER CIVI	10	61	59
AMERICAN RAILWAY INDUSTRY, THE CORLISS	02	56	72
AMERICAN RAILWAY SIGNALING PRINCIPALS	06	55	53
AMERICAN RR POLITICS,1914-20:RATES WAGES	02	69	60
AMERICAN SHORT LINE RAILWAY GUIDE LEWIS	W	75	09R
AMERICAN SHORTLINE GUIDE LEWIS	01	80	15
AMERICAN SHORTLINE RAILWAY GUIDE LEWIS	12	75	61
AMERICAN SINGLE LOCOMOTIVES AND THE PIO	11	76	58
AMERICAN SINGLE-AXEL LOCO-"PIONEER" WHIT	02	74	36
AMERICAN STEAM LOCOMOTIVE V1: EVOLUTION	08	68	52
AMERICAS COLORFUL RAILROADS BALL	03	79	13R
AMERICAS RAILROADS: 2ND GENERATION BALL	03	81	16
AMTRAK AFT-1 TURBO OLD 97 CONRAIL H36-34	12	77	12R
AMTRAK CAR AND LOCOMOTIVE SPOTTER (REV)	SU	76	07R
AMTRAK CAR SPOTTER, INCLUDING AUTOTRAIN	04	74	60
AN OLD RAILROAD TOWN DEEGAN	08	57	77
AND NOW ITS MAIL TIME SHAW	06	75	60
AND TO THINK IT ONLY COST A NICKLE! STEI	06	76	47
ANDROSCOGGIN RIVER VALLEY WIGHT	03	68	50
APEX OF THE ATLANTICS WESTING	02	64	46
APPLICATION OF MODERN SCIENTIIC RESEARCH	08	55	66
ARCADE & ATTICA RAILROAD LEWIS	11	72	63
ARCATA & MAD RIVER: 100 YEARS BORDEN	01	55	68
ARCH AND ENG OF A WASH-NY CORRIDOR:PICTO	07	78	60
ARCHAEOLOGY OF THE CABLE CAR HANSCOM	04	71	48
ARCHAEOLOGY OF THE CABLE CAR. HANSCOM	06	71	55
ARGENTINE CENTRAL HOLLENBACK	02	62	55
ARID DOMAIN (ATSF AND LAND GRANTS)	12	54	56
ARIZONA RAILROADS:PAST & PRESENT GLOVER	10	65	61
ARTHUR E STILWELL (KCM&O) BRYANT	06	72	63
ARTHUR KONYOT:WHITE RIDER REICHMANN	04	62	59
ARTICULATED CARS OF N AMERICA CHARLTON	04	67	49
ARTICULATED LOCOMOTIVES WIENER	07	71	61
ATLANTA AND THE OLD SOUTH KURTZ	03	70	52
ATLANTIC COAST LINE:STEAM LOCOS & SHIPS	03	67	54
ATMOSPHERIC RAILWAYS: VICTORIAN VENTURE	05	68	50
ATWOODS CAT OF US & CANADIAN TRANS TOKEN	01	66	33
AURORA 'N' ELGIN (CA&E) JOHNSON	05	66	62
B&M, B&L, AND ERM BRADLEY	06	73	53
B&O IN THE CIVIL WAR SMITH	08	66	47
B&O POWER:STEAM DIESEL ELECTRIC 1829-'64	02	65	60
B&O RR STANDARD PLANS FOR MOW & CONSTRUC	03	78	60
B&O STEAM & ELECTRIC LOCO DIAGRAMS STAUF	11	65	54
B&RB-THE CANARSIE RAILROAD FAUSSER	07	77	47
BACKWOODS RAILROADS OF THE WEST STEINHEI	04	64	60
BADGER TRACTION	01	70	29

Railroad/Railfan

Stephans' Railroad Directory

LITERATURE REVIEWS

RAILROAD PROTOTYPE BOOKS	M	Y	P
BALDWIN CATALOG OF LOCOMOTIVES 1915 REPR	05	73	54
BALDWIN LOCO WORKS LOGGING LOCOS 1913	01	74	61
BALDWIN LOCO WORKS NARROW GAUGE LOCOS'76	01	74	61
BALDWIN LOCO WORKS RECORD 78 REPRINT	03	65	62
BALDWIN LOCO WORKS VAUCLAIN COMPDS 1900	01	74	61
BALDWIN LOCO WORKS:RECORD #89 (REPRINT)	08	64	46
BALDWIN LOCOMOTIVE WORKS:1881 CATALOG RE	10	60	52
BALDWIN RECORD #79:PACIFIC TYPE LOCOS RP	12	65	64
BALTIMORE & ITS STREETCARS:POSTWAR YEARS	05	85	15
BALTIMORE STREETCARS 1905-1963 SACHS	05	83	13
BANGOR STREET RAILWAY HESELTINE	10	76	56
BART AT MID-POINT:SF BOLD NEW TRANSIT PR	01	69	40
BART OFF AND RUNNING STRAPAC	04	73	55
BEAUTY OF RAILWAYS ELLIS	08	61	33
BEAUTY OF RR BRIDGES IN N AMERICA-THEN &	11	87	25
BELLS & WHISTLES IN OLD PERRY (N&SV)	SU	75	10R
BELLS & WHISTLES IN OLD PERRY (PECO)	SU	75	10R
BELLS & WHISTLES IN OLD PERRY (PVRR)	SU	75	10R
BELLS & WHISTLES IN OLD PERRY (SR&W)	SU	75	10R
BENT ZIGZAG & CROOKED:OHIOS LAST NARROW	08	60	51
BERKSHIRE STREET RAILWAY CUMMINGS	11	73	41
BERLIN STREET RAILWAY CUMMINGS	11	65	41
BESSEMER & LAKE ERIE RR:1869-1969 BEAVER	02	70	52
BESSEMER STORY, THE (B&LE)	06	55	53
BEST FRIEND OF CHARLESTON (SCC&RR) LANGL	09	70	50
BIBLIOGRAPHY OF RAILROAD LITERATURE	10	54	60
BIG 4 ROUTE (CCC&SL) PABST	02	64	50
BIG BLOW--UP TURBINES KEEKLEY	11	78	55
BIG FOUR, THE (CENTRAL PACIFIC) LEWIS	10	38	37
BIG IVY, THE (NOVEL) MCCAGUE	04	56	73
BIG SPENDERS BEEBE	09	66	51
BIRNEY CAR COX	11	66	46
BLACK RIVER & WESTERN STORY SMITH	12	73	61
BLACKSTONE VALLEY LINE (P&W) LEWIS	02	74	60
BLUE RIDGE TROLLEY:HAGERSTOWN & FREDERIC	08	70	40
BLUEBIRDS & MINUTEMEN 1974-84 (B&M) NELL	03	87	19
BOB AND THE RAILROAD (CHILDRENS) TOUSEY	02	42	52
BONANZA RAILROADS KNEISS	03	42	130
BOOK OF DANIEL DREW-1ST WALL ST SPECULAT	09	65	50
BOSTON CAPITALISTS & WESTERN RAILROADS	09	67	56
BRADFORD & FOSTER BROOK PEG LEG RAILROAD	05	75	61
BRADFORD BORDELL AND KINZUA WOODS	11	71	57
BRADSHAWS AUGUST 1914 CONTINENTAL GUIDE	09	72	55
BRANCH LINE ALBUM:SECOND SERIES WHITEHOU	02	66	62
BRASS POUNDERS HARLOW	12	62	46
BRIDGES AND THEIR BUILDERS	02	42	51
BRIEF HISTORY OF THE MODESTO & EMPIRE TR	04	57	55
BRILL DECK ROOF TROLLEY CARS FOESIG	11	73	41
BROAD STREET STATION, PHILADELPHIA (PRR)	01	77	56
BROOKLYN TROLLEYS GRELLER	05	87	15
BROTHERHOOD OF SLEEPING CAR PORTERS, THE	10	46	61
BUDD RDC IN CANADA CORLEY	05	68	50
BUFFALO & LAKE ERIE TRACTION CO GORDON	03	78	29
BUFFALO & SUSQUEHANNA RY PIETRAK	04	67	51
BUILDING & OPERATING MODEL RAILWAYS JANE	04	69	50

RAILROAD PROTOTYPE BOOKS	M	Y	P
BUILDING THE CANADIAN WEST HEDGES	03	41	79
BULLIED:LAST GIANT OF STEAM DAY-LEWIS	10	64	42
BURLINGTON NORTHERN ANNUAL 1972 WAGNER	05	73	55
BURLINGTON NORTHERN ANNUAL 1974-75 WAGNE	F	75	09R
BURLINGTON NORTHERN ANNUAL 1976-77 WAGNE	11	78	11R
BURLINGTON ROUTE:HISTORY OF BURLINGTON L	11	65	52
BURLINGTON WEST: A COLONIZATION HISTORY	02	42	51
BUSES ANNUAL 1965 SMITH	04	65	45
BUSES, TROLLEYS, AND TRAMS HAMLYN	02	68	40
BUSTED AND STILL RUNNING (B&SR) MEAD	05	71	60
BUSTED AND STILL RUNNING:B&SR MEAD	02	69	60
BY RAIL TO THE BOARD WALK GLADRICH	07	87	22
C&NW POWER:MODERN STEAM-DIESEL 1900-1971	03	73	58
C&O POWER:STEAM & DIESEL 1900-65 SHUSTER	03	66	62
C&O: SUPERPOWER TO DIESELS DIXON	07	85	14
C&TS: HISTORIC PRESERVATION STUDY WILSON	01	81	18
CAB-FORWARD CHURCH	02	70	52
CAB-FORWARD: STORY OF SP ARTICULATED LOC	06	73	53
CAB-IN-FRONT:50 YEAR STORY OF UNCONVENTI	04	60	46
CABLE CAR DRUMMOND	08	67	52
CABLE CAR CARNIVAL BEEBE & CLEGG	10	51	91
CABLE CAR IN AMERICA HILTON	01	72	41
CABLE CARS OF SAN FRANCISCO	02	69	43
CABLE CARS OF SAN FRANCISCO (SFM)	06	71	55
CALGARY MUNICIPAL RY COX	04	64	38
CALIFORNIA WESTERN RAILROAD, THE BORDEN	02	58	74
CALIFORNIAS ELECTRIC RYS:ILLUSTRATED HIS	09	87	16
CALIFORNIAS RAILROAD ERA 1850-1911 MCAFE	05	74	60
CALL OF THE IRON TRAIL (POEMS) INGRAHAM	08	60	50
CALVACADE OF THE RAILS MORSE	07	40	72
CAMBRIAS TROLLEYS (SCA) ROHERBECK	05	77	52
CAMELBACK LOCOMOTIVES ALBRECHT	07	71	61
CANADIAN CAR BUILDERS	04	72	55
CANADIAN ELEC SR RYS & INTERURBAN LINES	04	72	55
CANADIAN NATIONAL RAILWAYS (2 VOLS) STEV	04	63	49
CANADIAN NATIONAL RAILWAYS STORY DORIN	07	76	11
CANADIAN NATIONAL STEAM POWER CLEGG	06	70	66
CANADIAN PACIFIC IN THE ROCKIES (4 VOLS)	03	80	13
CANADIAN PACIFIC RAILWAY DORIN	03	75	61
CANADIAN PACIFIC: BRIEF HISTORY MCDOUGAL	09	68	57
CANADIAN RAILWAY PROBLEM THOMSON	11	39	94
CANADIAN RAILWAYS IN PICTURES LEGGET	11	78	55
CANADIAN STEAM MORGAN	06	62	37
CANADIAN TRANSPORTATION ECONOMICS CURRIE	03	68	48
CANAJOHARIE & CATSKILL RAILROAD	07	74	60
CANAL BOATS, INTERURBANS & TROLLEYS AMBE	07	86	12
CANNEL CARRIER (OHIO & KENTUCKY) SULZER	03	47	75
CAR BUILDERS DICTIONARY 1869 GREGG	07	72	60
CAR BUILDERS DICTIONARY, 1906 GREGG	03	72	39
CAR BUILDERS' CYCLOPEDIA 15TH EDITION	04	41	51
CAR BUILDERS' CYCLOPEDIA 19TH EDITION	06	54	102
CAR BUILDERS' DICTIONARY 1888 (REPRINT)	09	71	59
CAR NAMES & CONSISTS WAYNER	08	63	45
CAREERS IN AMERICAN RAILROAD INDUSTRY	12	60	59
CARS OF PACIFIC ELECTRIC,INTERURBAN & DE	12	65	37

Railroad/Railfan

LITERATURE REVIEWS

RAILROAD PROTOTYPE BOOKS	M	Y	P
CARS OF PE VOL 1:CITY & SUBURBAN CARS RE	01	76	28
CARS OF PE,CITY AND SUBURBAN CARS SWETT	04	65	45
CARS OF SACRAMENTO NORTHERN SWETT	04	64	38
CARS STOP HERE:BRIEF HIS OF ST RY TUSCON	09	72	40
CASEY JONES LEE	01	40	56
CASEY JONES' LOCKER SHAW	06	60	42
CASS COLLECTION KILLORAN	05	83	16
CASSIER'S MAGAZINE AUG 1899 (REPRINT)	10	61	51
CATALOGUE OF FUNICULAR RYS OF N AMERICA	12	76	48
CATALOGUE OF STEAM LOCOMOTIVE TYPES LONG	10	73	57
CATARACT TRACTION:RYS OF HAMILTON MILLS	05	72	62
CATENARY THROUGH COUNTIES: STORY OF M&SC	02	68	40
CATSKILL SOUVENIR 1879 (U&D) HELMER	04	70	58
CENTENNIAL HISTORY OF SOUTH CAROLINA RR	02	44	138
CENTRAL AMERICAN HOLIDAY BEST	04	61	56
CENTRAL MASS B&M HISTORICAL	08	76	60
CENTRAL PACIFIC & SOUTHERN PACIFIC RRS	10	63	40
CENTURIES OF THE NORTH WOODS (C&NW) :EAS	11	87	36
CENTURY OF CHICAGO STREETCARS 1858-1958	01	65	43
CENTURY OF RAILROADING IN CRAWFORD NOTCH	01	76	61
CENTURY OF READING MOTIVE POWER, A	09	41	82
CENTURY OF SP LOCOMOIVES DUNSCOMB	10	63	40
CENTURY OF SP STEAM LOCOMOTIVES DUNSCOMB	10	68	48
CERA'S EARLY BULLETINS 1-19 1938-40 REPR	04	78	27
CHALLENGER LOCOMOTIVES KRATVILLE	01	83	16
CHANGE AT PARK STREET UNDER (BS) CUDAHY	02	73	39
CHARLES MORGAN & DEV OF SOUTHERN TRANSPO	11	68	50
CHESAPEAKE BEACH RAILWAY WILLIAMS	01	76	29
CHESSIE'S ROAD TURNER	02	61	47
CHESSIE'S ROAD (C&O) TURNER	04	57	55
CHICAGO & ILLINOIS MIDLAND WALLIN	03	81	17
CHICAGO AURORA & ELGIN RR COMPANY REPRIN	06	78	55
CHICAGO ELEVATED RR: CONSOLIDATIONS OF O	03	68	35
CHICAGO GREAT WESTERN: 2-8-0 CONSOLIDATIO	02	78	39
CHICAGO'S PASSENGER TRAINS OLMSTED	11	83	24
CHICAGOS RAPID TRANSIT: V1 ROLLING STOCK	06	73	62
CHICAGOS RAPID TRANSIT:ROLLING STOCK 47-	04	78	09R
CHIEF WAWATAM-STORY OF A HAND-BOMBER	05	77	56
CHIEF WAY REFERENCE SERIES SYSTEM STDS	11	78	55
CHOCOLATE TOWN TROLLEYS (HT) STEINMETZ	12	67	36
CHUNK SWITCH BACK RAILWAY (MCH) GARDNER	06	75	61
CINCINNATI & LAKE ERIE RR, OHIO INTERURB	05	75	57
CINCINNATI GEORGETOWN & PORTSMOUTH RR	03	78	29
CINCINNATI GEORGETOWN & PORTSMOUTH RR	06	73	62
CINCINNATI LOCOMOTIVE BUILDERS 1845-1868	05	66	46
CINCINNATI STREETCARS #1 HORSECARS & STE	10	68	31
CINCINNATI STREETCARS #2 INCLINES WAGNER	03	69	30
CINCINNATI STREETCARS #3 CABLE CARS & EA	03	70	36
CINCINNATI STREETCARS #4 MILCREEK VALLEY	04	71	56
CINCINNATI STREETCARS #8 THROUGH 1930	11	80	19
CINCINNATI STREETCARS #9 STREAMLINERS &	03	85	15
CINCINNATI STREETCARS:1895-1911 WAGNER	05	72	62
CINCINNATI STREETCARS:1912-1922 WRIGHT	03	74	57
CINDERS & SMOKE (D&RGW) OSTERWALD	12	65	64
CINDERS & TIMBER (D&NE) HARRISON	02	70	54

RAILROAD PROTOTYPE BOOKS	M	Y	P
CIRCUS PHEALN	08	63	46
CIRCUS KINGS:OUR RINGLING FAMILY STORY	08	60	51
CIRCUS TRAIN SELBY-LOWNDES	04	65	50
CIRCUS: CINDERS TO SAWDUST O'BRIAN	06	62	40
CITY & INTERURBAN CARS BRILL '11 REPRINT	04	64	38
CITY AND INTERURBAN CARS 1913 BRILL REPR	01	67	45
CITY MAKERS:STORY OF S CAL'S FIRST BOOM	05	66	46
CIVIL WAR CAREER OF THOMAS A SCOTT, THE	12	41	85
CIVIL WAR RAILROADS ADBILL	10	61	60
CIVIL WAR RAILROADS & MODELS ALEXANDER	04	78	60
CIVIL WAR RAILROADS:PICTORIAL HIST OF IR	04	62	59
CLANG! CLANG! THE STORY OF TROLLEYS REID	11	64	44
CLARKE'S HISTORY OF EARLY RY NOVA SCOTIA	04	38	55
CLASSIC SHORTLINE RAILROAD PHOTOS GREENE	12	69	52
CLEAR THE TRACK ASSN OF AMERICAN RRS	02	57	71
CLEAR THE TRACK: TRUE STORIES OF RRING	09	52	139
CLEAR THE TRACKS! (DL&W HOGGER) BROMLEY	12	43	98
CLEVE SOUTHWESTERN & COLUMBUS TROLLEY	05	82	08
CLEVELAND RY: OPERATION & MAINTENANCE RE	07	67	40
CLEVELAND SOUTHWESTERN & COLUMBUS RY CO	01	83	12
CLEVELAND STREETCARS PART 2 MORSE	01	65	43
CLEVELAND, SOUTHWESTERN & COLUMBUS RY	06	63	39
CLIMAX PATENT GEARED LOCOMOTIVE 1924 REP	02	64	48
CLIMAX:UNUSUAL STEAM LOCOMOTIVE TABER	04	61	56
CLOUD CLIMBING RAILROAD NEAL	09	67	56
CLOUD-CLIMBING RR: STORY OF A&SM NEAL	03	68	48
CNJ, A PICTORIAL REVIEW GARDNER	06	74	11
COACH TRAINS AND TRAVEL DORIN	11	75	60
COACH, CABBAGE & CABOOSE (ATSF) MCCALL	09	80	14
COLLECTED COLORADO RAIL ANNUAL	01	75	56
COLLECTIVE BARGAINING INTHE RAILROAD IND	02	55	68
COLLECTORS BOOK OF RAILROADIANNA BAKER	09	78	11R
COLLECTORS BOOK OF THE LOCOMOTIVE ALEXAN	04	67	50
COLLIS POTTER HUNTINGTON EVANS	06	56	46
COLONEL MORGAN JONES SPENCE	04	72	63
COLORADO & SOUTHERN: NORTHERN DIVISION	03	67	54
COLORADO ANNUAL #4 1966	10	66	54
COLORADO ANNUAL #6 1968 HAUCK	09	68	57
COLORADO ANNUAL #7 CHILI 1969	12	69	52
COLORADO ANNUAL #7 CHILI LINE HAUCK	09	69	57
COLORADO ANNUAL #9 RHINE	11	71	57
COLORADO MIDLAND CAFKY	07	65	54
COLORADO RAILROADS HAUCK	12	61	43
COLORADO RAILROADS (MAPS) BY TRAINS MAG	04	44	81
COLORADO RAILROADS: CHRONOLOGICAL DEVELO	07	75	61
COLORADO ROAD (C&S AND FW&D) WAGNER	08	71	60
COLORADOS MOUNTAIN RAILROADS V1 LEMASSEN	06	64	55
COLORADOS MOUNTAIN ROADS V2 LEMASSENA	10	66	53
COMMODORE VANDERBILT LANE	07	42	73
COMMUTER RAILROADS DORIN	02	71	54
COMMUTER TRAINS TO GRAND CENTRAL TERMINA	09	87	14
COMPENDIUM OF SIGNALS KARL	05	72	55
CONCORD MAYNARD & HUDSON ST RY CUMMINGS	03	68	35
CONTROVERSIAL MARK HOPKINS LATTA	03	55	53
COPPER SPIKE JANSON	07	76	61

Railroad/Railfan

LITERATURE REVIEWS

RAILROAD PROTOTYPE BOOKS		M	Y	P
COPPER WIRES, CLERESTORIES & COMMUTERS		09	69	39
CORDWOOD LTD:HISTORY OF V&SRY	HEARN	10	66	53
CORNER OF HICKORY & THIRD (ONE MANS MEMO		10	67	37
CORTLAND COUNTY TRACTION	KING	08	65	63
COTTON BELT LOCOMOTIVES	STRAPAC	05	78	13R
COUDERSPORT & PORT ALLEGANY AND NY&P		08	73	61
COVERED BRIDGES OF THE MID-ATLANTIC STAT		06	60	43
COVERED WAGONS	YOUNG	12	77	09R
COW TRAIN CARNIVAL	BEEBE & CLEGG	05	54	114
CREDIT VALLEY RAILWAY	FILBY	08	76	60
CREST OF THE CONTINENT (CP)	INGERSOLL	06	70	66
CROOKEDEST RAILROAD IN THE WORLD (MT&MW)		08	54	104
CROOKEDEST RAILROAD IN THE WORLD. (MT&MW)		06	61	59
CROSS ISLAND:STORY OF HUNTINGTON RR	SEYF	09	77	52
CROSS TIES THROUGH CAROLINA:STORY OF NC		06	69	55
CRYSTAL RIVER PICTORIAL (COLORADO)	MCCOY	01	75	35
CURVED SIDE CARS BUILT BY CINCY CAR CO		11	65	41
CZ: STORY OF CALIFORNIA ZEPHYR	ZIMMERMAN	W	76	10R
D-DAY ON THE WESTERN PACIFIC	STAFF	01	83	18
DAIRY ROUTE: HIST OF E&B	GUSTAFSON	04	68	36
DALTON GANG:END OF AN OUTLAW ERA	PREECE	10	63	41
DANIEL WILLARD RIDES THE LINE	WILLARD	02	39	95
DANVILLE & SUNBURY TRANSIT CO	GORDON	11	68	39
DANVILLE TRACTION & POWER CO	TOSH	08	73	52
DATE NAILS COMPLETE	WISWELL	07	77	59
DAWN OF THE DIESEL AGE	KIRKLAND	01	85	19
DAY THEY SHOOK THE PLUM TREE (TM)	LEWIS	10	63	40
DAYLIGHT THROUGH THE MOUNTAIN	WALKER	06	58	68
DAYS OF THE NORTH SHORE LINE	CAMPBELL	11	86	19
DAYTON COVINGTON & PIQUA TRACTION CO	GOR	11	72	53
DECADE OF THE TRAINS, 1940'S	BALL	05	78	10R
DECADE OF THE TRAINS-THE 1940'S	BALL	07	78	60
DECLINE OF STEAM	GIFFORD	08	65	55
DELAWARE & HUDSON	SHAUGHNESSY	04	68	51
DELAWARE VALLEY RAILS	PAWSON	05	83	16
DELORIMER & ANGUS (CP)	LAVALLEE	07	67	50
DEMOCRACY'S RAILROADS (MICHIGAN)	PARKS	12	72	54
DENVER & RIO GRANDE WESTERN RR (REPRINT)		05	78	61
DENVER SOUTH PARK & PACIFIC		04	77	60
DENVER SOUTH PARK & PACIFIC	KINDIG	06	60	42
DENVER SOUTH PARK & PACIFIC: HISTORY		07	51	45
DENVER TRAMWAYS	GRIFFITH	08	62	49
DEPARTMENT OF TRANSPORTATION	DAVIS	09	70	50
DEPLETION MYTH:HISTORY OF RR USE OF TIMB		01	72	11
DEPOT DAYS	STIMSON	05	73	54
DESERT RIDER, THE	SCOTT	12	55	54
DESIGN OF HIGH SPEED DIESEL ENGINES	HOWA	10	66	54
DESTINATION LOOP (CHICAGO)	CUDAHY	09	83	14
DESTINATION TOPOLOBAMPO: KCM&O	KERR	02	69	60
DETROIT MONROE & TOLEDO SHORT LINE RY		10	87	27
DETROIT STREET RYS V1 CITY LINES 1893-22		12	78	53
DETROIT STREET RYS V2 CITY LINES 1922-56		01	81	16
DETROIT: ITS TROLLEYS & INTERURBANS		12	76	48
DEVELOPMENT OF THE AMERICAN INDUSTRIES,T		08	42	96
DEVELOPMENT OF THE LOCOMOTIVE ENGINE		12	36	50
DEVELPOMENT OF THE LOCOMOTIVE ENGINE SIN		05	71	60
DEVER SOUTH PARK & PACIFIC	POOR	05	49	127
DIE DAY IN LA	SWETT	12	64	41
DIESEL AND ELECTRIC TRAINS	COOPER	11	64	50
DIESEL BUILDERS: F-M & L-H	KIRKLAND	07	86	13
DIESEL ENGINE MANUAL	AUDEL	09	36	78
DIESEL LOCOMOTIVES	ALLAN	02	64	48
DIESEL LOCOMOTIVES OF NEW HAVEN RR	CAVAN	09	81	16
DIESEL LOCOMOTIVES OF NYC SYSTEM	EDSON	01	80	17
DIESEL LOCOMOTIVES: MECHANICAL EQUIPMENT		04	44	80
DIESEL SPOTTERS GUIDE	PINKEPANK	06	67	53
DIESEL SPOTTERS GUIDE-UPDATE	PINKEPANK	07	80	17
DIESEL YEARS	OLMSTED	W	75	08R
DIESEL YEARS	OLMSTEAD	12	75	53
DIESELS OF ESPEE:V1 ALCO PA'S	CORTANI	SP	76	08R
DIESELS OF THE ESPEE VOL 1	CHATHAM	05	76	62
DIESELS WEST:EVOLUTION OF POWER ON BURLI		04	64	61
DILWORTH STORY, THE (DIESEL LOCOS)	RECK	04	55	52
DINING IN THE DINER:GREAT RR RECIPES	HOL	02	66	62
DINING ON RAILS:ENC OF RAILROAD CHINA		05	84	14
DINKY (FICTION)	REESE	01	65	62
DIRECT CURRENT TRACTION MOTOR	LIGHTBAND	08	70	52
DIRECTORY OF RY OFFICIALS & YRBK 1957-58		04	58	48
DIRECTORY OF RY OFFICIALS & YRBK 1958-59		04	59	82
DIRECTORY OF RY OFFICIALS & YRBK 1959-60		06	60	42
DL&W IN THE 19TH CENTURY	TABER	09	77	60
DO LINES	LEWIS	07	78	07R
DOCUMENTS PROVE SUPERIOR OF RY TO CANALS		12	36	53
DOMELINERS	DORIN	11	73	60
DONNER PASS: SP SIERRA CROSSING	SIGNOR	05	86	11
DOODLEBUG COUNTRY:RAIL MOTOR CAR ON CL 1		05	83	15
DOODLEBUGS (ATSF)	MCCALL	03	78	61
DOODLEBUGS, THE	MCCALL	03	79	12R
DOUBLEHEADED:2 GENERATIONS OF RY ENTHUSI		06	64	57
DOWN AT THE DEPOT: AMER RR STATIONS 1831		07	70	42
DOWN BRAKES:HISTORY OF RY ACCIDENTS SAFE		08	62	56
DUMMY (B&M)	MCLIN	06	74	60
DUNELAND ELECTRIC:S SHORE LINE IN TRANSI		09	85	08
EAGLE BOOK OF TRAINS	ALLEN	04	58	48
EARLY AMERICAN STEAM LOCOS:1ST 7 DECADES		04	63	50
EARLY ELECTRIC CARS OF PHILLY:1885-1911		02	70	35
EARLY HISTORY OF ANN ARBOR CAR-FERRIES		11	50	135
EARLY HISTORY OF LONG ISLAND RR 1834-190		08	59	69
EARLY HISTORY OF TRANSPORTATION OREGON		08	44	101
EARLY MOTIVE POWER OF THE B&O RR	BELL	12	75	61
EAST BROAD TOP	RAINEY	09	82	14
EAST CAROLINA RAILWAY	BRIDGERS	02	74	60
EAST SHORE & SUBURBAN RY	HANSON	10	61	51
EASTERN MASS ST RYS:OPEN & CLOSED CARS		04	65	45
EASTERN STEAM PICTORIAL:ANTHRACITE ROADS		04	67	50
EBT: TO THE MINES AND BACK	GRENARD	01	81	16
ECHOES DOWN THE CANYON:WP JOURNAL '68-86		12	87	30
ECONOMICS OF REGULATION:THEORY & PRACTIC		01	66	64
ECONOMICS OF TRANSPORTATION IN AMERICA,		09	40	66
ECONOMICS OF TRANSPORTATION REVISED	LOCK	08	66	46

Railroad/Railfan

LITERATURE REVIEWS

RAILROAD PROTOTYPE BOOKS		M	Y	P
ED NOWAK'S NYC	ZIMMERMAN	07	84	18
EDAVILLE RAILROAD	MOODY	06	48	114
EIGHT WHEEL TYPE LOCOS BUILT BY ALCO		08	63	45
EL CENTENARIO DEL FERRO CARRIL MEXICANO		07	73	61
EL PASO ELEC TRANSPORTATION DIV: TENTATI		04	76	58
ELECTRIC CARES IN ELECTRIC CITY	MOWERS	07	65	41
ELECTRIC CARS AND TRUCKS (1895 BRILL)REP		01	72	41
ELECTRIC INTERURBAN RYS IN AMERICA HILTO		10	60	40
ELECTRIC LOCOMOTIVE ROSTERS	WAYNER	08	65	62
ELECTRIC RAILROADS OF INDIANA	MARLETTE	08	60	33
ELECTRIC RAILROADS OF INDIANA	.MARLETTE	09	82	12
ELECTRIC RAILWAY	PARK	04	73	55
ELECTRIC RAILWAY CAR TRUCKS	CAHRLTON	02	68	40
ELECTRIC RAILWAY CARS & TRUCKS 1905 REPR		03	73	58
ELECTRIC RAILWAY DICTIONARY (1911) REPRI		10	72	52
ELECTRIC RAILWAY PIONEER	DEMORO	01	84	24
ELECTRIC RAILWAYS OF MICHIGAN		08	60	33
ELECTRIC RAILWAYS OF NORTHEASTERN OHIO		01	66	33
ELECTRIC RY DIRECTORY MCGRAW HILL 1924 R		10	71	53
ELECTRIC TRACTION ENGINEERING	BINNEY	02	56	72
ELECTRIC TRAMWAYS OF HOBART (TASMANIA)		04	62	55
ELECTRIC TRANSPORTATION	THOMPSON	08	40	66
ELECTRIFICATION BY GE		03	78	29
ELEMENTS OF DIESEL ENGINEERING	ADAMS	07	36	87
ELEMENTS OF RAILWAY SIGNALING		01	55	68
ELEMENTS OF TRANSPORT	EATON	09	68	57
ELEVATED & SUBWAY CARS OF IRT & PREDICES		08	73	52
ELMIRA & CHEMUNG VALLEY TROLLEYS	GORDON	01	72	41
ELMIRA TROLLEYS	KING	04	62	54
EMPIRE THAT MISSOURI PACIFIC SERVES, THE		08	57	77
END OF THE LINE, THE	MORGAN	02	56	72
END OF TRACK	KYNER	05	37	41
ENGINE THAT LOST ITS WHISTLE, THE	CROSS	05	46	138
ENGINE-DRIVING LIFE:STIRRING ADVENTURES		02	69	60
ENGINEERING EXPERIMENT STATION	ILL UNIV	02	56	72
ENTERPRISE DENIED (RR STUDY 1897-1917)		12	71	48
ERA OF INTERURBANS IN WINNIPEG 1902-1939		02	72	50
ERA OF STREETCARS IN WINNIPEG 1851-1955		01	72	41
ERIE LACKAWANA STORY	CARLETON	03	75	59
ERIE LACKAWANNA EAST	ZIMMERMANN	11	75	60
ERIE LACKAWANNA MEMORIES-FINAL YEARS COO		11	87	26
ERIE PICTORIAL REVIEW	GARDNER	10	74	61
ERIE POWER	WESTING	05	71	60
ERIE RAILROAD, ROCHESTER DIV	GORDON	02	66	38
ERIE RAILROAD: PICTORAL REVIEW V2	GARDNE	10	75	60
ERIE RR: ROCHESTER DIVISION	GORDON	12	65	56
ERIE STEAM LOCOMOTIVE DIAGRAMS	STAUFER	11	65	54
ERIE-LACKAWANNA EAST QP#3	ZIMMERMANN	W	75	09R
ERIR RAILROAD-PICTORIAL REVIEW	GARDNER	F	75	09R
ESSAYS IN TRANSPORTATION	INNIS	07	42	74
ESSAYS ON "INHERENT ADVANTAGES" RY SERVI		05	55	54
EUGENE DEBS:REBEL LABOR LEADER-PROPHET		10	66	54
EUGENE V DEBS SPEAKS	TUSSEY	05	73	54
EVERYWHERE WEST THE BURLINGTON ROUTE		03	77	60
EVOLUTION OF RAILWAYS, THE	LEE	03	38	47
EVOLUTION OF THE RAILWAYS, THE	LEE	05	44	144
EXTRA 6706 WEST (C&NW) :EAST END PRODUCT		11	87	37
EXTRA SOUTH	REID	10	64	42
EXTRA SOUTH 2ND EDITION	REID	03	87	16
FACTS ON FILE YEARBOOK VOL III 1943		07	44	138
FACTS ON FILE, PERSON'S INDEX VOLUME 5		10	46	61
FAIRMOUNT PARK TROLLEY:UNIQUE PHILLY EXP		11	70	39
FALL & RISE OF STEAM	COOKE	09	84	17
FAMOUS AMERICAN TRAINS	REYNOLDS	01	35	88
FARES PLEASE (REPRINT)	MILLER	06	61	49
FAREWELL TO STEAM	PLOWDEN	03	67	54
FAREWELL TO STEAM IN CANADA	MIKA	04	66	50
FASCINATING RAILROAD BUSINESS	HENRY	07	42	73
FAST TRAINS! BUSY TRAINS! (CHILDREN)	MAL	12	56	74
FASTEST HOUND DOG IN THE STATE OF MAINE		10	54	60
FIDDLE HILL (NOVEL)	MCGAUGE	06	61	59
FIDDLETOWN & COPPEROPOLIS (CARTOONS)		10	60	52
FIFTY BEST OF PRR	DAVIS	10	78	65
FIFTY MILLION ACRES: KANSAS LAND POLICY		11	54	55
FIFTY YEARS OF PROGRESSIVE TRANS:TTCO		11	75	56
FIFTY YEARS OF PROGRESSIVE TRANSIT	BROML	SP	76	07R
FINAL YEARS, THE (NYO&W)	KRAUSE	12	77	12R
FINAL YEARS: NYO&W	KRAUSE	10	77	58
FINEST PICTURES OF AMERICAN RR SCENES		04	43	155
FIRST BOOK OF TRAINS (PRIMER-KIDS)	WATTS	12	56	74
FIRST FIVE YEARS OF RR ERA IN COLORADO		01	50	118
FIRST IRON PASSENGER CARS	LUCAS	08	62	56
FIRST PASSENGER RAILWAY, THE	LEE	11	44	56
FIRST QUARTER CENTURY OF STEAM LOCOS IN		02	60	38
FIRST QUARTER CENTURY OF STEAM LOCOS NA		02	57	70
FIRST STEAM WEST OF BIG MUDDY (SJ&GI)		03	71	58
FIRST TRAIN TO GREENPORT IN 1844	WOOD	05	44	146
FIRST TRANSCONTINENTAL RR: CENTRAL PACIF		09	50	65
FOCUS:RAILROAD IN TRANSITION 1947-1967		02	70	52
FOGG AND STEAM	CLODFELTER	09	79	14
FOREST GLEN TROLLEY & EARLY DEV OF SILVE		03	76	23
FORGOTTEN MEN OF CRIPPLE CREEK	SPELL	04	61	57
FORMATION & HIST OF CONN & CR&L (REV)		04	76	58
FORMATION & HIST OF CONN COMPANY 2ND ED		01	83	14
FORMATION OF THE NEW ENGLAND RR SYSTEMS		03	38	47
FORT WAYNE'S TROLLEYS	BRADLEY	10	64	41
FORTY FEET BELOW:CHICAGO FREIGHT TUNNELS		05	83	14
FORWARD IS THE MOTTO OF TODAYS STREET RY		03	85	15
FOX & ILLINOIS UNION RY CO		01	78	45
FR FOREIGN RAILROAD BOOKS		08	67	52
FR 1948 BRITISH RAILWAY LOCOMOTIVES		08	67	52
FR 60 YEARS OF WESTERN EXPRESS RUNNING		11	73	60
FR ALL ABOARD WITH EM FRIMBO	WHITAKER	02	75	57
FR ALONG THE LINE IN VICTORIA--AUSTRALIA		08	67	52
FR ALWAYS A TRAM IN SIGHT (BLACKPOOL)		11	72	53
FR AMERICAN-BRITISH DICTIONARY TO TRAVEL		05	73	54
FR ASPINALL ERA	BULLEID	03	68	50
FR AUSTRIAN TRAVEL WONDERLAND	DAVIES	07	74	60
FR BALLYCASTLE RAILWAY	PATTERSON	06	67	54
FR BALLYCASTLE RAILWAY	PATTERSON	10	68	51

LITERATURE REVIEWS

RAILROAD PROTOTYPE BOOKS	M	Y	P
FR BOOK OF SPLENDID TRAINS: BRITISH	02	39	95
FR BRADSHAWS APRIL 1910 RAILWAY GUIDE RE	05	69	57
FR BRANCH LINES (BRITISH) NOCK	08	58	64
FR BRIGHTON ELECTRIC LINE (AUSTRALIA)	09	67	34
FR BRITAIN'S BIG FOUR GREENLEAF	05	49	123
FR BRITAINS NEW RAILWAY NOCK	10	66	54
FR BRITAINS RAILWAYS AT WAR NOCK	05	72	55
FR BRITAINS RAILWAYS UNDER STEAM SNELL	06	66	55
FR BRITISH BRANCH LINES VALLANCE	09	65	51
FR BRITISH IRON & STEEL INDUSTRY GALE	06	67	54
FR BRITISH LOCO NAMES OF THE 20TH CENTUR	03	68	51
FR BRITISH LOCO NAMES OF THE 20TH CENTYR	06	64	57
FR BRITISH LOCOMOTIVES 1829-1963	12	63	14
FR BRITISH LOCOMOTIVES 1948-50	01	73	59
FR BRITISH LOCOMOTIVES ILLUSTRATED BELL	09	33	50
FR BRITISH RAIL LOCOMOTIVES	03	68	51
FR BRITISH RAIL MAINLINE GRADIANT PROFIL	01	67	50
FR BRITISH RAILWAY BRIDGES WALTERS	02	64	50
FR BRITISH RAILWAY HISTORY V1 1830-76	08	55	66
FR BRITISH RAILWAY SIGNALING KICHENSIDE	10	64	44
FR BRITISH RAILWAY STATIONS DENTON	12	65	64
FR BRITISH RAILWAY TUNNELS BLOWER	06	66	56
FR BRITISH RAILWAYS NEWLANDS	04	37	55
FR BRITISH RAILWAYS DIESEL LOCOS ALLAN	06	64	57
FR BRITISH RAILWAYS IN ACTION NOCK	06	57	67
FR BRITISH RAILWAYS IN TRANSITION NOCK	10	64	44
FR BRITISH RAILWAYS LOCOS & OTHER MOTIVE	07	65	55
FR BRITISH RAILWAYS MAINLINE DIESELS CAR	10	64	44
FR BRITISH RY ACCIDENTS OF 20TH CENTURY	07	67	50
FR BRITISH RYS: STANDARD STEAM LOCOS	06	67	54
FR BRITISH STEAM LOCOS FROM 1825 TO 1925	06	64	55
FR BRITISH STEAM RAILWAY LOCOS V2:1925	04	67	50
FR BRITISH STEAM RAILWAYS NOCK	08	62	56
FR BRITISH TRAINS OF YESTERDAY--PRE 1923	05	67	50
FR BRITISH TRAMWAYS & PRESERVED TRAMCARS	07	69	41
FR BRITISH TRANSPORT 1956 BRITISH TRANSP	12	57	33
FR BRITISH TRANSPORT 1959	12	60	59
FR BRITISH TROLLEYBUSES SYMONS	04	68	36
FR BUILDER FRAN SVERIGES JARNVAGAR: SWED	11	66	49
FR BY RAIL TO THE END OF THE EARTH WESTC	01	70	54
FR BYGONE LIGHT RAILS OF EUROPE LAURSON	07	78	60
FR CALLANDER & OBAN RAILWAY THOMAS	06	67	54
FR CALLANDER & OBAN RAILWAY. THOMAS	10	68	51
FR CAMBRIAN RYS 1852-1888 CHRISTIANSEN	08	68	55
FR CAVALCADE REFLECTIONS & RETROSPECT	08	76	40
FR CAVAN & LEITRIM RAILWAY FLANAGAN	06	67	54
FR CAVAN & LEITRIM RAILWAY. FLANAGAN	08	68	55
FR CENTUARY OF LOCOS: NEW S WALES AUSTRA	05	67	50
FR CENTURY OF NEW SOUTH WALES TRAMCARS 2	03	69	30
FR CENTURY ON NEW SOUTH WALES TRAMCARS 1	10	63	36
FR CONTINENTAL MAIN LINES NOCK	06	64	57
FR COOKS CONTINENTAL TIMETABLE COOK	05	70	58
FR DAMPFLOKOMOTIVEN IM DEUTSCHLAND HARTM	08	75	31
FR DAWN OF WORLD RAILWAYS 1800-1850 NOCK	11	72	63
FR DESIRE OF TRAMCARS JOWITT	07	70	40

RAILROAD PROTOTYPE BOOKS	M	Y	P
FR DESTINATION EAGLEHAWK (AUSTRALIA)	01	70	29
FR DESTINATION VALLEY (AUSTRALIA) DAVIES	09	67	34
FR EACH A GLIMPSE (BRITISH LOCOS) GIFFOR	09	70	50
FR EARLY BRITISH RAILWAYS BARMAN	06	55	53
FR EARLY RAILWAYS SNELL	01	65	62
FR ELECTRIC EUSTON TO GLASGOW NOCK	01	75	47
FR ELECTRIC RAILWAY THAT NEVER WAS--BRIT	09	70	44
FR EMETT'S DOMAIN TRAINS, TRAMS & ENGLIS	11	54	55
FR ENGINE PASS: NEW ZEALAND RAILWAYS LEI	04	68	52
FR ENGINE SHED BOOK ALLAN	06	64	57
FR ENJOY EUROPE BY RAIL FARQUHR	05	66	45
FR EURAILPASS TRAVEL GUIDE BAXTER	08	72	62
FR EUROPES GREATEST TRAMWAY NETWORK VAND	02	71	45
FR EXPRESS TRAINS:ENGLISH & FOREIGN FOXW	01	65	62
FR FACTS & FIGURES ABOUT ENGLISH RY 1957	04	58	48
FR FAIRWELL TO STEAM VOL1:TANK ENGINES	11	74	37
FR FAMOUS LOCOMOTIVES OF THE WORLD HAMIL	02	64	46
FR FAMOUS RAILROAD STATIONS OF THE WORLD	07	54	124
FR FAMOUS TRAINS OF THE WORLD CARTER	12	63	12
FR FAMOUS UNDERGROUND RAILWAYS OF WORLD	12	63	42
FR FESTINIOG RAILWAY REVIVAL (WELSH)	04	64	62
FR FIRST STOP CENTRAL (BRITISH) KEENAN	08	64	59
FR FLYING SCOTSMAN PEGLER	03	70	52
FR FORGOTTEN RYS:EAST MIDLANDS (BRITISH)	05	74	60
FR FRENCH MINOR RAILWAYS DAVIES	06	67	54
FR FRENCH STEAM LOCOMOTIVES GLOVER	07	75	41
FR FUTURE OF BRITANS RAILWAYS CALVERT	07	67	51
FR FUTURE RAILWAYS & GUIDED TRANSPORT UK	09	73	61
FR GOLDEN AGE OF STEAM NOCK	11	75	34
FR GRAND EUROPEAN EXPRESS:STORY WAGON/LI	12	63	12
FR GREASLEY PACIFICS PART 1 NOCK	07	74	60
FR GREAT BRITISH TRAMWAY WORKS BETT	10	63	36
FR GREAT CENTRAL V3:FAY SETS THE PACE	07	66	47
FR GREAT CENTRAL:DOM OF WATKIN 1864-1899	02	64	50
FR GREAT EASTERN RAILWAY ALLEN	03	68	50
FR GREAT NORTHERN LOCO ENGINEERS V1 1846	07	67	51
FR GREAT NORTHERN RAILWAY NOCK	10	66	54
FR GREAT RAILWAY BAZAAR	12	75	61
FR GREAT RAILWAY JOURNEYS OF THE WORLD	01	66	62
FR GREAT RAILWAY JOURNIES OF THE WORLD	01	83	15
FR GREAT STEAM TRECK (S AFRICAN STEAM)	09	80	14
FR GREAT TRAIN ROBERY OF 1963 GOSLING	09	65	51
FR GREAT TRAINS MORGAN	02	74	60
FR GREAT TRAINS OF THE WORLD BLASSINGAME	05	55	53
FR GREAT TRAINS. MORGAN	03	75	59
FR GREAT TRANS-CONTINENTAL RY GUIDE-REPR	08	71	60
FR GREAT WESTERN ALBUM RILEY	06	67	54
FR GREAT WESTERN COACHES 1890-1954 HARRI	12	66	50
FR GREAT WESTERN RAILWAY IN 20TH CENTURY	12	64	36
FR GREAT WESTERN RY IN 19TH CENTURY NOCK	08	63	45
FR GREAT WESTERN RY STARS, CASTLES & KIN	10	68	51
FR GREAT WESTERN SCENE (BRITISH) EARLEY	06	72	63
FR GREEN LINES (AUSTRALIAN) HENDERSON	08	67	43
FR GRICER IN TURKEY TAYLORSON	08	76	40
FR HIGHLAND RAILWAY NOCK	12	65	63

Stephans Railroad Directory

Railroad/Railfan

LITERATURE REVIEWS

RAILROAD PROTOTYPE BOOKS	M	Y	P
FR HIGHLAND RAILWAY VALLANCE	10	68	51
FR HIGHLIGHTS OF STEAM TRIP (AUSTRALIAN)	05	74	60
FR HIST OF GREAT WESTERN RY V1 1833-1863	11	64	50
FR HIST OF SOUTHERN RY (BRITISH) MARSHAL	06	64	57
FR HISTORIC RAIL DISASTERS NOCK	12	69	52
FR HISTORIC RAILWAY DISASTERS NOCK	05	67	50
FR HISTORIC WAGON DWGSS IN 4MM SCALE ROC	12	65	64
FR HISTORICAL LOCOMOTIVE DRAWINGS IN 4MM	10	64	44
FR HISTORY OF BRITISH RY DOWN TO YR 1830	01	39	28
FR HISTORY OF KEIGHLEY & WORTH VALLEY RY	01	75	35
FR HISTORY OF RUSSIAN RAILWAYS WESTWOOD	11	64	48
FR HISTORY OF SCOTLAND: GREAT NORTH RY	02	41	75
FR HISTORY OF THE WORLDS SUBWAYS BOBRICK	05	82	08
FR HOLIDAY CARAVANNING: COMPLETE GUIDE	06	67	54
FR HONGKONG TRAMWAYS ATKINSON	04	71	56
FR HOW I BECAME AN ENGINE DRIVER MCKILLO	03	55	53
FR HOW THE UNDERGROUND WORKS GARBUTT	07	68	37
FR HUNGARIAN RAILROADS KALLA-BISHOP	02	74	60
FR HUNGARIAN RAILROADS. KALLA-BISHOP	08	75	31
FR HUNSLET HUNDRED ROLT	10	68	51
FR I TRIED TO RUN A RAILWAY FIENNES	03	68	50
FR IMPACT OF RAILWAYS ON VICTORIAN CITY	09	69	57
FR INDIAN NARROW GAUGE RAILWAYS HUGHES	12	69	52
FR INLAND EMPIRE:DC CORBIN & SPOKANE FAH	12	65	62
FR INSIDE UNDERGROUND RAILWAYS (BRITISH)	07	65	41
FR INTRODUCTION TO RAILWAY BRAKING BROAD	09	69	57
FR IRISH LOCOMOTIVES CLEMENTS	03	68	51
FR ISLE OF WRIGHT ALBUM KICHENSIDE	03	68	51
FR JANE'S FREIGHT CONTAINERS 1972-73 FIN	04	73	59
FR JANE'S WORLD RAILWAYS SAMPSON	08	68	52
FR JANE'S WORLD RAILWAYS 1970	10	70	48
FR JANE'S WORLD RAILWAYS 1970-71 SAMPSON	06	71	51
FR JANE'S WORLD RAILWAYS 1971-72 SAMPSON	05	72	54
FR JANE'S WORLD RAILWAYS 1972-73	04	73	58
FR JANE'S WORLD RAILWAYS 9TH ED SAMPSON	12	66	50
FR JANE'S WORLD RYS & RAPID TRANSIT 1977	11	77	60
FR JOHANNESBURGH TRAMWAYS SPIT	05	77	52
FR JUNGLE ROUTE, THE (BRAZIL-BOTAVIA)	10	40	71
FR KEIGHLEY & WORTH VALLEY STOCKBOOK UK	10	76	25
FR LAST STEAM LOCOMOTIVE ENG:RA RIDDLES	03	71	58
FR LAST STEAM LOCOMOTIVES OF EASTERN EUR	06	75	49
FR LEEDS TRAMS (BRITISH) YOUNG	02	75	39
FR LIGHT RAILWAYS OF FIRST WORLD WAR DAV	05	68	50
FR LIVERPOOL & MANCHESTER RY OPERATIONS	09	74	61
FR LIVERPOOL TRANSPORT V1 1830-1900 HORN	07	76	21
FR LMS ALBUM DORMAN	03	68	51
FR LMS ALBUM #3 STEPHENSON	05	75	49
FR LMS LOCOMOTIVES:COMPLETE LIST OF LOND	08	66	48
FR LNER 2-8-2 & 2-6-2 CLASSES CLAY	06	73	53
FR LNER LOCOS 1938 (LONDON & NORTHEASTER	09	38	37
FR LOCO SHED BOOK (BRITISH) ALLAN	12	64	36
FR LOCO SPOTTERS ALBUM 1968 KICHENSIDE	03	68	51
FR LOCO SPOTTERS ANNUAL 1966 KICHENSIDE	06	66	55
FR LOCO SPOTTERS ANNUAL 1967 KICHENSIDE	01	67	52
FR LOCOMOTIVE ENGINEERS ALBUM:SAGA STEAM	12	65	63

RAILROAD PROTOTYPE BOOKS	M	Y	P
FR LOCOMOTIVES AT THE GROUPING JOHNSTON	09	67	56
FR LOCOS AT THE GROUPING: GREAT WESTERN	03	68	51
FR LOCOS AT THE GROUPING:SOUTHERN RY	06	66	56
FR LOCOS OF THE LNER, A PICTORIAL RECORD	06	48	113
FR LONDON & NORTH WESTERN RY PRECURSOR F	10	68	51
FR LONDON & SOUTH WESTERN NOCK	08	66	47
FR LONDON & SOUTH WESTERN RY VOL 2 GROWT	10	74	61
FR LONDON RAILWAYS COURSE	10	65	40
FR LONDON TRANSPORT RAILWAYS	02	64	42
FR LONDON'S TERMINI JACKSON	12	69	52
FR LONDON'S UNDERGROUND HOWSON	07	82	13
FR LONDONS TRAMWAY SUBWAY	04	76	58
FR LOST PLEASURES OF GREAT TRAINS PAGE	01	76	61
FR LOUGH SWILLY RAILWAY PATTERSON	06	67	54
FR LUNATIC EXPRESS (EAST AFRICA) MILLER	05	72	55
FR LYNTON & BARNSTAPLE RAILWAY PRIDEAUX	08	68	55
FR MAIN LINE ALBUM (BRITISH) WHITEHOUSE	07	65	54
FR MAJESTY OF BRITISH STEAM HEIRON	03	74	61
FR MASTER BUILDERS OF STEAM (UK) BULLE	06	64	57
FR MELBORNE TRAMWAYS KEENAN	12	87	29
FR MELBOURNES' TRAMWAYS IN 1974 KEENAN	12	74	56
FR METRE-GAUGE RY IN S & E SWITZERLAND	12	74	59
FR MIDLAND & SOUTH WESTERN JUNCTION RY	10	68	51
FR MIDLAND COMPOUNDS	10	68	51
FR MIDLAND MAINLINE 1875-1922 BARNES	04	70	58
FR MIDLAND RAILWAY (BRITISH) ELLIS	10	66	54
FR MIDLAND STEAM (BRITISH) TUPLIN	06	74	60
FR ML2 STORY (AUSTRALIAN) BERMINGHAM	07	83	15
FR MODERN AUSTRALIAN & NEW ZEALAND TRAIN	04	67	50
FR MODERN TRAMWAY REVIEW (BRITISH) JOYCE	04	65	45
FR MODERNIZATION & RE-EQUIPMENT BRITISH	12	55	55
FR MOSTLY SCOTTISH STEAM MIDDLEMASS	07	76	11
FR NAMIB NARROW-GAUGE (S AFRICA) MOIR	08	67	52
FR NO 4220: ROUND TRIP TO STAMMERSDORF	02	75	39
FR NORTH EASTERN STEAM (BRITISH) ALLEN	01	71	47
FR NORTH WESTERN ALBUM (BRITISH) DORMAN	12	65	63
FR NORTHWESTERN STEAM (BRITISH) TUPLIN	06	64	57
FR OBSERVERS BOOK OF BRITISH STEAM LOCOS	SU	76	09R
FR ON RAILS UNDER PARIS PRIGMORE	09	71	49
FR ORIENT EXPRESS: STORY OF WORLDS MOST	11	67	56
FR PAINTED ENGINES (BRITISH) RUSSELL	06	66	56
FR PASSENGER TRANSPORT 1967	03	68	51
FR PASSENGERS NO MORE (BRITISH) DANIELS	04	74	60
FR PERTINENT DATA PRINCIPAL RR OF WORLD	02	56	72
FR PICTORIAL ENCYCLOPEDIA OF RAILWAYS EL	01	78	61
FR PICTORIAL HIST OF ELECTRIC LOCOMOTIVE	10	70	48
FR PICTURE STORY OF WORLD RAILWAYS JOHNS	01	67	50
FR PIONEER PERIOD OF EUROPEAN RAILROADS	03	47	75
FR PROCEED TO PETERBOROUGH (AUSTRALIA)	03	71	58
FR RAIL & ROAD IN EAST AFRICA HAZLEWOOD	12	65	64
FR RAIL STEAM & SPEED NOCK	03	71	58
FR RAILROADING IN EIGHTEEN COUNTRIES GRA	04	56	73
FR RAILROADS OF NEW ZEALAND LEITCH	11	72	63
FR RAILROADS OF NORTH AFRICA BRANT	04	72	63
FR RAILROADS OF THE USSR	06	62	40

Railroad/Railfan

LITERATURE REVIEWS

RAILROAD PROTOTYPE BOOKS	M	Y	P
FR RAILS ACROSS PANAMA SCHOTT	08	67	52
FR RAILS TO THE RISING SUN (JAP) SMALL	02	66	62
FR RAILWAY ACCIDENTS OF GREAT BRITAIN &E	11	70	44
FR RAILWAY ADVENTURE (TALYLLYN RY ENGLAN	10	54	60
FR RAILWAY ANTHOLOGY WHITEHOUSE	06	66	55
FR RAILWAY BOOK: HDBK FOR SPOTTERS & OTH	12	63	14
FR RAILWAY CARRAGES 1839-1939 KITCHENSID	03	65	62
FR RAILWAY CARRIAGE ALBUM KITCHENSIDE	10	66	54
FR RAILWAY CARRIAGES 1839-1939 KITCHENSI	03	66	63
FR RAILWAY CARRIAGES ON THE BRITISH ISLE	06	66	55
FR RAILWAY COLOUR ALBUM ALLAN	03	68	51
FR RAILWAY DESIGN SINCE 1830 V2 1914-69	01	70	54
FR RAILWAY DIRECTORY & YEARBOOK 1978	08	78	67
FR RAILWAY DIRECTORY AND YEAR BOOK 1971	06	71	51
FR RAILWAY DIRECTORY AND YEAR BOOK 1972	04	72	63
FR RAILWAY ENGINES OF THE WORLD REGD	11	34	95
FR RAILWAY ENTHUSIASTS BED SIDE BOOK VAL	05	67	50
FR RAILWAY ENTHUSIASTS ENCYCLOPEDIA NOCK	06	69	55
FR RAILWAY FOUNDRY LEADS REDMAN	11	72	62
FR RAILWAY HERALDRY (BRITISH) DOW	08	74	60
FR RAILWAY HOLIDAY IN BAVARIA PRICE	06	67	54
FR RAILWAY HOLIDAY IN FRANCE BEHREND	11	64	50
FR RAILWAY HOLIDAY IN ITALY KALLA-BISHOP	06	68	60
FR RAILWAY HOLIDAY IN NORTHERN GERMANY	07	66	47
FR RAILWAY HOLIDAY IN SPAIN ROWE	06	67	54
FR RAILWAY HOLIDAY IN SWITZERLAND BEHREN	07	66	46
FR RAILWAY KING: GEO HUDSON & BUSINESS M	10	64	42
FR RAILWAY RELICS & REGALIA (BRITISH)	10	76	58
FR RAILWAY WORLD ANNUAL 1975 WILLIAMS	08	75	31
FR RAILWAYMANS DIESEL ANNUAL (UK) BOLT	06	64	57
FR RAILWAYS AND THE (BRITISH) NATION PEA	10	64	44
FR RAILWAYS OF AUSTRALIA NOCK	02	72	51
FR RAILWAYS OF RHODESIA CROXTON	06	74	60
FR RAILWAYS OF SOUTH AFRICA NOCK	10	71	47
FR RAILWAYS OF SOUTHERN AFRICA DAY	04	64	61
FR RAILWAYS OF THE ANDES FAWCETT	06	64	57
FR RAILWAYS OF THE CINEMA (BRITISH) HUNT	01	70	54
FR RAILWAYS OF THE MODERN AGE NOCK	12	77	61
FR RAILWAYS OF THE WORLD 1964	10	64	41
FR RAILWAYS OF THE WORLD OVER ALLEN	04	57	55
FR RAILWAYS THEN AND NOW NOCK	11	75	34
FR RAILWAYS THROUGH THE MOUNTAINS OF EUR	06	68	60
FR RAILWAYS TO THE END OF 19TH CENTURY	03	66	63
FR RAILWAYS:BRIT RY FROM BEGINNING TO'60	11	65	54
FR RAILWAYS:THE TWENTIETH CENTURY SIMMON	08	70	52
FR RAPID TRANSIT RAILWAYS OF THE WORLD	02	72	50
FR REFLECTIONS ON A BRITISH RY CAREER	06	67	54
FR REGIONAL HIST OF RYS OF GREAT BRIT V1	10	68	51
FR REGIONAL HIST OF RYS OF GREAT BRIT V4	06	67	54
FR REGIONAL HIST OF RYS OF GREAT BRITAIN	08	68	55
FR RISE OF MIDLAND RAILWAY 1844-1874 UK	10	66	54
FR ROYAL TRAINS OF THE BRITISH ISLES SLA	05	75	62
FR RUSSIAN LOCOMOTIVE TYPES WESTWOOD	04	61	57
FR RUSSIAN STEAM LOCOMOTIVES LEFLEMING	08	61	33
FR RUSSIAN STEAM LOCOMOTIVES LE FLEMING	06	69	55

RAILROAD PROTOTYPE BOOKS	M	Y	P
FR RYS IN THE FORMATIVE YEARS 1851-1895	11	74	60
FR SCOTTISH LOCOMOTIVE HISTORY 1831-1923	06	71	51
FR SCOTTISH RAILWAY HISTORY IN PICTURES	10	68	51
FR SCOTTISH RAILWAYS NOCK	06	57	67
FR SCOTTISH RAILWAYS. NOCK	06	55	53
FR SEATON TRAMWAY PRICE	02	75	39
FR SEVERN VALLEY STREAM (BRITISH) NABARR	08	72	62
FR SIMPLE HISTORY OF THE STEAM ENGINE	10	70	48
FR SLIGO LEITRIM & NORTHERN COUNTIES RY	01	71	47
FR SNAEFELL MOUNTAIN RAILWAY 1895-1970	09	71	49
FR SNOWDON MOUNTAIN RAILWAY RANSOME-WALL	03	68	51
FR SOUTH AMERICAN STEAM FINCH	07	75	41
FR SOUTH AMERICAN STEAM CHRISTIAN	02	72	51
FR SOUTH WESTERN RAILWAY, THE ELLIS/ALLE	08	57	77
FR SOUTHERN STEAM NOCK	06	67	54
FR SOUTHERN STEAM. NOCK	10	68	51
FR SOUTHWESTERN RAILWAY (BRITISH) ELLIS	10	64	44
FR SOUTHWOLD RAILWAY (BRITISH) TAYLOR	02	66	62
FR SPRINGBURN STORY THOMAS	10	64	44
FR SPRINGBURN STORY. THOMAS	10	68	51
FR STANIER BLACK FIVE (BRITISH) CLAY	10	72	62
FR STANIER LOCOMOTIVES HARESNAPE	08	70	52
FR STEAM IN EUROPE WHITEHOUSE	04	67	50
FR STEAM LOCOMOTIVE OF EASTERN EUROPE RD	02	74	60
FR STEAM LOCOMOTIVES (BRITISH) WILLIAMS	03	65	62
FR STEAM LOCOMOTIVES IN EASTERN EUROPE	04	67	50
FR STEAM LOCOMOTIVES IN INDUSTRY-BRITISH	09	68	58
FR STEAM LOCOMOTIVES OF BRITISH RAILWAYS	11	76	53
FR STEAM LOCOMOTIVES OF EAST AFRICAN RYS	11	74	11
FR STEAM LOCOMOTIVES OF EASTERN EUROPE	09	68	58
FR STEAM NOSTALGIA (BRITISH) NABARRO	10	76	25
FR STEAM OVER BELFAST LOUGH ARNOLD	10	70	48
FR STEAM RAILWAYS IN RETROSPECT NOCK	09	66	52
FR STERLING SINGLES LEECH	09	68	58
FR STOCKTON & DARLINGTON RY 1825-1975	02	76	61
FR STONE BLOCKS AND IRON RAILS GREEN	06	67	54
FR STORY OF NEW STREET, THE (BRITISH RY)	01	55	68
FR STORY OF PASSENGER TRANSPORT IN BRITA	03	68	51
FR SUDAN TRANSPORT:HIST RY MARINE & RIVR	01	66	63
FR SWINDON STEAM (BRITISH) COOK	06	75	49
FR SWISS TRAVEL WONDERLAND ALLEN	10	72	63
FR SWITZERLAND'S AMAZING RAILWAYS ALLEN	05	55	53
FR THE DELTICS:A SYMPOSIUM ALLEN	02	73	61
FR THE PERMANENT WAY GREENLEAF	05	49	123
FR THIRD WOODHEAD TUNNEL, THE (BRITISH)	01	55	68
FR THOMAS NEWCOMEN:PREHISTORY OF THE STE	10	68	51
FR THROUGH SIBERIA BY TRAIN ZONN	10	76	25
FR TITLED TRAINS OF THE WESTERN BRITISH	07	75	41
FR TO THE GREAT OCEAN: TAMING OF SIBERIA	11	65	54
FR TRAINS 'SIXTY-EIGHT SNELL	03	68	51
FR TRAINS ANNUAL 1964 (BRITISH) ALLEN	06	64	57
FR TRAINS ANNUAL 1965 ALLAN	01	65	62
FR TRAINS ANNUAL 1966 ALLAN	06	66	55
FR TRAINS ANNUAL 1967 KICHENSIDE	01	67	52
FR TRAINS OF THE WORLD RIVERIAN	02	67	52
FR TRAINS ANNUAL ALLEN	08	63	45

STEPHANS_RAILROAD_DIRECTORY

492

Railroad/Railfan

LITERATURE REVIEWS

RAILROAD PROTOTYPE BOOKS		M	Y	P
FR TRAINS: 20TH ANNIVERSARY EDITION	HENR	11	54	55
FR TRAMCARS	PRICE	02	64	42
FR TRAMS OF SOUTH YORKSHIRE & HUMBERSIDE		11	75	56
FR TRAMWAY HEYDAY (BRITISH)	JOYCE	04	65	45
FR TRAMWAY MEMORIES	JOYCE	04	68	36
FR TRAMWAYS OF EASTERN EUROPE	TAPLIN	02	74	59
FR TRAMWAYS OF KENT VOL1-WEST KENT		01	73	38
FR TRAMWAYS OF PORTUGAL: VISITORS GUIDE		01	73	38
FR TRAMWAYS OF THE WORLD	JOYCE	07	66	33
FR TROLLEYS TO SALISBURY BEACH	CUMMINGS	07	66	33
FR TWILIGHT OF WORLD STEAM	ZIEL	01	74	61
FR VALE OF RHEIDOL LIGHT RAILWAY	DAVIES	12	64	36
FR VICTORIAN RAILWAYMEN	KINGSFORD	01	72	37
FR VICTORIAN STATIONS (BRITISH)	BIDDLE	01	75	56
FR VINTAGE STEAM (BRITISH)	KITE	04	70	58
FR WELSH HIGHLAND RAILWAY	LEE	06	67	54
FR WELSH HIGHLAND RAILWAY (MORE)	LEE	06	67	54
FR WEST HIGHLAND RAILWAY	THOMAS	10	68	51
FR WEST OF THE TARARUS (AUSTRALIAN)	HOY	08	74	60
FR WHEN STEAM WAS KING	STEWART	01	71	47
FR WORLD OF SOUTH AMERICAN STEAM		07	74	44
FR WORLD RAILWAY LOCOMOTIVES: CONCISE EN		06	60	42
FR WORLD RAILWAYS 1953		10	54	60
FR WORLD'S RAILWAYS 1962-1963	SAMPSON	12	62	46
FR WORLD'S RAILWAYS 3RD EDITION	SAMPSON	12	55	55
FR WORLD'S RY---1894 WORLDS FAIR REPRINT		11	74	59
FR WORLDS UNDERGROUND RAILWAYS		04	65	45
FREIGHT CARS ROLLING	SAGLE	06	61	60
FREIGHT RATES, INTER-REGIONAL TARIFF IS		09	42	67
FREIGHT TRAIN	REICHERT	10	57	37
FREIGHT TRAIN HANDLING SUPREME		08	43	77
FREIGHT TRAIN HANDLING SUPREME	CONNOR	09	47	74
FREIGHT YARD, THE	STEVER	12	58	64
FRIENDLY SOO, THE	SUPREY	02	55	68
FRISCO FOLKS:STORIES OF STEAM DAYS ON FR		12	61	42
FROM CAB TO CABOOSE:50 YEARS OF RAILROAD		08	64	46
FROM COAST TO COAST WITH JACK LONDON A#1		11	70	44
FROM HORSE TO STEEL RAILS	WARDWELL	04	56	67
FROM HORSE-CARS TO STREAMLINERS	MILLER	07	41	71
FROM MINE TO MARKET (N&W COAL TRANSPORTA		02	55	67
FROM OMNIBUS TO MOTOR BUS: HISTORY OF SH		07	70	40
FROM THE HILLS TO THE HUDSON(PA&HR)LUCAS		01	45	77
FULTON COUNTY NARROW GAUGE		12	43	101
FUN AND WORK OF RAILROADING	MURPHY	04	69	50
GALVESTON-HOUSTON ELECTRIC RY	WOODS	01	83	12
GARDEN SPOT TROLLEYS	CUMMINGS	04	78	27
GATEWAY TO THE NORTHWEST (MITR)	DONOVAN	03	55	53
GENERAL AMERICAN TRANSPORTATION: WHAT IT		07	42	74
GENERAL RIDES AGAIN (A&W)	ATKINSON	10	62	39
GEO STEPHENSON: ENGINEER AND HIS LETTERS		03	74	61
GEORGIAN LOCOMOTIVE	BRYANT	10	62	39
GHOST LUMBER TOWNS OF CENTRAL PENNSYLVAN		04	71	49
GHOST RAILROADS OF INDIANA	SULZER	03	71	40
GHOST RAILROADS OF KENTUCKY	SULZER	05	68	50
GHOST RAILWAYS OF INDIANA	SULZER	07	71	61

RAILROAD PROTOTYPE BOOKS		M	Y	P
GILPIN GOLD TRAM	FERRELL	11	71	57
GILPIN TRAIN, THE	HOLLENBACK	08	59	69
GILPIN TRAM	HOLLENBACK	02	62	55
GIT ON BOARD:FOLK SONGS FOR GROUP SINGIN		12	65	63
GM&O NORTH	OLMSTED	SP	77	12R
GOLD RUSH NARROW GAUGE (WP&Y)	MARTIN	06	70	66
GOLDEN BOOK OF TRAINS, THE	WERNER	11	54	55
GOLDEN SPIKE	MILLER	05	74	60
GOLDEN SPIKE:A CENTENNIAL REMEMBRANCE		07	69	58
GONE BUT NOT FORGOTTEN: THE M&OL	PALMER	05	67	50
GOODBYE TO THE INTERURBAN-AMER HERITAGE		08	66	63
GOODBYE, GARCIA, ADIOS	DEDERA	09	77	61
GOULDS MILLIONS	O'CONNOR	06	62	40
GOV OPERATIONS OF THE RAILROADS 1918-20		06	76	55
GOVERNMENT OWNERSHIP OF RAILROADS		01	40	57
GRAND CENTRAL:WORLDS GREATEST RY TERMINA		01	78	60
GRAND TRUNK RAILWAY OF CANADA, THE CURRI		08	58	64
GRAND TRUNK WESTERN	DORIN	03	78	25
GRAND TRUNK WESTERN RR	DORIN	12	77	60
GRANT LOCOMOTIVE WORKS CATALOG 1871 FERR		03	72	39
GRASS BETWEEN THE RAILS (MILW BRANCH)		12	73	61
GREAT DAYS OF THE CIRCUS	HUBBARD	10	62	38
GREAT HORSESHOE WRECK (CP 1907)	BEAUMONT	11	76	58
GREAT IRON TRAIL:1ST TRANSCONTINENTAL RR		02	63	37
GREAT KICKING HORSE BLUNDER (CP)	PUGSLEY	10	73	57
GREAT LAKES CAR FERRIES	HILTON	12	62	46
GREAT LOCOMOTIVE CHASE, THE	ROBERTS	08	56	72
GREAT POEMS FROM RAILROAD MAGAZINE	WAYNE	05	68	50
GREAT RAILROAD PAINTINGS	GOLDSBOROUGH	05	78	10R
GREAT RAILROAD PAINTINGS	.GOLDSBOROUGH	10	77	61
GREAT RAILROAD STORIES OF THE WORLD		04	55	53
GREAT RICHMOND TERMINAL	KLEIN	08	70	52
GREAT ROCK ISLAND ROUTE	GARDNER	09	75	61
GREAT SOUTHWEST STRIKE, THE	ALLEN	09	42	67
GREAT THIRD RAIL		08	62	49
GREAT THIRD RAIL (CA&E) REPRINT		07	67	40
GREAT TRAIN ROBBERIES OF THE WEST	BLOCK	12	59	55
GREAT TRAINS OF ALL TIME	HUBBARD	02	63	36
GREAT YELLOW FLEET (REEFERS)	WHITE	01	87	25
GRIERSIN'S RAID	BROWN	08	55	66
GROWING UP WITH TRAINS:S CAL ALBUM	STEIN	09	83	15
GT HERITAGE, STEAM IN NEW ENGLAND	HASTIN	03	79	11R
GUERNEVILLE BRANCH, THE	STINDT	06	56	61
GULF TO ROCKIES (FW&D + C&S 1861-1898)		08	54	105
GULF, MOBILE AND OHIO, THE	LEMLY	07	54	123
HANDBOOK OF AMERICAN RAILROADS	LEWIS	06	57	67
HARRY BIDWELL, LAST OF THE GREAT RR STOR		04	60	45
HARTFORD & SPRINGFIELD STREET RAILWAY CO		01	76	28
HARVEY GIRLS, THE (NOVEL)	ADAMS	01	43	86
HAWAIIAN RAILROADS:MEMOIR OF COMMON CARR		06	64	55
HAWAIIAN TRAMWAYS:STORY OF HONOLULU RAPI		08	60	33
HEADLIGHTS & MARKERS:ANTHOLOGY OF RR STO		03	69	50
HEADLIGHTS AND MARKERS	DONOVAN	05	46	136
HEAR THAT LONESOME WHISTLE BLOW	BROWN	06	78	62
HEAR THE TRAIN BLOW	BEEBE	05	54	112

Railroad/Railfan

LITERATURE REVIEWS

RAILROAD PROTOTYPE BOOKS		M	Y	P
HEISLER LOCOMOTIVE 1891-1941	KLINE	09	82	14
HENRY VARNUM POOR	CHANDLER	06	57	67
HERBS HOT BOX OF RR SLANG PLUS HEROS OF		02	76	61
HERE COMES THE TROLLEY!	GURLEY	10	64	41
HETCH HETCHY AND ITS DAM RAILROAD	WURM	01	74	61
HG&DSR AND GR&ISR	CUMMINGS	10	63	37
HIAWATHA STORY (MILW)	SCRIBBINS	12	70	62
HIGH IRON	BALLARD	11	54	55
HIGH IRON '72	PINCUS	12	72	54
HIGH IRON CO 1971	ROWLAND	01	72	37
HIGH IRON, A BOOK OF TRAINS	BEEBE	01	39	26
HIGH IRON: MAIN LINE STEAM 1972-3 PINCUS		10	74	62
HIGH ROAD TO PROMONTORY:BUILDING CPA ACR		08	69	32
HIGH TENSION (NOVEL)	WISTER	09	38	37
HIGHBALL: A PAGEANT OF TRAINS	BEEBE	04	46	73
HIGHBALL:PAGENT OF TRAINS (REPRINT) BEEB		06	62	37
HIGHWAY COSTS (WHO SHOULD PAY THEM) BEHL		10	56	57
HILL CITY TROLLEYS-SR OF LYNCHBURG VA		01	78	45
HISTORIC ALPINE TUNNEL (SOP)	HELMERS	08	64	44
HISTORIC SOUTHERN PACIFIC CARS	WAYNER	04	74	60
HISTORICAL GUIDE TO N AMERICAN RRS DRURY		07	86	16
HISTORICAL SKETCHES OF EARLY RAILROADING		08	62	57
HISTORY OF AT&SF RAILWAY	BRYANT	06	75	60
HISTORY OF BROTHERHOOD CARMEN OF AMERICA		06	42	95
HISTORY OF BROTHERHOOD RY & STEAMSHIP CL		08	65	55
HISTORY OF GREAT WESTERN RY V2 1863-1921		04	65	51
HISTORY OF HUDSON VALLEY RAILWAY	NESTLE	12	67	36
HISTORY OF KNOXVILLE ST RY SYSTEM	BEL	06	75	06
HISTORY OF LOUISVILLE & NASHVILLE RR		02	73	60
HISTORY OF MACK MOTOR CARS & LOCOMOTIVES		06	60	43
HISTORY OF PASS & THROUGH CAR SERV PRR		10	74	62
HISTORY OF PRR FT WAYNE SHOPS	RICE	04	67	52
HISTORY OF SAN LUIS OBISPO TELEGRAM-TRIB		08	56	72
HISTORY OF ST LOUIS CAR CO-QUALITY SHOPS		01	79	61
HISTORY OF TEXAS RAILROADS, A	REED	11	42	71
HISTORY OF THE 3101 (CP)	BEST	01	67	52
HISTORY OF THE BROTHERHOOD OF MOW EMPLOY		04	56	73
HISTORY OF THE CIRCUS IN AMERICA CHINDAH		08	62	57
HISTORY OF THE ELECTRIC LOCOMOTIVE	HAUT	01	70	29
HISTORY OF THE ILLINOIS CENTRAL	STOVER	01	76	61
HISTORY OF THE KANSAS CENTRAL RY, A		01	55	68
HISTORY OF THE LEBANON VALLEY RAILROAD		07	44	136
HISTORY OF THE LOCOS OF THE READING CO.		10	46	61
HISTORY OF THE LV RAILROAD	ARCHER	09	78	12R
HISTORY OF THE NORTH PENNSYLVANIA RR		07	44	136
HISTORY OF THE RAILROAD HAND CAR (REP)		04	76	60
HOLLYWOOD IN THE MOTHER LODE (SIE) JENSE		10	74	61
HOOT TOOT & WHISTLE:STORY OF HT&W CARMAN		04	64	61
HORNY TOAD MAN (ATSF)	DILS	07	67	51
HORSECARS, CABLE CARS & OMNIBUSES	WHITE	12	74	56
HOW THE LOCOMOTIVE WORKS AND WHY	SELLS	12	36	54
HOW TO GET A JOB THAT TAKES YOU TRAVELIN		06	57	67
HOW WE BUILT THE UP RAILWAY & OTHER RY P		05	65	52
HOW YOUNG GOT THE VOTES	FORTUNE	11	54	55
HUDSON RIVER DAY LINE	RINGWALD	10	65	61

RAILROAD PROTOTYPE BOOKS		M	Y	P
HUEY THE ENGINEER	STUART	02	61	47
HURRICANE ROAD (FEC)	SMILEY & WHITE	02	55	67
HYDE PK DIV OF DEDHAM-NORWOOD-E WALPOLE		01	78	44
I LOVE YOU HONEY, BUT THE SEASONS OVER		10	61	60
I REMEMBER PENNSY	WOOD	02	74	37
ILLINOIS CENTRAL IN IOWA	DONOVAN	12	62	48
ILLUSTRATED BOOK OF AMERICAN FOLKLORE, T		08	59	69
ILLUSTRATED HISTORY OF ST LOUIS CAR CO		01	79	61
IMPRESSIONS OF STEAM	JORGENSEN	06	64	56
IMPRESSIONS OF THE TERMINAL PROVIDENCE R		12	60	59
IMPROVING LONDON'S TRANSPORT		09	47	75
IN PERSUIT OF THE GENERAL:HISTORY OF CIV		01	66	63
INDIANA REVISITED	NEDDEN	09	72	40
INSIDE A DIESEL LOCOMOTIVE	COOPER	03	65	62
INSIDE MUNI (SFM)	MC KANE	09	82	14
INTEGRAL TRAIN SYSTEMS	KNEILING	10	69	59
INTERCITY ELECTRIC RAILWAY INDUSTRY IN C		02	67	46
INTERMOUNTAIN RAILROADS:STD & NAR GAUGE		02	63	37
INTERMOUNTAIN RAILROADS:STD & NARROW GAU		02	64	50
INTERURBAN ERA	MIDDLETON	12	61	52
INTERURBAN ERA IN HOLLAND MICHIGAN REKEN		05	83	15
INTERURBAN GOES MODERN & OTHER EARLY CER		04	78	27
INTERURBAN LIMITED	MAGUIRE	01	66	33
INTERURBAN RAILWAY & TERMINAL CO:BLACK L		02	73	39
INTERURBAN RAILWAYS OF THE BAY AREA TRIM		05	78	48
INTERURBAN TO MILWAUKEE (CNS&M)		08	63	41
INTERURBANS OF THE EMPIRE STATE		09	49	83
INTERURBANS OF UTAH	SWETT	09	74	51
INTERURBANS WITHOUT WIRES	KEILTY	03	80	12
IOWA TROLLEYS REVISED	CERA	07	75	59
IRON HORSE (HUBBARD REVIEW)	COMSTOCK	03	72	39
IRON HORSE AT WAR	VALLE	01	79	62
IRON HORSE, THE	NATHAN & ERNST	05	37	41
IRON HORSES (1859-1900)	ALEXANDER	01	42	68
IRON HORSES ACROSS THE GARDEN STATE GALL		01	87	24
IRON HORSES OF THE SANTA FE TRAIL WORLEY		06	66	54
IRON HORSES TO PROMONTORY (CPA)	BEST	08	69	32
IRON MEN AND COPPER WIRES (SCEC) MEYERS		07	84	17
IRON ROAD TO EMPIRE (ROCK ISLAND) HAYES		06	54	103
IRON ROADS: RAILWAYS OF NOVA SCOTIA STEP		05	73	54
IRONS AND STEEL TODAY	DEARDEN	09	40	66
ITHACA STREET RAILWAY	COX	07	72	39
ITHACA-AUBURN SHORT LINE	PALMER	09	78	53
JAMES J. HILL	HOLBROOK	12	55	54
JAMES MILLHOLLAND & EARLY RR ENGINEERING		02	68	61
JAMES WATT	ROLT	02	64	46
JAMES WATT:PIONEER OF MECHANICAL POWER		11	64	50
JAMESTOWN & CHAUTAUQUA LAKE TROLLEYS		09	74	51
JERSEY CENTRAL ALBUM	CARTER	04	64	61
JERSEY CENTRAL STORY	CARLTON	03	77	60
JERSEY CENTRAL TRACTION CO	EID	05	83	14
JH THOMAS: A LIFE FOR UNITY		12	64	35
JIM FISK: CAREER OF IMPROBABLE RASCAL		08	59	69
JOHNSTOWN FLOOD	MCCULLOUGH	08	68	52
JOHNSTOWN TRACTION CO 1882-1960 ROHRBECK		06	76	47

Railroad/Railfan

LITERATURE REVIEWS

RAILROAD PROTOTYPE BOOKS		M	Y	P
JOURNEY TO AMTRAK	EDMONSON	08	72	63
KANSAS QUARTERLY:AMERICAN RAILROADS		12	70	62
KATY NORTHWEST	HOFSOMMER	10	76	58
KATY NORTHWEST	HOFSOMMER	09	78	12R
KATY RAILROAD & THE LAST FRONTIER MASTER		06	78	61
KEEP 'EM ROLLING	WATSON	03	85	14
KEEPING THE RAILROADS RUNNING:50 Y /NYC		08	75	61
KEUKA LAKE MEMORIES	GORDON	01	68	63
KEY ROUTE PART 2 TRANS BAY COMMUTING SFM		07	86	12
KEY ROUTE:TRANSBAY COMMUTING BY TRAIN/FE		07	85	14
KEY SYSTEM ALBUM	WALKER	11	78	54
KEYSTONE STEAM & ELECTRIC (PRR)	EDSON	03	75	61
KITE ROUTE:STORY OF D&IRR	JONES	11	87	24
L&N STEAM LOCOMOTIVES	PRINCE	04	60	46
L&N STEAM LOCOMOTIVES REVISED 1968	PRINC	03	70	52
LA RAILWAYS PRE-HUNTINGTON CARS 1890-'02		08	63	41
LABYRINTH (FICTION)	DUNCAN	11	67	59
LACKAWANNA HERITAGE 1947-1952	KRAUSE	11	78	12R
LACKAWANNA RAILROAD #2	GARDNER	12	76	54
LAKE SHORE ELECTRIC	CHRISTIANSEN	10	64	41
LAKE SUPERIOR IRON ORE RAILROADS	DORIN	11	69	56
LANGUAGE OF THE RAILS	ADAMS	02	78	58
LARAMIE PLAINS LINE	HOLLENBACK	02	62	55
LAST BROAD GAGE, THE	BROWN	08	55	66
LAST DECADE OF BUFFALO TROLLEYS		01	74	59
LAST MILE: A STREETCAR NAMED CHARLES		05	73	61
LAST OF STEAM	COLLIAS	04	61	56
LAST OF THE YELLOW CARS (LAR)	WOOTON	12	63	42
LAST STEAM LOCOS OF WESTERN EUROPE	RANSO	08	63	42
LAST TRAIN FROM ATLANTA	HOEHLING	08	59	67
LAST WHISTLE (OS)	WAGNER	12	74	59
LAUREL LINE (L&WV)	HENWOOD	09	86	12
LAW AND LOCOMOTIVES (WISCONSIN)	HUNT	12	59	55
LEE COUNTY CENTRAL ELECTRIC RY	KEISTER	07	67	40
LEHIGH VALLEY RAILROAD:A PICTORIAL REV 1		12	75	61
LEHIGH VALLEY RAILROAD:RT OF THE BLACK D		06	78	20
LEHIGH VALLEY TRANSIT CO ST LOUIS CARS		04	62	54
LET'S OPERATE A RAILROAD	ROXBURY	12	57	33
LETS LOOK AT TRAINS	CARTER	05	66	46
LEWISTON AUGUSTA & WATERVILLE STREET RY		10	64	41
LEWISTON-CLARKSTON TRANSIT		03	76	23
LIBERTY BELL ROUTES 1000 SERIES INTERURB		02	65	40
LIBERTY BELL ROUTES HEAVY INTERURBAN CAR		06	71	55
LIFE & TIMES OF AMER BLUE YODELER, J ROD		09	82	15
LIFE & TIMES OF PACIFIC ELECTRIC	WALKER	03	84	12
LIFE AND DECLINE OF THE AMERICAN RAILROA		07	70	42
LIFE ON A LOCOMOTIVE (C&NW)	WILLIAMS	01	72	37
LIFE ON THE HEAD END	ADAMS	02	57	71
LIGHT RAILWAYS:THEIR RISE AND DECLINE		11	64	50
LIGHTNING ROUT (MONTGOMERY AL)		03	76	23
LIMA: THE HISTORY	HIRSIMAKI	09	87	18
LIMITEDS ALONG THE LAKEFRONT:IC IN CHICA		05	87	19
LINCOLN LAND TRACTION (IT)	JOHNSON	12	65	37
LINCOLN'S RAILROAD MAN: HERMAN HAUPT		09	69	57
LINCOLNS JOURNEY TO GREATNESS:12 DAY INA		10	60	52
LINES OF PACIFIC ELECTRIC-WESTERN DIV		10	64	41
LINES OF PACIFIC ELECTRIC:NORTHERN & EAS		10	76	56
LINES WEST (GN)	WEST	02	68	60
LIST OF PRINCIPAL RAILROADS IN THE US		02	57	71
LITTLE ENGINES AND BIG MEN	LATHROP	03	55	53
LITTLE JEWEL (SOO)	ABBEY	05	85	16
LITTLE MIAMI RAILROAD	BLACK	07	40	72
LITTLE RAILWAYS OF THE WORLD	SHAW	04	59	82
LITTLE RED ENGINE GOES TRAVELING	ROSS	12	56	74
LITTLE TRAIN, THE (CHILDREN)	GREENE	12	58	64
LOCAL LINES OF PE:PASADENA, LONG BEACH		10	62	48
LOCO PROFILE #9:CAMELS & CAMELBACK	REED	09	71	59
LOCO ROSTERS OF NORTH AMERICA 12-1973		09	74	60
LOCO ROSTERS OF NORTH AMERICA JUNE 1973		02	74	60
LOCOMOTIVE 4501 (S)	MORGAN	04	69	48
LOCOMOTIVE ADVENTURE V2:RUNNING EXPERIEN		02	66	62
LOCOMOTIVE ADVENTURE:50 YEARS WITH STEAM		08	63	42
LOCOMOTIVE ADVERTISING IN AMER 1850-1900		02	61	47
LOCOMOTIVE CYCLOPEDIA	SIMMONS-BOARDMAN	11	38	74
LOCOMOTIVE CYCLOPEDIA 10TH EDITION		02	39	94
LOCOMOTIVE CYCLOPEDIA OF AMER PRACT 15TH		08	57	77
LOCOMOTIVE CYCLOPEDIA OF AMER PRACTICE		07	72	60
LOCOMOTIVE DICTIONARY (1906) REPRINT	GRE	10	72	62
LOCOMOTIVE ENGINEER,1863-1963:CENT OF LA		08	64	44
LOCOMOTIVE ENGINEERS & FIREMAN'S MANUAL		09	43	130
LOCOMOTIVE ENGINEERS & FIREMANS MANUAL		07	42	74
LOCOMOTIVE PANORAMA VOL 1	COX	02	66	62
LOCOMOTIVE QUARTRERLY V1 NUMBER 1		W	76	08R
LOCOMOTIVE TROLLEY & RAIL CAR BUILDERS		02	67	46
LOCOMOTIVE, THE	LOEWY	09	37	65
LOCOMOTIVES & LOCOMOTIVE BUILDING REPRIN		12	63	14
LOCOMOTIVES 1-999 NEW JERSEY CENTRAL CAR		01	79	62
LOCOMOTIVES AND CARS SINCE 1900	LUCAS	06	60	42
LOCOMOTIVES IN MY LIFE	WOOD	W	75	08R
LOCOMOTIVES IN OUR LIVES 1890-1951		07	54	121
LOCOMOTIVES IN RETIREMENT	FENTON	04	61	56
LOCOMOTIVES OF DM&IR	KING	05	85	19
LOCOMOTIVES OF NYC LINES	MAY	11	66	49
LOCOMOTIVES OF THE ATSF SYSTEM		12	39	125
LOCOMOTIVES OF THE DICKSON MFG CO	BEST	01	67	50
LOCOMOTIVES OF THE JERSEY CENTRAL		06	58	68
LOCOMOTIVES OF THE JERSEY CENTRAL 1-999		03	80	13
LOCOMOTIVES OF THE READING 1836-1923	WAR	10	63	41
LOCOMOTIVES OF THE WESTERN PACIFIC		05	55	53
LOCOMOTIVES ON PARADE	HUNGERFORD	04	41	51
LOCOMOTIVES THAT BALDWIN BUILT	WESTING	01	67	50
LOCOMOTIVES, LOCALS & LIMITEDS	OLMSTED	05	78	11R
LOGGING ALONG THE DENVER & RIO GRANDE		06	72	63
LOGGING RAILROADS OF THE WEST	ADAMS	12	61	42
LONDON & PORT STANLEY RAILWAY	TORRENS	01	85	17
LONDON TRANSPORT: TRAMS & TROLLEYBUSES		04	67	49
LONG ISLAND RAILROAD	KRAMER	06	78	20
LONG ISLAND RAILROAD PART 1 S SIDE RY		10	62	37
LONG ISLAND RAILROAD PART 2: COMP HISTOR		06	64	56
LONG ISLAND RAILROAD PART 3 1863-80 EXPA		03	67	54

LITERATURE REVIEWS

RAILROAD PROTOTYPE BOOKS	M	Y	P
LONG ISLAND RAILROAD PART 4 COMPREHENSIV	05	69	57
LONG ISLAND RAILROAD PART 5 SAYFRIED	10	72	52
LONG ISLAND RAILROAD PART 6 GOLDEN AGE	06	76	55
LONG LOOK AT STEAM OLMSTED	07	65	54
LONG SUMMER OF GEORGE ADAMS (FICTION)	02	62	55
LOST GLORY LOGAN	04	78	61
LOST GLORY, GREAT DAYS OF AMERICAN RYS	09	77	20
LOUISIANA STREET & INTERURBAN RAILWAYS	10	63	36
LOUISVILLE & NASHVILLE RAILROAD HERR	08	60	50
LOUISVILLE & NASHVILLE RAILROAD, THE	08	43	78
LOUISVILLE & NASHVILLE RR (1850-1963)5TH	11	64	48
LUCIUS BEEBE READER CLEGG	03	68	48
LURE OF STEAM TREACY	05	67	50
MA & PA, A VANISHING RAILROAD KENDALL	03	72	39
MA&PA:HISTORY OF MARYLAND & PENN RR HILT	12	63	12
MAIL BY RAIL: POSTAL TRANSPORTATION SERV	01	53	118
MAIN LINE TO OBLIVION CARSON	01	72	37
MAINE CENTRAL STEAM LOCOMOTIVES ROBERTSO	01	78	61
MAINE TWO-FOOTERS, THE MOODY	12	59	55
MAINES FAST ELECTRIC RR: PLR CUMMINGS	07	68	37
MAINLINE MEXICO EDMONDSON	04	65	50
MAKENS GUIDE TO MEXICAN TRAIN TRAVEL MAK	11	73	60
MAKIN' TRACKS MAYER	06	76	55
MALLET ARTICULATED LOCOMOTIVES (REPRINT)	10	62	39
MALLET TO MOGUL HOGAN	01	76	60
MAN FROM STEAMTOWN: STORY OF NELSON BLOU	11	67	56
MAN HAUPT, THE (PRR) WARD	04	74	60
MAN WHO LIVES IN PARADISE, THE GILBERT	12	55	54
MANAGING A TRANSPORT BUSINESS BARRY	06	65	52
MANCHESTER & ONEIDA RAILWAY, THE DONOVAN	04	58	48
MANO MAJRA SINGH	12	56	74
MANSIONS ON RAILS: ORIV RY CAR BEEBE	12	59	55
MANSIONS ON RAILS: PRIVATE RAILWAY CARS	02	59	61
MANSIONS ON RAILS:FOLKLORE OF PRIVATE RR	02	60	38
MANY FACES OF PENNSY K4 PENNYPACKER	09	87	16
MARKET STREET RY REVISITED:BEST OF INSID	01	73	38
MARQUETTE COOKE	05	76	55
MASTERING MOMENTUM SILLCOX	10	41	77
MATCHES FUMES & RAILS STEPHENS	10	78	65
MCCLOUD RIVER RAILROAD: GOLD SPIKE SPECI	02	56	72
MCCULLOCH'S WONDER (KVRR) SANFORD	04	78	12
MCGRAW ELECTRIC RY DIRECTORY (REPRINT)	02	71	45
MEGALOPOLIS UNBOUND PELL	12	66	50
MEMORIES OF A MT SHORTLINE: STORY OF TF	12	76	55
MEMORIES OF NYC DIESELS-ELECTRIC POWER 2	01	84	29
MEN AND IRON (HISTORY OF NYC) HUNGERFORD	07	38	29
MEN AND THE MOUNTAIN, THE BREMONT	12	55	55
MEN OF ERIE HUNGERFORD	12	47	119
MEN OF SCIENCE & INVENTION BLOW	06	61	60
MEN OF WEALTH FLYNN	09	41	83
MERIDAN WATERBURY & CONNECTICUT RIVER RR	01	55	68
METROPOLITAN TRANSPORTATION:1980	12	63	42
MEXICAN NARROW GAUGE BEST	04	69	48
MIDLAND ROUTE: A COLORADO MIDLAND GUIDE	09	81	19
MIDLAND STORY, THE (C&IM)	06	55	53

RAILROAD PROTOTYPE BOOKS	M	Y	P
MILE-HIGH TROLLEYS 2ND EDITION	10	75	51
MILITARY RAILWAY SERVICE JOURNAL MAURER	10	56	57
MILWAUKEE IN IOWA DONOVAN	11	64	50
MILWAUKEE RAILS OLMSTED	01	82	19
MILWAUKEE ROAD ELECTRIFICATION BRAIN	02	62	56
MILWAUKEE ROAD UNDER WIRE ZIMMERMANN	03	74	61
MILWAUKEE ROAD WEST WOOD	12	72	54
MIND THE DOORS PLEASE:STORY OF TORONTO S	05	84	12
MINERAL BELT VOL 1,OLD SOUTH PARK-DENVER	07	79	12
MINING CAMP DAYS BILLEB	12	68	58
MINING TOWN TROLLEYS (W-B) FRANCAVIGLIA	01	85	17
MINISINK VALLEY EXPRESS (PJM&NY) BEST	08	56	72
MINISINK VALLEY EXPRESS (PJM&NY) BEST	02	68	61
MISSABE ROAD (DM&IR) KING	11	72	62
MIXED TRAIN DAILY: SHORT-LINE RAILROADS	12	47	119
MOBILE HISTORY OF ATLANTA INTERURBANS	07	82	12
MODERN RAILWAY, THE PARMALEE	10	40	72
MODERN RAILWAYS:ENGINEERING EQUIPMENT OP	12	60	59
MOGULES, MOUNTAINS AND MEMORIES (B&M)	11	80	19
MOGULS & IRON MEN:STORY 1ST TRANS CONT R	12	64	35
MOHAWK THAT REFUSED TO ABDICATE & OTHER	SP	76	10R
MONON ROUTE HILTON	12	78	65
MONON ROUTE. HILTON	01	80	18
MONORAILS BOTZOW	08	60	33
MONTANA'S TROLLEYS BOOK 1: HELENA MYERS	11	70	39
MONTANA'S TROLLEYS--III SWETT	04	71	56
MONTANA'S TROLLEYS:BUTTE, ANACONDA, BAP	01	71	30
MONTREAL CITY PASSENGER RY CO LAVALLEE	08	62	49
MONTREALS ELECTRIC STREETCARS BINNS	12	74	56
MORE CLASSIC TRAINS DUBIN	08	74	60
MORE RAIL CLASSICS JONES	10	77	61
MORE UNUSUAL RAILROADS DAY	12	63	14
MORLEYS (ATSF) CLEAVELAND	09	72	54
MORRIS COUNTY TRACTION COMPANY LOWENTHAL	11	84	20
MORRISTOWN & ERIE RAILROAD TABER	04	68	51
MOTHER LODE SHORTLINE (SIE)	07	71	61
MOTIVE POWER OF UNION PACIFIC KRATVILLE	02	60	38
MOTIVE POWER RECOGNITION 2: EMU'S MARSDE	09	82	14
MOUNT LOWE, RAILWAY IN THE CLOUDS SEIMS	02	78	48
MOUNT LOWE: RAILWAY IN THE CLOUDS SEIMS	12	77	10R
MOUNTAINS, THE FARRELL	01	79	12R
MR PULLMANS ELEGANT PALACE CAR BEEBE	04	62	59
MR. THURTLE'S TROLLEYS PRATT	02	48	118
MT LOWE PICTORIAL (PE) MOREAU	09	63	39
MULE CAR AND TROLLEY EVERETT	09	85	08
MULE TO MARTA VOL 1 (ATLANTA GA)	07	76	21
MUNCY VALLEY LIFELINE (W&NB) TABER	04	69	50
MY IRON JOURNEY (AUTOBIOGRAPHY KUHLER)	09	67	54
MY LIFE WITH LOCOMOTIVES RIVINGTON	08	63	45
N&W RAILWAY: POCAHONTAS COAL CARRIER PRI	01	82	19
NA STEAM LOCOMOTIVES: THE NORTHERNS BROW	SP	76	06R
NANTASKET BEACH BRANCH:NYNH&H ELECTRIFIC	05	83	14
NAPA VALLEY ROUTE (SF&NV) SWETT	10	75	51
NARROW GAGE RAILROADS OF COLORADO BEEBE	01	47	139
NARROW GAUGE COUNTRY LIND	06	64	56

LITERATURE REVIEWS

RAILROAD PROTOTYPE BOOKS		M	Y	P
NARROW GAUGE IN A KINGDOM (HAWAII)	CONDE	05	72	55
NARROW GAUGE IN THE ROCKIES	BEEBE/CLEGG	04	58	48
NARROW GAUGE IN THE ROCKIES.	BEEBE/CLEGG	12	58	64
NARROW GAUGE LOCOMOTIVES B 1877 REPRINT		05	68	50
NARROW GAUGE NOSTALGIA	TURNER	08	66	46
NARROW GAUGE PORTRAIT S PACIFIC COAST		03	76	61
NARROW GAUGE RAILS TO PORTMADOC	BOYD	01	50	116
NARROW GAUGE RAILWAYS IN AMERICA	FLEMING	01	50	118
NARROW GAUGE RAILWAYS OF CANADA	LAVALLEE	12	72	54
NARROW GAUGE TO CENTRAL & SILVER PLUME		11	72	62
NARROW GAUGE TO THE CUMBRES	OSTERWALD	12	72	55
NARROW GAUGE TO THE REDWOODS(NPC)	GRAVES	10	67	51
NASHVILLE CHATTANOOGA & ST LOUIS RY: HIS		03	68	50
NATCHEZ ROUTE:A MISS CENTRAL RR ALBUM		F	75	10R
NEBRASKA STREET & INTERURBAN RAILWAYS PH		05	75	57
NELSON STREET RAILWAY (BC)	PARKER	08	62	49
NEVADA COUNTY NARROW GAUGE	BEST	09	65	50
NEVADA NORTHERN:SAGEBRUSH SHORT LINE	ALL	07	65	55
NEVER ON WEDNESDAY (D&RGW)	LOVEMAN	11	81	09
NEVER VICTORIOUS, NEVER DEFEATED	NOVEL	12	54	57
NEW ENGLAND ALCOS IN TWILIGHT	HARTLEY	11	84	20
NEW ENGLAND COUNTRY DEPOTS	LEWIS	05	73	54
NEW ENGLAND DIESELS	ALBERT	05	78	61
NEW ENGLANDS RR PAST, PRESENT & FUTURE		08	78	67
NEW HAVEN RAILROAD: ITS RISE & FALL	WELL	03	70	52
NEW HAVEN RR:A FOND LOOK BACK	PAVLUCIK	09	79	16
NEW JERSEY SHORTLINE RAILROADS	JOHNSON	02	60	38
NEW MEXICO'S RAILROADS	MYRICK	02	71	54
NEW NORTHERN OHIO'S INTERURBANS	CHRISTIA	09	84	15
NEW ORLEANS & CARROLLTON RAIL ROAD	GUIBE	12	76	48
NEW RAILS TO OLD TOWNS:REGION (CH-P)		07	69	58
NEW VISION LOCOMOTIVE, THE	LOEWY	01	40	56
NEW YORK & LONG BRANCH RR SIGNAL BOOK		05	76	55
NEW YORK CENTRAL CARS	WAYNER	02	73	61
NEW YORK STATE RAILWAYS	KING	09	70	44
NEW YORK STATE RAILWAYS.	KING	05	76	22
NEW YORK SUBWAYS		08	63	40
NEW YORK, NEW HAVEN & HARTFORD ELECTRIFI		06	70	40
NEXT STATION WILL BE V 4 1910 NRNJ		09	76	60
NEXT STATION WILL BE... VOL 4 NRNJ		F	76	12R
NEXT STATION WILL BE..1910 NJ & NY DEPOT		07	75	61
NEXT STATION WILL BE:1910 NJ & NY DEPOTS		09	74	60
NEXT STOP GRAND CENTRAL:TRIP THROUGH TIM		12	87	29
NIAGARA ST CATHARINES & TORONTO RY	MILLS	01	69	40
NICHOLS' STANDARD RAILROAD TEXTBOOK		06	41	29
NICKEL PLATE ROAD, THE	HAMPTON	06	48	111
NICKEL PLATE STORY	REHOR	06	66	54
NIGHT PASSAGE (NOVEL)	FOX	10	56	57
NIGHT TRAIN	DUKE	06	62	37
NILES CARS (CATALOG REPRINT 1905)		09	82	13
NINETY FOUR YEARS OF ROCHESTER RYS VOL 2		05	76	23
NORFOLK & BRISTOL STREET RAILWAY	MURRAY	02	63	49
NORFOLK & WESTERN STEAM: LAST 25 YEARS		06	73	52
NORTH AMERICA BY RAIL	MORRIS	07	77	58
NORTH AMERICAN HUDSONS	STAGNER	10	87	27

RAILROAD PROTOTYPE BOOKS		M	Y	P
NORTH ARKANSAS LINE (M&A)	FAIR	02	70	54
NORTHEAST RAILROAD SCENE V2: L&HR	PENNIS	12	77	11R
NORTHEAST RAILROAD SCENE: VOL 1 LV		F	76	11R
NORTHERN AND THE MIKE:TALE OF TWO LOCOS		08	66	48
NORTHERN OHIO TRACTION REVISITED	BLOWER	10	70	44
NORTHERN OHIOS INTERURBAN & RAPID TRANSI		08	65	63
NORTHERN PACIFIC RAILWAY OF MCGEE & NIXO		03	86	19
NORTHERN PACIFIC SUPERSTEAM ERA 1925-45		01	86	14
NORTHERN PACIFIC: MAIN STREET OF THE NOR		04	69	48
NORTHERN RAILS: COMPLETE ME,NH & VT	SMIT	10	67	52
NORTHERNS (4-8-4)	FARRELL	05	76	55
NORTHWEST RAIL PICTORIAL	WING	01	84	25
NORTHWESTERN IN IOWA (C&NW)	DONOVAN	06	63	50
NORTHWESTERN PACIFIC RR:REDWOOD EMPIRE R		05	65	51
NORTHWESTERN PENNSYLVANIA RAILWAY	SIEBER	11	76	57
NOT&L STORY	BLOWER	03	67	47
NSO, OLD DOMINION & CONNECTIONS	PRINCE	10	73	33
NSC&T ELECTRIC RAILWAY IN PICTURES	PANKO	05	85	15
NWI GUIDE TO RAILROAD PHOTOGRAPHY	SCHMID	SP	76	09R
NYC EARLY STEAM POWER V2 1831-1916	STAUF	10	67	51
NYC SYSTEMS, GONE, BUT NOT FORGOTTEN	CAV	01	85	19
NYC'S LATER POWER 1910-1968	STAUFER	05	83	17
NYS&W: ALBUM OF 1910 DEPOT PHOTOS	TILTON	07	73	61
O&W: LONG LIFE-SLOW DEATH OF NYO&W		04	60	46
OAKDALE-MCDONALD STREET RAILWAY	GALBRAIT	02	69	43
OCEAN LINERS OF THE 20TH CENTURY	NEWELL	04	64	61
OCEAN TO OCEAN:S FLEMINGS EXP THRU CANAD		08	68	52
OFF WITH THE OLD, ON WITH THE NEW (B&LE)		02	56	72
OFFICIAL CAR RECORDS:PACIFIC ELECTRIC RY		06	65	33
OFFICIAL REGISTER OF PASSENGER TRAIN EQU		10	56	57
OHIO TROLLEY TRAILS	CHRISTIANSON	03	72	56
OHIO TROLLEYS	MORSE	02	61	39
OIL INDUSTRY AND TRANSPORTATION		04	44	80
OIL LAMPS AND IRON PONIES		01	50	116
OLD SWITCHBACK RAILROAD	LENTZ	09	46	61
OLIPHANT'S EARNING POWER OF RAILROADS		03	47	75
ON THE NARROW GAUGE	WHITEHOUSE	12	64	36
ON THE OLD LINES	ALLEN	06	58	68
ON THE RAILROAD	HENRY	10	36	76
ONE WAY TO ELDORADO	NOBLE	10	54	60
OPEN THROTTLE:STORIES OF RRS & RR MEN		01	67	49
OPERATIONS SANTA FE	ARMITAGE	03	49	123
OUR GM SCRAPBOOK	KALMBACH	04	72	62
OUTDOORS WITH THE CAMERA	SHERMAN	08	42	96
OUTLOOK FOR THE RAILROADS	TYLER	10	60	52
OVER THE RAILS BY STEAM	THURLOW	04	66	51
OVER THE RAILS TO WOODSTOCK (WO)	MEAD	04	68	51
OVERLAND LIMITED	BEEBE	04	64	60
OVERLAND SLIM, THE MAVERICK (HOBO)		08	58	64
PA BOOK	YOUNG	03	76	61
PA BOOK VOL1 (RAILROADING SERIES)	YOUNG	05	76	62
PA BOOK, THE	YOUNG	SU	76	08R
PACIFIC COAST SHAY:STRONG MAN OF THE WOO		05	65	51
PACIFIC ELECTRIC BIG RED CARS	PHILLIPS	07	67	40

Stephans' Railroad Directory

Railroad/Railfan

LITERATURE REVIEWS

RAILROAD PROTOTYPE BOOKS		M	Y	P
PACIFIC ELECTRIC IN POMONA	SWETT	12	69	43
PACIFIC ELECTRIC IN TRANSITION 1911 REPR		08	68	37
PACIFIC TOURIST (REPRINT 1870)	SHEARER	08	70	52
PALMETTO TRACTION:ELEC RYS OF S CAROLINA		11	78	54
PAN AMERICAN HIGHWAY GUIDE	JAHN	10	69	59
PARDON ME..IS THAT THE CHATTANOOGA CHOO-		02	77	61
PASSENGER CAR PLANS REVISED	WALTHERS	11	73	60
PASSENGER EQUIPMENT DIAGRAMS:NYC SYSTEM		12	66	51
PASSENGER TERMINALS & TRAINS (REPRINT)		08	69	33
PASSENGER TRAIN ANNUAL 2	KEEFE	08	77	09R
PASSENGER TRAIN ANNUAL NO 2	KEEFE	08	77	15
PASSENGER TRANSPORT IN THE US 1920-1950		09	44	136
PASSENGERS MUST NOT RIDE ON FENDERS TTCO		08	74	50
PCC CARS OF BOSTON 1937-67	ANDERSON	06	68	41
PCC CARS OF NORTH AMERICA	COX	10	63	36
PCC CARS OF NORTH AMERICA	.COX	08	63	41
PCC FROM COAST TO COAST	SCHNEIDER	07	84	19
PCC:THE CAR THAT FOUGHT BACK	CARLSON	09	81	17
PENINSULA SERVICE (SP COMMUTER TRAINS)		02	58	74
PENNSY POWER II	STAUFER	07	69	58
PENNSY POWER:STEAM & ELEC LOCOS 1900-57		04	63	50
PENNSY STEAM & SEMAPHORES	WESTING	09	75	61
PENNSY: A TO T	CARLESON	10	62	38
PENNSYLVANIA RAILROADS K4'S	ALBRECT	05	68	50
PENNSYLVANIA RR: THE EARLY YEARS	BROOKS	12	64	36
PENNSYLVANIAS BLUE RIBBON FLEET OF E-W F		02	76	61
PEOPLES RAILWAY (SFM)	PERLES	03	82	16
PEOPLES RAILWAY, HISTORY OF MUNI OF SF		09	81	15
PERE MARQUETTE RAILROAD COMPANY	IVES	11	70	43
PGE: RAILWAY TO THE NORTH	RAMSEY	10	64	42
PHANTOM BRAKEMAN, THE (SHORT STORIES) HU		12	59	55
PHILADELPHIA IN MOTION	BOORSE	10	76	56
PHOTOGRAPHIC OCCUPATIONS	LEYSON	02	41	97
PHOTOGRAPHY: ITS SCIENCE AND PRACTICE		06	42	94
PHOTOGRAPHY:ITS PRINCIPLES & PRACTICE 4T		01	43	87
PICTORIAL ENCYCLOPEDIA OF RAILWAYS ELLIS		08	68	52
PICTORIAL HISTORY OF C&O TRAIN & AUTO FE		02	56	72
PICTORIAL HISTORY OF THE WILD WEST HORAN		12	55	54
PICTURE HISTORY OF US TRANSPORTATION, A		08	59	67
PIEDMONT & NORTHERN:GREAT ELECTRIC SYSTE		04	75	10
PIEDMONT PRODIGY (P&N)	LYNCH	10	54	60
PIGGYBACK: HIGHWAY STYLE		08	56	72
PIKES PEAK BY RAIL	HOLLENBACK	02	63	37
PIKES PEAK COG RAILROAD (M&PP)	ABBOTT	12	72	54
PIKES PEAK TROLLEYS:CO SPRINGS STREETCAR		11	85	20
PINE ACROSS THE MOUNTAIN (MCRI)	HAUFT	03	72	40
PINO GRANDE: LOGGING RAILROADS OF M-CL		04	67	51
PIONEER ARIZONA RAILROADS	MYRICK	12	68	59
PIONEER RAILROAD: CHICAGO & NORTHWESTERN		04	49	107
PIONEER RAILROADS	BOWMAN	08	54	105
PIONEER: CHICAGOS FIRST LOCOMOTIVE		08	76	40
PIONEER: LIGHT PASSENGER LOCO OF 1851		04	65	50
PITCH PINE AND PROP TIMBER	KLINE	02	72	51
PITTSBURG SHAWMUT & NORTHERN RR CO PIETR		05	70	58
PITTSBURGH & LAKE ERIE RAILROAD	MCLEAN	07	81	17

RAILROAD PROTOTYPE BOOKS		M	Y	P
PITTSBURGH TROLLEY PICTORIAL		12	71	48
PLATTSBURGH TRACTION COMPANY	BORRUP	07	72	39
POCKET GUIDE TO AMERICAN LOCOS	LUCAS	06	54	102
PORTRAIT OF A SILVER LADY (CZ)	MACGREGOR	02	78	10R
PORTRAIT OF A SILVER LADY (THE CZ)	MACGR	04	78	60
PORTRAIT OF THE RAILS:STEAM TO DIESEL		03	73	58
PORTRAITS OF THE IRON HORSE	KUHLER	11	76	58
PORTRAITS OF THE IRON HORSE	HENRY/KUHLER	01	38	63
POWERED VEHICLES: HISTORICAL REVIEW		08	75	62
PRAIRIE OASIS	HOFSOMMER	11	75	60
PRAIRIE RAILS (C&NW)	OLMSTED	11	79	12
PRESERVED CANADIAN RAILWAY EQUIPMENT COR		04	73	58
PRINCIPLES OF INLAND TRANSPORTATION		07	41	70
PROFANE JUNCTION (NOVEL)	WHITE	04	59	82
PROGRESS ON RAILS	WALKER	05	65	52
PROPOSED SOUTHEASTERN RR	MITCHELL	08	63	46
PROVOCATIVE PEN OF LUCIUS BEEBE ESQ		11	67	56
PRR: FLEET OF MODERNISM	GARDNER	07	74	44
PRUNE COUNTRY RAILROADING	HOLMES	09	86	14
PUBLIC SERVICE VEHICLES	KAYE	06	64	46
PUBLIC TRANSPORTATION IN CA SANTA CLARA		05	82	08
PUGET SOUND ELECTRIC RAILWAY	SWETT	04	61	44
PULLMAN & PRIVATE CAR PICTORIAL	WAYNER	08	75	61
PULLMAN AND PRIVATE CAR PICTORIAL	WAYNER	07	72	60
PULLMAN CO: PRIVATE CAR & SPECIAL TRAIN		04	75	62
PULLMAN IN EUROPE	BEHREND	06	63	50
PULLMAN PANORAMA VOL 1	WAYNER	12	67	51
PULLMAN STRIKE, THE	LINDSEY	04	43	06
QUEEN & CRESCENT ROUTE (CNO&TP)	GARDNER	04	77	60
QUEST FOR CRISIS	SITES	08	63	42
QUICK REVIEW OF EAST BROAD TOP	MANNIX	02	61	47
QUICKEST ROUTE (N&WO)	FARNHAM	11	73	60
QUIZ, JR. SCHOOL AND COLLEGE SERVICE		02	56	72
RAIL CITY: CHICAGO USA	DOUGLAS	07	82	13
RAIL FACTS AND FEATS	MARSHALL	07	74	60
RAIL FICTION CLASSICS	JONES	02	75	57
RAIL ODDITIES ASSOCIATION OF AMER RRS.		08	57	77
RAIL ROUTES SOUTH:LOUISVILLES FIGHT FOR		03	70	54
RAIL TRANSPORT AND THE WINNING OF WARS		10	56	57
RAIL VENTURES	SWANSON	07	83	16
RAILBOOK BIBLIOGRAPHY 1948-1972	HUDSON	M	74	13R
RAILBOOK BIBLIOGRAPHY: 1948-1972	HUDSON	06	73	52
RAILROAD ALBUM	O'CONNELL	07	54	124
RAILROAD AND THE CITY	CONDIT	11	77	61
RAILROAD AND THE SPACE PROGRAM	MAZLISH	05	66	46
RAILROAD AVENUE	HUBBARD	11	45	59
RAILROAD AVENUE:GREAT STORIES LEGENDS OF		03	65	60
RAILROAD BOOK: TRAINS IN AMERICA	FELDMAN	11	78	56
RAILROAD CABOOSE:100 YEAR HISTORY, LORE		07	68	43
RAILROAD CAR JOURNAL #4 CABOOSES	KRATVIL	12	72	55
RAILROAD COMES OF AGE (SCC&RR)	LANGLEY	09	70	50
RAILROAD COMPETITION IN OIL TRADE	HARPER	01	42	69
RAILROAD CRISIS	CUNNINGHAM	09	39	73
RAILROAD ENGINEERS & AIRPLANE PILOTS	GRE	04	65	51
RAILROAD IN ALASKA 2ND SECTION 1914-64		12	66	50

Railroad/ Railfan

LITERATURE REVIEWS

RAILROAD PROTOTYPE BOOKS	M	Y	P
RAILROAD IN THE CLOUDS:AL 1914-44 WILSON	01	79	14R
RAILROAD INDUSTRY, THE	11	40	75
RAILROAD LEADERS 1845-1890 COCHRAN	10	54	60
RAILROAD MANAGEMENT WYCKOFF	04	77	60
RAILROAD MANUAL ALLIS-CHAMBERS MFG	12	55	55
RAILROAD MEN:BOOK OF PHOTOGRAPHS & STORI	04	62	59
RAILROAD MERGERS & ABANDONMENTS CONANT	08	65	55
RAILROAD MONOPOLY, THE SHOTT	07	52	135
RAILROAD PANORAMA KALMBACH	07	44	139
RAILROAD PASSENGER CAR, THE MENCKEN	04	58	48
RAILROAD POLICE, THE DEWHURST	04	56	73
RAILROAD POST OFFICE HISTORY MCKEE	11	72	61
RAILROAD POTPOURRI HILL	SP	75	15R
RAILROAD POTPOURRI .HILL	02	75	57
RAILROAD RENAISSANCE IN THE ROCKIES ATHE	06	58	68
RAILROAD SAGA OF JEFF KEENAN KEENAN	04	76	60
RAILROAD SCENE MIDDLETON	10	69	59
RAILROAD SONGS OF YESTERDAY MCCLINTOCK	08	43	76
RAILROAD STATION (REPRINT) MEEKS	02	76	61
RAILROAD STATION, THE MEEKS	04	57	55
RAILROAD THAT CAME OUT OF THE NIGHT KYPE	03	78	60
RAILROAD THAT DIED AT SEA:FEC KEY WEST E	02	69	61
RAILROAD THAT LIGHTED S CALIFORNIA--SJ&L	06	65	52
RAILROAD THAT RAN BY THE TIDE (IL) FEAGA	12	72	54
RAILROAD WITH 3 GAUGES:CG&P AND F&BE	10	87	26
RAILROAD--WHAT IS IT, WHAT IT DOES ARMST	10	78	65
RAILROAD:TRAINS & TRAIN PEOPLE IN AM CUL	04	77	60
RAILROADER, THE COTTRELL	11	40	76
RAILROADERS WALKER	03	84	13
RAILROADIANA COLLECTORS PRICE GUIDE BAKE	09	77	61
RAILROADIANS OF AMERICA BOOK 2 LUCAS	11	40	75
RAILROADING AFTER A CENTURY OF PROGRESS	09	33	50
RAILROADING AROUND THE WORLD FARRINGTON	02	56	72
RAILROADING COAST TO COAST FARRINGTON	06	77	56
RAILROADING FROM THE HEAD END	06	43	160
RAILROADING THROUGH CAJON PASS WALKER	12	78	50
RAILROADING WEST, CONTEMPORARY GLIMPSE	SP	76	08R
RAILROADING WEST: A CONTEMPORARY GLIMPSE	03	76	61
RAILROADMAN (CHAUNCEY DEL FRENCH) FRENCH	07	38	29
RAILROADS BALL	03	86	17
RAILROADS & AMERICAN ECONOMIC GROWTH FOG	03	65	61
RAILROADS AND PUBLIC WELFARE JOHNSON	09	46	61
RAILROADS AND RIVERS CLARK	11	39	93
RAILROADS AND THE ROCKIES:RECORD IN COLO	04	64	61
RAILROADS AT WORK ASSN OF AMERICAN RRS	02	57	71
RAILROADS IN CRISIS	12	39	124
RAILROADS IN CRISIS (ADDITIONAL COMMENTS	01	40	57
RAILROADS IN LEHIGH RIVER VAL 1836-1953	10	57	37
RAILROADS IN OKLAHOMA	06	78	55
RAILROADS IN THE DAYS OF STEAM MCCREADY	10	60	52
RAILROADS IN THE LEHIGH VALLEY	12	63	12
RAILROADS IN THE STREETS OF SYRACUSE PAL	06	71	51
RAILROADS OF ARIZONA VOL 1(SOUTHERN RDS)	W	75	07R
RAILROADS OF ARIZONA VOL 1:SOUTHERN RDS	01	76	61
RAILROADS OF CANADA LEGGETT	02	74	60

RAILROAD PROTOTYPE BOOKS	M	Y	P
RAILROADS OF NEVADA & E CALIFORNIA VOL 1	06	63	50
RAILROADS OF NEVADA & E CALIFORNIA VOL 2	06	64	56
RAILROADS OF NEW JERSEY HYER	07	75	51
RAILROADS OF OKLAHOMA	04	43	156
RAILROADS OF PENNSYLVANIA: 3 COLOR MAP	04	43	157
RAILROADS OF THE BLACK HILLS FIELDER	02	65	60
RAILROADS OF THE HOUR FARRINGTON	08	59	73
RAILROADS OF THE SOUTH, THE STOVER	06	56	47
RAILROADS OF THE WOODS LABBE	10	61	59
RAILROADS OF YOSEMITE VALLEY JOHNSON	05	67	50
RAILROADS TODAY AND YESTERDAY BUEHR	04	58	48
RAILROADS, GREAT AMERICAN ADVENTURE OGBU	08	77	08R
RAILROADS: AN AMERICAN JOURNEY BALL	01	76	60
RAILROADS: AN AMERICAN JOURNEY. BALL	SP	75	12R
RAILROADS:GREAT AMERICAN ADVENTURE OGBUR	08	77	61
RAILRODIANA KLAMKIN	07	76	60
RAILS BALL	05	82	08
RAILS ACROSS THE MIDLANDS COOK	12	64	36
RAILS AROUND GOLD HILL CAFKY	06	56	46
RAILS AROUND GOTHAM CARLETON	11	81	09
RAILS FROM THE WEST:BIOGRAPHY OF T JUDAH	08	69	32
RAILS IN RICHMOND MCKENNEY	01	87	24
RAILS IN THE NORTH WOODS ALLEN	09	73	61
RAILS IN THE NORTHEAST HILL	12	78	65
RAILS IN THE SHADOW OF MT SHASTA SIGNOR	09	84	16
RAILS OVER THE HORIZON LANDIS	02	39	95
RAILS THROUGH DIXIE:CLASSIC ALBUM OF SOU	05	66	45
RAILS THROUGH THE CLAY JACKSON	06	63	39
RAILS TO CARRY COPPER (MA) CHAPPELL	05	74	60
RAILS TO OCHOCO COUNTRY:CITY OF PRINEVIL	12	68	58
RAILS TO THE BLUE RIDGE (W&OD) HARWOOD	03	70	52
RAILS TO THE BLUE RIDGE: W&OD RR HARWOOD	12	63	42
RAILS TO THE HIGH COUNTRY LIND	10	62	38
RAILS TO THE NORTH STAR:100 YEARS OF RR	01	67	49
RAILS UNDER THE MIGHTY HUDSON CUDAHY	03	76	23
RAILS WEST ADBILL	04	61	57
RAILS, SAGEBRUSH, AND PINE FARRELL	02	68	60
RAILWAY AGE, THE ANDREWS	10	38	39
RAILWAY ART ELLIS	02	78	58
RAILWAY ENGINEER: STORY OF GEO STEPHENSN	08	42	97
RAILWAY KING, THE LAMBERT	02	36	89
RAILWAY PICTURE GALLERY ADAMS	06	63	50
RAILWAY SIGNALLING TAYLOR	01	50	119
RAILWAY SIGNALLING SYSTEMS (REVISED) DAY	04	64	62
RAILWAY STAMPS BURKHALTER	12	71	48
RAILWAY TO THE MOON (MWCOG) KIDDER	01	70	54
RAILWAYS IN WARTIME CARTER	12	64	35
RAILWAYS OF CANADA COLES PUBLISHING	04	71	48
RAMBLE INTO THE PAST ON EAST BROAD TOP	10	72	63
RAND MCNALLY HANDY RR ATLAS OF THE US	11	86	20
RAPID TRANSIT BOSTON CLARKE	11	71	51
RAPID TRANSIT CAR AND LAYOUT DESIGN	06	66	41
RAPID TRANSIT IN THE CLEVELAND AREA	06	66	41
RAPID TRANSIT LINES IN BOSTON	08	66	63
RATTLING HOME FOR CHRISTMAS REYNARD	02	42	52

Railroad/Railfan

LITERATURE REVIEWS

RAILROAD PROTOTYPE BOOKS	M	Y	P
RAYONIER INC:RRING IN THE NORTHWEST PINE	10	64	44
READING POWER PICTORIAL PENNYPACKER	07	74	43
READING STEAM PICTORIAL PENNYPACKER	10	64	42
READING'S T1:AN UNUSUAL NORTHERN DIRKES	12	87	30
READINGS VICTORIAN STATIONS LEWIS	10	77	09R
RECENT LOCOMOTIVES (1886) REPRINT GREGG	01	73	58
RECOLLECTIONS OF W&LE AT NORWALK OHIO	01	71	47
RED ARROW (PSTC) DEGRAW	03	73	58
RED ARROW: FIRST 100 YEARS 1848-1948	01	86	14
RED CAR DAYS:MEMORIES OF PE LONG	05	84	13
RED FOR DANGER ROLT	07	67	50
RED FOR DANGER. ROLT	10	77	61
RED TRAINS IN EAST BAY (SFM) FORD	03	78	29
RED TRAINS REMEMBERED FORD	01	81	16
REDWOOD RAILWAYS KNEISS	04	57	55
REDWOODS IRON HORSES & THE PACIFIC (CW)	06	64	56
REMARKABLE 6G1 ZIMMERMANN	02	78	57
REMARKABLE 6G1 QP#6 ZIMMERMANN	05	78	12R
REMEMBER WHEN TROLLEY WIRES SPANNED COUN	03	81	17
REMINISCENSES OF JOHN B JERVIS FITZSIMON	03	72	40
RENAISSANCE 6060 (CN) PERRY	10	74	61
REPRIEVE FOR THE IRON HORSE:AMTRAK EXPER	04	75	61
RHODE ISLAND COMPANY PART 1:EQUIPMENT RO	02	66	38
RHYMES FOR RAILROADERS KELLY	12	39	124
RHYMES OF THE RAILS SIMMONS	01	79	62
RICHMOND (CA) STREET CARS 1900-33 HANSON	12	68	39
RICHMOND JUNCTION (FICTION) MEERSE	01	76	61
RIDE A MILE & SMILE THE WHILE:HIST PSRY	02	78	48
RIDE THE BIG RED CARS CRUMP	06	63	39
RIDE THE RATTLER TO ROMANCE (FICTION)	08	74	60
RIDE THE SANDY RIVER CORNWALL	08	73	61
RIDE THROUGH GARDEN OF CANADA (HG&B) BLA	12	67	36
RIDING THE PENNSY TO RUIN	11	71	57
RIDING THE RAILS MATHEWS	04	74	60
RIGHT-OF-WAY:GUIDE TO ABANDONED RR IN US	04	73	58
RIGHTS OF TRAINS FORMAN	05	46	138
RIGHTS OF TRAINS JOSSERAND	10	61	59
RIGHTS OF TRAINS 5TH EDITION JOSSERAND	04	58	48
RIO GRANDE CAR PLANS WAYNER	11	69	56
RIO GRANDE GLORY DAYS LATHROP	09	76	60
RIO GRANDE GLORY DAYS .LATHROP	W	76	10R
RIO GRANDE IN THE ROCKIES (D&RGW) HILL	04	78	10R
RIO GRANDE...TO THE PACIFIC LEMASSENA	04	75	53
RIO GRANDE:MAINLINE OF THE ROCKIES BEEBE	10	62	37
RISE AND FALL OF AN EMPIRE:HOOSIER ELEC	05	68	42
RIVERSIDE & ARLINGTON ELECTRIC RY SWETT	06	63	39
RIVERSIDE LINE: STORY OF CAMDEN & TRENTO	11	81	12
ROAD AND RAIL WALKER	08	43	77
ROAD FROM UPPER DARBY COX	09	67	34
ROAD OF THE CENTURY, THE (NYC) HARLOW	08	47	116
ROAD TO PARADISE (STRR) MOEDINGER	10	72	63
ROAD TO PARADISE: STORY OF STRASBURG RR	09	66	52
ROAD TO PARADISE:STORY OF STRASBURG RR	08	62	57
ROARING U50'S..UP TWIN DIESELS KEEKLEY	07	79	14
ROBERT YOUNG, POPULIST OF WALL STREET	11	69	56

RAILROAD PROTOTYPE BOOKS	M	Y	P
ROCHESTER HORSE CARS AND TROLLEYS 1862--	08	75	45
ROCHESTER LOCKPORT & BUFFALO RR 1908-31	02	64	42
ROCHESTER SYRACUSE & EASTERN GORDON	04	62	54
ROCHESTER SYRACUSE & EASTERN MCFARLANE	10	61	51
ROCK ISLAND IN IOWA DONOVAN	04	64	62
ROCK-A-BYE BABY:HISTORY OF RVA TABER	04	73	58
RODDIS LINE (LOGGING) HUSTON	08	72	63
ROLLING WHEELS:FACT & FICTION AN ANTHOLO	06	60	43
ROMANCE AND HISTORY OF THE RAILROADS	02	42	52
ROMANCE OF TIME, THE PALMER	06	55	53
ROSTERS UNLIMITED VOL 1 CLACK	12	63	14
ROUNDHOUSE, PARADISE & MR PICKERING PERR	08	66	47
ROUTE OF THE ELECTROLINERS V2 (CNS&M)	06	64	46
ROUTE OF THE ORANGE LIMITED, THE GORDON	02	56	72
ROUTE OF THE WARBONNETS (ATSF) MCMILLAN	09	78	12R
ROUTE OF THE WARBONNETS (ATSF) MCMILLAN	08	78	66
ROYAL BLUE LINE (R&SB) GORDON	12	62	53
RR IN THE CLOUDS:AL IN THE AGE OF STEAM	03	78	25
RUDOLF DIESEL:PIONEER OF AGE OF POWER	06	65	52
RULER OF THE READING: LIFE OF F.B. GOWEN	02	48	117
RUN OF THE 20TH CENTURY (NYC) HUNGERFORD	05	71	60
RURAL RAILROADS:TRAILS TO RAILS CORLISS	01	78	61
RUTLAND ROAD SHAUGHNESSY	12	64	34
RY REVOLUTION:GEO & RBT STEPHENSON ROLT	08	62	56
SACRAMENTO NORTHERN SWEET	04	63	33
SACRAMENTO NORTHERN (REPRINT) SWETT	06	71	55
SACRAMENTO NORTHERN ALBUM SWETT	08	64	59
SACRAMENTO NORTHERN: SPECIAL # 26 WILCOX	05	82	08
SAGA OF BEN HOLLADAY: GIANT OF THE OLD W	06	60	43
SAGA OF THE STEAM PLOUGH BONNETT	08	65	56
SAN DIEGOS SOUTH BAY INTERURBAN (SD&S)	12	87	29
SAN FRANCISCO BAY FERRYBOATS (SP) HARLAN	11	67	59
SAN FRANCISCO CABLE CAR COLORING BOOK	02	76	61
SAN FRANCISCO MUNICIPAL RY:1912-44 SEVER	12	68	39
SAN FRANCISCO STREET CARS 1944-64 (SFM)	12	68	39
SAN FRANCISCOS DECORATED CABLE CARS STIN	10	75	60
SANDUSKY MILAN & NORWALK ELECTRIC RAILWY	04	64	38
SANTA FE DIESELS AND CARS WAYNER	08	74	43
SANTA FE MOTIVE POWER MCMILLAN	07	86	14
SANTA FE RAILWAY: TRAIN ALBUM OF PHOTOS	04	46	75
SANTA FE TRAIL, THE LOOK	12	47	118
SANTA FE'S BIG THREE:LIFE STORY OF WORLD	04	73	58
SANTA FE'S DIESEL FLEET MC MILLAN	F	76	10R
SANTA FE: THE RR THAT BUILT AN EMPIRE	04	46	72
SANTA FES DIESEL FLEET MCMILLAN	12	75	53
SAPBUSH RUN, INFORMAL HISTORY BR&U	03	49	125
SASKATCHEWANS PIONEER ST CARS: RMRY HATC	07	72	39
SCHEMATIC TRACK DIAGRAMS OF EL RY SHEPPA	10	76	58
SCHEMATIC TRACK DIAGRAMS OF THE EL	SU	75	11R
SEA BEACH TO CONEY ISLAND (NY&SB) FAUSER	11	80	19
SEARCH FOR STEAM COLLIAS	12	72	54
SEARCH FOR STEAM. COLLIAS	W	74	12R
SECOND DIESELS SPOTTERS GUIDE PINKEPANK	10	73	57
SELECTED ROLLING STOCK OF CNS&M	05	68	42
SELECTIVE SURVEY OF LIT ON TRANSPORTATIO	10	68	48

Stephans Railroad Directory

Railroad/Railfan

LITERATURE REVIEWS

RAILROAD PROTOTYPE BOOKS		M	Y	P
SEMI-CONVERTIBLE CARS OF BOSTON ELEVATED		04	64	38
SHAY LOCOMOTIVE:TITAN OF THE TIMBER	KOCH	08	71	60
SHAYS ON SWITCHBACKS:HIST OF LMSRY	WHITE	02	64	46
SHERMAN HILL	EHERNBERGER	03	75	59
SHERMAN HILL (UP)	EHERNBERGER	11	79	14
SHIPS AND NARROW GAUGE RAILS:STORY PCOA		11	64	48
SHORE LINE ELECTRIC RY PART 2	CUMMINGS	06	62	29
SHORT HAUL TO THE BAY (NPIER)	HENWOOD	04	70	58
SHORT HISTORY OF THE STEAM ENGINE, A		08	39	69
SHORT LINE JUNCTION	WAGNER	12	56	74
SHORT TROLLEY ROUTES IN LEHIGH VALLEY	KU	09	68	42
SHORTLINES OF ARKANSAS	HULL	11	69	56
SIERRA RAILWAY	DEANE	04	61	56
SIGNALING	WALTERS	01	41	121
SILK ALONG STEEL: STORY OF SOMRR	LEWIS	01	77	56
SILVERTON TRAIN, THE	HUNT	12	55	55
SILVERTON: TRIP TO YESTERDAY (D&RGW) STO		09	68	57
SINGING RAILS	PEASE	01	50	120
SINGLE-LINE RAILWAYS:HANDBOOK OF MANAGEM		08	66	48
SITUATION IN FLUSHING (MI) (CS&M)	LOVE	02	66	62
SKUNK RAILROAD (WP)	TRANS-ANGLO	02	66	38
SKUNK RAILROAD-FT BRAGG TO WILLITS (CW)		12	64	36
SLIM PRINCESS, THE (CA&C)	HUNGERFORD	12	56	74
SLOW TIRED & EASY RR (ST&E)	DAVIS	05	77	56
SMALL HOOSIER LINES	NEDDEN	07	75	59
SMOKE ABOVE THE PLAINS: UP KANSAS DIVISN		05	66	45
SMOKE ACROSS THE PRAIRIE (UP)EHERNBERGER		05	65	52
SMOKE DOWN THE CANYONS (UP) EHERNBERGER		11	66	48
SMOKE OVER THE DIVIDE:UP WYOMING DIVISIO		11	65	52
SMOKE STEAM & CINDERS (PRR)	SHAFER	07	77	58
SMOKE TRAILS IN REBEL LAND	STOWE	09	70	50
SNOW FIGHTING EQIP:EASTERN MASS ST RY CO		08	65	63
SNOWPLOW:CLEANING MOUNTAIN RAILS	BEST	03	67	54
SOME CLASSIC TRAINS	DUBIN	12	64	34
SOUTH PACIFIC COAST	MAC GREGOR	03	69	50
SOUTH PARK LINE: CONCISE HISTORY	CHAPPEL	10	75	60
SOUTH SHORE, THE LAST INTERURBAN	MIDDLET	03	71	40
SOUTH SHORE: QUINCY-BOSTON	CLARKE	08	72	51
SOUTH SHORE:QUINCY-BOSTON (MBTA)	CLARKE	10	76	56
SOUTHERN PACIFIC 1901-85	HOFSOMMER	05	87	16
SOUTHERN PACIFIC MOTIVE POW ANNUAL 1967		12	68	59
SOUTHERN PACIFIC MOTIVE POW ANNUAL 1974		04	78	11R
SOUTHERN PACIFIC MOTIVE POW ANNUAL 66-67		06	67	53
SOUTHERN PACIFIC MOTIVE POW ANNUAL 74-76		11	77	55
SOUTHERN PACIFIC REVIEW 1977	STRAPAC	05	79	13
SOUTHERN PACIFIC REVIEW 1978-79	STRAPAC	05	80	18
SOUTHERN PACIFIC REVIEW 1983-85	STRAPAC	11	86	19
SOUTHERN PACIFIC'S FIRST CENTURY	SP	04	56	73
SOUTHERN RAILWAY PANORAMA	KRAMER	01	79	14R
SOUTHERN RAILWAY SYSTEM:STEAM LOCOS & BO		07	65	54
SOUTHERN STEAM SPECIALS	EAGLESON	01	71	47
SOUTHERN: PS4 CLASS PACIFIC DRAWINGS		12	74	59
SP OF MEXICO AND THE WEST COAST ROUTE		07	87	23
SP STEAM LOCOMOTIVES:PICTORAL ANTHOLOGY		02	63	37
SPEED LIMIT 20:STORY OF NARROW GAUGE BRA		06	64	57

RAILROAD PROTOTYPE BOOKS		M	Y	P
SPIRIT OF THE SOUTH SHORE	RAIR	07	85	14
SPLENDOR OF STEAM	ELLIS	07	67	51
SPOKANE PORTLAND & SEATTLE RY	WOOD	03	75	59
SPSF MOTIVE POWER '86 PREPARE TO MERGE		09	87	17
ST CHARLES STREET CAR-NO&C RR (REVISED)		01	79	61
ST LOUIS CABLE RAILWAYS	KATZ	09	65	39
ST LOUIS CAR COMPANY ALBUM	YOUNG	11	84	20
STAIRWAY TO THE STARS, CO ARGENTINE CENT		05	79	12
STAMPEDE CITY STREETCARS:STORY OF CMRY		01	76	28
STARK'S LAST INTERURBANS (SERR)	EAKIN	09	84	15
STATE, INVESTOR, & RAILROAD: THE B&A SAL		01	68	63
STATEN ISLAND MIDLAND RY		08	60	33
STATEN ISLAND RAPID TRANSIT		06	66	40
STATIONS WEST: STORY OF OREGON RAILWAYS		06	73	53
STEAM & THUNDER IN TIMBER,SAGA FORREST R		03	80	14
STEAM AGE IN WESTERN ONTARIO	GEORGE	07	77	58
STEAM AND ELECTRIC LOCOMOTIVE DIAGRAMS		09	65	52
STEAM IN THE ALLEGHENIES:WESTERN MARYLND		05	80	17
STEAM IN THE SIXTIES	ZIEL	02	68	59
STEAM LOCO DIAGRAMS OF C&O RR	STAUFER	06	65	52
STEAM LOCOMOTIVE	TUPLIN	01	76	60
STEAM LOCOMOTIVE IN 1838: R STEPHENSON'S		05	68	50
STEAM LOCOMOTIVE IN TRAFFIC, THE		01	50	120
STEAM LOCOMOTIVE PLAN MANUAL & ALBUM CAR		12	59	55
STEAM LOCOMOTIVE, THE	JOHNSON	12	42	47
STEAM LOCOMOTIVES & HISTORY:G AND WPR		04	73	58
STEAM LOCOMOTIVES CYCLOPEDIA VOL 1 WESTC		04	61	56
STEAM LOCOMOTIVES OF BURLINGTON ROUTE		03	65	61
STEAM LOCOMOTIVES OF BURLINGTON RT CORBI		08	60	50
STEAM LOCOMOTIVES OF FRISCO LINE STAGNER		04	78	10R
STEAM LOCOMOTIVES OF THE FRISCO LINE STA		08	77	61
STEAM LOCOS & HIST:G AND WPR	PRINCE	08	62	56
STEAM ON THE ANTHRACITE ROADS	EAGLESON	SU	75	11R
STEAM PASSENGER SERVICE DIRECTORY 1984		09	84	19
STEAM PIKES ALONG TURN PIKES:PICTORIAL P		11	69	56
STEAM POWER OF THE NYC SYSTEM 1915-1955		12	61	42
STEAM POWER:C&NW 1848-1956 CLASSES A-Z		12	65	62
STEAM POWERED PASSENGER TRAINS OF YESTER		12	71	49
STEAM ROAD ELECTRIFICATION	OHIO BRASS	10	67	37
STEAM STEEL & STARS AMERICAS LAST STEAM		07	87	20
STEAM TRAINS OF THE SOO	SUPREY	04	63	50
STEAM TRAINS OF THE SOO.	SUPREY	10	77	10R
STEAM TRAINS ON THE SOO (2ED ED)	SUPREY	12	64	36
STEAM-POWERED PASS TRAINS OF YESTERDAY		12	73	61
STEAMCARS TO THE COMSTOCK	BEEBE & CLEGG	10	57	37
STEAMING UP! AUTO BIO OF SAM VAUCLAIN		12	73	61
STEAMS FINEST HOUR	MORGAN	04	60	46
STEEL RAILS	STEVERS	02	34	89
STEEL RAILS TO SUNRISE (LI) (BEEBE REV)		05	66	46
STEEL RAILS TO THE SUNRISE:THE LIRR	ZIEL	11	65	50
STEEL RAILS TO VICTORY	ZIEL	10	71	47
STEEL TRAILS AND IRONHORSES	BUCHANAN	12	55	55
STEELWAYS OF NEW ENGLAND	HARLOW	04	46	74
STEUBENVILLE, EAST LIVERPOOL, & BEAVER V		03	69	30
STOLEN TRAIN, THE (ANDREWS RAILDERS)		11	54	55

Stephans' Railroad Directory

Railroad/Railfan

LITERATURE REVIEWS

RAILROAD PROTOTYPE BOOKS		M	Y	P
STORY OF AMERICAN RAILROADS, THE	HOLBROOK	02	48	116
STORY OF GREEN BAY & WESTERN	SPECHT	02	67	52
STORY OF MANSFIELD TRANSIT SYSTEM	BRASHA	02	72	50
STORY OF METRO (WASHINGTON DC)	DEITER	05	86	10
STORY OF OHIO RAILROADS, THE		07	54	124
STORY OF PASSENGER FARES, THE	FREED	11	42	72
STORY OF STEAMTOWN & EDAVILLE	ZIEL	11	65	54
STORY OF SUSQUEHANNA & NEW YORK	KASEMAN	07	65	55
STORY OF SUSQUEHANNA & NEW YORK (REPRINT)		06	64	57
STORY OF SUSQUEHANNA & NEW YORK.	KASEMAN	03	80	16
STORY OF THE CALIFORNIA ZEPHYR	ZIMMERMAN	04	76	60
STORY OF THE SUSQUEHANNA & NEW YORK		12	41	85
STORY OF THE WEST RIVER RAILROAD	MORSE	11	39	94
STORY OF TUNNELS, THE	BLACK	03	38	47
STRANGE PEOPLE (CIRCUS)	EDWARDS	08	62	57
STREAMLINE ERA	REED	11	75	60
STREAMLINE ERA.	REED	F	76	11R
STREAMLINED STEAM QP#1	QUADRENT PRESS	01	73	59
STREAMLINED STEAM:REVIEW #1	ARCHER	04	73	58
STREATOR CONNECTION	OLMSTED	01	82	19
STREET AND INTERURBAN RYS OF NEW ENGLAND		11	73	41
STREET CARS & INTERURBANS OF YESTERDAY		10	60	40
STREET CARS OF BOSTON V1 CLOSED HORSE,EL		11	73	41
STREET CARS OF BOSTON V2 OPEN HORSE & EL		06	75	06
STREET CARS OF BOSTON V4 TYPE 4 SEMI-CON		07	76	21
STREET CARS OF BOSTON V5 ARTICULATED & C		09	77	52
STREET RAILWAY ERA IN SEATTLE	BLANCHARD	04	69	46
STREET RAILWAYS OF BIRMINGHAM	HUDSON	11	76	57
STREET RAILWAYS OF CONNECTICUT		02	61	38
STREET RAILWAYS OF ST PETERSBURG FL	BUCK	11	83	23
STREET RAILWAYS OF TRENTON	GUMMERE	07	87	20
STREET RYS OF MIAMI AREA	RIDOLPH	05	82	08
STREETCARS OF BIRMINGHAM	HUDSON	10	71	53
STREETCARS OF FORT SMITH ARKANSAS	WINTER	09	82	13
STREETCARS OF NEW ORLEANS 1831-1956 V2		11	65	41
STUDY OF PRR K4 LOCOMOTIVE	ALBRECHT	11	77	60
SUDBURY STREETCARS (SCCE)	KNOWLES	09	84	14
SUGAR TRAINS PICTORIAL	CONDE	02	76	61
SUGAR TRAINS: NARROW GAUGE RAILS OF HAWA		03	74	61
SUGAR TRAMP	MORGAN	SU	76	09R
SUGAR TRAMP (GWS)	MORGAN	08	76	60
SUMMER SAUNTERINGS BY THE B&L		03	71	58
SUPER POWER STEAM LOCOMOTIVES	COOKE	06	67	53
SURFACE CARS OF BOSTON 1903-'63	COX	04	64	38
SURFACE CARS OF PHILADELPHIA: 1911-65	CO	02	66	38
SURFACE CARS OF PHILADELPHIA:1911-65	COX	12	65	37
SUSQUEHANNA	KRAUSE	11	80	22
SYMPHONY IN STEAM (4-4-0)	GLEYSTEEN	06	66	54
SYRACUSE & SUBURBAN RAILROAD	JOHNSON	07	68	37
SYSTEM OF (STEAM) STREET RYS OF PHILADEL		11	71	51
SYSTEM OF WIDE CABLE RAILWAYS REPRINT		06	68	41
T-O-O-O-O-O-OT! (CHILDREN)	LAWELL	12	58	64
TAXATION OF RAILROADS IN NEW JERSEY, THE		12	41	85
TEACHER'S KIT: A STUDY OF RY TRANSPORTAT		08	56	72
TECHNOLOGICAL CHANGE & LABOR IN RR INDUS		10	70	48

RAILROAD PROTOTYPE BOOKS		M	Y	P
TEXAS ELECTRIC ALBUM	VARNEY	03	76	23
THE BEST FRIEND (OF CHARLESTON)	WILLIAMS	10	69	59
THE WITTS:AFFEC LOOK AT TOTONTOS RED ROC		01	83	14
THEN CAME THE RAILROADS	CLARK	08	58	64
THEY FELLED THE REDWOODS	JOHNSTON	02	67	50
THEY MOVED MILLIONS (NYMTA)	DAVIS	11	85	20
THIRD RAILS PANTOGRAPHS & TROLLEY POLES		01	74	59
THIRTY POUND RAILS	CHODA	04	57	55
THIS IS BART	FIREMENS FUND	11	65	41
THIS WAS RAILROADING	ABDILL	04	59	82
THOSE DAYLIGHT 4-8-4'S	CHURCH	02	70	52
THOSE DAYLIGHT 4-8-4'S (SP)	CHURCH	06	77	56
THOSE PORTLAND TROLLEY YEARS	LABBE	05	82	08
THREE BARRELS OF STEAM (4-10-2)	BOYTON	12	73	61
THREE FEET ON THE PANHANDLE (PRR)	KOEHLER	01	84	26
THREE LITTLE LINES (RAILS AMONG PEAKS)		02	57	71
THROTTLING THE RAILROADS	CARSON	06	72	63
THROUGH BY RAIL (CHILDRENS)	HALL	01	39	28
THROUGH COVERED BRIDGES TO CONCORD	MEAD	01	71	47
THROUGH THE HEART OF OHIO:CD&M ELECTRIC		11	85	20
THROUGH THE HEART OF OHIO:D&MEC	BRASHARE	03	74	57
THUNDER IN THE MOUNTAINS (MSPC)	JOHNSTON	11	68	50
THUNDER LAKE NARROW GAUGE '93-'41	HUSTON	08	61	33
TIDEWATER TERMINALS OF EL RAILWAY	SHEPHA	SU	76	08R
TIME OF THE TROLLEY	MIDDLETON	02	68	59
TIMETABLE COLLECTOR	GARDNER	03	77	60
TO HELL IN A DAY COACH: EXASPERATED LOOK		05	68	50
TO THE MOUNTAINS BY RAIL (NYO&W)	WAKEFIE	03	71	58
TOLEDO & INDIANA RAILWAY	KING	05	83	14
TOLEDO PORT CLINTON & LAKESIDE RY	HILTON	08	64	59
TORONTO CIVIC RAILWAY:ILLUSTRATED HIST		11	87	23
TORONTO GREY & BRUCE RY	MCILWRAITH	06	64	57
TORONTO TROLLEY CAR STORY 1921-61	SWETT	02	62	38
TOURS OF DISCOVERY:SF MUNI ALBUM	PERLES	05	85	15
TRACING THE ROUTE OF MARTHAS VINEYARD RR		06	72	63
TRACK GOING BACK	DEGOLYER	10	69	59
TRACKING GHOST RAILROADS IN COLORADO		05	76	55
TRACKING GHOST RRS IN COLORADO	ORMES	F	75	10R
TRACKLESS TROLLEYS OF BOSTON	CLARKE	09	70	44
TRACKLESS TROLLEYS OF F&LSR	CLARKE	12	75	49
TRACKS OF NY #2: BROOKLYN ELEVATED RRS		11	75	56
TRACTION CLASSICS 2:INTERURBANS X FAST X		09	85	10
TRACTION CLASSICS-INTERURBANS-WOOD & STE		03	84	12
TRACTION CLASSICS: INTERURBAN FREIGHT		05	86	10
TRACTION ON THE GRAND	MILLS	09	78	53
TRACTIONS OF THE ORANGE EMPIRE (PE)	SWET	03	68	35
TRAFFIC MANAGEMENT	WILSON	07	41	70
TRAGEDY AT EDEN (D&RG WRECK)	HELMERS	09	71	59
TRAGIC TRAIN:CITY OF SAN FRANCISCO	DENEV	02	78	57
TRAILS OF THE IRON HORSE	RUSSELL	01	77	65
TRAIN ROBBERS AND TRAIN ROBBERIES	PINKER	02	71	55
TRAIN THAT NEVER CAME BACK & OTHER STORY		12	54	57
TRAIN TIME (DA)	GIBSON	08	75	61
TRAIN WATCHERS GUIDE TO CHICAGO	SZWAJKAR	06	69	55
TRAIN WRECK!	GRISWOLD	03	70	52

LITERATURE REVIEWS

RAILROAD PROTOTYPE BOOKS		M	Y	P
TRAIN WRECKS:PICTORIAL HIST OF ACCIDENTS		01	69	60
TRAINS		01	37	90
TRAINS	DAY	02	71	55
TRAINS ALBUM #5-#9	KALMBACH	04	45	105
TRAINS ALBUM OF GREAT NORTHERN RAILWAY		09	47	75
TRAINS AND THE MEN WHO RUN THEM	UHL	02	55	68
TRAINS IN STORY AND PICTURES	BROWN	01	36	87
TRAINS IN TRANSITION	BEEBE	01	42	68
TRAINS OF NORTHERN NEW ENGLAND	KRAUSE	09	77	60
TRAINS OF NORTHERN NEW ENGLAND	.KRAUSE	03	78	25
TRAINS OF NORTHERN NEW ENGLAND.	KRAUSE	02	78	09R
TRAINS OF PENNSYLVANIA DUTCH COUNTRY DEN		01	67	52
TRAINS ROLLING	MCBRIDE	08	54	107
TRAINS TO RUSSIAN RIVER (NWP)	STINDT	07	74	60
TRAINS TRACKS AND TRAVEL	VAN METRE	11	39	93
TRAINS VOLUME 1 (NOV 40 TO OCT 41) BOUND		03	42	131
TRAINS WE RODE VOL 1	BEEBE	01	66	62
TRAINS WE RODE VOL II	BEEBE	02	67	50
TRAINS, ELECTRONIC AGE EDITION	HENRY	10	57	37
TRAINS, TRACKS AND TRAVEL	METRE	07	36	87
TRAINS, TRACKS AND TRAVEL	VANMETRE	09	32	273
TRAINS, TRACKS AND TRAVEL	VAN METRE	02	39	94
TRAINS, TRACKS AND TRAVEL 6TH	VAN METRE	11	44	57
TRAINS, TRACKS, AND TRAVEL	VAN METRE	03	47	75
TRAMCAR TREASURY	GILL	08	64	59
TRAMS AND TRAMWAYS	CARTER	12	63	42
TRANSIT BOSTON 1850-1970	BOSTON ST RY	04	71	56
TRANSIT TO WETERSFIELD	BORRUP	02	71	45
TRANSITS STEPCHILD:THE TROLLEY COACH		03	74	57
TRANSPORTATION & ECONOMICS	PEGRUM	01	69	60
TRANSPORTATION CENTURY	MOTT	09	67	56
TRANSPORTATION CORRIDORE IN NW INDIANA		01	79	61
TRANSPORTATION UNIFORMS OF THE WORLD		06	40	75
TRANSPORTATION: A TOUR OF MUSEUMS SIMMON		12	70	62
TRANSPORTATION:ECONOMICS & FOREIGN POLIC		12	63	12
TRAVEL ON SOUTRN ANTEBELLUM RDS 1828-60		06	75	61
TRAVELERS OFFICIAL RY GUIDE 1869-REPRINT		02	70	54
TRAVELING BY TROLLEY IN MISSISSIPPI BROO		07	84	17
TRAVELTOWN	BEST	12	56	74
TREASURY OF RAILROAD FOLKLORE, A		04	54	124
TRENTON-PRINCETON TRACTION CO & PA-NJ RY		11	66	46
TROLLEY CAR TREASURY	ROWSOME	02	57	70
TROLLEY CAR TREASURY.	ROWSOME	11	68	39
TROLLEY COACH IN NORTH AMERICA	SEBREE	04	75	10
TROLLEY DAYS IN PASADENA (PE)	SEIMS	09	83	14
TROLLEY DAYS IN SEATTLE (S&RV)	BLANCHARD	02	66	38
TROLLEY DAYS IN THE TONAWANDAS	LLOYD	10	70	44
TROLLEY LINES IN QUEENS COUNTY	SAYFRIED	02	61	39
TROLLEY TALK VII	WAGNER	07	86	13
TROLLEY TALK VOL VIII		07	87	20
TROLLEY THROUGH THE COUNTRYSIDE	CHANDLER	04	64	38
TROLLEY TIMETABLE PANORAMA	GARDNER	07	68	37
TROLLEY TO THE PAST	YOUNG	11	83	23
TROLLEY TRAILS THROUGH GREATER CLEVELAND		12	75	49
TROLLEY TRAILS THROUGH THE WEST	WILSON	05	43	126
TROLLEY TRAILS THROUGH THE WEST VOL 10		05	83	14
TROLLEY TRAILS THROUGH THE WEST VOL 6		11	80	19
TROLLEY TRAILS VOL 7, NORTHERN CALIFORNI		11	80	19
TROLLEY--TRIUMPH OF TRANSPORT	MOEDINGER	01	72	41
TROLLEYGRAMS (USR)	BORRUP	07	83	14
TROLLEYS & STREET CARS ON AMER POSTCARDS		11	80	19
TROLLEYS ACROSS THE SAND DUNES (PPNJT)		03	78	29
TROLLEYS ALONG THE TURNPIKE	CUMMINGS	09	76	57
TROLLEYS DOWN THE MOHAWK VALLEY (FJ&G)		01	69	60
TROLLEYS FROM THE MINES	ALBERT	01	81	16
TROLLEYS IN THE VALLEY (AUGUSTA GA)		10	72	52
TROLLEYS OF BERKS COUNTY PA	FOESIG	03	71	40
TROLLEYS OF CHESTER COUNTY PA	BOWMAN	06	75	06
TROLLEYS OF LOWER DELAWARE VALLEY, PA		10	70	44
TROLLEYS OF MNES VOL 5	CUMMINGS	02	70	35
TROLLEYS OF MONTGOMERY COUNTY PA	FOESIG	10	68	31
TROLLEYS OF THE EMPIRE STATE		07	50	117
TROLLEYS OF THE PA DUTCH COUNTRY	DENNY	04	75	10
TROLLEYS OF THE TRIPLE CITIES	KING	06	77	49
TROLLEYS TO AUGUSTA MAINE	CUMMINGS	03	70	36
TROLLEYS TO CANOBIE LAKE PARK (MNES)		11	67	28
TROLLEYS TO CAYUGA LAKE PARK	KING	06	78	55
TROLLEYS TO HAMPTON BEACH	CUMMINGS	04	67	49
TROLLEYS TO SALISBURY BEACH V 2	CUMMINGS	05	66	62
TROLLEYS TO THE CASINO: EH&A	CUMMINGS	11	70	39
TROLLEYS TO THE SURF:STORY OF LAPR	MYERS	11	76	57
TROLLEYS TO YORK BEACH	CUMMINGS	09	65	39
TROLLEYS: THE FORGOTTEN TRANSPORTATION		12	68	39
TROLLEYS:RIDING & REMEMBERING ELEC INTER		11	76	57
TROY & NEW ENGLAND RY CO 1895-1925	VIENS	05	77	52
TRUE ADVENTURES OF RAILROADERS	MORGAN	12	54	56
TS TRAIN SHED CYCLOPEDIAS	GREGG	03	73	59
TS INDEX TO VOLUMES 1-42		07	77	59
TS#01 LOCOMOTIVES 1922 CYCLOPEDIA		03	73	59
TS#02 SWITCHING LOCOS 1930 CYCLOPEDIA		03	73	59
TS#03 BOX/STOCK/REEFER CARS 1931 CAR BLD		03	73	59
TS#04 RULES & REGULATIONS 1848 REPRINT		07	73	62
TS#05 GONDOLAS & HOPPERS 1940 CAR BUILDE		07	73	62
TS#06 PASSENGER LOCOS 1930 LOCO CYCLOPED		07	73	62
TS#07 BUILDINGS & STRUCTURES OF US ROADS		01	74	61
TS#09 WAR & STANDARD LOCOS & CARS 1919		01	74	61
TS#10 RAIL MOTOR CARS OF 1930	GREGG	01	74	61
TS#11 CABOOSE CARS 1879-1943	GREGG	04	74	61
TS#12 TANK CARS 1922-1943	GREGG	04	74	60
TS#13 BUILDINGS & STRUCTURES OF AM RRS 2		04	74	60
TS#14 4-8-4S AND OTHER HEAVY PASSENGER L		06	74	60
TS#15 HEAVY TRACTION 1922-1941	GREGG	06	74	61
TS#16 FAMOUS PASSENGER TRAINS 1943	GREGG	06	74	61
TS#17 BOX STOCK & FLAT CARS 1943 CAR BLD		11	74	59
TS#18 LOCOMOTIVES FROM 1916 LOCO DIRECTO		11	74	59
TS#19 BLDS & STRUCTURES OF AM RDS 1893 3		11	74	59
TS#20 DIESEL-ELECTRIC LOCOS OF 1920-38		11	74	59
TS#21 PASSENGER CARS 1943 CAR BUILDERS C		07	75	62
TS#22 STEAM LOCOS & TENDERS 1938 CYCLO#2		04	75	62
TS#23 LOCOS & TENDERS 1938 LOCO CYCLO #2		07	75	62

Railroad/Railfan

LITERATURE REVIEWS

RAILROAD PROTOTYPE BOOKS	M	Y	P
TS#24 BUILDINGS & STRUCTURES US ROADS #4	07	75	62
TS#25 ELECTRIC MOTOR CARS 1888-1928 GREG	08	75	45
TS#26 RAILWAY SERVICE CARS 1928-43 GREGG	09	75	61
TS#27 SIGNALS & SIGNAL SYMBOLS 1911 REPR	09	75	62
TS#28 CARS, SCALES & GATES-BUDA CATALOG	09	75	62
TS#29 FREIGHT CARS OF 1892 GREGG	12	75	61
TS#30 RAIL MOTOR CARS 1919-1928 GREGG	12	75	62
TS#31 LOCOMOTIVES 1927 CYCLOPEDIA (1) GR	12	75	62
TS#32 LOCOMOTIVE TENDERS & TRUCKS PART 2	03	76	61
TS#33 BUILDINGS & STRUCTURES OF AM RR 5	03	76	61
TS#34 SHAYS AND OTHER GEARED LOCOS FROM	03	76	61
TS#35 FREIGHT CARS PART 1 1919 CAR BUILD	07	76	62
TS#36 FREIGHT CARS PART 2 1919 CAR BUILD	07	76	62
TS#37 INDUSTRIAL & FOREIGN 1930 LOCO CYL	07	76	62
TS#38 BUILDINGS & STRUCTURES 7 1893	11	76	58
TS#40 LOCO CABS & FITTINGS 1 1927 LOCO C	11	76	58
TS#41 LOCO CABS & FITTINGS 2 1927 LOCO C	11	76	58
TS#50 LOCOS OF 40'S & 50'S PART 4 GREGG	03	77	60
TS#51 LOCOS OF 40'S & 50'S PART 5 GREGG	03	77	60
TS#52 STEAM LOCOS 1919 LOCO CYCLOPEDIA	07	77	58
TS#53 STEAM LOCOS 1919 LOCO CYCLOPEIDA	07	77	58
TS#54 BRIDGES & TRESTLES GREGG	11	77	60
TS#55 FREIGHT & PASSENGER CARS 1 GREGG	11	77	60
TS#57 FREIGHT & PASSENGER CARS 2 GREGG	11	77	60
TS#58 LOCOS OF 40'S & 50'S DIESEL PART 7	03	78	61
TS#59 FREIGHT AND PASSENGER CARS PART 3	03	78	61
TS#60 LOCOS OF 40'S & 50'S DIESEL PART 8	03	78	61
TS#61 BOX STOCK & REEFERS 1	07	78	60
TS#62 FLATS GONDOLAS & HOPPERS 2	07	78	60
TS#63 DUMP CARS TANKS CABOOSES & PASSENG	07	78	60
TS#64 LOCOS OF THE 40'S & 50'S DIESELS	12	78	65
TS#65 PASSENGERS, POSTALS & MOTOR CARS	12	78	65
TS#66 LOCOS OF THE 40'S & 50'S ELECTRICS	12	78	65
TT '28:ELEC RY SERVICES OF TTCO 1928 BRO	09	68	42
TUCKERTON RR:CHRONICAL OF TRANSPORT TO N	06	74	58
TUMULT IN THE MOUNTAINS:LUMBERING IN WV	02	65	60
TUNNEL 13 (SP) CHIPMAN	12	77	61
TURBINES WEST (UP) LEE	12	76	54
TURBINES WESTWARD (UP) LEE	W	76	12R
TWEETSIE COUNTRY (ET&WNC) FARRELL	05	77	56
TWEETSIE: THE BLUE RIDGE STEMWINDER	08	59	69
TWENTY-FOUR INCH GAGE RR AT BRIDGTON ME	03	42	131
TWILIGHT OF STEAM LOCOMOTIVES ZIEL	02	64	46
TWILIGHT ON THE NARROW GAUGE KRAMER	02	77	61
TWILIGHT ON THE NARROW GAUGE QP#5 KRAMER	SP	77	10R
TWIN CITIES RAILFAN'S GUIDE WEISTER	11	78	09R
TWIN CITY RAPID TRANSIT PICTORIAL (TCRT)	05	85	16
TWO MILLION MILES OF TRAIN TRAVEL ALLEN	03	66	62
TWO-FOOT CYCLOPEDIA VOL2:SR&RL #23 JANSE	09	78	58
ULSTER & DELAWARE BEST	11	72	62
UNDER PENNSY WIRES CARLETON	04	78	10R
UNDER PENNSY WIRES (2ND ED) CARLETON	07	82	12
UNION PACIFIC 3985 BOTKIN	11	85	22
UNION PACIFIC 8444 KINDIG	05	79	10
UNION PACIFIC RAILROAD:CASE OF PREMATURE	08	61	33

RAILROAD PROTOTYPE BOOKS	M	Y	P
UNION PACIFIC STREAMLINERS RANKS	05	75	61
UNION PACIFIC: HELL ON WHEELS ! CARSON	08	69	32
UNION PACIFIC:BUILDING OF 1ST TRANSCONTI	07	69	58
UNION STREET RAILWAY CUMMINGS	01	84	24
UNION STREET RAILWAY (USR) CUMMINGS	01	81	16
UNITED RAILWAYS OF OREGON HALLGREN	06	62	29
UNIVERSAL DIRECTORY OF RAILWAY OFFICIALS	02	38	61
UNIVERSAL DIRECTORY OF RY OFFIC/YEARBOOK	05	44	146
UNIVERSAL DIRECTORY OF RY OFFICIALS 47TH	02	42	52
UNIVERSAL DIRECTORY OF RY OFFICIALS/YRBK	09	41	83
UNUSUAL LOCOMOTIVES CARTER	12	60	59
UNUSUAL RAILWAYS WILSON	12	63	14
UP MOTIVE POWER REVIEW 1968-77 WAGNER	03	80	15
UP STEAM LOCOMOTIVE DIRECTORY KOENIGSBUR	02	68	60
UP STEAM LOCOS INCLUDING OSL OWRR&N LA&L	06	61	60
UP-COUNTRY LINE (BC&M) MEAD	10	75	60
UPTOWN, DOWNTOWN FISCHLER	10	77	41
UTILITY CARS OF PHILADELPHIA:1892-1971	04	72	55
VALLEY & SILETZ RAILROAD CULP	04	59	82
VALLEY RAILWAYS SIEBERT	07	83	14
VANCOUVER ISLAND RAILROADS TURNER	12	73	61
VANDERBILT LEGEND, THE ANDREWS	04	41	51
VANDERBUILTS AND THEIR FORTUNES	06	62	37
VANHORNES ROAD (CP) LAVALLEE	06	76	55
VANISHING DEPOT BYE	SP	75	14R
VANISHING MARKERS FISHER	02	77	60
VANISHING MARKERS. FISHER	SP	77	10R
VENTURA COUNTY RAILWAY MAGUIRE	12	61	52
VERMONT'S COVERED BRIDGE ROAD (SJ&LCO)	SP	75	13R
VERMONTS COVERED BRIDGE RD (SJ&LC) LEWIS	03	75	61
VICTORY RODE THE RAILS: CIVIL WAR TURNER	07	54	121
VINTAGE STEAM ROBERTS	11	67	56
VIRGINIA & TRUCKEE, CITY & COMSTOCK TIME	07	49	109
VIRGINIA & TRUCKEE: A STORY OF VIRGINIA	12	55	54
VIRGINIA RAILROADS IN THE CIVIL WAR JOHN	02	62	54
VIRGINIAN RAILROAD REID	02	62	54
VOCATIONAL AND PROFESSIONAL MONOGRAPHS	08	57	77
WABASH IN IOWA DONOVAN	03	65	62
WAITING FOR THE 5:05 GROW	11	77	60
WALNUT CREEK'S UNIQUE OLD STATION MURDOC	08	74	60
WASHINGTON & OLD DOMINION RR WILLIAMS	09	71	49
WATER LEVEL ROUTE (NYC) KNOLL	10	77	11R
WATER LEVEL ROUTE (NYC) KNOLL	06	77	56
WAY TO GO:COMING REVIVAL OF US RAIL PASS	06	74	59
WE HAD A SHORE FAST LINE BORGNIS	11	80	19
WE HAD A SHORE FAST LINE (AC&S) BORGNIS	09	81	16
WEEKS MILLS "Y" OF THE 2 FOOTER THURLOW	04	66	51
WELLSVILLE ADDISON & GALETON RR LEWIS	05	72	55
WEST JERSEY RAILS WEST JERSEY NRHS	03	85	16
WEST JERSEY RAILS II NRHS	09	86	12
WEST PENN TRACTION	09	68	42
WEST SIDE--NARROW GAUGE IN SIERRA FARREL	11	80	21
WESTCHESTERS FORGOTTEN RY ARCARA	02	63	49
WESTCHESTERS FORGOTTEN RY (NYW&B) ARCARA	07	73	50
WESTCHESTERS FORGOTTON RAILWAY (NYW&B)	10	62	48

LITERATURE REVIEWS

RAILROAD PROTOTYPE BOOKS

Title	Author	M	Y	P
WESTERN INCIDENTS ON THE UP	SEYMOUR	02	71	55
WESTERN MARYLAND DIESELS	JAHN	03	80	16
WESTERN MARYLAND STEAM POWER	PRICE	09	85	08
WESTERN NY AND PENNSYLVANIA RAILROAD		09	43	161
WESTERN PACIFICS DIESEL YEARS	STRAPAC	07	81	16
WESTERN RAIL TRAIL	MCKILLOP	02	63	37
WESTERN TRAINS	STEINHEIMER	04	66	50
WESTWARD TO PROMONTORY:BUILD UP ACROSS		08	69	32
WHAT CITIZENS SHOULD KNOW ABOUT ARMY ENG		08	42	96
WHAT YOU SHOULD KNOW ABOUT ILLINOIS RRS		12	57	33
WHEELS ROLLING WEST	STYFFE	07	79	13
WHEN BEAUTY ROAD THE RAILS	BEEBE	04	63	49
WHEN E MICH RODE THE RAILS 2:DETROIT TO		07	87	20
WHEN EASTERN MICHIGAN RODE THE RAILS DUL		07	85	14
WHEN MCQUEEN WAS KING	LYONS	02	57	70
WHEN OKLAHOMA TOOK THE TROLLEY	CHANDLER	05	81	16
WHEN THE STEAM RAILROADS ELECTRIFIED		SU	75	12R
WHEN THE STEAM RAILROADS ELECTRIFIED MID		05	75	56
WHEN THE WESTCHESTER WAS NEW (NYW&B)		05	65	36
WHERE ARE THE RAILROADS & SUBWAYS GOING?		04	62	29
WHERE TO WATCH TRAINS	LADD	08	77	61
WHISTLE ON THE WIND (FICTION)	SHIPLEY	08	62	57
WHITE FRONT TRAINS OF SAN FRANCISCO	SMAL	03	72	56
WHITE PASS & YUKON ROUTE: PICTORIAL HIST		11	80	20
WHO MADE ALL THE STREETCARS GO? BALTIMOR		12	73	50
WHO'S WHO IN RAILROADING (NORTH AMERICA)		12	40	68
WHO'S WHO IN RAILROADING N AMERICA 13TH		02	56	72
WHOSE FEATHER BED?	MATTESON	06	65	53
WILD RIVER WILDERNESS (LOGGING)	WIGHT	02	72	51
WILDCATTING ON THE MOUNTAIN	KLINE	04	71	49
WILKES-BARRE & HAZLETON RY	QUINBY	05	73	61
WILKES-BARRE RYS CO	ROHRBECK	11	75	56
WILL NOT RUN FEBUARY 22ND	STINNET	06	57	67
WILLIAM STANIER:ENGINEERING BIOGRAPHY		03	65	62
WINCHESTER & WESTERN RAILROAD	WINNEMORE	05	76	55
WM:FIREBALLS & BLACK DIAMONDS	COOK	03	82	15
WORK OF GIANTS:BUILDING 1ST TRANSCONTENT		02	63	37
WORKIN' ON THE RAILROAD	REINHARDT	11	70	44
WORKING ON THE TRACKS	MOORE	12	56	74
WORLD FAMOUS HORSESHOE CURVE & ALTOONA		12	73	61
WRECK OF OLD 97 (S)	CLEMMER	02	64	50
WW&F TWO FOOTER:HAIL & FAREWELL	THURLOW	04	66	51
WYMORE STORY (CB&Q)	KISTLER	12	71	49
YALE SCIENTIFIC MAGAZINE	SPRING 1939	08	39	68
YELLOW CARS OF LOS ANGELES (LAR)	WALKER	08	77	23
YORK COUNTY TROLLEYS	ROHRBECK	01	79	61

RAILROAD LITERATURE BY ROAD

Title	Author	M	Y	P
REPRIEVE FOR THE IRON HORSE:AMTRAK EXPER		04	75	61
JOURNEY TO AMTRAK	EDMONSON	08	72	63
ARCH AND ENG OF A WASH-NY CORRIDOR:PICTO		07	78	60
AMTRAK CAR SPOTTER, INCLUDING AUTOTRAIN		04	74	60
AMTRAK CAR AND LOCOMOTIVE SPOTTER (REV)		SU	76	07R

RAILROAD LITERATURE BY ROAD

RD	Title	Author	M	Y	P
A&A	ARCADE & ATTICA RAILROAD	LEWIS	11	72	63
A&H	THIRD RAILS PANTOGRAPHS & TROLLEY POLES		01	74	59
A&MR	ARCATA & MAD RIVER: 100 YEARS	BORDEN	01	55	68
A&SM	CLOUD-CLIMBING RR: STORY OF A&SM	NEAL	03	68	48
A&W	GENERAL RIDES AGAIN (A&W)	ATKINSON	10	62	39
AC&S	WE HAD A SHORE FAST LINE (AC&S)	BORGNIS	09	81	16
ACL	ATLANTIC COAST LINE:STEAM LOCOS & SHIPS		03	67	54
AL	RR IN THE CLOUDS:AL IN THE AGE OF STEAM		03	78	25
	RAILROAD IN THE CLOUDS:AL 1914-44	WILSON	01	79	14R
	RAILROAD IN ALASKA 2ND SECTION 1914-64		12	66	50
	ALASKA RAILROAD IN PICTURES	PRINCE	07	66	46
	ALASKA RAILROAD	FITCH	02	68	59
	ALASKA RAILROAD	:PENTREX	12	87	34
ALCO	ALCO ROTARY PLOW 1909 (REPRINT)		01	74	61
	ALCO USRA LOCOMOTIVES 1919 REPRINT		01	74	61
ALGE	ALGOMA EASTERN RAILWAY	WILSON	04	78	61
ARC	STAIRWAY TO THE STARS, CO ARGENTINE CENT		05	79	12
	ARGENTINE CENTRAL	HOLLENBACK	02	62	55
ATSF	ROUTE OF THE WARBONNETS (ATSF)	MCMILLAN	08	78	66
	SANTA FE DIESELS AND CARS	WAYNER	08	74	43
	SANTA FE MOTIVE POWER	MCMILLAN	07	86	14
	SANTA FES DIESEL FLEET	MCMILLAN	12	75	53
	ROUTE OF THE WARBONNETS (ATSF)	MCMILLAN	09	78	12R
	SANTA FE'S DIESEL FLEET	MC MILLAN	F	76	10R
	SANTA FE'S BIG THREE:LIFE STORY OF WORLD		04	73	58
	OPERATIONS SANTA FE	ARMITAGE	03	49	123
	SANTA FE: THE RR THAT BUILT AN EMPIRE		04	46	72
	SANTA FE RAILWAY: TRAIN ALBUM OF PHOTOS		04	46	75
	SANTA FE TRAIL, THE	LOOK	12	47	118
	HISTORY OF AT&SF RAILWAY	BRYANT	06	75	60
	HORNY TOAD MAN (ATSF)	DILS	07	67	51
	IRON HORSES OF THE SANTA FE TRAIL	WORLEY	06	66	54
	LOCOMOTIVES OF THE ATSF SYSTEM		12	39	125
	MORLEYS (ATSF)	CLEAVELAND	09	72	54
	ARID DOMAIN (ATSF AND LAND GRANTS)		12	54	56
	COACH, CABBAGE & CABOOSE (ATSF)	MCCALL	09	80	14
	DOODLEBUGS (ATSF)	MCCALL	03	78	61
	CHIEF WAY REFERENCE SERIES SYSTEM STDS		11	78	55
B&A	STATE, INVESTOR, & RAILROAD: THE B&A SAL		01	68	63
B&FB	BRADFORD & FOSTER BROOK PEG LEG RAILROAD		05	75	61
B&H	TWENTY-FOUR INCH GAGE RR AT BRIDGTON ME		03	42	131
B&L	SUMMER SAUNTERINGS BY THE B&L		03	71	58
B&LE	OFF WITH THE OLD, ON WITH THE NEW (B&LE)		02	56	72
	BESSEMER STORY, THE (B&LE)		06	55	53
	BESSEMER & LAKE ERIE RR:1869-1969	BEAVER	02	70	52
B&LET	BUFFALO & LAKE ERIE TRACTION CO	GORDON	03	78	29
B&M	MOGULS, MOUNTAINS AND MEMORIES (B&M)		11	80	19
	BLUEBIRDS & MINUTEMEN 1974-84 (B&M)	NELL	03	87	19
	B&M, B&L, AND ERM	BRADLEY	06	73	53
	DUMMY (B&M)	MCLIN	06	74	60
B&O	RAILROADING AFTER A CENTURY OF PROGRESS		09	33	50
	B&O POWER:STEAM DIESEL ELECTRIC 1829-'64		02	65	60
	B&O STEAM & ELECTRIC LOCO DIAGRAMS	STAUF	11	65	54
	B&O IN THE CIVIL WAR	SMITH	08	66	47
	B&O RR STANDARD PLANS FOR MOW & CONSTRUC		03	78	60

LITERATURE REVIEWS

RD	RAILROAD LITERATURE BY ROAD		M	Y	P
	EARLY MOTIVE POWER OF THE B&O RR	BELL	12	75	61
B&RB	B&RB-THE CANARSIE RAILROAD	FAUSSER	07	77	47
B&SQU	BUFFALO & SUSQUEHANNA RY	PIETRAK	04	67	51
B&SR	BUSTED AND STILL RUNNING (B&SR)	MEAD	05	71	60
	BUSTED AND STILL RUNNING:B&SR	MEAD	02	69	60
B&WD	TROLLEYS ALONG THE TURNPIKE	CUMMINGS	09	76	57
BART	THIS IS BART	FIREMENS FUND	11	65	41
	BART AT MID-POINT:SF BOLD NEW TRANSIT PR		01	69	40
	BART OFF AND RUNNING	STRAPAC	04	73	55
BB&K	BRADFORD BORDELL AND KINZUA	WOODS	11	71	57
BC&M	UP-COUNTRY LINE (BC&M)	MEAD	10	75	60
BCRW	+ BCR STEAM WITH 2860 & 3716 :GREG SCHOL		10	87	12
	BRITISH COLUMBIA RAILWAY	PENTREX	09	86	26
BELL	STREET CARS OF BOSTON V4 TYPE 4 SEMI-CON		07	76	21
	STREET CARS OF BOSTON V5 ARTICULATED & C		09	77	52
	SEMI-CONVERTIBLE CARS OF BOSTON ELEVATED		04	64	38
BERR	TRACKS OF NY #2:BROOKLYN ELEVATED RRS		11	75	56
BERS	BERKSHIRE STREET RAILWAY	CUMMINGS	11	73	41
BLW	BALDWIN LOCO WORKS VAUCLAIN COMPDS 1900		01	74	61
	BALDWIN LOCO WORKS NARROW GAUGE LOCOS'76		01	74	61
	BALDWIN LOCO WORKS LOGGING LOCOS 1913		01	74	61
BN	BURLINGTON NORTHERN ANNUAL 1974-75 WAGNE		F	75	09R
	BURLINGTON NORTHERN ANNUAL 1976-77 WAGNE		11	78	11R
	BURLINGTON NORTHERN ANNUAL 1972	WAGNER	05	73	55
	BURLINGTON NORTHERN RR CLASSICS (1 TO 5)		11	86	32
BR&U	SAPBUSH RUN, INFORMAL HISTORY BR&U		03	49	125
BR&W	BLACK RIVER & WESTERN STORY	SMITH	12	73	61
BS	CHANGE AT PARK STREET UNDER (BS)	CUDAHY	02	73	39
BSRY	BERLIN STREET RAILWAY	CUMMINGS	11	65	41
BZ&C	BENT ZIGZAG & CROOKED:OHIOS LAST NARROW		08	60	51
C&CA	CANAJOHARIE & CATSKILL RAILROAD		07	74	60
C&CL	THROUGH COVERED BRIDGES TO CONCORD	MEAD	01	71	47
C&IM	MIDLAND STORY, THE (C&IM)		06	55	53
	CHICAGO & ILLINOIS MIDLAND	WALLIN	03	81	17
C&LE	CINCINNATI & LAKE ERIE RR, OHIO INTERURB		05	75	57
C&NW	PRAIRIE RAILS (C&NW)	OLMSTED	11	79	12
	PIONEER RAILROAD: CHICAGO & NORTHWESTERN		04	49	107
	STEAM POWER:C&NW 1848-1956 CLASSES A-Z		12	65	62
	LIFE ON A LOCOMOTIVE (C&NW)	WILLIAMS	01	72	37
	NORTHWESTERN IN IOWA (C&NW)	DONOVAN	06	63	50
	C&NW POWER:MODERN STEAM-DIESEL 1900-1971		03	73	58
	CENTURIES OF THE NORTH WOODS (C&NW) :EAS		11	87	36
	EXTRA 6706 WEST (C&NW) :EAST END PRODUCT		11	87	37
C&O	STEAM LOCO DIAGRAMS OF C&O RR	STAUFER	06	65	52
	PICTORIAL HISTORY OF C&O TRAIN & AUTO FE		02	56	72
	C&O: SUPERPOWER TO DIESELS	DIXON	07	85	14
	CHESSIE'S ROAD (C&O)	TURNER	04	57	55
	C&O POWER:STEAM & DIESEL 1900-65 SHUSTER		03	66	62
	C&O 614 COAL TRAINS	GREG SCHOLL	03	86	06
C&PA	COUDERSPORT & PORT ALLEGANY AND NY&P		08	73	61
C&S	COLORADO & SOUTHERN: NORTHERN DIVISION		03	67	54
	COLORADO ROAD (C&S AND FW&D)	WAGNER	08	71	60
C&TR	RIVERSIDE LINE: STORY OF CAMDEN & TRENTO		11	81	12
C&TS	NARROW GAUGE TO THE CUMBRES	OSTERWALD	12	72	55
	C&TS: HISTORIC PRESERVATION STUDY WILSON		01	81	18

RD	RAILROAD LITERATURE BY ROAD		M	Y	P
CA&C	SLIM PRINCESS, THE (CA&C)	HUNGERFORD	12	56	74
CA&E	GREAT THIRD RAIL (CA&E) REPRINT		07	67	40
	AURORA 'N' ELGIN (CA&E)	JOHNSON	05	66	62
	CHICAGO AURORA & ELGIN RR COMPANY REPRIN		06	78	55
CASS	CASS COLLECTION	KILLORAN	05	83	16
CB&Q	WYMORE STORY (CB&Q)	KISTLER	12	71	49
	STEAM LOCOMOTIVES OF BURLINGTON RT CORBI		08	60	50
	STORY OF THE CALIFORNIA ZEPHYR ZIMMERMAN		04	76	60
	STEAM LOCOMOTIVES OF BURLINGTON ROUTE		03	65	61
	BURLINGTON WEST: A COLONIZATION HISTORY		02	42	51
	BURLINGTON ROUTE:HISTORY OF BURLINGTON L		11	65	52
	NORTHERN AND THE MIKE:TALE OF TWO LOCOS		08	66	48
	CZ: STORY OF CALIFORNIA ZEPHYR ZIMMERMAN		W	76	10R
	EVERYWHERE WEST THE BURLINGTON ROUTE		03	77	60
	DIESELS WEST:EVOLUTION OF POWER ON BURLI		04	64	61
CBE	CHESAPEAKE BEACH RAILWAY	WILLIAMS	01	76	29
CBELT	COTTON BELT LOCOMOTIVES	STRAPAC	05	78	13R
CCC&SL	BIG 4 ROUTE (CCC&SL)	PABST	02	64	50
CCSR	CINCINNATI STREETCARS #9 STREAMLINERS &		03	85	15
CCTR	CORTLAND COUNTY TRACTION	KING	08	65	63
CD&M	THROUGH THE HEART OF OHIO:CD&M ELECTRIC		11	85	20
CG&P	CINCINNATI GEORGETOWN & PORTSMOUTH RR		06	73	62
	CINCINNATI GEORGETOWN & PORTSMOUTH RR		03	78	29
CGW	CHICAGO GREAT WESTERN:2-8-0 CONSOLIDATIO		02	78	39
CH-P	NEW RAILS TO OLD TOWNS:REGION (CH-P)		07	69	58
CHESS	CHESSIE'S ROAD	TURNER	02	61	47
CLI	OVER UNDER AROUND & THROUGH THE CLINCHFI		09	85	60
CM&H	CONCORD MAYNARD & HUDSON ST RY	CUMMINGS	03	68	35
CMI	MIDLAND ROUTE: A COLORADO MIDLAND GUIDE		09	81	19
	COLORADO MIDLAND	CAFKY	07	65	54
CMRY	STAMPEDE CITY STREETCARS:STORY OF CMRY		01	76	28
	CALGARY MUNICIPAL RY	COX	04	64	38
CN	RENAISSANCE 6060 (CN)	PERRY	10	74	61
	WHISTLE ON THE WIND (FICTION)	SHIPLEY	08	62	57
	CANADIAN NATIONAL STEAM POWER	CLEGG	06	70	66
	CANADIAN NATIONAL RAILWAYS (2 VOLS) STEV		04	63	49
	CANADIAN NATIONAL RAILWAYS STORY	DORIN	07	76	11
	+ SNOW PLOW WITH CN F7'S :GREG SCHOLL VI		10	87	13
	SNOW PLOW WITH CN F7'S :GREG SCHOLL VIDE		12	87	36
CNJ	JERSEY CENTRAL ALBUM	CARTER	04	64	61
	JERSEY CENTRAL STORY	CARLTON	03	77	60
	LOCOMOTIVES OF THE JERSEY CENTRAL		06	58	68
	LOCOMOTIVES 1-999 NEW JERSEY CENTRAL CAR		01	79	62
	LOCOMOTIVES OF THE JERSEY CENTRAL 1-999		03	80	13
	CNJ, A PICTORIAL REVIEW	GARDNER	06	74	11
	BIG LITTLE RAILROAD (CNJ) EVERYTHING VID		05	85	20
CNO&TP	QUEEN & CRESCENT ROUTE (CNO&TP)	GARDNER	04	77	60
CNS&M	SELECTED ROLLING STOCK OF CNS&M		05	68	42
	ROUTE OF THE ELECTROLINERS V2 (CNS&M)		06	64	46
	INTERURBAN TO MILWAUKEE (CNS&M)		08	63	41
	DAYS OF THE NORTH SHORE LINE	CAMPBELL	11	86	19
COL	NARROW GAUGE TO CENTRAL & SILVER PLUME		11	72	62
CONN	FORMATION & HIST OF CONN COMPANY 2ND ED		01	83	14
	FORMATION & HIST OF CONN & CR&L (REV)		04	76	58
CP	VANHORNES ROAD (CP)	LAVALLEE	06	76	55

Railroad/ Railfan

LITERATURE REVIEWS

RD	RAILROAD LITERATURE BY ROAD	M	Y	P
	HISTORY OF THE 3101 (CP) BEST	01	67	52
	GREAT KICKING HORSE BLUNDER (CP) PUGSLEY	10	73	57
	GREAT HORSESHOE WRECK (CP 1907) BEAUMONT	11	76	58
	BIG FOUR, THE (CENTRAL PACIFIC) LEWIS	10	38	37
	CANADIAN PACIFIC IN THE ROCKIES (4 VOLS)	03	80	13
	CANADIAN PACIFIC: BRIEF HISTORY MCDOUGAL	09	68	57
	CREST OF THE CONTINENT (CP) INGERSOLL	06	70	66
	CANADIAN PACIFIC RAILWAY DORIN	03	75	61
	DELORIMER & ANGUS (CP) LAVALLEE	07	67	50
	CP'S LAGGAN SUB RAIL INNOVATIONS	05	87	20
	# "THE CANADIAN" (CP) :RAIL INNOVATIONS	12	87	33
CPA	RAILS FROM THE WEST:BIOGRAPHY OF T JUDAH	08	69	32
	IRON HORSES TO PROMONTORY (CPA) BEST	08	69	32
	HIGH ROAD TO PROMONTORY:BUILDING CPA ACR	08	69	32
	CENTRAL PACIFIC & SOUTHERN PACIFIC RRS	10	63	40
	FIRST TRANSCONTINENTAL RR: CENTRAL PACIF	09	50	65
CPR	RAILS TO OCHOCO COUNTRY:CITY OF PRINEVIL	12	68	58
CRW	CLEVELAND RY: OPERATION & MAINTENANCE RE	07	67	40
CS&M	SITUATION IN FLUSHING (MI) (CS&M) LOVE	02	66	62
CSCO	CLEVE SOUTHWESTERN & COLUMBUS TROLLEY	05	82	08
	CLEVELAND, SOUTHWESTERN & COLUMBUS RY	06	63	39
	CLEVELAND SOUTHWESTERN & COLUMBUS RY CO	01	83	12
CSS&SB	SPIRIT OF THE SOUTH SHORE RAIR	07	85	14
	SOUTH SHORE, THE LAST INTERURBAN MIDDLET	03	71	40
	DUNELAND ELECTRIC:S SHORE LINE IN TRANSI	09	85	08
CTA	CHICAGOS RAPID TRANSIT: V1 ROLLING STOCK	06	73	62
	CHICAGOS RAPID TRANSIT:ROLLING STOCK 47-	04	78	09R
CUMV	AMERICAN SINGLE-AXEL LOCO-"PIONEER" WHIT	02	74	36
CVRY	CREDIT VALLEY RAILWAY FILBY	08	76	60
CW	REDWOODS IRON HORSES & THE PACIFIC (CW)	06	64	56
	SKUNK RAILROAD-FT BRAGG TO WILLITS (CW)	12	64	36
	CALIFORNIA WESTERN RAILROAD, THE BORDEN	02	58	74
D&H	DELAWARE & HUDSON SHAUGHNESSY	04	68	51
D&IRR	KITE ROUTE:STORY OF D&IRR JONES	11	87	24
D&MEC	THROUGH THE HEART OF OHIO:D&MEC BRASHARE	03	74	57
D&NE	CINDERS & TIMBER (D&NE) HARRISON	02	70	54
D&RG	TRAGEDY AT EDEN (D&RG WRECK) HELMERS	09	71	59
D&RGS	COLORADO ANNUAL #7 CHILI LINE HAUCK	09	69	57
D&RGW	PORTRAIT OF A SILVER LADY (THE CZ) MACGR	04	78	60
	RIO GRANDE IN THE ROCKIES (D&RGW) HILL	04	78	10R
	RIO GRANDE...TO THE PACIFIC LEMASSENA	04	75	53
	RIO GRANDE GLORY DAYS .LATHROP	W	76	10R
	SILVERTON: TRIP TO YESTERDAY (D&RGW) STO	09	68	57
	RIO GRANDE CAR PLANS WAYNER	11	69	56
	RIO GRANDE GLORY DAYS LATHROP	09	76	60
	LOGGING ALONG THE DENVER & RIO GRANDE	06	72	63
	NEVER ON WEDNESDAY (D&RGW) LOVEMAN	11	81	09
	COLORADO ANNUAL #7 CHILI 1969	12	69	52
	CINDERS & SMOKE (D&RGW) OSTERWALD	12	65	64
	DENVER & RIO GRANDE WESTERN RR (REPRINT)	05	78	61
	# CHAMA TURN (D&RGW) :GREEN FROG	12	87	33
	# WORK TRAIN TO SILVERTON (D&RGW) :GREEN	12	87	33
	# TWILIGHT OF THE RIO GRANDE NARROW GAUG	12	87	33
D&ST	DANVILLE & SUNBURY TRANSIT CO GORDON	11	68	39
DA	TRAIN TIME (DA) GIBSON	08	75	61

RD	RAILROAD LITERATURE BY ROAD	M	Y	P
DC&P	DAYTON COVINGTON & PIQUA TRACTION CO GOR	11	72	53
DL&W	LACKAWANNA RAILROAD #2 GARDNER	12	76	54
	LACKAWANNA HERITAGE 1947-1952 KRAUSE	11	78	12R
	ALONG THE LACKAWANNA-A PICTORIAL REVIEW	07	76	60
	CLEAR THE TRACKS! (DL&W HOGGER) BROMLEY	12	43	98
	DL&W IN THE 19TH CENTURY TABER	09	77	60
	LACKAWANNA LEGACY RUN 8 VIDEO	11	85	24
DM&IR	MISSABE ROAD (DM&IR) KING	11	72	62
	LOCOMOTIVES OF DM&IR KING	05	85	19
DMT	DETROIT MONROE & TOLEDO SHORT LINE RY	10	87	27
DNEW	HYDE PK DIV OF DEDHAM-NORWOOD-E WALPOLE	01	78	44
DSP&P	MINERAL BELT VOL 1,OLD SOUTH PARK-DENVER	07	79	12
	DENVER SOUTH PARK & PACIFIC	04	77	60
	DENVER SOUTH PARK & PACIFIC: HISTORY	07	51	45
	DEVER SOUTH PARK & PACIFIC POOR	05	49	127
	DENVER SOUTH PARK & PACIFIC KINDIG	06	60	42
DST	DETROIT STREET RYS V2 CITY LINES 1922-56	01	81	16
	DETROIT STREET RYS V1 CITY LINES 1893-22	12	78	53
DT&PC	DANVILLE TRACTION & POWER CO TOSH	08	73	52
DUL	WHEN EASTERN MICHIGAN RODE THE RAILS DUL	07	85	14
E	MEN OF ERIE HUNGERFORD	12	47	119
	ERIE STEAM LOCOMOTIVE DIAGRAMS STAUFER	11	65	54
	ERIE RR: ROCHESTER DIVISION GORDON	12	65	56
	ERIE RAILROAD, ROCHESTER DIV GORDON	02	66	38
	ERIE PICTORIAL REVIEW GARDNER	10	74	61
	ERIE POWER WESTING	05	71	60
	ERIR RAILROAD-PICTORIAL REVIEW GARDNER	F	75	09R
	ERIE RAILROAD: PICTORAL REVIEW V2 GARDNE	10	75	60
E&B	DAIRY ROUTE: HIST OF E&B GUSTAFSON	04	68	36
EBT	RAMBLE INTO THE PAST ON EAST BROAD TOP	10	72	63
	QUICK REVIEW OF EAST BROAD TOP MANNIX	02	61	47
	EBT: TO THE MINES AND BACK GRENARD	01	81	16
	EAST BROAD TOP RAINEY	09	82	14
ECRY	EAST CAROLINA RAILWAY BRIDGERS	02	74	60
ED	EDAVILLE RAILROAD MOODY	06	48	114
EH&A	TROLLEYS TO THE CASINO: EH&A CUMMINGS	11	70	39
EL	SCHEMATIC TRACK DIAGRAMS OF THE EL	SU	75	11R
	TIDEWATER TERMINALS OF EL RAILWAY SHEPHA	SU	76	08R
	SCHEMATIC TRACK DIAGRAMS OF EL RY SHEPPA	10	76	58
	ERIE LACKAWANNA EAST ZIMMERMANN	11	75	60
	ERIE-LACKAWANNA EAST QP#3 ZIMMERMANN	W	75	09R
	ERIE LACKAWANA STORY CARLETON	03	75	59
	ERIE LACKAWANNA MEMORIES-FINAL YEARS COO	11	87	26
EMD	OUR GM SCRAPBOOK KALMBACH	04	72	62
EMSR	SNOW FIGHTING EQIP:EASTERN MASS ST RY CO	08	65	63
EPEC	EL PASO ELEC TRANSPORTATION DIV: TENTATI	04	76	58
ES&S	RICHMOND (CA) STREET CARS 1900-33 HANSON	12	68	39
	EAST SHORE & SUBURBAN RY HANSON	10	61	51
ET&WNC	TWEETSIE COUNTRY (ET&WNC) FARRELL	05	77	56
F&BE	RAILROAD WITH 3 GAUGES:CG&P AND F&BE	10	87	26
F&IU	FOX & ILLINOIS UNION RY CO	01	78	45
F&LSR	TRACKLESS TROLLEYS OF F&LSR CLARKE	12	75	49
FCM	EL CENTENARIO DEL FERRO CARRIL MEXICANO	07	73	61
FEC	RAILROAD THAT DIED AT SEA:FEC KEY WEST E	02	69	61
	HURRICANE ROAD (FEC) SMILEY & WHITE	02	55	67

Railroad/Railfan

LITERATURE REVIEWS

RD	RAILROAD LITERATURE BY ROAD	M	Y	P
FJ&G	TROLLEYS DOWN THE MOHAWK VALLEY (FJ&G)	01	69	60
FPT	FAIRMOUNT PARK TROLLEY:UNIQUE PHILLY EXP	11	70	39
FRIS	STEAM LOCOMOTIVES OF FRISCO LINE STAGNER	04	78	10R
	STEAM LOCOMOTIVES OF THE FRISCO LINE STA	08	77	61
	FRISCO FOLKS:STORIES OF STEAM DAYS ON FR	12	61	42
FW&D	GULF TO ROCKIES (FW&D + C&S 1861-1898)	08	54	105
G	STEAM LOCOMOTIVES & HISTORY:G AND WPR	04	73	58
	STEAM LOCOS & HIST:G AND WPR PRINCE	08	62	56
GB&W	STORY OF GREEN BAY & WESTERN SPECHT	02	67	52
GCT	GILPIN TRAM HOLLENBACK	02	62	55
	GILPIN GOLD TRAM FERRELL	11	71	57
GHE	GALVESTON-HOUSTON ELECTRIC RY WOODS	01	83	12
GM&O	GULF, MOBILE AND OHIO, THE LEMLY	07	54	123
	GM&O NORTH OLMSTED	SP	77	12R
GN	TRAINS ALBUM OF GREAT NORTHERN RAILWAY	09	47	75
	LINES WEST (GN) WEST	02	68	60
GTC	GRAND TRUNK RAILWAY OF CANADA, THE CURRI	08	58	64
GTW	GRAND TRUNK WESTERN DORIN	03	78	25
	GT HERITAGE, STEAM IN NEW ENGLAND HASTIN	03	79	11R
	GRAND TRUNK WESTERN RR DORIN	12	77	60
	LAST BREATH OF FIRE HOPEWELL PRODUCTIONS	09	87	29
GWS	SUGAR TRAMP (GWS) MORGAN	08	76	60
H&F	BLUE RIDGE TROLLEY:HAGERSTOWN & FREDERIC	08	70	40
H&SSR	HARTFORD & SPRINGFIELD STREET RAILWAY CO	01	76	28
HG&B	RIDE THROUGH GARDEN OF CANADA (HG&B) BLA	12	67	36
HG&DSR	HG&DSR AND GR&ISR CUMMINGS	10	63	37
HH	HETCH HETCHY AND ITS DAM RAILROAD WURM	01	74	61
HORT	HAWAIIAN TRAMWAYS:STORY OF HONOLULU RAPI	08	60	33
HRC	NARROW GAUGE IN A KINGDOM (HAWAII) CONDE	05	72	55
HT	CHOCOLATE TOWN TROLLEYS (HT) STEINMETZ	12	67	36
HT&W	HOOT TOOT & WHISTLE:STORY OF HT&W CARMAN	04	64	61
HU	CROSS ISLAND:STORY OF HUNTINGTON RR SEYF	09	77	52
HVRY	HISTORY OF HUDSON VALLEY RAILWAY NESTLE	12	67	36
I-ASL	ITHACA-AUBURN SHORT LINE PALMER	09	78	53
IC	HISTORY OF THE ILLINOIS CENTRAL STOVER	01	76	61
	ILLINOIS CENTRAL IN IOWA DONOVAN	12	62	48
	LIMITEDS ALONG THE LAKEFRONT:IC IN CHICA	05	87	19
IL	RAILROAD THAT RAN BY THE TIDE (IL) FEAGA	12	72	54
IR&T	INTERURBAN RAILWAY & TERMINAL CO:BLACK L	02	73	39
IRT	ELEVATED & SUBWAY CARS OF IRT & PREDICES	08	73	52
ISRY	ITHACA STREET RAILWAY COX	07	72	39
IT	LINCOLN LAND TRACTION (IT) JOHNSON	12	65	37
JCTR	JERSEY CENTRAL TRACTION CO EID	05	83	14
JTC	JOHNSTOWN TRACTION CO 1882-1960 ROHRBECK	06	76	47
KCM&O	ARTHUR E STILWELL (KCM&O) BRYANT	06	72	63
	DESTINATION TOPOLOBAMPO: KCM&O KERR	02	69	60
KS	KEY SYSTEM ALBUM WALKER	11	78	54
	KEY ROUTE:TRANSBAY COMMUTING BY TRAIN/FE	07	85	14
KSRS	HISTORY OF KNOXVILLE ST RY SYSTEM BEL	06	75	06
KVRR	MCCULLOCH'S WONDER (KVRR) SANFORD	04	78	12
L&HR	NORTHEAST RAILROAD SCENE V2: L&HR PENNIS	12	77	11R
L&N	PARDON ME..IS THAT THE CHATTANOOGA CHOO-	02	77	61
	L&N STEAM LOCOMOTIVES PRINCE	04	60	46
	LOUISVILLE & NASHVILLE RAILROAD HERR	08	60	50
	HISTORY OF LOUISVILLE & NASHVILLE RR	02	73	60
	LOUISVILLE & NASHVILLE RAILROAD, THE	08	43	78
	LOUISVILLE & NASHVILLE RR (1850-1963)5TH	11	64	48
	L&N STEAM LOCOMOTIVES REVISED 1968 PRINC	03	70	52
	# PACIFIC PRINCESS (L&N):BERKSHIRE VIDEO	11	87	36
	# LIGHT PACIFIC:SECOND SECTION (L&N):LAS	10	87	13
	# LIGHT PACIFIC (L&N) :LASTING IMPRESSIO	10	87	13
	# PACIFIC THROUGH THE CUMBERLANDS :LASTI	10	87	13
L&PS	LONDON & PORT STANLEY RAILWAY TORRENS	01	85	17
L&WV	LAUREL LINE (L&WV) HENWOOD	09	86	12
L-CTR	LEWISTON-CLARKSTON TRANSIT	03	76	23
LA&W	LEWISTON AUGUSTA & WATERVILLE STREET RY	10	64	41
LAPR	TROLLEYS TO THE SURF:STORY OF LAPR MYERS	11	76	57
LAR	YELLOW CARS OF LOS ANGELES (LAR) WALKER	08	77	23
	LA RAILWAYS PRE-HUNTINGTON CARS 1890-'02	08	63	41
	LAST OF THE YELLOW CARS (LAR) WOOTON	12	63	42
LCCE	LEE COUNTY CENTRAL ELECTRIC RY KEISTER	07	67	40
LI	STEEL RAILS TO SUNRISE (LI) (BEEBE REV)	05	66	46
	STEEL RAILS TO THE SUNRISE:THE LIRR ZIEL	11	65	50
	LONG ISLAND RAILROAD PART 6 GOLDEN AGE	06	76	55
	LONG ISLAND RAILROAD PART 1 S SIDE RY	10	62	37
	LONG ISLAND RAILROAD PART 2: COMP HISTOR	06	64	36
	LONG ISLAND RAILROAD KRAMER	06	78	20
	LONG ISLAND RAILROAD PART 4 COMPREHENSIV	05	69	57
	LONG ISLAND RAILROAD PART 3 1863-80 EXPA	03	67	54
	LONG ISLAND RAILROAD PART 5 SAYFRIED	10	72	52
	EARLY HISTORY OF LONG ISLAND RR 1834-190	08	59	69
LMSRY	SHAYS ON SWITCHBACKS:HIST OF LMSRY WHITE	02	64	46
LPL	LARAMIE PLAINS LINE HOLLENBACK	02	62	55
LSE	LAKE SHORE ELECTRIC CHRISTIANSEN	10	64	41
LV	HISTORY OF THE LV RAILROAD ARCHER	09	78	12R
	LEHIGH VALLEY RAILROAD:RT OF THE BLACK D	06	78	20
	LEHIGH VALLEY RAILROAD:A PICTORIAL REV 1	12	75	61
	NORTHEAST RAILROAD SCENE: VOL 1 LV	F	76	11R
	ACE OF BLACK DIAMONDS HOPEWELL PRODUCT	03	86	06
LVT	LEHIGH VALLEY TRANSIT CO ST LOUIS CARS	04	62	54
	LIBERTY BELL ROUTES 1000 SERIES INTERURB	02	65	40
	LIBERTY BELL ROUTES HEAVY INTERURBAN CAR	06	71	55
M	MONON ROUTE. HILTON	01	80	18
	MONON ROUTE HILTON	12	78	65
M&A	NORTH ARKANSAS LINE (M&A) FAIR	02	70	54
M&E	MORRISTOWN & ERIE RAILROAD TABER	04	68	51
M&ET	BRIEF HISTORY OF THE MODESTO & EMPIRE TR	04	57	55
M&OL	GONE BUT NOT FORGOTTEN: THE M&OL PALMER	05	67	50
M&ONE	MANCHESTER & ONEIDA RAILWAY, THE DONOVAN	04	58	48
M&PP	PIKES PEAK COG RAILROAD (M&PP) ABBOTT	12	72	54
M&SC	CATENARY THROUGH COUNTIES: STORY OF M&SC	02	68	40
M-CL	PINO GRANDE: LOGGING RAILROADS OF M-CL	04	67	51
MA	RAILS TO CARRY COPPER (MA) CHAPPELL	05	74	60
MA&PA	MA&PA:HISTORY OF MARYLAND & PENN RR HILT	12	63	12
	MA & PA, A VANISHING RAILROAD KENDALL	03	72	39
MASSC	CENTRAL MASS B&M HISTORICAL	08	76	60
MBTA	SOUTH SHORE:QUINCY-BOSTON (MBTA) CLARKE	10	76	56
MC	MAINE CENTRAL STEAM LOCOMOTIVES ROBERTSO	01	78	61
MCH	CHUNK SWITCH BACK RAILWAY (MCH) GARDNER	06	75	61
MCPR	MONTREAL CITY PASSENGER RY CO LAVALLEE	08	62	49

Railroad/Railfan

LITERATURE REVIEWS

RD	RAILROAD LITERATURE BY ROAD	M	Y	P
MCRI	PINE ACROSS THE MOUNTAIN (MCRI) HAUFT	03	72	40
	MCCLOUD RIVER RAILROAD: GOLD SPIKE SPECI	02	56	72
MCTC	MORRIS COUNTY TRACTION COMPANY LOWENTHAL	11	84	20
MCV	CINCINNATI STREETCARS #4 MILCREEK VALLEY	04	71	56
MILW	HIAWATHA STORY (MILW) SCRIBBINS	12	70	62
	GRASS BETWEEN THE RAILS (MILW BRANCH)	12	73	61
	MILWAUKEE ROAD ELECTRIFICATION BRAIN	02	62	56
	MILWAUKEE RAILS OLMSTED	01	82	19
	MILWAUKEE ROAD UNDER WIRE ZIMMERMANN	03	74	61
	MILWAUKEE ROAD WEST WOOD	12	72	54
MISSC	NATCHEZ ROUTE:A MISS CENTRAL RR ALBUM	F	75	10R
MITR	GATEWAY TO THE NORTHWEST (MITR) DONOVAN	03	55	53
MKT	KATY RAILROAD & THE LAST FRONTIER MASTER	06	78	61
	KATY NORTHWEST .HOFSOMMER	09	78	12R
	KATY NORTHWEST HOFSOMMER	10	76	58
MNES	TROLLEYS OF MNES VOL 5 CUMMINGS	02	70	35
	TROLLEYS TO CANOBIE LAKE PARK (MNES)	11	67	28
MP	EMPIRE THAT MISSOURI PACIFIC SERVES, THE	08	57	77
MSPC	THUNDER IN THE MOUNTAINS (MSPC) JOHNSTON	11	68	50
MSSRY	MARKET STREET RY REVISITED:BEST OF INSID	01	73	38
MT&MW	CROOKEDEST RAILROAD IN THE WORLD (MT&MW)	08	54	104
	CROOKEDEST RAILROAD IN THE WORLD. (MT&MW)	06	61	59
MTL	MOUNT LOWE: RAILWAY IN THE CLOUDS SEIMS	12	77	10R
	MOUNT LOWE, RAILWAY IN THE CLOUDS SEIMS	02	78	48
MV	TRACING THE ROUTE OF MARTHAS VINEYARD RR	06	72	63
MW&CR	MERIDAN WATERBURY & CONNECTICUT RIVER RR	01	55	68
MWCOG	RAILWAY TO THE MOON (MWCOG) KIDDER	01	70	54
N&BSR	NORFOLK & BRISTOL STREET RAILWAY MURRAY	02	63	49
N&SV	BELLS & WHISTLES IN OLD PERRY (N&SV)	SU	75	10R
N&W	STEAM STEEL & STARS AMERICAS LAST STEAM	07	87	20
	NORFOLK & WESTERN STEAM: LAST 25 YEARS	06	73	52
	N&W RAILWAY: POCAHONTAS COAL CARRIER PRI	01	82	19
	# AWSOME A-PART 1 (N&W) :BERKSHIRE VIDEO	11	87	36
	# THE MIGHTY J (N&W) :BERKSHIRE VIDEOGRA	11	87	36
	18 WHEELS OF STEEL. (N&W) :HOPWELL PRODUC	10	87	13
	FROM MINE TO MARKET (N&W COAL TRANSPORTA	02	55	67
	MIGHTY "J" PART 1,2,3 (N&W) SUNDAY RIVER	09	84	20
	N&W STEAM IN ACTION VIDEO	07	84	21
	N&W J 611 JMJ PRODUCTIONS	03	83	12
	BRIDGES TO BUFFALO HOPWELL PRODUCTIONS	11	85	23
	NORFOLK & WESTERN 611 VIDEO RAILS	05	86	13
	# 18 WHEELS OF STEEL (N&W) :HOPWELL PROD	09	87	28
	# N&W 1218 REBUILT & ROANOKE BOUND :GREG	09	87	28
	# 1218 FREIGHT (N&W) :MIAN LINE	09	87	28
	# VIDEO CLASSICS 1218 (N&W) :VIDEO CLASS	09	87	28
	# COAL TRAIN (N&W) :MAIN LINE	09	87	29
	N&W A 1218 JMJ	09	87	29
	# THE A AND THE J (N&W) :TRACKSIDE VIDEO	12	87	33
	# 1218:A NEW BEGINNING (N&W) :TRACKSIDE	12	87	33
N&WO	QUICKEST ROUTE (N&WO) FARNHAM	11	73	60
NBCS	NELSON STREET RAILWAY (BC) PARKER	08	62	49
NC&SL	NASHVILLE CHATTANOOGA & ST LOUIS RY: HIS	03	68	50
NCN	NEVADA COUNTY NARROW GAUGE BEST	09	65	50
NGRR	# NEW GEORGA RAILROAD :GREEN FROG	12	87	32
NKP	NICKEL PLATE STORY REHOR	06	66	54

RD	RAILROAD LITERATURE BY ROAD	M	Y	P
	NICKEL PLATE ROAD, THE HAMPTON	06	48	111
	# BERKSHIRE--BEST OF BREED (NKP) :BERKSH	11	87	36
	# SEVEN SIX FIVE (NKP) :LASTING IMPRESSI	10	87	13
	LIFE BEGINS AT FORTY HOPEWELL PRODUCTION	01	87	36
NN	NEVADA NORTHERN:SAGEBRUSH SHORT LINE ALL	07	65	55
NO&C	ST CHARLES STREET CAR-NO&C RR (REVISED)	01	79	61
	NEW ORLEANS & CARROLLTON RAIL ROAD GUIBE	12	76	48
NOPS	LAST MILE: A STREETCAR NAMED CHARLES	05	73	61
NOT&L	NORTHERN OHIO TRACTION REVISITED BLOWER	10	70	44
	NOT&L STORY BLOWER	03	67	47
NP	NORTHERN PACIFIC SUPERSTEAM ERA 1925-45	01	86	14
	NORTHERN PACIFIC RAILWAY OF MCGEE & NIXO	03	86	19
	NORTHERN PACIFIC: MAIN STREET OF THE NOR	04	69	48
NPC	NARROW GAUGE TO THE REDWOODS(NPC) GRAVES	10	67	51
NPIER	SHORT HAUL TO THE BAY (NPIER) HENWOOD	04	70	58
NPR	NORTHWESTERN PENNSYLVANIA RAILWAY SIEBER	11	76	57
NRNJ	NEXT STATION WILL BE... VOL 4 NRNJ	F	76	12R
	NEXT STATION WILL BE V 4 1910 NRNJ	09	76	60
NSC&T	NSC&T ELECTRIC RAILWAY IN PICTURES PANKO	05	85	15
	NIAGARA ST CATHARINES & TORONTO RY MILLS	01	69	40
NSO	# N&W + SOU = NS DIESELS :JMJ	10	87	13
NWP	TRAINS TO RUSSIAN RIVER (NWP) STINDT	07	74	60
	NORTHWESTERN PACIFIC RR:REDWOOD EMPIRE R	05	65	51
NY&LB	NEW YORK & LONG BRANCH RR SIGNAL BOOK	05	76	55
NY&SB	SEA BEACH TO CONEY ISLAND (NY&SB) FAUSER	11	80	19
NYC	WATER LEVEL ROUTE (NYC) KNOLL	10	77	11R
	RAILROADS IN THE STREETS OF SYRACUSE PAL	06	71	51
	RUN OF THE 20TH CENTURY (NYC) HUNGERFORD	05	71	60
	STEAM POWER OF THE NYC SYSTEM 1915-1955	12	61	42
	WATER LEVEL ROUTE (NYC) KNOLL	06	77	56
	PASSENGER EQUIPMENT DIAGRAMS:NYC SYSTEM	12	66	51
	ROAD OF THE CENTURY, THE (NYC) HARLOW	08	47	116
	KEEPING THE RAILROADS RUNNING:50 Y /NYC	08	75	61
	MEN AND IRON (HISTORY OF NYC) HUNGERFORD	07	38	29
	LOCOMOTIVES OF NYC LINES MAY	11	66	49
	MEMORIES OF NYC DIESELS-ELECTRIC POWER 2	01	84	29
	NYC'S LATER POWER 1910-1968 STAUFER	05	83	17
	NYC SYSTEMS, GONE, BUT NOT FORGOTTEN CAV	01	85	19
	NYC EARLY STEAM POWER V2 1831-1916 STAUF	10	67	51
	NEW YORK CENTRAL CARS WAYNER	02	73	61
	DIESEL LOCOMOTIVES OF NYC SYSTEM EDSON	01	80	17
	ED NOWAK'S NYC ZIMMERMAN	07	84	18
NYMTA	THEY MOVED MILLIONS (NYMTA) DAVIS	11	85	20
NYNH&H	NANTASKET BEACH BRANCH:NYNH&H ELECTRIFIC	05	83	14
	NEW HAVEN RAILROAD: ITS RISE & FALL WELL	03	70	52
	NEW YORK, NEW HAVEN & HARTFORD ELECTRIFI	06	70	40
	NEW HAVEN RR:A FOND LOOK BACK PAVLUCIK	09	79	16
	DIESEL LOCOMOTIVES OF NEW HAVEN RR CAVAN	09	81	16
NYO&W	TO THE MOUNTAINS BY RAIL (NYO&W) WAKEFIE	03	71	58
	O&W: LONG LIFE-SLOW DEATH OF NYO&W	04	60	46
	FINAL YEARS: NYO&W KRAUSE	10	77	58
	FINAL YEARS, THE (NYO&W) KRAUSE	12	77	12R
NYS&W	SUSQUEHANNA KRAUSE	11	80	22
	NYS&W: ALBUM OF 1910 DEPOT PHOTOS TILTON	07	73	61
NYW&B	WESTCHESTERS FORGOTTEN RY (NYW&B) ARCARA	07	73	50

Railroad/Railfan

LITERATURE REVIEWS

RD	RAILROAD LITERATURE BY ROAD	M	Y	P
	WHEN THE WESTCHESTER WAS NEW (NYW&B)	05	65	36
	WESTCHESTERS FORGOTTON RAILWAY (NYW&B)	10	62	48
O&K	CANNEL CARRIER (OHIO & KENTUCKY) SULZER	03	47	75
O-MS	OAKDALE-MCDONALD STREET RAILWAY GALBRAIT	02	69	43
ODOM	NSO, OLD DOMINION & CONNECTIONS PRINCE	10	73	33
OS	LAST WHISTLE (OS) WAGNER	12	74	59
P&LE	PITTSBURGH & LAKE ERIE RAILROAD MCLEAN	07	81	17
P&N	PIEDMONT & NORTHERN:GREAT ELECTRIC SYSTE	04	75	10
	PIEDMONT PRODIGY (P&N) LYNCH	10	54	60
P&O	CENTURY OF RAILROADING IN CRAWFORD NOTCH	01	76	61
P&W	BLACKSTONE VALLEY LINE (P&W) LEWIS	02	74	60
P*	PULLMAN CO: PRIVATE CAR & SPECIAL TRAIN	04	75	62
PA&HR	FROM THE HILLS TO THE HUDSON(PA&HR)LUCAS	01	45	77
PCOA	SHIPS AND NARROW GAUGE RAILS:STORY PCOA	11	64	48
PD&Y	TROLLEYS TO YORK BEACH CUMMINGS	09	65	39
PE	TROLLEY DAYS IN PASADENA (PE) SEIMS	09	83	14
	RED CAR DAYS:MEMORIES OF PE LONG	05	84	13
	PACIFIC ELECTRIC BIG RED CARS PHILLIPS	07	67	40
	PACIFIC ELECTRIC IN TRANSITION 1911 REPR	08	68	37
	TRACTIONS OF THE ORANGE EMPIRE (PE) SWET	03	68	35
	PACIFIC ELECTRIC IN POMONA SWETT	12	69	43
	OFFICIAL CAR RECORDS:PACIFIC ELECTRIC RY	06	65	33
	LINES OF PACIFIC ELECTRIC:NORTHERN & EAS	10	76	56
	MT LOWE PICTORIAL (PE) MOREAU	09	65	39
	LOCAL LINES OF PE:PASADENA, LONG BEACH	10	62	48
	LINES OF PACIFIC ELECTRIC-WESTERN DIV	10	64	41
	LIFE & TIMES OF PACIFIC ELECTRIC WALKER	03	84	12
	CARS OF PE,CITY AND SUBURBAN CARS SWETT	04	65	45
	CARS OF PACIFIC ELECTRIC,INTERURBAN & DE	12	65	37
	CARS OF PE VOL 1:CITY & SUBURBAN CARS RE	01	76	28
PECO	BELLS & WHISTLES IN OLD PERRY (PECO)	SU	75	10R
PGE	PGE: RAILWAY TO THE NORTH RAMSEY	10	64	42
PJM&NY	MINISINK VALLEY EXPRESS (PJM&NY) BEST	08	56	72
	MINISINK VALLEY EXPRESS (PJM&NY) BEST	02	68	61
PLR	MAINES FAST ELECTRIC RR: PLR CUMMINGS	07	68	37
PLTC	PLATTSBURGH TRACTION COMPANY BORRUP	07	72	39
PM	PERE MARQUETTE RAILROAD COMPANY IVES	11	70	43
PPNJT	TROLLEYS ACROSS THE SAND DUNES (PPNJT)	03	78	29
PRR	REMARKABLE 661 ZIMMERMANN	02	78	57
	PRR: FLEET OF MODERNISM GARDNER	07	74	44
	UNDER PENNSY WIRES (2ND ED) CARLETON	07	82	12
	THREE FEET ON THE PANHANDLE (PRR)KOEHLER	01	84	26
	UNDER PENNSY WIRES CARLETON	04	78	10R
	REMARKABLE 661 QP#6 ZIMMERMANN	05	78	12R
	PENNSY STEAM & SEMAPHORES WESTING	09	75	61
	RIDING THE PENNSY TO RUIN	11	71	57
	PENNSYLVANIA RAILROADS K4'S ALBRECT	05	68	50
	PENNSY POWER II STAUFER	07	69	58
	WORLD FAMOUS HORSESHOE CURVE & ALTOONA	12	73	61
	PENNSYLVANIAS BLUE RIBBON FLEET OF E-W F	02	76	61
	STUDY OF PRR K4 LOCOMOTIVE ALBRECHT	11	77	60
	SMOKE STEAM & CINDERS (PRR) SHAFER	07	77	58
	PENNSY POWER:STEAM & ELEC LOCOS 1900-57	04	63	50
	PENNSYLVANIA RR: THE EARLY YEARS BROOKS	12	64	36
	PENNSY: A TO T CARLESON	10	62	38

RD	RAILROAD LITERATURE BY ROAD	M	Y	P
	I REMEMBER PENNSY WOOD	02	74	37
	HISTORY OF PASS & THROUGH CAR SERV PRR	10	74	62
	HISTORY OF PRR FT WAYNE SHOPS RICE	04	67	52
	KEYSTONE STEAM & ELECTRIC (PRR) EDSON	03	75	61
	MAN HAUPT, THE (PRR) WARD	04	74	60
	MANY FACES OF PENNSY K4 PENNYPACKER	09	87	16
	BROAD STREET STATION, PHILADELPHIA (PRR)	01	77	56
	+ MORE DIESELS ROAR ON THE FORMER PENNSY	10	87	13
	FIFTY BEST OF PRR DAVIS	10	78	65
	K4 RESTORATION & RETURN TO SERVICE MARK1	09	87	29
PRT	SURFACE CARS OF PHILADELPHIA:1911-65 COX	12	65	37
	SURFACE CARS OF PHILADELPHIA: 1911-65 CO	02	66	38
PS&N	PITTSBURG SHAWMUT & NORTHERN RR CO PIETR	05	70	58
PSER	PUGET SOUND ELECTRIC RAILWAY SWETT	04	61	44
PSRY	RIDE A MILE & SMILE THE WHILE:HIST PSRY	02	78	48
PSTC	RED ARROW (PSTC) DEGRAW	03	73	58
PVRR	BELLS & WHISTLES IN OLD PERRY (PVRR)	SU	75	10R
R	READING POWER PICTORIAL PENNYPACKER	07	74	43
	READINGS VICTORIAN STATIONS LEWIS	10	77	09R
	READING'S T1:AN UNUSUAL NORTHERN DIRKES	12	87	30
	RULER OF THE READING: LIFE OF F.B. GOWEN	02	48	117
	READING STEAM PICTORIAL PENNYPACKER	10	64	42
	HISTORY OF THE LOCOS OF THE READING CO.	10	46	61
	LOCOMOTIVES OF THE READING 1836-1923 WAR	10	63	41
	CENTURY OF READING MOTIVE POWER, A	09	41	82
R&AE	RIVERSIDE & ARLINGTON ELECTRIC RY SWETT	06	63	39
R&SB	ROYAL BLUE LINE (R&SB) GORDON	12	62	53
RAL	RED ARROW: FIRST 100 YEARS 1848-1948	01	86	14
RBC	CIRCUS KINGS:OUR RINGLING FAMILY STORY	08	60	51
RG	RIO GRANDE:MAINLINE OF THE ROCKIES BEEBE	10	62	37
RI	ROCK ISLAND IN IOWA DONOVAN	04	64	62
	GREAT ROCK ISLAND ROUTE GARDNER	09	75	61
	IRON ROAD TO EMPIRE (ROCK ISLAND) HAYES	06	54	103
RIC	RHODE ISLAND COMPANY PART 1:EQUIPMENT RO	02	66	38
RL&B	ROCHESTER LOCKPORT & BUFFALO RR 1908-31	02	64	42
RMRY	SASKATCHEWANS PIONEER ST CARS: RMRY HATC	07	72	39
RS&E	ROCHESTER SYRACUSE & EASTERN MCFARLANE	10	61	51
	ROCHESTER SYRACUSE & EASTERN GORDON	04	62	54
RU	RUTLAND ROAD SHAUGHNESSY	12	64	34
RVA	ROCK-A-BYE BABY:HISTORY OF RVA TABER	04	73	58
RY	RAYONIER INC:RRING IN THE NORTHWEST PINE	10	64	44
S	SOUTHERN: PS4 CLASS PACIFIC DRAWINGS	12	74	59
	SOUTHERN RAILWAY PANORAMA KRAMER	01	79	14R
	SOUTHERN STEAM SPECIALS EAGLESON	01	71	47
	SOUTHERN RAILWAY SYSTEM:STEAM LOCOS & BO	07	65	54
	WRECK OF OLD 97 (S) CLEMMER	02	64	50
	LOCOMOTIVE 4501 (S) MORGAN	04	69	48
	SOUTHERN STYLE (SOUTHERN) TRACKSIDE VID	01	86	31
S&NY	STORY OF SUSQUEHANNA & NEW YORK. KASEMAN	03	80	16
	STORY OF SUSQUEHANNA & NEW YORK KASEMAN	07	65	55
	STORY OF SUSQUEHANNA & NEW YORK(REPRINT)	06	64	57
	STORY OF THE SUSQUEHANNA & NEW YORK	12	41	85
S&RV	TROLLEY DAYS IN SEATTLE (S&RV) BLANCHARD	02	66	38
SCA	CAMBRIAS TROLLEYS (SCA) ROHERBECK	05	77	52
SCC&RR	RAILROAD COMES OF AGE (SCC&RR) LANGLEY	09	70	50

STEPHANS_RAILROAD_DIRECTORY

Railroad/Railfan

LITERATURE REVIEWS

RD	RAILROAD LITERATURE BY ROAD	M	Y	P
	BEST FRIEND OF CHARLESTON (SCC&RR) LANGL	09	70	50
SCCE	SUDBURY STREETCARS (SCCE) KNOWLES	09	84	14
SCEC	IRON MEN AND COPPER WIRES (SCEC) MEYERS	07	84	17
SCHEN	TROLLEYS: THE FORGOTTEN TRANSPORTATION	12	68	39
SD&S	SAN DIEGOS SOUTH BAY INTERURBAN (SD&S)	12	87	29
SEL&B	STEUBENVILLE, EAST LIVERPOOL, & BEAVER V	03	69	30
SERR	STARK'S LAST INTERURBANS (SERR) EAKIN	09	84	15
SF&NV	NAPA VALLEY ROUTE (SF&NV) SWETT	10	75	51
SFM	PEOPLES RAILWAY (SFM) PERLES	03	82	16
	RED TRAINS IN EAST BAY (SFM) FORD	03	78	29
	TOURS OF DISCOVERY:SF MUNI ALBUM PERLES	05	85	15
	SAN FRANCISCOS DECORATED CABLE CARS STIN	10	75	60
	SAN FRANCISCO STREET CARS 1944-64 (SFM)	12	68	39
	SAN FRANCISCO MUNICIPAL RY:1912-44 SEVER	12	68	39
	PEOPLES RAILWAY, HISTORY OF MUNI OF SF	09	81	15
	INSIDE MUNI (SFM) MC KANE	09	82	14
	KEY ROUTE PART 2 TRANS BAY COMMUTING SFM	07	86	12
	CABLE CARS OF SAN FRANCISCO (SFM)	06	71	55
SIE	SIERRA RAILWAY DEANE	04	61	56
	HOLLYWOOD IN THE MOTHER LODE (SIE) JENSE	10	74	61
	MOTHER LODE SHORTLINE (SIE)	07	71	61
SIMRY	STATEN ISLAND MIDLAND RY	08	60	33
SJ&E	RAILROAD THAT LIGHTED S CALIFORNIA--SJ&E	06	65	52
SJ&GI	FIRST STEAM WEST OF BIG MUDDY (SJ&GI)	03	71	58
SJ&LC	VERMONTS COVERED BRIDGE RD (SJ&LC) LEWIS	03	75	61
SJ&LCO	VERMONT'S COVERED BRIDGE ROAD (SJ&LCO)	SP	75	13R
SLE	SHORE LINE ELECTRIC RY PART 2 CUMMINGS	06	62	29
SLO	HISTORY OF SAN LUIS OBISPO TELEGRAM-TRIB	08	56	72
SM&N	SANDUSKY MILAN & NORWALK ELECTRIC RAILWY	04	64	38
SN	SACRAMENTO NORTHERN: SPECIAL # 26 WILCOX	05	82	08
	SACRAMENTO NORTHERN (REPRINT) SWETT	06	71	55
	SACRAMENTO NORTHERN ALBUM SWETT	08	64	59
	SACRAMENTO NORTHERN SWETT	04	63	33
	CARS OF SACRAMENTO NORTHERN SWETT	04	64	38
SOMRR	SILK ALONG STEEL: STORY OF SOMRR LEWIS	01	77	56
SOO	STEAM TRAINS OF THE SOO. SUPREY	10	77	10R
	STEAM TRAINS OF THE SOO SUPREY	04	63	50
	STEAM TRAINS ON THE SOO (2ED ED) SUPREY	12	64	36
	LITTLE JEWEL (SOO) ABBEY	05	85	16
	FRIENDLY SOO, THE SUPREY	02	55	68
SOP	SOUTH PARK LINE: CONCISE HISTORY CHAPPEL	10	75	60
	HISTORIC ALPINE TUNNEL (SOP) HELMERS	08	64	44
SP	TRAGIC TRAIN:CITY OF SAN FRANCISCO DENEV	02	78	57
	SOUTHERN PACIFIC REVIEW 1983-85 STRAPAC	11	86	19
	RAILS IN THE SHADOW OF MT SHASTA SIGNOR	09	84	16
	SOUTHERN PACIFIC 1901-85 HOFSOMMER	05	87	16
	SOUTHERN PACIFIC MOTIVE POW ANNUAL 1974	04	78	11R
	SOUTHERN PACIFIC MOTIVE POW ANNUAL 66-67	06	67	53
	SAN FRANCISCO BAY FERRYBOATS (SP) HARLAN	11	67	59
	SOUTHERN PACIFIC MOTIVE POW ANNUAL 1967	12	68	59
	THREE BARRELS OF STEAM (4-10-2) BOYTON	12	73	61
	SOUTHERN PACIFIC REVIEW 1977 STRAPAC	05	79	13
	SOUTHERN PACIFIC REVIEW 1978-79 STRAPAC	05	80	18
	TUNNEL 13 (SP) CHIPMAN	12	77	61
	SOUTHERN PACIFIC MOTIVE POW ANNUAL 74-76	11	77	55

RD	RAILROAD LITERATURE BY ROAD	M	Y	P
	THOSE DAYLIGHT 4-8-4'S (SP) CHURCH	06	77	56
	PENINSULA SERVICE (SP COMMUTER TRAINS)	02	58	74
	SOUTHERN PACIFIC'S FIRST CENTURY SP	04	56	73
	SP STEAM LOCOMOTIVES:PICTORAL ANTHOLOGY	02	63	37
	HISTORIC SOUTHERN PACIFIC CARS WAYNER	04	74	60
	CAB-FORWARD: STORY OF SP ARTICULATED LOC	06	73	53
	CHARLES MORGAN & DEV OF SOUTHERN TRANSPO	11	68	50
	CENTURY OF SP STEAM LOCOMOTIVES DUNSCOMB	10	68	48
	CENTURY OF SP LOCOMOIVES DUNSCOMB	10	63	40
	DIESELS OF THE ESPEE VOL 1 CHATHAM	05	76	62
	DONNER PASS: SP SIERRA CROSSING SIGNOR	05	86	11
	DIESELS OF ESPEE:V1 ALCO PA'S CORTANI	SP	76	08R
	SP-I:BAY AREA COMMUTERS SUNDAY RIVER	05	85	21
	SP-II: SMALL ENGINES SUNDAY RIVER	05	85	21
	SP-III: PACIFICS TO MOUNTAINS SUNDAY RIV	05	85	21
	SP-IV: THE BIG ONES SUNDAY RIVER	05	85	21
SP&S	SPOKANE PORTLAND & SEATTLE RY WOOD	03	75	59
SPC	SOUTH PACIFIC COAST MAC GREGOR	03	69	50
	NARROW GAUGE PORTRAIT S PACIFIC COAST	03	76	61
SPM	SP OF MEXICO AND THE WEST COAST ROUTE	07	87	23
SPSF	SPSF MOTIVE POWER '86 PREPARE TO MERGE	09	87	17
SR&RL	TWO-FOOT CYCLOPEDIA VOL2:SR&RL #23 JANSE	09	78	58
	RIDE THE SANDY RIVER CORNWALL	08	73	61
SR&W	BELLS & WHISTLES IN OLD PERRY (SR&W)	SU	75	10R
ST&E	SLOW TIRED & EASY RR (ST&E) DAVIS	05	77	56
STRR	ROAD TO PARADISE (STRR) MOEDINGER	10	72	63
	ROAD TO PARADISE: STORY OF STRASBURG RR	09	66	52
	ROAD TO PARADISE:STORY OF STRASBURG RR	08	62	57
SY&S	SYRACUSE & SUBURBAN RAILROAD JOHNSON	07	68	37
T&IRY	TOLEDO & INDIANA RAILWAY KING	05	83	14
T&NE	TROY & NEW ENGLAND RY CO 1895-1925 VIENS	05	77	52
TAT	ACROSS NY BY TROLLEY:3RD AVE RAILWAY SYS	09	84	16
TCRT	TWIN CITY RAPID TRANSIT PICTORIAL (TCRT)	05	85	16
TCRY	TORONTO CIVIC RAILWAY:ILLUSTRATED HIST	11	87	23
TF	MEMORIES OF A MT SHORTLINE: STORY OF TF	12	76	55
TG&B	TORONTO GREY & BRUCE RY MCILWRAITH	06	64	57
TLL	THUNDER LAKE NARROW GAUGE '93-'41 HUSTON	08	61	33
TM	DAY THEY SHOOK THE PLUM TREE (TM) LEWIS	10	63	40
TPC&L	TOLEDO PORT CLINTON & LAKESIDE RY HILTON	08	64	59
TTCO	PASSENGERS MUST NOT RIDE ON FENDERS TTCO	08	74	50
	TT '28:ELEC RY SERVICES OF TTCO 1928 BRO	09	68	42
	FIFTY YEARS OF PROGRESSIVE TRANS:TTCO	11	75	56
TUCK	TUCKERTON RR:CHRONICAL OF TRANSPORT TO N	06	74	58
U&D	ULSTER & DELAWARE BEST	11	72	62
	CATSKILL SOUVENIR 1879 (U&D) HELMER	04	70	58
UP	UNION PACIFIC 3985 BOTKIN	11	85	22
	UNION PACIFIC STREAMLINERS RANKS	05	75	61
	TURBINES WESTWARD (UP) LEE	W	76	12R
	WESTERN INCIDENTS ON THE UP SEYMOUR	02	71	55
	UP STEAM LOCOMOTIVE DIRECTORY KOENIGSBUR	02	68	60
	UNION PACIFIC:BUILDING OF 1ST TRANSCONTI	07	69	58
	WESTWARD TO PROMONTORY:BUILD UP ACROSS	08	69	32
	UNION PACIFIC: HELL ON WHEELS ! CARSON	08	69	32
	ROARING U50'S..UP TWIN DIESELS KEEKLEY	07	79	14
	UNION PACIFIC 8444 KINDIG	05	79	10

Railroad/Railfan

LITERATURE REVIEWS

RD	RAILROAD LITERATURE BY ROAD		M	Y	P
	SHERMAN HILL (UP)	EHERNBERGER	11	79	14
	UP MOTIVE POWER REVIEW 1968-77	WAGNER	03	80	15
	SMOKE ABOVE THE PLAINS: UP KANSAS DIVISN		05	66	45
	UP STEAM LOCOS INCLUDING OSL OWRR&N LA&L		06	61	60
	UNION PACIFIC RAILROAD:CASE OF PREMATURE		08	61	33
	TURBINES WEST (UP)	LEE	12	76	54
	SMOKE ACROSS THE PRAIRIE (UP)	EHERNBERGER	05	65	52
	SMOKE OVER THE DIVIDE:UP WYOMING DIVISIO		11	65	52
	SMOKE DOWN THE CANYONS (UP)	EHERNBERGER	11	66	48
	HOW WE BUILT THE UP RAILWAY & OTHER RY P		05	65	52
	MOTIVE POWER OF UNION PACIFIC	KRATVILLE	02	60	38
	BIG BLOW--UP TURBINES	KEEKLEY	11	78	55
	UP STEAM EXPRESS: THE 3985 CHALLENGER		01	85	22
	UP 6900'S THE CENTENNIALS	VIDEO RAILS	09	85	60
USR	TROLLEYGRAMS (USR)	BORRUP	07	83	14
	UNION STREET RAILWAY	CUMMINGS	01	84	24
	UNION STREET RAILWAY (USR)	CUMMINGS	01	81	16
V	VIRGINIAN RAILROAD	REID	02	62	54
V&S	VALLEY & SILETZ RAILROAD	CULP	04	59	82
V&SRY	CORDWOOD LTD:HISTORY OF V&SRY	HEARN	10	66	53
V&T	VIRGINIA & TRUCKEE, CITY & COMSTOCK TIME		07	49	109
	VIRGINIA & TRUCKEE: A STORY OF VIRGINIA		12	55	54
VCO	VENTURA COUNTY RAILWAY	MAGUIRE	12	61	52
VIA	+ F-UNITS WINTER IN CANADA :GREG SCHOLL		10	87	12
W	WABASH IN IOWA	DONOVAN	03	65	62
W&LE	RECOLLECTIONS OF W&LE AT NORWALK OHIO		01	71	47
W&NB	MUNCY VALLEY LIFELINE (W&NB)	TABER	04	69	50
W&OD	RAILS TO THE BLUE RIDGE (W&OD)	HARWOOD	03	70	52
	WASHINGTON & OLD DOMINION RR	WILLIAMS	09	71	49
	RAILS TO THE BLUE RIDGE: W&OD RR	HARWOOD	12	63	42
W-B	MINING TOWN TROLLEYS (W-B)	FRANCAVIGLIA	01	85	17
W-BRY	WILKES-BARRE RYS CO	ROHRBECK	11	75	56
WA&G	WELLSVILLE ADDISON & GALETON RR	LEWIS	05	72	55
WB&H	WILKES-BARRE & HAZLETON RY	QUINBY	05	73	61
WI&W	WINCHESTER & WESTERN RAILROAD	WINNEMORE	05	76	55
WM	WESTERN MARYLAND STEAM POWER	PRICE	09	85	08
	WM:FIREBALLS & BLACK DIAMONDS	COOK	03	82	15
	WESTERN MARYLAND DIESELS	JAHN	03	80	16
	STEAM IN THE ALLEGHENIES:WESTERN MARYLND		05	80	17
WNY&P	WESTERN NY AND PENNSYLVANIA RAILROAD		09	43	161
WO	OVER THE RAILS TO WOODSTOCK (WO)	MEAD	04	68	51
WP	PORTRAIT OF A SILVER LADY (CZ)	MACGREGOR	02	78	10R
	WESTERN PACIFICS DIESEL YEARS	STRAPAC	07	81	16
	SKUNK RAILROAD (WP)	TRANS-ANGLO	02	66	38
	LOCOMOTIVES OF THE WESTERN PACIFIC		05	55	53
	D-DAY ON THE WESTERN PACIFIC	STAFF	01	83	18
	ECHOES DOWN THE CANYON:WP JOURNAL '68-86		12	87	30
WP&Y	WHITE PASS & YUKON ROUTE: PICTORIAL HIST		11	80	20
	GOLD RUSH NARROW GAUGE (WP&Y)	MARTIN	06	70	66
WSL	WEST SIDE--NARROW GAUGE IN SIERRA	FARREL	11	80	21
WW&F	WW&F TWO FOOTER:HAIL & FAREWELL	THURLOW	04	66	51
WWVR	CANAL ROUTE (WWVR)	LASTING IMPRESSION	05	84	15

512

RAILROAD MODEL BOOKS		M	Y	P
ADVANCED MODEL RAILROADING	HERTZ	02	56	72
BOOK OF RULES FOR MODEL RAILROADERS		07	44	139
BRIDGE & TRESTLE HANDBOOK FOR MRRERS		03	73	59
BUILDING A MODEL PASSENGER TRAIN		01	41	121
COLLECTING MODEL TRAINS	HERTZ	06	57	67
EASY TO BUILD MODEL RR FREIGHT CARS	KALM	07	72	61
ELECTRICAL HANDBOOK FOR MODEL RAILROADER		06	56	46
FUN WITH A MODEL RAILROAD	SAGLE	11	44	57
GREENBERGS PRICE GUIDE TO LIONEL TRAINS		12	77	61
HANDBOOK OF OLD AMERICAN TOYS, A	HERTZ	06	48	114
HO RAILROAD THAT GROWS (2ED EDITION)	KAL	02	73	61
IDEAS AND STANDARDS FOR HO TROLLEY LAYOU		03	69	30
LIONEL TRAINS:STD OF THE WORLD 1900-1945		06	77	56
MODEL CARS AND LOCOMOTIVES	BEAL & TAYLOR	02	41	91
MODEL RAILROADER CYCLOPEDIA 1941 EDITION		01	41	121
MODEL RAILROADER CYCLOPEDIA 1944 EDITION		04	44	81
MODEL RAILROADING	LIONEL	11	51	95
MODEL RAILROADING HANDBOOK	SCHLECHER	11	75	61
MODEL RAILROADS	ALEXANDER	02	41	90
MODEL RAILWAY ENGINES	MINNS	02	70	54
MODEL RAILWAYS 1838-1939	ELLIS	08	63	46
MODEL RAILWAYS AS A PASTIME	POLLINGER	10	60	52
RIDING THE TINPLATE RAILS	HERTZ	04	45	105
ROLLING STOCK PLAN BOOK (REVISED)	CARSTE	12	61	43
SCALE MODEL RAILROADING	WHITE	01	65	59
SEVEN FOOT MODEL TRAIN BOOK	RIGBY	06	51	123
SO YOU WANT TO BUILD A LIVE STEAM LOCOMO		01	75	35
TOY COLLECTOR	HERTZ	03	70	54
TRACTION GUIDEBOOK FOR MODEL RAILROADERS		10	74	44
TRACTION PLANBOOK & PHOTO ALBUM	CARSTENS	11	64	44
WORLD LOCOMOTIVE MODELS	DOW	01	74	61

RAILROAD VIDEOS	M	Y	P
+ VIDEO NEW ARRIVALS +	09	87	28
+ "THE CANADIAN" (CP) :RAIL INNOVATIONS	12	87	33
+ 1218 FREIGHT (N&W) :MAIN LINE	09	87	28
+ 1218:A NEW BEGINNING (N&W) :TRACKSIDE	12	87	33
+ 18 WHEELS OF STEEL (N&W) :HOPWELL PROD	09	87	28
+ AWSOME A-PART 1 (N&W) :BERKSHIRE VIDEO	11	87	36
+ BCR STEAM WITH 2860 & 3716 :GREG SCHOL	10	87	12
+ BERKSHIRE--BEST OF BREED (NKP) :BERKSH	11	87	36
+ CHAMA TURN (D&RGW) :GREEN FROG	12	87	33
+ COAL TRAIN (N&W) :MAIN LINE	09	87	29
+ COLLIER CROSSING :DAYLIGHT PRODUCTIONS	12	87	34
+ DIESELS '86 :GREEN FROG	12	87	33
+ F-UNITS WINTER IN CANADA :GREG SCHOLL	10	87	12
+ FANS FILMAKERS & STEAM TRAINS :DAYLIGH	12	87	34
+ GREAT RAILWAY JOURNEYS :PENTREX	11	87	36
+ LIGHT PACIFIC (L&N) :LASTING IMPRESSIO	10	87	13
+ LIGHT PACIFIC:SECOND SECTION (L&N):LAS	10	87	13
+ MORE DIESELS ROAR ON THE FORMER PENNSY	10	87	13
+ N&W + SOU = NS DIESELS :JMJ	10	87	13
+ N&W 1218 REBUILT & ROANOKE BOUND :GREG	09	87	28
+ NEW GEORGA RAILROAD :GREEN FROG	12	87	32
+ PACIFIC PRINCESS (L&N):BERKSHIRE VIDEO	11	87	36
+ PACIFIC THROUGH THE CUMBERLANDS :LASTI	10	87	13
+ PART ONE: FAIRWELL TO STEAM :NORTHLAND	12	87	34
+ ALONG THE RIO GRANDE (D&RGW) :GREEN FR	12	87	33

LITERATURE REVIEWS

RAILROAD VIDEOS		M	Y	P
# PART TWO: RAILROADERS	:NORTHLAND HOME	12	87	34
# RAILS WIRES & PANTOGRAPHS	:RAIL INNOVA	12	87	34
# SEVEN SIX FIVE (NKP)	:LASTING IMPRESSI	10	87	13
# SNOW PLOW WITH CN F7'S	:GREG SCHOLL VI	10	87	13
# STEAM IN THE 50'S	:GREEN FROG	12	87	32
# THE A AND THE J (N&W)	:TRACKSIDE VIDEO	12	87	33
# THE MIGHTY J (N&W)	:BERKSHIRE VIDEOGRA	11	87	36
# THUNDER ON CHRISTAINSBURG MT	:MAIN LINE	09	87	28
# TWILIGHT OF THE RIO GRANDE NARROW GAUG		12	87	33
# VIDEO CLASSICS 1218 (N&W)	:VIDEO CLASS	09	87	28
# WORK TRAIN TO SILVERTON (D&RGW)	:GREEN	12	87	33
##DESIGN YOUR OWN TRAIN##COMPUTER PROGRM		11	87	16
18 WHEELS OF STEEL.(N&W)	HOPWELL PRODUC	10	87	13
4070-THE VALLEY LINE	HOPWELL	07	80	19
4449 : RETURN OF THE DAYLIGHT	VIDEO	11	84	24
4449 DAYLIGHT DELIGHT	HOPEWELL	03	85	17
ACE OF BLACK DIAMONDS	HOPEWELL PRODUCT	03	86	06
ALASKA RAILROAD	:PENTREX	12	87	34
ALCOS IRON ORE & MORE	MARK I	01	87	36
BERKSHIRES MONTAGE SERIES: VOL 1	:BERKSH	12	87	35
BERKSHIRES MONTAGE SERIES: VOL 2	:BERKSH	12	87	35
BIG LITTLE RAILROAD (CNJ)	EVERYTHING VID	05	85	20
BRIDGES TO BUFFALO	HOPWELL PRODUCTIONS	11	85	23
BRITISH COLUMBIA RAILWAY	PENTREX	09	86	26
BURLINGTON NORTHERN RR CLASSICS (1 TO 5)		11	86	32
C&O 614 COAL TRAINS	GREG SCHOLL	03	86	06
CANAL ROUTE (WWVR)	LASTING IMPRESSION	05	84	15
CAPITOL LIMITED '79	HOPEWELL	07	80	19
CP'S LAGGAN SUB	RAIL INNOVATIONS	05	87	20
DIESELS ROAR ON THE FORMER PENNSY	JMJ	05	87	20
EYE ON TRAINS VOL III	VIDEOPERIODICALS	07	86	16
FR BRITISH: TITFIELD THUNDERBOLT		12	53	06
661 AN AMERICAN CLASSIC	AVANTI PROD	01	85	21
GLORY MACHINES	HERRON RAIL SERVICES	07	85	15
GLORY MACHINES II.	:HERRON RAIL SERVICES	10	87	15
K4 RESTORATION & RETURN TO SERVICE	MARK1	09	87	29
LACKAWANNA LEGACY	RUN 8 VIDEO	11	85	24
LAST BREATH OF FIRE	HOPEWELL PRODUCTIONS	09	87	29
LIFE BEGINS AT FORTY	HOPEWELL PRODUCTION	01	87	36
LINES INTO LOUISVILLE	LASTING IMPRESSION	05	86	13
MAJESTIC MIKADO	BERKSHIRE VIDEOGRAPHY	03	87	26
MARCH TO HINTON	VIDEO RAILS	03	86	06
MIGHTY "J" PART 1,2,3 (N&W)	SUNDAY RIVER	09	84	20
MINES MILLS AND METRO TRANSIT	GLORIA MUN	07	87	25
N&W A 1218	JMJ	09	87	29
N&W J 611	JMJ PRODUCTIONS	03	83	12
N&W STEAM IN ACTION VIDEO		07	84	21
NORFOLK & WESTERN 611	VIDEO RAILS	05	86	13
OVER UNDER AROUND & THROUGH THE CLINCHFI		09	85	60
PCC TRILOGY	EMPIRE VIDEO	01	86	31
PHOENIX ENGINE (2 PARTS)	HOPEWELL	03	82	17
RAILFAIR SACRAMENTO 1981	YOUNGSOUND	03	82	17
RAINHILL: 150 YEARS ON THE MAIN LINE		03	82	17
ROPES AND RAILS	TRANSIT GLORIA MUNDI	07	87	25
SNOW PLOW WITH CN F7'S	:GREG SCHOLL VIDE	12	87	36

RAILROAD VIDEOS		M	Y	P
SNOW TRAIN	ROGER HOLMES	05	86	14
SOUTH AFRICAN STEAM COLLECTION	GREG SCHO	03	87	26
SOUTHERN STYLE (SOUTHERN)	TRACKSIDE VID	01	86	31
SP-I:BAY AREA COMMUTERS	SUNDAY RIVER	05	85	21
SP-II: SMALL ENGINES	SUNDAY RIVER	05	85	21
SP-III: PACIFICS TO MOUNTAINS	SUNDAY RIV	05	85	21
SP-IV: THE BIG ONES	SUNDAY RIVER	05	85	21
STREAMLINERS OF YESTERYEAR	VIDEO RAILS	07	87	24
TRAIN DISPATCHER VIDEO GAME	SIGNAL	07	85	12
UP 6900'S THE CENTENNIALS	VIDEO RAILS	09	85	60
UP STEAM EXPRESS: THE 3985 CHALLENGER		01	85	22
WORLDS FAIR DAYLIGHT 1984	VIDEO RAILS	03	85	17

Railroad/ Railfan

BILL OF LADING — GENERAL RAILROADING

This section is the catch-all for all those miscellaneous items that do not clearly fall into a specific category. We initially attempted to divide this into model related and prototype related but finally gave up as many were both. This section really has to be "read" to get the full benefit from it. Many items appear here as well as under a specific heading.

We have specified non-fiction narratives as a separate subsection. Railroad also had interesting fiction. These stories are listed here. If space permitted the authors last name was noted at the end of the descriptor line.

The people section identifies interesting things about real railroad people as well as authors who have became experts of today.

Collecting as an entity to Railroading is addressed here—from models to full size equipment, from stamps to dishes to timetables.

Tinplate & Toy Trains had few entries in Railroad so they are included here.

Lastly Railroad Photography techniques are in this section.

MANIFEST — GENERAL RAILROADING

DETAILED CONSIST	PAGE
GENERAL RAILROADING	515
GENERAL RAILROADING NON-FICTION	543
RAILROAD PEOPLE	560
GENERAL RAILROADING FICTION	566
RAILROADANIA COLLECTING	575
PHOTOGRAPHY	576
TOY AND TINPLATE TRAINS	576

GENERAL RAILROADING

GENERAL RAILROADING	M	Y	P
A FEW OF THE COMPONENTS OF CONRAIL PHOTO	06	76	48
AAR COMPLY WITH STANDARDIZED SPECIFICATI	06	38	74
AAR: MORE DETAILS ABOUT	08	38	94
ABANDONED RAILROADS	05	34	131
ABANDONED RAILROADS AND RR STATIONS	04	34	133
ABANDONED RR PROJECTS-DIED BEFORE BIRTH	04	32	30
ABANDONED RR: RIGHT OF WAYS? WHAT HAPPEN	10	38	61
ABBREVIATIONS OF SOME RAILROADS	08	37	58
ACE 3000:DISCUSSION	01	82	24
ACE AND 614	05	85	61
ACE PUTS STEAM TO THE TEST (ACE 3000)	05	85	34
ADVANCEMENTS/PROMOTIONS IN RAILROADING	02	30	472
ADVERTISING: WARTIME/VARIOUS ROADS	05	43	08
AERIAL SURVEYS FOR CANADIAN RAILWAYS	04	50	46
AFTER THE GRASSHOPPERS WE HAD JIM HILL	12	78	20
AIR COMPRESSOR LUBRICATION OF STEAM LOCO	10	51	58
AIR COMPRESSORS ON DIESEL LOCOMOTIVES	02	53	52
AIR COMPRESSORS: STEAM LOCOMOTIVE CARE	09	48	73
AIR DISTRIBUTION IN STEAM LOCOMOTIVES	10	48	60
AIR FILTERS & BRAKE VENT VALVES	06	51	62
AIR LINE ROUTES	12	37	55
AIR POLLUTION AND MASS TRANSIT	01	72	05
AIRBRAKE SYSTEMS	12	48	63
AIRCONDITIONED TRAINS	08	46	55
AIRLINES VS RAILROADS: READER COMMENTS	11	50	119
AIRLINES WINNING THE PASSENGER BATTLE	07	50	12
ALASKA MUSEUM LINE	01	74	09
ALCO COUNTRY--C&NW	08	77	43R
ALCO'S 50,000 LOCOMOTIVE	10	40	22
ALGOMA CENTRAL RAILROAD TOUR	12	72	22
ALL QUIET ON THE QUINCY: OPEN LETTER	07	47	48
ALPINE PASS-ABANDONED 20 YEARS-REVISITED	03	38	64
ALPINE TUNNEL ROUTE DSP&P	06	41	06
ALTOONA'S K4 UNDER STEAM (PRR)	07	87	42
AMERICA'S FASTEST TRAINS-LISTING	06	33	44
AMERICA'S FIRST RAILROADS	10	33	33
AMERICA'S MILITARY RAILROADS	06	37	48
AMERICAN LOCOMOTIVE COMPANY	10	48	27
AMERICAN RAIL SPEED RECORD 183.8 MPH NYC	11	66	14
AMERICAN SHORT LINE RAILROAD ASSOCIATION	10	44	78
AMERICAS FIRST BIG TRAIN ROBBERY	12	33	34
AMES MONUMENT	11	36	27
AMTRAK IMPROVED SCHEDULE FOR 1975	01	75	50
AMTRAK PROBLEMS ON THE SP	06	75	42
AMTRAK TRIVIA QUIZ	05	76	19
AMUSEMENT PARK RAILROAD "ROCKET"	04	48	85
AMUSEMENT PARK ROLLER COASTERS	12	49	70
ANDREWS CIVIL WAR RAID	01	32	146
ANDREWS RAID APRIL 12, 1862	07	65	52
ANNUAL SPEED SURVEY 1941	01	42	95
ANNUAL SPEED SURVEY 1942	03	43	10
ANNUAL SPEED SURVEY 1943	03	44	66
ANNUAL SPEED SURVEY 1944	03	45	35
ANNUAL SPEED SURVEY 1945	03	46	40
ANNUAL SPEED SURVEY 1946	04	47	78

GENERAL RAILROADING	M	Y	P
ANNUAL SPEED SURVEY 1948	04	49	08
ANNUAL SPEED SURVEY 1949	04	50	14
ANNUAL SPEED SURVEY 1950	04	51	18
ANNUAL SPEED SURVEY 1951	04	52	14
APRIL 27 AT NORTH FORK (PHOTO SESSION)	09	85	20
AR ABANDONED RAILROADS	07	34	133
AR BRADFORD ELDRED & CUBA RAILROAD	07	34	133
AR KANSAS CITY & MEMPHIS RAILWAY	07	34	133
AR KANSAS CITY NORTHWEST	07	34	133
AR TALLULAH FALLS RAILWAY	07	34	133
ARCH-BAR TRUCKS	12	42	87
ARMISTICE OF WWI SIGNED IN RAIL CAR	05	66	35
ARMY RAILROADERS--MILITARY RAILWAY SERVI	02	43	24
ARMY RAILROADING	01	52	54
ART OF DRIFTING	08	43	48
ART OF RAILROAD WRECKING (DISMANTLING)	07	34	28
ARTIST WITH A CAMERA	10	50	12
ASHVILLE TRAINS ON THE SOUTHERN	10	77	46R
ASSISTANCE TO FARMERS	12	29	55
ASSOCIATION OF AMERICAN RAILROADS	05	39	67
ATC AND ATS	SU	76	05R
ATLANTA BEFORE AMTRAK	F	75	51R
ATLANTIC TYPE LOCOMOTIVES	12	36	55
ATSF STATION MASTER RECALLS LAND RUSH	02	31	447
ATSF WITHDRAWS "CHIEF" NAMES FROM A	05	74	36
AUCTION-JOURNEY'S END FOR PACKAGES	12	51	74
AUCTIONS OF BANKRUPT RRS: HOW THEY WORK	03	36	85
AUTO-TRAIN FIRST OF THE NEW	03	72	04
AUTOGRAPHED LOCOMOTIVES	07	50	06
AUTOMATED SLIDE SHOWS 1	05	86	22
AUTOMATED SLIDE SHOWS 2	07	86	19
AUTOMATIC AIR BRAKE OPERATION	06	66	31
AUTOMATIC FARE COLLECTION ON IC	04	65	10
AUTOMATIC TICKET SELLING MACHINES NYC/LI	12	46	77
AUTOMATIC TRAIN CONTROL: CONTINOUS	06	40	71
AUTOMATIC TRAIN CONTROL: INTERMITTENT	06	40	71
AUTOMATIC TRAIN CONTROLS	02	30	385
AUTOMATIC TRAIN RECORDER SYSTEM: 1921	10	53	117
AUTOMATIC TRAIN STOP	09	50	42
AUTOMATION IN RAILROAD INDUSTRY	10	61	42
AVERAGE FREIGHT CREW	12	31	94
AX FALLS ON PASSENGER TRAINS	07	79	20
B&O MUSEUM AT BALTIMORE MD	08	77	56
BACK YARD RAILROAD	07	39	87
BALDWIN CENTIPEDES	04	73	26
BALDWIN GREAT EDDYSTONE PLANT 100 ANNIV	08	31	33
BALDWIN LOCOMOTIVE WORKS	12	72	20
BANK NOTES WITH TRAINS	09	53	06
BARLOW PLAN: CO-OPERATIVE SYSTEM	01	47	10
BARNUM ORIGINATES MOVING CIRCUS BY RAIL	02	34	37
BATTLE OF THE "ATLANTIC" READER COMMENTS	05	86	05
BATTLE OF THE BLIZZARD GN 1949	12	49	28
BATTLE OF THE GAUGES	12	31	80
BATTLE OF THE GAUGES READER COMMENTS	02	32	426
BATTLE OF THE ROYAL GORGE	12	38	71

Railroad/ Railfan

GENERAL RAILROADING

GENERAL RAILROADING	M	Y	P
BAXTER PASS UINTAH RAILWAY COLORADO	07	40	73
BEACH RAILWAYS OF NEW JERSEY	09	45	62
BEAR CREEK SCENIC RAILROAD VISIT	09	69	16
BEEF (LIVESTOCK) MOVING	12	49	16
BELL TYPE LOCOMOTIVES	02	46	56
BELLS ON STEAM LOCOMOTIVES	12	44	37
BIG ROCK CANDY MOUNTAIN-STORY BEHIND WOR	08	63	32
BIGGER AND FEWER RAILROADS	08	64	39
BILLION DOLLAR SHORT LINE: V&T	09	41	06
BIRNEY CARS	08	44	90
BIRTH OF A LOCOMOTIVE	10	42	06
BLACK SMOKE AND STEAM LOCOMOTIVES	11	78	16
BLACK SMOKE IN STEAM LOCOMOTIVES	03	51	52
BLUE CHINA RAILROAD SETTING OF THE B&O	03	77	47
BOILER BRACING OF STEAM LOCOMOTIVES	11	51	56
BOILER CHECKS ON STEAM LOCOMOTIVES	09	49	50
BOILER CONSTRUCTION	03	43	93
BOILER EXPLOSION D&H 4-6-6-4 1941	02	65	13
BOILER MAINTENANCE AND INSPECTION: STEAM	04	42	57
BOILER PRESSURE GAUGE	07	46	46
BOMBARDIER ACQUIRES ALCO	07	84	26
BONEHEADS--RAILROAD MISTAKES	06	38	60
BONNEVILLE RAILROAD PROJECT	05	46	73
BOOMER'S BAG OF TRICKS	10	41	06
BOOMERS	10	39	06
BOOSTERS FOR STEAM LOCOMOTIVES	12	42	36
BOX CAR ART	07	39	30
BOX-TOP RAILROAD: GENERAL MILLS CEREAL	12	47	120
BRAKE SHOES--THEIR STORY	04	70	36
BRAKE SYSTEMS QUESTIONS ON	04	60	30
BRAKE VENT VALVES	06	51	62
BRAKES ON STEAM LOCOMOTIVES	05	38	13
BRAKES: AB TYPE	02	57	43
BRAKES: AB TYPE VERSUS K2 TRIPLE	12	39	118
BRAKES: AIR BRAKE OPERATION	11	42	58
BRAKES: AIR BRAKE REVOLUTION	11	30	529
BRAKES: LA CHATELIERAUX WATER BRAKE	10	52	65
BRAKES: LOAD-COMPENSATING AIR BRAKES	11	48	55
BRAKES: MODERN AIR BRAKE--LAP VALVE??	02	57	46
BRANCH LINES ARE RAILROAD LIABILITIES	12	72	12
BRAZING SPEEDS UP CYLINDER REPAIRS	01	44	34
BRIDGE OF SIZE-SCOTLAND'S FORTH BRIDGE	10	36	77
BRIDGE TO FAME--UP GEORGETOWN LOOP	07	86	32
BRIDGES--280,000 IN US & CANADA	05	37	43
BRIDGES: STEEL ACROSS THE RIVERS	01	48	08
BRILL	02	48	87
BRITISH COLUMBIAS ELECTRIC LINES	10	46	99
BROTHERHOOD OF LOCOMOTIVE ENGINEERS	05	36	45
BROTHERHOOD RAILWAY CARMEN OF AMERICA	01	46	62
BUDD COMPANY	10	49	12
BUFFALO-HUNTING EXCURSION-SPECIAL TRAINS	11	30	536
BUILDER PLATE COLLECTING	10	67	18
BUILDERS PLATE PHOTOGRAPH L&N	10	67	04
BUILDERS PLATE PHOTOGRAPHS	10	67	01
BUILDERS PLATES-HOW TO TELL THEM	02	74	38

GENERAL RAILROADING	M	Y	P
BUREAU OF RAILWAY ECONOMICS LIBRARY	10	40	31
BURLINGTON ROUTE: AURORA--1948	F	75	18R
BURLINGTON SPECIAL-ACROSS 4 STATES FAST!	09	31	259
C&E HOLDS MIDGET RECORD PRIV STEAM LINES	11	30	494
C&O #614 4-8-4 STEAMS FOR SAFETY	01	81	45
C&O UNLOADING MACHINE (FOR COAL)	02	39	88
CAB SIGNALS	10	52	48
CABOOSE COOKERY	03	72	10
CABOOSE COOKERY-A VANISHING ART PHOTOS	06	55	13
CABOOSE IN A GHOST TOWN UP #3303	08	78	53
CABOOSE RESTAURANT	03	68	36
CABOOSE RIDING PASSES IN THE 1880'S O&LC	10	75	36
CABS OF STEAM LOCOMOTIVES	10	43	10
CAGNEY STEAM LOCOMOTIVES BEING BUILT AGA	04	60	06
CAJON PASS PHOTO ESSAY	01	44	66
CALCULATING SPEED OF TRAIN	04	41	49
CALIFORNIA STATE RR MUSEUM PHOTO ESSAY	02	78	44
CALIFORNIA ZEPHYR (WP)	11	49	15
CALIFORNIA ZEPHYR--25 TH ANNIVERSARY	02	74	22
CAMELBACKS' LAST ROUNDHOUSE	10	54	11
CAMERA STUDIES IN COLOR	01	79	33
CAMP DIX RAILROAD USA	08	38	20
CANADA RAILROAD: STEEL ACROSS CANADA	08	33	80
CANADA RAILWAY SYSTEMS PART 1	11	47	12
CANADA RAILWAY SYSTEMS PART 2	12	47	12
CANADA RED RIVER VALLEY-CANADIAN PACIFIC	05	34	90
CANADA'S FIRST RAILWAY C&SL 1836	08	36	132
CANADIAN PACIFIC PRESIDENT BEATTY	06	31	376
CANADIAN RAILWAYS 150 YEARS OLD	05	78	12
CANADIAN STEAM SHORTLINE (PARK ROAD)	09	66	36
CANADIANS DEMAND COMPLETION OF PGE	02	31	407
CANYON WAR (HILL VS HARRIMAN)	10	56	22
CANYON WAR D&RG VS ATSF	08	32	22
CAPITAL LIMITED PHOTO CONTEST WINNERS	01	80	33
CAR INSPECTOR: QUALIFICATIONS	05	42	61
CAR TRUCKS: 110 YEARS OF	06	42	98
CAREY, BILL-RAILROAD BUILDER	01	31	273
CARRIERS OF COMMUTER TRAFFIC IN NYC	08	31	48
CASCADE TUNNEL GN	11	49	48
CASCADE TUNNEL: AIR-COOLING FOR DIESELS	02	57	33
CASEY JONES ANNIVERSARY (75)	11	75	10
CASEY JONES MEMORIES	05	66	62
CASEY JONES MUSEUM	08	56	27
CASEY JONES ORIGINAL SONG	05	66	35
CASEY JONES WRECK READER COMMENTS	08	78	04
CASEY JONES WRECK REPORT ADDENDUM	06	78	05
CASEY JONES'S TRIP TO THE PROMISED LAND	12	32	94
CAST-IRON WHEELS ROLL INTO OBLIVION	03	69	18
CENSUS OF TRANSPORTATION: INTERESTING FA	05	40	86
CENTENNIAL ALBUM OF PRR 1846-1946 PHOTOS	04	46	10
CENTENNIAL SUMMER-RETURN OF DDA40X	03	85	51
CENTRALIZED TRAFFIC CONTROL	10	42	54
CENTRALIZED TRAFFIC CONTROL (SP)	11	44	100
CERA'S 45TH YEAR	07	84	23
CEYLON'S NARROW GAGE (2 1/2') RAILROAD	12	36	21

516

Railroad/Railfan

GENERAL RAILROADING

GENERAL RAILROADING	M	Y	P
CHART OF ALTITUDES/GRADES OF WORLD RRS	08	35	84
CHART OF COAT-LAPEL EMBLEMS	04	43	121
CHEAPER FUEL FOR ENGINES-NP MINES COAL	02	31	335
CHECKING 90000 ENGINE PARTS S #1408	04	41	55
CHEROKEE STRIP LAND RUSH	02	31	447
CHICAGO LOCOMOTIVE BUILDERS	03	73	26
CHICAGO RAILROAD FAIR 1948	09	48	11
CHILDS GRAVE ON FRIS ROW ELDORADO OK	06	31	420
CHINESE AND US RAILROAD CONSTRUCTION	05	49	32
CHURCHILL FUNERAL TRAIN	10	65	24
CHURCHILL: SEAPORT/END OF CN	06	54	14
CINCINATIAN STREAMLINER OF THE B&O	06	47	08
CINCINATTI SUBWAY READER COMMENTS	10	62	08
CINCINATTI'S UNUSED SUBWAY	08	62	21
CIRCUS FREAKS AND RAILROAD FARES	02	61	33
CIRCUS RAILROADING	07	46	12
CIRCUS RAILROADING: 1872 PT BARNUM	11	44	142
CIRCUS TRAIN ROLLING	09	71	12
CIRCUS TRAIN TRAVELING & LIVING	09	72	04
CIRCUS TRAINS AND WRECKS	03	65	12
CIRCUS TRAINS: 100 YEARS OF	04	56	12
CIRCUS UNLOADING: UNLOADING CARS	01	53	134
CIRCUS: TRAVEL BY TRAINS	02	30	330
CIRCUSES USE RAILROADS FOR TRANSPORT	07	34	39
CITIZENS' ARMED INVASION OF MEXICO	05	51	74
CITY OF IRON HORSES: PATTERSON NJ	06	33	34
CITY OF NEW ORLEANS TRAIN (IC)	12	47	36
CITY OWNED STEAM ROAD-THE SKAGIT-SEATTLE	02	37	58
CIVIL WAR "GONE WITH THE WIND"	01	40	59
CIVIL WAR RAIL ALBUM	11	53	56
CLASSIFICATION OF INFO ON SWITCH LISTS	07	44	77
CLASSROOM RAILROADING	03	50	54
CLEARANCE CAR ON PRR	08	58	70
CLUB FOR EVERY RAILFAN	02	67	14
CLUBS: HOW TO ORGANIZE A RAILROAD CLUB	12	40	112
CN BUILDS NEW 100 MILE BRANCH LINE	03	38	48
CN GOES ACROSS CONTINENT IN 67 HOURS!	07	31	604
COAL	09	43	64
COAL SMOKE:TOUREST RAILROADS IN MONTANA	03	80	46
COALING UP TENDERS	06	60	24
COAST TO COAST RAILROAD?--GEORGE GOULD	06	37	38
COLLECTING ENGINE PICTURES	01	31	212
COLLECTING RAILROAD TIMETABLES	12	34	76
COLLECTING RAILROAD-PICTURE STAMPS	01	31	216
COLLVER SPECIAL--WRECK HIRAM GA	02	50	28
COLONIST CARS	04	48	76
COLORADO MIDLAND: MEMORIES	08	42	06
COLORADO'S "SWITZERLAND TRAIL" DB&W	07	41	47
COLORFUL JOINT LINE--DENVER TO PUEBLO	10	87	56
COMMERCIAL HIGHWAY TRAFFIC WAGES	04	35	30
COMMERCIAL WATERWAYS	05	35	91
COMMODORE CORNELIUS VANDERBILT-PRES NYC	11	36	04
COMMON CARRIER PROBLEMS	05	38	06
COMMON CARRIER STEAM POWER ROSTERS 1961	02	61	56
COMMUTER RAILROAD COPS ICG	12	76	43
COMMUTERS TO CAPE COD?	01	80	55
COMPETITION FROM BUS AND AIR TRAFFIC	03	31	491
COMPUTERS DONT RUN EVERYTHING ON UP	11	78	12
CONCRETE ROADBEDS	11	31	595
CONDITIONING COMPRESSED AIR FOR STEAM LO	09	45	48
CONDUCTOR JIM BULLARD & REVENUE ON RI	05	30	161
CONEY ISLAND AMUSEMENT PARK-ROCKY ROAD T	12	49	74
CONGRESSIONAL LTD VS TOKAIDO BULLET SERV	06	68	08
CONRAIL STREAMLINING OF OPERATIONS	07	76	44
CONRAILS TOP BRASS	07	76	49
CONSTRUCTING A MODEL RAILROAD	03	32	476
CONTINENTAL CODE	05	33	60
CONTRIBUTING PHOTOS	11	87	30
CONTROL CIRCUITS FOR DIESEL LOCOMOTIVES	11	52	56
COORS AND A RAILROAD	01	85	36
CORREGIDOR-US OPERATES RR ON THE ISLAND	03	37	10
COST OF BUILDING A RAILROAD	09	33	47
COST OF FIR TIES	09	33	47
COST OF RAIL	09	33	47
COST TO AIR-CONDITION A RAILROAD CAR	10	37	67
COUNTERBALANCING STEAM LOCOMOTIVE DRIVER	07	50	58
COUNTERFEIT SUBWAY TOKENS IN NYC	08	68	34
COUNTRY NEEDS FEATHERBEDDING!	08	64	28
COUPLER: DEVELOPMENT OF	05	41	06
COUPLER: MILLER HOOK TYPE	08	53	120
COUPLERS	05	41	06
COUPLERS: AUTOMATIC	01	30	237
COUPLERS: HISTORY OF	01	30	233
COUPLERS: JANNEY	01	30	240
COUPLERS: LINK AND PIN	01	30	233
COUPLERS: MILLER HOOK	01	30	244
COUPLERS: PHOTO OF FIRST	01	30	241
COUPLERS: TITELOCK (FOR DIESELS)	07	48	69
CP BUILT 1056 LOCOMOTIVES	03	67	38
CP HIGH-PRESSURE LOCO	07	31	531
CRANE WATERMARK: 1892 REPRODUCED	03	51	138
CRANE WATERMARKS--MORE!	06	51	135
CREATURES FROM CLEBURNE-SOWS EAR/SILK PU	05	85	44
CROOKED CANYON LINE RCBH&W	01	34	94
CROSS COMPOUND AIR COMPRESSOR ON STEAM L	08	51	52
CROSSHEADS ON STEAM LOCOMOTIVES	11	44	46
CROSSTIE PRESERVATION	12	50	57
CROWN SHEET PROTECTION FOR STEAM LOCOS	07	42	59
CYLINDER BUSHINGS OF STEAM LOCOMOTIVES	05	51	54
CYLINDERS OF STEAM LOCOMOTIVES	01	50	70
D&H 150 YEARS OLD PHOTO ESSAY	07	73	20
D&RG "SCENIC LIMITED"	01	39	60
DAVID FINK TALKS ABOUT MAINE CENTRAL	05	83	28
DAYLIGHT TO THE 1984 WORLDS FAIR	09	84	50
DEADMANS CONTROL AND LACK OF FIREMEN	09	66	10
DEATH VALLEY SCOTTY'S GREAT RUN	07	31	561
DECORATING TRAINS FOR SPECIAL OCCASIONS	06	58	26
DEGREE OF A CURVE ON A RAILROAD TRACK	07	52	138
DELANO: PORTRAIT OF A RAILROAD TOWN (LV)	03	48	12
DEPOTS ARE PASSING	11	67	33

Railroad/Railfan

STEPHANS_RAILROAD_DIRECTORY

GENERAL RAILROADING

GENERAL RAILROADING	M	Y	P
DESCHUTES RIVER OR RAISING A DIESEL 1954	09	54	10
DESIGN PROCEDURES FOR STEAM LOCOMOTIVES	10	42	06
DEVELOPMENT OF THE LOCOMOTIVE 1825-1829	04	31	116
DEVELOPMENT OF THE LOCOMOTIVE 1830-31	05	31	280
DEVELOPMENT OF THE LOCOMOTIVE 1832	06	31	412
DEVELOPMENT OF THE LOCOMOTIVE 1832-1837	07	31	542
DEVELOPMENT OF THE LOCOMOTIVE 1839-1846	08	31	88
DEVELOPMENT OF THE LOCOMOTIVE 1847-1854	09	31	184
DEVELOPMENT OF THE LOCOMOTIVE 1857-1872	10	31	452
DEVELOPMENT OF THE LOCOMOTIVE 1880-1893	11	31	568
DEVELOPMENT OF THE LOCOMOTIVE 1892-1901	12	31	78
DEVELOPMENT OF THE LOCOMOTIVE 1903-1920	01	32	238
DEVELOPMENT OF THE LOCOMOTIVE 1924-1925	02	32	398
DEVELOPMENT OF THE LOCOMOTIVE 1925	03	32	565
DIAMOND STACKS	04	38	22
DICK JENSEN'S ENGINES	11	87	69
DID STEAM ENGINES REALLY OUTLAST DIESELS	02	73	44
DIESEL COLOR SCHEMES	12	72	56
DIESEL COOLING SYSTEMS	07	52	58
DIESEL FIELD-SERVICE ENGINEER (REFUELER)	10	72	35
DIESEL FIREMAN	08	59	34
DIESEL FUEL OIL SYSTEMS 1	04	52	70
DIESEL FUEL OIL SYSTEMS 2	05	52	58
DIESEL LOCOMOTIVE FUTURE REPLACEMENTS	06	62	47
DIESEL LOCOMOTIVES IN MEXICO	08	71	48
DIESEL REPAIR SHOP PHOTO ESSAY COLLINWOO	06	71	60
DIESEL VERSUS STEAM	03	39	07
DIESEL YARD GOATS IN THE EAST	09	71	20
DIESEL-ELECTRIC FREIGHT RUN: NEW IRON HO	06	41	31
DIESELS AND STEAM LOCOS PHOTO ESSAY	08	47	34
DIFFERENCES IN RAILROAD OPERATION US/CAN	08	61	35
DIGGING FOR A SUBWAY IN NYC	04	65	43
DINING CAR PROBLEM	08	47	56
DINING CARS-ONE AMERICAN RD MAKES MONEY	12	63	18
DINNER IN THE DINER	10	65	17
DISASTER AT STEAMTOWN--BELLOWS FALLS VT	05	82	22
DISC BRAKES FOR RAILROADS	01	51	68
DISPATCHER	02	56	30
DISPATCHER--TRAIN SHEET BLUES	10	56	63
DISPATCHER-FEMALE IN INDIANAPOLIS	01	52	60
DO RAILROADS REALLY WANT FASTER TRAINS?	10	67	34
DOT RAIL SPEED RECORD VEHICLE PHOTO	10	74	24
DOUBLE DECK STREETCARS	06	43	102
DOUBLE END LOCOMOTIVES	04	58	26
DOUBLE-ENDERS: NEVER POPULAR IN N AMERIC	12	43	58
DOWN MEMORY LANE PYNN	02	43	44
DRAPING LINCOLN'S FUNERAL CAR	02	32	325
DRIVE FOR PASSENGER BUSINESS	06	64	13
DRIVING BOX DESIGN IN STEAM LOCOMOTIVES	07	51	56
DUTIES OF ASSISTANT SUPERINTENDENT	02	66	30
DUTIES OF CREW DISPATCHER	04	55	33
DUTIES OF FIREMAN	07	32	507
DUTIES OF FIRMEAN	01	38	59
DUTIES OF RAILLROAD PRESIDENT	03	55	30
DUTIES OF ROUNDHOUSE FOREMAN	01	55	37

GENERAL RAILROADING	M	Y	P
DUTIES OF TRAINMASTER	02	66	30
DYNAMOMETER CAR.	07	47	56
EARLY CTC INSTALLATIONS	07	66	38
EARLY DAYS IN THE WASHINGTON TERRITORY	09	37	31
EARLY RAILROAD TROUP MOVEMENTS	02	41	27
EASING UP THE SLACK (FAM)	04	78	16
EASY ACCESS: TERM USED IN PASS COACHES	05	40	94
EBT PHOTO ESSAY	03	74	41
EDDY CLOCKS--WILSON EDDY	08	38	94
EIGHT-WHEEL LOCOMOTIVES	02	36	38
ELECTRIC HUMP YARD OPERATION	02	61	29
ELECTRIC LINE LINGO	10	43	112
ELECTRIC LINES INDEX 1943-1958	04	59	46
ELECTRIC LOCOS & LINES	07	44	11
ELECTRIC RAIL TERMS 1	11	42	95
ELECTRIC RAIL TERMS 2	12	42	151
ELECTRIC RAIL TERMS E-E	01	43	152
ELECTRIC RAIL TERMS EL-IG	02	43	149
ELECTRIC RAIL TERMS IM-SE	03	43	147
ELECTRIC RAIL TERMS: SE-WO	04	43	148
ELECTRIC RAILWAY STAMPS	02	36	92
ELECTRIC TRACTION: SPRAGUE, FRANK FOUNDR	08	40	07
ELECTRIC VERSUS STEAM RAILROADS	10	33	86
ELECTRIFICATION PROBLEMS (MILW)	12	75	07
ELECTRIFICATION VS DIESEL POWER	10	47	48
ELECTROLINER	07	47	104
ELECTRONIC DINING CAR CONCEPT	08	47	56
ELECTRONIC YARDMASTER	03	55	43
EMBLEMS OF RAILROAD LABOR GROUPS	04	43	121
EMD'S ON ARARAT GRADE IN PA	SU	76	13R
EMERGENCY POTOMAC CROSSING	12	46	68
EMERGENCY POTOMAC RIVER CROSSING WW II	12	46	68
EMMETT KELLEY BORN IN CABOOSE MYTH	04	66	37
EMPIRE BUILDER OF THE GN	07	47	80
EMPLOYEES' TIMETABLES	06	42	81
EMPLOYEES: MASTER MECHANIC VS TRAINMASTR	05	36	85
ENGINE MESSENGER PHOTO ESSAY	06	44	28
ENGINEER MESSENGER: DELIVERED USED LOCOS	09	47	79
ENGINEERS' BROTHERHOOD	05	36	45
ENGINEERS--THEN & NOW READER COMMENTS	05	87	05
EQUIPMENT TRUST CERTIFICATES-WHAT ARE TH	12	78	19
ERIE RAILROAD MOVES 51 CARS OF SALT	12	29	122
ERIE WAR, THE GREAT	03	52	44
ESSAY FROM ARARAT PENNSYLVANIA	F	76	47R
ESTIMATING TRAIN SPEED	03	66	25
ET BRAKE EQUIPMENT (ENGINE & TENDER)	11	50	58
EUCALYPTUS BOOM AND BUST	10	50	74
EUREKA NEVADA RY COLLECTS FROM UNCLE SAM	02	38	26
EVOLUTION OF IC LOGO	07	67	34
EVOLUTION OF THE FREIGHT TRUCK 1832-1900	06	42	102
EXCERPTS FROM AG&WIT RULE BOOK--1858	01	66	10
EXCURSIONS AND THE INDUSTRY	03	38	06
EXPECTED LIFE EXPECTANCY OF RAILROADERS	01	76	12
EXPLORING AMERICA:A PASSAGE BY RAIL	05	83	38
EXPLORING AMERICA:PASSAGE BY RAIL,KURALT	09	83	39

GENERAL RAILROADING

GENERAL RAILROADING	M	Y	P
EXPLORING AMERICA:PASSAGE BY RAIL.KURALT	07	83	36
EXPLOSIVES AS RAILROAD CARGO	05	50	40
EXPRESS PACKAGE SERVICE HISTORY	10	48	94
EXPRESS TRUCK ROBBERIES--HIGH IRON LAW	03	50	27
EXTRA 454 SOUTH ON CV	05	78	18R
F7 UNITS EMD	07	49	68
FACTORS INVOLVED MAKING RR FREIGHT RATE	02	48	75
FAIRWELL TO LUXURY RAIL TRAVEL	03	68	16
FAIRWELL TO THE FRISCO	11	80	51
FAIRWELL TO THE STILLWELLS	SP	75	52R
FAKE TRAIN-PICTURE STAMPS	03	38	68
FAMOUS PEOPLE DIEING ON TRAINS	02	76	08
FANTASTIC TRAINS-SOME FLOPS/SOME GOOD	12	34	51
FANTRIP: BUFFALO 225 FANS/1000 MILES	12	40	28
FANTRIP: GTW 2-8-2	04	69	16
FAREWELL TO STEAM PRR#5436 "BROADWAY LTD	07	33	60
FASTER PASSENGER TRAINS	06	66	23
FASTEST COAST TO COAST--CR & ATSF	11	87	40
FEATHER RIVER CANYON: CENTRAL TRAFFIC CO	11	46	10
FEDERAL WARTIME CONTROL OF RAILROADS	10	38	07
FEEDWATER TREATMENT	04	46	57
FEMALE HOBOS	09	39	49
FEMALE PRESIDENTS OF RAILROADS	06	35	46
FIRE: RAILROAD MENACE	05	45	70
FIREBOX: HEART OF THE LOCOMOTIVE	08	45	08
FIREDOORS ON STEAM LOCOMOTIVES	07	44	65
FIRELESS COOKERS IN PENNSYLVANIA	05	69	25
FIRELESS--HOW THEY WORK	07	79	40
FIREWORKS AND RAINBOW WARS-PAINT SCHEMES	09	86	58
FIRING AN OIL-BURNER LOCOMOTIVE	08	50	44
FIRING UP THE BLUE RIDGE..IN THE RAIN	10	75	23
FIRST AUTOMATIC COUPLERS	08	61	34
FIRST DEFINITE STEP TOWARDS PACIFIC RR	08	30	115
FIRST RAIL ROLLING-MILL IN CANADA	04	78	10
FIRST RAILROAD NUMBERED PATENT: WHEELS	01	47	52
FIRST RAILROAD STRIKE	08	46	136
FIRST RAILROAD STRIKE B&TRR 1855	07	78	07
FIRST RAILROAD STRIKE SEPT 2 1916	08	35	126
FIRST STEAM TRAIN IN US: 1820/1828	08	35	83
FIRST TELEGRAPH MESSAGE (NOT BY MORSE)	04	64	29
FIRST TRIP ON BART IMPRESSIONS	12	73	49
FIRST US-CANADIAN BOARDER RR CROSSING	02	61	31
FIVE MILES FOR A NICKEL (NBCS)	03	69	31
FLASH FLOOD AT MOJAVE GAP (ATSF)	01	78	26
FLEXTRAIN DEVELOPMENT	03	72	37
FLOATING FREIGHT YARDS: GREAT LAKES RR	03	43	110
FLUE REMOVAL AND INTERNAL INSPECTION	05	47	63
FLYING DUDE-NYNH&H TRAIN FOR WEALTHY	05	65	22
FLYING START OF THE STREAMLINER ERA	07	68	20
FLYING SWITCH	04	38	54
FLYING SWITCHES	12	54	41
FORD'S RAILROAD (DT&I)	07	38	09
FORGOTTEN LOCOMOTIVES	01	73	18
FORGOTTEN RULES--STANDARD RULEBOOKS	08	47	06
FORGOTTEN TROLLEYS OF CAMBRIA COUNTY PA	05	48	94

GENERAL RAILROADING	M	Y	P
FORNEY LOCOMOTIVES: THEIR HISTORY	06	45	08
FORNEY'S IRON HORSE	01	36	37
FORT GEORGE AMUSEMENT PARK-3RD RAIL THRI	12	49	70
FORT RILEY KANSAS	12	58	26
FOSTORIA OHIO: HOT INTERLOCKING JOB	05	68	30
FOUR TRACK FAREWELL--CR RAIL TRAIN	05	82	54
FPD: FROM PUBLISHERS DESK	F	75	03R
FPD: LET'S PAINT THEM OLD!	01	87	04
FPD: 150 YEARS OF RAILROADS	08	77	03R
FPD: 460 NEVER CROSSED THE ATLANTIC	09	87	04
FPD: 50 YEARS OF PUBLISHING	05	83	03
FPD: ABANDONED LINES	05	81	03
FPD: AMTRAK TO CHICAGO	09	85	04
FPD: AMTRAK'S CATCH 22	11	79	03
FPD: AUTO TRAIN	F	75	03R
FPD: BRITISH STEAM	01	83	03
FPD: CAMERA BAGS ARE HEAVY	11	82	03
FPD: CAMP GRANT TROUP TRAINS	09	82	03
FPD: CATBIRD SEAT ON THE ERIE	05	84	03
FPD: CLUB NEWSLETTERS	09	84	03
FPD: COLLECTABLE TRIVIA	01	79	03R
FPD: COLOR FILM	09	78	03R
FPD: COLOR SCHEMES	07	82	03
FPD: COLORADO MEMORIES	11	78	03R
FPD: COMPUTER PHOTO FILING	07	84	04
FPD: FAREWELL TO A GIANT-661	03	84	03
FPD: FAVORITE RAILROAD 2 (NYC)	09	81	03
FPD: FIGHTING THE PHOENIX	12	87	05
FPD: FILING THOSE NEGATIVES	03	82	03
FPD: FILM & VIDEO CONVERSION	01	86	04
FPD: GLUTTONY, GOURMET DINING/FAST FOOD	09	83	03
FPD: HOME VIDEO TAPES	01	80	04
FPD: MEN WHO STYLED THE STREAMLINERS	07	86	03
FPD: MUSEUM CONTRIBUTIONS	05	86	03
FPD: NARROW GAUGE THOUGHTS	12	77	03R
FPD: NORTHWEST PASSAGE IS A TROLLEY LINE	01	84	03
FPD: PAPER RAILROADIANA	10	77	03R
FPD: PHOTO SWAPPING	05	85	03
FPD: PRESERVING OUR RAILROADIANA	09	79	03
FPD: RAILFAN & RAILROAD COMBINED	05	79	03
FPD: RAILFAN/RAILROAD	03	79	03R
FPD: RAILFANS TENTH ANNIVERSARY	11	84	04
FPD: RAILPHOTOS	SU	76	02R
FPD: RAILPHOTOS II	F	76	03R
FPD: RAILROAD PAINTINGS	11	86	04
FPD: RAILROAD POSTCARDS	07	79	03
FPD: RAILROADIANA	09	86	03
FPD: RAPID TRANSIT	03	85	03
FPD: ROAD NAMES CHANGING	03	81	03
FPD: ROOSEVELT ROAD REVISITED	01	85	04
FPD: RULE BOOKS	09	80	03
FPD: SECAM ISN'T A PAL OF NTSC	10	87	05
FPD: SHORT LINES HAVE SHORT LIVES,SOMETI	07	86	03
FPD: SOUND MOVIES	02	78	03R
FPD: SPLICING MOVIE FILM	11	83	03

Railroad/ Railfan

STEPHANS' RAILROAD DIRECTORY

GENERAL RAILROADING

GENERAL RAILROADING	M	Y	P
FPD: STEAM POWER HAS MEANT TO PULSATE	03	87	04
FPD: STEAMTOWN MOVE TO SCRANTON	07	83	03
FPD: SUBWAY GRAFFITI	11	80	04
FPD: SUSQUEHANNA, THE REAL LIFE PHOENIX	05	87	04
FPD: THAT FAVORITE RAILROAD	07	81	03
FPD: THE BLUE COMET	01	82	03
FPD: THE NEW SUSQUEHANNA	01	81	03
FPD: THE O&W	W	76	03R
FPD: THE RAILROAD FAIR	07	78	03R
FPD: THE SUSKIE (NYS&W)	03	80	03
FPD: THE T1 IS A FREIGHT ENGINE	03	86	04
FPD: THEY EVEN NAME DIESELS	10	87	05
FPD: TOURIST RAILROADS	SP	77	03R
FPD: TROLLEYS	SP	76	03R
FPD: TROUP TRAINS 1	04	78	03R
FPD: VIEW FROM THE CAB	11	85	04
FPD: VINTAGE RAILROAD BOOKS	07	80	03
FPD: WASHINGTON HOLDS THE CARDS	07	85	03
FR FOREIGN RAILROAD	08	33	40
FR 2-10-4'S OF TUBARAO BRAZIL	09	79	44
FR 39 HOUR DAY IN NEW ZEALAND	09	77	45
FR 4-8-2 S AFRICAN 19D'S CORRECTION	F	75	64R
FR AFRICA UGANDA RAILWAY 1898	04	35	91
FR APT-E RUN OF 152.3 MPH IN BRITAN	12	75	12
FR APT-E TEST PROGRAM (BRITISH HI-SPEED)	11	75	05
FR ARTIC: LAPLAND'S ELECTRIC RAILWAY	10	39	69
FR AUSTRALIA: GAGES USED IN	06	38	75
FR AUSTRALIA: RRING 'NEATH SOUTH CROSS	11	30	538
FR AUSTRALIAN DESERT RAIL TRAVEL	07	73	11
FR AUSTRALIAN RAILROADS	05	48	44
FR AUSTRIA--THE MURTALBAHN	W	74	48R
FR AUTOMATED RAILWAYS IN EUROPE	11	74	51
FR AUTOMATIC TRAIN OPERATION IN LONDON	11	64	42
FR BALDWIN 4-8-0'S STILL IN SERVICE	06	71	22
FR BERMUDA BUILDS ITS FIRST RAILWAY	07	31	530
FR BERMUDA: DELIVERY SERVICE VIA BIKE	12	40	127
FR BRAZIL: MADEIRA-MAMORE RAILWAY	08	33	40
FR BRAZIL: MADEIRA-MAMORE RR: AMAZON	05	53	70
FR BRAZILIAN RAILROAD: RAILWAY OF DEATH	08	63	15
FR BRISTOL & GLOUCESTER RY "PHILADELPHIA	07	35	63
FR BRITISH : EAST AFRICA UGANDA RAILWAY	04	35	91
FR BRITISH INSIGNIA OF BRITISH RAILWAYS	12	33	45
FR BRITISH POLICYS ON BELLS/WHISTLES/LIG	07	66	39
FR BURMA RAILROADS	07	45	114
FR CALCUTTA'S STREETCAR SYSTEM	12	66	38
FR CEYLON: NARROW GAUGE LINES	12	36	21
FR CHILE: BALDWIN BUILDS LOCOS FOR CHILE	01	39	62
FR CHINA RAIL-FLIGHT FOR FREEDOM	05	45	32
FR CHINESE RAILWAYS	02	39	124
FR CHITTARANJAN LOCO WORKS INDIA LAST EN	08	72	62
FR COAL HAULING IN RUSSIA	05	77	10
FR CORREGIDOR PHILLAPEANS TROLLEY LINE N	08	69	31
FR COSTA RICA NORTHERN RY (BANANA LINE)	07	37	35
FR COUPLING OF BRITISH ROLLING STOCK	12	65	26
FR CUBA'S FIRST LOCOMOTIVE	05	36	79
FR CUBA: HERSHEY CUBAN RAILWAY	11	46	95
FR CUBA: STEAM AND MORE!	07	82	26
FR CZECHOSLOVAKIA: CONQUEROR'S BRIDGE	01	49	42
FR DENMARK: WARTIME	07	40	19
FR DENMARK: WORLD WAR II ACTIVITIES	07	40	19
FR DUTCH RAILWAYS: WARTIME	08	40	67
FR ECUADOR GUAYAQUIL & QUITO RAILWAY	08	34	42
FR ECUADOR: GUAYAQUIL & QUITO RAILWAY	11	35	91
FR EMD INVADES ENGLAND	03	86	25
FR ENGLAND SOMERSAULT SEMAPHORE ORIGIN	08	33	130
FR ENGLAND SWANSEA & MUMBLES RAILWAY	03	35	15
FR ENGLAND: ELECTRIC TOKEN BLOCK SYSTEM	10	60	32
FR ETHIOPIA RAILROAD	11	35	56
FR ETHIOPIA: WRECKED IN	09	42	70
FR EUROPE ON RAILS: BERLIN/BASLE/MILAN/N	05	30	222
FR EUROPE ON RAILS: GOLDEN ARROW	05	30	223
FR EUROPE ON RAILS: ORIENT EXPRESS	05	30	223
FR EUROPE ON WHEELS	05	30	218
FR EUROPE'S HI SPEED PASSENGER TRAINS	06	30	442
FR EUROPE: FREIGHT TRAINS	06	31	369
FR EUROPE: SMALLEST RAILROAD 8 MILES	05	32	194
FR FEDERATED MALAY STATES RAILWAY	04	37	68
FR FERROCARRIL CUZCO-SANTA ANA PERU	12	71	59
FR FIRST RAILWAY ON EUROPEAN CONTINENT	01	65	30
FR FLYING SCOTSMAN VISITS AMERICA	03	70	24
FR FOREIGN RAILWAYS PHOTO ESSAY	10	62	50
FR FOREIGN TIMETABLES	05	36	96
FR FRANCE DEACUVILLE ROADS--WAR RAILROAD	05	30	273
FR FRANCE WORLD WAR 1 OPERATIONS	05	30	273
FR FRANCE--A CENTURY OF FRENCH RAILWAYS	05	37	122
FR FRANCO-ETHIOPIAN RAILWAY PHOTOS	12	35	43
FR FRENCH "MISTRAL" WORLD'S FASTEST TRAI	06	62	13
FR FRENCH COALBURNERS	03	75	34
FR FRENCH FLYING DUTCHMAN--ROBOT TRAIN	10	55	11
FR FRENCH LOCO ERECTION IN 72 1/2 HOURS	07	69	32
FR FRENCH LOCOMOTIVE ALARM BELLS	08	77	12
FR GERMAN PASS MILEAGE EXCEEDS AMERICAN	08	36	121
FR GERMAN SPEED RUN 130.5 MPH	11	31	565
FR GERMAN STEAM POWER READER COMMENTS	10	70	06
FR GERMANY'S FINEST TRAIN RHEINGOLD XPRE	11	31	567
FR GERMANY: 100 YEARS OF RAILROADING	12	35	90
FR GERMANY: LANGAN LINE--MONORAILS	06	31	437
FR GREAT RAILWAY RACE ENGLAND-SCOTLAND	08	35	68
FR HIGH SPEED GERMAN ELECTRIC LINES 1903	10	74	05
FR HIGHWHEELING ASIATIC ROYALTY	06	31	411
FR HISTORY OF EUROPE: AZUR COAST PLM XPR	05	30	218
FR HISTORY OF EUROPE: COMPAIGNE IN WAGON	05	30	218
FR HISTORY OF OXFORD & AYLESBURY TRAMRD.	03	36	45
FR IMPRESSIONS OF GERMAN STEAM	06	74	28
FR IN SEARCH OF STEAM IN ASIA	07	80	37
FR IN SEARCH OF STEAM IN CUBA	01	80	32
FR IN SEARCH OF STEAM IN EQUADOR	05	81	20
FR IN SEARCH OF STEAM IN INDIA	09	80	18
FR IN SEARCH OF STEAM IN PERU (BALDWINS)	05	82	36
FR IN SEARCH OF STEAM IN SOUTHERN AFRICA	03	80	18

Railroad/Railfan

GENERAL RAILROADING

GENERAL RAILROADING	M	Y	P
FR IN SEARCH OF STEAM IN TYRKEY	09	81	22
FR IN SEARCH OF STEAM NORTHERN AFRICA	05	80	56
FR IN SEARCH OF STEAM: SPAIN UPDATE	05	85	06
FR IN SEARCH OF STEAM:FAST STEAM-GERMANY	07	84	56
FR IN SEARCH OF STEAM:MORE IN SPAIN	03	85	56
FR IN SEARCH OF STEAM:S AFRICAS 4-8-4'S	05	85	32
FR IN SEARCH OF STEAM:SPAIN COAL-TRAINS	01	85	26
FR INDIA & AFRICA: RRING IN THE JUNGLE	10	32	340
FR INDIA HAS OVER 9000 STEAMERS	07	72	20
FR INDIA IS STILL BUILDING STEAM POWER	07	67	20
FR INDIA KHYBER PASS RAILWAY	06	34	38
FR INDIA: TICKETLESS TRAVEL	07	42	56
FR INDIAN RAILWAYS GIRDED FOR WAR	11	43	128
FR INDUCTION MOTOR DEVELOPMENT IN BRITAN	01	76	15
FR IRELAND BALLYBUNION MONORAIL	09	33	39
FR IRISH RAILS IN PEACE & WAR	06	73	34
FR ITALY SETTEBELLO GLAMOUROUS TRAIN	10	62	62
FR ITALY: LIST OF RAILROADS IN	10	43	71
FR JAMAICAS FIRST RAILFAN TRIP	12	66	18
FR JAPAN "TOKAIDO RAILWAY" 159 MPH	12	63	43
FR JAPAN'S POST WAR RAIL SERVICE	12	46	48
FR JAPAN'S RAILROADS	06	49	72
FR JAPAN: A JUICEFAN'S PARADISE	04	51	95
FR JAPAN: FIRST TRAIN TO TOKYO	10	53	102
FR JAPANESE "HONEYMOON EXPRESS"	10	67	30
FR LAST GASP OF STEAM IN FRANCE	04	72	14
FR LIST OF TRAMWAYS IN AUSTRALIA	07	50	121
FR LIST OF TRAMWAYS IN NEW ZEALAND	07	50	120
FR LOCO KEEPS SAME NUMBER--4 OWNERS	04	34	65
FR LONG-NECKED OIL CAN (FRENCH RAILROAD)	07	77	09
FR LOWEST ELEVATION RR JISR EL MAJAME IS	01	78	48
FR MADEIRA-MAMORE RR (MAD MARY) BRAZIL	08	33	40
FR MADELEINE & I RIDE THE CAB (FRANCE)	09	75	14
FR MALLORCA RAILWAYS (MEDITERRANEAN)	01	76	21
FR MIDGET RAILWAY (GERMANY) ROMNEY HYTHE	12	78	15
FR MIXED TRAIN IN IRAN	06	74	04
FR MULE POWERED ROADS IN S AMERICA PHOTO	03	67	22
FR NEW ZEALAND RAIL TERMS	03	53	132
FR NEW ZEALAND RAILWAYS 1867 TO ?	08	37	33
FR NICARAGUA LURES THE BOOMER	06	30	403
FR NO MORE BELGIAN STEAM	04	67	64
FR NORWAY WORLDS MOST NORTHERN RAILROAD	06	78	57
FR OLDEST RAILWAY: TANFIELD BRANCH UK	06	65	38
FR ORIENT EXPRESS	05	75	03
FR ORIENT EXPRESS ADVENTURE RIDES	10	62	14
FR ORIENT EXPRESS READER COMMENTS	12	62	10
FR OVERSEAS WHEEL ARRANGEMENTS	04	60	57
FR PACHYDERM TYPE MOTIVE POWER INDIA	01	72	16
FR PANAMA RAILROAD	04	37	56
FR PARIS-METRO GREAT MODERN SUBWAY SYSTE	05	68	34
FR PERU RAILROAD IN THE SKY ELEV 15,665'	08	30	06
FR PERU'S HIGHEST STANDARD GAGE	09	36	78
FR PERU: CENTRAL RY OF PERU	04	40	82
FR PHILIPPINO STEAM	02	61	16
FR PRESENT DAY STEAM POWER 1966--BOLIVIA	11	66	18

GENERAL RAILROADING	M	Y	P
FR QUAINT WATER TOWERS	09	78	02
FR QUEEN OPENS NEW LONDON SUBWAY	06	69	36
FR RAIL EMPLOYEE QUALIFICATIONS IN NZ	10	73	12
FR RAILFANNING IN CHINA	11	79	47
FR RAILROADING IN NEW ZEALAND	02	77	05
FR RAILROADING TODAY IN CENTRAL AMERICA	01	74	22
FR RAILROADS IN SOUTH AMERICA W/5.5 GAGE	01	36	86
FR RED TIES ON BRITISH PORTERS	04	67	32
FR RIDING THE TRANS-SIBERIAN	01	76	15
FR RT PASSED FIREMAN: BRITISH TERM	10	59	36
FR RUSSIA: NEW FRONTIER FOR BOOMERS	09	31	211
FR RUSSIAN RAILWAYS: BIGGEST RAIL SYSTEM	05	46	34
FR RUSSIAS NATIONALIZED RAILWAY SYSTEM	06	60	30
FR S AFRICA-IN STEAMY SWAZILAND	03	77	32
FR S AMER GUAYAQUIL & QUITO RY, ECUADOR	04	34	96
FR S&D 150 ANNIVERSARY ENGLAND	04	76	15
FR SCOTLAND FORTH BRIDGE RAILWAY COMPANY	10	36	77
FR SCOTTISH RAILWAY: ONE IN A MILLION	08	61	29
FR SNO ALL FEMALE PASSENGER COACHES	02	75	08
FR SNO BRITANS ELECTRIC "SCOTS"	04	75	12
FR SNO BRITISH APT-E TRAIN	04	74	08
FR SNO BRITISH PULLMAN CARS READER INFO	03	75	12
FR SNO ENGLAND: FIRST TRAINS IN ENGLAND	06	63	24
FR SNO EUROPE'S HIGHEST RAILWAY	01	75	55
FR SNO EUROPEAN LUXURY: ORIENT EXPRESS	04	57	45
FR SNO FIRST MAIL TRAIN ENGLAND 1830	02	75	51
FR SNO FIRST RAILWAY IN NEW ZEALAND	04	71	62
FR SNO IRELANDS FIRST RAILWAY (1834)	08	74	57
FR SNO JAPAN: TOKAIDO LINE	10	63	30
FR SNO PRINCIPAL RAILWAYS IN ITALY 1938	02	74	53
FR SNO ROAD WITH LARGEST NUMBER TUNNELS	10	75	53
FR SNO THE FLYING HAMBURGER 1932 GERMAN	03	73	43
FR SNO TOKAIDO LINE IN JAPAN	04	65	55
FR SNO VATICAN CITY RAILWAY.	06	62	42
FR SNO VATICAN RAILWAY	02	63	06
FR SNO WORSDELL BROTHERS OF BRITAN	09	72	52
FR SNO WRECK OF "ROYAL SCOT" 1931	02	74	53
FR SOUTH AFRICA BLUE TRAIN	08	63	30
FR SOUTH AFRICA: NEW RAILWAY SPANS	06	31	334
FR SOUTH AFRICAS 19D'S (4-8-2'S)	SU	75	28R
FR SOUTH AMERICAN STEAM IN 1979	07	79	17
FR SPEED RECORDS IN EUROPE	05	66	10
FR STEAM ERA ENDING IN LONDON	07	71	40
FR STEAM IN ASIA	03	73	39
FR STEAM IN BRAZIL	08	72	21
FR STEAM IN BRAZIL 1976	08	76	32
FR STEAM IN COSTA RICA 1973	10	73	38
FR STEAM IN EASTERN EUROPE	11	79	45
FR STEAM IN EL SALVADOR 1973	10	73	36
FR STEAM IN EUROPE 1979	09	79	17
FR STEAM IN FORMOSA	12	62	27
FR STEAM IN GERMANY TODAY 1973	11	73	37
FR STEAM IN GUATEMALA 1973	10	73	36
FR STEAM IN GUATEMALA READERS COMMENTS	08	71	04
FR STEAM IN HONDURAS 1973	10	73	37

Railroad/Railfan

GENERAL RAILROADING

GENERAL RAILROADING	M	Y	P
FR STEAM IN NICARAGUA 1973	10	73	38
FR STEAM IN THE CANEFIELDS	11	71	40
FR STEAM IN THE CARIBBEAN	12	68	13
FR STEAM IN VENEZUELA	07	77	21
FR STEAM IS DEAD IN FRANCE-LONG LIVE STE	02	73	40
FR STEAM LOCOMOTIVE MEN-RHEINE GERMANY	09	74	18
FR STEAM POWER IN GERMANY TODAY	07	70	20
FR STEAM POWER IN HUNGARY	03	75	30
FR STEAM POWER IN SWITZERLAND	12	70	29
FR STEAM POWER IN SWITZERLAND TODAY	02	70	37
FR STEAM TODAY IN GUATEMALA	07	71	22
FR SURINAM NARROW-GAUGE RAILROADS	05	78	14
FR SWEDEN: LAND CRUISE TO MIDNIGHT SUN	07	51	39
FR SWEDEN: MIDNIGHT SUN CRUISE TRAIN	07	51	39
FR SWEDENS AND RAILROADING	12	50	16
FR SWEDISH RAILWAYS	06	56	33
FR SWEDISH STATE RY: ARCTIC CIRCLE TRIP	07	51	39
FR TRACK REPAIR TRAIN IN USSR 1MI IN 4HR	02	73	05
FR TRAINS STOPPED FOR ANTS & FIREFLYS	11	76	09
FR TRINIDAD GOV'T RAILWAYS	03	31	568
FR TWILIGHT OF STEAM IN GUATEMALA	09	72	19
FR US STEAM IN FRANCE TODAY	07	69	20
FR USSR: SOVIET UNION RR FOR KIDS BY KID	12	38	57
FR VATICAN RAILWAY COMMENTS	02	63	06
FR VATICAN STATE RAILROAD	11	50	36
FR WALES: FESTINIOG RY/OLDEST NARROW GAG	07	38	56
FR WOODBURNERS IN THAILAND	05	73	38
FR:TURKEY TODAY	06	77	20
FRD FAMOUS RAILROAD DIASTERS	05	34	89
FRD FIRST BIG ELECTRIC WRECK OCT 28 1906	12	36	120
FRD FLAMING DEATH ON THE HUDSON	07	34	76
FRD FREAK BOILER EXPLOSION NYNH&H 1890	08	34	41
FRD MEXICO'S BIGGEST RR DISASTER 06/1881	03	36	51
FRD THE ASHTABULA CATASTROPHE	09	34	40
FRD THE FIRTH OF TAY TRAGEDY	06	34	22
FRD THE PROSPECT PA WRECK OF 1872 PRR	05	34	89
FRD THE TRAGEDY AT ANGOLA	08	34	78
FREAK ACCIDENT-LOCO ON BOX CAR PLUG DOOR	10	75	40
FREAK MAIN LINE AP	10	31	393
FREE SLACK ACTION IN TRAINS	08	49	48
FREEDOM TRAIN 1947--THE FIRST!	10	75	04
FREEDOM TRAIN IS LANDMARK-RR SECURITY	05	48	104
FREEDOM TRAIN PHOTO CONTEST WINNERS	10	77	28R
FREIGHT BUSINESS- HOW TO GET M&A	01	41	65
FREIGHT CAR INTERCHANGING IN US	02	76	47
FREIGHT CARS ON THE HIGHWAY	01	51	06
FREIGHT CARS RIDE THE WAVES	03	72	47
FREIGHT INSPECTOR	06	44	133
FREIGHT--MOVING CHRISTMAS TREES	12	31	29
FREIGHT--UNUSUAL SHIPMENTS	12	31	24
FREIGHT: WHERE IS IT????	08	48	54
FREQUENCY OF FREIGHT TRAINS DISCUSSION	04	64	29
FRICTION & LUBRICATION OF STEAM LOCOS	12	43	70
FRIENDS OF A MUSEUM IN NEED	09	85	43
FRISCO CUTS RATE TO FIGHT BUS COMPETITIO	05	31	161

GENERAL RAILROADING	M	Y	P
FRIST RAIL MILL IN AMERICA	01	36	87
FROG WAR PRR VS D&BB 1876	10	32	353
FROG WARS	03	53	62
FROM THE PACIFIC TO ATLANTIC IN 100 MIN.	02	32	334
FRUSTRATIONS OF RAILFANNING	SU	76	43R
FUNERAL TRAIN-ULYSSES S GRANT JULY 1885	09	35	57
FUNERAL TRAINS AND SUBURBAN CEMETERY	12	71	13
FUSEE RULES FOR SLOW MOVING TRAINS	01	78	06
FUSEES	08	51	12
G.I. RAILS	03	52	96
GAGE COCKS & WATER GLASSES IN STEAM LOCO	10	44	67
GANDY DANCERS LIVE LONGER	08	63	22
GANDY-DANCERS: GOOD-BYE	08	57	48
GASOLINE ALLEY-RAIL PHOTOGRAPHER SEGMENT	11	87	47
GATEWAY YARD (P&LE)	10	58	18
GAUGES IN RAILROAD HISTORY	11	39	74
GENERAL AGENT--HIS JOB	06	30	411
GENERAL YARDMASTER	01	44	10
GERMAN PASSENGER MILEAGE EXCEEDS AMERICN	08	36	121
GHOST TOWN RHYOLITE NV	10	76	02
GIRL "OP" WRITES FINEST "FIST"	01	31	252
GIRL ON A COAL PILE--BR&W	01	79	08
GN & NP COMPLETE 230 MILE OREGON TO CALI	02	32	397
GOLD COUNTRY IRON TRAIL WP&Y	10	31	378
GOLDEN SPIKE	12	39	122
GOOD-BYE CALIFORNIA ZEPHYR (WP)	07	70	32
GOULD-FISK WANT TO ADD A&SU TO ERIE	03	33	16
GRAHAM CUTOFF	09	51	42
GRAND JCT COLORADO CAPSULE HISTORY	12	78	45
GRAVY TRAIN: CATTLE MOVING	04	53	38
GREAT DAYS OF CIRCUS TRAINS	07	75	10
GREAT FREIGHT '79 FAN TRIP C&TS	01	80	38
GREAT LAKES RAILROADING	03	43	110
GREAT LAKES RAILROADING: FLOATING FRT YD	03	43	110
GREAT LOCOMOTIVE SHUFFLE-1974	SP	75	43R
GREAT NORTHERN AND JIM HILL (FOUNDER)	02	37	34
GREAT NORTHERN RADIO PROGRAM-EMPIRE BLDR	02	32	388
GREAT STEAM EXHIBITION	F	76	22R
GREATEST CONCENTRATION OF STEAM--GWS	03	72	22
GREEN FRUIT (GFX) TRAINS OF ATSF	01	38	59
GUARD RAILS--3 TYPES	10	31	426
GUS PHILLIPS CALLS KING BORIS III	06	38	66
HAGERSTOWN MARYLAND: EARLY RAILROAD CENT	08	53	11
HAND CLEARING IC ROW 1936 REMSEN IA PHOT	01	76	06
HARVEY GIRLS OF 1870'S--WHO WERE THEY?	04	62	48
HARVEY GIRLS USE TO BE QUEENS OF RAILS	08	69	10

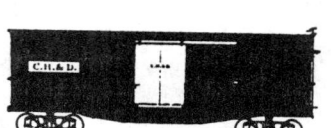

GENERAL RAILROADING

GENERAL RAILROADING	M	Y	P
HATS: SECTION 77 = FREE HATS TO TRAINMEN	11	46	43
HAULING HIGH HAZARD-DYNAMITE/EXPLOSIVES	06	30	369
HAWAIIAN RAILWAY PROJECT	10	68	44
HE "STOLE" A MONUMENT	11	36	27
HE BOUGHT 8 SHORTLINES-SAMUEL PINSLY	04	67	61
HEADLIGHTS: THEIR HISTORY	07	41	18
HEAVIEST LOAD CARRIED ON D&H FOR 208 MI.	11	35	87
HEENAN MINISTER OF LABOR-CP HOGGER	08	31	25
HERE COMES 765! 2-8-4 NKP #765	01	80	42
HERE COMES CONRAIL: THE NE WILL NEVER BE	SU	75	38R
HERITAGE OF "RAILROAD" MAGAZINE	09	79	32
HERITAGE OF "RAILROAD" MAGAZINE 2	03	80	32
HERITAGE OF "RAILROAD" MAGAZINE 3	07	80	24
HEROES OF CP	07	35	76
HI-FI RAILROAD RECORDINGS	10	60	50
HIGH COST OF PERISHABLE HAULING-LOSSES!	01	31	169
HIGH SPEED AT PUEBLO CO--DOT TEST GROUND	05	75	59
HIGH SPEED OPERATION IN LARGE CITIES	02	47	99
HIGH-SPEED MASS TRANSIT	05	65	35
HIGH-SPEED TRAINS: STEAM OR DIESEL DEBAT	06	43	52
HIGHBALL-ORIGIN OF TERM	11	31	488
HIGHBALLING IN HAWAII	10	46	84
HIGHBALLING THE BROADWAY LIMITED	12	29	88
HIGHBALLING THE T-BONE	12	49	16
HIGHWAY TO YESTERDAY--THE RAILROAD DEPOT	01	76	13
HILL AGAINST HARRIMAN 1910	01	35	90
HILL-HARRIMAN CANYON WAR IN OREGON	10	56	22
HILLS MAKE RAILROADS INTERESTING	07	40	73
HISTORY OF UDEY:ROUTE OF FIRE-BULLS	06	68	18
HOBBLE SKIRT CARS	02	44	74
HOBO SIGN LANGUAGE	04	67	30
HOBO SIGNAL SYSTEM & SIGNS	12	70	42
HOBO SIGNAL SYSTEM & SIGNS ADENDUM	01	71	06
HOME IN A F-UNIT	03	84	60
HOPEFUL TREND IN RR INDUSTRY-LABOR SECRE	04	31	62
HORSE-CAR DAYS	02	46	08
HORSE-ERA RAILROADING AT HARBORSIDE	02	78	50R
HORSES: TRAIN RIDE BEST TRANSPORTATION	08	54	20
HOSTLER HELPER	04	38	54
HOTBOX ALARMS--CHEMICALS USED	11	50	64
HOTSHOT FREIGHT LV	11	40	06
HOUSTON UNION STATION	09	52	14
HOW A RAILROAD MOVIE IS MADE	08	33	92
HOW MANY RAILROADS IN THE US-ALL TIME	06	61	33
HOW MILITARY AFFECTED RAILROAD TIMETABLE	05	51	28
HOW THE N&W #1218 WAS SAVED	09	87	45
HUMP RIDER GONE-MECHANICAL DEVICES HERE	08	30	83
HUMP YARD: DEFINITION	02	38	56
HUMP-BACKED LOCOMOTIVES	12	35	38
I NEVER PLANNED TO BE A RAILFAN-MARRIED	05	86	50
IC SETTLEMENT OF DAMAGES--C JONES WRECK	07	66	40
ICC AND PASSENGER TRAINS	03	68	06
ICE RAILWAYS IN CANADA	05	67	32
IDEAL FREIGHT CREW	06	34	70
ILLINOIS CENTRAL ON MY MIND	01	87	75

GENERAL RAILROADING	M	Y	P
IMPROVEMENTS IN RAILROADING	01	37	77
IN GLORY DAYS OF INTERURBANS (C&LE)	09	74	46
IN SEARCH OF STEAM:PORTAGE LA PRAIRIE CP	11	83	42
IN THE GREAT DAYS OF STEAM RAILROADING	09	54	21
IN THE HOLE--FOR HOUSING	12	46	47
INDEX OF ELECTRIC LINE ARTICLES IN RAILR	01	68	42
INDEX TO LANTERN ARTICLES	08	43	61
INFORMATION MAN--TICKET SELLER/CLERK/ETC	12	38	62
INJECTOR ECONOMY IN STEAM LOCOS	12	47	74
INJECTORS AND GOVERNORS FOR DIESEL LOCOS	06	52	54
INSPECTION LOCOMOTIVES: THEIR HISTORY	04	45	08
INSTRUCTION CAR SP #111 (ROLLING CLASSRM	09	41	16
INTERMITTENT TRAIN CONTROL	10	50	53
INTERNATIONAL COMPLICATIONS US/CANADA	08	47	77
INTERSTATE COMMERCE COMMISSION	02	36	82
INTERSTATE COMMERCE COMMISSION	08	38	06
INVENTION-HAMMOCK FOR DAY COACH	10	35	98
INVENTION-SQUIRT AT LOOSE ANIMALS	10	35	99
IRON HORSE RAMBLES (READING)	11	79	56
IRON ORE ALCOS AND MORE (E&LS)	11	85	60
IRON SPIKE AT GOLD CREEK NP	12	33	84
IVAN AND THE OSS (4-8-4'S)	11	84	53
JAMES BOYS: READER MEMORIES	08	47	126
JAMES O'NEILL GEN MANAGER GREAT NORTHERN	05	32	214
JANNEY COUPLERS & MILLER HOOKS	10	62	08
JAY GOULD MADE A HUNDRED MILLION	07	36	26
JOB DESCRIPTIONS	01	32	260
JOB QUALIFICATION (SHORT) READERS COMENT	02	61	08
JOHN HENRY REAL STORY	08	65	08
JOHNSON BAR, THE STORY OF	11	30	602
JOHNSTON PA FLOOD MAY 31 1889 PRR PHOTOS	06	49	13
JOHNSTOWN FLOOD PHOTO ESSAY	08	39	119
JOINT LINE-DENVER TO PUEBLO	05	78	46R
JONES, CASEY: MEMORIAL TO	11	47	116
JUBILEE AT EDAVILLE PHOTO ESSAY	10	71	40
K4 & PENNSY HEADLIGHTS READER COMMENTS	10	87	08
KEEPING TAB ON COMMUTER TRAINS	02	66	34
KENOVA WV AND COAL	04	78	50R
KIMBALL, OHIO 1974 N&W	W	74	30R
KIMBALL, OHIO: 1957 NKP	W	74	26R
KIMBALL, OHIO:1974 CHESSIE	W	74	30R
KIMBALL,OHIO:1957 B&O	W	74	26R
KING OF THE HOBOS--MAURY GRAHAM	05	77	08
KING OF THE SUBWAY LOCKERS	12	67	35
KINGS DINER ON PANAMA LIMITED	07	67	10
KIT CARSON COLORADO: GHOST TOWN/REASONS	08	54	108
L&N "PAN AMERICA" ON THE RAILROAD	04	37	118
LACKAWANNA ENGINEERS OVERCOME OBSTACLES	12	29	136
LADY ENGINEER ON BN	09	77	05
LADY SLEEPS ON TRAIN NIGHTLY FOR $12/WEE	12	76	08
LADY SWITCHTENDER ON PRR	04	54	18
LAND GRANT LEGEND PART 1 IC	08	51	28
LAND GRANT LEGEND PART 2	09	51	64
LAND GRANT LEGEND PART 3	10	51	68
LAND GRANT LEGEND PART 4	11	51	30

Railroad/ Railfan

STEPHANS' RAILROAD DIRECTORY

GENERAL RAILROADING

GENERAL RAILROADING	M	Y	P
LAND GRANT LEGEND PART 5 OF 5	12	51	40
LAND GRANT RAILROADS	11	40	75
LANTERNS	01	53	34
LARGEST ACTIVE STEAM LOCOMOTIVE UP #8444	03	75	18
LARGEST COLLECTION OF ACTIVE STEAM IN US	09	70	19
LARGEST FIVE RAILROADS IN US 1965	12	66	27
LASER TRACK INSPECTOR	01	70	36
LAST OF THE CABLE CARS	11	45	90
LAST OF THE INTERURBANS	02	55	38
LAST OF THE NARROW GAUGES	08	41	06
LAST OF THE NARROW-GAGES	01	37	46
LAST RUN OF BERKSHIRE EXPRESS	08	71	20
LAST RUN OF MP "TEXAS EAGLE"	01	71	38
LAST STOCK ROUNDUP AT PARLIN COLORADO	F	76	42R
LAST SURVIVOR OF PLANNED CRASH OF 1896	05	67	33
LAST TRAIN ROBBED BY GUNPOINT 10,1960	04	61	13
LAST YEARS OF CANADIAN PACIFIC STEAM	10	69	18
LEADER OF LOST CAUSES-EUGENE VICTOR DEBS	12	37	43
LEHIGH VALLEY JOINS RANKS OF BANKRUPT RD	06	73	23
LEVERS OF STEAM LOCOMOTIVES	10	43	64
LI ROAD DOG NAMED "ROXIE" 1915	04	62	48
LIBERATION OF PRR #1361 CLASS K4	01	86	62
LIBRARIES: ASSOC OF AMER RR/BUREAU OF TR	10	54	43
LIBRARY: LARGEST RAILROAD--WASHINGTON DC	10	40	31
LIDGERWOOD METHOD OF RE-TURNING WWHEELS	02	44	52
LIGHTWEIGHT TRAINS: AEROTRAIN/TRAIN X	06	56	30
LIMA LOCOMOTIVE WORKS: 60 YEARS	12	39	06
LIMITED FAST TRAINS: WHY CALLED THAT?	03	36	87
LINCOLN PIN: DEVELOPMENT OF COUPLER	05	41	06
LINCOLN SAVED RI BRIDGE-MISSISSIPPI RIVE	02	31	328
LINK AND PIN COUPLER	02	39	128
LINK AND PINS (4 VARIETIES) PHOTOS	05	41	11
LINK PIN COUPLERS & REPLACEMENT	01	65	31
LINK, PIN, AND DRAWBAR ASSEMBLY PHOTO	05	41	13
LIONEL TRAIN VALUE APPRECIATION	03	78	06
LIST OF 4-6-6-4 LOCOS BUILT & OWNERS	10	64	25
LIST OF ABANDONED CANADIAN ELECTRIC TRAC	12	43	156
LIST OF ACROYMNS RELATING TO RAILROADS	09	66	57
LIST OF ACTIVE WOOD BURNING LOCOMOTIVES	06	60	29
LIST OF AMERICAS 25 LONGEST ROADS 1964	04	64	28
LIST OF B&M NAME LOCOMOTIVES	12	71	30
LIST OF BIGGEST MOST POWERFUL US LOCOS	03	65	56
LIST OF CAMELBACK LOCOMOTIVES & OWNERS	10	66	38
LIST OF CANADIAN ENGINES W/BIBLICAL NAME	09	76	51
LIST OF CANADIAN RAILROADS 1939	10	74	45
LIST OF CANADIAN RDS NOT LISTED IN OFF G	02	64	38
LIST OF CAR BUILDERS IN CANADAA	12	55	38
LIST OF CAR BUILDERS IN UNITED STATES	12	55	38
LIST OF CITIES WITH CABLE CAR SERVICE	04	60	48
LIST OF COUNTIES WITHOUT RAILROADS	01	47	130
LIST OF COVERED BRIDGES AS OF 1941	04	43	128
LIST OF CP BUILT LOCOMOTIVES	03	67	44
LIST OF CP STEAM LOCOMOTIVES	03	66	52
LIST OF DEMONSTRATORS & WHO BOUGHT THEM	02	65	33
LIST OF DIESEL PASS-LOCO NYC AUG 18 1948	01	49	70

GENERAL RAILROADING	M	Y	P
LIST OF DIESEL PASS-LOCO PRR AUG 18 1948	01	49	70
LIST OF DIESELS OPERATED PRIVATELY-CANAD	10	65	54
LIST OF DL&W NAMED & NUMBERED LOCOMOTIVE	07	65	33
LIST OF ELECTRIC INTERURBANS-CANADA	09	43	124
LIST OF ELECTRIC LINES 1945	12	45	94
LIST OF ELECTRIC LINES ARTICLES IN RR	11	75	56
LIST OF ELECTRIC LINES IN 1950 CORRECTIO	05	50	99
LIST OF ELECTRIC LINES IN ARKANSAS 1947	12	75	56
LIST OF ELECTRIC LINES IN CALIFORNIA '39	04	74	43
LIST OF ELECTRIC LINES IN CANADA/NEWFOUN	05	43	123
LIST OF ELECTRIC LINES IN FLORIDA	12	46	105
LIST OF ELECTRIC LINES IN ILLINOIS 1940	11	77	24
LIST OF ELECTRIC LINES IN INDIANA 1940	11	77	24
LIST OF ELECTRIC LINES IN IOWA 1945	03	78	52
LIST OF ELECTRIC LINES IN IOWA 1945 ADD	08	78	56
LIST OF ELECTRIC LINES IN KANSAS 1945	10	75	53
LIST OF ELECTRIC LINES IN LOUISIANA 1945	12	75	56
LIST OF ELECTRIC LINES IN MARYLAND 1945	05	76	25
LIST OF ELECTRIC LINES IN MEXICO 1945	02	78	50
LIST OF ELECTRIC LINES IN MINN 1945	07	78	56
LIST OF ELECTRIC LINES IN MISSISSIPPI 45	12	75	56
LIST OF ELECTRIC LINES IN MISSOURI 1945	03	78	52
LIST OF ELECTRIC LINES IN N AMER: ABANDO	03	47	93
LIST OF ELECTRIC LINES IN NEBRASKA 1945	03	78	52
LIST OF ELECTRIC LINES IN NEW ENGLAND 45	03	76	55
LIST OF ELECTRIC LINES IN OKLAHOMA 1945	10	75	53
LIST OF ELECTRIC LINES IN ONTARIO 1944	02	76	46
LIST OF ELECTRIC LINES IN PA 1945	05	76	25
LIST OF ELECTRIC LINES IN TENNESSEE 1945	12	75	56
LIST OF ELECTRIC LINES IN TEXAS	11	44	88
LIST OF ELECTRIC LINES IN TEXAS 1945	10	75	53
LIST OF ELECTRIC LINES IN UNITED STATES	05	43	117
LIST OF ELECTRIC LINES IN WISC 1946	07	78	56
LIST OF ELECTRIC LINES NYS/ABANDONED/	02	45	104
LIST OF ELECTRIC RAILROADS CONNECTICUT	04	47	72
LIST OF ELECTRIC RAILWAY PUBLICATIONS	02	49	83
LIST OF ELECTRIC RAILWAYS IN VIRGINIA	03	50	81
LIST OF ELECTRIC ROADS IN 1950 ADDS/CORR	07	50	120
LIST OF ELECTRIC ROADS IN WEST VIRGINA	09	48	107
LIST OF ELECTRIC STREET CAR BUILDERS	01	78	44
LIST OF ELECTRIC/INTERURBAN ROADS BY STA	01	48	99
LIST OF ELECTRICS IN OHIO	11	52	90
LIST OF ELECTRICS INTO GRAND CENTRAL TER	12	58	34
LIST OF ELECTRICS/INTERURBANS IN CANADA	01	48	101
LIST OF ELECTRIFIED CLASS 1 ROADS 1941	06	74	21
LIST OF ELEVATIONS OF ROCKY MT ROADS	05	76	25
LIST OF EMPLOYEES' MAGAZINES	07	40	72
LIST OF ENGINES ORDERED IN 1929 VS 1940	05	41	42
LIST OF FREIGHT CARS: MOST COMMON TYPES	07	37	52
LIST OF GRAND CAVALCADE OF STEAM LOCOS	04	76	21
LIST OF HEAVY PACIFICS & SPECIFICATIONS	03	69	48
LIST OF HEAVY STEAM-ROAD ELECTRIFICATION	02	50	76
LIST OF HIGHEST ALTITUDES AND ROADS	09	35	80
LIST OF HIGHEST ALTITUDES BY CONTINENTS	01	45	43
LIST OF INTERURBANS IN CHICAGO	08	59	75

GENERAL RAILROADING

GENERAL RAILROADING	M	Y	P
LIST OF INTERURBANS IN ILLINOIS 1900-25	09	53	76
LIST OF INTERURBANS IN INDIANA 1900-1925	09	53	76
LIST OF INTERURBANS IN IOWA--REVENUES	04	49	92
LIST OF INTERURBANS IN MICHIGAN 1900-25	09	53	76
LIST OF INTERURBANS IN OHIO 1900-1925	09	53	76
LIST OF INTERURBANS WHO WANT TO ABANDON	02	55	43
LIST OF LARGEST FREIGHT TERMINALS	07	47	121
LIST OF LARGEST LOCOS-BY WEIGHT	03	37	59
LIST OF LARGEST PASSENGER STATIONS	07	47	121
LIST OF LARGEST RAIL YARDS 1941	12	75	56
LIST OF LOCO BUILDERS IN CANADA	12	55	38
LIST OF LOCO BUILDERS IN NORTH AMERICA	06	57	44
LIST OF LOCO BUILDERS IN UNITED STATES	12	55	38
LIST OF LOCO BUILDERS IN VIRGINIA	06	57	45
LIST OF LOCO BUILDERS: STEAM (NOT GEARED	12	57	44
LIST OF LOCO TYPES IN SERVICE BY YEAR	11	69	29
LIST OF LOCOMOTIVES IN IDAHO 1972	11	72	56
LIST OF LOCOMOTIVES ON PC 2-1-75	12	76	51
LIST OF LOCOMOTIVES UNION ARMY CIVIL WAR	06	67	48
LIST OF LOCOMOTIVES: DEATH VALLEY SPECIA	08	40	61
LIST OF LOCOS AND HOW THEY GOT NAMES	02	36	88
LIST OF LOCOS NUMBERED SAME AS WHEEL ARR	06	47	130
LIST OF LOCOS OF HRRR W/NAMES AND NUMBER	03	51	28
LIST OF LOCOS ON DISPLAY AT WORLD'S FAIR	02	34	89
LIST OF LOCOS ON PERMANENT DISPLAY	12	52	126
LIST OF LOCOS OPERATED IN CANADA <1840	08	57	44
LIST OF LOCOS TO BE BUILT IN 1943	09	43	76
LIST OF LOCOS WITH RELIGIOUS NAMES CANAD	09	47	135
LIST OF LOGGING RAILROADS	08	55	51
LIST OF LOGGING RAILROADS IN CANADA	08	55	51
LIST OF LOGGING RAILROADS IN THE US	08	55	50
LIST OF LOGGING RAODS IN WEST VIRGINIA	04	57	46
LIST OF LONGEST RAIL TUNNELS	04	60	30
LIST OF MAJOR INTERURBAN ROUTES MIDWEST	09	53	79
LIST OF MINIMUM CLEARANCES OF TUNNELS	07	49	67
LIST OF MISSOURI STREET CAR & INTERURBAN	06	65	39
LIST OF MOTHER HUBBARB LOCOS CORRECTION	05	43	139
LIST OF NAMES FOR RF&P 4-8-2 LOCOS	10	76	46
LIST OF NORTH AMERICAN TUNNELS 1+ MILES	06	46	41
LIST OF PASS STEAM RR INTO CHICAGO/DATE	10	49	58
LIST OF PASSENGER STATIONS 1946 & ROADS	11	71	31
LIST OF PCC CARS IN USE BY ROADS/#S OF	06	46	135
LIST OF PERSONAL SIGNALS USED AMONG RRER	12	58	40
LIST OF PLACES NAMED FOR RR PRESIDENTS	02	65	25
LIST OF POTOMAC REGION ELECTRIC/TROLLEYS	04	46	118
LIST OF PUBLICATIONS FOR ELECTIC LINES	05	45	138
LIST OF PULLMAN "CASCADE" SERIES	08	40	61
LIST OF PULLMAN CASCADE SERIES (ADDS)	10	40	71
LIST OF RAILFAN CLUB PUBLICATIONS	03	70	46
LIST OF RAILFAN CLUBS,MUSEUMS,TOURIST RD	06	74	23
LIST OF RAILORAD CENTERS: 10 LARGEST US	07	36	80
LIST OF RAILRIADS IN ILLINOIS	03	34	87
LIST OF RAILROAD "COMPANY" MAGAZINES	02	34	88
LIST OF RAILROAD EMPLOYEE MAGAZINES	08	64	30
LIST OF RAILROAD EMPLOYEE PUB: ATSF/UP	06	39	56
LIST OF RAILROAD GAGES & COUNTRIES	05	55	32
LIST OF RAILROAD MEMORABILIA IN THE US	12	57	41
LIST OF RAILROAD STATIONS ON NATL REGIST	12	76	49
LIST OF RAILROAD STREET/AVE/SQ/TOWNS	04	52	134
LIST OF RAILROAD YARDS: 10 LARGEST	06	39	55
LIST OF RAILROADING OCCUPATIONS-10 LARGE	04	42	66
LIST OF RAILROADS & COLOR OF PASS EQUIP	06	34	87
LIST OF RAILROADS & COLOR OF PASS STOCK	08	34	84
LIST OF RAILROADS 1935 ABANDONED MILEAGE	08	36	71
LIST OF RAILROADS ABANDONED IN 1941	06	42	89
LIST OF RAILROADS AND MAIN LINE ALTITUDE	01	36	81
LIST OF RAILROADS ANTHRACITE	03	35	84
LIST OF RAILROADS ANTHRACITE (CORRECTION	06	35	87
LIST OF RAILROADS BITUMINOUS	03	35	84
LIST OF RAILROADS BITUMINOUS (CORRECTION	06	35	87
LIST OF RAILROADS BURNING HARD COAL	05	40	91
LIST OF RAILROADS CONTROLLED BY B&O	09	41	78
LIST OF RAILROADS CONTROLLED BY US STEEL	04	42	64
LIST OF RAILROADS ENTERING ST LOUIS MO	10	43	72
LIST OF RAILROADS EXEMPT ICC FARE REDUCT	09	36	74
LIST OF RAILROADS IN ALABAMA (STEAM)	06	35	83
LIST OF RAILROADS IN ALABAMA: MOBILE	04	40	77
LIST OF RAILROADS IN ALASKA	06	38	77
LIST OF RAILROADS IN ALASKA	02	37	77
LIST OF RAILROADS IN ALASKA	04	35	86
LIST OF RAILROADS IN ALASKA	05	33	134
LIST OF RAILROADS IN ALASKA 1918	09	76	52
LIST OF RAILROADS IN ALASKA: MILEAGE	09	48	81
LIST OF RAILROADS IN AMERICA-NARROW GAGE	01	37	71
LIST OF RAILROADS IN ARIZONA (STEAM)	04	36	87
LIST OF RAILROADS IN ARIZONA PAST & PRES	06	62	46
LIST OF RAILROADS IN ARKANSAS (STEAM)	01	36	82
LIST OF RAILROADS IN CALIFORNIA (STEAM)	12	34	82
LIST OF RAILROADS IN CALIFORNIA (ADDS)	03	35	85
LIST OF RAILROADS IN CALIFORNIA (JUICE)	09	40	60
LIST OF RAILROADS IN CALIFORNIA: NARROW	10	39	86
LIST OF RAILROADS IN CALIFORNIA: STEAM	02	33	83
LIST OF RAILROADS IN CANADA	03	34	85
LIST OF RAILROADS IN CANADA--CORRECTIONS	06	38	78
LIST OF RAILROADS IN CANADA: THEIR MILES	04	38	50
LIST OF RAILROADS IN COLORADO (STEAM)	11	34	92
LIST OF RAILROADS IN CONNECTICUT (STEAM)	05	35	85
LIST OF RAILROADS IN DELAWARE	12	37	54
LIST OF RAILROADS IN DELAWARE	08	36	76
LIST OF RAILROADS IN DELAWARE (STEAM)	04	35	83
LIST OF RAILROADS IN DELAWARE (ADDITION)	06	35	87
LIST OF RAILROADS IN DETROIT 1940	03	76	56
LIST OF RAILROADS IN FLORIDA--STEAM	06	34	85
LIST OF RAILROADS IN GEORGIA (ADDITION)	06	35	87
LIST OF RAILROADS IN GEORGIA (STEAM)	04	35	85
LIST OF RAILROADS IN HAWAII	04	35	83
LIST OF RAILROADS IN IDAHO (STEAM)	03	36	85
LIST OF RAILROADS IN ILLINOIS: CHICAGO	10	36	75
LIST OF RAILROADS IN INDIANA (STEAM)	06	36	84
LIST OF RAILROADS IN IOWA	02	34	87

Railroad/Railfan

GENERAL RAILROADING

GENERAL RAILROADING	M	Y	P
LIST OF RAILROADS IN KANSAS (STEAM)	05	35	86
LIST OF RAILROADS IN KENTUCKY (STEAM)	10	37	69
LIST OF RAILROADS IN LOUISIANA (STEAM)	11	37	53
LIST OF RAILROADS IN MAINE	03	36	87
LIST OF RAILROADS IN MAINE (STEAM)	05	35	85
LIST OF RAILROADS IN MARYLAND (STEAM)	08	36	76
LIST OF RAILROADS IN MASSACHUSETTS-STEAM	10	34	86
LIST OF RAILROADS IN MEXICO & CENTRAL AM	10	73	34
LIST OF RAILROADS IN MICHIGAN (STEAM)	07	35	85
LIST OF RAILROADS IN MICHIGAN (DETROIT)	07	39	83
LIST OF RAILROADS IN MINNESOTA--STEAM RD	04	34	83
LIST OF RAILROADS IN MISSOURI (STEAM)	02	36	88
LIST OF RAILROADS IN MISSOURI (STEAM)	09	34	87
LIST OF RAILROADS IN MONTANA	08	37	58
LIST OF RAILROADS IN MONTANA 1930	02	75	50
LIST OF RAILROADS IN N AMER: LONGEST	08	36	76
LIST OF RAILROADS IN N DAKOTA 1930	05	78	57
LIST OF RAILROADS IN NEBRASKA	08	37	58
LIST OF RAILROADS IN NEBRASKA 1939	10	74	46
LIST OF RAILROADS IN NEVADA (STEAM)	11	34	94
LIST OF RAILROADS IN NEW ENGLAND STATES	07	33	80
LIST OF RAILROADS IN NEW HAMPSHIRE	03	36	87
LIST OF RAILROADS IN NEW HAMPSHIRE-STEAM	01	35	86
LIST OF RAILROADS IN NEW JERSEY	01	34	91
LIST OF RAILROADS IN NEW JERSEY (STEAM)	09	35	86
LIST OF RAILROADS IN NEW MEXICO (STEAM)	03	35	87
LIST OF RAILROADS IN NEW YORK STATE	07	34	92
LIST OF RAILROADS IN NEW YORK-MANHATTAN	04	37	49
LIST OF RAILROADS IN NORTH CAROLINA (STE	08	34	90
LIST OF RAILROADS IN NORTH CAROLINA-STEA	02	35	87
LIST OF RAILROADS IN NORTH DAKOTA	07	37	56
LIST OF RAILROADS IN NORTH DAKOTA--STEAM	07	34	93
LIST OF RAILROADS IN NOVA SCOTIA (STEAM)	12	34	85
LIST OF RAILROADS IN OHIO (STEAM)	02	35	86
LIST OF RAILROADS IN OHIO: CINCINNATI	06	36	81
LIST OF RAILROADS IN OHIO: CINCINNATI-CO	08	36	76
LIST OF RAILROADS IN OKLAHOMA (STEAM)	09	34	83
LIST OF RAILROADS IN OREGON (STEAM)	06	35	87
LIST OF RAILROADS IN PENNSYLVANIA--STEAM	05	34	83
LIST OF RAILROADS IN PENNSYLVANIA-NARROW	05	35	84
LIST OF RAILROADS IN QUEBEC (STEAM)	01	35	84
LIST OF RAILROADS IN QUEBEC IN 1935	12	75	57
LIST OF RAILROADS IN ST LOUIS 1941	08	74	56
LIST OF RAILROADS IN TENNESSEE (STEAM)	04	36	94
LIST OF RAILROADS IN TEXAS (STEAM)	08	34	87
LIST OF RAILROADS IN THE CARIBBEAN	12	68	13
LIST OF RAILROADS IN US/CANADA:STREAMLIN	01	38	61
LIST OF RAILROADS IN US: 1 & 2 MILE ROAD	06	59	37
LIST OF RAILROADS IN US: LONGEST MILEAGE	11	37	51
LIST OF RAILROADS IN UTAH (STEAM)	05	37	39
LIST OF RAILROADS IN VERMONT (STEAM)	12	34	87
LIST OF RAILROADS IN VIRGINIA--STEAM RDS	07	34	90
LIST OF RAILROADS IN WASHINGTON STATE	10	33	43
LIST OF RAILROADS IN WEST VIRGINIA-STEAM	10	34	85
LIST OF RAILROADS IN WISCONSIN	04	35	85
LIST OF RAILROADS IN WISCONSIN	12	33	88
LIST OF RAILROADS LARGEST MAIN LINE MILE	01	35	81
LIST OF RAILROADS MISSISSIPPI TO PAC ADD	11	35	86
LIST OF RAILROADS MISSISSIPPI TO PACIFIC	08	35	85
LIST OF RAILROADS NOT IN OFFICIAL GUIDE2	10	62	54
LIST OF RAILROADS NOT IN OFFICIAL GUIDE3	12	62	54
LIST OF RAILROADS NOT LISTED IN OFFICIAL	08	62	28
LIST OF RAILROADS OPERATING STREAMLINERS	04	41	45
LIST OF RAILROADS PENINSULAR	04	36	94
LIST OF RAILROADS THAT ISSUED CURRENCY	07	42	105
LIST OF RAILROADS UNDER GRAVEYARDS	08	50	125
LIST OF RAILROADS UNDER GRAVEYARDS ADDS	09	50	129
LIST OF RAILROADS UNDER GRAVEYARDS B&O	11	50	140
LIST OF RAILROADS UNDER GRAVEYARDS MORE!	03	51	128
LIST OF RAILROADS UNDER GRAVEYARDS-2 ADD	04	51	130
LIST OF RAILROADS USING CAMELBACK LOCOS	03	43	99
LIST OF RAILROADS USING HUDSON LOCOS ADD	05	43	91
LIST OF RAILROADS USING I/C TRAIN CONTRL	04	34	86
LIST OF RAILROADS W/EMPLOYEE MAGAZINES	04	39	80
LIST OF RAILROADS W/EMPLOYEEES MAGAZINES	01	35	87
LIST OF RAILROADS W/LOCO/FRT/PASS/MISC C	03	34	89
LIST OF RAILROADS W/PASS SERV NY TO CHIC	12	37	52
LIST OF RAILROADS W/PASSENGER SERV 1959	08	59	38
LIST OF RAILROADS W/POST OFFICE CAR 1959	08	59	38
LIST OF RAILROADS WITH 4-6-4 TYPE LOCOS	04	38	55
LIST OF RAILROADS WITH HIGHEST ALTITUDES	02	37	75
LIST OF RAILROADS WITH LOCO FEMININE NAM	08	44	131
LIST OF RAILROADS WITH MOTHER HUBBARBS	05	38	75
LIST OF RAILROADS-DATE OPENED/COUNTRY	06	58	39
LIST OF RAILROADS-SHORTEST <1 MILE 1959	08	59	38
LIST OF RAILROADS: 15 LARGEST 1935 INCOM	09	36	71
LIST OF RAILROADS: ABAND TRACK 1922-1935	10	36	70
LIST OF RAILROADS: ATLANTIC TO PACIFIC C	08	38	90
LIST OF RAILROADS: LONGEST RUNS 07-36 80	09	36	77
LIST OF RAILROADS: NON-PULLMAN STD SLEEP	08	40	62
LIST OF RAILRODS IN CANADA QUEBEC	02	36	84
LIST OF RAILRODS IN MISSISSIPPI (STEAM)	12	35	87
LIST OF RAILRODS IN SOUTH DAKOTA	07	37	56
LIST OF RDS NOT IN OFFICIAL GUIDE REVISE	02	64	39
LIST OF RETIRED LOCOS IN DISPLAY USA	03	53	128
LIST OF RETIRED LOCOS ON DISPLAY---MORE!	12	53	124
LIST OF RETIRED LOCOS ON DISPLAY-MORE!!!	09	53	121
LIST OF RETITED LOCOS ON DISPLAY-MORE	04	53	128
LIST OF RI MOTOR CARS	04	66	22
LIST OF ROADS CONTROLLED BY ACL 1940	05	75	51
LIST OF ROADS HAVING 4-6-4 1940	03	75	12
LIST OF ROADS IN CN SYSTEM	10	75	52
LIST OF ROADS IN SP IN 1940	07	75	52
LIST OF ROADS MAKING UP CONRAIL	07	76	50
LIST OF ROADS NOT IN OFFICIAL GUIDE 5	04	63	38
LIST OF ROADS NOT IN OFFICIAL GUIDE 8	08	63	57
LIST OF ROADS NOT IN OFFICIAL GUIDE	12	63	52
LIST OF ROADS NOT IN OFFICIAL GUIDE 9	10	63	58
LIST OF ROADS NOT LISTED IN OFF GUIDE 4	02	63	50
LIST OF ROSTERS PUBLISHED IN RAILROAD	09	67	58

526

Railroad/Railfan

GENERAL RAILROADING

GENERAL RAILROADING	M	Y	P
LIST OF SALARIES PAID RR PRESIDENTS 1964	04	64	30
LIST OF SHORT LINE MILEAGE BY STATE	09	69	30
LIST OF SHORT LINES IN THE "ASLRA"	10	44	88
LIST OF SHORTLINE RAILROADS (D-F)	10	77	34
LIST OF SHORTLINE RAILROADS (F-G)	01	78	54
LIST OF SHORTLINE RAILROADS (G)	03	78	54
LIST OF SHORTLINE RAILROADS (G-I)	10	78	57
LIST OF SHORTLINE RAILROADS (I-K)	07	78	62
LIST OF SHORTLINE RAILROADS (L)	01	79	51
LIST OF SHORTLINE RAILROADS (L-M)	11	78	57
LIST OF SHORTLINE RAILROADS (M)	07	79	29
LIST OF SHORTLINES (A-B)	04	75	47
LIST OF SHORTLINES (B-C)	06	75	52
LIST OF SHORTLINES (C)	10	75	43
LIST OF SHORTLINES (CH-CO)	11	75	49
LIST OF SHORTLINES DICTRICT OF COLUMBIA	08	59	55
LIST OF SHORTLINES IN ALABAMA	02	67	48
LIST OF SHORTLINES IN ALABAMA 1971	07	71	52
LIST OF SHORTLINES IN ALASKA 1967	03	67	64
LIST OF SHORTLINES IN ARIZONA 1967	04	67	39
LIST OF SHORTLINES IN ARIZONA 1971	10	71	46
LIST OF SHORTLINES IN ARKANSAS	06	64	48
LIST OF SHORTLINES IN ARKANSAS 1967	05	67	54
LIST OF SHORTLINES IN ARKANSAS 1972	03	72	58
LIST OF SHORTLINES IN CALIFORNIA	08	64	60
LIST OF SHORTLINES IN CALIFORNIA 1967	06	67	50
LIST OF SHORTLINES IN CALIFORNIA 1972	03	72	59
LIST OF SHORTLINES IN CANADA	02	66	54
LIST OF SHORTLINES IN CANADA 1971	05	71	57
LIST OF SHORTLINES IN COLORADO	10	64	62
LIST OF SHORTLINES IN COLORADO 1967	07	67	64
LIST OF SHORTLINES IN COLORADO 1972	07	72	59
LIST OF SHORTLINES IN CONNECTICUT 1972	06	72	50
LIST OF SHORTLINES IN DISTRICT OF COLUMB	09	67	65
LIST OF SHORTLINES IN DISTRICT OF COLUMB	12	59	34
LIST OF SHORTLINES IN FLORIDA 1967	10	67	50
LIST OF SHORTLINES IN FLORIDA 1972	08	72	57
LIST OF SHORTLINES IN GEORGA 1965	02	65	54
LIST OF SHORTLINES IN GEORGA 1967	11	67	46
LIST OF SHORTLINES IN GEORGIA 1972	10	72	44
LIST OF SHORTLINES IN IDAHO 1965	01	65	63
LIST OF SHORTLINES IN IDAHO 1967	12	67	48
LIST OF SHORTLINES IN IL 1967	03	68	52
LIST OF SHORTLINES IN ILLINOIS	10	59	68
LIST OF SHORTLINES IN ILLINOIS 1973	01	73	52
LIST OF SHORTLINES IN INDIANA	12	62	60
LIST OF SHORTLINES IN INDIANA 1968	02	68	62
LIST OF SHORTLINES IN IOWA 1965	02	65	58
LIST OF SHORTLINES IN IOWA 1967	01	68	56
LIST OF SHORTLINES IN IOWA 1973	05	73	56
LIST OF SHORTLINES IN KANSAS 1965	04	65	36
LIST OF SHORTLINES IN KANSAS 1968	04	68	48
LIST OF SHORTLINES IN KANSAS 1973	08	73	13
LIST OF SHORTLINES IN KENTUCKY 10-1964	04	65	53
LIST OF SHORTLINES IN KENTUCKY 1968	05	68	52
LIST OF SHORTLINES IN KENTUCKY 1973	10	73	61
LIST OF SHORTLINES IN LOUISIANA 1965	05	65	50
LIST OF SHORTLINES IN LOUISIANA 1968	06	68	50
LIST OF SHORTLINES IN LOUISIANA 1973	07	73	58
LIST OF SHORTLINES IN MAINE 1968	07	68	56
LIST OF SHORTLINES IN MAINE 1973	06	73	11
LIST OF SHORTLINES IN MARYLAND 1968	09	68	44
LIST OF SHORTLINES IN MARYLAND 1974	01	74	45
LIST OF SHORTLINES IN MASSACHUSETTS '73	10	73	13
LIST OF SHORTLINES IN MASSACHUSETTS 1968	09	68	50
LIST OF SHORTLINES IN MICHIGAN 1965	06	65	55
LIST OF SHORTLINES IN MICHIGAN 1968	10	68	38
LIST OF SHORTLINES IN MICHIGAN 1974	03	74	46
LIST OF SHORTLINES IN MINNESOTA 1965	07	65	53
LIST OF SHORTLINES IN MINNESOTA 1968	12	68	48
LIST OF SHORTLINES IN MINNESOTA 1973	11	73	62
LIST OF SHORTLINES IN MISSISSIPPI 1965	08	65	65
LIST OF SHORTLINES IN MISSISSIPPI 1969	03	69	38
LIST OF SHORTLINES IN MISSISSIPPI 1974	05	74	59
LIST OF SHORTLINES IN MISSOURI 1965	09	65	54
LIST OF SHORTLINES IN MISSOURI 1969	02	69	46
LIST OF SHORTLINES IN MONTANA 1965	12	65	28
LIST OF SHORTLINES IN MONTANA 1969	05	69	50
LIST OF SHORTLINES IN NEBRASKA 1965	11	65	55
LIST OF SHORTLINES IN NEBRASKA 1969	03	69	66
LIST OF SHORTLINES IN NEBRASKA 1974	08	74	55
LIST OF SHORTLINES IN NEW HAMPSHIRE 1969	05	69	50
LIST OF SHORTLINES IN NEW HAMPSHIRE 1974	08	74	55
LIST OF SHORTLINES IN NEW JERSEY	02	59	44
LIST OF SHORTLINES IN NEW JERSEY 1969	07	69	48
LIST OF SHORTLINES IN NEW JERSEY 1974	10	74	48
LIST OF SHORTLINES IN NEW MEXICO 1969	07	69	54
LIST OF SHORTLINES IN NEW YORK 1963	04	64	52
LIST OF SHORTLINES IN NEW YORK 1969	08	69	50
LIST OF SHORTLINES IN NEW YORK 1975	12	75	53
LIST OF SHORTLINES IN NORTH CAROLINA	08	64	36
LIST OF SHORTLINES IN NORTH CAROLINA '69	10	69	50
LIST OF SHORTLINES IN OHIO 1969	12	69	44
LIST OF SHORTLINES IN OKLAHOMA 1966	03	66	59
LIST OF SHORTLINES IN OKLAHOMA 1970	01	70	10
LIST OF SHORTLINES IN OREGON 1966	04	66	58
LIST OF SHORTLINES IN OREGON 1970	02	70	50
LIST OF SHORTLINES IN PENNSYLVANIA	05	66	48
LIST OF SHORTLINES IN PENNSYLVANIA 1970	03	70	62
LIST OF SHORTLINES IN RHODE ISLAND 1970	04	70	52
LIST OF SHORTLINES IN SOUTH CAROLINA	06	66	48
LIST OF SHORTLINES IN SOUTH CAROLINA '70	05	70	50
LIST OF SHORTLINES IN SOUTH DAKOTA 1966	08	66	64
LIST OF SHORTLINES IN TENNESSEE 1966	08	66	64
LIST OF SHORTLINES IN TENNESSEE 1970	07	70	41
LIST OF SHORTLINES IN TEXAS 1966	09	66	46
LIST OF SHORTLINES IN TEXAS 1970	11	70	40
LIST OF SHORTLINES IN UTAH 1970	12	70	60
LIST OF SHORTLINES IN VERMONT 1970	12	70	56
LIST OF SHORTLINES IN VIRGINIA 1966	10	66	52

Railroad/Railfan

GENERAL RAILROADING

GENERAL RAILROADING	M	Y	P
LIST OF SHORTLINES IN VIRGINIA 1971	04	71	51
LIST OF SHORTLINES IN WASHINGTON 1971	06	71	37
LIST OF SHORTLINES IN WASHINGTON DC 1972	06	72	50
LIST OF SHORTLINES IN WASHINGTON STATE	08	62	29
LIST OF SHORTLINES IN WEST VIRGINIA 1966	12	66	54
LIST OF SHORTLINES IN WEST VIRGINIA 1971	02	71	59
LIST OF SHORTLINES IN WISCONSIN 1966	01	66	66
LIST OF SHORTLINES IN WISCONSIN 1971	05	71	58
LIST OF SHORTLINES IN WYOMING 1966	11	66	62
LIST OF SHORTLINES IN WYOMING 1971	06	71	37
LIST OF SHORTLINES OF CONNECTICUT 1967	08	67	64
LIST OF SHORTLINES OF DELAWARE & MARYLAN	11	64	62
LIST OF SHORTLINES STARTING WITH (A)	03	75	44
LIST OF STANDARD ENGINE WHISTLE SIGNALS	05	45	30
LIST OF STATIONS WITH STREET NUMBERS	05	43	138
LIST OF STEAM & TROLLEY LINES IN WASH ST	10	78	47
LIST OF STEAM ENGINES--CANADIAN RY MUSEU	09	65	31
LIST OF STEAM IN US 1963	12	63	62
LIST OF STEAM LOCO ORDERED 1947/ROAD/BLD	05	48	69
LIST OF STEAM LOCO ORDERS FOR 1945	04	46	60
LIST OF STEAM LOCOMOTIVE BUILDERS	01	73	10
LIST OF STEAM LOCOMOTIVE BUILDERS (US)	11	66	40
LIST OF STEAM LOCOMOTIVE BUILDERS ADDS	03	73	09
LIST OF STEAM LOCOMOTIVE ORDERS 1941	04	42	88
LIST OF STEAM LOCOMOTIVES 1940 DELIV '41	04	42	92
LIST OF STEAM LOCOMOTIVES NDEM	01	71	26
LIST OF STEAM LOCOS ON D&RGW 1966	04	66	48
LIST OF STEAM LOCOS ON DISPLAY	10	59	31
LIST OF STEAM LOCOS ON DISPLAY 1959	10	59	48
LIST OF STEAM RAILROADS IN IDAHO 1935	09	75	56
LIST OF STEAM RAILROADS IN MISSISSIP '35	01	76	39
LIST OF STEAM ROADS IN ARIZONA 1937	07	76	51
LIST OF STEAM ROADS IN CALIFORNIA 1934	10	73	59
LIST OF STEAM ROADS IN INDIANA 1930	11	75	43
LIST OF STEAM ROADS IN KENTUCKY 1935	06	75	30
LIST OF STEAM ROADS IN LOUISIANA IN 1930	12	74	58
LIST OF STEAM ROADS IN MARYLAND 1930	03	75	10
LIST OF STEAM ROADS IN MICHIGAN IN 1934	09	73	41
LIST OF STEAM ROADS IN SOUTH DAKOTA 1938	07	75	53
LIST OF STEAM ROADS IN UTAH 1935	05	75	51
LIST OF STEAM SUPER-LOCOMOTIVES	10	66	19
LIST OF STREAMLINED TRAINS ADDITTIONS	06	41	29
LIST OF STREAMLINED TRAINS IN OPERATION	02	37	79
LIST OF STREET & INTERURBANS CANADA 1956	04	56	54
LIST OF STREET & INTERURBANS CUBA 1956	04	56	55
LIST OF STREET & INTERURBANS IN 1952	03	52	73
LIST OF STREET & INTERURBANS IN US 1956	04	56	54
LIST OF STREET & SUBURBAN RYS-CANADIAN E	09	43	125
LIST OF STREET RAILWAYS CORRECTIONS	06	60	38
LIST OF STREET RY/INTERURBANS IN CANADA	02	50	75
LIST OF STREET RY/INTERURBANS IN US 1950	02	50	73
LIST OF STREETCAR BUILDERS IN CANADA	01	69	32
LIST OF STREETCARS ABANDONED 1947-1948	03	49	79
LIST OF STREETCARS/INTERURBAN N AMER '58	10	58	48
LIST OF SUPER-RAILROADS	08	56	38

GENERAL RAILROADING	M	Y	P
LIST OF TEN LARGEST AMERICAN RAILROADS	01	39	65
LIST OF THE LARGEST RAILROADS N. AMERICA	05	34	81
LIST OF TRACKAGE CANADIAN ELECT-STEAM OP	09	43	125
LIST OF TRAINS NAMED FOR RAILROAD MEN	04	40	138
LIST OF TRAINS WITH FEMININE NAMES	12	55	38
LIST OF TRAINS WITH SAME NAME ON DIF RDS	01	69	33
LIST OF TROLLEY LINES IN GEORGA 1978	01	78	45
LIST OF TROLLEY LINES IN GEORGIA	12	49	80
LIST OF TROLLEY LINES IN GEORGIA ADDS/CO	06	50	91
LIST OF TROLLEY LINES IN NEVADA	04	76	53
LIST OF TROLLEY LINES IN W VA CORRECTION	12	48	101
LIST OF TROLLEY LINES IN WEST VIRGINIA	09	48	110
LIST OF TROLLEYS IN ALABAMA	05	51	102
LIST OF TROLLEYS IN CANADA (ALL-TIME)	10	52	78
LIST OF TUNNELS: AMERICA'S LONGEST	01	30	248
LIST OF TUNNELS: WORLD'S LONGEST	01	30	248
LIST OF UP ENGINHOUSES	06	71	59
LIST OF US RAILROADS IN BANKRUPTCY 1974	12	74	57
LIST OF WATER TRACK PAN LOCATIONS BY RD	11	69	22
LIST OF WHEEL ARRANGEMENTS/NAMES-EXPANDE	03	69	25
LIST OF WORLD TROLLEY MUSEUMS	12	72	47
LITTLE GIANT DELUXE D&RGW	05	50	76
LITTLE KNOWN DIESEL LOCO BUILDERS	01	73	31
LITTLE RED CABOOSE	12	41	06
LIVE STEAM--WESTERN PACIFIC JR ELKO NEVA	01	48	75
LIVE STEAMERS	08	52	50
LIVESTOCK FEEDING	06	49	65
LOAD REGULATORS FOR DIESEL LOCOMOTIVES	04	53	56
LOADING CIRCUS TRAINS	04	76	08
LOCO IN THE MOVIES V&T #22 BALDWIN 1875	08	37	37
LOCOMOTIVE BELL RINGING RULES	06	62	42
LOCOMOTIVE BELLS: ROMANCE	09	49	08
LOCOMOTIVE BOILERS PART 2	04	43	90
LOCOMOTIVE BUILDERS IN CANADA ADDITIONS	05	78	58
LOCOMOTIVE DESIGN AND DEVELOPMENT	01	51	50
LOCOMOTIVE DEVELOPMENT OF 1937	12	37	06
LOCOMOTIVE ENGINEER--DUTIES	07	32	507
LOCOMOTIVE ENGINEERS RESPONSABILITIES	10	75	05
LOCOMOTIVE INSPECTION LAWS	09	69	31
LOCOMOTIVE MILE	06	41	27
LOCOMOTIVE ODDITIES	08	48	10
LOCOMOTIVE ODDITIES	04	34	34
LOCOMOTIVE ODDITIES: CORRECTION 08/48	11	48	137
LOCOMOTIVE OF THE FUTURE-STREAMLINED!	08	31	90
LOCOMOTIVE TANKS	08	41	60
LOCOMOTIVE TESTING PLANT	08	36	91
LOCOMOTIVE TYPES: CORRECTIONS	09	37	65
LOCOMOTIVE TYPES: FIRSTS/READER COMMENTS	04	49	129
LOCOMOTIVE WHISTLE ORIGINATION	05	78	57
LOCOMOTIVES AND CURVES	02	43	50
LOCOMOTIVES IN MOVIES: EP&S #1	05	39	47
LOCOMOTIVES ON DISPLAY AT 1893 WORLDS FA	11	74	04
LOCOMOTIVES ON PARADE--NAT MUS OF TRANSP	12	62	06
LOGGING LOCOMOTIVES PHOTO ESSAY	04	51	53
LOGGING RAILROADS	05	41	52

GENERAL RAILROADING

GENERAL RAILROADING	M	Y	P
	08	55	13
LOGGING ROAD CRB&L	02	39	78
LOGGING WOODBURNERS IN MAINLINE SERVICE	04	68	18
LOGO EVOLUTION OF GN	09	67	26
LONE TREE-CHANGES RAILROAD ROUTE UP	03	38	37
LONG ISLAND CARS GET BEAUTY TREATMENT	01	71	40
LONGEST STREIGHT STRECH OF TRACK	10	78	47
LOSS OF MAIL KILLS PASSENGER TRAINS	01	68	18
LOUISIANA SHORTLINE SKETCHBOOK	04	78	34R
LOW STEAM: STEAMING QUALITIES	12	49	48
LOWEST ELEVATION RAILROAD TRACKS SP	10	78	49
LS CINCINNATI CAR PAPERS-OLIN LIBRARY DC	07	75	56
LS READING ARCHIVES TO ELEUTHERIAN MILLS	09	75	04
LUMBER PIKES: MICHIGAN	07	53	51
LUNCH PREPARATION (RAILROAD COACH)	10	47	71
MAKE DIESEL LOCOMOTIVES SAFER	01	76	53
MALLET LOCOMOTIVES	01	32	194
MALLET LOCOMOTIVES	08	55	26
MALLET LOCOMOTIVES: THEIR HISTORY	03	44	08
MAN O'WAR	11	47	66
MAN WHO MADE RAILROADING SAFE--MR COFFIN	04	38	57
MAN WHO STOLE A STREET RY-LOCK/STOCK/BAR	06	74	55
MANHATTANS EARLY RPO LINES	06	48	90
MANUFACTURER OF AMUSEMENT PARK RR EQUIP	05	46	76
MANUSCRIPT TICKET: DEFINED	07	42	67
MAP OF 37 UNITED STATES STREAMLINERS	02	40	120
MASS TRANSPORTATION BY SUBWAY/ELEVATED	02	47	99
MASTER CAR "RE"-BUILDERS	W	74	35R
MASTER OF THE NIGHT L&HR 1976	F	76	26R
MASTER OF THE NIGHT N&W STEAM 1955	F	76	26R
MATTER OF PRIORITIES: HOW SPEND SUPER BO	SU	76	42R
MAUCH CHUNK OLDEST RR SOLD FOR SCRAP	12	37	59
MCKAY & ALDUS LOCO WORKS BRIEF HISTORY	02	62	50
MEALS AT ALL HOURS (RAIL BOARDING HOUSE)	09	74	21
MEALS-DINING CAR SERVICE FINANCIAL LOSS	03	33	128
MEASURING SPEED AND CUT-OFF	09	44	57
MECHANICAL LUBRICATORS ON STEAM LOCOS	10	46	49
MEET BURKE, MIKE:SILVERTON AUTHOR	11	81	18
MEN WHO STYLED STREAMLINERS	11	84	32
MEN WHO STYLED STREAMLINERS 2 END TOUCH	01	85	48
MERGER OF CB&Q, NP, GN TO FORM BN	12	71	12
METROPOLITANS-SUBWAYS & ELEVATEDS	02	38	05
MEXICAN STEAM	06	61	16
MEXICAN STEAM ROUNDUP	01	71	20
MEXICO CITY TERMINAL	12	69	16
MEXICO USES "OLD" ENGINES	01	41	78
MICROWAVE COMMUNICATION (ADVANTAGES OF)	02	51	52
MID-CONTINENT RAILWAY MUSEUM VISIT	09	75	32
MIDGET RAILROADING	02	32	400
MIDGET RAILROADING (AMUSEMENT PARK ROAD)	12	63	32
MIDWEST CENTRAL MUSEUM VISIT	08	69	34
MIDWESTERN INTERURBANS: RISE AND FALL OF	09	53	74
MIKADO LOCOMOTIVES	08	37	41
MILE-A-MINUTE BOXCARS	08	50	10
MILE-A-MINUTE RUNS-NORTH AMERICA	02	39	07
MILITARY LOCOMOTIVES	10	53	62

GENERAL RAILROADING	M	Y	P
MILITARY RAILROADS	06	37	48
MILITARY TROLLEY LINE ON CORREGIDOR	05	69	41
MILITAY ARTILLERY	02	43	30
MILWAUKEE ROAD ELECTRIFICATION ENDING	05	73	22
MINNEAPOLIS & ST LOUIS	05	36	33
MINNESOTA TRANSFER	05	54	52
MINUTEMAN CONVENTION '86 (NRHS RRE NMRA)	11	86	56
MISSING ONE LOCOMOTIVE-FIRST HAND INFO	02	66	06
MISSING: ONE LOCOMOTIVE	12	65	24
MIXED TRAIN ON G IN 1974	11	74	26
MKT SHORT WAVE RADIO	04	48	66
MO-PAC'S NAVY (CAR FLOATS)	11	82	40
MODELING IN THE ULTIMATE SCALE	03	87	60
MODERN LOGGING ROAD	05	41	52
MODERN LOUISVILLE YARD OF FAM	10	78	12
MODERNIZATION-NEW EQUIPMENT & GADGETS	03	65	17
MODERNIZED LINGO OF THE RAILS	02	65	36
MODERNIZED RAILWAY TRAVEL-MR. PULLMAN	04	37	05
MOGUL COUNTRY FAREWELL	03	54	33
MOGUL-THE HISTORY	05	36	41
MOJAVE CALIFORNIA-RR TOWN SINCE 1876	08	50	62
MONEY-BOX PLOT--FORGED RR TICKETS	08	68	38
MONORAIL FOR AIRPORT PARKING DALLAS TX	09	70	44
MONORAIL FOR LONG ISLAND COMMUTERS?	06	31	437
MONORAIL FOR LOS ANGELES	12	53	88
MONORAIL PHOTO ESSAY NY WORLDS FAIR	05	65	30
MONORAIL SEATTLE WORLDS FAIR READER COM	12	62	36
MONORAIL--CONSIDERED FOR NYC	06	31	437
MONORAIL-NY WORLDS FAIR	12	63	38
MONORAILS	09	47	98
MONTREAL--RAILROAD METROPOLIS	08	52	14
MONTREALS BIG CENTURYS	09	82	52
MONTREALS ENDANGERED ELECTRICS (CN)	11	80	46
MORE & MORE AUTOS RIDE THE RAILS	10	65	58
MORE SECURITY FOR RAILROADERS-RETIREMENT	11	46	30
MORSE CODE	05	33	60
MORSE CODE/CONTINENTAL CODE COMPARISON C	05	33	60
MOST WRECKS IN A US CITY--DUNKIRK NY	09	73	08
MOTION PICTURE "UNION PACIFIC" UP	03	39	55
MOTOR AND WHEEL PROBLEMS OF DIESEL LOCOS	07	53	40
MOVIES: HOLLYWOOD TRAINS	11	47	119
MOVIES: MOVIE STATION	03	48	69
MOVIES: ROCK ISLAND TRAIL 90 MIN WESTERN	07	50	76
MOVING CIRCUS ANIMALS/WILD ANIMALS	07	32	448
MP WHITE RIVER DIVISION SCALING GANG	07	35	44
MR BRADSHAW BUYS THE SILVERTON	11	81	38
MR NIXONS MYSTERIOUS ERIE PACIFIC FILMS	03	80	29
MR TRAVIS ON PAINTING LOCOMOTIVES (BAR)	03	85	48
MRS HOWARDS HOTEL ROWLESBURG WV B&O	SP	75	64R
MULLIGAN STEW	08	36	110
MULTIPLE THROTTLE ON STEAM LOCOMOTIVES	10	49	49
MY NARROW-GAGE ALBUM PART 2	08	39	46
MYSTERY OF THE THIRTEEN UP HOLDUP	03	34	33
N&W CHANGES GAUGES JUNE 1 1886	07	35	46
NAME CHANGES OF RAILWAY AGE--4!	10	31	428

Railroad/Railfan

GENERAL RAILROADING

GENERAL RAILROADING	M	Y	P
NAMED FOR RAILROAD PRESIDENTS	02	65	24
NAMES OF CITIES: ALFRECHA/CORNING/UZ	05	48	133
NAMES OF CITIES: CHAMBERS MILLS/MCCRACKN	05	48	134
NARROW GAGE LORE	06	38	07
NARROW GAUGE CIRCLES	10	77	36R
NARROW GAUGE RAILROADS IN US 1961	02	62	48
NARROW GAUGE ROADS OF MAINE	09	35	41
NARROW-GAGE: BECOMING OBSOLETE	08	41	06
NASA RESIDENT RAILROADER--DAVID HOFFMAN	09	82	29
NATIONAL CITY LINES-GM EFFORTS TO BUSES	06	74	54
NATIONALIZATION OF US PASSENGER ON UPSWI	12	73	27
NATIONALIZATION OF US RAILROADS	04	65	10
NAVY AND RAILROADS	11	49	38
NAVY RAILROAD	06	47	115
NAVY RAILROADS MARINE OPERATIONS USN	08	59	18
NEED FOR MULTIPLE UNITS ON ATSF	02	63	31
NELSON BLOUNT STORY	06	67	19
NEW COAL AGE & US RAILS	01	78	09
NEW ENGLAND'S BIGGEST FREIGHT POWER	03	30	489
NEW HOPE & IVYLAND PHOTO ESSAY	08	76	02
NEW ICC POLICY? MINIMUM PASSENGER STDS	07	68	60
NEW JERSEY HISTORICAL SOCIETY-RR EXHIBIT	07	50	86
NEW JERSEY TAXES (CNJ)	05	45	78
NEW LIFE FOR OLD ENGINES & CARS (MUSEUM)	01	70	30
NEW MOUNTAIN RAILWAY (ZOO NARROW GAUGE)	02	61	48
NEW YORK CITY SUBWAY FARE RAISE FROM 15C	07	66	37
NEW YORK HARBOR: TUGS/CARFLOATS/BARGES	09	45	08
NEW YORK STATES TRACTION LINES	02	45	101
NEW YORK SUBWAY CARS	07	73	46
NEW YORK TO SAN FRANSISCO IN 81.5 HOURS	09	32	191
NEW YORK TRANSIT TRAVEL RECORD 15 HRS 40	07	69	39
NEW YORK TROLLEY PHOTO ESSAY	04	74	48
NEWFOUNDLAND'S NARROW GAGE RR	08	38	70
NIGHT BEFORE THE ARROWS	07	85	32
NIGHT CHIEF: DUTIES/MEMORIES	04	54	34
NIGHT RIDE ON FREEDOM TRAIN (1975)	11	75	20
NO ONE WANTS HIGH SPEED PASSENGER TRAINS	07	68	06
NON-RAILROADER FIRED 42 STEAM LOCOMOTIVE	05	67	40
NON-STOP RUNS: 200 MILES/53 TRAINS	06	39	59
NORTH AMERICA'S FIRST RAILWAY	05	42	24
NORTH AMERICA'S MILE-A-MINUTE RUNS	10	36	20
NORTH AMERICA'S MILE-A-MINUTE TRAIN RUNS	04	38	07
NORTHERN PACIFIC "OLD BETSY" COMES BACK	09	33	40
NORTHERN PACIFIC CONDUCTOR #1 (SWEETMAN)	04	40	72
NOSTALGIA QUIPS FROM OLD ISSUES	12	67	21
NOT ON THE HIGHWAY MAPS: LOMBARD MONT	10	40	122
NP CONDUCTOR RIDES 961 MILES CONTINUOUSLY	05	31	219
NRHS 50TH ANNIVERSARY CONVENTION	01	86	45
NRHS COLORADO RAILS '82	11	82	34
NRHS CONVENTION 1964	12	64	56
NRHS RICHMOND CONVENTION 1983	11	83	37
NRHS ROANOKE CONVENTION 1987	11	87	42
NW CORRIDOR-1.75 BILLION TRACK JOB	07	77	55
NYC PRESIDENT VANDERBILT	11	36	04
O&W UBOAT (NYO&W)	07	85	60
OAHU RAILWAY 172 MILES 3' GAUGE TRACK	05	35	37
OCEAN SHORE RAILWAY REBORN	12	35	69
ODD COMBINATION OF DIESEL MOTIVE POWER	06	75	09
ODD RUN TRAINS "FEMALES CHEAP"	02	61	28
OFFICIAL REPORT OF CASEY JONES WRECK	03	78	36
OGDEN-SALT LAKE AREA: GATEWAY TO PACIFIC	07	53	13
OLD 0-4-0 VULCAN BURIED FOR YEARS RUNS A	06	62	34
OLD COLORADO MIDLAND	08	36	39
OLD RAILROAD RULES	11	67	30
OLD SAN DIEGO & ARIZONA	05	73	18
OLIVER AMERICAN TRADING CO & HIS LOCOS	11	37	05
ON THE NIGHT FREIGHT	11	37	18
ON THE RAILROAD WITH CHARLES KURALT	05	83	60
ON THE ROAD WITH SP 4449 (4-8-4)	W	75	36R
ONCE EVERY HUNDRED YEARS:PROMONTORY PT	08	69	14
ONE BIG RAIL UNION?	01	70	06
ONE HUNDRED YEARS OF STANDARD TIME-ALLEN	11	83	51
ONE MAN MUSEUMS	10	66	56
ONE PRESIDENT/2 RR-SUPREMACY STRUGGLE	11	35	111
ONE TOWN INTERURBAN LINE (BBLR)	02	71	60
ONE-MAN RR (STD GAUGE/NARROW GAUGE)	03	35	77
OPEN JAW FARES	04	42	63
OPERATED BUT NOT BUILT-BIG HILL CP	06	30	321
OPERATING RATIO	05	33	75
OPERATING RATIO	11	41	52
OPERATION LIFESAVER-TRAINS CANT STOP!!	03	81	51
ORDER OF RAILWAY CONDUCTORS	03	44	58
ORDER: D-FORM R	01	30	209
OREGONS LAST LOGGERS	08	77	18R
ORIGIN OF STANDARD GAGE- MORE COMMENTS	04	49	125
ORIGINS OF RAIL TERMS	10	49	12
OVERSIZE SHIPMENTS PHOTO ESSAY	11	43	88
OWEGO CONNECTION-LV & D&H	SP	76	18R
P&W CHALLENGES PRR ON TRACK CONDITIONS	05	75	37
PACIFIC TYPE LOCOMOTIVE SET TO MUSIC	06	31	410
PACIFIC TYPE LOCOMOTIVE-"THE FIRST"	07	36	47
PACIFIC TYPE LOCOMOTIVES	06	36	90
PAINT ON RAILROADS	06	44	74
PAINT: 100'S OF USES/ALL PURPOSE PRESERV	06	44	74
PASSENGER BUSINESS	01	30	210
PASSENGER ELIMINATION ON NYC & PENNSY	04	68	10
PASSENGER PROBLEM, THE: SUGGESTIONS	06	47	44
PASSENGER REVENUE 1969 VS 1944	09	69	30
PASSENGER SERVICE SELLING	08	30	50
PASSENGER TRAFFIC REVITALIZATION	03	47	125
PASSENGER TRAIN BLUES: AN EDITORIAL	10	64	06
PASSENGER TRAIN CRISIS	01	65	46
PASSENGER TRAIN FARE DISCREPANCIES	03	68	08
PASSENGER TRAIN NAMED FOR WOMEN	07	46	32
PASSENGER TRAIN SURVEY 1967	06	67	13
PASSENGER TRAIN SURVEY 1968	06	68	24
PASSENGER TRAIN SURVEY 1968 (DECEMBER)	12	68	50
PASSENGER TRAIN SURVEY 1968 READER COMME	07	68	10
PASSING SIDINGS	11	66	42
PATERSON NJ 4 FAMOUS LOCO PLANTS!	06	33	34

Railroad/ Railfan

GENERAL RAILROADING

GENERAL RAILROADING	M	Y	P
PATTERNS OF A GREAT INDUSTRY PHOTO ESSAY	02	55	17
PAY CAR HISTORY	02	56	20
PAY CAR: ROLLING BANK	08	43	06
PAY OR NO, THEY GO! (PASSENGER TRAINS)	10	64	13
PAY RATES FOR LOCOMOTIVE ENGINEERS/FIREM	08	61	36
PEANUT BUTCHER ON CN 1919	10	67	10
PEANUT BUTCHER-SP'S LAST	04	67	25
PECOS LEGENDS (SP)	07	49	42
PELLEY, JOHN J-TRACK HAND TO PRES NYNH&H	12	29	01
PENN CENTRAL'S GREAT AUCTION SALE	07	72	28
PENN STATION--MANHATTAN MONUMENT	08	71	28
PENN VIEW MOUNTAIN RR VISIT	09	72	45
PENNSY HOGS	11	74	38
PENNSY PULLED A FAST ONE-PRESERVE #7002	09	85	36
PER-DIEM RULE	05	48	62
PERU'S RAILWAY STAMPS	06	37	37
PETROLEUM	07	44	70
PETTICOAT JUNCTION TRAIN INFORMATION	06	64	36
PHOTO EXHIBIT--O WINSTON LINK	01	84	63
PHOTO FREIGHTS	03	86	51
PHOTO VISIT TO STEAMTOWN (BELLOWS FALLS)	09	68	42
PICTURESQUE PENN-CENTRAL	SU	76	34R
PILOT: 110 YEARS OF LOCOMOTIVE HISTORY	07	42	06
PINS AND AXLES ON STEAM LOCOMOTIVES	02	47	56
PIONEER RAILROAD BUILDER G.M. DODGE	05	33	87
PIPE-LINE CROSSINGS:60 YRS BATTLE	01	36	18
PISTON ROD PARTING IN STEAM LOCOMOTIVES	05	49	48
PITTSBURGH TROLLEY WRECK DEC 24 1917	03	36	89
PLAIN HEROIC BREED DL&W 1905 ADAIR	04	34	68
PLANES VS RAILROADS PASSENGER SERVICE	02	31	376
PLIGHT OF THE RAILROADS-CRYING WOLF!	12	73	02
PLOT TO KILL LINCOLN BY TRAIN WRECK	06	65	40
PNEUMATIC TUBE TRAINS	10	69	10
POLING METHOD OF SWITCHING CARS	12	46	80
POOLING SYSTEM OF LOCOMOTIVE OPERATIONS	04	45	77
POPPET VALVES ON STEAM LOCOMOTIVES	01	47	45
PORTERS UNION DISOLVED	06	78	05
POST-WAR CHALLENGE OF ELECTRIC LINES	01	45	64
POUGHKEEPSIE BRIDGE BURNS L&HR	W	74	18R
POWDER CAR DISASTER KINGS MILLS OH 1890	11	77	26
PREAMBLE EXPRESS	SP	75	16R
PRESENT-DAY RAILROAD WAR 1966	09	66	49
PRESERVING YOUR RAILROADIANA	09	79	03
PRESIDENT OF BROTHERHOOD OF RR TRAINMEN	07	31	523
PRESIDENT'S SPECIAL	11	45	08
PRESIDENTIAL ASSASINATIONS & THE RAILROA	04	64	06
PRESIDENTIAL CAMPAIGNING BY RAILS	08	56	12
PRESSURE WELDING RAILS	06	49	63
PRIVATE OWNERSHIP DESIGNATED BY "X"	07	37	57
PRIVATE OWNERSHIP/NON-REV DESIGNATION X	02	38	56
PRIVATE TROLLEY MRS. CHAPIN'S	07	40	80
PRIVATELY OWNED PASSENGER CARS: MANSIONS	11	39	06
PRO & CONRAIL	W	75	28R
PROBLEMS OF SUBWAY BUILDING	04	68	31
PROPOSED CHICAGO-NEW YORK ELECTRIC LINE	05	33	78
PROPOSED DENVER COLORADO CANYON & PACIFI	09	33	78
PROSPERITY SPECIAL 2-10-2 SP BALDWIN	01	47	26
PRR BOOK-KEEPING SYSTEM	02	31	370
PRR ELECTRIC LINE	07	35	126
PRR GIANT LOCOMOTIVES	11	35	44
PRR SPEEDS UP ELECTRIFICATION	04	31	118
PUBLICS OPINION OF THE RAILROADS	12	36	05
PULLMAN LEAVES RAILROAD BUSINESS	07	79	21
PULLMAN PORTERS JOB REQUIREMENTS & DESCR	07	76	05
PULLMAN STRIKE MYSTERY	08	33	48
PULLMANS ON THE HILL	05	82	47
PUSH PULL ON MBTA UPDATE	07	79	20
PUSH-BUTTON RAILROADING	12	55	12
PUSH-BUTTON YARDS	10	58	20
PUT STEAM IN YOUR VACATION	05	66	20
QUICK PROMOTION: YOUNG CONDUCTORS	02	42	07
RACEHORSE MOVEMENT BY TRAIN	06	43	08
RADIO & TV IN MODERN RAILROADING	04	58	20
RADIO A THREAT TO THE TELEGRAPH??	06	30	331
RADIO TALK	SP	76	27R
RAIL AUTOMATION, THEN AND NOW	02	69	50
RAIL COMMISSIONS TO TRAVEL AGENTS	10	67	30
RAIL DETECTOR CAR HELPS FIND RAIL DEFECT	07	34	57
RAIL FAILURES	11	38	12
RAIL FARRY-HAIL TO THE CHIEF	SP	76	45R
RAIL LAWSUITS-NITTY GRITTY PICKY CASES	10	37	28
RAIL MERGER COMMENTS	12	61	58
RAIL MUSEUM SAFARI	02	72	39
RAIL PASSENGER INCREASES ON WEST COAST	12	72	28
RAIL PASSENGER SERVICE NEEDS POS THINKIN	07	65	26
RAIL POLISHER SPECIAL (TRACTION IN NY)	05	67	45
RAIL PROBLEMS--"SHELLY" RAIL	09	52	61
RAIL WORK RECORDS FOR TRAVELING BOOMERS	10	63	06
RAIL-HIGHWAY STEEL FREIGHT CONTAINERS	07	31	578
RAIL-PICTURE ENVELOPES	04	41	70
RAIL-WAGON MODEL	04	32	134
RAILFAN TOUR (6000 MILES) JULY 1938	11	38	75
RAILFAN TOUR--5800 MILES	07	38	06
RAILFAN-IN THE BEGINNING	11	84	72
RAILFANNING CALIFORNIA STYLE	W	74	31R
RAILFANNING THE ELECTRICS (DL&W)	07	81	50
RAILFANS I HAVE KNOWN-MAC FARLAND ET AL	01	78	30
RAILFANS: ASSETS OR LIABILITIES?	08	64	33
RAILPASS--21 DAY US TRIP	10	78	20
RAILROAD BULL--THOMAS FURLONG	02	66	45
RAILROAD CHICKEN-YARD COLONY PHOTO ESSAY	05	42	111
RAILROAD CLUBS: JOBS	05	39	118
RAILROAD DOGS	06	43	144
RAILROAD DOGS	08	43	151
RAILROAD DRAMA	11	38	60
RAILROAD ENGINEERS DWINDLING NUMBERS	06	67	35
RAILROAD EXHIBITS AT WORLDS FAIR 1939	07	40	06
RAILROAD FAN MOVEMENT	07	37	23
RAILROAD FICTION AUTHORS	09	71	42
RAILROAD FICTION BOOK LIST 1	02	37	104

GENERAL RAILROADING

GENERAL RAILROADING	M	Y	P
RAILROAD FICTION WRITERS	02	76	09
RAILROAD HISTORY AWARDS 1982 (R&LHS)	09	82	60
RAILROAD HISTORY AWARDS 1983	09	83	60
RAILROAD HISTORY AWARDS 1984 (R&LHS)	09	84	61
RAILROAD HISTORY AWARDS 1985 (R&LHS)	09	85	61
RAILROAD HISTORY AWARDS 1986 5TH ANNUAL	09	86	60
RAILROAD HISTORY AWARDS 1987 (R&LHS)	09	87	60
RAILROAD JOBS: 128 DIFFERENT	05	54	14
RAILROAD LANGUAGE--IMPORTANT WORDS	06	30	469
RAILROAD LANGUAGE: SLANGS/SEMI-TECHICAL	01	30	317
RAILROAD LINGO	10	32	366
RAILROAD LINGO	04	40	32
RAILROAD MAGAZINE HISTORY	01	73	02
RAILROAD MAGAZINE--ITS HISTORY	12	60	29
RAILROAD MEN TO CITY MAYORS	02	31	400
RAILROAD MERGERS & CONSOLIDATIONS	07	39	07
RAILROAD MOVIES OF 1939	06	39	129
RAILROAD MOVIES: PROPS USED IN	06	41	59
RAILROAD MUSEUM-STATE OF PENNSYLVANIA	09	75	24
RAILROAD MUT NAMED "OWNEY" 1897	12	77	04
RAILROAD NAVY	08	59	19
RAILROAD PASSENGER BUSINESS	06	39	07
RAILROAD PASSES: WHO CAN GET ONE?	05	36	80
RAILROAD PIPE DREAMS--INVENTIONS	10	35	91
RAILROAD POCKET WATCH MAIN FEATURES	01	76	40
RAILROAD POWER PLANTS	10	44	72
RAILROAD PRESIDENTS WOMEN	09	53	73
RAILROAD RECORDING LOOOONG LIST (AUDIO)	10	60	51
RAILROAD RHYTHM	06	47	106
RAILROAD RULES	07	51	16
RAILROAD RUNS-120 TO 150 MILES NON-STOP	10	36	28
RAILROAD RUNS-150 TO 180 MILES NON STOP	10	36	27
RAILROAD RUNS-30 TO 60 MILES NON-STOP	10	36	33
RAILROAD RUNS-60 TO 90 MILES NON-STOP	10	36	31
RAILROAD RUNS-90 TO 120 MILES NON-STOP	10	36	30
RAILROAD RUNS-LESS THAN 30 MILES NONSTOP	10	36	35
RAILROAD RUNS-LIST OF MILE-A-MINUTE	10	36	20
RAILROAD RUNS-MORE THAN 180 MILE NONSTOP	10	36	27
RAILROAD SCANNER REVIEW REGENCY ELECRTON	SP	75	08R
RAILROAD SCRAPBOOKS	09	34	27
RAILROAD SCRIPT	11	69	10
RAILROAD SEPARATION OF PASSENGERS BY SEX	01	73	02
RAILROAD SONGS & POETRY LIST	07	37	123
RAILROAD STRIKEBREAKERS	05	73	10
RAILROAD TRADEMARKS	12	31	54
RAILROAD TRADEMARKS-MORE!	04	32	126
RAILROAD UNDER THE ARTIC ICE CAP	11	64	13
RAILROAD VS RAILWAY	11	33	88
RAILROAD WATCH REQUIREMENTS	11	34	96
RAILROAD WATCHES	10	41	119
RAILROAD WATCHES SPECIFICATIONS (WRIST)	01	66	20
RAILROAD WATCHES--RAILROAD TIME KEEPER	07	35	90
RAILROAD WOMEN	04	42	74
RAILROADERS IN BRONZE	11	37	40
RAILROADING 65 YEARS AGO (1866) RICHMOND	10	31	409
RAILROADING BELOW SEA LEVEL	08	66	22
RAILROADING BY TIMETABLES--HISTORY	05	51	25
RAILROADING FEATURED IN EXPO '86	09	86	39
RAILROADING IN CANADA C&SL	06	32	325
RAILROADING IN THE FUTURE	03	37	05
RAILROADING ODDITIES	01	32	223
RAILROADING THROUGH TOWN NAMES	05	48	06
RAILROADING WITH RITTASE PHOTO ESSAY	04	55	10
RAILROADING: A HAZARDOUS OCCUPATION	SU	76	13R
RAILROADS ADOPTED STANDARD TIME IN 1872	03	42	71
RAILROADS AND DRUG TESTING	01	87	05
RAILROADS AND THE VOLCANO-MT ST HELENS	11	80	44
RAILROADS BIGGEST RIVAL--AUTOMOBILES	09	35	76
RAILROADS BUCK BREADLINE-SPENDING POLICY	03	31	481
RAILROADS FIGHT UNFAIR MOTOR TRUCK COMP	02	31	321
RAILROADS GO AFTER PUBLIC'S GOOD WILL	07	31	493
RAILROADS IN CANADA--10 LARGEST	05	33	72
RAILROADS IN MISSOURI-KANSAS CITY	09	37	61
RAILROADS IN THE MOVIES	09	37	07
RAILROADS IN THE NEWSREEL	01	48	108
RAILROADS IN THE WORLD 15 LARGEST	01	35	81
RAILROADS NOT LISTED IN OFFICIAL GUIDE	08	62	27
RAILROADS OFFER AID FOR THE FARMERS	12	29	55
RAILROADS ON BANK NOTES	09	53	06
RAILROADS ON PARADE: NY WORLD'S FAIR	04	39	68
RAILROADS PAID FOR HANDLING MAIL HOW?	01	51	74
RAILROADS THAT VANISHED	02	35	69
RAILROADS USING MOTHER HUBBARD LOCOS COR	07	38	79
RAILROADS VERSUS AIRPLANE SAFETY/FATALIT	09	38	53
RAILROADS VERSUS OTHER TRANSPORTATION	05	39	07
RAILROADS VS RAILWAYS: DIFFERENT TERMS	05	40	91
RAILROADS VS TRUCKS	02	39	126
RAILROADS WHICH CARRY THE MOST COAL-TOP3	02	39	94
RAILROADS: BIGGER AND FEWER	07	39	07
RAILROADS: DEVELOP ADMINISTRATIVE PERSON	05	51	06
RAILS	11	38	07
RAILS IN THE WILDERNESS	12	60	48
RAILWAY CAR USED TO TEST HELICOPTER PHOT	02	33	87
RAILWAY EXPRESS AGENCY	04	36	21
RAILWAY EXPRESS AGENCY-PURPOSE	01	39	59
RAILWAY FERRIES-93 YEARS ON SF BAY	01	65	13
RAILWAY GUIDE 1852	09	37	136
RAILWAY MAIL SERVICE	12	38	83
RAILWAY MEDALS	06	40	117
RAPID TRANSIT: NEW TRENDS	02	57	28
RAT-HOLE DIVISION CINCINNATI SOUTHERN	01	39	07
RATON MOUNTAIN WHAT A MOUNTAIN!	03	34	40
RATON MOUNTAIN: WHERE/TUNNEL	01	36	86
RAWLINGS BUYS A RAILROAD FOR $301 WRB	01	39	29
REA SHIPS BEES TO CANADA & SOUTH	10	55	37
READINGS PASSENGER PROBLEM	11	64	46
REAL RAILROADS FOR CHILDREN SOVIET UNION	12	38	57
REASONS FOR DIESELIZATION	12	48	48
REBUILDING STEAM LOCOS FT ESTIS VA 1965	02	65	28
RECALLING THE GRAND MANNER OF RAIL DININ	SP	77	24R

GENERAL RAILROADING

GENERAL RAILROADING	M	Y	P
RECEIVER VS TRUSTEE	08	36	74
RECEIVERSHIP VS TRUSTEESHIP	01	42	60
RECIPE FOR A CLASS I RAILROAD NYC	11	50	15
RECORDS: THE HIGHEST/STEEPEST/FASTEST/OL	05	40	131
RED CABOOSE LODGE STRASBURG PA	01	71	36
RED TAPE IN SELLING PASSENGER FARES	03	65	29
REDBALL TERMINAL	11	41	06
REDSKINS HOLD RIGHT-OF-WAY ATSF 1883	02	33	18
REFLECTOSCOPE: SPERRY SUPERSONIC-EXPLAIN	03	49	89
REGISTRATION OF ID MARKS ON FREIGHT CARS	03	53	64
REGULATING BUS COMPETITION RRS CONCERNED	01	31	161
REGULATIONS OF RAILROAD WATCHES	11	46	65
RELIGIOUS SERVICES ON PASSENGER TRAINS	05	65	43
REMEMBER THE DAYS... PHOTO ESSAY	06	55	27
REPAIR TOOLS: WELDING	03	44	94
RESISTANCE: FRICTION & AIR IN STEAM LOCO	05	44	68
RESTORING A 2-8-4 (PM #1225)	12	73	30
RESURRECTION OF R #2102 4-8-4	03	86	33
RETIRED MOTORMANS PARADISE	08	60	44
RETIREMENT: CROSSER BILL	11	46	30
RETRACKING THE APOLLOS	F	76	51R
RETURN OF THE "CENTURY"?	SP	76	48R
REUSING RAILROAD STATIONS	10	77	53
REVITALIZING PASSENGER TRAFFIC	12	46	12
REVIVAL OF THE VIRGINIA & TRUCKEE	08	76	41
RICHARDSON DESERT COMPARTMENT	08	46	128
RICHMONDS TRIPLE CROSSING	11	83	34
RIDE 66 MILES FOR A NICKEL ON NYCE	04	33	81
RIDE BEHIND A WOODBURNER	05	76	37
RIDE TRAINS FOR FUN	06	64	20
RIDING ASEA "MIGHTY MOUSE" SWEDENS COMPA	10	77	25R
RIDING DOWN THE HIGH IRON PHOTO ESSAY	04	49	78
RIDING HERD ON FREIGHT CARS	05	31	248
RIDING IN STYLE (PRIVATE CAS)	07	67	36
RIDING ON PLANES VERSUS TRAINS	11	32	563
RIGHTS OF TRAINS	07	51	16
RO-RAILER-RUNS ON TRACKS & PAVED ROADS	06	31	400
ROAD BACK TO PROSPERITY	04	31	62
ROAD FOREMAN VS ROUNDHOUSE FOREMAN	06	32	337
ROAD HOGS TRUCK TRAFFIC	03	35	15
ROAD NAMES CHANGING	03	81	03
ROCHESTER NEW YORK VIGNETTE	01	51	12
ROCK ISLAND'S PART IN NEW MOVIE	07	50	76
ROCKET 150 YEAR BIRTHDAY	01	81	22
ROD PACKINGS ON STEAM LOCOMOTIVES	09	47	64
RODS AND BUSHINGS OF STEAM LOCOMOTIVES	06	45	52
ROGERS LOCOMOTIVE WORKS	02	46	99
ROLLER BEARING HISTORY	03	40	125
ROLLING IN THE MONEY BANGOR & AROOSTOOK	12	38	07
ROLLING WITH RADIO-RADIO EQUIPPED TRAINS	05	30	246
ROMANCE OF STATION BELLS	12	50	71
ROSEVILLE YARD SP SACRAMENTO CA	10	71	28
ROTARY PLOW (UP)	04	74	24
ROUGH TOUGH TEHACHAPI LOOP (ATSF)	04	69	32
ROYAL BLUE LINE	06	36	45

GENERAL RAILROADING	M	Y	P
ROYAL HUDSON SOUTH--SOUTHERN #2839	03	80	42
ROYAL TRAIN GEORGE VI & ELIZABETH 1939	09	39	75
RPO ROUTE: THE SHORTEST/12 MILES	08	41	34
RPO-GRAVEYARD RUN	10	77	21
RR LAND GRANTS 1	08	51	28
RR LAND GRANTS 2	09	51	64
RR LAND GRANTS 3	10	51	68
RR LAND GRANTS 4	11	51	30
RR LAND GRANTS 5	12	51	40
RT: RAILROAD TERMS DEFINITIONS	09	65	00
RT: "B" END OF CAR DEFINITION	03	66	27
RT: 16 RAILTERMS	07	33	135
RT: 19Y & 19R TRAIN ORDERS	08	67	30
RT: ABSOLUTE BLOCK & ABSOLUTE SIGNAL	03	66	26
RT: ACRYONMS DEALING WITH RAILROADS	09	66	57
RT: ADJUSTED TONNAGE DEFINED	04	43	96
RT: AIR LINE	10	32	349
RT: AIR PRESSURE	05	44	68
RT: ARTICULATED LOCOMOTIVE	03	66	28
RT: ARTICULATED LOCOMOTIVE	03	65	47
RT: ARTICULATED LOCOMOTIVES	11	69	28
RT: ASHTRAY FREIGHT	02	56	39
RT: AUTOMATIC REDUCING VALVE	07	66	38
RT: AUTOMATIC RETARDER	10	56	39
RT: AUTOMATIC TRAIN IDENTIFICATION	09	66	33
RT: BALLING THE JACK	09	54	27
RT: BARNEY (MECHANICAL MULE)	02	56	42
RT: BATTING 'EM OUT	07	77	49
RT: BEANERY	04	75	12
RT: BEE/STINGER	04	54	60
RT: BELL-BOTTOM BRAKEMAN	05	76	24
RT: BELPAIRE FIREBOX	08	64	30
RT: BINDLE STIFF	04	75	12
RT: BIRD CAGE	04	67	33
RT: BLIND	04	34	82
RT: BLIND SIDE OF A TRACK	03	66	26
RT: BOOMER (HOW TERM ORIGINATED)	08	57	72
RT: BOOSTER DEFINED	04	55	35
RT: BRAKE POSITION "LAP"	05	69	31
RT: BRAKE VAN (BRITISH TERM)	11	65	25
RT: BRAKEHEAD	04	78	55
RT: BRAKING POWER	03	54	123
RT: BROTHER-IN-LAW (FARE INDICATOR FAKE)	02	50	58
RT: BRUCK (COMBINATION BUS-TRUCK)	08	56	41
RT: BULL	04	75	12
RT: BULLGINE	03	72	62
RT: CAB SIGNAL	11	71	38
RT: CABOOSE HOP	03	66	28
RT: CAMELBACK NAME DERIVATION	02	66	32
RT: CANDLE LAMPS	05	67	29
RT: CAR RETARDER	05	66	34
RT: CAR TOAD	05	76	24
RT: CARLINES	11	71	38
RT: CAT	06	54	58
RT: CAT CRACKED	12	56	30

Railroad/Railfan

GENERAL RAILROADING

GENERAL RAILROADING	M	Y	P
RT: CAT-WHISKERS	01	55	38
RT: CHALKED HAT	08	56	38
RT: CINDER SNAPPER	03	72	62
RT: CINDER SNAPPER	07	77	49
RT: CLASS I & CLASS II RAILROADS	02	72	61
RT: CLASS I RAILROAD DEFINED	06	59	36
RT: COD (ORIGINATION OF TERM)	10	56	45
RT: COMMODITY RATE	02	57	45
RT: COMMODITY RATE-SPECIAL FREIGHT RATE	04	55	36
RT: COMPROMISE CARS	02	57	46
RT: CONDUCTOR ORIGINS	09	66	33
RT: CONGO CAR	10	66	35
RT: CONTINUOUS BRAKE	08	62	31
RT: CONTRABAND BAGGAGE	10	56	45
RT: CORNFIELD MEET	08	72	58
RT: CORNFIELD MEET (HEAD ON COLLISION)	06	55	34
RT: COUPON STATION	10	64	26
RT: COUPON STATION	04	69	29
RT: COW & CALF UNITS	03	68	24
RT: COW AND CALF W/SLUG ADDED	10	59	38
RT: CROSSTIE	02	73	49
RT: CROWN SHEETS (STEAM LOCOMOTIVES)	06	71	44
RT: CURVEMASTER RAIL	05	70	37
RT: CUTS & FILLS	08	73	57
RT: D-FORM ORDERS	12	73	52
RT: DEAD MAN'S HOLE	12	64	55
RT: DECELOSTAT CONTROL FEATURE	04	47	48
RT: DECORATE	03	65	48
RT: DEGREE OF CURVES	07	47	64
RT: DEMURRAGE (PENALTY PAYMENT)	04	59	37
RT: DINGDONG	04	75	12
RT: DINGER	07	77	49
RT: DINGER	04	78	55
RT: DISTANT SIGNAL	03	71	60
RT: DO NOT HUMP (FRAGILE MATERIAL)	10	55	35
RT: DOG CATCHER	04	67	33
RT: DOLLY BAR	04	67	33
RT: DOWNER/ROLLERS/SNOWDOZER/GROUT/ETC	11	50	128
RT: DRONE CABE	05	76	24
RT: DUAL FUEL	02	57	44
RT: DUNNAGE (BRACING/STAGING/SHELVING)	06	56	38
RT: DUTCH CLOCK	05	66	34
RT: DUTCH CLOCK	12	70	44
RT: ELECTRIC RAIL TERMS 1	11	42	95
RT: ELECTRIC RAIL TERMS 2	12	42	151
RT: ELECTRIC RAIL TERMS E-E	01	43	152
RT: ELECTRIC RAIL TERMS EL-IG	02	43	149
RT: ELECTRIC RAIL TERMS IM-SE	03	43	147
RT: ELECTRIC RAIL TERMS SE-WO	04	43	148
RT: ENGINE	10	42	59
RT: EURAILPASS	07	66	38
RT: EXHAUST LAP	10	55	36
RT: FAIR-WEATHER CARS	10	62	35
RT: FAN TRACK	11	43	63
RT: FANTAIL ENGINE	04	63	56
RT: FARES (STANDARD VERSUS DIFFERENTIAL)	10	59	36
RT: FIGURE EIGHT (PATTERN)	12	58	36
RT: FISH HORN	09	54	29
RT: FIVE POINTED STAR INDICATES	08	55	41
RT: FLANGE LUBRICATOR-GADGET APPLIES GRE	12	55	38
RT: FLASH WALL (OIL-BURNING LOCOS)	06	56	39
RT: FLASH WALL (OIL STEAM LOCOS)	03	66	29
RT: FLYING SWITCH	12	54	41
RT: FOGMAN (BRITISH)	05	72	56
RT: FREIGHT CAR LETTERING (LT/LD/CAPY)	05	71	52
RT: FRICTION	05	44	68
RT: FROZEN RAIL JOINT	04	46	52
RT: FUSEE	06	62	45
RT: GANDY DANCER	10	64	26
RT: GANDY DANCER	03	70	37
RT: GANDY DANCER (HOW TERM ORIGINATED)	12	55	66
RT: GANDY DANCER ORIGINATION	11	70	42
RT: GANDY DANCER.	04	75	12
RT: GIN POLE	04	67	33
RT: GRASSHOPPERS	02	57	47
RT: GRAVEYARD WATCH	05	76	24
RT: GRAVITY	05	44	69
RT: GUMSHOE	07	77	49
RT: HANDI-TALKIES	03	71	60
RT: HAY BURNER	07	77	49
RT: HAYBURNER	05	76	24
RT: HEADER HEATER SYSTEM	04	76	53
RT: HERDER	04	78	55
RT: HIGH-CUBE CARS	11	64	35
RT: HIGHBALL	08	59	35
RT: HOBO BASKET	04	58	44
RT: HOGHEAD	04	39	74
RT: HOGHEAD	02	75	50
RT: HOME SIGNAL	03	71	60
RT: HORSEPOWER OF STEAM LOCOS: FORMULA	04	54	62
RT: HOT HOLE CARS	11	71	38
RT: HOUSE TRACK	11	43	62
RT: HUMP (ARTIFICIAL KNOLL)	03	55	30
RT: HYDROSTATIC LUBRICATORS	08	66	34
RT: INTERLINE HAUL	02	57	40
RT: INTERLOCKING	01	65	29
RT: INTERLOCKING-SYSTEM TO INSURE SAFE H	02	55	27
RT: IRON HORSE-STEAM LOCO/WHO FIRST CALL	03	55	30
RT: JERK SOUP	05	76	24
RT: JERKWATER	03	53	139
RT: JERKWATER	04	58	41
RT: JIMMY JOHN	12	63	62
RT: JOHNSON BAR	05	65	06
RT: JOIN THE BIRDS	04	56	43
RT: JUMBO CAR	12	58	40
RT: KANGAROO COURT	07	54	63
RT: KANGAROO COURT	05	76	24
RT: KICK (SWITCHING TERM)	04	55	35
RT: KICKER	04	78	55
RT: KING SNIPE	10	76	47

Stephans' Railroad Directory

Railroad/Railfan

GENERAL RAILROADING

GENERAL RAILROADING	M	Y	P
RT: KISS 'N' RIDE FACILITY	03	68	25
RT: LADDER TRACK	11	43	62
RT: LEASE VS OPERATING CONTRACT	01	44	40
RT: LEFT-LEAD ENGINE (STEAM)	02	74	53
RT: LIGHTNING SLINGER	10	76	47
RT: LIGHTNING SLINGER	04	78	55
RT: LIMITED (PASSENGER TRAINS)	02	58	45
RT: LIMITED CUT-OFF DEFINED	05	45	64
RT: LIST OF DEFINITIONS	10	32	366
RT: LIZARD SCORCHER	04	78	55
RT: LNRC ON REEFERS	09	66	32
RT: LOCOMOTIVE BOOSTER	02	66	28
RT: MALLET ARTICULATED LOCOMOTIVE	03	66	28
RT: MANIFEST/TIME/WAY FREIGHT	04	32	69
RT: MARS LIGHT (HEADLIGHT)	04	59	36
RT: MEANING OF "T" IN LOCOMOTIVES	03	72	63
RT: MOLYGREASE	02	57	46
RT: MORE RAILROAD TERMS	01	33	136
RT: MUD DRUM (STEAM LOCOMOTIVES)	03	71	60
RT: MUDHOP	10	76	47
RT: MULE	04	67	33
RT: MUX--TELETYPE PRINTER	01	53	133
RT: NUT-SPLITTER	04	78	55
RT: OFFICIAL RAILWAY EQUIPMENT REGISTER	03	65	45
RT: OPERATING RATIO (%)	04	57	41
RT: OPERATING RATIO DEFINED	08	47	63
RT: OPERATING RATIO-% EXPENSE TO REVENUE	08	55	39
RT: ORDER NOTIFY FREIGHT SHIPMENT	02	43	59
RT: ORPHAN RAILROAD	04	58	45
RT: OS	03	75	12
RT: PEA VINE RAILWAYS	03	70	37
RT: PEDDLER	02	59	39
RT: PEDDLER	04	67	33
RT: PEDDLER CAR	05	45	62
RT: PERCENT OF CUT-OFF (LOCOMOTIVES)	12	43	79
RT: PIE-BOOK	12	78	47
RT: PIG-MAULER	10	76	47
RT: PINCH BAR	06	62	42
RT: POCATELLO YARD MASTER	06	61	34
RT: POCKET, DOG CHART & GLAND	02	60	35
RT: POSITIVE VS PERMISSIVE BLOCKS	06	57	43
RT: POSSUM BELLY	10	56	45
RT: POWER INTERLOCKING	08	66	31
RT: PRIOR CLASSIFICATION	08	57	41
RT: PULL THE PIN	10	76	47
RT: PULLED PLOW	06	46	73
RT: PUT ON THE NOSEBAG	12	78	47
RT: QUANTOMETER	02	58	40
RT: RABBIT	04	67	33
RT: RAIL SLANG LIST 6-61 DEFINITIONS	06	61	58
RT: RAILROAD COCOON DEFINED	10	55	33
RT: RAILROAD DROP	02	71	36
RT: RAILROAD GAGE	10	56	44
RT: RAILROAD NAVY	10	56	45
RT: RAILROAD VS RAILWAY	11	71	38

GENERAL RAILROADING	M	Y	P
RT: RED CAP	03	75	10
RT: RED LIGHT DISTRICT ORIGINS	04	63	36
RT: REDCAPS--ORIGIN OF TERM	02	47	124
RT: RELAY TRAIN	06	58	36
RT: RESISTANCE	05	44	69
RT: RIDING THE BLIND (HOBOES)	12	57	40
RT: RIDING THE BLINDS	12	66	28
RT: RIDING THE RODS	12	66	28
RT: RIP TRACK	11	43	63
RT: RULE 29	08	58	40
RT: RULE 6 WORDING (DRUGS & INTOXICANTS)	11	65	23
RT: RULING GRADE	08	58	40
RT: RULING GRADE	02	68	29
RT: RUN-THROUGH	06	72	60
RT: SCISSORBILL	09	54	28
RT: SCIZZOR-BILL	04	75	12
RT: SCOWS AND LIGHTERS	04	52	76
RT: SD (STOP DELAYED)	04	57	39
RT: SECONDARY FLAGMAN	09	65	30
RT: SEE AMERICA FIRST (HILL 1912)	02	58	44
RT: SHIMMYSHAKER	11	51	63
RT: SHOO-FLY	04	61	35
RT: SHOO-FLY	03	72	63
RT: SHORTLINE	12	76	06
RT: SHUFFLE THE DECK	10	76	47
RT: SIDE DOOR PULLMAN	10	71	45
RT: SIX DEGREE CURVE	02	45	70
RT: SKELTONIZING (TRACKWORK TERM)	10	56	45
RT: SLANGS AND SEMI-TECHNICAL	01	30	317
RT: SLIP COUCH (BRITISH TERM)	02	59	35
RT: SMOKING OVER	03	72	62
RT: SOFT BELLIES	10	76	47
RT: SPOTBOARD-GUIDE USED BY SECTION MEN	10	57	44
RT: STATION ORDER BOARD	02	66	29
RT: STATION-DEPOT-TERMINAL	02	65	31
RT: STCC MEANING	04	78	19
RT: STEAM DUMMY	08	75	58
RT: STEAM LAP	10	55	36
RT: STEAM-WINDER	12	78	47
RT: STOP-OFF VERSUS PART-LOAD CARS	09	44	64
RT: STRAIGHT PLAN VS AVERAGE AGREEMENT	06	46	73
RT: STROBEACON-TRADENAME ELECTRONIC LAMP	06	58	37
RT: SUBGRADE-USED IN RAILROAD TRACK WORK	04	57	44
RT: SUN KINK--ABNORMAL BEND IN RAIL	10	54	40
RT: SUPER-RAILROADS (MERGER)	08	56	38
RT: SUPERIOR TRAIN	06	66	32
RT: T/OB TONNAGE PER OPERATIVE-BRAKE	03	76	56
RT: TALGO	01	65	29
RT: TALLOWPOT	04	39	74
RT: TALLOWPOT	02	75	50
RT: TALLOWPOT--LOCOMOTIVE FIREMAN	05	54	80
RT: TALLOWPOTS (FIREMEN)	12	70	44
RT: TANK & SADDLE-TANK DEFINITIONS	02	67	25
RT: TANK LOCOMOTIVE	12	69	28
RT: TANK LOCOMOTIVE	12	66	27

Railroad/Railfan

GENERAL RAILROADING

GENERAL RAILROADING	M	Y	P
RT: TANK TOWN	04	58	41
RT: TEAM TRACK	11	43	63
RT: TEAM TRACK	08	67	30
RT: THOUSAND-MILER	04	75	12
RT: THROTTLE FEAVER	12	61	58
RT: TICKETFAX SYSTEM	06	55	33
RT: TON-MILE	04	75	11
RT: TRACTIVE EFFORT	10	72	53
RT: TRACTIVE FORCE FORMULA	02	59	38
RT: TRAIN-HANDLING INDICATOR	04	70	34
RT: TRAIN-PERFORMANCE CALCULATOR	04	55	36
RT: TRANSPORTATION EXCISE TAXES	08	57	39
RT: TRAP CAR	02	70	40
RT: TRAPEZE ARTIST	12	78	47
RT: TRAVELING GRUNT	04	75	12
RT: TRICK (TELEGRAPH SERVICE)	12	74	57
RT: TRIMMER ENGINE MOVEMENT	10	57	43
RT: TROLLEY "BROTHER-IN-LAW"	08	72	58
RT: TRUCK RAIL DEFINED	08	57	42
RT: TTX (TRAILER TRAIN)	12	67	24
RT: TUNNEL MASK	10	64	26
RT: TYPES OF PASSENGER DEPOTS	01	65	29
RT: UHF DEAD MAN CONTROL	08	67	31
RT: UNIT TRAIN	10	67	30
RT: VARNISH	04	75	12
RT: VARNISH (PASSENGER CARS)	12	59	18
RT: VISQUEEN POLYETHLENE-NEW FILM/CELLOP	06	58	37
RT: WABASH	04	75	12
RT: WABASHING	03	73	41
RT: WANIGAN CAR	12	78	47
RT: WASHOUT (STOP SIGNAL)	02	55	28
RT: WASP EXCLUDER	02	68	29
RT: WATER JACKET	12	69	28
RT: WATER SCOOP	01	66	26
RT: YELLOW FLAG	02	63	31
RT: ZULU (EMIGRANT FAMILY BOXCAR)	06	56	38
RT: ZULU CAR	03	72	62
RULE 93	01	30	209
RULE 99	01	30	207
RULES FROM 1855 RULE BOOK	04	70	13
RULES ON TRAINS MEETING ON SINGLE TRACK	04	66	35
RULES--THIS RULES BUSINESS	07	51	16
RULES: SP RULEBOOK #1	07	40	18
RUNNING GEAR FAILURES OF STEAM LOCOS	11	43	52
RUTLAND REVIVAL: OGDENSBURG BRIDGE & POR	F	75	30R
RUTLAND TRAIN--LIFE AFTER STEAMTOWN?	07	86	55
RUTTAN SYSTEM: HEATING/COOLING DEVICE	05	42	64

GENERAL RAILROADING	M	Y	P
SAFETY FEATURES-AUTO BLOCK/MILLER PLATFO	03	37	122
SAFETY FIRST PHOTO ESSAY	07	69	14
SAFETY FIRST--MYTH ON RAILROADS	08	61	13
SAFETY VALVES ON STEAM LOCOMOTIVES	06	48	46
SAGA OF HIGH-T (RAIL)	12	65	18
SAGINAW SOUTHBOUND-D&M MUSEUM CONSIST	05	80	24
SAILROADING: DEVELOPED IN MIDWEST 1875	10	40	112
SALARIES IN RAILROAD INDUSTRY	10	32	355
SALVAGING C&NW BRIDGE-SHAWANO-OCONTO JCT	07	38	123
SAN DIEGO: THE HARD WAY PHOTO ESSAY	05	53	34
SAN FRANCISCO CABLE CARS	11	45	90
SAN JUAN EXPRESS	06	60	35
SAND: USE OF SAND FOR LOCOS/COST	06	47	85
SANDBOX: ORIGINS	09	46	87
SANDING THE RAILS: HELPS ABNORMAL CONDIT	03	42	64
SANDY RIVER FIGHTS TO STAY IN OPERATION	11	31	536
SANTA FE SKYWAY SAGA	11	85	57
SAVING RAILROAD STATIONS	W	75	13R
SAWMILL & RR IN NW CALIFORNIA NEVER RAN!	01	35	39
SCALE RAILROADS	07	37	67
SCHOOL ON WHEELS (NC&SL)	05	53	06
SEA-GOING RAILROAD MILW	03	41	87
SEARS ROEBUCK & COMPANY: HISTORY OF	04	58	25
SEASHORE TROLLEY MUSEUM AT 40	09	79	51
SECTION CARS: THEIR HISTORY	03	42	06
SEGREGATION ON NEW ORLEANS STREETCARS	08	69	31
SELLING FREIGHT SERVICE	09	31	296
SELLING PASSENGER SERVICE	08	30	50
SENIORITY BEGANS AT FORTY: JOBS ON RR	08	44	50
SERVICE INDICATIONS OF STARS/BARS	12	46	82
SEVEN CARS PAINTED BLACK-LINCOLN FUNERAL	12	62	18
SEVEN KINDS OF TRANSPORTATION-BOAZ WV	02	38	69
SHANNON CONVENTION (ORWO) 1888 STRIKE	02	51	38
SHE'LL BE COMIN' ROUND THE MOUNTAIN	06	72	24
SHIPPING WITHOUT CONTAINERS W/MULTIGUAGE	01	67	29
SHOCKPROOF SHIPPING FOR DAMAGE CONTROL	02	48	68
SHOE PROTECTION - GANDY DANCER "TAMPERS"	04	67	08
SHORTEST PASSENGER RUN	04	64	29
SHRINERS AND STREAMLINERS	12	50	38
SIDETRACKING COMPETITION	09	31	295
SIGN LANGUAGE OF TRAIN & YARD CREWS	06	56	38
SIGNALING & ELECTRONICS 2	11	47	78
SILK TRAINS ON CP	06	77	10
SILK TRAINS READER INFORMATION	06	65	07
SILK TRAINS--NO DELAYS	04	65	13
SILVERTON LINE	06	69	13
SIMPLIFIED MORSE	06	51	65
SINGLE TRACK MAIN LINE CP	02	44	08
SINGLE-DRIVER LOCOMOTIVES	11	37	73
SISTERS OF THE ROAD (FEMALE HOBOS)	08	70	64
SIVER ENGINE "AMERICA" GERMAN SILVER	11	45	77
SIX HOUR DAY-PLAN TO HELP UNEMPLOYED	04	31	01
SKUNK CW #M100	12	47	60
SKYBUS DISCUSSIONS	04	71	53
SKYSCRAPER STATION (CLEVELAND)	06	51	19

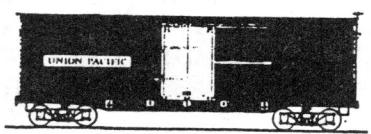

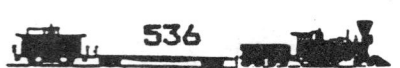

Railroad/Railfan

GENERAL RAILROADING

GENERAL RAILROADING	M	Y	P
SKYTRAIN TO VANCOUVERS EXPO	09	86	24
SLACK ACTION IN TRAINS	08	49	48
SLEEPING CAR MILEAGE LISTINGS	01	72	56
SLIM GAUGE	10	67	53
SLOGAN "STOP LOOK & LISTEN": ORIGIN	02	59	35
SLOGAN: SAFETY FIRST LESEUR 1905	10	56	40
SLOW BOAT TO CHINA BASIN (ATSF TUBS)	11	84	49
SLUDGE REMOVAL IN STEAM LOCOMOTIVES	06	47	80
SNO SHORT NOTES ON	05	65	42
SNO "DUTCH CLOCK" TRAIN SPEED MONITOR	12	70	44
SNO "THERMOS BOTTLE" ENGINES	02	62	50
SNO "TOONERVILLE TROLLEY"	11	75	42
SNO "TRAIN II" COMPUTER CONTROL	03	76	55
SNO 15 TOP REVENUE ROADS 1967	01	68	26
SNO 2' GAGE RAILROADS IN UNITED STATES	01	33	98
SNO 2-8-8-4 VS BIG BOY LOCO SPECS	12	71	58
SNO 2.5 BILLION GOLD SHIPMENT BY RAIL	06	74	09
SNO 4-6-2 LARGEST PACIFIC READER COMMENT	06	69	08
SNO 4-8-4-8-4 C&O 500 SERIES TURBINES	08	68	31
SNO 99 VS 100 YEAR LEASES	02	67	26
SNO AIR AND HAND BRAKES	10	66	37
SNO AIR BRAKE OPERATION ON AIR FAILURE	04	65	57
SNO ALASKA RAILROADS	05	65	42
SNO AMTRAK & AIR FARES	12	74	31
SNO ANIMALS USED IN SWITCHING CARS	08	55	39
SNO ARCHEOLOGICAL FINDS IN SUBWAY EXCAVA	03	71	36
SNO AUTOMATIC CAR IDENTIFICATION	10	69	34
SNO AUTOMATIC COUPLER DEVELOPMENT	11	73	57
SNO AUTOMATIC COUPLERS & THE LINK PIN	07	71	13
SNO BALTIMORE STREETCAR MUSEUM	07	71	48
SNO BELL-RINGER HEATER	06	59	36
SNO BENGUELA RY AFRICA EUCALYPTIS WOOD	01	74	48
SNO BI-LINGUAL ROADS 1966 (NONE)	01	66	25
SNO BIBLE-TRAIN MYSTERY	03	67	12
SNO BIDDING FOR RUNS	01	75	54
SNO BLIND PERSONS: PAY FULL FARE?	04	58	39
SNO BOILER EXPLOSIONS IN COLLISIONS	12	72	59
SNO BUFFALO AND TELEGRAPH POLES	04	69	10
SNO BUREAU OF EXPLOSIVES	07	71	43
SNO CAB FORWARD LOCO DEVELOPMNT NPC 1901	08	75	57
SNO CABOOSE STOVE HISTORY	12	70	08
SNO CALIFORNIA RAILWAY MUSEUM	09	76	51
SNO CANADIAN RAIL MILEAGE ABANDONMENT	01	67	27
SNO CANADIAN RAILWAY MUSEUM	09	65	31
SNO CANADIAN RAILWAY MUSEUM	08	76	51
SNO CHICAGO'S SOUTHWEST TRANSIT PROJECT	07	85	26
SNO CMI:WILLIAM GOAT'S LIFETIME PASS	02	70	10
SNO CN:INDIAN "MISS ONTARIO" MURDER	09	70	66
SNO CONDUCTOR'S PUNCHES	12	57	59
SNO COPPER TOKENS: PAY FOR CORDWOOD	08	53	63
SNO CORONATION SCOT 38T '39 WORLDS FAIR	07	73	38
SNO COUPLERS-COMPATIMATIC COUPLER	01	69	31
SNO DAVENPORT LOCOMOTIVE WORKS	09	71	39
SNO DIESEL TRAINS STARTING BRUSH FIRES	09	69	30
SNO DIFFERENT RAILROADS WITH SAME NAME	02	66	31
SNO DUPLEX STEAM LOCOMOTIVES	10	64	27
SNO DUTCH CLOCK SPEED CONTROL ON ATSF	09	74	42
SNO E: 4-WAY RADIO INSTALLATION	01	49	62
SNO EARLY RAIL DEVELOPMENT 1848-54	09	65	31
SNO ELECTRIC FREIGHT LINES IN ALASKA	04	68	33
SNO ELECTRIC PASSENGER LINES IN ALASKA	11	68	38
SNO ELECTRIFIED TRACK/MILES OF TRACK	04	32	69
SNO ELECTRONIC TICKET COLLECTORS	11	66	38
SNO ENGINEERS HANDLING THE FUEL SHORTAGE	04	74	43
SNO FAST FREIGHT SERVICE CHICAGO-NY	11	75	43
SNO FIBERGLASS TELEGRAPH POLES	12	56	29
SNO FIREMEN CALLED TALLOWPOTS	12	70	44
SNO FIRST & LARGEST TANK CARS	01	66	25
SNO FIRST CIRCUS ON TRANSCONTINENTAL LIN	08	69	08
SNO FIRST CIRCUS TRAINS	02	74	52
SNO FIRST FATAL RAILWAY ACCIDENT	12	75	58
SNO FIRST HANDBRAKES	10	65	27
SNO FIRST ISSUE OF RAILROAD MANS MAGAZIN	10	68	35
SNO FIRST RAIL CHARTER IN US--NEW JERSEY	04	61	34
SNO FIRST RAILROAD FATALITY	11	65	23
SNO FIRST TELEPHONE USE ON RAILROADS	09	73	42
SNO FIRST TRAINS TO GREAT LAKES	07	73	39
SNO FIRST TRANSCONTINENTAL RR IN PANAMA	09	77	54
SNO FIRST TROOPS ON TRAINS	11	70	42
SNO FIRST TV RECEPTION ON TRAINS (B&O)	07	74	39
SNO FIRST USE OF PAPER CUPS (DL&W) 1909	12	76	27
SNO FORM 19 VERSUS FORM 31 DIFFERENCES	11	38	72
SNO FORNEY MUSEUM	07	76	50
SNO FOX TRUCKS	10	75	54
SNO FUEL CONSERVATION MEASURES OF RRS	03	74	33
SNO FUEL CONSUMPTION OF VARIOUS DIESELS	07	73	39
SNO GAUGES OF EARLY CANADIAN RAILWAYS	08	77	56
SNO GLASS USED IN TRAINS	07	69	34
SNO GOVERNMENT REGULATIONS ON STARTING R	11	72	54
SNO GRAND CENTRAL (NY) TRIPARTITE AGREEM	05	72	56
SNO GRAND CENTRAL'S RED CARPET (NY CITY)	04	68	26
SNO GRAVITY CARS	05	75	02
SNO HAZARDOUS WASTE HAULING BY TANK CARS	01	75	04
SNO HOTBOX PROBLEMS	01	55	36
SNO HOTBOXES-STILL A SERIOUS PROBLEM	10	55	32
SNO ICE RAILWAYS	05	67	32
SNO INTERNAL RAIL FORCE MEASUREMENT	05	75	51
SNO KINZUA BRIDGE HISTORY	11	65	23
SNO LAND BRIDGE ATSF/PC	08	68	08
SNO LAND BRIDGE:UP & N&W PROPOSAL	10	68	35
SNO LARGEST DRIVING WHEELS--MATHER DIXON	02	74	54
SNO LARGEST LOCO FLEETS IN 1948	05	70	38
SNO LAW OFFICER BUST ON "ON TIME" AMTRAK	06	75	57
SNO LINCOLN WRITING GETTYSBURG ADDRESS	05	74	06
SNO LOCO CABS: DO ALL HAVE WINDOWS?	04	55	33
SNO LOCOMOTIVE "WILLIAM PENN"	09	66	57
SNO LOCOMOTIVE MILES (DIFFERENT TYPES)	10	74	45
SNO LOST CAR AGENTS	08	73	06
SNO LOUISIANA SUGAR PLANTATIONS 1966	07	66	37
SNO MARTIN VAN BURENS DISLIKE OF RAILROA	12	68	59

Railroad/Railfan

STEPHANS_RAILROAD_DIRECTORY

GENERAL RAILROADING

GENERAL RAILROADING	M	Y	P
SNO MASON-DIXON LINE (NOT A RAILROAD!)	10	67	31
SNO MERGING OF RAILROADS AN OLD STORY	06	69	39
SNO MICROFILMING RECORDS	03	55	29
SNO MOGUL COUNTRY FAREWELL-COMMENTS	06	54	06
SNO MOVING SIDEWALK	07	54	64
SNO MUNICIPALLY OWNED CANADIAN RAILROADS	05	68	26
SNO N&W:2-8-8-2 CLASS Y6B LOCOMOTIVES	02	71	36
SNO NATIONAL GEOGRAPHIC RAIL ARTICLES	10	71	44
SNO NERVE GAS ON US RAILROADS	09	70	10
SNO NEW YORK WORLD'S FAIR	08	39	69
SNO NEWFOUNDLANDS FIRST RAILWAYS	06	78	57
SNO NEWSPAPER PUBLISHED ON GN TRAIN 1913	12	76	26
SNO NEWSPAPERS PRINTED ON BOARD A TRAIN	11	66	39
SNO NORTHEAST CORRIDOR CONSTRUCTION	01	67	08
SNO NP:FREE PASSES	07	69	10
SNO NYC:HORSE MAN LEADING TRAINS IN 1941	05	68	58
SNO OFFICIAL GUIDE REVAMPED PUBLICATION	05	74	04
SNO OLDEST US RAILROADS	06	66	31
SNO ON AIR HOSE MATERIALS	04	71	62
SNO ON HOW TRAINS ROUND CURVES W/FIXED W	11	65	24
SNO ORANGE EMPIRE RY MUSEUM	10	76	47
SNO PC:HOPPER CARS MARKED "TOC"	10	68	35
SNO PER DIEM RATE OF CAR SERVICE	09	72	52
SNO PLANS FOR TRANSCONTINENTAL RAIL SYST	12	72	59
SNO PNEUMATIC TIRES ON RAILROAD CARS	07	68	27
SNO PORTABLE CAR STOPS "PORTA-STOP" PHOT	12	57	40
SNO PRESIDENT PRIVILEDGES ON RAILROADS	03	54	121
SNO PREVENTING WATER FROM FREEZING IN ST	12	76	25
SNO PRR LONGEST & HEAVIEST TRAIN	03	67	31
SNO PRR:4-4-4-4 CLASS T1 STEAM LOCOMOTIV	02	71	36
SNO PRR:THE WORLDS HEAVIEST ORE TRAIN	02	67	08
SNO RACIAL DISCRIMINATION	02	55	07
SNO RADAR STOP WATCHES PROTECT FREIGHT	06	72	60
SNO RAIL BIKES	10	70	20
SNO RAIL PAY PRACTICES IN 1899	08	67	08
SNO RAILROAD CAR JOURNALS	08	57	40
SNO RAILROAD HALL OF FAME	10	70	20
SNO RAILROAD LAND GRANTS	10	66	36
SNO RAILROAD SCRIPT (MONEY)	05	70	37
SNO RAILROAD SCRIPT ON CANADIAN ROADS	01	67	28
SNO RAILROAD WATCHES: SPECIFICATIONS	08	59	37
SNO RAILROADING IN HAWAII	02	67	56
SNO RAILROADS FIRST WAR ROLLS	08	69	27
SNO RAILROADS RUN ON FROZEN WATER	10	66	36
SNO RAILROADS USE OF MICROWAVE TRANSMISS	05	74	47
SNO RENT-A-TRAIN (IC)	08	68	30
SNO RIGHT OF WAY DISPOSITION ON ABANDONM	11	72	54
SNO RINGLEMANN TESTS FOR LOCO SMOKE	11	75	41
SNO ROAD WITH LARGEST SUBURBAN FLEET	03	68	24
SNO ROCK BOLTING	02	59	39
SNO ROCK SLIDES: WAYS TO PREVENT	10	56	39
SNO S STATE WITH MOST RAIL MILES 1866 GA	11	76	42
SNO SAND: PREVENTS SLIPPING-HOW?	12	54	43
SNO SEASHORE TROLLEY MUSEUM-OLDEST IN US	01	71	50
SNO SHAYS--THE LARGEST EVER BUILT	11	65	61
SNO SHORTLINES IN TWO GAUGES	02	64	35
SNO SINGLE TRACKING	05	74	46
SNO SMOKE BOX PAINT TYPES	11	65	24
SNO SP: DIESEL-HYDRAULIC LOCOMOTIVES	06	68	29
SNO STAFF SYSTEM & MACHINES CONTROL	09	70	30
SNO STANDARD TIME ADOPTED	02	72	61
SNO STARS AND BARS ON CONDUCTORS UNIFORM	03	72	63
SNO STEAMTOWN ARRIVES IN SCRANTON	05	84	28
SNO STEAMTOWN IN SCRANTON UPDATE	09	84	28
SNO STEAMTOWN USA:FINANCIAL UPDATE	03	87	30
SNO STEAMTOWN-BELLOWS FALLS VT	09	65	30
SNO STEAMTOWN:ROAD OF ANTHRACITE	09	87	32
SNO STORY BEHIND "GOULDS SIGNAL" POEM	07	67	33
SNO SUBMARINE "TORSK" SINKS TRAIN (WWII)	08	73	04
SNO SUBWAYS: FIRST ONES	03	55	30
SNO SWEDISH TRAIN SUSPENSION SYSTEM	09	70	30
SNO TALGO: WHAT DOES WORD MEAN	01	55	36
SNO TELEPHONE DISPATCHING OF TRAINS	06	77	52
SNO TELEPHONE TRAIN DISPATCHING	09	53	68
SNO TELEVISION IN YARD OPERATIONS	02	55	30
SNO TENDER HEADLIGHTS	11	54	36
SNO TERM "STOP, LOOK, LISTEN" ORIGIN	10	72	53
SNO TICKET PUNCHES: VARIOUS/DISTINCTIVE	10	54	42
SNO TOONERVILLE TROLLEY CARTOONS	01	71	48
SNO TOY TRAIN ON US CHRISTMAS STAMP	10	71	09
SNO TRACK PAN WATER KEPT FROM FREEZING	08	71	45
SNO TRAIN EXHIBITS AT NY WORLD FAIR 1939	11	70	42
SNO TRAIN MODIFICATIONS FOR US PRESIDENT	02	71	39
SNO TRAIN ORDER ORIGINATION	05	75	52
SNO TRAIN ORDERS: 19 VS 31	12	59	34
SNO TRAIN/AIR PLANE COLLISIONS	09	66	32
SNO TRAINMENS UNIFORMS	07	69	35
SNO TRAINS BEING HIT BY LIGHTING	06	63	25
SNO TRANSCONTINENTAL RR UNDER ONE ROAD?	05	65	42
SNO TRANSCONTINENTAL TRAIN RUNS	04	72	66
SNO TUNNEL BUILDING PHILOSOPHY OF US RDS	12	65	27
SNO TUNNEL DANGERS IN EARLY YEARS	08	69	56
SNO TURBOLINERS ON AMTRAK	12	74	30
SNO TYPES OF COUPLERS MANUAL & AUTOMATIC	10	66	35
SNO TYPES OF ELECTRIFICATION--EAST COAST	12	63	63
SNO US OWNED MILEAGE IN CANADA	06	38	72
SNO US PRESIDENTS DEALINGS WITH RAILROAD	12	68	30
SNO US RAILROADS MAKING MONEY	08	74	56
SNO VARIOUS MAJOR ROADS W/EQUIPMENT	10	32	346
SNO VERT-A-PACK CARS OF SP	01	71	50
SNO VIRGINIA CIVIL WAR ERA RAILROADS	05	76	24
SNO WASH LIE TO DERAIL TRAIN? CCE	06	76	04
SNO WASHING OF LOCOS	02	57	40
SNO WATCHES: 21 JEWEL/TESTED FOR ACCURAC	10	54	40
SNO WATER OPERATED FUNICULAR RAILWAYS	03	71	18
SNO WAYBILLS: WHO ORIGINATES	02	56	37
SNO WEIGHT OF FREIGHT TRAINS 1974	07	74	39
SNO WESTERN UNION: OWNS RAILROAD CARS	08	59	34
SNO WESTINGHOUSE AIR BRAKE CO--HISTORY	09	67	27
SNO WESTINGHOUSE, GEORGE: INVENTED...	04	56	42

Railroad/Railfan

GENERAL RAILROADING

GENERAL RAILROADING	M	Y	P
SNO WHAT IS A SHORTLINE	12	76	06
SNO WHEEL SLIPPING--MOISTURE	02	55	27
SNO WHEELS AND INTERCHANGE SERVICE	10	54	39
SNO WHEELS: HOW KEPT IN PRECISION TRIM	10	55	37
SNO WHISTLE BLASTS FOR GRADE CROSSINGS	10	71	45
SNO WHY PITTSBURGH MAY NOT HAVE LAST "H"	06	62	46
SNO WHY RAPID TRANSIT ROOFS DONT LEAK?	07	76	55
SNO WORLD WAR I: US GOV'T OWNED RRS WHEN	08	56	43
SNO WORLDS STEEPEST GRADES (LONG DIST)	11	68	34
SNO Y & R ORDERS READER COMMENTS	10	67	32
SNO: STEAMTOWN TO SCRANTON PA	07	83	26
SNOW PHOTO ESSAY	03	47	86
SNOW BLOCKADES IN THE WEST 1949	12	49	28
SNOW CLEARING	01	38	05
SNOW CLEARING IN COLORADO D&RGW	01	31	241
SNOW CLEARING ON YELLOWSTONE LINE UP	02	54	64
SNOW CLEARING--BLIZZARDS	03	31	529
SNOW DAY ON NYC	03	81	43
SNOW FIGHTING ON THE WESTERN PRAIRIES	03	31	529
SNOW ON RAILS PHOTO ESSAY	12	65	13
SNOW ON THE REID NEWFOUNDLAND RY 1905-6	02	32	338
SNOW REMOVAL D&RGW USING ROTARY PLOWS	01	31	241
SNOW--THE WAR AGAINST	01	38	05
SNOWPLOWS	03	83	34
SNOWSHOTS OF SP STEAM	03	72	16
SNOWSTORMS & GN COOK D&RG CMI	09	34	93
SOCIAL SECURITY FOR RAILROAD MEN	06	54	67
SOLAR ENERGY ON RAILROADS	06	77	08
SOLAR ENERGY ON SOUTHERN	04	78	17
SOO LINE-UNLUCKIEST BIG RAILROAD	09	38	07
SOO SOUTH OF SCHILLER	SP	77	50R
SOUND OF PROFESSIONAL QUALITY	07	79	56
SOUTH OF THE RIO GRANDE (PHOTO ESSAY)	08	61	30
SOUTH PARK'S LAST RUN	08	37	96
SOUTHERN PACIFIC LINES SABOTAGED	04	40	92
SOUTHERN PENN RR-VANDERBILT'S FOLLY	01	38	45
SP RESCUES SHIPWRECKED SAILORS	10	66	16
SP TRAIN YARD AT ROSEVILLE CALIFORNIA	10	40	47
SPEED IN THE LONG AGO (1800'S)	09	36	17
SPEED WAR CENTRAL VERSUS PENNSYLVANIA RR	12	34	08
SPEEDERMEN: FIGHT FOREST FIRES	02	30	395
SPEEDING UP DEAD FREIGHT-MOVE TONS STEEL	04	31	10
SPOKANE: A CITY SERVED BY 6 RAILROADS	06	53	12
SPRING LOADED WHEELS TO ACCOMODATE GAUGE	04	60	27
SPRING RIGGING AND EQUALIZATION	04	45	68
STAGED WRECKS FOR STATE FAIRS	04	33	39
STAMPS DEPICT ENGINE HISTORY	12	33	44
STANDARD GAGE: WHY 4 FEET 8.5 INCHES??	10	47	69
STANDARD GAUGE CARS ON SLIM GAUGE ROADS	03	34	131
STATION AGENT PHOTO ESSAY	12	39	57
STATION AGENT N&W	07	54	71
STATION AGENT (ANITA GALE) CP	04	62	30
STATION BELLS	12	50	71
STATION MASTER DE LUXE--BILL EGAN	08	30	01
STATIONMASTER: O'NEILL 36 YRS ST LOUIS	04	47	122
STATUES AND BUSTS OF RAILROAD MEN	11	37	40
STEAM DAYS IN NH (PAINTING COLLECTION)	05	74	31
STEAM DAYS ON THE WHEELING ROAD	03	74	28
STEAM ENGINES AND ZERO TEMPERATURES	04	65	34
STEAM ENGINES STILL HAULING COAL (WMC)	02	66	66
STEAM EXPO AND GRAND PARADE	09	86	32
STEAM FROM ALTOONA (PRR)	12	63	25
STEAM HOGGERS	11	76	53
STEAM IN MEXICO 1964	04	64	54
STEAM IN MEXICO 1971	04	71	30
STEAM IN MEXICO 1973	10	73	35
STEAM IN THE CANEFIELDS	11	71	40
STEAM IN THE CAROLINAS TODAY (1961)	12	61	35
STEAM LOCO DEVELOPMENT 120 YEARS	06	75	22
STEAM LOCOMOTIVE POWER	12	51	57
STEAM LOCOMOTIVE SCRAPPING PHOTO ESSAY	01	53	110
STEAM LOCOMOTIVE TYPES	07	37	59
STEAM ON DIRT ROADS	06	62	42
STEAM PASSENGER TRAINS-WHERE TO FIND 'EM	08	63	24
STEAM POWER IN ALABAMA	02	59	62
STEAM POWER SOUTH OF THE BORDER	03	67	17
STEAM POWER TODAY (1956)	08	56	66
STEAM RAILROADING IN MEXICO PHOTO ESSAY	04	65	38
STEAM RETURNS TO MCCLOUD RIVER	11	82	28
STEAM STILL SERVES STERLING 1960	SP	77	44R
STEAM SWITCHERS IN THE EAST	03	71	20
STEAM TO COOL CARS ON MILW	09	73	42
STEAM TRAINS AND AIR POLLUTION GRIPES	01	73	49
STEAM TURBINE READER COMMENTS	05	70	08
STEAM VERSUS DIESEL	02	35	28
STEAM VS DIESEL LOCOMOTIVES	05	34	80
STEAM VS JUICE READER DISCUSSION	01	32	279
STEAM VS JUICE CONTROVERSY	07	33	65
STEAM-WAGON	11	40	84
STEAMING TO SACRAMENTO-MUSEUM OPENING	09	81	32
STEAMS FINEST HOUR	02	73	26
STEAMTOWN IN SCRANTON OPENING	01	85	32
STEAMTOWN MOVING? (TO SCRANTON PA)	01	83	24
STEAMTOWN NATIONAL HISTORIC SITE	01	87	40
STEAMTOWN RAILFAN WEEKEND	04	78	14R
STEAMTOWN SCRANTON 1985 NOTES	07	85	28
STEAMTOWN SURPRISES	03	81	38
STEAMTOWN TO MOVE TO KINGSTON NY IN 1981	07	79	18
STEAMTOWN USA UPDATE	03	87	30
STEAMTOWN USA VISIT BY MADELEINE SINETY	12	75	28
STEAMTOWN: REMEMBERING BELLOWS FALLS VT	05	84	60
STEEL ACROSS THE RIVERS PART 2 BRIDGES	02	48	10
STEEL CITY COMMUTING (PITTSBURGH)	11	81	33
STEEL GANG IN TROPICAL JUNGLES PANAMA	08	39	73
STEEL TO THE WEST-TRANSCONTINENTAL ROAD	08	30	115
STEEPEST RAILWAY GRADE IN THE WORLD	05	66	35
STEPHENSON LOCO FIRST RUN REENACTMENT	04	76	15
STEPHENSON LOCOMOTIVE WORKS COMPANY	04	36	44
STILL SOME STEAM IN MEXICO 1966	02	66	20
STOPPING STEAM LOCO WITH LOCKED DRIVERS	02	66	29

Railroad/Railfan

GENERAL RAILROADING

GENERAL RAILROADING	M	Y	P
STOPPING TRAINS AT FLAGSTOPS READER INFO	12	63	64
STORY BEHIND POEM "ESSEX JUNCTION"	10	67	30
STORY BEHIND POEM "WRECK ON THE C&O"	11	67	30
STORY BEHIND THE POEM-WILL LIGHTS BE WHI	04	66	36
STRANGE CREATURES--HORSE W/13' MANE	04	61	08
STREAMLINE TRAINS	03	35	43
STREET AND INTERURBAN RAILWAY OF 1950	02	50	70
STREET CAR THRILLS	04	36	39
STREET CAR VILLAGE--MADE INTO APTS PHOTO	06	38	78
STREETCAR POST OFFICES	09	38	60
STREETCAR POST OFFICES	09	54	46
STREETCARS ON DISPLAY	04	60	51
STRIKE CURTAILING DETAIL PAINTING LOCOS	08	62	32
STRIKE OF 1855	08	35	126
STRIKE OF 1877	08	59	46
STRIKE OF 1877-IRREGULAR EMPLOY/SLOW PAY	02	36	05
STRIKES IN THE 1850'S	08	46	136
STUB SWITCHES	09	54	28
STUDENT OPERATOR ADVISE	07	43	72
SUBJECT TO CHANGE WITHOUT NOTICE PART 1	05	51	28
SUBJECT TO CHANGE WITHOUT NOTICE PART 2	06	51	37
SUBURBAN TRAINS OF YESTERDAY	11	73	26
SUBWAY FAIR CHEATS	06	77	48
SUBWAY SERVICE SCHOOL	04	53	48
SUBWAYS	01	40	69
SUBWAYS IN THE UNITED STATES: FIRSTS	07	52	68
SUBWAYS OF THE WORLD	02	64	16
SUGAR CANE RAILROADS	04	57	22
SUGAR-CANE HAULING	11	42	32
SUGAR-PLANTATION RAILROADS	04	57	22
SUN KINK: ABNORMAL BEND IN RAILS	02	42	43
SUN SETS ON THE HUMP RIDER	12	60	16
SUNNYSIDE YARD NEW YORK CITY NY PRR	05	48	10
SUPER-LOCOMOTIVES (STEAM)	10	66	19
SUPERHEATERS ON STEAM LOCOMOTIVES	07	43	58
SUPERINTENDENT'S JOB	10	39	106
SUPERINTENDENTS--WHAT THEY DO? VARIOUS	08	32	56
SUPERSTITIONS	04	49	42
SUPRISING SURVIVORS: ALCO'S CENTURY 430	05	86	38
SWITCH KEYS	03	68	18
SWITCHING ENGINES ON WESTERN RAILS	05	65	26
TALES OF A LANKY TEXAN--2-10-4	02	78	26R
TAMING THE CANYON (FEATHER RIVER CANYON)	11	46	10
TANK CARS MOVE OIL	07	43	08
TAPE RECORDED MUSIC IN PASSENGER TRAIN S	02	58	06
TARIFF PREPARATION	02	48	75
TAUNTON LOCO WORKS BRIEF HISTORY	02	62	50
TEHACHAPI LOOP CALIFORNIA	02	49	12
TELEGRAPH CODES FOR TRAIN CONTROL 1910	10	78	48
TELEGRAPH OPERATORS: WHAT DOES "30" MEAN	12	35	83
TELEGRAPH: 1840-1940 EQUIPMENT PHOTO ESS	03	47	28
TELEGRAPH: ITS HISTORY	03	47	08
TELEGRAPHONE: PARTS OF	02	42	60
TELEGRAPHY ON RAILROADS	03	47	08
TEN MILES OF TRACK LAID IN ONE DAY 1869	05	36	83
TEN-WHEELER "THE CHESAPEAKE" LOCOMOTIVE	09	36	65
TENOR EMPLOYEE ON SECTION GANG	04	61	33
TEXAS RAILROADS: LAWS GOVERNING OWNERSHI	03	34	88
TFO TIMING THE FAST ONES	01	39	21
TFO ANN RUTLEDGE B&O	11	39	29
TFO BOARDWALK FLYER	01	39	21
TFO BURLINGTON-ROCK ISLAND STREAMLINERS	12	40	50
TFO CHAMPION	03	40	80
TFO CONGRESSIONAL PRR	02	40	78
TFO CRUSADER READING LINES	05	40	29
TFO MERCURY NYC	09	39	53
THANKS, DAD: RAILFAN TRIBUTE	01	83	46
THE 1027'S THEY DIDN'T SHOW YOU!	05	87	38
THE FOUR-YEAR-OLD RAILFAN	11	82	33
THIRTY YEARS OF STEAM PHOTOGRAPHY	09	67	36
THOSE HARVEY GIRLS OF ATSF	12	64	13
THOUSAND MILES BY TROLLEY	12	37	116
THREAT TO PRIVATE OPERATION OF RAILROADS	08	61	47
THROTTLE CONTROL FOR DIESEL LOCOMOTIVES	12	52	59
TICKET TO CHARLOTTSVILLE	03	80	37
TIES: THEIR HISTORY	06	52	44
TILLY FOSTER IRON MINE: HISTORY	01	53	63
TIME AND RAILROAD WATCHES	05	52	30
TIME AND TIMEKEEPING	07	35	90
TIME BEGAN AT KIPTON: 1891 WRECK INSPIRE	01	66	18
TIMETABLES AND SCHEDULES	06	51	37
TIMETABLES OCTOBER 1825-1935	06	35	40
TIMETABLES-FOREIGN	05	36	96
TIMKEN ROLLER-BEARINGS	03	40	125
TIPS: CONDUCTOR-SO YOU'RE GONNA BE BRAIN	08	43	124
TIPS: ENGINEERS---TRAIN HANDLING	06	45	32
TIPS: MACHINIST	11	43	116
TIPS: NEWS DISPATCHER	09	43	130
TIPS: STUDENT FIREMAN	10	43	102
TIPS: SWITCHMAN	12	43	92
TIPS: TOWERMAN	08	44	102
TIRE SETTING ON WHEELS	11	49	60
TMG TRAINS THAT ARE MAKING GOOD	10	36	88
TMG 20TH CENTURY LIMITED NYC PASS TRAIN	09	38	66
TMG BLUE COMET CNJ PASSENGER TRAIN	11	36	24
TMG BROADWAY LIMITED PRR PASSENGER TRAIN	09	38	66
TMG BURLINGTON ZEPHYR PASSENGER TRAIN	03	37	21
TMG CANADIAN PACIFIC STREAMLINER	07	37	60
TMG CHALLENGER UP/C&NW	10	36	88
TMG CITY OF MEXICO PASSENGER TRAIN	05	38	63
TMG CONGRESSIONAL PASSENGER TRAIN	10	37	51
TMG DAYLIGHT PASSENGER TRAIN	08	37	27
TMG EGYPTIAN ZIPPER C&EI	11	38	124
TMG EL CAPITAN ATSF PASSENGER TRAIN	07	38	66
TMG EMPIRE BUILDER PASSENGER TRAIN	06	38	22
TMG EMPIRE STATE EXPRESS NYC PASS TRAIN	02	38	48
TMG FLYING YANKEE B&M PASSENGER TRAIN	12	37	70
TMG GEORGE WASHINGTON PASSENGER TRAIN	12	36	25
TMG GREEN DIAMOND IC PASSENGER TRAIN	11	37	35
TMG HIAWATHA MILW PASSENGER TRAIN	02	37	54

STEPHANS_RAILROAD_DIRECTORY

Railroad/Railfan

GENERAL RAILROADING

GENERAL RAILROADING	M	Y	P
TMG HIAWATHA, THE NEW PHOTOS	12	38	73
TMG ILLINOIS CENTRAL MS-1 ACCELERATED FR	08	38	23
TMG MOUNTAINEER NYO&W PASSENGER TRAIN	10	38	52
TMG ORANGE BLOSSOM SPECIAL	04	38	63
TMG REBEL GM&N STREAMLINED DIESEL-ELECT	01	37	122
TMG ROCKETS RI PASSENGER TRAINS	01	38	67
TMG ROYAL BLUE PASSENGER TRAIN	06	37	85
TMG SILVER METEOR (SAL) PHOTO ESSAY	04	39	25
TMG SILVER METEOR (SAL) PHOTO ESSAY	05	39	25
TMG SUPER CHIEF PASSENGER TRAIN-LUXURY	09	37	52
TMG THE 400 PASSENGER TRAIN	05	37	61
TMG UNION PACIFIC STREAMLINERS	03	38	25
TO CAPTURE A CABOOSE	01	80	31
TOLEDO: CITY OF MANY TRAINS	11	53	18
TOM THUMB RAILROADS	01	39	67
TOMBSTONE SHAPED LIKE A CABOOSE	12	67	06
TOONERVILLE TROLLEY--HISTORY OF CARTOON	02	38	120
TOUGH GUYS--DAYLIGHT MOVIE	09	86	44
TOWN-OPERATED STEAM RAILROAD	10	40	07
TRACK SCALE	01	46	60
TRACK SQUEEZE PRACTICES-STUPIDITY!	02	75	13
TRACK TORPEDOES	06	50	36
TRACKAGE RIGHTS: 7% SHARED BY 2+ ROADS	10	41	24
TRACTIVE FORCE: SAME DIMENSIONS WHY DIFF	10	35	82
TRAFFIC MANAGER	07	41	07
TRAFIC PROBLEMS OF MEGALOPOLIS	01	65	44
TRAIN CREW COLLECTION ON EL	04	67	10
TRAIN DISPATCHERS	04	64	20
TRAIN DISPATCHERS IN COMMUTER SERVICE	02	68	33
TRAIN FERRY FIRST BUILT & OPERATED	11	77	25
TRAIN HANDLING ADVICE TO NEW ENGINEERS	06	45	32
TRAIN HOOP ORDERS	09	41	19
TRAIN NAMED FOR ACTRESS:DOLLY VARDEN	09	32	239
TRAIN ORDERS 19 VERSUS 31	02	30	471
TRAIN ORDERS: FORMS	04	34	79
TRAIN PERFORMANCE SIMULATION USE ON SP	01	68	10
TRAIN RIDING CAT	11	76	08
TRAIN RIDING SURVEY	06	66	20
TRAIN ROBBER GENE BUNCH 1888	07	69	34
TRAIN TALK (PRR) COMMUNICATION	10	44	55
TRAIN TELEPHONES	02	42	54
TRAIN TRAVELS NOWHERE AT 42 MPH	03	78	37
TRAIN VS AUTO RACE OF 1913	03	77	46
TRAIN VS BUS VS GAS-ELECTRIC CARS	01	39	62
TRAIN-AUTO CRASH OF 1901 WESTBURY NY	09	76	05
TRAIN-DEFINITION OF A TRAIN	12	29	99
TRAIN-WRECKING AS A SPORT	02	37	108
TRAINMAN'S HAND LANTERN LANGUAGE OF OWN	01	53	34
TRAINMASTER ON RB&BB CIRCUS	01	78	08
TRAINMASTER/SUPERINTENDENT-HOW TO BECOME	09	33	45
TRAINS CALLED "CANNON BALL"	08	65	17
TRAINS CHANGE TO STANDARD TIME 9/30/1945	03	46	73
TRAINS NAMED FOR WOMEN (ADDS/CORRECTS)	10	46	125
TRAINS NAMED FOR WOMEN W/PHOTOS/HISTORY	07	46	32
TRAINS STOPPED BY AN ANT (SOUTHERN)	06	66	32
TRAINS USED IN TV SERIES"WILD WILD WEST"	01	66	25
TRAINS WITH BRAINS-CREWLESS LOCOS	04	63	19
TRANSPORTATION ACT OF 1940	08	41	71
TRANSPORTATION FACTORY	04	39	07
TRAVELING SCHOOLS IN CANADIAN WILDERNESS	06	31	332
TREES AS WINDBREAKS SP	01	70	08
TROJAN HORSEPOWER: DIESELIZATION	10	48	12
TROLLEY LINES OF WEST VIRGINIA	09	48	107
TROLLEY MUSEUMS	08	67	37
TROLLEY/INTERURBAN INDEX PRIOR TO 1942	04	59	46
TROLLEYVILLE USA	10	66	25
TROOP TRAINS: HISTORY OF RAILWAY TROOP	02	41	27
TROY NY: SHOWCASE OF ELECTRIC OPERATION	12	55	42
TRUCK SPRINGING OF DIESEL LOCOMOTIVES	06	53	54
TRUCKING AMERICA'S RAW DEAL	01	35	42
TRUCKING COSTS MORE!	02	35	18
TRUST COMPANIES AND RAILROAD EQUIPMENT	03	36	85
TUGS-CHESSIE'S FAIRBANKS-MORSE FAREWELL	07	84	34
TUNNELS-RAILROADS WITH PLENTY OF THEM	02	39	94
TUNNELS-WORLD'S FIFTEEN LONGEST	01	36	80
TURBOTRAINS ON CN	06	67	14
TURNTABLE: HISTORY	04	43	08
TWIN CITIES: RAILROADS OF THE	02	54	16
TWO RIVAL ENGINE BLDRS MASON & TAUNTON	02	34	38
TWO VIEWPOINTS ON RAIL PASSENGER SERVICE	11	66	56
ULTIMATE SCALE RAILROADING READER COMMEN	12	87	12
UNDER CHICAGO STREETS CHICAGO TUNNEL RY	11	33	94
UNDERGROUND ELECTRIC FEED CABLES	05	40	91
UNION PACIFIC HERALD EVOLUTION	02	74	06
UNION PACIFIC HISTORICAL MUSEUM	07	76	22
UNION STATIONS COUNTRY WIDE	11	71	24
UNIONS STOP FIGHTING REPEAL FULL CREW LA	06	65	54
UNIQUE CITIES: LOMBARD MONTANA	10	41	75
UNIQUE GRAVE MARKER (WHISTLE OF N&W)	12	42	64
UNITED STATES & CANADA RR COOPERATION	08	47	77
UNITED STATES RAILWAY ASSOC	10	38	07
UNUSUAL LAWS ON RAILROADS	06	61	35
US GOVERNMENT SUSIDIZES AUTO COMMUTERS	06	65	60
US PRESIDENTS THAT WORKED FOR THE RR	12	62	31
US ROADS SLIPPING ON TRACK REPLACEMENT	12	73	51
USE OF PC LOCOS TO STEAL PRODUCE CARS	08	74	04
VALVE GEAR ACCELERATOR ON STEAM LOCOS	07	49	58
VAN SWERINGEN EMPIRE ARTICLE SENTURE	10	71	15
VANCOUVER ISLAND TODAY	09	78	49R
VANDENBERG'S BLUE ALCO (MRS1)	03	86	30
VANISHING FAN TRIPS	08	64	49
VANISHING PASSENGER TRAINS	06	62	17
VANS TO COMMUTERS TO STOP RAILRIDING SP	12	76	42
VARIETY OF GAUGES CAUSES PROBLEMS	12	31	80
VENTURA COUNTY RR QUESTION	03	77	46
VERMONT RAILWAYS TENTH ANNIVERSARY	03	74	02
VIA AND THE BUSMAN	03	82	22
VISIT TO STRASBURG RAIL ROAD	05	69	18
VISTA DOME TRAVELER--NEW HORIZONS	02	48	28
WAR BETWEEN ENGLISH/AMERICAN RAILROADERS	07	33	86

Railroad/Railfan

GENERAL RAILROADING

GENERAL RAILROADING	M	Y	P
WAR LESSONS FOR RAILROADS	01	42	06
WAR PRODUCTION BOARD & LOCOMOTIVES	03	85	41
WAR PRODUCTION BOARD AND DIESELS	01	86	36
WAR PRODUCTION BOARD READER INFORMATION	07	85	06
WAR RAILROAD-DEACUVILLE ROADS, FRANCE	05	30	273
WARTIME RAIL ADVERTISING	05	43	08
WARTIME RAILROADING PHOTO ESSAY	07	42	51
WARTIME RAILROADING-MANY STORIES	02	36	33
WASHINGTON DC METRO PROBLEMS	01	71	28
WATCHES WHICH PASS RAILROAD INSPECTION	06	32	332
WATCHES: HISTORY OF	05	52	31
WATCHES: SWISS VS AMERICAN/SPECIFICATION	06	56	39
WATER FOR THE LOCOS-EXPENSIVE/NECESSARY	05	31	239
WATER FREEZING PROBLEMS: HOW TO AVOID	12	40	58
WATER POWER VERSUS OIL	10	47	48
WATER STOP	10	55	12
WATER STORAGE FOR LOCOMOTIVE USE	03	40	106
WATER TOWER VIGNETTE	12	63	17
WAX SEALERS IN OLD DEPOTS	03	73	52
WEED BURNERS AND HOW THEY WORK	05	54	81
WEED KILLERS: CHEMICAL	04	54	62
WEEDS: HISTORY OF WAYS RAILROADS REMOVED	04	43	130
WEEKEND IN HOUSTON: 1948	11	79	33
WEIGHT OF STEAM EVAPORATED 1 LB WATER	12	29	99
WELDED BOILERS ON STEAM LOCOMOTIVES	03	47	66
WELDING TORCHES IN ENGINE SHOPS	05	45	54
WEST PENN RAILWAYS	12	42	83
WESTERN COAL RUSH ON	07	77	02
WESTERN RAILFAN VACATION	07	78	26R
WHALE-OIL TO ELECTRIC: STORY OF LANTERNS	09	76	11
WHAT A RR LOOKS LIKE IN STRIKE-PHOTO ESS	05	73	24
WHAT ARE DATE NAILS?	07	76	12
WHAT IS A GOOD LOOKING LOCOMOTIVE?	03	48	46
WHAT IS A GOOD LOOKING STEAM ENGINE? REP	06	72	30
WHAT IS THE MACO GHOST?	04	61	35
WHAT REALLY HAPPENED TO WINTON?	01	85	61
WHATS WRONG WITH RAILROADS-LABOR VIEW	10	63	24
WHATS WRONG WITH RAILROADS-MANAGEMENT VI	10	63	28
WHEEL ARRANGEMENTS (STEAM/DIESEL/ELECTRC	10	59	61
WHEEL SLIDING	02	49	57
WHEELING THE BIG TOP	07	46	12
WHEELING THE FRUITERS-CALIF CITRUS CROPS	11	30	486
WHEELS AND DRIVING BOXES OF STEAM LOCOS	04	44	67
WHEELS: PRECISION TRIM/NOT REMOVING TRUC	11	54	56
WHEELS: THEIR HISTORY	03	43	45
WHEN BOILERS BLOW UP	06	37	06
WHEN RADIO RULED THE RAIL NOVEMBER 1930	04	31	112
WHEN RAILROADS "MADE" MONEY	07	42	96
WHEN STEAM ACHIEVED METROLINER SPEEDS	05	70	21
WHEN THE US PRESIDENT RIDES THE RAILS	05	31	213
WHERE ARE THE PENN STATION EABLES?	05	72	36
WHERE PASSENGERS RIDE THE CABOOSE	10	73	26
WHICH RR DID MOST FOR STEAM POWER?	08	64	48
WHISTLE-STOP WINNER--SENATOR HOWARD BAKE	03	73	50
WHISTLE-STOPPING (JOHN ANDERSON CAMPAIGN	05	81	28

GENERAL RAILROADING	M	Y	P
WHISTLES: STEAM WHISTLE RECORDING	11	51	10
WHITE MOUNTAIN SCENIC RAILROAD	03	69	26
WHO INVENTED THE LOCO? BELL/HEADLITE/COW	01	34	48
WHO INVENTED THE LOCO? BOILER	01	34	42
WHO INVENTED THE LOCO? DRIVING WHEELS	01	34	44
WHO INVENTED THE LOCO? LEADING TRUCKS	01	34	46
WHO INVENTED THE LOCO? PISTONS/CYLINDERS	01	34	49
WHO INVENTED THE LOCO? WHISTLE	01	34	47
WHO OWNS THE RR? EMPLOYEE VS EXECUTVE	05	31	168
WHO'S THE BOSS? WHO RUNS THE RAILROAD??	06	31	321
WHO'S YOUR BOSS? VAN SWERINGEN CONTINUE	08	31	80
WHO'S YOUR BOSS? VAN SWERINGEN EMPIRE	07	31	481
WHO'S YOUR BOSS? 4 10 JOBS PER MAN	09	31	289
WHY DO THEY BUY DIESEL LOCOMOTIVES? EDIT	08	61	06
WHY WE'RE GOING DIESEL	12	48	48
WHYTE'S LOCOMOTIVE CLASSIFICATION	09	35	81
WINANS LOCOMOTIVES-HISTORY OF	11	36	69
WINDMILL USED TO PUMP WATER UP	03	34	96
WINDS OF CHANGE ON AMTRAK	11	81	36
WIZARD OF OZ AND TOY TRAIN CONSPIRACY	03	78	06
WOMEN AND RAILS SHORT NOTE ARTICLE	04	76	06
WOMEN HOBOS	04	67	30
WOMEN RAILROAD PRESIDENTS	09	53	73
WOODEN RAILROAD (OREGON)	06	69	17
WOODSTOCK'S LAST RUN	07	33	29
WORLD WAR II ADVERTISING	05	43	08
WORLD WAR II EMPLOYMENT PROBLEMS	08	44	50
WORLD WAR II OPERATIONS FOR RAILROADS	01	42	06
WORLD'S CROOKEDEST PIKE MT&MW	06	32	320
WORLD'S FAIR: RAILROADING AT	07	40	06
WORLD'S GREATEST RAILROAD MAN	06	36	27
WORLD'S SLOWEST TRAIN "GOLD RUSH LTD"	03	31	527
WORLDS OLDEST TRAIN	08	63	30
WRECK DAMAGES FOR RR FROM EMPLOYEES	07	77	04
WRECK OF OLD 97 9-1903 S	11	69	29
WRECK THAT MADE RAILROADING SAFE	03	37	122
WRECKMASTERS	12	63	57
WWI ARMISTICE CAR FATE	08	72	59
YANKEE CLIPPER NY TO BOSTON NYNH&H	05	30	209
YARD SWITCHES	08	41	67
YARDMASTER DUTIES	11	52	61
YEAR ROUND STEAM PASSENGER LINE	02	64	26
YEARS FOR MINUTES: PASSENGER SCHEDULES	01	50	10

Railroad/ Railfan

GENERAL RAILROADING

RAILROAD NON-FICTION	M Y P
110 MILES IN 12 HOURS (WP&Y) HENRY	06 45 24
2-10-4 FIRING CP 1929	10 78 09
38 TONS OF GOLD IN ONE TRAIN	04 63 28
4449: HOMEWARD BOUND	12 77 46R
525 MILES IN 443 MINUTES	10 31 394
6262 COMES THROUGH, THE (SP) EDWARDS	08 54 77
7600 MILES BY RAIL (NRHS CONV & BACK)	01 66 38
A NEW BRAKE VALVE... (PRR) LEE	03 53 12
A SECOND IN '25	03 49 08
AFFAIR AT RICHMOND TRIPLE CROSSING	11 83 58
AFFAIR AT STONE CREEK, THE HUBBARB	04 51 74
ALONG THE BOOMER TRAIL MOORE	12 77 34
AMERICA'S FIRST BIG TRAIN ROBBERY DAVIS	12 33 34
AMTRAK VS BRAY BOULDER (WRECK)	01 83 44
AMTRAKING ACROSS THE COUNTRY	11 76 10
AN ENGINE MET HERSELF NP 1906	02 33 79
ANNUAL SPEED SURVEY 1947	04 48 06
APPALACHIAN ODYSSEY S #2716	11 82 49
APPRENTICE TRIPS BEFORE HIRING AS HOGGER	12 60 36
ASHLEY INTERLUDE IC & L&N 1957	09 80 44
ATSF ENTERS THE SPACE AGE	09 82 26
B&O: DANIEL WILLARD SAVES	02 30 321
BAD MAN OF THE CIMARRON LATHROP	06 46 116
BAILED HAY IN THE TUNNEL (ATSF)	10 78 08
BEAR IN THE BAGGAGE CAR HUBBARD	04 76 44
BEGINNING & END OF CP EDRANS MANITOBA	08 78 03
BELIEVE IT OR NOT...	10 48 06
BELOW SEA LEVEL DAYS AT SALTON, CA	08 66 27
BERK GOES TO WORK NKP 2-8-4	09 80 26
BIG O, THE (ORDER OF RY CONDUCTORS)	03 44 58
BIGGEST KETTLE EVER BUILT	09 48 97
BILLY RICHARDSONS LAST RIDE	10 68 32
BLACK DIAMONDS FIRST RUN (LV)	10 77 07
BLIZZARD, BATH & BREAKFAST (C&NW)	11 44 99
BLOW THAT WHISTLE HAYWIRE MAC	11 51 10
BLOW THE MAN DOWN HARRIS	06 53 06
BLOWING UP A TUNNEL ON THE UP	05 78 32
BN TO GOODLAND KANSAS	05 82 53
BOB BRUHIN REMONISES ON THE KATY	02 67 13
BOOMER IN MEXICO SMITH	08 61 40
BOOMER'S DIARY, A BURTON	12 42 06
BOOMER--A THING OF THE PAST	12 29 39
BOOMERS AND HOME GUARDS HUBBARD	12 76 44
BOOMERS DIARY	10 74 27
BOXCAR DEPOT IN WILDERNESS (HBRR)	02 70 51
BOXCAR NAVY ROHDE	09 45 08
BOXCAR WEEKEND	W 76 30R
BREAKMAN SB BROOKE REMONISES	09 67 10
BROAD PASS BEAR, THE GALE	04 52 12
BULL SESSION FOUNTAIN	06 50 06
BUM GUESS KNAPKE	07 46 06
BUYING DIESELS READER COMMENTS	10 61 06
C&O #614 4-8-4 STEAMS FOR SAFETY 2	03 81 47
C&O #614 STEAMS FOR SAFETY (REBUILD)	01 81 45
CABOOSE COOKERY	12 66 08

RAILROAD NON-FICTION	M Y P
CABOOSE FOR CHRISTMAS (C&O)	01 46 118
CALIFORNIA OPERATION LIFESAVER	09 87 52
CARNEGIE SCOTCH BERRY	08 46 36
CASEY JONES'S FIREMAN--SLIM WEBB	03 36 36
CENTENNIALS!	03 81 30
CERTIFIED HEROES-BRONZE METALS	12 34 67
CHALLENGER ON SHERMAN HILL FAN TRIP	11 85 38
CHESSIE SAFETY EXPRESS--FIRST CLASS	03 82 36
CHICAGO & ALTON RAILROAD AT YOUNG AGE	11 35 130
CHOLLY CLOCKER'S COOLIES ARMES	05 49 32
CIRCUS AT CHANUTE MCGUIRE	12 49 12
CIRCUS BOOMER COMMENTS	08 61 44
CITY OF TRAIN ROBBERS	08 54 108
CLARK'S CUPOLAS COMSTOCK	07 48 06
COAST TO COAST ON AMTRAK & D&RGW	05 81 38
COMMOTION AT KEDDIE CA (WP) 6-'81 WRECK	01 82 55
CONVERTIBLE CABOOSE COPE	11 53 06
COOKING ON A COAL SHOVEL	08 63 06
COWBOY VS RAILROADER HOIG	12 53 106
CP REMEMBERENCES OF BERT LANNING	06 72 13
CP REVELSTOKE RUN 1928	01 78 10
CTC COMES TO GARNET	08 75 11
CUSTOMER IS SOMETIMES WRONG, THE TEXINO	04 52 06
D&RGW MEMORIES 56 YEARS AGO 1-1916	08 72 46
DAVID GOODYEAR COLLECTION OF LOCO PHOTOS	11 65 56
DEAD ENGINES JAY	06 48 06
DEAR SON REARDON	09 48 06
DEATH OF A DEPOT NP MONTESANO WA	05 71 51
DIESEL FIELD SERVICE ENGINEER	10 72 35
DINING CARS-72 YEARS OF EXPERIENCE	08 78 27
DISPATCHER, OR OPERATOR? JOSSERAND	07 53 06
DIXON IL, THE IC & 25 YEARS	05 80 60
DOGS & ELEPHANTS ON THE ROAD	03 76 11
DOODLEBUG RPO ON THE READING	09 79 38
DOWN THE HOLE-GRAND CENTRAL TERMINAL	06 50 12
DRIVING WHEELS	07 66 34
ED EDMONDS REMONISES ON T&SH	01 67 54
ENGINE CAB HEROES	05 35 58
ENGINE HOUSE MYSTERY (B&A)	01 66 29
ENGINE MESSENGER	11 65 18
ENGINE SERVICE & CARING FOR YOUR LOCO	02 67 08
ENGINEER RC RUCKER REMONISES	09 67 10
ENGINEER'S DESERT MONUMENT (ATSF) COOPER	08 46 128
ENGINEERS BICYCLE VITRY	03 78 41
ENGINES LOST IN QUICKSAND	03 34 132
ENIGMATIC TRAIN RULES	12 70 36
ERIE "LAKE CITIES"	12 40 06
ERIE FIGHTS RAILROAD FOR 6 FOOT GAUGE	01 33 36
ERIE: AT THE END OF THE RUN	12 40 06
ESCAPE FROM WINTER 2:EASTBOUND ON AMTRAK	05 85 51
ESCAPE FROM WINTER-BROADWAY & SWEST LTD	03 85 34
EVERYTHING IS MODERN NOW FORBES	06 52 06
EXPLICIT DISPATCHER	04 49 06
EXTRA WEST ON THE BELL (ATSF OTTAWA JCT)	01 49 33
FAST HAZARDOUS HAND CAR RIDE 1901 D&RG	10 76 13

Railroad/Railfan

GENERAL RAILROADING

RAILROAD NON-FICTION		M	Y	P
FIFTY YEARS IN THE CAB (NP)	BRADFORD	10	44	08
FIFTY YEARS ON THE RAILS:LIGHTNING SLING		09	42	38
FIRE IN TUNNEL 9 WP	JOSSERAND	05	54	65
FIRST RUN WRECK OF GLEN HARDMAN B&O		08	72	10
FLANGED DESTINY	DULIN	09	49	71
FLIGHT OF CENTURY (20TH CNTURY LTD) NYC		05	31	219
FOLLOW THAT JET: PHILADELPHIA TRAILER JE		05	82	26
FOR HIRE:ONE RED CABOOSE (RG)		05	87	41
FORTY-TWO YEARS A TOWERMAN	THOMAS	08	44	102
FOSTORIA OHIO ALL TRAINS STOP HERE!		08	49	24
FOUR COWLS OVER TEHACHAPI (CAB RIDE)		05	86	32
FR 39 HOUR DAY IN NEW ZEALAND		09	77	45
FR CABOOSE CHAPLAIN (IRANIAN STATE RY)		10	45	06
FR CP INVISIBLE HOGGER		12	77	08
FR FIRING WITH BRIQUETTES (FRANCE)		04	73	20
FR FLIGHT INTO EGYPT	GLEDHILL	03	51	34
FR FLUTE-PLAYER ON FRENCH ROAD		02	78	11
FR GUATEMALA RAILROADING WHILE ON TOUR		07	73	09
FR HE BOUGHT A LOCOMOTIVE (FRENCH)		08	73	28
FR INDIA: FANTRIP IN C.B.I.	KORST	10	47	84
FR JOINING THE RAILROAD IN INDIA		02	67	10
FR MY 41 YEARS OF STEAM (FRANCE)		07	72	41
FR MY LAST STEAM RUN (FRENCH)		12	72	26
FR RM AFRICAN RAIL MEMORIES		09	74	05
FR RM AUSTRALIA: OILER AND HIS HAIRCUT		12	50	128
FR RM BRITISH RAILWAYS: LEAMINGTON SPA		03	50	132
FR RM EGYPT: RUNAWAY FREIGHT LOCOMOTIVE		11	53	116
FR RM ENGLAND: CALEDONIAN RAILWAY 1916		10	49	137
FR RM INDIAN RYS: PEOPLE HANG ON SIDES		04	52	128
FR RM SOUTH AFRICA: ROYAL TOUR/1ST MOUNT		10	49	132
FR RM SOUTH MANCHURIAN RR EXPLOSION 1931		03	51	123
FR RM: ENGLISH RY "ROYAL GEORGE" LOCO		04	50	128
FR RM: INDIAN GOV'T RR MOVES LOCO		05	52	138
FR SIBERIAN RAIL PROBLEMS		08	78	07
FR THE WORST TRAIN WRECK MODANE FRANCE		10	77	24
FRD THE "CORNFIELD MEET" AT SILVER CREEK		11	34	66
FRD THE WRECK AT SPUYTEN DEVIL		12	35	45
FRD TWO BOSTON & PROVIDENCE WRECKS		10	34	89
FREEDOM TRAIN READING T1 POWERED CAB RID		W	76	51R
FREEDOM TRAIN: LETTERS TO UNCLE JOE		12	47	06
FREIGHT HOPPING ON D&RGW 1960		02	71	06
FREIGHT RIDING HOBOS		05	76	06
FROM SCALE TO PROTOTYPE		01	51	100
GATHERING OF PRIVATE VARNISH		03	87	54
GEARED FOR TONNAGE (N&W)		09	44	08
GIFT FOR STEAMTOWN 2-4-2T VULCAN X-B&M		05	71	40
GOD BLESS AMERICA		03	49	06
GOLD ROBBERY ON CMI 1903		01	67	63
GOLDEN SPIKE (NP)	COOPER	12	40	80
GREASY HILL-RETALIATION AGAINST RAILROAD		09	48	129
GREAT SEEKONK CASE, THE	HARLOW	04	48	104
GREATEST MAIL-TRAIN ROBBERY (MILW)		03	53	36
HALCEY BUILDS WORKING LOCO MODEL PRISION		11	39	65
HAM OPERATOR	STEPHENSON	04	70	38
HAND-FIRED COAL BURNERS AT VANCOUVER BC		03	77	08

RAILROAD NON-FICTION		M	Y	P
HARVEY GIRL	WHITE	02	45	78
HAUNTED CABOOSE (SP)		04	60	21
HE THROWS THE BOOK (ARNOLD)	THOMPSON	11	51	08
HEADLIGHTS AND MOONSHINE	MCCARTHY	12	47	10
HEADS FOR ST PAUL		09	49	32
HELL BENT FOR SEATTLE		05	76	08
HERE COMES THE MAIL	RUNEY	09	48	66
HI, MISS FRISCO!	QUAST	05	48	106
HIGH WATER (UP) FLOODED IN CALIFORNIA		02	43	119
HIGH-WHEELED WOODBURNERS (1902)		02	61	24
HIGHBALLING THE BROADWAY LIMITED		12	29	88
HOG ON ATSF "FAST MAIL" 1951		05	78	07
HOLDUPS THAT MISFIRED	MAGUIRE	02	59	22
HOME TOWN BUM	SMITH	08	51	06
HORROR SCOPE	HEROLD	10	49	06
HORSE SAVED BY "BIG HOOK"	MCCARTY	05	46	06
HOW TO CRACK A NUT WITH A LOCOMOTIVE		12	77	19
HUMAN CROSSING GUARDS (ENDICOTT NY) EL		02	70	08
HUMAN ELEMENT, THE (OF RAILROADING)		08	39	108
HUNCHES: RAILROAD MEN HAVE PREMONITIONS		02	41	60
HUSBAND-WIFE ENGINE CREW (R)	WHITE	09	44	82
I DELIVER DIESELS	MCELHINNEY	02	59	18
I FIRED THE 50000 (ERIE)	GOOBECK	01	74	26
I HAVE ALWAYS LOVED TRAINS--WALT DISNEY		10	65	13
I HELPED TO REBUILD STEAM LOCOMOTIVES		02	72	22
I LEFT MY HEART AT MUNI METRO		05	83	22
I PREFER STEAM--PENNINGTON, WP ENGINEER		11	65	32
I WRECKED 146 LOCOMOTIVES (ST FAIR WRECK		04	33	39
IC HOGGER RIDES THE READER		08	63	28
ICC LOCOMOTIVE INSPECTOR		09	65	24
ICG AT GIBSLAND LA		04	78	38R
INCIDENT ON SALUDA (FOULED UNITS)		07	85	56
IR HAMLEY, DAVID:X MODELER #123		03	73	30
IRM 1987 RAILFAN WEEKEND		12	87	73
JAY GOULD RAILROAD TYCOON: LEE MEMORIES		06	48	129
JERSEY CENTRAL-40 YEARS IN THE CAB		07	65	13
JESSE JAMES BANK ROBBER, THE TRUE STORY		09	32	198
JOE BALDWIN'S GHOST LIGHT (ACL9		07	46	45
JOHN DAVERN REMONISES (FIRST LOCO RUN)		01	67	10
JOHN LAW REMEMBERS RATON NM 1921		10	69	06
JUMBO PT BARNUMS ELEPHANT KILLED BY TRAI		03	76	11
KNOW YOUR ATOMS	HEROLD	04	50	06
LAST OF THE BOOMERS (C&S)	RANCK	08	68	20
LAST OF THE JESSE JAMES GANG		03	36	52
LEADING THE HOTSHOT (ELECTRIC LINES)		08	48	86
LEE CHRISTMAS HOGHEAD-DICTATOR HONDURAS		05	34	04
LEST WE FORGET SP: SANTA ANA LOCAL		10	53	06
LETTER FOR THE OLD CHIEF	JOHNSTON	03	52	12
LETTER FROM KOREA...	BENJAMIN	07	52	10
LETTER TO MY NEPHEW		04	43	63
LEWIS MINCHNER REMONISES ON M&SL		01	67	54
LIFE IN THE CAB AT 90 MPH A TURBOLINER		12	76	12
LIFE ON OLD SP TRAIN-FERRIES		01	67	47
LOCOMOTIVE EYE APPEAL		12	48	06
LOCOMOTIVE REPAIR TRICKS		02	67	60

Railroad/Railfan

GENERAL RAILROADING

RAILROAD NON-FICTION		M	Y	P
LONG ISLAND'S NUMBER 3 TRAINMAN		05	46	112
LONG ROAD, THE "SPEED"	WARREN	08	39	33
LOOK WHERE YOU'RE GOING UP	HUFFSMITH	02	39	128
LOST ENGINE, LOST TRAIN, LOST RAILROAD		02	49	08
MARQUETTE, JULIUS L: OLDEST RR TRAINMAN		11	48	06
MATTER OF PRESTIGE, A	MURPHY	03	52	06
MEET ON THE DESERT	KNAPKE	12	61	46
MEMORIES ON A&CR 1908 ASTORIA OR		09	72	09
MISSING "31" ORDER (IC)	KRAMER	02	73	52
MISSING CAR FROM MIDDLE OF TRAIN		10	78	08
MIXED TRAIN 1921		04	61	19
MIXED TRAINS & NATIVE WOMEN (UPPER MICH)		06	71	25
MORSE MEANDERINGS	DULIN	08	52	06
MOTOR EXTRA 830 WEST (WP)	JOSSERAND	03	45	78
MOUNTAIN DISPATCHER (WP)	JOSSERAND	04	44	08
MR. MORGAN AND THE BEAVER	CADIEUX	09	52	06
MY DEAR SON	REARDON	06	49	06
MY FAVORITE MOTIVE POWER IS "S T E A M"		03	66	31
MY NARROW-GAGE ALBUM	LATHROP	05	40	06
MY NARROW-GAGE ALBUM (D&RGW)	LATHROP	05	39	28
MY NARROW-GAGE ALBUM: PART 3	LATHROP	12	39	28
MYSTERY ON CP 1947		05	78	50
NARROW GAGE GLORY DAYS	LATHROP	11	46	44
NARROW-GAGE GLORY DAYS PART 2	LATHROP	12	46	80
NARROW-GAGE GLORY DAYS PART 3	LATHROP	01	47	94
NARROW-GAGE GLORY DAYS PART 4	LATHROP	02	47	44
NC&SL "TENNESEE" LOCO--THE SOUTHS FINEST		07	35	37
NEVADA NORTHERN	THOMAS	07	48	40
NEVADA NORTHERN (AUTHOR COMMENTS)		07	48	134
NIGHT CHIEF	JOSSERAND	04	54	34
NIGHT CHIEF DISPATCHER (WP)	JOSSERAND	11	75	12
NIGHT TRAIN		10	62	13
NIGHT TRAIN		06	75	58
NOW...WE'LL TELL YOU! (CNJ)	COMSTOCK	02	48	08
OLD COLORADO MIDLAND, THE		08	36	39
OLD DAYS ON THE DIAMOND JO		03	36	39
OLD JOHN (ATSF)	DULIN	12	52	10
OLD NUMBER NINE (OREGON)	WEAVER	02	48	06
OLIVER C. PERRY THE LONE WOLF BANDIT		11	32	460
ONE NIGHT ON A SOUTHBOUND LIMITED		04	64	13
OPEN SWITCH SABOTAGE		07	66	10
OPENING A NEWSSTAND?	MAYBROOKE	11	52	12
OPPORTUNITY ON THE RAILROAD	CLUTTER	07	52	06
OUR OWN LINGO	KNAPKE	06	61	56
OUR READERS RATE THE RAILROADS	COMSTOCK	03	48	06
OUTSIDE THE RULE BOOK: LOGGING & HOODOOS		08	60	38
PACIFIC EXPRESS MESSENGER		11	42	06
PALACE PIE-CARD (COOKING ON CABOOSES)		05	46	135
PANIC OF 1893 ON ATSF		06	64	39
PANTOGRAPHS DOWN!	HARRISON	01	51	86
PEANUT ROASTER		04	54	91
PEELING PAINT-OLD RAILROAD STATIONS		04	63	13
PHANTOM RAILWAY TRAIN	WALKER	05	52	06
PICNIC TRAINS	SMITH	10	61	34
PICNIC TRAINS		10	75	12

RAILROAD NON-FICTION		M	Y	P
POCAHONTAS DIVISION (N&W)	HOCK	04	45	39
POCAHONTAS DIVISION (N&W)	HOCK	03	45	08
POCATELLO YARDMASTER (OSL)	MC CLINTOCK	01	77	42
POPOVER STOPOVER NJRT	QUINBY	09	49	74
PORTAGE LA PRAIRIE 1959 STEAM		11	83	42
PREMONITIONS OF DISASTER		11	73	29
PRR SPIRIT OF ST LOUIS WRECK (JAN ISSUE)		04	73	09
PUSH-PULL MEET	CLIFFORD	04	54	106
RACE FOR THE MAIL CONTRACT MP 1908		01	78	28
RACE THAT COST 44 LIVES, A		04	36	81
RAIL DOG	CLAPP	03	47	06
RAIL DOG ON MONON 1939		03	72	11
RAIL'S END		08	39	42
RAILFANNING BRITISH COLUMBIA		09	86	41
RAILROAD BOARDING HOUSE		01	67	18
RAILROAD JIM	DAUGHERTY	04	44	26
RAILROAD JIM PART 2	DAUGHERTY	05	44	48
RAILROAD JIM PART 3	DAUGHERTY	06	44	86
RAILROAD JIM PART 4	DAUGHERTY	07	44	50
RAILROAD PURCHASED FOR $1.00 (BCH&P)		10	69	08
RAILROAD SCOUTS PART 1	DELLINGER	05	48	28
RAILROAD SCOUTS PART 2	DELLINGER	06	48	62
RAILROADS OFFER AID FOR THE FARMERS		12	29	55
RAILS THROUGH THE WILDERNESS	HASELTINE	03	78	38
RAWHIDING ON NKP--CARL CRONE		03	67	10
RECOLLECTIONS OF HOBO LIFE	SANDERS	02	47	119
REFLECTIONS ON A TRAIN RIDE		02	63	13
RI FIRING STEAM LOCOS AT GUN POINT		01	67	63
RIDING ASEA "MIGHTY MOUSE" SWEDENS COMPA		10	77	25R
RIDING THE GEORGETOWN LOOP 1908		07	79	41
RIDING THE HUMP 1919 IHB		06	61	54
RIDING THE SHARKS		SP	76	30R
RIDING THE SP #4449		11	84	58
RIGHT-HAND SIDE: ENGINEER		05	43	128
RIGHT-HAND SIDE: LACK ENGINEER TELLS		01	30	161
RINGLING-B&B CIRCUS TRAIN		07	66	06
RM 1920 MP CHESTER MO LOCOMO MESSENGER		04	74	08
RM 1922 HOBO TO CAR INSPECTOR		06	74	04
RM 1927 MISSISSIPPI RIVER FLOOD		04	74	03
RM 1954 TALE OF STAMINA ON MP		05	76	10
RM A&PA: 1887 STICKUP		07	49	124
RM A&SU: BRAKEMAN MEMORIES		10	49	131
RM AC&HB 1920 2-8-0 FIRING		11	75	09
RM ACL: BROKEN LEVER		07	53	119
RM ACL: DEPOT AT CLEWISTON FL EMBARRASSI		10	58	06
RM AE: BALED ALFALFA HAY-MORE PER SEASON		07	49	137
RM AL ROBBING THE COOK CAR		08	78	06
RM AL: 180 MOOSE KILLED--FEAR DEEP SNOW		12	55	65
RM AL: BROAD PASS BEAR		04	52	12
RM AL: SAVES LIVES OF 3 MEN IN SNOWSLIDE		07	50	127
RM ALB&C HOW TO FIX YOUR STEAM LOCO		12	73	36
RM ALGC: USUALLY A WATER SHORTAGE		06	50	134
RM ANDREW GOTTO REMEMBERS 65 YEARS		02	69	10
RM ATSF 1921 LINE INSPECTION & SCARE		07	76	07
RM ATSF 1921 SUPERINTENDENT PASS STOLEN		11	76	08

Railroad/Railfan

GENERAL RAILROADING

RAILROAD NON-FICTION	M	Y	P
RM ATSF 1955 BEAM OVER TRACKS CASSADY KS	12	73	02
RM ATSF AN ATSF FAMILY 1870-1929	06	75	11
RM ATSF CALIFORNIA LIMITED SERVICE PLUS	05	51	130
RM ATSF ELECTRICAL COMMUNICATIONS IN '30	11	78	07
RM ATSF LOVE TRIANGLE	11	75	09
RM ATSF SPECIAL TRAIN 1919 BELVIDERE KS	01	76	07
RM ATSF TEXAS ICE STORM 1940	04	78	23
RM ATSF ZULU CARS IN 1918 E MAHONEY	01	74	07
RM ATSF: LOCATING & CONSTRUCTION ENGINE	02	49	103
RM ATSF: OTTAWA KANSAS/TAKES FIRE TO TRU	01	54	113
RM ATSF: PRAIRIE FIRE 1880-1890'S	12	49	121
RM ATSF: RAIL MOTOR CAR AND LEGHORN	11	53	121
RM ATSF: SIDE DOOR CABOOSES	10	55	56
RM ATSF: SPARES TO KATY--	11	48	134
RM B&M 1886-1917	08	75	04
RM B&M 1901 HOOSIC TUNNEL THOUGHTS	09	74	05
RM B&M ENGINEER HARVEY CLOUGH REMEMBERS	12	66	14
RM B&O ENGINEERING IN 1898	08	75	05
RM B&O: 2 CONVICTS IN LOCO TENDER	02	53	128
RM B&O: CAR INSPECTOR 51 YRS/TUNNEL AWAR	06	49	128
RM B&O: EMPLOYEE FINDS ICE AGE HORSE	03	54	14
RM B&O: FOLKLORE	05	49	134
RM B&O: FREIGHT TRAIN JUMPS TRACK/GRASSH	12	52	123
RM B&O: LAST PASS TRAIN #40-41	10	51	135
RM B&O: LATE TRAIN-EMERGENCY OPERATION	12	50	127
RM B&O: MARCH 1893 LAST CAP WORN BY READ	01	50	128
RM B&O: SECTION CREW RESCUE AGED WOMEN	12	51	121
RM B&O: SLEEPING CAR PASSENGERS AWAKENED	06	56	04
RM BAR: 1918 MEMORIES	11	53	116
RM BAR: CONDUCTOR'S JOB	05	54	10
RM BAR: DSETERMINATION OF JOHN PARKER	04	53	137
RM BC&SA: 1912 YELLOW JACKETS	10	57	76
RM BEERCAN RESCUE ON SD&EA	12	65	10
RM BELL: CAR OPEATED UNDER OWN POWER	10	54	71
RM BERT LANG ON CP IN 1932	11	72	10
RM BFR FIRING	08	75	05
RM BH&FP: 1881 SLIM GAGE/CB&Q ABSORBED	03	49	128
RM BRLC: UNUSUAL LUMBER ROAD	01	54	119
RM BUGGY WRECK ON HV BY P SOUTHWORTH	06	69	29
RM BYGONE CABOOSE DAYS	03	74	10
RM C&O: FISHERMAN FLAG TRAINS/70T BURY T	11	48	136
RM C&E: SOON TO BE RUNNING AGAIN	01	50	132
RM C&EI: 1902 ST ELMO/ST LOUIS DIVISIONS	11	49	127
RM C&EI: 2 BOYS RUN IN FRONT OF LOCO	08	49	137
RM C&EI: FIGHTING/AWOL SOLDIERS KILLS	08	52	121
RM C&EI: LOCO TOPPLES INTO PIT	03	51	135
RM C&EI: TOY TRAIN NEARLY FATAL TO TIM R	10	54	06
RM C&EI: TRAINMASTER/COMPLICATED TIMESLP	10	49	132
RM C&NW BLIZZARD OF '79	05	80	62
RM C&NW ENCOUNTERS WITH THE FALCON	05	80	61
RM C&NW: 6 MILE WALK THROUGH BLIZZARD	03	51	135
RM C&NW: BRAKEMAN'S DEVOTION TO BOY NOT	06	58	38
RM C&NW: COME & WORK A MONTH RAILROAD	02	54	117
RM C&NW: KATE SHELLEY'S HEROISM	01	50	124
RM C&NW: PRAIRIE FIRE 1950 10 MILE PATH	08	50	131

RAILROAD NON-FICTION	M	Y	P
RM C&NW: RUBBER GASKETS STOLEN/RETURNED	09	50	128
RM C&NW: SHOWDOWN CHICAGO YARDS	08	49	138
RM C&O: CONDUCTOR/63 YEARS OF RAILROADNG	09	52	129
RM C&O: EQUIPMENT--READER OPINIONS	04	49	136
RM C&O: MARCH 1876-OCT 1906 MEMORIES	10	49	125
RM C&O: MOTHER CAT AND HER YOUNG	10	51	141
RM CABLE CAR DAYS IN NEW YORK	10	51	88
RM CAN BANNING ONTARIO 1905	03	71	09
RM CANADIAN TAILS OF 1908 WRECK/CIRCUS/B	02	75	08
RM CAPR: FIELD DRAFTSMAN	06	53	116
RM CB&Q CABOOSE RIDING BULLDOG	04	75	07
RM CB&Q: AIRBRAKE LESSON	02	53	119
RM CB&Q: AURORA DIVISION/SUPERIOR OFFICE	04	51	121
RM CB&Q: BILLY SUNDAY PREACHER	09	50	131
RM CB&Q: DUKE VS BRAKEMAN	09	51	133
RM CB&Q: FAST MAIL #7, #8	06	53	114
RM CB&Q: FRANK BULLARD REMEMBERED	10	50	132
RM CB&Q: ICE CREAM SHORTAGE/PAY	07	52	131
RM CB&Q: JESSE JAMES' BROTHER/AGENT	09	49	137
RM CB&Q: PASS BRAKEMAN/LANTERNS	02	50	129
RM CB&Q: PASSENGER EXTRA BOARD	05	54	08
RM CB&Q: SKIPPED REGULAR SCHEDULED STOPS	02	54	105
RM CBELT FOUR GENERATIONS ON THE ROAD	08	74	07
RM CC WHISMAN EXPERIENCES ON L&N	08	65	10
RM CGA: 1900'S MCCARTNEY COULD BE RICH	09	52	133
RM CGA: 1910 RUNAWAY	08	52	137
RM CGW: NORTH END FREIGHTS	03	54	12
RM CH HERRICK ON ATSF IN 1893	09	69	08
RM CHAIN DOORS ON FIRE BOXES ON B&M	10	66	10
RM CHARLEY CONE AND THE GN	01	65	10
RM CHT OPERATIONS REMEMBERED	01	74	13
RM CIRCUS: MEMORIES	06	56	06
RM CIRCUSES AND THE RAILROADS	05	51	134
RM CL: BLUE RIDGE MOUNTAINS	11	54	75
RM CLARENCE COFFMAN ON THE GM&N	02	65	08
RM CMT: READER AUTOMOTIVE MEMORIES	08	49	130
RM CN TRADING TALES	01	72	09
RM CN: 340 MINK--MINK INDUSTRY BUILDING	10	55	04
RM CN: ABE LINCOLN STORY	12	55	06
RM CN: CREW CLERK	04	58	10
RM CN: GLENCOE MEMORIES	12	56	57
RM CN: NATION-WIDE STRIKE/PRINCE EDWARD	01	51	126
RM CN: RAILROADING AT -68 DEGREES	09	50	124
RM CN: SMITHER BC CANADA	09	50	133
RM CN: TIMETABLES	08	51	137
RM CNS&M: INTERURBAN TO CAMP/SEATLESS CA	07	53	85
RM COR: LOST ENGINE IN 1888	11	52	123
RM CP 1903 MOOSE JAW SASK	05	75	11
RM CP 1920 FIRING NELSON BC HAWKINS	12	75	06
RM CP 1920 MEMORIES OF CP STEAM	07	74	09
RM CP 1922 NORTH OF THE BORDER	07	78	10
RM CP 1924 MYSTERIOUS EXPLOSION	08	75	06
RM CP 1925 ENGINEERS PROMOTION	07	78	10
RM CP 1925 NIGHT WATCHMAN KETTLE VALLEY	05	75	08
RM CP 1926 HAND FIRED COALBURNERS	09	74	10

STEPHANS' RAILROAD DIRECTORY

Railroad/ Railfan

GENERAL RAILROADING

RAILROAD NON-FICTION	M	Y	P
RM CP 1926 NIGHT WATCHMAN PROCTOR BC	05	74	10
RM CP 1927 "ALIBI IKE" WOOLEY	01	75	06
RM CP 1927 FIRING	11	75	08
RM CP 1927 FIRING 3200 SERIES CAMELBACKS	02	75	07
RM CP 1927 FIRING ROSSLAND BC	09	76	09
RM CP 1928 ELEPHANTS ON THE TRACK	11	76	06
RM CP 1929 GOLDEN BC	08	74	09
RM CP 1947 SLOCAN LAKE FIRING	10	76	14
RM CP COBURG ONTARIO 1934	10	71	11
RM CP EMERGENCY HOGGER ON 2-10-2'S 1925	06	75	11
RM CP FIREMAN IN 1920	11	78	07
RM CP FIRING A ROGERS 4-4-0 1927	11	74	10
RM CP HOW TO HAND FIRE	12	74	05
RM CP KELOWNA BC 1928 COW JUMPING OVER M	07	75	06
RM CP NELSON BC--LIFE IN RAILWAY SHACK	04	77	07
RM CP PROCTOR BC CAUGHT BETWEEN TWO CARS	04	74	07
RM CP SMOKE IN TUNNELS MT MCDONALD BC	01	74	06
RM CP SNOW 22 FEET DEEP	06	78	48
RM CP TRAINMEN REMINISCENCE	09	68	08
RM CP VIOLATION OF RULE "G" LANNING	11	73	07
RM CP: 19 YR OLD ARMHAND LOCKED ON PULLM	12	50	123
RM CP: AUG 1908 MEMORIES	02	55	76
RM CP: CALGARY TRAINMAN	05	55	67
RM CP: CIRCUS MEMORIES	08	56	76
RM CP: CP #30 LOCO IN FILM CANADIAN PACI	02	49	101
RM CP: KETTLE VALLEY ROUTE MEMORIIES	02	51	128
RM CP: NICHOLAS MORANT PHOTOGRAPHER	04	55	06
RM CP: NOT OUTDATED/STEAM, DIESELS	08	50	124
RM CP: TRAIN #51	12	52	138
RM CPM&O: WINTER 1953/LAST ROUNDUP	05	54	117
RM CTA: RED STREETCARS NOW GREEN/BUSES	10	54	70
RM CTA: WOMEN SLEEPS ON CARS EVERY NIGHT	06	53	90
RM D&H: CHAMPLAIN DIV/BELL CORD	07	51	128
RM D&H: FIREMAN MEMORIES	07	50	136
RM D&NE: 11 MILES/FREIGHT LINE	07	54	120
RM D&RG 1916 SNOW STORM	11	75	06
RM D&RGW 1930 ALAMOSO COLORADO	05	74	07
RM D&RGW: 27 MILES HISTORIC RAIL ABANDON	03	49	127
RM D&RGW: MYSTERY OF TOBEY	07	51	132
RM DEXTER BARTLETT ON THE GN IN 1903	08	68	06
RM DINING CAR MEALS	01	51	127
RM DL&W 1926 WHITE TERROR IN POCONOS	09	75	07
RM DL&W READER MEMORIES	03	82	07
RM DL&W: LOCO #1131, #789 MEMORIES	12	55	06
RM DT&I: 1915/BOOMER MEMORIES	05	50	137
RM DT&I: BOOMER EXPERIENCES	09	50	129
RM DT&I: STEAM POWER/SOME SCRAPPED	08	53	119
RM DT&I: WYNN MEMORIES	10	50	137
RM DWC: EARLY 1900'S MEMORIES	02	56	11
RM E&NA: DATA SUPPLEMENT	09	51	127
RM E: CUBA TO HUNTS NY CONSTRUCTION 1906	04	51	140
RM E: MARION-KENT DIV GANDY DANCER 1920S	09	49	136
RM E: PHYSICIAN & FIREMAN	10	49	128
RM E: SMALL CITY AGENT	10	51	138
RM ENGINE TERMINALS 1953 AGAIN IN 1974	01	74	52

RAILROAD NON-FICTION	M	Y	P
RM ENGINEER REMINISCENCESES	10	64	48
RM ENGINEER WS GILES--A NEER MISS DL&W	12	66	31
RM EP&S 1930 CALLBOY ON A BIG HORSE	03	74	13
RM EY&C: LAST PASSENGER RUN	12	52	128
RM F&C: KENTUCKY CARDINAL/PASS TO FRT	05	53	129
RM FE&MV: NOW PART OF C&NW/1890/1888	12	55	06
RM FIREMANS SHOVELING RECORD READER INFO	08	77	06
RM FIRING IN ONE DAY (1912)	02	63	06
RM FOG MCCLINTOCK	11	48	128
RM FOSTER WISCONSIN-NAMED FOR WC FOSTER	01	51	132
RM FR&NE: LOCOS/MAN HUNTS/ENG KILLS 2	03	53	133
RM FR&NE: PHANTOM TRAIN	11	54	72
RM FRANK VAN HORN EXCITING EXPERIENCE	04	65	08
RM FRIS: 1880 FEMALE TELEGRAPHER	08	54	14
RM FRIS: TRAIN BLOCKS SHERIFF-CONDUCTOR	09	53	124
RM G AUGUSTA GA 1917 RAILROAD SHOP LIFE	02	74	08
RM G GALE ON BATTERY JARS ON AL	05	71	09
RM G: 300 SERIES LOCO HUNCH SEPT 1925	12	52	120
RM GEORGE CLEMENT REMEMBERS 1870'S	12	68	10
RM GEORGE GALE ON AL THAW OF 1946	08	71	12
RM GEORGE GALE ON UP & WP	08	70	10
RM GIL LATHROP ON THE DR&G	12	65	08
RM GM&O: AMATEUR RADIO OPERATERS HELP	05	52	138
RM GM&O: FARMER TO GENERAL SUPERINTENDEN	12	55	11
RM GM&O: TOOK ENGINE HOME WEEKEND	09	50	140
RM GN: 1898 SNOW SLIDE	04	54	115
RM GN: AVERAGE CAR KILLED/1ST BY GN	03	54	77
RM GN: CALLBOY MEMORIES	09	54	07
RM GN: GERTIE ANDERSON LEGEND	10	49	128
RM GN: LID OPERATOR	08	50	123
RM GN: MARCH 1 1901 AVALANCHE	08	59	71
RM GN: MINNEAPOLIS JUNCTTION	02	53	127
RM GN: N DAKOTA VILLAGE GROCERY COMPLAIN	03	54	08
RM GN: OIL-BURNING LANTERNS/ELECTRIC LMP	08	53	118
RM GN: ROTARY SNOWPLOW	05	49	132
RM GN: SAVES CRITICALLY ILL GIRL	08	50	127
RM GN: WILMAR DIVISON/STEALS CABOOSE	05	49	126
RM GO AINSWORTH BY GONE DAYS ON RI 1902	09	69	54
RM GRA: 1ST AMERICAN RAIL LINE	10	54	09
RM GSL WORK DAYS 1969---90 HR WEEKS	11	71	13
RM GT DEATH AT THE DRAWBRIDGE	09	78	40
RM GTP 1912 BUSH JOBS	10	71	11
RM GTP AT HUNT ONTARIO 1912	11	71	11
RM GTW IN 1900 MEMORIES	01	72	10
RM GW: KENYON MINNESOTA	01	54	112
RM H&LB: 1906 TRIP/ONLY 1 LOCO & FLATCAR	08	51	131
RM H&LB: BUMPERLESS TRACK	04	53	125
RM HBRR: 1929/"POP" THE NEWS BUTCHER	08	54	06
RM HE RAILROADED IN 1906	12	77	07
RM HE&WT: CIVIL WAR	05	50	125
RM HJ BROCK FIREMAN & ENGINEER TRIP PREP	07	65	10
RM I WISH I KNEW THE ANSWER-1920	10	60	42
RM IC: 1888/FIREMAN MEMORIES	03	52	122
RM IC: DISPATCHER RACE TRACK DIVISION	09	52	123
RM IC: MIXED TRAIN IN MISSISSIPPI	05	53	136

Railroad/ Railfan

GENERAL RAILROADING

RAILROAD NON-FICTION	M	Y	P
RM IC: NOV 7 1921/TRAIN ROBBERY	10	55	57
RM IC: WALL LAKE IOWA MOVES TRAIN FOR CH	04	53	125
RM IDEAL CREW AND TRAIN	12	77	10
RM IMPROVEMENTS	04	49	131
RM JACK HAGGERTY REMEMBERS THE B&M	03	69	10
RM JE MCFALL REMINISCENCESES	10	65	10
RM JOHN LAWS ON ATSF IN 1923	11	72	10
RM JT STITT REMINISCENCESES	10	65	10
RM L&A: CAR DRIVES DOWN TRACK	05	53	122
RM L&N PLAYING FOOTBALL SEMI-PRO 1923	11	74	08
RM L&N RATTLE SNAKES IN THE CAB 1923	10	73	02
RM L&N: "GULFWIND" AND COLT	06	54	111
RM L&N: 1906 MEMORIES	02	53	118
RM L&N: BLACKLISTING BROTHERHOOD MEN	08	50	133
RM L&N: DIXIE FLYERS UNCOUPLED-FREAK MIS	03	52	128
RM L&N: FAST MERCHANDISE SPECIAL/SUPERST	08	49	129
RM L&N: PAY CAR MEMORIES	04	56	07
RM L&N: PAYS WAGES AFTER 50 YEARS	08	54	114
RM L&N: RATTLER RIDES	02	51	139
RM L&N: SPUR LINE FREIGHT TRAIN	02	51	129
RM L&N: TRAIN DISPATCHER	05	52	128
RM LA&SL: 1907 TELEGRAHER OPERATOR MEMOR	02	59	71
RM LAR: DESCANSO MEMORIES	10	53	94
RM LAST OF THE BOOMERS 1920	10	75	06
RM LE&DR: MEN MUST ATTEND CHURCH.	02	51	136
RM LE&W: 1890 MEMORIES	10	56	75
RM LEAVENWORTH KS RAILROAD MEMORIES	09	78	09
RM LEAVINES 50 YEARS OF SERVICE REMEMBER	05	67	10
RM LEL: LIMA OHIO STREETCARS/MEMORIES	03	54	118
RM LI: JUVENILE DELINQUENTS	08	54	12
RM LI: MYSTERY TUNNEL	05	49	133
RM LOCKED INSIDE A BOILER	10	66	10
RM LOCOS ASSIGNED TO REGULAR CREWS	10	51	122
RM LOGGING ROAD STAR TO RATS	01	49	116
RM LOOKOUT MOUNTAIN STEAM ROAD	01	51	127
RM LS&MS: 1912 TELEGRAPH DEPARTMENT MEMO	12	57	10
RM LS&MS: SUNDAY PASSENGER TRAINS	07	49	138
RM LS&MS: YMCA/"GOT RELIGION"	05	49	130
RM LSEL: FONDLY REMEMBERED	02	52	82
RM LSEL: READER EXPERIENCES	03	52	79
RM LUCIAN H "TEX" PLATT'S EXPERIRNCES	08	65	08
RM LV: REFUELING OF A DIESEL LOCO PROBLE	04	52	133
RM M&BIG: CHRISTMAS DAY 1952	01	54	106
RM M&CIN: ATHEN CITIZENS TEAR UP TRACK	04	50	126
RM M&MG: 1893 BAD LUCK	07	50	130
RM M&MI: PONTOON BRIDGE	11	52	62
RM M&O IN THE 1880'S	10	71	10
RM M&SP: CAR INSPECTOR JOURNAL BOX	05	53	127
RM MAX MOORE REMINISCENCESES	12	65	29
RM MC: LOCO ENGINEER MEMORIES	11	50	132
RM MCKEEN MOTOR CARS	04	50	122
RM MEMORIES OF EXCURSION TRAINS 1900	03	76	53
RM MEMORIES OF THE JOHNSTOWN FLOOD 1889	08	66	34
RM MEXICO: ENGINEER IN 1890'S	06	50	123
RM MICHC: FLAGMAN ON ROBBED TRAIN	05	55	68
RM MILW 0-6-0 CHICAGO SWITCHING	08	74	05
RM MILW: 22 MILES OF WILD RIDE--MEMORIES	04	50	138
RM MILW: COAST DIVISION LOCO #2509, 3012	01	55	07
RM MILW: JOE EMERY BOOMER MOBRIDGE SD	10	48	129
RM MILW: LA CROSSE DIV/ADVENTUROUS FIRIN	02	57	52
RM MILW: OLYMPIC PENINSULA BRANCH	09	50	135
RM MKT: 4-6-0 LOCO #66 MEMORIES	01	51	128
RM MKT: SHORT-WAVE RADIOS	05	49	127
RM MORSE CODE: NO REVISIONS	11	51	133
RM MOTHER HUBBARBS: ELECTRICIAN MEMORIES	01	51	125
RM MP DRAG FREIGHT LITTLE ROCK AK 1973	01	74	55
RM MP: BOZO TEXINO MEMORRIES	12	50	121
RM MP: CALLED INTO PRESIDENTS PRIV CAR	07	54	120
RM MP: CIVIL WAR GHOSTS	01	54	112
RM MP: GRANDPA'S ENGINE	07	50	129
RM MP: MEMORIES	06	45	126
RM MP: SHOVEL BELONGS TO FIREMEN	06	51	136
RM MSRY: COMPRESSED AIR CARS	02	51	75
RM MV: BATH-HOUSE	10	55	38
RM MWCOG: JUNE 1928 DEDICATION	07	49	132
RM MXC: 1892/NATIVE THIEVES	01	50	124
RM N&L: "LITTLE HOOK" PASSENGER TRAIN	07	49	14
RM N&W SPECIALIZED COAL TRAINS	10	75	42
RM NAVY AMMO LEONARDO PIERS NEW JERSEY	12	74	03
RM NC&SL: SOUTH BERLIN TENN	03	49	128
RM NEW YORK SUBWAYS: OCTOBER 1904	11	52	102
RM NFALLS: GARBAGE CHUTE AND OPEN CARS	10	54	70
RM NKP: HERRICK ILL NS-1 TRAIN/TOWN FIRE	01	53	123
RM NKP: INDIAN TERRITORY 1888	09	52	135
RM NKP: LOCAL FREIGHT #61 & TAFFY (HORSE	06	51	124
RM NN: GLORY HOLE	01	49	120
RM NN: TRAIN RUNAWAY COPPER FLATS	12	48	122
RM NP & UP: VILLAGERS ROLLUP AWNINGS	07	51	127
RM NP: 1910 WRECK MEMORIES COCOLALLA ID	01	49	111
RM NP: DUCK-HUNTING	10	51	131
RM NP: TELEGRAPH OPERATOR BRIGHT IDEAS	06	53	113
RM NP: UMPYNA CAR RUNAWAY NOV 5 1908	02	57	54
RM NYC EXCITING DROP ANDERSON IN 1926	01	76	12
RM NYC: 6 WK OLD INFANT DOESN'T GO HUNGR	12	50	124
RM NYC: CROTON TO GRAND CENTRAL TERMINAL	09	51	123
RM NYC: ERIE DIVISION 1917	06	59	11
RM NYC: INDIANA DIVISION LINCOLN SPOKE H	05	50	131
RM NYC: PAYS PRR MUDHOP FOR TELEGRAPHY	08	54	10
RM NYC: PUTNAM DIV MORSE OPERATOR	08	52	129
RM NYC: PUTNAM DIVISON/PICTURE CAPTIONS	04	49	138
RM NYC: SAVES WOMANS LIFE	05	50	129
RM NYC: SNOWSTORM AT NORTH YARDS	12	51	127
RM NYC: SUPERINTENDENT DINING CARS	02	53	131
RM NYCS: BMT-BRIGHTONBEACH EXPRESS--MUTT	03	55	56
RM NYCS: SUBWAY TRAIN RESCUES PEOPLE	02	59	37
RM NYNH&H: 1925 BLIZZARD	02	51	125
RM NYNH&H: LOSES MANS SHOES	02	53	127
RM NYNH&H: SHOW TRAIN	07	49	128
RM NYNH&H: SIGNAL TOWERMAN TRAVELS	06	49	126
RM NYNH&H: STATION AGENT/MISSING TRAIN	05	53	122

Railroad/Railfan

GENERAL RAILROADING

RAILROAD NON-FICTION	M Y P
RM OLD BOOMERS DON'T DIE	03 75 03
RM OLD CONDUCTORS RECALL...	03 76 07
RM OLD DAYS ON THE SIGNAL GANG	06 77 06
RM OLD LOG ROADS IN FL & LA	12 71 10
RM ON THE TEXAS PANHANDLE	12 78 09
RM ON: WINTER 1953/BAD WEATHER	05 54 117
RM ONE HELLUVA BANKER	12 74 08
RM OPERATORS: SLEEPING ON THE JOB	10 51 128
RM ORIGIN OF WABASHING (CB&Q)	07 76 08
RM P&R: MORE READER MEMORIES	06 44 121
RM P&R: READER MEMORIES	05 44 120
RM P&R: WALKOUT	03 49 138
RM P&WV: CARNEGIA PA TRAIN RUNS OVER BIL	08 50 124
RM PAY CARS: TRAINMASTER/BOOMERS	02 56 04
RM PE: HOLD-UP N HOLLYWOOD CA	02 53 76
RM PE: TRANSFERRED OCTOBER 1 1953	03 54 116
RM PGE: ROCK SLIDE DELAYS 1ST TRAIN	02 57 50
RM PHILADELPHIA SUBWAY-ELEVATED	01 75 48
RM PM 1910 WATER TANK COLLAPSE	07 76 07
RM PM DORAN SIDING J CANAVAN	12 73 10
RM PRR: AIR HOSE W/MISSING CROSS-PIN	10 53 115
RM PRR: CAR LOAD OF PASSENGER LOSE SHOES	05 53 126
RM PRR: CONWAY PA HUMPS/BOOMER/GUNNIES	12 48 121
RM PRR: CP DIVISION/UNLUCKY 13	11 51 131
RM PRR: CUMBERLAND VALLEY--DUMB MAN	07 51 136
RM PRR: JOHNSTOWN FLOODS 1889 MEMORIES	07 54 118
RM PRR: KING RANCH	11 53 117
RM PRSL: SUMMER 1951/CARS PARK ON LINE	12 52 127
RM R: READER MEMORIES	05 44 120
RM R: SUBORDINATE TELLS OFF SUPER	06 53 115
RM RAILROAD US MAIL MESSENGERS	01 50 134
RM RAILROADING IN THE '90S READ	11 73 10
RM REEFER COOLING OFF!	08 64 10
RM REMEMBER THOSE DAYS?	08 74 10
RM RG: CONDUCTOR KILLED/EMERGENCY STOP	08 53 122
RM RG: FINAL RUN SAN JUAN	07 51 119
RM RI: 0-4-0T SWITCHER HISTORY	01 52 131
RM RI: DES MOINES BRIDGE FIRE	12 56 08
RM RI: QUEENIE (MASCOT OF LOCO 761)	02 49 108
RM ROY GALE ON GTP WILDERNESS IN 1911	06 70 08
RM RU: RUTLAND VT COMPANY COOPERATES	06 51 127
RM RW&O ROME NY 1910 KIDS & GANDYDANCERS	02 74 06
RM S 1905 TRAILING BEHIND A MULE	02 75 05
RM S AND L&N 1922 NIGHT IN THE YARD	06 76 08
RM S JELLICO TN 1920	05 75 04
RM S: 2 GIRLS/PRES PALATIAL RAILROAD CAR	05 50 132
RM S: CONDUCTORS NAMES ON CABOOSE	02 52 121
RM S: MURPHY BRANCH/NEGRO COOK MEMORIES	09 49 127
RM S: SELMA ALABAMA PAYMASTER/XTRA MONEY	07 49 135
RM SA&AP: NOW SP/CALLBOY MEMORIES	05 54 122
RM SD&AE: COMMERICAL AGENT/MEMORIES	08 49 135
RM SE&WV: NOW PART OF C&O/WEST VIRGINIA	01 55 07
RM SILK TRAIN MEMORIES 1	04 65 06
RM SILK TRAIN MEMORIES 2 & 3	04 65 08
RM SL&H: ABANDONED 1944/RINGLING LINE	01 49 114

RAILROAD NON-FICTION	M Y P
RM SLOW TRAIN TO PORTLAND MAINE (GT)	12 74 06
RM SNOW PLOWING IN 1929	09 77 09
RM SP 1912 AND 200' BELOW SEA LEVEL	10 71 12
RM SP LOGGING ENGINEER	06 76 11
RM SP&S: TUNNEL UNDER GREENWOOD CEMETARY	08 50 125
RM SP: 1890'S BEAR AT SWITCH	05 53 125
RM SP: 1905 STAFF SYSTEM OF OPERATING	02 51 131
RM SP: 2 GIRL COUSINS RUN OVER BY TRAIN	11 52 136
RM SP: BEOWAWE NEVADA LUCINDA DUNCAN	12 58 10
RM SP: CAB-IN-FRONT LOCOS	03 55 06
RM SP: COAST DIVISION WHISKEY BOXCAR	08 56 76
RM SP: DINING-CAR WAITER	05 50 134
RM SP: FREIGHT TRAIN/BOYS AGE 10 & 8 ON	07 50 137
RM SP: GLAMIS TO BERTRAM CALIFORNIA	07 51 133
RM SP: JOHN HUMISTON/LOCO AIRBRAKES	03 53 137
RM SP: LOCO #300 CLASS A6 DRAFTING MEMOR	03 54 12
RM SP: MCKEEN MOTOR CARS	05 51 129
RM SP: MOGULS/AMERICANS/CORNFIELD FRT YD	06 54 116
RM SP: RIVER DEPOT LOS ANGELES	03 51 129
RM SP: ROSEVILLE CALIF YARDS/PIGEON	01 53 123
RM SP: RUNAWAY WRECK 6 KILLED	03 53 125
RM SP: SAN JOAQUIN DIV UNUSUAL SETUP	06 51 122
RM SP: STUDENTS NOW RIDE TRAIN, NOT BUS	07 49 128
RM SP: TRAIN BAGGAGE MAN REMEMBERS	06 49 132
RM SP: VIOLATION OF RULES NECESSARY	05 50 134
RM SP: WATSONVILLE JCT, CA SUPERSTITION	06 51 125
RM SR&D: 5' GAGE/238 MILES/MEMORIES	04 57 73
RM SR&RL: MEMORIES	06 56 74
RM STEAMBOATS: ALBATROSS/PELICAN	12 48 122
RM STEINWAY LINES: NYC TROLLEY MEMORIES	11 52 101
RM STREET-CAR PAINTERS, TRAVELING	12 50 93
RM STRR: EQUIP/1880'S MEMORIES	05 52 130
RM STUDENT TELAGRAPH OPERATOR	07 74 07
RM T&D: SUPERINTENDENT OF LINE	04 53 119
RM T&P ENGINEER ON DIESELIZATION	04 49 136
RM T&P: CALLBOY	12 50 129
RM T&P: MONAHAN'S WELL	07 54 117
RM T&P: RACE WITH DEATH 1910	12 50 125
RM T&T: GEN MANAGERS DAUGHTER	04 53 116
RM TAT: BATTERY CAR MEMORIES	12 50 95
RM TCRT: MAN HELD UP TWICE ONE NIGHT	08 53 77
RM TELEGRAPHY A LOST ART	03 74 12
RM TENNC IN 1930 MEMORIES	01 72 09
RM TMEX: FRIENDLY RAILROAD	04 53 129
RM TRAIN MAROONED IN MISS FLOOD 1927	08 74 03
RM TROTTING CARS	06 52 127
RM TUNNEL CAVE IN CLOSE CALL DT&I	09 66 58
RM TURTLE ON THE TRACK	09 77 11
RM TV&G: 1890 PASSENGER BRAKEMAN	08 57 71
RM UP TRAIN HIT BY A TORNADO 1977	09 78 12
RM UP: GREEN FLAGS/WHITE FLAGS	09 50 129
RM UP: NAVAJO INDIANS EMPLOYED	12 50 124
RM UP: SHERMAN HILL/WORK TRAIN	01 54 120
RM V&T: ABOUT TO BE ABANDONED/PASSENGERS	09 49 131
RM V&T: GOLD HILL NEVADA JAN 5 1888	06 54 118

Railroad/ Railfan

GENERAL RAILROADING

RAILROAD NON-FICTION	M	Y	P
RM V&T: READER DEBATES	01	52	125
RM V&T: SINGLE TRACK DESERT LINE	09	51	123
RM VB: RUNAWAY TROLLEY	01	49	95
RM W 1909 ENGINES GOT BIGGER	05	74	04
RM W WILFORD ON AC&HB OF 1917	05	71	08
RM W&LE: 1916/DRAG FREIGHT/BOWMAN	08	50	129
RM W&N: PEANUT BUTCHER/72 MI/73 STATIONS	01	55	66
RM W&OD: READER CORRECTIONS	01	50	138
RM W: #14 DES MOINES-ST LOUIS ATTRACTS B	04	49	128
RM WALKING CAR ROOFS CP 1920 MOUNTAIN DV	05	76	12
RM WC: LOCO ENGINEER & BRAKEMAN	03	52	122
RM WESTERN US BRASS POUNDER 1880	02	75	04
RM WILLIAM BAKER REMINISCENCESES	06	65	09
RM WP BLIZZARD IN THE SIERRAS 1943	06	76	04
RM WP: 55 ANNIV/LEONARD TOMASSO-WHAT HAP	03	55	71
RM WP: CIRCUS CALLIOPE	02	51	131
RM WP: NARROW ESCAPE	12	50	131
RM WP: NUDIST TRY TO RENT TRAIN	11	53	106
RM WP: WAYLAND CHURCH RECIEVES LOCO BELL	12	50	132
RM WRB: RHODE ISLAND/"YELLOW DOG" BRANCH	03	49	130
RM ZULU CARS	12	66	13
RM: AJ BARNARD REMINISCENCES	05	66	10
RM: NEWS BUTCHER	01	53	124
RM: OLDTIMER 1891/1894/1899/1938	09	52	121
ROAD TO YESTERDAY F HUBBARD	01	74	24
ROCK ISLAND AT GIBSLAND LA	04	78	42R
ROEBLING, THE RAILROADER	07	45	63
ROLLING THE CITRUS GOLD DELLINGER	12	48	18
ROMANCE, ADVENTURE, GLORY: 1900 STYLE	03	76	02
ROOM WITH A VIEW-IZAAK WALTON HOTEL MT	SP	76	40R
ROUNDHOUSE FORMAN-A DAY IN THE LIFE	05	78	39R
ROUNDHOUSE RUCKUS PART 2 SPROUT	08	51	100
RR IN OLD WEST-CONSTRUCTION TRAIN 1867	04	78	16
RT SPEEDWALK: CONVEYOR, MOVES PEOPLE	04	56	42
RUNAWAY--GN WINTER OF 1913 BRIEN	07	53	10
RUNNING LATE 1928	02	78	08
SAGA OF HARVEY GIRLS	03	76	12
SAGA OF THE SPURS PART 1	10	51	48
SALT SPRAY ON THE RAILS	08	43	08
SAWMILL RAILROADING SMITH	04	59	30
SCOOP FEAVER (FIREMEN ON MP)	05	70	29
SCOOPS & THROTTLES ON KVRR 1926	05	78	10
SCRANTON RAILFAN WEEKEND 1985	03	86	56
SCRAP-IRON SPECIAL PARRY	06	59	29
SCRAPBOOK-AMER SOC CIVIL ENG 1878 STORY	05	78	08
SCULPTURED ON A TOMBSTONE	09	36	35
SEASONING THE HAM: STUDENT OPERATOR	07	43	72
SELF-APPOINTED TRAIN MASTER (IC)	04	78	18
SETOUTS AND PICKUPS TIDBITS OF INFORMATI	02	34	47
SHAUGHNESSY'S SPECIAL BERRY	12	44	63
SKY-PILOT OF THE RAILS MAGUIRE	01	47	06
SKYLINE DISPATCHER (S) SANDLIN'S STORY	05	46	08
SMART BOOMER--BEDWELL APPRENTICESHIP	10	76	05
SMOKE ORDERS KNAPKE	10	57	74
SNO GTP:STATION LIFE 1921	01	71	10

RAILROAD NON-FICTION	M	Y	P
SNO GTW TRAVELING DOCTOR	09	75	06
SNO HOBOS AND RR EXPERIENCES	06	67	37
SNO MP:JIM POAGUE REMEMBERS THE 20'S	03	72	08
SNO MP:MISREAD ORDERS	01	70	59
SNO SP:RUSHED ORDERS	01	70	59
SNO TCRT: PCC CAR #299 HISTORY	02	54	105
SNOWBOUND IN IOWA BUTTS	10	59	24
SNOWPLOW JOB KNAPKE	03	45	116
SNOWTIME SAFARI-AMTRAK/VIA JOURNEY TO NO	03	87	39
SNUFFY (DOG) MCGUIRE	10	48	81
SO LONG 614, CHESSIE SAFETY EXPRESS	03	82	34
SOME RULES ARE FUNDEMENTAL MCMASTERS	05	50	10
SOMNAMBULISTIC IRON HORSES POMMER	11	49	08
SON OF A BITCH, YA PULLED OUT A DRAWBAR!	01	70	57
SOUTHERN BERKSHIRE #2716	11	82	60
SPECIAL AGENT FOR RI	01	70	52
SPONSOR IDENTIFICATION (45 SECOND WHISTL	01	49	08
STALLED IN A BLIZZARD (NYNH&H) ?????	03	46	06
STEAM DAYS ON THE GRAND TRUNK	06	60	21
STEAMTOWN RAILFAN WEEKEND 1981	03	82	60
STRANGER THAN FICTION	11	33	80
STRANGER THAN FICTION: 3 WHEELED LOCO ET	01	33	43
STREET CAR THRILLS	04	36	39
STUBENVILLE IN INTERCHANGE MEALS 25 CENT	03	76	10
STUDENT FIREMAN	06	57	62
STUDENT TRIP THE OLD-TIMER	01	43	88
SUCCESSFUL CHALLENGER (UP) PALMER	05	45	47
SUNK WITHOUT TRACE (CP)	08	34	58
SUNSET EXPRESS (SP) TODD	04	46	66
SUPERSTITIONS	04	49	42
SWITCHING AGREEMENT (E/DL&W IN WAYLAND)	04	53	06
TALES OF A LANKY TEXAN---2-10-4	02	78	26R
TAMING SALUDA (WNC) MONROE	11	44	10
TAX COLLECTING FROM RAILROAD 1907 CANADA	08	64	50
TEAMSTERS OF LONG AGO	05	77	08
TEHACHAPI WEEKEND	SP	77	29R
TELEGRAPH OPERATOR GN 36 HR TOUR 1890	07	71	12
TEN-WHEELER STORY	08	60	35
TERROR AT LOOKOUT MOUNTAIN MONROE	12	51	06
TERROR IN CAB C&O 1914	06	70	52
THAT FIRST NIGHT (ATSF) DULIN	03	53	06
THE WOULD-BE JESSE JAMES (BLACK JACK)	08	45	54
THEN AND NOW (SP) KNAPKE	04	46	06
THEY BURN BY NIGHT	08	51	12
THEY BURNED UNION STATION OSPRING	08	59	46
THEY CALL IT HUNCH-INTUITION	03	33	96
THEY DELAYED THE ZEPHYR	10	77	09
THEY DIDN'T GET THE RAILROAD	02	64	52
THOMAS WOLFE & THE ASHEVILLE SPECIAL	01	79	20
THOSE SURPRISING TRIPS (PHOTOGRPHIC)	10	52	137
THREE MILLION MILES ON THE BR&P MOORE	09	43	08
TIPS: I'D RATHER BE A SWITCHMAN #3	06	43	126
TONNAGE TRAP	04	71	45
TOO MUCH SOLAR ENERGY	04	78	14
TORNADO AT OAKDALE WIS JULY 1907 MILW	05	78	09

Railroad/ Railfan

GENERAL RAILROADING

RAILROAD NON-FICTION		M	Y	P
TRACKSIDE GOLD	HARRIS	12	47	91
TRAGIC TALE OF A TRAINMAN'S TEETH	KNAPKE	11	44	85
TRAILS & RAILS IN DEAITH VALLEY		12	44	50
TRAIN ROBBERY FOR $65 IN PENNIES PRR		10	78	08
TRAIN THAT NEVER CAME BACK, THE	CLARK	04	52	107
TRAIN WRECKER WHO TERRIFIED EUROPE, THE		11	33	34
TRAIN-SHEET BLUES		10	56	63
TRAIN-WATCHING		10	65	21
TRAPPED IN A BOILER	SPOTT	12	47	58
TRAVELING SALESMAN 1888	WATKINS	02	39	128
TROJAN HORSEPOWER: READER COMMENTS		03	49	131
TROLLEYING DOWN MEMORY LANE	BOOTH	07	52	80
TTR A $1400 PASSENGER	SPRINGFIELD	06	33	49
TTR A BAD TEN MINUTES	NASH	04	54	104
TTR A BAD TEN MINUTES	TEMPLE	06	31	345
TTR A BOOMER HERO	WADLEY	04	32	93
TTR A BOOMER IN AFRICA	"HAYWIRE MAC"	06	38	84
TTR A BOOMER IN OLD MEXICO	DAVISON	05	38	39
TTR A BOOMER IN SPAIN	DUNKEE	05	39	82
TTR A BRAKEMAN USED HIS HEAD	WADLEY	08	31	49
TTR A CAR TOAD'S APOLOGY	STODDARD	11	31	514
TTR A CARLOAD OF MULES	OVERLEY	08	55	53
TTR A CARLOAD OF MULES	OVERLEY	03	36	76
TTR A CIVIL WAR ADVENTURE	JONES	10	34	66
TTR A COMEDY OF ERRORS	MOORE	02	37	120
TTR A CONSPIRACY IN A WORTHY CAUSE	BEACH	07	39	36
TTR A COUPLE OF THRILLERS NYNH&H/BFR		01	33	80
TTR A DANGEROUS ASSIGNMENT	THENAN	06	41	73
TTR A DOZEN CHRISTMAS THRILLS BY A DOZEN		01	37	38
TTR A DUBIOUS HERO	SMITH	09	39	43
TTR A FATHER-SON SECTION GANG (CP)	PLANT	12	42	76
TTR A FIGHT I'LL NEVER FORGET	ABSTON	10	37	74
TTR A FLYING LOOP IN A COACH	DUNKLE	01	35	114
TTR A FLYING SWITCH FOR THE REBELS		08	34	42
TTR A FRIENDLY LITTLE DEVIL	CLARK	08	32	66
TTR A GHOST IN THE TANK	ROBERTS	10	33	118
TTR A GHOST ON THE TRACK	WILKINS	09	34	78
TTR A GOOD MEMORY	MCGUIRE	06	47	06
TTR A GRAVEYARD RUN (NOVELETTE)	SAMPLES	06	39	42
TTR A GUARDIAN ANGEL ON THE CRUMMY		12	33	56
TTR A HAND-CAR RACES THE MAIL	WYBERG	06	41	86
TTR A HEADLIGHT MEET	JOSSERAND	01	39	56
TTR A HOGHEAD "OVER THERE"	BARRETT	09	40	73
TTR A LOST LANGUAGE	PALMER	06	40	89
TTR A LUCKY OUTFIT	WEBSTER	10	38	74
TTR A LUCKY SLIDE	MCCLANAHAN	09	31	240
TTR A MAIN LINE ON THE ICE (NP BIDGE)		04	32	85
TTR A MEET WITH A GRIZZLY	RUTER	06	31	339
TTR A MEMORABLE TRIP (CB&Q)	BENIS	01	42	26
TTR A MIDNIGHT VISITOR	REISS	05	39	80
TTR A MIRACLE IN TWO SECTIONS	FRASER	09	35	126
TTR A MIXUP ON THE PACIFIC ELECTRIC		12	32	34
TTR A NARROW-GAGE IN THE BLACK HILLS		02	39	67
TTR A NIGHT I'LL NEVER FORGET (ATSF)		03	45	103
TTR A ONE-DAY CITY OF 30,000	DAVIS	06	34	71
TTR A PECULIAR ACCIDENT	RAYMOND	04	41	89
TTR A PERILOUS LOOP-THE-LOOP	SHAW	06	32	419
TTR A RAIL OUT-NO FLAG!	PARRY	03	35	36
TTR A RAILFAN IN THE WAR ZONE	AUSTIN	08	38	64
TTR A RAILROAD GIRL IN MEXICO	JEFFORDS	03	37	82
TTR A RAMBLING OP	JOHNSTON	12	45	72
TTR A ROVING NUT-SPLITTER	REEVES	07	41	79
TTR A RUSH COAL DELIVERY	"SILENT SLIM"	02	37	117
TTR A SCORPION IN EVERY POT	VOSS	03	39	37
TTR A SMASH HIT ON THE LEHIGH	MOSER	09	48	100
TTR A STAFF-OPERATOR'S STORY (SP)	HECOX	03	40	70
TTR A STRANGE RAILROAD ROMANCE	MINER	01	34	77
TTR A TASTE OF RAILROADING	ROONEY	05	48	80
TTR A TORCH ON WHEELS	DEARNESS	07	40	97
TTR A TRIP ON THE RABBIT	HINDS	01	50	98
TTR A TURTLE DELAYED THE "CENTURY"		04	37	109
TTR A VERY CLOSE CALL	FOWLER	11	30	526
TTR A WASHOUT ON THE "MOP"	DAVIS	06	31	338
TTR A WOMEN AT THE KEY		03	33	24
TTR A WRECKLESS WRECK	BLISS	05	33	64
TTR ABOUT TO BLOW UP	HEMNESS	09	31	241
TTR ACCIDENT AT WINSLOWS CROSSING		11	48	62
TTR ACCORDING TO THE RULE	PYNE	02	47	113
TTR ADVENTURES OF A BOOMER OP	HASELTINE	12	35	74
TTR ADVENTURES OF ENGINE 3041	JAMES	08	43	100
TTR AFFAIR AT STONE CREEK (S)		12	74	20
TTR ALASKA SWITCHES (AL)	HARRIS	09	46	101
TTR ALL IN THE GAME	GOLDSWORTHY	02	31	421
TTR ALL IT TAKES IS NERVE	RIDGELEY	12	38	42
TTR ALL MARKERS LOST	BOLDS	02	50	84
TTR AMBULANCE TRAIN	NICIPHOR	07	37	18
TTR AMBUSHED BY REVOLUTIONISTS	GRIFFITH	07	34	65
TTR AN ADAMS EXPRESS MYSTERY	STREIGHT	05	37	86
TTR AN AMATEUR DETECTIVE (NYC)	ADAIR	05	45	38
TTR AN ELECTRIC RUNAWAY (PE)	FELIX	03	33	33
TTR AN EMERGENCY STOP	RHOADS	03	31	592
TTR AN ENGINEER'S BIGGEST THRILL	MOORE	01	38	34
TTR AN ETERNITY IN SECONDS	BROWN	04	44	100
TTR AN EXCITING FIRST NIGHT	MACCABE	11	30	592
TTR AN EYE FOR AN EYE	CHILDS	03	31	586
TTR AN INFORMAL ORDER	CAMERON	02	50	78
TTR AN IRON PIKE IN BORNED	TAYLOR	06	35	91
TTR AN OCEAN OF HOGS	WYNN	05	31	193
TTR AN OLD TIMER'S THRILL	NICHOLS	01	32	244
TTR AN OLD-TIMER'S STORY	ESKEW	07	36	53
TTR AN UNLUCKY LOCOMOTIVE	EARP	05	34	66
TTR ANGUS WOOD'S RELIC	BERRY	07	51	114
TTR ANYTHING FOR A LAUGH	KNAPKE	12	62	34
TTR AUTOMATIC BLOCK	SAMMONS	11	40	50
TTR AUTOMATIC TRAIN CREWS	BOOTH	01	39	53
TTR BABOON SIGNALMAN	LAING	07	31	574
TTR BABY, THAT'S COAL OUTSIDE!	LESLIE	08	50	74
TTR BAD ORDER LOCOMOTIVE	BEST	04	31	45
TTR BANANAS AND BULLETS	RODALES	11	38	40
TTR BANGOR & AROOSTOOK	HIGGINS	08	45	77

Stephans' Railroad Directory

Railroad / Railfan

GENERAL RAILROADING

RAILROAD NON-FICTION		M	Y	P
TTR BAY RUM, CHURCH-BELL AND FARMER	EARP	05	32	224
TTR BEANERY BLOCKADE	JOSSERAND	08	47	102
TTR BEATING THE TIMECARD	GUNNISON	02	44	115
TTR BEEF TALLOWS AND LIMBURGER	BURNS	04	35	53
TTR BEFORE THE ENGINES WERE POOLED	LATHR	07	68	23
TTR BEFORE THE RAILROAD CAME	DRAPER	12	45	83
TTR BESIEGED BY LONGHORNS	SAMPLE	05	31	199
TTR BIG JOHNS JONES OF THE I-GN	TEXINO	02	35	51
TTR BIG MEN, LITTLE ENGINES	LATHROP	05	54	46
TTR BIG NOISE IN QUIET HOLLAND	LESLIE	04	49	72
TTR BILL JEFFERS BAILING-WIRE MOIKE		12	39	93
TTR BILL KRETLEY'S FAST RUN	DRUMMOND	11	36	47
TTR BILL RILEY'S HOG TRAIN	EARP	04	31	99
TTR BILLY JOINS THE BIRDS	BOSTWICK	08	38	59
TTR BLACK DIAMONDS	WALKER	06	31	354
TTR BLACK HILLS HIGH LINE	COAN	07	49	106
TTR BLIZZARD OF '88 (NYC)	DANIELS	03	41	61
TTR BLOOMIN' BLUNDERS	SPROUT	06	52	108
TTR BLUE BLAZE	THOMAS	06	31	342
TTR BLUE VITRIOL (RGW)	LATHROP	04	43	79
TTR BOB CURTIS'S MIRACLE W&LE	WESTCOTT	04	33	79
TTR BOGUS PASSES	CHAMBERS	10	34	74
TTR BOILER EXPLOSION (C&NW)	STOCKWELL	07	38	45
TTR BOOMER CLERK		11	30	610
TTR BOOMER DAYS ARE HERE AGAIN (MP)		07	42	87
TTR BOOMER KINGSNIPE	ROACH	06	50	110
TTR BOOMER MEETS GIRL	FUNKHOUSER	08	39	07
TTR BOOMER'S BEGINNING	BARNETT	01	47	88
TTR BOOMER'S LUCK	ROACH	06	37	74
TTR BOOMERS	ROACH	07	50	102
TTR BOOMERS AND BOLSHEVIKS	SLAVEN	01	34	81
TTR BOOMERS AND THEIR WOMEN	HAYWIRE MAC	12	57	28
TTR BOOMERS I HAVE KNOWN	HAYWIRE MAC	01	39	48
TTR BOOMERS IN A BLIZZARD	ROACH	03	53	100
TTR BOOMERS IN THE TROPICS	MOORE	05	36	54
TTR BOOMERS MISS NO MEALS	FUNKHOUSER	09	38	38
TTR BOOMERS, NORTHBOUND	HAYWIRE MAC	04	54	26
TTR BOOMING AROUND PART 1 OF 4	WALLACE	05	49	60
TTR BOOMING AROUND PART 2	WALLACE	06	49	116
TTR BOOMING AROUND PART 3	WALLACE	07	49	110
TTR BOOMING AROUND PART 4	WALLACE	08	49	100
TTR BOOTS AND SADDLES	CORSON	01	40	46
TTR BOXCAR ART	HECOX	07	39	20
TTR BOXCAR BLUES	DULIN	03	51	06
TTR BRANCHLINE LOCAL	MURDOCK	09	51	90
TTR BRASS HAT AND BURRO (RI)	ROACH	12	44	90
TTR BRASS POUNDER (B&O)	GRASSLEY	06	44	66
TTR BRIEF TALES FROM BRITISH RAILS		04	34	87
TTR BRIGANDS OF THE OLD "ESPEE"	DAVIS	11	31	492
TTR BROKEN LINKS	BURNS	04	36	103
TTR BROWNIES OFF THE RECORD	MCCARTY	10	52	68
TTR BUCCANEERING DAYS	GREVE	11	43	76
TTR BUCKING THE REBEL BLOCKADE	SMALL	11	49	72
TTR BUM'S RUSH	BEATTIE	12	54	74
TTR BUMS I HAVE KNOWN (SP)	JOSSERAND	06	42	69

RAILROAD NON-FICTION		M	Y	P
TTR BURIED ALIVE	PARRY	06	36	17
TTR BURIED ALIVE	DUNLAP	01	51	83
TTR BURIED TO THE STACK (IC)	PARKER	01	42	72
TT BABY BORN ON NY SUBWAY		02	65	38
TT RAILROAD SALOON	LATHROP	09	67	18
TTR TRUE TALES OF THE RAILS		12	29	144
TTR "DISREGARDING" ORDERS	WESTCOTT	12	36	81
TTR "FROG" SMITH REMINISCENCES		02	66	32
TTR "GHOSTS" ON THE RAIL	WAMSLEY	01	38	44
TTR "GOOD THIS DAY ONLY"	MARSHALL	08	33	54
TTR "LET 'ER BLOW UP!"	LEWIS	02	36	51
TTR "MILE-A-MINUTE" MURPHY'S GREAT RIDE		11	34	72
TTR "PEACE TO THE MAJOR!"	CROSS	04	31	66
TTR "PICK UP ONE TIGER"	TREANOR	11	30	612
TTR "REACH FOR THE CEILING!"	WRIGHT	07	31	575
TTR "SINK THE BRIDGE"	MCCABE	02	32	357
TTR "WE DON'T NEED TIMETABLES"	JAMES	12	40	75
TTR $17 TRAIN ROBBERY	O'CONNELL	10	42	67
TTR $199 FOR ONE TURKEY!	WILLIAMS	11	31	509
TTR 'BO MONEY	HAYWIRE MAC	03	39	44
TTR 136 SWITCH KEYS	EVERSOLE	05	43	62
TTR 200 YEARS ON THE READING	NEVEIL	03	51	75
TTR 3 1/2 MILLION LIVES LOST	DE LANEY	06	50	80
TTR 30 BELOW ZERO RI 1908	MOORE	01	68	58
TTR 50 MILES ON THE COWCATCHER	HAND	07	33	76
TTR 50 YEARS ON THE HIGH IRON	BUTCHER	07	40	90
TTR 54 YEARS ON THE A&S THE OLDTIMER		03	55	61
TTR 59 YEARS IN THE CAB	MOONEY	11	33	104
TTR 61 HOURS OF RAWHIDING	REARDON	02	45	112
TTR CABOOSE CAVORTINGS	SPROUT	09	50	66
TTR CABOOSE HUSTLER	HAYWIRE MAC	10	56	28
TTR CALAMITY JANE (NP)	BERRY	01	46	86
TTR CALAMITY JANE AND THE DISPATCHER		07	35	50
TTR CALAMITY'S CLOSE CALL	CHILDS	01	35	121
TTR CALLBOY	KNAPKE	09	40	83
TTR CALLBOY (MILW)	MOREHEAD	09	44	84
TTR CALLBOY AND BOOMER	LYNCH	01	53	64
TTR CALLING-ON SIGNAL	CHURCH	01	71	61
TTR CAMP-MEETING SPECIAL	SMITH	02	63	26
TTR CANAL AND MADISON	WHITE	03	43	69
TTR CAPTIAN ANSLEY'S REWARD	PEACE	05	34	61
TTR CAR DEPARTMENT	HORTON	12	49	108
TTR CAR KNOCKER (B&O)	MOHR	07	44	87
TTR CASEY JONES TOLD ME TO JUMP	WEBB	11	54	38
TTR CASEY'S WIDOW RECALLS	RHODES	05	33	63
TTR CAUGHT ON THE RUN	MORGAN	01	45	48
TTR CHAPERONING A MOGUL	PUGH	03	43	78
TTR CHARLIE BOONE AND THE 5508 (MP)		02	76	18
TTR CHASED BY BURNING CARS		12	36	84
TTR CHASING THE RED (ATSF) MCGUIRE & MAC		09	44	92
TTR CHECKERS ON THE NIGHT TRICK (CPM&O)		09	44	89
TTR CHICAGO TO NY IN 15 HOURS	FRENCH	04	32	95
TTR CHRISTMAS AT LONE PINE	MCCARTY	01	52	90
TTR CINDERS	ROACH	01	49	74
TTR CIRCUS EXTRA (MP)	ROACH	07	46	68

Railroad/Railfan

GENERAL RAILROADING

RAILROAD NON-FICTION		M	Y	P
TTR CITIZENS' ARMED INVASION OF MEXICO		05	51	74
TTR CIVIL WAR MEMORIES	LT. STARON	03	38	120
TTR CLEAR BLACK-GRAY HAIR	LOCKABEY	07	47	47
TTR CLOSE TRACKS	HALL	03	30	593
TTR COALBURG CUTOFF	ROACH	03	51	64
TTR COMPANY SOAP	BURNS	10	34	73
TTR CONFESSIONS OF A BOOMER CROOK	HOLMES	10	32	409
TTR CONFESSIONS OF A BOXCAR	SAL 18386	04	38	82
TTR CONVICTS USE RAILROADS TO ESCAPE		03	32	466
TTR COPIES	PALMER	10	47	74
TTR COPPER-WIRE DEATH	LEKSTROM	02	31	424
TTR CORNFIELD MEET (CH&D)	WARD	05	43	74
TTR CORNFIELD MEET (NP)	MUNCH	09	44	90
TTR COTTON BELT BLUES	ROACH	08	32	58
TTR COUNTERFEIT (CPM&O)	GLOVER	07	44	96
TTR COWCATCHER BRAKEMAN	SAMPLES	06	43	85
TTR CRAZY SIGNALS	JAY	03	50	66
TTR CREAMED PEAS	GOLDSWORTHY	05	37	85
TTR CUSTODIAN OF CLOCKS	HOLDEN	02	40	66
TTR DAUGHTERS OF THE ROAD	MAXWELL	09	39	49
TTR DC&N VERSUS GREAT NORTHERN	RALPH	09	41	56
TTR DEAD ENGINE	JAY	02	47	06
TTR DEAD MAN'S CURVE IC	LOWELL	06	33	51
TTR DEAD MEN BUILD NO FIRES	MITCHELL	01	33	75
TTR DEAD TO THE WORLD	ZIENER	08	34	46
TTR DEAR EDITOR	JOSSERAND	04	50	109
TTR DEATH AT THE THROTTLE	MCCLINTOCK	03	49	44
TTR DEATH AVALANCHE (GN)	CORY	09	45	78
TTR DEATH ON A PASSING TRACK	BURNS	01	32	247
TTR DEBUNKING THE BOOMER CHF DISPATCHER		08	43	106
TTR DEMON OF THE RASCAN	CLARK	05	30	241
TTR DESERT DETOUR (ATSF)	IZOR	07	45	138
TTR DESERT MEMORIES	PALMER	02	42	66
TTR DESERT MEMORIES (SP)	PALMER	01	41	45
TTR DESERT OPERATOR (SP)	PALMER	05	42	70
TTR DID I TIE UP THE ROAD?	O'BRIEN	08	43	92
TTR DINING-CAR CONDUCTOR (GN)	DULMAGE	10	41	84
TTR DINNER PAIL (ATSF)	MCGUIRE	09	45	81
TTR DISASTER AT JAMES CREEK	LEE	06	36	20
TTR DISPATCHING TRAINS WHILE ASLEEP		11	36	45
TTR DIVISON POINT (CP)	PALMER	07	43	91
TTR DO YOU REMEMBER?	GORDON	11	39	35
TTR DOCTOR OF AILING LOCOMOTIVES	CARTER	09	36	46
TTR DOLLAR A DIVISION	MILBURN	10	58	28
TTR DON'T EVER LEAVE ME	YOUNG	05	51	83
TTR DON'T FORGET THE MEAT	MURDOCK	08	49	64
TTR DONE IN OILS	KENNEY	03	50	84
TTR DONT TRADE WATER FOR STEAM		04	64	24
TTR DOODLEBUG TRANSPORTATION	BEATTY	12	33	53
TTR DOTS AND DASHES FROM THE PAST	TREAT	10	51	92
TTR DOUBLE TRACK DEBUT (ATSF)	CLEVENGER	05	47	06
TTR DOUBLEHEADING TO DISASTER	NP	02	33	34
TTR DOWN BETWEEN	CULPERRER	03	31	589
TTR DOWN BY THE DEPOT (D&RGW)	LATHROP	01	68	20
TTR DOWN THE BRANCH	KNAPKE	05	40	102

RAILROAD NON-FICTION		M	Y	P
TTR DOWNHILL AT NINETY MILES PER HOUR		02	55	44
TTR DOXEY DEPOT HOLDS THE MAIN RI	DENTON	04	33	78
TTR DRAWBAR FLAGGING (PRR)	HAYWIRE MAC	10	44	107
TTR DROPS AND DRAWBARS	VOORHEIS	01	43	107
TTR DROVERS' PASS (RU)	BERRY	05	45	34
TTR DYNAMITE IN THE FIREBOX	KUHLER	12	77	11
TTR EACH IN HIS TIME	KNAPKE	02	49	50
TTR EARLY DAYS IN MONTANA	HARTWELL	12	36	75
TTR EARTHQUAKE	HUNKINS	10	40	78
TTR EARTHQUAKE	MERRILL	04	38	79
TTR EASING HIM DOWN THE HILL	PUGSLEY	08	32	68
TTR EASY MONEY (MP)	DELLINGER	10	44	92
TTR EASY MONEY (RI)	JEWEL	02	43	79
TTR EAT MESELF STRIKE	ARMES	03	48	74
TTR EIGHT RAILROAD BROTHERS	WATERS	09	34	69
TTR EIGHT-YEAR-OLD OP (TC)	FIELDS	01	46	67
TTR ELECTION NIGHT	BEACH	06	40	86
TTR EMERGENCY ENGINEER	MOFFETT	06	34	77
TTR ENCOUNTERS WITH SEMAPHORES	PALMER	01	43	118
TTR END OF STEEL	CROYN	05	48	74
TTR ENGINE ON A JOY RIDE	ROBERTS	12	33	52
TTR ENGINE SEIZED BY CRIMINALS 1914		04	32	84
TTR EXCURSION TRAIN (D&RGW 1915)	LATHROP	02	68	25
TTR EXPERIENCES 'WAY BACK	PURKESS	12	47	121
TTR EXPLOSION (PRR)	HAYWIRE MAC	06	44	60
TTR EXTRA GANG TIMEKEEPER (NP)	GILBERT	02	53	66
TTR FAKE TEST ON OLD RIO GRANDE	LATHROP	09	68	59
TTR FAMOUS RUN OF THE OLD 97 C&A	BURNS	02	33	30
TTR FATHER-SON CREWS (ATSF)	MCGUIRE	07	43	86
TTR FEEDING THE CHAIN GANG	PATERSON	05	32	221
TTR FEEDING THE CREW THE "GOOD OLD DAYS"		08	72	10
TTR FEMALE HOBO & THE SAND HOUSE (SP)		11	68	06
TTR FIDO TAKES TO THE RAILS	WILSON	07	51	79
TTR FIFTY YEARS AGO	REED	07	41	84
TTR FIFTY YEARS AGO (MC)	SAVAGE	07	54	52
TTR FILLING A BOILER W/BUCKETS	STOCKWELL	02	38	115
TTR FIREBOY	SLEDGE	12	43	113
TTR FIRING BEGINS AT 42 (PRR)	CORNELL	09	45	85
TTR FIRING OVER SUPAI	REARDON	12	45	66
TTR FIRST ROTARY IN THE MIDWEST	SMITH	03	34	99
TTR FIVE DAYS IN A SNOWDRIFT	PORTER	07	33	68
TTR FIVE DAYS ON A SNOWOUND TRAIN	PORTER	08	55	54
TTR FLAG NUMBER FIVE	GAGE	10	31	384
TTR FLAGGING BIRD CAGES	HILL	04	31	106
TTR FLYING SPIKES	WHITE	06	49	98
TTR FORGOTTEN LIMA LOCOS	JERNSTROM	02	73	53
TTR FORGOTTON ENGINE RACES DEATH	WILKINS	01	35	118
TTR FORTITUDE	KNAPP	03	39	48
TTR FORTY CENTS A HEAD (S)	SANDLIN	08	46	66
TTR FORTY HOURS ON DUTY	HOEFFEL	10	31	370
TTR FOUR MIRACLES	CLOUSER	05	38	35
TTR FOUR TRAIN ROBBERIES -- NO LOOT		09	73	11
TTR FOUR TRAIN ROBBERIES 4 MISSES	READER	11	73	06
TTR FOUR-TRAIN WRECK	BARNES	12	43	102
TTR FOURTH COOK	LATHROP	09	49	88

Railroad/ Railfan

GENERAL RAILROADING

RAILROAD NON-FICTION		M	Y	P
TTR FREAK RUNAWAYS	JOSSERAND	04	41	91
TTR FREE GASOLINE	"CUPID" CHILDS	12	35	73
TTR FREIGHT CHARGES COLLECT	LURIAN	08	50	84
TTR FREIGHT RACKETEERS	LOCKE	01	45	58
TTR FREIGHT RACKETEERS (MP)	WARREN	11	42	73
TTR FRISCO PRESS AGENT	DRAPER	02	47	92
TTR FROM SCALE TO PROTOTYPE	KESSEL	01	51	100
TTR FRONTIER VENGEANCE	SHERWOOD	10	31	364
TTR FROZEN STIFF	FOUNTAIN	11	50	08
TTR GALVESTON FLOOD	STRONG	05	40	98
TTR GASOLINE GOATS ON THE LOGGING PIKE		04	48	88
TTR GEARED ENGINES ON WOOD RAILS	SMITH	06	62	49
TTR GENERAL GRAY'S SPECIAL (WW II)		01	69	41
TTR GEORGEVILLE BRIDGE (BFR)	GRASSLEY	08	46	72
TTR GETTING OVER THE ROAD WITH A BOOMER		10	49	66
TTR GHOST IN THE TOWER	WESTCOTT	11	31	521
TTR GIRL IN WHITE FLANNEL NIGHTGOWN (VA)		02	73	48
TTR GIRL OPERATOR (MP)	JASSERAND	04	39	35
TTR GOLD TRAINS	CONNOLLY	08	45	64
TTR GOLDEN SPIKE (NP)	COOPER	12	40	78
TTR GONE WITH THE BIRDS	FUNKHOUSER	11	38	32
TTR GOSSIP AND SMILES	KILPATRICK	05	52	100
TTR GRAND CENTRAL MEMORIES(NYNH&H)	MILLER	11	41	63
TTR GRAVEL PIT EXPRESS	ESHNAUR	10	46	95
TTR GRAVITY CAR	FAWCETT	04	44	89
TTR GREEN LIGHTS REPLACE WHITE (PRR)	MAC	08	44	82
TTR GREENHORN FIREMAN	GABBERT	10	42	74
TTR GRUDGES AGAINST THE RAILROAD	BERRY	12	37	63
TTR HAIR AND RATE CUTTING	BERRY	08	51	81
TTR HALF A CENTURY AGO	BRADFORD	03	44	85
TTR HALF AN INCH FROM DEATH	TIMMERMAN	11	31	518
TTR HALF-PINT HOGGER (SP)	WELCH	09	43	83
TTR HAM OPERATOR	WOOD	09	42	86
TTR HARD CONDUCTOR (FRIS)	DELLINGER	07	44	98
TTR HARD-SHELL FIREBOY		09	31	243
TTR HE FOOLED THE MOUNTIES	GILMOUR	08	31	51
TTR HE FORGOT THE ORDER	FLETCHER	10	43	92
TTR HE TIED UP THE RAILROAD	HUBBARD	05	74	30
TTR HE WANTED TO GET WARM	VAUGHAN	05	38	38
TTR HEAD END COLLISION	SAVAGE	09	49	96
TTR HEAD ON! N TONAWANDA NY WRECK	HURLEY	06	32	417
TTR HELPER TOWN (D&RG)	HAYWIRE MAC	01	41	38
TTR HEREABOUTS & ELSEWHERE RAILROADS		10	51	06
TTR HI, BUB!	HEROLD	09	51	06
TTR HIGH SPOTS AND LOW JOINTS	BURNS	03	36	73
TTR HIGH WATER	ELLIS	11	48	93
TTR HIGHBALLING THE LIBERTY BELL		07	36	62
TTR HIGHBALLING THE WHALES	CONROY	12	40	71
TTR HIRED, MIRED, AND FIRED	QUINBY	03	55	40
TTR HOBO	MEAD	01	40	37
TTR HOBOES ON THE HIGH IRON	SMITH	12	70	40
TTR HOBOS AND HOT COTTON	ROACH	03	47	111
TTR HOG IN A MUDHOLE	DELLINGER	01	38	31
TTR HOG-BACK FRIEGHT (PRR)	DIXON	08	42	108
TTR HOGGER FOR A DAY (B&H)	OSGOOD	07	38	49

RAILROAD NON-FICTION		M	Y	P
TTR HOGGER TALK	CLODFELTER	02	44	116
TTR HOGHEADS EXTRAORDINARY	MOORE	06	37	78
TTR HOLD ALL TRAINS EAST AND WEST	EVANS	09	42	80
TTR HOLDUP (ATSF)	KING	05	46	92
TTR HOME ON THE RAILS (PTS)	PINNEO	05	42	81
TTR HOMESTEADING	ROACH	06	51	84
TTR HOODOO ENGINE	HUFFSMITH	06	36	19
TTR HOODOO NUMBER	RASMUSSEN	04	41	86
TTR HOOPS AND HOOKEY	BLEDSOE	08	51	70
TTR HORNY TOAD WRECK ATSF	BROWN	07	33	73
TTR HORSE MEDICINE	SNYDER	02	30	461
TTR HORSE RACE (NH)	REILLY	12	41	88
TTR HORSEPLAY	JOHNSTON	06	46	78
TTR HOT BABBITT	BURNS	09	31	236
TTR HOT FREIGHT	GOLDSWORTHY	11	30	595
TTR HOT RAILS (ATSF)	MCGUIRE	10	44	100
TTR HOT TIMES ON THE HORNY TOAD	CLARK	03	32	507
TTR HOURS OF SERVICE (NP)	BRADFORD	10	45	86
TTR HOW "SLIPPERY BILL" GOT HIS NAME		01	38	38
TTR HOW I BEGAN RAILROADING A SYMPOSIUM		02	57	72
TTR HOW I LOST MY NERVE	DEEGAN	11	34	77
TTR HOW NOT TO RUN A RAILROAD	BURNS	04	34	98
TTR HUDSON DIVISION BRAKEMAN NYC	HASSETT	06	53	62
TTR HUDSON DIVISION BRAKEMAN PART 2 NYC		07	53	88
TTR HUNTING GREENER PASTURES	SHORT	09	37	96
TTR I BRUSHED THE PEARLY GATES (WABASH)		08	40	87
TTR I DISOBEYED THE DISPATCHER	AIRD	11	40	46
TTR I MARRIED A TRAIN DISPATCHER		06	56	48
TTR I REMEMBER	RAMSEY	05	54	74
TTR I REMEMBER ABE LINCOLN (IC)	DODGE	06	44	64
TTR I REMEMBER JIM ROOT-HERO OF 70 YEARS		12	64	37
TTR I RIDE THE ENGINE	MCGUIRE	12	46	08
TTR I SHOULD HAVE "DOUBLED" DOWN HILL		07	39	33
TTR I STOLE $1,000,000 FROM BOX CARS		10	31	321
TTR I STOPPED THE WHITE TRAIN	MCMASTERS	12	48	76
TTR I WAS A DISPATCHER FOR FIVE MINUTES		10	56	60
TTR I WAS A NEWS BUTCHER IN 1906 ON MKT		02	71	61
TTR I WAS A PULLMAN STRIKER	PARKER	04	45	80
TTR I WORK ON A WRECKING CREW (GT)	DENAR	10	68	20
TTR ICY RAILS (MC&C)	FROST	08	46	71
TTR IF I KNEW YOU WERE COMING	BARNES	01	52	104
TTR IN THE DAYS OF THE OLD EIGHTY-FIVE		06	48	81
TTR INJUN BURY 'UM DEEP	GODSEY	02	51	103
TTR INTERNATIONAL BOOMER	HOME	03	45	94
TTR INTO THE DITCH!-SOUTHERN RY-	BATES	01	33	81
TTR IPECAC IN REAL LIFE	KNIGHT	09	31	238
TTR IRON HORSE THIEF	LAIRD	07	51	10
TTR IT WAS A CLOSE CALL (CB&Q)	BEMIS	03	41	66
TTR IT WAS NOT A GHOST	BENTZ	06	31	348
TTR JAWBONE	THOMAS	12	49	64
TTR JEFFERS MADE ME A BOOMER(UP)	KEENLYNE	02	43	66
TTR JIM BEEMAN'S BAD MEN D&RG	DRUMMOND	02	33	36
TTR JINX SWITCHES	MORRISON	07	33	74
TTR JUDGEMENT DAY FOR MAIL THIEFS		02	66	08
TTR JUICE LINE UNDER SEA	ROWELL	01	35	112

Railroad/Railfan

GENERAL RAILROADING

RAILROAD NON-FICTION		M	Y	P
TTR JUST A BOOMER	HARWOOD & STAMP	03	34	101
TTR JUST AS WIDE	HAYWIRE MAC	09	41	66
TTR KEEP 'EM RUNNING	BENNITT	12	51	104
TTR KENNEDY'S LAST HOLDUP	FINLEY	08	30	107
TTR KID OPERATOR (ATSF)	JOHNSTON	06	45	64
TTR KID SWITCHMAN	ROACH	08	52	68
TTR KING OF THE THROTTLE-PULLERS (SP)		12	41	98
TTR KING SNIPE (ATSF)	MCGUIRE	07	46	75
TTR LADY BRAKEMAN	LEGERTS	06	41	77
TTR LADY TRAIN DISPATCHER	ALBRECHT	01	55	25
TTR LAP ORDERS	JOSSERAND	09	42	89
TTR LAST DAYS OF NARROW GAGE (RGW)		12	41	91
TTR LAST MILE FOR CASEY JONES	ATHANAS	07	49	82
TTR LATE BUT ON TIME	STEEVES	08	31	52
TTR LEAKY THROTTLE	STOCKWELL	10	38	81
TTR LEGEND OF BOOMER (A DOG) (IC)		03	74	57
TTR LEVER SEVENTEEN	DAVIS	01	31	260
TTR LIFE IN THE MAIL CARS	HUBBELL	08	49	78
TTR LIGHTING SLINGER	FRANCISCO	11	43	66
TTR LIGHTNING SLINGER	NEVILLE	04	54	78
TTR LIKE A FLYING TRAPEZE (CGW)	SMITH	04	39	43
TTR LINK AND PIN	BUTLER	02	56	50
TTR LINK-AND-PIN BRAKEMAN	PIERCE	04	44	92
TTR LINK-AND-PIN DAYS	HOUGHTON	11	40	55
TTR LOCKED HORNS	REHBEIN	08	34	49
TTR LOCO LEAVES A TRAIN BEHIND		04	76	09
TTR LOCOMOTIVE PARADE	CHESTER	07	39	20
TTR LOCOMOTIVES TO BURN	WALLENBERGER	01	45	56
TTR LONG FLAGSTOP	KIMBALL	08	47	89
TTR LOOKING BACK	KENNEY	02	51	06
TTR LOST CRUMMY (MP)	ROACH	01	46	80
TTR LOST FREIGHT TRAIN	MARTIN	12	42	72
TTR LOST IN THE WRECK	YATES	02	32	360
TTR LOST: ONE CAR OF "PRINTER'S INK"		01	34	75
TTR LUCKY BRAKEMAN (IOWA CENTRAL)	BURNET	08	41	77
TTR LURE OF THE RAILS	BLEDSOE	05	54	90
TTR MAIN LINE MEET	THOMAS	10	31	376
TTR MAINE CENTRAL MEMORIES	MANKS	11	44	60
TTR MARRIED BY TELEGRAPH	GILLEN	04	37	110
TTR MARYLAND DIVISION TALLOWPOTS		12	43	108
TTR MEASURE OF A MAN	WOODS	01	49	106
TTR MEET WITH A CANAL BOAT	GALLIHER	09	32	209
TTR MEMORIES OF A MORSE MAN (BFR)	FOSTER	07	46	79
TTR MEMORIES OF AN OLD DISPATCHER		11	35	69
TTR MEMORIES OF MAINE	TODD	10	49	80
TTR MEMORIES OF OLD ALTON	RODRIGES	05	37	87
TTR MEMORIES OF THE BURLINGTON STRIKE		10	36	41
TTR MENTAL LAPSES	KNAPKE	06	54	107
TTR MILEPOST 78	BURLINGAME	11	48	102
TTR MINIATURE TRUE TALES	BEERS/KIMBALL	12	37	69
TTR MISHAP OF THE 122	KILPATRICK	08	48	06
TTR MIXED ORDERS	RIDGELEY	03	39	52
TTR MODESTY TO THE WINDS	KALFUS	08	37	51
TTR MORE DESERT MEMORIES	PALMER	06	41	67
TTR MORSE MISSING	DULIN	05	51	14

RAILROAD NON-FICTION		M	Y	P
TTR MORSEMAN IN MEXICO	FOSTER	12	46	59
TTR MOST EXCITING DAY-HALIFAX SHIP EXPLO		08	74	38
TTR MOUNTAIN OF WHEAT	FRASER	12	29	148
TTR MOUNTAIN RAILROADING	KING	12	48	106
TTR MUDDY SHOE TELLS TALE IN COURT		01	49	98
TTR MUDHOP	FERGUSON	06	43	81
TTR MULLIGAN STEW	MARTIN	08	36	110
TTR MY BIGGEST CHRISTMAS THRILL-18 TALES		12	31	30
TTR MY BOX CAR DAYS	ARDEEN FOLSOM	09	71	27
TTR MY CIVIL WAR THRILLS	THOMAS	11	32	476
TTR MY FIRST RAILROAD JOB	A SYMPOSIUM	06	57	34
TTR MY FIRST RUN	TYLER	01	44	78
TTR MY FIRST TRAIN ORDER (SP)	HILL	10	32	407
TTR MY FIRST TRAIN ORDER (MP)	MILLS	07	44	93
TTR MY FREE RIDE, CHICAGO TO DENVER		07	37	11
TTR MY GREATEST MOMENT	GILLILAN	06	31	344
TTR MY GREATEST SCARE	ANDREWS	05	31	178
TTR MY HAPPIEST CHRISTMAS	BUTLER	01	36	126
TTR MY HEART'S ON THE SOO LINE	MILLER	06	43	70
TTR MY HOODOO MAIL RUN	MOORE	06	54	62
TTR MY MOST EXCITING DAY	BARTH	10	40	75
TTR MY MOST PERILOUS TRIP	FRANKLIN	05	34	57
TTR MY PARLOR-CAR HOME	GRAVES	06	37	81
TTR MY RAILROAD CAREER	COLLIER	06	51	100
TTR MY RIDE UNDER A LOCOMOTIVE	TEXINO	11	36	49
TTR MY SIX BIGGEST THRILLS	FANT	03	35	29
TTR MY WEEKLY SPECIAL	HEDGECOCK	10	38	76
TTR MY WILDEST RIDE	DEATON	07	32	555
TTR MYSTERU OF CAR 907 (UP)	HUBBARD	05	75	50
TTR NARROW-GAGE MEMORIES	LATHROP	09	37	89
TTR NARROW-GAGE VACATION (RGS)	VOSS	01	46	71
TTR NATURE IS WONDERFUL	MCGUIRE	04	50	78
TTR NEEDLES ON THE OLD A&P (ATSF)		08	42	100
TTR NEW ENGLAND HURRICANE (NYNH&H)	EASTON	07	42	75
TTR NEW MAN (NYC)	JOHNS	12	44	104
TTR NEW NUMBERS BRING OLD MEMORIES		04	53	68
TTR NEW WAY TO FILL A BOILER		07	32	491
TTR NEWS BUTCHER	BENNETT	06	40	97
TTR NIGHT JOBS (TELEGRAPH SERVICE)	PALME	12	56	50
TTR NIGHT ROUNDHOUSE FOREMAN	O'CONNELL	04	74	22
TTR NIGHT YARDMASTER	ROACH	09	47	110
TTR NO DRAMA	EARP	12	29	144
TTR NO MORE WHISKERS	PUGSLEY	01	52	78
TTR NO PLACE FOR A TRAMP	ARIZA	03	49	96
TTR NON REVENUE TRIP	PARRY	03	47	100
TTR NOSTALGIA	MCCLINTOCK	11	47	96
TTR NOT ON THE ORDER HOOP	COLLIER	04	45	91
TTR NOT ON THE TIMECARD	MASO	04	47	108
TTR NOT ON THE TIMETABLE	HILLER	10	52	92
TTR NOVICE FOR A NIGHT	CLEVENGER	06	46	92
TTR NUTS AND BOLTS	THOMAS	11	51	96
TTR NY 1050-MILE FREE RIDE	GILLAM	03	38	114
TTR OFF THE RECORD	MARVIN	02	39	62
TTR OLD DAYS IN THE NORTHWEST(NP/GN)	CADY	07	38	47
TTR OLD DAYS ON THE PERE MARQUETTE		05	41	73

Railroad/Railfan

GENERAL RAILROADING

RAILROAD NON-FICTION		M	Y	P
TTR OLD DAYS ON THE SOUTHERN	REED	11	41	68
TTR OLD HEAD	MARVIN	07	40	99
TTR OLD TIMES ON THE C&A	DEEGAN	09	35	123
TTR OLD-TIME TELEGRAPHER	RAYMOND	06	47	91
TTR ON THE CARPET	WAMSLEY	03	38	112
TTR ON THE COMPANY'S TIME	GARRY	09	34	73
TTR ON THE OLD COLORADO MIDLAND	DRUMMOND	11	32	487
TTR ON THE PICKET LINE	WHITE	01	48	94
TTR ON THE WRONG TRACK	RAYMOND	06	41	83
TTR ON THROUGH THE NIGHT	MCCARTY	12	53	80
TTR ONCE IN A LIFETIME	WHITE	06	40	99
TTR ONCE IN A LIFETIME	SPRINGFIELD	02	56	68
TTR ONE ARMED HOGGER	SMITH	08	64	26
TTR ONE DROP TOO MANY	WALKER	03	33	30
TTR ONE FOOT IN HEAVEN (IRISH LINE)	HUGH	03	69	34
TTR ONE IN A MILLION	KOHL	04	40	57
TTR ONE NIGHT OF TERROR	GIROURARD	01	30	306
TTR ONE PERILOUS RIDE	NEVILLE	07	41	89
TTR ONE WILD GOAT	WEBER	09	32	213
TTR ONE-MAN RODEO (MP)	ROACH	04	46	89
TTR OPEN SWITCH (ATSF)	TURK	10	41	78
TTR OPEN SWITCHES	FRASER	11	39	40
TTR ORDEAL OF FIRE	MCKENZIE	02	34	90
TTR ORDERS ARE ORDERS	EARP	11	30	588
TTR OUT OF CONTROL	EVANS	02	38	109
TTR OUTSIDE THE LAW	MCCLINTOCK	09	46	62
TTR PAID FOR--NOT EARNED	MCGUIRE	01	43	112
TTR PANAMA RAILROADING	ROACH	02	50	64
TTR PANAMA: READER COMMENTS		06	50	134
TTR PANHANDLE RAILROADING	LOCKE	05	44	106
TTR PASSENGER LOCO HITS A TANK TRUCK		06	76	14
TTR PAUL BUNYAN'S TOOTHPICKS	FROG SMITH	06	71	40
TTR PAY DAY	SILENT SLIM	01	45	115
TTR PAY-CAR	"HAYWIRE MAC"	08	62	53
TTR PEG-LEG'S WILD RIDE	CRUNCLETON	06	30	448
TTR PHANTOM SWITCHING	CHAPMAN	09	37	88
TTR PIG TROUGH FOR A THIRSTY HOG	DEEGAN	01	55	54
TTR PIG-TAIL OPERATOR	BOWLES	04	48	82
TTR PISTOL-PACKING CYCLISTS	HUBBARD	03	74	15
TTR PITY THE SECTION BOSS (ATSF)	MCGUIRE	06	42	73
TTR PORT CHAW	MCCLINTOCK	10	47	104
TTR POTATO PIKE	TODD	05	49	96
TTR POWER PUSHER	STEINMETZ	10	48	74
TTR PREACHING HOGGER	MONROE	05	47	77
TTR PREMONITION	SEIDEL	11	40	62
TTR PREMONITIONS (S)	MONROE	08	44	76
TTR PRESIDENT TAFT'S UNDELIVERED LETTER		11	48	76
TTR PRESIDENTIAL SPECIAL	LATHROP	07	41	72
TTR PREWAR CALICO	MCGUIRE	01	48	116
TTR PRICE OF CARELESSNESS (C&O)	PATTERSON	10	45	92
TTR PROMOTING THE ORIENT	DRAPER	11	49	104
TTR PROTECTED BY SNAKES	DIAZ	02	32	361
TTR PUBLICITY AGENT	FOUNTAIN	05	50	92
TTR PULLMAN IN THE RIVER (NP)	BERRY	07	46	73
TTR PUTTING THE BLACK ON THE WHITE	TYLER	11	44	81

RAILROAD NON-FICTION		M	Y	P
TTR QUEER RAILROAD CHARACTERS	DAVIS	06	31	414
TTR QUOTATIONS YOURS	MCGUIRE	08	48	104
TTR RACE TO THE SWITCH (CP)	LANNING	02	73	31
TTR RACE TRACK PART 1	LATHROP	07	48	72
TTR RACE TRACK PART 2	LATHROP	08	48	78
TTR RACE TRACK PART 3	LATHROP	09	48	118
TTR RACE TRACK PART 4	LATHROP	10	48	117
TTR RACE WITH FLAMING DEATH	BROWN	01	55	46
TTR RACING A TORNADO (GN)	SHAFER	09	32	215
TTR RACING THE GRIM REAPER	WILLIAMS	12	34	95
TTR RAIL-DOG (NP)	MARVIN	05	42	79
TTR RAILROAD BLACKSMITH (RU)	BERRY	03	46	88
TTR RAILROAD BULL	MOREHEAD	04	47	101
TTR RAILROAD FEAVER (B&A)	ROBERTS	03	66	23
TTR RAILROAD HASHER	WISSMATH	05	41	68
TTR RAILROAD ISLAND	SWANSON	10	46	06
TTR RAILROAD LUCK (C&O)	KELLY	04	39	40
TTR RAILROAD OR RAMBLE	DRUMMOND	03	43	82
TTR RAILROAD PRESIDENTS I'VE KNOWN	BERRY	08	36	107
TTR RAILROAD STREET	MCGUIRE	11	49	118
TTR RAILROAD WOMAN (NKP)	DICKS	11	41	58
TTR RAILROADERS STICK TOGETHER	ROONEY	08	38	57
TTR RAILROADIN' PICTURES	BURTON	09	38	42
TTR RAILROADING AT ITS WORST	DAVIS	04	31	36
TTR RAILROADING IN OLD MEXICO	GRIFFITH	03	34	97
TTR RAILROADING WITH VILLA	FOWLER	06	31	351
TTR RAILS AT CHOW	HARLOW	10	48	104
TTR RAILS I HAVE KNOWN	JASSERAND	02	40	62
TTR RAILS OF YESTERDAY	HUFF	03	42	46
TTR RAILS THROUGH SLIPPER SWAMP	CLARK	08	44	85
TTR RAILS THROUGH THE WILDERNESS		04	34	90
TTR RAILWAY MAIL CROOK	MOORE	07	32	553
TTR RAILWAY MAIL PIRATES	HENDERSON	04	31	34
TTR RAILWAY NON-COM	CASTLE	09	47	117
TTR RAMBLING REMINISCENCES	ORVIN	09	50	94
TTR RANDOM THOUGHTS OF A LINE OP	DULIN	01	48	111
TTR READY FOR PROMOTION	MCGUIRE	07	47	96
TTR RECOLLECTIONS	WRIGHT	06	48	118
TTR RECOLLECTIONS OF JESSE JAMES	BURNS	04	37	117
TTR RED BUCK	MARTIN	09	36	51
TTR RED CAP DAYS	ATKINS	07	49	96
TTR RED EYE AT MALVERN JUNCTION	YOUNG	06	31	356
TTR RED RAILS	JAMES	04	35	45
TTR RELIEF AGENT	MORRISON	09	52	96
TTR REMEMBER THE CALLBOY?	KNAPKE	08	56	62
TTR REMEMBER THE OLD PAY CAR?	HAYWIRE MAC	04	39	46
TTR REMINDER OF THE PAST	MACK	02	49	88
TTR RIDERLESS RUNAWAYS	CHILDS	11	31	551
TTR RIDING HOME IN KOREA 1945		05	68	06
TTR RIDING THE DL&G	SQUIRES	04	43	72
TTR RIDING THE FREIGHT	SOUTHCOTT	04	36	100
TTR RIDING THE RODS	HILKER	02	56	54
TTR RIGHT OF TRACK (FRISCO)	SALLY	11	44	76
TTR RIGHT TRAIN, WRONG RAILROAD (D&RG)		10	44	104
TTR RILEY GOES OVER THE TOP	MORAN	08	52	96

GENERAL RAILROADING

RAILROAD NON-FICTION		M	Y	P
TTR RIO GRANDE MEMORIES	LATHROP	06	52	68
TTR RIO GRANDE MEMORIES PART 2	LATHROP	07	52	70
TTR ROAD FOREMAN (ATSF)	MCGUIRE	02	46	74
TTR ROCK ISLAND RUSH	KENNEDY	05	40	106
TTR ROLLING WHEELS	"HAYWIRE MAC"	06	62	30
TTR ROMANCE, ADVENTURE, GLORY	RELLY	08	38	61
TTR ROMANCE, ADVENTURE, GLORY	RELYEA	08	56	35
TTR ROOSEVELT RIDES	REPPARD	07	35	51
TTR ROUNDHOUSE BLUES		05	65	24
TTR ROUNDHOUSE FOREMAN	CURTIN & MONROE	03	37	75
TTR ROUNDHOUSE MYSTERY (B&A)	ROBERTS	02	71	52
TTR ROUNDHOUSE RATS PART 1	LATHROP	05	47	84
TTR ROUNDHOUSE RATS PART 2	LATHROP	06	47	72
TTR ROUNDHOUSE RATS PART 3	LATHROP	07	47	72
TTR ROUNDHOUSE RATS PART 4	LATHROP	08	47	68
TTR ROUNDHOUSE RUCKUS	SPROUT	07	51	70
TTR RULE G	HAYWIRE MAC	06	40	93
TTR RUN WITHOUT COAL!	SMITH	08	31	54
TTR RUNAWAY (JM&I)	THOMPSON	07	42	91
TTR RUNAWAY CARS (ATSF)	IJAMES	09	43	94
TTR RUNAWAY ROTARY	THE OLDTIMER	04	54	111
TTR RUNAWAY TANKS	FRASER	07	32	556
TTR RUNNING A RED BOARD (1929)	LANNING	03	75	13
TTR RUNNING BLIND	PARRY	12	47	66
TTR RUNNING THE GAUNTLET	WEBSTER	01	36	121
TTR RUNNING WILD	DAVIS	07	31	569
TTR RUNNING WILD (ATSF)	TURK	02	41	115
TTR RUNNING WILD ON A JUICE LINE	WILSON	01	33	78
TTR SAFETY IS OF FIRST IMPORTANCE		11	46	72
TTR SAFETY MEASURE (NP)	FLETCHER	11	45	60
TTR SAGA OF THE ELEPHANTS	HUBBARB	04	56	28
TTR SAGA OF THE SPURS PART 2	LORENZINO	11	51	66
TTR SALIDA MEMORIES (D&RGW)	KENNEDY	08	40	80
TTR SALTY SPUDS	SABROWSKY	11	31	519
TTR SANDHOG	ARMES	10	46	76
TTR SANDHOUSE PARTIES	LATHROP	11	68	18
TTR SANTA FE ROADMASTER	FLACK	03	42	52
TTR SAVED BY A HUNCH (CN)	PARRY	07	44	82
TTR SAVED BY A MITTEN	CHRISTENSON	10	40	83
TTR SAVED BY AN ECHO	EMERSON	11	32	485
TTR SCISSOR-BILL'S SHORT FLAG	FRASER	08	30	110
TTR SEALED, LOCKED AND CLEATED	CASE	11	31	515
TTR SECTION BOSS	MCGUIRE	11	44	72
TTR SECTION FOREMAN OR BUTCHER	FLACK	12	51	10
TTR SELLING BOXCARS (MP)	ROACH	05	45	41
TTR SENTIMENTAL EPISODES	DULIN	04	51	06
TTR SERVICE LETTERS	HAYWIRE MAC	02	55	24
TTR SEVENTH NUMBER TWO	WRIGHT	03	50	92
TTR SEVENTY-EIGHT YEARS AGO	LEE	02	35	44
TTR SHELL SIDING	HINDS	12	48	115
TTR SHOE STRING CONTROL	CHILDS	01	31	270
TTR SHORT-LINE BOOMER	AREND	05	41	79
TTR SHUT-EYE (SP)	JOSSERAND	12	44	95
TTR SIERRA STORM	JOSSERAND	12	54	44
TTR SIGNAL MAINTAINER	MATTHIAS	10	54	51
TTR SIGNAL OIL (MKT)	ROACH	11	45	70
TTR SIGNAL OIL VS ALCOHOL	NUTT	10	48	113
TTR SILVER RUN TUNNEL	WILLIAMS	07	32	558
TTR SINGING BRAKEMAN	CUNNINGHAM	03	48	102
TTR SINGLE-TRACK GAME TRAIL	HUTCHINSON	04	45	95
TTR SIXTEEN HOURS LATE (BR&P)	EARL	02	41	110
TTR SKOOKUM FEVER (MA)	KING	12	52	100
TTR SLEEPING BEAUTIES (B&M)	TYLER	12	44	100
TTR SLEEPING ON THE JOB (W&LE)	BATTLES	08	40	85
TTR SLIM GORDON'S ALIBI	LEE	11	33	107
TTR SMOKING OVER THE SOUTH PARK	DOOLEY	08	54	96
TTR SNAP JUDGMENT (NYC)	LASS	10	41	81
TTR SNOW ON THE RAILS	TREAT	11	47	08
TTR SNOW SHOVELERS	ARMES	01	48	80
TTR SNOWBOUND WITH BERNHARDT	DONOVAN	12	32	36
TTR SNOWFLAKER	BUCK	10	50	89
TTR SO YOU'RE A PASSENGER CONDUCTOR	EARP	05	48	84
TTR SOD HUTS AND THE SANTA FE	BOLDS	04	48	59
TTR SOLDIER SPECIAL	VAN PELTE	12	49	68
TTR SOME HAD LUCK	PUGSLEY	02	49	70
TTR SOUTH PARK MEMORIES		06	34	73
TTR SOUVENIRS OF THE SOUTHERN	MILLS	07	52	96
TTR SPARE BOARD	TYLER	04	44	84
TTR SPEED WITHOUT SAFETY	MARDEN	11	37	121
TTR SPLIT SWITCH	EATON	10	42	83
TTR SPLIT-SECOND DECISION	HUBBARD	07	74	24
TTR START TOWARD THE RIGHT SEAT BOX		11	52	66
TTR STEEL RAILS THROUGH THE TALL CANE		04	57	23
TTR STICK 'EM UP	SHUTT & STOUT	07	47	86
TTR STILL A HOGGER AT 82	DOLAN	05	55	38
TTR STOLEN HOG BUTCHERING STORY		02	71	11
TTR STORE DEPARTMENT	HORTON	03	49	84
TTR STORM IN LOUISIANA	FOSS	05	44	115
TTR STORMY BOYER'S CAP	ROONEY	08	39	21
TTR STORMY'S MILLION-DOLLAR CAP	ARNDT	10	39	48
TTR STRANGE CARGO	MOORE	08	37	45
TTR STRANGER THAN TRUTH	THOMPSON	04	51	84
TTR STRANGER THAN TRUTH PART 2	THOMPSON	05	51	86
TTR STRANGER THAN TRUTH PART 3 OF 3		06	51	06
TTR STRINGS AND BRASS	DULIN	07	50	82
TTR STUDENT BRAKEMAN	MOREHEAD	02	52	06
TTR STUDENT FIREMAN	REARDON	03	47	78
TTR STUDENT OPERATOR (CONCLUSION)		09	74	04
TTR SUBMERGING "THE SNAKE"	BLISS	08	39	17
TTR SUDS	SHALER	06	34	80
TTR SWAMP ANGLE		12	60	46
TTR SWELLHEAD	SMITH	06	54	104
TTR SWITCH-STAND MEET (SP)	LOVELACE	11	42	80
TTR TALES FROM THE INDIAN NATION		03	52	84
TTR TAMING A RAWHIDER	TAMM	08	33	56
TTR TANK STOP HOLDUP (CB&Q)	LOCKE	09	43	90
TTR TEA-TRAIN WRECK (NP)	WOOLDRIDGE	03	41	56
TTR TEAMWORK	SMITH	01	51	78
TTR TEARS ON A TRAIN SHEET	OVERLEY	03	35	33
TTR TELEGRAPH GIRL	MILLER	03	54	60

Railroad/ Railfan

GENERAL RAILROADING

RAILROAD NON-FICTION		M	Y	P
TTR TELEGRAPHER ALARM CLOCK STORY		09	68	10
TTR TEN DAYS IN A SNOWSHED (GN)	WIGHTMAN	03	40	62
TTR TEN MILES IN TWO DAYS	ROACH	03	38	116
TTR TEN SECONDS TO SPARE	BEEBE	10	40	73
TTR TENDERFOOT BOOMER	FOSTER	05	47	100
TTR TERMINAL TALLOWPOT (JT)	ALLEN	11	45	65
TTR TEXAS & PACIFIC ADVENTURE	ROACH	04	49	96
TTR THANKS FOR BREAKING THE RULE!(NYNH&H)		06	45	71
TTR THAT'S RAILROADING	DELLINGER	06	31	335
TTR THE "BULLMAN" CAR	OWNBY	11	30	522
TTR THE 999 MEETS THE 666	THOMAS	02	34	92
TTR THE ABC SYSTEM	THOMAS	08	48	69
TTR THE BEER THAT VANISHED	MOORE	10	36	47
TTR THE BEST LAID PLANS	SMITH	12	50	08
TTR THE BIG HILL (CP)	NIBLOCK	07	42	79
TTR THE BOOMER OF YESTERDAY	FUNKHOUSER	11	37	116
TTR THE BOOMER TRAIL	MOORE	10	35	04
TTR THE BOOMER'S BAG O' TRICKS	HWIRE MAC	09	54	42
TTR THE BOY "OP"	MILLER	10	36	39
TTR THE BOYS GO HUNTING	FARROW	02	44	110
TTR THE BRAKEMAN'S ALIBI	X.BOOMER	12	38	53
TTR THE BRAVE ENGINEER		03	36	99
TTR THE BRIDGE FELL TWICE	CARTER	02	36	44
TTR THE BROKEN WHEEL	DONNELLY	02	32	349
TTR THE BUG AND I PART 1	KILEY	04	50	56
TTR THE BUG AND I PART 2	KILEY	05	50	66
TTR THE BUG AND I PART 3 OF 4	KILEY	06	50	68
TTR THE BUG AND I PART 4 OF 4	KILEY	07	50	68
TTR THE BUMS' RUSH	SCHONEMANN	11	32	482
TTR THE CALIENTE MYSTERY (LA&SL)	SNYDER	06	33	53
TTR THE CALLBOY	WILLIAMS	09	39	46
TTR THE CAR THAT VANISHED	JOSSERAND	09	38	44
TTR THE CASE OF THE CONTRABAND	QUAIL	08	54	64
TTR THE COMPLIMENT (CB&Q)	HOELL	02	46	70
TTR THE CROSSING GATE FIGHT	ROACH	12	37	65
TTR THE CURSE OF ALPINE TUNNEL	LATHROP	04	55	48
TTR THE DEATH ORDER	SNYDER	08	39	24
TTR THE DEVIL'S SLIDE	DUNKLE	04	34	96
TTR THE DOLLAR BACK	PAINE	01	40	99
TTR THE DRESSED BEEF SPECIAL	BURNS	03	32	514
TTR THE DUKE	REISS	11	39	43
TTR THE DYNAMITE KIT	BANKS	06	31	340
TTR THE DYNAMITER	NOWELS	12	39	85
TTR THE FIGHT AT 6X	DOOLING	06	32	414
TTR THE FIRST RAILROAD CLOWN	ROACH	09	48	84
TTR THE FLAG ARTIST	ALLEN	04	32	97
TTR THE FLAGMAN'S MULE C&O	OVERLEY	07	34	60
TTR THE FLYING HAND-CAR	DOUGHTEN	11	37	124
TTR THE GENERAL MANAGER'S STORY PART 1		02	52	60
TTR THE GENERAL MANAGER'S STORY PART 2		03	52	60
TTR THE GENERAL MANAGER'S STORY PART 3-3		04	52	80
TTR THE GHOST OF BLACK ASH SWAMP	ADAIR	04	33	73
TTR THE GLORIOUS FOURTH (D&RG)	DUNLAP	08	41	73
TTR THE GOOD PROVIDER (BOOMERS)	MAC	03	40	67
TTR THE GOULD BLACKBALL SYSTEM	RICHMOND	05	34	64
TTR THE GRAY GHOST (SP)	PALMER	06	45	75
TTR THE GREAT HINCKLEY FIRE	ROOT	01	37	32
TTR THE GREAT JOHNSTOWN FLOOD	RIDENOUR	09	36	40
TTR THE GREAT OLD SOUTH PARK DSP&P		12	33	46
TTR THE GREAT SLIDE (GN)	BRODY	03	46	78
TTR THE GYPSY'S PROPHECY	OVERLEY	07	36	57
TTR THE HAUNTED WIRE	BAGGETT	03	31	590
TTR THE HOMESTEAD RACKET (ATSF)	DRAPER	08	46	78
TTR THE HOODOO THIRD TRICK	BLISS	03	33	28
TTR THE JONAH	WEBSTER	06	46	88
TTR THE KETTLE VALLEY EXPRESS MYSTERY		12	34	96
TTR THE KID KNEW HIS RAILROAD		03	36	99
TTR THE LARK (SP)	ROONEY	09	46	117
TTR THE LAST OF THE LK&W	EARP	05	35	72
TTR THE LEDGER ARTIST	JAMES	05	52	74
TTR THE LITTLE BLACK BAG (RI)	HOWE	02	41	106
TTR THE LITTLE RED CABOOSE "HAYWIRE MAC"		04	38	71
TTR THE LOST RATTLER (ATSF)	BIGGS	07	54	40
TTR THE LUCKIEST WECK	BURNS	11	31	523
TTR THE MAIL CRASHES THROUGH	WILLIAMSON	02	34	94
TTR THE MAKING OF A BOOMER	FUNKHOUSER	06	39	29
TTR THE MARVELOUS DETOUR	WOLF	05	35	77
TTR THE MATRIMONIAL LOCAL	ALLREAD	01	31	257
TTR THE MILLION-DOLLAR HOG C&O	SCOTT	02	33	27
TTR THE MISSING SWITCH PIN	BOYD	06	31	350
TTR THE MISSING TOOL CHECK	DEEGAN	11	35	67
TTR THE MISSING WHEEL	SNOW	01	40	42
TTR THE MYSTERIOUS HAND	HARRISON	08	56	57
TTR THE NIGHT FIREMAN	GIFFORD	05	31	196
TTR THE NUTTY NOTION	CASTLE	07	48	94
TTR THE O.R.C. KID	ROACH	01	47	110
TTR THE OLD DISPATCHER'S STORY	LA COUR	10	37	79
TTR THE OPPORTUNITY I MISSED	LATHROP	06	43	91
TTR THE OTHER CHEEK	CRAWFORD	04	31	76
TTR THE PEANUT BUTCHER	STANLEY	10	54	18
TTR THE PHANTOM RIDER		09	31	245
TTR THE PULLMAN STRIKE MYSTERY	DEEGAN	08	33	48
TTR THE PUNJAB AMIL	PENDEXTER	05	33	61
TTR THE SILENT ALARM	WELDY	01	32	245
TTR THE SILENT LAND	KNAPKE	12	47	86
TTR THE SKELETON JACK	BRICE	07	31	567
TTR THE SKIPPER USES HIS HEAD	DRUMMOND	04	36	98
TTR THE SNITCH (ATSF)	MCGUIRE	03	46	84
TTR THE SPEED OF DEATH	WEBSTER	12	34	90
TTR THE SPOTTER GETS SPOTTED CB&Q	SMITH	03	33	34
TTR THE ST. CHARLES RIVER WRECK	BALL	04	37	115
TTR THE STATIONMASTER'S TALE	DAVIS	08	34	50
TTR THE STOLEN JAIL	BANKS	12	29	151
TTR THE STRANGE CASE OF CONDUCTOR KEENE		07	34	64
TTR THE SUPER LIKED FRIED CHICKEN	ROACH	02	48	82
TTR THE SUPERINTENDENT'S STORY	BEDWELL	12	55	52
TTR THE SWITCHMAN'S BOOTS (USSC)		04	46	82
TTR THE TALLOWPOT HERO	MARTIN	04	31	42
TTR THE TAMING OF WISEHEAD	FUNKHOUSER	05	36	64
TTR THE THREAT (GT)	GREANEY	10	45	138

Railroad/ Railfan

GENERAL RAILROADING

RAILROAD NON-FICTION		M	Y	P
TTR THE TORRENT OF TERROR	SEAMAN	11	31	510
TTR THE TOWERMAN AT RO	NEVILLE	10	42	79
TTR THE TRAIL TO NAYARIT	MCHALE	07	34	68
TTR THE TRAIN ORDER WAS PERFECT	OLDTIMER	12	38	49
TTR THE TROLLEY RACKET	DEEGAN	05	36	61
TTR THE UMBRELLA FLAGMAN (S)	KENDALL	04	42	99
TTR THE UNWELCOME FIREMAN	BETHEL	02	30	464
TTR THE WHISTLE	GRESS	11	34	79
TTR THE WOMAN ON THE CREW	DELLINGER	10	31	367
TTR THE WORLD'S FASTEST INTERURBAN	HAY	01	34	79
TTR THE WORLD'S OLDEST NEWSBUTCHER		09	50	92
TTR THE WRECK AT SNAKE CURVE	DIAZ	05	31	188
TTR THE WRECK AT ST THOMAS	HAYHOE	01	36	125
TTR THE WRECK AT THAXTON	SIMMONS	03	36	70
TTR THERE WAS A WAR ON	BUCK	05	50	106
TTR THEY CALLED HIM WOOSTER	ATHANAS	05	49	88
TTR THEY CALLED ME HAM	SNYDER	08	37	48
TTR THIRTY MILES IN SIX MINUTES!	THOMAS	12	31	88
TTR THIRTY YEARS ON THE TRACK	MCGUIRE	10	50	66
TTR THOSE OLD FAMILIAR SIGNS	WILSON	01	50	78
TTR THOUSAND DOLLARS FOR A LADDER		02	42	64
TTR THOUSAND MILER	JOHNS	08	74	11
TTR THREE HUNCHES	CONNOR	09	41	62
TTR THREE IN A ROW	BALLENGER	03	39	41
TTR THREE MILES AN HOUR	HYNING	12	38	51
TTR THREE NARROW ESCAPES	PUCKETT	10	32	408
TTR THREE TIMES AND SAFE (GN)	WEBSTER	05	46	88
TTR THREE-WAY FLAGGING (ATSF)		08	44	83
TTR THRILLED BY A VOICE	CARTER	01	30	310
TTR THROUGH HELL-ON WHEELS	LOGAN	09	34	76
TTR THROUGH THE REBEL LINES	DIAZ	11	31	516
TTR TICKETS, PLEASE! (NYC)	JOHNS	04	46	76
TTR TIEING UP THE RAILROAD	HUGHES	10	38	78
TTR TIMBERLAND INFERNO	GAGE	10	31	360
TTR TIME FREIGHTS (CN)	POWERS	02	46	66
TTR TNT FOR FUEL	KUHLER	10	32	405
TTR TO THE RESCUE	ATHANAS	02	48	110
TTR TOO DAMN BUSY (CN)		03	69	52
TTR TOO MANY DOGS	ERWIN	12	38	45
TTR TOPPING THE ROYAL SCOT	FRASER	11	38	42
TTR TORPEDOES!	WESTCOTT	09	32	210
TTR TOUGHEST TOWN IN THE WEST	DRUMMOND	12	32	31
TTR TRACK FOREMAN	VAN WINKLE	01	44	82
TTR TRACK-WALKER	DEEGAN	08	36	115
TTR TRAIN DETAINERS	REDDING	02	38	113
TTR TRAIN DISPATCHER	JASSERAND	03	38	123
TTR TRAIN DISPATCHER'S TROUBLES (S)	FOSS	02	43	75
TTR TRAIN ON THE HIGHWAY	GRANBERG	01	51	06
TTR TRAIN ORDERS FOR A HANDCAR (L&NW)		04	39	49
TTR TRAIN WAS THREE YEARS LATE (ATSF)		08	42	109
TTR TRAIN WRECK & A DATE WITH A GIRL		06	69	16
TTR TRAIN-ORDER SLIP-UP	HILLER	02	55	65
TTR TRAIN-WRECKING BABOON	BIGGS	01	55	59
TTR TRAINMASTER RIDES TO-NIGHT	JOHNS	04	31	124
TTR TRAPPED IN A SNOWSHED	MURPHY	02	31	426
TTR TRAVELING AUDITOR PART 1	JAMES	11	50	72
TTR TRAVELING AUDITOR PART 2	JAMES	12	50	58
TTR TRAVELING OP	SCHAEFFER	03	47	42
TTR TRAVELING OP PART 2	SCHAEFFER	04	47	56
TTR TRIALS OF A SUB	STUART	04	40	67
TTR TRIP TO GLORY (CGW)	KATTENBERG	04	42	94
TTR TUG-OF-WAR	HOPSON	04	41	84
TTR TUMBLING BOX CARS	CONNOR	01	31	263
TTR TURKEY CREEK BOOMS AGAIN	JOHNSTON	02	51	98
TTR TWELVE WEEKS ON THE PIKE	KILPATRICK	12	50	112
TTR TWENTY YEARS OF ACCIDENTS	GUNNISON	09	38	46
TTR TWO BOOMERS (SP)	HOELL	05	46	81
TTR TWO DAYS ON THE TURNTABLE	SISK	09	35	125
TTR TWO FEET FROM DEATH	GIROUARD	05	31	182
TTR TWO INCHES FROM DEATH	SEAMAN	03	30	588
TTR TWO MONTHS OVERDUE	SQUIRES	03	44	82
TTR TWO PAY-DAY THRILLS	SAMPLE	01	31	266
TTR TWO SCARED STIFFS	SABROWSKY	05	30	237
TTR TWO WORDS MISSING	EVERSOLE	09	42	95
TTR TWO-FOOT GAGE	MOODY	05	39	77
TTR TWO-FOOT GAGE (F&M)	SAVAGE	03	46	92
TTR UNCLE BILL'S BLUNDERS	BROWN	12	52	70
TTR UNCLE NAT	HINDS	12	47	104
TTR UNDER THE CARS	HILKER	04	32	98
TTR UNNECESSARY WORK	RIDGELEY	02	39	76
TTR UP AGAINST IT (GT)	PARRY	09	45	72
TTR VANISHED CONDUCTOR UTE PARK NM 1920		12	76	05
TTR VIGILANTES OF THE HIGH IRON	MAGUIRE	02	48	100
TTR WABASH WASHOUT SILENT SLIM	ROACH	08	45	70
TTR WAR PASSENGER	WATSON	02	35	48
TTR WE LIKE LIVING BY THE LINE	WINTER	09	51	95
TTR WEST JERSEY & SEASHORE	ALBERTSON	07	45	80
TTR WEST OF THE WATER TOWER (ROBBERY)		04	73	60
TTR WHAT IS A TRAIN?	PARKER	02	45	120
TTR WHAT WAS IT?	SPRIEGEL	10	37	81
TTR WHAT WOULD YOU DO?	GLOVER	05	44	112
TTR WHEN A MAN FORGETS	CRAWFORD	02	31	418
TTR WHEN A TANK TRAIN BUSTS LOOSE		01	32	241
TTR WHEN AIR BRAKES WERE NEW		10	33	120
TTR WHEN GUS LENBERG PRAYED	ROONEY	06	49	80
TTR WHEN I WAS A BOOMER OP	BEDWELL	04	37	112
TTR WHEN THE BUNCH WENT WEST	LAKEWOOD	04	31	40
TTR WHEN THE LINK-AND-PIN WENT OUT	WARD	10	34	77
TTR WHEN THE N&W CHANGED ITS GAGE		07	35	46
TTR WHEN VILLA CROSSED THE BORDER	TUMA	11	35	64
TTR WHEN YOU AND I WERE YOUNG	"OLD-TIMER"	07	42	147
TTR WHILE THE ANGEL WATCHED	KNAPKE	11	50	80
TTR WHO TO BLAME?	SISK	05	35	78
TTR WHY ENGINEERS GET GRAY	CHILDS	03	32	513
TTR WHY THE TRAIN WAS LATE		09	74	40
TTR WILD ENGINEERS "HIGHBALL JOHN"	BURNS	06	35	88
TTR WIRE TESTS ON THE BOOMER TRAIL	ARIZA	06	46	137
TTR WIRE TRAIN	MERRITT	10	39	41
TTR WIRELESS RAILROADING	ROONEY	06	38	94
TTR WOMAN OP	MOREHEAD	01	44	88

Railroad/Railfan

GENERAL RAILROADING

RAILROAD NON-FICTION		M	Y	P
TTR WOOD-BURNERS	BERRY	04	36	95
TTR WOOD-BURNING DAYS IN NEW ENGLAND		10	43	76
TTR WORSE AND WORSER	THOMAS	10	50	94
TTR WRECK OF THE 216	THORNE	07	51	06
TTR WRECK OF THE CANNON BALL-C&O-SANDERS		01	33	76
TTR WRECKER CREW (NP)	ALLEN	10	55	24
TTR WRECKING BOSS	WC "CAP" WHITE	08	35	32
TTR WRECKING MASTER	RANDALL	06	55	43
TTR WRECKS AND RUNAWAYS	VOORHEES	06	41	88
TTR WRONG DESTINATION	FOSS	01	43	115
TTR YANKING THE HOOK AROUND	BROWN	05	50	86
TTR YELLOW FEVER	JAMES	08	50	56
TTR YOU CAN'T ROB A MAIL CAR	MOORE	06	51	74
TTR YOUTH IN THE SADDLE	ERWIN	06	38	90
TTR YULETIDE RUNAWAY (D&RG)	SIBLEY	01	42	80
TTR ZULUS	THOMAS	09	52	66
TUNNEL COLLAPSE MYSTERY C&O 1925		10	78	10
TUNNEL TROUBLES PRR	LEE	08	53	06
TWENTY MINUTES	BUCK	01	53	06
TWO HOURS AT HUNTER TOWER, NEWARK NJ		08	77	48R
TWO THOUSAND MILES BY TROLLEY		04	61	18
UNION PACIFIC: POCATELLO NIGHT YARDMASTR		12	40	19
UNION PACIFIC: POCATELLO-BIG RAIL CENTER		12	40	19
VIA: A NIGHT TO REMEMBER		01	82	30
VOLUNTEER FIREMAN--CUYAHOGA VALLEY LINE		07	80	55
WABASH WESTWARD "CITY OF ST LOUIS" RIDE		01	84	59
WANDERLUST	SWAN	07	45	08
WANDERLUST 2 MALDEN YARDS	SWAN	03	77	38
WANDERLUST 4 A BOOMERS LIFE HISTORY		05	77	11
WANDERLUST 5 LIFE STORY OF A BOOMER		06	77	34
WANDERLUST PART 2		08	45	116
WANDERLUST PART 3	SWAN	09	45	114
WANDERLUST PART 3	MAXWELL SWAN	04	77	34
WANDERLUST PART 4 CONCLUSION	SWAN	10	45	108
WANDERLUST-BOOMERS LIFE STORY	MAX SWAN	02	77	10
WEEKEND FIREMAN ON C&NW 4-6-0		SU	75	46R
WELCOMING COMMITTEE--WESTERN STYLE		04	48	93
WET GRAIN SACKS IN THE TUNNEL 1921 ATSF		06	78	11
WHAT ABOUT THAT WRECK?		03	48	10
WHAT MOTIVATED THE BOOMERS?	KNAPKE	09	73	26
WHEN I WAS A TRAIN AUDITOR	AIRD	05	42	116
WHEN I WAS AN ICC LOCOMOTIVE INSPECTOR		01	67	38
WHIP, THE (MELODRAMA)	O'CONNOR	12	48	10
WHISTLING HOGGERS (SOUTHERN)	MONROE	05	45	10
WHITE FLAGS ON A 2-10-0 (CP)		10	77	23
WHY THE TRAIN WAS LATE (GT)		02	45	74
WILD HOGGERS AND NO BRAKES	SMITH	10	59	26
WOODBURNING ENGINE TRUE STORIES		02	60	17
WORK TRAINS	KNAPKE	10	61	20
WORKING ON THE RAILROAD	ALLEN	10	52	06
WRCKING BOSS'S WIFE	BRUNNER	04	59	18
WRECK OF OLD 97, THE SONG AND HOGGER		01	34	37
WRECKING BOSS ON THE SOUTHERN	WHITE	11	77	13
WRECKING BOSS: DAVID GOODMAN		01	72	32
WRECKING ENGINEER: ATSF RECALLS BIG HOOK		06	42	06

RAILROAD NON-FICTION		M	Y	P
WRECKS TO ORDER BY "HEAD ON JOE"		08	77	10
Y COMES TO BABAHATCHIE, THE		02	43	106
YULE CABOOSE	THOMAS	01	52	10

RAILROAD PEOPLE		M	Y	P
33 "RAIL" SONS IN 5 FAMILIES		04	31	95
ALLEN, WILLIAM: 100 YEARS OF STD TIME		11	83	51
ASHLEY, JIM-RAILFAN WHO WANTED TO OWN RR		10	38	64
BEATTY, ED PRESIDENT OF CP		06	31	376
BECKER, HENRY E: CENTERVILLE & SOUTHWEST		11	48	66
BEDWELL, HARRY REMEMBERED BY READER		09	75	04
BEGGS, EUGENE: FOUNDER/MFG OF MINI STEAM		08	49	41
BELL, HARVEY W.: BELL GEARED LOCOS		02	46	57
BELMONT, AUGUST P: RAILROAD TYCOON		02	56	46
BEMIS, FRANK: LEDGE WALKER B&M		01	71	10
BERGOFF, PEARL L. STRIKE-BREAKER		06	35	34
BLOUNT, NELSON: HIS STORY		06	67	19
BOLLMAN, WENDELL: DESIGNER/CONST ENGINEE		07	46	54
BRADY, DIAMOND JIM: RR SUPPLY SALESMAN		09	33	38
BULLARD, JIM-CONDUCTOR RI		05	30	161
BUNCH, GENE: TRAIN ROBBER		07	69	34
CAREY, BILL-RAILROAD BUILDER		01	31	273
CARROLL, CHARLES: B&O DIRECTOR 1827		03	77	58
CARTER, CHARLES F. (OBITUARY)		03	40	112
CARTER, HENRIETTA: RAILFANETTE		04	41	76
CHRISTMAS, LEE HOGHEAD-HONDURAS DICTATR		05	34	04
CHRYSLER, CHARLES:MILLION $ MULLIGAN"		08	76	11
CLAPPER MELVIN "COON": FOREMAN OF H&BTOP		01	54	06
CLEMENTSON, CHARLES E: USRA		07	39	19
COFFIN, LORENZO S. REV: RR SAFETY CRUSAD		09	47	130
COFFIN, LORENZO S.--SAFETY CRUSADOR		04	38	57
CONNOLLY , "HEAD ON" JOE:WRECK SPECIALIS		06	62	42
COOK, G.W.: SNOWSTORMS D&RG		09	34	93
COUP, WC: REVOLUTIONIZED CIRCUS TRAVEL		02	30	330
CRAWFORD, GRIFF-TRAIN DISPATCHER-HIS LIF		06	30	379
CROOKS, WILLIAM: RAILROAD CHIEF ENGINEER		07	76	51
CUMMINGS, CAPT ALBERT:SWITCH & SIGNAL IN		01	65	64
DAFT, LEO:FIRST PRACTICAL ELECTRIC LOCO		04	62	47
DAVIS, SAM: CONFEDERATE SPY		03	53	135
DEBS, EUGENE VICTOR-LEADER OF LOST CAUSE		12	37	43
DELLINGER, E.S. WRITER-MOP/FRISCO WORKER		05	33	65
DELLINGER, ES: AUTHOR		05	76	06
DICKENS, AUGUSTUS: CHARLES' BROTHER		04	68	26
DIESEL, DR RUDOLPH: MYSTERIOUS DISAPPEAR		06	57	43
DIESEL, DR. RUDOLPH		05	43	78
DIESEL, RUDOLF: INVENTOR OF LOCOMOTIVES		04	55	19
DIESEL, RUDOLPH: WILSON REMEMBERS		10	57	18
DISNEY, WALT: LOVER OF TRAINS		10	65	06
DOAK, BILL-FARMER/MUDHOP/SECRETARY LABOR		03	31	561
DODGE, G.M. PIONEER RAILROAD BUILDER		05	33	87
DOWNS, LARRY SECTION BOSS'S SON		12	32	107
DOYLE, SANLEY:FROM BOOMER TO SUPREME CT		06	66	58
DRANEY, JOHN: LOCOMOTIVE ENGINEER		01	30	161
DRAYTON, JOHN:MAN WITH 8000 IDEAS		02	63	25

560

Railroad/Railfan

GENERAL RAILROADING

RAILROAD PEOPLE	M	Y	P
DUDLEY, C.B.: AUTHORITY ON STEEL RAILS	07	47	12
DUMOIS, ANGELO: FATHER OF SUGAR RAILROAD	04	57	22
DWINELL, LANE: GOVERNOR OF NEW HAMPSHIRE	08	55	64
EARP, JAMES W-CONDUCTOR CRI&P-HIS LIFE	05	30	256
EASLEY, JOE: "RAILROAD"MAGAZINE CARTOONS	04	72	33
EASLEY, JOE: RAILROAD ILLUSTRATOR	08	51	126
EASLEY, JOE: RAILROAD MAGAZINE ARTIST	12	67	25
EDDY, WILSON--MASTER MECHANIC"EDDY CLOCK	08	38	94
EDMONDSON, THOMAS: RAILROAD TICKETS	08	75	58
EGAN, BILL-STATION MASTER DELUXE	08	30	01
EIFFEL, ALEXANDRE RAILROAD BRIDGE BLDR	08	72	11
ELROD, ROBERT S: FIREMAN HONORED BY PRES	05	39	24
ELSTE, GEORGE W: SAFETY SUPER B&O	10	50	10
ERTHAL, FRANK: LI TRAINMAN	05	46	112
EVANS, JOHN: DENVER'S GREATEST RAILROADER	09	48	18
FALKNER, WILLIAM C: RAILROAD BUILDR GM&O	03	54	22
FARR, EDWARD: LOCO ENGINEER READING RR	04	36	81
FE FAMOUS ENINEERS	01	34	57
FE "LUCKY BILL" HOCKENBERGER UP	08	34	65
FE CHARLIE FROTHINGHAM C&NW	05	34	29
FE CY WARMAN D&RG	01	34	57
FE DANIEL WILLARD B&O	06	34	27
FE DENNIS CASSIN NYC&HR	04	34	126
FE FRANK MCMANAMY C&WM	03	34	39
FE JOHN CAVINS C&O	07	34	59
FE MATT H SHAY ERIE	02	34	105
FE TULL WATERS	09	34	68
FINK, DAVID: MC PRESIDENT ON GUILFORD	05	83	28
FLAGLER, HENRY M: 1830-1913 TRAIN NAMED	04	40	138
FLYING DUTCHMAN: ENGINEER JOHN GULMYER	01	38	58
FRENCH, EDWARD SANBORN: PRESIDENT B&M	01	46	31
FURLONG, THOMAS: RAILROAD BULL	02	66	45
GARCIA, JESUS HERO OF NACOZARI (MEXICO)	10	33	70
GARLICK, JEHU: TINPLATE PIONEER	12	46	116
GATES, CHARLES--"BET A MILLION"	10	62	36
GERARD, CAPTAIN JH: TRAIN ROBBER	08	61	34
GN GENERAL MANAGER, JAMES H. O'NEILL	05	32	214
GOULD, GEORGE: COAST TO COAST RAILROAD	06	37	38
GOULD, JAY: RAILROAD MANIPULATOR	07	36	26
GOULD, JAY: SHORT NOTE ON	09	66	32
GRAHAM, MAURY: ELECTED KING OF HOBOS	05	77	08
GRESBY, HERBERT: WORLDS FASTEST STEAM LOC	10	76	47
GULMYER, JOHN: FLYING DUTCHMAN	01	38	58
GUTHRIE, JAMES: PRESIDENT OF L&N 1859	06	78	57
HALCEY, CARL: PRISONER BUILDS LOCO MODE	11	39	65
HALL, HAROLD NSO VP RETIRES	12	87	46
HALLIDIE, ANDREW SMITH: MANY INVENTIONS	11	45	90
HAND, NELLIE: HEROINE DEC 11 1905	10	52	65
HAND, NELLIE: P&R HEROINE OF 1905	04	75	11
HARNDEN, WILLIAM F: RAILWAY EXPRESS AGEN	10	48	94
HARRIMAN, EDWARD HENRY: GREATEST RR MAN	06	36	27
HARVEY, FRED: HARVEY HOUSES	04	58	44
HAUPT, GENERAL WILLIAM: PRR & CIVIL WAR	03	74	33
HAYS, MILTON D: PRESIDENT OF TWO RAILROAD	11	35	111
HAYWIRE MAC SEE MCCLINTOCK, HARRY OBIT	10	57	57

RAILROAD PEOPLE	M	Y	P
HEENAN, PETER "THE PEACEFUL" LABOR MINIS	08	31	25
HEINEKEN, DR JOHN: C&AM WRECK 1855	10	73	58
HENNESSEY, JOHN J: MASTER CAR BUILDER	04	58	39
HENRY, JAWN (JOHN) NEGRO STEEL DRIVER	09	34	66
HILL, JIM: FOUNDER OF GN	12	78	20
HILL, JIM: GREAT NORTHERN FOUNDED BY HIM	02	37	34
HILL, SAM: FAMOUS HOGGER	04	57	38
HOBO RIDING THE RODS PHOTO	12	75	04
HOGAN, CHARLES: 65 YEARS OF RAILROADING	03	30	481
HOWE, WILLIAM: VALVE GEAR INVENTOR	09	75	59
HUNT, JOEL: CIVIL ENGINEER	03	77	47
HYLAN, JOHN F.-TRAINMAN TO JUDGE IN NYC	02	31	400
IR INTERESTING RAILFAN IR	01	77	00
IR ALBRECHT, HARRY: HISTORIAN #71	11	68	30
IR ALEXANDER, EDWIN: COLLECTOR AUTHOR #12	02	63	18
IR ALLEN, CECIL: 2 MILLION MILES #39	03	66	18
IR ALLEN, GARY: PHOTOGRAPHER #104	08	71	38
IR ALLEN, RICHARD: D&H PHOTOGRAPHER #155	11	75	33
IR APPEL, WALTER: WEEKLY HOBBY WRITER #78	06	69	26
IR ARCARA, ROGER: RAIL GENERAL KNOW #192	12	78	54
IR ARONE, FRED: RAILROADIANA #54	06	67	38
IR ARPAN, ROY: RADIO RAILFAN #159	03	76	13
IR AUDIBERT, J HOWARD: PHOTOGRAPHER #136	04	74	38
IR BAILEY, FREDERICK: STEAMTOWN FOUND#160	04	76	23
IR BARR, HOWARD: PHOTOGRAPHER #69	09	68	20
IR BARRIGER, JOHN: RAIL EXECUTIVE #14	06	63	34
IR BEEBE, LUCIUS: AUTHOR #3	08	61	17
IR BEST, JERRY: AUTHOR RAILFAN #16	10	63	32
IR BOGLE, COL JAMES: HISTORIAN #49	01	67	22
IR BRADLEY, JAMES: COLLECTOR #127	07	73	31
IR BRAMSON, SETH: FL LARGEST COLLECTR#148	04	75	26
IR BRIDGES, WAYNE: C&A PUMP HOUSE #150	06	75	34
IR BROWN, JAMES: CANADIAN FAN #27	03	65	32
IR BRUCW, RUSSELL: FOREIGN PHOTOGRAP #186	06	78	12
IR BYE, RANULPH: RAIL PAINTER #142	10	74	37
IR CARLETON, PAUL: RAILFAN PUBLISHER #29	05	65	38
IR CARTER, WARREN: RAILFAN #31	07	65	34
IR CASTNER, CHARLES: KENTUCKY ROADS #128	08	73	22
IR CHARLTON, E HARPER: TRACTION #52	04	67	36
IR CHEESBOROUGH, TOM: CAMERAMAN #135	03	74	36
IR CHRISTIANSEN, HARRY: CTS OFFICIAL #119	11	72	34
IR CLARK, FRED JR #169	01	77	12
IR CLAYTOR, W GRAHAM: RAIL SUPER #86	02	70	28
IR CLEGG, CHARLES: PHOTOGRAPHER #62	02	68	20
IR CLODFLTER, FRANK: S RY ENGINEER #164	08	76	12
IR COLE, NORMAN: ENGINEER & CONDUCTOR#144	12	74	32
IR COLEMAN, ALFRED: ENTREPRENEUR #115	07	72	32
IR COMSTOCK, HENRY: PAINTER #70	10	68	24
IR CONIGLIO, JOHN: RAIL PHOTOGRAPHER #194	05	79	47
IR COOK, DICK: LOCO ENGINEER STAFF #167	11	76	18
IR CORTANI, ROGER: PACIFIC NEWS ED #146	02	75	54
IR CRUMP, SPENCER: AUTHOR/PUBLISHER #88	04	70	30
IR CUMMINGS, DOUG: NRHS CHAPTER PRES #80	08	69	22
IR DAVIS, OWEN: RAILROADIANNA EXPERT #5	10	61	10
IR DEGOLYER, EVERETT: AUTHOR #34	10	65	31

Railroad/ Railfan

GENERAL RAILROADING

RAILROAD PEOPLE		M	Y	P
IR DEMORO, HARRE:TROLLEYS	#103	07	71	34
IR DENLINGER, DONALD:CABOOSE MOTEL	#132	12	73	22
IR DONOVAN, FRANK: AUTHOR "TRAINS"	#19	04	64	32
IR DUBIN ART, AUTHOR	#21	08	64	34
IR DUKE, DONALD:EDITOR PAC RY JOURNAL	#15	08	63	20
IR DUNSCOMB, GUY:RAIL HOBBIEST	#139	07	74	55
IR EAGLESTON, MICHAEL PHOTOGRAPHER	#72	12	68	34
IR EDMONSTON, JAMES:DIESEL EXPERT	#111	03	72	29
IR EHRLICH, BRONETTE:NRHS	#26	02	65	34
IR EMERICK, JACK:STEAM LOCO BUFF	#75	03	69	20
IR ENTRINGER, ROSEMARY:M ED TRAINS	#11	12	62	33
IR FERRELL, MALLORY: AUTHOR	#133	01	74	38
IR FESCO, JACK:ENGINEER/FAN	#73	01	69	26
IR FINK, DANIEL: PHOTOGRAPHER	#116	08	72	27
IR FISHER, CHARLIE: RL&HS FOUNDER	#6	02	62	29
IR FISHER, RALPH*B&M BREAKMAN	#179	11	77	19
IR FISTELL, IRA:RAIL RADIO PERSONAL	#96	12	70	24
IR FOSS, GILBERT: BEAR CREAK RR	#66	06	68	32
IR FOX, JOSEPH: CYCLOPEDIA RR LORE	#130	10	73	52
IR GARDE, PAUL:COLORADO PHOTOGRAPHER	#37	01	66	21
IR GARLAND, BARRY:SIERRA MT CLUB	#157	01	76	16
IR GERHART, GEORGE:MARRIED TO AMTRAK	#143	11	74	20
IR GIL, EARL:MORRIS COUNTY CENTRAL	#131	11	73	43
IR GOLSON, WILBER:LE BUFF	#13	04	63	34
IR GRAVES, ROY: ENGINEMAN	#81	09	69	26
IR GREENE, HOWARD:ORGANIZATION HEAD	#109	01	72	29
IR GRIFFITHS, HANK:RAIL CAMERA ARTIST	#30	06	65	34
IR GUIDO, FRANCIS:RAILFAN & LECTURER	#33	09	65	34
IR GUTOHRLEIN, ADOLF:PHOTOGRAPHER	#32	08	65	24
IR HAERTLEIN, JEFF:CABOOSE OWNER	#168	12	76	18
IR HARDY, GRAHAME:TRANSPORTATION COL	#1	04	61	60
IR HART, GEORGE: READING SPECIALIST	#7	02	62	33
IR HASTINGS, PHILIP:AUTHOR	#85	01	70	17
IR HASWELL, ANTHONY:PASS RR SERVICE	#67	07	68	30
IR HAUCK, CORNELIUS:COL RR MUSEUM	#188	08	78	12
IR HEDGE, JOHN:WHISTLE COLLECTOR	#196	01	80	46
IR HELCK, PETER:RAIL PAINTER	#154	10	75	16
IR HESS, BOB:BLACK DIAMOND FARM	#22	10	64	34
IR HOGAN, ROBERT:STEAM PHOTOGRAPHER	#113	05	72	28
IR HOLLEY, NOEL:ELECTRIC RAILROADING	#184	04	78	35
IR HOLST, JACK:NRHS PACIFIC NW CHAP	#114	06	72	36
IR HOLTON, JAMES:RAILROAD PAINTER	#183	03	78	12
IR HORN, GEORGE:RAPID TRANSIT	#94	10	70	35
IR HUBBARD, FREEMAN: EDITOR	#100	04	71	22
IR JANSSEN, OTTO:FOUNDER NARP	#137	05	74	42
IR JENSEN, OLIVER:AMERICAN HERITAGE	#162	06	76	16
IR JERNSTROM, BILL:PHOTOGRAPHER	#40	04	66	30
IR JOHNSON, RON:SCHOOL TEACHER	#166	10	76	16
IR JOHNSTON, HENRY:AUTHOR	#43	07	66	27
IR JONES, CLINTON:STEAM LOCO OWNER	#74	02	69	27
IR JONES, WILLIAM:COLORADO RR MUSEUM	#170	02	77	16
IR KALMBACH, ALBERT:TRAINS PUBLISHER	#2	06	61	31
IR KESSEL, WILLIAM:BCR VETERAN	#134	02	74	26
IR KIMBALL, WARD:GRIZZLY FLATS RR	#28	04	65	25
IR KING, NATHAN:CAR REPAIR MAN	#108	12	71	33
IR KOCH, MICHAEL:SHAY EXPERT	#110	02	72	30
IR KRAMBECK, WESLEY:RI RAILFAN	#180	12	77	12
IR KUHLER, OTTO:PAINTER DESIGNER	#18	02	64	30
IR KYPER, FRANK:EBT FAN	#165	09	76	14
IR LANGLEY, ALBERT:NRHS DEVOTEE	#98	02	71	32
IR LAUGHLIN, DOROTHY: TOURIST ROAD	#55	07	67	28
IR LAVALLEE, OMER:RAIL HISTORIAN	#48	12	66	32
IR LEVIN, RUBEN:EDITOR OF "LABOR"	#53	05	67	24
IR LEWIS, IRENE:LIVE-STEAMER BUILDER	#47	11	66	34
IR LEWIS, ROBERT:PRES STONE HARBOR	#50	02	67	30
IR LIND, DON:MUSEUM BUILDER	#175	07	77	14
IR LINDEN, ROBERT:CONDUCTOR	#99	03	71	29
IR LLOYD, ARTHUR:EXCURSIONS	#44	08	66	36
IR LYONS, THOMAS:PHOTOGRAPHER-FAN	#151	07	75	42
IR MAGUIRE, STEPHEN:TRANSIT TOPICS	#58	10	67	24
IR MCGUIRE, RAMONA:ROAD RIDER	#161	05	76	14
IR MEANEY, FRANCIS:NATT PRESIDENT	#174	06	77	41
IR MIDCAP, WILLIAM: ENGINEER & FAN	#60	12	67	28
IR MIDDLEBROOK, PHIL:RETIRED HOGGER	#65	05	68	22
IR MIDDLETON, WILLIAM:CIVIL ENG R FAN	#84	12	69	30
IR MILLER, KRISTOFER:RAIL MUSEUM	#95	11	70	30
IR MOEDINGER, WILLIAM: PULLMAN COND	#56	08	67	24
IR MONAGHAN, DAN:PASSENGER TRAIN CON	#172	04	77	13
IR MORANT, NICHOLAS:PHOTOGRAPHER	#118	10	72	20
IR MORGAN, DAVID: EDITOR OF "TRAINS"	#5	12	61	39
IR MORGAN, WILLIAM:GIRLS & TRAINS	#190	10	78	23
IR MURDOCK, RICHARD:SP ENGINEER	#117	09	72	32
IR MURWAY, RICHARD: ED LOCO ENGINEER	#57	09	67	23
IR NEUBAUER, JAMES:RI STEAM POWER	#120	12	72	36
IR NIXON, RON:RAIL PHOTOGRAPHER	#76	04	69	24
IR NORWOOD, JOHN:PHOTOGRAPHER	#171	03	77	11
IR OATES, JOSEPH:SCL SUPERVISOR-FAN	#176	08	77	16
IR OST, MELVILLE:RR ENTHUSIASTS PRES	#158	02	76	14
IR PAGE, HERMAN:SEMINARY & RAILS	#149	05	75	40
IR PEGLER, ALAN:ENGLISH DRIVER	#87	03	70	20
IR PENNYPACKER, BERT:AUTHOR	#91	07	70	36
IR PLOMER, JAMES:AFRICAN BORN FAN	#185	05	78	22
IR PLOMER, JAMES:REVISITED	#185	06	78	26
IR PLUMMER, ROGER:EX-HOGGER	#163	07	76	24
IR PONTIN, JACK:ENGINEER & PHOTOGRAP	#24	12	64	29
IR PRICE, GRATTAN:SHENANDOAH CENTRAL	#101	05	71	30
IR PURDIE, WILLIAM:S MASTER MECHANIC	#121	01	73	27
IR QUIMBY, EJ:ERA FOUNDER	#8	06	62	26
IR RAMSDELL, ALICE: RAIL COLLECTOR	#61	01	68	23
IR RAPP, WILLIAM:RAILROAD STATIONS	#124	04	73	28
IR REDDEN, ROBERT:PHOTOGRAPHER--FAN	#178	10	77	14
IR REICH, SY: ROSTER KING	#59	11	67	34
IR REID, H:PHOTOGRAPHER & AUTHOR	#17	12	63	44
IR REYNOLDS, RICHARD:SIERRA FAN TRIP	#189	09	78	26
IR RICHARDSON, BOB:RAILROAD PHOTOS	#20	06	64	26
IR RINKE, HERMAN:REA SECRETARY	#68	08	68	24
IR ROBINSON, DON:SIGNAL MAN	#105	09	71	34
IR RODWELL, DIANNE:CABOOSE DEVOTEE	#193	01	79	23
IR ROHRER, EVERETT:FAN MODELER	#129	09	73	56
IR RUFFELL, RAY:ENGLISH RAILFAN	#173	05	77	22

Railroad/Railfan

GENERAL RAILROADING

Stephans' Railroad Directory

RAILROAD PEOPLE		M	Y	P
IR SAGLE, LAWRENCE: B&O EXPERT	#97	01	71	32
IR SAUNDERS, IVAN: B&O STEAMERS	#79	07	69	36
IR SCRIBBINS, JIM: TIMETABLES	#38	02	66	24
IR SHEDD, THOMAS: MODERN RAILROADS ED	#51	03	67	34
IR SIMS, RONALD: TROLLEYS & INTERURB	#138	06	74	16
IR SKIDMORE, MERRILL: RR FACT & FICT	#82	10	69	36
IR SMITH, DWIGHT: PHOTOGRAPHER	#106	10	71	37
IR SOLOMON, THOMAS: RAIL PAINTER	#177	09	77	12
IR SPAUGH, BISHOP HERBERT: CABOOSE	#112	04	72	42
IR SPRINGER, FRED: PHOTOGRAPHER	#125	05	73	30
IR STAFF, VIRGIL: PHOTOGRAPHER	#92	08	70	20
IR STAHL, CARROLL: 4' GAUGE RR	#45	09	66	26
IR STAUFER, ALVIN: RAIL ARTIST	#25	01	65	36
IR STEINHEIMER, RICHARD: PHOTOGRAPHER	#181	01	78	13
IR STEUERNAGEL, ELMER: BUILDER PLATES	#89	05	70	26
IR STINDT, FRED: RAIL PHOTOGRAPHER	#10	10	62	27
IR SULZER, ELMER: GHOST RR WRITER	#141	09	74	25
IR SUMMERS, BETTY: ARTIST	#153	09	75	26
IR SWETT, IRA: ORGANIST-AUTHOR	#107	11	71	32
IR TAIBI, JOHN: THE LENSMEN	#140	08	74	33
IR THOMAS, EDISON: RAIL HISTORIAN	#35	11	65	28
IR TOWLER, ERNIE: RAIL PAINTER	#182	02	78	26
IR TRELOAR, ELMER: RAIL LINGUIST	#90	06	70	35
IR TUTWILER, DAVID: RAIL PAINTER	#191	11	78	37
IR UCKLEY, JOHN: HUMAN-INTEREST PHOT	#145	01	75	20
IR VIEKMAN, WILLIAM: OWNER & COLLECTOR	#41	05	66	30
IR VOLLRATH, HAROLD: TRAIN DISPATCHER	#83	11	69	32
IR WAGNER, WILLIAM: NRHS BULLETIN ED	#147	03	75	24
IR WALKER, CHARD: CAJON PASS	#126	06	73	28
IR WALSH, THOMAS: MEXICAN RY AUTHOR	#187	07	78	16
IR WALTERS, COLE: CHARLESTON NRHS	#122	02	73	22
IR WEBBER, WILLIAM: PHOTOGRAPHER	#102	06	71	34
IR WEBER, ARTHUR: FAN TRIP PROMOTER	#77	05	69	34
IR WEST, HARWELL: BRASS POUNDER	#156	12	75	24
IR WHITAKER, ROGERS: RAILFAN MILEAGE R	#9	08	62	25
IR WHITE, ELWOOD: LOGGING ROADS	#46	10	66	28
IR WHITE, JOHN: SMITHSONIAN	#93	09	70	26
IR WILMUNDER, HAL: RAILROAD OWNER	#36	12	65	30
IR WINTERS, CHARLES: WEEKEND ENGINEER	#195	07	79	47
IR WITHUHN, BILL: ENGINEER FAN	#152	08	75	20
IR WOOD, DON: PHOTOGRAPHER	#63	03	68	28
IR WURM, TED: RAILROADIANA	#64	04	68	22
IR YOUNG, BILL: SHORTLINE EXPERT	#23	11	64	30
IR ZIEL, RON: AUTHOR-PHOTOGRAPHER	#42	06	66	34
JACKSON, KIRBY C. PRR OLDEST LIVE VETERN		07	32	500
JAMES, JESSE JR: SON OF TRAIN ROBBER		09	51	133
JAMES, JESSE SHORT NOTE		05	66	13
JAMES, JESSE--TRAIN ROBBER		09	32	198
JANNEY, ELI H: AUTOMATIC COUPLER INVENTR		08	53	61
JONES, CASEY		12	38	71
JONES, CASEY AND FAMILY		03	48	132
JONES, CASEY SURVIVORS OF WRECK		08	67	08
JONES, CASEY-TRIP TO THE PROMISED LAND		12	32	94
JONES, CASEY: RELATIVES		07	33	139
JONES, CASEY: LEGEND DEBUNKED		02	76	06

RAILROAD PEOPLE	M	Y	P
JOSEPH REYNOLDS-"DIAMOND JO" REYNOLDS	03	36	39
JUDAH, THEODORE D: CONSTRUCTION ENGINEER	10	35	73
KAUKE, PHILLIPS: NEEDLES DISTRICT VETERAN	01	84	41
KETCHUM, JERRY: FRIS DEPOT PASS REPRESEN	05	48	106
KING, JB--WHO WAS HE?	06	61	35
KNAPKE, BILL: HE'S WRITING A BOOK AT 95	10	64	46
KUHLER, OTTO--PAINTER	08	77	02
KURALT, CHARLES: EXPLORING AMERICA A PASS	05	83	38
LAWSON, THOMAS: AUTHOR SHORT LINE EXPERT	04	63	08
LEIPER, THOMAS: FIRST RR IN UNITED STATES	08	60	26
LINCOLN, ABRAHAM-RAILROAD LAWYER TO PRES	02	31	328
LOEWY, RAYMOND REDISCOVERED	07	78	18R
MAGUIRE, STEVE: EDITOR, MAGISTRATE, CONDU	11	65	64
MALLET, ANATOLE INVENTOR OF MALLET LOCO	01	32	194
MALLET, ANATOLE: INVENTOR OF LOCOMOTIVES	08	55	26
MANN, COLONEL WILLIAM: CARBUILDER/BLACKM	06	59	24
MATTHIAS BALDWIN-WHO WAS HE?	02	77	57
MATUSCHKA, SYLVESTER--SEMAPHORES//WRECKS	09	33	76
MCCLINTOCK, HARRY: GREAT RAIL SINGER	09	72	42
MCCOY ELIJAH: INVENTOR OF OIL CUP & MORE	01	76	08
MCMILLAN, ROBERT TP&W PRESIDENT INTERVIE	07	83	54
MCQUEEN, WALTER: SCHENECTADY LOCO WORKS	04	60	28
MEARS, OTTO: BUILDS MOUNTAIN RR (SNO)	02	41	76
MEET "RAILS AFTER DARK"	07	85	16
MEET ANDREESEN, LA VERNE: SNOWPLOWS	03	83	22
MEET APPEL, WALTER: RAILNEWS	W	76	57R
MEET BAILEY, T BRAMWELL: SOUTH PARIS SWIT	09	85	27
MEET BALKIN, MARK: RAIL SOUND RECORDER	07	79	60
MEET BENDER, HENRY: RAILFANNING IN CHINA	11	79	53
MEET BENSON, TED: PHOTO CONTEST WINNER	10	77	57R
MEET BLABEY, E.H. II-OB&PA	F	75	59R
MEET BLAIR KOOISTRA: BN ALCOS	03	79	57R
MEET BLEDSOE, STEVEN: 13 YEAR OLD PHOTOGR	05	84	19
MEET BOHI, CHARLES: DEPOTS	05	84	20
MEET BOYD, RON: RIO GRANDE ZEPHYR ARTIST	05	81	16
MEET BROWN, P H SPIKE: MUSEUM TRAIN	F	76	57R
MEET BROWN, RANDOLPH: ICC EXAMINER & AUTHO	W	75	59R
MEET BURTON, CHARLES: LAKE SUPERIOR & IS	07	85	19
MEET CADY, RON: DETROIT & MACKINAC	07	78	57R
MEET CAVANAUGH, EH: FL9'S	12	77	53R
MEET CHARLES FELSTEAD: CP PHOTOGRAPHER	03	79	57R
MEET CLEMENS, DAVID: PHOTOGRAPHER	W	76	57R
MEET CLOUSE, KEITH: P&LE RIVER BOATS	11	86	22
MEET CLOUSER, WILLIAM: TRACTION	W	74	60R
MEET CLOVIS BUTTERWORTH: CUMBRES & TOLTEC	11	78	56R
MEET COATES, WES: LACKAWANNA ELECTRICS	07	81	19
MEET COURTNEY, ROBERT: KCS F UNITS	11	83	28
MEET CRAFT, JOHN: MISSISSIPPIAN & MAGNOLA	12	87	39
MEET CROSBY, JIM: ALCO SHORT LINES	03	82	21
MEET CUPPER, DANIEL: LIBERATION OF PRR K4	01	86	25
MEET CURRY, BRUCE: RUTLAND REVIVAL	SU	75	59R
MEET DAMATO, CHRIS: TEXAS TRANSPORTATION	05	78	57R
MEET DELVECCHIO, MICHAEL: VCR BASICS	07	87	16
MEET DI CENSO, ALFRED: VIDEOS	03	86	20
MEET DONALD KAPLAN: STILL INTERURBANS	11	78	56R

Railroad/Railfan

GENERAL RAILROADING

RAILROAD PEOPLE	M	Y	P
MEET DORFLINGER,DON:PHOTO CONTEST WINNER	10	77	57R
MEET DORN,DICK-OREGONS LOGGERS	08	77	57R
MEET DURFEE, ROGER:AKRON & BARBERTON BEL	01	84	13
MEET EAGLESON, MIKE: INTERNATIONAL STEAM	09	79	57
MEET EDWARDS, DOUG:AKRON & BARBERTON BEL	01	84	10
MEET FISHER, LARRY: DDAX UP #6923	03	81	21
MEET FLANARY, JOHN: APPALACHIAN ODYSSEY	11	82	36
MEET GAYDEK, JERRY: SAGANAW BOUND	05	80	57
MEET GELETZKE, CHARLES:D&TSL AUTHORITY	07	81	20
MEET GRIFFITHS, HENRY:STEAM ON CAMAS PRAI	02	78	57R
MEET HARMEN,ROBERT & GAYLE:COL & WYOMING	SU	76	57R
MEET HARROP, DB: CENTENNIAL SUMMER	03	85	22
MEET HART, BOB: PHOTOGRAPHER	07	85	18
MEET HARWOOD,HERBERT: RUBBER TIRED SWITCH	02	78	57R
MEET HASTINGS, PHILIP: WEEKEND IN HOUSTON	11	79	53
MEET HENLEY, MARK: MCCLOUD RIVER	11	82	36
MEET HOFFMAN,DAVID: NASA RESIDENT RAILRO	09	82	29
MEET HOLMES, ROGER: TP&W TIP UP	07	83	22
MEET HUDDLESTON,GENE: KENOVA COAL	04	78	57R
MEET HUTCHINGS, RICHARD: SAGINAW SOUTHBOND	05	80	57
MEET ILLMAN, JOHN: CHURCHILL-LYNN LAKE	03	83	22
MEET JAY MILLER: HOUSTON BELT & TERMINAL	01	79	57R
MEET JOHNSEN, KENNETH: WASHINGTON CENTRAL	09	87	20
MEET JOHNSON,RONALD: MAINE CENTRAL	07	78	57R
MEET JOLITZ, BILL:GREAT FREIGHT '79	01	80	57
MEET JOSEPH OATES:CREATURES OF BONE VAL	11	78	65R
MEET KAMISHER, JOEL: WHISTLE-STOPPING	05	81	19
MEET KARSTEN,BOB: LOUISIANA SHORT LINES	04	78	57R
MEET KATTAU, HAL:CARTOONIST	SU	76	57R
MEET KAUFFMAN, MIKI: MCCLOUD RIVER	11	82	36
MEET KELCEC,TOM:SNOUTS & TUNNEL MOTORS	SP	75	58R
MEET KELLER,RON: APACHE RAILWAY	07	79	60
MEET KELLY, BRUCE: BN "FUNNEL"	12	87	38
MEET KILLIAN,CHUCK: FIVE ALCOS AND A MACK	05	79	60
MEET KING, PAUL: TEXAS STATE RAILROAD	05	84	16
MEET KOZMA, LES:GMD1 AUTHOR	05	84	20
MEET KRARMER,KEN: NIAGARA JUNCTION	F	76	57R
MEET KRAUSE,JOHN:PHOTO SAMPLING	F	75	59R
MEET LANKENAU, WALTER: CONTRIBUTING EDIT	11	84	26
MEET LEFFER, DOUG: PELLETS & PULPWOOD	03	80	57
MEET LENARDSON, BOB:LUDINGTON & NORTHERN	01	81	20
MEET LEWIS, ED: STRASBURG RAILROAD	09	78	57R
MEET LLOYD, GORDEN: FRUSTRATIONS OF RAILF	F	76	57R
MEET LUSTIG, DAVID: EAGLE MOUNTAIN RR	09	83	10
MEET MALINOSKY,BOB: BOXCAR WEEKEND	W	76	57R
MEET MARRE,LOUIS:LIMA BUFF	W	74	60R
MEET MCKENZIE, WILLIAM: ORIN CUTOFF	05	80	57
MEET MCLLWAIN,MORGAN:L&N/MONON MERGER	SU	75	59R
MEET MEISE,JOHN: MARYLAND MIDLAND	11	85	25
MEET MITCHELL, RICHARD: ATSF TO THE BAY	07	86	22
MEET MOHOWSKI,ROBERT: STILLWELLS	SP	75	58R
MEET MONROE, GREGORY: COORS AUTHOR	01	85	22
MEET MONTE VARDE, DAVID: ALCO SHORT LINES	03	82	21
MEET MORGAN,GARY: GEORGETOWN LOOP	07	79	60
MEET MOYERS, JERRY:UP CENTENNIALS	F	75	59R
RAILROAD PEOPLE	M	Y	P
MEET NAZAROW,GREG:REAWAKENING OF A GIANT	01	83	21
MEET NELLIGAN, TOM:AMTRAK RDC FLEET	01	80	56
MEET NETT, BRUCE:VIA-A NIGHT TO REMEMBER	01	82	10
MEET NIXON, RONALD:ERIE PACIFICS	03	80	57
MEET OLAH, DAN :PUGET SOUND & SNOQUALMIE	05	86	20
MEET PALMER, JERRY: JOINT LINE	05	78	57R
MEET PANZA, JAMES:SOO SOUTH OF SCHILLER	SP	77	57R
MEET PAPP, ALBERT: PHOTOGRAPHER	07	85	17
MEET PENNYPACKER, BERT:DOODLEBUG RPO	09	79	57
MEET PINCUS, HOWARD: PHOTOGRAPHER	07	85	17
MEET PISKOR, RON:GREENBRIER C&O #614	03	81	22
MEET PORTER, JAY: CENTURY 430 PHOTOGRAPHS	05	86	19
MEET POWELL, GARY: IOWA RAILROAD	07	84	22
MEET REISLER, HAL:L&N U25B	05	81	17
MEET RETENBERG, BILL:WESTERN RAILFAN VACA	07	78	57R
MEET RINEHART, LLOYD:TP&W TIP UP	07	83	20
MEET ROBIN, MAX: BOOK REVIEWER & PHOTOGRAP	08	77	57R
MEET ROEHM, PETER: KAYLOR CHRONICALS-PRR	07	82	18
MEET ROONEY,BILL:GREENVILLE & NORTHERN	SP	77	57R
MEET ROSE, TED: RR WATERCOLORS	01	87	27
MEET ROWLAND, WILLIAM:FRIENDS OF RR MUSE	09	85	27
MEET RUDINSKY,MIKE: SP BOOK REVIEWER	05	78	57R
MEET SANDERS, DALE:WP BUFF	05	79	60
MEET SAVIO, TOM: PRIVATE CAR OWNERS CONVE	03	87	10
MEET SCANCARELLI, JIM: GASOLINE ALLEY	11	87	28
MEET SCHAEPPI,BILL:WEEKEND FIREMAN	SU	75	59R
MEET SCHMIDT, BOB:ROARIN' ELGIN	12	77	53R
MEET SCOTT HARTLEY: CENTRAL VERMONT	03	79	57R
MEET SHAUGHNESSY,JIM: BOAZ TO BLUE RIDGE	SP	75	58R
MEET SHAVER,CARL: KENOVA COAL	04	78	57R
MEET SHEPPARD, JAMES:CAROLINA MIXED	11	86	25
MEET SISTRUNK, JOHN:HARTFORD & SLOCOMB	11	86	26
MEET SMERK, GEORGE:TRACTION EXPERT	05	82	14
MEET STEINBRENNER, RICHARD:C&NW ALCOS	08	77	57R
MEET SULLIVAN,TODD: CAMAS PRAIRIE	12	77	53R
MEET TITSWORTH, JIM:CADILLAC & LAKE CITY	05	82	18
MEET TOM DEJOSEPH: SPERRY RAIL SERVICE	01	79	57R
MEET TOMASIC, KEVIN: P&LE RIVER BOATS	11	86	22
MEET TURNER,ROBERT: VANCOUVER ISLAND	09	78	57R
MEET TUTHILL, SEAWARD:CAL RAILFAN	W	74	61R
MEET VALENTINE,BILL:B&M HILLSBORO BRANCH	SU	76	57R
MEET WADE,JIM:GREENVILLE & NORTHERN	SP	77	57R
MEET WALLACE, MAX:FLORIDA CENTRAL	10	87	28
MEET WALTER ROBBINS--HISTORIAN	11	68	56
MEET WEINSTOCK,CHARLES:PASSENGER TRAINS	SP	76	58R
MEET WILSON, JEFF:CORNITH & COUNCE	05	83	18
MEET WISE, BOB: TUSCOLA & SAGINAW BAY	03	84	16
MEET WOOD,DON:PHOTOGRAPHER	W	74	61R
MEET YAGER, DICK:LOCOMOTIVE RESTORER	W	75	59R
MEET YOUNG, J.J.-PHOTOGRAPHER	SP	76	58R
MEET YUNKURTH, CHUCK: RAIL PHOTOGRAPHER	SP	76	58R
MEET ZIMMERMANN, KARL:ROYAL HUDSONS	W	75	59R
MILE-A-MINUTE MURPHY (CHARLES) (LI)	08	70	34
MOORE, WILLIAM: PC NEW PRESIDENT	12	70	10
MURPHY, CHARLES: "MILE-A-MINUTE" BICYCLE	04	55	35

Railroad/Railfan

GENERAL RAILROADING

RAILROAD PEOPLE	M	Y	P
NEUHART, DAVID:GIANT AMONG MOTIVE POWER	04	74	28
NEUHART, DAVID--UP LOCOMOTIVE BUILDER	F	75	38R
NEWELL, EVELYN:FIRST FEMALE MEMBER BLE	07	75	02
O'NEILL, JAMES H., GENERAL MANAGER GN	05	32	214
O'NEILL, RAY: STATIONMASTER 36 YEARS	04	47	122
OBITUARY BALL, DON:PHOTOGRAPHER	01	87	73
OBITUARY BARRIGER,JOHN WALKER:RR EXEC	SP	77	59R
OBITUARY BARRINGER, JOHN:RR PRESIDENT	03	77	03
OBITUARY BLOUNT, NELSON: STEAMTOWN FOUND	12	67	59
OBITUARY COWEN, JOSHUA LIONEL	12	65	06
OBITUARY DONOVAN, FRANK: RAIL HISTORIAN	12	70	10
OBITUARY HARDY, GRAHAME: RAILROADANIA DE	10	68	54
OBITUARY HARLOW, ALVIN:AUTHOR	04	64	10
OBITUARY HASTINGS, PHILLIP:RAIL PHOTOGRA	05	87	62
OBITUARY HOLBROOK, STEWART: AUTHOR	12	64	10
OBITUARY HUBBARD,FREEMAN: "RAILROAD"	01	82	22
OBITUARY KALMBACH, ALBERT: PUBLISHER	03	82	64
OBITUARY KNAPKE, BILL: BY WILLIAM JENNER	07	69	08
OBITUARY KNAPKE, WILLIAM:SP CONDUCTOR	05	69	57
OBITUARY KUHLER, OTTO:EUOLOGY	11	77	12
OBITUARY LATHROP, GIL:AUTHOR	07	69	06
OBITUARY LAVELLE, JOSEPH: STEAM LOCO PHO	10	68	10
OBITUARY LOWEY, RAYMOND:FATHER OF S-LINE	11	86	36
OBITUARY LUCAS, WALTER: RR HISTORIAN	12	67	59
OBITUARY LUCIUS, BEEBE	05	66	17
OBITUARY MAGUIRE,STEPHEN: TRANSIT TOPICS	01	82	22
OBITUARY MCCLINTOCK, HARRY 1882-1957	10	57	57
OBITUARY PERRY, OLIVER-TRAIN BANDIT	11	30	521
OBITUARY QUIMBY, EJ:ERA FOUNDER	05	82	03
OBITUARY RINKE, HERMAN:ERA SECRETARY	09	76	56
OBITUARY SAGLE, LAWRENCE B&O MUSEUM CURA	08	75	10
OBITUARY TABER, THOMAS:RAILROADIANS OF A	08	75	10
OBITUARY TABER,TOM & EULOGY	F	75	13R
OBITUARY WITBECK BILL:SE LOUISIANA NRHS	06	72	39
OLIVER, HOWARD: RAN HIS TRAINS IN MEXICO	11	37	05
OMAN, JOSEPH-TOWER MAN	11	30	562
ONTARIO LINES PEOPLE (SHORT NOTES)	07	82	63
PACKER, ASA: 1805-1879 TRAIN NAMED FOR	04	40	138
PANGBORN, FOUR GENERATIONS GROOMED C&SL	06	32	325
PEASE, EDWARD: BRITISH PIONEER	07	75	54
PEASE, EDWARD: ENGLISH RAIL PROMOTER	09	74	43
PELLEY, JOHN J-TRACK HAND TO PRES NYNH&H	12	29	01
PERRY, OLIVER C-LONE WOLF BANDIT	11	32	460
PHILLIPS, GUS-CALLS KING BORIS III	06	38	66
PINSLEY, SAMUEL--HE BOUGHT 8 SHORTLINES	04	67	61
PULLMAN FAMILY HOME "CAROLANDS"	06	50	126
PULLMAN, GEORGE MORTIMER: MODERNIZES TRA	04	37	05
RAILROAD BUILDER (PIONEER) G.M. DODGE	05	33	37
RAILROAD BUILDER-BILL CAREY	01	31	273
RAILROAD PRESIDENTS WOMEN	06	35	46
RAWLINGS, ROY--BUYS WRB FOR $301	01	39	29
RODGERS, JIMMY: GREAT RAIL SINGER	09	72	42
ROEBLING, JOHN A: WIRE CABLE/RAILROAD MA	07	45	63
ROGERS, THOMAS (SHORT NOTE ON)	11	74	51
ROGERS, THOMAS: ROGERS LOCOMOTIVE WORKS	11	76	43
ROSS WINANS-WINANS' LOCOMOTIVES	11	36	69
SCHERE, ALFRED: SECTION BOSS PHOTO ESSAY	06	40	77
SEARS, RICHARD W: FOUNDER SEARS ROEBUCK	04	58	25
SEQUIN, MARC: FRENCH ENG & SCIENTIST	08	76	52
SHAUGHNESSY, THOMAS:CP PRESIDENT	09	77	55
SHE IS NUMBER TWO--A FIREMAN JACKIE BIGA	01	76	02
SHELLEY, KATE: RAILROAD HEROINE OF 1881	04	72	07
SMITH, DWIGHT:CASS SCENIC RAILWAY EXEC	05	83	54
SPRAGUE, FRANK J: FATHER OF ELEC TRACTIO	08	40	07
STEEL DRIVER JAWN (JOHN) HENRY	09	34	66
STEPHENSON, GEORGE: 1ST PRESIDENT OF CP	09	75	06
STEPHENSON, GEORGE: PIONEER LOCO COMPANY	04	36	44
STEPHENSON, JOHN: MASTER CAR-BUILDER	09	45	41
STEVENS, COL JOHN: FATHER OF AMERICAN RR	02	57	42
STEVENS, COL JOHN:FATHER OF AMERICAN RR	06	65	39
STEVENS, JOHN: LOCOMOTIVE BICENTENNIAL	08	76	10
STILLWELL, ARTHUR E: FATHER OF KCS	04	57	32
STRIKE-BREAKER PEARL L. BERGOFF	06	35	34
STROMBECKER, JE:STROMBECK-BECKER COMPANY	10	36	83
SWEETMAN, FRED: 1ST NP CONDUCTOR	04	40	72
TACK, CARL:RAILROAD INVENTOR-351 PATENTS	08	71	12
THOMPSON,AC:ONE ARMED THREE FINGERED MAN	01	65	60
THORNTON, SIR HENRY WORTH-PRESIDENT CN	11	30	481
TIMKEN, HENRY SR: ROLLER BEARINGS	03	40	125
TREVITHICK, GEORGE:WHO WAS HE?	11	78	49
VAN HORNE, WILLIAM CORNELIUS CP	08	35	43
VAN SWERINEN, ORIS & MANTIS	07	31	481
VANDERBILT, COMMODORE CORNELIUS	11	36	04
VANDERBILT, COMMODORE: 1794-1877 TRAIN N	04	40	138
VAUCLAIN, SAMUEL:ENGINEER AT BALDWIN LOC	05	77	54
VAUGHAN, GUY A: MODEL BUILDER/VERMONTER	08	48	72
VERNOR, JOHN-RODE FIRST PASSENGER TRAIN	02	31	321
VIRGIL STAFF ON GIRLS IN RAILROAD PHOTOS	06	71	10
VOHLAND, PHYLLIS: FEMALE DISPATCHER	01	52	60
VOLK, MAGNUS:ELECTRIC RAILWAY PIONEER	03	76	56
VON BORRIES, AUGUST:PIONEER IN LOCO COMP	02	78	51
VON SIEMENS, ERNST: 1ST PRACTICAL ELECTR	12	74	58
WALSCHAERT, EGIDE: VALVE GEAR INVENTOR	05	75	52
WATKINS, SAMUEL TAYLOR: PREACHING HOGGER	05	47	77
WEBB, SLIM: CASEY JONES' FIREMAN	03	36	36
WEBSTER WAGNER SLEEPING CAR INVENTOR	12	35	45
WESTINGHOUSE, GEORGE--BRAKES	05	38	19
WESTINGHOUSE, GEORGE-AIRBRAKE WIZARD	11	30	529
WHISTLER, GEORGE W: RUSSIA'S RAILROAD	04	52	52
WHITNEY, ALEXANDER F. PRES BROTHERHOOD	07	31	523
WILLARD, DANIEL: CHIEF OF THE B&O	02	30	321
WILLIAM FREDERICK HARNDEN RAILWAY EXPRES	04	36	21

GENERAL RAILROADING

RAILROAD FICTION		M	Y	P
$50,000 RACE, THE	HAYES	09	33	52
'BO MONEY	HILKER	06	34	05
'BOES ARE 'BOES	PUGSLEY	02	36	52
20 MILES AN HOUR!	EARP	01	34	118
230 GRAND IN A SUITCASE	ELSTON	09	34	04
31 TURNS 13	CHILDS	08	31	29
90 MINUTES LATE	CRAWFORD	09	32	217
A MAN'S JOB	LATHROP	07	45	127
A MANS JOB	LATHROP	11	70	45
A MANS'S JOB	PARRY	03	67	48
A MEET WITH 86	WATERS	01	31	289
AGAINST ORDERS	JORDAN	07	32	524
AGAINST ORDERS	BEDWELL	09	54	16
AGAINST ORDERS-TELEGRAPH SERVICE-BEDWELL		01	73	39
AGE LIMIT	PACKARD	07	66	58
AGENT FOR A DAY	SNYDER	02	37	81
ALIBI ARTIST	EARP	06	64	52
ALIBI ARTIST, THE	EARP	08	34	53
ALL GOD'S CHILLUN GOT SHOES	SAUMS	11	48	117
ALPINE PASS (SOUTH PARK LINE)	LATHROP	08	64	40
ALWAYS INVENTING THINGS	EARP	04	34	58
AMATEUR BOOMER	SWAINE	01	33	93
ANGEL OF CANYON PASS	TYLER	02	73	54
ANGEL OF CANYON PASS, THE	TYLER	04	36	24
ANOTHER BROWN	THOMPSON	04	37	31
ANOTHER DAY ANOTHER DOLLAR	PARKER	10	74	09
ANOTHER DAY, ANOTHER DOLLAR	PARKER	02	42	30
ANOTHER DAY, ANOTHER DOLLAR (R)	PARKER	04	67	41
ANYTHING CAN HAPPEN	LIVINGSTON	08	37	16
ANYTHING'S LIABLE TO HAPPEN	BEDWELL	02	40	34
ANYTHING'S LIABLE TO HAPPEN (R)	BEDWELL	06	57	54
AULD LANG SYNE	SNYDER	09	35	108
AVALANCHE	PUGSLEY	03	52	106
AVALANCHE	DELLINGER	02	34	06
AVALANCHE (CANADIAN PACIFIC)	PUGSLEY	04	62	36
AVALANCHE WARNING	BEDWELL	07	76	32
BACK IN CIRCULATION	BEDWELL	09	40	88
BACK IN CIRCULATION	BIDWELL	06	60	46
BACK ON THE BOARD	WINGO	04	53	104
BACK ON THE MAIN	TYLER	12	31	58
BACK ON THE MAIN (REPRINT)	TYLER	10	64	58
BACK TO THE FARM	HASKELL	01	78	52
BAGGAGE-CAR GOAT	SWAINE	06	33	30
BALL OF FIRE	HULL	07	71	56
BALLAST SCORCHER	MOSLER	09	77	39
BALLAST SCORCHER, THE	HAYES	02	35	70
BALLAST SCORCHER, THE (NOVELET)	DELLINGER	01	40	76
BANANA EXPRESS, THE	MEEK	12	32	21
BANDIT & THE SUNDAY SCHOOL TEACHER	HUBBA	02	75	30
BEACON LIGHTS	DELLINGER	01	34	06
BEANERY QUEEN	MCLARN	10	55	66
BEANERY QUEEN (REPRINT)	MCLARN	03	76	37
BEAVERS FLOODED THE TRACK	HUBBARD	03	76	34
BEGINNER'S LUCK	MARTIN	01	35	33
BEGINNING OF A BOOMER	WELLS	09	31	221

RAILROAD FICTION		M	Y	P
BENNIE BOOMS ON	DENTON	08	31	56
BENNY THE BUM	NIELSON	02	35	66
BIG BROTHER	MCLARN	09	53	104
BIG ENGINES	JOHNS	08	75	34
BIG ENGINES (NOVELETTE)	JOHNS	06	44	32
BIG GRAIN RUSH, THE ENGINE PICTURE KID		08	35	117
BIG HILL, THE	PUGSLEY	03	36	04
BIG HOLE, THE	PUGSLEY	04	54	92
BIGGER AND BETTER CLAIMS	LIVINGSTON	02	30	367
BIGGER AND BETTER EFFICIENCY	DAVIS	03	37	14
BINDLE'S PALACE	LATHROP	01	38	18
BLACK HAND	CRAWFORD	06	30	380
BLACKBALLED	HAYES	07	32	513
BLACKLISTED	SAMPLES	02	37	04
BLACKLISTED	DELLINGER	05	76	40
BLANKET STIFFS	MARTIN	04	35	07
BLAZE OF GLORY	PARRY	07	68	38
BLAZING RACE	AUSTIN	10	31	412
BLIND CROSSING	LANE	02	41	98
BLIND CROSSING (ENGINE SERVICE)	LANE	10	69	43
BLOCK SIGNALS (NOVELETTE)	DELLINGER	07	39	38
BLOOD AND STEAM PART 1 OF 4	WATERS	12	29	14
BLOOD AND STEAM PART 2 OF 4	WATERS	01	30	278
BLOOD AND STEAM PART 3 OF 4	WATERS	02	30	438
BLOOD AND STEAM PART 4 OF 4	WATERS	03	30	602
BLUE CHIP RUN	PARRY	02	46	44
BLUE CHIP RUN (REPRINT)	PARRY	02	70	43
BLUE FLAG	CRAWFORD	08	32	31
BLUE ICE	PARRY	12	43	30
BONEHEAD	HAYES	09	32	241
BOOMER FIREMAN	KEITH	07	41	30
BOOMER FIREMAN (REPRINT)	KEITH	04	68	38
BOOMER FIREMAN (REPRINT)	KEITH	08	62	34
BOOMER INK-SLINGER	HASKELL	09	36	80
BOOMER JIM'S LAST RUN	BRANDHORST	12	33	58
BOOMER JONES--GHOST DETECTOR	EARP	06	52	88
BOOMER PILOT	JOHNS	07	31	594
BOOMER PILOT (REPRINT)	JOHNS	10	45	56
BOOMER PUP	FAIRES	11	34	48
BOOMER TRAILS	DELLINGER	11	32	510
BOOMER, DON'T LIE	MORGAN	10	51	110
BOOMERS COME TO TOWN, THE	EARL DAVIS	07	35	100
BOOMERS EASTBOUND	ROACH	12	51	92
BOOMERS EXPAND, THE	DAVIS	03	36	100
BOOMERS' FAST LINE, THE	DAVIS	07	36	100
BOOMERS' PARADISE	ROACH	07	32	434
BOOMERS--NORTHBOUND	MCCLINTOCK	12	72	49
BORN TO THE RAILS	DELLINGER	12	55	56
BOSS OF SEVENTEEN	SCISM	12	47	42
BOSS OF THE EXTRA GANG	SWEET	10	37	58
BOX CAR BLUES		11	32	456
BOXCAR MARY	MARTIN	11	36	61
BOXCARS ARE TEMPERAMENTAL	JACKSON	06	71	56
BRAKE CLUBS AND BAYONETS	DELLINGER	07	33	88
BRAKEHEAD HENNESSEY	SAMPLES	08	35	52

GENERAL RAILROADING

RAILROAD FICTION		M	Y	P
BRAKEMAN COMES BACK	DELLINGER	08	48	114
BRAKEMAN'S LUCK	HARGIS	04	34	42
BRANCH LINE BUZZARD, THE	WATERS	08	31	106
BRANCH-LINE HOGGER	SAMPLES	03	41	36
BRANCH-LINE OPERATOR	DELLINGER	11	42	48
BRANCH-LINE OPERATOR (REPRINT)	DELLINGER	02	66	40
BRASS BUTTONS	PUGSLEY	08	36	60
BRASS BUTTONS (REPRINT)	PUGSLEY	04	64	40
BRASS HAT	BRANDHORST	06	34	102
BRASS HAT (NOVELETTE)	JOHNS	11	43	24
BRASS POUNDER	FAIRES	09	33	115
BRASS POUNDING GIRL	DELLINGER	08	77	34
BROKEN COUPLERS	DELLINGER	02	46	108
BROKEN COUPLERS (REPRINT)	DELLINGER	08	68	42
BROKEN DRAWBAR, THE	EARP	11	37	64
BROKEN LINKS	DELLINGER	03	34	46
BROKEN RAILS	SCOTT	12	32	48
BROTHERHOOD MAN	SAMPLES	07	35	07
BUILT FOR THE NEW YORK CENTRAL		12	34	60
BULKHEAD HENNESSEY	DELLINGER	08	76	24
BULL TROUBLE	PUGSLEY	08	47	42
BULLETIN 990	WILLIAMS	02	43	12
BULLETIN 990 (REPRINT)	WILLIAMS	06	68	42
BURLINGTON HILL (HISTORICAL)	SAMPLES	01	44	46
BURNING BRAKES	DELLINGER	05	44	82
BURNING MOUNTAIN	STODDARD	09	31	161
BURNING MOUNTAIN (REPRINT)	STODDARD	01	66	34
BURNING MOUNTAIN (REPRINT)	STODDARD	10	78	34
BUSSES COME TO TOWN, THE	DAVIS	10	35	104
BUTTERMILK AND BALLAST	ROACH	03	32	555
BY WHOSE HAND?	FAIRES	12	32	58
CALL BOY CONFESSES, A		06	32	409
CALL OF THE CAB (NOVELETTE)	JOHNS	06	43	24
CAMPBELL'S WEDDING RACE	BEDWELL	06	59	54
CAN'T BE DONE?	EARP	01	32	164
CANADIAN NATIONAL (HISTORICAL)	DELLINGER	09	42	06
CANADIAN PACIFIC (HISTORICAL)	SAMPLES	11	41	82
CAP WHEELER'S GRAVY TRAIN	SWEET	09	34	48
CARELESS ROAD, THE	BEDWELL	02	39	32
CARELESS ROAD, THE (REPRINT)	BEDWELL	06	58	48
CASH PRIZES FOR TITLES	FRASER	01	32	206
CASHMERE GOAT, THE	LIVINGSTON	07	38	104
CHANCE-TAKERS, THE	DELLINGER	03	38	80
CHANCES	DELLINGER	07	34	04
CHARGES COLLECT	IND	06	31	422
CHECK AND DOUBLE CHECK	MAXWELL	01	31	225
CHEE-AINS	SAMPLES	09	37	38
CHICALOON CHICANERY	ENGINE PICTURE KID	10	36	50
CHINOOK CHARLIE COMES HOME	MARTIN	12	60	52
CHINOOK CHARLIE COMES HOME	MARTIN	05	36	99
CHRISTMAS AT CRAGHEAD	LATHROP	12	73	38
CHRISTMAS AT CRAGHEAD (NOVELET)	LATHROP	01	42	26
CHRISTMAS COMES TO THE PRAIRIE CENTRAL		01	43	48
CHRISTMAS MAIL	THOMPSON	01	34	66
CHRISTMAS TEST	HILKER	01	35	16
CINDER CRUNCHERS	WALKER	11	32	556
CINDER KID, THE	CHAPMAN	02	32	290
CIRCUMSTANTIAL EVIDENCE	EARP	06	34	124
CIRCUS DAZE	ENGINE PICTURE KID	07	36	04
CIRCUS JINX	GIROUARD	09	34	90
CIRCUS SPECIAL, THE	PACKARD	11	36	112
CIRCUS TRAIN	PACKARD	08	66	40
CIRCUS-TRAIN ELEPHANT		01	76	55
CIVIL WAR	LESLIE	12	33	06
CLEAR BOARD	WILSON	03	35	20
CLEAR BOARD	SHERWOOD	05	32	234
CLEAR BOARD (REPRINT)	SHERWOOD	09	78	37
CLEAR IRON	TYLER	02	34	52
CLEOPATRA RIDES	SCOTT	06	34	114
CLOSING DAYS	SNYDER	04	36	108
CLOSING DAYS (REPRINT)	SNYDER	02	64	32
CLOUDBURST	SCOTT	03	33	64
CODE OF THE BOOMER	BEDWELL	05	40	40
CODE OF THE BOOMER (REPRINT)	BEDWELL	10	57	48
CODED WIRES	CRAWFORD	01	34	50
COLD STEEL	LESLIE	06	31	394
COLOR-BLIND	MARTIN	10	56	49
COLORADO MIDLAND	BRANDHORST	09	33	89
COMMUTER	MCCLARY	09	36	28
COMPLETE EVIDENCE	GABLE	01	30	220
CONDUCTOR WATSON'S RETIREMENT	MILLS	10	47	40
CONDUCTORETTE	ROHDE	01	45	96
CONDUCTORETTE (YULETIDE STORY)	ROHDE	01	69	28
CONTRACTA BRAKEMAN, THE	EARP	10	39	94
COPY 10	PALMER	04	46	46
COPY 10 (TELEGRAPH SERVICE)	PALMER	03	69	40
CORN IN EGYPT	PUGSLEY	05	51	106
CORNFIELD MEET	EARP	09	31	254
COUNT YOUR CHICKENS	SWEET	05	37	107
COUNTRY STATION AGENT, THE	SMITH	01	30	262
CRAZY WITH THE HEAT	HAYES	04	32	54
CREEPING SHADOWS	DELLINGER	05	33	06
CROSSINGS	DELLINGER	01	35	46
DAMN HOBO	DELLINGER	04	35	112
DANGER OVERHEAD	HARGEST	01	33	120
DANGER SIGNALS PART 1 OF 5	JOHNS	05	32	146
DANGER SIGNALS PART 2 OF 5	JOHNS	06	32	374
DANGER SIGNALS PART 3 OF 5	JOHNS	07	32	530
DANGER SIGNALS PART 4 OF 5	JOHNS	08	32	94
DANGER SIGNALS PART 5 OF 5	JOHNS	09	32	254
DAREDEVIL DAN	DELLINGER	03	33	04
DARK DOOM	AKERS	05	30	202
DEAD MAN'S CAB	THOMPSON	05	32	196
DEADHEAD PASSENGER, THE	MAXWELL	11	33	58
DEADHEAD, THE (NOVELET)	DELLINGER	12	40	84
DEAR MISTER THORNWHISTLE	WINGO	08	52	106
DEATH CLEARS THE MAIN	LESLIE	02	32	342
DEATH TRAPS	DELLINGER	12	36	86
DEATH VALLEY DAYS	SNYDER	12	35	125
DEATH WATCH AT DEXTER	HAYES	12	31	44

Stephans' Railroad Directory

Railroad/Railfan

GENERAL RAILROADING

RAILROAD FICTION		M	Y	P
DEATH'S RIGHT-OF-WAY	BOWERS	03	33	36
DEBT OF HONOR, A	LIVINGSTON	12	36	39
DELAY AT MESQUITE	BEDWELL	02	59	50
DEMON OF THE RAIL	DEATON	07	31	606
DERAILED HOT SHOT	ROBINSON	12	31	98
DERAILS PART 1 OF 3	DELLINGER	05	30	166
DERAILS PART 2 OF 3	DELLINGER	06	30	414
DESERT DIVISION	WILLIAMS	11	68	40
DESERT DIVISION, THE	WILLIAMS	09	40	38
DESERT FREIGHT THE ENGINE PICTURE KID		06	33	73
DESERT JOB (AN EDDIE SAND STORY)	BEDWELL	02	60	46
DESERT JOB PART 1	BEDWELL	05	45	90
DESERT JOB PART 2 (EDDIE SAND)	BEDWELL	06	45	86
DESERT SHADOWS "BOOMER BILL" HAYES		11	34	04
DESERT STEEL	DELLINGER	09	31	196
DEVIL'S SINKHOLE, THE	FAIRES	07	33	04
DIAMOND STACKS	LATHROP	11	33	06
DINING CAR GOAT	HUBBARD	06	76	42
DIRTY WORK ON THE SIDING!	REEVES	02	32	381
DIVISION MOTHER (NOVELET)	LATHROP	08	40	92
DOG'S LIFE, A	DELLINGER	12	37	80
DOLLARS ON ICE	ROHDE	04	48	112
DON'T TAKE NO FOR AN ANSWER	DELLINGER	02	72	52
DOUBLE-CROSS AT EDEN	LATHROP	03	31	551
DOWN TO SANTA FE	SAMPLES	12	38	88
DYNAMITE DAN	EARP	01	31	201
DYNAMITE KELLY	ATHANAS	12	48	128
DYNAMITE TRAIL PART 1 OF 2	LATHROP	04	32	02
DYNAMITE TRAIL PART 2 OF 2	LATHROP	05	32	242
EASY MONEY	DELLINGER	08	34	04
EDUCATING POP MILLER	BEATER	07	33	124
EFFICIENCY EXPERT	GIROUARD	07	32	488
EMERGENCY RUN	JOHNS	08	33	66
EMERGENCY RUN (PENNSY 7003)	JOHNS	10	60	44
EMERGENCY STOP	STODDARD	05	32	208
EMPTIES COME BACK	JOHNS	03	43	28
EMPTIES COMING BACK	JOHNS	04	75	54
END OF THE LINE (ENGINE SERVICE)	WATERS	10	70	52
END OF THE RUN	FOSTER	05	33	100
ENGINE DISPATCHER	COLFER	05	40	111
ENGINE DISPATCHER (REPRINT)	COLFER	09	67	48
ENGINE FAILURE	WATERS	05	78	34
ENGINE FAILURE	WATERS	12	32	02
ENGINE HE LOVED, THE	PACKARD	03	34	116
ENGINE PICTURE KID IN ALASKA, THE		08	36	122
ENGINE PICTURE KID IN ETHIOPIA		01	36	04
ENGINE PICTURE KID IN HOLLYWOOD		02	36	22
ENGINE WIPER	PACKARD	05	66	36
ENGINE WIPER, THE	PACKARD	01	36	111
EPIC OF A LAZY MAN, THE	FREY	08	35	98
EVERGREEN AND IRON	DELLINGER	12	31	01
EVERGREEN DRAG, THE ENGINE PICTURE KID		12	35	60
EX-BRAKEMAN	MASKELL	02	32	419
EXPERIENCE	ROHDE	05	49	74
EXTRA ACES	AKERS	05	31	285

RAILROAD FICTION		M	Y	P
EXTRA FARE THE ENGINE PICTURE KID		04	33	67
FALL GUY	HARRISON	05	52	112
FALL GUY (REPRINT)	HARRISON	09	75	39
FASTER FREIGHT	THOMPSON	01	38	103
FEMALE OP, THE	TEMPLE	05	36	119
FERRY TRAIN (MOSTLY FACTUAL)	SMITH	02	62	40
FIERY COMET, THE	HULL	07	48	102
FIRED AGAIN	LAYNG	11	37	24
FLAMING DEATH	DELLINGER	07	31	498
FLAT WHEEL	WATERS	06	34	28
FLAT-WHEEL	WATERS	02	63	38
FOAMY WATER	LATHROP	11	39	48
FOGBOUND	JOHNS	07	43	46
FOGBOUND (REPRINT)	JOHNS	02	67	38
FOOL FOR LUCK, A	PARRY	03	34	104
FOOTBOARD YARDMASTER	DELLINGER	02	61	42
FOOTBOARD YARDMASTER, THE	DELLINGER	07	36	16
FORGOTTEN FAVORS	SAMPLES	01	38	76
FOUL-UP	PUGSLEY	06	53	94
FOUR-TRACK STUFF	JOHNS	05	41	26
FREE WHEELING	GARRY	12	33	74
FRESH FROM THE CORNROW	DELLINGER	05	38	86
FRISCO HOTSHOT	CAFFREY	03	40	99
FRISCO HOTSHOT (HOBO STORY)	CAFFREY	01	65	48
FROG PROMOTERS, THE	COIL	08	53	82
FULL TONNAGE (NOVELET)	LATHROP	11	40	86
FUSEE FRANK, FLAGMAN	EARP	07	31	515
GANDY DANCER	KELLY	04	50	100
GANGSTERS OF THE RAILS PART 1 OF 5	DELLI	11	30	498
GANGSTERS OF THE RAILS PART 3	DELLINGER	01	31	184
GANGSTERS OF THE RAILS PART 4	DELLINGER	02	31	449
GANGSTERS OF THE RAILS PART 5	DELLINGER	03	31	606
GANGSTERS OF THE RAILS PART 6	DELLINGER	04	31	140
GENERAL MANAGER COMES TO BAXTER, THE		07	37	44
GENERAL MANAGERS ORDER	SWEET	03	70	40
GENIUS, THE	DRAWBAR	05	37	66
GHOST BELL, THE	DEATON	03	30	546
GHOST OF PETER MATAVICH, THE	WALLACE	07	51	92
GIRL AT LOUP GAROU, THE	DELLINGER	05	34	30
GIRL IN THE CANYON	DELLINGER	06	78	34
GIRL IN THE ZULU CAR	TITUS	09	36	04
GIRL IN ZULU CAR	TITUS	04	66	40
GLORIFIED STREET CARS	LATHROP	03	34	76
GLORY BOUND	JOHNS	10	33	90
GLORY HUNTER, THE	DELLINGER	08	38	32
GLORY TRAIL, THE	FAIRES	05	35	100
GOAT MCGUIRE AND THE DYNAMITE EXTRA		10	50	116
GOD OF HIGH IRON (NOVELETTE)	TYLER	03	30	490
GODS OF HIGH IRON	BEDWELL	02	58	52
GODS OF IRON	DELLINGER	04	37	78
GOLD RUSH SPECIAL, THE	THOMPSON	12	33	68
GOOD MARKETS	SMITH	01	41	80
GOOD SAMARITAN, THE	EARP	02	39	96
GOOFY GARVIN		02	32	368
GRAPEFRUIT SPECIAL, THE	LIVINGSTON	09	37	23

Railroad/Railfan

GENERAL RAILROADING

RAILROAD FICTION

Title	Author	M	Y	P
GRASSHOPPER SMASHUP	ROACH	09	31	171
GRAVEYARD TRICK, THE	DELLINGER	09	36	94
GREATEST ENGINEER IN THE WORLD, THE		02	35	07
GREEN RIVER	TEXINO	09	32	186
GREEN TIMBER	LATHROP	06	37	98
GREENHORN WINS HIS SPURS, A	HARRIS	12	46	40
GRIEVANCE IN GRUB	ROHDE	01	47	36
GRIEVANCE MAN (NOVELETTE)	SAMPLES	12	42	96
GROUCHY JOINS THE HUMAN RACE	FUNKHOUSER	03	36	57
GROUNDED WEST	HAYES	03	32	498
HALIBUTOSIS	PUGSLEY	05	50	110
HAM AND EGGS	BALL	07	37	117
HAM FACTORY DAYS	SNYDER	03	36	63
HAM, THE	BEDWELL	05	39	17
HANDICAPS	DELLINGER	07	37	78
HARANAHAN'S NEW BOSS	MCGUIRE	11	48	42
HARD WAY	MCCLINTOCK	10	61	52
HARD WAY, THE	ROHDE	12	44	26
HARD-BOILED EGG, THE	ANDERTON	07	35	61
HARVEY HOUSE GIRL	DELLINGER	03	35	54
HASH-HOUSE	ROHDE	08	71	61
HAUNTED DIVISION, THE	JOHNS	06	33	04
HE KNEW THE RULES, BUT-(NOVELET)	LATHROP	06	41	92
HELL FOR DINNER	WATERS	09	32	146
HELL FOR DINNER (REPRINT)	WATERS	06	63	40
HELL ON WHEELS	LATHROP	11	30	568
HELPER TROUBLE	GOOBECK	04	41	104
HELPER TROUBLE (ENGINE SERVICE)	GOOBECK	01	70	42
HH HONK AND HORACE	HARTE	05	30	285
HH DARK ARE THE PLOTS TO OFFICIALDOM		05	30	285
HH FINE REVENUE & FINE FEATHERS	HARTE	06	30	456
HH HIGH ROMANCE -FISHERMANS FANCY	HARTE	08	30	125
HIGH IRON FEUD	CHILDS	05	32	184
HIGH SPEED FIREMAN		09	32	269
HIGH WATER	THOMPSON	07	33	51
HIGH WHEELER	DELLINGER	02	44	86
HIGH-PRICE LOYALTY	WALKER	12	31	102
HIGH-WHEELER	DELLINGER	06	69	42
HIGHBALL ARTISTS	HAYES	07	36	70
HIGHBALL DAT CASH!	AKERS	09	31	302
HIGHBALL NO. 10!	KNIGHT	06	32	356
HIGHBALLING THE APPLES BILL THE BOOMER		02	33	117
HIGHBALLING THE MOONBEAM TRAIL	TYLER	05	30	184
HIGHLY INFLAMMABLE (NOVELETTE)	DELLINGER	07	42	26
HIS BROTHER'S SON	PARRY	02	43	88
HIS LAST QUARTER	HEASLEY	05	34	70
HIS LAST RUN	GABLE	10	32	332
HOBO LOCAL	FUNKHOUSER	10	65	42
HOBO LOCAL, THE	FUNKHOUSER	01	44	23
HOBO RIDER, THE	SCOTT	04	34	72
HOBO'S SECRET, THE	DELLINGER	10	36	98
HOCUS POCUS STUFF	HULL	08	50	102
HOG LAW	DELLINGER	09	35	06
HOG'S BACK	PUGSLEY	06	74	36
HOG'S BACK, THE	PUGSLEY	10	34	96
HOGGER'S BOY	SAMPLES	06	37	16
HOGGERS ARE STUBBORN	LAYNG	05	37	74
HOGGERS ARE STUBBORN (REPRINT)	LAYNG	09	74	36
HOKUM VALLEY LINE	TEXINO	08	33	59
HOLIDAY WEEK-END	BEDWELL	12	59	48
HOME GUARD, THE	SAMPLES	06	39	84
HOME ON THE RAILS ENGINE PICTURE KID		06	36	50
HOME-GROUND PIKE	LATHROP	03	46	120
HOODOO SPECIAL, THE	DELLINGER	09	33	04
HORNED TOAD DETOUR, THE	TYLER	11	30	549
HORSE SENSE	HUBBARD	07	76	14
HORSE SENSE	MURDOCK	07	54	67
HORSESHOES	PUGSLEY	08	35	102
HOT RETAINERS!	GOLDSWORTHY	10	31	397
HOT SHOT SILK	BLISS	04	32	74
HOT SHOT! COMPOSITE STORY BY TEN AUTHORS		04	34	45
HOT WHEELS	HAYES	07	34	95
HOTBOX EXPERT, THE	EARP	12	37	33
HOTSHOT SILK TRAIN	BLISS	06	70	42
HOURS OF SERVICE (NOVELETTE)	JOHNS	08	43	22
HOW SLIPPERY BUCK FED THE MULTITUDE	EARP	02	38	36
HUMAN ELEMENT, THE	SAMPLES	02	38	80
HUNDRED PERCENT HALEY	ADAMS	09	39	30
HUNDRED-PERCENTER, THE	MURDOCK	05	55	25
I REMEMBER WHEN	MAXWELL	02	30	342
IF NOT PAID-	JOHNSEN	11	32	539
IMPERIAL PASS	BEDWELL	02	77	34
IMPERIAL VALLEY (SP NOVELET)	DELLINGER	10	41	88
IN A BLAZE OF GLORY	PARRY	10	44	43
IN SEARCH OF THE SUN	BEDWELL	01	39	34
IN SEARCH OF THE SUN (REPRINT)	BEDWELL	04	58	52
IN THE CLEAR	SWEET	04	38	100
IN THE DAYS OF THE BOOMERS	JOHNS	04	42	30
INCIDENT ON THE MAIN LINE	SOMERVILLE	09	48	50
INDEFINITE LEAVE OF ABSENCE	WATERS	08	61	53
INDEFINITE LEAVE OF ABSENCE, AN	WATERS	06	30	352
INTERFERENCE	CRAWFORD	04	35	123
IRON CAMEL, THE	MILLER	08	33	122
IRON HORSES	THOMPSON	07	32	460
IRON MIKE	LATHROP	10	35	55
IRON MIKE (REPRINT)	LATHROP	02	65	42
IRON TRAIL TO GLORY	TYLER	02	33	06
IRON-ORE DRAG	PARRY	09	70	52
ISLAND LAND	KNAPKE	06	73	24
JACOB'S LADDER	PUGSLEY	06	36	60
JACOBS LADDER	PUGSLEY	12	64	42
JAWBONE	BEDWELL	11	47	40
JAZZING UP THE SERVICE	ROACH	12	32	44
JIM HILL ROAD (NOVELET)	DELLINGER	08	41	92
JIM WORLEY'S BIG GUN	LESLIE	03	33	100
JINX RUN	WALLACE	02	51	82
JOB INSURANCE	SWEET	11	35	74
JOBS	GABLE	09	34	58
JOE SHOWS THE BRASS HAT	KAVANAUGH	08	31	117
JUDGEMENT RUN, THE	THOMPSON	03	32	483

Stephans' Railroad Directory

Railroad/Railfan

GENERAL RAILROADING

RAILROAD FICTION		M	Y	P
KEEP YOUR RETAINERS UP	PUGSLEY	09	71	60
KID SWITCHMAN, THE	BEDWELL	02	57	58
KILLER MCGOON	SLATTERY	10	47	112
KING FOR A DAY THE ENGINE PICTURE KID		06	35	15
KING FOR A TRIP	ARSENAU	11	52	104
KLONDIKE SMITH'S BRIGHT IDEA	DEEGAN	09	33	66
LACE FOR LENA	PUGSLEY	01	36	24
LADY HOGGER, THE THE ENGINE PICTURE KID		10	34	58
LANDSLIDE	DELLINGER	12	32	66
LANGUAGE OF THE KEY	LIVINGSTON	10	41	48
LANGUAGE OF THE KEY (REPRINT)	LIVINGSTON	11	67	04
LANTERN IN HIS HAND	BEDWELL	01	77	21
LASSITUDE AND LONGITUDE	BEDWELL	07	39	94
LAST OF THE BOOMERS	MCCLINTOCK	12	71	52
LAST QUARTER, THE	STODDARD	07	31	551
LAST ROCKAWAY, THE	LATHROP	09	36	56
LAST RUN	PARRY	02	56	56
LAUGH OR LOSE	BAYLOR	09	46	44
LAW OF HIGH IRON, THE	DELLINGER	08	36	04
LAW OF THE BIG WOODS	MCGILLIVARY	01	34	58
LIFE BEGINS AT SEVENTY	MARTIN	01	40	102
LIFE BEGINS ON THE 8.40		02	35	21
LIFE SAVER, THE	WELLS	03	31	578
LIGHTNING SLINGER	LIVINGSTON	12	40	37
LIGHTNING SLINGER (REPRINT)	LIVINGSTON	11	64	52
LIGHTNING SLINGER (REPRINT)	LIVINGSTON	06	75	38
LIGHTNING SLINGER, THE	KAVANAUGH	01	32	232
LINDY HOPPER, THE ENGINE PICTURE KID		09	35	114
LINK AND PIN	SAMPLES	04	36	54
LINKED AND PINNED ENGINE PICTURE KID		07	37	04
LION TAMER	DELLINGER	06	35	98
LITTLE ACTION	TITUS	08	72	40
LIVE DEADHEADS	EARP	03	37	32
LOCAL WEST	ROACH	09	44	46
LOCAL WEST (REPRINT)	ROACH	12	67	40
LOCH NESS MONSTER, THE	THOMAS	06	35	22
LONESOME WHISTLE	MOSLER	06	39	19
LONESOME WHISTLE (REPRINT)	MOSLER	05	67	36
LONG ROAD	MOSLER	12	69	38
LONG ROAD	DERAGON	01	75	28
LONG ROAD, THE	DERAGON	04	55	38
LONG ROAD, THE ("RAILROAD TOWN")	MOSLER	08	39	32
LONGHORN LANNIGAN	SAMPLES	04	35	56
LOOSE JOURNALS	JORDAN	04	33	117
LOOSE JOURNALS (TRAIN-FERRY)	JORDAN	10	62	40
LOST LOCOMOTIVE	SOMERVILLE	11	49	90
LOST LOCOMOTIVE (REPRINT)	SOMERVILLE	03	71	52
LOST RIVER	LESLIE	05	34	102
LOST-ONE LOCOMOTIVE	THOMPSON	12	29	64
LOUISVILLE & NASHVILLE (HISTORICAL NOVEL		02	42	84
LUCK OF THE IRISH	MCGUIRE	06	48	102
LURE OF THE RAILS PART 1 OF 2	DELLINGER	01	30	172
LURE OF THE RAILS PART 2 OF 2	DELLINGER	02	30	405
LUTHER LEGHORN	SMITH	12	29	128
MADMAN AT THE THROTTLE, A	WALKER	07	32	492

RAILROAD FICTION		M	Y	P
MAGIC OF THE RAILS	DELLINGER	08	33	04
MAIL PIRATE	HAYS	08	30	37
MAIN LINE BLUES	MASKELL	05	31	267
MAIN LINE MANNERS	GOLDSWORTHY	06	32	352
MAIN-LINE RUNNER	PARRY	08	43	62
MAIN-LINE RUNNER (REPRINT)	PARRY	12	62	38
MAIN-LINE RUNNER (CNR)	PARRY	08	67	44
MAJOR'S WATCH, THE (NOVELET)	DELLINGER	11	39	96
MAKE WAY FOR THE EASTBOUND	TYLER	10	54	18
MAKE WAY FOR THE EASTBOUND (R)	TYLER	02	74	32
MAKING OF A HAND, THE	SCISM	05	47	46
MAN BUILDER	LESLIE	07	33	40
MAN FAILURE	HAYES	02	33	40
MAN OF IMAGINATION	SWEET	05	65	60
MAN OF IMAGINATION,A	SWEET	12	37	28
MAN UP AHEAD	JOHNS	04	76	34
MAN UP AHEAD, THE	JOHNS	08	44	26
MAN WHO COULD HANDLE TRAINS, A	BEDWELL	11	36	30
MAN WHO COULD HANDLE TRAINS, A .	BEDWELL	08	56	48
MAN WHO COULDN'T BE FIRED, THE	DELLINGER	01	39	80
MAN'S JOB, A	PARRY	05	42	98
MAN'S JOB, A	BRANDHORST	06	33	62
MARKER LAMPS	WHITE	03	44	106
MASK OF CHING WO PART 1 OF 6	BRAND	08	30	62
MASK OF CHING WO PART 4 OF 6	BRAND	11	30	614
MASK OF CHING WO PART 6 CONCLUSION	BRAND	01	31	301
MASTER MANIAC THE ENGINE PICTURE KID		08	34	72
MASTER MECHANIC'S BLOOD	LATHROP	11	35	120
MATRIMONY LOCAL	HULL	06	47	26
MATT PASSES THE BUCK	WAMSLEY	12	34	73
MATTER OF TECHNIQUE	ADAMS	10	65	50
MATTER OF TECHNIQUE, A	ADAMS	08	44	70
MAWRICE ADDS A POSTSCRIPT	LATHROP	05	31	203
MEET ON FIVE-MILE TRESTLE, A	WATERS	04	54	52
MEET ON THE SUNSET ROUTE, A	NORTON	04	39	71
MEET ORDERS WITH HELL	LESLIE	04	32	87
MEET WITH NUMBER 86	WATERS	03	73	45
MEN IN POWER	DAVIS	03	35	98
MIDDLE ORDER	DELLINGER	09	73	33
MIDDLE ORDER, THE	DELLINGER	06	54	36
MILEAGE HOG	DELLINGER	02	36	98
MILEPOST 40	WATERS	09	45	30
MISSING MULES	EARP	12	36	60
MISSING WITNESS, THE	WATERS	03	45	56
MISSING-ONE VICTIM	CHILDS	02	31	412
MISSING: ONE CRUMMY	CROSS	01	32	210
MIXED ORDERS	DELLINGER	10	32	372
MONKEY MOTION THE ENGINE PICTURE KID		05	34	74
MOONSHINE (AN EDDIE SAND STORY)	BEDWELL	08	58	54
MOUNTAIN HOGGER	MURDOCK	05	53	112
MOUNTAIN HOGGER (REPRINT)	MURDOCK	09	72	26
MOUNTAIN JOB	SAMPLES	10	36	04
MOUNTAIN STANDARD TIME PART 1	BEDWELL	01	49	122
MOUNTAIN STANDARD TIME PART 2	BEDWELL	02	49	112
MOUNTAIN TIME PART 1	BEDWELL	02	75	20

Railroad/Railfan

GENERAL RAILROADING

RAILROAD FICTION		M	Y	P
MOUNTAIN TIME PART 2	BEDWELL	03	75	42
MOXLEY PUTS ONE OVER	HOFFMAN	01	30	194
MR. BROWN'S SYSTEM	JACKSON	04	49	114
MR. MANIFEST MISSES	CRAWFORD	04	32	38
MR. POTTS GETS HIS TRAIN	MCCLARY	01	37	72
MULE POWER	CRAWFORD	03	33	71
MULESHOE MALONEY	EARP	06	33	55
MURDER AT SPIRE, THE	BOOMER BILL	06	30	333
MYSTERIOUS HEADLIGHT	CRAWFORD	06	32	403
MYSTERY OF MILEPOST 40	WATERS	02	69	36
NARROW-GAGE MAN	LATHROP	12	54	24
NASTY NINE	HULL	02	50	92
NEW ASSISTANT TRAINMASTER, THE	DELLINGER	04	39	82
NEW FIREMAN	SCHNEIDER	07	73	52
NEW TRAINMASTER, THE	EARP	06	36	70
NEXT TRAIN, THE	PARKE	05	33	54
NICE WORK, MIKE!	LAYNG	03	39	66
NIGHT FOREMAN	DAVIS	10	37	39
NIGHT OF PLUNDER PART 1	BEDWELL	11	74	29
NIGHT OF PLUNDER PART 2	BEDWELL	12	74	38
NIGHT OPERATOR	TYLER	01	71	54
NIGHT OPERATOR	BEDWELL	08	57	66
NIGHT OPERATOR	PACKARD	06	66	42
NIGHT OPERATOR, THE	PACKARD	08	38	98
NIGHT PEDDLER, THE	JOHNS	05	30	298
NIGHT RUN	JOHNS	01	45	80
NIGHT TRICK	TYLER	01	53	90
NIGHT TRICK AT ARMADILLO	BEDWELL	04	59	60
NIGHT YARDMASTER	LATHROP	07	78	40
NIGHT YARDMASTER (NOVELETTE)	LATHROP	11	42	108
NINETY DAYS TO SOBER UP	PUGSLEY	12	36	28
NO BILLING	HOELL	10	46	114
NO JOB FOR AN AMATEUR	CRAWFORD	07	34	48
NO MORE BLACK CATS	SAMPLES	04	38	116
NO SCRAPPING ALLOWED		08	32	118
NO-BILL	DAVIS	01	35	97
NORTH OF NOWHERE	THOMPSON	12	32	120
NOT A WHEEL TURNING	ALFRED	03	49	70
NOT IN THE BOOK	WILLIAMS	06	42	118
NOT IN THE BOOK (REPRINT)	WILLIAMS	03	68	42
NOT IN THE CONTRACT PART 1	BIDWELL	05	73	44
NOT IN THE CONTRACT PART 2	BIDWELL	06	73	42
NOT IN THE CONTRACT PART 1	BEDWELL	06	46	42
NOT IN THE CONTRACT PART 2	BEDWELL	07	46	110
NOT ON THE MANIFEST	ENGINE PICTURE KID	01	34	99
NOT ON THE TIME CARD	EARP	11	34	57
NOTHING BUT THE RULES	EARP	07	35	67
NUT, THE	SHERWOOD	09	31	226
OBLIGING OP, THE	GIROUARD	10	32	329
OBSERVATIONS OF A COUNTRY AGENT	SMITH	02	30	425
OBSERVATIONS OF A STATION AGENT	SMITH	05	30	225
OFFICIAL APPRECIATION	BEDWELL	10	39	52
OFFICIALS ALWAYS REIGN	EARP	10	46	44
OHKAY SHOOTS THE BULL	CRAWFORD	08	31	62
OIL FOR INVASION	PARRY	04	44	58

RAILROAD FICTION		M	Y	P
OILCAN JOHHNY	TEXINO	05	33	48
OLD DEPENDABLE	PARRY	05	46	124
OLD FOUR-EYES	KNIGHT	05	31	226
OLD GIRL WENT OUT IN A BLAZE OF GLORY		04	77	19
OLD HELL BENDER	DELLINGER	09	34	100
OLD IRON HORSE, THE	MARTIN	08	35	74
OLD MOGUL MOUNTAIN	BEDWELL	07	38	32
OLD MOGUL MOUNTAIN (REPRINT)	BEDWELL	10	56	30
OLD-TIMER	LATHROP	11	34	26
ON A FOGBOUND NIGHT	JOHNS	05	74	50
ON COMPANY TIME	DAVIS	12	35	98
ON OVERLOOKING TRAIN ORDERS	CAMERON	04	51	110
ON THE BLACKLIST	DELLINGER	07	38	80
ON THE CARPET	WICKERSHAM	06	54	76
ON THE CARPET (NOVELETTE)	JOHNS	10	43	36
ON THE NIGHT WIRE	BEDWELL	01	37	91
ON THE NIGHT WIRE (REPRINT)	BEDWELL	06	56	52
ON THE ROAD TO TOKIO	ENGINE PICTURE KID	11	44	36
ON THE WRONG TRACK	DENTON	11	32	551
ON TIME!	TYLER	03	31	514
ONCE A BOOMER	THOMPSON	09	37	120
ONCE TOO OFTEN	DEL FRENCH	12	38	76
ONCE TOO OFTEN (REPRINT)	DEL FRENCH	07	69	42
ONCE TOO OFTEN (REPRINT)	DEL FRENCH	12	78	59
ONE OF THE GANG	WILLIAMS	12	41	106
OPEN DRAWBRIDGE, THE	ROACH	08	31	99
OPEN GATE, THE	DELLINGER	04	43	104
OPEN GATE, THE (REPRINT)	DELLINGER	05	77	34
OPEN SEASON FOR BULLS	PUGSLEY	07	31	546
OPNE KNUCKLE	PUGSLEY	01	51	112
ORDERS AT CANYON	JOHNS	07	40	104
ORDERS AT CANYON (REPRINT)	JOHNS	07	67	42
ORDERS AT CANYON (REPRINT)	JOHNS	01	74	30
OREGON CENTRAL (NOVELET)	DELLINGER	05	42	28
OTHER LETTER, THE	CRAWFORD	12	31	63
OUTSIDE THE LAW	MCCLINTOCK	04	72	56
OVER THE SAWLOG	SWEET	06	37	64
OVERTIME	SWEET	09	37	102
OVERTIME	LATHROP	04	40	98
OVERTIME (STOCK TRAIN)	LATHROP	05	70	42
OWSLEY AND THE 1601	PACKARD	10	66	42
PACIFIC ELECTRIC (EDDIE SAND)	BEDWELL	08	59	56
PACIFIC ELECTRIC (NOVELET)	BEDWELL	01	41	88
PASS TO SEATTLE	BEDWELL	11	76	28
PASSING OF THE RED CABOOSE, THE	BRYNE	05	30	183
PAYMENT ON ACCOUNT		02	32	377
PEAVINE RAILROAD, THE	SCHAFNITT	09	32	248
PEN UP DE WOMEN!	AKERS	02	31	466
PENSIONED	DELLINGER	05	37	18
PERFECT FIREMAN, THE	EARP	10	33	50
PERFECT STATION AGENT, THE	LIVINGSTON	09	38	111
PERFECT TIMECARD, THE	EARP	08	36	96
PERFIDIOUS GANDY	ARMES	10	48	46
PHANTOM BRASS	JACOBI	08	34	66
PHANTOM BRASS (TELEGRAPH SERVICE)	JACOBI	12	61	32

GENERAL RAILROADING

RAILROAD FICTION		M	Y	P
PHANTOM CITY	DELLINGER	01	36	42
PHANTOM ENGINE	WARMAN	10	71	54
PHANTOM OF THE HIGH IRON	LESLIE	11	32	434
PHANTOM ORDERS	CRAWFORD	02	34	66
PICKANINNIES AND PILLS	HULL	11	46	80
PICKED CREW	MOSLER	07	70	43
PICKED CREW, THE	MOSLER	05	43	94
PICKLED CREW	ROACH	10	31	401
PIECE OF STRING, A	CADY	01	50	92
PIG IRON	TITUS	06	36	04
POKRY GOES UP	CRAWFORD	03	30	577
PORK CHOP SPECIAL	SAXON	11	33	110
PORKY PLAYS POLITICS	CRAWFORD	04	33	107
PORKY REPLIES	CRAWFORD	01	31	176
PRESIDENT'S SPECIAL, THE	SWEET	04	33	98
PRESIDENT'S SPECIAL, THE	SLAWSON	04	52	118
PRIDE OF PEDRO SARAGOSSO, THE	JOHNSTON	08	49	32
PRIDE OF THE T&B	FUNKHOUSER	07	41	94
PRIORITY SPECIAL	BEDWELL	03	72	41
PRIVATE CAR	KELLY	05	75	43
PRIVATE CAR	KELLEY	05	71	46
PRIVATE CAR, THE	KELLY	06	50	98
PRIVATE SPOTTER, THE	EARP	11	38	46
PRIVILEGED CHARACTER ENGINE PICTURE KID		10	35	74
PROBLEM AT MUD CREEK	EVERETT	08	69	42
PROFANE ANGEL AND THE GLORY TRAIN	CURTIS	07	50	88
PULLMAN CONDUCTOR	HULL	01	46	36
PULLMAN PERIL	AKERS	05	32	270
PUTTIN' THE CARS AWAY	ROACH	05	32	265
RABBIT'S FOOT	DELLINGER	10	34	04
RAIL-FICTION'S MOST POULAR CHARACTER		10	42	53
RAILFAN	SAMPLES	05	39	102
RAILROAD AVENUE (NOVELET)	SAMPLES	04	40	06
RAILROAD BLOOD (NOVELETTE)	LATHROP	02	40	96
RAILROAD CRAZY	LATHROP	04	70	44
RAILROAD DRUMMER	TYLER	12	34	100
RAILROAD ENGINEER	TYLER	10	33	55
RAILROAD FICTION BOOKS LIST #2		05	37	104
RAILROAD FICTION-MORE!		07	37	125
RAILROAD GIRL	DELLINGER	06	38	28
RAILROAD MAN	ROBERTS	09	69	44
RAILROAD MAN	BRANDHORST	04	34	06
RAILROAD NICKNAMES	EARP	03	32	496
RAILROAD OR RAMBLE	DAVIS	12	66	40
RAILROAD PHONOGRAPH RECORDS		09	37	99
RAILROAD POETRY--A LIST		07	37	124
RAILROAD ROMEO, A	EARP	03	30	520
RAILROAD SONGS--A LIST		07	37	123
RAILROAD TOWN	MOSLER	03	39	24
RAILROAD TOWN (REPRINT)	MOSLER	01	67	32
RAILROAD TRAINMAN	DELLINGER	08	37	64
RAILROAD WIDOW, THE	HARTE	03	31	625
RAILROAD WOMEN	SAMPLES	10	39	108
RAILROAD-CRAZY	LATHROP	08	36	77
RAILROADED	ANDERTON	06	30	430

RAILROAD FICTION		M	Y	P
RAILROADERS ALL	LESLIE	11	33	70
RAILROADERS ARE TOUGH	MCCLINTOCK	12	65	41
RAILROADERS ARE TOUGH	HAYWIRE MAC	04	43	48
RAILROADERS DON'T CELEBRATE	BEDWELL	12	58	50
RAILROADIN' FOOL, A	FOSTER	08	32	81
RAILROADMAN	LATHROP	10	44	34
RAILROADMAN (REPRINT)	LATHROP	07	74	20
RAILS TO THE FRONT	DELLINGER	06	33	94
RAILWAY CONDUCTOR	DELLINGER	10	37	84
RATTLER RACKET, THE	TYLER	08	31	123
RATTLESNAKE MORSE	SNYDER	05	33	57
RATTLESNAKE MOUNTAIN	DELLINGER	12	33	96
RATTLETRAP TRANSIT (HANK & HORACE)	HARTE	11	31	556
RAWHIDE RUN	MCCLINTOCK	06	65	42
RAWHIDE RUN "HAYWIRE MAC"	MCCLINTOCK	06	42	50
RAWHIDER	DELLINGER	11	36	78
RAWHIDER (REPRINT)	DELLINGER	09	44	68
RAWHIDER (REPRINT)	DELLINGER	07	75	34
RAWHIDER, THE	CROSS	02	31	337
READY IN FIVE MINUTES		03	78	34
READY IN FIVE MINUTES	SNYDER	06	37	122
READY IN FIVE MINUTES (REPRINT)	SNYDER	07	65	39
RECORD PERFECT	EARP	01	47	120
RED BLOCK	SHERWOOD	07	31	584
RED BOARD	WEBSTER	11	33	122
RED FLAG	EARP	12	32	91
RED HOGAN, HOGGER	THOMPSON	06	31	383
RED LANTERN OIL	MAXWELL	08	32	41
RED OR GREEN?	THOMPSON	11	32	490
REDBALL WEST	DELLINGER	09	38	82
REDEMPTION FOR SLIM	DELLINGER	12	29	75
REEFERS	THOMPSON	02	34	106
REINDEER SPECIAL THE ENGINE PICTURE KID		01	35	124
REPORT TO THE G.M.	LIVINGSTON	12	42	50
RESTLESS FEET	BEDWELL	10	58	50
RESTLESS FEET (NOVELETTE)	BEDWELL	08	42	52
RETAINERS UP	PUGSLEY	03	50	110
RETURN OF CASEY JONES, THE	JOHNS	04	33	04
RETURN OF EDDIE SAND	DALLENGER	04	61	04
RETURN OF EDDIE SAND, THE	BEDWELL	02	44	22
RETURN OF JESSE JAMES	SCOTT	11	33	50
RETURN OF REDBALL	DELLINGER	12	34	20
RETURN OF THE ENGINE PICTURE KID		11	40	22
RIDERS OF THE IRON TRAIL	LAYNG	10	32	290
RIDERS OF THE IRON TRAIL PART 1	LAYING	07	65	42
RIDERS OF THE IRON TRAIL PART 2	LAYNG	08	65	44
RIDERS OF THE IRON TRAIL PART 3	LAYNG	09	65	40
RIDIN' WILD	WILLETS & CLARK	12	29	123
RIDING ON A CARD	SNYDER	04	37	122
RIGHT-OF-WAY	BRANDHORST	08	34	94
RIGHTS OVER EVERYTHING		04	35	99
RIO GRANDE	SAMPLES	05	36	04
ROAD HOGS (SOL MCCOOL STORY)	LIVINGSTON	12	39	66
ROAD TO ADDIS ABABA, THE	DELLINGER	03	36	04
ROAD TO GLORY PART 1 OF 2	JOHNS	10	31	338

Railroad/Railfan

GENERAL RAILROADING

RAILROAD FICTION		M	Y	P
ROAD TO GLORY PART 2 OF 2	JOHNS	11	31	570
ROAD TO YESTERDAY, THE	TYLER	02	36	61
ROAD'S END	JOHNS	03	31	541
ROADMASTER'S STORY	SPEARMAN	11	72	42
ROARING ROAD, THE	LAYNG	01	33	50
ROCKING CHAIR, THE	MILLS	12	45	49
ROLL 'EM, RAILROADER!	AKERS	08	32	70
ROLLING DOWN TO RENO	ENGINE PICTURE KID	04	36	119
ROLLING STONE, THE	SILENT SLIM	12	43	84
ROLLING WHEELS	HULL	02	47	72
ROLLING WHEELS	MCCLINTOCK	11	66	30
ROLLING WHEELS	HAYWIRE MAC	06	41	42
ROLLING WHEELS PART 2 OF 4	WATERS	08	30	138
ROMANCE ON THE HIGH IRON	ARMES	02	71	56
ROUNDHOUSE CAT	HUBBARD	02	76	34
ROUNDHOUSE FOREMAN	EARP	12	35	113
ROUNDHOUSE FOREMAN	PARRY	10	40	35
ROUNDHOUSE FOREMAN (REPRINT)	PARRY	05	68	43
ROUNDHOUSE GOAT	DAVIS	10	34	48
ROUNDHOUSE MURDER PART 1 OF 3	WATERS	11	31	465
ROUNDHOUSE MURDER PART 2 OF 3	WATERS	12	31	112
ROUNDHOUSE MURDER PART 3 OF 3	WATERS	01	32	264
RULE 108	CRAWFORD	11	30	577
RULE 99	DELLINGER	03	51	96
RULE 6	SAMPLES	10	38	84
RULE 6	CRAWFORD	10	31	385
RULEBOOK'S LAST TRIP	MILLS	04	45	31
RULEBOOK'S LAST TRIP (REPRINT)	MILLS	10	78	51
RULES AND THE REDHEAD	HULL	09	49	108
RUNAWAY HOG (GEORGIA RAMBLER)	WATERS	06	45	44
RUNNING SPECIAL	JOHNS	03	34	06
RUNNING WILD	LESLIE	10	33	06
RUNT RYAN-SQUARE PEG	EARP	05	30	257
RUNT, THE	WALLACE	03	42	78
RUSTED RAILS	LATHROP	08	33	98
RUSTY STEEL	THOMPSON	04	38	86
SABOTAGE	SLOMAN	12	45	45
SAGA OF SEATTLE SLIM, THE	MARTIN	05	35	119
SAM DRAPER'S LAST STAND	MURDOCK	11	51	112
SANDHOUSE CHATTER	SHERWOOD	10	43	150
SANTA FE TRAIL, THE	HAYES	06	34	46
SAUCE FOR THE GOOSE	SWEET	02	37	62
SCRAP HEAP	WELLS	11	31	524
SCREAMING WHEELS	BEDWELL	03	77	27
SECOND-TRICK DISPATCHER	BEDWELL	02	76	48
SECRET WEAPON	ENGINE PICTURE KID	12	44	95
SECRETS OF THE BRASS KEY	ADAIR	09	31	247
SENIORITY	SWEET	04	37	39
SENIORITY RIGHTS	MCCARTY	05	33	123
SENIORITY RIGHTS (REPRINT)	MCCARTY	04	65	46
SENTIMENTAL VALUE	LIVINGSTON	11	35	98
SERVICE EXPEDITER, THE	EARP	05	39	50
SHADOWS OF THE FREIGHTS	HAYS	12	29	111
SHOO-FLY	TAYLOR	12	31	68
SHOO-FLY (REPRINT)	TAYLOR	04	63	52
SHOOTIN' AIR	WILLETS & CLARK	02	30	381
SHOWDOWN	DELLINGER	05	72	48
SHOWDOWN, THE	DELLINGER	04	45	106
SIDE-DOOR PULLMAN	HARTE	06	31	445
SIDE-ROD BENDER, THE	MAXWELL	02	31	385
SIDETRACK THE OLD ONES	DELLINGER	06	32	340
SIDETRACK THE OLD ONES (R)	DELLINGER	04	78	38
SIDETRACKED	BETHEL	02	33	69
SIDETRACKED STUDENT	EARP	06	51	108
SIGN ON THE REEFER, THE	DELLINGER	03	37	86
SIGNAL TOWER GIRL	MARTIN	06	40	103
SILVER CROSS, THE	DELLINGER	02	35	96
SILVER SWITCH KEY, THE PART 1 OF 5	WELLS	04	31	17
SILVER SWITCH KEY, THE PART 2 OF 5	WELLS	05	31	291
SILVER SWITCH KEY, THE PART 3 OF 5	WELLS	06	31	453
SILVER SWITCH KEY, THE PART 4 OF 5	WELLS	07	31	616
SILVER SWITCH KEY, THE PART 5 OF 5	WELLS	08	31	134
SING US A SONG	MCCLINTOCK	09	47	42
SINGLE TRACK	SNYDER	10	32	356
SIXTY YEARS - AND OUT	PACKARD	07	34	106
SKELETON CREW	DELLINGER	02	53	94
SKELETON CREW (REPRINT)	DELLINGER	04	71	57
SKIMPY TIMBERS	DELLINGER	03	46	56
SLAVE DRIVER, THE	REEVES	03	31	497
SLEEPWALKER, THE	MURPHY	09	52	110
SLIPPERY BUCK (BOOMER JONES STORY)	EARP	09	41	100
SLIPPERY BUCK SLIPS	EARP	10	35	63
SLIPPERY BUCK'S ALIBI	EARP	10	36	58
SLIPPERY BUCK'S BALLROOM RUN	EARP	04	35	20
SLIPPERY BUCK'S CIRCUS ROBBERY	EARP	02	48	54
SLOW-MOTION SWITCHER	DERAGON	01	55	22
SLOWPOKE, THE	ROACH	10	33	125
SMART BOOMER	BEDWELL	11	71	58
SMART BOOMER (REPRINT)	BEDWELL	10	76	40
SMILING SMITH SITS IN	TYLER	08	30	92
SMOKE GETS IN YOUR EYES	JOHNS	10	42	16
SMOKE ORDERS (NOVELET)	DELLINGER	10	40	86
SMOKE SCREEN	DELLINGER	06	39	66
SMOKY MARY		02	32	363
SNAKE IN THE GRASS	WATERS	06	31	361
SNAKY AND I GO RUNNING	SABROWSKY	07	31	553
SNAP JUDGEMENT	LAYNG	02	33	95
SNAP JUDGEMENT (REPRINT)	LAYNG	08	63	50
SNOW ON THE HIGH IRON	BEDWELL	12	76	34
SNOW ON THE IRON	SAMPLES	01	37	04
SNOW ON THE IRON (NOVELET)	DELLINGER	02	41	38
SNOW ON THE IRON (PART 1)	DELLINGER	12	75	38
SNOW ON THE IRON (PART 2)	DELLINGER	01	76	34
SNOW ORDERS	CREAGAN	11	32	502
SNOWBALL SPECIAL, THE	JORDAN	01	32	252
SNOWBOUND AT MUSKEG	SWEET	11	69	40
SNOWED IN	DELLINGER	01	33	02
SNOWPLOW JOB	KNAPKE	04	75	23
SNOWSLIDE	NORWOOD	03	54	100
SNOWSLIDE (ENGINE SERVICE)	NORWOOD	12	70	46

Railroad/Railfan

Stephans Railroad Directory

GENERAL RAILROADING

RAILROAD FICTION		M	Y	P
SOAPSTONE LIMITED, THE	ENG PICTURE KID	11	35	47
SOUTH PARK BOGIE	LATHROP	09	51	106
SOUTHWEST PASSAGE	DELLINGER	12	35	04
SOUVENIRS	THOMAS	03	44	48
SOUVENIRS FOR THE SUPER	EARP	02	36	73
SOUVENIRS FOR THE SUPER	THOMAS	10	68	40
SPECIAL ATTENTION TO EVERYBODY	AKERS	06	30	363
SPECIAL CAR	HULL	05	46	50
SPEED CRAZY	LAYNG	03	33	106
SPEED FOR SECOND NUMBER 3	DELLINGER	11	45	104
SPEED LIMITS	DELLINGER	04	34	102
SPOTBOARDS	EARP	12	38	32
SPOTTER	PACKARD	09	66	40
SPOTTER, THE	PACKARD	09	35	96
SPREAD RAILS	THE ENGINE PICTURE KID	09	33	72
SPUR TO NOWHERE	MORAN	02	52	88
SPUR TO NOWHERE (REPRINT)	MORAN	03	74	44
SQUARE PEG, THE	DELLINGER	11	38	86
STACK OF RED, A	WATERS	06	32	292
STEAM AND STEEL PART 1 OF 4	DELLINGER	01	32	167
STEAM AND STEEL PART 2 OF 4	DELLINGER	02	32	404
STEAM AND STEEL PART 3 OF 4	DELLINGER	03	32	532
STEAM AND STEEL PART 4 OF 4	DELLINGER	04	32	100
STEEL ACROSS THE DESERT	DELLINGER	11	34	98
STEVE MAGILL'S PAST	FAIRES	10	34	107
STOCK EXTRA	NICHOLS	04	69	38
STOCK EXTRA	NICHOLS	11	45	79
STOLEN SENIORITY	EARP	06	38	96
STONY ISLAND SERVICE	EVERETT	03	38	36
STOP! LOOK! LISTEN!	BRADLEY	10	51	100
STORY WITHOUT A TITLE	EARP	04	32	49
STREAK OF RUST, THE	MITCHELL	03	33	83
STREAMLINE COMES TO TOWN, THE		03	35	06
STREAMLINE SYMPHONY	LAYNG	09	38	28
STRIKE ORDER	BOWERS	01	33	83
STUDENT BRAKEMAN	BEDWELL	04	60	36
STUDENT BRAKEMAN	SAMPLES	11	37	80
STUDENT BRAKEMAN, THE (NOVELET)	BEDWELL	06	40	34
STUDENT FIREMAN (NOVELET)	DELLINGER	03	40	32
STUDENT SECTION BOSS	ARMES	11	75	17
STUDENT SECTION FOREMAN	ARMES	08	51	114
STUDENT SWITCHMAN	PARRY	08	41	38
SUCH A BUSINESS!	CRAWFORD	05	31	256
SUMERTIME SNOW	EARP	02	35	55
SUN AND SILENCE	BEDWELL	04	38	34
SUN AND SILENCE (REPRINT)	BEDWELL	04	56	58
SUNSET SPECIAL, THE	MARTIN	02	37	98
SUPER SERVICE	THE ENGINE PICTURE KID	05	35	50
SUPER'S ERROR, THE	SNYDER	01	37	107
SUPER-STREAMLINER (BOOMER JONES)	EARP	08	40	38
SURPRISE FOR PEDRO, A	HILLER	12	52	114
SWITCH KEY	MOORE	11	65	42
SWITCH SHANTY TALK	HAYWIRE MAC	08	73	30
SWITCH-KEY	MOORE	12	41	60
SWITCH-SHANTY YARN, A	HAYWIRE MAC	08	55	24
SWITCHMAN	BEDWELL	11	77	34
SWITCHMAN, THE	BEDWELL	04	39	52
T-SERIES MAIL KEY, THE	DELLINGER	06	36	102
TALLOWPOT! PART 1 OF 3	LATHROP	08	31	01
TALLOWPOT! PART 2 OF 3	LATHROP	09	31	264
TALLOWPOT! PART 3 OF 3	LATHROP	10	31	430
TALLOWPOT'S RETURN, THE	ROACH	01	34	106
TAMING BEEFY BONNER	EARP	02	33	102
TANK CARS ROLLING (NOVELET)	HAYES	03	42	88
TAXPAYERS' MONEY	LIVINGSTON	06	35	55
TELEGRAFTER, BEWARE!	LOVETT	01	33	27
TEST RUN	JOHNS	10	67	42
TEST RUN	PARRY	01	50	106
TEST RUN, THE	JOHNS	09	42	104
THANKSGIVING ORDERS	CRAWFORD	11	31	502
THAT SPECK O' HUMAN	BLEDSOE	01	30	271
THEY CALLED HIM "MOONBEAM"	BEDWELL	12	39	98
THIRD TRICK	SNYDER	09	33	63
THIRD TRICK	BEDWELL	11	73	51
THIRD TRICK, THE	BEDWELL	06	55	30
THREE TESTS AND ONE TRAINMASTER	EARP	06	30	390
THROTTLE ARTIST (NOVELETTE)	LATHROP	09	43	44
THROUGH HELL AND HIGH WATER	ROBERTS	02	33	110
THUNDERING RAILS	BEDWELL	09	76	36
TICKET TO DESTRUCTION	DELLINGER	11	50	100
TIE RAFTERS	DELLINGER	07	40	34
TIME ELEMENT	JACKSON	05	48	110
TIMETABLE TROUBLES	EARP	09	32	250
TINHORN BRAKEMAN (NOVELETTE)	DELLINGER	09	39	82
TONNAGE HOUND	EARP	09	37	66
TONY'S TIN GOD	LATHROP	12	39	75
TONY'S TIN GOD (REPRINT)	LATHROP	08	70	41
TOO LONG IN THE DESERT	BIDWELL	08	60	46
TOO MANY COPS	HULL	01	48	46
TOO MUCH BRAINS	EARP	08	32	38
TOO PERFECT	ROHDE	08	45	30
TOP MAN	MCDONALD	07	54	102
TORNADO	DELLINGER	11	35	07
TORPEDO TRAIN	THOMPSON	11	33	98
TOWER MAN (EDDIE SANDS)	BEDWELL	10	59	54
TOWER MAN (PACIFIC ELEC NOVELET)	BEDWELL	05	41	92
TRACKSIDE GRAVE	MCLARN	11	54	22
TRACKSIDE GRAVE (REPRINT)	MCLARN	10	73	29
TRACKSIDE GRAVE (NOVELET)	LATHROP	09	41	30
TRACKWALKER'S TALE, THE	MARTIN	09	35	66
TRAIL TO YESTERDAY	FUNKHOUSER	03	41	106
TRAIL TO YESTERDAY (REPRINT)	FUNKHOUSER	03	66	40
TRAINMASTER	MCLARN	08	54	32
TRAINMASTER	LIVINGSTON	07	44	40
TRAINMASTER (REPRINT)	LIVINGSTON	09	68	34
TRAVEL, BLACK BOY, TRAVEL	AKERS	07	31	610
TRAVELING GRUNT, THE	DAVIS	05	35	61
TRAVELING GRUNT, THE	MCLARN	02	55	32
TRIAL BY SHOVEL	HERBER	03	53	114
TRICK AT EAGLE'S NEST, THE	FRASER	05	36	110

Railroad / Railfan

GENERAL RAILROADING

RAILROAD FICTION		M	Y	P
TRICK AT EAGLES NEST	FRASER	06	61	40
TROUBLE AT KILGORE	PHELPS	07	52	118
TROUBLE IN THE CANYON	TYLER	10	52	104
TROUBLES MADE TO ORDER	NORWOOD	12	50	98
TRURO	CAMERON	10	49	114
TURKEY TRICK, THE	LESLIE	12	32	115
TWENTY MINUTES LATE	FREY	07	77	34
TWILIGHT OF THE BOOMERS (REPRINT)	MCCLIN	04	73	32
TWIN TREES	LATHROP	09	50	106
TWO DOGS ONE WAYBILL	HUBBARD	05	76	34
TWO HOURS OFF DUTY	HOLLAND	08	32	74
TWO IMPORTANT RAIL OFFICIALS	ARMES	07	49	72
TWO-TIMING BLONDE	TITUS	06	67	42
TWO-WAY RULES	LIVINGSTON	02	68	42
TWO-WAY RULES (SOL MCCOOL)	LIVINGSTON	05	39	91
UNBROKEN SEALS	DELLINGER	03	49	104
UNCLE NASTY WHEEL	BAYLOR	03	47	55
UNCLE TOM'S CABIN	ENGINE PICTURE KID	05	36	70
UNDER TWO FLAGS	WATERS	02	45	34
UNFORESEEN CONTINGENCY	ARMES	09	51	86
UNWORTHY BROTHER, THE	DAVIS	11	31	543
VACATION AT MUSKEG	SWEET	02	31	360
VANDERBILT ROAD (HISTORICAL)	SAMPLES	04	41	18
VANISHING TAIL LIGHTS	MILLS	03	44	116
VARNISH ON THE SIGNAL	MILLS	08	45	37
VENGEANCE	DELLINGER	05	35	07
VENUS AT THE PUMP		02	32	374
VINEGAR BILL	LATHROP	11	44	124
WANDERLUST	BEDWELL	06	76	35
WANDERLUST (AN EDDIE SAND STORY)	BEDWELL	04	57	56
WARTIME MEMORIES OF '98	KANE	09	33	70
WASHOUT!	DELLINGER	09	32	154
WASTED YEARS	DELLINGER	04	33	54
WATCH THAT BOX	HAMILTON	05	51	12
WATERMELON TIME	LIVINGSTON	05	37	96
WEAK LINK, THE	WATERS	03	32	524
WESTBOUND JINX	JOHNS	01	33	106
WESTBOUND MAIN	DEEVER	04	47	32
WESTERN UNION KID, THE	TYLER	05	34	15
WHEELING THE HOTSHOTS	DELLINGER	12	49	88
WHEELING THE HOTSHOTS (REPRINT)	DELLINGER	01	79	27
WHEN DESTINY CALLS	DELLINGER	08	35	06
WHEN HOBOES RODE	TYLER	06	35	68
WHEN IT RAINS	SWEET	10	33	72
WHEN REDWOOD WENT DRY	CROSS	08	30	16
WHEN THE CHIPS ARE DOWN	TYLER	12	68	42
WHEN THE CHIPS WERE DOWN	TYLER	07	45	38
WHEN THE CLOCK STRIKES TWELVE		03	55	34
WHEN THE CLOCK STRIKES TWELVE	DELLINGER	04	74	20
WHEN THE HOBOES RODE		02	32	353
WHEN THERE'S TRAFFIC TO MOVE	BEDWELL	05	38	44
WHEN THERE'S TRAFFIC TO MOVE (R)	BEDWELL	12	56	60
WHERE IS MY GAL TONIGHT?	ENG PICTURE KID	07	35	54
WHILE THE BLIZZARD RAGED	GIROUARD	11	30	545
WHILE THE FLAGMAN SLEPT	MITCHELL	09	33	68

RAILROAD FICTION		M	Y	P
WHIRLWIND RIGGS	DELLINGER	07	47	34
WHISTLE FOR THE CROSSING	MOORE	05	49	116
WHISTLE ON THE LEVEE	DELLINGER	12	45	103
WHISTLE ON THE LEVEE (REPRINT)	DELLINGER	10	63	44
WHITECLIFF PASS (NOVELETTE)	SAMPLES	03	39	78
WHY THE LIMITED WAS LATE	MARTIN	08	37	118
WIDE-AWAKE SLEEPY	ROACH	04	33	48
WIDE-OPEN THROTTLE	SOMERVILLE	10	72	30
WILD POWER	DAVIDSON	01	32	198
WILLY'S FIRST TRIP	SCOTT	08	46	100
WITH THE WIRES DOWN	BEDWELL	10	38	40
WITH THE WIRES DOWN (REPRINT)	BEDWELL	12	57	48
WOLVES OF THE RAIL	JOHNS	03	32	434
WOMEN AND BOXCARS	JACKSON	03	48	116
WORLD'S LONGEST NICKNAME, THE	TEXINO	04	32	64
WORN-OUT MATERIAL	WILLIAMS	11	41	26
WORN-OUT MATERIAL (REPRINT)	WILLIAMS	05	69	42
WORTHY BROTHERS	DELLINGER	08	32	02
WORTHY BROTHERS (REPRINT)	DELLINGER	02	78	14
WRECKING MASTER	PACKARD	03	65	40
WRECKING MASTER, THE	PACKARD	03	35	122
WRECKING RACKET, THE	ENGINE PICTURE KID	07	34	70
YARDMASTER	MCLARN	05	54	36
YARDMASTER	BIDWELL	01	72	44
YARDMASTER'S STORY, THE	BEDWELL	08	39	82
YELLOW MAIL STORY	SPEARMAN	07	72	52
YOUNG RUNNER	MURDOCK	01	52	114

GENERAL MISCELLANEOUS TOPICS	M	Y	P
* COLLECTING RAILROAD ITEMS *			
BANK NOTE WITH TRAIN COLLECTING	09	53	06
BUILDER PLATE COLLECTING	10	67	18
BUILDER PLATE COLLECTING: LOCOMOTIVE	07	67	36
BUTTON COLLECTING: UNIFORMS	09	67	29
BUTTON COLLECTION: RAILROAD PHOTO	04	65	33
CHRISTMAS CARDS: RAILROAD	01	41	52
DATE NAIL COLLECTING (SHORT NOTE)	04	74	10
DATE NAILS: COLLECTING	03	79	43R
DATE NAILS: WHAT ARE THEY?	07	76	12
DINNERWARE PLATES MP:CAPITAL BLDS OF STS	04	50	139
ENVELOPES: RAIL-PICTURE	04	41	70
LANTERNS: RAILROAD	08	66	59
LETTERHEAD: GRIZZLY FLATS RAILROAD	10	41	44
MEDALS: RAILROAD	06	40	117
MONEY: RAILROAD "MONEY"	07	42	96
PASS COLLECTING: ANNUAL	09	69	34
PASSES 1878 EXAMPLES PHOTO	09	69	04
PASSES: F&CC "GOLD BELT LINE" 1900	04	42	18
PASSES: SCIOTO VALLEY RAILWAY	05	42	107
PICTURES: ENGINE COLLECTING	01	31	212
PLAYING CARD COLLECTING (RAILROAD)	12	63	62
POST OFFICE MARKS: RAILWAY	01	39	134
POSTCARDS: RAILROAD	07	79	03

Railroad/ Railfan

STEPHANS_RAILROAD_DIRECTORY

GENERAL RAILROADING

GENERAL MISCELLANEOUS TOPICS	M	Y	P
POSTMARKS: COLLECTING RY POSTMARKS/STAMP	06	34	94
PRESERVING YOUR RAILROADIANA	09	79	03
SCRAPBOOKS: RAILROAD	09	34	27
STAMP: FRENCH--PAUL DOUMER, SON RAIL LAB	11	47	134
STAMPS: 125 YEARS OF RAIL TRANSPORTATION	06	52	131
STAMPS: 15 ANNIV OF TURKISH REPUBLIC	03	39	132
STAMPS: 1944 3 CENT STAMP	08	44	68
STAMPS: 35TH ANNIV OF INDO-CHINESE RY	03	39	133
STAMPS: BULGARIA'S 50TH ANNIVERSARY RR	08	39	127
STAMPS: CASEY JONES APRIL 29 1950	08	50	135
STAMPS: CHILE 10 PESOS	10	40	131
STAMPS: COLLECTING RAILROAD POSTAGE STAM	01	31	216
STAMPS: COLLECTING STAMPS & RY POSTMARKS	06	34	94
STAMPS: COMPLETION OF MOSCOW SUBWAY	03	39	136
STAMPS: DEPICT ENGINE HISTORY	12	33	44
STAMPS: ECUADOR PRR LOCOMOTIVE	11	40	123
STAMPS: ELECTRIC RAILWAY STAMPS	02	36	92
STAMPS: FAKE TRAIN PICTURE STAMPS	03	38	68
STAMPS: FEATURED 6 TIMES ON US STAMPS	08	44	67
STAMPS: FOREIGN POSTAGE STAMPS	12	37	133
STAMPS: GERMAN SHOW MOTIVE POWER DEVELOP	12	35	90
STAMPS: INDIA'S NEW TRANSP SERIES STAMPS	04	38	129
STAMPS: JUGOSLAVIA CENTARY OF RAILROADS	08	39	126
STAMPS: KAHULUI RAILROAD (HAWAIIAN ISLAN	02	41	139
STAMPS: LOCOMOTIVE PICTURE STAMPS	06	35	65
STAMPS: LOCOMOTIVES ON (OLDEST)	03	70	37
STAMPS: MANCHUKUA EXPANDING RR SYSTEM	03	40	118
STAMPS: MEXICO 20 CENTAUQS	02	42	137
STAMPS: MEXICO AIRMAIL JESUS GARCIA MEMO	04	58	69
STAMPS: NETHERLANDS 100TH ANNIV (2 STAMP	01	40	141
STAMPS: NEW ZEALAND 100 YRS OF TRANSPORT	09	40	64
STAMPS: NEW ZEALAND RAILROAD STAMPS	08	37	33
STAMPS: NEWFOUNDLAND	08	38	75
STAMPS: NICARAGUA 75TH ANNIV 1937	11	40	136
STAMPS: NORTH AMERICA'S RAIL PICTURE STA	07	38	117
STAMPS: PERU'S LOCOMOTIVE STAMPS	09	36	78
STAMPS: PERU'S RAILWAY STAMPS	06	37	37
STAMPS: PICTURING LOCOMOTIVES COLLECTING	08	65	60
STAMPS: ROMANIA 70 YEARS OF RYS (6 STAMP	12	39	137
STAMPS: RUSSIAN RAILWAY STAMPS	07	37	119
STAMPS: TOY TRAINS ON US CHRISTMAS STAMP	10	71	09
STAMPS: VARIOUS COUNTRIES & ISSUES	11	75	11
SWITCH KEY COLLECTING	03	68	18
SWITCH LOCK AND KEY	03	42	117
TABLEWARE: COLLECTING RAILROAD MUGS	08	43	72
TABLEWARE: RAIL DINING COLLECTING	SP	77	24R
TABLEWARE: TRAINS	01	40	132
TIMETABLES: COLLECTING RAILROAD TIMETABL	12	34	76
TRAIN ORDERS: UNUSUAL	07	39	73
TRAIN-ORDER COLLECTIONS	06	69	18
WEATHERVANE REPLICA OF "WILLIAM MASON" P	08	46	99

* TOY TRAINS & TINPLATE *

	M	Y	P
TINPLATE RAILROADING CONSTRUCTION	06	35	138
TINPLATERS AND TINPLATE MANUFACTURERS	06	37	90

GENERAL MISCELLANEOUS TOPICS	M	Y	P
TOY-TRAIN BUSINESS	01	53	120

* PHOTOGRAPHY *

	M	Y	P
30,000 ENGINE PICTURES-LAVELLE HAS!!	12	31	107
AUTOMATED SLIDE SHOWS	05	86	22
AUTOMATED SLIDE SHOWS 2	07	86	19
BACKGROUND CLUTTER	03	80	56
BASIC RAILFAN CAMERA TECHNIQUES	SP	75	60R
BUYING A NEW CAMERA	07	84	13
BUYING A SLIDE PROJECTOR	11	81	20
CAMERA BASICS -- REVIEW	09	80	57
CAMERA SET UP LOCATIONS	F	76	56R
CAMERA STUDIES IN COLOR	01	79	33
COMPUTER PHOTO FILING	07	84	04
CONCERNING VIDEOS--READER DEBATE	09	84	04
CONCERNING VIDIO'S	05	84	20
CONTINUING PHOTO EDUCATION	07	85	20
CONTRIBUTING PHOTOS	11	87	30
CONTRIBUTIONS TO PHOTO LINE SECTION	01	79	56R
CROPPING YOUR SLIDES	F	75	58R
DARK SIDE PHOTOGRAPHS	01	82	11
DEPTH OF FIELD	03	79	60R
DEVELOPING FILM	10	77	58R
DISCOUNT CAMERA SHOPS	01	83	50
EARLIEST KNOWN RAILROAD PHOTO	06	57	36
EKTAGRAPHIC SLIDE PROJECTORS	03	82	19
EXPOSURE, A WORD ON	03	80	56
F8 AND BE THERE	11	85	28
FEEEDOM TRAIN PHOTO CONTEST WINNERS	10	77	28R
FILING THOSE SLIDES	01	86	20
FILTER FUSSING CONTINUED	11	78	57R
FILTERS FOR BLACK & WHITE FILM REVISITED	07	78	60R
FILTERS FOR BLACK & WHITE PHOTOS	04	78	58R
FUJICHROME?	01	87	28
FULL DAYLIGHT PHOTOS	03	83	18
FULL DAYLIGHT REVISITED	09	83	16
GROUP NIGHT PHOTO SESSIONS	09	78	60R
GRUBBY DAY PICTURES	W	76	58R
GRUBBY DAY PICTURES--MORE!	09	86	20
HOW ENGINE BUILDERS MAKE PHOTOS	02	35	137
HOW TO TAKE GOOD RAILROAD PHOTOS	06	33	80
ILFORD XP-1 FILM	07	82	14
K200 AND K64 FILM READER COMMENTS	09	87	05
K200 AND THE KODAK BLIMP	05	87	22
K200 MORE ABOUT KODACHROME 200	10	87	16
LARGE FORMAT CAMERAS FOR RAILROAD PHOTOS	SP	76	13R
LIGHT DAMAGES SLIDES!	05	82	13
LIGHTING THE TRIPLE CROSSING	11	83	26
LOCKING CABLE RELEASES	SU	76	56R
MASTER OF THE NIGHT--O WINSTON LINK	F	76	26R
METERING WITH FILTERS	11	79	44
MOVIE MISHAPS	11	80	24
MOVIES MORE!	03	81	23
MOVIES VS MOTOR DRIVES READER COMMENT	01	85	05
MOVING TRAINS PHOTOGRAPHY	01	36	92

Railroad/Railfan

GENERAL RAILROADING

GENERAL MISCELLANEOUS TOPICS

Title	M	Y	P
NEW FILMS FROM KODAK	03	87	53
NIGHT BEFORE THE ARROWS-RAILS AFTER DARK	07	85	32
NIGHT PHOTO SESSION 4-24 AT NORTH FORK	09	85	20
NIGHT RAILFAN PHOTOGRAPHY	SP	76	57R
PHOTO FREIGHTS	03	86	51
PHOTO LINE FOR FAN TRIP PHOTOS	W	75	58R
PHOTOGRAPHING LOCOMOTIVES	11	46	134
PHOTOGRAPHING THE SHORT LINE	08	49	92
PHOTOGRAPHING YOUR MODELS	08	35	141
PHOTOS FOR PUBLICATION	SP	77	58R
PLAYING WITH 24MM WIDE ANGLES	01	81	55
RAIL MOVIES	08	77	58R
RAIL RECORDS- PHOTOS AS RECORDS	12	52	06
RAILCAMERA HOBBY: HOW TO GET GOOD PICTUR	09	40	127
RAILFAN MOVIES	11	52	06
RAILFANNING WITH VIDEOTAPE	05	80	53
SHOOT YOUR WIFE	11	82	56
SHOOTING RAILROAD PEOPLE	05	78	60R
SHOP PHOTOGRAPHER	12	51	131
SHUTTER SPEED -- ALL IMPORTANT	11	78	57R
SHUTTER SPEEDS VS TRAIN SPEEDS	03	84	24
SLIDE KILLERS	05	81	60
SLIDE KILLERS REVISITED	07	81	60
SLIDE LONGEVITY	09	82	17
SLIDE PROJECTING SKILLS	07	83	19
SLIDE PROJECTORS	12	77	54R
SLIDE SHOW PREPERATION	11	75	58
SPEED GRAPHIC--ACTION PHOTOGRPHY	03	55	32
STRANGE LIGHT READINGS	09	84	24
SUPER CAMERA REPAIR COSTS	11	79	44
SUPER CAMERAS	09	79	60
TAKING PHOTOS OF SMALL ROADS	06	31	406
TAPE/SLIDE PRESENTATIONS 1	01	85	64
TAPE/SLIDE PRESENTATIONS 2	03	85	19
TAPE/SLIDE PRESENTATIONS 3	05	85	22
TELEPHOTO EXTENDERS	11	79	44
TELEPHOTO MENTALITY	11	86	28
TELEPHOTOS	05	79	57
THIRTY YEARS OF STEAM PHOTOGRAPHY	09	67	36
TRACKSIDE CAMERAMAN	02	57	48
VARIABLES IN PHOTOGRAPHY	05	83	19
VCR BASICS-I	07	87	14
VCR BASICS-II	09	87	22
WELL-PREPARED TRAVELING PHOTOGRAPHER	12	87	19
WESTERN PHOTOGRAPHY TECHNIQUES	09	81	20
WIDE ANGLE READER COMMENTS	09	81	06
WORLD'S LARGEST CAMERA	09	42	125
WRECK PHOTOGRAPHY	11	51	135

GENERAL RAILROAD ADDITIONS

Title	M	Y	P
100 YEARS OF STEAM (NYC)	09	53	44
100 YEARS OF STEAM ON LACKAWANNA	06	65	13
1800 MPH AIR TRAVEL VS TRAIN TRAVEL	11	67	10
2-6-0 MOGUL HISTORY READER UPDATE	12	62	37
2-8-2 MIKADO TYPE LOCOMOTIVES	12	59	24
30,000 ENGINE PICTURES TAKEN BY LAVELLE	12	31	107
320,000 RAIL JOBS OPEN AUGUST 1942	08	42	43
36 YEARS OF ENGINE PICTURES	12	43	136
4-4-0 GENERAL STOLEN AGAIN 1967	01	68	60
4-4-2 PRR #460 FASTEST 226 MILE RUN	08	31	75
4-4-2 READING CAMELBACKS--GLORY & DISAST	10	72	47
4-6-2 PRR #1737 CLASS K4S HISTORY OF	05	35	46
4-6-4 HUDSON TYPE LOCOS	04	59	22
4-8-0 LOCOMOTIVES	03	37	28
4-8-2 MOUNTAIN TYPE LOCOS	08	59	26
4-8-4 NORTHERN TYPE LOCOS	12	58	18
4449: HOMEWARD BOUND	12	77	46R
645 MILES FOR 87 CENTS BR&E	11	38	58
70 YEARS AGO IN OKLAHOMA	04	64	35
8444 TO NEW ORLEANS UP WORLDS FAIR SPECI	09	84	48
85 MILES IN 67 MINUTES MILW#6402 DOES IT	11	34	34
LIST OF LARGEST RAILROADS BY MILEAGE	08	33	85
LIST OF LONGEST RAILROADS: CB&Q CORRECTI	11	32	471
LIST OF RAILROADS IN ARIZONA: PAST/PRESE	06	62	46
LIST OF RAILROADS W/COLOR OF PASS EQUIP	08	33	85
LIST OF ROADS NOT IN OFFICIAL GUIDE 6	06	63	60
LIST OF SHORTLINES IN VERMONT	03	33	138
SNO INITIALS AND THE ROAD THEY STAND FOR	12	32	101
SNO INITIALS OF RAILROADS.	01	33	100
SNO LARGEST LOCOMOTIVES	07	32	506
SNO LARGEST RAILROADS	09	32	231
SNO LARGEST RAILROADS IN US-15 LARGEST	10	32	346
SNO MAIN YARDS OF VARIOUS ROADS	12	32	103
SNO MAXIMUM HEIGHT/WIDTH LIMITS ON ROADS	06	32	333
SNO MEXICAN RAILROAD: MODERN STREAMLINER	03	54	122
SNO MEXICAN RAILROADS: PHOTO ESSAY	05	52	70
SNO MEXICO: RECENT DEVELOPMENTS (1952)	06	52	62
SNO NEW JERSEY'S BEACH RAILWAYS	09	45	62
SNO NEW YORK TO CHICAGO-3 ROADS/MILEAGE	09	33	50
SNO RAIL GAUGE MATCHING ROMAN CHARIOTS	04	32	136
SNO RAIL TICKET PRINTER MACHINE	08	52	63
SNO RAILROAD MILEAGE	03	33	91
SNO RAILROAD MILEAGE: CN VS CP	03	33	92
SNO RAILROAD TRADEMARKS	12	31	54
SNO RAILROADS USING AUTO TRAIN CONTROLS	03	33	91
SNO RAILWAY MILEAGE OF THE WORLD	01	33	97
SNO ROADS/CLASS/SERIES NYC/B&A	04	32	72
SNO ROCKY MOUNTAIN TRACK	12	32	102
SNO SEATRAIN SERVICE	01	52	71
SNO SHORT LINES	10	44	78
SNO SHORTEST REGULAR PASSENGER RUN IN US	10	60	32
SNO SHORTEST ROUTE NYC TO ST LOUIS	12	32	104
SNO SHORTEST ROUTES--VARIOUS	06	32	333
SNO SHORTEST ROUTES: CHICAGO TO ST PAUL	07	32	506
TUNNEL MASK: ENGINEERS (SOUTHERN) PHOTO	02	41	12

Railroad/ Railfan

BILL OF LADING APPENDIX

The appendix is a reference in itself. It has 3 sections---Railroads, Builders and Manufacturers. Part A contains a listing of all RAILROADS that we have come across since we started our indexing project. Part B contains all the BUILDERS of prototype equipment and Part C all the MANUFACTURERS of models. All of the roads, builders or manufacturers appearing in this directory appear in this appendix. However all of the entries in this appendix may NOT appear in this directory, some may only appear in a previous volume. There are two listings: one alphabetically followed by its assigned abbreviation and one alphabetical by abbreviation followed by the road, builder or manufacturers name. By knowing one you can find the other. Some entries are followed by a (O). This is an obsolete abbreviation and is being phased out.

A note on the roads: Don't count them -- We list 4988 roads. (2445 more than Volume 1!) That number boggles our mind! The interesting fact is that we are still adding to the list. Don't forget this listing only covers roads sufficiently well known to have something published about them!

MANIFEST APPENDIX

ROADNAME-ABBREVIATION APPENDIX	A2
ABBREVIATION-ROADNAME APPENDIX	A34
BUILDER-ABBREVIATION APPENDIX	A67
ABBREVIATION-BUILDER APPENDIX	A69
MANUFACTURER-ABBREVIATION APPENDIX	A71
ABBREVIATION-MANUFACTURER APPENDIX	A76

APPENDIX A (RAILROADS)

ROADS ALPHABETICALLY W/ABBREVIATIONS	A
ABBEVILLE SOUTHERN	ABS
ABERDEEN & BRIAR PATCH	ABP
ABERDEEN & ROCKFISH RAILROAD	A&R
ABERDEEN BISMARCK & NORTHWESTERN	AB&NW
ABILENE & SOUTHERN RAILWAY	A&SO
ABILENE STREET RAILWAY COMPANY	ABI
ABITIBI PULP & PAPER COMPANY	ABIT
ABITIBI SOUTHERN	ABSO
ACME RED RIVER & NORTHERN	AR&N
ACTON (NASHUA ACTON & BOSTON RR)	NA&B
ADDISON RAILROAD	ADD
ADIRONDACK & ST LAWRENCE	A&STL
ADIRONDACK & ST LOUIS	AD&SL
ADIRONDACK RAILROAD	ADIR
AGAR	AG*
AGRICO CHEMICAL (PIERCE PLANT)	AGR
AGUA PRIETA SONORA MEXICO PACIFIC RY	APSM
AHNAPEE & WESTERN RAILWAY	A&W
AKRON & BARBERTON BELT RAILROAD	A&BB
AKRON & CHICAGO JUNCTION RAILROAD CO	A&CJ
AKRON BEDFORD & CLEVELAND	AB&CL
AKRON CANTON & YOUNGSTOWN RAILROAD	AC&Y.
AKRON CANTON & YOUNGSTOWN RAILWAY	AC&Y
AKRON UNION PASSENGER DEOPT	AUPD
AKRON YOUNGSTOWN & CINCINNATI	AY&C
ALABAMA & FLORIDA	A&F
ALABAMA & VICKSBURG	A&V
ALABAMA & WESTERN FLORIDA	A&WF
ALABAMA BIRMINGHAM & COAST	ALB&C
ALABAMA BY-PRODUCTS	AB-P
ALABAMA CENTRAL RAILROAD	ALC
ALABAMA DRYDOCK & SHIPBUILDING	AD&S
ALABAMA FLORIDA & ATLANTIC	AF&A
ALABAMA GREAT SOUTHERN	AGC
ALABAMA MIDLAND	AMID
ALABAMA POWER COMPANY	APC
ALABAMA STATE DOCKS TERMINAL	ASDT
ALABAMA STATE DOCKS TERMINAL RAILWAY	TRASD.
ALABAMA TENNESSEE & NORTHERN RAILROAD	AT&N
ALAMEDA BELT LINE	AB
ALAMOGORDO & SACRAMENTO MOUNTAIN (O)	A&SN
ALAMOGORDO & SACRAMENTO MOUNTAIN RR	A&SMT
ALAMOGORDO & SACRAMENTO MOUNTAIN RY	A&SMT
ALAMOGORDO & SACRAMENTO MOUNTIAN RY	A&SM.
ALAMOGORDO & SACREMENTO MOUNTIAN RR CO	A&SM
ALASKA ANTHRACITE RAILROAD	AKAC
ALASKA RAILROAD	AL
ALBANY & HUDSON ELECTRIC RAILWAY	A&H
ALBANY & NORTHERN RAILWAY	A&N
ALBANY & SCHENECTADY RAILROAD COMPANY	A&SCH
ALBANY & SUSQUEHANNA RAILROAD	A&SU
ALBANY & SYRACUSE RAILROAD	A&SY
ALBANY & W. STOCKBRIDGE	A&WS
ALBANY FLORIDA & NORTHERN RAILWAY	AF&N
ALBANY PASSENGER TERMINAL	APT
ALBANY PORT DISTRICT TERMINAL	APDT
ALBANY RAILWAY	ALB
ALBANY STREET RAILWAY	ALBS
ALBERNI PACIFIC LUMBER COMPANY	ALBP
ALBERTA & GREAT WATERWAYS RAILWAY	A&GWW
ALBERTA RESOURCES RAILWAY	AR
ALBION & SOUTHEASTERN	AL&SE
ALBION MINES	AM
ALBUQUERQUE EASTERN	AEA
ALCAN	ALCA
ALCOA	ALC*
ALCOA ORE COMPANY	AOC
ALCOA TERMINAL	AT
ALEXANDER RAILROAD	ALEX
ALEXANDRIA LONDON & HAMPSHIRE	AL&H
ALFRED & SLOAN	AL&SL
ALGIERS WINSLOW & WESTERN RAILWAY	AW&W
ALGOMA	ALG
ALGOMA CENTRAL & HUDSON BAY RAILWAY	AC&HB
ALGOMA CENTRAL RAILWAY	ALGC
ALGOMA EASTERN RAILWAY	ALGE
ALHAMBRA & PASADENA	A&P

ROADS ALPHABETICALLY W/ABBREVIATIONS	A
ALIQUIPPA & SOUTHERN RAILROAD	AL&S
ALLEGHENY & KINZUA	A&K
ALLEGHENY & SOUTH SIDE RAILWAY	A&SS
ALLEGHENY & WESTERN	AL&W
ALLEGHENY CENTRAL	AC
ALLEGHENY PORTAGE	AP
ALLEGHENY RAILROAD	ALY
ALLEGHENY VALLEY RAILROAD	ALV
ALLENTOWN	ALLEN
ALLENTOWN & SLATINGTON STREET RY CO	A&SSRY
ALLIED CHEMICAL (BRUNNER MOND)	ACBM
ALLIED CHEMICAL (SOLVAY)	ALL
ALMA & JONQUIERES RAILWAY	A&J
ALMANOR RAILROAD	ALM
ALTA	ALTA
ALTADENA	ALT
ALTON & EASTERN	A&E
ALTON & SANGAMON	AL&SA
ALTON & SOUTHERN RAILROAD	A&S
ALTON & SOUTHERN RAILWAY	A&S.
ALTON RAILROAD (B&O)	ARR
ALTOONA & LOGAN VALLEY RAILWAY	A&LV
ALTOONA JUNIATA & NORTHERN	AJ&N
ALTOONA NORTHERN	ANO
ALTUS WICHITA & HOLLIS	AW&H
ALUMINUM ORE COMPANY	AO
AMADOR CENTRAL RAILROAD	AMC
AMALGAMATED SUGAR	AMS
AMARILLO STREET RAILWAY COMPANY	ACRS
AMERICAN CAN COMPANY	ACC
AMERICAN CAST IRON PIPE	ACIP
AMERICAN COMMERCIAL BARGE LINES	ACBL
AMERICAN COMPRESSED STEEL	ACS
AMERICAN CYANAMID COMPANY	ACY
AMERICAN GRAINS	AG
AMERICAN PIPE & CONSTRUCTION	AP&C
AMERICAN RAILWAY EXPRESS	REA,
AMERICAN REDWOOD LUMBER	AMRL
AMERICAN REFRIGERATED TRANSIT	ART
AMERICAN REFRIGERATED TRANSIT	ART*
AMES & COLLEGE RAILWAY	A&CRY
AMHERST & BELCHERTOWN	A&B
AMHERST INDUSTRIES	AI
AMOSKEAG MANUFACTURING COMPANY	AMO
AMSTERDAM & ROCTON STREET RAILWAY	A&RS
AMTRAK	A
ANACONDA ALUMINUM	ANAL
ANACONDA COPPER MINING CO STREET RY	SRDAC
ANACONDA STREET RAILWAY (MONTANA)	ASRY
ANDROSCOGGIN & KENNEBEC	AND&K
ANDROSCOGGIN RAILROAD	AND
ANGEL'S FLIGHT RAILWAY	AF
ANGELINA & NECHES RIVER RAILROAD	A&NR
ANGELINA LUMBER COMPANY	ANG
ANN ARBOR RAILROAD	AA
ANNA QUARRIES	AQ
ANNAPOLIS & ELK RIDGE	A&ER
ANNAPOLIS SHORT LINE	ASL
ANNAPOLIS WASHINGTON & BALTIMORE	AW&B
ANROSCOGGIN & KENNEBEC	A&KEN
ANTELOPE & WESTERN	AN&W
ANTOINE VALLEY	ANTV
APACHE RAILWAY	APA
APALACHICOLA NORTHERN RAILROAD	AN
APPALACHIAN POWER COMPANY	APO
APPOMATTOX	APP
AQUITAINE	AQU
ARCADE & ATTICA RAILROAD	A&A
ARCADIA & BETSEY RIVER	A&BR
ARCATA & MAD RIVER RAILROAD	A&MR
ARCATA TRANSPORTATION COMPANY	ARCT
ARGENT LUMBER	ARL
ARGENTINE CENTRAL	ARC
ARIZONA & CALIFORNIA	A&C
ARIZONA & SOUTHEASTERN	AR&S
ARIZONA & UTAH	A&U

APPENDIX A (RAILROADS)

ROADS ALPHABETICALLY W/ABBREVIATIONS

Road	Abbr
ARIZONA CENTRAL RAILROAD	ARI
ARIZONA EASTERN RAILWAY	AE
ARIZONA LUMBER & TIMBER COMPANY	AL&T
ARIZONA SOUTHERN	ASO
ARKANSAS & LOUISIANA	A&L
ARKANSAS & LOUISIANA MISSOURI RAILWAY	A&LM
ARKANSAS & MISSOURI	AK&MO
ARKANSAS & OZARKS RAILROAD	A&O
ARKANSAS & WESTERN RAILWAY	A&WRY
ARKANSAS VALLEY INTERURBAN RAILWAY	AVI
ARKANSAS WESTERN RAILWAY	AW
ARLINGTON & FAIRFAX AUTO RAILROAD	A&FA
ARMCO CHEMICAL COMPANY	ACH
ARMCO STEEL	AS
ARMOUR	A*
ARNAUD	ARN
AROOSTOOK VALLEY RAILROAD	AV
ARTEMUS-JELLICO	AJ
ARTIC OIL WORKS	AOW*
ASARCO MEXICANA	AME
ASBESTOS & DANVILLE	A&DA
ASHBURNHAM	ASH
ASHERTON & GULF	A&GU
ASHEVILLE & SPARTANBURG	AV&SB
ASHLAND & WESTERN	ASH&W
ASHLAND COAL & IRON	AC&I
ASHLEY DREW & NORTHERN RAILWAY	AD&N
ASPHALT BELT	ABELT
ASSOCIATION OF AMERICAN RAILROADS	AAR
ASTORIA & COLUMBIA RIVER RAILROAD	A&CR
ATCHISON & TOPEKA	A&T
ATCHISON TOPEKA & SANTA FE RAILWAY	ATSF
ATKINSON CONSTRUCTION COMPANY	ATKC
ATL HIGHLANDS RED BANK & L BR ELEC	AHRB
ATLANTA & EDGEWOOD STREET RAILWAY	A&ES
ATLANTA & LAGRANGE RAILROAD	A&LG
ATLANTA & ST ANDREWS BAY RAILWAY	A&STAB
ATLANTA & WEST POINT RAILROAD	A&WP
ATLANTA BIRMINGHAM & ATLANTIC	AB&A
ATLANTA BIRMINGHAM & COAST (O)	AB&CO.
ATLANTA BIRMINGHAM & COAST RAILROAD	AB&C
ATLANTA CITY STREET RAILWAY	ACSR
ATLANTA CONSOLIDATED STREET RAILWAY	ACSRY
ATLANTA NORTHERN	ATNO
ATLANTA STONE MOUNTAIN & LITHONIA RY	ASM&L
ATLANTA TERMINAL COMPANY	ATC
ATLANTIC & DANVILLE RAILROAD	A&D
ATLANTIC & DANVILLE RAILWAY COMPANY	A&D.
ATLANTIC & EAST CAROLINA RAILWAY	A&EC
ATLANTIC & GREAT WESTERN	A&GW
ATLANTIC & GULF	A&G
ATLANTIC & LAKE SUPERIOR RAILROAD	A&LS
ATLANTIC & NORTH CAROLINA RAILROAD	A&NC
ATLANTIC & PACIFIC	A&PA
ATLANTIC & ST LAWRENCE	A&SL
ATLANTIC & SUBURBAN RAILWAY	A&SB
ATLANTIC & WESTERN RAILWAY	A&WE
ATLANTIC & YADKIN	A&Y
ATLANTIC CITY & SHORE	AC&S
ATLANTIC CITY & SUBURBAN TRACTION CO	AC&ST
ATLANTIC CITY RAILROAD	ACRR
ATLANTIC CITY TRANSPORTATION	ACT
ATLANTIC COAST ELECTRIC RAILWAY	ACE
ATLANTIC COAST LINE	ACL
ATLANTIC COAST LINE OF SOUTH CAROLINA	ACLC
ATLANTIC COAST LINE RR CO OF VIRGINIA	ACLV
ATLANTIC COAST ST JOHNS & INDIAN RIV	ACJ&IR
ATLANTIC GULF & WEST INDIES TRANSIT	AG&WIT
ATLANTIC KNOXVILLE & NORTHERN	AK&N
ATLANTIC MISSISSIPPI & OHIO	AM&O
ATLANTIC NORTHERN	ATN
ATLANTIC PORT RAILWAY	APRY
ATLANTIC SHORE LINE RAILWAY	ASHL
ATLANTIC STEEL COMPANY	ATS
ATLANTIC SUWANEE RIVER & GULF	ASR&G
ATTICA & ALLEGHENY VALLEY	A&AV
ATTICA & BUFFALO RAILROAD	A&BUF

ROADS ALPHABETICALLY W/ABBREVIATIONS

Road	Abbr
ATTICA & FREEDOM RAILROAD	AT&F
ATTICA & SOUTHERN	AT&SO
AUBURN & ROCHESTER	A&ROC
AUBURN & SYRACUSE	A&SYR
AUBURN & SYRACUSE ELECTRIC	A&SE
AUBURN BRANCH	AUB
AUGUSTA & FLORIDA RAILWAY	A&FL
AUGUSTA & SUMMERVILLE RAILROAD	A&SRR
AUGUSTA RAILROAD	AU
AUGUSTA SAVANNAH MACON & NORTHERN	ASM&N
AUGUSTA SOUTHERN	AUS
AUGUSTA TRAMWAY & TRANSFER	AT&T
AUGUSTA UNION STATION COMPANY	AUSC
AUGUSTA WATERVILLE & GARDINER	AW&G
AURORA BRANCH	AUR
AURORA ELGIN & FOX RIVER ELECTRIC	AE&FR
AURORA ELGIN & FOX RIVER ELECTRIC (O)	AE&FRE
AURORA PLAINFIELD & JOLIET	AP&J
AUSTIN & NORTHWESTERN	A&NW
AUSTIN CITY RAILROAD (RAILWAY?)	ACR
AUSTRIAN FEDERAL RAILWAY	AFR
AUTO TRAIN	ATR
AVONDALE SHIPYARDS	AVS
AVOYELLES RAILROAD	AVOY
AZUSA LINE	AZ
BABCOCK & WILCOX	B&WI
BABY RUTH	BR*
BAGDAD LAND & LUMBER COMPANY	BL&L
BAKERSFIELD & KERN ELECTRIC	B&KE
BALDWIN LOCOMOTIVE WORKS	BLW
BALLSTON TERMINAL RAILROAD	BTRR
BALTIMORE & ANNAPOLIS RAILROAD	B&AN
BALTIMORE & ANNAPOLIS SHORT LINE	B&ASL
BALTIMORE & CUMBERLAND VALLEY	B&CV
BALTIMORE & EASTERN RAILROAD	B&E
BALTIMORE & HAMPDEN ELECTRIC	B&HE
BALTIMORE & HARRISBURG	B&HB
BALTIMORE & HARRISBURG RY EXTENSION	B&HBE
BALTIMORE & HARRISBURG RY WESTERN EXT	B&HWE
BALTIMORE & LEHIGH RAILROAD	B&LEH
BALTIMORE & LEHIGH RAILWAY	B&LEH.
BALTIMORE & NORTHERN ELECTRIC RY	B&NE
BALTIMORE & OHIO & CHICAGO	B&O&C
BALTIMORE & OHIO CHICAGO TERMINAL RR	B&OCT
BALTIMORE & OHIO RAILROAD	B&O
BALTIMORE & OHIO SOUTHWESTERN RR	B&OSW.
BALTIMORE & OHIO SOUTHWESTERN RY	B&OSW
BALTIMORE & OHIO TERMINAL RAILROAD	B&OHT
BALTIMORE & POTOMAC	B&POT
BALTIMORE BELT RAILROAD COMPANY	BBELT
BALTIMORE CARROLL & FREDERICK	BC&FR
BALTIMORE CHESAPEAKE & ATLANTIC	BC&A
BALTIMORE CITY PASSENGER RAILWAY	BCPR
BALTIMORE PITTSBURGH & CHICAGO	BP&C
BALTIMORE TRANSIT COMPANY	BALT
BAMBERG ERHART & WALTERBORO RAILROAD	BE&W
BAMBERGER ELECTRIC	BE
BAMBERGER RAILROAD	BAM
BANGOR & AROOSTOOK	BAR
BANGOR & AROOSTOOK (O)	B&AR
BANGOR & KATAHDIN IRON WORKS	B&K
BANGOR & PISCATAQUIS	B&PI
BANGOR & PISCATAQUIS CANAL	B&PIC
BANGOR OLD TOWN & MILFORD	BOT&M
BANGOR RAILWAY & ELECTRIC COMPANY	BR&E
BARNEGAT RAILROAD	BARN
BARNES & TUCKER COAL COMPANY	B&T
BARRE & CHELSEA RAILROAD	B&CH
BARTLESVILLE INTERURBAN	BI
BARTLETT & ALBANY	B&AL
BARTLETT & WESTERN	B&WE
BARTLETT WESTERN	BW
BASIC REFRACTORIES	BAS
BATH & HAMMONDSPORT (O)	BA&H
BATH & HAMMONDSPORT RAILROAD	B&HA
BATTEN KILL RAILROAD	BKRR
BATTLE CREEK & STURGES RAILWAY CO	BC&S

A3

STEPHANS' RAILROAD DIRECTORY

APPENDIX A (RAILROADS)

ROADS ALPHABETICALLY W/ABBREVIATIONS	A
BAUXITE & NORTHERN RAILWAY	B&N
BAY AREA RAPID TRANSIT	BART
BAY COLONY	BCO
BAY DE NOQUET & MARQUETTE	BDN&M
BAY LINE	A&STAB.
BAY POINT & CLAYTON RAILROAD	BP&CT
BAY SOL	BS*
BAY STATE STREET RAILWAY	BSS
BAY TERMINAL	BAYT
BEACH MOUNTAIN RAILROAD	BEEC
BEAR CREEK RAILROAD	BEAR
BEAR LAKE & EASTERN	BL&E
BEAUFORT & MOREHEAD RAILROAD	BE&M
BEAUMONT & GREAT NORTHERN	B&GN
BEAUMONT SOUR LAKE & PORT ARTHUR TRAC	BSL&PA
BEAUMONT SOUR LAKE & WESTERN	BSL&W
BEAVER DAM RAILWAY	BDAM
BEAVER MEADE & ENGLEWOOD RAILROAD	BM&E
BEAVER MEADOW RAILROAD	BM
BEAVER MEADOW TRESKOW & NEW BOSTON RR	BMT&NB
BEAVER PENROSE & NORTHERN	BP&N
BECCO	B*
BECKER SAND & GRAVEL	BS&GR
BEDFORD & BILLERICA RAILROAD	B&BI
BEDFORD & BLOOMFIELD RAILROAD	B&BL
BEDFORD BELT RAILWAY	BEDB
BEDFORD RAILROAD	BED
BEECH CREEK CLEARFIELD & SOUTHWESTERN	BCC&S
BEECH CREEK RAILWAY	BC
BEECH MOUNTAIN RAILROAD	BEEC.
BELFAST & MOOSEHEAD LAKE RAILROAD	B&ML
BELL'S GAP RAILROAD	BGRR
BELLAIRE & SOUTHWESTERN	B&SW
BELLAIRE ZANESVILLE & CINCINNATI RR	BZ&C
BELLEFIELD BOILER PLANT	BBP
BELLEFONTAINE	BEL
BELLEFONTE CENTRAL RAILROAD	BEC
BELLEVUE & CASCADE	B&C
BELLINGHAM BAY & BRITISH COLUMBIA RY	BB&BC
BELMONT & BUFFALO	B&B
BELT RAILWAY COMPANY OF CHICAGO	BRC
BELTON RAILROAD	BELT
BELVIDERE-DELAWARE RAILROAD	BD
BEMIS LUMBER COMPANY	BEM
BENNETSVILLE & CHERAW RAILROAD	BE&CH
BENNINGTON & GLASTENBURY	B&G
BENNINGTON & RUTLAND	B&R
BENNINGTON & WOODFORD ELECTRIC RY	B&WEL
BENSON	BEN
BENTLY-KNIGHT ELECTRIC RAILWAY SYSTEM	B-KE
BERKSHIRE BACON	BEB*
BERKSHIRE STREET RAILWAY	BERS
BERLIN & BRIDGEPORT ELECTRIC ST RY	B&BE
BERLIN & NORTHERN RAILWAY	B&NO
BERLIN STREET RAILWAY	BSRY
BERWIND WHITE COAL MINING COMPANY	BWC
BESSEMER	BESS
BESSEMER & LAKE ERIE RAILROAD	B&LE
BETHLEHEM MINES	BETH
BEVIER & SOUTHERN RAILROAD	B&S
BF GOODRICH	BFGR
BIDDEFORD & SACO	BID&S
BIG CREEK & TELOCASET RAILROAD	BC&T
BIG FORK & NORTHERN	BF&N
BIG FOUR ROUTE	BFR
BIG HORN LUMBER COMPANY	BHL
BIG LEVEL & KINZUA RAILROAD	BL&K
BIG RIVER LUMBER COMPANY	BRLC
BIG TREES & PACIFIC	BT&P
BILLERICA & BEDFORD RAILROAD	BI&B
BILLINGS TRACTION	BILT
BILLMEYER & SMALL'S	BI&SM
BINGHAM & GARFIELD RAILWAY COMPANY	B&GA
BINGHAMTON	BING
BIRDS HILL SAND COMPANY	BHS
BIRMINGHAM & ATLANTIC	B&AT
BIRMINGHAM & GULF RY & NAVIGATION CO	B&GR

ROADS ALPHABETICALLY W/ABBREVIATIONS	A
BIRMINGHAM & SOUTHEASTERN RAILROAD	BI&S
BIRMINGHAM BELT RAILROAD	BBRR
BIRMINGHAM COLUMBUS & ST ANDREWS	BC&SA
BIRMINGHAM ELECTRIC COMPANY	BIR
BIRMINGHAM RAIL & LOCO COMPANY	BR&L
BIRMINGHAM SLAG	BSL
BIRMINGHAM SOUTHERN RAILROAD	BIS
BIRMINGHAM TERMINAL COMPANY	BIRM
BIRMINGHAM TRANSIT COMPANY	BIRT
BIRMINGHAM-TUSCALOOSA RY & UTILITIES	BTR&U
BISMARCK WASHBURN & GREAT FALLS	BW&GF
BLACK HILLS & FORT PIERRE	BH&FP
BLACK HILLS CENTRAL RAILROAD	BHC
BLACK LICK & YELLOW CREEK RAILROAD	BL&YC
BLACK MESA & LAKE POWELL RAILROAD	BM&LP
BLACK MOUNTAIN RAILROAD	BMT
BLACK RIVER & UTICA RAILROAD	BR&U
BLACK RIVER & WESTERN RAILROAD	BR&W
BLAIRSTOWN RAILWAY	BL
BLAIRSVILLE & INDIANA	B&I
BLATZ	BL*
BLATZ OLD HEIDELBERG	BOH*
BLAW-KNOX CORPORATION-UNION STEEL DIV	B-K
BLISSFIELD RAILROAD	BLISS
BLOEDALL-DONOVAN LUMBER MILLS	BDLM
BLOEDEL STEWART & WELSH LTD	BS&W
BLOOMER RAILROAD	BLRR
BLOOMSBURG & SOUTHERN	BL&S
BLOOMSBURG & SULLIVAN	B&SU
BLUE MOUNTAIN & READING	BM&R
BLUE RIDGE & ATLANTIC RAILROAD	BR&A
BLUE RIDGE RAILWAY	BR
BLUE SPRINGS ORANGE CITY & ATLANTIC	BSOC&A
BLUFF CITY ELECTRIC STREET RY CO	BCES
BODIE & BENTON RAILWAY	BOD&B
BODIE RAILWAY & LUMBER COMPANY	BODRL
BOEING RAILROAD	BOE
BOISE & INTERURBAN RAILWAY	B&IRY
BOISE & WESTERN	BOI&W
BOISE RAILROAD	BRR
BOISE VALLEY RAILWAY	BVRY
BOMBARDIER	BOM
BONHOMIE & HATTIESBURG SOUTHERN RR	B&HS
BONLEE & WESTERN	BO&W
BOOTH KELLY LUMBER COMPANY	BKL
BORATE & DAGGETT RAILROAD	B&D
BORDEN CHEMICAL	BORC
BORK COMPANY	BORK
BOSQUES DE CHIHUAHUA	BDC
BOSTON & ALBANY	B&A
BOSTON & ALBANY RAILROAD OF GEORGIA	B&AGA
BOSTON & LOWELL RAILROAD	B&L
BOSTON & MAINE	B&M
BOSTON & NEW YORK AIR LINE	B&NY
BOSTON & NORTHERN STREET RAILWAY	B&NSR
BOSTON & PROVIDENCE	B&P
BOSTON & THOMPSON RAILROAD	B&TRR
BOSTON & WORCESTER RAILROAD	B&WO
BOSTON BARRE & GARDNER	BB&G
BOSTON CLINTON & FITCHBURG	BC&F
BOSTON CLINTON FITCHBURG & NEW BEDFORD	BCF&NB
BOSTON CONCORD & MONTREAL RAILROAD	BC&M
BOSTON ELEVATED LINES	BELL
BOSTON ELEVATED RAILWAY	BELL.
BOSTON HARTFORD & ERIE	BH&E
BOSTON HOOSAC TUNNEL & WESTERN	BHT&W
BOSTON LOWELL & NASHUA	BL&N
BOSTON METALS COMPANY	BMC
BOSTON NORWICH & NEW LONDON	BN&NL
BOSTON RAPID TRANSIT	BRT
BOSTON REVERE BEACH & LYNN	BRB&L
BOSTON SUBWAY	BS
BOSTON WINTHROP & POINT SHIRLEY	BW&PS
BOSTON WINTHROP & SHORE RAILROAD	BW&S
BOURK DONALDSON TAYLOR POTATOES	BDTP*
BOWDON RAILWAY & TRANSPORTATION CO	BOW
BOYNE CITY GAYLORD & ALPENA RAILROAD	BCG&A

A4

APPENDIX A (RAILROADS)

ROADS ALPHABETICALLY W/ABBREVIATIONS	A
BOYNE CITY RAILROAD	BOYN
BOYTON BICYCLE RAILWAY	BBRY
BRADFORD & FOSTER BROOK RAILWAY	B&FB
BRADFORD & WESTERN PENNSYLVANIA	B&WP
BRADFORD BORDELL & KINZUA	BB&K
BRADFORD BORDELL & SMETHPORT	BB&S
BRADFORD ELDRED & CUBA	BE&C
BRADFORD RICHBURG & CUBA	BR&C
BRADFORD STEAM RAILROAD	BRAD
BRADSHAW MOUNTAIN	BRMT
BRAINERD & NORTHERN MINNESOTA	B&NM
BRANDON RAILROAD	BRRR
BRANDYWINE TRANSIT	BWT
BRANDYWINE VALLEY RAILROAD	BVRR
BRANFORD ELECTIRC RAILWAY	BERY
BRANFORD RAILROAD	BRAR
BRANFORD STEAM RAILROAD	BSRR
BRANTFORD WATERLOO & LAKE ERIE RAILWAY	BW&LE
BRASWELL SAND & GRAVEL	BS&G
BRATTLEBORO & WHITEHALL	B&W
BREWSTER PHOSPHATE	BP
BREWSTER PHOSPHATES	BREP
BRIDGEPORT TRAMWAY	BRID
BRIDGTON & HARRISON RAILWAY	B&H
BRIDGTON & SACO RIVER RAILROAD	B&SR
BRIDGTON RAILROAD & DEVELOPMENT	BR&D
BRIGANTINE BEACH RAILROAD	BBER
BRIGANTINE BECAH RAILROAD	BRIGB
BRIGHT HOPE	BH
BRILLION & FOREST JUNCTION	B&FJ
BRIMSTONE RAILROAD	BRI
BRINSON RAILWAY	BRIN
BRISTOL & NORFOLK STREET RAILWAY	BR&N
BRISTOL & NORTH WESTERN	B&NW
BRISTOL BELT LINE RAILWAY COMPANY	BBLR
BRISTOL ELIZABETHTON & NORTH CAROLINA	BE&NC
BRISTOL RAILROAD	BRIS
BRISTOL TRACTION	BT
BRITISH COLUMBIA ELECTRIC RAILWAY	BCE
BRITISH COLUMBIA HYDRO & POWER AUTHOR	BCH&P
BRITISH COLUMBIA RAILWAY	BCRW
BRITISH COLUMBIA YUKON RAILWAY	BCRY
BRITISH RAILWAYS	BRW
BRITISH YUKON NAVIGATION COMPANY	BYNC
BRITISH YUKON RAILWAY	BYRY
BROCKINGS & PEACH ORCHARD	B&PO
BROCKVILLE & OTTAWA	B&OT
BRODERICK WOOD PRODUCTS	BWP
BROOKLYN & QUEENS TRANSIT	B&Q
BROOKLYN & ROCKAWAY BEACH	B&RB
BROOKLYN BATH & CONEY ISLAND RAILROAD	BB&CI
BROOKLYN BATH & WEST END	BB&WE
BROOKLYN CITY & NEWTON RAILROAD CO	BC&N
BROOKLYN CITY RAILROAD COMPANY	BCRR
BROOKLYN EASTERN DISTRICT TERMINAL	BEDT
BROOKLYN ELEVATED RAILROAD	BERR
BROOKLYN HEIGHTS RAILROAD	BHRR
BROOKLYN MANHATTAN TRANSIT COMPANY	BMTC
BROOKLYN NAVY YARD	BNY
BROOKLYN RAPID TRANIST	BRRT
BROOKLYN RAPID TRANSIT ELEVATED CO.	BRTE
BROOKLYN RAPID TRANSIT SUBWAY LINES	BRTS
BROOKSVILLE & HUDSON	BR&H
BROOKVILLE & MAHONING	B&MA
BROWARD COUNTY PORT AUTHORITY	BCPA
BROWN COUNTY	BRO
BROWNSTONE & MIDDLETOWN	BR&M
BRUCE MINES & ALGONQUIN	BM&A
BRUNSWICK & BIRMINGHAM	BR&B
BRUNSWICK & WESTERN	BR&WE
BRUNSWICK TRACTION COMPANY	BTC
BUCK MOUNTAIN	BUCK
BUCKEYE CENTRAL SCENIC RAILROAD	BCSR
BUCKEYE STEEL CASTINGS COMPANY	BSC

ROADS-ALPHABETICALLY W/ABBREVIATIONS	A
BUCKHANNON & NORTHERN	BUCK&N
BUCKSPORT & BANGOR	BU&BA
BUDLONG	BDL*
BUFFALO & ERIE RAILWAY COMPANY	B&ERIE
BUFFALO & GENEVA RAILROAD	BUF&G
BUFFALO & LAKE ERIE TRACTION	B&LET
BUFFALO & LAKE HURON RAILWAY	B&LH
BUFFALO & LOCKPORT	BUF&L
BUFFALO & ROCHESTER RAILROAD	B&ROCH
BUFFALO & ST MARYS	B&SM
BUFFALO & SUSQUEHANNA (O)	B&SQU
BUFFALO & SUSQUEHANNA RAILROAD	B&SQ
BUFFALO & SUSQUEHANNA RAILWAY	B&SQ.
BUFFALO ALLEGHENY & PITTSBURG	BA&PI
BUFFALO ATTICA & ARCADE RAILROAD	BA&A
BUFFALO BAYO BRAZOS & COLORADO RY	BBB&C
BUFFALO BRADFORD & PITTSBURGH	BB&P
BUFFALO CHAUTAUQUA LAKE & PITTSBURGH	BCL&P
BUFFALO CORREY & PITTSBURGH	BC&P
BUFFALO CREEK & GAULEY RAILROAD	BC&G
BUFFALO CREEK RAILROAD	BCR
BUFFALO LAKE ERIE & CLEVELAND	BLE&C
BUFFALO LOCKPORT & ROCHESTER	BL&R
BUFFALO ROCHESTER & PACIFIC	BR&PA
BUFFALO ROCHESTER & PITTSBURG RAILWAY	BR&P
BUFFALO RUN BELLEFONTE & BALD EAGLE RR	BRB&BE
BUFFALO SLAG COMPANY	BUSC
BUFFALO ST MARYS & SOUTHWESTERN	BM&S
BUFFALO SUSQUEHANNA & WESTRN ALLEGHENY	BS&WA
BUFFALO TERMINAL	BUT
BUFFALO UNION CAROLINA RAILROAD	BUC
BUICK	BUI
BULERICA & BEDFORD	B&BED
BULL FROG BEER	BFB*
BULLFROG GOLDFIELD RAILROAD	BG
BUNKER HILL & SULLIVAN MINE & COAL CO	BH&SM&C
BURLINGTON	CB&Q.
BURLINGTON (O)	B
BURLINGTON & LAMOILLE VALLEY	B&LAM
BURLINGTON & LAMOILLE VALLEY (O)	B&LAMV
BURLINGTON & MISSOURI	B&MI
BURLINGTON & MISSOURI RIVER RAILROAD	B&MR
BURLINGTON & MT HOLLY	B&MH
BURLINGTON & NORTHWESTERN	BU&NW
BURLINGTON & WESTERN	BU&W
BURLINGTON CEDAR RAPIDS & MINNESOTA	BCR&M
BURLINGTON CEDAR RAPIDS & NORTHERN	BCR&N
BURLINGTON ELECTRIC	BUR
BURLINGTON NORTHERN	BN
BURLINGTON NORTHERN (MANITOBA) LTD	BN(M)
BURLINGTON REFRIGERATOR EXPRESS	BRE
BURLINGTON-ROCK ISLAND	BURI
BURNS BIGGS LUMBER COMPANY	BB
BURNSVILLE & EASTERN	B&EA
BUSH TERMINAL RAILROAD	BUSH
BUTLER & PITTSBURGH	B&PITT
BUTLER COUNTY RAILROAD	BUTCO
BUTTE ANACONDA & PACIFIC RAILWAY	BA&P
ST LOUIS SOUTHWESTERN (COTTON BELT)	CBELT.
CADDO & CHOCTAW	CA&CH
CADILLAC & LAKE CITY RAILWAY	C&LC
CADILLAC & NORTHEASTERN	CA&NE
CADIZ RAILROAD	CAD
CAHUENGA VALLEY	CVA
CAIRO & FULTON RAILROAD	C&F
CAIRO & KANAWANHA VALLEY RAILROAD	C&KV
CAIRO ARKANSAS & TEXAS	CA&T
CAIRO RAILROAD	CAI
CAIRO TRUMAN & SOUTHERN	CT&S
CALAIS STREET RAILWAY	CALS
CALCASIEU PAPER COMPANY	CAPC
CALDOR & NORTHERN	C&NO
CALGARY MUNICIPAL RAILWAY	CMRY
CALIFORNIA & NEVADA	CA&N
CALIFORNIA & NORTHERN	CAL&N
CALIFORNIA & OREGON COAST	C&OC
CALIFORNIA CENTRAL	CCE

A5

APPENDIX A (RAILROADS)

ROADS ALPHABETICALLY W/ABBREVIATIONS	A
CALIFORNIA EASTERN	CE
CALIFORNIA ELECTRIC RAILWAY	CER
CALIFORNIA MIDLAND RAILROAD	CAM
CALIFORNIA NORTHWESTERN RAILWAY CO	CNW
CALIFORNIA PACIFIC	CAPA
CALIFORNIA RAILWAY	CARY
CALIFORNIA SOUTHERN	CAS
CALIFORNIA SOUTHERN & REDONDO BEACH	CS&RB
CALIFORNIA STREET CABLE RR COMPANY	CSCR
CALIFORNIA STREET LINE	CSCR.
CALIFORNIA WESTERN NORTH	CWN
CALIFORNIA WESTERN RR & NAV CO	CW
CALTRANS	CAL
CALUMET & HECLA CONSOLIDATED COPPER	C&HC
CALUMET & SOUTHEASTERN	CA&SE
CAMAS PRAIRIE RAILROAD	CAPR
CAMBRIA & INDIANA RAILROAD	C&I
CAMDEN & AMBOY RAILROAD	C&AM
CAMDEN & ATLANTIC RAILROAD	C&AT
CAMDEN & BURLINGTON COUNTY	C&BCO
CAMDEN & TRENTON RAILWAY	C&TR
CAMDEN COUNTY RAILROAD	CCRR
CAMDEN GLOUSTER & MT EPHRAIM	CG&ME
CAMINO CABLE & NORTHERN	CC&N
CAMINO PLACERVILLE & LAKE TAHOE RR	CP&LT
CAMP LEJEUNE RAILROAD	CLRR
CAMP MANUFACTURING COMPANY	CMFG
CAMPBELL'S CREEK RAILROAD	CCR
CANADA & GULF TERMINAL RAILWAY	C&GT
CANADA & ST LOUIS RAILWAY CO	C&STL
CANADA ATLANTA	CA
CANADA EASTERN	CEAST
CANADA SOUTHERN BRIDGE COMPANY	CSB
CANADA SOUTHERN LINE	CSLI
CANADA SOUTHERN RAILWAY	CSLI.
CANADA SOUTHERN RAILWAY	CSOR
CANADIAN COLLIERIES LIMITED	CAC
CANADIAN COPPER COMPANY	CCOC
CANADIAN FOREST PRODUCTS	CFP
CANADIAN GOVERNMENT RAILWAY	CGR
CANADIAN NATIONAL RAILWAY	CN
CANADIAN NORTHERN QUEBEC RAILWAY CO	CNQ
CANADIAN NORTHERN RAILWAY	CAN
CANADIAN PACIFIC	CP
CANADIAN PACIFIC GREAT WESTERN	CPGE
CANADIAN REFRACTORIES	CRE
CANADIAN SOUTHERN RAILROAD COMPANY	CS
CANAJOHARIE & CATSKILL RAILROAD	C&CA
CANAL & CLAIBORNE RAILROAD	CA&CL
CANANEA RIO YAQUI Y PAIFICO	CYR&P
CANANEA YANQUI RIVER & PACIFIC RR	CYR&P.
CANARISE & ROCKAWAY BEACH	C&RB
CANASTOTA NORTHERN	CANO
CANEY FORK & WESTERN	CF&W
CANMORE MINES	CMM
CANON CITY & ROYAL GORGE	CC&RG
CANON CITY FLORENCE & ROYAL GORGE	CCF&RG
CANTON & CARTHAGE	C&C
CANTON RAILROAD	C
CANYON CREEK RAILROAD	CYC
CAPE BRETON STEAM RAILWAY	CBSR
CAPE BRETON TRAMWAYS	CBT
CAPE COD CENTRAL	CC
CAPE COD RAILROAD	CCOD
CAPE COD REGIONAL TRANS AUTHORITY	CCRTA
CAPE FEAR & NORTHERN	CF&N
CAPE FEAR RAILWAYS	CF
CAPE GIRARDEAU & CHESTER RAILROAD	CG&C
CAPE GIRARDEAU NORTHERN	CGN
CAPE MAY DELAWARE BAY & SEWELLS POINT	CMDB&S
CAPITAL CITY ELECTRICAL RY (ALABAMA)	CCER
CAPITAL TRANSIT COMPANY	CTC
CARBON COUNTY RAILWAY	CARB
CARBON STREET RAILWAY	CSRY
CARGILL INCORPORATED	CAR
CARILLON & GRENVILLE	C&G

ROADS ALPHABETICALLY W/ABBREVIATIONS	A
CARLTON & COAST	C&CO
CARLTON LOGGING COMPANY	CLC
CARNATION	CAR≠
CAROLINA & NORTHWESTERN RAILWAY	C&N
CAROLINA & YADKIN RIVER RAILROAD	C&YR
CAROLINA & YADKIN RIVER RAILWAY	C&YR.
CAROLINA CLINCHFIELD & OHIO RAILROAD	CC&O
CAROLINA CLINCHFIELD & OHIO RAILWAY	CC&O.
CAROLINA NITROGEN DIV OF GRACE CHEM	CND
CAROLINA POWER & LIGHT	CP&L
CAROLINA RAILROAD	KCRR
CAROLINA SOUTHERN RAILWAY	CARS
CAROLINA WESTERN RAILROAD	CAW
CARRABELLE TALLAHASSEE & GEORGIA	CT&G
CARROLLTON RAILROAD	CARR
CARROLTON & WORTHVILLE	C&WO
CARSON & COLORADO RAILROAD	CA&C
CARSON & COLORADO SOUTHERN PACIFIC	C&CSP
CARTHAGE & ADIRONDACK	C&AD
CARTHAGE ROAD	CARTH
CARTIAGE PAPER MAKERS	CPM
CARTIER RAILWAY	CART
CASCADE	CASC
CASPER SOUTH FORK & EASTERN	CSF&E
CASS SCENIC	CASS
CASSVILLE & EXETER RAILWAY (MISSOURI)	C&E
CASSVILLE & WESTERN	CV&W
CATASAUQUA & FOGELSVILLE	C&FOG
CATAWISSA	CAT
CATHELS & SORENSON	C&SO
CATSKILL & CANAJOHARIE	CA&CH
CATSKILL & TANNERSVILLE RAILROAD	C&TA
CATSKILL MOUNTAIN RAILROAD	CMT.
CATSKILL MOUNTAINS RAILWAY SYSTEMS	CMT
CAYUGA & SUSQUEHANNA RAILROAD	C&SU
CAYUGA LAKE	CAYL
CAYUGA SOUTHERN	CAYS
CAZENOVIA SOUTHERN	CAZS
CD JOHNSON LUMBER COMPANY	JL
CEDAR RAPIDS & IOWA CITY RAILWAY	CR&IC
CENTRAL APPALACHIAN COAL COMPANY	CACC
CENTRAL CALIFORNIA TRACTION COMPANY	CCT
CENTRAL CANADA RAILWAY	CCAN
CENTRAL FOUNDRY	CFO
CENTRAL ILLINOIS RAILWAY	CILL
CENTRAL INDIANA RAILWAY	CIN
CENTRAL IOWA TRANSPORTATION COOP	CITC
CENTRAL MASSACHUSETTS	CMA
CENTRAL MEXICANO	CMEX
CENTRAL MILITARY TRACT	CEMT
CENTRAL NEW ENGLAND & WESTERN	CNE&W
CENTRAL NEW ENGLAND RAILROAD	CNE
CENTRAL NEW YORK & NORTHERN	CNY&N
CENTRAL NEW YORK & WESTERN	CNY&W
CENTRAL NEW YORK RAILROAD	CNY
CENTRAL NEW YORK SOUTHERN RAILROAD	CNYS
CENTRAL OF GEORGIA	CGA
CENTRAL PACIFIC RAILROAD (1861)	CPA
CENTRAL PACIFIC RAILWAY (1899)	CPA.
CENTRAL RAILROAD OF GEORGIA	CGA.
CENTRAL RAILROAD OF LONG ISLAND	CRLI
CENTRAL RAILROAD OF NEW JERSEY	CNJ
CENTRAL RAILROAD OF OREGON	CRO
CENTRAL RAILWAY OF ARKANSAS	CRARK
CENTRAL RAILWAY OF CALIFORNIA	CRYOC
CENTRAL RAILWAY OF CANADA	CRYC
CENTRAL RAILWAY OF PERU	CRWP
CENTRAL RR & BANKING CO OF GEORGIA	CRR&B
CENTRAL RR & BANKING CO OF GEORGIA(O)	CRB
CENTRAL RR & CANAL CO OF GEORGIA	CRR&C
CENTRAL TRACTION COMPANY	CET
CENTRAL VALLEY	CEV
CENTRAL VERMONT (CN) RAILWAY	CV
CENTRAL WAREHOUSE COMPANY	CWC
CENTRAL WEST VIRGINIA & SOUTHERN	CWV&S
CENTRE & CLEARFIELD	CE&C
CERRILLOS COAL RAILROAD	CECR

A6

APPENDIX A (RAILROADS)

ROADS ALPHABETICALLY W/ABBREVIATIONS	A
CERVECERIA CUAHTEMOC	CECU
CHAGRIN FALLS & EASTERN ELECTRIC RY	CF&E
CHAMAS PRAIRIE RAILROAD	CHP
CHAMPION FIBRE	CFI
CHAMPLAIN & CONNECTICUT RAILROAD	C&CON
CHAMPLAIN & OGDENSBURG RAILROAD	C&OG
CHAMPLAIN & ST LAWRENCE	C&SL
CHAREAU MARTIN WINE	CMW*
CHARLES CITY WESTERN RAILWAY	CCW
CHARLESTON & HAMBURG RAILROAD	C&HB
CHARLESTON & SAVANNAH	CH&SO
CHARLESTON & WESTERN CAROLINA RAILWAY	C&WC
CHARLESTON CINCINNATI & CHICAGO	CC&CH
CHARLESTON UNION STATION COMPANY	CUST
CHARLEVOIX & MICHIGAN CENTRAL	C&MC
CHARLOTTE MONROE & COLUMBIA	CM&C
CHARTIERS VALLEY RAILROAD	CHVR
CHATAM IRON & METAL	CI&M
CHATEAUGAY RAILROAD	CHAT
CHATHAM & LEBANON VALLEY RAILROAD	C&LV
CHATHAM WALLACEBURG & LAKE ERIE	CW&LE
CHATTACHOOCEE & GULF	C&GU
CHATTAHOOCHEE & EAST PASS	C&EP
CHATTAHOOCHEE INDUSTRIAL RAILROAD	CI
CHATTAHOOCHEE VALLEY RAILWAY	CHV
CHATTANOOGA ROME & NORTHERN	CR&S
CHATTANOOGA STATION COMPANY	CHSC
CHATTANOOGA TRACTION COMPANY	CHTR
CHAUTAUQUA TRACTION COMPANY	CHT
CHEAT RIVER COAL & LUMBER RAILROAD	CRC
CHEHALIS WESTERN RAILROAD	CHWE
CHERAW & CHESTER RAILWAY	C&CRY
CHERAW & COALFIELD	CH&C
CHERAW & DARLINGTON	CH&DA
CHERRELYN LINE (COLORADO)	CHER
CHERRY RIVER BOOM & LUMBER	CRB&L
CHESAPEAKE & OHIO RAILROAD	C&O
CHESAPEAKE & OHIO RAILWAY	C&O.
CHESAPEAKE & WESTERN RAILROAD	C&W
CHESAPEAKE BEACH RAILWAY	CBE
CHESAPEAKE OHIO & SOUTHWESTERN	CO&SW
CHESAPEAKE SHENANDOAH & WESTERN	CS&W
CHESAPEAKE WESTERN RAILWAY	CHW
CHESHIRE	CHE
CHESSIE SYSTEM	CHESS
CHESTER & BECKET RAILROAD	C&B
CHESTER & LENOIR	CH&L
CHESTER DARBY & PHILADELPHIA RAILWAY	CD&P
CHESTER PERRYVILLE & ST GENEVIEVE	CP&SG
CHESTER TRACTION COMPANY	CTRC
CHESTERFIELD	CHES
CHESTNUT RIDGE RAILWAY	CRI
CHESUNCOOK CHAMBERLAIN	CCH
CHESWICK & HARMAR RAILROAD	C&H
CHICAGO & AIR LINE	C&AL
CHICAGO & ALTON RAILROAD	C&A
CHICAGO & ATLANTIC	CH&A
CHICAGO & AURORA	C&AU
CHICAGO & BLOCK COAL	C&BC
CHICAGO & CALUMET RIVER RAILWAY	C&CR
CHICAGO & CALUMET TERMINAL RAILWAY	C&CT
CHICAGO & EASTERN ILLINOIS RAILROAD	C&EI
CHICAGO & EASTERN ILLINOIS RAILWAY	C&EI
CHICAGO & ERIE	CH&E
CHICAGO & GALENA	C&GA
CHICAGO & GRAND TRUNK	CH&GT
CHICAGO & GREAT SOUTHERN	C&GS
CHICAGO & ILLINOIS MIDLAND RAILWAY	C&IM
CHICAGO & ILLINOIS WESTERN RAILROAD	C&IW
CHICAGO & INDIANA COAL RAILWAY	C&IC
CHICAGO & INDIANAPOLIS AIR LINE RY	C&IAL
CHICAGO & INDIANAPOLIS TERMINAL CO	C&IT
CHICAGO & INTERURBAN TRACTION CO	C&ITR
CHICAGO & JOLIET	C&J
CHICAGO & MILWAUKEE	CH&M
CHICAGO & MILWAUKEE ELECTRIC RAILWAY	C&ME
CHICAGO & NORTH WESTERN RAILWAY	C&NW

ROADS ALPHABETICALLY W/ABBREVIATIONS	A
CHICAGO & NORTHERN PACIFIC	C&NP
CHICAGO & NORTHERN RAILROAD	CH&N
CHICAGO & NORTHWESTERN BELT	C&NWB
CHICAGO & PACIFIC	CH&P
CHICAGO & ROCK ISLAND	C&RI
CHICAGO & SOUTH SIDE RAPID TRANSIT	C&SSRT
CHICAGO & SOUTHEASTERN RAILWAY	C&SE
CHICAGO & TOMAH	C&TOM
CHICAGO & WABASH VALLEY	C&WV
CHICAGO & WEST MICHIGAN RAILS	C&WM
CHICAGO & WEST TOWNS RAILWAY	C&WT
CHICAGO & WESTERN INDIANA BELT	C&WIB
CHICAGO & WESTERN INDIANA RAILROAD	C&WI
CHICAGO ALTON & ST LOUIS	CA&SL
CHICAGO ATTICA & SOUTHERN	CA&SO
CHICAGO AURORA & ELGIN RAILROAD	CA&E
CHICAGO BELLEVUE CASCADE & WESTERN	CBC&W
CHICAGO BLUFFTON & CINCINNATI RR	CB&C
CHICAGO BRIDGE & IRON	CB&I
CHICAGO BURLINGTON & KANSAS CITY	CB&KC
CHICAGO BURLINGTON & QUINCY RAILROAD	CB&Q
CHICAGO CENTRAL	CHIC
CHICAGO CENTRAL & PACIFIC	CC&P
CHICAGO CINCINNATI & LOUISVILLE	CC&L
CHICAGO CITY RAILWAYS	CHC
CHICAGO DANVILLE & VINCENNES RAILROAD	CD&V
CHICAGO DECORAH & MINNESOTA	CD&MI
CHICAGO DETROIT & CANADA GRAND JCT RY	CD&C
CHICAGO EL	CEL
CHICAGO FREIGHT CAR COMPANY	CFC
CHICAGO GRAVEL COMPANY	CG
CHICAGO GREAT WESTERN RAILWAY	CGW
CHICAGO GREAT WESTERN RAILROAD	CGW.
CHICAGO HARLEM & BATAVIA	CH&B
CHICAGO HEIGHTS TERMINAL TRANSFER RR	CHTT
CHICAGO INDIANAPOLIS & LOUISVILLE RY	M.
CHICAGO INDPOLIS & LOUISVILLE RY (O)	CI&L
CHICAGO JUNCTION	CJ
CHICAGO KALAMAZOO & SAGINAW RAILWAY	CK&SA
CHICAGO KANSAS & WESTERN	CK&W
CHICAGO LAKE SHORE & EASTERN	CLS&E
CHICAGO LAKE SHORE & SOUTH BEND	CLS&SB
CHICAGO LOCOMOTIVE WORKS	CLW
CHICAGO MADISON & NORTHERN	CM&N
CHICAGO MILL & LUMBER COMPANY	CM&LC
CHICAGO MILWAUKEE & GARY	CM&G
CHICAGO MILWAUKEE & PUGET SOUND	CM&P
CHICAGO MILWAUKEE & ST PAUL	CMSP
CHICAGO MILWAUKEE ST PAUL & OMAHA	CMSP&O
CHICAGO MILWAUKEE ST PAUL & PACIFIC	MILW
CHICAGO MISSOURI & WESTERN	CM&W
CHICAGO NEW YORK AIR LINE RAILROAD	CNYE
CHICAGO NEW YORK ELECTRIC AIR LINE RR	CNYE.
CHICAGO NORTH SHORE & MILWAUKEE	CNS&M
CHICAGO OUTER BELT	COB
CHICAGO PEORIA & ST LOUIS RAILROAD	CP&SL
CHICAGO PEORIA & ST LOUIS RY CO OF IL	CP&SL.
CHICAGO PRODUCE TERMINAL	CPTE
CHICAGO RAPID TRANSIT COMPANY	CRT
CHICAGO REGIONAL TRANSIT AUTHORITY	CRTA
CHICAGO RIVER & INDIANA RAILROAD	CR&I
CHICAGO ROCK ISLAND & GULF	CRI&G
CHICAGO ROCK ISLAND & PACIFIC RR	RI
CHICAGO SANITARY DISTRICT	CHSD
CHICAGO SHORT LINE RAILWAY	CSL
CHICAGO SOUTH BEND & NORTHERN INDIANA	CSB&NI
CHICAGO SOUTH SHORE & SOUTH BEND RR	CSS&SB
CHICAGO SOUTH SHORE & SOUTH BEND RY	CSS&SB.
CHICAGO SOUTHERN	CHSO
CHICAGO SPRINGFIELD & ST LOUIS	CS&STL
CHICAGO ST LOUIS & WESTERN	CSL&W
CHICAGO ST PAUL & FORD DU LAC	CSP&FL
CHICAGO ST PAUL & KANSAS CITY	CSP&KC
CHICAGO ST PAUL MINNEAPOLIS & OHIO	CSPM&O
CHICAGO ST PAUL MINNEAPOLIS & OMAHA	CPM&O
CHICAGO SUBWAYS	CSUB
CHICAGO SURFACE LINES	CSLS

APPENDIX A (RAILROADS)

ROADS ALPHABETICALLY W/ABBREVIATIONS	A
CHICAGO TERMINAL TRANSFER RAILROAD	CTT
CHICAGO TERRE HAUTE & SOUTHEASTERN RY	CTH&SE
CHICAGO TRANSIT AUTHORITY	CTA
CHICAGO TUNNEL RAILWAY COMPANY	CT
CHICAGO UNION STATION	CUST
CHICAGO UNION TRACTION	CUTR
CHICAGO UNION TRANSFER RAILWAY CO	CHUT
CHICAGO WEST PULLMAN & SOUTHERN RR	CWP&S.
CHICAGO WEST PULLMAN & SOUTHERN RY	CWP&S
CHICAGO WEST UNION TFR	CWU
CHICO ELECTRIC RAILWAY (CALIF)	CERY
CHIHUAHUA MINERAL	CHMI
CHIHUAHUA-PACIFIC	CH-P
CHIHUAHUA-PACIFIC (0)	C-P
CHIPPAWAH RIVER & MENOMONIE RAILWAY	CR&M
CHIPPEWA FALLS & WESTERN	CF&WE
CHOCTAW COAL & RAILWAY COMPANY	CC&RC
CHOCTAW NEWCASTLE & WESTERN	CN&W
CHOCTAW OKLAHOMA & GULF RAILROAD	CO&G
CHUMBRES & TOLRIC SCENIC RAILROAD	C&T
CIMMARRON & NORTHWESTERN	CI&NW
CINCINNATI & EASTERN RAILWAY	CIN&E
CINCINNATI & LAKE ERIE RAILROAD	C&LE
CINCINNATI & MUSKINGUM VALLEY	C&MV
CINCINNATI & WESTWOOD RAILROAD	C&WW
CINCINNATI ATLANTIC & COLUMBUS	C&CI
CINCINNATI FLEMINGON & SOUTHEASTERN	CF&SE
CINCINNATI GEORGETOWN & PORTSMOUTH RR	CG&P
CINCINNATI HAMILTON & DAYTON	CH&D
CINCINNATI LAWRENCE & AURORA	CL&A
CINCINNATI LEBANON & NORTHERN RAILWAY	CL&N
CINCINNATI NEW ORLEANS & TEXAS PACIFC	CNO&TP
CINCINNATI NEWPORT & COVINGTON RY	CN&C
CINCINNATI NORTHERN	CINO
CINCINNATI RAPID TRANSIT	CIRT
CINCINNATI SAGINAW & MACKINAW	CS&M
CINCINNATI SOUTHERN	CSO
CINCINNATI STREET RAILWAY	CCSR
CINCINNATI UNION TERMINAL	CIUT
CINCINNATI VAN WERT & MICHIGAN	CVW&M
CISCO & NORTHEASTERN RAILWAY	C&NE
CITADEL CEMENT COMPANY	CIT
CITIES SERVICE COMPANY	CSC
CITIZENS TRACTIONS OF OIL CITY	CTR
CITY & SUBURBAN RAILWAY	C&SR
CITY ISLAND RAILROAD (MONORAIL)	CIM
CITY OF BALTIMORE	CBA
CITY OF CALGARY TRANSIT	COCT
CITY OF PRINEVILLE RAILWAY	CPR
CITY OF SEATTLE	CITYS
CITY OF WINNIPEG HYDRO	CWH
CITY PASSENGER RAILWAY (ATLANTIC CITY	CPRY
CITY POINT	CPT
CITY RAILWAY OF DAYTON	CRY
CITY UTILITIES COMPANY	CU
CJ LAVINO & COMPANY	CJL&C
CLAIBORNE & POLK MILITARY RAILROAD	C&PM
CLAREDON & PITTSFORD RAILROAD	C&PI
CLAREMONT & CONCORD RAILROAD	CL&C
CLAREMONT & CONCORD RAILWAY	CL&C.
CLAREMONT RAILWAY	CLAR
CLAREMONT UNIVERSITY & FERRIES ST RR	CU&F
CLARION RIVER RAILWAY	CLA
CLAY STREET HILL RAILROAD COMPANY	CSHR
CLEMENT LUMBER COMPANY	CLE
CLEVELAND & BEREA RAILWAY	CL&B
CLEVELAND & CANTON	CL&CA
CLEVELAND & CHAGRIN FALLS ELECTRIC RY	C&CFE
CLEVELAND & CHAGRIN FALLS RAILWAY	C&CF
CLEVELAND & EASTERN ELECTRIC RAILWAY	C&EE
CLEVELAND & EASTERN TRACTION COMPANY	C&ET
CLEVELAND & ELYRIA STREET RAILROAD	CL&E
CLEVELAND & NEWBURGH RAILROAD	C&NRR
CLEVELAND & SOUTHERN	CL&SO
CLEVELAND & SOUTHWESTERN RAILWAY	C&SW
CLEVELAND & SOUTHWESTERN TRACTION CO	C&SWT
CLEVELAND & TOLEDO	C&TOL

ROADS ALPHABETICALLY W/ABBREVIATIONS	A
CLEVELAND AKRON & CINCINNATI RY CO	CA&CIN
CLEVELAND AKRON & COLUMBUS	CA&COL
CLEVELAND ASHLAND & MANSFIELD RY	CA&M
CLEVELAND BEREA & ELYRIA STREET RY	CB&E
CLEVELAND BEREA ELYRIA & OBERLIN RY	CBE&O
CLEVELAND CANTON & SOUTHERN	CC&S
CLEVELAND CINCINNATI CHIC & ST LOUIS	CCC&SL
CLEVELAND COLUMBUS & CINCINNATI RR	CC&CIN
CLEVELAND COLUMBUS CINCIN & INDIANAPL	CCC&I
CLEVELAND ELECTRIC ILLUMINATING CO	CEI
CLEVELAND ELYRIA & WESTERN RAILWAY	CE&W
CLEVELAND LORAIN & WHEELING RAILROAD	CL&W
CLEVELAND MEDINA & SOUTHERN RAILWAY	CM&S
CLEVELAND PAINESVILLE & ASHTABULA	CP&A
CLEVELAND RAILWAYS	CRW
CLEVELAND RAPID TRANSIT	CLRT
CLEVELAND SOUTHWESTERN & COLUMBUS RY	CSCO
CLEVELAND SOUTHWESTERN RY & LIGHT CO	CSW
CLEVELAND TERMINAL & VALLEY	CT&V
CLEVELAND TRANSIT	CLRT.
CLEVELAND TUSCARAWAS VALLEY & WHEELING	CTV&W
CLEVELAND UNION TERMINAL (NYC)	CUT
CLEVELAND WOOSTER & MAHONING VALLEY	CW&MV
CLEVELAND YOUNGSTOWN & EASTERN RY	CY&E
CLIFFSIDE RAILROAD	CLIF
CLINCHFIELD COAL	CLI
CLINCHFIELD NORTHERN RY OF KENTUCKY	CNRY
CLINCHFIELD RAILROAD	CL.
CLINCHFIELD RAILWAY	CL
CLINTON & OKLAHOMA WESTERN	C&OW
CLINTON & VICKSBURG	C&V
CLINTON DAVENPORT & MUSCATINE RAILWAY	CD&MU
CLOVER HILL	CH
CLOVER LEAF	TSL&W
CLOVER LEAF (TOLEDO ST LOUIS & CINCI)	TSL&C
CLOVER VALLEY RAILROAD	CLV
CMSTP&P	MILW
COAHUILA & ZACATECAS RAILWAY	C&Z
COAL & IRON	C&IR
COAL BELT ELECTRIC RAILWAY	CBER
COAL FIELDS RAILWAY	COAL
COAST ENGINE & EQUIPMENT COMPANY	CE&EC
COBOURG & PETERBOROUGH	C&P
CODY & MOORE RAILWAY	C&MRY
COEUR D'ALENE RAILWAY & NAVIGATION	CDR&N
COG DEPOT & IRON SPRINGS	CD&IS
COLEBROOK VALLEY RAILROAD	COLV
COLFAX NORTHERN	COLN
COLLEGE INN	CI*
COLLIER STREETCAR	COLSC
COLLINS & GLENNVILLE	C&GL
COLLINS & REIDSVILLE	C&R
COLORADO & EASTERN	C&EST
COLORADO & NORTHWESTERN	C&NWT
COLORADO & SOUTHEASTERN RAILROAD	COL&SE
COLORADO & SOUTHERN RAILWAY	C&S
COLORADO & WYOMING RAILWAY	C&WY
COLORADO CENTRAL	COL
COLORADO COLUMBUS & MEXICAN RAILROAD	CC&M
COLORADO FUEL & IRON COMPANY	CF&IC
COLORADO KANSAS	CK
COLORADO KANSAS & OKLAHOMA RAILROAD	CK&O
COLORADO MIDLAND	CMI
COLORADO RAILROAD	COLRR
COLORADO SPRINGS & CRIPPLE CR DIST RY	CS&CC
COLORADO SPRINGS & INTERURBAN RY CO	CS&I
COLORADO SPRINGS & MANITOU ST RY	CS&MS
COLORADO SPRINGS DISTRICT RAILWAY	CCD
COLORADO SPRINGS RAPID TRANSIT	CSRT
COLORADO WYOMING & EASTERN	CW&E
COLUMBIA & COWLITZ RAILWAY	CO&C
COLUMBIA & MILLSTADT RAILROAD	C&MI
COLUMBIA & PUGET SOUND RAILROAD	C&PS
COLUMBIA & WESTERN	CO&W
COLUMBIA NEWBERRY & LAURENS RAILROAD	CN&L
COLUMBIA PARK & SOUTHERN	CP&S
COLUMBIA PARK & SOUTHWESTSERN	CP&SW

A8

APPENDIX A (RAILROADS)

ROADS ALPHABETICALLY W/ABBREVIATIONS

Road	Abbr
COLUMBIA RAPID TRANSIT	COLRT
COLUMBIA SOURS	CS*
COLUMBIA UNION STATION COMPANY	COUS
COLUMBUS & GREENVILLE RAILWAY	C&GR
COLUMBUS & ROME RAILROAD	C&RO
COLUMBUS & SOUTHERN	CO&SO
COLUMBUS & SOUTHERN OHIO ELECTRIC CO	C&SOE
COLUMBUS DELAWARE & MARION ELECTRIC	CD&M
COLUMBUS HOCKING VALLEY & TOLEDO RY	CHV&T
COLUMBUS LANCASTER & WELLSTON	CL&WE
COLUMBUS RAILWAY & LIGHT COMPANY	CR&LC
COLUMBUS SANDUSKY & HOCKING	CS&H
COLUMBUS TRANSIT COMPANY	COLT
COLUMBUS URBANA & WESTERN	CU&W
COLUMBUS WELLSTON & SOUTHERN	CW&S
COLUSA & LAKE RAILROAD	C&L
COMM DE TRANSPORT URBAINE DE MONTREAL	CTDM
COMMERCIAL & RR BANK OF VICKSBURG	C&RBV
COMMONWEALTH AVE STREET RAILWAY	CASR
COMMONWEALTH EDISON	CED
COMOX LOGGING & RAILWAY COMPANY	CLR
COMOX LUMBER & RAILROAD COMPANY	CL&R
CONCORD & CLAREMONT	C&CL
CONCORD & MONTREAL	C&MO
CONCORD MAYNARD & HUDSON STREET RY	CM&H
CONCORD RAILROAD	CONC
CONCORD STREET RAILWAY	CST
CONDON KINZUA & SOUTHERN RAILROAD	CK&S
CONEMAUGH & BLACK LICK RAILROAD	C&BL
CONESTOGA TRACTION COMPANY	CTCO
CONEY ISLAND & BROOKLYN RAILROAD CO	CI&B
CONNECTICUT & PASSUMPSIC RIVERS	C&PR
CONNECTICUT CENTRAL	CONNC
CONNECTICUT COMPANY	CONN
CONNECTICUT DEPT OF TRANSPORTATION	CDOT
CONNECTICUT RAILROAD	CONNR
CONNECTICUT RAILWAY & LIGHTING CO	CR&L
CONNECTICUT RIVER RAILROAD	COR
CONNECTICUT VALLEY	CTVY
CONNECTICUT WESTERN RAILROAD	COW
CONNELLSVILLE & STATE LINE	CO&SL
CONNOR STEEL DIVISION	CSD
CONNOTON VALLEY RAILWAY	CONV
CONQUISTA COAL RAILWAY	CCRY
CONRAIL	CR
CONSOLIDATED CHICAGO ALTONA &SOUTHERN	CA&S
CONSOLIDATED KANSAS & SIDELL	CK&S
CONSOLIDATED ROCK PRODUCTS	CRP
CONSUMERS COMPANY	CONS
CONSUMERS POWER	CON
CONTINENTAL STEEL	CONT
CONWAY SCENIC	CONW
COOPERATIVE TRANSIT COMPANY	COOPT
COOPERSTOWN & CHARLOTTE VALLEY RY	C&CV
COORS BREWERY	CB
COOS BAY LUMBER	CBL
COPLAY EGYPT & IRONTON STREET RY	CE&I
COPPER HILL & NORTH WESTERN	CH&NW
COPPER RANGE RAILROAD	CRA
COPPER RIVER & NORTHWESTERN (O)	CR&N
COPPER RIVER & NORTHWESTERN RAILWAY	CR&NW
COPPERWELD STEEL COMPANY	CWST
CORAL GABLES RAPID TRANSIT	CGRT
CORINTH & COUNCE RAILROAD	CO&CO
CORNWALL & LEBANON RAILROAD	CO&L
CORNWALL & MT HOPE	C&MH
CORNWALL RAILROAD	CORN
CORNWALL STREET RY LIGHT & POWER CO	CSRL&P
CORNWALLIS VALLEY RAILWAY	CWV
CORONADO RAILROAD (CALIFORNIA)	CO
CORPUS CHRISTIE SAN DIEGO & RIO GRANDE	CCSDRG
CORTEZ MINES LIMITED	CML
CORTLAND COUNTY TRACTION	CCTR
CORVALLIS & EASTERN	COR&E
COTTON BELT	CBELT
COTTON PLANT-FARGO RAILWAY	CP-F
COUDERSPORT & PORT ALLEGHENY RAILROAD	C&PA
COUNCIL BLUFFS & ST JOE	CB&SJ
COUNTRY CLUB BEER	CCB*
COVINGTON & CINCINNATI	C&CIN
COVINGTON & OHIO	CO&O
COVINGTON FLEMINGSBURG & ASHLAND	CF&A
COVINGTON FLEMINGSBURG & POUND GAP	CF&PG
COWICHAN NARROW GAUGE	CNG
COWICHAN VALLEY RAILROAD	CVRR
COWLITZ CHEHALIS & CASCADE	CC&C
CRAB ORCHARD & EGYPTIAN	CO&E
CRAIG MOUNTAIN RAILWAY	CM
CRAWFORDSVILLE & WESTERN TRACTION CO	CR&W
CREDIT VALLEY RAILWAY	CVRY
CRESCENT CITY & SMITH RIVER	CC&SR
CRESCENT CITY RAILROAD COMPANY	CRESC
CRESTBOOK FOREST INDUSTRIES	CRFI
CRIPPLE CREEK & COLORADO SPRINGS RY	CC&CS
CRIPPLE CREEK DISTRICT RAILWAY	CCDRY
CROSSETT WESTERN COMPANY (LUMBER RD)	CROSW
CROWN WILLAMETTE PAPER	CWP
CROWN ZELLERBACH	CZ
CROWN ZELLERBACH--CANADA	CZ.
CRYSTAL CITY & UVALDE RAILROAD	CS&U
CRYSTAL RIVER & SAN JUAN RAILROAD	CR&SJ
CRYSTAL RIVER RAILROAD	CRRR
CSX TRASNPORTATION	CSX
CUBA OIL & MOLASSES COMPANY	CMOX
CUMBERLAND & MANCHESTER RAILROAD	C&M
CUMBERLAND & PENNSYLVANIA RAILROAD	C&PE
CUMBERLAND & WESTERNPORT ELECTRIC	C&WE
CUMBERLAND COUNTY POWER & LIGHT CO	CCP&L
CUMBERLAND RAILWAY & COAL COMPANY	CUM
CUMBERLAND VALLEY RAILROAD	CUMV
CUMBRES & TOLEC SCENIC RAILROAD	C&TS
CURRENT RIVER RAILROAD	CUR
CUSHING STONE	CUS
CUTLER & SAVIDGE	CU&S
CUYAHOGA VALLEY LINES (O)	CUY
CUYAHOGA VALLEY LINES.	CVL
CUYAHOGA VALLEY RAILWAY	CUY
DAIRYMENS EXPRESS	DE*
DAKOTA MINNESOTA & EASTERN	DME
DAKOTA PACIFIC RAILROAD	DPA
DAKOTA RAIL	DARA
DAKOTA SOUTHERN	DKS
DAKOTA WYOMING & MISSOURI RIVER RR	DW&MR
DALLAS RAILWAY & TERMINAL	DR&T
DAN PATCH ELECTRIC RAILROAD	DPE
DANSVILLE & MT MORRIS RAILROAD	D&MM
DANVILLE & NEW RIVER	D&NR
DANVILLE & POTTSVILLE	D&P
DANVILLE & SUNBURY TRANSIT COMPANY	D&ST
DANVILLE & WESTERN	DA&W
DANVILLE MOCKSVILLE & SOUTHWESTERN	DM&S
DANVILLE TRACTION & POWER COMPANY	DT&PC
DARDANELLE & RUSSELLVILLE RAILROAD	D&R
DARDANELLE OLA & SOUTHERN	DO&S
DARIEN & WESTERN	D&WE
DAUPHIN & SUSQUEHANNA	D&SQ
DAVENPORT & ROCK ISLAND RY BRIDGE CO	D&RIB
DAVENPORT ROCK ISLAND & NORTH WESTERN	DRI&N
DAVENPORT ROCK ISLAND BRIDGE RY &TERM	D&RIBT
DAVIES JOHNSON LUMBER COMPANY	DJL
DAWES SILICA MINING	DSM
DAWSON BRADFORD & MT PLEASANT RR	DB&MP
DAYTON & TROY ELECTRIC	D&TE
DAYTON & UNION RAILROAD CO	D&U
DAYTON & XENIA TRACTION	D&XT
DAYTON COVINGTON & PIQUA TRACTION CO.	DC&P
DAYTON LEBANON & NORTHERN	DL&NO
DC TRANSIT	DCT
DCCRR	DCCRR
DEADWOOD CENTRAL	DWC
DEATH VALLEY RAILROAD	DV
DEBARDELEBEN COAL CORPORATION	DBC
DECATUR SULLIVAN & MATTOON	DS&M
DEDHAM-NORWOOD-E WAPOLE LINE	DNEW

APPENDIX A (RAILROADS)

ROADS ALPHABETICALLY W/ABBREVIATIONS	A
DEEP CREEK RAILROAD	DC
DEEP ROCK	DR*
DEEPWATER	DWAT
DEERFIELD RIVER RAILROAD	DRRR
DEERFIELD VALLEY RAILROAD	DVRR
DEITCH COMPANY	DEI
DEL NORTE SOUTHERN RAILWAY	DNS
DELAWARE & BOUND BROOK RAILROAD	D&BB
DELAWARE & EASTERN RAILROAD	D&E
DELAWARE & HUDSON CANAL COMPANY	D&HCC
DELAWARE & HUDSON COAL COMPANY	D&HC
DELAWARE & HUDSON GRAVITY RAILROAD	D&HG
DELAWARE & HUDSON RAILROAD COMPANY	D&H
DELAWARE & MARION ELECTRIC COMPANY	D&MEC
DELAWARE & NORTHERN RAILROAD	D&N
DELAWARE & NORTHERN RAILWAY	D&N.
DELAWARE & ULSTER RAILROAD	D&UL
DELAWARE BAY & CAPE MAY RAILROAD	DB&CM
DELAWARE LACK SCHUYKILL & SUSQUEHANNA	DLS&S
DELAWARE LACKAWANNA & WESTERN	DL&W
DELAWARE OTSEGO SYSTEM	DO
DELAWARE RIVER JOINT COMMISSION	DRJC
DELAWARE RIVER PORT AUTHORITY	DRPA
DELAWARE SHORE RAILROAD	DSH
DELAWARE SUSQUEHANNA & SCHUYLKILL	DS&S
DELAWARE VALLEY RAILROAD	DVA
DELAWARE VALLEY RAILWAY	DVA
DELMARVA POWER & LIGHT	DP&L
DELRAY CONNECTING RAILROAD	DE
DELRAY TERMINAL	DET
DELTA BULK TERMINALS	DBT
DELTA SOUTHERN	DES
DELTA VALLEY & SOUTHERN RAILWAY	DV&S
DENISON & SHERMAN RAILWAY	D&SH
DENISON & WASHITA	D&W
DENKMAN LUMBER COMPANY	DLC
DENVER & CHEYENNE	D&CH
DENVER & INTERMOUNTAIN RAILROAD	D&I
DENVER & INTERURBAN RAILROAD	D&IRR
DENVER & INTERURBAN RAILROAD (O)	D&IN
DENVER & NEW ORLEANS	D&NO
DENVER & RIO GRANDE RAILROAD	D&RG
DENVER & RIO GRANDE WESTERN RAILROAD	D&RGW
DENVER & SALT LAKE RAILROAD	D&SL
DENVER & SALT LAKE RAILWAY	D&SL.
DENVER BOULDER & WESTERN	DB&W
DENVER COLORADO CANYON & PACIFIC	DCC&P
DENVER ENID & GULF	DE&G
DENVER LEADVILLE & ALMA	DL&A
DENVER LEADVILLE & GUNNISON RAILROAD	DL&G
DENVER NORTHWESTERN & PACIFIC	DN&P
DENVER PACIFIC RAILROAD COMPANY	DP
DENVER SOUTH PARK & PACIFIC	DSP&P
DENVER TEXAS & FORT WORTH	DT&FW
DENVER TRAMWAY	DTM
DENVER UNION TERMINAL RAILWAY	DUTR
DENVER UTAH & PACIFIC	DU&P
DEPARTMENT OF DEFENSE	DOD
DEQUEEN & EASTERN RAILROAD	DQ&E
DES MOINES & CENTRAL	DM&C
DES MOINES & CENTRAL IOWA RAILWAY	DM&CI
DES MOINES & FORT DODGE	DM&FD
DES MOINES & MINNESOTA	DM&MI
DES MOINES TERMINAL COMPANY	DMTC
DES MOINES UNION RAILWAY	DMU
DES MOINES VALLEY RAILROAD	DMV
DESERET-WESTERN RAILWAY	DW
DETROIT & LIMA NORTHERN	D&LN
DETROIT & MACKINAC RAILWAY	D&M
DETROIT & ST JOSEPH	D&SJ
DETROIT & TOLEDO SHORE LINE RAILROAD	D&TSL
DETROIT BAY CITY & ALPENA	DBC&A
DETROIT BAY CITY & WESTERN	DBC&W
DETROIT CARO & SANDUSKY	DC&S
DETROIT DIESEL EDISON	DED
DETROIT EDISON	DEED
DETROIT EEL RIVER & ILLINOIS	DER&I

ROADS ALPHABETICALLY W/ABBREVIATIONS	A
DETROIT GRAND HAVEN & MILWAUKEE	DGH&M
DETROIT HILLSDALE & SOUTHWESTERN RY	DH&S
DETROIT MACKINAC & MARQUETTE	DM&M
DETROIT MONROE TOLEDO SHORT LINE	DMT
DETROIT PONTIAC & MACKINAC	DP&M
DETROIT RIVER TUNNEL COMPANY	DRT
DETROIT SOUTHERN	DSO
DETROIT STREET RAILWAY	DST
DETROIT TERMINAL RAILROAD	DT
DETROIT TOLEDO & IRONTON	DT&I
DETROIT TOLEDO & MILWAUKEE	DT&M
DETROIT UNITED LINES	DUL
DETROIT UNITED RAILWAYS	DUL.
DEVCO RAILWAY	D
DEVIL'S LAKE & CHAUTAUQUA	DL&C
DEVILS LAKE & NORTHERN	DL&N
DEXTER & NORTHERN	DX&N
DIAMOND & CALDOR RAILROAD	D&CA
DIAMOND JO LINE	C&F.
DIAMOND VALLEY	DIA
DICK CONSTRUCTION CO	DCCO
DICK CONSTRUCTION COMPANY	DICK
DIERKS FOREST INDUSTRIES	DFI
DISMAL SWAMP RAILROAD	DS
DISTRICT OF COLUMBIA TRANSIT	DCT.
DIXIE SAND & GRAVEL	DS&G
DOMINION ATLANTIC RAILWAY	DA
DOMINION FOUNDRIES & STEEL	DF&S
DOMINION OF CANADA	DOC
DONALDSONVILLE & NAPOLEONVILLE RY	D&NRY
DONIPHAN KENSETT & SEARCY RAILWAY	DK&S
DONORA SOUTHERN RAILROAD	DOS
DOUGLAS AUGUSTA & FLORIDA	DA&F
DOUGLAS AUGUSTA & GULF RAILWAY	DA&G
DOVER & SOUTHBOUND	D&SO
DOW CHEMICAL	DC*
DOWLING & CAMP	DO&C
DOWN TOWN RAILROAD COMPANY	DTRR
DRY FORK	DF
DRY ICE REFRIGERATOR LINE	DICX
DUBLIN & SOUTHWESTERN	D&SW
DUBLIN & WRIGHTSVILLE	D&WV
DUBUQUE	D*
DUDGEMONA BAYOU LUMBER COMPANY	DBL
DUKE POWER COMPANY	DPC
DULUTH & IRON RANGE	D&IR
DULUTH & NORTHEASTERN RAILROAD	D&NE
DULUTH & NORTHERN MINNESOTA RAILROAD	D&NM
DULUTH MISSABE & IRON RANGE RAILWAY	DM&IR
DULUTH MISSABE & NORTHERN	DM&N
DULUTH MISSABE & WESTERN	DM&W
DULUTH MISSISSIPPI RIVER & NORTHERN	DMR&N
DULUTH RAINY LAKE & WINNIPEG	DRL&W
DULUTH SOUTH SHORE & ATLANTIC	DSS&A
DULUTH ST CLOUTH GLENCOE & MANKATO RY	DSCG&M
DULUTH STREET RAILWAY	DSRY
DULUTH UNION DEPOT & TRANSFER	DUD&T
DULUTH UNION DEPOT & TRANSFER (O)	DUP&T.
DULUTH VIRGINIA & RAINY LAKE	DV&RL
DULUTH WINNIPEG & PACIFIC RAILROAD	DW&P.
DULUTH WINNIPEG & PACIFIC RAILWAY	DW&P.
DULUTH WINNIPEG & WESTERN RAILWAY	DW&W
DUNCANNON BLOOMFIELD & LOYSVILLE	DB&L
DUNCANNON LANDISBURG & BROADTOP RR	DL&B
DUNKIRK ALLEGHENY VALLEY & PITTSBURGH	DAV&P
DUNKIRK WARREN & PITTSBURGH	DW&PIT
DUPONT (EI DUPONT)	DU*
DUQUESNE SLAG PRODUCTS COMPANY	DQSP
DURANGO & SILVERTON	D&SI
DURBAN TRAMWAYS COMPANY (CANADA)	DTW
DURHAM & SOUTHERN RAILWAY	D&S
DURHAM UNION STATION COMPANY	DUSC
DUTCHESS & COLUMBIA RAILROAD COMPANY	D&C
DUTCHESS COUNTY RAILROAD COMPANY	DU
DYERSBURG-MEMPHIS	D-M
EAGLE LAKE & WEST BRANCH	EL&WB
EAGLE MOUNTAIN RAILROAD	EMT

A10

APPENDIX A (RAILROADS)

ROADS ALPHABETICALLY W/ABBREVIATIONS	A
EAGLE PITCHER LEAD COMPANY	EPLC
EAGLES MERE RAILROAD	EMRR
EAST & WEST COAST RAILROAD (FLORIDA)	E&WC
EAST BARRE & CHELSEA	EB&C
EAST BRANCH & LINCOLN	EB&L
EAST BROAD TOP	EBT
EAST BROAD TOP RAILROAD & COAL CO	EBT&CC
EAST CAMDEN & HIGHLAND RAILROAD	EC&H
EAST CAROLINA RAILWAY	ECRY
EAST ERIE COMMERCIAL RAILROAD	EEC
EAST FLORIDA	EF
EAST FLORIDA LIVE OAK & ROWLANDS BLUFF	EFLORB
EAST JERSEY RAILROAD & TERMINAL	EJR&T
EAST JORDAN & SOUTHERN RAILROAD	EJ&S
EAST LINE & RED RIVER	EL&RR
EAST LORAIN STREET RAILWAY	ELS
EAST MAHANOY	EMA
EAST OAKLAND RAILROAD COMPANY	EORC
EAST PENNSYLVANIA RAILROAD	EP
EAST SHORE & SURBURBAN RAILWAY CO	ES&S
EAST ST LOUIS & CARONDELET	ESL&C
EAST ST LOUIS & SUBURBAN RAILWAY	ESL&S
EAST ST LOUIS JUNCTION RAILROAD	ESLJ
EAST TENNESSEE & GEORGIA RAILROAD CO	ET&G
EAST TENNESSEE & VIRGINIA RAILROAD CO	ET&V
EAST TENNESSEE & WESTERN N CAROLINA	ET&WNC
EAST TENNESSEE VIRGINIA & GEORGIA	ETV&GA
EAST TENNESSEE VIRGINIA & GULF	ETV&G
EAST TROY MUNICIPAL RAILWAY	ETRR
EAST TROY RAILROAD	ETRR.
EAST WASHINGTON RAILWAY	EW
EASTERN (EASTERN MINNESOTA??)	EAST
EASTERN KENTUCKY	EKY
EASTERN KENTUCKY SOUTHERN	EKS
EASTERN MASSACHUSETTS STREET RY	EMSR
EASTERN MICHIGAN RAILWAYS	EMRY
EASTERN NEW YORK RAILWAY	ENY
EASTERN OHIO TRACTION	EOT
EASTERN RAILROAD	ERM.
EASTERN RAILROAD OF MASSACHUSETTS	ERM
EASTERN SHORE	ESH
EASTMAN KODAK COMPANY	EK
EBERLE TANNING	ET
ED HINES WESTERN PINE COMPANY	EHWP
EDAVILLE RAILROAD	ED
EDGMOOR & MANETTA RAILWAY	E&M
EDMODNTON TRANSIT	ETR
EDMONTON DONVOGA & BRITISH COLUMBIA RY	ED&BC
EDMONTON YUKON & PACIFIC	EY&P
EDVAVILLE RAILROAD	ER
EDWARD HINES LUMBER COMPANY	EHLC
EEL RIVER & EUREKA	ER&E
EL DORADO & WESSON RAILWAY	ED&W
EL PASO & JUAREZ ELECTRIC CO (TEXAS)	EP&J
EL PASO & SOUTHWESTERN	EP&S
EL PASO CITY LINES	EPCL
EL PASO ELECTRIC COMPANY	EPEC
EL PASO SOUTHERN	EPS
EL PASO UNION PASSENGER DEPOT	EPUP
EL POTOSI & CHIHUAHUA	ELP&C
ELBERTON SOUTHERN RAILWAY	ESRY
ELDORADO MARION & SOUTHWESTERN	EM&SW
ELDORADO RAILROAD	ELD
ELECTO MOTIVE CORPORATION	EMCB
ELECTRIC SHORT LINE RAILWAY	ESL
ELECTRO-MOTIVE CORPORATION	E-M
ELGIN & BELVIDERE INTERURBAN	E&B
ELGIN JOLIET & EASTERN RAILWAY	EJ&E
ELGIN JOLIET & WESTERN	EJ&W
ELI LILLY PHARMACEUTICAL	ELP
ELIZABETH & SOMERVILLE	E&S
ELIZABETHPORT & SOMERVILLE RAILROAD	E&S
ELIZABETHTON & NORTH CAROLINA	E&NC
ELIZABETHTOWN & SOMERVILLE RAILROAD	E&S.
ELK & HIGHLAND	E&H
ELK RIVER COAL & LUMBER	ERC&L
ELK RUN COAL	ERC

ROADS ALPHABETICALLY W/ABBREVIATIONS	A
ELKHART & WESTERN	E&W
ELKHART METALS	EM
ELKTON & GUTHRIE	E&G
ELMIRA CORTLAND & NORTHERN	EC&N
ELMIRA LIGHT HEAT & POWER COMPANY	ELH&P
ELY THOMAS LUMBER	ETL
ELYRIA GRAFTON & SOUTHERN RAILWAY	EG&S
EMMITSBURG RAILROAD	EMM
EMORY RIVER RAILROAD	ER
EMPIRE DETROIT DIV OF CYCLOPS STEEL	E-D
EMPIRE SUGAR COMPANY	ESC
EMPIRE TRANSPORTATION COMPANY	ETCO
EMPORIUM & MT JEWITT	E&MJ
ENSLEY OPEN HEARTH	EOH
EPSOM SALTS MONORAIL	ES
EREX	EREX
ERIE	E
ERIE & KALAMAZOO	E&K
ERIE & MICHIGAN RY & NAVIGATION CO	E&M
ERIE & ONTARIO RAILWAY COMPANY	E&O
ERIE & PITTSBURG	E&PT
ERIE & WYOMING VALLEY RAILROAD CO	E&WV
ERIE COMMERCIAL RAILROAD	ECRR
ERIE LACKAWANNA	EL
ERIE MINING COMPANY	EMC
ERIE WABASH & ST LOUIS	EW&STL
ERIE WESTERN	EWE
ESCANABA & LAKE SUPERIOR RAILROAD	E&LS
ESCANABA & LAKE SUPERIOR RAILWAY	EL&S.
ESPEE	SP.
ESQUIMALT & NANAIMO FAMILY LINES RY	E&N
ESSEX TERMINAL RAILWAY	ETE
ESTACADO & GULF	ES&G
ETHIOPIAN GOVERNMENT RAILWAYS	EG
ETNA & MONTROSE	E&MO
EUCLID RAILROAD	EUC
EUREKA & KALAMATH RIVER RAILROAD	E&KR
EUREKA & PALISADE RAILWAY	E&P
EUREKA HILL RAILROAD	EH
EUREKA NEVADA RAILWAY	EN
EUREKA SOUTHERN	ESO
EUREKA SPRINGS RAILROAD	ESP
EUROPEAN & NORTH AMERICAN RAILROAD	E&NA
EUSTIS	EU
EVANSVILLE & CRAWFORD	E&C
EVANSVILLE & INDIANAPOLIS	EV&I
EVANSVILLE & OHIO VALLEY RAILWAY	E&OV
EVANSVILLE & PEORIA	EV&P
EVANSVILLE & TERRE HAUTE RAILROAD	E&TH
EVANSVILLE BELT RAILWAY	EBRY
EVANSVILLE INDIANAPOLIS & TERRE HAUTE	EI&TH
EVANSVILLE SUBURBAN & NEWBURG	ES&N
EVANSVILLE WASHINGTON & BRAZIL	EW&B
EVANSVILLE WASHINGTON & WORTHINGTON	EW&W
EVERETT PIPE & STEEL	EVP&S
EVERETT RAILROAD	EV
EWAUNA BOX COMPANY	EBC
EXCELSIOR BRICK	EB
EXETER HAMPTON & AMESBURY STREET RY	EH&A
EXPO '67 RAPID TRANSIT, MONTREAL	EXPO
FAIRBANKS MORSE	F-M
FAIRCHILD & NORTHEASTERN	F&N
FAIRFIELD WORKS TENNESSEE COAL & IRON	FWTC&I
FAIRHAVEN & SOUTHERN	F&S
FAIRMONT & QUARRYVILLE	F&Q
FAIRMOUNT PARK TRANSIT	FPT
FAIRPORT PAINESVILLE & EASTERN RY	FP&E
FALCONBRIDGE NICKEL MINES	FNM
FALL BROOK COAL COMPANY	FB
FALL BROOK RAILROAD	FBRR
FALL BROOK RAILWAY	FBRR.
FALL RIVER LINE	FRL
FAMILY LINES	FAM
FAMOCO	FAM.
FAR ROCKAWAY BRANCH RAILROAD	FRB
FARMRAIL	FARM
FARMVILLE & POWHATAN	F&P

A11

APPENDIX A (RAILROADS)

ROADS ALPHABETICALLY W/ABBREVIATIONS	A
FEATHER RIVER LUMBER COMPANY	FR
FEATHER RIVER RAILROAD	FR.
FEATHER RIVER RAILWAY	FR .
FEATHER RIVER RAILWAY (O)	FRRY
FEDERAL BARGE LINES	FBL
FEDERAL VALLEY RAILROAD	FV
FELICIANA EASTERN RAILROAD	FE
FELICITY & BETHEL RAILROAD	F&BE
FENNIMORE & WOODMAN	F&W
FERDINAND RAILROAD	FERD
FERNANDINA & AMELIA BEACH	F&AB
FERNANDINA & JACKSONVILLE	F&J
FERNANDINA MUNICIPAL RAILWAY	FMU
FERNWOOD COLUMBIA & GULF RAILROAD	FC&GU
FERROCARILLES DE VALLE DE MEXICO	FVM
FERROCARILLES NACIONALES DE MEXICO	FNDM
FERROCARNIL DEL PACIFICO	FDP
FERROCARRI MEXICANO	FCM
FERROCARRIL CHIHUAHUA PACIFICO	CH-P.
FERROCARRIL DE CHIHUAHUA AL PACI (O)	FDC&P
FERROCARRIL DE CHIHUAHUA AL PACIICO	CH-P
FERROCARRIL DEL SURESTE	FDES
FERROCARRIL OCCIDENTAL DE MEXICO	FCOM
FERROCARRIL URBANO	FU
FERROCARRIL CHIHUAHUA AL PACIFI (O)	FCAP
FERROCARRILES UNIDOS DE YUCAT (O)	FUCY
FERROCARRILES UNIDOS DE YUCATAN	FUDY
FERROCARRILES UNIDOS DE YUCATAN.	URY.
FERROCARRILES UNIDOS DEL SURESTE	FDES.
FERROCARRILL DE SONORA	FDSO
FERROCCARRI SONORA BAJA CALIFO	FSBC
FILTRATION PLANT RAILWAY	FPL
FISHER ELECTRIC RAILWAY	FERS
FITCHBURG & LEOMINISTER STREET RY	F&LSR
FITCHBURG RAILROAD	FRR
FITCHBURG RAILROAD (O)	FI
FIVE MILE BEACH RAILWAY	FMB
FLAMBEAU PAPER	FP
FLEMINGSBURG & NORTHERN	FL&N
FLEMINGSBURG & NORTHWESTERN RAILROAD	F&NW
FLINT & PERE MARQUETTE	F&PM
FLINT RIVER & NORTH EASTERN	FR&NE
FLORA LOGGING COMPANY	FLC
FLORDIA POWER & LIGHT	FP&L
FLORENCE & CRIPPLE CREEK RAILROAD CO	F&CC
FLORENCE RAILROAD	FLRR
FLORIDA	F
FLORIDA & WEST INDIA SHORT LINE	F&WI
FLORIDA ALABAMA & GEORGIA	FA&G
FLORIDA CENTRAL & GULF	FC&G
FLORIDA CENTRAL & PENINSULAR	FC&P
FLORIDA CENTRAL & WESTERN	FC&W
FLORIDA CENTRAL RAILROAD	FC
FLORIDA EAST COAST RAILROAD	FEC
FLORIDA INTERURBAN RAPID TRANSIT CO	FIRT
FLORIDA MIDLAND	FM
FLORIDA RAILWAY & NAVIGATIONS	FR&N
FLORIDA SOUTHERN	FS
FLORIDA SOUTHWESTERN	FSW
FLORIDA TRANSIT	FT
FLORIDA TRANSIT & PENINSULAR	FT&P
FONDA JOHNSTOWN & GLOVERSVILLE RR	FJ&G
FOOTE MINERALS	FMIN
FORD MOTOR COMPANY	FMC
FORD MOTOR COMPANY (O)	FOMOCO
FORDYCE & PRINCETON RAILROAD	F&PR
FORE RIVER RAILROAD	FOR
FOREST GROVE TRANSPORTATION	FGT
FORT BRAGG & SOUTHEASTERN RR CO	FB&S
FORT COLLINS MUNICIPAL RAILWAY (CO)	FCMR
FORT DODGE DES MOINES & SOUTHERN RY	FDM&S
FORT DODGE STREET RAILWAY	FDS
FORT EUSTIS MILITARY RAILROAD	FEM
FORT HAMILTON	FH
FORT HOWARD PAPER COMPANY	FHP
FORT LUCINDA RAILROAD	FTL
FORT MYERS SOUTHERN RAILWAY	FMSR

ROADS ALPHABETICALLY W/ABBREVIATIONS	A
FORT ORANGE PAPER COMPANY	FOP
FORT SMITH & SOUTHERN	FS&S
FORT SMITH & VAN BUREN RAILWAY	FS&VB
FORT SMITH & WESTERN RAILROAD	FS&W
FORT SMITH SUBIACO & ROCK ISLAND RR	FSS&RI
FORT STREET UNION DEPOT	FSUD
FORT WAYNE & CHICAGO	FW&C
FORT WAYNE & WABASH VALLEY TRACTION	FW&WV
FORT WAYNE-LIMA	FWL
FORT WILLIAMS ELECTRIC	FWE
FORT WORTH & DENVER CITY RAILWAY	FW&DC
FORT WORTH & DENVER RAILWAY	FW&D
FORT WORTH BELT RAILWAY	FWB
FORT WORTH TRANSIT	FWT
FOX & ILLINOIS UNION RAILWAY CO.	F&IU
FRANKFORD TACONY & HOLMESBURG RAILWAY	FT&H
FRANKFORT & CINCINNATI RAILROAD	F&C
FRANKFORT & CINCINNATI RAILWAY	F&C.
FRANKLIN & CAROLINA RAILROAD	F&CRR
FRANKLIN & LEBANON TRACTION CO	F&L
FRANKLIN & MEGANTIC	F&M
FRANKLIN ELECTRIC STREET RAILWAY CO	FES
FRANKLIN RAILROAD	FRANK
FREDERICK-MIDDLETOWN	F-MT
FREDERICKSBURG POTOMAC & PIEDMONT	FP&P
FREEHOLD & JAMESBURG AGRICULTURAL	F&JA
FREEPORT	FRE
FREMONT & ELKHORN VALLEY RAILROAD	F&EV
FREMONT & INDIANA	F&I
FREMONT ELKHORN & MISSOURI VALLEY RR	FE&MV
FRENCH RAILWAYS	FRW
FRIENDSHIP	FRI
FRISCO	FRIS
FRISCO MANDARIN	FRM
FRUIT GROWERS EXPRESS	FGEX
FRUIT GROWERS EXPRESS (O)	FGE*
FULTON COUNTY NARROW GAUGE	FCN
FULTON RAILWAY	FRY
FULTON STREET RAILWAY	FSRY
GAINESVILLE & GULF	G&G
GAINESVILLE & NORTHWESTERN	GV&NW
GAINESVILLE JEFFERSON & SOUTHERN	GJ&S
GAINESVILLE MIDLAND RAILROAD	GMI
GALENA & CHICAGO UNION	G&CU
GALENA & SOUTHERN WISCONSIN	G&SW
GALES CREEK & WILSON RIVER RAILROAD	GC&WR
GALESBURG & GREAT EASTERN RAILROAD	G&GE
GALLATIN VALLEY ELECTRIC	GVE
GALT PRESTON & HESPELER RAILWAY	GP&H
GALVESTON & WESTERN RAILROAD	G&W
GALVESTON HOUSTON & HENDERSON RR	GH&H
GALVESTON HOUSTON ELECTRIC RY	GHE
GALVESTON WHARF COMPANY	GWHC
GALVESTON WHARVES TERMINAL	GWH
GARDEN CITY RAILWAY COMPANY	GARC
GARDEN CITY WESTERN RAILWAY	GCW
GARDINER INC	GAR
GARY & WESTERN RAILROAD	G&WE
GARY RAILWAY	GARY
GATX	GA*
GAYLORD PAPER COMPANY	GAYP
GE SCHENECTADY INDUSTRIAL RAILROAD	GESI
GEARY STREET CABLE RAILROAD COMPANY	GSC.
GEARY STREET CABLE RAILWAY	GSC
GENERAL AMERICAN PFAUDLER CORP	GPEX
GENERAL ANILINE FILM	GAF
GENERAL CRUSHED STONE	GCS
GENERAL ELECTRIC	GE
GENERAL IRON WORKS	GIW
GENERAL LOGGING COMPANY	GLC
GENERAL MINING ASSN OF NOVA SCOTIA	GMA
GENERAL MOTORS	GM
GENESEE & WYOMING (O)	G&Y
GENESSEE & WYOMING (O)	G&W.
GENESSEE & WYOMING RAILROAD	G&WY

A12

APPENDIX A (RAILROADS)

ROADS ALPHABETICALLY W/ABBREVIATIONS	A
GENEVA & ITHACA	G&I
GENEVA ITHACA & ATHENS RAILROAD	GI&A
GENEVA ITHACA & SAYRE	GI&S
GEORGES CREEK & CUMBERLAND	GC&C
GEORGES VALLEY	GV
GEORGETOWN & GRAY'S PEAK	G&GP
GEORGETOWN BRECKENRIDGE & LEADVILLE	GB&L
GEORGETOWN RAILROAD	GTN
GEORGETOWN ROWLEY & IPSWICH ST RY	GR&ISR
GEORGETOWN STEEL	GTS
GEORGIA & FLORDIA RAILWAY	G&F.
GEORGIA & FLORIDA RAILROAD	G&F
GEORGIA & WEST POINT	G&WP
GEORGIA ASHBURN SYLVESTER & CAMILLA	GAS&C
GEORGIA COAST & PIEDMONT RAILROAD	GC&P
GEORGIA FLORIDA & ALABAMA	GF&A
GEORGIA MARBLE	GAM
GEORGIA MIDLAND & GULF	GM&G
GEORGIA NORTHERN RAILWAY	GNO
GEORGIA POWER COMPANY	GPC
GEORGIA RAILROAD	G
GEORGIA SOUTHERN & FLORDIA RAILWAY	GS&F
GEORGIA SOUTHWESTERN & GULF RAILROAD	GS&G
GEORGIA-PACIFIC CORPORATION	G-P
GERBERS BABY FOOD	GERB#
GERMAN FEDERAL RAILWAY	GFR
GETTYSBURG & HARRISBURG	G&H
GETTYSBURG ELECTRIC	GET
GETTYSBURG RAILROAD	GETTY
GIFFORD-HILL	G-H
GILFORD TRANSPORTATION COMPANY	GIL
GILMORE & PITTSBURGH RAILROAD	G&P
GILMORE INDUSTRIAL CENTER	GIC
GILPIN COUNTY TRAMWAY COMPANY	GCT
GILPIN RAILROAD	GI
GLASSBORO & MILLVILLE	G&MV
GLEN HAVEN CANNING FACTORY	GHCF
GLENFIELD & WESTERN	GL&W
GLENMORE DISTILLERIES	GDIS
GLENMORE DISTRIBUTORS	GD
GLOSTER & SOUTHERN RAILWAY	GL&S
GO TRANSIT	GOTR
GODCHAUX SUGAR	GS
GOLD COAST RAILROAD	GC
GOLDEN CIRCLE RAILROAD COMPANY	GCRR
GOLDEN CITY & SAN JUAN	GC&SJ
GOLDFIELD RAILROAD	GO
GOLDSBORO UNION STATION (O)	GUST
GOLDSBORO UNION STATION COMPANY	GUSC
GOODPASTURE GRAIN	GG
GOODYEAR	GY#
GOSHEN SOUTH BEND & CHICAGO RAILWAY	GSB&C
GOSHEN VALLEY	GOSH
GOVERNMENT OF ONTARIO TRANSIT	GOT
GRACE CHEMICAL	GCH
GRAFTON & UPTON RAILROAD	G&U
GRAHAM COUNTY RAILROAD	GCO
GRAND FALLS CENTRAL RAILWAY	GFC
GRAND RAPIDS & INDIANA RAILWAY	GR&I
GRAND RAPIDS & NORTH WESTERN RAILROAD	GR&NW
GRAND RAPIDS GRAND HAVEN & MICHIGAN RY	GRGHM
GRAND RAPIDS GRAND HAVEN & MUSKEGON RY	GRGH&M
GRAND RAPIDS RAILWAY	GRRAP
GRAND RIVER RAILWAY	GRRY
GRAND RIVER VALLEY RAILROAD	GR
GRAND TRUCK CORPORATION	GTCO
GRAND TRUCK RAILROAD	GT.
GRAND TRUNK OF CANADA	GTC
GRAND TRUNK PACIFIC	GTP
GRAND TRUNK RAILWAY SYSTEM	GT
GRAND TRUNK WESTERN RAILROAD COMPANY	GTW.
GRAND TRUNK WESTERN RAILWAY	GTW
GRANITE MOUNTAIN QUARRIES	GMQ
GRANITE RAILWAY	GRA
GRASSE RIVER RAILROAD	GRR
GRAY'S RUN RAILROAD	GRAY
GRAYSONIA NASHVILLE & ASHDOWN RR	GN&A

ROADS ALPHABETICALLY W/ABBREVIATIONS	A
GRAYVILLE & MATTOON RAILROAD	GR&M
GREAT CENTRAL	GCE
GREAT FALLS & OLD DOMINION	GF&OD
GREAT LAKES NAVAL STATION	GLN
GREAT LAKES STEEL CORPORATION	GLS
GREAT NORTHERN OF CANADA	GNC
GREAT NORTHERN RAILWAY	GN
GREAT PLAINS RAILWAY	GP
GREAT SLAVE LAKE RAILWAY	GSL
GREAT SOUTHWEST RAILROAD	GSW
GREAT SWAMP RAILWAY	GSRY
GREAT WESTERN OF CANADA	GWC
GREAT WESTERN RAILWAY	GW
GREAT WESTERN SUGAR	GWS
GREATER WINNIPEG WATER DISTRICT RY	GWWD
GREEN BAY & LAKE PEPIN	GB&LP
GREEN BAY & WESTERN RAILROAD COMPANY	GB&W
GREEN BAY MILWAUKEE & CHICAGO	GBM&C
GREEN BAY ROUTE	GB&W.
GREEN BAY ROUTE (O)	GBR
GREEN BAY WINONA & ST PAUL RAILWAY	GBW&SP
GREEN COVE SPRINGS & MELROSE	GCS&M
GREEN MOUNTAIN RAILROAD	GMT
GREEN RIVER STEEL COMPANY	GRSC
GREENBRIER & EASTERN	GB&E
GREENBRIER CHEAT & ELK	GC&E
GREENSBURG & HEMPFIELD ELECTRIC RY	G&HE
GREENVILLE & MIAMI	G&MI
GREENVILLE & NORTHERN RAILWAY	G&N
GREENVILLE STEEL CAR COMPANY	GSCC
GREENWICH & JOHNSONVILLE RAILWAY	G&J
GRIZZLY FLATS RAILROAD	GF
GROTON & STONINGTON TRCTION COMPANY	G&ST
GROTON STONINGTON STREET RAILWAY	GSSR
GROVES COMPANY	GCOM
GUALALA RAILWAY	GUA
GUIGNARD BRICK	GB
GUILFORD TRANSPORTATION INDUSTRY	GTI
GULF	G#
GULF & CHICAGO RAILROAD	G&C
GULF & INTERSTATE RAILROAD	G&IR
GULF & MISSISSIPPI	G&MIS
GULF COAST LINES	GCL
GULF COLORADO & SANTA FE	GC&SF
GULF LINE RAILWAY	GL
GULF MOBILE & NORTHERN	GM&N
GULF MOBILE & OHIO	GM&O
GULF PORTS TERMINAL	GPT
GULF POWER COMPANY	GPCO
GULF TEXAS & WESTERN	GT&W
GULFPORT & MISSISSIPPI COAST TRACTION	G&M
GUNN & BLACK RAILROAD	G&B
HABCO LORAM	HALO
HACKENSACK & LODI	H&L
HACKENSACK & NEW YORK RAILROAD	H&NY
HAGERSTOWN & FREDERICK RAILWAY	H&F
HALIFAX CITY RAILROAD	HALC
HALL & MANNING	H&MA
HALLETT DOCK	HADK
HALTON COUNTY RADIAL RAILWAY	HCR
HAMERSLEY IRON	HIR
HAMILTON & DUDAS STREET RAILWAY	H&DS
HAMILTON & NORTHWESTERN RAILWAY	H&NW
HAMILTON GRINSBY & BEAMVILLE ELEC RY	HG&B
HAMILTON STREET RAILWAY	HST
HAMMERMILL PAPER COMPANY	HAMPC
HAMMOND & LITTLE RIVER LUMBER COMPANY	H&LR
HAMMOND LUMBER COMPANY	HLC
HAMPDEN RAILROAD	HAMP
HAMPTON & BRANCHVILLE RAILROAD	H&B
HAMS	HAMS#
HANCOCK & CALUMET RAILWAY	H&C
HANNA NICKEL SMELTING	HNSM
HANNIBAL & ST JOSEPH	H&SJ
HANNIBAL CONNECTING RAILROAD	HANC
HARBOR BELT LINE RAILROAD-CALIFORNIA	HBLR
HARDWICK & WOODBURY RAILWAY	H&W

STEPHANS_RAILROAD_DIRECTORY

A13

APPENDIX A (RAILROADS)

ROADS ALPHABETICALLY W/ABBREVIATIONS	A
HARLEM & MANHATTAN CABLE	H&MC
HARLEM TRANSFER COMPANY	HTR
HARRINGTON LUMBER COMPANY	HRLC
HARRISBURG & WESTERN	H&WE
HARRISBURG PORSMOUTH MT JOY & LANCAST	HPM
HARRISBURG RYS	H
HART & HORNING COMPANY	H&HC
HARTFORD & CONNECTICUT VALLEY	H&CV
HARTFORD & CONNECTICUT WESTERN	H&CW
HARTFORD & NEW HAVEN	H&NH
HARTFORD & SLOCOMB RAILROAD	H&S
HARTFORD & SPRINGFIELD STREET RY CO	H&SSR
HARTFORD & WETHERSFIELD HORSE RY	H&WH
HARTFORD EASTERN	HE
HARTFORD ELECTRIC LIGHT COMPANY	HELC
HARTFORD MANCHESTER & ROCKVILLE TRAMWY	HM&R
HARTWELL RAILWAY	HAR
HARVARD BRANCH	HB
HASSINGER	HAS
HAVERHILL GEORGETOWN & DANVERS ST RY	HG&DSR
HAVERHILL MERRIMAC & AMESBURY ST RY	HM&A
HAWAIIAN RAILROAD COMPANY	HRC
HAWKINSVILLE & FLORIDA SOUTHERN	H&FS
HAWKINSVILLE & WESTERN	HA&W
HAYDEN COAL COMPANY	HAYC
HAYDENVILLE BRANCH RAILROAD	HAY
HAYT'S CORNERS OVID & WILLARD	HCO&W
HAZELTON & BEAVER MEADOWS	H&BM
HAZELTON-SUGAR LOAF	HSL
HAZLETON	HA
HECLA & TORCH LAKE	H&TL
HEINZ 57	HZ
HEINZ 57 (O)	HZ*
HELENA LIGHT & RAILWAY	HL&R
HELENA PARKIN & NORTHERN RAILWAY	HP&N
HELENA SOUTHERN	HESO
HELENA SOUTHWESTERN RAILROAD	HES
HELLENIC STATE RAILWAYS	HSR
HENDERSON LUMBER COMPANY	HENL
HERCULES POWDER COMPANY	HPC
HEREFORD RAILWAY	HERE
HERSHEY CUBAN RAILWAY	HC
HERSHEY TRANSIT	HT
HETCH HETCHY RAILROAD	HH
HIBISCUS & HELICONIA	H&H
HICKGAS COMPANY	HGC
HIGH POINT THOMASVILLE & DENTON RR	HPT&D
HIGHLAND PARK & FRUITVALE AVE RR	HP&FV
HIGHLAND RAILROAD	HIGH
HILL CITY RAILWAY	HILLC
HILLCREST LUMBER COMPANY LTD	HLCL
HILLCREST OSBORNE	HOS
HILLCREST WSR.	HWSR
HILLSBORO & NORTH EASTERN RAILWAY	H&NE
HILLSDALE COUNTY RAILWAY	HIL
HIMMTEBERG-HARRISON LUMBER CO	HHL
HINES LUMBER COMPANY	EHLC
HINESVILLE FLEMINGTON & WESTERN	HF&W
HINKLEY LOCOMOTIVE WORKS	HLW
HOBART SOUTHERN	HS
HOBO RAILROAD	HOBO
HOBOKEN MANUFACTURERS RAILROAD	HM
HOBOKEN SHORE RAILROAD (HM)	HSH
HOCKEN VALLEY SCENIC RAILWAY	HVS
HOCKING VALLEY RAILROAD	HV
HOERNER-WALDORF PAPER PRODUCTS	H-WPP
HOLLIS & EASTERN RAILROAD	H&E
HOLTEN INTER-URBAN RAILWAY COMPANY	HI
HOMESTAKE MINING COMPANY	HMC
HONOLULU RAPID TRANSIT COMPANY	HORT
HOOD RIVER RAILROAD	HOOD
HOOPPOLE YORKTOWN & TAMPOCO	HY&T
HOOSAC & WILMINGTON	H&WI
HOOSAC TUNNEL & WILMINGTON RAILROAD	HT&W
HOOSAC VALLEY STREET RAILWAY	HVSR
HOPE VALLEY RAILROAD	HOPE
HOPKINSVILLE & SOUTHERN	H&SO

ROADS ALPHABETICALLY W/ABBREVIATIONS	A
HORNELLSVILLE & COHOCTON VALLEY	HV&CV
HORTON LUMBER & TIMBER COMPANY	HL&T
HORWITH RAILROAD	HRR
HOT SPRINGS RAILROAD	HOTS
HOUGHTON & ONTONAGON	H&O
HOUGHTON CHASSELL & SOUTHWESTERN	HC&SW
HOUSASTONIC	HO
HOUSE OF DAVID	HD
HOUSTON & BRAZOS VALLEY (MP)	H&BV
HOUSTON & TEXAS	H&T
HOUSTON & TEXAS CENTRAL	H&TC
HOUSTON BELT & TERMINAL RAILWAY CO.	HB&T
HOUSTON CENTRAL ARKANSAS & NORTHERN	HCA&N
HOUSTON EAST & WEST TEXAS	HE&WT
HOUSTON ELECTRIC COMPANY	HECO
HOUSTON NORTH SHORE (MP)	HNS
HOWARD TERMINAL RAILWAY	HTRY
HUDSON & BOSTON CORPORATION	H&BC
HUDSON & BROAD TOP MOUNTAIN	H&BT
HUDSON & MANHATTAN RAILROAD	H&M
HUDSON & MANHATTAN SUBWAY	H&M.
HUDSON & MOWHAK	H&MO
HUDSON BAY RAILROAD	HBRR
HUDSON BAY RAILWAY	HBRR.
HUDSON COAL COMPANY	HCC
HUDSON CONNECTING RAILROAD COMPANY	HCRR
HUDSON RIVER & BOSTON	HR&B
HUDSON RIVER RAILROAD & TERMINAL	HRRR
HUDSON VALLEY ELECTRIC RAILROAD	HVE
HUDSON VALLEY RAILWAY	HVRY
HUENEME MALIBU & PORT LOS ANGELES RY	HM&PLA
HULL ELECTRIC RAILWAY (ONTARIO)	HER
HUMBOLDT BAY & TRINIDAD	HB&TD
HUMMELSTOWN & CAMPBELLTOWN STREET RY	H&CT
HUNTER PACKING COMPANY	HPC*
HUNTINGTON & BROAD TOP MOUNTAIN RR	H&BTM
HUNTINGTON & BROAD TOP MT RR & COAL CO	HU&BT
HUNTINGTON & BROAD TOP RAILROAD	H&BTOP
HUNTINGTON RAILROAD	HU
HUNTSVILLE & LAKE OF BAYS RAILROAD	H&LB
HUNTSVILLE & LAKE OF BAYS RAILWAY	H&LB.
HURON & EASTERN RAILWAY	HU&E
HURON BAY & IRON RANGE	HB&IR
HURON CITY RAILWAY	HCRY
HUTCHINSON & NORTHERN RAILWAY COMPANY	H&N
HYDRO ELECTRIC POWER COMMISSION	HEPC
IBERIA ST MARY & EASTERN	ISM&E
ICE FULTON TRIANGLE	IFT
IDAHO & WASHINGTON NORTHERN RAILROAD	I&WN
IDAHO SOUTHERN	ISO
ILLINOIS CENTRAL GULF	ICG
ILLINOIS CENTRAL RAILROAD	IC
ILLINOIS MIDLAND RAILWAY	IM
ILLINOIS NORTHERN RAILROAD	IN.
ILLINOIS NORTHERN RAILWAY	IN
ILLINOIS RIVER PACKET CO	IRPC
ILLINOIS SLAG & BALLAST	IS&B
ILLINOIS TERMINAL RAILROAD COMPANY	IT
ILLINOIS TERMINAL RAILROAD SYSTEMS	IT.
ILLINOIS TRACTION RAILWAY	ITR
ILLINOIS TUNNEL COMPANY	ITCO
ILLINOIS VALLEY TRACTION	IVT
ILWACO RAILWAY & NAVIGATION COMPANY	IL
IMPERIAL IRRIGATION DISTRICT	IRD
IMPERIAL SUGAR	IMPX
INDEPENDENCE & MONMOUTH	I&M
INDIAN HILL & IRON RANGE RAILROAD	IH&IR
INDIAN VALLEY RAILROAD	IV
INDIANA & MICHIGAN ELECTRIC	I&ME
INDIANA & OHIO	I&OH
INDIANA COLUMBUS & EASTERN TRACTION	IC&E
INDIANA HARBOR BELT RAILROAD	IHB
INDIANA HI-RAIL CORPORATION	IHRC
INDIANA NORTHERN RAILWAY	INN
INDIANA RAILROAD	I
INDIANA SERVICE CORPORATION	INDSC
INDIANA SOUTHERN	INS

A14

APPENDIX A (RAILROADS)

ROADS ALPHABETICALLY W/ABBREVIATIONS	A
INDIANAPOLIS & CINCINNATTI TRACTION CO	I&C
INDIANAPOLIS & EASTERN	I&E
INDIANAPOLIS CINCINNATI & LAFAYETTE RR	IC&LRR
INDIANAPOLIS DELPHI & CHICAGO	ID&C
INDIANAPOLIS RAILWAYS	IRW
INDIANAPOLIS UNION RAILWAY	IU
INGALLS SHIPBUBILDING	IS
INGERSOLL RAND POWERED LOCOMOTIVES	IRP
INLAND EMPIRE SYSTEM	IES
INLAND LIME & STONE	IL&S
INLAND PAPER COMPANY	IEPC
INLAND STEEL CO	ISC*
INSPERATION CONSOLIDATION COPPER CO	ICCO
INTER-CITY RAPID TRANSIT (OHIO)	ICRT
INTER-MOUNTAIN RAILWAY	INMT
INTER-URBAN RAILWAY	IUR
INTERBUROUGH RAPID TRANSIT COMPANY	IRT
INTERCOLONIAL CANADA RAILWAY	ICO
INTERCOLONIAL RAILROAD	ICO
INTERCOLONIAL RAILWAY	ICO
INTERLAKE STEEL	ILST
INTERMOUNTAIN RAILWAY	INMT
INTERNATIONAL GREAT NORTHERN (MP)	I-GN
INTERNATIONAL MILLING	IMI
INTERNATIONAL MINERALS & CHEMICAL	IM&C
INTERNATIONAL RAILWAY (CANADA)	IRY
INTERNATIONAL RW OF CENTRAL AMERICA	IRCA
INTERSTATE PUBLIC SERV CO OF INDIANA	IPSI
INTERSTATE RAILROAD	INTER
INTERSTATE STREET RAILWAY	ISR
INTERURBAN RAILWAY & TERMINAL	IR&T
IOLA & NORTHERN RAILROAD	I&N
IOLA & ST JOSEPH CANAL & RAILROAD	I&JC
IOWA CENTRAL	IOWAC
IOWA CENTRAL & WESTERN RAILWAY	IC&W
IOWA INTERSTATE	IOIS
IOWA POWER & LIGHT	IP&L
IOWA RAILROAD CORPORATION	IRRC
IOWA TERMINAL RAILROAD COMPANY	IOWA
IOWA TERMINAL RAILWAY	IOWA
IOWA TRANSFER RAILWAY	IOWAT
IRON MOUNTAIN RAILWAY	IMT
IRON ORE CO OF CANADA	IOCC
IRONTON RAILROAD	IR
ISLAND CREEK COAL	ICC
ISLAND RAILROAD	IRR
ISLAND TERMINAL COMPANY	ITC
ISLAND TUG & BARGE LIMITED	IT&B
ISTHMUS CANAL COMMISSION	ISTCC
ITASCA RAILROAD	ITAS
ITHACA & ATHENS	I&A
ITHACA & OSWEGO	I&OS
ITHACA & OWEGO	I&O
ITHACA AUBURN & WESTERN	IA&W
ITHACA STREET RAILWAY	ISRY
ITHACA TRACTION CORPORATION	ITH
ITHACA-AUBURN SHORT LINE	I-ASL
ITTX	ITTX
JACKASS & WESTERN	J&W
JACKSON COUNTY GRAIN	JCG
JACKSONVILLE & ATLANTIC	J&A
JACKSONVILLE & HAVANA	J&H
JACKSONVILLE & SOUTHWESTERN	J&S
JACKSONVILLE BELT	JB
JACKSONVILLE GAINESVILLE & GULF	JG&G
JACKSONVILLE MAYPORT & PABLO RY & NAV	JM&P
JACKSONVILLE PENSACOLA & MOBILE	JP&M
JACKSONVILLE ST AUGUSTINE & HALIFAX R	JA&HR
JACKSONVILLE ST AUGUSTINE & INDIAN RI	JA&IR
JACKSONVILLE TAMPA & KEY WEST	JT&KW
JACKSONVILLE TERMINAL COMPANY	JT
JACKSONVILLE TRACTION COMPANY	JVT
JAMES RIVER COMPANY	JR
JAMESTOWN & FRANKLIN	JA&F
JAMESTOWN CHAUTAUQUA & LAKE ERIE	JC&LE
JAMESTOWN STREET RAILWAY	JSRY
JAMESTOWN WESTFIELD & NORTHWESTERN RR	JW&N

ROADS ALPHABETICALLY W/ABBREVIATIONS	A
JAPAN NATIONAL RAILWAY	JNR
JAPANESE NATIONAL RAILWAYS	JN
JAY STREET CONNECTING RAILROAD	JS
JEFFERSON & LAKE PONTCHARTRAIN RR	J&LP
JEFFERSON & NORTHWESTERN RAILROAD	J&NW
JEFFERSON MADISON & INDIANAPOLIS RR	JM&I
JEFFERSON RAILROAD	J
JEFFERSON SOUTHWESTERN RAILROAD	JSW
JEROME & SOUTHWESTERN	J&SW
JERSEY CENTRAL	CNJ
JERSEY CENTRAL (O)	JCE
JERSEY CENTRAL TRACTION	JCTR
JERSEY CITY	JCITY
JERSEY CITY & ALBANY	JC&A
JERSEY CITY TERMINAL	JCET
JERSEY SHORE & ANTES FORT RAILROAD	JS&AF
JERSEYVILLE & EASTERN RAILROAD	J&E
JIM WALTER RESOURCES INC	JWR
JOE CUSHING RAILROAD	JCRR
JOHNSON LUMBER	JL
JOHNSONBURG	JO
JOHNSTOWN & SOMERSET	J&SS
JOHNSTOWN & STONY CREEK RAILROAD	J&SC
JOHNSTOWN EBENSBURG & NORTHERN	JE&N
JOHNSTOWN PASSENGER RAILWAY	JP
JOHNSTOWN TERMINAL RAILWAY COMPANY	JTT
JOHNSTOWN TRACTION CO	JTC
JOLIET & CHICAGO	J&C
JOLIET UNION DEPOT COMPANY	JUD
JONES & LAUGHLIN STEEL	J&L
JOPLIN UNION DEPOT COMPANY	JUDC
JUNCTION CITY & FORT RILEY RAILWAY	JC&FR
JUNCTION CITY-HORTON WOODEN RAILROAD	JC
KAHN'S SONS' REFRIGERATION	KSR*
KAHUKU PLANTATION COMPANY	KP
KAHULUI RAILROAD	KA
KAISER BAUXITE	KB
KAISER STEEL	KST
KALAMAZOO LAKE SHORE & CHICAGO	KLS&C
KANAWHA & MICHIGAN	K&M
KANAWHA CENTRAL RAILWAY	KAC
KANAWHA GLEN JEAN & EASTERN	KGJ&E
KANE	K
KANE & ELK	K&E
KANKAKEE & SENECA	K&SEN
KANKAKEE & URSANA TRACTION COMPANY	K&U
KANSAS & ARKANSAS VALLEY	K&AV
KANSAS & MISSOURI RY & TERMINAL CO	K&MR&T
KANSAS & NEVADA RY & TERMINAL CO	K&N
KANSAS & OKLAHOMA	K&O
KANSAS & SIDELL	K&SID
KANSAS CITY & BEATRICE	KC&B
KANSAS CITY & EASTERN	KC&E
KANSAS CITY & INDEPENDENCE AIR LINE RR	KC&IAL
KANSAS CITY & PACIFIC	KC&P
KANSAS CITY & SOUTHERN RAILROAD	KC&S
KANSAS CITY CLINTON & SPRINGFIELD	KCC&S
KANSAS CITY CONNECTING RAILROAD	KCC
KANSAS CITY ELDORADO & SOUTHERN	KSE&S
KANSAS CITY ELEVATED RAILWAY	KCERY
KANSAS CITY FORT SCOTT & GULF RAILROAD	KCFSG
KANSAS CITY FORT SCOTT & MEMPHIS	KCFS&M
KANSAS CITY FORT SMITH & GULF	KCFS&G
KANSAS CITY FORT SMITH & SOUTHERN	KCFS&S
KANSAS CITY KAW VALLEY	KCKW
KANSAS CITY KAW VALLEY & WESTERN	KCKV&W
KANSAS CITY MEMPHIS & BIRMINGHAM	KCM&B
KANSAS CITY MEXICO & ORIENT RAILROAD	KCM&O.
KANSAS CITY MEXICO & ORIENT RAILWAY	KCM&O
KANSAS CITY NEVADA & FORT SMITH RR CO	KCN&FS
KANSAS CITY NORTHWESTERN RAILWAY	KCN
KANSAS CITY PITTSBURGH & GULF RAILWAY	KCP&G
KANSAS CITY PUBLIC SERVICE	KCPS
KANSAS CITY PUBLIC SERVICE (O)	KSPS
KANSAS CITY SHREVEPORT & GULF	KCS&G

A15

APPENDIX A (RAILROADS)

ROADS ALPHABETICALLY W/ABBREVIATIONS	A
KANSAS CITY SHREVEPORT & GULF TERMINAL	KCS&GT
KANSAS CITY SOUTHERN RAILWAY	KCS
KANSAS CITY SOUTHERN TRANSPORT CO	KCST
KANSAS CITY SPRINGFIELD & MEMPHIS	KCS&M
KANSAS CITY ST JOSEPH & COUNCIL BLUFF	KCSJCB
KANSAS CITY ST LOUIS & CHICAGO	KCSL&C
KANSAS CITY SUBURBAN BELT RAILROAD	KCSB
KANSAS CITY TERMINAL RAILWAY	KCT
KANSAS CITY WYANDOTTE & NORTHWESTERN	KCW&NW
KANSAS OKLAHOMA & GULF RAILWAY	KO&G
KANSAS UTILITIES COMPANY	KUC
KARSHNER	KARS
KASLO & SLOCAN	K&SL
KATY NORTHWEST	MKT
KATY NORTHWEST (MKT) (O)	KATY
KAULLUMBER COMPANY	KAUL
KEATING & SMETHPORT	K&S
KEESEVILLE AUSABLE CHASM &L CHAMPLAIN	KAC&LC
KEEWEENAW CENTRAL RAILROAD	KWNC
KELLEY'S CREEK & NORTH WESTERN RR	KC&NW
KELLEY'S CREEK RAILROAD	KC
KELLYS ISLAND LIME & TRANSPORT CO.	KIL&T
KENDALL & ELDRED	K&EL
KENNEBEC CENTRAL	KCE
KENNEBEC WHARF & COAL	KW&C
KENNECOTT COPPER COMPANY	KE
KENTUCKY & INDIANA BRIDGE & RR CO.	K&IB
KENTUCKY & INDIANA TERMINAL RAILROAD	K&IT
KENTUCKY & TENNESSEE RAILROAD	K&T
KENTUCKY & TENNESSEE RAILWAY	K&T
KENTUCKY IMPROVEMENT COMPANY	KICO
KENTUCKY MIDLAND	KM
KENTUCKY ORDINACE WORKS	KYOW
KENTUCKY TRACTION & TERMINAL	KT&T
KENTUCKY UNION RAILWAY	KURY
KENTUCKY UTILITIES COMPANY	KTU
KENTUCKY WEST TENNESSEE	KWT
KEOKUK & DES MOINES	K&DM
KEOKUK & WESTERN	K&W
KEOKUK UNION DEPOT COMPANY	KUDC
KERR-MCGEE	K-M
KERSEY	KER
KETTLE VALLEY RAILROAD	KVRR
KEWAUNEE GREEN BAY & WESTERN RAILROAD	KGB&W
KEWEENAW CENTRAL RAILWAY	KEWC
KEY SYSTEM OF SAN FRANCISCO	KS
KEY WEST ELECTRIC COMPANY	KWE
KEY WEST STREET-CAR ASSOCIATION	KWS
KEYSTONE	KEY
KIAMICHI VALLEY RAILROAD	KIAM
KINGAN RELIABLE HAM	KRH*
KINGFIELD & DEAD RIVER	K&DR
KINGS LAKE SHORE RAILROAD	KLS
KINGSTON & ADELPHI RAILROAD	K&AR
KINGSTON BRIDGE & TERMINAL COMPANY	KB&TC
KINGSTON PORTSMOUTH & CATARAQUI	KP&C
KINKORA & NEW LISBON	K&NL
KINMOND BROTHERS MONTREAL	KBM
KINSTON LUMBER COMPANY	KINL
KINSTON-CAROLINA RAILROAD	KCRR
KINZUA	KI
KINZUA & TIONA	K&TI
KINZUA CREEK & KANE	KC&K
KINZUA HEMLOCK	KH
KINZUA VALLEY	KV
KIRBY LUMBER COMPANY	KLC
KISHACOQUILLAS VALLEY RAILROAD	KISH
KISO FOREST JAPAN	KF
KITCHENER WATERLOO RAILWAY	KW
KITTY HAWK CENTRAL	KHC
KLAMATH NORTHERN RAILWAY	KLN
KLICKITAT LOG & LUMBER COMPANY	KL&L
KLIPNOCKIE	KLI
KLONDIKE MINES RAILWAY	KMRY
KNICKERBOCKER LIME	KL
KNOX & LINCOLN	K&L
KNOX RAILROAD	KN

ROADS ALPHABETICALLY W/ABBREVIATIONS	A
KNOXVILLE & OHIO RAILROAD	K&OH
KNOXVILLE POWER & LIGHT	KP&L
KNOXVILLE STREET RAILWAY SYSTEM	KSRS
KOLOA PLANTATION	KOLOA
KOPPERS	K*
KOPPERS COMPANY	KOP
KOSCIVSKO & SOUTHEASTERN	K&SE
KOSMOS TIMBER COMPANY	KTC
KRAFT	KRA*
KREY PACKING	KP*
KUERT CONCRETE	KUCO
KUMPE-HAUSER CORPORATION	K-HC
KUSHEQUA	KU
KYLE RAILWAYS INC	KYRR
L&N SHOPS	L&NS
LA CROSSE & MILWAUKEE	LC&MI
LA CROSSE & SOUTHEASTERN RAILWAY	LC&SE
LA JOLLA LINE (CALIFORNIA)	LJ
LA JUNTA INDUSTRIAL PARK	LJIP
LA SALLE & BUREAU COUNTY RAILROAD	LS&B
LAC LA BELLE & CALUMET RAILROAD	LLB&C
LACHINE JACQUES CARTIER & MAISSONNEUVE	LJC&M
LACKAWANNA	DL&W.
LACKAWANNA (DL&W) (O)	LACK
LACKAWANNA & BLOOMSBURG	L&B
LACKAWANNA & MONTROSE	LACK&M
LACKAWANNA & PITTSBURG	L&P
LACKAWANNA & SOUTHWESTERN	L&SW
LACKAWANNA & WYOMING VALLEY RAILWAY	L&WV
LACKAWAXEN & STOURBRIDGE	LA&S
LACLEDE STEEL COMPANY	LSCO
LACOMBE & BLINDMAN VALLEY	L&BV
LACOMBE & NORTH WESTERN	LC&NW
LACROSSE & MILWAUKEE	LA&M
LAFAYETTE & MONON RAILWAY	L&MRY
LAFAYETTE STREET RAILWAY (INDIANA)	LISRY
LAHAINA KAANAPALI & PACIFIC	LK&P
LAKE CHAMPLAIN & MORIAH RAILROAD	LC&M
LAKE CHAMPLAIN & ST LAWRENCE JUNCTION	LC&LJ
LAKE COUNTY RAILROAD (LOGGING)	LCRR
LAKE ERIE & DETROIT RIVER	LE&DR
LAKE ERIE & EASTERN RAILROAD	LE&E
LAKE ERIE & FORT WAYNE RAILROAD	LE&FW
LAKE ERIE & NORTHERN RAILWAY (CP)	LE&N
LAKE ERIE & PITTSBURGH RAILROAD	LE&P
LAKE ERIE & WESTERN	LE&W
LAKE ERIE BOWLING GREEN & NAPOLEON RY	LEBG&N
LAKE ERIE FRANKLIN & CLARION RAILROAD	LEF&C
LAKE ERIE WOOSTER & MUSKINGUM VALLEY	LEWMV
LAKE GEORGE & MUSKEGON RIVER RAILROAD	LG&MR
LAKE HURON & NORTHERN ONTARIO	LH&NO
LAKE ONTARIO SHORE RAILROAD	LOSRR
LAKE SHORE & MICHIGAN SOUTHERN	LS&MS
LAKE SHORE & MICHIGAN SOUTHERN (O)	LS&MC
LAKE SHORE & TUSCARAWAS VALLEY	LS&TV
LAKE SHORE ELECTRIC INTERURBAN	LSE
LAKE SHORE ELECTRIC RAILWAY	LSEL
LAKE SHORE RAILROAD	LSH
LAKE SUPERIOR & ISHPEMING RAILROAD	LS&I
LAKE SUPERIOR & ISHPEMING RAILWAY	LS&I.
LAKE SUPERIOR & MISSISSIPPI	LS&M
LAKE SUPERIOR TERMINAL & TRANSFER RY	LST&T
LAKE TAHOE RAILWAY & TRANSPORTATION	L&R
LAKE TERMINAL RAILROAD	LT
LAKE WHATCOM RAILWAY	LWRY
LAKE WINICO ST JOSEPH CANAL & RR CO	LW&JC
LAKEFRONT DOCK & RAILROAD TERMINAL	LD&RT
LAKELAND	L
LAKESIDE & MARBLEHEAD RAILROAD	L&MA
LAMAR QUEENS & NORTHERN	LQ&N
LAMOILLE VALLEY	LAV
LAMOILLE VALLEY RAILWAY CORP	LVRC
LANCASTER & CHESTER RAILWAY	L&C
LANCASTER & HAMDEN	L&H
LANCASTER & READING NARROW GAGE RR	L&RNG
LANCASTER & YORK FURNACE STREET RY	L&YF
LANCASTER (OHIO) STREET RAILWAY	LOSRY

STEPHANS' RAILROAD DIRECTORY

A16

APPENDIX A (RAILROADS)

ROADS ALPHABETICALLY W/ABBREVIATIONS	A
LANCASTER EPHRATA & LEBANON TRACTION	LE&L
LANCASTER LOCOMOTIVE WORKS	LLW
LANCASTER OXFORD & SOUTHERN	LO&S
LANCASTER TRACTION & POWER COMPANY	LT&P
LAONA & NORTHERN RAILWAY	L&NO
LARAMIE HAHN'S PEAK & PACIFIC	LHP&P
LARAMIE NORTH PARK & WESTERN	LNP&W
LARAMIE PLAINS LINES	LPL
LAS VEGAS & TONOPAH RAILROAD	LV&T
LASKO	LAS
LATROBE & LIGONIER	L&L
LAUHOFF GRAIN	LG
LAUREL & TALLAHOMA WESTERN RAILWAY	L&TWRY
LAUREL FORK & SAND HILL	LF&SH
LAUREL LINE (LACKAWANNA & WYOMING VALLEY)	L&WV.
LAUREL LINE	LALN
LAUREL RIVER & HOT SPRINGS	LR&HS
LAURINBURG & SOUTHERN RAILROAD	LA&SO
LAWNDALE RAILWAY & INDUSTRIAL	LA
LAWRENCEBURG & MISSISSIPPI	L&MISS
LAWRENCEVILLE & EVERGREEN	L&E
LAWTON RAILWAY & LIGHTING	LR&L
LEAVENWORTH & OLATHE	L&OL
LEAVENWORTH & TOPEKA	L&T
LEAVENWORTH DEPOT & RAILROAD	LD&R
LEAVENWORTH KANSAS & WESTERN	LK&W
LEAVENWORTH TOPEKA & WESTERN	LT&W
LEBANON SPRINGS	LS
LEBANON VALLEY RAILWAY	LVRY
LEE COUNTY CENTRAL ELECTRIC RAILWAY	LCCE
LEE TIDEWATER CYPRESS COMPANY	LTC
LEETONIA & CHERRY VALLEY	L&CV
LEHIGH & HUDSON RIVER RAILROAD	L&HR
LEHIGH & HUDSON RIVER RAILWAY COMPANY	L&HR
LEHIGH & MAHANOY	L&M
LEHIGH & NEW ENGLAND RAILROAD	L&NE
LEHIGH & NEW ENGLAND RAILWAY	L&NE.
LEHIGH & SUSQUEHANNA	L&SQ
LEHIGH LUZERNE	LL
LEHIGH NAVIGATION COAL COMPANY	LNCC
LEHIGH PORTLAND CEMENT COMPANY	LPC
LEHIGH VALLEY	LV
LEHIGH VALLEY TRANSIT	LVT
LEIPER	LEI
LENAWEE CENTRAL	LCE
LENAWEE COUNTY RAILROAD	LCO
LENORA MT SICKLER RAILWAY	LMSRY
LEONA HEIGHTS RAILROAD	LH
LEONARDS STORE	LST
LEVIS & KENNEBEC RAILWAY	L&K
LEWIS RUN RAILWAY	LRRY
LEWISTON & CRAIGMONT	L&CR
LEWISTON & YOUNGSTOWN FRONTIER	L&YFR
LEWISTON AUGUSTA & WATERVILLE ST RY	LA&W
LEWISTON-CLARKSON TRANSIT	L-CTR
LEXINGTON & DANVILLE RAILROAD	L&DV
LEXINGTON & EASTERN RAILWAY	LX&E
LEXINGTON & FRANKFORT RAILROAD	L&FF
LEXINGTON & OHIO	LX&O
LIBBY'S	LIB#
LIGONIER & LATROBE RAIL ROAD	L&LA
LIGONIER VALLEY RAILROAD	LIG
LIHUE PLANTATION COMPANY LTD	LP
LIMA & DEFIANCE RAILROAD	LI&DE
LIMA ELECTRIC RAILWAY	LEL
LIMA HAMILTON CORPORATION	L-HC
LIMA LOCOMOTIVE WORKS	LILW
LIMA NORTHERN	LN
LIMA STONE COMPANY	LSC
LIMA STREET MOTOR & POWER COMPANY	LSM&PC
LIME ROCK RAILROAD	LRRR
LINCOLN STONE QUARRY	LSQ
LINCOLN TRACTION COMPANY	LTR
LINDELL RAILWAY	LIND
LINVILLE RIVER RAILWAY	LR
LINWOOD STREET RAILWAY	LSR

ROADS ALPHABETICALLY W/ABBREVIATIONS	A
LIPSETT STEEL COMPANY	LISC
LIQUID CARBONIC DRY ICE	LCDI#
LITCHFIELD & MADISON RAILWAY	LI&M
LITTLE EMMA SILVER MINE	LESM
LITTLE FALLS & DOLGEVILLE RAILROAD	LF&D
LITTLE KANAWHA RAILROAD	LK
LITTLE MIAMI RAILROAD (OHIO)	LMRR
LITTLE RIVER & ARKANSAS VALLEY	LR&AV
LITTLE RIVER RAILROAD	LITRI
LITTLE SCHUYLKILL NAV RR & COAL CO.	LSCH
LIVE OAK & CHARLOTTE'S HARBOR RR CO	LO&CH
LIVE OAK & GULF	LO&G
LIVE OAK & PERRY	LO&P
LIVE OAK & ROWLAND'S BLUFF	LO&RB
LIVE OAK PERRY & GULF RAILROAD	LOP&G
LIVE OAK PERRY & GULF RAILWAY	LOP&G.
LIVE OAK PERRY & SOUTH GEORGIA RY	LOP&SG
LIVE OAK TAMPA & CHARLOTTES HARBOR	LOT&CH
LIVE OAK TAMPA & HOWLAND'S BLUFF	LOT&HB
LIVE POULTRY TRANSPORT COMPANY	LPT
LIVONIA AVON & LAKEVILLE RAILROAD	LA&L
LOCK CITY ELECTRIC RAILWAY	LCER
LOCKS & CANALS COMPANY LOWELL MASS	L&CC
LODI BRANCH	LODI
LODI RAILROAD	LOD
LONDON & PORT STANLEY RAILWAY	L&PS
LONDON STREET RAILWAY	LSRY
LONE STAR STEEL COMPANY	LSSC
LONG BELL RAILROAD	LB
LONG ISLAND CITY & MANHATTAN BEACH RY	LIC&MB
LONG ISLAND RAILROAD	LI
LONG WHARF	LW
LONGVIEW PORTLAND & NORTHERN RAILWAY	LP&N
LONGVIEW SWITCHING COMPANY	LSWC
LOOP & LOOKOUT	L&LO
LORAIN & CLEVELAND RAILWAY	L&CRY
LORAIN & ELYRIA RAILROAD	L&ERR
LORAIN & WESTERN VIRGINIA RAILWAY	L&WVA
LORAIN ASHLAND & SOUTHERN	LAS&S
LORAIN COUNTY LINE	LCOL
LORAIN STREET RAILROAD	LSRR
LORAIN STREET RAILWAY	LSRR.
LORAMA RAILROAD	LOR
LORBERRY CREEK	LC
LORTON & OCCOQUAN	L&O
LOS ANGELES & EAGLE ROCK VALLEY	LA&ERV
LOS ANGELES & GLENDALE	LA&G
LOS ANGELES & LONG BEACH	LA&LB
LOS ANGELES & PACIFIC RR	LA&P
LOS ANGELES & REDONDO	LA&R
LOS ANGELES & SALT LAKE RAILROAD (UP)	LA&SL
LOS ANGELES & SAN DIEGO BEACH RY	LA&SDB
LOS ANGELES & SAN GABRIEL VALLEY	LA&SG
LOS ANGELES & SAN PEDRO	LA&SP
LOS ANGELES COUNTY	LAC
LOS ANGELES INDEPENDENT RAILROAD	LAIR
LOS ANGELES JUNCTION RAILWAY	LAJ
LOS ANGELES PACIFIC RAILWAY COMPANY	LAPR
LOS ANGELES PASADENA & GLENDALE	LAP&G
LOS ANGELES RAILWAY	LAR
LOS ANGELES TERMINAL	LAT
LOS ANGELES TRANSIT LINES	LATR
LOS ANGELES UNION PASSENGER TERMINAL	LAUPT
LOUIS SANDS' ROAD	LSAN
LOUISA RAILROAD	LOU
LOUISIANA & ARKANSAS KANSAS CITY SOUTH	L&AKS
LOUISIANA & ARKANSAS RAILWAY COMPANY	L&A
LOUISIANA & DELTA	L&D
LOUISIANA & MISSOURI RIVER	L&MR
LOUISIANA & NORTH WEST RAILROAD	L&NW
LOUISIANA & PINE BLUFF RAILWAY	L&PB
LOUISIANA & TEXAS	LO&T
LOUISIANA CYPRESS LUMBER COMPANY	LCL
LOUISIANA EASTERN RAILROAD	LE
LOUISIANA LONGLEAF LUMBER COMPANY	LLLC
LOUISIANA MIDLAND RAILROAD	LM
LOUISIANA MIDLAND RAILWAY	LM

A17

APPENDIX A (RAILROADS)

ROADS ALPHABETICALLY W/ABBREVIATIONS	A
LOUISIANA NEW ALBANY & CHICAGO	LNA&CH
LOUISIANA NEW ORLEANS & TEXAS	LNO&T
LOUISIANA RAILROAD & NAVIGATION CO.	LR&N
LOUISIANA SOUTHERN RAILWAY	LOS
LOUISIANA STATE PENITENTIARY	LPEN
LOUISVILLE & ATLANTIC RAILROAD	L&AT
LOUISVILLE & FRANKFORT	L&F
LOUISVILLE & INTERURBAN	L&I
LOUISVILLE & NASHVILLE	L&N
LOUISVILLE & WADLEY RAILROAD	L&WRR
LOUISVILLE & WADLEY RAILWAY	L&WRR.
LOUISVILLE CINCINNATI & CHARLESTON RR	LC&C
LOUISVILLE CINCINNATI & LEXINGTON RR	LC&L
LOUISVILLE HENDERSON & ST LOUIS RY	LH&SL
LOUISVILLE NEW ALBANY & CHICAGO	LNAC
LOUISVILLE NEW ALBANY & CORYDON RR	LNA&C
LOUISVILLE NEW ALBANY & SALEM	LNA&S
LOUISVILLE RAILWAY (KENTUCKY)	LRY
LOWELL & ANDOVER	L&AND
LOWVILLE & BEAVER RIVER RAILROAD	L&BR
LOYAL	LO
LUDINGTON & NORTHERN RAILWAY	LU&N
LUDLOW & SOUTHERN	L&S
LUKENS STEEL	LUS
LUMER ROADS IN GENERAL	LUMB
LYKENS VALLEY	LYK
LYNCHBURG & DANVILLE	LY&D
LYNCHBURG TRACTION & LIGHT COMPANY	LT&L
LYNN & BOSTON RAILROAD	L&B
LYONS-IOWA CENTRAL	L-IC
LYSTUL-LAWSON LUMBER COMPANY	LLL
M.K.T.	MKT*
M.U.N.X.	MUNX*
MA BROWN	MAB*
MACK TRUCK COMPANY	MTC
MACMILLAN BLOEDEL LIMITED	MBL
MACMILLAN BLOEDEL LUMBER COMPANY	MBL.
MACOMB & WESTERN ILLINOIS	M&WI
MACOMB INDUSTRY & LITTLETON	MI&L
MACON & BIRMINGHAM RAILROAD	M&BI
MACON & BIRMINGHAM RAILWAY	M&BI.
MACON & BRUNSWICK	M&BR
MACON & DUBLIN	M&DU
MACON DUBLIN & SAVANNAH RAILROAD	MD&S
MAD RIVER & LAKE ERIE	MR&LE
MADEIRA-MAMORE RAILWAY (BRAZIL)	M-M
MADERA SUGAR PINE COMPANY	MSPC.
MADISON & INDIANAPOLIS	M&I
MADRID	MAD
MAGMA ARIZONA RAILROAD	MA
MAHANOY & SHAMOKIN	M&SH
MAHONING COAL RAILROAD COMPANY	MAH
MAID OF THE MIST INCLINE	MOMI
MAINE CENTRAL RAILROAD	MC
MAINE CENTRAL SHOPS	MCS
MAINE POTATO	MP*
MAINSTEE & NORTHEASTERN RAILWAY	M&NRY
MALDEN & MELROSE	MA&ME
MALONE & ST LAURENCE RAILWAY COMPANY	M&SLRY
MAMMOTH CAVE RAILROAD	MCA
MANAHAWKEN & LONG BEACH TRANPORT CO	M&LB
MANAHAWKEN & LONG BEACH TRANSIT	M&LB.
MANASSAS GAP RAILROAD	MGAP
MANATEE CRATE COMPANY	MANC
MANATEE LIGHT & TRACTION COMPANY	ML&TC
MANCHESTER & ONEIDA RAILWAY	M&ONE
MANCHESTER DORSET & GRANVILLE	MD&G
MANCHESTER LOCOMOTIVE WORKS	MLW
MANCHESTER STREET RAILWAY	MSRW
MANDEVILLE NORTHERN	MAN
MANHATTAN & QUEENS TRACTION COMPANY	M&QT
MANHATTAN CITY & INTERURBAN RAILWAY	MC&I
MANHATTAN ELECTRIC	MAE
MANHATTAN ELEVATED COMPANY	MEC
MANHATTEN ALMA & BURLINGAME	MA&B
MANILA RAILWAY (PHILIPPINES)	MRW
MANISTEE & GRAND RAPIDS	M&GR

ROADS ALPHABETICALLY W/ABBREVIATIONS	A
MANISTEE & NORTH EASTERN RAILWAY	M&NE
MANISTIQUE & LAKE SUPERIOR RAILROAD	M&LS
MANITOBA & SASKATCHEWAN MINE	M&SM
MANITOU & PIKE'S PEAK RAILWAY	M&PP
MANITOWOC GREEN BAY & WESTERN	MGB&W
MANN'S CREEK RAILROAD	MCR
MANSFIELD COLDWATER & LAKE MICHIGAN	MC&LM
MANUFACTURERS JUNCTION RAILWAY	MJ
MANUFACTURERS RAILWAY OF ST LOUIS	MFG
MARCELLUS & OTISCO LAKE	M&OL
MARENGO MILWAUKEE & NORTHERN	MM&N
MARIANNA & BLOUNTSTOWN RAILROAD	M&BL
MARIETTA & CINCINNATI	M&CIN
MARIETTA & NORTH GEORGIA	M&NG
MARIETTA COLUMBUS & CLEVELAND	MC&C
MARIETTA HOCKING & NORTHERN RAILROAD	MH&N
MARIETTA WILLIAMSTOWN & PARKERSBURG	MW&P
MARINETTE TOMAHAWK & WESTERN RAILROAD	MT&W
MARINETTE TOMAHAWK & WESTERN RAILWAY	MT&W.
MARION & EASTERN	MA&E
MARION POWER SHOVEL COMPANY	MPS
MARION RAILWAY	MAR
MARION RIVER CARRY RAILROAD	MRC
MARITIME RAILWAY	MARY
MARKET STREET RAILWAY (SAN FRANCISCO)	MSSRY
MARKET STREET SUBWAY	MSS
MARQUETTE & HURON MOUNTAIN RAILROAD	M&HM
MARQUETTE & ONTONAGON	M&ON
MARQUETTE & SOUTHEASTERN	M&SE
MARQUETTE & WESTERN	M&W
MARQUETTE CEMENT	MCEM
MARTHA'S VINEYARD RAILROAD	MV
MARTINSBURG STREET RAILWAY	MSRY
MARYLAND & DELAWARE	M&D
MARYLAND & DELAWARE COAST RAILWAY	M&DC
MARYLAND & DELAWARE SEACOAST	M&DSC
MARYLAND & PENNSYLVANIA RAILROAD	MA&PA
MARYLAND CENTRAL	MDCE
MARYLAND DELAWARE & VIRGINIA RY	MD&V
MARYLAND DEPT OF TRANSPORTATION	MDOT
MARYLAND MARC	MARC
MARYLAND MIDLAND	MMI
MARYSVILLE & BIG SANDY	M&BS
MASCOT & WESTERN	MA&W
MASON & OCEANA RAILWAY	M&OC
MASON CITY & CLEAR LAKES RAILROAD	MC&CL
MASON CITY & FORT DODGE	MC&FD
MASONITE CORPORATION	MCORP
MASSACHUETTS BAY TRANSPORTATION AUTHO	MBTA
MASSACHUSETTS BAY TERMINAL AUTHORITY	MBTA
MASSACHUSETTS CENTRAL	MASSC
MASSACHUSETTS NORTHEASTERN STREET RY	MNES
MASSACHUSETTS STREET RAILWAY	MASS
MASSENA TERMINAL RAILROAD	MATE
MATERIAL SERVICE CORPORATION	MSCO
MATHIESON ALKALI WORKS	MAT*
MATTAGAMI RAILROAD	MAT
MATTOON RAILWAY	MATT
MAUCH CHUNK & LEIGHTON	MC&L
MAUCH CHUNK SWITCH-BACK RAILROAD	MCH
MAXTON ALMA & SOUTHBOUND RAILROAD	MA&S
MCCLOUD RIVER LUMBER COMPANY	MRIL
MCCLOUD RIVER RAILROAD	MCRI
MCKEAN & BUFFALO	M&B
MCKEESPORT & YOUGHIOGHENY RAILROAD	M&Y
MCKEESPORT CONNECTING RAILROAD	MCKC
MCNARY-MAVERICK RAILROAD	MMA
MEAD RUN	MR
MEADOW CREEK COAL COMPANY	MCCC
MEADOW RIVER LUMBER RAILROAD	MRL
MEADVILLE TRACTION CO LINE (PA)	MTCL
MEDFORD & CRATE LAKE RAILROAD	M&CLRR
MEDFORD COAST RAILWAY	MCOR
MEDINA & DARIEN	ME&D
MEDIX RUN COAL COMPANY	MRCC
MEIGS RAILROAD (MASSACHUSETTS)	MEIGS
MEMPHIS & CHARLESTON	M&CH

STEPHANS RAILROAD DIRECTORY

A18

APPENDIX A (RAILROADS)

ROADS ALPHABETICALLY W/ABBREVIATIONS	A
MEMPHIS & CHARLESTON RAILWAY	M&CT
MEMPHIS DALLAS & GULF	MD&GU
MEMPHIS EL PASO & PACIFIC RAILROAD	MEP&P
MEMPHIS PARIS & GULF	MP&G
MEMPHIS UNION STATION COMPANY	MUS
MENDHAM & MORRISTOWN EXTESION RY CO	M&ME
MERCHANTS BISCUITS	MB#
MERCHANTS DESPATCH (O)	MDT#
MERCHANTS DESPATCH TRANS CORP CHICAGO	MDTCC
MERIDAN & BIGBEE RAILROAD	M&BIG
MERIDAN & CROMWELL RAILROAD	M&CRR
MERIDAN & WATERBURY RAILROAD	M&WB
MERIDAN WATERBURY & CONNECTICUT RIVER	MW&CR
MESABE SOUTHERN	MSO
METAL PROCESSING INC	MPI
METRO ATLANTA RAPID TRANSIT AUTHORITY	MARTA
METRO-NORTH (NY CITY)	M-N
METROPOLITAN AREA EXPRESS OF PORTLAND	MAX
METROPOLITAN COACH COMPANY	MCL
METROPOLITAN RADIAL LINE	MRAD
METROPOLITAN RAILROAD (WASHINGTON DC)	MDC
METROPOLITAN STREET RAILWAY (OKLAHOMA)	MSOK
METROPOLITAN TRANSIT AUTHORITY BOSTON	MTA
MEXICAN CENTRAL	MXC
MEXICAN EASTERN	MEXE
MEXICAN NATIONAL RAILWAY	MNRY
MEXICAN PACIFIC	MDP
MEXICAN RAILWAY COMPANY	MEX.
MEXICAN SL & INDUST RR (VARIOUS)	MSL&IR
MEXICANO (MEXICAN RAILWAY)	MEX
MEXICO CITY STREETCARS	MCI
MEXICO CITY TRAMWAYS	MCT
MIAMI BEACH RAILWAY	MBE
MICH-CAL (MICHIGAN-CALIFORNIA) (O)	MICH-CAL
MICHIGAN AIR LINE RAILWAY	MAL
MICHIGAN ALKALI	MA#
MICHIGAN CENTRAL	MICHC
MICHIGAN EAST & WEST	ME&W
MICHIGAN ELECTRIC	MIEL
MICHIGAN LIMESTONE OPERATIONS	MLO
MICHIGAN NORTHERN	MN
MICHIGAN RAILROAD	MRR
MICHIGAN RAILWAY CO	MRR.
MICHIGAN SOUTHERN	MICHS
MICHIGAN SOUTHERN & NORTHRN INDIANA RR	MS&NI
MICHIGAN SUBURBAN TRACTION COMPANY	MSTC
MICHIGAN-CALIFORNIA LUMBER COMPANY	M-CL
MID SOUTH RAIL	MIDSR
MIDDLE FORK RAILROAD	MF
MIDDLE TENNESSEE RAILROAD	MTRR
MIDDLEBURG & SCHOHARIE	MD&SC
MIDDLETOWN & CINCINNATI	M&CIN
MIDDLETOWN & NEW JERSEY RAILROAD	M&NJ
MIDDLETOWN & NEW JERSEY RAILWAY	M&NJ
MIDDLETOWN & UNIONVILLE RAILROAD	M&U
MIDDLETOWN MERIDAN & WATERBURY RR	MM&W
MIDDLETOWN UNIONVILLE & WATER GAP RR	MU&WG
MIDLAND CONNECTING	MIDCO
MIDLAND CONTINENTAL RAILROAD	MIDC
MIDLAND ELECTRIC COAL COMPANY	MECC
MIDLAND OF INDIANA	MIND
MIDLAND OF NOVA SCOTIA	MONS
MIDLAND RAILROAD OF NEW JERSEY	MNJ
MIDLAND RAILWAY	MIDL
MIDLAND RAILWAY OF MANITOBA	MM
MIDLAND TERMINAL RAILWAY	MIT
MIDLAND VALLEY RAILROAD	MIV
MIDWAY RAILROAD COMPANY	MID
MIDWEST CENTRAL RAILROAD	MWC
MILFORD MATAMORAS & NEW YORK	MM&NY
MILITARY RAILWAY SERVICE	MRS
MILL CREEK & MINE HILL NAV & RR CO	MC&MHN
MILL CREEK VALLEY LINES	MCV
MILL SPRING CURRENT RIV & BAINESVILLE	MSCR&B
MILL VALLEY & MT TAMALPAIS	MV&MT
MILLEN & SOUTHWESTERN RAILROAD	M&SW
MILLER MILL COMPANY INC.	MMCI

ROADS ALPHABETICALLY W/ABBREVIATIONS	A
MILSTEAD RAILROAD	MIL
MILWAUKEE	MILW
MILWAUKEE & MISSISSIPPI	M&MI
MILWAUKEE & NORTHERN	M&N
MILWAUKEE & ST PAUL	MI&SP
MILWAUKEE ELECTRIC LINES SYSTEM	ME
MILWAUKEE ELECTRIC RAILWAY & LIGHT	MER&L
MILWAUKEE ELECTRIC RY & TRANSPORT CO	MER&T
MILWAUKEE LAKE SHORE & WESTERN	MLS&W
MILWAUKEE RAPID TRANSIT	MRTR
MILWAUKEE RAPID TRANSIT & SPEEDRAIL CO	MRT&S
MILWAUKEE ST PAUL & PACIFIC	MSP&P
MILWAUKEE STREET RAILWAYS	MIST
MINARETS & WESTERN RAILWAY	MI&W
MINE HILL & SCHUYLKILL HAVEN	MH&SH
MINE HILL RAILROAD	MHRR
MINERAL RAILWAY OF CHIHUAHUA	MRCH
MINERAL RANGE RAILROAD	MIN
MINERAL ROCK TRAMWAY	MRT
MINERALES NACIONAL DE MEXICO	MNDM
MINGO VALLEY RAILROAD	MINV
MINNEAPOLIS & PACIFIC	M&PAC
MINNEAPOLIS & RAINY RIVER RAILROAD	M&RR
MINNEAPOLIS & ST CLOUD	MI&SC
MINNEAPOLIS & ST CROIX	M&SCR
MINNEAPOLIS & ST LOUIS RAILROAD	M&SL
MINNEAPOLIS & ST PAUL	M&SP
MINNEAPOLIS ANOKA & CUYUNA RANGE RR	MA&CR
MINNEAPOLIS EASTERN RAILWAY	MERY
MINNEAPOLIS INDUSTRIAL RAILWAY	MIIR
MINNEAPOLIS LYNDALE & MINNESOTA	ML&M
MINNEAPOLIS NORTHFIELD & SOUTHERN RY	MN&S
MINNEAPOLIS RED LAKE & MANITOBA	MRL&M
MINNEAPOLIS ST PAUL & ASHLAND RY	MSP&AS
MINNEAPOLIS ST PAUL & ATLANTIC	MSP&A
MINNEAPOLIS ST PAUL & SAULTE ST MARIE	SOO
MINNEAPOLIS ST PAUL ROCH & DUBUQUE E	MPR&DE
MINNEAPOLIS ST PAUL ROCHESTR & DUBUQU	MSPR&D
MINNEAPOLIS STE MARIE & ATLANTIC	MSM&A
MINNESOTA & INTERNATIONAL RAILWAY	M&IRY
MINNESOTA & NORTH WISCONSIN	M&NW
MINNESOTA & NORTHWESTERN RAILROAD	MI&NW
MINNESOTA & PACIFIC	MI&PAC
MINNESOTA CENTRAL RAILROAD	MCRY.
MINNESOTA CENTRAL RAILROAD (O)	MINNC
MINNESOTA CENTRAL RAILWAY	MCRY
MINNESOTA DAKOTA & WESTERN RAILWAY	MD&W
MINNESOTA MINING & MANUFACTURING	3M#
MINNESOTA TRANSFER RAILWAY	MITR
MINNESOTA VALLEY RAILROAD	MINNV
MINNESOTA WESTERN RAILROAD	MW.
MINNESOTA WESTERN RAILWAY	MW
MINX	MINX
MISKEGON TRACTION & LIGHTING COMPANY	MT&L
MISSISQUOI & CLYDE RIVERS	M&CR
MISSISSIPPI & LA FOURACHE RAILWAY	M&LF
MISSISSIPPI & MISSOURI	MI&MO
MISSISSIPPI & SKUNA VALLEY RAILROAD	M&SV
MISSISSIPPI CENTRAL RAILROAD	MISSC
MISSISSIPPI EXPORT RAILROAD	MEXP
MISSISSIPPI RAILROAD MUSEUM	MRRM
MISSISSIPPI RIVER & BONNE TERRE	MR&BT
MISSISSIPPI VALLEY PUBLIC SERVICE CO	MVPSC
MISSISSIPPI VALLEY TERMINAL COMPANY	MVT
MISSISSIPPIAN RAILWAY	MI
MISSOULA BELT LINE	MIBL
MISSOURI & ARKANSAS RAILROAD	M&A
MISSOURI & ARKANSAS RAILWAY COMPANY	M&A.
MISSOURI & ILLINOIS BRIDGE & BELT RY	M&IB&B
MISSOURI & NORTH ARKANSAS	M&NA
MISSOURI KANSAS & EASTERN	MK&E
MISSOURI KANSAS TEXAS	MKT
MISSOURI PACIFIC RAILROAD SYSTEM	MP.
MISSOURI PACIFIC RAILWAY COMPANY	MP
MISSOURI PORTLAND CEMENT	MPCE
MISSOURI RIVER & NORTHWESTERN RAILWAY	MR&NW
MISSOURI SOUTHERN RAILROAD	MS

A19

APPENDIX A (RAILROADS)

ROADS ALPHABETICALLY W/ABBREVIATIONS	A
MISSOURI VALLEY RAILROAD	MVRR
MISSOURI-ILLINOIS RAILROAD	M-I
MKT OF TEXAS	MKTX
MOBILE & GULF RAILROAD	M&G
MOBILE & OHIO	M&O
MOBILE CHEMICAL	MOBCH
MOBILE GAS	MG#
MOBILE JACKSON & KANSAS CITY	MJ&KC
MOCTEZUMA BREWERY	MB
MODELTRONICS	MTR
MODERA SUGAR PINE COMPANY	MSPC
MODESTO & EMPIRE TRACTION	M&ET
MOFFAT ROAD (DENVER NW & PACIFIC)	DN&P
MOHAWK & HUDSON RAILROAD	MH&H
MOHAWK & HUDSON RIVER	M&HR
MOHAWK & MALONE RAILWAY	M&M
MOHAWK VALLEY	MHV
MOIRA & BOMBAY	M&BO
MOJAVE NORTHERN	MOJN
MOLINE TIMBER CO	MTI
MONADNOCK NORTHERN	MONO
MONARCH	MOA#
MONCTON TRAMWAYS ELECTRICITY & GAS CO	MTE&G
MONMOUTH COUNTY ELECTRIC	MCE
MONO LAKE RAILWAY & LUMBER COMPANY	MLR
MONOCACY VALLEY	MOV
MONOLITH PORTLAND CEMENT	MPC
MONON	M
MONONGAHELA CONNECTING RAILROAD	MCO
MONONGAHELA RAILROAD	MON.
MONONGAHELA RAILWAY	MON
MONONGAHELA WEST PENN	MWP
MONROE RAILROAD COMPANY	MONR
MONSON RAILROAD	MO
MONTAGUE STEEL COMPANY	MSC
MONTANA RAILROAD	MONTA
MONTANA SOUTHERN	MSN
MONTANA WESTERN RAILWAY	MOW
MONTANA WYOMING & SOUTHERN	MW&S
MONTCLAIR & GREENWOOD LAKE	M&GL
MONTCLAIR RAILWAY OF NEW JERSEY	MRNJ
MONTEREY & SALINAS VALLEY	M&SVA
MONTEREY &MEXICAN GULF (MEXICO)	M&MG
MONTEZUMA LUMBER COMPANY	MONTL
MONTFORT & GATINEAU RAILWAY CO (O)	M&GYR
MONTFORT & GATINEAU RAILWAY COMPANY	M&GRY
MONTFORT COLONIZATION RAILWAY CO	MCOL
MONTOUR LAND COMPANY	MLCO
MONTOUR RAILROAD	MONT
MONTOUR RAILWAY	MONT
MONTPELIER & BARRE RAILROAD	M&BA
MONTPELIER & WELLS RIVER RAILROAD	M&WR
MONTREAL & ATLANTA (CP)	M&AT
MONTREAL & CHAMPLAIN	M&C
MONTREAL & LACHINE	M&L
MONTREAL & PLATTSBURG	M&P
MONTREAL & SOREL	M&S
MONTREAL & SOUTHERN COUNTIES RAILWAY	M&SC
MONTREAL CITY PASSENGER RAILWAY CO	MCPR
MONTREAL HARBOR COMMISSION	MHC
MONTREAL ICE RAILWAY	MIRW
MONTREAL PORTLAND & BOSTON	MP&B
MONTREAL TRAMWAYS CORPORATION	MTWC
MONTREAL TRANSIT	MT
MONTREAL TRANSPORTATION COMMISSION	MT.
MOOSEHEAD LAKE RAILROAD	MHL
MOPAC	MOP
MOREHEAD & MORGAN FORK RAILROAD	M&MF
MOREHEAD & NORTH FORK RAILROAD	M&NF
MORGON'S LOUISIANA & TEXAS RAILROAD	ML&T
MORRIS BRANCH	MORB
MORRIS COUNTY CENTRAL	MCC
MORRIS COUNTY CONNECTING RAILWAY	MCCO
MORRIS COUNTY TRACTION COMPANY	MCTC
MORRISON-KNUDSEN	M-K
MORRISSEY FERNIE & MICHEL	MF&M
MORRISTOWN & CUMBERLAND GAP	M&CG

ROADS ALPHABETICALLY W/ABBREVIATIONS	A
MORRISTOWN & ERIE RAILROAD	M&E
MORSE & ORY	M&ORY
MOSCOW CAMDEN & ST AUGUSTINE RAILROAD	MC&SA
MOSHASSUCK VALLEY RAILROAD	MOVA
MOTLEY COUNTY RAILROAD	MCRR
MOUNT CARBON & PORT CARBON	MC&PC
MOUNT CARBON RAILWAY	MCRW
MOUNT GRETNA NARROW-GAUGE	MG
MOUNT HOOD RAILROAD	MH
MOUNT HOOD RAILWAY	MH.
MOUNT HOPE MINERAL RAILROAD	MHM
MOUNT JEWELL & SMETHPORT	MJ&S
MOUNT JEWETT CLERMONT & NORTHERN	MJC&N
MOUNT JEWETT KINZUA & RITERVILLE RR	MJK&R
MOUNT LOWE	MTL
MOUNT MCGREGOR RAILWAY	MMG
MOUNT MCKAY & KAKABEKA FALLS RAILWAY	MM&KF
MOUNT RAINIER SCENIC RAILROAD	MRSR
MOUNT TAMALPAIS & MUIR WOODS	MT&MW
MOUNT TOM INCLINE RAILWAY	MTTI
MOUNT UNCOONUNICH	MTU
MOUNT VERNON ELECTRIC RAILWAY	MVE
MOUNT WASHINGTON	MTW
MOUNT WASHINGTON COG	MWCOG
MOUNTAIN CENTRAL	MTCE
MOUNTAIN ICE COMPANY	MIC
MOWER LUMBER COMPANY	MLC
MUD BAY LOGGING COMPANY	MBLC
MUNCIE & WESTERN RAILROAD	M&WE
MUNCIE STREET RAILWAY	MUNC
MUNICIPAL RAILWAY OF SAN FRANCISCO	MSF
MUNCY CREEK RAILROAD	MUN
MUNICIPAL DOCKS	MD
MUNICIPAL RAILWAY	MUNRY
MUNISING	MU
MUNISING MARQUETTE & SOUTHEASTERN RY	MM&S
MUNSIE STREET RAILWAY	MSR
MUSCATINE & TIPTON	M&TI
MUSKINGUM ELECTRIC RAILROAD	MEL
MUSKOGEE ELECTRIC TRACTION	MET
MYSTIC TERMINAL COMPANY	MTCO
NACIONALES DE MEXICO	NDM
NAHMA & NORTHERN	N&N
NANSEMOND LAND LUMBER & NARROW GAGE RY	NLL
NANTUCKET CENTRAL	NANC
NANTUCKET RAILROAD	NRR
NAPA VALLEY RAILROAD	NVR
NAPIERVILLE JUNCTION RAILWAY	NJ
NAPORANO IRON & METAL	NI&M
NARRAGANSETT PIER RAILROAD	NPIER
NASA	NASA
NASHUA & LOWELL RAILROAD	N&L
NASHUA ACTON & BOSTON RAILROAD	NA&B
NASHVILLE & CHATTANOOGA RAILROAD	N&CH
NASHVILLE & CLARKSVILLE RAILROAD	N&CRR
NASHVILLE & KNOXVILLE RAILROAD	N&K
NASHVILLE & SPARKS RAILROAD	N&SP
NASHVILLE CHATTANOOGA & ST LOUIS RY	NC&SL
NASHVILLE INTERURBAN RAILWAY	NIR
NASHVILLE-FRANKLIN RAILWAY (TENN)	N-F
NATCHEZ & HAMBURG RAILROAD	N&H
NATCHEZ & SOUTHERN RAILWAY	NA&S
NATCHEZ URANIA & RUSTON RAILWAY	NU&R
NATCHITOCHES & RED RIVER VALLEY RY	N&RRV
NATIONAL ALUMINATE COMPANY	NAC#
NATIONAL CITY & OTAY	NC&O
NATIONAL HARBOURS BOARD	NHB
NATIONAL IRON WORKS	NIW
NATIONAL LOCOMOTIVE	NL
NATIONAL OF TEHUANTEPEC (MEXICO)	NDET
NATIONAL PLATE GLASS CO	NPGC
NATIONAL RAILWAYS OF MEXICO	NRWM
NATIONAL TRANSCONTINENTAL	NTRC
NATIONALES DE MEXICOS	NDEM
NAUGATUCK RAILROAD (CONNECTICUT)	NAU
NAVAJO MINE RAILROAD	NMR
NAVEL ORDINANCE DEPOT	NOD

STEPHANS' RAILROAD DIRECTORY

APPENDIX A (RAILROADS)

ROADS ALPHABETICALLY W/ABREVIATIONS	A
NEBRASKA & LAKE SUPERIOR RAILROAD	N&SLRR
NEKOOSA PAPER COMPANY	NPCO
NELSON & ALBEMARLE RAILWAY	N&A
NELSON BC STREET RAILWAYS	NBCS
NELSON ELECTRIC TRAMWAY	NETR
NESCOPEC	NES
NESQUEHONING	N
NESSON LUMBER COMPANY	NESL
NEVADA & CALIFORNIA RAILROAD	N&CA
NEVADA CALIFORNIA OREGON RAILROAD	NCO
NEVADA CENTRAL RAILROAD	NC
NEVADA CITY NARROW GAUGE	NCNG
NEVADA COPPER BELT	NCBT
NEVADA COUNTY NARROW-GAUGE RAILROAD	NCN
NEVADA COUNTY TRACTION	NCT
NEVADA NORTHERN RAILWAY COMPANY	NN
NEVADA TRANSIT COMPANY	NTCO
NEW ALBANY & CORYDON	NA&C
NEW ALBANY & LOUISVILLE ELECTRIC	NA&LE
NEW ALBANY & SALEM	NA&SA
NEW BEDFORD & TAUNTON RAILROAD	NB&T
NEW BERLIN & WINFIELD	NB&W
NEW BRUNSWICK & CANADA	NB&C
NEW BRUNSWICK POWER COMPANY	NBP
NEW CANAAN	NCA
NEW CASTLE & FRENCHTOWN	NC&F
NEW CASTLE STREET RAILWAY (PA)	NCS
NEW CORNELIA BRANCH	NCB
NEW CORNELIA COPPER COMPANY	NCC
NEW ENGLAND LACKAWANNA & PITTSBURGH	NEL&P
NEW ENGLAND RAILROAD	NERR
NEW GEORGIA RAILROAD	NGR
NEW HAVEN & NORTHAMPTON	NH&NI
NEW HAVEN & SHORE LINE	NHSL
NEW HAVEN & SHORT LINE	NH&SL
NEW HAVEN MIDDLETOWN & WILLIMANTIC	NHM&W
NEW HAVEN RAILROAD	NH
NEW HAVEN SHORE LINE RAILWAY	NHSL.
NEW HOPE & IVYLAND RAILROAD	NH&I
NEW IBERIA & NORTHERN	NI&N
NEW JERSEY & NEW YORK RAILROAD	NJ&NY
NEW JERSEY & PENNSYLVANIA	NJ&P
NEW JERSEY CENTRAL	CNJ.
NEW JERSEY DEPT OF TRANSPORTATION	NJDOT
NEW JERSEY INDIANA & ILLINOIS RR	NJI&I
NEW JERSEY JUNCTION RAILROAD	NJJ
NEW JERSEY MIDLAND RAILWAY	NJM
NEW JERSEY RAILROAD & TRANSPORTATION	NJR&T
NEW JERSEY RAPID TRANIST .	NJTR.
NEW JERSEY SOUTHERN RAILWAY	NJS
NEW JERSEY TRANSIT	NJTR
NEW JERSEY ZINC	NJZ
NEW LONDON NORTHERN	NLN
NEW LONDON STREET RAILWAY	NLSRY
NEW LONDON WILLIMANTIC & PALMER RR	NLW&P
NEW LONDON WILLIMANTIC & SPRINGFIELD	NLW&S
NEW MEXICO & COLORADO	NM&C
NEW MEXICO & SOUTHERN PACIFIC	NM&SP
NEW MEXICO CENTRAL RAILROAD	NMC
NEW MEXICO CENTRAL RAILWAY	NMC.
NEW MEXICO LUMBER COMPANY	NMLC
NEW MEXICO MIDLAND	NMM
NEW ORANGE FOUR JUNCTION RAILROAD	NOF
NEW ORLEANS & CARROLLTON RAIL ROAD	NO&C
NEW ORLEANS & LOWER COAST RAILROAD	NO&LC
NEW ORLEANS & NORTH WESTERN	NO&NW
NEW ORLEANS & NORTHEASTERN RAILROAD	NO&N
NEW ORLEANS CITY & LAKE RAILROAD	NOC&L
NEW ORLEANS CITY RAILROAD	NOC
NEW ORLEANS PACIFIC RAILWAY	NOP
NEW ORLEANS PUBLIC BELT RAILROAD	NOPB
NEW ORLEANS PUBLIC SERVICE	NOPS
NEW ORLEANS RAILWAY	NORL
NEW ORLEANS RAILWAY & LIGHT COMPANY	NOR&LC
NEW ORLEANS TERMINAL COMPANY	NOT
NEW ORLEANS TEXAS & MEXICO	NOT&M
NEW ORLEANS UNION PASSENGER TERMINAL	NOUPT

ROADS ALPHABETICALLY W/ABREVIATIONS	A
NEW SOUTH WALES GOVERNMENT RAILROAD	NSW
NEW SOUTH WALES GOVERNMENT RAILWAY	NSWG
NEW YORK & BOSTON RAILROAD	NY&B
NEW YORK & BROOKLYN BRIDGE	NY&BB
NEW YORK & ERIE	NY&E
NEW YORK & GREENWOOD LAKE RAILROAD	NY&GL
NEW YORK & HARLAEM RAILROAD CO	NY&H
NEW YORK & HARLEM RAILROAD	NY&H.
NEW YORK & LAKE ERIE	NY&LE
NEW YORK & LONG BRANCH RAILROAD	NY&LB
NEW YORK & MAHOPAC RAILROAD COMPANY	NY&M
NEW YORK & MANHATTAN BEACH RAILWAY	NY&MB
NEW YORK & MASSACHUETTS RAILWAY	NY&MA
NEW YORK & NEW ENGLAND RAILROAD	NY&NE
NEW YORK & NORTHERN	NY&N
NEW YORK & OSWEGO MIDLAND RAILROAD	NY&OM
NEW YORK & OTTAWA	NY&O
NEW YORK & PENNSYLVANIA	NY&P
NEW YORK & QUEENS COUNTY RAILWAY	NY&QC
NEW YORK & SEA BEACH RAILROAD	NY&SB
NEW YORK AUBURN & LANSING RAILROAD	NYA&L
NEW YORK BAY RIDGE & JAMAICA	NYBR&J
NEW YORK BOSTON & NORTHERN	NYB&N
NEW YORK BROOKLYN & JAMAICA	NYB&J
NEW YORK BROOKLYN & MANHATTAN BEACH	NYB&MB
NEW YORK CENTRAL & HUDSON RIVER (O)	NYC&H
NEW YORK CENTRAL & HUDSON RIVER RR	NYC&HR
NEW YORK CENTRAL & NORTHERN	NYC&N
NEW YORK CENTRAL & WESTERN	NYC&W
NEW YORK CENTRAL RAILROAD	NYC
NEW YORK CHICAGO & ST LOUIS (O)	NYC&SL
NEW YORK CHICAGO & ST LOUIS RAILROAD	NKP.
NEW YORK CITY & NORTHERN	NYC&N.
NEW YORK CITY ELEVATED RAILROAD	NYCE
NEW YORK CITY RAPID	NYCR
NEW YORK CITY SUBWAY-ELEVATED LINES	NYCS
NEW YORK CITY THIRD AVENUE ELEVATED	NYCTAE
NEW YORK CITY TRANSIT AUTHORITY	NYCTA
NEW YORK CONNECTING RAILROAD	NYCRR
NEW YORK DOCK RAILWAY	NYD
NEW YORK ELEVATED LINES	NYCS.
NEW YORK HEAT LIGHT & POWER COMPANY	NYHL
NEW YORK LAKE ERIE & WESTERN	NYLE&W
NEW YORK METRO TRANSIT AUTHORITY	NYMTA
NEW YORK NEW HAVEN & HARTFORD RAIL RD	NYNH&H
NEW YORK NINTH AVENUE RAILWAY	NYNA
NEW YORK ONTARIO & WESTERN	NYO&W
NEW YORK PENNSYLVANIA & OHIO RAILROAD	NYP&O
NEW YORK PENNSYLVANIA OHIO & DETROIT	NYPO&D
NEW YORK PHILADELPHIA & NORFOLK	NYP&N
NEW YORK PITTSBURGH & CHICAGO RR	NYP&C
NEW YORK PORT AUTHORITY	NYPA
NEW YORK PROVIDENCE & BOSTON RAILROAD	NYP&B
NEW YORK RAILWAYS	NYRY
NEW YORK RUTLAND & MONTREAL	NYR&M
NEW YORK STATE RAILWAYS	NYRY.
NEW YORK SUBWAY-EL CARS	NYCS
NEW YORK SUSQUEHANNA & WESTERN	NYS&W
NEW YORK WEST SHORE & BUFFALO	NYWS&B
NEW YORK WESTCHESTER & BOSTON RY	NYW&B
NEW YORK WESTCHESTER & PUTNAM	NYW&P
NEW YORK WOODHAVEN & ROCKAWAY RR	NYW&R
NEWARK & BLOOMFIELD RAILROAD	N&BF
NEWARK & MARION RAILROAD	N&M
NEWARK SUBWAYS	NSUB
NEWAUKUM VALLEY	NV
NEWBURGH & SOUTH SHORE RAILWAY	N&SS
NEWBURGH DUTCHESS & CONNECTICUT	ND&C
NEWFOUNDLAND LIGHT & POWER COMPANY	NFL&P
NEWFOUNDLAND RAILROAD	NF
NEWFOUNDLAND RAILWAY	NF.
NEWPORT & PROVIDENCE	N&P
NEWPORT & RICHFORD	NP&R
NEWPORT & SHERMANS VALLEY RAILROAD	N&SV
NEWPORT NEWS & HAMPTON RAILWAY	NN&H
NEWPORT NEWS RAILWAY & LIGHT	NNR&L
NEWTON & BOSTON STREET RAILWAY	N&BS

STEPHANS' RAILROAD DIRECTORY

A21

APPENDIX A (RAILROADS)

ROADS ALPHABETICALLY W/ABREVIATIONS	A
NEWTON & NORTHWESTERN	NT&NW
NEZPERCE & IDAHO RAILROAD COMPANY	NEZ&I
NEZPERCE RAILROAD	NEZ
NIAGARA CENTRAL	NIAGC
NIAGARA ESCARPMENT INCLINED PLANE	NEIP
NIAGARA FALLS	NFALLS
NIAGARA FALLS WESLEY PARK & CLIFTON T	NFWP&C
NIAGARA GEORGE RAILROAD	NGRR
NIAGARA JUNCTION RAILWAY	NJUN
NIAGARA PORTAGE INCLINE PLANE	NPIP
NIAGARA ST CATHERINES & TORONTO NAV	NSC&TN
NIAGARA ST CATHERINES & TORONTO RY	NSC&T
NICHOLAS FAYETTE & GREENBRIAR	NF&G
NICHOLSON TERMINAL & DOCK	NT&D
NICKEL PLATE	NKP
NIPISSING CENTRAL	NIPC
NOR-OESTE DE MEXICO	NODX
NORANDA MINES	NM
NORFOLK & ATLANTIC TERMINAL	N&AT
NORFOLK & BRISTOL STREET RAILWAY	N&BSR
NORFOLK & CAROLINA	N&C
NORFOLK & OCEAN VIEW	N&OV
NORFOLK & PETERSBURG	N&PB
NORFOLK & PORTSMOUTH BELT LINE RR	N&PBL
NORFOLK & PORTSMOUTH TRACTION COMPANY	N&PT
NORFOLK & VIRGINIA BEACH	N&VB
NORFOLK & WESTERN RAILWAY	N&W
NORFOLK BELT LINE	NORB
NORFOLK CITY RAILROAD	NCI
NORFOLK CITY RAILWAY	NCI.
NORFOLK FRANKLIN & DANVILLE RAILROAD	NF&D.
NORFOLK FRANKLIN & DANVILLE RAILWAY	NF&D
NORFOLK RAILWAY & LIGHT COMPANY	NR&LC
NORFOLK SOUTHERN RAILROAD	NSO .
NORFOLK SOUTHERN RAILWAY	NSO
NORFOLK TERMINAL RAILWAY	NTRY
NORFOLK WILLOUGHBY SPIT & OLD POINT RR	NWSOP
NORTH & SOUTH RAILROAD CO OF GEORGIA	N&SG
NORTH & SOUTH RAILROAD OF WYOMING	N&S
NORTH AMERICAN CAR CORPORATION	NATX
NORTH AMERICAN COAL	NAC
NORTH AMERICAN DESPATCH	NAD#
NORTH AMERICAN DISPATCH	NAD
NORTH BEACH LINES (ST AUGUSTINE FL)	NBL
NORTH BRANCH CANAL COMPANY	NBCC
NORTH BRANCH TRANSIT	NBTR
NORTH BRITISH RAILWAY	NBRY
NORTH CAROLINA STATE PORTS AUTHORITY	NCSPA
NORTH CENTRAL TEXAS	NCTX
NORTH CHARLESTON TERMINAL COMPANY	NCTC
NORTH COAST LINES	NCL
NORTH COUNTY RAILROAD CORP	NCRR
NORTH DAKOTA RAILWAY	NDRY
NORTH JERSEY	NJER
NORTH JERSEY ELECTRIC LINES	NJEL
NORTH JERSEY RAPID TRANSIT	NJRT
NORTH LOUISANA & GULF RAILROAD	NL&G
NORTH PACIFIC COAST	NPC
NORTH PENNSYLVANIA RAILROAD	NPA
NORTH POLE ROUTE	NPOLE
NORTH SHORE RAILROAD	NS
NORTH SHORE RAILWAY	NS.
NORTH STAR & MIFFLIN	NS&M
NORTH STAR STEEL COMPANY	NSSC
NORTH YAKIMA & VALLEY RAILWAY	NY&V
NORTH YONGE	NYO
NORTH-WEST RAILROAD	N-W
NORTHAMPTON & BATH RAILROAD	N&B
NORTHAMPTON TRANSIT	NT
NORTHEAST OKLAHOMA RAILROAD	NO
NORTHERN & NORTH WESTERN	N&NW
NORTHERN ALBERTA RAILWAYS	NA
NORTHERN CAMBIA STREET RAILWAY	NCAM
NORTHERN CENTRAL RAILWAY	NCE
NORTHERN COLONIZATION RAILWAY CO.	NCRY
NORTHERN CONSTRUCTION CO OF MONTREAL	NCCM
NORTHERN CROSS RAILROAD	NCR

ROADS ALPHABETICALLY W/ABREVIATIONS	A
NORTHERN DAKOTA RAILWAY	ND
NORTHERN ELECTRIC RAILWAY	NE
NORTHERN INDIANA & SOUTHERN MICHIGAN	NI&SM
NORTHERN INDIANA DOCK	NID
NORTHERN INDIANA RAILWAY COMPANY	NI
NORTHERN LACKAWANNA	NLACK
NORTHERN MICHIGAN RAILROAD	NMICH
NORTHERN NEW BRUNSWICK & SEABOARD RY	NNB&S
NORTHERN NEW YORK RAILROAD	NNY
NORTHERN OHIO RAILROAD	NOH
NORTHERN OHIO RAILWAY	NOH.
NORTHERN OHIO RAILWAY & LIGHT COMPANY	NOR&L
NORTHERN OHIO TRACTION & LIGHT	NOT&L
NORTHERN PACIFIC RAILROAD	NPRR
NORTHERN PACIFIC RAILWAY	NP
NORTHERN PACIFIC TERMINAL	NPTR
NORTHERN RAILROAD	NORTH
NORTHERN RAILROAD OF NEW JERSEY	NRNJ
NORTHERN RAILWAY	NORTH.
NORTHERN RAILWAY OF CANADA	NRC
NORTHERN RAILWAY OF NEW JERSEY	NRNJ.
NORTHERN REDWOOD LUMBER COMPANY	NRLC
NORTHERN REFRIGERATOR LINE	NR
NORTHERN TEXAS TRANSPORTATION COMPANY	NTTC
NORTHPORT TRACTION COMPANY	NPTC
NORTHWESTERN	NW
NORTHWESTERN LINES	NWL
NORTHWESTERN OHIO RAILWAY	NORY
NORTHWESTERN OKLAHOMA	NWO
NORTHWESTERN PACIFIC RAILROAD	NWP
NORTHWESTERN PENNSYLVANIA RAILROAD	NPR
NORTHWESTERN REFRIGERATOR LINE	NRL#
NORTHWESTERN STEEL & WIRE	NS&W
NORTHWESTERN TERMINAL RAILROAD	NTRR
NORTHWOOD PULP & TIMBER	NP&T
NORWICH & WORCESTER RAILROAD	N&WO
NORWOOD & ST LAWRENCE RAILROAD	N&SL
NOS-OESTE DE MEXICO	NODM
NOVA SCOTIA LIGHT & POWER COMPANY	NSC
NOVA SCOTIA RAILWAY	NSRY
NOVA SCOTIA TRAMWAY & POWER COMPANY	NST&PC
NOYAN RAILROAD (CANADA)	NOY
OAHU RAILWAY	ORY
OAHU RAILWAY & LAND COMPANY	OR&LC
OAHU RAILWAY & TERMINAL WAREHOUSING	OR&TW
OAK GROVE & GEORGETOWN	OG&G
OAKDALE-MC DONALD STREET RAILWAY	O-MS
OAKLAND & ANTIOCH	O&AN
OAKLAND & EAST SIDE RAILWAY	O&ES
OAKLAND ANTLOCK & EASTERN	OA&E
OAKLAND CABLE RAILWAY COMPANY	OCRY
OAKLAND TERMINAL RAILWAY	OT
OCEAN CITY ELECTRIC RAILROAD (NJ)	OCER
OCEAN CITY RAILROAD	OCCRR
OCEAN CITY WESTERN	OCW
OCEAN SHORE RAILROAD	OS
OCEAN SHORE RAILWAY	OS.
OCILLO SOUTHERN	OCS
OCONEE & WESTERN	O&W
OCTORARO RAILWAY	OCT
OGDEN LOGAN & IDAHO RAILWAY COMPANY	OL&I
OGDEN UNION RAILWAY & DEPOT COMPANY	OUR&D
OGDENSBURG & LAKE CHAMPLAIN RAILROAD	O&LC
OGDENSBURG & NORWOOD RAILWAY	O&N
OGDENSBURG BRIDGE & PORT AUTHORITY	OB&PA
OHIO & INDIANA	OH&IN
OHIO & INDIANA STONE COMPANY	O&IS
OHIO & KENTUCKY RAILWAY	O&K.
OHIO & MISSISSIPPI RAILROAD	O&M.
OHIO & MISSISSIPPI RAILWAY	O&M
OHIO & MORENCI	OH&MO
OHIO & PENNSYLVANIA	OH&PA
OHIO CENTRAL LINES	OHIOC
OHIO ELECTRIC RAILWAY	OER
OHIO MIDLAND POWER & LIGHT COMPANY	OM
OHIO POWER COMPANY	OPC
OHIO PUBLIC SERVICE COMPANY	OPS

APPENDIX A (RAILROADS)

ROADS ALPHABETICALLY W/ABREVIATIONS	A	ROADS ALPHABETICALLY W/ABREVIATIONS	A
OHIO RAILROAD	OHIO	ORLEANS KENNER TRACTION	OKT
OHIO RAPID TRANSIT COMAPNY	RTOH.	ORLEANS RAILROAD	ORL
OHIO RIVER	OR	ORLEANS WEST BADEN & FRENCH LICK SPRGS	OWB&FL
OHIO RIVER & WESTERN	OR&W	ORO DAM	ORO
OHIO SEAMLESS TUBE	OST*	OSAGE RAILWAY	OSA
OHIO SOUTHERN	OSO	OSBORNE BAY & WARF	OSB&W
OHIO VALLEY	OV	OSCAR MEYER	OM*
OIL CITY & PITHOLE RAILWAY	OC&P	OSHAWA RAILWAY	OSH
OIL CITY STREET RAILWAY COMPANY	OILC	OSTRANDER RAILWAY & TIMBER CO	ORTC
OIL CREEK & ALLEGHENY	OC&A	OSTRICH FARM	OF
OIL CREEK RAILROAD	OILCR	OTIS RAILROAD	OTIS
OIL FIELDS SHORT LINES	OFSL	OTSEGO & HERKIMER	O&H
OKLAHOMA & ARKANSAS	O&A	OTTAWA & GATINEAU	O&G
OKLAHOMA & RICH MOUNTAIN	O&RM	OTTAWA & PRESCOTT	O&P
OKLAHOMA CENTRAL	OC	OTTAWA ELECTRIC RAILWAY	OEL
OKLAHOMA CITY ADA-ATOKA RAILWAY	OCITY	OTTAWA NORTHERN & WESTERN	OTN&W
OKLAHOMA CITY JUNCTION RAILWAY	OCJR	OTTAWA TRANSPORTATION COMMISSION	OTCO
OKLAHOMA RAILWAY	ORW	OVERLAND DISPATCH	OD
OKLAHOMA SOUTHWESTERN	OSW	OVERTON RAILROAD	OVER
OKMULGEE NORTHERN	ONO	OWASCO RIVER RAILWAY	ORRY
OLD AUGUSTA RAILROAD	OARR	OWENS & NELSON LOGGING ROAD	O&NL
OLD COLONY & FALL RIVER RAILROAD	OC&FR	PABST BEER	PAB*
OLD COLONY RAILROAD	OCO	PACIFIC & ARCTIC RAILWAY & NAVIGATION	P&AR
OLD DOMINION LINE	ODOM	PACIFIC & EASTERN	P&EAST
OLD DUTCH CLEANSER	ODC*	PACIFIC & IDAHO NORTHERN	P&IN
OLEAN	O	PACIFIC COAST AGGREGATES COMPANY	PCAC
OLEAN BRADFORD & WARREN	OB&W	PACIFIC COAST RAILROAD	PCOAST
OLIN CHEMICAL DIVISION	OLCH	PACIFIC COAST RAILWAY	PCOA
OLIVER IRON MINING COMPANY	OIM	PACIFIC COAST TERMINAL	PCTR
OLYMPIA NARROW GAGE RAILROAD	ONG	PACIFIC ELECTRIC RAILWAY	PE
OMAHA & COUNCIL BLUFFS RAILWAY	O&CB	PACIFIC ELECTRIC RAILWAY OF MEXICO	PERM
OMAHA & REPUBLICAN VALLEY	O&RV	PACIFIC FRUIT GROWERS EXPRESS	PFE
OMAHA KANSAS CITY & EASTERN	OKC&E	PACIFIC FRUIT GROWERS EXPRESS (O)	PFE*
OMAHA LINCOLN & BEATRICE RAILWAY	OL&B	PACIFIC GAS & ELECTRIC	PG&E
OMAHA ROAD	CPM&O	PACIFIC GREAT EASTERN RAILWAY	PGE
ONEIDA & WESTERN	ON&W	PACIFIC LINES	PL
ONEONTA & MOHAWK RAILWAY	O&MH	PACIFIC LUMBER COMPANY	PLC
ONEONTA & MOHAWK VALLEY	O&MV	PACIFIC MOBILE & OHIO	PM&O
ONEONTA COOPERSTOWN & RICHFIELD SPRGS	OC&RS	PACIFIC NORTHWEST TRACTION COMPANY	PNW
ONIEDA RAILWAY	ONRY	PACIFIC PORTLAND CEMENT CO. CONSOLID.	PPC
ONTARIO & QUEBEC RAILWAY	O&Q	PACIFIC RAILROAD COMPANY	PRRCO
ONTARIO & SAN ANTONIA HEIGHTS RR CO	O&SA	PACIFIC RAILROAD OF MEXICO	PRWM
ONTARIO CENTRAL	ONCE	PACIFIC RAILWAY OF MEXICO	PRWM
ONTARIO EASTERN	ONE	PACOLET MILLS MANUFACTURING	PMM
ONTARIO LINES-MIDLAND/CENTRAL/EASTERN	OLN	PADUCAH & ILLINOIS RAILROAD	P&IR
ONTARIO MIDLAND RAILROAD	ONMI	PADUCHA & LOUISVILLE	PA&L
ONTARIO NORTHLAND RAILWAY	ON	PAGE MILK	PGM*
ONTARIO SIMCOE & HURON	OS&H	PAINESVILLE & EASTERN	PA&E
OPELOUSAS GULF & NORTHEASTERN RAILWAY	OG&NE	PAINESVILLE WOOSTER & OHIO	PW&O
ORANGE & ALEXANDRIA	O&AL	PAJURO VALLEY CONSOLIDATED RAILROAD	PAJV
ORANGE & FREDERICKSBURG RAILROAD	O&FRR	PALESTINE LAKE ZURICH & WAUCONDA	PLZ&W
ORANGE ALEXANDRIA & MANASSAS	O&AM	PANA & SPRINGFIELD RAILROAD CO	P&SRR
ORANGE BELT	OB	PANAMA CANAL COMPANY	PAN.
ORANGE COUNTY RAILROAD	OCRR	PANAMA RAILROAD	PAN
ORANGE MOUNTAIN TRACTION	OMT	PANHANDLE & SANTA FE RAILWAY	P&SF
OREGON & CALIFORNIA RAILROAD	O&C	PARIS & DECATUR RAILROAD	P&D
OREGON & EUREKA	O&E	PARIS & MOUNT PLEASANT RAILROAD	P&MP
OREGON & NAVIGATION COMPANY	OR&NC	PARIS & TERRE HAUTE	P&TH
OREGON & NORTHWESTERN RAILROAD	O&NW	PARK UTAH CONSOLIDATED MINES	PUCM
OREGON & PACIFIC	O&PA	PARKER & KANSAS CITY RAILROAD	P&KC
OREGON & WASHINGTON TERRITORY RAILWAY	O&WT	PARR TERMINAL RAILROAD	PARR
OREGON AMERICAN	OA	PARSONS & PACIFIC	P&P
OREGON CALIFORNIA & EASTERN RAILROAD	OC&E.	PASADENA CITY	PCI
OREGON CALIFORNIA & EASTERN RAILWAY	OC&E	PASADENA RAILWAY	PARW
OREGON ELECTRIC RAILWAY COMPANY	OE	PASSAIC & NEW YORK	P&NY
OREGON PACIFIC	OPA	PATAPSCO & BLACK RIVERS RAILROAD	P&BRRR
OREGON PACIFIC & EASTERN RAILWAY	OP&E	PATAUSCO & BACK RIVERS RAILROAD	P&BR
OREGON PORTAGE RAILROAD	OP	PATERSON & HUDSON RIVER RAILROAD	PA&HR
OREGON RAILROAD & NAVIGATION COMPANY	URWO	PATH VALLEY RAILROAD	PVRR
OREGON RAILWAYS & NAVIGATION COMPANY	URWO.	PATTEN & SHERMAN	P&SH
OREGON SHORT LINE	OSL	PATTERSON & HUDSON RIVER	P&HR
OREGON STEAM NAVIGATION COMPANY	OSN	PATTERSON & PASSAIC RAILROAD	P&PRR
OREGON TRUNK RAILWAY	OTRY	PATTERSON & WESTERN	P&WE
OREGON WASHINGTON PORTLAND & R	OWP&R	PATTERSON CENTRAL ELECTRIC	PCE
OREGON WASHINGTON RR & NAVIGATION CO	OWR&N	PATTERSON EXTENSION	PEXT
OREGON WATER POWER	OWP	PATTERSON HEIGHTS STREET RAILWAY CO.	PHSR
OREGONIAN RAILWAY	OREG	PATTERSON NEW JERSEY RAILROAD	PNJRR

APPENDIX A (RAILROADS)

ROADS ALPHABETICALLY W/ABREVIATIONS	A
PAUL SMITH RAILROAD	PSRR
PAWNEE RAILROAD	PAWN
PEABODY COAL	PCOAL
PEABODY SHORT LINE	PSL
PEACH BOTTOM RAILROAD	PBRR
PEAKER SERVICES INC	PSVI
PEARL RIVER VALLEY RAILROAD	PRV
PECOS VALLEY & NORTHEASTERN	PV&N
PECOS VALLEY SOUTHERN RAILWAY	PVS
PEEKSKILL LIGHTING & RAILROAD COMPANY	PL&RR
PEERLESS BEER	PB*
PEG LEG	PLEG
PEKIN LINCOLN & DECATUR	PL&D
PELHAM PARK RAILROAD (MONORAIL)	PPR
PEMBERTON & HIGHTSTOWN	P&HT
PEMBERTON & NEW YORK	PE&NY
PEMBERTON & SEASHORE	PE&SS
PEMBINA VALLEY RAILWAY	PVRY
PEMIGEWASSET VALLEY	PEMV
PEND OREILLE VALLEY RAILROAD	POV
PENINSULA TERMINAL RAILROAD COMPANY	PTER
PENINSULAR RAILWAY	PERY
PENN CENTRAL	PC
PENN CENTRAL RAILROAD	PCRR
PENN HAVEN & WHITE HAVEN	PH&WH
PENN ROAD SEA SHORE	PRSS
PENN VIEW MOUNTAIN RAILROAD	PVMT
PENNSBORO & HARRISVILLE RAILROAD	P&H
PENNSBORO & HARRISVILLE RITCHIE CO RY	P&HRR
PENNSYLVANIA & ATLANTIC RAILROAD	PA&AT
PENNSYLVANIA & DELAWARE RAILROAD	PA&D
PENNSYLVANIA & MARYLAND STREET RW	P&MSR
PENNSYLVANIA & NEW YORK CANAL & RR	P&NYC
PENNSYLVANIA & NEW YORK RAILROAD	PA&NY
PENNSYLVANIA & NORTHWESTERN	PA&NW
PENNSYLVANIA & PACIFIC	PA&P
PENNSYLVANIA COAL COMPANY	PCCO
PENNSYLVANIA DETROIT RAILROAD	PD
PENNSYLVANIA GLASS SAND COMPANY	PGS
PENNSYLVANIA MERCHANDISE	PM*
PENNSYLVANIA MIDLAND	PMID
PENNSYLVANIA OHIO & DETROIT RR CO	PO&D
PENNSYLVANIA POUGHKEEPSIE & BOSTON	PP&B
PENNSYLVANIA POWER & LIGHT COMPANY	PAP&L
PENNSYLVANIA RAILROAD	PRR
PENNSYLVANIA READING SEASHORE LINES	PRSL
PENNSYLVANIA RR OF MARYLAND	PRRMD
PENNSYLVANIA STATE RAILROAD	PAS
PENNSYLVANIA-PACIFIC RAILROAD	P-P
PENOBSCOT & KENNEBEC	P&KE
PENOLES MEXICANNA	PMEX
PENSACOLA & ATLANTIC	P&A
PENSACOLA & GEORGIA	P&G
PENSACOLA & PERDIDO	P&PE
PENSACOLA ALABAMA & TENNESSEE	PA&T
PENSACOLA ELECTRIC COMPANY	PENE
PENSACOLA MOBILE & NEW ORLEANS	PM&NO
PEOPLES ELECTRIC STREET RAILWAY	PEOP
PEOPLES RAILWAY	PEOP.
PEORIA & EASTERN RAILWAY	P&EA
PEORIA & OQUQWKA	P&OQ
PEORIA & PEKIN UNION RAILWAY	P&PU
PEORIA ATLANTA & DECATUR	PA&DEC
PEORIA DECATUR & EVANSVILLE RAILROAD	PD&E
PEORIA GATEWAY RAILROAD	PG
PEORIA TERMINAL COMPANY	PETE
PEQUEST & WALKILL	P&WAL
PERE MARQUETTE RAILWAY	PM
PERMIAN BASIN RAILROAD	PERB
PERRY COUNTY RAILROAD	PECO
PERU & INDIANAPOLIS	P&I
PETALUMA & SANTA ROSA RAILROAD	P&SR
PETERBOROUGH RADIAL RAILWAY	PETR
PETERSBURG & SEA ISLE	P&SI
PETERSBURG RAILROAD COMPANY	PET
PETRO-TEX	PT*
PHELPS DODGE CORPORATION	P-D

ROADS ALPHABETICALLY W/ABREVIATIONS	A
PHILADELPHIA & BRIGANTINE	P&B
PHILADELPHIA & CAMDEN FERRY COMPANY	P&CF
PHILADELPHIA & COLUMBIA RAILROAD	P&C
PHILADELPHIA & ERIE RAILROAD	P&ERR
PHILADELPHIA & GERMANTOWN RAILWAY	P&GT
PHILADELPHIA & LONG BRANCH RAILWAY	P&LB.
PHILADELPHIA & NEWTON CONNECTING RR	P&NC
PHILADELPHIA & READING	P&R
PHILADELPHIA & READING COAL & IRON	P&RC
PHILADELPHIA & SEASHORE	P&SS
PHILADELPHIA & WEST CHESTER TRACTION	P&WC
PHILADELPHIA & WESTERN RAILROAD	P&WR
PHILADELPHIA & WESTERN RAILWAY	P&WR.
PHILADELPHIA & WESTERN STREET RAILWAY	P&WS
PHILADELPHIA BALTIMORE & WASHINGTON RR	PB&W
PHILADELPHIA BELT LINE RAILROAD	PHBL
PHILADELPHIA BETHLEHEM & NEW ENGLAND	PB&NE
PHILADELPHIA COKE COMAPNY	PCC
PHILADELPHIA GERMANTOWN & CHEST. HILL	PG&CH
PHILADELPHIA GERMANTOWN & NORRISTOWN	PG&N
PHILADELPHIA MARLTON & MEDFORD	PM&M
PHILADELPHIA NEWTON & NEW YORK RR	PN&NY
PHILADELPHIA RAPID TRANSIT	PRT
PHILADELPHIA READING & NEW ENGLAND	PR&NE
PHILADELPHIA SUBURBAN TRANS COMPANY	PSTC
PHILADELPHIA SUBWAYS	PSW
PHILADELPHIA TRANSPORTATION COMPANY	PTC
PHILADELPHIA WILMINGTON & BALTIMORE	PW&B
PHILADEPHIA & LONG BRANCH RAILROAD	P&LB
PHILLIPS & RANGELEY	P&RA
PHOENIX STREET RAILWAY	PSRY
PICKENS RAILROAD	PI
PICKERING LUMBER	PLU
PICTOU COUNTY ELECTRIC COMPANY	PCEC
PIEDMONT & CUMBERLAND	P&CU
PIEDMONT & NORTHERN RAILWAY	P&N
PIGEON RIVER RAILROAD	PIGR
PILLSBURY	PILL
PINAFORE PARK	PP
PINE CREEK RAILROAD	PCR
PINEHURST ELECTRIC RAILWAY	PIER
PINSLY	PIN
PIONEER & FAYETTE RAILROAD	P&F
PIONEER PENNSYLVANIA COAL COMPANY	PPCO
PIONEER VALLEY RAILROAD	PIONV
PIRAEUS ATHENS PELOPONNESUS (GREECE)	PAPG
PITHOLE VALLEY RAILROAD	PHV
PITTSBURGH & BIRMINGHAM PASSENGER RY	P&BPR
PITTSBURGH & BUTLER	P&BU
PITTSBURGH & BUTLER STREET RAILWAY	P&BS
PITTSBURGH & CARNEGIE RAILROAD	P&CA
PITTSBURGH & CASTLE SHANNON INCLINE	P&CS
PITTSBURGH & LAKE ERIE RAILROAD	P&LE
PITTSBURGH & MOON RIVER	P&MR
PITTSBURGH & MOON RUN	P&MOR
PITTSBURGH & OHIO VALLEY RAILWAY	P&OV
PITTSBURGH & SHAWMUT RAILROAD	PI&SH
PITTSBURGH & SUSQUEHANNA	P&S
PITTSBURGH & WEST VIRGINIA RAILWAY	P&WV
PITTSBURGH & WESTERN RAILROAD CO	P&WRR
PITTSBURGH ALLEGHENY & MCKEES ROCKS	PA&MR
PITTSBURGH BESSEMER & LAKE ERIE	PB&LE
PITTSBURGH BINGHAMTON & EASTERN	PB&E
PITTSBURGH CHARTIERS & YOUGHIOGHENY	PC&Y
PITTSBURGH CINCINNATI & ST LOUIS RR	PC&SL
PITTSBURGH CINCINNATI CHIC & ST LOUIS	PCC&SL
PITTSBURGH CLEVELAND & TORONTO	PC&T
PITTSBURGH COMMUTER	PAT
PITTSBURGH COUNTY	PCO
PITTSBURGH FT WAYNE & CHICAGO RAILWAY	PFW&C
PITTSBURGH HARMONY BUTLER & N CASTLE	PHB&NC
PITTSBURGH LACKAWANNA & NORTHEASTERN	PL&N
PITTSBURGH LISBON & WESTERN RAILROAD	PL&W.
PITTSBURGH LISBON & WESTERN RAILWAY	PL&W
PITTSBURGH MARION & CHICAGO RAILROAD	PM&C.
PITTSBURGH MARION & CHICAGO RAILWAY	PM&C
PITTSBURGH MARS & BUTLER RAILWAY	PM&B

A24

APPENDIX A (RAILROADS)

ROADS ALPHABETICALLY W/ABREVIATIONS	A
PITTSBURGH MCKEESPORT & YOUNGIOGHENY	PM&Y
PITTSBURGH OHIO VALLEY & CINCINNATI	POV&C
PITTSBURGH PLATE GLASS	PPG
PITTSBURGH RAILWAYS	PIT
PITTSBURGH SHAWMUT & NORTHERN RR CO	PS&N
PITTSBURGH SHENANGO & LAKE ERIE	PS&LE
PITTSBURGH SOUTHERN	PS
PITTSBURGH TITUS & BUFFALO	PT&B
PITTSBURGH WESTMORELAND & SOMERSET	PW&S
PITTSBURGH YOUNGSTOWN & ASHTABULA RY	PY&A
PITTSBURGH YOUNGSTOWN & CHICAGO	PY&C
PITTSTON HAWLEY GRAVITY COMPANY	PHG
PLACERVILLE & LAKE TAHOE	P&LT
PLANT SYSTEM	PSY
PLATTSBURGH TRACTION COMPANY	PLTC
PLYMOUTH & MIDDLEBOROUGH RAILROAD	P&M
POCONO NORTHEAST RAILWAY	PONE
POINT COMFORT & NORTHERN RAILWAY	PC&N
POINT PLEASANT NEW JERSEY TRANSIT	PPNJT
POINT SHIRLEY STREET RAILWAY	PSS
POLK-CLAIBORNE MILITARY RAILROAD	P-C
POMEROY & NEWARK	PO&NE
POMEROY & STATELINE RAILROAD	P&SL
PONTCHARTRAIN RAILROAD	PONT
PONTIAC PACIFIC JUNCTION RAILWAY	PPJ
PONTIAC-PONTIAC JUNCTION RAILWAY	P-PJ
PORT ANGELES PACIFIC	PAP
PORT AUTHORITY OF ALLEGHENY COUNTY	PAAC
PORT AUTHORITY TRANS HUDSON	PATH
PORT AUTHORITY TRANSIT (PITTSBURGH)	PATP
PORT BIENVILLE RAILROAD	PB
PORT COMFORT & NORTHERN	PC&NO
PORT DALHOUSE ST CATHERINES & THOROLD	PDSC&T
PORT EVERGLADES BELT LINE RAILROAD	PEV
PORT EVERGLADES RAILWAY	PTE
PORT HOPE LINDSAY & BEAVERTON	PHL&B
PORT HURON & DETROIT RAILROAD	PH&D
PORT HURON & NORTHWESTERN	PH&NW
PORT ISABEL & RIO GRANDE VALLEY RR	PI&RGV
PORT ISABEL & RIO GRANDE VALLEY RY	PI&RGV.
PORT JARVIS & MONTICELLO RAILWAY	PJ&M
PORT JERVIS MONTICELLO & NEW YORK RR	PJM&NY
PORT MANATEE	PMA
PORT OF PALM BEACH DISTRICT	POPB
PORT OF TACOMA	POT
PORT OF TILLAMOOK BAY RAILROAD	POTB
PORT ORAM RAILROAD	PORAM
PORT ORANGE RAILROAD	PORR
PORT ROYAL & AUGUSTA RAILWAY	PR&A
PORT ROYAL & WESTERN CAROLINA RAILWAY	PR&WC
PORT STANLEY INCLINE RAILWAY	PSIRY
PORT TERMINAL RAILROAD ASSOCIATION	PTRA
PORT TOWNSEND & PUGET SOUND	PT&PS
PORT TOWNSEND RAILROAD	PTO
PORT TOWNSEND SOUTHERN	PTS
PORT UTILITIES COMMISSION RAILWAY	PUC
PORTAGE CREEK & RICH VALLEY	PC&RV
PORTAGE RAILROAD	PO
PORTER	POR
PORTERFIELD & ELLIS	P&EL
PORTERVILLE NORTHEASTERN	PNE
PORTLAND & CAPE ELIZABETH RAILWAY	P&CE
PORTLAND & KENNEBEC	P&K
PORTLAND & OGDENSBURG RAILROAD LINE	P&O
PORTLAND & ROCHESTER RAILROAD	P&RO
PORTLAND & RUMFORD FALLS RAILROAD	P&RF
PORTLAND ELECTRIC POWER COMPANY	PEPC
PORTLAND ELECTRIC RAILWAY	PEL
PORTLAND LEWISTON INTERURBAN RAILROAD	PLR
PORTLAND LEWISTON RAILWAY	PLR.
PORTLAND LOCOMOTIVE WORKS	PLW
PORTLAND PUBLIC DOCKS	PPD
PORTLAND RAILROAD COMPANY	P.
PORTLAND RAILWAY LIGHT & POWER COMPANY	PRL&P
PORTLAND RAILWAYS	P
PORTLAND SACO & PORTSMOUTH	PS&P
PORTLAND TERMINAL RAILROAD	PLTER

ROADS ALPHABETICALLY W/ABREVIATIONS	A
PORTLAND TERMINAL RAILROAD COMPANY	PT
PORTLAND TRACTION COMPANY	PTR
PORTLAND TRI-MET	PTRM
PORTLAND UNION RAILWAY STATION COMPANY	PUSC
PORTSMOUTH & ROANOKE RAILROAD	P&ROAN
PORTSMOUTH DOVER & YORK STREET RAILWAY	PD&Y
POTATO CREEK RAILROAD	POTCR
POTEAU & CAVANAL MOUNTAIN	P&CM
POTEAU VALLEY	PV
POTOMAC EDISON	PED
POTOMAC ELECTRIC POWER	PEP
POTOMAC FREDERICKSBURG & PIEDMONT	PF&P
POTOMIC REGION LINES	PRL
POTTSDAM & WATERTOWN	P&WAT
POTTSTOWN RAILWAY	POTT
POUGHKEEPSIE & CONNECTICUT RAILROAD	P&CRR
POUGHKEEPSIE & EASTERN RAILROAD CO	P&E
POUGHKEEPSIE BRIDGE COMPANY	PBC
POUGHKEEPSIE HARTFORD & BOSTON	PH&B
POWDER RIVER RAILROAD	PRI
POWELL STREET RAILWAY	PSTRY
PRAIRIE CENTRAL	PACY
PRATTSBURGH RAILWAY	PR
PRECISION NATIONAL	PNA
PRESCOTT & ARIZONA CENTRAL	P&AC
PRESCOTT & EASTERN	PR&EA
PRESCOTT & MT UNION RAILWAY	P&MU
PRESCOTT & NORTHEASTERN	P&NE
PRESCOTT & NORTHWESTERN RAILROAD	P&NW
PRESIDIO & FERRIES RAILROAD COMPANY	P&FRR
PRESTON RAILROAD	PRES
PRINCE EDWARD ISLAND	PEI
PRINCETON FAST LINE	PFL
PRINCETON-BLUEFIELD	P-B
PRODUCTS TANK LINE	PX
PROFILE & FRANCONIA NOTCH RAILROAD	P&FN
PROFILE NORTHERN	PN
PROVIDENCE & BEDFORD	P&BED
PROVIDENCE & DANIELSON RAILWAY COMPANY	P&DRY
PROVIDENCE & DANIELSON STREET RAILWAY	P&DRY
PROVIDENCE & SPRINGFIELD	P&SP
PROVIDENCE & WORCESTER RAILROAD	P&W
PROVIDENCE WARREN & BRISTOL RAILROAD	PW&BRR
PUBLIC BELT ROAD	PBR
PUBLIC SERVICE COORDINATED TRANSPORT	PSCT
PUBLIC SERVICE OF COLORADO	PSC
PUBLIC SERVICE OF INDIANA	PSI
PUBLIC SERVICE OF NEW JERSEY	PSNJ
PUBLIC SERVICE RAILWAY CO UNION LINE	PSRW
PUEBLO & ARKANSAS VALLEY	P&AV
PUEBLO UNION DEPOT & RAILROAD	PUD&R
PUGET SOUND & SNOQUALMIE VALLEY RR	PS&SV
PUGET SOUND ELECTRIC RAILWAY	PSER
PULLMAN COMPANY	PLM
PULLMAN COMPANY (O)	P*
PURDUE UNIVERSITY	PU
PUTNAM LUMBER COMPANY	PUT
QUABOG TRANSFER COMPANY	QT
QUAKAKE	QU
QUAKER OATS	QO
QUAKERTOWN & BETHLEHEM RAILROAD	Q&B
QUAKERTOWN & EASTERN RAILROAD	Q&E
QUANAH ACME & PACIFIC RAILWAY	QA&P
QUEBEC & GOSFORD WOODEN RAILWAY	Q&GW
QUEBEC & LAKE ST JOHN RAILWAY	Q&LSJ
QUEBEC CENTRAL RAILWAY	QC
QUEBEC CITADEL INCLINE PLANE	QCIP
QUEBEC DISTRICT RAILWAY	QDRY
QUEBEC IRON & TITANIUM	QI&T
QUEBEC MONTREAL & SOUTHERN RAILWAY	QM&S
QUEBEC MONTREAL OTTAWA & OCCIDENTAL RY	QMO&O
QUEBEC NORTH SHORE & LABRADOR RAILWAY	QNS&L
QUEBEC RAILWAY LIGHT & POWER COMPANY	QRL&P
QUEBEC SOUTHERN RAILWAY	QSRY
QUEEN ANNE'S RAILROAD COMPANY	QA
QUEENSBORO BRIDGE RAILWAY COMPANY	QBRW
QUEENSLAND GOV. RAILWAYS	QG

STEPHANS' RAILROAD DIRECTORY

A25

APPENDIX A (RAILROADS)

ROADS ALPHABETICALLY W/ABREVIATIONS	A
QUINCY & TORCH LAKE (SAME AS QM)	Q&TL
QUINCY MINING COMPANY	QM
QUINCY RAILROAD	Q
QUINCY SOYBEAN COMPANY	QS
QUINCY WESTERN RAILWAY COMPANY	QW
QUOCHITA & NORTH WESTERN	Q&NW
RAHWAY VALLEY RAILROAD	RV
RAIL TO WATER TRANSPORT CORP.	RWTC
RAILBOX	RB
RAILCAR MAINTENANCE COMPANY	RMCO
RAILROAD WEED CONTROL INC	RWCX
RAILWAY EXPRESS	REA
RAILWAY EXPRESS.	REA#
RAILWAY TRANSFER CITY OF MINNEAPOLIS	RTCM
RAILWORKS	RW
RALEIGH & CHARLESTON	R&C
RALSTON PURINA	RP#
RANGELY PHILLIPS & INDUSTRY RAILROAD	RP&I
RAPID CITY BLACK HILLS & WESTERN	RCBH&W
RAPID RAILWAY	RAP
RAPID TRANSIT COMPANY OF OHIO	RTOH
RAQUETTE LAKE RAILWAY	RL
RARITAN & DELAWARE BAY	R&DB
RARITAN RIVER RAILROAD	RR
RATH BLACK HAWK	RBH#
RAUB CENTRAL POWER	RCP
RAY & GILA VALLEY RAILROAD CO	R&GV
RAYMONDVILLE & WADDINGTON	R&W
RAYONIER & NAVIGATION COMPANY	RAY
RAYONIER RAILWAY	RY
READER RAILROAD	RRR
READING & COLUMBIA	R&COL
READING & LEHIGH	R&L
READING IRON COMPANY	RICO
READING RAILROAD COMPANY	R
READING STREET RAILWAY	RSR
RED ARROW LINES	RAL
RED RIVER & GULF RAILROAD	RR&G
RED RIVER LUMBER COMPANY	RRLC
RED SPRINGS & NORTHERN	RS&N
REDONDO RAILROAD	RE
REDSTONE RAILROAD	REDR
REGINA MUNICIPAL RAILWAY	RMRY
REGIONAL TRANSIT AUTHORITY CHICAGO	CRTA.
REGISTER & GLENVILLE	R&G
REICHHOLD CHEMICAL	RC
REINEGOLD	RG#
RENO & PITHOLE	R&P
RENSSELAER & SARATOGA RAILROAD	R&SA
REPUBLIC STEEL CORPORATION	RST
RESERVE MINING COMPANY	RMC
REW CITY & ELDRED	RC&E
RHINEBECK & CONNECTICUT RAILROAD CO	R&CO
RHODE ISLAND COMPANY	RIC
RHODE ISLAND SUBURBAN RAILWAY	RISR
RICHELIEU DRUMMOND & ATHABASKA	RD&A
RICHLAND & PETERSBURG	R&PB
RICHMOND & ALLEGHENY RAILROAD	R&A
RICHMOND & CHESAPEAKE BAY	R&CB
RICHMOND & DANVILLE	R&D
RICHMOND & PETERSBURG	R-P.
RICHMOND FREDERICKSBURG & POTONIC RR	RF&P
RICHMOND LOCOMOTIVE & MACHINE WORKS	RL&MW
RICHMOND TERMINAL RAILWAY	RT
RICHMOND-PETERSBURG RAILROAD COMPANY	R-P
RIDEAU CANAL TRAMWAY	RCT
RIDGEFIELD PARK	RIDP
RINGLING BROTHERS CIRCUS	RBC
RIO GRANDE	RG
RIO GRANDE & SOUTHWESTERN	RG&S
RIO GRANDE CITY	RGC
RIO GRANDE EASTERN	RGE
RIO GRANDE SOUTHERN	RGS
RIO GRANDE WESTERN	RGW
RIVER TERMINAL RAILWAY	RIVT
RIVERSIDE & ARLINGTON ELECTRIC RY	R&AE
RIVERSIDE BRIDGEBORO MT HOLLY & ATL S	RBMH

ROADS ALPHABETICALLY W/ABREVIATIONS	A
RIVERSIDE PARK RAILWAY	RPRY
ROANOKE RAILWAY & ELECTRIC COMPANY	RR&E
ROANOKE RIVER RAILWAY	ROR
ROARING CAMP & BIG TREES RAILROAD	RC&BT
ROBBINS RAILROAD	ROB
ROBERVAL & SAGUENAY RAILWAY	R&S
ROBY & NORTHERN RAILWAY	R&N
ROCHESTER & EASTERN	R&E
ROCHESTER & EASTERN RAPID RAILWAY	R&ER
ROCHESTER & GENESSEE VALLEY RAILROAD	RO&GV
ROCHESTER & SODUS BAY RAILWAY	R&SB
ROCHESTER & SOUTHERN	RO&SO
ROCHESTER & SUBURBAN	R&SUB
ROCHESTER & SYRACUSE RAILROAD	R&SRR
ROCHESTER CITY & BRIGHTON	RC&B
ROCHESTER ELECTRIC	ROCHE
ROCHESTER GAS & ELECTRIC	RG&E
ROCHESTER HORNELLSVILLE & LACKAWANNA	RH&L
ROCHESTER LOCKPORT & BUFFALO RAILROAD	RL&B
ROCHESTER LOCKPORT & NIAGARA FALLS	RL&NF
ROCHESTER NEW YORK & PENNSYLVANIA	RNY&P
ROCHESTER NUNDA & PENNSYLANIA	RN&PA
ROCHESTER NUNDA & PITTSBURGH	RN&P
ROCHESTER RAILWAY	ROCH
ROCHESTER SYRACUSE & EASTERN	RS&E
ROCHESTER TRANSIT CORPORATION	RTC
ROCHESTER TROLLEY LINES	RTL
ROCK ISLAND	RI
ROCK ISLAND SOUTHERN RAILWAY CO.	RIS
ROCK PORT LANGDON & NORTHERN	RPL&N
ROCKAWAY RAILWAY COMPANY	RRY
ROCKAWAY VALLEY MFG & CONSTRUCTION CO	RVAM
ROCKAWAY VALLEY RAILROAD	RVA
ROCKCASTLE RAILROAD	RCR.
ROCKCASTLE RIVER RAILROAD	RCR
ROCKDALE SANDOW & SOUTHERN RAILROAD	RS&S
ROCKFORD & INTERURBAN RAILWAY	R&IR
ROCKFORD ILLINOIS ELECTRIC COMPANY	RIE
ROCKINGHAM RAILROAD	ROCKRR
ROCKLAND CENTRAL	RLC
ROCKPORT RAILROAD	ROC
ROCKPORT THOMASTON & CAMDEN ST RY	RT&C
ROCKTON & RION RAILWAY	R&R
ROCKY MOUNTAIN & SANTA FE RAILWAY	RM&SF
ROCKY SPRINGS PARK	RSP
ROGUE RIVER VALLEY	RRV
ROME & CLINTON	R&CL
ROME & NORTHERN	R&NO
ROME & WATERTOWN	R&WAT
ROME WATERTOWN & OGDENSBURG	RW&O
ROOT REFINING COMPANY	RF
ROSCOE SNYDER & PACIFIC RAILWAY	RS&P
ROSECRANS	RO
ROWLAND SPRINGS RAILROAD	RS
ROWLESBURG & SOUTHERN	RO&S
ROY GREENE	ROY
ROYAL BLUE LINE	RBL
RUMFORD FALLS & RANGELEY LAKES	RF&RL
RUSSIAN DECAPODS	RD
RUTLAND & BURLINGTON	R&B
RUTLAND RAILROAD	RU
RUTLAND RAILWAY	RU.
SABDERSVILLE	SAB
SABINE RIVER & NORTHERN RAILROAD	SR&N
SACKETS HARBOR & ELLISBURG	SH&E
SACRAMENTO AUBURN & NORTHERN	SA&N
SACRAMENTO CITY LINES	SCLS
SACRAMENTO ELECTRIC GAS & RAILWAY CO	SEG&RY
SACRAMENTO NORTHERN RAILWAY	SN
SACRAMENTO RT METRO	SRTM
SACRAMENTO SOUTHERN	SSO
SACRAMENTO VALLEY & EASTERN RAILWAY	SV&E
SACRAMENTO VALLEY RAILROAD	SAV
SAGINAW & MT PLEASANT	S&MP
SAGINAW UNION STATION RAILWAY (MICH)	SUS
SAGIWAN LOGGING	SL
SALEM FALLS CITY & WESTERN RAILWAY	SFC&W

STEPHANS' RAILROAD DIRECTORY

A26

APPENDIX A (RAILROADS)

ROADS ALPHABETICALLY W/ABBREVIATIONS	A
SALEM RAILROAD	SALEM
SALEM VALLEY	SALV
SALT LAKE & LOS ANGELES RAILWAY	SL&LA
SALT LAKE & UTAH	SL&U
SALT LAKE CITY UNION DEPOT & RR CO	SLCUD
SALT LAKE GARFIELD & WESTERN RAILWAY	SLG&W
SAN ANTONIO & ARKANSAS PASS	SA&AP
SAN ANTONIO PUBLIC SERVICE	SAPS
SAN ANTONIO SOUTHERN (MP)	SAS
SAN ANTONIO TRACTION COMPANY	SATC
SAN ANTONIO UVALDE & GULF RAILROAD	SAU&G
SAN BENITO & RIO GRANDE VALLEY	SB&RGV
SAN BERDO & LOS ANGELES	SB&LA
SAN BERNARDINO ARROWHEAD & WATERMAN	SBA&W
SAN BERNARDINO VALLEY TRACTION	SBVT
SAN DIEGO & ARIZONA EASTERN RAILWAY	SD&AE
SAN DIEGO & ARIZONA RAILROAD	SD&A
SAN DIEGO & CUYAMACA	SD&C
SAN DIEGO & SOUTH EASTERN RY CO.	SD&S
SAN DIEGO CUYAMACA & EASTERN	SDC&E
SAN DIEGO ELECTRIC RAILWAY	SDE
SAN DIEGO OLD TOWN & PALM BEACH	SDOT&P
SAN DIEGO PACIFIC BEACH & LA JOLLA	SDPB&L
SAN DIEGO SOUTH EASTERN RAILWAY	SDS
SAN DIEGO TRANSIT	SDT
SAN FRANCISCO & NAPA VALLEY RAILROAD	SF&NV
SAN FRANCISCO & NORTH PACIFIC RY CO	SF&NP
SAN FRANCISCO & NORTHWESTERN RY CO	SF&N
SAN FRANCISCO & SAN JOAQUIN VALLEY	SF&SJV
SAN FRANCISCO & SAN JOSE	SF&SJ
SAN FRANCISCO & SAN MATEO	SF&SM
SAN FRANCISCO BELT LINE RAILROAD	SFB
SAN FRANCISCO MUNICIPAL RAILWAY	SFM
SAN FRANCISCO NAPA & CALISTOGA RY	SFN&C
SAN FRANCISCO OAKLAND & SAN JOSE	SFO&SJ
SAN FRANCISCO TAMALPAIS & BOLINAS	SFT&B
SAN FRANCISCO VALLEJO & NAPA	SFV&N
SAN FRANCISCO-SACRAMENTO RAILROAD	SF-S
SAN GABRIEL VALLEY RAPID TRANSIT	SGV
SAN JACINTO RAILWAY COMPANY	SJRY
SAN JOACHIN LUMBER	SJL
SAN JOAQUIN & EASTERN RAILROAD	SJ&E
SAN JOSE RAILROAD	SJRR
SAN JUAN CENTRAL	SJC
SAN JUAN PACIFIC	SJP
SAN LUIS CENTRAL RAILROAD	SLC
SAN LUIS OBISPO & SANTA MARIA VALLEY	SLO&SM
SAN LUIS OBISPO RAILWAY	SLO
SAN LUIS SOUTHERN	SLS
SAN LUIS VALLEY	SLV
SAN LUIS VALLEY SOUTHERN	SLVS
SAN MANUEL ARIZONA RAILROAD	SMA
SAN PEDRO LOS ANGELES & SALT LAKE RR	SPLASL
SAN RAFAEL & SAN QUENTIN	SR&SQ
SAND SPRINGS RAILWAY	SSP
SANDERSVILLE RAILROAD	SAND
SANDUSKY & COLUMBUS SHORT LINE	S&CSL
SANDUSKY & INTERURBAN	S&I
SANDUSKY & INTERURBAN	S&INT
SANDUSKY FREMONT & SOUTHERN	SF&S
SANDUSKY MILAN & HURON	SM&H
SANDUSKY MILAN & NORWALK ELECTRIC RY	SM&N
SANDUSKY NORWALK & MANSFIELD ELECT RY	SN&M
SANDUSKY NORWALK & SOUTHERN	SN&S
SANDUSKY NORWALK & SOUTHERN	SN&SO
SANDUSKY STREET RAILWAY	SSRY
SANDWICH WINDSOR & AMERSTBURG ELECTRIC	SW&A
SANDY RIVER & ELKHAM	SR&ELK
SANDY RIVER & RANGELEY LAKES RAILROAD	SR&RL
SANDY RIVER RAILROAD	SRV
SANDY VALLEY & ELKHORN	SV&ELK
SANDY VALLEY & ELKHORN (O)	SV&E.
SANFORD & EVERGLADES RAILROAD	S&EG
SANFORD & ST PETERSBURG	S&SP
SANFORD TRACTION	SANT

ROADS ALPHABETICALLY W/ABBREVIATIONS	A
SANTA BARBARA & SUBURBAN	SB&S
SANTA CRUZ & FELTON	SC&F
SANTA CRUZ & WATSONVILLE	SC&W
SANTA CRUZ RAILROAD COMPANY	SCRR
SANTA CRUZ-WATSONVILLE RAILROAD	SC&W
SANTA FE	ATSF.
SANTA FE (O)	SF
SANTA FE CENTRAL	SFC
SANTA FE PRESCOTT & PHOENIX	SFP&P
SANTA FE RATON & EASTERN RAILROAD	SFR&E
SANTA MARIA VALLEY RAILROAD	SMV
SAPULPA UNION	SU
SARANAC & LAKE PLACID	S&LP
SARATOGA & ENCAMPMENT RAILWAY	S&ERY
SARATOGA & SCHENECTADY RAILROAD	SA&SC
SARATOGA & SCHUYLERSVILLE	SAR&S
SARATOGA MT MCGREGOR & LAKE GEORGE RR	SMG&LG
SASKATOON MUNICIPAL RAILWAY	SMRY
SAUCELITO TERMINAL	STER
SAVANNAH & ATLANTA RAILWAY COMPANY	S&A
SAVANNAH & NORTHWESTERN	S&NW
SAVANNAH & SOUTHERN	S&SO
SAVANNAH & STATESBORG RAILROAD	S&SRR
SAVANNAH ALBANY & GULF	SA&G
SAVANNAH FLORIDA & WESTERN	SF&W
SAVANNAH GRIFFIN & NORTH ALABAMA	SG&NA
SAVANNAH RIVER TERMINAL	SRTC
SAVANNAH STATE DOCKS	SSD
SAWYER RIVER	SAR
SCHENECTADY & TROY	SCH&T
SCHENECTADY LOCOMOTIVE WORKS	SLW
SCHENECTADY RAILWAY COMPANY	SCHEN
SCHLITZ BEER	SCH*
SCHOHARIE VALLEY RAILROAD	SVAL
SCHUYLER RAILWAY	SCHUY
SCHUYLKILL & SUSQUEHANNA	S&S
SCHUYLKILL VALLEY NAVIGATION & RR	SVN
SCHWARGEHILD SULZBERGER	S&S*
SCIATO VALLEY SOUTHERN	SVS
SCIOTO VALLEY TRACTION	SVT
SCOTT & BEARSKIN LAKE	S&BL
SCRANTON & BINGHAMTON	S&B
SCRANTON DUNMORE & MOOSIC LAKE	SD&ML
SCRANTON TRACTION	SCRA
SCRANTON TRACTION COMPANY	STRC
SCRANTON TROLLEY COMPANY	STC
SD WARREN PAPER COMPANY	SDW
SE MINERAL	SEMIN
SEA CLIFF INCLINED RAILWAY COMPANY	SCIR
SEA VIER RAILROAD	SVRR
SEABOARD AIR LINE	SAL
SEABOARD AIR LINE. (O)	SEA.
SEABOARD COAST LINE	SCL
SEABOARD RAILROAD	SEA
SEABOARD SYSTEM	SBD
SEASHORE ELECTRIC MUSEUM	SEM
SEATRAIN LINES	SEAT
SEATTLE & NORTH COAST	S&NC
SEATTLE & RANIER VALLEY RAILROAD	S&RV
SEATTLE & WALLA WALLA	S&WW
SEATTLE COAL & TRANSPORTATION COMPANY	SC&T
SEATTLE COLUMBIA & PUGET SOUND RAILWY	SC&PS
SEATTLE ELECTRIC COMPANY	SEL
SEATTLE LAKE SHORE & EASTERN	SLS&E
SEATTLE MUNICIPAL RAILWAY	SEAM
SEATTLE MUNICIPAL STREET RAILWAY SYST	SMST
SEATTLE TACOMA INTERURBAN	STI
SEATTLE TERMINAL	SET
SEAVIEW TRANSPORTATION	STR
SEBASTICOOK & MOOSEHEAD LAKE	S&ML
SECOND AVE RAILROAD COMPANY	SARR
SECRETARIA DE COMUNICATIONES Y OBRAS P	SCOP
SEEKONK	SEE
SELMA ROME & DALTON	SR&D
SEWARD PENINSULA RAILROAD	SPEN
SEWELL VALLEY RAILROAD	SEWV
SHADE GAP ELECTRIC RAILWAY	SGER

A27

APPENDIX A (RAILROADS)

ROADS ALPHABETICALLY W/ABBREVIATIONS	A
SHAKER HEIGHTS RAPID TRANSIT	SHRT
SHAMOKIN & TREVERTON	S&T
SHAMOKIN SUNBURY & LEWISBURG	SS&L
SHAWMUT & NORTHERN	SH&N
SHAWMUT CONNECTING	SHAWC
SHAWNEE TECUMSEH TRACTION	STT
SHEBOYGAN RAILWAY LIGHT & POWER CO.	SRL&P
SHEFFIELD & TIONESTA RAILWAY	S&TI
SHELBURNE FALLS & COLRAIN STREET RY	SF&CS
SHELL CHEMICAL CORPORATION	SCMX
SHELL OIL	SHO*
SHENANDOAH CENTRAL	SCEN
SHENANGO & ALLEGHENY	S&AL
SHENANGO & BEAVER VALLEY	S&BV
SHEPAUG LITCHFIELD & NORTHERN	SL&N
SHEPAUG RAILROAD COMPANY	SHEP
SHEPAUG VALLEY RAILROAD COMPANY	SHEPV
SHERBROOKE EASTERN TOWNSHIP &KENNEBEC	SET&K
SHERMAN'S VALLEY & BROAD TOP RAILROAD	SV&BT
SHIP RAILWAY OF CHICNECTO	SRC
SHIPPERS CAR LINE	SCL*
SHIPYARD RAILWAY	SHIP
SHORE FAST LINE	SFL
SHORE LINE ELECTRIC RAILWAY COMPANY	SLE
SHORTLINE RAILROAD (OHIO)	SLOR
SHREVEPORT & PACIFIC RAILROAD	SH&P
SHREVEPORT & RED RIVER VALLEY RAILWAY	S&RRV
SIDELL & OLNEY RAILROAD	SID&O
SIDNEY & LOWE RAILROAD	S&LRR
SIERRA NEVADA WOOD & LUMBER COMPANY	SNW&L
SIERRA PACIFIC	SIEP
SIERRA RAILROAD	SIE
SIERRA RAILROAD OF CALIFORNIA	SOC
SIERRA RAILWAY	SIE.
SIERRA VALLEYS	SIEV
SILVER CITY PINOS ALTOS & MOGOLLON	SCPA
SILVER KING COALITION MINES COMPANY	SKM
SILVER PEAK RAILROAD	SILP
SILVER SPRINGS OCALA & GULF	SSO&G
SILVERTON GLADSTONE & NORTHERLY RR	SG&N
SILVERTON NORTHERN RAILROAD	SNO
SILVERTON RAILROAD	SILV
SIMPSON TIMBER COMPANY	STC
SINCLAIR	S*
SINGER MANUFACTURING COMPANY	SING
SINNEMAHONING VALLEY	SINV
SIOUX CITY & MORNINGSIDE STREET RY	SC&MS
SIOUX CITY & PACIFIC	SC&PA
SIOUX CITY ELEVATED RAILWAY	SCERY
SIOUX CITY RAPID TRANSIT COMPANY	SCRT
SIOUX CITY TERMINAL RAILWAY	SCT
SIOUX CITY TRACTION COMPANY	SCIT
SIOUX CITY TRANSIT COMPANY	SICT
SIOUX FALLS & NORTHERN	SIF&N
SIOUX FALLS TRACTION SYSTEM	SFTS
SISTRUNK & JORDAN	S&J
SKAGIT RAILWAY	SR,
SKAGIT RIVER RAILWAY	SR
SKANEATELES RAILROAD	SKA
SKANEATELES SHORT LINE RAILROAD	SSL
SLAVE FALLS RAILWAY	SFRY
SMETHPORT	SMETH
SMETHPORT & OLEAN	S&OL
SMOKY MOUNTAIN COMPANY	SMT
SOMERS LUMBER COMPANY	SLCO
SOMERSET	SOM
SOMERVILLE & EASTON	S&EA
SONOMA VALLEY PRISMOIDAL RAILROAD	SVP
SONOMA VALLEY RAILROAD	SONV
SONORA BAJA CALIFORNIA RAILROAD	SBC
SONORA BAJA CALIFORNIA RAILWAY	SBC.
SOO LINE	SOO
SOUTH ATLANTIC & OHIO	SA&O
SOUTH BRANCH	SB
SOUTH BRANCH VALLEY	SBV
SOUTH BRANCH VALLEY RAILROAD	SB.
SOUTH BROOKLYN RAILWAY	SBR

ROADS ALPHABETICALLY W/ABBREVIATIONS	A
SOUTH BUFFALO RAILROAD	SBUF
SOUTH CAROLINA CANAL & RAILROAD	SCC&RR
SOUTH CAROLINA ELECTRIC & GAS	SCE&G
SOUTH CAROLINA RAILROAD	SOCA
SOUTH CENTRAL TENNESSEE RAILROAD	SCTR
SOUTH CHICAGO & WEST INDIANA RAILROAD	SC&WI
SOUTH DAKOTA CENTRAL RAILWAY	SDCEN
SOUTH EAST KANSAS RAILROAD	SEK
SOUTH EAST MICHIGAN TRANSIT	SEMT
SOUTH EASTERN & PHILLIPSBURG RAILROAD	SE&P
SOUTH EASTERN (SOUTH CAROLINA)	SESC
SOUTH EASTERN COAL COMPANY	SECX
SOUTH EASTERN PA TRANSIT AUTHORITY	SEPTA.
SOUTH EASTERN PA TRANSPORTATION AUTH	SEPTA
SOUTH EASTERN RAILWAY (CANADA)	SE
SOUTH EASTON & PHILLIPSBURG RAILROAD	SE&PH
SOUTH FLORDIA	SOF
SOUTH FORK-PORTAGE RAILWAY	SFP
SOUTH GEORGIA RAILROAD	SG
SOUTH GEORGIA RAILWAY	SG.
SOUTH HOPKINS COAL COMPANY	SHC
SOUTH IOWA RAILWAY	SIOR
SOUTH JERSEY RAILROAD	SJR
SOUTH JERSEY RAPID TRANSIT LINES	SJRTL
SOUTH LAKE RAILROAD	SLRR
SOUTH LOGAN RAILWAY	SLR
SOUTH MANCHESTER RAILROAD	SOMRR
SOUTH OMAHA TERMINAL RAILWAY	SOT
SOUTH PACIFIC COAST	SPC
SOUTH PARK	SOP
SOUTH PENNSYLVANIA RAILROAD	SPA
SOUTH SHORE & SOUTH BEND	SS&SB
SOUTH SHORE RAILWAY (LOUISIANA)	SS
SOUTH SHORE RAPID TRANSIT	SSRT
SOUTH SIDE & NORFOLK & PETERSBURG	SSNP
SOUTH SIDE RAILROAD OF LONG ISLAND	SSLI
SOUTH SIDE TRACTION COMPANY	SOS
SOUTH WESTERN RAILROAD	SW
SOUTHEAST OKLAHOMA INDUSTRIAL AUTHOR	SOIA
SOUTHEASTERN OHIO TRACTION	SEOT
SOUTHEASTERN PENNSYLVANIA TRANS AUTH	SPTA
SOUTHERN APPALACHIAN RAILWAY	SARY
SOUTHERN CAL EDISON CO (CALIFORNIA)	SCEC
SOUTHERN CALIFORNIA RAILROAD	SCAL
SOUTHERN CALIFORNIA RAILWAY	SCAL.
SOUTHERN CAMBRIA RAILWAY	SCA
SOUTHERN CEMENT COMPANY	SCC
SOUTHERN CENTRAL	SCE
SOUTHERN COLORADO POWER COMPANY	SCP
SOUTHERN ELECTRIC GENERATING	SEG
SOUTHERN INDIANA RAILWAY	SIND
SOUTHERN INDUSTRIAL RAILWAY	SIN
SOUTHERN IOWA RAILWAY	SIRY
SOUTHERN KANSAS	SK
SOUTHERN MARYLAND RAILROAD	SMD
SOUTHERN NEW ENGLAND RAILROAD	SNE
SOUTHERN NEW JERSEY	SNJ
SOUTHERN NEW YORK POWER & RAILWAY CO	SNYP
SOUTHERN NEW YORK RAILWAY	SNY
SOUTHERN PACIFIC LINES	SPL
SOUTHERN PACIFIC OF CALIFORNIA	SPCAL
SOUTHERN PACIFIC OF MEXICO RAILROAD	SPM
SOUTHERN PACIFIC OF NEW MEXICO	SPNM
SOUTHERN PACIFIC RAILROAD	SP
SOUTHERN PACIFIC RR CO OF TEXAS	SPTEX
SOUTHERN PACIFIC SANTA FE	SPSF
SOUTHERN PENNSYLVANIA RAILROAD	SPA.
SOUTHERN PINE LUMBER COMPANY	SPLU
SOUTHERN RAILWAY	S
SOUTHERN RAILWAY CO OF MISSISSIPPI	SMISS
SOUTHERN RIO GRANDE	SRG
SOUTHERN SAN LUIS VALLEY RAILROAD	SSLV
SOUTHERN TRANS-CONTINENTAL RAILWAY	SOTC
SOUTHERN UTAH RAILWAY	SUR
SOUTHEASTERN RAILROAD	SEAST
SOUTHINGTON & PLANTSVILLE TRAMWAY CO	S&PT
SOUTHWEST FOREST INDUSTRIES	SFI

STEPHANS' RAILROAD DIRECTORY

A28

APPENDIX A (RAILROADS)

ROADS ALPHABETICALLY W/ABBREVIATIONS

Road	Abbr
SOUTHWEST PORTLAND CEMENT	SWPC
SOUTHWEST RAILWAY CONSTRUCTION CO	SRCC
SOUTHWEST VIRGINIA RAILROAD	SWV
SOUTHWESTERN ELECTRIC POWER COMPANY	SWEP
SOUTHWESTERN INTERURBAN	SWIU
SOUTHWESTERN RAILROAD OF NEW MEXICO	SWNM
SOUTHWESTERN RAILWAY COMPANY	SWRY
SOUTHWESTERN SYSTEM (OHIO)	SWS
SPARKS WESTERN RAILWAY	SPW
SPENCER RAILROAD	SRR
SPENCER STEEL WIRE COMPANY	SSWC
SPENCERVILLE & ELGIN	SPEG
SPERRY RAIL SERVICE	SPS
SPOKANE & INLAND ELECTRIC RAILWAY	S&IE
SPOKANE & INLAND EMPIRE	S&IE.
SPOKANE COEUR D'ALENE & PALOUSE	SCA&P
SPOKANE FALLS & NORTHERN RAILWAY	SF&NO
SPOKANE INTERNATIONAL RAILROAD	SPI
SPOKANE INTERNATIONAL RAILWAY	SPI
SPOKANE PORTLAND & SEATTLE RAILROAD	SP&S
SPOKANE PORTLAND & SEATTLE RAILWAY	SP&S.
SPRING CREEK RAILWAY	SCRY
SPRINGFIELD & NORTHWESTERN	SF&NW
SPRINGFIELD ELECTRIC RAILWAY	SERY
SPRINGFIELD HAVANA & PEORIA	SH&PE
SPRINGFIELD RAILROAD	SPRR
SPRINGFIELD SOUTHERN	SPRS
SPRINGFIELD TERMINAL RAILWAY	ST
SPUYTEN DUYVIL & PORT MORRIS RAILROAD	SD&PM
SQUAW CREEK COAL COMPANY	SCCC
ST AUGUSTINE & SOUTH BEACH	SA&SB
ST CATHERINES STREET RAILWAY	SCS
ST CHARLES STREET RAILROAD	SCHS
ST CLAIR TUNNEL CO	SCTC
ST CLOUD & SUGAR BELT	SC&SB
ST CROIX & PENOBSCOTT RAILROAD	SC&PRR
ST ELIZABETH HOSPITAL	SEH
ST FRANCOIS COUNTY RAILROAD COMPANY	SFCRR
ST JOHN & MAINE RAILWAY	SJ&M
ST JOHN & OPHIR	SJ&O
ST JOHNS & INDIAN RIVER	SJ&IR
ST JOHNS & LAKE EUSTIS	SJ&LE
ST JOHNS ELECTRIC COMPANY	SJE
ST JOHNS RIVER TERMINAL RAILWAY CO	SJRT
ST JOHNS STREET RAILWAY	SJ
ST JOHNSBURY & LAKE CHAMPLAIN RR	SJ&LC
ST JOHNSBURY & LAMOILLE COUNTY RR	SJ&LCO
ST JOSEPH & COUNCIL BLUFFS	SJ&CB
ST JOSEPH & DES MOINES	SJ&DM
ST JOSEPH & GRAND ISLAND (UP)	SJ&GI
ST JOSEPH & ST LOUIS	SJ&SL
ST JOSEPH BELT RAILWAY	SJB
ST JOSEPH TERMINAL RAILROAD	SJT
ST JOSEPH VALLEY RAILROAD	SJV.
ST JOSEPH VALLEY RAILWAY	SJV
ST LAURENCE & ADIRONDACK RAILWAY CO	SL&ARY
ST LAURENT & VILLAGE D'INDUSTRIE	SL&VD
ST LAWRENCE & ADIRONDACK RAILROAD	SL&AD
ST LAWRENCE & ATLANTIC	SL&A
ST LAWRENCE & INDUSTRY VILLAGE RY	SL&IV
ST LAWRENCE & OTTAWA	SL&O
ST LAWRENCE INTERNATIONAL RR & LAND	SLI
ST LAWRENCE RAILROAD	STL
ST LOUIS & ADIRONDACK	STL&A
ST LOUIS & CAIRO SHORTLINE	SL&C
ST LOUIS & HANNIBAL	SL&H
ST LOUIS & IRON MOUNTAIN RAILROAD	SL&IM
ST LOUIS & KANSAS CITY	SL&KC
ST LOUIS & NORTH ARKANSAS RAILROAD	SL&NA
ST LOUIS & SAN FRANCISCO RAILWAY	FRIS,.
ST LOUIS & SOUTHWESTERN	CBELT
ST LOUIS & SUBURBAN	SL&SU
ST LOUIS ALTON & TERRE HAUTE RAILROAD	SLA&TH
ST LOUIS ARKANSAS & TEXAS RAILWAY	SLA&T
ST LOUIS BROWNSVILLE & MEXICO	SLB&M
ST LOUIS EL RENO & WESTERN RAILWAY	SLER&W
ST LOUIS IRON MOUNTAIN & SOUTHERN	SLIM&S
ST LOUIS KANSAS CITY & CHICAGO	SLKC&C
ST LOUIS KANSAS CITY & NORTHERN	SLKC&N
ST LOUIS KANSAS CITY SHORT LINE	SLKC
ST LOUIS KEOKUK & NORTHWESTERN	SLK&N
ST LOUIS LAWRENCE & DENVER	SLL&D
ST LOUIS LAWRENCE & WESTERN	SLL&W
ST LOUIS MATERIALS & SAND COMPANY	SLM&SC
ST LOUIS MEMPHIS & SOUTHEATERN RR	SLM&S
ST LOUIS PUBLIC SERVICE	SLPS
ST LOUIS REEFER EXPRESS	SLRE#
ST LOUIS ROCKY MOUNTAIN & PACIFIC RY	SLRM&P
ST LOUIS SAN FRANCISCO RAILWAY	FRIS
ST LOUIS SOUTHWESTERN (COTTON BELT)	CBELT,
ST LOUIS STURGIS & BATTLE CREEK RR CO	SLS&BC
ST LOUIS VANDALIA & TERRE HAUTE	SLV&TH
ST LOUIS WATER WORKS RAILWAY	SLWW
ST MARIES RIVER RAILROAD	SMR
ST MARYS & SOUTHWESTERN	SM&S
ST MARYS RAILROAD	SM
ST PAUL & DULUTH	SP&DUL
ST PAUL & PACIFIC RAILROAD COMPANY	SP&P
ST PAUL MINNEAPOLIS & MANITOBA	SPM&M
ST PAUL UNION DEPOT	SPUD
ST PETERSBURG MUNICIPAL RAILWAY (FL)	SPMRY
ST REGIS PAPER COMPANY	SRPC
STALEY SYSTEM OF ELECTRIFIED RW	SSE
STAMFORD STREET RAILWAY	STAM
STANDARD GRAVEL	STG
STANDARD SLAG COMPANY	SSCO
STANDARD STEEL DIV-BALDWIN LIMA HAMIL	STDS
STANSTEAD SHEFFORD & CHAMBLY RAILWAY	SS&C
STARK ELECTRIC RAILROAD	SERR
STARKE & SIMPSON CITY	S&SC
STATE BELT RAILROAD	SBELT
STATE LINE & SULLIVAN RAILROAD	SL&S
STATE UNIVERSITY RAILROAD	SURR
STATEN ISLAND MIDLAND RAILWAY	SIMRY
STATEN ISLAND RAILROAD	SI
STATEN ISLAND RAILWAY	SI.
STATEN ISLAND RAPID TRANSIT RAILWAY	SIRT
STATENVILLE RAILROAD OF GEORGIA	STAT
STATESBORO NORTHERN RAILWAY	SNRY
STATESVILLE & WESTERN	ST&W
STAUFFER CHEMICAL	SCH
STEEL COMPANY OF CANADA	SCOC
STEELTON & HIGHSPIRE RAILROAD	S&H
STEINWAY LINES	STEIN
STERLING IRON & RAILWAY	SI&R
STERLING MOUNTAIN RAILROAD	SMRR
STEUBENVILLE E LIVERPOOL & BEAVER VAL	SEL&B
STEWART RAILROAD	STEWRR
STEWARTSTOWN RAILROAD	STEW
STOCKHAM VALVES & FITTINGS	SV&F
STOCKTON & COPPEROPLIS RAILWAY	S&CRY
STOCKTON TERMINAL	STTER
STOCKTON TERMINAL (O)	STTE
STOCKTON TERMINAL & EASTERN RAILROAD	ST&E
STONE CANYON & PACIFIC	SC&P
STONE CANYON RAILWAY	SC
STONE HARBOR & WILDWOOD	SH&W
STONE HARBOR RAILROAD	SH
STONE HARBOR TERMINAL RAILROAD	SHT
STONE MOUNTAIN SCENIC RAILROAD	SMS
STOURBRIDGE LINE	STLN
STRASBURG RAILROAD	STRR
STRATTON & COMPANY	ST&C
STREET RAILWAY DEPT OF ANACONDA COPPR	SRDAC
STROUDS CREEK & MUDDLETY RAILROAD	SC&M
STROUDSBURG PASSENGER RAILWAY	SPR
SUALMATZ LUMBER CO	SUL
SUBURBAN TRACTION	SUBT
SUD-PACIFICO DE MEXICO	SPM.
SUDBURY COPPER CLIFF ELECTRIC RAILWAY	SCCE
SUFFOLK & CAROLINA	S&CA
SUFFOLK TRACTION	SUFT
SUGAR LAND	SUGL
SUGAR PINE LUMBER COMPANY	SPLC

APPENDIX A (RAILROADS)

ROADS ALPHABETICALLY W/ABBREVIATIONS	A
SUGAR RUN	SUGR
SULLIVAN COUNTY RAILROAD	SCO
SUMMIT & NORTHEASTERN RAILWAY	S&NE
SUMPTER VALLEY RAILWAY (OREGON)	SV
SUMTER & CHOCTAW RAILWAY	S&C
SUN OILS	SO*
SUNBURY & LEWISTOWN	SB&LT
SUNBURY & SELINGROVE STREET RY CO	S&SS
SUNBURY HAZELTON & WILLES BARRE	SH&WB
SUNCOOK VALLEY RAILROAD	SUNV
SUNSET RAILWAY	SURY
SUPERIOR STONE COMPANY	SSC
SURESTE RAILWAY (MEXICO)	SRM
SURRY SUSSEX & SOUTHHAMPTON	SS&S
SUSQUEHANNA	NYS&W
SUSQUEHANNA (O)	SES
SUSQUEHANNA & NEW YORK RAILWAY	S&NY
SUSQUEHANNA & WESTERN	S&W
SUSQUEHANNA CONNECTING RAILROAD	SUSC
SUSQUEHANNA RIVER & WESTERN RAILROAD	SR&W
SUTTON STREET WIRE ROPE RAILROAD	SSWR
SWAMP RABBIT	SWR
SWATARA & COLD SPRINGS	S&CS
SWAYNE LUMBER COMPANY	SWL
SWIFT	SW*
SWIFT & COMPANY	SW&C
SYDNEY & LOUISBURG RAILWAY	S&L
SYDNEY MINES	SMINE
SYLVANIA CENTRAL RAILROAD (PRIOR 1903)	SYC.
SYLVANIA CENTRAL RAILWAY (AFTER 1903)	SYC
SYLVANIA RAILWAY	SYC
SYRACUSE & BALDWINSVILLE	SY&B
SYRACUSE & CHENANGO VALLEY	S&CV
SYRACUSE & EASTERN	S&E
SYRACUSE & EASTSIDE RAILWAY COMPANY	S&ES
SYRACUSE & ONONDAGA	S&O
SYRACUSE & ROCHESTER RAILROAD	S&R
SYRACUSE & SUBURBAN RAILROAD	SY&S
SYRACUSE & UTICA DIRECT	S&UD
SYRACUSE & UTICA RAILROAD	S&U
SYRACUSE BINGHAMTON & NEW YORK	SB&NY
SYRACUSE LAKE SHORE & NORTHERN	SLS&N
SYRACUSE PHOENIX & OSWEGO	SP&O
RALLAHASSEE & ST MARKS	T&SM
T.R. MILLER COMPANY	TRM
TACOMA & COLUMBIA RIVER RAILWAY	T&CR
TACOMA & LAKE CITY RR & NAV CO	T&CR
TACOMA LAKE CITY RR & NAVIGATION CO	T&CR.
TACOMA LAKE PARK & COLUMBIA RIVER RY	TLP&CR
TACOMA MUNICIPAL BELT LINE RAILWAY	TMB
TACOMA RAILWAY & POWER COMPANY	TR&PC
TACUBAYA RAILROAD	TACR
TALBOTTON RAILROAD	TAL
TALLADEGA & COOSA VALLEY	T&CV
TALLAHASEE	TALL
TALLAHASSE PENSACOLA & GULF RAILROAD	TP&G
TALLULAH FALLS RAILWAY	TF
TAMA & TOLEDO	T&TO
TAMALPAIS & MUIR WOODS RAILWAY	T&MW
TAMAQUA HAZLETON & NORTHERN	TH&N
TAMPA & KEY WEST	T&KW
TAMPA & THONOTOSASSA	T&TH
TAMPA UNION STATION COMPANY	TUSCO
TANANA VALLEY RAILROAD	TANV
TATUM LUMBER COMPANY	TL
TAUNTON & MIDDLEBORO RAILROAD	TA&M
TAUNTON BRANCH RAILROAD	TBRR
TAUTON LOCOMOTIVE WORKS	TLW
TAVARES & GULF RAILROAD	T&GU
TAYLOR MOUNTAIN & BEAVER CREEK	TM&BC
TECOPA	TEC
TEMISCOUATA RAILWAY	TEM
TEMISKAMING & NORTHERN ONTARIO RY	T&NON
TENNESSEE & ALABAMA	T&A
TENNESSEE & COOSA	T&C
TENNESSEE & NORTH CAROLINA RAILWAY	T&NC
TENNESSEE ALABAMA & GEORGIA RAILWAY	TA&G

ROADS ALPHABETICALLY W/ABBREVIATIONS	A
TENNESSEE CENTRAL RAILROAD	TENNC.
TENNESSEE CENTRAL RAILWAY	TENNC
TENNESSEE COAL & IRON	TC&I
TENNESSEE ELECTRIC POWER COMPANY	TEPC
TENNESSEE KENTUCKY & NORTHERN	TK&N
TENNESSEE RAILROAD	T
TENNESSEE RAILROAD (O)	TNRR
TENNESSEE STATE LINE RAILROAD	TSL
TENNESSEE VALLEY AUTHORITY	TVA
TENNESSEE VALLEY RAILROAD	TVRR
TENNESSEE VIRGINIA & GEORGIA	TV&G
TERMINAL RAILROAD ASSOC OF ST LOUIS	TRA
TERMINAL RAILROAD OF NEW ORLEANS	TRNO
TERMINAL RAILWAY ALABAMA STATE DOCKS	TRASD
TERRE HAUTE & INDIANAPOLIS	TH&I
TERRE HAUTE & LOGANSPORT	TH&L
TERRE HAUTE & PEORIA	TH&P
TERRE HAUTE & SOUTHEASTERN	TH&SE
TERRE HAUTE INDIANAPOLIS & EASTERN	THI&E
TEXACO	T*
TEXARKANA & FORT SMITH	T&FS
TEXARKANA SHREVEPORT & NATCHEZ RY	TS&N
TEXARKANA UNION STATION TRUST	TUST
TEXAS & NEW ORLEANS RAILROAD COMPANY	T&NO
TEXAS & NORTHERN RAILWAY	T&N
TEXAS & PACIFIC	T&P
TEXAS & ST LOUIS RAILWAY CO OF ARKANSA	T&SLA
TEXAS CENTRAL RAILROAD	TC
TEXAS CITY TERMINAL RAILWAY	TCT
TEXAS ELECTRIC RAILWAY	TE
TEXAS EXPORT	TEX
TEXAS MIDLAND	TM
TEXAS OKLAHOMA & EASTERN RAILROAD	TO&E
TEXAS PACIFIC MISSOURI PAC TERM RR NO	TPMP
TEXAS PACIFIC RAILROAD COMPANY	TP
TEXAS SHORT LINE RAILWAY	TEXSL
TEXAS SOUTH-EASTERN RAILROAD	TSE
TEXAS STATE RAILROAD	TEXS
TEXAS TRACTION	TEXTR
TEXAS TRANSPORTATION COMPANY	TTC
TEXAS TRUCK RAILROAD	TEXT
TEXAS WESTERN NARROW GAGE RAILROAD	TW
TEXAS WESTERN RAILWAY COMPANY	TW.
TEXAS-MEXICAN RAILWAY COMPANY	TMEX
TEXAS-NEW MEXICO RAILWAY	T-NMR
TEXAX TRACTION (O)	TTR
THAILAND RAILWAYS	TRW
THATCHER'S INLET RAILROAD	TIR
THIRD AVENUE RAILWAY SYSTEM	TAT
THIRD AVENUE TRANSIT RAILROAD COMPANY	TAT.
THOMASTON TRAMWAY COMPANY	TTY
THORNTON & ALEXANDRIA RAILROAD CO	T&AL
THUNDER LAKE LUMBER COMPANY	TLL
THUNDERBIRD COLLIERIES	THC
THURMONT-FREDERICK	T-F
THURSO & NATION VALLEY	T&NV
TICHY TRAIN GROUP	TTG
TIDEWATER & DEEPWATER	T&DW
TIDEWATER & SOUTHERN TRANSIT COMPANY	T&ST
TIDEWATER & WESTERN	T&W
TIDEWATER RAILWAY	TIDE
TIDEWATER SOUTHERN RAILROAD	TS.
TIDEWATER SOUTHERN RAILWAY	TS
TIFFIN FOSTORIA & EASTERN RAILWAY	TF&E
TIMKEN ROLLER BEARING COMPANY	TRB
TIOGA CENTRAL	TIC
TIOGA LUMBER COMPANY	TLCO
TIONESTA VALLEY & HICKORY	TV&H
TIONESTA VALLEY & SALMON CREEK	TV&SC
TIONESTA VALLEY RAILWAY	TIV
TIVOLI BEER	TB*
TOLDEO-DETROIT RAILROAD	T-DR
TOLEDO & EASTERN RAILROAD	T&EA
TOLEDO & ILLINOIS	T&ILL
TOLEDO & INDIANA RAILWAY	T&IRY
TOLEDO & OHIO	T&O
TOLEDO & OHIO CENTRAL	T&OC

A30

APPENDIX A (RAILROADS)

ROADS ALPHABETICALLY W/ABBREVIATIONS	A
TOLEDO & SOUTH HAVEN	T&SH
TOLEDO & WESTERN	T&WE
TOLEDO ANGOLA & WESTERN RAILWAY	TA&W
TOLEDO ANN ARBOR & CADILLAC RAILWAY	TAA&C
TOLEDO ANN ARBOR & JACKSON	TAA&J
TOLEDO BOWLING GREEN & SOUTHERN TRACT	TBG&ST
TOLEDO CANADA SOUTHERN & DETROIT RY	TCS&D
TOLEDO CINCINNATI & ST LOUIS	TC&SL
TOLEDO CLEVELAND LAKE SHORE ELECTRIC	TCLSE
TOLEDO COLUMBUS & OHIO RIVER RR CO	TC&OR
TOLEDO DELPHOS & BURLINGTON	TD&B
TOLEDO EDISON	TED
TOLEDO ELECTRIC RAILWAY	TERY
TOLEDO FOSTORIA & FINDLEY	TF&F
TOLEDO FREMONT & NORWALK	TF&N
TOLEDO FREMONT & NORWALK	TF&NK
TOLEDO PEORIA & WARSAW	TP&WAR
TOLEDO PEORIA & WESTERN RAILROAD	TP&W
TOLEDO PEORIA & WESTERN RAILWAY	TP&W.
TOLEDO PORT CLINTON & LAKESIDE	TPC&L
TOLEDO RAILWAY & LIGHT COMPANY	TR&L
TOLEDO ST LOUIS & CINCINNATI	TSL&C
TOLEDO ST LOUIS & KANSAS CITY RR CO	TSL&KC
TOLEDO ST LOUIS & WESTERN	TSL&W
TOLEDO TERMINAL RAILROAD	TT
TOLEDO WABASH & WESTERN	TW&W
TOMAH & LAKE ST CROIX	T&LSC
TOMBSTONE SOUTHERN	TOMBS
TONAWANDA GENESEE VALLEY & PINE CREEK	TGV&PC
TONAWANDA RAILROAD	TONAW
TONAWANDA VALLEY & CUBA RAILROAD CO	TV&C
TONAWANDA VALLEY EXTENSION RR CO	TVE
TONAWANDA VALLEY RAILROAD	TV
TONAWANDA WISCOY & GENESEE VALLEY	TW&GV
TONOPAH & GOLDFIELD RAILROAD	T&GO
TONOPAH & GREENWATER RAILROAD	T&GW
TONOPAH & TIDEWATER RAILROAD	T&T
TONOPAH RAILROAD	TON
TOOELE VALLEY RAILWAY	TOV
TORONTO & MIMICO ELECTRIC RAILWAY	T&MERY
TORONTO & NIPISSING RAILWAY	T&NRY
TORONTO & YORK RADIAL RAILWAY	T&YR
TORONTO CIVIC RAILWAY	TCRY
TORONTO GRAY & BRUCE RAILWAY	TG&B
TORONTO HAMILTON & BUFFALO RAILWAY	TH&B
TORONTO RAILWAY CO	TRCO
TORONTO RAPID TRANSIT	TRT
TORONTO SARNIA & LAKE HURON	TS&LH
TORONTO SIMCOE & LAKE HURON	TS&LH
TORONTO TERMINALS RAILWAY	TTRY
TORONTO TRANSIT COMMISSION	TTCO
TORONTO TRANSPORTATION COMMISSION	TCO.
TORRINGTON & WINCHESTER STREET RAILWAY	T&WS
TOWANDA MONROETON SHIPPERS LIFELINE	TMSL
TOWNSVILLE RAILROAD	TOWN
TRAILER TRAIN	TTR
TRANS CAR SERVICES	TCS
TRANSKENTUCKY TRANSPORTATION SYS INC	TTI
TREASURE ISLAND	TI
TREMONT STREET LINE	TRSL
TREMOUNT & GULF RAILWAY	TR&G
TRENTON PRINCETON TRACTION	TPT
TRESCKOW	TR
TRI CITY TRACTION	TCTR
TRI-CITY RAILWAY COMPANY	T-CR
TRIAD CHEMICAL	TRC
TRINITY & BRAZOS VALLEY	T&BV
TRONA RAILWAY	TRO
TROPICANA	TROP
TROY & BOSTON	T&B
TROY & GREENFIELD	T&G
TROY & NEW ENGLAND RAILWAY COMPANY	T&NE
TROY CITY RAILWAY	TROYC
TROY SARATOGA & NORTHERN	TS&NO
TROY UNION RAILROAD	TU
TUCKERTON RAILROAD	TUCK

ROADS ALPHABETICALLY W/ABBREVIATIONS	A
TULIA GRAIN TERMINAL	TGT
TULSA-SAPULPA UNION RAILWAY	TSU
TUSCALOOSA BELT RAILWAY	TUS
TUSCALOOSA RAILWAY & UTILITIES COMPANY	TR&U
TUSCAMBIA & DECATUR	T&D
TUSCARORA VALLEY	TUV
TUSCOLA & SAGINAW BAY	T&SB
TUSCON CORNELIA & GILA BEND RAILROAD	TC&GB
TUSCUMBIA COURTLAND & DEACTUR RY	TC&D
TUSCUMBIA RAILRAOD	TUSC
TUSCUMBIA RAILWAY	TUSC.
TUSKEGEE RAILROAD	TUSK
TWIN BRANCH RAILROAD	TB
TWIN CITY RAPID TRANSIT	TCRT
TWIN MOUNTAIN & POTOMAC RAILROAD	TM&P
TWIN SEAMS MINING COMPANY	TSM
TWIN TREES MINES RAILWAY	TTM
TYLER TAP RAILROAD	TTAP
TYRONE & CLEARFIELD	T&CL
UINTAH RAILROAD	U
UINTAH RAILWAY	U.
ULSTER & DELAWARE	U&D
ULTIMA THULE ARKADELPHIA & MISSISSIPP	UTA&M
ULVALDE & NORTHERN RAILWAY	U&N
UNADILLA VALLEY RAILWAY	UV
UNCANOONUC INCLINE RAILWAY	UIRY
UNIDOS DE YUCATAN	UDEY
UNIDOS DEL SURESTE (MEXICO)	UDES
UNION CANAL	UCA
UNION CARBIDE	UNC
UNION CARBIDE.	UC*
UNION ELECTRIC RAILWAY	UE
UNION FREIGHT RAILROAD	UF
UNION IRON WORKS	UIW
UNION PACIFIC COAL COMPANY	UPCC
UNION PACIFIC DENVER & GULF	UPD&G
UNION PACIFIC RAILROAD	UP
UNION RAILROAD	URR
UNION RAILROAD OF OREGON	URO
UNION RAILWAY (TENNESSEE)	URYT
UNION REFRIGERATED TRANSIT	URTX*
UNION STOCK YARD & TRANSFER	USY&T
UNION STOCK YARD & TRANSIT COMPANY	USY&T.
UNION STREET RAILWAY	USR
UNION TANK CAR COMPANY	UTCC
UNION TANK LINE	UTL*
UNION TANK LINE.	UTLX
UNION TERMINAL COMPANY (TEXAS)	UTCO
UNION TERMINAL RAILWAY COMPANY	UT
UNION TRACTION COMPANY	UTC
UNION TRANSPORTAION CO	UTRC
UNION WARF & PLANK WALK COMPANY	UW&PW
UNITED COMMERCIAL COMPANY INC	UC-MX
UNITED COMPANY (OREGON)	UNIC
UNITED ELECTRIC COAL	UEC
UNITED ELECTRIC RAILWAY COMPANY	UERC
UNITED ELECTRIC RAILWAYS (RI)	UERY
UNITED RAILROADS OF SAN FRANCISCO	URSF
UNITED RAILWAY OF ST LOUIS	URSL
UNITED RAILWAYS & ELECTRIC	UR&E
UNITED RAILWAYS OF OREGON	URWO
UNITED RAILWAYS OF YUCATAN	URY
UNITED RAILWAYS OF YUCATAN (0)	YU.
UNITED STATES AIR FORCE	USAF
UNITED STATES ARMY	USA
UNITED STATES ATOMIC ENERGY COMMISSIO	USAEC
UNITED STATES BORAX	USBOR
UNITED STATES DEPT OF TRANSPORTATION	USDOT
UNITED STATES ISTHMIAN CANAL COMMISS	ISTCC
UNITED STATES ISTHMIAN CANAL COMM (0)	US
UNITED STATES MILITARY RAILROAD	USM
UNITED STATES NAVAL AMMUNITION DEPOT	USNAD
UNITED STATES NAVY	USN
UNITED STATES PIPE & FOUNDRY	USP&F
UNITED STATES RAILROAD ADMINISTRATION	USRA
UNITED STATES RAILWAY EQUIP MFG	USREM
UNITED STATES STEEL CORPORATION	USSC

APPENDIX A (RAILROADS)

ROADS ALPHABETICALLY W/ABBREVIATIONS	A
UNITED STATES SUGAR	USS
UNITED STATES WAR DEPARTMENT	USWD
UNITED TRACTION COMPANY	UNTR
UNITED TRACTION STREET RAILWAY	UTSR
UNITY RAILWAY	UN
UNIVERSAL EXPLORATION COMPANY	UXL
UNIVERSITY OF ILLINOIS	UI
UNIVERSITY OF MINNESOTA INTER-CAMPUS	UM
UPJOHN COMPANY	UJC
UPPER COOS & HEREFORD	UC&H
UPPER COOS RAILROAD	UCRR
UPPER MERION & PLYMOUTH RAILROAD	UM&P
URBAN TRANSPORTATION DEVELOPMENT CORP	UTDC
UTAH & NORTHERN	UT&N
UTAH BELT	UB
UTAH CENTRAL RAILROAD	UC
UTAH COAL ROUTE	UCR
UTAH COPPER DIV OF KENNECOTT COPPER C	UCKC
UTAH IDAHO CENTRAL RAILROAD	UIC
UTAH NORTHERN	UNO
UTAH POWER & LIGHT	UP&L
UTAH RAILWAY COMPANY	UTAH
UTAH TERMINAL COMPANY	UTAHT
UTICA & BLACK RIVER	U&BR
UTICA & SCHENECTADY RAILROAD	U&SRR
UTICA CLINTON & BINGHAMTON	UC&B
UTICA ITHACA & ELMIRA RAILROAD	UI&E
UTICA ITHACA & ELMIRA RAILWAY	UI&E.
UTLX	U*
UVALDE & NORTHERN (TEXAS)	UV&N
UWANTA EGG	UE*
VACUUM WINE & SPIRITS CANNING CORP	VW&S
VALDOSTA MOULTRIE & WESTERN	VM&W
VALDOSTA SOUTHERN RAILROAD	VS
VALDOSTA SOUTHERN RAILWAY	VS
VALLEY & SILETZ RAILROAD	V&S
VALLEY CITY STREET & INTERURBAN RY	VCS&I
VALLEY RAILROAD	VAL
VALLEY RAILWAYS	VAL.
VANCOUVER VICTORIA & EASTERN RY & NAV	VV&E
VANDALIA RAILROAD	VA
VENANGO RIVER RAILROAD	VR
VENICE SHORE LINE	VSL
VENICE SHORT LINE	VSL.
VENTURA COUNTY RAILWAY	VCO
VEPCO	VEPCO
VERMONT & MASSACHUETTS	V&M
VERMONT CENTRAL	VTC
VERMONT NORTHERN	VN
VERMONT RAILWAY	VER
VERMONT VALLEY	VV
VERONIA SOUTH PARK & SUNSET STEAM RR	VSP&S
VIA	VIA
VICKSBURG & JACKSON RAILROAD	V&J
VICKSBURG SHREVEPORT & PACIFIC	VS&P
VICKSBURG STREET RAILWAY (MISSISSIPPI)	VB
VICTORIA & SYDNEY RAILWAY	V&SRY
VICTORIA LUMBER COMPANY	VLC
VICTORY PARK RAILWAY	VIP
VIET NAM RAILWAYS	VNR
VINELAND	VIN
VIRGINIA & CAROLINA SOUTHERN RAILROAD	V&CS
VIRGINIA & MARYLAND	V&MA
VIRGINIA & RAINY LAKE	V&RL
VIRGINIA & SOUTHERN	V&SO
VIRGINIA & SOUTHWESTERN RAILROAD	V&SW
VIRGINIA & TENNESSEE	V&TEN
VIRGINIA & TRUCKEE RAILROAD	V&T
VIRGINIA & TRUCKEE RAILWAY	V&T.
VIRGINIA ANTHRACITE & COAL RY CO	VA&C
VIRGINIA BLUE RIDGE RAILWAY	VBR
VIRGINIA CAROLINA RAILROAD	VAC
VIRGINIA CENTRAL RAILWAY	VC
VIRGINIA ELECTRIC & POWER COMPANY	VE&PC
VIRGINIA POCAHONTAS	VP
VIRGINIA PUBLIC SERVICE COMPANY	VPS
VIRGINIA RAILWAY & POWER COMPANY	VR&P
VIRGINIA TRANSIT	VT
VIRGINIA-TENNESSEE RAILROAD	V-T
VIRGINIA.....	VEPCO.
VIRGINIAN & WESTERN	V&W
VIRGINIAN RAILWAY	V
VISALIA ELECTRIC RAILROAD	VE
VULCAN DETINNING	VD
VULCAN MATERIALS	VM
W&S	W&S
W.T. SMITH LUMBER COMPANY	WTSL
WABASH CHESTER & WESTERN	WC&W
WABASH PITTSBURGH TERMINAL	WPT
WABASH RAILROAD COMPANY	W.
WABASH RAILWAY	W
WABASH ST LOUIS & PACIFIC RAILWAY	WSL&P
WABASH TERMINAL RAILWAY	WT
WABASH VALLEY	WVA
WACO BEAUMONT TRINITY & SABINE RY	WBT&S
WAHPETON-BRECKENRIDGE STREET RY CO	W-BS
WAIALUA PLANTATION	WAI
WAITESBORO & WESTERN	WA&W
WALLA WALLA & COLUMBIA RIVER RAILROAD	WW&CR
WALLA WALLA VALLEY RAILWAY	WWV
WALLACE STONE	WAST
WALLKILL VALLEY RAILROAD	WAV
WAMPUM & STATE LINE	WA&SL
WANAMAKER KEMPTON & SOUTHERN	WK&S
WANAMIE MINING COMPANY	WMC
WARE SHOALS RAILROAD	WAS
WARNER SAND & GRAVEL	WS&G
WARREN & FARNSWORTH	W&F
WARREN & FRANKLIN RAILWAY	W&FRY
WARREN & OUACHITA VALLEY RAILWAY	W&OV
WARREN & SALINE RIVER RAILROAD	W&SR
WARREN & VENANGO	W&V
WARREN PAPER COMPANY	WPC
WARREN-BISBEE RAILWAY	W-B
WARRENTON RAIL ROAD	WAR
WARRIOR RIVER TERMINAL RAILROAD	WRTRR
WARWICK RAILROAD	WA
WARWICK RAILWAY	WA
WARWICK VALLEY RAILROAD	WA.
WASHINGTON & CHESAPEAKE BEACH	W&CB
WASHINGTON & COLUMBIA RIVER RAILROAD	W&CR
WASHINGTON & LINCOLNTON RAILROAD	W&L
WASHINGTON & OLD DOMINION RAILROAD	W&OD
WASHINGTON & OLD DOMINION RAILWAY	W&OD.
WASHINGTON & PITTSBURGH	WA&P
WASHINGTON & POTOMAC RAILROAD	W&POT
WASHINGTON & WAYNESBURG	WA&WA
WASHINGTON ALEXANDRIA & MT VERNON RY	WA&MV
WASHINGTON ARLINGTON & FALLS CHURCH	WA&FC
WASHINGTON BALTIMORE & ANNAPOLIS ELEC	WB&AE
WASHINGTON BRANDYWINE & POINT LOOKOUT	WB&PL
WASHINGTON CENTRAL RAILROAD	WCRC
WASHINGTON CITY VIRGINIA MID & GR SOU	WCVM&GS
WASHINGTON COUNTY RAILROAD	WCO
WASHINGTON IDAHO & MONTANA RAILWAY	WI&M
WASHINGTON POTOMAC & CHESAPEAKE RY	WP&C
WASHINGTON RAILWAY & ELECTRIC COMPANY	WRY&E
WASHINGTON RUN RAILROAD	WASHR
WASHINGTON SOUTHERN RAILWAY COMPANY	WSO
WASHINGTON TERMINAL COMPANY	WASHT
WASHINGTON WATER POWER COMPANY	WWPC
WASHINGTON WESTMINSTER & GETTYSBURG	WW&G
WASHINGTON-VIRGINIA RAILWAY	WVRY
WASHITA & SANTA FE	W&SFE
WASHOE COUNTY RAILROAD	WCRR
WATER GAP RAILROAD	WG
WATERBURY & MILLDALE	W&MD
WATERLOO CEDAR FALLS & NORTHERN RY	WCF&N
WATERLOO RAILROAD	WLOO
WATERLOO-WELLINGTON	W-W
WATERTOWN & ROME	WAT&R
WATERTOWN & SIOUX FALLS RAILWAY	W&SF
WATERTOWN RAILROAD COMPANY	WRCO
WATERVIET TURNPIKE	WVT

A32

APPENDIX A (RAILROADS)

ROADS ALPHABETICALLY W/ABBREVIATIONS	A
WATERVIET TURNPIKE & HORSE RAILWAY	WT&H
WATERVILLE & FAIRFIELD HORSE RAILROAD	WV&FH
WATERVILLE & FAIRFIELD RY & LIGHT CO	WV&F
WATERVILLE & OAKLAND STREET RAILWAY	W&O
WATERVILLE ELECTRIC LIGHT & POWER CO	WELP
WATERVILLE FAIRFIELD & OAKLAND RY	WF&O
WATERVILLE RAILWAY	WAT
WAUKEGAN ROCKFORD & ELGIN	WR&E
WAUPACA GREEN BAY RAILWAY	WGB
WAYCROSS & FLORIDA	WC&F
WAYCROSS AIR LINE	WAL
WAYNESBURG & WASHINGTON RAILROAD	W&WA
WAYNESBURG SOUTHERN	WS
WEATHERFORD MINERAL WELLS & NORTHWEST	WMW&N
WEBBER FALLS	WF
WEEMS ELECTRIC	WEL
WELLAND	WELL
WELLAND & PORT COLBORNE	W&PC
WELLSVILLE & BUFFALO RAILROAD CORP	W&B
WELLSVILLE ADDISON & GALETON RAILROAD	WA&G
WELLSVILLE BOLIVAR & ELDRED	WB&EL
WEST CHESTER KENNETT SQUARE & WILMING	WCKS
WEST CHICAGO STREET RAILROAD COMPANY	WCS
WEST COAST RAILWAY	WCRT
WEST END CHEMICAL COMPANY	WECC
WEST END STREET RAILWAY (BOSTON)	WESR
WEST FELICIANA RAILROAD COMPANY	WFE
WEST JERSEY & SEASHORE RAILROAD	WJ&S
WEST PALM BEACH TERMINAL	WPBT
WEST PENN & PITTSBURG RAILWAY	WP&P
WEST PENN RAILWAY COMPANY	WPA
WEST PITTSTON-EXETER RAILROAD	WPE
WEST POINT ROUTE	WPR
WEST RIVER RAILROAD	WR
WEST SHORE RAILROAD	WSH
WEST SIDE & YONKERS RAILWAY	WS&Y
WEST SIDE LUMBER COMPANY	WSL
WEST SIDE RAILROAD (OF ELMIRA)	WSRR
WEST SIDE RAILWAY (ELMIRA NY)	WSRR.
WEST TENNESSEE RAILROAD	WTRR
WEST VIRGINIA CENTRAL & PITTSBURGH RR	WVC&P
WEST VIRGINIA MIDLAND RAILROAD	WVM
WEST VIRGINIA NORTHERN RAILROAD	WVN
WEST VIRGINIA PULP & PAPER COMPANY	WVPP
WESTBROOK WINDHAM & NAPLES RAILWAY	WW&N
WESTCHESTER & WESTERN	WE&W
WESTERN & ALLEGHENY	W&AL
WESTERN & ATLANTIC	W&A
WESTERN ALLEGHENY RAILROAD	WARR
WESTERN ALLEGHENY RAILWAY	WARR.
WESTERN BRICK COMPANY	WBC
WESTERN COAL & COKE COMPANY	WC&C
WESTERN COUNTIES ON NOVA SCOTIA	WCNS
WESTERN ENERGY COMPANY	WEC
WESTERN FOREST INDUSTRIES	WFI
WESTERN FRUIT EXPRESS	WFE*
WESTERN INSURANCE & TRANSPORTATION CO	WI&TC
WESTERN MARYLAND	WM
WESTERN NEW YORK & PENNSYLVANIA	WNY&P
WESTERN NORTH CAROLINA RAILROAD	WNC
WESTERN NOVA SCOTIA POWER COMPANY	WNSP
WESTERN OF MASSACHUSETTS	WMASS
WESTERN OHIO RAILROAD	WOHIO
WESTERN PACIFIC	WP
WESTERN PACIFIC & RIO GRANDE	WP&RG
WESTERN RAILROAD CORPORATION	WRC
WESTERN RAILROAD OF ALASKA	WRRA
WESTERN RAILWAY OF ALABAMA	WRA
WESTERN RAILWAY OF MASSACHUSETTS	WRM
WESTERN RAILWAY OF MEXICO	WROM
WESTERN UNION TELEGRAPH CO	WUT*
WESTERN VERMONT	WV
WESTFIELD PLANTAION	WPL
WESTFIELD RAILROAD	WES
WESTINGHOUSE	WE*
WESTINGHOUSE ELECTRIC	WE
WESTMINISTER	WEST
WESTMONT INCLINED PLANE	WIP
WESTMORELAND COAL COMPANY	WCC
WESTON & BROOKER CRUSHED STONE CO	W&BCS
WESTVACO	WV*
WEYERHAEUSER LUMBER COMPANY	WTC
WEYERHAEUSER TIMBER COMPANY.	WTC.
WHARTON & NORTHERN RAILROAD	W&NO
WHEELING & LAKE ERIE RAILROAD	W&LE
WHEELING & LAKE ERIE RAILWAY COMPANY	W&LE.
WHEELING PITTSBURGH STEEL	WPS
WHEELING RAILWAY COMPANY	WRY
WHEELING TRACTION COMPANY	WHTR
WHIPPANY & PASSAIC RIVER RAILROAD	W&PR
WHIPPANY RIVER RAILROAD	WIPR
WHITE DEER & LOGANTON RAILROAD	WD&L
WHITE DEER VALLEY RAILROAD	WDV
WHITE MOUNTAIN CENTRAL RAILROAD	WMCE
WHITE PASS & YUKON ROUTE	WP&Y
WHITE RIVER LUMBER	WRL
WHITE RIVER RAILROAD	WRRR
WHITE SULPHUR SPRING & YELLOWSTONE PK	WSS&YP
WHITE TOP	WTP
WHITE WATER VALLEY RAILROAD	WWVR
WHITEHALL CEMENT	WHC
WHITMER & STEEL LUMBER COMPANY	W&SL
WHITNEYVILLE & MACHIASPORT	WV&M
WICHITA & MIDLAND VALLEY	W&MV
WICHITA & WESTERN	W&WE
WICHITA FALLS & NORTHWESTERN	WF&N
WICHITA FALLS & SOUTHERN	WF&S
WICHITA NORTHWESTERN RAILWAY	WNW
WICHITA UNION TERMINAL RAILWAY	WUTR
WICHITA VALLEY RAILWAY	WIV
WILD GOOSE RAILROAD	WGRR
WILKES BARRE & EASTERN	WB&E
WILKES BARRE & HAZELTON RAILWAY	WB&H
WILKES-BARRE & WYOMING VALLEY TRACTION	WB&WVT
WILKES-BARRE CONNECTING RAILROAD	W-BC
WILKES-BARRE RAILWAY	W-BRY
WILLAMETTE IRON & STEEL COMPANY	WI&S
WILLIAM MASON	WMM
WILLIAMETTE VALLEY & COAST	WV&C
WILLIAMSPORT & NORTH BRANCH RAILROAD	W&NB.
WILLIAMSPORT & NORTH BRANCH RAILWAY	W&NB
WILLIAMSTOWN	WI
WILLIAMSTOWN & REDFIELD	W&R
WILMINGTON & BALTIMORE RAILROAD	W&BA
WILMINGTON & NORTHERN	W&N
WILMINGTON & READING	WIL&R
WILMINGTON & WELDEN RAILWAY	W&WR
WILMINGTON & WELDEN RAILWAY (0)	W&NR
WILMINGTON & WESTERN	W&W
WILMINGTON BRUNSWICK & SOUTHPORT	WB&S
WILSON	W*
WINANS LOCOMOTIVES	WL
WINCHESTER & POTOMAC	WI&P
WINCHESTER & WESTERN RAILROAD	WI&W
WINCHESTER STREET RAILWAY	WSRY
WINDSOR & ANNAPOLIS RAILWAY	W&AN
WINFIELD ELECTRIC RAILWAY	WINF
WINFIELD RAILROAD	WRR
WINIFREDE RAILROAD	WINI
WINNIPEG ELECTRIC COMPANY	WELC
WINNIPEG HYDRO TRAMWAY	WHT
WINNIPEG SELKIRK & LAKE WINNIPEG	WS&LW
WINONA & WARSAW RAILWAY	WI&W
WINONA INTERURBAN RAILWAY	WINO
WINONA RAILROAD	WIN
WINSLOW & RICHLAND	W&RL
WINSTON & BONE VALLEY	W&BV
WINSTON SALEM SOUTHERN	WSS
WINSTON-SALEM SOUTHBOUND RAILWAY	WSSB
WINSTON-SALEM TERMINAL COMPANY	WSTC
WISCASSET & QUEBEC	W&Q
WISCASSET WATERVILLE & FARMINGTON	WW&F
WISCONSIN & MICHIGAN	W&M
WISCONSIN & NORTHERN	WI&N

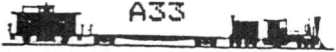

A33

APPENDIX A (RAILROADS)

ROADS ALPHABETICALLY W/ABBREVIATIONS	A
WISCONSIN & SOUTHERN	WIS&S
WISCONSIN CENTRAL	WC
WISCONSIN IOWA & NEBRASKA	WI&NE
WISCONSIN MINNESOTA & PACIFIC	WM&P
WISCONSIN POWER & LIGHT	WP&L
WOBURN BRANCH	WB
WOLFBORO RAILROAD	WORR
WOOD RIVER BRANCH RAILROAD	WRB
WOODARD WALKER LUMBER COMPANY	WWL
WOODSTOCK RAILWAY	WO
WOODWARD IRON COMPANY RAILROAD	WWI
WOONSOCKET & PASCOAG	W&P
WORCESTER & CONNECTICUT EASTERN	W&CE
WORCESTER & NORWICH	WO&N
WORCESTER & WEBSTER STREET RAILWAY	W&WSRY
WORCESTER NASHUS & ROCHESTER	WN&R
WRIGHTSVILLE & SUN HILL RAILROAD CO	W&SH
WRIGHTSVILLE & TENNILLE RAILROAD	W&T
WSE (BINGHAMTON NY)	WSE
WYANDOTTE SOUTHERN RAILROAD	WYS
WYANDOTTE TERMINAL RAILROAD	WYT
YAKIMA TRACTION COMPANY	YTC
YAKIMA VALLEY TRANSPORTATION CO (O)	YAV
YAKIMA VALLEY TRANSPORTATION COMPANY	YVT
YAKUTAT & SOUTHERN RAILWAY	Y&SO
YALE SHORT LINE	YALE
YAMPA VALLEY RAILROAD	YVA
YANCEY RAILROAD	Y
YANKEETOWN DOCK	YD
YANKTON NORFOLK & SOUTHERN	YN&S
YARMOUTH & ANNAPOLIS RAILWAY	Y&A
YAZOO & MISSISSIPPI VALLEY	Y&MV
YELLOW RIVER RAILROAD	YR
YELLOWSTONE PARK RAILROAD	YSP
YORK HARBOR & BEACH RAILROAD	YH&B
YORK PENNA. RAILWAYS	YP
YORK RAILWAY	YKRY
YORK SOUTHERN RAILROAD	YSO
YORK UTILITIES RAILWAY COMPANY	YUC
YOSEMITE MOUNTAIN & SUGAR PINE	YM&SP
YOSEMITE SHORT LINE	YSL
YOSEMITE VALLEY RAILROAD	YV
YOUNGSTOWN & NORTHERN RAILROAD	Y&N
YOUNGSTOWN & OHIO RIVER	Y&OR
YOUNGSTOWN & SOUTHERN RAILWAY	Y&S
YOUNGSTOWN & SUBURBAN	Y&SU
YOUNGSTOWN STEEL	YS
YREKA RAILROAD	YREKA
YREKA WESTERN RAILROAD	YW
YUCATAN RAILWAY (O)	YU
YUCATAN RAIWLAY	URY.
ZALEV BROTHERS LIMITED	ZB
ZANESVILLE & WESTERN	Z&W
ZANESVILLE MARIETA & PARKERSBURG	ZM&P
ZERBE VALLEY	ZV

STEPHANS' RAILROAD DIRECTORY

A	ABBREVIATIONS ALPHABETICALLY W/ROADS
A	AMTRAK
A&A	ARCADE & ATTICA RAILROAD
A&AV	ATTICA & ALLEGHENY VALLEY
A&B	AMHERST & BELCHERTOWN
A&BB	AKRON & BARBERTON BELT RAILROAD
A&BR	ARCADIA & BETSEY RIVER
A&BUF	ATTICA & BUFFALO RAILROAD
A&C	ARIZONA & CALIFORNIA
A&CJ	AKRON & CHICAGO JUNCTION RAILROAD CO
A&CR	ASTORIA & COLUMBIA RIVER RAILROAD
A&CRY	AMES & COLLEGE RAILWAY
A&D	ATLANTIC & DANVILLE RAILROAD
A&D.	ATLANTIC & DANVILLE RAILWAY COMPANY
A&DA	ASBESTOS & DANVILLE
A&E	ALTON & EASTERN
A&EC	ATLANTIC & EAST CAROLINA RAILWAY
A&ER	ANNAPOLIS & ELK RIDGE
A&ES	ATLANTA & EDGEWOOD STREET RAILWAY
A&F	ALABAMA & FLORIDA
A&FA	ARLINGTON & FAIRFAX AUTO RAILROAD
A&FL	AUGUSTA & FLORIDA RAILWAY
A&G	ATLANTIC & GULF
A&GU	ASHERTON & GULF
A&GW	ATLANTIC & GREAT WESTERN
A&GWW	ALBERTA & GREAT WATERWAYS RAILWAY
A&H	ALBANY & HUDSON ELECTRIC RAILWAY
A&J	ALMA & JONQUIERES RAILWAY
A&K	ALLEGHENY & KINZUA
A&KEN	ANROSCOGGIN & KENNEBEC
A&L	ARKANSAS & LOUISIANA
A&LG	ATLANTA & LAGRANGE RAILROAD
A&LM	ARKANSAS & LOUISIANA MISSOURI RAILWAY
A&LS	ATLANTIC & LAKE SUPERIOR RAILROAD
A&LV	ALTOONA & LOGAN VALLEY RAILWAY
A&MR	ARCATA & MAD RIVER RAILROAD
A&N	ALBANY & NORTHERN RAILWAY
A&NC	ATLANTIC & NORTH CAROLINA RAILROAD
A&NR	ANGELINA & NECHES RIVER RAILROAD
A&NW	AUSTIN & NORTHWESTERN
A&O	ARKANSAS & OZARKS RAILROAD
A&P	ALHAMBRA & PASADENA
A&PA	ATLANTIC & PACIFIC
A&R	ABERDEEN & ROCKFISH RAILROAD
A&ROC	AUBURN & ROCHESTER
A&RS	AMSTERDAM & ROCTON STREET RAILWAY
A&S	ALTON & SOUTHERN RAILROAD
A&S.	ALTON & SOUTHERN RAILWAY
A&SB	ATLANTIC & SUBURBAN RAILWAY
A&SCH	ALBANY & SCHENECTADY RAILROAD COMPANY
A&SE	AUBURN & SYRACUSE ELECTRIC
A&SL	ATLANTIC & ST LAWRENCE
A&SM	ALAMOGORDO & SACREMENTO MOUNTIAN RR CO
A&SM.	ALAMOGORDO & SACREMENTO MOUNTIAN RY
A&SMT	ALAMOGORDO & SACREMENTO MOUNTAIN RY
A&SMT.	ALAMOGORDO & SACREMENTO MOUNTAIN RR
A&SN	ALAMOGORDO & SACREMENTO MOUNTAIN (O)
A&SO	ABILENE & SOUTHERN RAILWAY
A&SRR	AUGUSTA & SUMMERVILLE RAILROAD
A&SS	ALLEGHENY & SOUTH SIDE RAILWAY
A&SSRY	ALLENTOWN & SLATINGTON STREET RY CO
A&STAB	ATLANTA & ST ANDREWS BAY RAILWAY
A&STAB.	BAY LINE
A&STL	ADIRONDACK & ST LAWRENCE
A&SU	ALBANY & SUSQUEHANNA RAILROAD
A&SY	ALBANY & SYRACUSE RAILROAD
A&SYR	AUBURN & SYRACUSE
A&T	ATCHISON & TOPEKA
A&U	ARIZONA & UTAH
A&V	ALABAMA & VICKSBURG
A&W	AHNAPEE & WESTERN RAILWAY
A&WE	ATLANTIC & WESTERN RAILWAY
A&WF	ALABAMA & WESTERN FLORIDA
A&WP	ATLANTA & WEST POINT RAILROAD
A&WRY	ARKANSAS & WESTERN RAILWAY
A&WS	ALBANY & W. STOCKBRIDGE
A&Y	ATLANTIC & YADKIN
A*	ARMOUR

A34

APPENDIX A (RAILROADS)

A	ABBREVIATIONS ALPHABETICALLY W/ROADS
AA	ANN ARBOR RAILROAD
AAR	ASSOCIATION OF AMERICAN RAILROADS
AB	ALAMEDA BELT LINE
AB&A	ATLANTA BIRMINGHAM & ATLANTIC
AB&C	ATLANTA BIRMINGHAM & COAST RAILROAD
AB&CL	AKRON BEDFORD & CLEVELAND
AB&CO.	ATLANTA BIRMINGHAM & COAST (O)
AB&NW	ABERDEEN BISMARCK & NORTHWESTERN
AB-P	ALABAMA BY-PRODUCTS
ABELT	ASPHALT BELT
ABI	ABILENE STREET RAILWAY COMPANY
ABIT	ABITIBI PULP & PAPER COMPANY
ABP	ABERDEEN & BRIAR PATCH
ABS	ABBEVILLE SOUTHERN
ABSO	ABITIBI SOUTHERN
AC	ALLEGHENY CENTRAL
AC&HB	ALGOMA CENTRAL & HUDSON BAY RAILWAY
AC&I	ASHLAND COAL & IRON
AC&S	ATLANTIC CITY & SHORE
AC&ST	ATLANTIC CITY & SUBURBAN TRACTION CO
AC&Y	AKRON CANTON & YOUNGSTOWN RAILWAY
AC&Y	AKRON CANTON & YOUNGSTOWN RAILROAD
ACBL	AMERICAN COMMERCIAL BARGE LINES
ACBM	ALLIED CHEMICAL (BRUNNER MOND)
ACC	AMERICAN CAN COMPANY
ACE	ATLANTIC COAST ELECTRIC RAILWAY
ACH	ARMCO CHEMICAL COMPANY
ACIP	AMERICAN CAST IRON PIPE
ACJ&IR	ATLANTIC COAST ST JOHNS & INDIAN RIV
ACL	ATLANTIC COAST LINE
ACLC	ATLANTIC COAST LINE OF SOUTH CAROLINA
ACLV	ATLANTIC COAST LINE RR CO OF VIRGINIA
ACR	AUSTIN CITY RAILROAD (RAILWAY?)
ACRR	ATLANTIC CITY RAILROAD
ACRS	AMARILLO STREET RAILWAY COMPANY
ACS	AMERICAN COMPRESSED STEEL
ACSR	ATLANTA CITY STREET RAILWAY
ACSRY	ATLANTA CONSOLIDATED STREET RAILWAY
ACT	ATLANTIC CITY TRANSPORTATION
ACY	AMERICAN CYANAMID COMPANY
AD&N	ASHLEY DREW & NORTHERN RAILWAY
AD&S	ALABAMA DRYDOCK & SHIPBUILDING
AD&SL	ADIRONDACK & ST LOUIS
ADD	ADDISON RAILROAD
ADIR	ADIRONDACK RAILROAD
AE	ARIZONA EASTERN RAILWAY
AE&FR	AURORA ELGIN & FOX RIVER ELECTRIC
AE&FRE	AURORA ELGIN & FOX RIVER ELECTRIC (O)
AEA	ALBUQUERQUE EASTERN
AF	ANGEL'S FLIGHT RAILWAY
AF&A	ALABAMA FLORIDA & ATLANTIC
AF&N	ALBANY FLORIDA & NORTHERN RAILWAY
AFR	AUSTRIAN FEDERAL RAILWAY
AG	AMERICAN GRAINS
AG&WIT	ATLANTIC GULF & WEST INDIES TRANSIT
AG*	AGAR
AGC	ALABAMA GREAT SOUTHERN
AGR	AGRICO CHEMICAL (PIERCE PLANT)
AHRB	ATL HIGHLANDS RED BANK & L BR ELEC
AI	AMHERST INDUSTRIES
AJ	ARTEMUS-JELLICO
AJ&N	ALTOONA JUNIATA & NORTHERN
AK&MO	ARKANSAS & MISSOURI
AK&N	ATLANTIC KNOXVILLE & NORTHERN
AKAC	ALASKA ANTHRACITE RAILROAD
AL	ALASKA RAILROAD
AL&H	ALEXANDRIA LONDON & HAMPSHIRE
AL&S	ALIQUIPPA & SOUTHERN RAILROAD
AL&SA	ALTON & SANGAMON
AL&SE	ALBION & SOUTHEASTERN
AL&SL	ALFRED & SLOAN
AL&T	ARIZONA LUMBER & TIMBER COMPANY
AL&W	ALLEGHENY & WESTERN
ALB	ALBANY RAILWAY
ALB&C	ALABAMA BIRMINGHAM & COAST
ALBP	ALBERNI PACIFIC LUMBER COMPANY
ALBS	ALBANY STREET RAILWAY

A	ABBREVIATIONS ALPHABETICALLY W/ROADS
ALC	ALABAMA CENTRAL RAILROAD
ALC*	ALCOA
ALCA	ALCAN
ALEX	ALEXANDER RAILROAD
ALG	ALGOMA
ALGC	ALGOMA CENTRAL RAILWAY
ALGE	ALGOMA EASTERN RAILWAY
ALL	ALLIED CHEMICAL (SOLVAY)
ALLEN	ALLENTOWN
ALM	ALMANOR RAILROAD
ALT	ALTADENA
ALTA	ALTA
ALV	ALLEGHENY VALLEY RAILROAD
ALY	ALLEGHENY RAILROAD
AM	ALBION MINES
AM&O	ATLANTIC MISSISSIPPI & OHIO
AMC	AMADOR CENTRAL RAILROAD
AME	ASARCO MEXICANA
AMID	ALABAMA MIDLAND
AMO	AMOSKEAG MANUFACTURING COMPANY
AMRL	AMERICAN REDWOOD LUMBER
AMS	AMALGAMATED SUGAR
AN	APALACHICOLA NORTHERN RAILROAD
AN&W	ANTELOPE & WESTERN
ANAL	ANACONDA ALUMINUM
AND	ANDROSCOGGIN RAILROAD
AND&K	ANDROSCOGGIN & KENNEBEC
ANG	ANGELINA LUMBER COMPANY
ANO	ALTOONA NORTHERN
ANTV	ANTOINE VALLEY
AO	ALUMINUM ORE COMPANY
AOC	ALCOA ORE COMPANY
AOW*	ARTIC OIL WORKS
AP	ALLEGHENY PORTAGE
AP&C	AMERICAN PIPE & CONSTRUCTION
AP&J	AURORA PLAINFIELD & JOLIET
APA	APACHE RAILWAY
APC	ALABAMA POWER COMPANY
APDT	ALBANY PORT DISTRICT TERMINAL
APO	APPALACHIAN POWER COMPANY
APP	APPOMATTOX
APRY	ATLANTIC PORT RAILWAY
APSM	AGUA PRIETA SONORA MEXICO PACIFIC RY
APT	ALBANY PASSENGER TERMINAL
AQ	ANNA QUARRIES
AQU	AQUITAINE
AR	ALBERTA RESOURCES RAILWAY
AR&N	ACME RED RIVER & NORTHERN
AR&S	ARIZONA & SOUTHEASTERN
ARC	ARGENTINE CENTRAL
ARCT	ARCATA TRANSPORTATION COMPANY
ARI	ARIZONA CENTRAL RAILROAD
ARL	ARGENT LUMBER
ARN	ARNAUD
ARR	ALTON RAILROAD (B&O)
ART	AMERICAN REFRIGERATED TRANSIT
ART*	AMERICAN REFRIGERATED TRANSIT
AS	ARMCO STEEL
ASDT	ALABAMA STATE DOCKS TERMINAL
ASH	ASHBURNAM
ASH&W	ASHLAND & WESTERN
ASHL	ATLANTIC SHORE LINE RAILWAY
ASL	ANNAPOLIS SHORT LINE
ASM&L	ATLANTA STONE MOUNTAIN & LITHONIA RY
ASM&N	AUGUSTA SAVANNAH MACON & NORTHERN
ASO	ARIZONA SOUTHERN
ASR&G	ATLANTIC SUWANEE RIVER & GULF
ASRY	ANACONDA STREET RAILWAY (MONTANA)
AT	ALCOA TERMINAL
AT&F	ATTICA & FREEDOM RAILROAD
AT&N	ALABAMA TENNESSEE & NORTHERN RAILROAD
AT&SO	ATTICA & SOUTHERN
AT&T	AUGUSTA TRAMWAY & TRANSFER
ATC	ATLANTA TERMINAL COMPANY
ATKC	ATKINSON CONSTRUCTION COMPANY
ATN	ATLANTIC NORTHERN
ATNO	ATLANTA NORTHERN

A35

APPENDIX A (RAILROADS)

A	ABBREVIATIONS ALPHABETICALLY W/ROADS
ATR	AUTO TRAIN
ATS	ATLANTIC STEEL COMPANY
ATSF	ATCHISON TOPEKA & SANTA FE RAILWAY
AU	AUGUSTA RAILROAD
AUB	AUBURN BRANCH
AUPD	AKRON UNION PASSENGER DEOPT
AUR	AURORA BRANCH
AUS	AUGUSTA SOUTHERN
AUSC	AUGUSTA UNION STATION COMPANY
AV	AROOSTOOK VALLEY RAILROAD
AV&SB	ASHEVILLE & SPARTANBURG
AVI	ARKANSAS VALLEY INTERURBAN RAILWAY
AVOY	AVOYELLES RAILROAD
AVS	AVONDALE SHIPYARDS
AW	ARKANSAS WESTERN RAILWAY
AW&B	ANNAPOLIS WASHINGTON & BALTIMORE
AW&G	AUGUSTA WATERVILLE & GARDINER
AW&H	ALTUS WICHITA & HOLLIS
AW&W	ALGIERS WINSLOW & WESTERN RAILWAY
AY&C	AKRON YOUNGSTOWN & CINCINNATI
AZ	AZUSA LINE
B	BURLINGTON (0)
B&A	BOSTON & ALBANY
B&AGA	BOSTON & ALBANY RAILROAD OF GEORGIA
B&AL	BARTLETT & ALBANY
B&AN	BALTIMORE & ANNAPOLIS RAILROAD
B&AR	BANGOR & AROOSTOOK (0)
B&ASL	BALTIMORE & ANNAPOLIS SHORT LINE
B&AT	BIRMINGHAM & ATLANTIC
B&B	BELMONT & BUFFALO
B&BE	BERLIN & BRIDGEPORT ELECTRIC ST RY
B&BED	BULERICA & BEDFORD
B&BI	BEDFORD & BILLERICA RAILROAD
B&BL	BEDFORD & BLOOMFIELD RAILROAD
B&C	BELLEVUE & CASCADE
B&CH	BARRE & CHELSEA RAILROAD
B&CV	BALTIMORE & CUMBERLAND VALLEY
B&D	BORATE & DAGGETT RAILROAD
B&E	BALTIMORE & EASTERN RAILROAD
B&EA	BURNSVILLE & EASTERN
B&ERIE	BUFFALO & ERIE RAILWAY COMPANY
B&FB	BRADFORD & FOSTER BROOK RAILWAY
B&FJ	BRILLION & FOREST JUNCTION
B&G	BENNINGTON & GLASTENBURY
B&GA	BINGHAM & GARFIELD RAILWAY COMPANY
B&GN	BEAUMONT & GREAT NORTHERN
B&GR	BIRMINGHAM & GULF RY & NAVIGATION CO
B&H	BRIDGTON & HARRISON RAILWAY
B&HA	BATH & HAMMONDSPORT RAILROAD
B&HB	BALTIMORE & HARRISBURG
B&HBE	BALTIMORE & HARRISBURG RY EXTENSION
B&HE	BALTIMORE & HAMPDEN ELECTRIC
B&HS	BONHOMIE & HATTIESBURG SOUTHERN RR
B&HWE	BALTIMORE & HARRISBURG RY WESTERN EXT
B&I	BLAIRSVILLE & INDIANA
B&IRY	BOISE & INTERURBAN RAILWAY
B&K	BANGOR & KATAHDIN IRON WORKS
B&KE	BAKERSFIELD & KERN ELECTRIC
B&L	BOSTON & LOWELL RAILROAD
B&LAM	BURLINGTON & LAMOILLE VALLEY
B&LAMV	BURLINGTON & LAMOILLE VALLEY (0)
B&LE	BESSEMER & LAKE ERIE RAILROAD
B&LEH	BALTIMORE & LEHIGH RAILROAD
B&LEH.	BALTIMORE & LEHIGH RAILWAY
B&LET	BUFFALO & LAKE ERIE TRACTION
B&LH	BUFFALO & LAKE HURON RAILWAY
B&M	BOSTON & MAINE
B&MA	BROOKVILLE & MAHONING
B&MH	BURLINGTON & MT HOLLY
B&MI	BURLINGTON & MISSOURI
B&ML	BELFAST & MOOSEHEAD LAKE RAILROAD
B&MR	BURLINGTON & MISSOURI RIVER RAILROAD
B&N	BAUXITE & NORTHERN RAILWAY
B&NE	BALTIMORE & NORTHERN ELECTRIC RY
B&NM	BRAINERD & NORTHERN MINNESOTA
B&NO	BERLIN & NORTHERN RAILWAY
B&NSR	BOSTON & NORTHERN STREET RAILWAY
B&NW	BRISTOL & NORTH WESTERN
B&NY	BOSTON & NEW YORK AIR LINE
B&O	BALTIMORE & OHIO RAILROAD
B&O&C	BALTIMORE & OHIO & CHICAGO
B&OCT	BALTIMORE & OHIO CHICAGO TERMINAL RR
B&OHT	BALTIMORE & OHIO TERMINAL RAILROAD
B&OSW	BALTIMORE & OHIO SOUTHWESTERN RY
B&OSW.	BALTIMORE & OHIO SOUTHWESTERN RR
B&OT	BROCKVILLE & OTTAWA
B&P	BOSTON & PROVIDENCE
B&PI	BANGOR & PISCATAQUIS
B&PIC	BANGOR & PISCATAQUIS CANAL
B&PITT	BUTLER & PITTSBURGH
B&PO	BROCKINGS & PEACH ORCHARD
B&POT	BALTIMORE & POTOMAC
B&Q	BROOKLYN & QUEENS TRANSIT
B&R	BENNINGTON & RUTLAND
B&RB	BROOKLYN & ROCKAWAY BEACH
B&ROCH	BUFFALO & ROCHESTER RAILROAD
B&S	BEVIER & SOUTHERN RAILROAD
B&SM	BUFFALO & ST MARYS
B&SQ	BUFFALO & SUSQUEHANNA RAILROAD
B&SQ.	BUFFALO & SUSQUEHANNA RAILWAY
B&SQU	BUFFALO & SUSQUEHANNA (0)
B&SR	BRIDGTON & SACO RIVER RAILROAD
B&SU	BLOOMSBURG & SULLIVAN
B&SW	BELLAIRE & SOUTHWESTERN
B&T	BARNES & TUCKER COAL COMPANY
B&TRR	BOSTON & THOMPSON RAILROAD
B&W	BRATTLEBORO & WHITEHALL
B&WE	BARTLETT & WESTERN
B&WEL	BENNINGTON & WOODFORD ELECTRIC RY
B&WI	BABCOCK & WILCOX
B&WO	BOSTON & WORCESTER RAILROAD
B&WP	BRADFORD & WESTERN PENNSYLVANIA
B*	BECCO
B-K	BLAW-KNOX CORPORATION-UNION STEEL DIV
B-KE	BENTLY-KNIGHT ELECTRIC RAILWAY SYSTEM
BA&A	BUFFALO ATTICA & ARCADE RAILROAD
BA&H	BATH & HAMMONDSPORT (0)
BA&P	BUTTE ANACONDA & PACIFIC RAILWAY
BA&PI	BUFFALO ALLEGHENY & PITTSBURG
BALT	BALTIMORE TRANSIT COMPANY
BAM	BAMBERGER RAILROAD
BAR	BANGOR & AROOSTOOK
BARN	BARNEGAT RAILROAD
BART	BAY AREA RAPID TRANSIT
BAS	BASIC REFRACTORIES
BAYT	BAY TERMINAL
BB	BURNS BIGGS LUMBER COMPANY
BB&BC	BELLINGHAM BAY & BRITISH COLUMBIA RY
BB&CI	BROOKLYN BATH & CONEY ISLAND RAILROAD
BB&G	BOSTON BARRE & GARDNER
BB&K	BRADFORD BORDELL & KINZUA
BB&P	BUFFALO BRADFORD & PITTSBURGH
BB&S	BRADFORD BORDELL & SMETHPORT
BB&WE	BROOKLYN BATH & WEST END
BBB&C	BUFFALO BAYO BRAZOS & COLORADO RY
BBELT	BALTIMORE BELT RAILROAD COMPANY
BBER	BRIGANTINE BEACH RAILROAD
BBLR	BRISTOL BELT LINE RAILWAY COMPANY
BBP	BELLEFIELD BOILER PLANT
BBRR	BIRMINGHAM BELT RAILROAD
BBRY	BOYTON BICYCLE RAILWAY
BC	BEECH CREEK RAILWAY
BC&A	BALTIMORE CHESAPEAKE & ATLANTIC
BC&F	BOSTON CLINTON & FITCHBURG
BC&FR	BALTIMORE CARROLL & FREDERICK
BC&G	BUFFALO CREEK & GAULEY RAILROAD
BC&M	BOSTON CONCORD & MONTREAL RAILROAD
BC&N	BROOKLYN CITY & NEWTON RAILROAD CO
BC&P	BUFFALO CORREY & PITTSBURGH
BC&S	BATTLE CREEK & STURGES RAILWAY CO
BC&SA	BIRMINGHAM COLUMBUS & ST ANDREWS
BC&T	BIG CREEK & TELOCASET RAILROAD
BCC&S	BEECH CREEK CLEARFIELD & SOUTHWESTERN
BCE	BRITISH COLUMBIA ELECTRIC RAILWAY

STEPHANS' RAILROAD DIRECTORY

APPENDIX A (RAILROADS)

A	ABBREVIATIONS ALPHABETICALLY W/ROADS	A	ABBREVIATIONS ALPHABETICALLY W/ROADS
BCES	BLUFF CITY ELECTRIC STREET RY CO	BL&K	BIG LEVEL & KINZUA RAILROAD
BCF&NB	BOSTON CLINTON FITCHBURG & NEW BEDFORD	BL&L	BAGDAD LAND & LUMBER COMPANY
BCG&A	BOYNE CITY GAYLORD & ALPENA RAILROAD	BL&N	BOSTON LOWELL & NASHUA
BCH&P	BRITISH COLUMBIA HYDRO & POWER AUTHOR	BL&R	BUFFALO LOCKPORT & ROCHESTER
BCL&P	BUFFALO CHAUTAUQUA LAKE & PITTSBURGH	BL&S	BLOOMSBURG & SOUTHERN
BCO	BAY COLONY	BL&YC	BLACK LICK & YELLOW CREEK RAILROAD
BCPA	BROWARD COUNTY PORT AUTHORITY	BL*	BLATZ
BCPR	BALTIMORE CITY PASSENGER RAILWAY	BLE&C	BUFFALO LAKE ERIE & CLEVELAND
BCR	BUFFALO CREEK RAILROAD	BLISS	BLISSFIELD RAILROAD
BCR&M	BURLINGTON CEDAR RAPIDS & MINNESOTA	BLRR	BLOOMER RAILROAD
BCR&N	BURLINGTON CEDAR RAPIDS & NORTHERN	BLW	BALDWIN LOCOMOTIVE WORKS
BCRR	BROOKLYN CITY RAILROAD COMPANY	BM	BEAVER MEADOW RAILROAD
BCRW	BRITISH COLUMBIA RAILWAY	BM&A	BRUCE MINES & ALGONQUIN
BCRY	BRITISH COLUMBIA YUKON RAILWAY	BM&E	BEAVER MEADE & ENGLEWOOD RAILROAD
BCSR	BUCKEYE CENTRAL SCENIC RAILROAD	BM&LP	BLACK MESA & LAKE POWELL RAILROAD
BD	BELVIDERE-DELAWARE RAILROAD	BM&R	BLUE MOUNTAIN & READING
BDAM	BEAVER DAM RAILWAY	BM&S	BUFFALO ST MARYS & SOUTHWESTERN
BDC	BOSQUES DE CHIHUAHUA	BMC	BOSTON METALS COMPANY
BDL*	BUDLONG	BMT	BLACK MOUNTAIN RAILROAD
BDLM	BLOEDALL-DONOVAN LUMBER MILLS	BMT&NB	BEAVER MEADOW TRESKOW & NEW BOSTON RR
BDN&M	BAY DE NOQUET & MARQUETTE	BMTC	BROOKLYN MANHATTAN TRANSIT COMPANY
BDTP*	BOURK DONALDSON TAYLOR POTATOES	BN	BURLINGTON NORTHERN
BE	BAMBERGER ELECTRIC	BN&NL	BOSTON NORWICH & NEW LONDON
BE&C	BRADFORD ELDRED & CUBA	BN(M)	BURLINGTON NORTHERN (MANITOBA) LTD
BE&CH	BENNETSVILLE & CHERAW RAILROAD	BNY	BROOKLYN NAVY YARD
BE&M	BEAUFORT & MOREHEAD RAILROAD	BO&W	BONLEE & WESTERN
BE&NC	BRISTOL ELIZABETHTON & NORTH CAROLINA	BOD&B	BODIE & BENTON RAILWAY
BE&W	BAMBERG ERHART & WALTERBORO RAILROAD	BODRL	BODIE RAILWAY & LUMBER COMPANY
BEAR	BEAR CREEK RAILROAD	BOE	BOEING RAILROAD
BEB*	BERKSHIRE BACON	BOH*	BLATZ OLD HEIDELBERG
BEC	BELLEFONTE CENTRAL RAILROAD	BOI&W	BOISE & WESTERN
BED	BEDFORD RAILROAD	BOM	BOMBARDIER
BEDB	BEDFORD BELT RAILWAY	BORC	BORDEN CHEMICAL
BEDT	BROOKLYN EASTERN DISTRICT TERMINAL	BORK	BORK COMPANY
BEEC	BEACH MOUNTAIN RAILROAD	BOT&M	BANGOR OLD TOWN & MILFORD
BEEC.	BEECH MOUNTAIN RAILROAD	BOW	BOWDON RAILWAY & TRANSPORTATION CO
BEL	BELLEFONTAINE	BOYN	BOYNE CITY RAILROAD
BELL	BOSTON ELEVATED LINES	BP	BREWSTER PHOSPHATE
BELL.	BOSTON ELEVATED RAILWAY	BP&C	BALTIMORE PITTSBURGH & CHICAGO
BELT	BELTON RAILROAD	BP&CT	BAY POINT & CLAYTON RAILROAD
BEM	BEMIS LUMBER COMPANY	BP&N	BEAVER PENROSE & NORTHERN
BEN	BENSON	BR	BLUE RIDGE RAILWAY
BERR	BROOKLYN ELEVATED RAILROAD	BR&A	BLUE RIDGE & ATLANTIC RAILROAD
BERS	BERKSHIRE STREET RAILWAY	BR&B	BRUNSWICK & BIRMINGHAM
BERY	BRANFORD ELECTIRC RAILWAY	BR&C	BRADFORD RICHBURG & CUBA
BESS	BESSEMER	BR&D	BRIDGTON RAILROAD & DEVELOPMENT
BETH	BETHLEHEM MINES	BR&E	BANGOR RAILWAY & ELECTRIC COMPANY
BF&N	BIG FORK & NORTHERN	BR&H	BROOKSVILLE & HUDSON
BFB*	BULL FROG BEER	BR&L	BIRMINGHAM RAIL & LOCO COMPANY
BFGR	BF GOODRICH	BR&M	BROWNSTONE & MIDDLETOWN
BFR	BIG FOUR ROUTE	BR&N	BRISTOL & NORFOLK STREET RAILWAY
BG	BULLFROG GOLDFIELD RAILROAD	BR&P	BUFFALO ROCHESTER & PITTSBURG RAILWAY
BGRR	BELL'S GAP RAILROAD	BR&PA	BUFFALO ROCHESTER & PACIFIC
BH	BRIGHT HOPE	BR&U	BLACK RIVER & UTICA RAILROAD
BH&E	BOSTON HARTFORD & ERIE	BR&W	BLACK RIVER & WESTERN RAILROAD
BH&FP	BLACK HILLS & FORT PIERRE	BR&WE	BRUNSWICK & WESTERN
BH&SM&C	BUNKER HILL & SULLIVAN MINE & COAL CO	BR*	BABY RUTH
BHC	BLACK HILLS CENTRAL RAILROAD	BRAD	BRADFORD STEAM RAILROAD
BHL	BIG HORN LUMBER COMPANY	BRAR	BRANFORD RAILROAD
BHRR	BROOKLYN HEIGHTS RAILROAD	BRB&BE	BUFFALO RUN BELLEFONTE & BALD EAGLE RR
BHS	BIRDS HILL SAND COMPANY	BRB&L	BOSTON REVERE BEACH & LYNN
BHT&W	BOSTON HOOSAC TUNNEL & WESTERN	BRC	BELT RAILWAY COMPANY OF CHICAGO
BI	BARTLESVILLE INTERURBAN	BRE	BURLINGTON REFRIGERATOR EXPRESS
BI&B	BILLERICA & BEDFORD RAILROAD	BREP	BREWSTER PHOSPHATES
BI&S	BIRMINGHAM & SOUTHEASTERN RAILROAD	BRI	BRIMSTONE RAILROAD
BI&SM	BILLMEYER & SMALL'S	BRID	BRIDGEPORT TRAMWAY
BID&S	BIDDEFORD & SACO	BRIGB	BRIGANTINE BECAH RAILROAD
BILT	BILLINGS TRACTION	BRIN	BRINSON RAILWAY
BING	BINGHAMTON	BRIS	BRISTOL RAILROAD
BIR	BIRMINGHAM ELECTRIC COMPANY	BRLC	BIG RIVER LUMBER COMPANY
BIRM	BIRMINGHAM TERMINAL COMPANY	BRMT	BRADSHAW MOUNTAIN
BIRT	BIRMINGHAM TRANSIT COMPANY	BRO	BROWN COUNTY
BIS	BIRMINGHAM SOUTHERN RAILROAD	BRR	BOISE RAILROAD
BKL	BOOTH KELLY LUMBER COMPANY	BRRR	BRANDON RAILROAD
BKRR	BATTEN KILL RAILROAD	BRRT	BROOKLYN RAPID TRANSIT
BL	BLAIRSTOWN RAILWAY	BRT	BOSTON RAPID TRANSIT
BL&E	BEAR LAKE & EASTERN	BRTE	BROOKLYN RAPID TRANSIT ELEVATED CO.

APPENDIX A (RAILROADS)

A	ABBREVIATIONS ALPHABETICALLY W/ROADS
BRTS	BROOKLYN RAPID TRANSIT SUBWAY LINES
BRW	BRITISH RAILWAYS
BS	BOSTON SUBWAY
BS&G	BRASWELL SAND & GRAVEL
BS&GR	BECKER SAND & GRAVEL
BS&W	BLOEDEL STEWART & WELSH LTD
BS&WA	BUFFALO SUSQUEHANNA & WESTRN ALLEGHENY
BS*	BAY SOL
BSC	BUCKEYE STEEL CASTINGS COMPANY
BSL	BIRMINGHAM SLAG
BSL&PA	BEAUMONT SOUR LAKE & PORT ARTHUR TRAC
BSL&W	BEAUMONT SOUR LAKE & WESTERN
BSOC&A	BLUE SPRINGS ORANGE CITY & ATLANTIC
BSRR	BRANFORD STEAM RAILROAD
BSRY	BERLIN STREET RAILWAY
BSS	BAY STATE STREET RAILWAY
BT	BRISTOL TRACTION
BT&P	BIG TREES & PACIFIC
BTC	BRUNSWICK TRACTION COMPANY
BTR&U	BIRMINGHAM-TUSCALOOSA RY & UTILITIES
BTRR	BALLSTON TERMINAL RAILROAD
BU&BA	BUCKSPORT & BANGOR
BU&NW	BURLINGTON & NORTHWESTERN
BU&W	BURLINGTON & WESTERN
BUC	BUFFALO UNION CAROLINA RAILROAD
BUCK	BUCK MOUNTAIN
BUCK&N	BUCKHANNON & NORTHERN
BUF&G	BUFFALO & GENEVA RAILROAD
BUF&L	BUFFALO & LOCKPORT
BUI	BUICK
BUR	BURLINGTON ELECTRIC
BURI	BURLINGTON-ROCK ISLAND
BUSC	BUFFALO SLAG COMPANY
BUSH	BUSH TERMINAL RAILROAD
BUT	BUFFALO TERMINAL
BUTCO	BUTLER COUNTY RAILROAD
BVRR	BRANDYWINE VALLEY RAILROAD
BVRY	BOISE VALLEY RAILWAY
BW	BARTLETT WESTERN
BW&GF	BISMARCK WASHBURN & GREAT FALLS
BW&LE	BRANTFORD WATERLOO & LAKE ERIE RAILWAY
BW&PS	BOSTON WINTHROP & POINT SHIRLEY
BW&S	BOSTON WINTHROP & SHORE RAILROAD
BWC	BERWIND WHITE COAL MINING COMPANY
BWP	BRODERICK WOOD PRODUCTS
BWT	BRANDYWINE TRANSIT
BYNC	BRITISH YUKON NAVIGATION COMPANY
BYRY	BRITISH YUKON RAILWAY
BZ&C	BELLAIRE ZANESVILLE & CINCINNATI RR
C	CANTON RAILROAD
C&A	CHICAGO & ALTON RAILROAD
C&AD	CARTHAGE & ADIRONDACK
C&AL	CHICAGO & AIR LINE
C&AM	CAMDEN & AMBOY RAILROAD
C&AT	CAMDEN & ATLANTIC RAILROAD
C&AU	CHICAGO & AURORA
C&B	CHESTER & BECKET RAILROAD
C&BC	CHICAGO & BLOCK COAL
C&BCO	CAMDEN & BURLINGTON COUNTY
C&BL	CONEMAUGH & BLACK LICK RAILROAD
C&C	CANTON & CARTHAGE
C&CA	CANAJOHARIE & CATSKILL RAILROAD
C&CF	CLEVELAND & CHAGRIN FALLS RAILWAY
C&CFE	CLEVELAND & CHAGRIN FALLS ELECTRIC RY
C&CI	CINCINNATI ATLANTIC & COLUMBUS
C&CIN	COVINGTON & CINCINNATI

A	ABBREVIATIONS ALPHABETICALLY W/ROADS
C&CL	CONCORD & CLAREMONT
C&CO	CARLTON & COAST
C&CON	CHAMPLAIN & CONNECTICUT RAILROAD
C&CR	CHICAGO & CALUMET RIVER RAILWAY
C&CRY	CHERAW & CHESTER RAILWAY
C&CSP	CARSON & COLORADO SOUTHERN PACIFIC
C&CT	CHICAGO & CALUMET TERMINAL RAILWAY
C&CV	COOPERSTOWN & CHARLOTTE VALLEY RY
C&E	CASSVILLE & EXETER RAILWAY (MISSOURI)
C&EE	CLEVELAND & EASTERN ELECTRIC RAILWAY
C&EI	CHICAGO & EASTERN ILLINOIS RAILROAD
C&EI	CHICAGO & EASTERN ILLINOIS RAILWAY
C&EP	CHATTAHOOCHEE & EAST PASS
C&EST	COLORADO & EASTERN
C&ET	CLEVELAND & EASTERN TRACTION COMPANY
C&F	CAIRO & FULTON RAILROAD
C&FOG	CATASAUQUA & FOGELSVILLE
C&G	CARILLON & GRENVILLE
C&GA	CHICAGO & GALENA
C&GL	COLLINS & GLENNVILLE
C&GR	COLUMBUS & GREENVILLE RAILWAY
C&GS	CHICAGO & GREAT SOUTHERN
C&GT	CANADA & GULF TERMINAL RAILWAY
C&GU	CHATTAHOOCEE & GULF
C&H	CHESWICK & HARMAR RAILROAD
C&HB	CHARLESTON & HAMBURG RAILROAD
C&HC	CALUMET & HECLA CONSOLIDATED COPPER
C&I	CAMBRIA & INDIANA RAILROAD
C&IAL	CHICAGO & INDIANAPOLIS AIR LINE RY
C&IC	CHICAGO & INDIANA COAL RAILWAY
C&IM	CHICAGO & ILLINOIS MIDLAND RAILWAY
C&IR	COAL & IRON
C&IT	CHICAGO & INDIANAPOLIS TERMINAL CO
C&ITR	CHICAGO & INTERURBAN TRACTION CO
C&IW	CHICAGO & ILLINOIS WESTERN RAILROAD
C&J	CHICAGO & JOLIET
C&KV	CAIRO & KANAWANHA VALLEY RAILROAD
C&L	COLUSA & LAKE RAILROAD
C&LC	CADILLAC & LAKE CITY RAILWAY
C&LE	CINCINNATI & LAKE ERIE RAILROAD
C&LV	CHATHAM & LEBANON VALLEY RAILROAD
C&M	CUMBERLAND & MANCHESTER RAILROAD
C&MC	CHARLEVOIX & MICHIGAN CENTRAL
C&ME	CHICAGO & MILWAUKEE ELECTRIC RAILWAY
C&MH	CORNWALL & MT HOPE
C&MI	COLUMBIA & MILLSTADT RAILROAD
C&MO	CONCORD & MONTREAL
C&MRY	CODY & MOORE RAILWAY
C&MV	CINCINNATI & MUSKINGUM VALLEY
C&N	CAROLINA & NORTHWESTERN RAILWAY
C&NE	CISCO & NORTHEASTERN RAILWAY
C&ND	CALDOR & NORTHERN
C&NP	CHICAGO & NORTHERN PACIFIC
C&NRR	CLEVELAND & NEWBURGH RAILROAD
C&NW	CHICAGO & NORTH WESTERN RAILWAY
C&NWB	CHICAGO & NORTHWESTERN BELT
C&NWT	COLORADO & NORTHWESTERN
C&O	CHESAPEAKE & OHIO RAILROAD
C&O.	CHESAPEAKE & OHIO RAILWAY
C&OC	CALIFORNIA & OREGON COAST
C&OG	CHAMPLAIN & OGDENSBURG RAILROAD
C&OW	CLINTON & OKLAHOMA WESTERN
C&P	COBOURG & PETERBOROUGH
C&PA	COUDERSPORT & PORT ALLEGHENY RAILROAD
C&PE	CUMBERLAND & PENNSYLVANIA RAILROAD
C&PI	CLAREDON & PITTSFORD RAILROAD
C&PM	CLAIBORNE & POLK MILITARY RAILROAD
C&PR	CONNECTICUT & PASSUMPSIC RIVERS
C&PS	COLUMBIA & PUGET SOUND RAILROAD
C&R	COLLINS & REIDSVILLE
C&RB	CANARISE & ROCKAWAY BEACH
C&RBV	COMMERCIAL & RR BANK OF VICKSBURG
C&RI	CHICAGO & ROCK ISLAND
C&RO	COLUMBUS & ROME RAILROAD
C&S	COLORADO & SOUTHERN RAILWAY
C&SE	CHICAGO & SOUTHEASTERN RAILWAY
C&SL	CHAMPLAIN & ST LAWRENCE

STEPHANS' RAILROAD DIRECTORY

A38

APPENDIX A (RAILROADS)

A	ABBREVIATIONS ALPHABETICALLY W/ROADS
C&SO	CATHELS & SORENSON
C&SOE	COLUMBUS & SOUTHERN OHIO ELECTRIC CO
C&SR	CITY & SUBURBAN RAILWAY
C&SSRT	CHICAGO & SOUTH SIDE RAPID TRANSIT
C&STL	CANADA & ST LOUIS RAILWAY CO
C&SU	CAYUGA & SUSQUEHANNA RAILROAD
C&SW	CLEVELAND & SOUTHWESTERN RAILWAY
C&SWT	CLEVELAND & SOUTHWESTERN TRACTION CO
C&T	CHUMBRES & TOLRIC SCENIC RAILROAD
C&TA	CATSKILL & TANNERSVILLE RAILROAD
C&TOL	CLEVELAND & TOLEDO
C&TOM	CHICAGO & TOMAH
C&TR	CAMDEN & TRENTON RAILWAY
C&TS	CUMBRES & TOLEC SCENIC RAILROAD
C&V	CLINTON & VICKSBURG
C&W	CHESAPEAKE & WESTERN RAILROAD
C&WC	CHARLESTON & WESTERN CAROLINA RAILWAY
C&WE	CUMBERLAND & WESTERNPORT ELECTRIC
C&WI	CHICAGO & WESTERN INDIANA RAILROAD
C&WIB	CHICAGO & WESTERN INDIANA BELT
C&WM	CHICAGO & WEST MICHIGAN RAILS
C&WO	CARROLTON & WORTHVILLE
C&WT	CHICAGO & WEST TOWNS RAILWAY
C&WV	CHICAGO & WABASH VALLEY
C&WW	CINCINNATI & WESTWOOD RAILROAD
C&WY	COLORADO & WYOMING RAILWAY
C&YR	CAROLINA & YADKIN RIVER RAILROAD
C&YR.	CAROLINA & YADKIN RIVER RAILWAY
C&Z	COAHUILA & ZACATECAS RAILWAY
C-P	CHIHUAHUA-PACIFIC (O)
CA	CANADA ATLANTA
CA&C	CARSON & COLORADO RAILROAD
CA&CH	CADDO & CHOCTAW
CA&CH	CATSKILL & CANAJOHARIE
CA&CIN	CLEVELAND AKRON & CINCINNATI RY CO
CA&CL	CANAL & CLAIBORNE RAILROAD
CA&COL	CLEVELAND AKRON & COLUMBUS
CA&E	CHICAGO AURORA & ELGIN RAILROAD
CA&M	CLEVELAND ASHLAND & MANSFIELD RY
CA&N	CALIFORNIA & NEVADA
CA&NE	CADILLAC & NORTHEASTERN
CA&S	CONSOLIDATED CHICAGO ALTONA &SOUTHERN
CA&SE	CALUMET & SOUTHEASTERN
CA&SL	CHICAGO ALTON & ST LOUIS
CA&SO	CHICAGO ATTICA & SOUTHERN
CA&T	CAIRO ARKANSAS & TEXAS
CAC	CANADIAN COLLIERIES LIMITED
CACC	CENTRAL APPALACHIAN COAL COMPANY
CAD	CADIZ RAILROAD
CAI	CAIRO RAILROAD
CAL	CALTRANS
CAL&N	CALIFORNIA & NORTHERN
CALS	CALAIS STREET RAILWAY
CAM	CALIFORNIA MIDLAND RAILROAD
CAN	CANADIAN NORTHERN RAILWAY
CANO	CANASTOTA NORTHERN
CAPA	CALIFORNIA PACIFIC
CAPC	CALCASIEU PAPER COMPANY
CAPR	CAMAS PRAIRIE RAILROAD
CAR	CARGILL INCORPORATED
CAR*	CARNATION
CARB	CARBON COUNTY RAILWAY
CARR	CARROLLTON RAILROAD
CARS	CAROLINA SOUTHERN RAILWAY
CART	CARTIER RAILWAY
CARTH	CARTHAGE ROAD
CARY	CALIFORNIA RAILWAY
CAS	CALIFORNIA SOUTHERN
CASC	CASCADE
CASR	COMMONWEALTH AVE STREET RAILWAY
CASS	CASS SCENIC
CAT	CATAWISSA
CAW	CAROLINA WESTERN RAILROAD
CAYL	CAYUGA LAKE
CAYS	CAYUGA SOUTHERN
CAZS	CAZENOVIA SOUTHERN
CB	COORS BREWERY
CB&C	CHICAGO BLUFFTON & CINCINNATI RR
CB&E	CLEVELAND BEREA & ELYRIA STREET RY
CB&I	CHICAGO BRIDGE & IRON
CB&KC	CHICAGO BURLINGTON & KANSAS CITY
CB&Q	CHICAGO BURLINGTON & QUINCY RAILROAD
CB&SJ	COUNCIL BLUFFS & ST JOE
CBA	CITY OF BALTIMORE
CBC&W	CHICAGO BELLEVUE CASCADE & WESTERN
CBE	CHESAPEAKE BEACH RAILWAY
CBE&O	CLEVELAND BEREA ELYRIA & OBERLIN RY
CBELT	COTTON BELT
CBER	COAL BELT ELECTRIC RAILWAY
CBL	COOS BAY LUMBER
CBSR	CAPE BRETON STEAM RAILWAY
CBT	CAPE BRETON TRAMWAYS
CC	CAPE COD CENTRAL
CC&C	COWLITZ CHEHALIS & CASCADE
CC&CH	CHARLESTON CINCINNATI & CHICAGO
CC&CIN	CLEVELAND COLUMBUS & CINCINNATI RR
CC&CS	CRIPPLE CREEK & COLORADO SPRINGS RY
CC&L	CHICAGO CINCINNATI & LOUISVILLE
CC&M	COLORADO COLUMBUS & MEXICAN RAILROAD
CC&N	CAMINO CABLE & NORTHERN
CC&O	CAROLINA CLINCHFIELD & OHIO RAILROAD
CC&O.	CAROLINA CLINCHFIELD & OHIO RAILWAY
CC&P	CHICAGO CENTRAL & PACIFIC
CC&RC	CHOCTAW COAL & RAILWAY COMPANY
CC&RG	CANON CITY & ROYAL GORGE
CC&S	CLEVELAND CANTON & SOUTHERN
CC&SR	CRESCENT CITY & SMITH RIVER
CCAN	CENTRAL CANADA RAILWAY
CCB*	COUNTRY CLUB BEER
CCC&I	CLEVELAND COLUMBUS CINCIN & INDIANAPL
CCC&SL	CLEVELAND CINCINNATI CHIC & ST LOUIS
CCD	COLORADO SPRINGS DISTRICT RAILWAY
CCDRY	CRIPPLE CREEK DISTRICT RAILWAY
CCE	CALIFORNIA CENTRAL
CCER	CAPITAL CITY ELECTRICAL RY (ALABAMA)
CCF&RG	CANON CITY FLORENCE & ROYAL GORGE
CCH	CHESUNCOOK CHAMBERLAIN
CCOC	CANADIAN COPPER COMPANY
CCOD	CAPE COD RAILROAD
CCP&L	CUMBERLAND COUNTY POWER & LIGHT CO
CCR	CAMPBELL'S CREEK RAILROAD
CCRR	CAMDEN COUNTY RAILROAD
CCRTA	CAPE COD REGIONAL TRANS AUTHORITY
CCRY	CONQUISTA COAL RAILWAY
CCSDRG	CORPUS CHRISTIE SAN DIEGO & RIO GRANDE
CCSR	CINCINNATI STREET RAILWAY
CCT	CENTRAL CALIFORNIA TRACTION COMPANY
CCTR	CORTLAND COUNTY TRACTION
CCW	CHARLES CITY WESTERN RAILWAY
CD&C	CHICAGO DETROIT & CANADA GRAND JCT RY
CD&IS	COG DEPOT & IRON SPRINGS
CD&M	COLUMBUS DELAWARE & MARION ELECTRIC
CD&MI	CHICAGO DECORAH & MINNESOTA
CD&MU	CLINTON DAVENPORT & MUSCATINE RAILWAY
CD&P	CHESTER DARBY & PHILADELPHIA RAILWAY
CD&V	CHICAGO DANVILLE & VINCENNES RAILROAD
CDOT	CONNECTICUT DEPT OF TRANSPORTATION
CDR&N	COEUR D'ALENE RAILWAY & NAVIGATION
CE	CALIFORNIA EASTERN
CE&C	CENTRE & CLEARFIELD
CE&EC	COAST ENGINE & EQUIPMENT COMPANY
CE&I	COPLAY EQYPT & IRONTON STREET RY
CE&W	CLEVELAND ELYRIA & WESTERN RAILWAY
CEAST	CANADA EASTERN
CECR	CERRILLOS COAL RAILROAD
CECU	CERVECERIA CUAHTEMOC
CED	COMMONWEALTH EDISON
CEI	CLEVELAND ELECTRIC ILLUMINATING CO
CEL	CHICAGO EL
CEMT	CENTRAL MILITARY TRACT
CER	CALIFORNIA ELECTRIC RAILWAY
CERY	CHICO ELECTRIC RAILWAY (CALIF)
CET	CENTRAL TRACTION COMPANY

A39

APPENDIX A (RAILROADS)

A	ABBREVIATIONS ALPHABETICALLY W/ROADS
CEV	CENTRAL VALLEY
CF	CAPE FEAR RAILWAYS
CF&A	COVINGTON FLEMINGSBURG & ASHLAND
CF&E	CHAGRIN FALLS & EASTERN ELECTRIC RY
CF&IC	COLORADO FUEL & IRON COMPANY
CF&N	CAPE FEAR & NORTHERN
CF&PG	COVINGTON FLEMINGSBURG & POUND GAP
CF&SE	CINCINNATI FLEMINGON & SOUTHEASTERN
CF&W	CANEY FORK & WESTERN
CF&WE	CHIPPEWA FALLS & WESTERN
CFC	CHICAGO FREIGHT CAR COMPANY
CFI	CHAMPION FIBRE
CFO	CENTRAL FOUNDRY
CFP	CANADIAN FOREST PRODUCTS
CG	CHICAGO GRAVEL COMPANY
CG&C	CAPE GIRARDEAU & CHESTER RAILROAD
CG&ME	CAMDEN GLOUSTER & MT EPHRAIM
CG&P	CINCINNATI GEORGETOWN & PORTSMOUTH RR
CGA	CENTRAL OF GEORGIA
CGA.	CENTRAL RAILROAD OF GEORGIA
CGN	CAPE GIRARDEAU NORTHERN
CGR	CANADIAN GOVERNMENT RAILWAY
CGRT	CORAL GABLES RAPID TRANSIT
CGW	CHICAGO GREAT WESTERN RAILWAY
CGW.	CHICAGO GREAT WESTERN RAILROAD
CH	CLOVER HILL
CH&A	CHICAGO & ATLANTIC
CH&B	CHICAGO HARLEM & BATAVIA
CH&C	CHERAW & COALFIELD
CH&D	CINCINNATI HAMILTON & DAYTON
CH&DA	CHERAW & DARLINGTON
CH&E	CHICAGO & ERIE
CH&GT	CHICAGO & GRAND TRUNK
CH&L	CHESTER & LENOIR
CH&M	CHICAGO & MILWAUKEE
CH&N	CHICAGO & NORTHERN RAILROAD
CH&NW	COPPER HILL & NORTH WESTERN
CH&P	CHICAGO & PACIFIC
CH&SO	CHARLESTON & SAVANNAH
CH-P	CHIHUAHUA-PACIFIC
CHAT	CHATEAUGAY RAILROAD
CHC	CHICAGO CITY RAILWAYS
CHE	CHESHIRE
CHER	CHERRELYN LINE (COLORADO)
CHES	CHESTERFIELD
CHESS	CHESSIE SYSTEM
CHIC	CHICAGO CENTRAL
CHMI	CHIHUAHUA MINERAL
CHP	CHAMAS PRAIRIE RAILROAD
CHSC	CHATTANOOGA STATION COMPANY
CHSD	CHICAGO SANITARY DISTRICT
CHSO	CHICAGO SOUTHERN
CHT	CHAUTAUQUA TRACTION COMPANY
CHTR	CHATTANOOGA TRACTION COMPANY
CHTT	CHICAGO HEIGHTS TERMINAL TRANSFER RR
CHUT	CHICAGO UNION TRANSFER RAILWAY CO
CHV	CHATTAHOOCHEE VALLEY RAILWAY
CHV&T	COLUMBUS HOCKING VALLEY & TOLEDO RY
CHVR	CHARTIERS VALLEY RAILROAD
CHW	CHESAPEAKE WESTERN RAILWAY
CHWE	CHEHALIS WESTERN RAILROAD
CI	CHATTAHOOCHEE INDUSTRIAL RAILROAD
CI&B	CONEY ISLAND & BROOKLYN RAILROAD CO
CI&L	CHICAGO INDPOLIS & LOUISVILLE RY (O)
CI&M	CHATAM IRON & METAL
CI&NW	CIMMARRON & NORTHWESTERN
CI*	COLLEGE INN
CILL	CENTRAL ILLINOIS RAILWAY
CIM	CITY ISLAND RAILROAD (MONORAIL)
CIN	CENTRAL INDIANA RAILWAY
CIN&E	CINCINNATI & EASTERN RAILWAY
CINO	CINCINNATI NORTHERN
CIRT	CINCINNATI RAPID TRANSIT
CIT	CITADEL CEMENT COMPANY
CITC	CENTRAL IOWA TRANSPORTATION COOP
CITYS	CITY OF SEATTLE
CIUT	CINCINNATI UNION TERMINAL
CJ	CHICAGO JUNCTION
CJL&C	CJ LAVINO & COMPANY
CK	COLORADO KANSAS
CK&O	COLORADO KANSAS & OKLAHOMA RAILROAD
CK&S	CONDON KINZUA & SOUTHERN RAILROAD
CK&S	CONSOLIDATED KANSAS & SIDELL
CK&SA	CHICAGO KALAMAZOO & SAGINAW RAILWAY
CK&W	CHICAGO KANSAS & WESTERN
CL	CLINCHFIELD RAILWAY
CL&A	CINCINNATI LAWRENCE & AURORA
CL&B	CLEVELAND & BEREA RAILWAY
CL&C	CLAREMONT & CONCORD RAILROAD
CL&C.	CLAREMONT & CONCORD RAILWAY
CL&CA	CLEVELAND & CANTON
CL&E	CLEVELAND & ELYRIA STREET RAILROAD
CL&N	CINCINNATI LEBANON & NORTHERN RAILWAY
CL&R	COMOX LUMBER & RAILROAD COMPANY
CL&SO	CLEVELAND & SOUTHERN
CL&W	CLEVELAND LORAIN & WHEELING RAILROAD
CL&WE	COLUMBUS LANCASTER & WELLSTON
CL.	CLINCHFIELD RAILROAD
CLA	CLARION RIVER RAILWAY
CLAR	CLAREMONT RAILWAY
CLC	CARLTON LOGGING COMPANY
CLE	CLEMENT LUMBER COMPANY
CLI	CLINCHFIELD COAL
CLIF	CLIFFSIDE RAILROAD
CLR	COMOX LOGGING & RAILWAY COMPANY
CLRR	CAMP LEJEUNE RAILROAD
CLRT	CLEVELAND RAPID TRANSIT
CLRT.	CLEVELAND TRANSIT
CLS&E	CHICAGO LAKE SHORE & EASTERN
CLS&SB	CHICAGO LAKE SHORE & SOUTH BEND
CLV	CLOVER VALLEY RAILROAD
CLW	CHICAGO LOCOMOTIVE WORKS
CM	CRAIG MOUNTAIN RAILWAY
CM&C	CHARLOTTE MONROE & COLUMBIA
CM&G	CHICAGO MILWAUKEE & GARY
CM&H	CONCORD MAYNARD & HUDSON STREET RY
CM&LC	CHICAGO MILL & LUMBER COMPANY
CM&N	CHICAGO MADISON & NORTHERN
CM&P	CHICAGO MILWAUKEE & PUGET SOUND
CM&S	CLEVELAND MEDINA & SOUTHERN RAILWAY
CM&W	CHICAGO MISSOURI & WESTERN
CMA	CENTRAL MASSACHUSETTS
CMDB&S	CAPE MAY DELAWARE BAY & SEWELLS POINT
CMEX	CENTRAL MEXICANO
CMFG	CAMP MANUFACTURING COMPANY
CMI	COLORADO MIDLAND
CML	CORTEZ MINES LIMITED
CMM	CANMORE MINES
CMOX	CUBA OIL & MOLASSES COMPANY
CMRY	CALGARY MUNICIPAL RAILWAY
CMSP	CHICAGO MILWAUKEE & ST PAUL
CMSP&O	CHICAGO MILWAUKEE ST PAUL & OMAHA
CMT	CATSKILL MOUNTAINS RAILWAY SYSTEMS
CMT.	CATSKILL MOUNTAIN RAILROAD
CMW*	CHAREAU MARTIN WINE
CN	CANADIAN NATIONAL RAILWAY
CN&C	CINCINNATI NEWPORT & COVINGTON RY
CN&L	COLUMBIA NEWBERRY & LAURENS RAILROAD
CN&W	CHOCTAW NEWCASTLE & WESTERN
CND	CAROLINA NITROGEN DIV OF GRACE CHEM
CNE	CENTRAL NEW ENGLAND RAILROAD
CNE&W	CENTRAL NEW ENGLAND & WESTERN
CNG	COWICHAN NARROW GAUGE
CNJ	CENTRAL RAILROAD OF NEW JERSEY
CNO&TP	CINCINNATI NEW ORLEANS & TEXAS PACIFC
CNQ	CANADIAN NORTHERN QUEBEC RAILWAY CO
CNRY	CLINCHFIELD NORTHERN RY OF KENTUCKY
CNS&M	CHICAGO NORTH SHORE & MILWAUKEE
CNW	CALIFORNIA NORTHWESTERN RAILWAY CO
CNY	CENTRAL NEW YORK RAILROAD
CNY&N	CENTRAL NEW YORK & NORTHERN
CNY&W	CENTRAL NEW YORK & WESTERN
CNYE	CHICAGO NEW YORK AIR LINE RAILROAD
CNYE.	CHICAGO NEW YORK ELECTRIC AIR LINE RR

A40

APPENDIX A (RAILROADS)

A	ABBREVIATIONS ALPHABETICALLY W/ROADS
CNYS	CENTRAL NEW YORK SOUTHERN RAILROAD
CO	CORONADO RAILROAD (CALIFORNIA)
CO&C	COLUMBIA & COWLITZ RAILWAY
CO&CO	CORINTH & COUNCE RAILROAD
CO&E	CRAB ORCHARD & EGYPTIAN
CO&G	CHOCTAW OKLAHOMA & GULF RAILROAD
CO&L	CORNWALL & LEBANON RAILROAD
CO&O	COVINGTON & OHIO
CO&SL	CONNELLSVILLE & STATE LINE
CO&SO	COLUMBUS & SOUTHERN
CO&SW	CHESAPEAKE OHIO & SOUTHWESTERN
CO&W	COLUMBIA & WESTERN
COAL	COAL FIELDS RAILWAY
COB	CHICAGO OUTER BELT
COCT	CITY OF CALGARY TRANSIT
COL	COLORADO CENTRAL
COL&SE	COLORADO & SOUTHEASTERN RAILROAD
COLN	COLFAX NORTHERN
COLRR	COLORADO RAILROAD
COLRT	COLUMBIA RAPID TRANSIT
COLSC	COLLIER STREETCAR
COLT	COLUMBUS TRANSIT COMPANY
COLV	COLEBROOK VALLEY RAILROAD
CON	CONSUMERS POWER
CONC	CONCORD RAILROAD
CONN	CONNECTICUT COMPANY
CONNC	CONNECTICUT CENTRAL
CONNR	CONNECTICUT RAILROAD
CONS	CONSUMERS COMPANY
CONT	CONTINENTAL STEEL
CONV	CONNOTON VALLEY RAILWAY
CONW	CONWAY SCENIC
COOPT	COOPERATIVE TRANSIT COMPANY
COR	CONNECTICUT RIVER RAILROAD
COR&E	CORVALLIS & EASTERN
CORN	CORNWALL RAILROAD
COUS	COLUMBIA UNION STATION COMPANY
COW	CONNECTICUT WESTERN RAILROAD
CP	CANADIAN PACIFIC
CP&A	CLEVELAND PAINESVILLE & ASHTABULA
CP&L	CAROLINA POWER & LIGHT
CP&LT	CAMINO PLACERVILLE & LAKE TAHOE RR
CP&S	COLUMBIA PARK & SOUTHERN
CP&SG	CHESTER PERRYVILLE & ST GENEVIEVE
CP&SL	CHICAGO PEORIA & ST LOUIS RAILROAD
CP&SL.	CHICAGO PEORIA & ST LOUIS RY CO OF IL
CP&SW	COLUMBIA PARK & SOUTHWESTSERN
CP-F	COTTON PLANT-FARGO RAILWAY
CPA	CENTRAL PACIFIC RAILROAD (1861)
CPA.	CENTRAL PACIFIC RAILWAY (1899)
CPGE	CANADIAN PACIFIC GREAT WESTERN
CPM	CARTIAGE PAPER MAKERS
CPM&O	CHICAGO ST PAUL MINNEAPOLIS & OMAHA
CPR	CITY OF PRINEVILLE RAILWAY
CPRY	CITY PASSENGER RAILWAY (ATLANTIC CITY
CPT	CITY POINT
CPTE	CHICAGO PRODUCE TERMINAL
CR	CONRAIL
CR&I	CHICAGO RIVER & INDIANA RAILROAD
CR&IC	CEDAR RAPIDS & IOWA CITY RAILWAY
CR&L	CONNECTICUT RAILWAY & LIGHTING CO
CR&LC	COLUMBUS RAILWAY & LIGHT COMPANY
CR&M	CHIPPAWAH RIVER & MENOMONIE RAILWAY
CR&N	COPPER RIVER & NORTHWESTERN (O)
CR&NW	COPPER RIVER & NORTHWESTERN RAILWAY
CR&S	CHATTANOOGA ROME & NORTHERN
CR&SJ	CRYSTAL RIVER & SAN JUAN RAILROAD
CR&W	CRAWFORDSVILLE & WESTERN TRACTION CO
CRA	COPPER RANGE RAILROAD
CRARK	CENTRAL RAILWAY OF ARKANSAS
CRB	CENTRAL RR & BANKING CO OF GEORGIA(O)
CRB&L	CHERRY RIVER BOOM & LUMBER
CRC	CHEAT RIVER COAL & LUMBER RAILROAD
CRE	CANADIAN REFRACTORIES
CRESC	CRESCENT CITY RAILROAD COMPANY
CRFI	CRESTBOOK FOREST INDUSTRIES
CRI	CHESTNUT RIDGE RAILWAY

A	ABBREVIATIONS ALPHABETICALLY W/ROADS
CRI&G	CHICAGO ROCK ISLAND & GULF
CRLI	CENTRAL RAILROAD OF LONG ISLAND
CRO	CENTRAL RAILROAD OF OREGON
CROSW	CROSSETT WESTERN COMPANY (LUMBER RD)
CRP	CONSOLIDATED ROCK PRODUCTS
CRR&B	CENTRAL RR & BANKING CO OF GEORGIA
CRR&C	CENTRAL RR & CANAL CO OF GEORGIA
CRRR	CRYSTAL RIVER RAILROAD
CRT	CHICAGO RAPID TRANSIT COMPANY
CRTA	CHICAGO REGIONAL TRANSIT AUTHORITY
CRW	CLEVELAND RAILWAYS
CRWP	CENTRAL RAILWAY OF PERU
CRY	CITY RAILWAY OF DAYTON
CRYC	CENTRAL RAILWAY OF CANADA
CRYOC	CENTRAL RAILWAY OF CALIFORNIA
CS	CANADIAN SOUTHERN RAILROAD COMPANY
CS&CC	COLORADO SPRINGS & CRIPPLE CR DIST RY
CS&H	COLUMBUS SANDUSKY & HOCKING
CS&I	COLORADO SPRINGS & INTERURBAN RY CO
CS&M	CINCINNATI SAGINAW & MACKINAW
CS&MS	COLORADO SPRINGS & MANITOU ST RY
CS&RB	CALIFORNIA SOUTHERN & REDONDO BEACH
CS&STL	CHICAGO SPRINGFIELD & ST LOUIS
CS&U	CRYSTAL CITY & UVALDE RAILROAD
CS&W	CHESAPEAKE SHENANDOAH & WESTERN
CS*	COLUMBIA SOURS
CSB	CANADA SOUTHERN BRIDGE COMPANY
CSB&NI	CHICAGO SOUTH BEND & NORTHERN INDIANA
CSC	CITIES SERVICE COMPANY
CSCO	CLEVELAND SOUTHWESTERN & COLUMBUS RY
CSCR	CALIFORNIA STREET CABLE RR COMPANY
CSCR.	CALIFORNIA STREET LINE
CSD	CONNOR STEEL DIVISION
CSF&E	CASPER SOUTH FORK & EASTERN
CSHR	CLAY STREET HILL RAILROAD COMPANY
CSL	CHICAGO SHORT LINE RAILWAY
CSL&W	CHICAGO ST LOUIS & WESTERN
CSLI	CANADA SOUTHERN LINE
CSLI.	CANADA SOUTHERN RAILWAY
CSLS	CHICAGO SURFACE LINES
CSO	CINCINNATI SOUTHERN
CSOR	CANADA SOUTHERN RAILWAY
CSP&FL	CHICAGO ST PAUL & FORD DU LAC
CSP&KC	CHICAGO ST PAUL & KANSAS CITY
CSPM&O	CHICAGO ST PAUL MINNEAPOLIS & OHIO
CSRL&P	CORNWALL STREET RY LIGHT & POWER CO
CSRT	COLORADO SPRINGS RAPID TRANSIT
CSRY	CARBON STREET RAILWAY
CSS&SB	CHICAGO SOUTH SHORE & SOUTH BEND RR
CSS&SB.	CHICAGO SOUTH SHORE & SOUTH BEND RY
CST	CONCORD STREET RAILWAY
CSUB	CHICAGO SUBWAYS
CSW	CLEVELAND SOUTHWESTERN RY & LIGHT CO
CSX	CSX TRASNPORTATION
CT	CHICAGO TUNNEL RAILWAY COMPANY
CT&G	CARRABELLE TALLAHASSEE & GEORGIA
CT&S	CAIRO TRUMAN & SOUTHERN
CT&V	CLEVELAND TERMINAL & VALLEY
CTA	CHICAGO TRANSIT AUTHORITY
CTC	CAPITAL TRANSIT COMPANY
CTCO	CONESTOGA TRACTION COMPANY
CTDM	COMM DE TRANSPORT URBAINE DE MONTREAL
CTH&SE	CHICAGO TERRE HAUTE & SOUTHEASTERN RY
CTR	CITIZENS TRACTIONS OF OIL CITY
CTRC	CHESTER TRACTION COMPANY
CTT	CHICAGO TERMINAL TRANSFER RAILROAD
CTV&W	CLEVELAND TUSCARAWAS VALLEY & WHEELING
CTVY	CONNECTICUT VALLEY
CU	CITY UTILITIES COMPANY
CU&F	CLAREMONT UNIVERSITY & FERRIES ST RR
CU&S	CUTLER & SAVIDGE
CU&W	COLUMBUS URBANA & WESTERN
CUM	CUMBERLAND RAILWAY & COAL COMPANY
CUMV	CUMBERLAND VALLEY RAILROAD
CUR	CURRENT RIVER RAILROAD
CUS	CUSHING STONE

APPENDIX A (RAILROADS)

A	ABBREVIATIONS ALPHABETICALLY W/ROADS
CUST	CHARLESTON UNION STATION COMPANY
CUST	CHICAGO UNION STATION
CUT	CLEVELAND UNION TERMINAL (NYC)
CUTR	CHICAGO UNION TRACTION
CUY	CUYAHOGA VALLEY LINES (O)
CUY	CUYAHOGA VALLEY RAILWAY
CV	CENTRAL VERMONT (CN) RAILWAY
CV&W	CASSVILLE & WESTERN
CVA	CAHUENGA VALLEY
CVL	CUYAHOGA VALLEY LINES.
CVRR	COWICHAN VALLEY RAILROAD
CVRY	CREDIT VALLEY RAILWAY
CVW&M	CINCINNATI VAN WERT & MICHIGAN
CW	CALIFORNIA WESTERN RR & NAV CO
CW&E	COLORADO WYOMING & EASTERN
CW&LE	CHATHAM WALLACEBURG & LAKE ERIE
CW&MV	CLEVELAND WOOSTER & MAHONING VALLEY
CW&S	COLUMBUS WELLSTON & SOUTHERN
CWC	CENTRAL WAREHOUSE COMPANY
CWH	CITY OF WINNIPEG HYDRO
CWN	CALIFORNIA WESTERN NORTH
CWP	CROWN WILLAMETTE PAPER
CWP&S	CHICAGO WEST PULLMAN & SOUTHERN RY
CWP&S.	CHICAGO WEST PULLMAN & SOUTHERN RR
CWST	COPPERWELD STEEL COMPANY
CWU	CHICAGO WEST UNION TFR
CWV	CORNWALLIS VALLEY RAILWAY
CWV&S	CENTRAL WEST VIRGINIA & SOUTHERN
CY&E	CLEVELAND YOUNGSTOWN & EASTERN RY
CYC	CANYON CREEK RAILROAD
CYR&P	CANANEA RIO YAQUI Y PAIFICO
CYR&P.	CANANEA YANQUI RIVER & PACIFIC RR
CZ	CROWN ZELLERBACH
CZ.	CROWN ZELLERBACH--CANADA
D	DEVCO RAILWAY
D&BB	DELAWARE & BOUND BROOK RAILROAD
D&C	DUTCHESS & COLUMBIA RAILROAD COMPANY
D&CA	DIAMOND & CALDOR RAILROAD
D&CH	DENVER & CHEYENNE
D&E	DELAWARE & EASTERN RAILROAD
D&H	DELAWARE & HUDSON RAILROAD COMPANY
D&HC	DELAWARE & HUDSON COAL COMPANY
D&HCC	DELAWARE & HUDSON CANAL COMPANY
D&HG	DELAWARE & HUDSON GRAVITY RAILROAD
D&I	DENVER & INTERMOUNTAIN RAILROAD
D&IN	DENVER & INTERURBAN RAILROAD (O)
D&IR	DULUTH & IRON RANGE
D&IRR	DENVER & INTERURBAN RAILROAD
D&LN	DETROIT & LIMA NORTHERN
D&M	DETROIT & MACKINAC RAILWAY
D&MEC	DELAWARE & MARION ELECTRIC COMPANY
D&MM	DANSVILLE & MT MORRIS RAILROAD
D&N	DELAWARE & NORTHERN RAILROAD
D&N.	DELAWARE & NORTHERN RAILWAY
D&NE	DULUTH & NORTHEASTERN RAILROAD
D&NM	DULUTH & NORTHERN MINNESOTA RAILROAD
D&NO	DENVER & NEW ORLEANS
D&NR	DANVILLE & NEW RIVER
D&NRY	DONALDSONVILLE & NAPOLEONVILLE RY
D&P	DANVILLE & POTTSVILLE
D&R	DARDANELLE & RUSSELLVILLE RAILROAD
D&RG	DENVER & RIO GRANDE RAILROAD
D&RGW	DENVER & RIO GRANDE WESTERN RAILROAD
D&RIB	DAVENPORT & ROCK ISLAND RY BRIDGE CO
D&RIBT	DAVENPORT ROCK ISLAND BRIDGE RY &TERM
D&S	DURHAM & SOUTHERN RAILWAY
D&SH	DENISON & SHERMAN RAILWAY

A	ABBREVIATIONS ALPHABETICALLY W/ROADS
D&SI	DURANGO & SILVERTON
D&SJ	DETROIT & ST JOSEPH
D&SL	DENVER & SALT LAKE RAILROAD
D&SL.	DENVER & SALT LAKE RAILWAY
D&SO	DOVER & SOUTHBOUND
D&SQ	DAUPHIN & SUSQUEHANNA
D&ST	DANVILLE & SUNBURY TRANSIT COMPANY
D&SW	DUBLIN & SOUTHWESTERN
D&TE	DAYTON & TROY ELECTRIC
D&TSL	DETROIT & TOLEDO SHORE LINE RAILROAD
D&U	DAYTON & UNION RAILROAD CO
D&UL	DELAWARE & ULSTER RAILROAD
D&W	DENISON & WASHITA
D&WE	DARIEN & WESTERN
D&WV	DUBLIN & WRIGHTSVILLE
D&XT	DAYTON & XENIA TRACTION
D*	DUBUQUE
D-M	DYERSBURG-MEMPHIS
DA	DOMINION ATLANTIC RAILWAY
DA&F	DOUGLAS AUGUSTA & FLORIDA
DA&G	DOUGLAS AUGUSTA & GULF RAILWAY
DA&W	DANVILLE & WESTERN
DARA	DAKOTA RAIL
DAV&P	DUNKIRK ALLEGHENY VALLEY & PITTSBURGH
DB&CM	DELAWARE BAY & CAPE MAY RAILROAD
DB&L	DUNCANNON BLOOMFIELD & LOYSVILLE
DB&MP	DAWSON BRADFORD & MT PLEASANT RR
DB&W	DENVER BOULDER & WESTERN
DBC	DEBARDELEBEN COAL CORPORATION
DBC&A	DETROIT BAY CITY & ALPENA
DBC&W	DETROIT BAY CITY & WESTERN
DBL	DUDGEMONA BAYOU LUMBER COMPANY
DBT	DELTA BULK TERMINALS
DC	DEEP CREEK RAILROAD
DC&P	DAYTON COVINGTON & PIQUA TRACTION CO.
DC&S	DETROIT CARO & SANDUSKY
DC*	DOW CHEMICAL
DCC&P	DENVER COLORADO CANYON & PACIFIC
DCCO	DICK CONSTRUCTION CO
DCCRR	DCCRR
DCT	DC TRANSIT
DCT.	DISTRICT OF COLUMBIA TRANSIT
DE	DELRAY CONNECTING RAILROAD
DE&G	DENVER ENID & GULF
DE*	DAIRYMENS EXPRESS
DED	DETROIT DIESEL EDISON
DEED	DETROIT EDISON
DEI	DEITCH COMPANY
DER&I	DETROIT EEL RIVER & ILLINOIS
DES	DELTA SOUTHERN
DET	DELRAY TERMINAL
DF	DRY FORK
DF&S	DOMINION FOUNDRIES & STEEL
DFI	DIERKS FOREST INDUSTRIES
DGH&M	DETROIT GRAND HAVEN & MILWAUKEE
DH&S	DETROIT HILLSDALE & SOUTHWESTERN RY
DIA	DIAMOND VALLEY
DICK	DICK CONSTRUCTION COMPANY
DICX	DRY ICE REFRIGERATOR LINE
DJL	DAVIES JOHNSON LUMBER COMPANY
DK&S	DONIPHAN KENSETT & SEARCY RAILWAY
DKS	DAKOTA SOUTHERN
DL&A	DENVER LEADVILLE & ALMA
DL&B	DUNCANNON LANDISBURG & BROADTOP RR
DL&C	DEVIL'S LAKE & CHAUTAUQUA
DL&G	DENVER LEADVILLE & GUNNISON RAILROAD
DL&N	DEVILS LAKE & NORTHERN
DL&NO	DAYTON LEBANON & NORTHERN
DL&W	DELAWARE LACKAWANNA & WESTERN
DLC	DENKMAN LUMBER COMPANY
DLS&S	DELAWARE LACK SCHUYLKILL & SUSQUEHANNA
DM&C	DES MOINES & CENTRAL
DM&CI	DES MOINES & CENTRAL IOWA RAILWAY
DM&FD	DES MOINES & FORT DODGE
DM&IR	DULUTH MISSABE & IRON RANGE RAILWAY
DM&M	DETROIT MACKINAC & MARQUETTE
DM&MI	DES MOINES & MINNESOTA

STEPHANS' RAILROAD DIRECTORY

A42

APPENDIX A (RAILROADS)

A	ABBREVIATIONS ALPHABETICALLY W/ROADS	A	ABBREVIATIONS ALPHABETICALLY W/ROADS
DM&N	DULUTH MISSABE & NORTHERN	DX&N	DEXTER & NORTHERN
DM&S	DANVILLE MOCKSVILLE & SOUTHWESTERN	E	ERIE
DM&W	DULUTH MISSABE & WESTERN	E&B	ELGIN & BELVIDERE INTERURBAN
DME	DAKOTA MINNESOTA & EASTERN	E&C	EVANSVILLE & CRAWFORD
DMR&N	DULUTH MISSISSIPPI RIVER & NORTHERN	E&G	ELKTON & GUTHRIE
DMT	DETROIT MONROE TOLEDO SHORT LINE	E&H	ELK & HIGHLAND
DMTC	DES MOINES TERMINAL COMPANY	E&K	ERIE & KALAMAZOO
DMU	DES MOINES UNION RAILWAY	E&KR	EUREKA & KALAMATH RIVER RAILROAD
DMV	DES MOINES VALLEY RAILROAD	E&LS	ESCANABA & LAKE SUPERIOR RAILROAD
DN&P	DENVER NORTHWESTERN & PACIFIC	E&M	EDGMOOR & MANETTA RAILWAY
DNEW	DEDHAM-NORWOOD-E WAPOLE LINE	E&M	ERIE & MICHIGAN RY & NAVIGATION CO
DNS	DEL NORTE SOUTHERN RAILWAY	E&MJ	EMPORIUM & MT JEWITT
DO	DELAWARE OTSEGO SYSTEM	E&MO	ETNA & MONTROSE
DO&C	DOWLING & CAMP	E&N	ESQUIMALT & NANAIMO FAMILY LINES RY
DO&S	DARDANELLE OLA & SOUTHERN	E&NA	EUROPEAN & NORTH AMERICAN RAILROAD
DOC	DOMINION OF CANADA	E&NC	ELIZABETHTON & NORTH CAROLINA
DOD	DEPARTMENT OF DEFENSE	E&O	ERIE & ONTARIO RAILWAY COMPANY
DOS	DONORA SOUTHERN RAILROAD	E&OV	EVANSVILLE & OHIO VALLEY RAILWAY
DP	DENVER PACIFIC RAILROAD COMPANY	E&P	EUREKA & PALISADE RAILWAY
DP&L	DELMARVA POWER & LIGHT	E&PT	ERIE & PITTSBURG
DP&M	DETROIT PONTIAC & MACKINAC	E&S	ELIZABETH & SOMERVILLE
DPA	DAKOTA PACIFIC RAILROAD	E&S	ELIZABETHPORT & SOMERVILLE RAILROAD
DPC	DUKE POWER COMPANY	E&S.	ELIZABETHTOWN & SOMERVILLE RAILROAD
DPE	DAN PATCH ELECTRIC RAILROAD	E&TH	EVANSVILLE & TERRE HAUTE RAILROAD
DQ&E	DEQUEEN & EASTERN RAILROAD	E&W	ELKHART & WESTERN
DQSP	DUQUESNE SLAG PRODUCTS COMPANY	E&WC	EAST & WEST COAST RAILROAD (FLORIDA)
DR&T	DALLAS RAILWAY & TERMINAL	E&WV	ERIE & WYOMING VALLEY RAILROAD CO
DR‡	DEEP ROCK	E-D	EMPIRE DETROIT DIV OF CYCLOPS STEEL
DRI&N	DAVENPORT ROCK ISLAND & NORTH WESTERN	E-M	ELECTRO-MOTIVE CORPORATION
DRJC	DELAWARE RIVER JOINT COMMISSION	EAST	EASTERN (EASTERN MINNESOTA??)
DRL&W	DULUTH RAINY LAKE & WINNIPEG	EB	EXCELSIOR BRICK
DRPA	DELAWARE RIVER PORT AUTHORITY	EB&C	EAST BARRE & CHELSEA
DRRR	DEERFIELD RIVER RAILROAD	EB&L	EAST BRANCH & LINCOLN
DRT	DETROIT RIVER TUNNEL COMPANY	EBC	EWAUNA BOX COMPANY
DS	DISMAL SWAMP RAILROAD	EBRY	EVANSVILLE BELT RAILWAY
DS&G	DIXIE SAND & GRAVEL	EBT	EAST BROAD TOP
DS&M	DECATUR SULLIVAN & MATTOON	EBT&CC	EAST BROAD TOP RAILROAD & COAL CO
DS&S	DELAWARE SUSQUEHANNA & SCHUYLKILL	EC&H	EAST CAMDEN & HIGHLAND RAILROAD
DSCG&M	DULUTH ST CLOUTH GLENCOE & MANKATO RY	EC&N	ELMIRA CORTLAND & NORTHERN
DSH	DELAWARE SHORE RAILROAD	ECRR	ERIE COMMERCIAL RAILROAD
DSM	DAWES SILICA MINING	ECRY	EAST CAROLINA RAILWAY
DSO	DETROIT SOUTHERN	ED	EDAVILLE RAILROAD
DSP&P	DENVER SOUTH PARK & PACIFIC	ED&BC	EDMONTON DONVOGA & BRITISH COLUMBIA RY
DSRY	DULUTH STREET RAILWAY	ED&W	EL DORADO & WESSON RAILWAY
DSS&A	DULUTH SOUTH SHORE & ATLANTIC	EEC	EAST ERIE COMMERCIAL RAILROAD
DST	DETROIT STREET RAILWAY	EF	EAST FLORIDA
DT	DETROIT TERMINAL RAILROAD	EFLORB	EAST FLORIDA LIVE OAK & ROWLANDS BLUFF
DT&FW	DENVER TEXAS & FORT WORTH	EG	ETHIOPIAN GOVERNMENT RAILWAYS
DT&I	DETROIT TOLEDO & IRONTON	EG&S	ELYRIA GRAFTON & SOUTHERN RAILWAY
DT&M	DETROIT TOLEDO & MILWAUKEE	EH	EUREKA HILL RAILROAD
DT&PC	DANVILLE TRACTION & POWER COMPANY	EH&A	EXETER HAMPTON & AMESBURY STREET RY
DTM	DENVER TRAMWAY	EHLC	EDWARD HINES LUMBER COMPANY
DTRR	DOWN TOWN RAILROAD COMPANY	EHWP	ED HINES WESTERN PINE COMPANY
DTW	DURBAN TRAMWAYS COMPANY (CANADA)	EI&TH	EVANSVILLE INDIANAPOLIS & TERRE HAUTE
DU	DUTCHESS COUNTY RAILROAD COMPANY	EJ&E	ELGIN JOLIET & EASTERN RAILWAY
DU&P	DENVER UTAH & PACIFIC	EJ&S	EAST JORDAN & SOUTHERN RAILROAD
DU‡	DUPONT (EI DUPONT)	EJ&W	ELGIN JOLIET & WESTERN
DUD&T	DULUTH UNION DEPOT & TRANSFER	EJR&T	EAST JERSEY RAILROAD & TERMINAL
DUL	DETROIT UNITED LINES	EK	EASTMAN KODAK COMPANY
DUL.	DETROIT UNITED RAILWAYS	EKS	EASTERN KENTUCKY SOUTHERN
DUP&T.	DULUTH UNION DEPOT & TRANSFER (O)	EKY	EASTERN KENTUCKY
DUSC	DURHAM UNION STATION COMPANY	EL	ERIE LACKAWANNA
DUTR	DENVER UNION TERMINAL RAILWAY	EL&RR	EAST LINE & RED RIVER
DV	DEATH VALLEY RAILROAD	EL&S.	ESCANABA & LAKE SUPERIOR RAILWAY
DV&RL	DULUTH VIRGINIA & RAINY LAKE	EL&WB	EAGLE LAKE & WEST BRANCH
DV&S	DELTA VALLEY & SOUTHERN RAILWAY	ELD	ELDORADO RAILROAD
DVA	DELAWARE VALLEY RAILROAD	ELH&P	ELMIRA LIGHT HEAT & POWER COMPANY
DVA .	DELAWARE VALLEY RAILWAY	ELP	ELI LILLY PHARMACEUTICAL
DVRR	DEERFIELD VALLEY RAILROAD	ELP&C	EL POTOSI & CHIHUAHUA
DW	DESERET-WESTERN RAILWAY	ELS	EAST LORAIN STREET RAILWAY
DW&MR	DAKOTA WYOMING & MISSOURI RIVER RR	EM	ELKHART METALS
DW&P	DULUTH WINNIPEG & PACIFIC RAILROAD	EM&SW	ELDORADO MARION & SOUTHWESTERN
DW&P.	DULUTH WINNIPEG & PACIFIC RAILWAY	EMA	EAST MAHANOY
DW&PIT	DUNKIRK WARREN & PITTSBURGH	EMC	ERIE MINING COMPANY
DW&W	DULUTH WINNIPEG & WESTERN RAILWAY	EMCB	ELECTO MOTIVE CORPORATION
DWAT	DEEPWATER	EMM	EMMITSBURG RAILROAD
DWC	DEADWOOD CENTRAL		

A43

APPENDIX A (RAILROADS)

A	ABBREVIATIONS ALPHABETICALLY W/ROADS
EMRR	EAGLES MERE RAILROAD
EMRY	EASTERN MICHIGAN RAILWAYS
EMSR	EASTERN MASSACHUSETTS STREET RY
EMT	EAGLE MOUNTAIN RAILROAD
EN	EUREKA NEVADA RAILWAY
ENY	EASTERN NEW YORK RAILWAY
EOH	ENSLEY OPEN HEARTH
EORC	EAST OAKLAND RAILROAD COMPANY
EOT	EASTERN OHIO TRACTION
EP	EAST PENNSYLVANIA RAILROAD
EP&J	EL PASO & JUAREZ ELECTRIC CO (TEXAS)
EP&S	EL PASO & SOUTHWESTERN
EPCL	EL PASO CITY LINES
EPEC	EL PASO ELECTRIC COMPANY
EPLC	EAGLE PITCHER LEAD COMPANY
EPS	EL PASO SOUTHERN
EPUP	EL PASO UNION PASSENGER DEPOT
ER	EDVAVILLE RAILROAD
ER	EMORY RIVER RAILROAD
ER&E	EEL RIVER & EUREKA
ERC	ELK RUN COAL
ERC&L	ELK RIVER COAL & LUMBER
EREX	EREX
ERM	EASTERN RAILROAD OF MASSACHUSETTS
ERM.	EASTERN RAILROAD
ES	EPSOM SALTS MONORAIL
ES&G	ESTACADO & GULF
ES&N	EVANSVILLE SUBURBAN & NEWBURG
ES&S	EAST SHORE & SURBURBAN RAILWAY CO
ESC	EMPIRE SUGAR COMPANY
ESH	EASTERN SHORE
ESL	ELECTRIC SHORT LINE RAILWAY
ESL&C	EAST ST LOUIS & CARONDELET
ESL&S	EAST ST LOUIS & SUBURBAN RAILWAY
ESLJ	EAST ST LOUIS JUNCTION RAILROAD
ESO	EUREKA SOUTHERN
ESP	EUREKA SPRINGS RAILROAD
ESRY	ELBERTON SOUTHERN RAILWAY
ET	EBERLE TANNING
ET&G	EAST TENNESSEE & GEORGIA RAILROAD CO
ET&V	EAST TENNESSEE & VIRGINIA RAILROAD CO
ET&WNC	EAST TENNESSEE & WESTERN N CAROLINA
ETCO	EMPIRE TRANSPORTATION COMPANY
ETE	ESSEX TERMINAL RAILWAY
ETL	ELY THOMAS LUMBER
ETR	EDMODNTON TRANSIT
ETRR	EAST TROY MUNICIPAL RAILWAY
ETRR.	EAST TROY RAILROAD
ETV&G	EAST TENNESSEE VIRGINIA & GULF
ETV&GA	EAST TENNESSEE VIRGINIA & GEORGIA
EU	EUSTIS
EUC	EUCLID RAILROAD
EV	EVERETT RAILROAD
EV&I	EVANSVILLE & INDIANAPOLIS
EV&P	EVANSVILLE & PEORIA
EVP&S	EVERETT PIPE & STEEL
EW	EAST WASHINGTON RAILWAY
EW&B	EVANSVILLE WASHINGTON & BRAZIL
EW&STL	ERIE WABASH & ST LOUIS
EW&W	EVANSVILLE WASHINGTON & WORTHINGTON
EWE	ERIE WESTERN
EXPO	EXPO '67 RAPID TRANSIT, MONTREAL
EY&P	EDMONTON YUKON & PACIFIC
F	FLORIDA
F&AB	FERNANDINA & AMELIA BEACH
F&BE	FELICITY & BETHEL RAILROAD
F&C	FRANKFORT & CINCINNATI RAILROAD
F&C.	FRANKFORT & CINCINNATI RAILWAY
F&CC	FLORENCE & CRIPPLE CREEK RAILROAD CO
F&CRR	FRANKLIN & CAROLINA RAILROAD
F&EV	FREMONT & ELKHORN VALLEY RAILROAD
F&I	FREMONT & INDIANA
F&IU	FOX & ILLINOIS UNION RAILWAY CO.
F&J	FERNANDINA & JACKSONVILLE
F&JA	FREEHOLD & JAMESBURG AGRICULTURAL
F&L	FRANKLIN & LEBANON TRACTION CO

A	ABBREVIATIONS ALPHABETICALLY W/ROADS
F&LSR	FITCHBURG & LEOMINISTER STREET RY
F&M	FRANKLIN & MEGANTIC
F&N	FAIRCHILD & NORTHEASTERN
F&NW	FLEMINGSBURG & NORTHWESTERN RAILROAD
F&P	FARMVILLE & POWHATAN
F&PM	FLINT & PERE MARQUETTE
F&PR	FORDYCE & PRINCETON RAILROAD
F&Q	FAIRMONT & QUARRYVILLE
F&S	FAIRHAVEN & SOUTHERN
F&W	FENNIMORE & WOODMAN
F&WI	FLORIDA & WEST INDIA SHORT LINE
F-M	FAIRBANKS MORSE
F-MT	FREDERICK-MIDDLETOWN
FA&G	FLORIDA ALABAMA & GEORGIA
FAM	FAMILY LINES
FAM.	FAMOCO
FARM	FARMRAIL
FB	FALL BROOK COAL COMPANY
FB&S	FORT BRAGG & SOUTHEASTERN RR CO
FBL	FEDERAL BARGE LINES
FBRR	FALL BROOK RAILROAD
FBRR.	FALL BROOK RAILWAY
FC	FLORIDA CENTRAL RAILROAD
FC&G	FLORIDA CENTRAL & GULF
FC&GU	FERNWOOD COLUMBIA & GULF RAILROAD
FC&P	FLORIDA CENTRAL & PENINSULAR
FC&W	FLORIDA CENTRAL & WESTERN
FCAP	FERROCARRILES CHIHUAHUA AL PACIFI (O)
FCM	FERROCARRI MEXICANO
FCMR	FORT COLLINS MUNICIPAL RAILWAY (CO)
FCN	FULTON COUNTY NARROW GAUGE
FCOM	FERROCARRIL OCCIDENTAL DE MEXICO
FDC&P	FERROCARRIL DE CHIHUAHUA AL PACI (O)
FDES	FERROCARRIL DEL SURESTE
FDES.	FERROCARRILES UNIDOS DEL SURESTE
FDM&S	FORT DODGE DES MOINES & SOUTHERN RY
FDP	FERROCARRIL DEL PACIFICO
FDS	FORT DODGE STREET RAILWAY
FDSO	FERROCARRILL DE SONORA
FE	FELICIANA EASTERN RAILROAD
FE&MV	FREMONT ELKHORN & MISSOURI VALLEY RR
FEC	FLORIDA EAST COAST RAILROAD
FEM	FORT EUSTIS MILITARY RAILROAD
FERD	FERDINAND RAILROAD
FERS	FISHER ELECTRIC RAILWAY
FES	FRANKLIN ELECTRIC STREET RAILWAY CO
FGE&	FRUIT GROWERS EXPRESS (O)
FGEX	FRUIT GROWERS EXPRESS
FGT	FOREST GROVE TRANSPORTATION
FH	FORT HAMILTON
FHP	FORT HOWARD PAPER COMPANY
FI	FITCHBURG RAILROAD (O)
FIRT	FLORIDA INTERURBAN RAPID TRANSIT CO
FJ&G	FONDA JOHNSTOWN & GLOVERSVILLE RR
FL&N	FLEMINGSBURG & NORTHERN
FLC	FLORA LOGGING COMPANY
FLRR	FLORENCE RAILROAD
FM	FLORIDA MIDLAND
FMB	FIVE MILE BEACH RAILWAY
FMC	FORD MOTOR COMPANY
FMIN	FOOTE MINERALS
FMSR	FORT MYERS SOUTHERN RAILWAY
FMU	FERNANDINA MUNICIPAL RAILWAY
FNDM	FERROCARRILES NACIONALES DE MEXICO
FNM	FALCONBRIDGE NICKEL MINES
FOMOCO	FORD MOTOR COMPANY (O)
FOP	FORT ORANGE PAPER COMPANY
FOR	FORE RIVER RAILROAD
FP	FLAMBEAU PAPER
FP&E	FAIRPORT PAINESVILLE & EASTERN RY
FP&L	FLORDIA POWER & LIGHT
FP&P	FREDERICKSBURG POTOMAC & PIEDMONT
FPL	FILTRATION PLANT RAILWAY
FPT	FAIRMOUNT PARK TRANSIT
FR	FEATHER RIVER LUMBER COMPANY
FR.	FEATHER RIVER RAILWAY
FR&N	FLORIDA RAILWAY & NAVIGATIONS

APPENDIX A (RAILROADS)

A	ABBREVIATIONS ALPHABETICALLY W/ROADS
FR&NE	FLINT RIVER & NORTH EASTERN
FR.	FEATHER RIVER RAILROAD
FRANK	FRANKLIN RAILROAD
FRB	FAR ROCKAWAY BRANCH RAILROAD
FRE	FREEPORT
FRI	FRIENDSHIP
FRIS	FRISCO
FRIS	ST LOUIS & SAN FRANCISCO RAILWAY
FRIS,	ST LOUIS & SAN FRANCISCO RAILWAY
FRL	FALL RIVER LINE
FRM	FRISCO MANDARIN
FRR	FITCHBURG RAILROAD
FRRY	FEATHER RIVER RAILWAY (O)
FRW	FRENCH RAILWAYS
FRY	FULTON RAILWAY
FS	FLORIDA SOUTHERN
FS&S	FORT SMITH & SOUTHERN
FS&VB	FORT SMITH & VAN BUREN RAILWAY
FS&W	FORT SMITH & WESTERN RAILROAD
FSBC	FERROCCARRI SONORA BAJA CALIFO
FSRY	FULTON STREET RAILWAY
FSS&RI	FORT SMITH SUBIACO & ROCK ISLAND RR
FSUD	FORT STREET UNION DEPOT
FSW	FLORIDA SOUTHWESTERN
FT	FLORIDA TRANSIT
FT&H	FRANKFORD TACONY & HOLMESBURG RAILWAY
FT&P	FLORIDA TRANSIT & PENINSULAR
FTL	FORT LUCINDA RAILROAD
FU	FERROCARRIL URBANO
FUCY	FERROCARRILES UNIDOS DE YUCAT (O)
FUDY	FERROCARRILES UNIDOS DE YUCATAN
FV	FEDERAL VALLEY RAILROAD
FVM	FERROCARILLES DE VALLE DE MEXICO
FW&C	FORT WAYNE & CHICAGO
FW&D	FORT WORTH & DENVER RAILWAY
FW&DC	FORT WORTH & DENVER CITY RAILWAY
FW&WV	FORT WAYNE & WABASH VALLEY TRACTION
FWB	FORT WORTH BELT RAILWAY
FWE	FORT WILLIAMS ELECTRIC
FWL	FORT WAYNE-LIMA
FWT	FORT WORTH TRANSIT
FWTC&I	FAIRFIELD WORKS TENNESSEE COAL & IRON
G	GEORGIA RAILROAD
G&B	GUNN & BLACK RAILROAD
G&C	GULF & CHICAGO RAILROAD
G&CU	GALENA & CHICAGO UNION
G&F	GEORGIA & FLORIDA RAILROAD
G&F.	GEORGIA & FLORDIA RAILWAY
G&G	GAINESVILLE & GULF
G&GE	GALESBURG & GREAT EASTERN RAILROAD
G&GP	GEORGETOWN & GRAY'S PEAK
G&H	GETTYSBURG & HARRISBURG
G&HE	GREENSBURG & HEMPFIELD ELECTRIC RY
G&I	GENEVA & ITHACA
G&IR	GULF & INTERSTATE RAILROAD
G&J	GREENWICH & JOHNSONVILLE RAILWAY
G&M	GULFPORT & MISSISSIPPI COAST TRACTION
G&MI	GREENVILLE & MIAMI
G&MIS	GULF & MISSISSIPPI
G&MV	GLASSBORO & MILLVILLE
G&N	GREENVILLE & NORTHERN RAILWAY
G&P	GILMORE & PITTSBURGH RAILROAD
G&ST	GROTON & STONINGTON TRCTION COMPANY
G&SW	GALENA & SOUTHERN WISCONSIN
G&U	GRAFTON & UPTON RAILROAD
G&W	GALVESTON & WESTERN RAILROAD
G&W.	GENESSEE & WYOMING (O)
G&WE	GARY & WESTERN RAILROAD
G&WP	GEORGIA & WEST POINT
G&WY	GENESSEE & WYOMING RAILROAD
G&Y	GENESSE & WYOMING (O)
G*	GULF
G-H	GIFFORD-HILL
G-P	GEORGIA-PACIFIC CORPORATION

A	ABBREVIATIONS ALPHABETICALLY W/ROADS
GA*	GATX
GAF	GENERAL ANILINE FILM
GAM	GEORGIA MARBLE
GAR	GARDINER INC
GARC	GARDEN CITY RAILWAY COMPANY
GARY	GARY RAILWAY
GAS&C	GEORGIA ASHBURN SYLVESTER & CAMILLA
GAYP	GAYLORD PAPER COMPANY
GB	GUIGNARD BRICK
GB&E	GREENBRIER & EASTERN
GB&L	GEORGETOWN BRECKENRIDGE & LEADVILLE
GB&LP	GREEN BAY & LAKE PEPIN
GB&W	GREEN BAY & WESTERN RAILROAD COMPANY
GB&W.	GREEN BAY ROUTE
GBM&C	GREEN BAY MILWAUKEE & CHICAGO
GBR	GREEN BAY ROUTE (O)
GBW&SP	GREEN BAY WINONA & ST PAUL RAILWAY
GC	GOLD COAST RAILROAD
GC&C	GEORGES CREEK & CUMBERLAND
GC&E	GREENBRIER CHEAT & ELK
GC&P	GEORGIA COAST & PIEDMONT RAILROAD
GC&SF	GULF COLORADO & SANTA FE
GC&SJ	GOLDEN CITY & SAN JUAN
GC&WR	GALES CREEK & WILSON RIVER RAILROAD
GCE	GREAT CENTRAL
GCH	GRACE CHEMICAL
GCL	GULF COAST LINES
GCO	GRAHAM COUNTY RAILROAD
GCOM	GROVES COMPANY
GCRR	GOLDEN CIRCLE RAILROAD COMPANY
GCS	GENERAL CRUSHED STONE
GCS&M	GREEN COVE SPRINGS & MELROSE
GCT	GILPIN COUNTY TRAMWAY COMPANY
GCW	GARDEN CITY WESTERN RAILWAY
GD	GLENMORE DISTRIBUTORS
GDIS	GLENMORE DISTILLERIES
GE	GENERAL ELECTRIC
GERB*	GERBERS BABY FOOD
GESI	GE SCHENECTADY INDUSTRIAL RAILROAD
GET	GETTYSBURG ELECTRIC
GETTY	GETTYSBURG RAILROAD
GF	GRIZZLY FLATS RAILROAD
GF&A	GEORGIA FLORIDA & ALABAMA
GF&OD	GREAT FALLS & OLD DOMINION
GFC	GRAND FALLS CENTRAL RAILWAY
GFR	GERMAN FEDERAL RAILWAY
GG	GOODPASTURE GRAIN
GH&H	GALVESTON HOUSTON & HENDERSON RR
GHCF	GLEN HAVEN CANNING FACTORY
GHE	GALVESTON HOUSTON ELECTRIC RY
GI	GILPIN RAILROAD
GI&A	GENEVA ITHACA & ATHENS RAILROAD
GI&S	GENEVA ITHACA & SAYRE
GIC	GILMORE INDUSTRIAL CENTER
GIL	GILFORD TRANSPORTATION COMPANY
GIW	GENERAL IRON WORKS
GJ&S	GAINESVILLE JEFFERSON & SOUTHERN
GL	GULF LINE RAILWAY
GL&S	GLOSTER & SOUTHERN RAILWAY
GL&W	GLENFIELD & WESTERN
GLC	GENERAL LOGGING COMPANY
GLN	GREAT LAKES NAVAL STATION
GLS	GREAT LAKES STEEL CORPORATION
GM	GENERAL MOTORS
GM&G	GEORGIA MIDLAND & GULF
GM&N	GULF MOBILE & NORTHERN
GM&O	GULF MOBILE & OHIO
GMA	GENERAL MINING ASSN OF NOVA SCOTIA
GMI	GAINESVILLE MIDLAND RAILROAD
GMQ	GRANITE MOUNTAIN QUARRIES
GMT	GREEN MOUNTAIN RAILROAD
GN	GREAT NORTHERN RAILWAY
GN&A	GRAYSONIA NASHVILLE & ASHDOWN RR
GNC	GREAT NORTHERN OF CANADA
GNO	GEORGIA NORTHERN RAILWAY
GO	GOLDFIELD RAILROAD
GOSH	GOSHEN VALLEY

STEPHANS' RAILROAD DIRECTORY

APPENDIX A (RAILROADS)

A	ABBREVIATIONS ALPHABETICALLY W/ROADS
GOT	GOVERNMENT OF ONTARIO TRANSIT
GOTR	GO TRANSIT
GP	GREAT PLAINS RAILWAY
GP&H	GALT PRESTON & HESPELER RAILWAY
GPC	GEORGIA POWER COMPANY
GPCO	GULF POWER COMPANY
GPEX	GENERAL AMERICAN PFAUDLER CORP
GPT	GULF PORTS TERMINAL
GR	GRAND RIVER VALLEY RAILROAD
GR&I	GRAND RAPIDS & INDIANA RAILWAY
GR&ISR	GEORGETOWN ROWLEY & IPSWICH ST RY
GR&M	GRAYVILLE & MATTOON RAILROAD
GR&NW	GRAND RAPIDS & NORTH WESTERN RAILROAD
GRA	GRANITE RAILWAY
GRAY	GRAY'S RUN RAILROAD
GRGH&M	GRAND RAPIDS GRAND HAVEN & MUSKEGON RY
GRGHM	GRAND RAPIDS GRAND HAVEN & MICHIGAN RY
GRR	GRASSE RIVER RAILROAD
GRRAP	GRAND RAPIDS RAILWAY
GRRY	GRAND RIVER RAILWAY
GRSC	GREEN RIVER STEEL COMPANY
GS	GODCHAUX SUGAR
GS&F	GEORGIA SOUTHERN & FLORIDA RAILWAY
GS&G	GEORGIA SOUTHWESTERN & GULF RAILROAD
GSB&C	GOSHEN SOUTH BEND & CHICAGO RAILWAY
GSC	GEARY STREET CABLE RAILWAY
GSC.	GEARY STREET CABLE RAILROAD COMPANY
GSCC	GREENVILLE STEEL CAR COMPANY
GSL	GREAT SLAVE LAKE RAILWAY
GSRY	GREAT SWAMP RAILWAY
GSSR	GROTON STONINGTON STREET RAILWAY
GSW	GREAT SOUTHWEST RAILROAD
GT	GRAND TRUNK RAILWAY SYSTEM
GT&W	GULF TEXAS & WESTERN
GT.	GRAND TRUCK RAILROAD
GTC	GRAND TRUNK OF CANADA
GTCO	GRAND TRUCK CORPORATION
GTI	GUILFORD TRANSPORTATION INDUSTRY
GTN	GEORGETOWN RAILROAD
GTP	GRAND TRUNK PACIFIC
GTS	GEORGETOWN STEEL
GTW	GRAND TRUNK WESTERN RAILWAY
GTW.	GRAND TRUNK WESTERN RAILROAD COMPANY
GUA	GUALALA RAILWAY
GUSC	GOLDSBORO UNION STATION COMPANY
GUST	GOLDSBORO UNION STATION (O)
GV	GEORGES VALLEY
GV&NW	GAINESVILLE & NORTHWESTERN
GVE	GALLATIN VALLEY ELECTRIC
GW	GREAT WESTERN RAILWAY
GWC	GREAT WESTERN OF CANADA
GWH	GALVESTON WHARVES TERMINAL
GWHC	GALVESTON WHARF COMPANY
GWS	GREAT WESTERN SUGAR
GWWD	GREATER WINNIPEG WATER DISTRICT RY
GY*	GOODYEAR
H	HARRISBURG RYS
H&B	HAMPTON & BRANCHVILLE RAILROAD
H&BC	HUDSON & BOSTON CORPORATION
H&BM	HAZELTON & BEAVER MEADOWS
H&BT	HUDSON & BROAD TOP MOUNTAIN
H&BTM	HUNTINGTON & BROAD TOP MOUNTAIN RR
H&BTOP	HUNTINGTON & BROAD TOP RAILROAD
H&BV	HOUSTON & BRAZOS VALLEY (MP)
H&C	HANCOCK & CALUMET RAILWAY
H&CT	HUMMELSTOWN & CAMPBELLTOWN STREET RY
H&CV	HARTFORD & CONNECTICUT VALLEY
H&CW	HARTFORD & CONNECTICUT WESTERN
H&DS	HAMILTON & DUDAS STREET RAILWAY
H&E	HOLLIS & EASTERN RAILROAD
H&F	HAGERSTOWN & FREDERICK RAILWAY
H&FS	HAWKINSVILLE & FLORIDA SOUTHERN
H&H	HIBISCUS & HELICONIA
H&HC	HART & HORNING COMPANY
H&L	HACKENSACK & LODI
H&LB	HUNTSVILLE & LAKE OF BAYS RAILROAD
H&LB.	HUNTSVILLE & LAKE OF BAYS RAILWAY

A	ABBREVIATIONS ALPHABETICALLY W/ROADS
H&LR	HAMMOND & LITTLE RIVER LUMBER COMPANY
H&M	HUDSON & MANHATTAN RAILROAD
H&M.	HUDSON & MANHATTAN SUBWAY
H&MA	HALL & MANNING
H&MC	HARLEM & MANHATTAN CABLE
H&MO	HUDSON & MOHWAK
H&N	HUTCHINSON & NORTHERN RAILWAY COMPANY
H&NE	HILLSBORO & NORTH EASTERN RAILWAY
H&NH	HARTFORD & NEW HAVEN
H&NW	HAMILTON & NORTHWESTERN RAILWAY
H&NY	HACKENSACK & NEW YORK RAILROAD
H&O	HOUGHTON & ONTONAGON
H&S	HARTFORD & SLOCOMB RAILROAD
H&SJ	HANNIBAL & ST JOSEPH
H&SO	HOPKINSVILLE & SOUTHERN
H&SSR	HARTFORD & SPRINGFIELD STREET RY CO
H&T	HOUSTON & TEXAS
H&TC	HOUSTON & TEXAS CENTRAL
H&TL	HECLA & TORCH LAKE
H&W	HARDWICK & WOODBURY RAILWAY
H&WE	HARRISBURG & WESTERN
H&WH	HARTFORD & WETHERSFIELD HORSE RY
H&WI	HOOSAC & WILMINGTON
H-WPP	HOERNER-WALDORF PAPER PRODUCTS
HA	HAZLETON
HA&W	HAWKINSVILLE & WESTERN
HADK	HALLETT DOCK
HALC	HALIFAX CITY RAILROAD
HALO	HABCO LORAM
HAMP	HAMPDEN RAILROAD
HAMPC	HAMMERMILL PAPER COMPANY
HAMS*	HAMS
HANC	HANNIBAL CONNECTING RAILROAD
HAR	HARTWELL RAILWAY
HAS	HASSINGER
HAY	HAYDENVILLE BRANCH RAILROAD
HAYC	HAYDEN COAL COMPANY
HB	HARVARD BRANCH
HB&IR	HURON BAY & IRON RANGE
HB&T	HOUSTON BELT & TERMINAL RAILWAY CO.
HB&TD	HUMBOLDT BAY & TRINIDAD
HBLR	HARBOR BELT LINE RAILROAD-CALIFORNIA
HBRR	HUDSON BAY RAILROAD
HBRR.	HUDSON BAY RAILWAY
HC	HERSHEY CUBAN RAILWAY
HC&SW	HOUGHTON CHASSELL & SOUTHWESTERN
HCA&N	HOUSTON CENTRAL ARKANSAS & NORTHERN
HCC	HUDSON COAL COMPANY
HCO&W	HAYT'S CORNERS OVID & WILLARD
HCR	HALTON COUNTY RADIAL RAILWAY
HCRR	HUDSON CONNECTING RAILROAD COMPANY
HCRY	HURON CITY RAILWAY
HD	HOUSE OF DAVID
HE	HARTFORD EASTERN
HE&WT	HOUSTON EAST & WEST TEXAS
HECO	HOUSTON ELECTRIC COMPANY
HELC	HARTFORD ELECTRIC LIGHT COMPANY
HENL	HENDERSON LUMBER COMPANY
HEPC	HYDRO ELECTRIC POWER COMMISSION
HER	HULL ELECTRIC RAILWAY (ONTARIO)
HERE	HEREFORD RAILWAY
HES	HELENA SOUTHWESTERN RAILROAD
HESO	HELENA SOUTHERN
HF&W	HINESVILLE FLEMINGTON & WESTERN
HG&B	HAMILTON GRINSBY & BEAMVILLE ELEC RY
HG&DSR	HAVERHILL GEORGETOWN & DANVERS ST RY
HGC	HICKGAS COMPANY
HH	HETCH HETCHY RAILROAD
HHL	HIMMTEBERG-HARRISON LUMBER CO
HI	HOLTEN INTER-URBAN RAILWAY COMPANY
HIGH	HIGHLAND RAILROAD
HIL	HILLSDALE COUNTY RAILWAY
HILLC	HILL CITY RAILWAY
HIR	HAMERSLEY IRON
HL&R	HELENA LIGHT & RAILWAY
HL&T	HORTON LUMBER & TIMBER COMPANY
HLC	HAMMOND LUMBER COMPANY

STEPHANS' RAILROAD DIRECTORY

A46

APPENDIX A (RAILROADS)

A	ABBREVIATIONS ALPHABETICALLY W/ROADS	A	ABBREVIATIONS ALPHABETICALLY W/ROADS
HLCL	HILLCREST LUMBER COMPANY LTD	IES	INLAND EMPIRE SYSTEM
HLW	HINKLEY LOCOMOTIVE WORKS	IFT	ICE FULTON TRIANGLE
HM	HOBOKEN MANUFACTURERS RAILROAD	IH&IR	INDIAN HILL & IRON RANGE RAILROAD
HM&A	HAVERHILL MERRIMAC & AMESBURY ST RY	IHB	INDIANA HARBOR BELT RAILROAD
HM&PLA	HUENEME MALIBU & PORT LOS ANGELES RY	IHRC	INDIANA HI-RAIL CORPORATION
HM&R	HARTFORD MANCHESTER & ROCKVILLE TRAMWY	IL	ILWACO RAILWAY & NAVIGATION COMPANY
HMC	HOMESTAKE MINING COMPANY	IL&S	INLAND LIME & STONE
HNS	HOUSTON NORTH SHORE (MP)	ILST	INTERLAKE STEEL
HNSM	HANNA NICKEL SMELTING	IM	ILLINOIS MIDLAND RAILWAY
HO	HOUSASTONIC	IM&C	INTERNATIONAL MINERALS & CHEMICAL
HOBO	HOBO RAILROAD	IMI	INTERNATIONAL MILLING
HOOD	HOOD RIVER RAILROAD	IMPX	IMPERIAL SUGAR
HOPE	HOPE VALLEY RAILROAD	IMT	IRON MOUNTAIN RAILWAY
HORT	HONOLULU RAPID TRANSIT COMPANY	IN	ILLINOIS NORTHERN RAILWAY
HOS	HILLCREST OSBORNE	IN.	ILLINOIS NORTHERN RAILROAD
HOTS	HOT SPRINGS RAILROAD	INDSC	INDIANA SERVICE CORPORATION
HP&FV	HIGHLAND PARK & FRUITVALE AVE RR	INMT	INTERMOUNTAIN RAILWAY
HP&N	HELENA PARKIN & NORTHERN RAILWAY	INMT.	INTER-MOUNTAIN RAILWAY
HPC	HERCULES POWDER COMPANY	INN	INDIANA NORTHERN RAILWAY
HPC*	HUNTER PACKING COMPANY	INS	INDIANA SOUTHERN
HPM	HARRISBURG PORSMOUTH MT JOY & LANCAST	INTER	INTERSTATE RAILROAD
HPT&D	HIGH POINT THOMASVILLE & DENTON RR	IOCC	IRON ORE CO OF CANADA
HR&B	HUDSON RIVER & BOSTON	IOIS	IOWA INTERSTATE
HRC	HAWAIIAN RAILROAD COMPANY	IOWA	IOWA TERMINAL RAILROAD COMPANY
HRLC	HARRINGTON LUMBER COMPANY	IOWA	IOWA TERMINAL RAILWAY
HRR	HORWITH RAILROAD	IOWAC	IOWA CENTRAL
HRRR	HUDSON RIVER RAILROAD & TERMINAL	IOWAT	IOWA TRANSFER RAILWAY
HS	HOBART SOUTHERN	IP&L	IOWA POWER & LIGHT
HSH	HOBOKEN SHORE RAILROAD (HM)	IPSI	INTERSTATE PUBLIC SERV CO OF INDIANA
HSL	HAZELTON-SUGAR LOAF	IR	IRONTON RAILROAD
HSR	HELLENIC STATE RAILWAYS	IR&T	INTERURBAN RAILWAY & TERMINAL
HST	HAMILTON STREET RAILWAY	IRCA	INTERNATIONAL RW OF CENTRAL AMERICA
HT	HERSHEY TRANSIT	IRD	IMPERIAL IRRIGATION DISTRICT
HT&W	HOOSAC TUNNEL & WILMINGTON RAILROAD	IRP	INGERSOLL RAND POWERED LOCOMOTIVES
HTR	HARLEM TRANSFER COMPANY	IRPC	ILLINOIS RIVER PACKET CO
HTRY	HOWARD TERMINAL RAILWAY	IRR	ISLAND RAILROAD
HU	HUNTINGTON RAILROAD	IRRC	IOWA RAILROAD CORPORATION
HU&BT	HUNTINGTON & BROAD TOP MT RR & COAL CO	IRT	INTERBUROUGH RAPID TRANSIT COMPANY
HU&E	HURON & EASTERN RAILWAY	IRW	INDIANAPOLIS RAILWAYS
HV	HOCKING VALLEY RAILROAD	IRY	INTERNATIONAL RAILWAY (CANADA)
HV&CV	HORNELLSVILLE & COHOCTON VALLEY	IS	INGALLS SHIPBUBILDING
HVE	HUDSON VALLEY ELECTRIC RAILROAD	IS&B	ILLINOIS SLAG & BALLAST
HVRY	HUDSON VALLEY RAILWAY	ISC*	INLAND STEEL CO
HVS	HOCKEN VALLEY SCENIC RAILWAY	ISM&E	IBERIA ST MARY & EASTERN
HVSR	HOOSAC VALLEY STREET RAILWAY	ISO	IDAHO SOUTHERN
HWSR	HILLCREST WSR.	ISR	INTERSTATE STREET RAILWAY
HY&T	HOOPPOLE YORKTOWN & TAMPOCO	ISRY	ITHACA STREET RAILWAY
HZ	HEINZ 57	ISTCC	ISTHMUS CANAL COMMISSION
HZ*	HEINZ 57 (O)	IT	ILLINOIS TERMINAL RAILROAD COMPANY
I	INDIANA RAILROAD	IT&B	ISLAND TUG & BARGE LIMITED
I&A	ITHACA & ATHENS	IT.	ILLINOIS TERMINAL RAILROAD SYSTEMS
I&C	INDIANAPOLIS & CINCINNATTI TRACTION CO	ITAS	ITASCA RAILROAD
I&E	INDIANAPOLIS & EASTERN	ITC	ISLAND TERMINAL COMPANY
I&JC	IOLA & ST JOSEPH CANAL & RAILROAD	ITCO	ILLINOIS TUNNEL COMPANY
I&M	INDEPENDENCE & MONMOUTH	ITH	ITHACA TRACTION CORPORATION
I&ME	INDIANA & MICHIGAN ELECTRIC	ITR	ILLINOIS TRACTION RAILWAY
I&N	IOLA & NORTHERN RAILROAD	ITTX	ITTX
I&O	ITHACA & OWEGO	IU	INDIANAPOLIS UNION RAILWAY
I&OH	INDIANA & OHIO	IUR	INTER-URBAN RAILWAY
I&OS	ITHACA & OSWEGO	IV	INDIAN VALLEY RAILROAD
I&WN	IDAHO & WASHINGTON NORTHERN RAILROAD	IVT	ILLINOIS VALLEY TRACTION
I-ASL	ITHACA-AUBURN SHORT LINE	J	JEFFERSON RAILROAD
I-GN	INTERNATIONAL GREAT NORTHERN (MP)	J&A	JACKSONVILLE & ATLANTIC
IA&W	ITHACA AUBURN & WESTERN	J&C	JOLIET & CHICAGO
IC	ILLINOIS CENTRAL RAILROAD	J&E	JERSEYVILLE & EASTERN RAILROAD
IC&E	INDIANA COLUMBUS & EASTERN TRACTION	J&H	JACKSONVILLE & HAVANA
IC&LRR	INDIANAPOLIS CINCINNATI & LAFAYETTE RR	J&L	JONES & LAUGHLIN STEEL
IC&W	IOWA CENTRAL & WESTERN RAILWAY	J&LP	JEFFERSON & LAKE PONTCHARTRAIN RR
ICC	ISLAND CREEK COAL	J&NW	JEFFERSON & NORTHWESTERN RAILROAD
ICCO	INSPERATION CONSOLIDATION COPPER CO	J&S	JACKSONVILLE & SOUTHWESTERN
ICG	ILLINOIS CENTRAL GULF	J&SC	JOHNSTOWN & STONY CREEK RAILROAD
ICO	INTERCOLONIAL RAILWAY	J&SS	JOHNSTOWN & SOMERSET
ICO	INTERCOLONIAL RAILROAD	J&SW	JEROME & SOUTHWESTERN
ICO.	INTERCOLONIAL CANADA RAILWAY	J&W	JACKASS & WESTERN
ICRT	INTER-CITY RAPID TRANSIT (OHIO)	JA&F	JAMESTOWN & FRANKLIN
ID&C	INDIANAPOLIS DELPHI & CHICAGO	JA&HR	JACKSONVILLE ST AUGUSTINE & HALIFAX R
IEPC	INLAND PAPER COMPANY	JA&IR	JACKSONVILLE ST AUGUSTINE & INDIAN RI

APPENDIX A (RAILROADS)

A	ABBREVIATIONS ALPHABETICALLY W/ROADS
JB	JACKSONVILLE BELT
JC	JUNCTION CITY-HORTON WOODEN RAILROAD
JC&A	JERSEY CITY & ALBANY
JC&FR	JUNCTION CITY & FORT RILEY RAILWAY
JC&LE	JAMESTOWN CHAUTAUQUA & LAKE ERIE
JCE	JERSEY CENTRAL (O)
JCET	JERSEY CITY TERMINAL
JCG	JACKSON COUNTY GRAIN
JCITY	JERSEY CITY
JCRR	JOE CUSHING RAILROAD
JCTR	JERSEY CENTRAL TRACTION
JE&N	JOHNSTOWN EBENSBURG & NORTHERN
JG&G	JACKSONVILLE GAINESVILLE & GULF
JL	JOHNSON LUMBER
JM&I	JEFFERSON MADISON & INDIANAPOLIS RR
JM&P	JACKSONVILLE MAYPORT & PABLO RY & NAV
JN	JAPANESE NATIONAL RAILWAYS
JNR	JAPAN NATIONAL RAILWAY
JO	JOHNSONBURG
JP	JOHNSTOWN PASSENGER RAILWAY
JP&M	JACKSONVILLE PENSACOLA & MOBILE
JR	JAMES RIVER COMPANY
JS	JAY STREET CONNECTING RAILROAD
JS&AF	JERSEY SHORE & ANTES FORT RAILROAD
JSRY	JAMESTOWN STREET RAILWAY
JSW	JEFFERSON SOUTHWESTERN RAILROAD
JT	JACKSONVILLE TERMINAL COMPANY
JT&KW	JACKSONVILLE TAMPA & KEY WEST
JTC	JOHNSTOWN TRACTION CO
JTT	JOHNSTOWN TERMINAL RAILWAY COMPANY
JUD	JOLIET UNION DEPOT COMPANY
JUDC	JOPLIN UNION DEPOT COMPANY
JVT	JACKSONVILLE TRACTION COMPANY
JW&N	JAMESTOWN WESTFIELD & NORTHWESTERN RR
JWR	JIM WALTER RESOURCES INC
K	KANE
K&AR	KINGSTON & ADELPHI RAILROAD
K&AV	KANSAS & ARKANSAS VALLEY
K&DM	KEOKUK & DES MOINES
K&DR	KINGFIELD & DEAD RIVER
K&E	KANE & ELK
K&EL	KENDALL & ELDRED
K&IB	KENTUCKY & INDIANA BRIDGE & RR CO.
K&IT	KENTUCKY & INDIANA TERMINAL RAILROAD
K&L	KNOX & LINCOLN
K&M	KANAWHA & MICHIGAN
K&MR&T	KANSAS & MISSOURI RY & TERMINAL CO
K&N	KANSAS & NEVADA RY & TERMINAL CO
K&NL	KINKORA & NEW LISBON
K&O	KANSAS & OKLAHOMA
K&OH	KNOXVILLE & OHIO RAILROAD
K&S	KEATING & SMETHPORT
K&SE	KOSCIVSKO & SOUTHEASTERN
K&SEN	KANKAKEE & SENECA
K&SID	KANSAS & SIDELL
K&SL	KASLO & SLOCAN
K&T	KENTUCKY & TENNESSEE RAILWAY
K&T .	KENTUCKY & TENNESSEE RAILROAD
K&TI	KINZUA & TIONA
K&U	KANKAKEE & URSANA TRACTION COMPANY
K&W	KEOKUK & WESTERN
K#	KOPPERS
K-HC	KUMPE-HAUSER CORPORATION
K-M	KERR-MCGEE
KA	KAHULUI RAILROAD
KAC	KANAWHA CENTRAL RAILWAY
KAC&LC	KEESEVILLE AUSABLE CHASM &L CHAMPLAIN
KARS	KARSHNER
KATY	KATY NORTHWEST (MKT) (O)
KAUL	KAULLUMBER COMPANY
KB	KAISER BAUXITE
KB&TC	KINGSTON BRIDGE & TERMINAL COMPANY
KBM	KINMOND BROTHERS MONTREAL
KC	KELLEY'S CREEK RAILROAD
KC&B	KANSAS CITY & BEATRICE
KC&E	KANSAS CITY & EASTERN
KC&IAL	KANSAS CITY & INDEPENDENCE AIR LINE RR
KC&K	KINZUA CREEK & KANE
KC&NW	KELLEY'S CREEK & NORTH WESTERN RR
KC&P	KANSAS CITY & PACIFIC
KC&S	KANSAS CITY & SOUTHERN RAILROAD
KCC	KANSAS CITY CONNECTING RAILROAD
KCC&S	KANSAS CITY CLINTON & SPRINGFIELD
KCE	KENNEBEC CENTRAL
KCERY	KANSAS CITY ELEVATED RAILWAY
KCFS&G	KANSAS CITY FORT SMITH & GULF
KCFS&M	KANSAS CITY FORT SCOTT & MEMPHIS
KCFS&S	KANSAS CITY FORT SMITH & SOUTHERN
KCFSG	KANSAS CITY FORT SCOTT & GULF RAILROAD
KCKV&W	KANSAS CITY KAW VALLEY & WESTERN
KCKW	KANSAS CITY KAW VALLEY
KCM&B	KANSAS CITY MEMPHIS & BIRMINGHAM
KCM&O	KANSAS CITY MEXICO & ORIENT RAILWAY
KCM&O.	KANSAS CITY MEXICO & ORIENT RAILROAD
KCN	KANSAS CITY NORTHWESTERN RAILWAY
KCN&FS	KANSAS CITY NEVADA & FORT SMITH RR CO
KCP&G	KANSAS CITY PITTSBURGH & GULF RAILWAY
KCPS	KANSAS CITY PUBLIC SERVICE
KCPS.	KANSAS CITY PUBLIC SERVICE
KCRR	KINSTON-CAROLINA RAILROAD
KCS	KANSAS CITY SOUTHERN RAILWAY
KCS&G	KANSAS CITY SHREVEPORT & GULF
KCS&GT	KANSAS CITY SHREVEPORT & GULF TERMINAL
KCS&M	KANSAS CITY SPRINGFIELD & MEMPHIS
KCSB	KANSAS CITY SUBURBAN BELT RAILROAD
KCSJCB	KANSAS CITY ST JOSEPH & COUNCIL BLUFF
KCSL&C	KANSAS CITY ST LOUIS & CHICAGO
KCST	KANSAS CITY SOUTHERN TRANSPORT CO
KCT	KANSAS CITY TERMINAL RAILWAY
KCW&NW	KANSAS CITY WYANDOTTE & NORTHWESTERN
KE	KENNECOTT COPPER COMPANY
KER	KERSEY
KEWC	KEWEENAW CENTRAL RAILWAY
KEY	KEYSTONE
KF	KISO FOREST JAPAN
KGB&W	KEWAUNEE GREEN BAY & WESTERN RAILROAD
KGJ&E	KANAWHA GLEN JEAN & EASTERN
KH	KINZUA HEMLOCK
KHC	KITTY HAWK CENTRAL
KI	KINZUA
KIAM	KIAMICHI VALLEY RAILROAD
KICO	KENTUCKY IMPROVEMENT COMPANY
KIL&T	KELLYS ISLAND LIME & TRANSPORT CO.
KINL	KINSTON LUMBER COMPANY
KISH	KISHACOQUILLAS VALLEY RAILROAD
KL	KNICKERBOCKER LIME
KL&L	KLICKITAT LOG & LUMBER COMPANY
KLC	KIRBY LUMBER COMPANY
KLI	KLIPNOCKIE
KLN	KLAMATH NORTHERN RAILWAY
KLS	KINGS LAKE SHORE RAILROAD
KLS&C	KALAMAZOO LAKE SHORE & CHICAGO
KM	KENTUCKY MIDLAND
KMRY	KLONDIKE MINES RAILWAY
KN	KNOX RAILROAD
KO&G	KANSAS OKLAHOMA & GULF RAILWAY
KOLOA	KOLOA PLANTATION
KOP	KOPPERS COMPANY
KP	KAHUKU PLANTATION COMPANY
KP&C	KINGSTON PORTSMOUTH & CATARAQUI
KP&L	KNOXVILLE POWER & LIGHT
KP#	KREY PACKING
KRA#	KRAFT
KRH#	KINGAN RELIABLE HAM
KS	KEY SYSTEM OF SAN FRANCISCO
KSE&S	KANSAS CITY ELDORADO & SOUTHERN
KSPS	KANSAS CITY PUBLIC SERVICE (O)
KSR#	KAHN'S SONS' REFRIGERATION
KSRS	KNOXVILLE STREET RAILWAY SYSTEM
KST	KAISER STEEL
KT&T	KENTUCKY TRACTION & TERMINAL
KTC	KOSMOS TIMBER COMPANY
KTU	KENTUCKY UTILITIES COMPANY
KU	KUSHEQUA

APPENDIX A (RAILROADS)

A	ABBREVIATIONS ALPHABETICALLY W/ROADS	A	ABBREVIATIONS ALPHABETICALLY W/ROADS
KUC	KANSAS UTILITIES COMPANY	LA&ERV	LOS ANGELES & EAGLE ROCK VALLEY
KUCO	KUERT CONCRETE	LA&G	LOS ANGELES & GLENDALE
KUDC	KEOKUK UNION DEPOT COMPANY	LA&L	LIVONIA AVON & LAKEVILLE RAILROAD
KURY	KENTUCKY UNION RAILWAY	LA&LB	LOS ANGELES & LONG BEACH
KV	KINZUA VALLEY	LA&M	LACROSSE & MILWAUKEE
KVRR	KETTLE VALLEY RAILROAD	LA&P	LOS ANGELES & PACIFIC RR
KW	KITCHENER WATERLOO RAILWAY	LA&R	LOS ANGELES & REDONDO
KW&C	KENNEBEC WHARF & COAL	LA&S	LACKAWAXEN & STOURBRIDGE
KWE	KEY WEST ELECTRIC COMPANY	LA&SDB	LOS ANGELES & SAN DIEGO BEACH RY
KWNC	KEEWEENAW CENTRAL RAILROAD	LA&SG	LOS ANGELES & SAN GABRIEL VALLEY
KWS	KEY WEST STREET-CAR ASSOCIATION	LA&SL	LOS ANGELES & SALT LAKE RAILROAD (UP)
KWT	KENTUCKY WEST TENNESSEE	LA&SO	LAURINBURG & SOUTHERN RAILROAD
KYOW	KENTUCKY ORDINACE WORKS	LA&SP	LOS ANGELES & SAN PEDRO
KYRR	KYLE RAILWAYS INC	LA&W	LEWISTON AUGUSTA & WATERVILLE ST RY
L	LAKELAND	LAC	LOS ANGELES COUNTY
L&A	LOUISIANA & ARKANSAS RAILWAY COMPANY	LACK	LACKAWANNA (DL&W) (O)
L&AKS	LOUISIANA & ARKANSAS KANSAS CITY SOUTH	LACK&M	LACKAWANNA & MONTROSE
L&AND	LOWELL & ANDOVER	LAIR	LOS ANGELES INDEPENDENT RAILROAD
L&AT	LOUISVILLE & ATLANTIC RAILROAD	LAJ	LOS ANGELES JUNCTION RAILWAY
L&B	LACKAWANNA & BLOOMSBURG	LALN	LAUREL LINE
L&B	LYNN & BOSTON RAILROAD	LAP&G	LOS ANGELES PASADENA & GLENDALE
L&BR	LOWVILLE & BEAVER RIVER RAILROAD	LAPR	LOS ANGELES PACIFIC RAILWAY COMPANY
L&BV	LACOMBE & BLINDMAN VALLEY	LAR	LOS ANGELES RAILWAY
L&C	LANCASTER & CHESTER RAILWAY	LAS	LASKO
L&CC	LOCKS & CANALS COMPANY LOWELL MASS	LAS&S	LORAIN ASHLAND & SOUTHERN
L&CR	LEWISTON & CRAIGMONT	LAT	LOS ANGELES TERMINAL
L&CRY	LORAIN & CLEVELAND RAILWAY	LATR	LOS ANGELES TRANSIT LINES
L&CV	LEETONIA & CHERRY VALLEY	LAUPT	LOS ANGELES UNION PASSENGER TERMINAL
L&D	LOUISIANA & DELTA	LAV	LAMOILLE VALLEY
L&DV	LEXINGTON & DANVILLE RAILROAD	LB	LONG BELL RAILROAD
L&E	LAWRENCEVILLE & EVERGREEN	LC	LORBERRY CREEK
L&ERR	LORAIN & ELYRIA RAILROAD	LC&C	LOUISVILLE CINCINNATI & CHARLESTON RR
L&F	LOUISVILLE & FRANKFORT	LC&L	LOUISVILLE CINCINNATI & LEXINGTON RR
L&FF	LEXINGTON & FRANKFORT RAILROAD	LC&LJ	LAKE CHAMPLAIN & ST LAWRENCE JUNCTION
L&H	LANCASTER & HAMDEN	LC&M	LAKE CHAMPLAIN & MORIAH RAILROAD
L&HR	LEHIGH & HUDSON RIVER RAILWAY COMPANY	LC&MI	LA CROSSE & MILWAUKEE
L&HR .	LEHIGH & HUDSON RIVER RAILROAD	LC&NW	LACOMBE & NORTH WESTERN
L&I	LOUISVILLE & INTERURBAN	LC&SE	LA CROSSE & SOUTHEASTERN RAILWAY
L&K	LEVIS & KENNEBEC RAILWAY	LCCE	LEE COUNTY CENTRAL ELECTRIC RAILWAY
L&L	LATROBE & LIGONIER	LCDI+	LIQUID CARBONIC DRY ICE
L&LA	LIGONIER & LATROBE RAIL ROAD	LCE	LENAWEE CENTRAL
L&LO	LOOP & LOOKOUT	LCER	LOCK CITY ELECTRIC RAILWAY
L&M	LEHIGH & MAHANOY	LCL	LOUISIANA CYPRESS LUMBER COMPANY
L&MA	LAKESIDE & MARBLEHEAD RAILROAD	LCO	LENAWEE COUNTY RAILROAD
L&MISS	LAWRENCEBURG & MISSISSIPPI	LCOL	LORAIN COUNTY LINE
L&MR	LOUISIANA & MISSOURI RIVER	LCRR	LAKE COUNTY RAILROAD (LOGGING)
L&MRY	LAFAYETTE & MONON RAILWAY	LD&R	LEAVENWORTH DEPOT & RAILROAD
L&N	LOUISVILLE & NASHVILLE	LD&RT	LAKEFRONT DOCK & RAILROAD TERMINAL
L&NE	LEHIGH & NEW ENGLAND RAILROAD	LE	LOUISIANA EASTERN RAILROAD
L&NE.	LEHIGH & NEW ENGLAND RAILWAY	LE&DR	LAKE ERIE & DETROIT RIVER
L&NO	LAONA & NORTHERN RAILWAY	LE&E	LAKE ERIE & EASTERN RAILROAD
L&NS	L&N SHOPS	LE&FW	LAKE ERIE & FORT WAYNE RAILROAD
L&NW	LOUISIANA & NORTH WEST RAILROAD	LE&L	LANCASTER EPHRATA & LEBANON TRACTION
L&O	LORTON & OCCOQUAN	LE&N	LAKE ERIE & NORTHERN RAILWAY (CP)
L&OL	LEAVENWORTH & OLATHE	LE&P	LAKE ERIE & PITTSBURGH RAILROAD
L&P	LACKAWANNA & PITTSBURG	LE&W	LAKE ERIE & WESTERN
L&PB	LOUISIANA & PINE BLUFF RAILWAY	LEBG&N	LAKE ERIE BOWLING GREEN & NAPOLEON RY
L&PS	LONDON & PORT STANLEY RAILWAY	LEF&C	LAKE ERIE FRANKLIN & CLARION RAILROAD
L&R	LAKE TAHOE RAILWAY & TRANSPORTATION	LEI	LEIPER
L&RNG	LANCASTER & READING NARROW GAGE RR	LEL	LIMA ELECTRIC RAILWAY
L&S	LUDLOW & SOUTHERN	LESM	LITTLE EMMA SILVER MINE
L&SQ	LEHIGH & SUSQUEHANNA	LEWMV	LAKE ERIE WOOSTER & MUSKINGUM VALLEY
L&SW	LACKAWANNA & SOUTHWESTERN	LF&D	LITTLE FALLS & DOLGEVILLE RAILROAD
L&T	LEAVENWORTH & TOPEKA	LF&SH	LAUREL FORK & SAND HILL
L&TWRY	LAUREL & TALLAHOMA WESTERN RAILWAY	LG	LAUHOFF GRAIN
L&WRR	LOUISVILLE & WADLEY RAILROAD	LG&MR	LAKE GEORGE & MUSKEGON RIVER RAILROAD
L&WRR.	LOUISVILLE & WADLEY RAILWAY	LH	LEONA HEIGHTS RAILROAD
L&WV	LACKAWANNA & WYOMING VALLEY RAILWAY	LH&NO	LAKE HURON & NORTHERN ONTARIO
L&WV.	LAUREL LINE	LH&SL	LOUISVILLE HENDERSON & ST LOUIS RY
L&WVA	LORAIN & WESTERN VIRGINIA RAILWAY	LHP&P	LARAMIE HAHN'S PEAK & PACIFIC
L&YF	LANCASTER & YORK FURNACE STREET RY	LI	LONG ISLAND RAILROAD
L&YFR	LEWISTON & YOUNGSTOWN FRONTIER	LI&DE	LIMA & DEFIANCE RAILROAD
L-CTR	LEWISTON-CLARKSON TRANSIT	LI&M	LITCHFIELD & MADISON RAILWAY
L-HC	LIMA HAMILTON CORPORATION	LIB+	LIBBY'S
L-IC	LYONS-IOWA CENTRAL	LIC&MB	LONG ISLAND CITY & MANHATTAN BEACH RY
LA	LAWNDALE RAILWAY & INDUSTRIAL	LIG	LIGONIER VALLEY RAILROAD
		LILW	LIMA LOCOMOTIVE WORKS

STEPHANS' RAILROAD DIRECTORY

APPENDIX A (RAILROADS)

A	ABBREVIATIONS ALPHABETICALLY W/ROADS
LIND	LINDELL RAILWAY
LISC	LIPSETT STEEL COMPANY
LISRY	LAFAYETTE STREET RAILWAY (INDIANA)
LITRI	LITTLE RIVER RAILROAD
LJ	LA JOLLA LINE (CALIFORNIA)
LJC&M	LACHINE JACQUES CARTIER & MAISSONNEUVE
LJIP	LA JUNTA INDUSTRIAL PARK
LK	LITTLE KANAWHA RAILROAD
LK&P	LAHAINA KAANAPALI & PACIFIC
LK&W	LEAVENWORTH KANSAS & WESTERN
LL	LEHIGH LUZERNE
LLB&C	LAC LA BELLE & CALUMET RAILROAD
LLL	LYSTUL-LAWSON LUMBER COMPANY
LLLC	LOUISIANA LONGLEAF LUMBER COMPANY
LLW	LANCASTER LOCOMOTIVE WORKS
LM	LOUISIANA MIDLAND RAILWAY
LM .	LOUISIANA MIDLAND RAILROAD
LMRR	LITTLE MIAMI RAILROAD (OHIO)
LMSRY	LENORA MT SICKLER RAILWAY
LN	LIMA NORTHERN
LNA&C	LOUISVILLE NEW ALBANY & CORYDON RR
LNA&CH	LOUISIANA NEW ALBANY & CHICAGO
LNA&S	LOUISVILLE NEW ALBANY & SALEM
LNAC	LOUISVILLE NEW ALBANY & CHICAGO
LNCC	LEHIGH NAVIGATION COAL COMPANY
LNO&T	LOUISIANA NEW ORLEANS & TEXAS
LNP&W	LARAMIE NORTH PARK & WESTERN
LO	LOYAL
LO&CH	LIVE OAK & CHARLOTTE'S HARBOR RR CO
LO&G	LIVE OAK & GULF
LO&P	LIVE OAK & PERRY
LO&RB	LIVE OAK & ROWLAND'S BLUFF
LO&S	LANCASTER OXFORD & SOUTHERN
LO&T	LOUISIANA & TEXAS
LOD	LODI RAILROAD
LODI	LODI BRANCH
LOP&G	LIVE OAK PERRY & GULF RAILROAD
LOP&G.	LIVE OAK PERRY & GULF RAILWAY
LOP&SG	LIVE OAK PERRY & SOUTH GEORGIA RY
LOR	LORAMA RAILROAD
LOS	LOUISIANA SOUTHERN RAILWAY
LOSRR	LAKE ONTARIO SHORE RAILROAD
LOSRY	LANCASTER (OHIO) STREET RAILWAY
LOT&CH	LIVE OAK TAMPA & CHARLOTTES HARBOR
LOT&HB	LIVE OAK TAMPA & HOWLAND'S BLUFF
LOU	LOUISA RAILROAD
LP	LIHUE PLANTATION COMPANY LTD
LP&N	LONGVIEW PORTLAND & NORTHERN RAILWAY
LPC	LEHIGH PORTLAND CEMENT COMPANY
LPEN	LOUISIANA STATE PENITENTIARY
LPL	LARAMIE PLAINS LINES
LPT	LIVE POULTRY TRANSPORT COPNPANY
LQ&N	LAMAR QUEENS & NORTHERN
LR	LINVILLE RIVER RAILWAY
LR&AV	LITTLE RIVER & ARKANSAS VALLEY
LR&HS	LAUREL RIVER & HOT SPRINGS
LR&L	LAWTON RAILWAY & LIGHTING
LR&N	LOUISIANA RAILROAD & NAVIGATION CO.
LRRR	LIME ROCK RAILROAD
LRRY	LEWIS RUN RAILWAY
LRY	LOUISVILLE RAILWAY (KENTUCKY)
LS	LEBANON SPRINGS
LS&B	LA SALLE & BUREAU COUNTY RAILROAD
LS&I	LAKE SUPERIOR & ISHPEMING RAILROAD
LS&I.	LAKE SUPERIOR & ISHPEMING RAILWAY
LS&M	LAKE SUPERIOR & MISSISSIPPI
LS&MC	LAKE SHORE & MICHIGAN SOUTHERN (O)
LS&MS	LAKE SHORE & MICHIGAN SOUTHERN
LS&TV	LAKE SHORE & TUSCARAWAS VALLEY
LSAN	LOUIS SANDS' ROAD
LSC	LIMA STONE COMPANY
LSCH	LITTLE SCHUYLKILL NAV RR & COAL CO.
LSCO	LACLEDE STEEL COMPANY
LSE	LAKE SHORE ELECTRIC INTERURBAN
LSEL	LAKE SHORE ELECTRIC RAILWAY
LSH	LAKE SHORE RAILROAD
LSM&PC	LIMA STREET MOTOR & POWER COMPANY

A	ABBREVIATIONS ALPHABETICALLY W/ROADS
LSQ	LINCOLN STONE QUARRY
LSR	LINWOOD STREET RAILWAY
LSRR	LORAIN STREET RAILROAD
LSRR.	LORAIN STREET RAILWAY
LSRY	LONDON STREET RAILWAY
LSSC	LONE STAR STEEL COMPANY
LST	LEONARDS STORE
LST&T	LAKE SUPERIOR TERMINAL & TRANSFER RY
LSWC	LONGVIEW SWITCHING COMPANY
LT	LAKE TERMINAL RAILROAD
LT&L	LYNCHBURG TRACTION & LIGHT COMPANY
LT&P	LANCASTER TRACTION & POWER COMPANY
LT&W	LEAVENWORTH TOPEKA & WESTERN
LTC	LEE TIDEWATER CYPRESS COMPANY
LTR	LINCOLN TRACTION COMPANY
LU&N	LUDINGTON & NORTHERN RAILWAY
LUMB	LUMER ROADS IN GENERAL
LUS	LUKENS STEEL
LV	LEHIGH VALLEY
LV&T	LAS VEGAS & TONOPAH RAILROAD
LVRC	LAMOILLE VALLEY RAILWAY CORP
LVRY	LEBANON VALLEY RAILWAY
LVT	LEHIGH VALLEY TRANSIT
LW	LONG WHARF
LW&JC	LAKE WIMICO ST JOSEPH CANAL & RR CO
LWRY	LAKE WHATCOM RAILWAY
LX&E	LEXINGTON & EASTERN RAILWAY
LX&O	LEXINGTON & OHIO
LY&D	LYNCHBURG & DANVILLE
LYK	LYKENS VALLEY
M	MONON
M&A	MISSOURI & ARKANSAS RAILROAD
M&A.	MISSOURI & ARKANSAS RAILWAY COMPANY
M&AT	MONTREAL & ATLANTA (CP)
M&B	MCKEAN & BUFFALO
M&BA	MONTPELIER & BARRE RAILROAD
M&BI	MACON & BIRMINGHAM RAILROAD
M&BI.	MACON & BIRMINGHAM RAILWAY
M&BIG	MERIDAN & BIGBEE RAILROAD
M&BL	MARIANNA & BLOUNTSTOWN RAILROAD
M&BO	MOIRA & BOMBAY
M&BR	MACON & BRUNSWICK
M&BS	MARYSVILLE & BIG SANDY
M&C	MONTREAL & CHAMPLAIN
M&CG	MORRISTOWN & CUMBERLAND GAP
M&CH	MEMPHIS & CHARLESTON
M&CIN	MARIETTA & CINCINNATI
M&CIN	MIDDLETOWN & CINCINNATI
M&CLRR	MEDFORD & CRATE LAKE RAILROAD
M&CR	MISSISQUOI & CLYDE RIVERS
M&CRR	MERIDAN & CROMWELL RAILROAD
M&CT	MEMPHIS & CHARLESTON RAILWAY
M&D	MARYLAND & DELAWARE
M&DC	MARYLAND & DELAWARE COAST RAILWAY
M&DSC	MARYLAND & DELAWARE SEACOAST
M&DU	MACON & DUBLIN
M&E	MORRISTOWN & ERIE RAILROAD
M&ET	MODESTO & EMPIRE TRACTION
M&G	MOBILE & GULF RAILROAD
M&GL	MONTCLAIR & GREENWOOD LAKE
M&GR	MANISTEE & GRAND RAPIDS
M&GRY	MONTFORT & GATINEAU RAILWAY COMPANY
M&GYR	MONTFORT & GATINEAU RAILWAY CO (O)
M&HM	MARQUETTE & HURON MOUNTAIN RAILROAD
M&HR	MOHAWK & HUDSON RIVER
M&I	MADISON & INDIANAPOLIS
M&IB&B	MISSOURI & ILLINOIS BRIDGE & BELT RY
M&IRY	MINNESOTA & INTERNATIONAL RAILWAY
M&L	MONTREAL & LACHINE
M&LB	MANAHAWKEN & LONG BEACH TRANPORT CO
M&LB.	MANAHAWKEN & LONG BEACH TRANSIT
M&LF	MISSISSIPPI & LA FOURACHE RAILWAY

STEPHANS' RAILROAD DIRECTORY

APPENDIX A (RAILROADS)

A	ABBREVIATIONS ALPHABETICALLY W/ROADS
M&LS	MANISTIQUE & LAKE SUPERIOR RAILROAD
M&M	MOHAWK & MALONE RAILWAY
M&ME	MENDHAM & MORRISTOWN EXTESION RY CO
M&MF	MOREHEAD & MORGAN FORK RAILROAD
M&MG	MONTEREY &MEXICAN GULF (MEXICO)
M&MI	MILWAUKEE & MISSISSIPPI
M&N	MILWAUKEE & NORTHERN
M&NA	MISSOURI & NORTH ARKANSAS
M&NE	MANISTEE & NORTH EASTERN RAILWAY
M&NF	MOREHEAD & NORTH FORK RAILROAD
M&NG	MARIETTA & NORTH GEORGIA
M&NJ	MIDDLETOWN & NEW JERSEY RAILWAY
M&NJ	MIDDLETOWN & NEW JERSEY RAILROAD
M&NRY	MAINSTEE & NORTHEASTERN RAILWAY
M&NW	MINNESOTA & NORTH WISCONSIN
M&O	MOBILE & OHIO
M&OC	MASON & OCEANA RAILWAY
M&OL	MARCELLUS & OTISCO LAKE
M&ON	MARQUETTE & ONTONAGON
M&ONE	MANCHESTER & ONEIDA RAILWAY
M&ORY	MORSE & ORY
M&P	MONTREAL & PLATTSBURG
M&PAC	MINNEAPOLIS & PACIFIC
M&PP	MANITOU & PIKE'S PEAK RAILWAY
M&QT	MANHATTAN & QUEENS TRACTION COMPANY
M&RR	MINNEAPOLIS & RAINY RIVER RAILROAD
M&S	MONTREAL & SOREL
M&SC	MONTREAL & SOUTHERN COUNTIES RAILWAY
M&SCR	MINNEAPOLIS & ST CROIX
M&SE	MARQUETTE & SOUTHEASTERN
M&SH	MAHANOY & SHAMOKIN
M&SL	MINNEAPOLIS & ST LOUIS RAILROAD
M&SLRY	MALONE & ST LAURENCE RAILWAY COMPANY
M&SM	MANITOBA & SASKATCHEWAN MINE
M&SP	MINNEAPOLIS & ST PAUL
M&SV	MISSISSIPPI & SKUNA VALLEY RAILROAD
M&SVA	MONTEREY & SALINAS VALLEY
M&SW	MILLEN & SOUTHWESTERN RAILROAD
M&TI	MUSCATINE & TIPTON
M&U	MIDDLETOWN & UNIONVILLE RAILROAD
M&W	MARQUETTE & WESTERN
M&WB	MERIDAN & WATERBURY RAILROAD
M&WE	MUNCIE & WESTERN RAILROAD
M&WI	MACOMB & WESTERN ILLINOIS
M&WR	MONTPELIER & WELLS RIVER RAILROAD
M&Y	MCKEESPORT & YOUGHIOGHENY RAILROAD
M-CL	MICHIGAN-CALIFORNIA LUMBER COMPANY
M-I	MISSOURI-ILLINOIS RAILROAD
M-K	MORRISON-KNUDSEN
M-M	MADEIRA-MAMORE RAILWAY (BRAZIL)
M-N	METRO-NORTH (NY CITY)
MA	MAGMA ARIZONA RAILROAD
MA&B	MANHATTAN ALMA & BURLINGAME
MA&CR	MINNEAPOLIS ANOKA & CUYUNA RANGE RR
MA&E	MARION & EASTERN
MA&ME	MALDEN & MELROSE
MA&PA	MARYLAND & PENNSYLVANIA RAILROAD
MA&S	MAXTON ALMA & SOUTHBOUND RAILROAD
MA&W	MASCOT & WESTERN
MA#	MICHIGAN ALKALI
MAB#	MA BROWN
MAD	MADRID
MAE	MANHATTAN ELECTRIC
MAH	MAHONING COAL RAILROAD COMPANY
MAL	MICHIGAN AIR LINE RAILWAY
MAN	MANDEVILLE NORTHERN
MANC	MANATEE CRATE COMPANY
MAR	MARION RAILWAY
MARC	MARYLAND MARC
MARTA	METRO ATLANTA RAPID TRANSIT AUTHORITY
MARY	MARITIME RAILWAY
MASS	MASSACHUSETTS STREET RAILWAY
MASSC	MASSACHUSETTS CENTRAL
MAT	MATTAGAMI RAILROAD
MAT#	MATHIESON ALKALI WORKS
MATE	MASSENA TERMINAL RAILROAD
MATT	MATTOON RAILWAY

A	ABBREVIATIONS ALPHABETICALLY W/ROADS
MAX	METROPOLITAN AREA EXPRESS OF PORTLAND
MB	MOCTEZUMA BREWERY
MB#	MERCHANTS BISCUITS
MBE	MIAMI BEACH RAILWAY
MBL	MACMILLAN BLOEDEL LIMITED
MBL.	MACMILLAN BLOEDEL LUMBER COMPANY
MBLC	MUD BAY LOGGING COMPANY
MBTA	MASSACHUSETTS BAY TRANSPORTATION AUTH
MBTA	MASSACHUSETTS BAY TERMINAL AUTHORITY
MC	MAINE CENTRAL RAILROAD
MC&C	MARIETTA COLUMBUS & CLEVELAND
MC&CL	MASON CITY & CLEAR LAKES RAILROAD
MC&FD	MASON CITY & FORT DODGE
MC&I	MANHATTAN CITY & INTERURBAN RAILWAY
MC&L	MAUCH CHUNK & LEIGHTON
MC&LM	MANSFIELD COLDWATER & LAKE MICHIGAN
MC&MHN	MILL CREEK & MINE HILL NAV & RR CO
MC&PC	MOUNT CARBON & PORT CARBON
MC&SA	MOSCOW CAMDEN & ST AUGUSTINE RAILROAD
MCA	MAMMOTH CAVE RAILROAD
MCC	MORRIS COUNTY CENTRAL
MCCC	MEADOW CREEK COAL COMPANY
MCCO	MORRIS COUNTY CONNECTING RAILWAY
MCE	MONMOUTH COUNTY ELECTRIC
MCEM	MARQUETTE CEMENT
MCH	MAUCH CHUNK SWITCH-BACK RAILROAD
MCI	MEXICO CITY STREETCARS
MCKC	MCKEESPORT CONNECTING RAILROAD
MCL	METROPOLITAN COACH COMPANY
MCO	MONONGAHELA CONNECTING RAILROAD
MCOL	MONTFORT COLONIZATION RAILWAY CO
MCOR	MEDFORD COAST RAILWAY
MCORP	MASONITE CORPORATION
MCPR	MONTREAL CITY PASSENGER RAILWAY CO
MCR	MANN'S CREEK RAILROAD
MCRI	MCCLOUD RIVER RAILROAD
MCRR	MOTLEY COUNTY RAILROAD
MCRW	MOUNT CARBON RAILWAY
MCRY	MINNESOTA CENTRAL RAILWAY
MCRY.	MINNESOTA CENTRAL RAILROAD
MCS	MAINE CENTRAL SHOPS
MCT	MEXICO CITY TRAMWAYS
MCTC	MORRIS COUNTY TRACTION COMPANY
MCV	MILL CREEK VALLEY LINES
MD	MUNICIPAL DOCKS
MD&G	MANCHESTER DORSET & GRANVILLE
MD&GU	MEMPHIS DALLAS & GULF
MD&S	MACON DUBLIN & SAVANNAH RAILROAD
MD&SC	MIDDLEBURG & SCHOHARIE
MD&V	MARYLAND DELAWARE & VIRGINIA RY
MD&W	MINNESOTA DAKOTA & WESTERN RAILWAY
MDC	METROPOLITAN RAILROAD (WASHINGTON DC)
MDCE	MARYLAND CENTRAL
MDOT	MARYLAND DEPT OF TRANSPORTATION
MDP	MEXICAN PACIFIC
MDT#	MERCHANTS DESPATCH (O)
MDTCC	MERCHANTS DESPATCH TRANS CORP CHICAGO
ME	MILWAUKEE ELECTRIC LINES SYSTEM
ME&D	MEDINA & DARIEN
ME&W	MICHIGAN EAST & WEST
MEC	MANHATTAN ELEVATED COMPANY
MECC	MIDLAND ELECTRIC COAL COMPANY
MEIGS	MEIGS RAILROAD (MASSACHUSETTS)
MEL	MUSKINGUM ELECTRIC RAILROAD
MEP&P	MEMPHIS EL PASO & PACIFIC RAILROAD
MER&L	MILWAUKEE ELECTRIC RAILWAY & LIGHT
MER&T	MILWAUKEE ELECTRIC RY & TRANSPORT CO
MERY	MINNEAPOLIS EASTERN RAILWAY
MET	MUSKOGEE ELECTRIC TRACTION
MEX	MEXICANO (MEXICAN RAILWAY)
MEX.	MEXICAN RAILWAY COMPANY
MEXE	MEXICAN EASTERN
MEXP	MISSISSIPPI EXPORT RAILROAD
MF	MIDDLE FORK RAILROAD
MF&M	MORRISSEY FERNIE & MICHEL
MFG	MANUFACTURERS RAILWAY OF ST LOUIS

A51

APPENDIX A (RAILROADS)

A	ABBREVIATIONS ALPHABETICALLY W/ROADS
MG	MOUNT GRETNA NARROW-GAUGE
MG*	MOBILE GAS
MGAP	MANASSAS GAP RAILROAD
MGB&W	MANITOWOC GREEN BAY & WESTERN
MH	MOUNT HOOD RAILROAD
MH&H	MOHAWK & HUDSON RAILROAD
MH&N	MARIETTA HOCKING & NORTHERN RAILROAD
MH&SH	MINE HILL & SCHUYLKILL HAVEN
MH.	MOUNT HOOD RAILWAY
MHC	MONTREAL HARBOR COMMISSION
MHL	MOOSEHEAD LAKE RAILROAD
MHM	MOUNT HOPE MINERAL RAILROAD
MHRR	MINE HILL RAILROAD
MHV	MOHAWK VALLEY
MI	MISSISSIPPIAN RAILWAY
MI&L	MACOMB INDUSTRY & LITTLETON
MI&MO	MISSISSIPPI & MISSOURI
MI&NW	MINNESOTA & NORTHWESTERN RAILROAD
MI&PAC	MINNESOTA & PACIFIC
MI&SC	MINNEAPOLIS & ST CLOUD
MI&SP	MILWAUKEE & ST PAUL
MI&W	MINARETS & WESTERN RAILWAY
MIBL	MISSOULA BELT LINE
MIC	MOUNTAIN ICE COMPANY
MICH-CAL	MICH-CAL (MICHIGAN-CALIFORNIA) (O)
MICHC	MICHIGAN CENTRAL
MICHS	MICHIGAN SOUTHERN
MID	MIDWAY RAILROAD COMPANY
MIDC	MIDLAND CONTINENTAL RAILROAD
MIDCO	MIDLAND CONNECTING
MIDL	MIDLAND RAILWAY
MIDSR	MID SOUTH RAIL
MIEL	MICHIGAN ELECTRIC
MIIR	MINNEAPOLIS INDUSTRIAL RAILWAY
MIL	MILSTEAD RAILROAD
MILW	MILWAUKEE
MIN	MINERAL RANGE RAILROAD
MIND	MIDLAND OF INDIANA
MINNC	MINNESOTA CENTRAL RAILROAD (O)
MINNV	MINNESOTA VALLEY RAILROAD
MINV	MINGO VALLEY RAILROAD
MINX	MINX
MIRW	MONTREAL ICE RAILWAY
MISSC	MISSISSIPPI CENTRAL RAILROAD
MIST	MILWAUKEE STREET RAILWAYS
MIT	MIDLAND TERMINAL RAILWAY
MITR	MINNESOTA TRANSFER RAILWAY
MIV	MIDLAND VALLEY RAILROAD
MJ	MANUFACTURERS JUNCTION RAILWAY
MJ&KC	MOBILE JACKSON & KANSAS CITY
MJ&S	MOUNT JEWELL & SMETHPORT
MJC&N	MOUNT JEWETT CLERMONT & NORTHERN
MJK&R	MOUNT JEWETT KINZUA & RITERVILLE RR
MK&E	MISSOURI KANSAS & EASTERN
MKT	MISSOURI KANSAS TEXAS
MKT*	M.K.T.
MKTX	MKT OF TEXAS
ML&M	MINNEAPOLIS LYNDALE & MINNESOTA
ML&T	MORGON'S LOUISIANA & TEXAS RAILROAD
ML&TC	MANATEE LIGHT & TRACTION COMPANY
MLC	MOWER LUMBER COMPANY
MLCO	MONTOUR LAND COMPANY
MLO	MICHIGAN LIMESTONE OPERATIONS
MLR	MONO LAKE RAILWAY & LUMBER COMPANY
MLS&W	MILWAUKEE LAKE SHORE & WESTERN
MLW	MANCHESTER LOCOMOTIVE WORKS
MM	MIDLAND RAILWAY OF MANITOBA
MM&KF	MOUNT MCKAY & KAKABEKA FALLS RAILWAY
MM&N	MARENGO MILWAUKEE & NORTHERN
MM&NY	MILFORD MATAMORAS & NEW YORK
MM&S	MUNISING MARQUETTE & SOUTHEASTERN RY
MM&W	MIDDLETOWN MERIDAN & WATERBURY RR
MMA	MCNARY-MAVERICK RAILROAD
MMCI	MILLER MILL COMPANY INC.
MMG	MOUNT MCGREGOR RAILWAY
MMI	MARYLAND MIDLAND
MN	MICHIGAN NORTHERN
MN&S	MINNEAPOLIS NORTHFIELD & SOUTHERN RY
MNDM	MINERALES NACIONAL DE MEXICO
MNES	MASSACHUSETTS NORTHEASTERN STREET RY
MNJ	MIDLAND RAILROAD OF NEW JERSEY
MNRY	MEXICAN NATIONAL RAILWAY
MO	MONSON RAILROAD
MOA*	MONARCH
MOBCH	MOBILE CHEMICAL
MOJN	MOJAVE NORTHERN
MOMI	MAID OF THE MIST INCLINE
MON	MONONGAHELA RAILWAY
MON.	MONONGAHELA RAILROAD
MONO	MONADNOCK NORTHERN
MONR	MONROE RAILROAD COMPANY
MONS	MIDLAND OF NOVA SCOTIA
MONT	MONTOUR RAILROAD
MONT.	MONTOUR RAILWAY
MONTA	MONTANA RAILROAD
MONTL	MONTEZUMA LUMBER COMPANY
MOP	MOPAC
MORB	MORRIS BRANCH
MOV	MONOCACY VALLEY
MOVA	MOSHASSUCK VALLEY RAILROAD
MOW	MONTANA WESTERN RAILWAY
MP	MISSOURI PACIFIC RAILWAY COMPANY
MP&B	MONTREAL PORTLAND & BOSTON
MP&G	MEMPHIS PARIS & GULF
MP*	MAINE POTATO
MP.	MISSOURI PACIFIC RAILROAD SYSTEM
MPC	MONOLITH PORTLAND CEMENT
MPCE	MISSOURI PORTLAND CEMENT
MPI	METAL PROCESSING INC
MPR&DE	MINNEAPOLIS ST PAUL ROCH & DUBUQUE E
MPS	MARION POWER SHOVEL COMPANY
MR	MEAD RUN
MR&BT	MISSISSIPPI RIVER & BONNE TERRE
MR&LE	MAD RIVER & LAKE ERIE
MR&NW	MISSOURI RIVER & NORTHWESTERN RAILWAY
MRAD	METROPOLITAN RADIAL LINE
MRC	MARION RIVER CARRY RAILROAD
MRCC	MEDIX RUN COAL COMPANY
MRCH	MINERAL RAILWAY OF CHIHUAHUA
MRIL	MCCLOUD RIVER LUMBER COMPANY
MRL	MEADOW RIVER LUMBER RAILROAD
MRL&M	MINNEAPOLIS RED LAKE & MANITOBA
MRNJ	MONTCLAIR RAILWAY OF NEW JERSEY
MRR	MICHIGAN RAILROAD
MRR.	MICHIGAN RAILWAY CO
MRRM	MISSISSIPPI RAILROAD MUSEUM
MRS	MILITARY RAILWAY SERVICE
MRSR	MOUNT RAINIER SCENIC RAILROAD
MRT	MINERAL ROCK TRAMWAY
MRT&S	MILWAUKEE RAPID TRANSIT & SPEEDRAIL CO
MRTR	MILWAUKEE RAPID TRANSIT
MRW	MANILA RAILWAY (PHILIPPINES)
MS	MISSOURI SOUTHERN RAILROAD
MS&NI	MICHIGAN SOUTHERN & NORTHRN INDIANA RR
MSC	MONTAGUE STEEL COMPANY
MSCO	MATERIAL SERVICE CORPORATION
MSCR&B	MILL SPRING CURRENT RIV & BAINESVILLE
MSF	MUNCIPAL RAILWAY OF SAN FRANCISCO
MSL&IR	MEXICAN SL & INDUST RR (VARIOUS)
MSM&A	MINNEAPOLIS STE MARIE & ATLANTIC
MSO	MESABE SOUTHERN
MSOK	METROPOLITAN STREET RAILWAY (OKLAHOMA)
MSP&A	MINNEAPOLIS ST PAUL & ATLANTIC
MSP&AS	MINNEAPOLIS ST PAUL & ASHLAND RY
MSP&P	MILWAUKEE ST PAUL & PACIFIC
MSPC	MODERA SUGAR PINE COMPANY
MSPC.	MADERA SUGAR PINE COMPANY
MSPR&D	MINNEAPOLIS ST PAUL ROCHESTR & DUBUQU
MSR	MUNSIE STREET RAILWAY
MSRW	MANCHESTER STREET RAILWAY
MSRY	MARTINSBURG STREET RAILWAY
MSS	MARKET STREET SUBWAY
MSSRY	MARKET STREET RAILWAY (SAN FRANCISCO)
MSTC	MICHIGAN SUBURBAN TRACTION COMPANY

STEPHANS' RAILROAD DIRECTORY

APPENDIX A (RAILROADS)

A	ABBREVIATIONS ALPHABETICALLY W/ROADS
MSW	MONTANA SOUTHERN
MT	MONTREAL TRANSIT
MT&L	MISKEGON TRACTION & LIGHTING COMPANY
MT&MW	MOUNT TAMALPAIS & MUIR WOODS
MT&W	MARINETTE TOMAHAWK & WESTERN RAILROAD
MT&W.	MARINETTE TOMAHAWK & WESTERN RAILWAY
MT.	MONTREAL TRANSPORTATION COMMISSION
MTA	METROPOLITAN TRANSIT AUTHORITY BOSTON
MTC	MACK TRUCK COMPANY
MTCE	MOUNTAIN CENTRAL
MTCL	MEADVILLE TRACTION CO LINE (PA)
MTCO	MYSTIC TERMINAL COMPANY
MTE&G	MONCTON TRAMWAYS ELECTRICITY & GAS CO
MTI	MOLINE TIMBER CO
MTL	MOUNT LOWE
MTR	MODELTRONICS
MTRR	MIDDLE TENNESSEE RAILROAD
MTTI	MOUNT TOM INCLINE RAILWAY
MTU	MOUNT UNCOONUNICH
MTW	MOUNT WASHINGTON
MTWC	MONTREAL TRAMWAYS CORPORATION
MU	MUNISING
MU&WG	MIDDLETOWN UNIONVILLE & WATER GAP RR
MUN	MUNCY CREEK RAILROAD
MUNC	MUNCIE STREET RAILWAY
MUNRY	MUNICIPAL RAILWAY
MUNX*	M.U.N.X.
MUS	MEMPHIS UNION STATION COMPANY
MV	MARTHA'S VINEYARD RAILROAD
MV&MT	MILL VALLEY & MT TAMALPAIS
MVE	MOUNT VERNON ELECTRIC RAILWAY
MVPSC	MISSISSIPPI VALLEY PUBLIC SERVICE CO
MVRR	MISSOURI VALLEY RAILROAD
MVT	MISSISSIPPI VALLEY TERMINAL COMPANY
MW	MINNESOTA WESTERN RAILWAY
MW&CR	MERIDAN WATERBURY & CONNECTICUT RIVER
MW&P	MARIETTA WILLIAMSTOWN & PARKERSBURG
MW&S	MONTANA WYOMING & SOUTHERN
MW.	MINNESOTA WESTERN RAILROAD
MWC	MIDWEST CENTRAL RAILROAD
MWCOG	MOUNT WASHINGTON COG
MWP	MONONGAHELA WEST PENN
MXC	MEXICAN CENTRAL
N	NESQUEHONING
N&A	NELSON & ALBEMARLE RAILWAY
N&AT	NORFOLK & ATLANTIC TERMINAL
N&B	NORTHAMPTON & BATH RAILROAD
N&BF	NEWARK & BLOOMFIELD RAILROAD
N&BS	NEWTON & BOSTON STREET RAILWAY
N&BSR	NORFOLK & BRISTOL STREET RAILWAY
N&C	NORFOLK & CAROLINA
N&CA	NEVADA & CALIFORNIA RAILROAD
N&CH	NASHVILLE & CHATTANOOGA RAILROAD
N&CRR	NASHVILLE & CLARKSVILLE RAILROAD
N&H	NATCHEZ & HAMBURG RAILROAD
N&K	NASHVILLE & KNOXVILLE RAILROAD
N&L	NASHUA & LOWELL RAILROAD
N&M	NEWARK & MARION RAILROAD
N&N	NAHMA & NORTHERN
N&NW	NORTHERN & NORTH WESTERN
N&OV	NORFOLK & OCEAN VIEW
N&P	NEWPORT & PROVIDENCE
N&PB	NORFOLK & PETERSBURG
N&PBL	NORFOLK & PORTSMOUTH BELT LINE RR
N&PT	NORFOLK & PORTSMOUTH TRACTION COMPANY
N&RRV	NATCHITOCHES & RED RIVER VALLEY RY
N&S	NORTH & SOUTH RAILROAD OF WYOMING
N&SG	NORTH & SOUTH RAILROAD CO OF GEORGIA
N&SL	NORWOOD & ST LAWRENCE RAILROAD
N&SLRR	NEBRASKA & LAKE SUPERIOR RAILROAD
N&SP	NASHVILLE & SPARKS RAILROAD
N&SS	NEWBURGH & SOUTH SHORE RAILWAY
N&SV	NEWPORT & SHERMANS VALLEY RAILROAD
N&VB	NORFOLK & VIRGINIA BEACH
N&W	NORFOLK & WESTERN RAILWAY

A	ABBREVIATIONS ALPHABETICALLY W/ROADS
N&WO	NORWICH & WORCESTER RAILROAD
N-F	NASHVILLE-FRANKLIN RAILWAY (TENN)
N-W	NORTH-WEST RAILROAD
NA	NORTHERN ALBERTA RAILWAYS
NA&B	NASHUA ACTON & BOSTON RAILROAD
NA&C	NEW ALBANY & CORYDON
NA&LE	NEW ALBANY & LOUISVILLE ELECTRIC
NA&S	NATCHEZ & SOUTHERN RAILWAY
NA&SA	NEW ALBANY & SALEM
NAC	NORTH AMERICAN COAL
NAC*	NATIONAL ALUMINATE COMPANY
NAD	NORTH AMERICAN DISPATCH
NAD*	NORTH AMERICAN DESPATCH
NANC	NANTUCKET CENTRAL
NASA	NASA
NATX	NORTH AMERICAN CAR CORPORATION
NAU	NAUGATUCK RAILROAD (CONNECTICUT)
NB&C	NEW BRUNSWICK & CANADA
NB&T	NEW BEDFORD & TAUNTON RAILROAD
NB&W	NEW BERLIN & WINFIELD
NBCC	NORTH BRANCH CANAL COMPANY
NBCS	NELSON BC STREET RAILWAYS
NBL	NORTH BEACH LINES (ST AUGUSTINE FL)
NBP	NEW BRUNSWICK POWER COMPANY
NBRY	NORTH BRITISH RAILWAY
NBTR	NORTH BRANCH TRANSIT
NC	NEVADA CENTRAL RAILROAD
NC&F	NEW CASTLE & FRENCHTOWN
NC&O	NATIONAL CITY & OTAY
NC&SL	NASHVILLE CHATTANOOGA & ST LOUIS RY
NCA	NEW CANAAN
NCAM	NORTHERN CAMBIA STREET RAILWAY
NCB	NEW CORNELIA BRANCH
NCBT	NEVADA COPPER BELT
NCC	NEW CORNELIA COPPER COMPANY
NCCM	NORTHERN CONSTRUCTION CO OF MONTREAL
NCE	NORTHERN CENTRAL RAILWAY
NCI	NORFOLK CITY RAILROAD
NCI.	NORFOLK CITY RAILWAY
NCL	NORTH COAST LINES
NCN	NEVADA COUNTY NARROW-GAUGE RAILROAD
NCNG	NEVADA CITY NARROW GAUGE
NCO	NEVADA CALIFORNIA OREGON RAILROAD
NCR	NORTHERN CROSS RAILROAD
NCRR	NORTH COUNTY RAILROAD CORP
NCRY	NORTHERN COLONIZATION RAILWAY CO.
NCS	NEW CASTLE STREET RAILWAY (PA)
NCSPA	NORTH CAROLINA STATE PORTS AUTHORITY
NCT	NEVADA COUNTY TRACTION
NCTC	NORTH CHARLESTON TERMINAL COMPANY
NCTX	NORTH CENTRAL TEXAS
ND	NORTHERN DAKOTA RAILWAY
ND&C	NEWBURGH DUTCHESS & CONNECTICUT
NDEM	NATIONALES DE MEXICOS
NDET	NATIONAL OF TEHUANTEPEC (MEXICO)
NDM	NACIONALES DE MEXICO
NDRY	NORTH DAKOTA RAILWAY
NE	NORTHERN ELECTRIC RAILWAY
NEIP	NIAGARA ESCARPMENT INCLINED PLANE
NEL&P	NEW ENGLAND LACKAWANNA & PITTSBURGH
NERR	NEW ENGLAND RAILROAD
NES	NESCOPEC
NESL	NESSON LUMBER COMPANY
NETR	NELSON ELECTRIC TRAMWAY
NEZ	NEZPERCE RAILROAD
NEZ&I	NEZPERCE & IDAHO RAILROAD COMPANY
NF	NEWFOUNDLAND RAILROAD
NF&D	NORFOLK FRANKLIN & DANVILLE RAILWAY
NF&D.	NORFOLK FRANKLIN & DANVILLE RAILROAD
NF&G	NICHOLAS FAYETTE & GREENBRIAR
NF.	NEWFOUNDLAND RAILWAY
NFALLS	NIAGARA FALLS
NFL&P	NEWFOUNDLAND LIGHT & POWER COMPANY
NFWP&C	NIAGARA FALLS WESLEY PARK & CLIFTON T
NGR	NEW GEORGIA RAILROAD
NGRR	NIAGARA GEORGE RAILROAD
NH	NEW HAVEN RAILROAD

A53

APPENDIX A (RAILROADS)

A	ABBREVIATIONS ALPHABETICALLY W/ROADS
NH&I	NEW HOPE & IVYLAND RAILROAD
NH&NI	NEW HAVEN & NORTHAMPTON
NH&SL	NEW HAVEN & SHORT LINE
NHB	NATIONAL HARBOURS BOARD
NHM&W	NEW HAVEN MIDDLETOWN & WILLIMANTIC
NHSL	NEW HAVEN & SHORE LINE
NHSL.	NEW HAVEN SHORE LINE RAILWAY
NI	NORTHERN INDIANA RAILWAY COMPANY
NI&M	NAPORANO IRON & METAL
NI&N	NEW IBERIA & NORTHERN
NI&SM	NORTHERN INDIANA & SOUTHERN MICHIGAN
NIA&C	NIAGARA CENTRAL
NID	NORTHERN INDIANA DOCK
NIPC	NIPISSING CENTRAL
NIR	NASHVILLE INTERURBAN RAILWAY
NIW	NATIONAL IRON WORKS
NJ	NAPIERVILLE JUNCTION RAILWAY
NJ&NY	NEW JERSEY & NEW YORK RAILROAD
NJ&P	NEW JERSEY & PENNSYLVANIA
NJDOT	NEW JERSEY DEPT OF TRANSPORTATION
NJEL	NORTH JERSEY ELECTRIC LINES
NJER	NORTH JERSEY
NJI&I	NEW JERSEY INDIANA & ILLINOIS RR
NJJ	NEW JERSEY JUNCTION RAILROAD
NJM	NEW JERSEY MIDLAND RAILWAY
NJR&T	NEW JERSEY RAILROAD & TRANSPORTATION
NJRT	NORTH JERSEY RAPID TRANSIT
NJS	NEW JERSEY SOUTHERN RAILWAY
NJTR	NEW JERSEY TRANSIT
NJTR.	NEW JERSEY RAPID TRANIST .
NJUN	NIAGARA JUNCTION RAILWAY
NJZ	NEW JERSEY ZINC
NKP	NICKEL PLATE
NKP.	NEW YORK CHICAGO & ST LOUIS RAILROAD
NL	NATIONAL LOCOMOTIVE
NL&G	NORTH LOUISANA & GULF RAILROAD
NLACK	NORTHERN LACKAWANNA
NLL	NANSEMOND LAND LUMBER & NARROW GAGE RY
NLN	NEW LONDON NORTHERN
NLSRY	NEW LONDON STREET RAILWAY
NLW&P	NEW LONDON WILLIMANTIC & PALMER RR
NLW&S	NEW LONDON WILLIMANTIC & SPRINGFIELD
NM	NORANDA MINES
NM&C	NEW MEXICO & COLORADO
NM&SP	NEW MEXICO & SOUTHERN PACIFIC
NMC.	NEW MEXICO CENTRAL RAILROAD
NMC.	NEW MEXICO CENTRAL RAILWAY
NMICH	NORTHERN MICHIGAN RAILROAD
NMLC	NEW MEXICO LUMBER COMPANY
NMM	NEW MEXICO MIDLAND
NMR	NAVAJO MINE RAILROAD
NN	NEVADA NORTHERN RAILWAY COMPANY
NN&H	NEWPORT NEWS & HAMPTON RAILWAY
NNB&S	NORTHERN NEW BRUNSWICK & SEABOARD RY
NNR&L	NEWPORT NEWS RAILWAY & LIGHT
NNY	NORTHERN NEW YORK RAILROAD
NO	NORTHEAST OKLAHOMA RAILROAD
NO&C	NEW ORLEANS & CARROLLTON RAIL ROAD
NO&LC	NEW ORLEANS & LOWER COAST RAILROAD
NO&N	NEW ORLEANS & NORTHEASTERN RAILROAD
NO&NW	NEW ORLEANS & NORTH WESTERN
NOC	NEW ORLEANS CITY RAILROAD
NOC&L	NEW ORLEANS CITY & LAKE RAILROAD
NOD	NAVEL ORDINANCE DEPOT
NODM	NOS-OESTE DE MEXICO
NODX	NOR-OESTE DE MEXICO
NOF	NEW ORANGE FOUR JUNCTION RAILROAD
NOH	NORTHERN OHIO RAILROAD
NOH.	NORTHERN OHIO RAILWAY
NOP	NEW ORLEANS PACIFIC RAILWAY
NOPB	NEW ORLEANS PUBLIC BELT RAILROAD
NOPS	NEW ORLEANS PUBLIC SERVICE
NOR&L	NORTHERN OHIO RAILWAY & LIGHT COMPANY
NOR&LC	NEW ORLEANS RAILWAY & LIGHT COMPANY
NORB	NORFOLK BELT LINE
NORL	NEW ORLEANS RAILWAY
NORTH	NORTHERN RAILROAD

A	ABBREVIATIONS ALPHABETICALLY W/ROADS
NORTH.	NORTHERN RAILWAY
NORY	NORTHWESTERN OHIO RAILWAY
NOT	NEW ORLEANS TERMINAL COMPANY
NOT&L	NORTHERN OHIO TRACTION & LIGHT
NOT&M	NEW ORLEANS TEXAS & MEXICO
NOUPT	NEW ORLEANS UNION PASSENGER TERMINAL
NOY	NOYAN RAILROAD (CANADA)
NP	NORTHERN PACIFIC RAILWAY
NP&R	NEWPORT & RICHFORD
NP&T	NORTHWOOD PULP & TIMBER
NPA	NORTH PENNSYLVANIA RAILROAD
NPC	NORTH PACIFIC COAST
NPCO	NEKOOSA PAPER COMPANY
NPGC	NATIONAL PLATE GLASS CO
NPIER	NARRAGANSETT PIER RAILROAD
NPIP	NIAGARA PORTAGE INCLINE PLANE
NPOLE	NORTH POLE ROUTE
NPR	NORTHWESTERN PENNSYLVANIA RAILROAD
NPRR	NORTHERN PACIFIC RAILROAD
NPTC	NORTHPORT TRACTION COMPANY
NPTR	NORTHERN PACIFIC TERMINAL
NR	NORTHERN REFRIGERATOR LINE
NR&LC	NORFOLK RAILWAY & LIGHT COMPANY
NRC	NORTHERN RAILWAY OF CANADA
NRL+	NORTHWESTERN REFRIGERATOR LINE
NRLC	NORTHERN REDWOOD LUMBER COMPANY
NRNJ	NORTHERN RAILROAD OF NEW JERSEY
NRNJ.	NORTHERN RAILWAY OF NEW JERSEY
NRR	NANTUCKET RAILROAD
NRWM	NATIONAL RAILWAYS OF MEXICO
NS	NORTH SHORE RAILROAD
NS&M	NORTH STAR & MIFFLIN
NS&W	NORTHWESTERN STEEL & WIRE
NS.	NORTH SHORE RAILWAY
NSC	NOVA SCOTIA LIGHT & POWER COMPANY
NSC&T	NIAGARA ST CATHERINES & TORONTO RY
NSC&TN	NIAGARA ST CATHERINES & TORONTO NAV
NSO	NORFOLK SOUTHERN RAILWAY
NSO .	NORFOLK SOUTHERN RAILROAD
NSRY	NOVA SCOTIA RAILWAY
NSSC	NORTH STAR STEEL COMPANY
NST&PC	NOVA SCOTIA TRAMWAY & POWER COMPANY
NSUB	NEWARK SUBWAYS
NSW	NEW SOUTH WALES GOVERNMENT RAILROAD
NSWG	NEW SOUTH WALES GOVERNMENT RAILWAY
NT	NORTHAMPTON TRANSIT
NT&D	NICHOLSON TERMINAL & DOCK
NT&NW	NEWTON & NORTHWESTERN
NTCO	NEVADA TRANSIT COMPANY
NTRC	NATIONAL TRANSCONTINENTAL
NTRR	NORTHWESTERN TERMINAL RAILROAD
NTRY	NORFOLK TERMINAL RAILWAY
NTTC	NORTHERN TEXAS TRANSPORTATION COMPANY
NU&R	NATCHEZ URANIA & RUSTON RAILWAY
NV	NEWAUKUM VALLEY
NVR	NAPA VALLEY RAILROAD
NW	NORTHWESTERN
NWL	NORTHWESTERN LINES
NWO	NORTHWESTERN OKLAHOMA
NWP	NORTHWESTERN PACIFIC RAILROAD
NWSOP	NORFOLK WILLOUGHBY SPIT & OLD POINT RR
NY&B	NEW YORK & BOSTON RAILROAD
NY&BB	NEW YORK & BROOKLYN BRIDGE
NY&E	NEW YORK & ERIE
NY&GL	NEW YORK & GREENWOOD LAKE RAILROAD
NY&H	NEW YORK & HARLAEM RAILROAD CO
NY&H.	NEW YORK & HARLEM RAILROAD
NY&LB	NEW YORK & LONG BRANCH RAILROAD
NY&LE	NEW YORK & LAKE ERIE
NY&M	NEW YORK & MAHOPAC RAILROAD COMPANY
NY&MA	NEW YORK & MASSACHUETTS RAILWAY
NY&MB	NEW YORK & MANHATTAN BEACH RAILWAY
NY&N	NEW YORK & NORTHERN
NY&NE	NEW YORK & NEW ENGLAND RAILROAD
NY&O	NEW YORK & OTTAWA
NY&OM	NEW YORK & OSWEGO MIDLAND RAILROAD
NY&P	NEW YORK & PENNSYLVANIA

A54

APPENDIX A (RAILROADS)

A	ABBREVIATIONS ALPHABETICALLY W/ROADS
NY&QC	NEW YORK & QUEENS COUNTY RAILWAY
NY&SB	NEW YORK & SEA BEACH RAILROAD
NY&V	NORTH YAKIMA & VALLEY RAILWAY
NYA&L	NEW YORK AUBURN & LANSING RAILROAD
NYB&J	NEW YORK BROOKLYN & JAMAICA
NYB&MB	NEW YORK BROOKLYN & MANHATTAN BEACH
NYB&N	NEW YORK BOSTON & NORTHERN
NYBR&J	NEW YORK BAY RIDGE & JAMAICA
NYC	NEW YORK CENTRAL RAILROAD
NYC&H	NEW YORK CENTRAL & HUDSON RIVER (O)
NYC&HR	NEW YORK CENTRAL & HUDSON RIVER RR
NYC&N	NEW YORK CENTRAL & NORTHERN
NYC&N.	NEW YORK CITY & NORTHERN
NYC&SL	NEW YORK CHICAGO & ST LOUIS (O)
NYC&W	NEW YORK CENTRAL & WESTERN
NYCE	NEW YORK CITY ELEVATED RAILROAD
NYCR	NEW YORK CITY RAPID
NYCRR	NEW YORK CONNECTING RAILROAD
NYCS	NEW YORK CITY SUBWAY-ELEVATED LINES
NYCS	NEW YORK SUBWAY-EL CARS
NYCS.	NEW YORK ELEVATED LINES
NYCTA	NEW YORK CITY TRANSIT AUTHORITY
NYCTAE	NEW YORK CITY THIRD AVENUE ELEVATED
NYD	NEW YORK DOCK RAILWAY
NYHL	NEW YORK HEAT LIGHT & POWER COMPANY
NYLE&W	NEW YORK LAKE ERIE & WESTERN
NYMTA	NEW YORK METRO TRANSIT AUTHORITY
NYNA	NEW YORK NINTH AVENUE RAILWAY
NYNH&H	NEW YORK NEW HAVEN & HARTFORD RAIL RD
NYO	NORTH YONGE
NYO&W	NEW YORK ONTARIO & WESTERN
NYP&B	NEW YORK PROVIDENCE & BOSTON RAILROAD
NYP&C	NEW YORK PITTSBURGH & CHICAGO RR
NYP&N	NEW YORK PHILADELPHIA & NORFOLK
NYP&O	NEW YORK PENNSYLVANIA & OHIO RAILROAD
NYPA	NEW YORK PORT AUTHORITY
NYPO&D	NEW YORK PENNSYLVANIA OHIO & DETROIT
NYR&M	NEW YORK RUTLAND & MONTREAL
NYRY	NEW YORK RAILWAYS
NYRY.	NEW YORK STATE RAILWAYS
NYS&W	NEW YORK SUSQUEHANNA & WESTERN
NYW&B	NEW YORK WESTCHESTER & BOSTON RY
NYW&P	NEW YORK WESTCHESTER & PUTNAM
NYW&R	NEW YORK WOODHAVEN & ROCKAWAY RR
NYWS&B	NEW YORK WEST SHORE & BUFFALO
O	OLEAN
O&A	OKLAHOMA & ARKANSAS
O&AL	ORANGE & ALEXANDRIA
O&AM	ORANGE ALEXANDRIA & MANASSAS
O&AN	OAKLAND & ANTIOCH
O&C	OREGON & CALIFORNIA RAILROAD
O&CB	OMAHA & COUNCIL BLUFFS RAILWAY
O&E	OREGON & EUREKA
O&ES	OAKLAND & EAST SIDE RAILWAY
O&FRR	ORANGE & FREDERICKSBURG RAILROAD
O&G	OTTAWA & GATINEAU
O&H	OTSEGO & HERKIMER
O&IS	OHIO & INDIANA STONE COMPANY
O&K	OHIO & KENTUCKY RAILWAY
O&LC	OGDENSBURG & LAKE CHAMPLAIN RAILROAD
O&M	OHIO & MISSISSIPPI RAILWAY
O&M.	OHIO & MISSISSIPPI RAILROAD
O&MH	ONEONTA & MOHAWK RAILWAY
O&MV	ONEONTA & MOHAWK VALLEY
O&N	OGDENSBURG & NORWOOD RAILWAY
O&NL	OWENS & NELSON LOGGING ROAD
O&NW	OREGON & NORTHWESTERN RAILROAD
O&P	OTTAWA & PRESCOTT
O&PA	OREGON & PACIFIC
O&Q	ONTARIO & QUEBEC RAILWAY
O&RM	OKLAHOMA & RICH MOUNTAIN
O&RV	OMAHA & REPUBLICAN VALLEY
O&SA	ONTARIO & SAN ANTONIA HEIGHTS RR CO
O&W	OCONEE & WESTERN
O&WT	OREGON & WASHINGTON TERRITORY RAILWAY
O-MS	OAKDALE-MC DONALD STREET RAILWAY

A	ABBREVIATIONS ALPHABETICALLY W/ROADS
OA	OREGON AMERICAN
OA&E	OAKLAND ANTLOCK & EASTERN
OARR	OLD AUGUSTA RAILROAD
OB	ORANGE BELT
OB&PA	OGDENSBURG BRIDGE & PORT AUTHORITY
OB&W	OLEAN BRADFORD & WARREN
OC	OKLAHOMA CENTRAL
OC&A	OIL CREEK & ALLEGHENY
OC&E	OREGON CALIFORNIA & EASTERN RAILWAY
OC&E.	OREGON CALIFORNIA & EASTERN RAILROAD
OC&FR	OLD COLONY & FALL RIVER RAILROAD
OC&P	OIL CITY & PITHOLE RAILWAY
OC&RS	ONEONTA COOPERSTOWN & RICHFIELD SPRGS
OCCRR	OCEAN CITY RAILROAD
OCER	OCEAN CITY ELECTRIC RAILROAD (NJ)
OCITY	OKLAHOMA CITY ADA-ATOKA RAILWAY
OCJR	OKLAHOMA CITY JUNCTION RAILWAY
OCO	OLD COLONY RAILROAD
OCRR	ORANGE COUNTY RAILROAD
OCRY	OAKLAND CABLE RAILWAY COMPANY
OCS	OCILLO SOUTHERN
OCT	OCTORARO RAILWAY
OCW	OCEAN CITY WESTERN
OD	OVERLAND DISPATCH
ODC*	OLD DUTCH CLEANSER
ODOM	OLD DOMINION LINE
OE	OREGON ELECTRIC RAILWAY COMPANY
OEL	OTTAWA ELECTRIC RAILWAY
OER	OHIO ELECTRIC RAILWAY
OF	OSTRICH FARM
OFSL	OIL FIELDS SHORT LINES
OG&G	OAK GROVE & GEORGETOWN
OG&NE	OPELOUSAS GULF & NORTHEASTERN RAILWAY
OH&IN	OHIO & INDIANA
OH&MO	OHIO & MORENCI
OH&PA	OHIO & PENNSYLVANIA
OHIO	OHIO RAILROAD
OHIOC	OHIO CENTRAL LINES
OILC	OIL CITY STREET RAILWAY COMPANY
OILCR	OIL CREEK RAILROAD
OIM	OLIVER IRON MINING COMPANY
OKC&E	OMAHA KANSAS CITY & EASTERN
OKT	ORLEANS KENNER TRACTION
OL&B	OMAHA LINCOLN & BEATRICE RAILWAY
OL&I	OGDEN LOGAN & IDAHO RAILWAY COMPANY
OLCH	OLIN CHEMICAL DIVISION
OLN	ONTARIO LINES-MIDLAND/CENTRAL/EASTERN
OM	OHIO MIDLAND POWER & LIGHT COMPANY
OM*	OSCAR MEYER
OMT	ORANGE MOUNTAIN TRACTION
ON	ONTARIO NORTHLAND RAILWAY
ON&W	ONEIDA & WESTERN
ONCE	ONTARIO CENTRAL
ONE	ONTARIO EASTERN
ONG	OLYMPIA NARROW GAGE RAILROAD
ONMI	ONTARIO MIDLAND RAILROAD
ONO	OKMULGEE NORTHERN
ONRY	ONIEDA RAILWAY
OP	OREGON PORTAGE RAILROAD
OP&E	OREGON PACIFIC & EASTERN RAILWAY
OPA	OREGON PACIFIC
OPC	OHIO POWER COMPANY
OPS	OHIO PUBLIC SERVICE COMPANY
OR	OHIO RIVER
OR&LC	OAHU RAILWAY & LAND COMPANY
OR&NC	OREGON & NAVIGATION COMPANY
OR&TW	OAHU RAILWAY & TERMINAL WAREHOUSING
OR&W	OHIO RIVER & WESTERN
OREG	OREGONIAN RAILWAY
ORL	ORLEANS RAILROAD
ORO	ORO DAM
ORRY	OWASCO RIVER RAILWAY
ORTC	OSTRANDER RAILWAY & TIMBER CO
ORW	OKLAHOMA RAILWAY
ORY	OAHU RAILWAY
OS	OCEAN SHORE RAILROAD
OS&H	ONTARIO SIMCOE & HURON

APPENDIX A (RAILROADS)

A	ABBREVIATIONS ALPHABETICALLY W/ROADS
OS.	OCEAN SHORE RAILWAY
OSA	OSAGE RAILWAY
OSB&W	OSBORNE BAY & WARF
OSH	OSHAWA RAILWAY
OSL	OREGON SHORT LINE
OSN	OREGON STEAM NAVIGATION COMPANY
OSO	OHIO SOUTHERN
OST*	OHIO SEAMLESS TUBE
OSW	OKLAHOMA SOUTHWESTERN
OT	OAKLAND TERMINAL RAILWAY
OTCO	OTTAWA TRANSPORTATION COMMISSION
OTIS	OTIS RAILROAD
OTN&W	OTTAWA NORTHERN & WESTERN
OTRY	OREGON TRUNK RAILWAY
OUR&D	OGDEN UNION RAILWAY & DEPOT COMPANY
OV	OHIO VALLEY
OVER	OVERTON RAILROAD
OWB&FL	ORLEANS WEST BADEN & FRENCH LICK SPRGS
OWP	OREGON WATER POWER
OWP&R	OREGON WASHINGTON PORTLAND & R
OWR&N	OREGON WASHINGTON RR & NAVIGATION CO
P	PORTLAND RAILWAYS
P&A	PENSACOLA & ATLANTIC
P&AC	PRESCOTT & ARIZONA CENTRAL
P&AR	PACIFIC & ARCTIC RAILWAY & NAVIGATION
P&AV	PUEBLO & ARKANSAS VALLEY
P&B	PHILADELPHIA & BRIGANTINE
P&BED	PROVIDENCE & BEDFORD
P&BPR	PITTSBURGH & BIRMINGHAM PASSENGER RY
P&BR	PATAUSCO & BACK RIVERS RAILROAD
P&BRRR	PATAPSCO & BLACK RIVERS RAILROAD
P&BS	PITTSBURGH & BUTLER STREET RAILWAY
P&BU	PITTSBURGH & BUTLER
P&C	PHILADELPHIA & COLUMBIA RAILROAD
P&CA	PITTSBURGH & CARNEGIE RAILROAD
P&CE	PORTLAND & CAPE ELIZABETH RAILWAY
P&CF	PHILADELPHIA & CAMDEN FERRY COMPANY
P&CM	POTEAU & CAVANAL MOUNTAIN
P&CRR	POUGHKEEPSIE & CONNECTICUT RAILROAD
P&CS	PITTSBURGH & CASTLE SHANNON INCLINE
P&CU	PIEDMONT & CUMBERLAND
P&D	PARIS & DECATUR RAILROAD
P&DRY	PROVIDENCE & DANIELSON RAILWAY COMPANY
P&DRY	PROVIDENCE & DANIELSON STREET RAILWAY
P&E	POUGHKEEPSIE & EASTERN RAILROAD CO
P&EA	PEORIA & EASTERN RAILWAY
P&EAST	PACIFIC & EASTERN
P&EL	PORTERFIELD & ELLIS
P&ERR	PHILADELPHIA & ERIE RAILROAD
P&F	PIONEER & FAYETTE RAILROAD
P&FN	PROFILE & FRANCONIA NOTCH RAILROAD
P&FRR	PRESIDIO & FERRIES RAILROAD COMPANY
P&G	PENSACOLA & GEORGIA
P&GT	PHILADELPHIA & GERMANTOWN RAILWAY
P&H	PENNSBORO & HARRISVILLE RAILROAD
P&HR	PATTERSON & HUDSON RIVER
P&HRR	PENNSBORO & HARRISVILLE RITCHIE CO RY
P&HT	PEMBERTON & HIGHTSTOWN
P&I	PERU & INDIANAPOLIS
P&IN	PACIFIC & IDAHO NORTHERN
P&IR	PADUCAH & ILLINOIS RAILROAD
P&K	PORTLAND & KENNEBEC
P&KC	PARKER & KANSAS CITY RAILROAD
P&KE	PENOBSCOT & KENNEBEC
P&LB	PHILADEPHIA & LONG BRANCH RAILROAD
P&LB.	PHILADELPHIA & LONG BRANCH RAILWAY
P&LE	PITTSBURGH & LAKE ERIE RAILROAD
P&LT	PLACERVILLE & LAKE TAHOE
P&M	PLYMOUTH & MIDDLEBOROUGH RAILROAD
P&MOR	PITTSBURGH & MOON RUN
P&MP	PARIS & MOUNT PLEASANT RAILROAD
P&MR	PITTSBURGH & MOON RIVER
P&MSR	PENNSYLVANIA & MARYLAND STREET RW
P&MU	PRESCOTT & MT UNION RAILWAY
P&N	PIEDMONT & NORTHERN RAILWAY
P&NC	PHILADELPHIA & NEWTON CONNECTING RR

A	ABBREVIATIONS ALPHABETICALLY W/ROADS
P&NE	PRESCOTT & NORTHEASTERN
P&NW	PRESCOTT & NORTHWESTERN RAILROAD
P&NY	PASSAIC & NEW YORK
P&NYC	PENNSYLVANIA & NEW YORK CANAL & RR
P&O	PORTLAND & OGDENSBURG RAILROAD LINE
P&OQ	PEORIA & OQUQWKA
P&OV	PITTSBURGH & OHIO VALLEY RAILWAY
P&P	PARSONS & PACIFIC
P&PE	PENSACOLA & PERDIDO
P&PRR	PATTERSON & PASSAIC RAILROAD
P&PU	PEORIA & PEKIN UNION RAILWAY
P&R	PHILADELPHIA & READING
P&RA	PHILLIPS & RANGELEY
P&RC	PHILADELPHIA & READING COAL & IRON
P&RF	PORTLAND & RUMFORD FALLS RAILROAD
P&RO	PORTLAND & ROCHESTER RAILROAD
P&ROAN	PORTSMOUTH & ROANOKE RAILROAD
P&S	PITTSBURGH & SUSQUEHANNA
P&SF	PANHANDLE & SANTA FE RAILWAY
P&SH	PATTEN & SHERMAN
P&SI	PETERSBURG & SEA ISLE
P&SL	POMEROY & STATELINE RAILROAD
P&SP	PROVIDENCE & SPRINGFIELD
P&SR	PETALUMA & SANTA ROSA RAILROAD
P&SRR	PANA & SPRINGFIELD RAILROAD CO
P&SS	PHILADELPHIA & SEASHORE
P&TH	PARIS & TERRE HAUTE
P&W	PROVIDENCE & WORCESTER RAILROAD
P&WAL	PEQUEST & WALKILL
P&WAT	POTTSDAM & WATERTOWN
P&WC	PHILADELPHIA & WEST CHESTER TRACTION
P&WE	PATTERSON & WESTERN
P&WR	PHILADELPHIA & WESTERN RAILROAD
P&WR.	PHILADELPHIA & WESTERN RAILWAY
P&WRR	PITTSBURGH & WESTERN RAILROAD CO
P&WS	PHILADELPHIA & WESTERN STREET RAILWAY
P&WV	PITTSBURGH & WEST VIRGINIA RAILWAY
P*	PULLMAN COMPANY (O)
P-B	PRINCETON-BLUEFIELD
P-C	POLK-CLAIBORNE MILITARY RAILROAD
P-D	PHELPS DODGE CORPORATION
P-P	PENNSYLVANIA-PACIFIC RAILROAD
P-PJ	PONTIAC-PONTIAC JUNCTION RAILWAY
P.	PORTLAND RAILROAD COMPANY
PA&AT	PENNSYLVANIA & ATLANTIC RAILROAD
PA&D	PENNSYLVANIA & DELAWARE RAILROAD
PA&DEC	PEORIA ATLANTA & DECATUR
PA&E	PAINESVILLE & EASTERN
PA&HR	PATERSON & HUDSON RIVER RAILROAD
PA&L	PADUCHA & LOUISVILLE
PA&MR	PITTSBURGH ALLEGHENY & MCKEES ROCKS
PA&NW	PENNSYLVANIA & NORTHWESTERN
PA&NY	PENNSYLVANIA & NEW YORK RAILROAD
PA&P	PENNSYLVANIA & PACIFIC
PA&T	PENSACOLA ALABAMA & TENNESSEE
PAAC	PORT AUTHORITY OF ALLEGHENY COUNTY
PAB*	PABST BEER
PACY	PRAIRIE CENTRAL
PAJV	PAJURO VALLEY CONSOLIDATED RAILROAD
PAN	PANAMA RAILROAD
PAN.	PANAMA CANAL COMPANY
PAP	PORT ANGELES PACIFIC
PAP&L	PENNSYLVANIA POWER & LIGHT COMPANY
PAPG	PIRAEUS ATHENS PELOPONNESUS (GREECE)
PARR	PARR TERMINAL RAILROAD
PARW	PASADENA RAILWAY
PAS	PENNSYLVANIA STATE RAILROAD
PAT	PITTSBURGH COMMUTER
PATH	PORT AUTHORITY TRANS HUDSON
PATP	PORT AUTHORITY TRANSIT (PITTSBURGH)
PAWN	PAWNEE RAILROAD
PB	PORT BIENVILLE RAILROAD
PB&E	PITTSBURGH BINGHAMTON & EASTERN
PB&LE	PITTSBURGH BESSEMER & LAKE ERIE
PB&NE	PHILADELPHIA BETHLEHEM & NEW ENGLAND
PB&W	PHILADELPHIA BALTIMORE & WASHINGTON RR
PB*	PEERLESS BEER

A56

APPENDIX A (RAILROADS)

A	ABBREVIATIONS ALPHABETICALLY W/ROADS
PBC	POUGHKEEPSIE BRIDGE COMPANY
PBR	PUBLIC BELT ROAD
PBRR	PEACH BOTTOM RAILROAD
PC	PENN CENTRAL
PC&N	POINT COMFORT & NORTHERN RAILWAY
PC&NO	PORT COMFORT & NORTHERN
PC&RV	PORTAGE CREEK & RICH VALLEY
PC&SL	PITTSBURGH CINCINNATI & ST LOUIS RR
PC&T	PITTSBURGH CLEVELAND & TORONTO
PC&Y	PITTSBURGH CHARTIERS & YOUGHIOGHENY
PCAC	PACIFIC COAST AGGREGATES COMPANY
PCC	PHILADELPHIA COKE COMAPNY
PCC&SL	PITTSBURGH CINCINNATI CHIC & ST LOUIS
PCCO	PENNSYLVANIA COAL COMPANY
PCE	PATTERSON CENTRAL ELECTRIC
PCEC	PICTOU COUNTY ELECTRIC COMPANY
PCI	PASADENA CITY
PCO	PITTSBURGH COUNTY
PCOA	PACIFIC COAST RAILWAY
PCOAL	PEABODY COAL
PCOAST	PACIFIC COAST RAILROAD
PCR	PINE CREEK RAILROAD
PCRR	PENN CENTRAL RAILROAD
PCTR	PACIFIC COAST TERMINAL
PD	PENNSYLVANIA DETROIT RAILROAD
PD&E	PEORIA DECATUR & EVANSVILLE RAILROAD
PD&Y	PORTSMOUTH DOVER & YORK STREET RAILWAY
PDSC&T	PORT DALHOUSE ST CATHERINES & THOROLD
PE	PACIFIC ELECTRIC RAILWAY
PE&NY	PEMBERTON & NEW YORK
PE&SS	PEMBERTON & SEASHORE
PECO	PERRY COUNTY RAILROAD
PED	POTOMAC EDISON
PEI	PRINCE EDWARD ISLAND
PEL	PORTLAND ELECTRIC RAILWAY
PENV	PENIGEWASSET VALLEY
PENE	PENSACOLA ELECTRIC COMPANY
PEOP	PEOPLES ELECTRIC STREET RAILWAY
PEOP.	PEOPLES RAILWAY
PEP	POTOMAC ELECTRIC POWER
PEPC	PORTLAND ELECTRIC POWER COMPANY
PERB	PERMIAN BASIN RAILROAD
PERM	PACIFIC ELECTRIC RAILWAY OF MEXICO
PERY	PENINSULAR RAILWAY
PET	PETERSBURG RAILROAD COMPANY
PETE	PEORIA TERMINAL COMPANY
PETR	PETERBOROUGH RADIAL RAILWAY
PEV	PORT EVERGLADES BELT LINE RAILROAD
PEXT	PATTERSON EXTENSION
PF&P	POTOMAC FREDERICKSBURG & PIEDMONT
PFE	PACIFIC FRUIT GROWERS EXPRESS
PFE*	PACIFIC FRUIT GROWERS EXPRESS (O)
PFL	PRINCETON FAST LINE
PFW&C	PITTSBURGH FT WAYNE & CHICAGO RAILWAY
PG	PEORIA GATEWAY RAILROAD
PG&CH	PHILADELPHIA GERMANTOWN & CHEST. HILL
PG&E	PACIFIC GAS & ELECTRIC
PG&N	PHILADELPHIA GERMANTOWN & NORRISTOWN
PGE	PACIFIC GREAT EASTERN RAILWAY
PGM*	PAGE MILK
PGS	PENNSYLVANIA GLASS SAND COMPANY
PH&B	POUGHKEEPSIE HARTFORD & BOSTON
PH&D	PORT HURON & DETROIT RAILROAD
PH&NW	PORT HURON & NORTHWESTERN
PH&WH	PENN HAVEN & WHITE HAVEN
PHB&NC	PITTSBURGH HARMONY BUTLER & N CASTLE
PHBL	PHILADELPHIA BELT LINE RAILROAD
PHG	PITTSTON HAWLEY GRAVITY COMPANY
PHL&B	PORT HOPE LINDSAY & BEAVERTON
PHSR	PATTERSON HEIGHTS STREET RAILWAY CO.
PHV	PITHOLE VALLEY RAILROAD
PI	PICKENS RAILROAD
PI&RGV	PORT ISABEL & RIO GRANDE VALLEY RR
PI&RGV	PORT ISABEL & RIO GRANDE VALLEY RY
PI&SH	PITTSBURGH & SHAWMUT RAILROAD
PIER	PINEHURST ELECTRIC RAILWAY
PIGR	PIGEON RIVER RAILROAD

A	ABBREVIATIONS ALPHABETICALLY W/ROADS
PILL	PILLSBURY
PIN	PINSLY
PIONV	PIONEER VALLEY RAILROAD
PIT	PITTSBURGH RAILWAYS
PJ&M	PORT JARVIS & MONTICELLO RAILWAY
PJM&NY	PORT JERVIS MONTICELLO & NEW YORK RR
PL	PACIFIC LINES
PL&D	PEKIN LINCOLN & DECATUR
PL&N	PITTSBURGH LACKAWANNA & NORTHEASTERN
PL&RR	PEEKSKILL LIGHTING & RAILROAD COMPANY
PL&W	PITTSBURGH LISBON & WESTERN RAILWAY
PL&W.	PITTSBURGH LISBON & WESTERN RAILROAD
PLC	PACIFIC LUMBER COMPANY
PLEG	PEG LEG
PLM	PULLMAN COMPANY
PLR	PORTLAND LEWISTON INTERURBAN RAILROAD
PLR.	PORTLAND LEWISTON RAILWAY
PLTC	PLATTSBURGH TRACTION COMPANY
PLTER	PORTLAND TERMINAL RAILROAD
PLU	PICKERING LUMBER
PLW	PORTLAND LOCOMOTIVE WORKS
PLZ&W	PALESTINE LAKE ZURICH & WAUCONDA
PM	PERE MARQUETTE RAILWAY
PM&B	PITTSBURGH MARS & BUTLER RAILWAY
PM&C	PITTSBURGH MARION & CHICAGO RAILWAY
PM&C.	PITTSBURGH MARION & CHICAGO RAILROAD
PM&M	PHILADELPHIA MARLTON & MEDFORD
PM&NO	PENSACOLA MOBILE & NEW ORLEANS
PM&O	PACIFIC MOBILE & OHIO
PM&Y	PITTSBURGH MCKEESPORT & YOUNGIOGHENY
PM*	PENNSYLVANIA MERCHANDISE
PMA	PORT MANATEE
PMEX	PENOLES MEXICANNA
PMID	PENNSYLVANIA MIDLAND
PMM	PACOLET MILLS MANUFACTURING
PN	PROFILE NORTHERN
PN&NY	PHILADELPHIA NEWTON & NEW YORK RR
PNA	PRECISION NATIONAL
PNE	PORTERVILLE NORTHEASTERN
PNJRR	PATTERSON NEW JERSEY RAILROAD
PNW	PACIFIC NORTHWEST TRACTION COMPANY
PO	PORTAGE RAILROAD
PO&D	PENNSYLVANIA OHIO & DETROIT RR CO
PO&NE	POMEROY & NEWARK
PONE	POCONO NORTHEAST RAILWAY
PONT	PONTCHARTRAIN RAILROAD
POPB	PORT OF PALM BEACH DISTRICT
POR	PORTER
PORAM	PORT ORAM RAILROAD
PORR	PORT ORANGE RAILROAD
POT	PORT OF TACOMA
POTB	PORT OF TILLAMOOK BAY RAILROAD
POTCR	POTATO CREEK RAILROAD
POTT	POTTSTOWN RAILWAY
POV	PEND OREILLE VALLEY RAILROAD
POV&C	PITTSBURGH OHIO VALLEY & CINCINNATI
PP	PINAFORE PARK
PP&B	PENNSYLVANIA POUGHKEEPSIE & BOSTON
PPC	PACIFIC PORTLAND CEMENT CO. CONSOLID.
PPCO	PIONEER PENNSYLVANIA COAL COMPANY
PPD	PORTLAND PUBLIC DOCKS
PPG	PITTSBURGH PLATE GLASS
PPJ	PONTIAC PACIFIC JUNCTION RAILWAY
PPNJT	POINT PLEASANT NEW JERSEY TRANSIT
PPR	PELHAM PARK RAILROAD (MONORAIL)
PR	PRATTSBURGH RAILWAY
PR&A	PORT ROYAL & AUGUSTA RAILWAY
PR&EA	PRESCOTT & EASTERN
PR&NE	PHILADELPHIA READING & NEW ENGLAND
PR&WC	PORT ROYAL & WESTERN CAROLINA RAILWAY
PRES	PRESTON RAILROAD
PRI	POWDER RIVER RAILROAD
PRL	POTONIC REGION LINES
PRL&P	PORTLAND RAILWAY LIGHT & POWER COMPANY
PRR	PENNSYLVANIA RAILROAD
PRRCO	PACIFIC RAILROAD COMPANY
PRRMD	PENNSYLVANIA RR OF MARYLAND

STEPHANS' RAILROAD DIRECTORY

A57

APPENDIX A (RAILROADS)

A	ABBREVIATIONS ALPHABETICALLY W/ROADS
PRSL	PENNSYLVANIA READING SEASHORE LINES
PRSS	PENN ROAD SEA SHORE
PRT	PHILADELPHIA RAPID TRANSIT
PRV	PEARL RIVER VALLEY RAILROAD
PRWM	PACIFIC RAILROAD OF MEXICO
PRWM	PACIFIC RAILWAY OF MEXICO
PS	PITTSBURGH SOUTHERN
PS&LE	PITTSBURGH SHENANGO & LAKE ERIE
PS&N	PITTSBURGH SHAWMUT & NORTHERN RR CO
PS&P	PORTLAND SACO & PORTSMOUTH
PS&SV	PUGET SOUND & SNOQUALMIE VALLEY RR
PSC	PUBLIC SERVICE OF COLORADO
PSCT	PUBLIC SERVICE COORDINATED TRANSPORT
PSER	PUGET SOUND ELECTRIC RAILWAY
PSI	PUBLIC SERVICE OF INDIANA
PSIRY	PORT STANLEY INCLINE RAILWAY
PSL	PEABODY SHORT LINE
PSNJ	PUBLIC SERVICE OF NEW JERSEY
PSRR	PAUL SMITH RAILROAD
PSRW	PUBLIC SERVICE RAILWAY CO UNION LINE
PSRY	PHOENIX STREET RAILWAY
PSS	POINT SHIRLEY STREET RAILWAY
PSTC	PHILADELPHIA SUBURBAN TRANS COMPANY
PSTRY	POWELL STREET RAILWAY
PSVI	PEAKER SERVICES INC
PSW	PHILADELPHIA SUBWAYS
PSY	PLANT SYSTEM
PT	PORTLAND TERMINAL RAILROAD COMPANY
PT&B	PITTSBURGH TITUS & BUFFALO
PT&PS	PORT TOWNSEND & PUGET SOUND
PT*	PETRO-TEX
PTC	PHILADELPHIA TRANSPORTATION COMPANY
PTE	PORT EVERGLADES RAILWAY
PTER	PENINSULA TERMINAL RAILROAD COMPANY
PTO	PORT TOWNSEND RAILROAD
PTR	PORTLAND TRACTION COMPANY
PTRA	PORT TERMINAL RAILROAD ASSOCIATION
PTRM	PORTLAND TRI-MET
PTS	PORT TOWNSEND SOUTHERN
PU	PURDUE UNIVERSITY
PUC	PORT UTILITIES COMMISSION RAILWAY
PUCM	PARK UTAH CONSOLIDATED MINES
PUD&R	PUEBLO UNION DEPOT & RAILROAD
PUSC	PORTLAND UNION RAILWAY STATION COMPANY
PUT	PUTNAM LUMBER COMPANY
PV	POTEAU VALLEY
PV&N	PECOS VALLEY & NORTHEASTERN
PVMT	PENN VIEW MOUNTAIN RAILROAD
PVRR	PATH VALLEY RAILROAD
PVRY	PEMBINA VALLEY RAILWAY
PVS	PECOS VALLEY SOUTHERN RAILWAY
PW&B	PHILADELPHIA WILMINGTON & BALTIMORE
PW&BRR	PROVIDENCE WARREN & BRISTOL RAILROAD
PW&O	PAINESVILLE WOOSTER & OHIO
PW&S	PITTSBURGH WESTMORELAND & SOMERSET
PX	PRODUCTS TANK LINE
PY&A	PITTSBURGH YOUNGSTOWN & ASHTABULA RY
PY&C	PITTSBURGH YOUNGSTOWN & CHICAGO
Q	QUINCY RAILROAD
Q&B	QUAKERTOWN & BETHLEHEM RAILROAD
Q&E	QUAKERTOWN & EASTERN RAILROAD
Q&GW	QUEBEC & GOSFORD WOODEN RAILWAY
Q&LSJ	QUEBEC & LAKE ST JOHN RAILWAY
Q&NW	QUOCHITA & NORTH WESTERN
Q&TL	QUINCY & TORCH LAKE (SAME AS QM)
QA	QUEEN ANNE'S RAILROAD COMPANY
QA&P	QUANAH ACME & PACIFIC RAILWAY
QBRW	QUEENSBORO BRIDGE RAILWAY COMPANY
QC	QUEBEC CENTRAL RAILWAY
QCIP	QUEBEC CITADEL INCLINE PLANE
QDRY	QUEBEC DISTRICT RAILWAY
QG	QUEENSLAND GOV. RAILWAYS
QI&T	QUEBEC IRON & TITANIUM
QM	QUINCY MINING COMPANY
QM&S	QUEBEC MONTREAL & SOUTHERN RAILWAY
QMO&O	QUEBEC MONTREAL OTTAWA & OCCIDENTAL RY
QNS&L	QUEBEC NORTH SHORE & LABRADOR RAILWAY
QO	QUAKER OATS
QRL&P	QUEBEC RAILWAY LIGHT & POWER COMPANY
QS	QUINCY SOYBEAN COMPANY
QSRY	QUEBEC SOUTHERN RAILWAY
QT	QUABOG TRANSFER COMPANY
QU	QUAKAKE
QW	QUINCY WESTERN RAILWAY COMPANY
R	READING RAILROAD COMPANY
R&A	RICHMOND & ALLEGHENY RAILROAD
R&AE	RIVERSIDE & ARLINGTON ELECTRIC RY
R&B	RUTLAND & BURLINGTON
R&C	RALEIGH & CHARLESTON
R&CB	RICHMOND & CHESAPEAKE BAY
R&CL	ROME & CLINTON
R&CO	RHINEBECK & CONNECTICUT RAILROAD CO
R&COL	READING & COLUMBIA
R&D	RICHMOND & DANVILLE
R&DB	RARITAN & DELAWARE BAY
R&E	ROCHESTER & EASTERN
R&ER	ROCHESTER & EASTERN RAPID RAILWAY
R&G	REGISTER & GLENVILLE
R&GV	RAY & GILA VALLEY RAILROAD CO
R&IR	ROCKFORD & INTERURBAN RAILWAY
R&L	READING & LEHIGH
R&N	ROBY & NORTHERN RAILWAY
R&NO	ROME & NORTHERN
R&P	RENO & PITHOLE
R&PB	RICHLAND & PETERSBURG
R&R	ROCKTON & RION RAILWAY
R&S	ROBERVAL & SAGUENAY RAILWAY
R&SA	RENSSELAER & SARATOGA RAILROAD
R&SB	ROCHESTER & SODUS BAY RAILWAY
R&SRR	ROCHESTER & SYRACUSE RAILROAD
R&SUB	ROCHESTER & SUBURBAN
R&W	RAYMONDVILLE & WADDINGTON
R&WAT	ROME & WATERTOWN
R-P	RICHMOND-PETERSBURG RAILROAD COMPANY
R-P.	RICHMOND & PETERSBURG
RAL	RED ARROW LINES
RAP	RAPID RAILWAY
RAY	RAYONIER & NAVIGATION COMPANY
RB	RAILBOX
RBC	RINGLING BROTHERS CIRCUS
RBH*	RATH BLACK HAWK
RBL	ROYAL BLUE LINE
RBMH	RIVERSIDE BRIDGEBORO MT HOLLY & ATL S
RC	REICHHOLD CHEMICAL
RC&B	ROCHESTER CITY & BRIGHTON
RC&BT	ROARING CAMP & BIG TREES RAILROAD
RC&E	REW CITY & ELDRED
RCBH&W	RAPID CITY BLACK HILLS & WESTERN
RCP	RAUB CENTRAL POWER
RCR	ROCKCASTLE RIVER RAILROAD
RCR.	ROCKCASTLE RAILROAD
RCT	RIDEAU CANAL TRAMWAY
RD	RUSSIAN DECAPODS
RD&A	RICHELIEU DRUMMOND & ATHABASKA
RE	REDONDO RAILROAD
REA	RAILWAY EXPRESS
REA*	RAILWAY EXPRESS.
REDR	REDSTONE RAILROAD
RF	ROOT REFINING COMPANY
RF&P	RICHMOND FREDERICKSBURG & POTOMIC RR
RF&RL	RUMFORD FALLS & RANGELEY LAKES
RG	RIO GRANDE
RG&E	ROCHESTER GAS & ELECTRIC
RG&S	RIO GRANDE & SOUTHWESTERN
RG*	REINEGOLD
RGC	RIO GRANDE CITY
RGE	RIO GRANDE EASTERN
RGS	RIO GRANDE SOUTHERN
RGW	RIO GRANDE WESTERN
RH&L	ROCHESTER HORNELLSVILLE & LACKAWANNA
RI	ROCK ISLAND
RIC	RHODE ISLAND COMPANY
RICO	READING IRON COMPANY

APPENDIX A (RAILROADS)

A	ABBREVIATIONS ALPHABETICALLY W/ROADS
RIDP	RIDGEFIELD PARK
RIE	ROCKFORD ILLINOIS ELECTRIC COMPANY
RIS	ROCK ISLAND SOUTHERN RAILWAY CO.
RISR	RHODE ISLAND SUBURBAN RAILWAY
RIVT	RIVER TERMINAL RAILWAY
RL	RAQUETTE LAKE RAILWAY
RL&B	ROCHESTER LOCKPORT & BUFFALO RAILROAD
RL&MW	RICHMOND LOCOMOTIVE & MACHINE WORKS
RL&NF	ROCHESTER LOCKPORT & NIAGARA FALLS
RLC	ROCKLAND CENTRAL
RM&SF	ROCKY MOUNTAIN & SANTA FE RAILWAY
RMC	RESERVE MINING COMPANY
RMCO	RAILCAR MAINTENANCE COMPANY
RMRY	REGINA MUNICIPAL RAILWAY
RN&P	ROCHESTER NUNDA & PITTSBURGH
RN&PA	ROCHESTER NUNDA & PENNSYLANIA
RNY&P	ROCHESTER NEW YORK & PENNSYLVANIA
RO	ROSECRANS
RO&GV	ROCHESTER & GENESSEE VALLEY RAILROAD
RO&S	ROWLESBURG & SOUTHERN
RO&SO	ROCHESTER & SOUTHERN
ROB	ROBBINS RAILROAD
ROC	ROCKPORT RAILROAD
ROCH	ROCHESTER RAILWAY
ROCHE	ROCHESTER ELECTRIC
ROCKRR	ROCKINGHAM RAILROAD
ROR	ROANOKE RIVER RAILWAY
ROY	ROY GREENE
RP&I	RANGELY PHILLIPS & INDUSTRY RAILROAD
RP#	RALSTON PURINA
RPL&N	ROCK PORT LANGDON & NORTHERN
RPRY	RIVERSIDE PARK RAILWAY
RR	RARITAN RIVER RAILROAD
RR&E	ROANOKE RAILWAY & ELECTRIC COMPANY
RR&G	RED RIVER & GULF RAILROAD
RRLC	RED RIVER LUMBER COMPANY
RRR	READER RAILROAD
RRV	ROGUE RIVER VALLEY
RRY	ROCKAWAY RAILWAY COMPANY
RS	ROWLAND SPRINGS RAILROAD
RS&E	ROCHESTER SYRACUSE & EASTERN
RS&N	RED SPRINGS & NORTHERN
RS&P	ROSCOE SNYDER & PACIFIC RAILWAY
RS&S	ROCKDALE SANDOW & SOUTHERN RAILROAD
RSP	ROCKY SPRINGS PARK
RSR	READING STREET RAILWAY
RST	REPUBLIC STEEL CORPORATION
RT	RICHMOND TERMINAL RAILWAY
RT&C	ROCKPORT THOMASTON & CAMDEN ST RY
RTC	ROCHESTER TRANSIT CORPORATION
RTCM	RAILWAY TRANSFER CITY OF MINNEAPOLIS
RTL	ROCHESTER TROLLEY LINES
RTOH	RAPID TRANSIT COMPANY OF OHIO
RTOH.	OHIO RAPID TRANSIT COMAPNY
RU	RUTLAND RAILROAD
RU.	RUTLAND RAILWAY
RV	RAHWAY VALLEY RAILROAD
RVA	ROCKAWAY VALLEY RAILROAD
RVAM	ROCKAWAY VALLEY MFG & CONSTRUCTION CO
RW	RAILWORKS
RW&O	ROME WATERTOWN & OGDENSBURG
RWCX	RAILROAD WEED CONTROL INC
RWTC	RAIL TO WATER TRANSPORT CORP.
RY	RAYONIER RAILWAY
CBELT	ST LOUIS & SOUTHWESTERN
CBELT,	ST LOUIS SOUTHWESTERN (COTTON BELT)
FRIS	ST LOUIS SAN FRANCISCO RAILWAY
FRIS,.	ST LOUIS & SAN FRANCISCO RAILWAY
NYS&W	SUSQUEHANNA
S	SOUTHERN RAILWAY
S&A	SAVANNAH & ATLANTA RAILWAY COMPANY
S&AL	SHENANGO & ALLEGHENY
S&B	SCRANTON & BINGHAMTON
S&BL	SCOTT & BEARSKIN LAKE
S&BV	SHENANGO & BEAVER VALLEY
S&C	SUMTER & CHOCTAW RAILWAY
S&CA	SUFFOLK & CAROLINA
S&CRY	STOCKTON & COPPEROPLIS RAILWAY
S&CS	SWATARA & COLD SPRINGS
S&CSL	SANDUSKY & COLUMBUS SHORT LINE
S&CV	SYRACUSE & CHENANGO VALLEY
S&E	SYRACUSE & EASTERN
S&EA	SOMERVILLE & EASTON
S&EG	SANFORD & EVERGLADES RAILROAD
S&ERY	SARATOGA & ENCAMPMENT RAILWAY
S&ES	SYRACUSE & EASTSIDE RAILWAY COMPANY
S&H	STEELTON & HIGHSPIRE RAILROAD
S&I	SANDUSKY & INTERURBAN
S&IE	SPOKANE & INLAND ELECTRIC RAILWAY
S&IE.	SPOKANE & INLAND EMPIRE
S&J	SISTRUNK & JORDAN
S&L	SYDNEY & LOUISBURG RAILWAY
S&LP	SARANAC & LAKE PLACID
S&LRR	SIDNEY & LOWE RAILROAD
S&ML	SEBASTICOOK & MOOSEHEAD LAKE
S&MP	SAGINAW & MT PLEASANT
S&NC	SEATTLE & NORTH COAST
S&NE	SUMMIT & NORTHEASTERN RAILWAY
S&NW	SAVANNAH & NORTHWESTERN
S&NY	SUSQUEHANNA & NEW YORK RAILWAY
S&O	SYRACUSE & ONONDAGA
S&OL	SMETHPORT & OLEAN
S&PT	SOUTHINGTON & PLANTSVILLE TRAMWAY CO
S&R	SYRACUSE & ROCHESTER RAILROAD
S&RRV	SHREVEPORT & RED RIVER VALLEY RAILWAY
S&RV	SEATTLE & RANIER VALLEY RAILROAD
S&S	SCHUYLKILL & SUSQUEHANNA
S&S#	SCHWARGEHILD SULZBERGER
S&SC	STARKE & SIMPSON CITY
S&SO	SAVANNAH & SOUTHERN
S&SP	SANFORD & ST PETERSBURG
S&SRR	SAVANNAH & STATESBORG RAILROAD
S&SS	SUNBURY & SELINGROVE STREET RY CO
S&T	SHAMOKIN & TREVERTON
S&TI	SHEFFIELD & TIONESTA RAILWAY
S&U	SYRACUSE & UTICA RAILROAD
S&UD	SYRACUSE & UTICA DIRECT
S&W	SUSQUEHANNA & WESTERN
S&WW	SEATTLE & WALLA WALLA
S#	SINCLAIR
S6INT	SANDUSKY & INTERURBAN
SA&AP	SAN ANTONIO & ARKANSAS PASS
SA&G	SAVANNAH ALBANY & GULF
SA&N	SACRAMENTO AUBURN & NORTHERN
SA&O	SOUTH ATLANTIC & OHIO
SA&SB	ST AUGUSTINE & SOUTH BEACH
SA&SC	SARATOGA & SCHENECTADY RAILROAD
SAB	SABDERSVILLE
SAL	SEABOARD AIR LINE
SALEM	SALEM RAILROAD
SALV	SALEM VALLEY
SAND	SANDERSVILLE RAILROAD
SANT	SANFORD TRACTION
SAPS	SAN ANTONIO PUBLIC SERVICE
SAR	SAWYER RIVER
SAR&S	SARATOGA & SCHUYLERSVILLE
SARR	SECOND AVE RAILROAD COMPANY
SARY	SOUTHERN APPALACHIAN RAILWAY
SAS	SAN ANTONIO SOUTHERN (MP)
SATC	SAN ANTONIO TRACTION COMPANY
SAU&G	SAN ANTONIO UVALDE & GULF RAILROAD
SAV	SACRAMENTO VALLEY RAILROAD
SB	SOUTH BRANCH
SB&LA	SAN BERDO & LOS ANGELES
SB&LT	SUNBURY & LEWISTOWN
SB&NY	SYRACUSE BINGHAMTON & NEW YORK
SB&RGV	SAN BENITO & RIO GRANDE VALLEY
SB&S	SANTA BARBARA & SUBURBAN
SB.	SOUTH BRANCH VALLEY RAILROAD
SBA&W	SAN BERNARDINO ARROWHEAD & WATERMAN
SBC	SONORA BAJA CALIFORNIA RAILROAD
SBC.	SONORA BAJA CALIFORNIA RAILWAY
SBD	SEABOARD SYSTEM
SBELT	STATE BELT RAILROAD

APPENDIX A (RAILROADS)

A	ABBREVIATIONS ALPHABETICALLY W/ROADS
SBR	SOUTH BROOKLYN RAILWAY
SBUF	SOUTH BUFFALO RAILROAD
SBV	SOUTH BRANCH VALLEY
SBVT	SAN BERNARDINO VALLEY TRACTION
SC	STONE CANYON RAILWAY
SC&F	SANTA CRUZ & FELTON
SC&M	STROUDS CREEK & MUDDLETY RAILROAD
SC&MS	SIOUX CITY & MORNINGSIDE STREET RY
SC&P	STONE CANYON & PACIFIC
SC&PA	SIOUX CITY & PACIFIC
SC&PRR	ST CROIX & PENOBSCOTT RAILROAD
SC&PS	SEATTLE COLUMBIA & PUGET SOUND RAILWY
SC&SB	ST CLOUD & SUGAR BELT
SC&T	SEATTLE COAL & TRANSPORTATION COMPANY
SC&W	SANTA CRUZ & WATSONVILLE
SC&W.	SANTA CRUZ-WATSONVILLE RAILROAD
SC&WI	SOUTH CHICAGO & WEST INDIANA RAILROAD
SCA	SOUTHERN CAMBRIA RAILWAY
SCA&P	SPOKANE COEUR D'ALENE & PALOUSE
SCAL	SOUTHERN CALIFORNIA RAILROAD
SCAL.	SOUTHERN CALIFORNIA RAILWAY
SCC	SOUTHERN CEMENT COMPANY
SCC&RR	SOUTH CAROLINA CANAL & RAILROAD
SCCC	SQUAW CREEK COAL COMPANY
SCCE	SUDBURY COPPER CLIFF ELECTRIC RAILWAY
SCE	SOUTHERN CENTRAL
SCE&G	SOUTH CAROLINA ELECTRIC & GAS
SCEC	SOUTHERN CAL EDISON CO (CALIFORNIA)
SCEN	SHENANDOAH CENTRAL
SCERY	SIOUX CITY ELEVATED RAILWAY
SCH	STAUFFER CHEMICAL
SCH&T	SCHENECTADY & TROY
SCH*	SCHLITZ BEER
SCHEN	SCHENECTADY RAILWAY COMPANY
SCHS	ST CHARLES STREET RAILROAD
SCHUY	SCHUYLER RAILWAY
SCIR	SEA CLIFF INCLINED RAILWAY COMPANY
SCIT	SIOUX CITY TRACTION COMPANY
SCL	SEABOARD COAST LINE
SCL*	SHIPPERS CAR LINE
SCLS	SACRAMENTO CITY LINES
SCMX	SHELL CHEMICAL CORPORATION
SCO	SULLIVAN COUNTY RAILROAD
SCOC	STEEL COMPANY OF CANADA
SCOP	SECRETARIA DE COMUNICATIONES Y OBRAS P
SCP	SOUTHERN COLORADO POWER COMPANY
SCPA	SILVER CITY PINOS ALTOS & MOGOLLON
SCRA	SCRANTON TRACTION
SCRR	SANTA CRUZ RAILROAD COMPANY
SCRT	SIOUX CITY RAPID TRANSIT COMPANY
SCRY	SPRING CREEK RAILWAY
SCS	ST CATHERINES STREET RAILWAY
SCT	SIOUX CITY TERMINAL RAILWAY
SCTC	ST CLAIR TUNNEL CO
SCTR	SOUTH CENTRAL TENNESSEE RAILROAD
SD&A	SAN DIEGO & ARIZONA RAILROAD
SD&AE	SAN DIEGO & ARIZONA EASTERN RAILWAY
SD&C	SAN DIEGO & CUYAMACA
SD&ML	SCRANTON DUNMORE & MOOSIC LAKE
SD&PM	SPUYTEN DUYVIL & PORT MORRIS RAILROAD
SD&S	SAN DIEGO & SOUTH EASTERN RY CO.
SDC&E	SAN DIEGO CUYAMACA & EASTERN
SDCEN	SOUTH DAKOTA CENTRAL RAILWAY
SDE	SAN DIEGO ELECTRIC RAILWAY
SDOT&P	SAN DIEGO OLD TOWN & PALM BEACH
SDPB&L	SAN DIEGO PACIFIC BEACH & LA JOLLA
SDS	SAN DIEGO SOUTH EASTERN RAILWAY
SDT	SAN DIEGO TRANSIT
SDW	SD WARREN PAPER COMPANY
SE	SOUTH EASTERN RAILWAY (CANADA)
SE&P	SOUTH EASTERN & PHILLIPSBURG RAILROAD
SE&PH	SOUTH EASTON & PHILLIPSBURG RAILROAD
SEA	SEABOARD RAILROAD
SEA.	SEABOARD AIR LINE. (O)
SEAM	SEATTLE MUNICIPAL RAILWAY
SEAST	SOUTHEASTERN RAILROAD
SEAT	SEATRAIN LINES

A	ABBREVIATIONS ALPHABETICALLY W/ROADS
SECX	SOUTH EASTERN COAL COMPANY
SEE	SEEKONK
SEG	SOUTHERN ELECTRIC GENERATING
SEG&RY	SACRAMENTO ELECTRIC GAS & RAILWAY CO
SEH	ST ELIZABETH HOSPITAL
SEK	SOUTH EAST KANSAS RAILROAD
SEL	SEATTLE ELECTRIC COMPANY
SEL&B	STEUBENVILLE E LIVERPOOL & BEAVER VAL
SEM	SEASHORE ELECTRIC MUSEUM
SEMIN	SE MINERAL
SEMT	SOUTH EAST MICHIGAN TRANSIT
SEOT	SOUTHEASTERN OHIO TRACTION
SEPTA	SOUTH EASTERN PA TRANSPORTATION AUTH
SEPTA.	SOUTH EASTERN PA TRANSIT AUTHORITY
SERR	STARK ELECTRIC RAILROAD
SERY	SPRINGFIELD ELECTRIC RAILWAY
SES	SUSQUEHANNA (O)
SESC	SOUTH EASTERN (SOUTH CAROLINA)
SET	SEATTLE TERMINAL
SET&K	SHERBROOKE EASTERN TOWNSHIP &KENNEBEC
SEWV	SEWELL VALLEY RAILROAD
SF	SANTA FE (O)
SF&CS	SHELBURNE FALLS & COLRAIN STREET RY
SF&N	SAN FRANCISCO & NORTHWESTERN RY CO
SF&NO	SPOKANE FALLS & NORTHERN RAILWAY
SF&NP	SAN FRANCISCO & NORTH PACIFIC RY CO
SF&NV	SAN FRANCISCO & NAPA VALLEY RAILROAD
SF&NW	SPRINGFIELD & NORTHWESTERN
SF&S	SANDUSKY FREMONT & SOUTHERN
SF&SJ	SAN FRANCISCO & SAN JOSE
SF&SJV	SAN FRANCISCO & SAN JOAQUIN VALLEY
SF&SM	SAN FRANCISCO & SAN MATEO
SF&W	SAVANNAH FLORIDA & WESTERN
SF-S	SAN FRANCISCO-SACRAMENTO RAILROAD
SFB	SAN FRANCISCO BELT LINE RAILROAD
SFC	SANTA FE CENTRAL
SFC&W	SALEM FALLS CITY & WESTERN RAILWAY
SFCRR	ST FRANCOIS COUNTY RAILROAD COMPANY
SFI	SOUTHWEST FOREST INDUSTRIES
SFL	SHORE FAST LINE
SFM	SAN FRANCISCO MUNICIPAL RAILWAY
SFN&C	SAN FRANCISCO NAPA & CALISTOGA RY
SFO&SJ	SAN FRANCISCO OAKLAND & SAN JOSE
SFP	SOUTH FORK-PORTAGE RAILWAY
SFP&P	SANTA FE PRESCOTT & PHOENIX
SFR&E	SANTA FE RATON & EASTERN RAILROAD
SFRY	SLAVE FALLS RAILWAY
SFT&B	SAN FRANCISCO TAMALPAIS & BOLINAS
SFTS	SIOUX FALLS TRACTION SYSTEM
SFV&N	SAN FRANCISCO VALLEJO & NAPA
SG	SOUTH GEORGIA RAILROAD
SG&N	SILVERTON GLADSTONE & NORTHERLY RR
SG&NA	SAVANNAH GRIFFIN & NORTH ALABAMA
SG.	SOUTH GEORGIA RAILWAY
SGER	SHADE GAP ELECTRIC RAILWAY
SGV	SAN GABRIEL VALLEY RAPID TRANSIT
SH	STONE HARBOR RAILROAD
SH&E	SACKETS HARBOR & ELLISBURG
SH&N	SHAWMUT & NORTHERN
SH&P	SHREVEPORT & PACIFIC RAILROAD
SH&PE	SPRINGFIELD HAVANA & PEORIA
SH&W	STONE HARBOR & WILDWOOD
SH&WB	SUNBURY HAZELTON & WILLES BARRE
SHAWC	SHAWMUT CONNECTING
SHC	SOUTH HOPKINS COAL COMPANY
SHEP	SHEPAUG RAILROAD COMPANY
SHEPV	SHEPAUG VALLEY RAILROAD COMPANY
SHIP*	SHIPYARD RAILWAY
SHO*	SHELL OIL
SHRT	SHAKER HEIGHTS RAPID TRANSIT
SHT	STONE HARBOR TERMINAL RAILROAD
SI	STATEN ISLAND RAILROAD
SI&R	STERLING IRON & RAILWAY
SI.	STATEN ISLAND RAILWAY
SICT	SIOUX CITY TRANSIT COMPANY
SID&O	SIDELL & OLNEY RAILROAD
SIE	SIERRA RAILROAD

A60

APPENDIX A (RAILROADS)

A	ABBREVIATIONS ALPHABETICALLY W/ROADS
SIE.	SIERRA RAILWAY
SIEP	SIERRA PACIFIC
SIEV	SIERRA VALLEYS
SIF&N	SIOUX FALLS & NORTHERN
SILP	SILVER PEAK RAILROAD
SILV	SILVERTON RAILROAD
SIMRY	STATEN ISLAND MIDLAND RAILWAY
SIN	SOUTHERN INDUSTRIAL RAILWAY
SIND	SOUTHERN INDIANA RAILWAY
SING	SINGER MANUFACTURING COMPANY
SINV	SINNEMAHONING VALLEY
SIOR	SOUTH IOWA RAILWAY
SIRT	STATEN ISLAND RAPID TRANSIT RAILWAY
SIRY	SOUTHERN IOWA RAILWAY
SJ	ST JOHNS STREET RAILWAY
SJ&CB	ST JOSEPH & COUNCIL BLUFFS
SJ&DM	ST JOSEPH & DES MOINES
SJ&E	SAN JOAQUIN & EASTERN RAILROAD
SJ&GI	ST JOSEPH & GRAND ISLAND (UP)
SJ&IR	ST JOHNS & INDIAN RIVER
SJ&LC	ST JOHNSBURY & LAKE CHAMPLAIN RR
SJ&LCO	ST JOHNSBURY & LAMOILLE COUNTY RR
SJ&LE	ST JOHNS & LAKE EUSTIS
SJ&M	ST JOHN & MAINE RAILWAY
SJ&O	ST JOHN & OPHIR
SJ&SL	ST JOSEPH & ST LOUIS
SJB	ST JOSEPH BELT RAILWAY
SJC	SAN JUAN CENTRAL
SJE	ST JOHNS ELECTRIC COMPANY
SJL	SAN JOACHIN LUMBER
SJP	SAN JUAN PACIFIC
SJR	SOUTH JERSEY RAILROAD
SJRR	SAN JOSE RAILROAD
SJRT	ST JOHNS RIVER TERMINAL RAILWAY CO
SJRTL	SOUTH JERSEY RAPID TRANSIT LINES
SJRY	SAN JACINTO RAILWAY COMPANY
SJT	ST JOSEPH TERMINAL RAILROAD
SJV	ST JOSEPH VALLEY RAILWAY
SJV.	ST JOSEPH VALLEY RAILROAD
SK	SOUTHERN KANSAS
SKA	SKANEATELES RAILROAD
SKM	SILVER KING COALITION MINES COMPANY
SL	SAGIWAN LOGGING
SL&A	ST LAWRENCE & ATLANTIC
SL&AD	ST LAWRENCE & ADIRONDACK RAILROAD
SL&ARY	ST LAURENCE & ADIRONDACK RAILWAY CO
SL&C	ST LOUIS & CAIRO SHORTLINE
SL&H	ST LOUIS & HANNIBAL
SL&IM	ST LOUIS & IRON MOUNTAIN RAILROAD
SL&IV	ST LAWRENCE & INDUSTRY VILLAGE RY
SL&KC	ST LOUIS & KANSAS CITY
SL&LA	SALT LAKE & LOS ANGELES RAILWAY
SL&N	SHEPAUG LITCHFIELD & NORTHERN
SL&NA	ST LOUIS & NORTH ARKANSAS RAILROAD
SL&O	ST LAWRENCE & OTTAWA
SL&S	STATE LINE & SULLIVAN RAILROAD
SL&SU	ST LOUIS & SUBURBAN
SL&U	SALT LAKE & UTAH
SL&VD	ST LAURENT & VILLAGE D'INDUSTRIE
SLA&T	ST LOUIS ARKANSAS & TEXAS RAILWAY
SLA&TH	ST LOUIS ALTON & TERRE HAUTE RAILROAD
SLB&M	ST LOUIS BROWNSVILLE & MEXICO
SLC	SAN LUIS CENTRAL RAILROAD
SLCO	SOMERS LUMBER COMPANY
SLCUD	SALT LAKE CITY UNION DEPOT & RR CO
SLE	SHORE LINE ELECTRIC RAILWAY COMPANY
SLER&W	ST LOUIS EL RENO & WESTERN RAILWAY
SLG&W	SALT LAKE GARFIELD & WESTERN RAILWAY
SLI	ST LAWRENCE INTERNATIONAL RR & LAND
SLIM&S	ST LOUIS IRON MOUNTAIN & SOUTHERN
SLK&N	ST LOUIS KEOKUK & NORTHWESTERN
SLKC	ST LOUIS KANSAS CITY SHORT LINE
SLKC&C	ST LOUIS KANSAS CITY & CHICAGO
SLKC&N	ST LOUIS KANSAS CITY & NORTHERN
SLL&D	ST LOUIS LAWRENCE & DENVER
SLL&W	ST LOUIS LAWRENCE & WESTERN
SLM&S	ST LOUIS MEMPHIS & SOUTHEASTERN RR

A	ABBREVIATIONS ALPHABETICALLY W/ROADS
SLM&SC	ST LOUIS MATERIALS & SAND COMPANY
SLO	SAN LUIS OBISPO RAILWAY
SLO&SM	SAN LUIS OBISPO & SANTA MARIA VALLEY
SLOR	SHORTLINE RAILROAD (OHIO)
SLPS	ST LOUIS PUBLIC SERVICE
SLR	SOUTH LOGAN RAILWAY
SLRE#	ST LOUIS REEFER EXPRESS
SLRM&P	ST LOUIS ROCKY MOUNTAIN & PACIFIC RY
SLRR	SOUTH LAKE RAILROAD
SLS	SAN LUIS SOUTHERN
SLS&BC	ST LOUIS STURGIS & BATTLE CREEK RR CO
SLS&E	SEATTLE LAKE SHORE & EASTERN
SLS&N	SYRACUSE LAKE SHORE & NORTHERN
SLV	SAN LUIS VALLEY
SLV&TH	ST LOUIS VANDALIA & TERRE HAUTE
SLVS	SAN LUIS VALLEY SOUTHERN
SLW	SCHENECTADY LOCOMOTIVE WORKS
SLWW	ST LOUIS WATER WORKS RAILWAY
SM	ST MARYS RAILROAD
SM&H	SANDUSKY MILAN & HURON
SM&N	SANDUSKY MILAN & NORWALK ELECTRIC RY
SM&S	ST MARYS & SOUTHWESTERN
SMA	SAN MANUEL ARIZONA RAILROAD
SMD	SOUTHERN MARYLAND RAILROAD
SMETH	SMETHPORT
SMG&LG	SARATOGA MT MCGREGOR & LAKE GEORGE RR
SMINE	SYDNEY MINES
SMISS	SOUTHERN RAILWAY CO OF MISSISSIPPI
SMR	ST MARIES RIVER RAILROAD
SMRR	STERLING MOUNTAIN RAILROAD
SMRY	SASKATOON MUNICIPAL RAILWAY
SMS	STONE MOUNTAIN SCENIC RAILROAD
SMST	SEATTLE MUNICIPAL STREET RAILWAY SYST
SMT	SMOKY MOUNTAIN COMPANY
SMV	SANTA MARIA VALLEY RAILROAD
SN	SACRAMENTO NORTHERN RAILWAY
SN&M	SANDUSKY NORWALK & MANSFIELD ELECT RY
SN&S	SANDUSKY NORWALK & SOUTHERN
SN&SO	SANDUSKY NORWALK & SOUTHERN
SNE	SOUTHERN NEW ENGLAND RAILROAD
SNJ	SOUTHERN NEW JERSEY
SNO	SILVERTON NORTHERN RAILROAD
SNRY	STATESBORO NORTHERN RAILWAY
SNW&L	SIERRA NEVADA WOOD & LUMBER COMPANY
SNY	SOUTHERN NEW YORK RAILWAY
SNYP	SOUTHERN NEW YORK POWER & RAILWAY CO
SO#	SUN OILS
SOC	SIERRA RAILROAD OF CALIFORNIA
SOCA	SOUTH CAROLINA RAILROAD
SOF	SOUTH FLORDIA
SOIA	SOUTHEAST OKLAHOMA INDUSTRIAL AUTHOR
SOM	SOMERSET
SOMRR	SOUTH MANCHESTER RAILROAD
SONV	SONOMA VALLEY RAILROAD
SOO	SOO LINE
SOP	SOUTH PARK
SOS	SOUTH SIDE TRACTION COMPANY
SOT	SOUTH OMAHA TERMINAL RAILWAY
SOTC	SOUTHERN TRANS-CONTINENTAL RAILWAY
SP	SOUTHERN PACIFIC RAILROAD
SP&DUL	ST PAUL & DULUTH
SP&O	SYRACUSE PHOENIX & OSWEGO
SP&P	ST PAUL & PACIFIC RAILROAD COMPANY
SP&S	SPOKANE PORTLAND & SEATTLE RAILROAD
SP&S.	SPOKANE PORTLAND & SEATTLE RAILWAY
SPA	SOUTH PENNSYLVANIA RAILROAD
SPA.	SOUTHERN PENNSYLVANIA RAILROAD
SPC	SOUTH PACIFIC COAST
SPCAL	SOUTHERN PACIFIC OF CALIFORNIA
SPE8	SPENCERVILLE & ELGIN
SPEN	SEWARD PENINSULA RAILROAD
SPI	SPOKANE INTERNATIONAL RAILWAY
SPI .	SPOKANE INTERNATIONAL RAILROAD
SPL	SOUTHERN PACIFIC LINES
SPLASL	SAN PEDRO LOS ANGELES & SALT LAKE RR
SPLC	SUGAR PINE LUMBER COMPANY
SPLU	SOUTHERN PINE LUMBER COMPANY

A61

APPENDIX A (RAILROADS)

A	ABBREVIATIONS ALPHABETICALLY W/ROADS
SPM	SOUTHERN PACIFIC OF MEXICO RAILROAD
SPM&M	ST PAUL MINNEAPOLIS & MANITOBA
SPM.	SUD-PACIFICO DE MEXICO
SPMRY	ST PETERSBURG MUNICIPAL RAILWAY (FL)
SPNM	SOUTHERN PACIFIC OF NEW MEXICO
SPR	STROUDSBURG PASSENGER RAILWAY
SPRR	SPRINGFIELD RAILROAD
SPRS	SPRINGFIELD SOUTHERN
SPS	SPERRY RAIL SERVICE
SPSF	SOUTHERN PACIFIC SANTA FE
SPTA	SOUTHEASTERN PENNSYLVANIA TRANS AUTH
SPTEX	SOUTHERN PACIFIC RR CO OF TEXAS
SPUD	ST PAUL UNION DEPOT
SPW	SPARKS WESTERN RAILWAY
SR	SKAGIT RIVER RAILWAY
SR&D	SELMA ROME & DALTON
SR&ELK	SANDY RIVER & ELKHAM
SR&N	SABINE RIVER & NORTHERN RAILROAD
SR&RL	SANDY RIVER & RANGELEY LAKES RAILROAD
SR&SQ	SAN RAFAEL & SAN QUENTIN
SR&W	SUSQUEHANNA RIVER & WESTERN RAILROAD
SR.	SKAGIT RAILWAY
SRC	SHIP RAILWAY OF CHICNECTO
SRCC	SOUTHWEST RAILWAY CONSTRUCTION CO
SRDAC	STREET RAILWAY DEPT OF ANACONDA COPPR
SRG	SOUTHERN RIO GRANDE
SRL&P	SHEBOYGAN RAILWAY LIGHT & POWER CO.
SRM	SURESTE RAILWAY (MEXICO)
SRPC	ST REGIS PAPER COMPANY
SRR	SPENCER RAILROAD
SRTC	SAVANNAH RIVER TERMINAL
SRTM	SACRAMENTO RT METRO
SRV	SANDY RIVER RAILROAD
SS	SOUTH SHORE RAILWAY (LOUISIANA)
SS&C	STANSTEAD SHEFFORD & CHAMBLY RAILWAY
SS&L	SHAMOKIN SUNBURY & LEWISBURG
SS&S	SURRY SUSSEX & SOUTHHAMPTON
SS&SB	SOUTH SHORE & SOUTH BEND
SSC	SUPERIOR STONE COMPANY
SSCO	STANDARD SLAG COMPANY
SSD	SAVANNAH STATE DOCKS
SSE	STALEY SYSTEM OF ELECTRIFIED RW
SSL	SKANEATELES SHORT LINE RAILROAD
SSLI	SOUTH SIDE RAILROAD OF LONG ISLAND
SSLV	SOUTHERN SAN LUIS VALLEY RAILROAD
SSNP	SOUTH SIDE & NORFOLK & PETERSBURG
SSO	SACRAMENTO SOUTHERN
SSO&G	SILVER SPRINGS OCALA & GULF
SSP	SAND SPRINGS RAILWAY
SSRT	SOUTH SHORE RAPID TRANSIT
SSRY	SANDUSKY STREET RAILWAY
SSWC	SPENCER STEEL WIRE COMPANY
SSWR	SUTTON STREET WIRE ROPE RAILROAD
ST	SPRINGFIELD TERMINAL RAILWAY
ST&C	STRATTON & COMPANY
ST&E	STOCKTON TERMINAL & EASTERN RAILROAD
ST&W	STATESVILLE & WESTERN
STAM	STAMFORD STREET RAILWAY
STAT	STATENVILLE RAILROAD OF GEORGIA
STC	SCRANTON TROLLEY COMPANY
STC	SIMPSON TIMBER COMPANY
STDS	STANDARD STEEL DIV-BALDWIN LIMA HAMIL
STEIN	STEINWAY LINES
STER	SAUCELITO TERMINAL
STEW	STEWARTSTOWN RAILROAD
STEWRR	STEWART RAILROAD
STG	STANDARD GRAVEL
STI	SEATTLE TACOMA INTERURBAN
STL	ST LAWRENCE RAILROAD
STL&A	ST LOUIS & ADIRONDACK
STLN	STOURBRIDGE LINE
STR	SEAVIEW TRANSPORTATION
STRC	SCRANTON TRACTION COMPANY
STRR	STRASBURG RAILROAD
STT	SHAWNEE TECUMSEH TRACTION
STTE	STOCKTON TERMINAL (0)

A	ABBREVIATIONS ALPHABETICALLY W/ROADS
STTER	STOCKTON TERMINAL
SU	SAPULPA UNION
SUBT	SUBURBAN TRACTION
SUFT	SUFFOLK TRACTION
SUGL	SUGAR LAND
SUGR	SUGAR RUN
SUL	SUALMATZ LUMBER CO
SUNV	SUNCOOK VALLEY RAILROAD
SUR	SOUTHERN UTAH RAILWAY
SURR	STATE UNIVERSITY RAILROAD
SURY	SUNSET RAILWAY
SUS	SAGINAW UNION STATION RAILWAY (MICH)
SUSC	SUSQUEHANNA CONNECTING RAILROAD
SV	SUMPTER VALLEY RAILWAY (OREGON)
SV&BT	SHERMAN'S VALLEY & BROAD TOP RAILROAD
SV&E	SACRAMENTO VALLEY & EASTERN RAILWAY
SV&E.	SANDY VALLEY & ELKHORN (0)
SV&ELK	SANDY VALLEY & ELKHORN
SV&F	STOCKHAM VALVES & FITTINGS
SVAL	SCHOHARIE VALLEY RAILROAD
SVN	SCHUYLKILL VALLEY NAVIGATION & RR
SVP	SONOMA VALLEY PRISMOIDAL RAILROAD
SVRR	SEA VIER RAILROAD
SVS	SCIATO VALLEY SOUTHERN
SVT	SCIOTO VALLEY TRACTION
SW	SOUTH WESTERN RAILROAD
SW&A	SANDWICH WINDSOR & AMERSTBURG ELECTRIC
SW&C	SWIFT & COMPANY
SW+	SWIFT
SWEP	SOUTHWESTERN ELECTRIC POWER COMPANY
SWIU	SOUTHWESTERN INTERURBAN
SWL	SWAYNE LUMBER COMPANY
SWNM	SOUTHWESTERN RAILWAY OF NEW MEXICO
SWPC	SOUTHWEST PORTLAND CEMENT
SWR	SWAMP RABBIT
SWRY	SOUTHWESTERN RAILWAY COMPANY
SWS	SOUTHWESTERN SYSTEM (OHIO)
SWV	SOUTHWEST VIRGINIA RAILROAD
SY&B	SYRACUSE & BALDWINSVILLE
SY&S	SYRACUSE & SUBURBAN RAILROAD
SYC	SYLVANIA CENTRAL RAILWAY (AFTER 1903)
SYC	SYLVANIA RAILWAY
SYC.	SYLVANIA CENTRAL RAILROAD (PRIOR 1903)
T	TENNESSEE RAILROAD
T&A	TENNESSEE & ALABAMA
T&AL	THORNTON & ALEXANDRIA RAILROAD CO
T&B	TROY & BOSTON
T&BV	TRINITY & BRAZOS VALLEY
T&C	TENNESSEE & COOSA
T&CL	TYRONE & CLEARFIELD
T&CR	TACOMA & COLUMBIA RIVER RAILWAY
T&CR	TACOMA & LAKE CITY RR & NAV CO
T&CR.	TACOMA LAKE CITY RR & NAVIGATION CO
T&CV	TALLADEGA & COOSA VALLEY
T&D	TUSCAMBIA & DECATUR
T&DW	TIDEWATER & DEEPWATER
T&EA	TOLEDO & EASTERN RAILROAD
T&FS	TEXARKANA & FORT SMITH
T&G	TROY & GREENFIELD
T&GD	TONOPAH & GOLDFIELD RAILROAD
T&GU	TAVARES & GULF RAILROAD
T&GW	TONOPAH & GREENWATER RAILROAD
T&ILL	TOLEDO & ILLINDIS
T&IRY	TOLEDO & INDIANA RAILWAY
T&KW	TAMPA & KEY WEST
T&LSC	TOMAH & LAKE ST CROIX
T&MERY	TORONTO & MIMICO ELECTRIC RAILWAY
T&MW	TAMALPAIS & MUIR WOODS RAILWAY
T&N	TEXAS & NORTHERN RAILWAY
T&NC	TENNESSEE & NORTH CAROLINA RAILWAY
T&NE	TROY & NEW ENGLAND RAILWAY COMPANY
T&NO	TEXAS & NEW ORLEANS RAILROAD COMPANY
T&NON	TEMISKAMING & NORTHERN ONTARIO RY
T&NRY	TORONTO & NIPISSING RAILWAY

A62

APPENDIX A (RAILROADS)

A	ABBREVIATIONS ALPHABETICALLY W/ROADS
T&NV	THURSO & NATION VALLEY
T&O	TOLEDO & OHIO
T&OC	TOLEDO & OHIO CENTRAL
T&P	TEXAS & PACIFIC
T&SB	TUSCOLA & SAGINAW BAY
T&SH	TOLEDO & SOUTH HAVEN
T&SLA	TEXAS & ST LOUIS RAILWAY CO OF ARKANSA
T&SM	RALLAHASSEE & ST MARKS
T&ST	TIDEWATER & SOUTHERN TRANSIT COMPANY
T&T	TONOPAH & TIDEWATER RAILROAD
T&TH	TAMPA & THONOTOSASSA
T&TO	TAMA & TOLEDO
T&W	TIDEWATER & WESTERN
T&WE	TOLEDO & WESTERN
T&WS	TORRINGTON & WINCHESTER STREET RAILWAY
T&YR	TORONTO & YORK RADIAL RAILWAY
T*	TEXACO
T-CR	TRI-CITY RAILWAY COMPANY
T-DR	TOLDEO-DETROIT RAILROAD
T-F	THURMONT-FREDERICK
T-NMR	TEXAS-NEW MEXICO RAILWAY
TA&G	TENNESSEE ALABAMA & GEORGIA RAILWAY
TA&M	TAUNTON & MIDDLEBORO RAILROAD
TA&W	TOLEDO ANGOLA & WESTERN RAILWAY
TAA&C	TOLEDO ANN ARBOR & CADILLAC RAILWAY
TAA&J	TOLEDO ANN ARBOR & JACKSON
TACR	TACUBAYA RAILROAD
TAL	TALBOTTON RAILROAD
TALL	TALLAHASEE
TANV	TANANA VALLEY RAILROAD
TAT	THIRD AVENUE RAILWAY SYSTEM
TAT.	THIRD AVENUE TRANSIT RAILROAD COMPANY
TB	TWIN BRANCH RAILROAD
TB*	TIVOLI BEER
TBG&ST	TOLEDO BOWLING GREEN & SOUTHERN TRACT
TBRR	TAUNTON BRANCH RAILROAD
TC	TEXAS CENTRAL RAILROAD
TC&D	TUSCUMBIA COURTLAND & DEACTUR RY
TC&GB	TUSCON CORNELIA & GILA BEND RAILROAD
TC&I	TENNESSEE COAL & IRON
TC&OR	TOLEDO COLUMBUS & OHIO RIVER RR CO
TC&SL	TOLEDO CINCINNATI & ST LOUIS
TCLSE	TOLEDO CLEVELAND LAKE SHORE ELECTRIC
TCO.	TORONTO TRANSPORTATION COMMISSION
TCRT	TWIN CITY RAPID TRANSIT
TCRY	TORONTO CIVIC RAILWAY
TCS	TRANS CAR SERVICES
TCS&D	TOLEDO CANADA SOUTHERN & DETROIT RY
TCT	TEXAS CITY TERMINAL RAILWAY
TCTR	TRI CITY TRACTION
TD&B	TOLEDO DELPHOS & BURLINGTON
TE	TEXAS ELECTRIC RAILWAY
TEC	TECOPA
TED	TOLEDO EDISON
TEM	TEMISCOUATA RAILWAY
TENNC	TENNESSEE CENTRAL RAILWAY
TENNC.	TENNESSEE CENTRAL RAILROAD
TEPC	TENNESSEE ELECTRIC POWER COMPANY
TERY	TOLEDO ELECTRIC RAILWAY
TEX	TEXAS EXPORT
TEXS	TEXAS STATE RAILROAD
TEXSL	TEXAS SHORT LINE RAILWAY
TEXT	TEXAS TRUCK RAILROAD
TEXTR	TEXAS TRACTION
TF	TALLULAH FALLS RAILWAY
TF&E	TIFFIN FOSTORIA & EASTERN RAILWAY
TF&F	TOLEDO FOSTORIA & FINDLEY
TF&N	TOLEDO FREMONT & NORWALK
TF&NK	TOLEDO FREMONT & NORWALK
TG&B	TORONTO GRAY & BRUCE RAILWAY
TGT	TULIA GRAIN TERMINAL
TGV&PC	TONAWANDA GENESEE VALLEY & PINE CREEK
TH&B	TORONTO HAMILTON & BUFFALO RAILWAY
TH&I	TERRE HAUTE & INDIANAPOLIS
TH&L	TERRE HAUTE & LOGANSPORT
TH&N	TAMAQUA HAZLETON & NORTHERN
TH&P	TERRE HAUTE & PEORIA
TH&SE	TERRE HAUTE & SOUTHEASTERN
THC	THUNDERBIRD COLLIERIES
THI&E	TERRE HAUTE INDIANAPOLIS & EASTERN
TI	TREASURE ISLAND
TIC	TIOGA CENTRAL
TIDE	TIDEWATER RAILWAY
TIR	THATCHER'S INLET RAILROAD
TIV	TIONESTA VALLEY RAILWAY
TK&N	TENNESSEE KENTUCKY & NORTHERN
TL	TATUM LUMBER COMPANY
TLCO	TIOGA LUMBER COMPANY
TLL	THUNDER LAKE LUMBER COMPANY
TLP&CR	TACOMA LAKE PARK & COLUMBIA RIVER RY
TLW	TAUTON LOCOMOTIVE WORKS
TM	TEXAS MIDLAND
TM&BC	TAYLOR MOUNTAIN & BEAVER CREEK
TM&P	TWIN MOUNTAIN & POTOMAC RAILROAD
TMB	TACOMA MUNICIPAL BELT LINE RAILWAY
TMEX	TEXAS-MEXICAN RAILWAY COMPANY
TMSL	TOWANDA MONROETON SHIPPERS LIFELINE
TNRR	TENNESSEE RAILROAD (O)
TO&E	TEXAS OKLAHOMA & EASTERN RAILROAD
TOMBS	TOMBSTONE SOUTHERN
TON	TONOPAH RAILROAD
TONAW	TONAWANDA RAILROAD
TOV	TOOELE VALLEY RAILWAY
TOWN	TOWNSVILLE RAILROAD
TP	TEXAS PACIFIC RAILROAD COMPANY
TP&G	TALLAHASSE PENSACOLA & GULF RAILROAD
TP&W	TOLEDO PEORIA & WESTERN RAILROAD
TP&W.	TOLEDO PEORIA & WESTERN RAILWAY
TP&WAR	TOLEDO PEORIA & WARSAW
TPC&L	TOLEDO PORT CLINTON & LAKESIDE
TPMP	TEXAS PACIFIC MISSOURI PAC TERM RR NO
TPT	TRENTON PRINCETON TRACTION
TR	TRESCKOW
TR&G	TREMOUNT & GULF RAILWAY
TR&L	TOLEDO RAILWAY & LIGHT COMPANY
TR&PC	TACOMA RAILWAY & POWER COMPANY
TR&U	TUSCALOOSA RAILWAY & UTILITIES COMPANY
TRA	TERMINAL RAILROAD ASSOC OF ST LOUIS
TRASD	TERMINAL RAILWAY ALABAMA STATE DOCKS
TRB	TIMKEN ROLLER BEARING COMPANY
TRC	TRIAD CHEMICAL
TRCO	TORONTO RAILWAY CO
TRM	T.R. MILLER COMPANY
TRNO	TERMINAL RAILROAD OF NEW ORLEANS
TRO	TRONA RAILWAY
TROP	TROPICANA
TROYC	TROY CITY RAILWAY
TRSL	TREMONT STREET LINE
TRT	TORONTO RAPID TRANSIT
TRW	THAILAND RAILWAYS
TS	TIDEWATER SOUTHERN RAILWAY
TS&LH	TORONTO SARNIA & LAKE HURON
TS&LH	TORONTO SIMCOE & LAKE HURON
TS&N	TEXARKANA SHREVEPORT & NATCHEZ RY
TS&NO	TROY SARATOGA & NORTHERN
TS.	TIDEWATER SOUTHERN RAILROAD
TSE	TEXAS SOUTH-EASTERN RAILROAD
TSL	TENNESSEE STATE LINE RAILROAD
TSL&C	TOLEDO ST LOUIS & CINCINNATI
TSL&KC	TOLEDO ST LOUIS & KANSAS CITY RR CO
TSL&W	TOLEDO ST LOUIS & WESTERN
TSM	TWIN SEAMS MINING COMPANY
TSU	TULSA-SAPULPA UNION RAILWAY
TT	TOLEDO TERMINAL RAILROAD
TTAP	TYLER TAP RAILROAD
TTC	TEXAS TRANSPORTATION COMPANY
TTCO	TORONTO TRANSIT COMMISSION
TTG	TICHY TRAIN GROUP
TTI	TRANSKENTUCKY TRANSPORTATION SYS INC
TTM	TWIN TREES MINES RAILWAY
TTR	TEXAX TRACTION (O)
TTR.	TRAILER TRAIN
TTRY	TORONTO TERMINALS RAILWAY

A63

APPENDIX A (RAILROADS)

A	ABBREVIATIONS ALPHABETICALLY W/ROADS
TTY	THOMASTON TRAMWAY COMPANY
TU	TROY UNION RAILROAD
TUCK	TUCKERTON RAILROAD
TUS	TUSCALOOSA BELT RAILWAY
TUSC.	TUSCUMBIA RAILRAOD
TUSC.	TUSCUMBIA RAILWAY
TUSCO	TAMPA UNION STATION COMPANY
TUSK	TUSKEGEE RAILROAD
TUST	TEXARKANA UNION STATION TRUST
TUV	TUSCARORA VALLEY
TV	TONAWANDA VALLEY RAILROAD
TV&C	TONAWANDA VALLEY & CUBA RAILROAD CO
TV&G	TENNESSEE VIRGINIA & GEORGIA
TV&H	TIONESTA VALLEY & HICKORY
TV&SC	TIONESTA VALLEY & SALMON CREEK
TVA	TENNESSEE VALLEY AUTHORITY
TVE	TONAWANDA VALLEY EXTENSION RR CO
TVRR	TENNESSEE VALLEY RAILROAD
TW	TEXAS WESTERN NARROW GAGE RAILROAD
TW&GV	TONAWANDA WISCOY & GENESEE VALLEY
TW&W	TOLEDO WABASH & WESTERN
TW.	TEXAS WESTERN RAILWAY COMPANY
U	UINTAH RAILROAD
U&BR	UTICA & BLACK RIVER
U&D	ULSTER & DELAWARE
U&N	ULVALDE & NORTHERN RAILWAY
U&SRR	UTICA & SCHENECTADY RAILROAD
U*	UTLX
U.	UINTAH RAILWAY
UB	UTAH BELT
UC	UTAH CENTRAL RAILROAD
UC&B	UTICA CLINTON & BINGHAMTON
UC&H	UPPER COOS & HEREFORD
UC*	UNION CARBIDE.
UC-MX	UNITED COMMERCIAL COMPANY INC
UCA	UNION CANAL
UCKC	UTAH COPPER DIV OF KENNECOTT COPPER C
UCR	UTAH COAL ROUTE
UCRR	UPPER COOS RAILROAD
UDES	UNIDOS DEL SURESTE (MEXICO)
UDEY	UNIDOS DE YUCATAN
UE	UNION ELECTRIC RAILWAY
UE*	UWANTA EGG
UEC	UNITED ELECTRIC COAL
UERC	UNITED ELECTRIC RAILWAY COMPANY
UERY	UNITED ELECTRIC RAILWAYS (RI)
UF	UNION FREIGHT RAILROAD
UI	UNIVERSITY OF ILLINOIS
UI&E	UTICA ITHACA & ELMIRA RAILROAD
UI&E.	UTICA ITHACA & ELMIRA RAILWAY
UIC	UTAH IDAHO CENTRAL RAILROAD
UIRY	UNCANOONUC INCLINE RAILWAY
UIW	UNION IRON WORKS
UJC	UPJOHN COMPANY
UM	UNIVERSITY OF MINNESOTA INTER-CAMPUS
UM&P	UPPER MERION & PLYMOUTH RAILROAD
UN	UNITY RAILWAY
UNC	UNION CARBIDE
UNIC	UNITED COMPANY (OREGON)
UNO	UTAH NORTHERN
UNTR	UNITED TRACTION COMPANY
UP	UNION PACIFIC RAILROAD
UP&L	UTAH POWER & LIGHT
UPCC	UNION PACIFIC COAL COMPANY
UPD&G	UNION PACIFIC DENVER & GULF
UR&E	UNITED RAILWAYS & ELECTRIC
URO	UNION RAILROAD OF OREGON
URR	UNION RAILROAD
URSF	UNITED RAILROADS OF SAN FRANCISCO
URSL	UNITED RAILWAY OF ST LOUIS
URTX*	UNION REFRIGERATED TRANSIT
URWO.	UNITED RAILWAYS OF OREGON
URY	UNITED RAILWAYS OF YUCATAN
URY.	YUCATAN RAIWLAY
URYT	UNION RAILWAY (TENNESSEE)
US	UNITED STATES ISTHMIAN CANAL COMM (O)
USA	UNITED STATES ARMY
USAEC	UNITED STATES ATOMIC ENERGY COMMISSIO
USAF	UNITED STATES AIR FORCE
USBOR	UNITED STATES BORAX
USDOT	UNITED STATES DEPT OF TRANSPORTATION
USM	UNITED STATES MILITARY RAILROAD
USN	UNITED STATES NAVY
USNAD	UNITED STATES NAVAL AMMUNITION DEPOT
USP&F	UNITED STATES PIPE & FOUNDRY
USR	UNION STREET RAILWAY
USRA	UNITED STATES RAILROAD ADMINISTRATION
USREM	UNITED STATES RAILWAY EQUIP MFG
USS	UNITED STATES SUGAR
USSC	UNITED STATES STEEL CORPORATION
USWD	UNITED STATES WAR DEPARTMENT
USY&T	UNION STOCK YARD & TRANSFER
USY&T.	UNION STOCK YARD & TRANSIT COMPANY
UT	UNION TERMINAL RAILWAY COMPANY
UT&N	UTAH & NORTHERN
UTA&M	ULTIMA THULE ARKADELPHIA & MISSISSIPP
UTAH	UTAH RAILWAY COMPANY
UTAHT	UTAH TERMINAL COMPANY
UTC	UNION TRACTION COMPANY
UTCC	UNION TANK CAR COMPANY
UTCO	UNION TERMINAL COMPANY (TEXAS)
UTDC	URBAN TRANSPORTATION DEVELOPMENT CORP
UTL*	UNION TANK LINE
UTLX	UNION TANK LINE.
UTRC	UNION TRANSPORTAION CO
UTSR	UNITED TRACTION STREET RAILWAY
UV	UNADILLA VALLEY RAILWAY
UV&N	UVALDE & NORTHERN (TEXAS)
UW&PW	UNION WARF & PLANK WALK COMPANY
UXL	UNIVERSAL EXPLORATION COMPANY
V	VIRGINIAN RAILWAY
V&CS	VIRGINIA & CAROLINA SOUTHERN RAILROAD
V&J	VICKSBURG & JACKSON RAILROAD
V&M	VERMONT & MASSACHUETTS
V&MA	VIRGINIA & MARYLAND
V&RL	VIRGINIA & RAINY LAKE
V&S	VALLEY & SILETZ RAILROAD
V&SO	VIRGINIA & SOUTHERN
V&SRY	VICTORIA & SYDNEY RAILWAY
V&SW	VIRGINIA & SOUTHWESTERN RAILROAD
V&T	VIRGINIA & TRUCKEE RAILROAD
V&T.	VIRGINIA & TRUCKEE RAILWAY
V&TEN	VIRGINIA & TENNESSEE
V&W	VIRGINIAN & WESTERN
V-T	VIRGINIA-TENNESSEE RAILROAD
VA	VANDALIA RAILROAD
VA&C	VIRGINIA ANTHRACITE & COAL RY CO
VAC	VIRGINIA CAROLINA RAILROAD
VAL	VALLEY RAILROAD
VAL.	VALLEY RAILWAYS
VB	VICKSBURG STREET RAILWAY (MISSISSIPPI)
VBR	VIRGINIA BLUE RIDGE RAILWAY
VC	VIRGINIA CENTRAL RAILWAY
VCO	VENTURA COUNTY RAILWAY
VCS&I	VALLEY CITY STREET & INTERURBAN RY
VD	VULCAN DETINNING
VE	VISALIA ELECTRIC RAILROAD
VE&PC	VIRGINIA ELECTRIC & POWER COMPANY
VEPCO	VEPCO
VEPCO.	VIRGINIA.....
VER	VERMONT RAILWAY
VIA	VIA
VIN	VINELAND
VIP	VICTORY PARK RAILWAY
VLC	VICTORIA LUMBER COMPANY
VM	VULCAN MATERIALS
VM&W	VALDOSTA MOULTRIE & WESTERN
VN	VERMONT NORTHERN
VNR	VIET NAM RAILWAYS
VP	VIRGINIA POCAHONTAS
VPS	VIRGINIA PUBLIC SERVICE COMPANY
VR	VENANGO RIVER RAILROAD
VR&P	VIRGINIA RAILWAY & POWER COMPANY
VS	VALDOSTA SOUTHERN RAILROAD

A64

APPENDIX A   (RAILROADS)

A	ABBREVIATIONS ALPHABETICALLY W/ROADS
VS .	VALDOSTA SOUTHERN RAILWAY
VS&P	VICKSBURG SHREVEPORT & PACIFIC
VSL	VENICE SHORE LINE
VSL.	VENICE SHORT LINE
VSP&S	VERONIA SOUTH PARK & SUNSET STEAM RR
VT	VIRGINIA TRANSIT
VTC	VERMONT CENTRAL
VV	VERMONT VALLEY
VV&E	VANCOUVER VICTORIA & EASTERN RY & NAV
VW&S	VACUUM WINE & SPIRITS CANNING CORP
W	WABASH RAILWAY
W&A	WESTERN & ATLANTIC
W&AL	WESTERN & ALLEGHENY
W&AN	WINDSOR & ANNAPOLIS RAILWAY
W&B	WELLSVILLE & BUFFALO RAILROAD CORP
W&BA	WILMINGTON & BALTIMORE RAILROAD
W&BCS	WESTON & BROOKER CRUSHED STONE CO
W&BV	WINSTON & BONE VALLEY
W&CB	WASHINGTON & CHESAPEAKE BEACH
W&CE	WORCESTER & CONNECTICUT EASTERN
W&CR	WASHINGTON & COLUMBIA RIVER RAILROAD
W&F	WARREN & FARNSWORTH
W&FRY	WARREN & FRANKLIN RAILWAY
W&L	WASHINGTON & LINCOLNTON RAILROAD
W&LE	WHEELING & LAKE ERIE RAILROAD
W&LE.	WHEELING & LAKE ERIE RAILWAY COMPANY
W&M	WISCONSIN & MICHIGAN
W&MD	WATERBURY & MILLDALE
W&MV	WICHITA & MIDLAND VALLEY
W&N	WILMINGTON & NORTHERN
W&NB	WILLIAMSPORT & NORTH BRANCH RAILWAY
W&NB.	WILLIAMSPORT & NORTH BRANCH RAILROAD
W&NO	WHARTON & NORTHERN RAILROAD
W&NR	WILMINGTON & WELDEN RAILWAY (0)
W&O	WATERVILLE & OAKLAND STREET RAILWAY
W&OD	WASHINGTON & OLD DOMINION RAILROAD
W&OD.	WASHINGTON & OLD DOMINION RAILWAY
W&OV	WARREN & OUACHITA VALLEY RAILWAY
W&P	WOONSOCKET & PASCOAG
W&PC	WELLAND & PORT COLBORNE
W&POT	WASHINGTON & POTOMAC RAILROAD
W&PR	WHIPPANY & PASSAIC RIVER RAILROAD
W&Q	WISCASSET & QUEBEC
W&R	WILLIAMSTOWN & REDFIELD
W&RL	WINSLOW & RICHLAND
W&S	W&S
W&SF	WATERTOWN & SIOUX FALLS RAILWAY
W&SFE	WASHITA & SANTA FE
W&SH	WRIGHTSVILLE & SUN HILL RAILROAD CO
W&SL	WHITMER & STEEL LUMBER COMPANY
W&SR	WARREN & SALINE RIVER RAILROAD
W&T	WRIGHTSVILLE & TENNILLE RAILROAD
W&V	WARREN & VENANGO
W&W	WILMINGTON & WESTERN
W&WA	WAYNESBURG & WASHINGTON RAILROAD
W&WE	WICHITA & WESTERN
W&WR	WILMINGTON & WELDEN RAILWAY
W&WSRY	WORCESTER & WEBSTER STREET RAILWAY
W*	WILSON
W-B	WARREN-BISBEE RAILWAY
W-BC	WILKES-BARRE CONNECTING RAILROAD
W-BRY	WILKES-BARRE RAILWAY
W-BS	WAHPETON-BRECKENRIDGE STREET RY CO
W-W	WATERLOO-WELLINGTON
W.	WABASH RAILROAD COMPANY
WA	WARWICK RAILROAD
WA .	WARWICK RAILWAY
WA&FC	WASHINGTON ARLINGTON & FALLS CHURCH
WA&G	WELLSVILLE ADDISON & GALETON RAILROAD
WA&MV	WASHINGTON ALEXANDRIA & MT VERNON RY
WA&P	WASHINGTON & PITTSBURGH
WA&SL	WAMPUM & STATE LINE
WA&W	WAITESBORO & WESTERN
WA&WA	WASHINGTON & WAYNESBURG
WA.	WARWICK VALLEY RAILROAD
WAI	WAIALUA PLANTATION
WAL	WAYCROSS AIR LINE

A	ABBREVIATIONS ALPHABETICALLY W/ROADS
WAR	WARRENTON RAIL ROAD
WARR	WESTERN ALLEGHENY RAILROAD
WARR.	WESTERN ALLEGHENY RAILWAY
WAS	WARE SHOALS RAILROAD
WASHR	WASHINGTON RUN RAILROAD
WASHT	WASHINGTON TERMINAL COMPANY
WAST	WALLACE STONE
WAT	WATERVILLE RAILWAY
WAT&R	WATERTOWN & ROME
WAV	WALLKILL VALLEY RAILROAD
WB	WOBURN BRANCH
WB&AE	WASHINGTON BALTIMORE & ANNAPOLIS ELEC
WB&E	WILKES BARRE & EASTERN
WB&EL	WELLSVILLE BOLIVAR & ELDRED
WB&H	WILKES BARRE & HAZELTON RAILWAY
WB&PL	WASHINGTON BRANDYWINE & POINT LOOKOUT
WB&S	WILMINGTON BRUNSWICK & SOUTHPORT
WB&WVT	WILKES-BARRE & WYOMING VALLEY TRACTION
WBC	WESTERN BRICK COMPANY
WBT&S	WACO BEAUMONT TRINITY & SABINE RY
WC	WISCONSIN CENTRAL
WC&C	WESTERN COAL & COKE COMPANY
WC&F	WAYCROSS & FLORIDA
WC&W	WABASH CHESTER & WESTERN
WCC	WESTMORELAND COAL COMPANY
WCF&N	WATERLOO CEDAR FALLS & NORTHERN RY
WCKS	WEST CHESTER KENNETT SQUARE & WILMING
WCNS	WESTERN COUNTIES ON NOVA SCOTIA
WCO	WASHINGTON COUNTY RAILROAD
WCRC	WASHINGTON CENTRAL RAILROAD
WCRR	WASHOE COUNTY RAILROAD
WCRT	WEST COAST RAILWAY
WCS	WEST CHICAGO STREET RAILROAD COMPANY
WCVM&S	WASHINGTON CITY VIRGINIA MID & GR SOU
WD&L	WHITE DEER & LOGANTON RAILROAD
WDV	WHITE DEER VALLEY RAILROAD
WE	WESTINGHOUSE ELECTRIC
WE&W	WESTCHESTER & WESTERN
WE*	WESTINGHOUSE
WEC	WESTERN ENERGY COMPANY
WECC	WEST END CHEMICAL COMPANY
WEL	WEEMS ELECTRIC
WELC	WINNIPEG ELECTRIC COMPANY
WELL	WELLAND
WELP	WATERVILLE ELECTRIC LIGHT & POWER CO
WES	WESTFIELD RAILROAD
WESR	WEST END STREET RAILWAY (BOSTON)
WEST	WESTMINISTER
WF	WEBBER FALLS
WF&N	WICHITA FALLS & NORTHWESTERN
WF&O	WATERVILLE FAIRFIELD & OAKLAND RY
WF&S	WICHITA FALLS & SOUTHERN
WFE	WEST FELICIANA RAILROAD COMPANY
WFE*	WESTERN FRUIT EXPRESS
WFI	WESTERN FOREST INDUSTRIES
WG	WATER GAP RAILROAD
WGB	WAUPACA GREEN BAY RAILWAY
WGRR	WILD GOOSE RAILROAD
WHC	WHITEHALL CEMENT
WHT	WINNIPEG HYDRO TRAMWAY
WHTR	WHEELING TRACTION COMPANY
WI	WILLIAMSTOWN
WI&M	WASHINGTON IDAHO & MONTANA RAILWAY
WI&N	WISCONSIN & NORTHERN
WI&NE	WISCONSIN IOWA & NEBRASKA
WI&P	WINCHESTER & POTOMAC
WI&S	WILLAMETTE IRON & STEEL COMPANY
WI&TC	WESTERN INSURANCE & TRANSPORTATION CO
WI&W	WINCHESTER & WESTERN RAILROAD
WI&W	WINONA & WARSAW RAILWAY
WIL&R	WILMINGTON & READING
WIN	WINONA RAILROAD
WINF	WINFIELD ELECTRIC RAILWAY
WINI	WINIFREDE RAILROAD
WINO	WINONA INTERURBAN RAILWAY
WIP	WESTMONT INCLINED PLANE

A65

APPENDIX A (RAILROADS)

A	ABBREVIATIONS ALPHABETICALLY W/ROADS
WIPR	WHIPPANY RIVER RAILROAD
WIS&S	WISCONSIN & SOUTHERN
WIV	WICHITA VALLEY RAILWAY
WJ&S	WEST JERSEY & SEASHORE RAILROAD
WK&S	WANAMAKER KEMPTON & SOUTHERN
WL	WINANS LOCOMOTIVES
WLOO	WATERLOO RAILROAD
WM	WESTERN MARYLAND
WM&P	WISCONSIN MINNESOTA & PACIFIC
WMASS	WESTERN OF MASSACHUSETTS
WMC	WANAMIE MINING COMPANY
WMCE	WHITE MOUNTAIN CENTRAL RAILROAD
WMM	WILLIAM MASON
WMW&N	WEATHERFORD MINERAL WELLS & NORTHWEST
WN&R	WORCESTER NASHUS & ROCHESTER
WNC	WESTERN NORTH CAROLINA RAILROAD
WNSP	WESTERN NOVA SCOTIA POWER COMPANY
WNW	WICHITA NORTHWESTERN RAILWAY
WNY&P	WESTERN NEW YORK & PENNSYLVANIA
WO	WOODSTOCK RAILWAY
WO&N	WORCESTER & NORWICH
WOHIO	WESTERN OHIO RAILROAD
WORR	WOLFBORO RAILROAD
WP	WESTERN PACIFIC
WP&C	WASHINGTON POTOMAC & CHESAPEAKE RY
WP&L	WISCONSIN POWER & LIGHT
WP&P	WEST PENN & PITTSBURG RAILWAY
WP&RG	WESTERN PACIFIC & RIO GRANDE
WP&Y	WHITE PASS & YUKON ROUTE
WPA	WEST PENN RAILWAY COMPANY
WPBT	WEST PALM BEACH TERMINAL
WPC	WARREN PAPER COMPANY
WPE	WEST PITTSTON-EXETER RAILROAD
WPL	WESTFIELD PLANTAION
WPR	WEST POINT ROUTE
WPS	WHEELING PITTSBURGH STEEL
WPT	WABASH PITTSBURGH TERMINAL
WR	WEST RIVER RAILROAD
WR&E	WAUKEGAN ROCKFORD & ELGIN
WRA	WESTERN RAILWAY OF ALABAMA
WRB	WOOD RIVER BRANCH RAILROAD
WRC	WESTERN RAILROAD CORPORATION
WRCO	WATERTOWN RAILROAD COMPANY
WRL	WHITE RIVER LUMBER
WRM	WESTERN RAILWAY OF MASSACHUSETTS
WROM	WESTERN RAILWAY OF MEXICO
WRR	WINFIELD RAILROAD
WRRA	WESTERN RAILROAD OF ALASKA
WRRR	WHITE RIVER RAILROAD
WRTRR	WARRIOR RIVER TERMINAL RAILROAD
WRY	WHEELING RAILWAY COMPANY
WRY&E	WASHINGTON RAILWAY & ELECTRIC COMPANY
WS	WAYNESBURG SOUTHERN
WS&G	WARNER SAND & GRAVEL
WS&LW	WINNIPEG SELKIRK & LAKE WINNIPEG
WS&Y	WEST SIDE & YONKERS RAILWAY
WSE	WSE (BINGHAMTON NY)
WSH	WEST SHORE RAILROAD
WSL	WEST SIDE LUMBER COMPANY
WSL&P	WABASH ST LOUIS & PACIFIC RAILWAY
WSO	WASHINGTON SOUTHERN RAILWAY COMPANY
WSRR	WEST SIDE RAILROAD (OF ELMIRA)
WSRR.	WEST SIDE RAILWAY (ELMIRA NY)
WSRY	WINCHESTER STREET RAILWAY
WSS	WINSTON SALEM SOUTHERN
WSS&YP	WHITE SULPHUR SPRING & YELLOWSTONE PK
WSSB	WINSTON-SALEM SOUTHBOUND RAILWAY
WSTC	WINSTON-SALEM TERMINAL COMPANY
WT	WABASH TERMINAL RAILWAY
WT&H	WATERVIET TURNPIKE & HORSE RAILWAY
WTC	WEYERHAEUSER LUMBER COMPANY
WTC.	WEYERHAEUSER TIMBER COMPANY.
WTP	WHITE TOP
WTRR	WEST TENNESSEE RAILROAD
WTSL	W.T. SMITH LUMBER COMPANY
WUT*	WESTERN UNION TELEGRAPH CO
WUTR	WICHITA UNION TERMINAL RAILWAY
WV	WESTERN VERMONT
WV&C	WILLIAMETTE VALLEY & COAST
WV&F	WATERVILLE & FAIRFIELD RY & LIGHT CO
WV&FH	WATERVILLE & FAIRFIELD HORSE RAILROAD
WV&M	WHITNEYVILLE & MACHIASPORT
WV*	WESTVACO
WVA	WABASH VALLEY
WVC&P	WEST VIRGINIA CENTRAL & PITTSBURGH RR
WVM	WEST VIRGINIA MIDLAND RAILROAD
WVN	WEST VIRGINIA NORTHERN RAILROAD
WVPP	WEST VIRGINIA PULP & PAPER COMPANY
WVRY	WASHINGTON-VIRGINIA RAILWAY
WVT	WATERVIET TURNPIKE
WW&CR	WALLA WALLA & COLUMBIA RIVER RAILROAD
WW&F	WISCASSET WATERVILLE & FARMINGTON
WW&G	WASHINGTON WESTMINSTER & GETTYSBURG
WW&N	WESTBROOK WINDHAM & NAPLES RAILWAY
WWI	WOODWARD IRON COMPANY RAILROAD
WWL	WOODARD WALKER LUMBER COMPANY
WWPC	WASHINGTON WATER POWER COMPANY
WWV	WALLA WALLA VALLEY RAILWAY
WWVR	WHITE WATER VALLEY RAILROAD
WYS	WYANDOTTE SOUTHERN RAILROAD
WYT	WYANDOTTE TERMINAL RAILROAD
Y	YANCEY RAILROAD
Y&A	YARMOUTH & ANNAPOLIS RAILWAY
Y&MV	YAZOO & MISSISSIPPI VALLEY
Y&N	YOUNGSTOWN & NORTHERN RAILROAD
Y&OR	YOUNGSTOWN & OHIO RIVER
Y&S	YOUNGSTOWN & SOUTHERN RAILWAY
Y&SO	YAKUTAT & SOUTHERN RAILWAY
Y&SU	YOUNGSTOWN & SUBURBAN
YALE	YALE SHORT LINE
YAV	YAKIMA VALLEY TRANSPORTATION CO (O)
YD	YANKEETOWN DOCK
YH&B	YORK HARBOR & BEACH RAILROAD
YKRY	YORK RAILWAY
YM&SP	YOSEMITE MOUNTAIN & SUGAR PINE
YN&S	YANKTON NORFOLK & SOUTHERN
YP	YORK PENNA. RAILWAYS
YR	YELLOW RIVER RAILROAD
YREKA	YREKA RAILROAD
YS	YOUNGSTOWN STEEL
YSL	YOSEMITE SHORT LINE
YSO	YORK SOUTHERN RAILROAD
YSP	YELLOWSTONE PARK RAILROAD
YTC	YAKIMA TRACTION COMPANY
YU	YUCATAN RAILWAY (O)
YU.	UNITED RAILWAYS OF YUCATAN (O)
YUC	YORK UTILITIES RAILWAY COMPANY
YV	YOSEMITE VALLEY RAILROAD
YVA	YAMPA VALLEY RAILWAY
YVT	YAKIMA VALLEY TRANSPORTATION COMPANY
YW	YREKA WESTERN RAILROAD
Z&W	ZANESVILLE & WESTERN
ZB	ZALEV BROTHERS LIMITED
ZM&P	ZANESVILLE MARIETA & PARKERSBURG
ZV	ZERBE VALLEY

APPENDIX B (BUILDERS)

BUILDERS ALPHABETICALLY W/ABREV	A
ALCO	ALCO
ALCO DUNKIRK	AD
ALCO GE	AGE
ALLIS CHALMERS	AC
ALTONA (PRR) SHOPS	AS
ALWEG	AL
AMERICAN CAR & FOUNDRY	ACF
AMERICAN CAR COMPANY	ACC
AMERICAN GK LOCO WORKS	A
AMERICAN HOIST & DERRICK CO	AHD
AMERICAN LOCOMOTIVE COMPANY	ALCO.
AMERICAN RAILBOX CAR CO	ARCC
AMERICAN REFRIGERATOR TRANSIT COMPANY	ART
AMOSKEAG MANUFACTURING COMPANY	AM
AND-KON INC	AKON
ASHLAND CAR WORKS	ACW
ATLAS CAR & MANUFACTURING COMPANY	AC&M
ATLAS INDUSTRIAL LOCOMOTIVES	AIL
ATSF SHOPS	ATSF
B&O SHOPS	B&O
BALDWIN	B
BALDWIN LIMA HAMILTON	BLH
BALDWIN-WESTINGHOUSE	BW
BARNEY & SMITH CO	BS
BERWICK	BER
BETHLAHAM STEEL CO	BSC
BETTENDORF COMPANY, THE	BET
BEYER PEACOCK & COMPANY LTD.	BP
BILLMEYER & SMALLS	B&S
BILLMEYER & SMITH	B&SM
BIRNEY	BIRN
BLOOMSBURG CAR MFG COMPANY	BCC
BOEING COMPANY	BOE
BOMBARDIER	BOM
BOOTH & COMPANY	BO
BORDEN STD TANK CAR CO	BSTC
BOSTON LOCOMOTIVE WORKS	BOL
BREEZE & KNEELAND LOCOMOTIVE WORKS	B&K
BRILL	BR
BROOKS LOCOMOTIVE WORKS	BLW
BROS	BROS
BUCHANAN	BUCH
BUCYRUS-ERIE	BE
BUDD	BUDD
BURNHAM WILLIAM SHOPS	BWS
BURROW CRANE INC.	BCI
CALUMET IRON WORKS	CIW
CANADIAN CAR & FOUNDRY	CCF
CANADIAN LOCOMOTIVE COMPANY (WORKS)	CLC
CANADIAN NATIONAL SHOPS	CN
CANADIAN PACIFIC SHOPS	CP
CARTER BROS CAR CO	CB
CATERPILLAR TRACTOR CO	CT
CB&Q SHOPS	CB&Q
CHARTER BROS CAR SHOPS	CBC
CHICAGO & NORTH WESTERN SHOPS	C&NW
CHICAGO MOTOR BUILDERS	CLB
CINCINATTI CAR COMPANY	CCC
CLIMAX MANUFACTURING COMPANY	CM
CN (CANADIAN NAT'L) SHOPS	CN.
CNJ SHOPS	CNJ
CONNETICUT CAR CO	CTC
COOK LOCOMOTIVE & MACHINE WORKS	CLW
CP SHOPS	CP
CRAWFORD LOCO WORKS	CRLW
CUMMINS ENGINE COMAPNY	CE
CUYAHOGA LOCOMOTIVE WORKS	CUY
D&H SHOPS	D&H
D&RGW SHOPS	D&RGW
DANFORTH COOKE & CO	DC&C
DANFORTH LOCOMOTIVE & MACHINE COMPANY	DAN
DANVILLE CAR CO	DCC
DAVENPORT BESLER	DB
DAVENPORT LOCO WORKS	DLW
DAVIS & GARTNER	D&G
DELAWARE LACKAWANNA & WESTERN	DL&W
DICKSON LOCOMOTIVE WORKS	D

BUILDERS ALPHABETICALLY W/ABREV	A
DIFFERETAIL CAR/STEEL CAR COMPANY	DC
DS INC	DSI
DU-WHE	DW
DUBS	DUBS
DUCYRES ERIE	DE
DUNKIRK	DUN
EASWICK & HARRISON	E&H
ELECTRO MOTIVE CORPORATION	EMCB
ELECTROMOTIVE DIVISION OF GE	EMD
ELLIS	ELLIS
ENGLISH ELECTRIC	EEL
ENTERPRISE RR EQUIPMENT CO	EE
ERIE	E
EVANS PRODUCTS CO.	EVANS
EVANS TRANSPORTATION GROUP	ETG
FAIRBANKS MORSE	FM
FAIRBANKS MORSE CANADA	CLC.
FAIRMONT RAILWAY MOTORS	FRM
FALLS CAR COMPANY	FCC
FATE-ROOTE-HEATH COMPANY	PLY.
FGE SHOPS	FGE
FILER & STOWELL	F&S
FMC CORP	FMC
FRISCO	FRIS
FRUEHAUF CORP	FC
G&B CAR COMPANY	G&B
GENERAL AMERICAN CAR COMPANY	GAC
GENERAL AMERICAN TRANSPORTATION CO	GAT
GENERAL ELECTRIC	GE
GENERAL MOTORS DIESEL LTD.	GMD
GENERAL MOTORS DIVISION LIMITED	GMDL
GEORGIA CAR & LOCOMOTIVE WORKS	GC&L
GILBERT CAR MANUFACTURING CO	GC
GILLINGHAM & WINANS	G&W
GLOVER MACHINE WORKS	GMW
GN SHOPS	GN
GRAND TRUNK SHOPS	GTS
GRANT LOCOMOTIVE WORKS	GLW
GREENVILLE CAR/STEEL CAR COMPANY	GSC
GUILFORD TRANSPORTATION CO	G
GUNDERSON BROTHERS	GB
H&B CAR CO	H&B.
HACKWORTH	HACK
HALL SCOTT	HS
HARLAN & HOLLINGSWORTH	H&H
HARRISON & WINANS & EASTWICK	HW&E
HASKELL & BAKER CAR COMPANY	H&B
HAWKER SIDDELEY LIMITED	HSI
HAYWARD BARTLETT & COMPANY	HB&C
HEISLER LOCOMOTIVE WORKS	H
HICKS LOCOMOTIVE WORKS	HICKS
HINKLEY & WILLIAMS	H&W
HINKLEY WORKS	HI
HOBARD (?) MILLS	HM
HOLMAN CAR COMPANY (HOLLMAN?)	HCC
ILLINOIS CENTRAL SHOPS	IC
ILLINOIS TERMINAL SHOPS	IT
INDUSTRIAL HOIST	IH
INDUSTRIAL WORKS	IW
INGALLS SHIP BUILDING COMPANY	I
INGERSOLL RAND	IR
INTERNATIONAL CAR CO	ICC
INTERNATIONAL GE COMPANY	IGE
INTERNATIONAL MOTOR COMPANY	IM
INTERNATIONAL POWER CO	IP
INTERNATIONAL RAILWAY CAR CO	IRC
ITEL CORP	ITEL
J. BLAINE WORCHESTOR	JBW
JACKSON & SHARP	J&S
JAVWITH SHOPS	JS
JERSEY CITY LOCOMOTIVE WORKS	JCLW
JEWETT CAR COMPANY	J
JOHN HAMMOND & SONS	JH
JOHN STEPHENSON CO	JSC
JORDAN	JORD
KEITH CAR & MANUFACTURING COMPANY	KCM
KILBORNE & JACOBS	KJ

STEPHANS' RAILROAD DIRECTORY

APPENDIX B (BUILDERS)

BUILDERS ALPHABETICALLY W/ABREV	A
KIMBALL MANUFACTURING CO	K
KINGSTON	KING
KITSON-MEYER	KM
KRAUSS-MAFFEI	K-M
KUHLMAR CAR COMPANY	KUHL
L&N SHOPS	L&N
LACONIA CAR COMPANY	LAC
LANCASTER LOCOMOTIVE WORKS	LLW
LENIOR CAR WORKS	LEN
LIBERTY CAR & EQUIPMENT COMPANY	LIB
LIMA	L
LIMA HAMILTON CORPORATION	LH
LIMA HAMILTON WESTINGHOUSE	LHW
LIMA MACHINE WORKS	LMW
LOWELL MACHINE SHOP	LMS
LV SHOPS	LV
MACK	MACK
MAGOR CAR COMPANY	MC
MAGUIRE-CUMMINGS	M-C
MANCHESTER LOCOMOTIVE WORKS	M
MANN BOUDOIR SLEEPING CAR	MANN
MARINE INDUSTRIES LTD	MI
MARION STEAM SHOVEL CO	MSS
MASON MACHINE WORKS	MMW
MCGUIRE CUMMINGS MFG COMPANY	MGC
MCKAY & ALDUS	M&A
MCKEEN	MCKEEN
MIDDLETOWN CAR WORKS	MCW
MIDWEST FREIGHT CAR	MFC
MIDWEST LOCOMOTIVE WORKS	MLWK
MILWAUKEE LOCO MFG CO	MLMC
MILWAUKEE SHOPS	MS
MISSOURI PACIFIC	MP
MISSOURI PACIFIC DESOTO SHOPS	MPDS
MKT SHOPS	MKT
MONTREAL LOCOMOTIVE WORKS	MLW
MORRISON-KNUDSEN	M-K
MOUNT CLAIRE SHOPS	MCS
MP SHOPS	MP
MT VERNON CAR MFG COMPANY	MVC
N&O SHOPS	N&O
N&W ROANOKE SHOPS	N&W
N&W SHOPS	N&W.
NATURAL STEEL CAR CO	NSC
NEW CASTLE	NC
NEW HAVEN	NH
NEW YORK CENTRAL SHOPS	NYC
NEW YORK LOCOMOTIVE WORKS	NYLW
NILES CAR & MFG. COMPANY	NILES
NJ LOCO & MACHINE COMPANY	NJ
NORRIS LOCOMOTIVE WORKS	NLW
NORTH AMERICAN CAR CO	NA
NP SHOPS	NP
O.S. JORDAN CO	OSJ
OHIO FALLS CAR CO	OF
OLD COLONY SHOPS	OCO
ORTNER CAR COMPANY	ORT
OSGOOD BRADLEY	OB
PAC CAR	PAC
PACIFIC CAR & FOUNDRY	PCF
PALACE AMERICAN CORP	PA
PETER WITT	WITT.
PFW&C SHOPS	PFW&C
PHILADELPHIA & READING SHOPS	P&R
PHINEAS DAVIS	PD
PITTSBURGH & LAKE ERIE SHOPS	P&LE
PITTSBURGH CAR & LOCOMOTIVE WORKS	PCLW
PLASSER AMERICAN	PLA
PLYMOUTH LOCOMOTIVE WORKS	PLY
PLYMOUTH-OLIVER	POL
PORTER	POR
PORTER BELL & COMPANY	PORB
PORTLAND LOCO CO	PL
PRESSED STEEL CAR COMAPNY	PSC
PRR JUNIATA SHOPS	PRR
PRR SHOPS	PRR
PULLMAN BRADLEY	PB

BUILDERS ALPHABETICALLY W/ABREV	A
PULLMAN CAR & MFG CORP CHICAGO	PLM
PULLMAN COMPANY	PLM.
PULLMAN STANDARD	PS
PULLMAN STEEL	PS .
READING SHOPS	R
REEDER	RE
RGS SHOPS	RGS
RHODE ISLAND & RICHMOND LOCO WORKS	RIR
RHODE ISLAND LOCO WORKS	RI
RICHMOND LOCO WORKS	RLW
ROANOKE SHOPS	N&W..
ROBERT STEPHENSON & CO LOCO WORKS	RS
RODGERS LOCOMOTIVE WORKS	ROG.
RODGERS OF PATERSON	RP
ROGERS	ROG
ROGERS KETCHUM & GROSVENOR	RK&G
ROHR	ROHR
ROME LOCO WORKS	RL
RUSSELL CAR & SNOW PLOW CO	RC&SP
SCHENECTADY LOCOMOTIVE WORKS	SLW
SEDALIA SHOPS	SS
SERVICE MOTOR TRUCK COMPANY	SMT
SHAY	SHAY
SHEFFIELD CAR CO	SHEF
SHEPHARP IRON WORKS	SIN
SIEMENS-HALSKE ELECTRIC CO (CHICAGO)	S-HEC
SMITH & JACKSON	S&J
SMITH & PERKINS	S&P
SOO SHOPS	SOO
SOUTH BALTIMORE CAR CO	SBCC
SOUTHERN PACIFIC WORKS	SPW
SOUTHERN SHOPS	SS .
SP SHOPS	SP .
SPERRY	SPER
SPOKANE PORTLAND & SEATTLE SHOPS	SP&S
ST CHARLES CAR COMPANY	SCC
ST LOUIS CAR COMPANY	SLC
STANDARD CAR COMPANY	SC
STANDARD STEEL CAR COMPANY	SSC
STANDARD TANK CAR COMPANY	STC
STEPHENSON LOCOMOTIVE WORKS	RS.
STRONG LOCOMOTIVE WORKS	STR
SYKES	SY
TANNER & DELANEY	T&D
TAUNTON LOCOMOTIVE WORKS	TLW
TAYLOR OB-CAR COMPANY	TAY
THIRD AVE TRANSIT SHOPS	TAT
THOMAS	THOM
THRALL CAR CO	THR
TOPEKA SHOPS	TS
TORONTO LOCOMOTIVE WORKS	TLW
TRA?ST EQUIPMENT COMPANY	TEC
UNION CAR COMPANY	UCC
UNION PALACE CAR CO	UPCC
UNION TERMINAL TRACTION CO OF INDIANA	UTCI
UNITED STATES RAILWAY EQUIPMENT CO	USRE
UP SHOPS	UP
VULCAN IRON WORKS	V
W MILWAUKEE SHOPS	MILW
WABASH	WAB
WASON CAR CO	WCC
WEST POINT FOUNDRIES	WPF
WESTERN WHEELED SCRAPER COMPANY	WWS
WESTINGHOUSE	W
WESTMINISTER IRON WORKS	WIW
WHEELING & LAKE ERIE	W&LE
WHITCOMB	WH
WHITEHEAD & KALES CO	W&K
WHITIN MACHINE WORKS	WHIT
WILLAMETTE IRON & STEEL	WIL
WILLIAM ROMANS	WR
WINANS	WI
WINTON	WINT
WITT, PETER	WITT
WT SNOW CONSTRUCTION CO	WT
YOUNGSTOWN STEEL DOOR CO	YSD

APPENDIX B (BUILDERS)

A	ABREV ALPHABETICALLY BY BUILDER
A	AMERICAN 6K LOCO WORKS
AC	ALLIS CHALMERS
AC&M	ATLAS CAR & MANUFACTURING COMPANY
ACC	AMERICAN CAR COMPANY
ACF	AMERICAN CAR & FOUNDRY
ACW	ASHLAND CAR WORKS
AD	ALCO DUNKIRK
AGE	ALCO GE
AHD	AMERICAN HOIST & DERRICK CO
AIL	ATLAS INDUSTRIAL LOCOMOTIVES
AKON	AND-KON INC
AL	ALWEG
ALCO	ALCO
ALCO.	AMERICAN LOCOMOTIVE COMPANY
AM	AMOSKEAG MANUFACTURING COMPANY
ARCC	AMERICAN RAILBOX CAR CO
ART	AMERICAN REFRIGERATOR TRANSIT COMPANY
AS	ALTONA (PRR) SHOPS
ATSF	ATSF SHOPS
B	BALDWIN
B&K	BREEZE & KNEELAND LOCOMOTIVE WORKS
B&O	B&O SHOPS
B&S	BILLMEYER & SMALLS
B&SM	BILLMEYER & SMITH
BCC	BLOOMSBURG CAR MFG COMPANY
BCI	BURROW CRANE INC.
BE	BUCYRUS-ERIE
BER	BERWICK
BET	BETTENDORF COMPANY, THE
BIRN	BIRNEY
BLH	BALDWIN LIMA HAMILTON
BLW	BROOKS LOCOMOTIVE WORKS
BO	BOOTH & COMPANY
BOE	BOEING COMPANY
BOL	BOSTON LOCOMOTIVE WORKS
BOM	BOMBARDIER
BP	BEYER PEACOCK & COMPANY LTD.
BR	BRILL
BROS	BROS
BS	BARNEY & SMITH CO
BSC	BETHLAHAM STEEL CO
BSTC	BORDEN STD TANK CAR CO
BUCH	BUCHANAN
BUDD	BUDD
BW	BALDWIN-WESTINGHOUSE
BWS	BURNHAM WILLIAM SHOPS
C&NW	CHICAGO & NORTH WESTERN SHOPS
CB	CARTER BROS CAR CO
CB&Q	CB&Q SHOPS
CBC	CHARTER BROS CAR SHOPS
CCC	CINCINATTI CAR COMPANY
CCF	CANADIAN CAR & FOUNDRY
CE	CUMMINS ENGINE COMAPNY
CIW	CALUMET IRON WORKS
CLB	CHICAGO MOTOR BUILDERS
CLC	CANADIAN LOCOMOTIVE COMPANY (WORKS)
CLC.	FAIRBANKS MORSE CANADA
CLW	COOK LOCOMOTIVE & MACHINE WORKS
CM	CLIMAX MANUFACTURING COMPANY
CN	CANADIAN NATIONAL SHOPS
CN.	CN (CANADIAN NAT'L) SHOPS
CNJ	CNJ SHOPS
CP	CANADIAN PACIFIC SHOPS
CRLW	CRAWFORD LOCO WORKS
CT	CATERPILLAR TRACTOR CO
CTC	CONNETICUT CAR CO
CUY	CUYAHOGA LOCOMOTIVE WORKS
D	DICKSON LOCOMOTIVE WORKS
D&G	DAVIS & GARTNER
D&H	D&H SHOPS
D&RGW	D&RGW SHOPS
DAN	DANFORTH LOCOMOTIVE & MACHINE COMPANY
DB	DAVENPORT BESLER
DC	DIFFERETAIL CAR/STEEL CAR COMPANY
DC&C	DANFORTH COOKE & CO
DCC	DANVILLE CAR CO
DE	DUCYRES ERIE

A	ABREV ALPHABETICALLY BY BUILDER
DL&W	DELAWARE LACKAWANNA & WESTERN
DLW	DAVENPORT LOCO WORKS
DSI	DS INC
DUBS	DUBS
DUN	DUNKIRK
DW	DU-WHE
E	ERIE
E&H	EASWICK & HARRISON
EE	ENTERPRISE RR EQUIPMENT CO
EEL	ENGLISH ELECTRIC
ELLIS	ELLIS
EMCB	ELECTRO MOTIVE CORPORATION
EMD	ELECTROMOTIVE DIVISION OF GE
ETG	EVANS TRANSPORTATION GROUP
EVANS	EVANS PRODUCTS CO.
F&S	FILER & STOWELL
FC	FRUEHAUF CORP
FCC	FALLS CAR COMPANY
FGE	FGE SHOPS
FM	FAIRBANKS MORSE
FMC	FMC CORP
FRIS	FRISCO
FRM	FAIRMONT RAILWAY MOTORS
G	GUILFORD TRANSPORTATION CO
G&B	G&B CAR COMPANY
G&W	GILLINGHAM & WINANS
GAC	GENERAL AMERICAN CAR COMPANY
GAT	GENERAL AMERICAN TRANSPORTATION CO
GB	GUNDERSON BROTHERS
GC	GILBERT CAR MANUFACTURING CO
GC&L	GEORGIA CAR & LOCOMOTIVE WORKS
GE	GENERAL ELECTRIC
GLW	GRANT LOCOMOTIVE WORKS
GMD	GENERAL MOTORS DIESEL LTD.
GMDL	GENERAL MOTORS DIVISION LIMITED
GMW	GLOVER MACHINE WORKS
GN	GN SHOPS
GSC	GREENVILLE CAR/STEEL CAR COMPANY
GTS	GRAND TRUNK SHOPS
H	HEISLER LOCOMOTIVE WORKS
H&B	HASKELL & BAKER CAR COMPANY
H&B.	H&B CAR CO
H&H	HARLAN & HOLLINGSWORTH
H&W	HINKLEY & WILLIAMS
HACK	HACKWORTH
HB&C	HAYWARD BARTLETT & COMPANY
HCC	HOLMAN CAR COMPANY (HOLLMAN?)
HI	HINKLEY WORKS
HICKS	HICKS LOCOMOTIVE WORKS
HM	HOBARD (?) MILLS
HS	HALL SCOTT
HSI	HAWKER SIDDELEY LIMITED
HW&E	HARRISON & WINANS & EASTWICK
I	INGALLS SHIP BUILDING COMPANY
IC	ILLINOIS CENTRAL SHOPS
ICC	INTERNATIONAL CAR CO
IGE	INTERNATIONAL GE COMPANY
IH	INDUSTRIAL HOIST
IM	INTERNATIONAL MOTOR COMPANY
IP	INTERNATIONAL POWER CO
IR	INGERSOLL RAND
IRC	INTERNATIONAL RAILWAY CAR CO
IT	ILLINOIS TERMINAL SHOPS
ITEL	ITEL CORP
IW	INDUSTRIAL WORKS
J	JEWETT CAR COMPANY
J&S	JACKSON & SHARP
JBW	J. BLAINE WORCHESTOR
JCLW	JERSEY CITY LOCOMOTIVE WORKS
JH	JOHN HAMMOND & SONS
JORD	JORDAN
JS	JAVWITH SHOPS
JSC	JOHN STEPHENSON CO
K	KIMBALL MANUFACTURING CO
K-M	KRAUSS-MAFFEI
KCM	KEITH CAR & MANUFACTURING COMPANY
KING	KINGSTON

APPENDIX B (BUILDERS)

A	ABREV ALPHABETICALLY BY BUILDER
KJ	KILBORNE & JACOBS
KM	KITSON-MEYER
KUHL	KUHLMAR CAR COMPANY
L	LIMA
L&N	L&N SHOPS
LAC	LACONIA CAR COMPANY
LEW	LENIOR CAR WORKS
LH	LIMA HAMILTON CORPORATION
LHW	LIMA HAMILTON WESTINGHOUSE
LIB	LIBERTY CAR & EQUIPMENT COMPANY
LLW	LANCASTER LOCOMOTIVE WORKS
LMS	LOWELL MACHINE SHOP
LMW	LIMA MACHINE WORKS
LV	LV SHOPS
M	MANCHESTER LOCOMOTIVE WORKS
M&A	MCKAY & ALDUS
M-C	MAGUIRE-CUMMINGS
M-K	MORRISON-KNUDSEN
MACK	MACK
MANN	MANN BOUDOIR SLEEPING CAR
MC	MAGOR CAR COMPANY
MCKEEN	MCKEEN
MCS	MOUNT CLAIRE SHOPS
MCW	MIDDLETOWN CAR WORKS
MFC	MIDWEST FREIGHT CAR
MGC	MCGUIRE CUMMINGS MFG COMPANY
MI	MARINE INDUSTRIES LTD
MILW	W MILWAUKEE SHOPS
MKT	MKT SHOPS
MLMC	MILWAUKEE LOCO MFG CO
MLW	MONTREAL LOCOMOTIVE WORKS
MLWK	MIDWEST LOCOMOTIVE WORKS
MMW	MASON MACHINE WORKS
MP	MISSOURI PACIFIC SHOPS
MPDS	MISSOURI PACIFIC DESOTO SHOPS
MS	MILWAUKEE SHOPS
MSS	MARION STEAM SHOVEL CO
MVC	MT VERNON CAR MFG COMPANY
N&O	N&O SHOPS
N&W	N&W ROANOKE SHOPS
N&W.	N&W SHOPS
N&W..	ROANOKE SHOPS
NA	NORTH AMERICAN CAR CO
NC	NEW CASTLE
NH	NEW HAVEN
NILES	NILES CAR & MFG. COMPANY
NJ	NJ LOCO & MACHINE COMPANY
NLW	NORRIS LOCOMOTIVE WORKS
NP	NP SHOPS
NSC	NATURAL STEEL CAR CO
NYC	NEW YORK CENTRAL SHOPS
NYLW	NEW YORK LOCOMOTIVE WORKS
OB	OSGOOD BRADLEY
OCO	OLD COLONY SHOPS
OF	OHIO FALLS CAR CO
ORT	ORTNER CAR COMPANY
OSJ	O.S. JORDAN CO
P&LE	PITTSBURGH & LAKE ERIE SHOPS
P&R	PHILADELPHIA & READING SHOPS
PA	PALACE AMERICAN CORP
PAC	PAC CAR
PB	PULLMAN BRADLEY
PCF	PACIFIC CAR & FOUNDRY
PCLW	PITTSBURGH CAR & LOCOMOTIVE WORKS
PD	PHINEAS DAVIS
PFW&C	PFW&C SHOPS
PL	PORTLAND LOCO CO
PLA	PLASSER AMERICAN
PLM	PULLMAN CAR & MFG CORP CHICAGO
PLM.	PULLMAN COMPANY
PLY	PLYMOUTH LOCOMOTIVE WORKS
PLY.	FATE-ROOTE-HEATH COMPANY
POL	PLYMOUTH-OLIVER
POR	PORTER
PORB	PORTER BELL & COMPANY
PRR	PRR JUNIATA SHOPS
PRR	PRR SHOPS
PS	PULLMAN STANDARD
PS .	PULLMAN STEEL
PSC	PRESSED STEEL CAR COMAPNY
R	READING SHOPS
RC&SP	RUSSELL CAR & SNOW PLOW CO
RE	REEDER
RGS	RGS SHOPS
RI	RHODE ISLAND LOCO WORKS
RIR	RHODE ISLAND & RICHMOND LOCO WORKS
RK&G	ROGERS KETCHUM & GROSVENOR
RL	ROME LOCO WORKS
RLW	RICHMOND LOCO WORKS
ROG	ROGERS
ROG.	RODGERS LOCOMOTIVE WORKS
ROHR	ROHR
RP	RODGERS OF PATERSON
RS	ROBERT STEPHENSON & CO LOCO WORKS
RS.	STEPHENSON LOCOMOTIVE WORKS
S&J	SMITH & JACKSON
S&P	SMITH & PERKINS
S-HEC	SIEMENS-HALSKE ELECTRIC CO (CHICAGO)
SBCC	SOUTH BALTIMORE CAR CO
SC	STANDARD CAR COMPANY
SCC	ST CHARLES CAR COMPANY
SHAY	SHAY
SHEF	SHEFFIELD CAR CO
SIW	SHEPHARP IRON WORKS
SLC	ST LOUIS CAR COMPANY
SLW	SCHENECTADY LOCOMOTIVE WORKS
SMT	SERVICE MOTOR TRUCK COMPANY
SOO	SOO SHOPS
SP	SP SHOPS
SP&S	SPOKANE PORTLAND & SEATTLE SHOPS
SPER	SPERRY
SPW	SOUTHERN PACIFIC WORKS
SS	SEDALIA SHOPS
SS .	SOUTHERN SHOPS
SSC .	STANDARD STEEL CAR COMPANY
STC	STANDARD TANK CAR COMPANY
STR	STRONG LOCOMOTIVE WORKS
SY	SYKES
T&D	TANNER & DELANEY
TAT	THIRD AVE TRANSIT SHOPS
TAY	TAYLOR OB-CAR COMPANY
TEC	TRA?ST EQUIPMENT COMPANY
THOM	THOMAS
THR	THRALL CAR CO
TLW	TAUNTON LOCOMOTIVE WORKS
TLW.	TORONTO LOCOMOTIVE WORKS
TS	TOPEKA SHOPS
UCC	UNION CAR COMPANY
UP	UP SHOPS
UPCC	UNION PALACE CAR CO
USRE	UNITED STATES RAILWAY EQUIPMENT CO
UTCI	UNION TERMINAL TRACTION CO OF INDIANA
V	VULCAN IRON WORKS
W	WESTINGHOUSE
W&K	WHITEHEAD & KALES CO
W&LE	WHEELING & LAKE ERIE
WAB	WABASH
WCC	WASON CAR CO
WH	WHITCOMB
WHIT	WHITIN MACHINE WORKS
WI	WINANS
WIL	WILLAMETTE IRON & STEEL
WINT	WINTON
WITT	WITT, PETER
WITT.	PETER WITT
WIW	WESTMINISTER IRON WORKS
WPF	WEST POINT FOUNDRIES
WR	WILLIAM ROMANS
WT	WT SNOW CONSTRUCTION CO
WWS	WESTERN WHEELED SCRAPER COMPANY
YSD	YOUNGSTOWN STEEL DOOR CO

APPENDIX C (MANUFACTURERS)

MANUFACTURERS ALPHABETICALLY W/ABREV	A	MANUFACTURERS ALPHABETICALLY W/ABREV	A
101 PRODUCTIONS	101P	BLUE LINE PRODUCTS	BL
20TH CENTURY SALES	20C	BOB PEARE ENGINEERING CORPORATION	BP
A-WEST	AW	BOB'S AIRCRAFT	BA
A. DEPIPPO	AD	BORDERTOWN PUBLISHING	BOR
A. MISENAR	AMIS	BOWSER	BOW
A.C. GILBERT	GIL	BOX CAR KEN	BCK
AB JAQUES	ABJ	BOYDE MODELS	BOY
AC MODEL	ACM	BRANCH LINE MODELS	BLM
ACACIA SCALE MODELS	ACSM	BRASS HAT MODELS	BHM
ACE MODEL RR EQUIPMENT CO	A	BRONSON	BR
ACI HOBBY	ACI	BUCKEYE MODLES	BUC
AHM	AHM.	BUILDERS IN SCALE	BSC
AHM-AIRFIX	AHMA	BUSCH	BU
AIM PRODUCTS	AIM	C&S SCALE INDUSTRIES	C&SS
AIRFIX	AIRF	C. BROMMER	CBRO
AKANE MODEL RAILROAD COMPANY	AK	CABOOSE INDUSTRIES	CAIN
AL ELLIS	AE	CADWELL INDUSTRIES	CI
ALAMOSA CAR SHOPS	ACS	CAL-SCALE	CAL
ALCO ENGINEERING	ALCOE	CAMBRON	CA
ALCO MODELS	ALCO	CAMERON	CA.
ALEXANDER & COMPANY	ALE	CAMINO SCALE MODELS	CAM
ALEXANDER SCALE MODELS	ALEX	CAMPBELL	C
ALEXANDER SCALE MODELS.	ALEZ.	CANADIAN PROTOTYPE REPLICAS	CAN
ALL-NATION HOBBY SHOP	AN	CANADIAN RAILWAY MODEL COMPANY	CRM
ALLEN F SEEBACH	AFS	CANNON & COMPANY	C&C
ALLOY FORMS	AL	CANNON SCALE MODELS	CSM
AMBROID	AMB	CANNONBALL CAR SHOPS	CCS
AMERICAN "N" BRASS	ANB	CANNONBALL PRODUCTS	CAP
AMERICAN BEAUTY LINES	ABL	CAPART INDUSTRIES	CAPI
AMERICAN FLYER	AF	CAR PART INDUSTRIES	CPI
AMERICAN GK LOCOMOTIVE WORKS	AGK	CAR SHOP	CS
AMERICAN MODEL TOYS INC	AMER	CARY LOCOMOTIVE WORKS	CLW
AMERICAN MODELS INC	AMI	CASCO ENCO CAR LINE	CECL
AMERICAN RAILROAD COMPANY	ARC	CASTOR PLASTICS	CAPL
AMERICAN RR MODELS	ARR	CENTRAL LINES MFG CO	CL
AMERICAN SCALE MODEL CORPORATION	ASMC	CENTRAL LOCO WORKS	CLWO
AMERICAN STANDARD CAR CO	ASC	CENTRAL VALLEY MODEL WORKS	CV
AMERICAN TRAIN & TRACK	ATT	CHANIS ENTERPRISES	CE
AMRO	AMRO	CHARLES DETTMANN	CD
APAG HOBBIES	APAG	CHAS C. MERZBACH COMAPNY	MER
ARBOUR MODELS	AM	CHB MODELS	CHB
ARDEN SCALE MODELS	ARD	CHESTER HOLLEY	CH
ARGY SPECIALTIES	ARGY	CHOOCH ENTERPRISES	CHO
ARISTO-CRAFT DISTINTIVE MINIATURES	ARISTO	CHRIS MAHON INDUSTRIES	CHM
ARROW MODELS	AROM	CHRISTOPH PRODUCTS COMPANY	CPC
ART FLEMING MODELS	AFM	CIBOLD CROSSING	CIC
ARVID ANDERSON	AA	CITY STREETS MODELS LTD	CSML
ASHLAND CAR WORKS	ACW	CJ ULRICH	U .
ASSOCIATED HOBBY MANUFACTURERS	AHM	CLASSIC MINIATURES	CMI
ASTER COMPANY	AST	CLEAR CREEK MODELS	CCM
ATA MODEL COMPANY	ATA	CLEVELAND MODELS & SUPPLY CO	CMS
ATHEARN	ATH	CLIFF LINE SCALE MODELS	CLIF
ATLANTIC SCALE MODELS	ATSM	CM SHOPS	CM
ATLAS INDUSTRIES INC	UN	COACH YARD	CY
ATLAS TOOL COMPANY	AT	COFFEE TABLE LAYOUTS	CTL
AURORA PLASTICS COMPANY	AUR	COLBER CORPORATION	COLB
AUTHENTICAST COMPANY	AUTH	COLLIER	CO
AYRES SCALE MODELS	ASM	COLLINS	COL
B&W SPECIALTIES	B&W	COLORADO MODEL MASTERPIECES	CMM
B/T ENTERPRISES	B/T	COLUMBIA CAR & FOUNDRY	CCF
BACHMANN INDUSTRIES	B	COLUMBIA VALLEY MODELS	CVM
BACK SHOP	BS	COMET METAL PRODUCTS	CMPR
BALBOA SCALE MODELS	BAL	COMET MODEL COMPANY	CMO
BALDWIN MODEL LOCO WORKS	BM	CON-COR COMPANY	CC
BARR-NIXON PRODUCTS	BN	CONCORD CAR WORKS	CCW
BART MODELS	BART	CONOVER MINIATURE	COMI
BAUMGARTEN MODEL RR EQUIP	BAU	CONRAD PRODUCTS	CPR
BAY STATE MODELS	BSM	CONTINENTAL MODELS	CM .
BEACH ISLAND MFG CO	BI	CONTINENTAL MONARCH MODEL CO	COMM
BEAVER CREEK MODELS	BCM	COOPER CRAFT	COC
BELL MODEL SHOPS	BELL	COPETOWN CAR WORKS	COCW
BELPAIRE SHOPS	BPS	CORNISA & SONS	C&S
BERG HOBBIES	BH	CORONADO SCALE MODELS	COM
BIMCO	BIM	COX HOBBIES INC	COX
BINKLEY MODELS	BIN	CRAFTSMAN KITS	CK
BLACK HAWK LOCO WORKS	BHLW	CRESCENT MODEL PRODUCTS	CMP
BLACKMAN PLASTICS	BLP	CROSSING GATE MODELS	CRGT

STEPHANS' RAILROAD_DIRECTORY

A71

APPENDIX C (MANUFACTURERS)

MANUFACTURERS ALPHABETICALLY W/ABREV	A
CRUMMY PRODUCTS	CP
CS RAFFING	CSR
CSC CORP	CSC
CUSTOM BRASS	CB
D.J. BAKER	DJB
DALE NEWTON COMPANY	DN
DALLAS MODEL CRAFT	DMC
DARR'S SCALE MODELS	DARR
DAVE'S MODEL TRAINS	DMT
DELAWARE VALLEY KITS	DVK
DENNIS	DE
DENNIS STORZEK MODELMAKER	DSM
DESIGN PRESERVATION MODELS	DPM
DESIGNS OF TOMORROW	DT
DETAIL ASSOCIATES	DA
DETAILS WEST	DW
DEVORT	DEV
DIA YONG MODELS COMPANY	DY
DIAMOND MODELS	DM
DIAMOND MOUNTAIN RAILROAD	DIM
DIAMOND SCALE CONSTRUCTION	DSC
DIMI-TRAINS	DIT
DMK REFINERY MODELS	DMK
DON FOWLER	DF
DON WINTER	DWI
DONG JIN MODEL WORKS	DJ
DURANGO PRESS	DP
DYNA-MODEL PRODUCTS COMPANY	D
E SUYDAM & COMPANY	S
E&B VALLEY RAILROAD	EBV
E&P ASSOCIATES	E&P
E.H. BESSEY	EHB
EARL FRANCIS MINIATURE TRAINS	EFMT
EAST PENN MODELS	EPM
EASTERN CAR WORKS	ECW
EASTERN TRACTION MODELS	ETM
ELECTRO-CRAFT APPLIANCES	ECA
ELECTRONIC SPECIALTY PRODUCTS	ESP
EMPIRE CITY MODELS	ECM
EMPIRE MIDLAND MODEL COMPANY	EMP
EMPIRE MODELS	EMM
ENGLISH	ENG
ENHORNING	ENH
EP ALEXANDER	EPA
ERNEST MFG COMPANY	EM
ES NIELSON	ESN
ETCETERA INC	ETC
EUROPA MODEL INTERNATIONAL	EMI
EUROTRAINS IMPORTERS	E
EVERETT SMITH	ES
EVERGREEN HILL DESIGNS	EHD
EVERGREEN ROUNDHOUSE	ER
EVERGREEN SCALE MODELS	ESM
EXPRESS WAGON CONSTRUCTION	EW
F.A. SIMONS	FAS
FAIRFIELD MODELS	FA
FAIRFIELD TRACTION MODELS	FTM
FALLER	FAL
FAMOUS MODEL COMPANY	FAM
FAR EAST DISTRIBUTORS(NW SHORT LINES)	FED
FAR EAST IMPORTERS	FEI
FINDEX-SYSTEMS INC	FS
FINE SCALE MINIATURES	F
FISCHERS HOBBY SERVICE	FHS
FLEISCHMANN	FL
FLYING 200	F2
FOMART	FO
FOMRAS MODELS	FOM
FORTY-NINTH STATE RR MODELS	FSM
FOWLER	DF.
FRANKLIN MODELS	FRM
FRED BRONNER	FB
FREDERICK MFG CO	FMC
FREW & GORDON LIMITED	F&G
FRONT RANGE PRODUCTS	FR
FRONTIER REPLICAS	FRR
FUJI MODELS	FM

MANUFACTURERS ALPHABETICALLY W/ABREV	A
FUJIYAMA KOGYO COMPANY LIMITED	FUJI
FULGAREX, S A	FUL
FUNARA & CAMERLENGO	F&C
G.O. MODEL WORKS COMPANY LIMITED	GOTO
GAMCO PRODUCTS	GP
GANDY DANCER RR MODELS	GD
GAUGE ONE AMERICA	G1
GEIGER	GEI
GEM MODEL RAILWAYS	GEM
GEM MODELS (IMPORTERS)	G
GEM-TONE	GT
GENERAL MODELS CORP.	GM
GENESEE MODEL RR CO	GEMO
GEORGE STOCK	GS
GESCHA	GES
GHB INTERNATIONAL	GHB
GILBERT, A.C.	GIL
GINGERBREAD SHOP	GBS
GLOBE MODELS	GLO
GOULD COMPANY	GC
GR SIGNALING	GRS
GRACELINE MODEL RAILROADS	GMR
GRANDT LINES	GL
GRANT LOCOMOTIVE WORKS	GLW
GREAT WESTERN MODEL LOCOS	GW
GREEN MAX	GMX
GSB RAIL ASSOCIATES	GSB
H-D SCALE MODELS	HDSM
H.P. PRODUCTS	HP
HALLMARK	H
HALLMARK KOREA MODELS	HK
HAMO-MODELL-FAHRZEEUGE	HAMO
HARRY GARRETT & COMPANY	HG
HARTLEY MODEL RAILROAD SUPPLY	HM
HAWK MODEL AEROPLANE CO	HA
HELJAN	HEL
HENNING SCALE MODELS	HSM
HENRY ZUHR INC	ZUHR
HERKIMER TOOL & MODEL WORKS	HERK
HERMAN ENTERPRISES	HERM
HERPA	HE
HETCH HETCHY SCALE MODELS	HHS
HEWAN	HEW
HI BALLER CORP	HIB
HI RAIL PRODUCTS	HR
HI-COUNTRY BRASS	HC
HIGH QUALITY MODEL DISTRIBUTORS	HIQ
HINES LINES	HIL
HISTORICAL SCALE MINIATURES	HSM
HL WOODSON	WO
HO EITNER	HOE
HO RAILROAD & TROLLEY SUPPLY CO.	HORT
HO TRAIN COMPANY	HOT
HO WEST	HOW
HOBBIES INC	HI
HOBBY BARN	HB
HOBBY HAVEN	HHA
HOBBY HOUSE INC	HH
HOBBY INDUSTRIES	HOI
HOBBY LINE	HL
HOBBY TECHNIQUES	HTE
HOBBYTOWN OF BOSTON	HOB
HOLGATE & REYNOLDS	H&R
HOPPER LIN	HLI
HORNBY	HOR
HOUSE OF FOUR WINDS	HFW
HOUSE OF TRAINS	HT
HOWARD MINIATURE LAMP COMPANY	HML
HOWELL DAY	HD
HOWELL INDUSTRIES	HI.
HP LINES	HPL
HUDSON MINIATURES INC	HMI
HUNTINGTON MODEL WORKS	HUNT
ICKEN MODEL LOCO CO	IMC
IDEAL AEROPLANE & SUPPLY	IA
IDEAL MODELS	IM
IMAI MODELS COMPANY LIMITED	I

APPENDIX C (MANUFACTURERS)

MANUFACTURERS ALPHABETICALLY W/ABREV	A
IMP/TAKARA	TAK
INDIANAPOLIS CAR COMPANY	IND
INDUSTRIAL MODEL WORKS	IMW
INLAND SCALE MODELS	ISM
INTERNATIONAL HOBBY CORP	IHC
INTERNATIONAL MODELS INC.	INT
IRON HORSE MODELS	IH
ISLE LABORATORIES	ISLE
IVERS MANUFACTURING	IE
IVES	IVES
J&J MODELS	J&J
J&M DISTRIBUTORS	J&M
J.C. MODELS	JC
J.C. ULRICH COMPANY INC.	U
JACK COLLIER	CO
JAMCO LIMITED	JAM
JANCO MODELS	JA
JEWEL MODELS	JM
JIM GRACES HOBBY CENTER	JGHC
JL MODELS	JL
JMC INTERNATIONAL	JMC
JOHN A. ENGLISH & COMPANY	JE
JOHN GRZYWNA	JG
JORDONS PRODUCTS	JP
JOUEF	J
JULIAN WOLFSOHN	JW
JUNECO SCALE MODELS	JSM
K&L HOUSE OF WOOD	K&L
K&P	K&P
K&W SHOPS	K&W
K-VAL CARS	KVAL
KADEE CO.	KD
KALAMAZOO TOY TRAIN WORKS	KTTW
KARLINE	KL
KASINER HOBBIES	KAS
KATO USA	KATO
KATSUMI MOKEITEN COMPANY LIMITED	KATS
KAW VALLEY SCALE MODELS	KAW
KAWAI	KW
KEMTRON	KEM
KEN KIDDER RAILROAD MODELS	KK
KEY IMPORTERS/KEY IMPORTS LIMITED	KEY
KEYSTONE LOCOMOTIVE WORKS	KLW
KIBRI	KIB
KIMBALL-KRAFT	KIK
KING MODELS	KM
KINSMAN SCALE MODELS	KSC
KLE-WE	KLE
KLEI-WE	KLE.
KOBRA MODELS	K
KODAMA SHISAKUSHO	KS
KOOK JEA MODELS	KJ
KOREA SCALE MODELS	KSM
KRAMER MODEL WORKS	KMW
KRIS MODEL TRAINS	KRIS
KUMATA MODELS (& CO LTD)	KUM
KURTZ-KRAFT	KKR
KWR INC	KWR
L&S HOBBY SERVICES	L&S
L.M. BLUM MODELS	LMB
LA BELLE WOODWORKING CO	LWC
LA MAY INDUSTRIES	LM
LABELLE LOCOMOTIVE WORKS COMPANY	LA
LACONIA (BINKLEY) INDUSTRIES	LAC
LADD MODEL WORKS	LADD
LAMBERT ASSOCIATES	L
LANE JONES COMPANY	LJ
LANG CINCINNATTI CARS	LC
LAUNCH PAD DISTRIBUTORS	LPD
LAWRENCE LABORATORY	LLA
LCM BLOSS	LCM
LEETOWN	LEE
LEHIGH MODEL PRODUCTS	LMP
LEHIGH VALLEY MODELS	LV
LESLIE BROTHERS	LB
LESNEY	LES
LGB	LGB

MANUFACTURERS ALPHABETICALLY W/ABREV	A
LIBERTY MODELS INC	LI
LIFELIKE	LL
LIGHTNING HOBBIES	LH
LILIPUT	LIL
LIMA	LIMA
LIMITED EDITIONS	LE
LINDBERG	LIND
LINDSAY PRODUCTS INC	LIN
LIONEL	LIO
LITTLE MINI SHOPS	LMS
LMB MODELS	LMB
LOBAUGH	LOB
LOCOMOTIVE COMPANY, THE	LOC
LOCOMOTIVE WORKSHOP, THE	LW
LOGGERS SUPPLY	LOG
LOUIS MARX COMPANY INC.	MX
LOWRY	LOW
LS LOC LTD	LSL
LW MODELS	LWM
LYKENS VALLEY MODELS	LVM
LYTLER & LYTLER	L&L
M. DALE NEWTON COMPANY	DN
M.B. AUSTIN	MBA
MAERKLIN	MKL
MAGNUS	MAGN
MAGNUSON MODELS INC	MMD
MAIN LINE MODELS	MLI
MAINLINE VARNEY	VM
MANN-MADE PRODUCTS	MANN
MANTUA METAL PRODUCTS	M
MARION PRODUCTS COMPANY	MAP
MARKLIN	MKL
MARNOLD	MAR
MASTER CREATIONS	MCR
MASTER MODEL PRODUCTS	MMP
MAX GRAY	MG
MCKEAN MODELS	MKM
MEECO	MEECO
MEGROW	ME
MERKER-FISCHER	MFI
MERLE FABER	MF
MERZBACH COMPANY, CHAS. C.	MER
MICRO CAST MIZUNO	MCM
MICRO ENGINEERING	MIC
MICRO-SCALE MODEL PRODUCTS	MSMP
MIDGAGE MODELS	MIM
MIDWEST HOBBY SHOP	MHS
MIDWEST RAIL WORKS	MRW
MIDWEST TROLLEY MUSEUM INC	MTM
MIDWESTERN TRAIN HOBBY	MTH
MIL-SCALE PRODUCTS	MSP
MILARKE	MIL
MILESTONE MODELS	MISM
MILLER MODELS	MILM
MILWAUKEE CAR WORKS DIV	MCW
MIN-SCALE MILL WORKS	MIN
MINI STRUCTURES	MIST
MINIATURE HOMES MFG. COMPANY	MHM
MINIATURE TOYS	MT
MINIATURE VEHICLE MFG CO	MV
MINIKITS	MK
MINITRIX	MTX
MIYAZAWA MOKEI	MMO
MLR MANUFACTURING COMAPNY	MLR
MODEL BUILDERS SUPPLY	MBS
MODEL BUILDERS SUPPLY.	MDS.
MODEL CRAFT MFG CO	MC
MODEL DIE CAST	MDC
MODEL ENGINEERING WORKS	MEW
MODEL EXPRESS	MDX
MODEL HOBBIES	MH
MODEL HOMEMAKER	MOH
MODEL MASTERPIECES MODEL	MM
MODEL POWER	MP
MODEL RAILROAD SHOP	MRS
MODEL RECITIFIER CORP	MRC
MODEL SHOP, THE	MOD

STEPHANS' RAILROAD DIRECTORY

A73

APPENDIX C (MANUFACTURERS)

MANUFACTURERS ALPHABETICALLY W/ABREV	A
MODEL STRUCUTRES COMPANY	MS
MODEL TRAMWAY SYSTEMS	MTS
MODELTON MFG COMPANY	MO
MODELTRONICS	MT
MONOGRAM	MONO
MONON SHOPS	MON
MOUNTAIN AUTOMATION	MA
MOUNTAIN STATES MODEL WORKS	MSMW
MR WEATHER	MW
MR. ROBERTS HOPPERS	MRH
MUIR MODELS INC	MU
MULTIPLEX MFG CO	MULTI
N&G RAILWAY SIGNAL CO	N&G
N.A.P. COMPANY	NAP
N.J. INTERNATIONAL	NJI
NAKAMURA SEIMITSU COMPANY LIMITED	NAKA
NANCO MODELS	NAN
NARROW GAUGE CAR SHOP	NGCS
NASON RAILWAYS	NR
NATIONAL CAR EAST	NCE
NATIONAL MOTOR COMPANY	NMC
NEW ENGLAND RAIL SERVICE	NRS
NEW ONE	NEW
NICKEL PLATE PRODUCTS	NPP
NIMCO	NIM
NIXON MODELS	NM
NOCH & COMPANY	NOCH
NOMA ELECTRIC CORPORATION	NOMA
NORTH JERSEY MODEL CAR CO	NJM
NORTHEASTERN SCALE MODELS	NSM
NORTHWEST SHORE LINE	NWSL
OHIO MODEL WORKS	OMW
OLDE HUFF 'N PUFF	OHP
OLYMPIA DISTRIBUTORS	OD
OLYMPIA PRECISION MODELS	OPM
OLYMPIC CASCADIAN	OC
OLYMPIC EXPRESS	OE
ORIENTAL LIMITED	OL
ORIGINAL WHISTLE STOP KIT CO	OWS
ORION MODELS	ORM
OVERLAND MODELS INC	OM
PACIFIC FAST MAIL	PFM
PACIFIC HO COMPANY	PHO
PACIFIC MODEL SUPPLIES	PMS
PACIFIC PIKE	PIKE
PACIFIC TRACTION	PT
PARAGON MODELS	PAR
PARK MODEL PRODUCTS	PMP
PARMELE & STURGES	PST
PB PRODUCTS	PBP
PEACH CREEK SHOPS	PCS
PEARCE TOOL	PTO
PECOS RIVER BRASS	PRBR
PEMCO INDUSTRIES INC	PCO
PENN LINE	PL
PENNSYLVANIA SCALE MODELS	PAM
PERFECT SCALE MODELS	PSM
PERIOD MINIATURES	PEM
PERMA-BILT	P-B
PETER BUILT LOCOMOTIVE WORKS	PBLW
PETERSON MOTOR TRUCKS	PMT
P&P MODELS	PGP
PIEDMONT SOUTHEASTERN SHOPS	PSS
PIKE STUFF	PIS
PIONEER COMAPNY	PC
PITTMAN ELECTRICAL DEVELOPMENT CO.	PIT
PLACER NEVADA & EL DORADO RR CO.	PNED
PLASTIC TOYS	PLAST
PLASTICVILLE	PLV
POCHER	POCH
POLA	POLA
POLK'S MODEL CRAFT	POLK
POLY MOLD CASTINGS	PMC
POTOMIC VALLEY GAUGE SUPPLY	PV
POWER SYSTEMS INC	PSI
PRATTS MODELS	PRA
PRECISION BRASS	PB

MANUFACTURERS ALPHABETICALLY W/ABREV	A
PRECISION INSTRUMENT	PI
PRECISION MASTERS INC	PMA
PRECISION MINIATURES	PM
PRECISION MODEL PRODUCTS	PMO
PRECISION MODELS INC	PRM
PRECISION MODELS OF CALIFORNIA	P
PRECISION SCALE COMPANY	PS
PREISEP	PR
PRITCHARD PATENT PRODUCE CO	PPP
PRM IMPORTS	PRB
PRO CUSTOM HOBBIES	PCH
PROTO POWER WEST	PPW
PROTOTYPE MODEL PRODUCTS	PMRR
PROTOTYPE MODLER INC	PMI
PUFFING BILLY MODELS	PBM
Q-CAR COMPANY	QCC
QUALITY CRAFT MODELS INC	QC
QUALITY PRODUCTS	QP
QUALITY SYSTEMS & TECHNOLOGY	QS&T
R ROBB LTD.	RRL
R&M INDUSTRY	R&M
R&T COMPANY	R&T
RABON RAILROAD	RAR
RAIL CHIEF PRODUCTS CO.	RCH
RAIL CRAFT MODELS	RC
RAIL LINE COMPANY	RL
RAIL MINIATURES	RMI
RAIL-ZIP	RZ
RAILHEAD	RH
RAILMASTER PRODUCTS	RMP
RAILROAD EQUIP CO	RRE
RAILWORKS	RW
RALPH TROXEL	RT
RAMAX	RAM
RAPIDO	RAP
RD DENISE	RDD
REAL LIKE SCALE MODELS	RLSM
RED BALL	RED
REGAL KITS	REK
REMINGTON LOCO WORKS	RNSM.
REMINGTON LOCOMOTIVE WORKS	RLW
REMINGTON N SCALE MINIATURES	RNSM
RENWAL PRODUCTS	REN
REVELL	RE
REX ENG & MFG CO	REX
REX S GAUGE MODELS	REXS
REYNOLDS RAILROAD PRODUCTS	RRR.
RHEOSTATE	RHE
RIB OF STIEHL	RS
RIBBONRAIL	RIB
RICHARD A LEE	RAL
RICHARD DATIN	RDA
RICHARD ORR	ORR
RICHARD-DENNIS MODELS	DE
RIOGRANDE MODELS	RGM
RIVAROSSI	RIV
RIX PRODUCTS	RIX
ROANOKE SHOPS	ROS
ROBERT L MILLER LABS	RLML
ROBERT LA REGINA	RLR
ROBERT SLOAN	ROSL
ROBINS RAILS INC	RRI
ROCK LANE MODELS	RLM
ROCKY MOUNTAIN MODELS	RM
ROK-AM (REPUBLIC OF KOREA-AMERICAN)	RA
ROKAL (GERMANY)	ROKAL
ROLLER BEARING MODELS	R
ROLLIN J LOBAUGH	LOB
ROLLINS HOUSE OF MINIATURES	RHM
ROSEBUD KITMASTER LTD.	RK
ROSEBUD PLASTICS CORP	RP
ROUNDHOUSE, THE	RD
ROWA	ROWA
ROYAL GEORGE SOUTHERN RAILROAD	RGSR
RR PROGRESS	RRP
RTR INDUSTRIES	RTR
RUSSELL MOBI-MODELS	RMM

APPENDIX C (MANUFACTURERS)

MANUFACTURERS ALPHABETICALLY W/ABREV	A
RUSSIAN RIVER RAILROAD COMPANY	RRR
S SOHO & COMPANY	SOHO
S&P DISTRIBUTORS	S&P
S.E. DANCE	SED
S.K. INTERNATIONAL	SKI
SAGINAW PATTERN MFG CO	SPM
SAKURA-TAKENO	SAK
SAMHONGSA COMPANY LIMITED	SAM
SAMPSON MODEL COMPANY	SMP
SAN JUAN ENGINEERING	SJE
SANDY RIVER CAR SHOPS	SR
SANGO MODEL RAILROAD WORKS	SMRW
SANGO MODEL RAILROAD WORKS (O)	SMW.
SATO MODELS	SAT
SCALE CRAFT ENGINEERING CO.	SCC
SCALE LOCOMOTIVE & SUPPLY	SLS
SCALE MODEL WEATHERING INC	SMW
SCALE MODELERS INDUSTRIES	SMI
SCALE MODELS	SCMO
SCALE RAILWAY EQUIPMENT COMPANY	SRE
SCALE SCENICS DIVISION	SSD
SCALE STRUCTURES LIMITED	SSL
SCALE-RAIL MINIATURES	SRA
SCENERY ("S"CENERY) UNLIMITED	SCU
SCENERY PRODUCTS	SCP
SCENERY UNLIMITED	SU
SCHRADER METAL SPECIALISTS	SMS
SCOTIA SCALE MODELS	SCSM
SEIKO MODELS	SE
SELLEY INC	SEL
SEQUOIA SCALE MODELS	SSMO
SHERLINE	SHL
SHERMAN DANCE	SD
SIERRA SOUTHERN PRODUCTS	SISP
SILVER LEAF RAPID TRANSIT MODELS	SLR
SILVER LEDGE MODELS	SLMO
SILVER STREAK	SS
SIMMONS SCALE MODELS INC	SISC
SIMPSON PRODUCT COMPANY	SIM
SLIM GAUGE PRODUCTIONS	SGP
SMALL SCALE PRODUCTS	SSP
SMART PRODUCTS INC	SPR
SMOKE STACK HOBBY KITS CO	SSHK
SMOKEY VALLEY RAILROAD	SV
SOUTH PARK PRODUCTIONS	SPPR
SOUTH SHORE SCALE MODELS	SSS
SOUTHERN TOOL & MANUFACTURING CO.	ST&M
SPRINGDALE STRANGLER CREEK	SSC
SPRINGTOWN CAR SHOPS	SPCS
SS LIMITED	SSL
STANDARD PRODUCTS	SP
STANDARD SCALE MODELS	STS
STAR CONTINENTAL KIT (MODELS)	SCK
STAR HOBBY PRODUCTS	SH
STAR LINE MODELS	SL
STAR MODELS	SMO
STATE LINE MODELS	SLM
STATE RAILROAD MODELS	SRM
STATE STREET MODELS	STST
STERLING MODELS	ST
STEWART HOBBIES INC	STEW
STEWART MODELS	STEWM
STROMBECK-BECKER MFG CO	SB
STRUCTURE COMPANY, THE	STC
SUGAR PINE MODELS	SUP
SUMMIT ENGINEERING	SEN
SUNCOAST MODELS	SC
SUNSET MODELS	SUN
SUNSHINE MODELS	SM
SUPER SCALE MODEL CORP.	SSM
SUPERIOR MODELS	SUM
SUPERQUICK	SQ
SUTHERLAND MODELS CASTERS INC	SMC
SUYDAM	S .
SYCAMORE HOLLOW STATION	SHS
TAKARA/IMP	TAK
TAURUS PRODUCTS	TP

MANUFACTURERS ALPHABETICALLY W/ABREV	A
TENSHODO MODEL COMPANY	TEN
TETSUDO MOKEISHA	TMK
THOMAS A YORKE ENTERPRISES	TY
THOMAS INDUSTRIES	TH
THRALL MFG CO	THM
TIGER VALLEY MODELS	TVM
TIMBERLINE MODELS	TIM
TK MODELS	TK
TOBY MODEL COMPANY LIMITED	TOBY
TOHO MODELS	TOHO
TOMALCO	TOM
TOMHAR MFG CO	TOMH
TOWN CRAFTS MODELS	TCM
TOY & HOBBY HOUSE	THH
TP PRODUCTS	TPPR
TRACKSIDE INDUSTRIES	TRI
TRACKSIDE SPECIALTIES	TSS
TRACTION HOUSE	TRH
TRACTION MODELS	TRM
TRAIN CRAFT PRODUCTS	TC
TRAIN MINIATURE OF CALIF	TMC
TRAIN MINIATURE OF ILLINOIS	TMI
TRAIN MINIATURES	TM
TRAIN MODELS	TMO
TRAINS OF TEXAS	TT
TRAINS, INC.	TI
TRAINSTUFF	TRS
TRIANGLE SCALE MODELS	TRIS
TRIX	TRIX
TROLLER	TR
TRU-SCALE MODELS	TSM
TRUXEL BROS ENTERPRISES	TBE
TSUBOMI	TS
TYCO INDUSTRIES	T
ULRICH	U
ULTRA SCALE	US
UNITED STATES TOY TRAIN COMPANY	USTT
UNIVERSAL MODEL PRODUCTS	UMP
US AIRFIX	USAI
US HOBBIES	USH
UTAH SCALE MODEL COMPANY	USM
V LINE LOCOMOTIVES INC	VL
V&T SHOPS	V&T
VALLAM ASSOCIATES	VAL
VALLEY CAR WORKS	VCW
VALLEY WORKS	VW
VAN HOBBIES	VAN
VANE JONES COMPANY	LJ
VARNEY	V
VARNEY MAINLINE	VM
VCM	VCM
VICOUNT MODEL RAILROAD PRODUCT CO	VMR
VIKING MODELS	VIK
VIRDEN	VI
VOLLMER	VOL
VOLTAMP	VOLT
W&T MODELS	W&T
WABASH VALLEY LINE	WVL
WAGNER CAR COMPANY	WC
WAHL	WAHL
WALKER MODEL SERVICE	WMS
WALLACE SCALE MODLES	WASM
WALTER S PARKS	WSP
WALTER SYRETT	WSY
WALTERS	WAL
WAYFREIGHT MODELS	WFM
WEBSTER MANUFACTURING COMPANY	WEB
WEEDEN	WEED
WEN-MAC	WMAC
WENTICO PRECISION MODELS	WPM
WESTCHESTER MODEL CO	WMC
WESTERFIELD	WD
WESTERN MODELS	WM
WESTERN RAILCRAFT	WR
WESTMORELAND CAR SUPPLY	WEC
WESTSIDE MODEL COMPANY	WSM
WESTWOOD	WEST

A75

APPENDIX C (MANUFACTURERS)

MANUFACTURERS ALPHABETICALLY W/ABREV	ABREV
WHEEL WORKS	WW
WHITE GROUND MODEL WORKS	WGM
WIKING	WIK
WILLIAM BROTHERS	WB
WILLIAMS REPRODUCTIONS LTD	WRL
WINSTON MINIATURE ENGINEERING CO	W
WISONSIN CENTRAL SUPPLY	WCS
WOODLAND SCENICS	WS
WOODSON	WO
WP CAR COMPANY	WPC
WR BROWN CORP	WRB
WRIGHT ENTERPRISES	WE
WS PARKS	WSP
YANK MODEL RESEARCH INC	YM
YE OLD HUFF 'N PUFF	YE
ZIMMER SCALE MODELS	ZSM
ZUHR	ZUHR

ABREV	ALPHABETICALLY BY MANUFACTURER
101P	101 PRODUCTIONS
20C	20TH CENTURY SALES
A	ACE MODEL RR EQUIPMENT CO
AA	ARVID ANDERSON
ABJ	AB JAQUES
ABL	AMERICAN BEAUTY LINES
ACI	ACI HOBBY
ACM	AC MODEL
ACS	ALAMOSA CAR SHOPS
ACSM	ACACIA SCALE MODELS
ACW	ASHLAND CAR WORKS
AD	A. DEPIPPO
AE	AL ELLIS
AF	AMERICAN FLYER
AFM	ART FLEMING MODELS
AFS	ALLEN F SEEBACH
AGK	AMERICAN GK LOCOMOTIVE WORKS
AHM	ASSOCIATED HOBBY MANUFACTURERS
AHM.	AHM
AHMA	AHM-AIRFIX
AIM	AIM PRODUCTS
AIRF	AIRFIX
AK	AKANE MODEL RAILROAD COMPANY
AL	ALLOY FORMS
ALCO	ALCO MODELS
ALCOE	ALCO ENGINEERING
ALE	ALEXANDER & COMPANY
ALEX	ALEXANDER SCALE MODELS
ALEZ.	ALEXANDER SCALE MODELS.
AM	ARBOUR MODELS
AMB	AMBROID
AMER	AMERICAN MODEL TOYS INC
AMI	AMERICAN MODELS INC
AMIS	A. MISENAR
AMRO	AMRO
AN	ALL-NATION HOBBY SHOP
ANB	AMERICAN "N" BRASS
APAG	APAG HOBBIES
ARC	AMERICAN RAILROAD COMPANY
ARD	ARDEN SCALE MODELS
ARGY	ARGY SPECIALTIES
ARISTO	ARISTO-CRAFT DISTINTIVE MINIATURES
AROM	ARROW MODELS
ARR	AMERICAN RR MODELS
ASC	AMERICAN STANDARD CAR CO
ASM	AYRES SCALE MODELS
ASMC	AMERICAN SCALE MODEL CORPORATION
AST	ASTER COMPANY
AT	ATLAS TOOL COMPANY
ATA	ATA MODEL COMPANY
ATH	ATHEARN
ATSM	ATLANTIC SCALE MODELS
ATT	AMERICAN TRAIN & TRACK
AUR	AURORA PLASTICS COMPANY
AUTH	AUTHENTICAST COMPANY
AW	A-WEST
B	BACHMANN INDUSTRIES
B&W	B&W SPECIALTIES
B/T	B/T ENTERPRISES
BA	BOB'S AIRCRAFT
BAL	BALBOA SCALE MODELS
BART	BART MODELS
BAU	BAUMGARTEN MODEL RR EQUIP
BCK	BOX CAR KEN
BCM	BEAVER CREEK MODELS
BELL	BELL MODEL SHOPS
BH	BERG HOBBIES
BHLW	BLACK HAWK LOCO WORKS
BHM	BRASS HAT MODELS
BI	BEACH ISLAND MFG CO
BIM	BIMCO
BIN	BINKLEY MODELS
BL	BLUE LINE PRODUCTS
BLM	BRANCH LINE MODELS
BLP	BLACKMAN PLASTICS
BM	BALDWIN MODEL LOCO WORKS
BN	BARR-NIXON PRODUCTS

APPENDIX C (MANUFACTURERS)

A	ABREV ALPHABETICALLY BY MANUFACTURER
BOR	BORDERTOWN PUBLISHING
BOW	BOWSER
BOY	BOYDE MODELS
BP	BOB PEARE ENGINEERING CORPORATION
BPS	BELPAIRE SHOPS
BR	BRONSON
BS	BACK SHOP
BSC	BUILDERS IN SCALE
BSM	BAY STATE MODELS
BU	BUSCH
BUC	BUCKEYE MODLES
C	CAMPBELL
C&C	CANNON & COMPANY
C&S	CORNISA & SONS
C&SS	C&S SCALE INDUSTRIES
CA	CAMBRON
CA.	CAMERON
CAIN	CABOOSE INDUSTRIES
CAL	CAL-SCALE
CAM	CAMINO SCALE MODELS
CAN	CANADIAN PROTOTYPE REPLICAS
CAP	CANNONBALL PRODUCTS
CAPI	CAPART INDUSTRIES
CAPL	CASTOR PLASTICS
CB	CUSTOM BRASS
CBRO	C. BROMMER
CC	CON-COR COMPANY
CCF	COLUMBIA CAR & FOUNDRY
CCM	CLEAR CREEK MODELS
CCS	CANNONBALL CAR SHOPS
CCW	CONCORD CAR WORKS
CD	CHARLES DETTMANN
CE	CHAMIS ENTERPRISES
CECL	CASCO ENCO CAR LINE
CH	CHESTER HOLLEY
CHB	CHB MODELS
CHM	CHRIS MAHON INDUSTRIES
CHO	CHOOCH ENTERPRISES
CI	CADWELL INDUSTRIES
CIC	CIBOLD CROSSING
CK	CRAFTSMAN KITS
CL	CENTRAL LINES MFG CO
CLIF	CLIFF LINE SCALE MODELS
CLW	CARY LOCOMOTIVE WORKS
CLWO	CENTRAL LOCO WORKS
CM	CM SHOPS
CM	CONTINENTAL MODELS
CMI	CLASSIC MINIATURES
CMM	COLORADO MODEL MASTERPIECES
CMO	COMET MODEL COMPANY
CMP	CRESCENT MODEL PRODUCTS
CMPR	COMET METAL PRODUCTS
CMS	CLEVELAND MODELS & SUPPLY CO
CO	COLLIER
CO	JACK COLLIER
COC	COOPER CRAFT
COCW	COPETOWN CAR WORKS
COL	COLLINS
COLB	COLBER CORPORATION
COM	CORONADO SCALE MODELS
COMI	CONOVER MINIATURE
COMM	CONTINENTAL MONARCH MODEL CO
COX	COX HOBBIES INC
CP	CRUMMY PRODUCTS
CPC	CHRISTOPH PRODUCTS COMPANY
CPI	CAR PART INDUSTRIES
CPR	CONRAD PRODUCTS
CRGT	CROSSING GATE MODELS
CRM	CANADIAN RAILWAY MODEL COMPANY
CS	CAR SHOP
CSC	CSC CORP
CSM	CANNON SCALE MODELS
CSML	CITY STREETS MODELS LTD
CSR	CS RAFFING
CTL	COFFEE TABLE LAYOUTS
CV	CENTRAL VALLEY MODEL WORKS
CVM	COLUMBIA VALLEY MODELS

A	ABREV ALPHABETICALLY BY MANUFACTURER
CY	COACH YARD
D	DYNA-MODEL PRODUCTS COMPANY
DA	DETAIL ASSOCIATES
DARR	DARR'S SCALE MODELS
DE	DENNIS
DE	RICHARD-DENNIS MODELS
DEV	DEVORT
DF	DON FOWLER
DF.	FOWLER
DIM	DIAMOND MOUNTAIN RAILROAD
DIT	DIMI-TRAINS
DJ	DONG JIN MODEL WORKS
DJB	D.J. BAKER
DM	DIAMOND MODELS
DMC	DALLAS MODEL CRAFT
DMK	DMK REFINERY MODELS
DMT	DAVE'S MODEL TRAINS
DN	DALE NEWTON COMPANY
DN	M. DALE NEWTON COMPANY
DP	DURANGO PRESS
DPM	DESIGN PRESERVATION MODELS
DSC	DIAMOND SCALE CONSTRUCTION
DSM	DENNIS STORZEK MODELMAKER
DT	DESIGNS OF TOMARROW
DVK	DELAWARE VALLEY KITS
DW	DETAILS WEST
DWI	DON WINTER
DY	DIA YONG MODELS COMPANY
E	EUROTRAINS IMPORTERS
E&P	E&P ASSOCIATES
EBV	E&B VALLEY RAILROAD
ECA	ELECTRO-CRAFT APPLIANCES
ECM	EMPIRE CITY MODELS
ECW	EASTERN CAR WORKS
EFMT	EARL FRANCIS MINIATURE TRAINS
EHB	E.H. BESSEY
EHD	EVERGREEN HILL DESIGNS
EM	ERNEST MFG COMPANY
EMI	EUROPA MODEL INTERNATIONAL
EMM	EMPIRE MODELS
EMP	EMPIRE MIDLAND MODEL COMPANY
ENG	ENGLISH
ENH	ENHORNING
EPA	EP ALEXANDER
EPM	EAST PENN MODELS
ER	EVERGREEN ROUNDHOUSE
ES	EVERETT SMITH
ESM	EVERGREEN SCALE MODELS
ESN	ES NIELSON
ESP	ELECTRONIC SPECIALTY PRODUCTS
ETC	ETCETERA INC
ETM	EASTERN TRACTION MODELS
EW	EXPRESS WAGON CONSTRUCTION
F	FINE SCALE MINIATURES
F&C	FUNARA & CAMERLENGO
F&G	FREW & GORDON LIMITED
F2	FLYING 200
FA	FAIRFIELD MODELS
FAL	FALLER
FAM	FAMOUS MODEL COMPANY
FAS	F.A. SIMONS
FB	FRED BRONNER
FED	FAR EAST DISTRIBUTORS(NW SHORT LINES)
FEI	FAR EAST IMPORTERS
FHS	FISCHERS HOBBY SERVICE
FL	FLEISCHMANN
FM	FUJI MODELS
FMC	FREDERICK MFG CO
FO	FOMART
FOM	FOMRAS MODELS
FR	FRONT RANGE PRODUCTS
FRM	FRANKLIN MODELS
FRR	FRONTIER REPLICAS
FS	FINDEX-SYSTEMS INC
FSM	FORTY-NINTH STATE RR MODELS
FTM	FAIRFIELD TRACTION MODELS
FUJI	FUJIYAMA KOGYO COMPANY LIMITED

A77

APPENDIX C (MANUFACTURERS)

A	ABREV ALPHABETICALLY BY MANUFACTURER
FUL	FULGAREX, S A
G	GEM MODELS (IMPORTERS)
G1	GAUGE ONE AMERICA
GBS	GINGERBREAD SHOP
GC	GOULD COMPANY
GD	GANDY DANCER RR MODELS
GEI	GEIGER
GEM	GEM MODEL RAILWAYS
GEMO	GENESEE MODEL RR CO
GES	GESCHA
GHB	GHB INTERNATIONAL
GIL	A.C. GILBERT
GIL	GILBERT, A.C.
GL	GRANDT LINES
GLO	GLOBE MODELS
GLW	GRANT LOCOMOTIVE WORKS
GM	GENERAL MODELS CORP.
GMR	GRACELINE MODEL RAILROADS
GMX	GREEN MAX
GOTO	G.O. MODEL WORKS COMPANY LIMITED
GP	GAMCO PRODUCTS
GRS	GR SIGNALING
GS	GEORGE STOCK
GSB	GSB RAIL ASSOCIATES
GT	GEM-TONE
GW	GREAT WESTERN MODEL LOCOS
H	HALLMARK
H&R	HOLGATE & REYNOLDS
HA	HAWK MODEL AEROPLANE CO
HAMO	HAMO-MODELL-FAHRZEEUGE
HB	HOBBY BARN
HC	HI-COUNTRY BRASS
HD	HOWELL DAY
HDSM	H-D SCALE MODELS
HE	HERPA
HEL	HELJAN
HERK	HERKIMER TOOL & MODEL WORKS
HERM	HERMAN ENTERPRISES
HEW	HEWAN
HFW	HOUSE OF FOUR WINDS
HG	HARRY GARRETT & COMPANY
HH	HOBBY HOUSE INC
HHA	HOBBY HAVEN
HHS	HETCH HETCHY SCALE MODELS
HI.	HOBBIES INC
HI.	HOWELL INDUSTRIES
HIB	HI BALLER CORP
HIL	HINES LINES
HIQ	HIGH QUALITY MODEL DISTRIBUTORS
HK	HALLMARK KOREA MODELS
HL	HOBBY LINE
HLI	HOPPER LIN
HM	HARTLEY MODEL RAILROAD SUPPLY
HMI	HUDSON MINIATURES INC
HML	HOWARD MINIATURE LAMP COMPANY
HOB	HOBBYTOWN OF BOSTON
HOE	HO EITNER
HOI	HOBBY INDUSTRIES
HOR	HORNBY
HORT	HO RAILROAD & TROLLEY SUPPLY CO.
HOT	HO TRAIN COMPANY
HOW	HO WEST
HP	H.P. PRODUCTS
HPL	HP LINES
HR	HI RAIL PRODUCTS
HSM	HENNING SCALE MODELS
HSM	HISTORICAL SCALE MINIATURES
HT	HOUSE OF TRAINS
HTE	HOBBY TECHNIQUES
HUNT	HUNTINGTON MODEL WORKS
I	IMAI MODELS COMPANY LIMITED
IA	IDEAL AEROPLANE & SUPPLY
IE	IVERS MANUFACTURING
IH	IRON HORSE MODELS
IHC	INTERNATIONAL HOBBY CORP
IM	IDEAL MODELS
IMC	ICKEN MODEL LOCO CO
IMW	INDUSTRIAL MODEL WORKS
IND	INDIANAPOLIS CAR COMPANY
INT	INTERNATIONAL MODELS INC.
ISLE	ISLE LABORATORIES
ISM	INLAND SCALE MODELS
IVES	IVES
J	JOUEF
J&J	J&J MODELS
J&M	J&M DISTRIBUTORS
JA	JANCO MODELS
JAM	JAMCO LIMITED
JC	J.C. MODELS
JE	JOHN A. ENGLISH & COMPANY
JG	JOHN GRZYWNA
JGHC	JIM GRACES HOBBY CENTER
JL	JL MODELS
JM	JEWEL MODELS
JMC	JMC INTERNATIONAL
JP	JORDONS PRODUCTS
JSM	JUNECO SCALE MODELS
JW	JULIAN WOLFSOHN
K	KOBRA MODELS
K&L	K&L HOUSE OF WOOD
K&P	K&P
K&W	K&W SHOPS
KAS	KASINER HOBBIES
KATO	KATO USA
KATS	KATSUMI MOKEITEN COMPANY LIMITED
KAW	KAW VALLEY SCALE MODELS
KD	KADEE CO.
KEM	KEMTRON
KEY	KEY IMPORTERS/KEY IMPORTS LIMITED
KIB	KIBRI
KIK	KIMBALL-KRAFT
KJ	KOOK JEA MODELS
KK	KEN KIDDER RAILROAD MODELS
KKR	KURTZ-KRAFT
KL	KARLINE
KLE	KLE-WE
KLE.	KLEI-WE
KLW	KEYSTONE LOCOMOTIVE WORKS
KM	KING MODELS
KMW	KRAMER MODEL WORKS
KRIS	KRIS MODEL TRAINS
KS	KODAMA SHISAKUSHO
KSC	KINSMAN SCALE MODELS
KSM	KOREA SCALE MODELS
KTTW	KALAMAZOO TOY TRAIN WORKS
KUM	KUMATA MODELS (& CO LTD)
KVAL	K-VAL CARS
KW	KAWAI
KWR	KWR INC
L	LAMBERT ASSOCIATES
L&L	LYTLER & LYTLER
L&S	L&S HOBBY SERVICES
LA	LABELLE LOCOMOTIVE WORKS COMPANY
LAC	LACONIA (BINKLEY) INDUSTRIES
LADD	LADD MODEL WORKS
LB	LESLIE BROTHERS
LC	LANG CINCINNATTI CARS
LCM	LCM BLOSS
LE	LIMITED EDITIONS
LEE	LEETOWN
LES	LESNEY
LGB	LGB
LH	LIGHTNING HOBBIES
LI	LIBERTY MODELS INC
LIL	LILIPUT
LIMA	LIMA
LIN	LINDSAY PRODUCTS INC
LIND	LINDBERG
LIO	LIONEL
LJ	LANE JONES COMPANY
LJ	VANE JONES COMPANY
LL	LIFELIKE
LLA	LAWRENCE LABORATORY
LM	LA MAY INDUSTRIES

A78

APPENDIX C (MANUFACTURERS)

A	ABREV ALPHABETICALLY BY MANUFACTURER	A	ABREV ALPHABETICALLY BY MANUFACTURER
LMB	LMB MODELS	MTS	MODEL TRAMWAY SYSTEMS
LMB	L.M. BLUM MODELS	MTX	MINITRIX
LMP	LEHIGH MODEL PRODUCTS	MU	MUIR MODELS INC
LMS	LITTLE MINI SHOPS	MULTI	MULTIPLEX MFG CO
LOB	LOBAUGH	MV	MINIATURE VEHICLE MFG CO
LOB	ROLLIN J LOBAUGH	MW	MR WEATHER
LOC	LOCOMOTIVE COMPANY, THE	MX	LOUIS MARX COMPANY INC.
LOG	LOGGERS SUPPLY	N&G	N&G RAILWAY SIGNAL CO
LOW	LOWRY	NAKA	NAKAMURA SEIMITSU COMPANY LIMITED
LPD	LAUNCH PAD DISTRIBUTORS	NAN	NANCO MODELS
LSL	LS LOC LTD	NAP	N.A.P. COMPANY
LV	LEHIGH VALLEY MODELS	NCE	NATIONAL CAR EAST
LVM	LYKENS VALLEY MODELS	NEW	NEW ONE
LW	LOCOMOTIVE WORKSHOP, THE	NGCS	NARROW GAUGE CAR SHOP
LWC	LA BELLE WOODWORKING CO	NIM	NIMCO
LWM	LW MODELS	NJI	N.J. INTERNATIONAL
M	MANTUA METAL PRODUCTS	NJM	NORTH JERSEY MODEL CAR CO
MA	MOUNTAIN AUTOMATION	NM	NIXON MODELS
MAGN	MAGNUS	NMC	NATIONAL MOTOR COMPANY
MANN	MANN-MADE PRODUCTS	NOCH	NOCH & COMPANY
MAP	MARION PRODUCTS COMPANY	NOMA	NOMA ELECTRIC CORPORATION
MAR	MARNOLD	NPP	NICKEL PLATE PRODUCTS
MBA	M.B. AUSTIN	NR	NASON RAILWAYS
MBS	MODEL BUILDERS SUPPLY	NRS	NEW ENGLAND RAIL SERVICE
MC	MODEL CRAFT MFG CO	NSM	NORTHEASTERN SCALE MODELS
MCM	MICRO CAST MIZUNO	NWSL	NORTHWEST SHORE LINE
MCR	MASTER CREATIONS	OC	OLYMPIC CASCADIAN
MCW	MILWAUKEE CAR WORKS DIV	OD	OLYMPIA DISTRIBUTORS
MDC	MODEL DIE CAST	OE	OLYMPIC EXPRESS
MDS.	MODEL BUILDERS SUPPLY.	OHP	OLDE HUFF 'N PUFF
MDX	MODEL EXPRESS	OL	ORIENTAL LIMITED
ME	MEGROW	OM	OVERLAND MODELS INC
MEECO	MEECO	OMW	OHIO MODEL WORKS
MER	CHAS C. MERZBACH COMAPNY	OPM	OLYMPIA PRECISION MODELS
MER	MERZBACH COMPANY, CHAS. C.	ORM	ORION MODELS
MEW	MODEL ENGINEERING WORKS	ORR	RICHARD ORR
MF	MERLE FABER	OWS	ORIGINAL WHISTLE STOP KIT CO
MFI	MERKER-FISCHER	P	PRECISION MODELS OF CALIFORNIA
MG	MAX GRAY	P-B	PERMA-BILT
MH	MODEL HOBBIES	PAM	PENNSYLVANIA SCALE MODELS
MHM	MINIATURE HOMES MFG. COMPANY	PAR	PARAGON MODELS
MHS	MIDWEST HOBBY SHOP	PB	PRECISION BRASS
MIC	MICRO ENGINEERING	PBLW	PETER BUILT LOCOMOTIVE WORKS
MIL	MILARKE	PBM	PUFFING BILLY MODELS
MILM	MILLER MODELS	PBP	PB PRODUCTS
MIM	MIDGAGE MODELS	PC	PIONEER COMAPNY
MIN	MIN-SCALE MILL WORKS	PCH	PRO CUSTOM HOBBIES
MISM	MILESTONE MODELS	PCO	PEMCO INDUSTRIES INC
MIST	MINI STRUCTURES	PCS	PEACH CREEK SHOPS
MK	MINIKITS	PEM	PERIOD MINIATURES
MKL	MARKLIN	PFM	PACIFIC FAST MAIL
MKL	MAERKLIN	PGP	PGP MODELS
MKM	MCKEAN MODELS	PHO	PACIFIC HO COMPANY
MLI	MAIN LINE MODELS	PI	PRECISION INSTRUMENT
MLR	MLR MANUFACTURING COMAPNY	PIKE	PACIFIC PIKE
MM	MODEL MASTERPIECES MODEL	PIS	PIKE STUFF
MMD	MAGNUSON MODELS INC	PIT	PITTMAN ELECTRICAL DEVELOPMENT CO.
MMO	MIYAZAWA MOKEI	PL	PENN LINE
MMP	MASTER MODEL PRODUCTS	PLAST	PLASTIC TOYS
MO	MODELTON MFG COMPANY	PLV	PLASTICVILLE
MOD	MODEL SHOP, THE	PM	PRECISION MINIATURES
MOH	MODEL HOMEMAKER	PMA	PRECISION MASTERS INC
MON	MONON SHOPS	PMC	POLY MOLD CASTINGS
MONO	MONOGRAM	PMI	PROTOTYPE MODLER INC
MP	MODEL POWER	PMO	PRECISION MODEL PRODUCTS
MRC	MODEL RECITIFIER CORP	PMP	PARK MODEL PRODUCTS
MRH	MR. ROBERTS HOPPERS	PMRR	PROTOTYPE MODEL PRODUCTS
MRS	MODEL RAILROAD SHOP	PMS	PACIFIC MODEL SUPPLIES
MRW	MIDWEST RAIL WORKS	PMT	PETERSON MOTOR TRUCKS
MS	MODEL STRUCUTRES COMPANY	PNED	PLACER NEVADA & EL DORRADO RR CO.
MSMP	MICRO-SCALE MODEL PRODUCTS	POCH	POCHER
MSMW	MOUNTAIN STATES MODEL WORKS	POLA	POLA
MSP	MIL-SCALE PRODUCTS	POLK	POLK'S MODEL CRAFT
MT	MINIATURE TOYS	PPP	PRITCHARD PATENT PRODUCE CO
MT	MODELTRONICS	PPW	PROTO POWER WEST
MTH	MIDWESTERN TRAIN HOBBY	PR	PREISEP
MTM	MIDWEST TROLLEY MUSEUM INC	PRA	PRATTS MODELS

STEPHANS' RAILROAD DIRECTORY

A79

APPENDIX C (MANUFACTURERS)

A	ABREV ALPHABETICALLY BY MANUFACTURER
PRB	PRM IMPORTS
PRBR	PECOS RIVER BRASS
PRM	PRECISION MODELS INC
PS	PRECISION SCALE COMPANY
PSI	POWER SYSTEMS INC
PSM	PERFECT SCALE MODELS
PSS	PIEDMONT SOUTHEASTERN SHOPS
PST	PARMELE & STURGES
PT	PACIFIC TRACTION
PTO	PEARCE TOOL
PV	POTOMIC VALLEY GAUGE SUPPLY
QC	QUALITY CRAFT MODELS INC
QCC	Q-CAR COMPANY
QP	QUALITY PRODUCTS
QS&T	QUALITY SYSTEMS & TECHNOLOGY
R	ROLLER BEARING MODELS
R&M	R&M INDUSTRY
R&T	R&T COMPANY
RA	ROK-AM (REPUBLIC OF KOREA-AMERICAN)
RAL	RICHARD A LEE
RAM	RAMAX
RAP	RAPIDO
RAR	RABON RAILROAD
RC	RAIL CRAFT MODELS
RCH	RAIL CHIEF PRODUCTS CO.
RD	ROUNDHOUSE, THE
RDA	RICHARD DATIN
RDD	RD DENISE
RE	REVELL
RED	RED BALL
REK	REGAL KITS
REN	RENWAL PRODUCTS
REX	REX ENG & MFG CO
REXS	REX S GAUGE MODELS
RGM	RIOGRANDE MODELS
RGSR	ROYAL GEORGE SOUTHERN RAILROAD
RH	RAILHEAD
RHE	RHEDSTATE
RHM	ROLLINS HOUSE OF MINIATURES
RIB	RIBBONRAIL
RIV	RIVAROSSI
RIX	RIX PRODUCTS
RK	ROSEBUD KITMASTER LTD.
RL	RAIL LINE COMPANY
RLM	ROCK LANE MODELS
RLML	ROBERT L MILLER LABS
RLR	ROBERT LA REGINA
RLSM	REAL LIKE SCALE MODELS
RLW	REMINGTON LOCOMOTIVE WORKS
RM	ROCKY MOUNTAIN MODELS
RMI	RAIL MINIATURES
RMM	RUSSELL MOBI-MODELS
RMP	RAILMASTER PRODUCTS
RNSM	REMINGTON N SCALE MINIATURES
RNSM.	REMINGTON LOCO WORKS
ROKAL	ROKAL (GERMANY)
ROS	ROANOKE SHOPS
ROSL	ROBERT SLOAN
ROWA	ROWA
RP	ROSEBUD PLASTICS CORP
RRE	RAILROAD EQUIP CO
RRI	ROBINS RAILS INC
RRL	R ROBB LTD.
RRP	RR PROGRESS
RRR	RUSSIAN RIVER RAILROAD COMPANY
RRR.	REYNOLDS RAILROAD PRODUCTS
RS	RIB OF STIEHL
RT	RALPH TROXEL
RTR	RTR INDUSTRIES
RW	RAILWORKS
RZ	RAIL-ZIP
S	E SUYDAM & COMPANY
S	SUYDAM
S&P	S&P DISTRIBUTORS
SAK	SAKURA-TAKENO
SAM	SAMHONGSA COMPANY LIMITED
SAT	SATO MODELS

A	ABREV ALPHABETICALLY BY MANUFACTURER
SB	STROMBECK-BECKER MFG CO
SC	SUNCOAST MODELS
SCC	SCALE CRAFT ENGINEERING CO.
SCK	STAR CONTINENTAL KIT (MODELS)
SCMO	SCALE MODELS
SCP	SCENERY PRODUCTS
SCSM	SCOTIA SCALE MODELS
SCU	SCENERY ("S"CENERY) UNLIMITED
SD	SHERMAN DANCE
SE	SEIKO MODELS
SED	S.E. DANCE
SEL	SELLEY INC
SEN	SUMMIT ENGINEERING
SGP	SLIM GAUGE PRODUCTIONS
SH	STAR HOBBY PRODUCTS
SHL	SHERLINE
SHS	SYCAMORE HOLLOW STATION
SIM	SIMPSON PRODUCT COMPANY
SISC	SIMMONS SCALE MODELS INC
SISP	SIERRA SOUTHERN PRODUCTS
SJE	SAN JUAN ENGINEERING
SKI	S.K. INTERNATIONAL
SL	STAR LINE MODELS
SLM	STATE LINE MODELS
SLMO	SILVER LEDGE MODELS
SLR	SILVER LEAF RAPID TRANSIT MODELS
SLS	SCALE LOCOMOTIVE & SUPPLY
SM	SUNSHINE MODELS
SMC	SUTHERLAND MODELS CASTERS INC
SMI	SCALE MODELERS INDUSTRIES
SMO	STAR MODELS
SMP	SAMPSON MODEL COMPANY
SMRW	SANGO MODEL RAILROAD WORKS
SMS	SCHRADER METAL SPECIALISTS
SMW	SCALE MODEL WEATHERING INC
SMW.	SANGO MODEL RAILROAD WORKS (O)
SOHO	S SOHO & COMPANY
SP	STANDARD PRODUCTS
SPCS	SPRINGTOWN CAR SHOPS
SPM	SAGINAW PATTERN MFG CO
SPPR	SOUTH PARK PRODUCTIONS
SPR	SMART PRODUCTS INC
SQ	SUPERQUICK
SR	SANDY RIVER CAR SHOPS
SRA	SCALE-RAIL MINIATURES
SRE	SCALE RAILWAY EQUIPMENT COMPANY
SRM	STATE RAILROAD MODELS
SS	SILVER STREAK
SSC	SPRINGDALE STRANGLER CREEK
SSD	SCALE SCENICS DIVISION
SSHK	SMOKE STACK HOBBY KITS CO
SSL	SCALE STRUCTURES LIMITED
SSL	SS LIMITED
SSM	SUPER SCALE MODEL CORP.
SSMO	SEQUOIA SCALE MODELS
SSP	SMALL SCALE PRODUCTS
SSS	SOUTH SHORE SCALE MODELS
ST	STERLING MODELS
ST&M	SOUTHERN TOOL & MANUFACTURING CO.
STC	STRUCTURE COMPANY, THE
STEW	STEWART HOBBIES INC
STEWM	STEWART MODELS
STS	STANDARD SCALE MODELS
STST	STATE STREET MODELS
SU	SCENERY UNLIMITED
SUM	SUPERIOR MODELS
SUN	SUNSET MODELS
SUP	SUGAR PINE MODELS
SV	SMOKEY VALLEY RAILROAD
T	TYCO INDUSTRIES
TAK	IMP/TAKARA
TAK	TAKARA/IMP
TBE	TRUXEL BROS ENTERPRISES
TC	TRAIN CRAFT PRODUCTS
TCM	TOWN CRAFTS MODELS
TEN	TENSHODO MODEL COMPANY
TH	THOMAS INDUSTRIES

APPENDIX C (MANUFACTURERS)

A	ABREV ALPHABETICALLY BY MANUFACTURER
THH	TOY & HOBBY HOUSE
THM	THRALL MFG CO
TI	TRAINS, INC.
TIM	TIMBERLINE MODELS
TK	TK MODELS
TM	TRAIN MINIATURES
TMC	TRAIN MINIATURE OF CALIF
TMI	TRAIN MINIATURE OF ILLINOIS
TMK	TETSUDO MOKEISHA
TMO	TRAIN MODELS
TOBY	TOBY MODEL COMPANY LIMITED
TOHO	TOHO MODELS
TOM	TOMALCO
TOMH	TOMHAR MFG CO
TP	TAURUS PRODUCTS
TPPR	TP PRODUCTS
TR	TROLLER
TRH	TRACTION HOUSE
TRI	TRACKSIDE INDUSTRIES
TRIS	TRIANGLE SCALE MODELS
TRIX	TRIX
TRM	TRACTION MODELS
TRS	TRAINSTUFF
TS	TSUBOMI
TSM	TRU-SCALE MODELS
TSS	TRACKSIDE SPECIALTIES
TT	TRAINS OF TEXAS
TVM	TIGER VALLEY MODELS
TY	THOMAS A YORKE ENTERPRISES
U	ULRICH
U	J.C. ULRICH COMPANY INC.
U .	CJ ULRICH
UMP	UNIVERSAL MODEL PRODUCTS
UN	ATLAS INDUSTRIES INC
US	ULTRA SCALE
USAI	US AIRFIX
USH	US HOBBIES
USM	UTAH SCALE MODEL COMPANY
USTT	UNITED STATES TOY TRAIN COMPANY
V	VARNEY
V&T	V&T SHOPS
VAL	VALLAM ASSOCIATES
VAN	VAN HOBBIES
VCM	VALLEY CAR WORKS
VCM	VCM
VI	VIRDEN
VIK	VIKING MODELS
VL	V LINE LOCOMOTIVES INC
VM	MAINLINE VARNEY
VM	VARNEY MAINLINE
VMR	VICOUNT MODEL RAILROAD PRODUCT CO
VOL	VOLLMER
VOLT	VOLTAMP
VW	VALLEY WORKS
W	WINSTON MINIATURE ENGINEERING CO
W&T	W&T MODELS
WAHL	WAHL
WAL	WALTERS
WASM	WALLACE SCALE MODLES
WB	WILLIAM BROTHERS
WC	WAGNER CAR COMPANY
WCS	WISONSIN CENTRAL SUPPLY
WD	WESTERFIELD
WE	WRIGHT ENTERPRISES
WEB	WEBSTER MANUFACTURING COMPANY
WEC	WESTMORELAND CAR SUPPLY
WEED	WEEDEN
WEST	WESTWOOD
WFM	WAYFREIGHT MODELS
WGM	WHITE GROUND MODEL WORKS
WIK	WIKING
WM	WESTERN MODELS
WMAC	WEN-MAC
WMC	WESTCHESTER MODEL CO
WMS	WALKER MODEL SERVICE
WO	WOODSON
WO	HL WOODSON

A	ABREV ALPHABETICALLY BY MANUFACTURER
WPC	WP CAR COMPANY
WPM	WENTZCO PRECISION MODELS
WR	WESTERN RAILCRAFT
WRB	WR BROWN CORP
WRL	WILLIAMS REPRODUCTIONS LTD
WS	WOODLAND SCENICS
WSM	WESTSIDE MODEL COMPANY
WSP	WS PARKS
WSP	WALTER S PARKS
WSY	WALTER SYRETT
WVL	WABASH VALLEY LINE
WW	WHEEL WORKS
YE	YE OLD HUFF 'N PUFF
YM	YANK MODEL RESEARCH INC
ZSM	ZIMMER SCALE MODELS
ZUHR	ZUHR
ZUHR	HENRY ZUHR INC

STEPHANS' RAILROAD DIRECTORY

A81

On the Historical Societies:

There is a long list of Historical Societies associated with railroads. I belong to 25 different ones just so I can maintain my periodical library. Most of these put out a magazine format publication that ranges from good to excellent. If you have an interest in a specific road I would strongly suggest that you join the appropriate society and contribute any special knowledge you have to it. In this way the base for "Your Road" grows to everyone's benefit.

Remember one thing about these societies. Most are ALL volunteer and ALL are non-profit. Be patient if you do not get an immediate response. Some key members are retired and they tend to give good response to letters received. Others hold down full time jobs and even if they had 25 hours in their day they tend to be slow. So keep that in mind. I have also found that some officers can be exceedingly helpful for your specific cause, others could care less. This is human nature. Do not fault the society for an unpleasant experience with one member.

On the following pages is information provided by various societies on their activities and their membership applications. All of these I find worthwhile and I highly recommend them. Following these is a listing of other societies and magazines that I currently belong or subscribe to. I consider all of these worthwhile too. There are other societies (I think I have all the currently available magazines.) that do exist but that I have not joined. I may not have joined because their publications are not something that lends itself to my indexing project or because I have not seen their publication yet. Eventually I will try them all. Do not let my tardiness in joining deter you if you have an interest--Go For It!!

On Magazines:

When I started this project I was aware of only four magazine titles. How wrong I was! Each of these have their good points and if you have an interest I urge you to subscribe. I get something out of each and every one of them. Some of the newer ones rely on subscriptions for their life-blood. If YOU do not support them, they will not be around. Their editors and publishers are extending an effort just for you. Support them.

MO PAC HISTORICAL SOCIETY	B2
TRACTION MAGAZINE	B4
SHORT & NARROW RAILS	B5
C&O HISTORICAL SOCIETY	B6
FREIGHT CAR JOURNAL	B7
MOTIVE POWER REVIEW	B7
SOCIETY/MAGAZINE LIST 1	334
RI TECHNICAL SOCIETY	335
GM&O HISTORICAL SOCIETY	336
EBT (FRIENDS OF)	369
SOCIETY/MAGAZINE LIST 2	481

The Missouri Pacific Historical Society, Inc. was organized in 1980 for the purpose of obtaining, preserving and sharing information and material relating to the Missouri Pacific Railroad and its subsidiaries to the society's members and others. The current M.P.H.S. is an outgrowth of a prior group which ran from 1974 to 1977. The society's area of interest include not only the Missouri Pacific Railroad, past to present, but its predecessor railroads including Texas & Pacific; Chicago & Eastern Illinois (after 1968 merger); St. Louis, Brownsville and Mexico; International-Great Northern; Gulf Coast Lines; St. Louis, Iron Mountain and Southern; New Orleans, Texas and Mexico; and the Missouri-Illinois.

Since its beginning the society has seen steady growth with members nationwide and overseas. It is a not-for-profit corporation chartered in the state of Missouri. Memberships are available in four classes to anyone interested in the Missouri Pacific story. Memberships are available as follows:

REGULAR - $12.00 annual dues.
CONTRIBUTING - $17.00 and over.
FOREIGN - $20.00 (air) $15.00 (surface).
STUDENT - (16 years & under) $10.00

Contributing memberships are for those individuals who desire to make a monetary contribution to the society in excess of regular dues amount.

Annual meetings began in 1981 and will be rotated throughout the Missouri Pacific system as feasible. In addition to the society's business, varied programs covering the Missouri Pacific and its history are given for the benefit of those attending.

The society publishes an illustrated quarterly magazine in April, July, October and January of each membership year. Each issue of the EAGLE contains current news and articles of historical interest. Rosters of equipment, technical information and data, and modeling projects are just a few of many items of interest published along with the business of the society. All members are urged to contribute material for publication. Memberships of all classes include a subscription to the EAGLE.

The M.P.H.S. membership year runs from February 1st to January 31st of each year. Each new member will receive all available issues of the EAGLE for the membership year in which he joins. Those who join before November 30th receive membership in the current membership year. Those received after December 1st will be for the following year.

A 12 month calendar is included with each membership. The first will be issued to all 1987 members in December 1987 for calendar year 1988.

MEMBERSHIP APPLICATION - MO-PAC HISTORICAL SOCIETY

Make check or money order payable to **MISSOURI PACIFIC HISTORICAL SOCIETY**, and mail to:

**Missouri Pacific
Historical Society
223 E. Main Street
Jackson, MO 63755**

☐ Regular Member
☐ Contributing Member
☐ Foreign Member
☐ Student

NAME *(Please Print)* _____

ADDRESS _____ ZIP CODE _____

HOW DID YOU FIND OUT ABOUT THE SOCIETY? _____
INTRODUCED BY "STEPHANS' RAILROAD DIRECTORY"

Please check the areas of your interest

☐ Historical
☐ Technical
☐ Motive Power
☐ Passenger Equipment
☐ Freight Equipment
☐ Modeling-Scale? _____ Period? _____
☐ Missouri Pacific
☐ Texas Pacific
☐ Gulf Coast Lines-Which Road? _____
☐ International-Great Northern
☐ Chicago & Eastern Illinois

Time period

☐ Pre 1900
☐ 1900 to 1930
☐ 1930 to 1950
☐ 1950 to 1962
☐ 1962 to 1976
☐ 1976 to present

Can you provide assistance, ie articles, photos, diagrams, etc., in any of the areas listed above?
☐ Yes ☐ No

Which one?

Would you be interested in participating in the societys operation?
☐ Yes ☐ No

What would you be willing to do?

B3

TRACTION
Prototype and Models

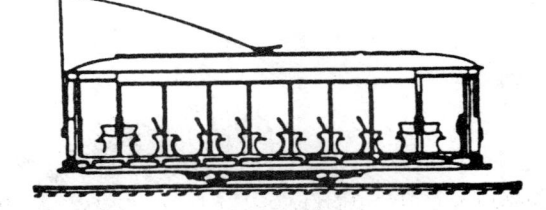

2020 Ninth St. S.W.   Canton, Ohio 44706

New

Volume 1   Number 1   Contents:

1 — Steve Bayard's Valley Railway Company, HO & O Scale
2 — Hutchinson & Northern
3 — Trolleyville U.S.A.

FEATURES:

Published by Railhead Publications

$2.95   Bi-monthly

Bi-monthly

36 to 44 pages each issue

High quality photo reproduction and easy to read type

Book reviews and informative letters from readers

Articles and photos by well-known and new authors and photographers

Presents articles covering lines from all the U.S. and many countries around the world

Scale drawings of cars, locomotives, buildings, maps, and more!

Prototypes (new, old, remnants), model articles, museum information.

INTRODUCED BY "STEPHANS' RAILROAD DIRECTORY"
ORDER FORM

☐ YES, I want a subscription to at the special price:
  ☐ 6 issues at $16.00   ☐ 12 issues at $30.00

Make checks payable to
Traction

Name _____

Address _____

City/State/Zip _____

Phone _____

SRRD

B4

Mail to: Box 526, Canton, Ohio 44701
Phone: (216) 454-7519

Experience the excitement of discovery in this unique publication exploring the farthest boundaries of railroad knowledge. This periodical seeks and finds information about popular Short and Narrow Gauge lines, along with the unknown.

The magazine presenting Railroad History for the Short-sighted & Narrow-minded Enthusiast

HORT AND NARROW RAILS

Brings you the best in Shortline and Narrow Gauge Prototype material.

Loaded with articles by noted authors such as Ross Grenard, Bill ensen, Ted Schnept, Charles Small, as well as many others.

s looking for suggestions and material to share with our readers.

6-44 pages of content per issue.

½ X 11, saddle-stitch.

.95

scription rates—6 issues: **$16.00**

12 issues: **$30.00**

lers—Minimum 5 copies, **25% discount**

k Issues Available

INTRODUCED BY "STEPHANS' RAILROAD DIRECTORY"
ORDER FORM

☐ YES, I want a subscription to at the special price:
    ☐ 6 issues at $16.00   ☐ 12 issues at $30.00

Make checks payable to
SHORT AND NARROW RAILS

Name _____

Address _____

City/State/Zip _____

Phone _____

SRRD

Mail to: Box 526, Canton, Ohio 44701
Phone: (216) 454-7519

CHESAPEAKE & OHIO... GEORGE WASHINGTON'S RAILROAD

...The C&O Historical Society invites you to experience the C&O story

About the Society...

The Chesapeake & Ohio Historical Society was established in 1969, and incorporated in 1975 under the laws of West Virginia as a nonprofit corporation. It has been recognized since 1977 as a nonprofit eleemosynary organization under paragraph 501(c)(3) of the Internal Revenue Code, so all contributions of material and money are tax-deductible charitable contributions.

The Society publishes a monthly magazine devoted to history, current news, and modeling information about the Chesapeake & Ohio, the Hocking Valley, and the Pere Marquette, as well as their predecessors. Other CSX Corporation railroad properties are covered to the extent that they interrelate with the C&O. The *Magazine* is printed on high-quality glossy paper, with scores of photos, maps, drawings, and illustrations. Each issue has a column devoted to modeling, often showing model photos, diagrams, "how-to" articles, and information on C&O-prototype models as they become available.

A major part of the Society's efforts goes into the production of books and pamphlets, which have received high praise from reviewers in the railfan and model railroad press, as well as from other magazines, newspapers, and periodicals. Recent titles have been *The Chesapeake and Ohio Diesel Review* (228 pages, over 300 photos), *Pere Marquette Power* (244 pages, over 300 photos), *C&O Alleghany Subdivision* (148 pages, 200 photos), and *Chessie's Road* (hardbound, 310 pages, 360 photos). Other books are in research, writing, and production stages now.

In the area of equipment preservation, the Society owns six former C&O passenger cars, which it is in the process of restoring for excursion train operation.

The C&O Historical Society is one of a very few one-railroad organizations that have a permanent, institutionalized archives facility housed in a safe, protected environment, and available for researchers. The society also operates a research service for members and others who write us with inquiries. Whenever possible, individual inquiries are answered and reproductions from the archives furnished. The collections contain over 40,000 negatives from which 8x10 prints can be ordered, over 5,000 mechanical drawings of C&O equipment, and over 15,000 civil engineering drawings, from which diazo prints can be ordered at reasonable rates. The society is engaged in indexing its collections by computer for easy user access. The Society also handles all inquiries received by the CSX Corporation pertaining to C&O history, and acts as its unofficial historical arm. It has received several grants from the company.

Although the C&O Historical Society is one of the largest organizations of its type in existence, its staff is entirely composed of volunteers, and its business is largely conducted through the mail. The membership has an opportunity to meet each year at the convention and annual meeting, which is held in a C&O city and includes displays, sales activities, model railroad tours, tours to C&O or former C&O facilities for photography, a business (directors') meeting, and a banquet with awards presentations and a prominent speaker. Past speakers have included the editors of *Trains* and *Railfan & Railroad* magazines, Chessie System Chairman John Collinson, CSX Chairman Hays Watkins, and numerous other railroad officials.

The Chesapeake & Ohio Railway

The Chesapeake & Ohio Railway traces its origin to the Louisa Railroad, begun during 1836 in Louisa County, Virginia, and to the James River and Kanawha Canal, begun also in Virginia in 1785. By 1850 the railroad has been built from Richmond to present-day Clifton Forge, Virginia, and renamed the Virginia Central. After extensive use and massive damage in the Civil War, the road was reorganized as the Chesapeake & Ohio, and was built across West Virginia to Huntington, on the Ohio River, in 1872 and 1873. In 1888 the main line was extended down the south bank of the Ohio and across that stream to Cincinnati. After the turn of the century another line was acquired from Cincinnati through Indiana to Chicago. Later, the Hocking Valley Railway was merged, and a line built between its road and the C&O, thus connecting the C&O with Great Lakes shipping at Toledo. In West Virginia and Kentucky extensive branch lines tapped the rich bituminous coal fields, from which the C&O's wealth has flowed. Coal was and is shipped primarily to Newport News, Virginia, for export and coastwise shipping, and to Toledo, Ohio, for Great Lakes shipping; it is used principally for metals production and power generation. In 1947 the C&O absorbed the Pere Marquette Railway, with which it had been affiliated since the Van Sweringen days of the 1930s. Today the former PM lines, mostly in Michigan, form an important source of merchandise freight revenues, including much lucrative automotive business.

Though primarily a freight railroad, the C&O long boasted a proud and superbly-operated passenger service. Even today, when the C&O has become just another part of the Chessie System—and now of CSX Transportation—the very name of "Chesapeake & Ohio" can conjure scenes of heavy coal drags behind massive motive power amid rugged mountains, or of polished engines pulling long standard passenger trains.

C&O locomotives

C&O steam locomotive design after the turn of the century reflected a need for greater and greater power to challenge its mountain districts with increasingly heavy trains. To meet the challenge, the railway's mechanical department produced some of the finest locomotives in America. The C&O had some 16 different wheel arrangements in service at one time, including the original Mountain (4-8-2) type, the heaviest and most powerful Hudson (4-6-4) type, and the most 2-8-4s of any railroad. It designed the most powerful steam locomotive of all time—the Allegheny (2-6-6-6) type—to carry coal over Alleghany Mountain. Yet amid this ruggedness, the C&O rostered some of the most beautiful locomotives of their age—locomotives that H. Stafford Bryant saw as the epitome of the stylish, dignified "Georgian" design.

The Pere Marquette

The Pere Marquette Railroad was created in 1900 from a group of Michigan lines that had grown up from a maze of lumber roads built in the preceding 30 years. It served local needs and carried some bridge traffic, but it was only after the C&O acquired control in 1923 and the road ended up in the back yard of the automobile industry that it became an important property. It was merged with the C&O in 1947.

The Hocking Valley

The Hocking Valley was an outgrowth of the old Columbus, Hocking Valley & Toledo. From 1899 until it absorbed into the C&O in 1930, it operated 320 miles of track, all in Ohio, carrying coal from the Hocking hills to Toledo and Great Lakes shipping. It later served the C&O as its coal outlet to the Great Lakes and the Midwest.

The railroaders

The image of the steam locomotive is still a powerful one in the collective memory of America, and no less so is that of the railroad man. A hero of his age, the idol of young boys, the epitome of the steadfast, courageous knight of the rail, the locomotive engineer holds a special place in the history of any railroad, just as he does in the lore of America. But then there were the gandy dancers, the construction men, the section workers, the agents and telegraph operators, and the great financial magnates... the story of the railroad is the story of men forging a new transportation link across the country, developing its resources, carrying people, raw materials, and finished goods, helping fight the wars, expand technology, and hastening the arrival of the "modern" age, which would have little use for them!

The C&O has its share of heros in all of these arenas, from financial titan Collis P. Huntington to brave engineer Billy Richardson and steel-driver John Henry. Their story is the heart of C&O history, an integral part which the C&O Historical Society does not neglect.

What are the Society's main goals?

We want to preserve data, equipment, and artifacts pertaining to the Chesapeake & Ohio Railway and integrate them into the overall regional history, and also use them as typical illustrations of the development of mechanical, civil engineering, construction, and transportation technology in America.

INTRODUCED BY "STEPHANS' RAILROAD DIRECTORY"

MEMBERSHIP APPLICATION:

Chessie

☐ Regular membership: $15.00
☐ Sustaining membership: $30.00 ($15.00 of which is a tax-deductible contribution)

NAME _____

ADDRESS _____

CITY, STATE _____ ZIP _____

I understand that I will receive a full year's issue of the Society's *Magazine*, member prices on all items sold by the Society, and other benefits as outlined in the By-laws.

Please mail this form, along with your check or money order, to: Dean R. Haschel, Membership
Rt. 1 — Box 70-F
Monterey, IN 46960

FREIGHT CARS JOURNAL

In 1988, Freight Cars Journal (FCJ) entered its 5th year of publication. FCJ is published quarterly on high-quality glossy paper for maximum photo reproduction. Contents include news, history and modeling of freight cars, builders, and related subjects of all eras and roads. Each issue is packed with data and photos. Various freight car rosters and scale drawings have appeared in past issues of Freight Cars Journal. Subscription is $15.00 per calendar year. Please send to:

Freight Cars Journal
P.O. Box 1458
Monrovia, CA 91016
INTRODUCED BY "STEPHANS' RAILROAD DIRECTORY"

Name_____

Address_____

City_____State_____

Postal Code_____

****

MOTIVE POWER REVIEW

Motive Power Review is a new magazine with its primary focus on contemporary locomotive news and recent history. MPR's content includes detailed photos, rosters, modeling suggestions, and resource guides. Printed on high-quality glossy paper for maximum photo reproduction. Subscription for 4 issues is $7.50. Please send check or money order to:

MOTIVE POWER REVIEW
P.O. BOX 2096
COVINA, CA 91722
INTRODUCED BY "STEPHANS' RAILROAD DIRECTORY"

Name_____

Address_____

City_____State_____

Postal Code_____

Continued on page 334

My research project has lead to my collecting a rather extensive library of railroad related periodicals. The following list shows all the titles that I am aware of. The dates listed with the title indicate the start and stop of publication. Those without a second date are still going strong.

TITLE	RUN
1:22.5 DIGEST	1981-1983
B&M BULLETIN	1971-
B&O ENG 5304, HIGH LIGHT	1978-1982
B&O RAILROADER	1972-1978?
B&O SENTINAL	1982-
BALDWIN	1944-1952
BALDWIN LOCOMOTIVES	1922-1943
BEE LINE (READING)	1978-
BURLINGTON BULLETIN (2)	1980-
C&O NEWSLETTER	1969-
CANADIAN RAIL	1937-
CAPITAL TRACTION QUARTERLY	1966-????
CENTRAL HEADLIGHT	1970-
DIAMOND (ERIE)	1972-
DISPATCHER	1956-1965
EAGLE MP PAC HIST SOC	1974-
EXTRA 2200 SOUTH (DOVER)	1967-
EXTRA 2200 SOUTH (PRE DOVER)	1961-1967
FINE SCALE MODELER	1982-
FINELINES	1964-1975
FLAGS DIAMONDS & STATUES	1980-
FREIGHT CAR JOURNAL	1983-
G SCALE NEWS	1983
GARDEN RAILWAYS	1984-
GARDEN RAILWAYS (SSB)	1982-1983
GM&O HISTORICAL NEWS	1974-
HEADLIGHTS	1938-
HIGH LINE (PHIL CHAPTER PRRT&HS)	1980-
HO MONTHLY (ETC)	1948-1964
JERSEY CENTRAL LINES	1981-
KEYSTONE	1968-
LESMAN, THE	1972-1977
LIGHT & INDUSRTIAL QUARTERLY	1982-1987
LIGHT LOCOMOTIVES	1982-????
LINES SOUTH	1983-
LIVE STEAM	1967-
LOCO PROFILES	
LOCOMOTIVE & RAILWAY PRESERVATION	1986-
LOCOMOTIVE QUARTERLY	1976-
LOG TRAIN	1982-
MAINLINE MODELER	1980-
MAINSTREETER (NP)	1982-
MINIATURE RAILROADING	1938-194?
MODEL BUILDER	1937-1949
MODEL RAILROADER	1934-
MODEL RAILROADER'S DIGEST	1936-194?
MODEL RAILROADING 1 (1001 IDEAS)	1968-1973
MODEL RAILROADING 2 (GW OF MRR)	1975-1979
MODEL RAILROADING 3	1979-
MODEL RAILROADING ENGINEERING	1969-????
MODEL RAILS	1969-????
MODELTEC	1984-
MODERN TRANSPORT HISTORY	1981-1983
MOTIVE POWER INTERNATIONAL	1973-1977
N&W ARROW	1974-1979?
NARROW GAUGE GAZETTE	1975-
NARROW GAUGE SOCIETY NEWSLETTER	1971-1972
NEW ENGLAND STATES LTD	1977-1982
NEW MEXICO RAILROADER	1962-1968?
NEWSLETTER OF UPPER CANADIAN	1952-
NKP NEWSLETTER	1966-
NMRA BULLETIN	1960-
NORTH WESTERN LINES (C&NW)	1973-
NRHS BULLETIN	1936-
NYNH&H SHORELINER	1970-
O SCALE NEWS 48 FT	1970-
O SCALE RAILROADING	1969-
O&W OBSERVER (FRANKLIN LAKES)	1969-????
O&W OBSERVER (MIDDLETOWN)	1965?-

TITLE	RUN
PACIFIC NEWS	1961-
PACIFIC RAILWAY JOURNAL	1954-1961
PENNSY JOURNAL	1981-1984
PROTOTYPE MODELER	1977-
PROTOTYPE MODELER HIGH IRON	1969-1973
PROTOTYPE MODELER NORTHWEST	1976-1977
PROTOTYPE MODELER SANTA FE	1977-1977
PROTOTYPE MODELER SOUTH WESTERN	1974-1977
PROTOTYPE MODELER WESTERN	1975-1977
PTJ	1967-
R&LHS BULLETIN	1921-
RAIL & TRANSIT	1975-????
RAIL CLASSICS	1972-
RAIL PROTOMODELS	1975-1975
RAILMODEL	1970-1971
RAILPACE	1982-
RAILROAD (RAILFAN) 1974-79	1974-1979
RAILROAD (RAILFAN/RAILROAD) 1979-	1979-
RAILROAD 1906-18	1906-1918
RAILROAD 1929-79	1929-1979
RAILROAD CAR JOURNAL	1971-1972
RAILROAD ENTHUSIAST 1	1934-1947
RAILROAD ENTHUSIAST 2	1963-
RAILROAD MODEL CRAFTSMAN	1933-
RAILROAD MODELER	1971-1980
RAILROADING 1 (STEAM LOCOMOTIVES)	1959-1960
RAILROADING 2 (STEAM LOCOS & RR T	1961-1967
RAILROADING 3 (RAILROADING)	1968-1975
RAILROADS ILLUSTRATED	????=????
RAILS NORTHEAST (PC RAILROADER)	1973-1975
RAILS NORTHEAST (RAILS NORTHEAST)	1976-1983
RAILS SOUTH	1978-
RAILWAY QUARTERLY	1977-1984
ROCK (ROCK ISLAND DIGEST)	1981-
ROCK, THE	1974-
S GAUGE HEARLD	1960-1978
S GAUGIAN	1962-
SANTA FE MODELER	1978-
SANTA FE ROUTE	1983-
SCALE COUPLER	1987-
SCALE MODEL TRACTION & MODELS	1979-
SHORT AND NARROW RAILS	1979-
SHORT LINE ANNUAL	1959-1965?
SHORT LINE RAILROADER (YOUNG)	1954-1960
SLIM GAUGE NEWS	1971-1974
SN3 MODELER	1983-
SOO, THE	1978-
SOUTHERN RAILFAN	1972-????
STEEL RAILS	1954-1956
STREAMLINER (UP HIST SOC)	1985-
STREET RAILWAY REVIEW	1973-1978?
TALL TIMBER SHORT LINES -TTSL	1985-
TALL TIMBER SHORT LINES-PLANFINDE	1983-1984
THE SHORT LINE	1973-
TIMBER TRANSFER (EBT)	1983-
TIMBERBEAST	1981-
TOY TRAINS	1951-1954
TRACTION & MODELS #1-219	1965-1985
TRACTION HERITAGE V1-V16#2	1968-1983
TRACTION-PROTOTYPE AND MODELS	1987-
TRAIN COLLECTORS QUARTERLY	1954-
TRAIN TALK	1984-1986
TRAINLINE (SP HIST SOC)	1982-
TRAINS	1940-
TROLLEY SPARKS	1944-????
TROLLEY TALK	1954-
TURNTABLE	1975-????
WESTERN RAILROADER	1937-
WHISTLE STOP (O GAUGE MODELER)	1950-1953

CATEGORY INDEX	PAGE
ABBREVIATION-BUILDER APPENDIX	A69
ABBREVIATION-MANUFACTURER APPENDIX	A76
ABBREVIATION-ROADNAME APPENDIX	A34
BAGGAGE CAR MODELS	276
BAGGAGE CAR PHOTOS	265
BOX CAR MODELS	285
BOX CAR PHOTOS	281
BOX CAR PLANS	281
BOX CAR PROTOTYPE DATA	279
BRIDGE & TUNNEL MODELS	368
BRIDGE & TUNNEL PHOTOS	348
BRIDGE & TUNNEL PLANS	348
BRIDGE & TUNNEL PROTOTYPE DATA	341
BUILDER-ABBREVIATION APPENDIX	A67
C&O HISTORICAL SOCIETY	B6
CABOOSE MODELS	299
CABOOSE PHOTOS	288
CABOOSE PHOTOS BY ROAD	290
CABOOSE PROTOTYPE DATA	287
COACH MODELS	276
COACH PHOTOS	268
COACH PLANS	262
COACH PROTOTYPE DATA	259
COMBINE MODELS	276
COMBINE PHOTOS	265
COMBINE PLANS	262
COMBINE PROTOTYPE DATA	259
COMMERCIAL BUILDING MODELS	368
COMMERCIAL BUILDING PHOTOS	349
COMMERCIAL BUILDING PROTOTYPE DATA	342
DEADHEADS	299
DIESEL LOCO PROTOTYPE DATA BY ROAD	185
DIESEL LOCOMOTIVE MODELS	254
DIESEL LOCOMOTIVE PHOTOS	187
DIESEL LOCOMOTIVE PHOTOS BY ROAD	215
DIESEL LOCOMOTIVE PLANS	254
DIESEL LOCOMOTIVE PROTOTYPE DATA	181
DIESEL LOCOMOTIVE PROTOTYPE DATA ADDS	256
DINER PHOTOS	265
DINER PLANS	262
DINER PROTOTYPE DATA	259
DISPATCHERS REPORT	277
DOME CAR PHOTOS	271
DOME CAR PROTOTYPE DATA	260
EBT (FRIENDS OF)	369
ELEC LOCO PROTOTYPE DATA BY ROAD	243
ELECTRIC LOCOMOTIVE MODELS	254
ELECTRIC LOCOMOTIVE PHOTOS	244
ELECTRIC LOCOMOTIVE PHOTOS BY ROAD	249
ELECTRIC LOCOMOTIVE PLANS	254
ELECTRIC LOCOMOTIVE PROTOTYPE DATA	242
EXPRESS CAR PHOTOS	265
EXPRESS CAR PROTOTYPE DATA	259
EXTRAS	180
FLAT CAR MODELS	285

CATEGORY INDEX	PAGE
FLAT CAR PHOTOS	282
FLAT CAR PLANS	281
FLAT CAR PROTOTYPE DATA	279
FREIGHT CAR JOURNAL	B7
FREIGHT CAR PHOTOS BY ROAD	283
GENERAL ELECTRONICS	483
GENERAL FREIGHT CAR MODELS	285
GENERAL FREIGHT CAR PHOTOS	283
GENERAL FREIGHT PLANS	281
GENERAL FREIGHT PROTOTYPE DATA	280
GENERAL LOCOMOTIVE PROTOTYPE DATA	256
GENERAL PASSENGER CAR PHOTOS	271
GENERAL PASSENGER CAR PLANS	262
GENERAL PASSENGER CAR PROTOTYPE DATA	260
GENERAL PROTOTYPE DATA	375
GENERAL RAILROADING	515
GENERAL RAILROADING FICTION	566
GENERAL RAILROADING NON-FICTION	543
GM&O HISTORICAL SOCIETY	336
GONDOLA MODELS	285
GONDOLA PHOTOS	282
GONDOLA PLANS	281
GONDOLA PROTOTYPE DATA	279
HISTORICAL SOCIETIES & MAGAZINES	B1
HISTORY OF...	406
HISTORY OF... SHORT NOTES	416
HISTORY OF... SHORT NOTES ADDITIONS	480
HOPPER MODELS	285
HOPPER PHOTOS	282
HOPPER PLANS	281
HOPPER PROTOTYPE DATA	279
LAYOUT BUILDING	483
LAYOUT DESIGN	483
LAYOUT OPERATION	483
LAYOUT PLANS	483
LAYOUT VISITS	483
LOCOMOTIVE PLANS (ALL) BY ROAD	255
MAGAZINE DEPOT	B7
MANUFACTURER-ABBREVIATION APPENDIX	A71
MO PAC HISTORICAL SOCIETY	B2
MODEL TRACKWORK	483
MODELING BOOK REVIEWS	512
MOTIVE POWER REVIEW	B7
MOW MODELS	299
MOW PHOTOS (NON-REVENUE)	293
MOW PLANS (NON-REVENUE)	288
MOW PROTOTYPE DATA (NON-REVENUE)	287
NON-REVENUE CAR PHOTOS BY ROAD	296
OBSERVATION CAR PHOTOS	268
OBSERVATION CAR PROTOTYPE DATA	259
PASSENGER CAR (ALL) PHOTOS BY ROAD	271
PASSENGER CAR (ALL) PROTO DATA BY ROAD	263
PHOTOGRAPHY	576
PROTOTYPE BOOK REVIEWS	485
PROTOTYPE BOOK REVIEWS BY ROAD	505

CATEGORY INDEX	PAGE
PROTOTYPE SPEED & SCHEDULES	373
PROTOTYPE TRACKWORK	371
RAILCAR PHOTOS	265
RAILCAR PROTOTYPE DATA	259
RAILROAD MAPS BY ROAD	478
RAILROAD PEOPLE	560
RAILROAD STRUCTURE MODELS	368
RAILROAD STRUCTURE PHOTOS	349
RAILROAD STRUCTURE PLANS	348
RAILROAD STRUCTURE PROTOTYPE DATA	342
RAILROADANIA COLLECTING	575
RDC CAR PROTOTYPE DATA	259
RDC MODELS	276
RDC PHOTOS	266
RDC PLANS	262
REFRIGERATOR CAR MODELS	285
REFRIGERATOR CAR PHOTOS	283
REFRIGERATOR CAR PLANS	281
REFRIGERATOR CAR PROTOTYPE DATA	279
RENT-A-KID PHOTOCOPIES	257
RI TECHNICAL SOCIETY	335
ROADNAME-ABBREVIATION APPENDIX	A2
ROSTERS BY ROAD	377
RPO MODELS	276
RPO PHOTOS	270
RPO PROTOTYPE DATA	260
SCENERY	483
SHORT & NARROW RAILS	B5
SIGNAL MODELS	368
SIGNAL PHOTOS	356
SIGNAL PLANS	348
SIGNAL PROTOTYPE DATA	343
SLEEPER PHOTOS	270
SLEEPER PLANS	262
SLEEPER PROTOTYPE DATA	260
SOCIETY/MAGAZINE LIST 1	334
SOCIETY/MAGAZINE LIST 2	481
SPECIAL CARS & TRAINS	372
STEAM LOCO PROTOTYPE DATA BY ROAD	036
STEAM LOCOMOTIVE MODELS	254
STEAM LOCOMOTIVE PHOTOS	053
STEAM LOCOMOTIVE PHOTOS BY ROAD	119
STEAM LOCOMOTIVE PLANS	254
STEAM LOCOMOTIVE PROTOTYPE DATA	010
STEAM LOCOMOTIVE PROTOTYPE DATA ADDS	256
STOCK CAR MODELS	285
STOCK CAR PHOTOS	283
STOCK CAR PLANS	281
STOCK CAR PROTOTYPE DATA	280
STRUCTURE, SIG & VEHIC PROTO DATA BY RD	345
STRUCTURE, SIGNAL & VEHICLE PHOTO BY RD	359
TANK CAR MODELS	285
TANK CAR PHOTOS	283
TANK CAR PLANS	281
TANK CAR PROTOTYPE DATA	280

CATEGORY INDEX	PAGE
TENDER MODELS	255
TENDER PHOTOS	180
TENDER PHOTOS BY ROAD	180
TENDER PLANS	255
TENDER PROTOTYPE DATA	179
TENDER PROTOTYPE DATA BY ROAD	179
TOY AND TINPLATE TRAINS	576
TRACTION MAGAZINE	B4
TRACTION MODELS	303
TRACTION PHOTOS	303
TRACTION PHOTOS BY ROAD	320
TRACTION PLANS	303
TRACTION PROTOTYPE DATA	301
TRACTION PROTOTYPE DATA BY ROAD	303
VEHICLE MODELS	368
VEHICLE PHOTOS	358
VEHICLE PROTOTYPE DATA	345
VIDEO REVIEWS	512
WRECKS AND DISASTERS	474

TAILCAR

For future volumes I am looking for some issues of selected publications. Below is a list of the titles I need to complete my reference library. Many titles are nearly complete, as an example in "Western Railroader" I only need issue #12. Many other titles are in similar shape. I would like to obtain original copies of the issues I am missing. Since I am really interested in content only just borrowing a copy would suffice. Photo copies are OK too. I have a copier and I intend to photocopy pertinent portions of borrowed issues. I try to return borrowed issues within one week of my receipt so your collection will not be tied up for months. If you can help with with my project please drop me a line. Earl Stephans, RD1 Box 101, Chenango Forks, NY 13746-9712.

TITLE

- B&O ENG 5304, HIGH LIGHT
- BALDWIN
- BEE LINE (READING)
- CANADIAN RAIL
- CAPITAL TRACTION QUARTERLY
- DISPATCHER
- EXTRA 2200 SOUTH (PRE DOVER)
- GARDEN RAILWAYS
- HEADLIGHTS
- HIGH LINE (PHIL CHAPTER PRRT&HS)
- JERSEY CENTRAL LINES
- LIGHT LOCOMOTIVES
- LINES SOUTH
- LIVE STEAM
- LOCO PROFILES
- LOG TRAIN
- MINIATURE RAILROADING
- MODEL BUILDER
- MODEL RAILROADER'S DIGEST
- MODEL RAILS
- MODERN TRANSPORT HISTORY
- N&W ARROW
- NEW MEXICO RAILROADER
- NEWSLETTER OF UPPER CANADIAN
- NKP NEWSLETTER
- NORTH WESTERN LINES (C&NW)
- NRHS BULLETIN
- NYNH&H SHORELINER

TITLE

- O SCALE NEWS 48 FT
- O&W OBSERVER (FRANKLIN LAKES)
- O&W OBSERVER (MIDDLETOWN)
- PTJ
- R&LHS BULLETIN
- RAIL & TRANSIT
- RAILPACE
- RAILROAD 1906-18
- RAILROAD 1929-79
- RAILROAD CAR JOURNAL
- RAILROAD ENTHUSIAST 1
- RAILROAD ENTHUSIAST 2
- RAILROAD MODEL CRAFTSMAN
- RAILS SOUTH
- ROCK, THE
- S GAUGIAN
- SANTA FE ROUTE
- SHORT LINE ANNUAL
- SHORT LINE RAILROADER (YOUNG)
- SOO, THE
- SOUTHERN RAILFAN
- TRACTION HERITAGE V1-V16#2
- TRAIN COLLECTORS QUARTERLY
- TRAINLINE (SP HIST SOC)
- TROLLEY SPARKS
- TROLLEY TALK
- TURNTABLE
- WESTERN RAILROADER

Nearly the last thing to be added to a book such as this is the index. When we did this one it came out shorter than expected. Since the printers run their jobs in multiples of pages we had two extras to fill. Thus these last two unplanned pages.

In addition to our Directories and magazine back issues we have a limited quantity of selected railroad related books. Below is a description of the titles we can currently supply. Send us your order. Please include $3.00 shipping and handling. If you pay too much for shipping of these we will send a refund with your package.

THE SUNRISE ROUTE by Michael Zimmerman is a history of the Railroads of Washington County, Maine. A delightful narrative covering 1842 to 1985. Included is a removeable timetable of the Washington County RR Monthly from January 1901, 50 pages of photographs, employee rosters, construction cost, etc. This book lists for $12.95, our price for this soft-bound book is only $6.00!

BUILD YOUR OWN CABLE-CAR by Alan Rose is a Perigee Book with a list price of $8.95. A Rainy Sunday afternoon, a few supplies and in 38 steps you can have a San Francisco cable car made from heavy cardstock! Our price is $2.00.

THE MODEL-BUILDING HANDBOOK by Brick Price is an excellent guide to tools, materials, kit-building, kit-bashing, scratchbuilding, painting, figure painting, super-detaiing, casting techniques, dioramas, displays and photography. This step-by-step guide can be yours for $4.50. List price on this book is $9.95.

MODEL RAILROADING HANDBOOK Volume II by Robert Schleicher has 177 pages and lists for $10.95. This book covers planning, building and operating all phases of model railroads. Locomotives and rolling stock are also covered. Your price is $5.00!

BALDWIN LOCOMOTIVE WORKS NARROW GAUGE LOCOMOTIVES is an 1876 reprint of the Baldwin record. This hard-bound book has 63 pages and contains full page builders photos with the specifications of each locomotive. Your price on this beauty is $5.00.

We also have a selection of non-railroad books. These are listed below:

Model Military, Model Cars or Model Planes by Consumer Guides $2.95 List $1.00 each.

Aircraft Album No. 6 lists for $4.95. This covers in words and pictures most all plane types that North American Aviation built $2.00

We have 4 different World War II Fact Files. Machine guns, Heavy Artillery, Anti-Tank Weapons and American Gunboats & Minesweepers. List $3.95 Your choice $1.50!